ALMOST A MIRACLE

The American Victory in the War of Independence

JOHN FERLING

OXFORD
UNIVERSITY PRESS

OXFORD

UNIVERSITY PRESS

Oxford University Press, Inc., publishes works that further
Oxford University's objective of excellence
in research, scholarship, and education.

Oxford New York
Auckland   Cape Town   Dar es Salaam   Hong Kong   Karachi
Kuala Lumpur   Madrid   Melbourne   Mexico City   Nairobi
New Delhi   Shanghai   Taipei   Toronto

With offices in
Argentina   Austria   Brazil   Chile   Czech Republic   France   Greece
Guatemla   Hungary   Italy   Japan   Poland   Portugal   Singapore
South Korea   Switzerland   Thailand   Turkey   Ukraine   Vietnam

Published by Oxford University Press, Inc.
198 Madison Avenue, New York, NY 10016

www.oup.com

First issued as an Oxford University Press paperback, 2009

Oxford is a registered trademark of Oxford University Press

Library of Congress Cataloging-in-Publication Data
Ferling, John E.
Almost a miracle : the American victory
in the War of Independence / John Ferling.
p. cm.
Includes bibliographical references and index.
ISBN 978-0-19-518121-0; 978-0-19-538292-1 (pbk.)
1. United States—History—Revolution, 1775–1783—Campaigns.
2. United States—History—Revolution, 1775–1783—Biography.
3. Generals—United States—Biography.
4. United States. Continental Army—Biography.
5. Soldiers—United States—History—18th century.
6. United States. Continental Army—Military life.
7. United States—Politics and government—1775–1783.
I. Title.
E230.F47 2007
973.3'3—dc22
2007009366

7 9 8
Printed in the United States of America
on acid-free paper

CONTENTS

ILLUSTRATIONS AND MAPS

Maps

PREFACE

M Y WORLD, and that of most Americans alive since 1939, was shaped to a
striking degree by war. Not least in importance for me was the incredible prosperity that resulted from America's victory in World War II.
It created opportunities for me that had not existed for my parents. My dad grew
up in a working-class family, completed high school in 1928, and, like his forebears, immediately went to work. That was the destiny of 90 percent of American
men of his generation. I graduated from high school a dozen years after World
War II and, like more than half of my classmates in a petrochemical-suffused
town on the Texas Gulf Coast, went on to college.

Eventually, I became a history professor. The more I studied American history,
the more convinced I became that my generation was not exceptional in having
been substantively influenced by war. Just as war had been instrumental in shaping
the world I inhabited, it had touched generation after generation of Americans. I
soon found myself devoting considerable time to America's wars in the courses
that I taught, and before long I began teaching seminars on the War of Independence and creating courses on U.S. military history. My first book dealt with the
experiences of a Loyalist in the American Revolution, including his services on behalf
of the British army. Over the years I never strayed far from the Revolutionary War.

Now I have done what I long intended to do: write a history of the War of
Independence. Of late, I've wanted to write a military history of the American
Revolution, seeing it as a companion to my political history of the Revolution,
A Leap in the Dark. I find the lure of the War of Independence to be ever more
irresistible. It was war on a grand scale. Near its end, John Adams remarked that

the American Revolution had set the world ablaze, and indeed the War of Independence grew to be a world war, with men fighting from Florida to Canada, from the Caribbean to Africa to India, and across broad reaches of the high seas. So vast was the war that hardly anyone living east of the Appalachian Mountains in North America was untouched. Proportionately, only one other American war, the Civil War, was more costly than the War of Independence. Many civilians perished, including Indians and the residents of some coastal towns, both of whom were deliberately targeted, and countless others fell victim to diseases that soldiers on both sides spread unwittingly. When the war broke out, no one could foresee its consequences—as Adams, again, pointed out in 1775—but many Americans believed they were fighting to create a new world filled with greater opportunities. By the fiftieth anniversary of independence, most free Americans believed—as I did about the American triumph in World War II—that victory in the Revolutionary War had created a better world, one in which they enjoyed advantages not available to their parents.

When victory was at hand, George Washington remarked that it was almost a miracle that the Americans had won the war, and I have used what he said as a title for this book. However, one could as easily argue that it was astonishing that Great Britain had not been driven from the North American colonies in defeat years earlier, or that it was truly remarkable that the conflict had not ended in a negotiated settlement, with no clear victor after years of bloodshed. This book seeks to explain why America won the war, and why the British, despite their many advantages, lost it. One of the book's themes is that the war came much closer to ending short of a great American victory than many now realize. The book also looks at how wars were waged in the eighteenth century. It explores how soldiers and civilians experienced the war. It assays leaders and looks for turning points. This war, like most wars, was filled with options and choices. Leaders chose whether, and when, to go to war. Men chose—if they had a choice—whether to serve. Soldiers under fire made choices about how, or whether, to fight. Soldiers also made choices about the treatment of captives and civilians. Governments chose their war aims. Generals, sometimes in concert with civilian officials, chose strategic plans and objectives.

Although I have written about aspects of the War of Independence for thirty years, some of my attitudes changed as I immersed myself in this conflict, seeking to look in as many nooks and crannies of hostilities as possible. I came to see both more flaws and greater virtues in Washington's leadership, arrived at a deeper appreciation of Nathanael Greene, and grew to see Charles Lee as an especially tragic figure, a man at once possessed of superlative soldierly qualities and laden with ruinous character defects. I came to a deeper appreciation of the difficulties faced by the commanding officers on each side. While the woes faced by American soldiers is a familiar story, I found that their experiences contained more shades of gray than is often realized. I was even more surprised by the plight of the British regulars. This was a very tough war, and the men in every army and navy involved in the conflict frequently faced appalling travail and surpassing hazards. Above all, I came to believe in the crucial importance of the war in the South in determining the outcome of the Revolutionary War. It is a part of this war that too often has been shortchanged. The story that follows is, in consequence, almost equally divided between the story of the war in the North to 1778 and the war in the South that ensued thereafter.

A note concerning style: I have left the spelling in all quotations as found in the documents, hoping by this means to convey to readers a sense of the writer and of the time.

YEARS WERE REQUIRED TO complete this book, and over time debts of gratitude have accumulated. Numerous scholars have generously responded to my queries, providing insights and information that were most helpful. I would like to thank Paul Kopperman, Caroline Cox, David Hackett Fischer, George A. Billias, Robert F. Jones, Stan Deaton, Nancy Hayward, Judith Van Buskirk, Holly Mayer, Walter Dornfest, Mary Thompson, Walter Todd, Ken Noe, Keith Bohannon, Steve Goodson, Peter Drummey, Sydney Bradford, Robert E. Mulligan Jr., John Maass, and Gregory Urwin. Three individuals read all or parts of the manuscript. Jim Sefcik helped with stylistic concerns, provided bibliographical guidance, and located documents for me in a faraway archive. Edward Lengel offered insights and direction on Washington and countless matters concerning the army, the war, and various battles. No one, however, was more helpful than my friend Matt deLesdernier, who often exchanged his hat as a successful businessman for that of copyeditor and historian, graciously sharing his profound knowledge of the Revolutionary War.

More than anyone can imagine, I am grateful for the gracious and always cheerful assistance provided by Angela Mehaffey and Laura Hartman at the Irvine S. Ingram Library of the University of West Georgia. They secured a veritable ton of books and articles for me on interlibrary loan. Elmira Eidson and Stacy Brown kept backup computer discs for me. For a fourth time Peter Ginna shepherded a book of mine from inception through the completion of the manuscript, and I often benefited from his insights and guidance. After he moved to another publishing house, Susan Ferber became my editor. I owe her a special—and an enormous—debt of gratitude. She picked up a manuscript that had been in the works for years, but from the beginning treated it as her very own. No writer can ask more from an editor, nor can any author ever expect to have an editor with more patience, energy, and enthusiasm than Susan brought to this task. I also wish to thank Brigit Dermott, my copy editor, for her help in getting the manuscript in better shape. For a fourth time Helen Mules has handled the production end of bringing a book of mine into existence, and as always she was a joy to work with.

My wife, Carol, bore the brunt of living with an all too often busy and distracted author. As always, she was understanding and supportive of my work.

September 26, 2006   *John Ferling*

ALMOST A MIRACLE

Introduction

"MY COUNTRY, MY HONOR, MY LIFE": BRAVERY AND DEATH IN WAR

OCTOBER 18, 1776. Captain William Glanville Evelyn, resplendent in his British uniform, stood tall in a coal-black landing barge, the first orange rays of daylight streaming over him and glistening on the calm waters of Pelham Bay above Manhattan. Men were all about him, in his craft and in countless others. They were soldiers, part of an operation that had begun hours earlier during the cold, dark night. Evelyn and his comrades could not have been happier to see the sun. Their feet and hands were numbed by a cruel autumn chill that penetrated even into their bones. As it grew lighter with each minute, the men, swaying gently in their landing boats, squinted toward the coast, searching for signs of the enemy. They saw nothing. The beach was deserted, and night still clung to the motionless trees in the interior.

The men were British regulars and their German allies, some four thousand strong. In each amphibious craft several soldiers struggled with long oars, grunting occasionally as they strained to row toward the coastline. In the center of most vessels, between the oarsmen, sat two lines of men facing one another, shivering and thinking anxiously about what might lie ahead. Now and then someone coughed nervously, and every so often muskets jostled together with a clatter, but otherwise all was silent. Officers stood fore and aft. Often one was an ensign, a young man likely still in his teens. Sometimes the other, like Evelyn, was a captain, a company commander. Evelyn, forward in a barge that carried men from the Fourth Foot, the King's Own Regiment, was a thirty-four-year-old veteran soldier. He had fought in Europe in a previous war, and in Massachusetts and on Long Island in this conflict.

Captain William Glanville Evelyn. Self-portrait made in September 1776. The commander of No. 7 company, Fourth Foot (King's Own Regiment) and a career soldier in the British army, Evelyn came to appreciate the capabilities of the rebel soldiers before he died fighting them.

Evelyn and his comrades had been sent to land at Pell's Point, a jagged, oblong splay of land that jutted toward Long Island Sound. Pell's Point was not especially important, but behind it lay roads that linked Manhattan Island to the mainland. The Continental army, the army of the new United States, had begun to evacuate Manhattan following a series of military disasters, hoping to find safety in the highlands north of New York City. The objective of Evelyn and his comrades was to advance rapidly and seal off the Continentals' exit, trapping the rebel soldiery on Manhattan Island. If Evelyn and his comrades succeeded, the American Revolution might be over.

A great crisis in America's fortunes was at hand. A Continental officer from Delaware thought the very "Fate of the Campaigns, & the American Army" was at stake. Only the "utmost exertions of desperate Valor" could save George Washington's army and the cause, Colonel John Haslet had written on the eve on the redcoats' landing.[1]

Though the British could not see them, Continental soldiers were not far from the beach at Pell's Point. Two days earlier Washington had posted four Massachusetts regiments at Eastchester, near the coast, to guard his flank. Washington had personally reconnoitered the area and concluded that the enemy was likely to land on the west coast of Long Island Sound, somewhere between New Rochelle and Pell's Point, hoping to cut off his retreat.[2] He had carefully chosen the units that he detached to Eastchester. If any rebels were veterans, these New England men were. Some had fought along the Concord Road on the first day of the war eighteen months earlier. Most had been soldiering for a year or more, and three of the regiments were led by experienced soldiers, men who had fought for Massachusetts in the French and Indian War in the 1750s. Many of the men had worked in the maritime trades before the war. They were tough men, accustomed to facing peril even in their civilian pursuits, and they were led by Colonel John Glover, whom Washington had come to think of as a reliable leader after seeing him in action in the fighting for New York. Glover and his men were not expected to defeat the British who landed. They were to stop them just long enough for the Continentals to make their escape from

Colonel John Glover. Anonymous facsimile of a pencil drawing by John Trumbull, date unknown. Though a latecomer to the popular protest movement, Glover served with dedication and valor for nearly the duration of the war.

Manhattan. In wartime, some men, at some times, are seen by their commanders as expendable, to be sacrificed for the greater good. Certain to be heavily outnumbered, Glover may have wondered if that was true of his mission.

As the first pale light of dawn crept over the horizon on this day, Glover had climbed a ridge in Eastchester and, with a spyglass, looked out toward Long Island Sound, nearly three miles away. He saw what he thought must have been two hundred landing barges headed for Pell's Point. In an instant, he knew that Washington had been correct. He also knew that the British would make landfall before he could get his units to the beach. He would have to make his stand in the interior. Moving urgently, Glover set his men in motion, marching them south along Split Rock Road, knowing that the British would have to advance inland on that same road.

As the Americans hurried toward battle, Captain Evelyn and his men splashed ashore. Although they landed unopposed, each man stole a hurried glance toward the interior. Nothing. No sign of the enemy. Some dared to believe that this day might pass without a battle.

Putting ashore four thousand men and six heavy cannon was time consuming. Immediately after the first men landed, pickets were set out all along the periphery of the beach to guard against a surprise attack. Those not assigned to that duty were put to work unloading supplies, horses, and the unwieldy artillery. Fires were built for the officers, some of whom brewed tea while waiting to go inland. Many of the men, wet from their chores at the beach, stood by idly in the dismaying cold. Around 9:00 a.m. Earl Cornwallis, with a sizeable force of light infantry, set off into the interior to secure the right flank along Split Rock Road. Simultaneously, a small advance force, a few more than one hundred men, was sent to explore the road itself and to determine whether any rebels were nearby.

By then, Glover's Continentals were in place. Leaving one regiment in reserve in the rear, Glover had posted his own advance unit of forty men on the road about a mile and a half inland from the beach. He stationed the remainder of his brigade, three regiments totaling about 650 men, at staggered intervals several hundred yards apart along both sides of Split Rock Road, each man hidden behind the ubiquitous stone wall property boundaries that dotted the landscape. The Continentals had a long wait for the looming battle. Thirty minutes passed. Then another thirty, more unnerving than the first. For many, the wait was worse than battle itself. As in all wars, when soldiers wait, they are preoccupied with thoughts of what might happen. Would they be captured, or wounded, or killed? Worst of all, perhaps, would they disgrace themselves before their comrades? To pass the time, the men checked their weapons, then anxiously examined them again, and again. They made certain they could easily get to their ammunition. Most said nothing, though a few talked a steady stream of bluster, good for impressing others, they hoped, and for steadying themselves. Not a few men prayed.

The mid-morning sky had turned a bright blue, adorned with filigree clouds, by the time Glover's "advance guard," as he called it, glimpsed the first British unit moving up Split Rock Road. Until then, time had crept by. Now the pace quickened. The Americans, in a cuff of trees along the road, braced and strained to see the enemy. Suddenly, they heard the heavy clump of hoof beats behind them. It was Glover. Drawing up, he, too, watched, and waited. He struggled to appear unflappable, though later he admitted that he was nearly overcome with fear. "[O]h! The anxiety of mind I was in," he recollected, knowing that "my country, my honour, my own life, and everything that was dear" hung in the balance. He wished that a general had been there to take responsibility.[3] Soon, the British were a thousand yards away. Then just 750. When the redcoats were only five hundred yards down the road, Glover, with calm authority, ordered his men to advance.

When merely fifty yards of open, lonely road separated the British from the Continentals, the redcoat commander ordered his men to fire. A crash resounded and a plume of acrid smoke rose from the British line. Not a single American was hit by the volley. The New Englanders immediately answered with fire of their own. They were better shots, or perhaps simply luckier. Four British regulars fell. Neither side moved. The British fired again. This time Continentals fell, but those still standing returned the fire. The Americans were amazingly "Calm & Steady," according to an American officer, as unperturbed as if shooting "at a flock of Pidgeons or Ducks and not in the least Daunted or Confused."[4] Each side got off five volleys. Several men were wounded and some, including two Continentals, were killed. Outnumbered, Glover ordered his men to fall back. They did so in an orderly manner, something only veterans were likely to do. Some remained and fired as their comrades drew back, then they hastened to the rear under a covering fire provided by those who had withdrawn first. For an instant, the British remained rooted in place, but thinking the rebels were fleeing in fright they loudly shouted "Huzzah," then broke into a run, charging after their prey. They charged into a trap. As the redcoats closed on their retreating foe, the most forward regiment of Glover's men raised up from behind a stone wall and directed a deadly fire at the British. Then the rebels sprang over the wall and charged their startled foe. In a flash, the British advance unit found itself outnumbered. The redcoats broke and fled.[5]

Captain Evelyn and the British still on the beach heard the exchanges of fire in the interior. Now there could be no mistake. This was to be a day of battle. It was not an unwelcome prospect for Evelyn. He was a soldier, a regular, a professional. Fighting was what he did, why he was in America, why he had chosen to remain in America. He believed in this war, thought it had to be, embraced it, and looked forward to combat with a zeal that many would find strange, even repugnant. It was on him now. Within moments of hearing the gunfire, the entire British force started inland. Their comrades needed help. There was a job to do. Rebels must be flushed out.

Born in Ireland in comfortable surroundings in 1742, the son of an Anglican vicar, young Evelyn had entered the British army late in the Seven Years' War, but in time to experience combat in Germany. During the peacetime military cutbacks that followed that war, he retired on half-pay. Still single—he never married—Evelyn lived with his parents until he was reappointed to the army four years later. Five months after the Boston Tea Party, the King's Own shipped out to the colonies. It was Evelyn's first trip to America. On June 13, 1774, six months almost to the day after the Boston Tea Party, he and his company disembarked in Boston. Now in his early thirties, Evelyn was a striking figure. At 5 feet 10 inches he stood several inches taller than most men in Britain's army. He was slight, with long black hair and soft features, including an almost delicate mouth. At a glance, he appeared more suited for a career in the law or the academy, but there was flintiness in his dark eyes that attested to tenacity and bravery.[6]

The men of the King's Own made a formidable, and gaudy, appearance as they marched from the harbor through Boston's cobblestone streets on that warm summer day. Every man wore a scarlet coat with blue lapels and cuffs edged in silver. The enlisted men wore blue breeches and red waistcoats. The officers, like Evelyn, dressed in red breeches and blue waistcoats edged with silver. The coats worn by all the men were bound and looped with regimental lace, white with a blue stripe. Evelyn and most of the men wore a red hat edged with white. Every officer wore a white wig and carried a sword. Most men bore a musket.[7]

It was akin to marching into the lions' den. Few Bostonians hid their hatred for what they regarded as Britain's army of occupation. Yet despite the enmity that he often encountered, as well as the need to sleep in tents on the Boston Common deep into the raw autumn until barracks at last were available, Evelyn found much that he liked about the city. He thought Boston was attractive and its climate good, at least until his first New England winter set in. The food was superb. There was an abundance of seafood, including turtle soup, which he relished. Madeira and tropical fruit, also among his favorites, were consistently available. He liked just about everything about Boston except the Bostonians. He cursed them as "Yankey scoundrels" and "a set of rascals and poltroons." He thought the Congregational clergy the worst of the bunch. They were a "set of sanctified villains" who preached sedition instead of Christianity, he said. The ordinary citizens were nearly as bad. They were troublemakers, sneaky, disorderly, and malicious. They were dishonest, too. When he visited their shops, Evelyn railed, they drove a hard bargain and usually cheated him. Boston's merchants, he declared, "would sell the Kingdom of Heaven" if they could turn a profit on the transaction.[8]

During his first year in Boston, Evelyn struggled to understand the American protest. Some of his conclusions were remarkably enlightened. He realized that almost all the colonists desired more control over their lives, and he appears not to have been especially put off by that, though he believed that the Americans' situation was far less "irksome" than they thought it to be. After only a few weeks in Boston he deduced that a considerable portion of the population sought American independence, though no one was saying any such thing publicly. He also concluded that a handful of "enterprizing, ambitious demagogues," led, he had no doubt, by Samuel Adams, had capitalized on the peoples' sentiments in order to gain a following. Evelyn was convinced that few of the firebrands believed that independence could be achieved in their lifetime, and he was no less certain that Adams and other troublemakers had no stomach for war. The goal of the provocateurs, he conjectured, was merely to "gain something towards" independence, pushing matters to the brink, gambling that the "tenderness and clemency" of the British would lead London to cave in before hostilities erupted and to grant greater autonomy to the American colonists.

Captain Evelyn hoped that would not be the case, and he did not believe it would be. In his first letter from America, written in the summer of 1774, he predicted that this crisis would not have a peaceful resolution. Britain would have to use force to quell the rebellion and keep America in a "state of dependency." He did not think it would be difficult to crush the colonial dissidents, and he hoped to be part of the military operation that took on the assignment. Six months after he arrived in Massachusetts, Evelyn was offered the opportunity to transfer to another regiment that was being sent out of America. He declined. He was convinced that the colonial radicals should be dealt with harshly and "made an example to future eyes," and he wished to be with the army when the battle came.[9]

His wish came true. On April 19, 1775, Evelyn and the King's Own were part of an operation to destroy a rebel arsenal in Concord, about twenty miles west of Boston. It was a bloody day. Though unharmed, Evelyn was shaken. He was astonished that the New Englanders were not "too great cowards" to fight, and thunderstruck that so many of them had rushed to battle and fought with incredible "daring." The "country is all in arms," he remarked with disbelief. Evelyn immediately prepared his will, choosing to leave his entire estate to Peggie Wright, a family servant to whom he had grown close during his half-pay residency at home, and who had accompanied him to America.[10]

Evelyn's attitude changed further after the Battle of Bunker Hill in June, in which the King's Own sustained heavy casualties. Once again, Evelyn emerged unscathed, but he now called the New England rebels "most dangerous enemies." Every man in Massachusetts between fifteen and fifty was soldiering, he exclaimed in a letter, and he no longer believed that the British army in America was adequate for putting down this "rebellious race" of Yankees. Massive reinforcements were needed, he went on, adding that the British army must take a heartless approach if it was to win this war. London must "lay aside that false humanity" and permit the army to put New England "to waste." With men dying all about him, Evelyn also grew more concerned with his own mortality. "I confess I cannot be without uneasiness" that "an unlucky ball" might someday find him, he remarked.[11]

Evelyn endured several uncomfortable weeks in Boston during the winter of 1775–1776. During part of the time he pulled duty on Bunker Hill, where he and his men slept in tents on the inhospitable ground. Early in 1776 he was sent south with his regiment in an unsuccessful operation to retake Charleston, South Carolina, but he rejoined the main army in July, just in time for the New York campaign. He saw considerable action that summer, and was cheered by the army's successes, though disappointed—or so he declared in the last letter that he wrote before Pell's Point—that the fast and "easy victory" on Long Island, and again at Manhattan, had not fully satisfied his primal, nearly inscrutable "eagerness and impetuosity" for battle.[12]

COLONEL GLOVER, the American commander at Pell's Point, was quite unlike Captain Evelyn. Twelve years older, Glover hailed from a humble background. The son and grandson of house carpenters in Salem, Massachusetts, young Glover had not reached school age when his father died. Thereafter, he and his three brothers were raised by their mother. By late adolescence Glover was earning a living as a shoemaker in Marblehead. He married at age twenty-two in a Congregational church and six months later he was a father. Ten other children followed. In his mid-twenties Glover opened a grog shop, or bar, and with his profits purchased a merchant ship. He made runs to the Caribbean, Spain, and Portugal, and to other British colonies in North America. He gradually acquired a small fleet of vessels, speculated in property, and by the mid-1760s was part of the local gentry. He lived in a large two-story house and was in the habit of wearing only clothing that was fashionable in London.

Like many merchants, Glover would have been adversely affected by Britain's attempted taxation of the colonists and its efforts to tighten its control of American trade outside the empire. But for several years he remained largely aloof from the American protest movement. Not until war approached was Glover's consciousness inflamed. He grew more active politically. Glover had always yearned to improve his status, and for many Americans winning renown as a soldier trumped possessing great wealth. Glover had served as a militiaman in the French and Indian War, rising from ensign to captain, and when Massachusetts reactivated its militia on the eve of the war with Great Britain he was elevated to the rank of lieutenant colonel. But neither Glover nor Marblehead's unit fought on the Concord Road or at Bunker Hill. The men were at sea plying their trade as fishermen. When Glover arrived at last to take part in the siege of Boston, his unit had already been taken into the new Continental army and he was recommissioned a colonel.[13]

Glover's men were mostly white, though some African Americans were in the ranks. They came to war bearing the look more of sailors than soldiers. The enlisted men wore blue jackets with leather buttons, white shirts, tarred breeches —to make them waterproof—blue stockings, and blue caps. The officers dressed all in white. Glover, fashionable as always, marched to New York in 1776 with two broadcloth coats—one trimmed in lace, the other with velvet—eight shirts from Holland, ten jackets, six pairs of trousers, and shoes with silver buckles. He was armed with two silver pistols, a Scottish sword, and a musket fitted with a bayonet made in Genoa. In his mid-forties at the time of Pell's Point, Colonel Glover may have looked more like the popular image of a soldier than did Evelyn. Short, thick, and sinewy, Glover had long, curly, reddish hair that was beginning to thin and gray, a perpetual five o'clock shadow, and a rugged visage that exuded power and authority. For much of the past twenty years he had commanded men on good voyages and bad. He was in the habit of leading, and of acting, under stress. Those who served under him were in the habit of following his direction.[14]

Much about Glover's background and activism suggest that economic self-interest had drawn him toward a role in the American rebellion, although what radiates from his few surviving letters is a vibrant nationalism and a yearning for American autonomy, the very sentiment that Evelyn had immediately sensed as the propulsive force driving the American protest. Glover spoke of the joy to be had in breathing "American Air." Freedom was at stake in this contest, he said repeatedly. The war would determine whether Americans were "freemen or slaves." To be a slave, he said, was "worse than Death." Like Evelyn, his thoughts often turned to death. There was a fatalism in his outlook. "We can but die in Conquering them—which will be dying Gloriously." But he wanted to live. Although he knew the "fate of War is very Uncertain," his dream was to go home "with Life and Laurels," and to live near his children and grandchildren far "from the Noise & Bustle of the World." His maxim was to "not leave too much to Chance." Fight hard, and hope for the best, he said.[15]

THE BRILLIANT MIDDAY SUN stood high in the sky over Pell's Point, transforming the bite of dawn into a comfortable fall day. The British army had moved inland after the exchanges between the rival advance units on Split Rock Road, though considerable time had been required to bring up baggage wagons and field pieces, and to contrive a plan of action. Evelyn and his men drew up near the stone walls where the British army's advance party had charged into an ambush. There they waited for ninety edgy minutes, wondering if the rebels were still behind the walls just ahead, and guessing how many might be hidden behind other walls further inland. Evelyn may have been keen for action, but even grizzled veterans grew anxious at the prospect of coming under fire. As the minutes passed unhurriedly, Evelyn likely spoke reassuringly to his men and, while unruffled, drank repeatedly from his canteen in a vain effort to slake the unquenchable thirst brought on by nerves. Finally, late in the morning, orders to make ready to advance were bawled out in English and German. With a rattle and clamor, thousands of men came to their feet, each lost for an instant in a final moment of reflection before stepping off into the crescendo of battle.

Then the order to advance! Thousands of men, accompanied by horse-drawn artillery, moved in the direction that the enemy was last known to have been deployed. Evelyn and his men were near the van of the British force. They moved ahead through the ragged fields, passing more than one stone wall. With each step the regulars strained for a glimpse of a Continental in his blue makeshift uniform. They saw nothing. They kept moving, advancing twenty-five more yards. Nothing. On they went. Some began to think that the rebels had abandoned the area.

Suddenly, without warning, a line of nearly 250 rebels rose up from behind stone walls only about thirty yards away. They fired in a staggered manner. The Americans to the right opened up, then as they ducked to reload, their brethren to the left, and then those in the center, laid down volleys. The British answered with small arms fire, although the artillery was rapidly brought forward. The cannon belched out a thunderous fire at the Continentals' stone barricade. The Americans got off seven volleys, taking a toll, before they—like the advance guard earlier in the morning—retreated. Just as earlier, the British, with a frightening shout, moved out hurriedly after the fleeing rebels. It was at moments like this that the British were usually at their best. Charge the provincials! Overtake them before they could reload! Fight the untrained Americans at close quarters with bayonets! It seldom was a match.

Evelyn came through the brief firefight in good shape. As the British charged, he was in, or near, the front ranks. He scaled the abandoned makeshift rampart and kept moving across the brown fields until he approached another stone wall. The regulars were going over it. Evelyn, striking in his vivid coat and red breeches, observable to all and clearly discernable as a British officer—the favorite target of the rebels—began to scale it, too. Ordinarily, he could have gotten over the wall quickly and effortlessly, but he was laden with cumbersome equipment. When he was almost over, more rebels raised up from behind still another stone wall not far away. Another entire regiment of Glover's men, about two hundred of them under Colonel William Shepard, a Westfield farmer, were poised with muskets trained on the moving, struggling line of advancing enemy soldiers. An explosive whomp of gunfire sounded.[16]

In an instant, Evelyn was hit, and hit again, and yet again. One bullet grazed his arm, but a second struck the upper part of his left thigh and a third shattered his right leg above the knee. He fell in a tangle at the base of that forsaken wall. Men were falling all about him to the terrible rebel fire, so many that the British broke and, for the second time on this day, retreated.

After the British fell back, another lull ensued for regrouping, a respite that lured out the ravening plunderers among the New England men. A Massachusetts soldier hurried to Evelyn, who lay in pain and shock at the wall. Despite the haze brought on by his wounds, Evelyn must have known that the rebel had not come to help. He would have felt the stranger rifling through his pockets, taking what he could, including possibly letters and keepsakes.[17] In his last seconds of consciousness, in the dusty weeds of a farm in a land far from home, Captain Evelyn must have known that he had lost everything.

The fighting at Pell's Point ended later in the afternoon. The Americans withdrew, yielding the area, but although outnumbered nearly six to one, they had held up the British long enough to permit the Continental army to escape

Manhattan Island. The British had lost nearly two hundred men on that blood-soaked day. The Americans reported only twenty-one men lost, a figure that surely was far too low, though no doubt existed that their losses were considerably fewer than those suffered by their foe.[18]

In the days that followed, Washington lavished praise on the men who had fought at Pell's Point. He spoke of their "merit and good behavior," and lauded Glover's "activity and industry," telling him: "you very well know the duty of a colonel" and "you know how to exact that duty from others."[19] Glover continued to serve and fight long after this engagement. His wife died while he was away with the army and his businesses, and personal finances, suffered from his prolonged absence. With his health deteriorating, the legacy of privation and stress from years spent in the field, Glover left the army in 1782, six years after the bloody fight at Pell's Point, and at last returned home. As he had dreamt, Glover came home a hero. In time, he regained his health and lived on for fifteen years, luxuriating in the life and laurels that he had hoped to enjoy at war's end.

On that bloody day at Pell's Point, Captain Evelyn had lain at the wall for several minutes until British soldiers assigned the gloomy task of finding the dead and wounded gathered him for the long agonizing wagon ride back down Split Rock Road to the beach. From there, Evelyn was taken in a landing barge to a hospital ship off shore, and still later, while his consciousness was obliterated from time to time by pain-numbing drugs, he was taken to an infirmary in Manhattan. The verdict of the army physicians who looked after him was instantaneous. His right leg must be amputated. Evelyn refused. Perhaps he believed that death was preferable to the career-ending loss of a limb. Perhaps he gambled that his doctors were wrong.

On November 6, nineteen days of wracking pain after he was wounded at that stone wall, Captain Evelyn died in Manhattan, overwhelmed by a massive infection. He had spent twenty-nine months in America. He had thought the American war just and necessary, and he had wanted to be part of it. In his final lucid moments, Evelyn perhaps drew some solace from the belief, widespread in British ranks late in 1776, that the American rebellion was on its last leg, and that his sacrifice had been in a winning cause.

Part One
Going to War, 1775–1776

1

"FEAR IS NOT AN AMERICAN ART": THE COMING OF THE WAR

WARFARE was woven into the fabric of life in colonial America. Not everyone was affected equally by war, but hardly any American escaped the sullen impact of hostilities. Wars were frequent, many men soldiered, and many soldiers died. Still other soldiers, the least fortunate in ways, came home from these wars, but not in one piece, physically or mentally. Nor were those who bore arms alone in experiencing the terrors of war. Civilians who dwelled on the exposed frontier in wartime lived with the constant fear of a possible surprise attack. Virtually every citizen in every generation in every colony paid war taxes, endured wartime scarcities, coped with war-induced inflation, and struggled through postwar economic busts. A handful of well-connected officials and businessmen profited handsomely in every conflict from lucrative war contracts. In the century and a half before 1776 it would have been difficult to find anyone born in the English colonies in North America who had not lost a loved one—a son, a father, a brother, a husband—to war. If one was lucky, the loss was temporary, only for a few months during the period of service. But sometimes it was forever.

In many colonies, generation after generation tasted war. Virginians fought four wars with their Indian neighbors during the first seventy-five years of the colony's existence, and after another seventy-five years, when George Washington was a young man in the 1750s, they were still fighting the Native Americans. The Puritans who founded New England went to war with the Indians within seven years of landing at Boston, again forty years later, and four additional times in the next seventy-five years.

Most of the Indian wars occurred because the English colonies expanded remorselessly, again and again encroaching on the Native Americans' lands and way of life. The first war in Virginia was fought over the low-lying region near the Chesapeake. Virginia's last war before the American Revolution was waged for possession of the green, rolling Shenandoah Valley and beyond, two hundred miles or more west of the colony's initial settlements. New England's seventeenth-century soldiers campaigned on the forbidding frontier just beyond the coastal littoral. Their eighteenth-century counterparts fought in the upper reaches of New York and Maine, and in Canada.

A new dimension was added to American warfare late in the seventeenth century. To that point, the Indians alone had been the enemy of the English settlers. Thereafter, Great Britain's wars, which were not infrequent, inexorably spilled across the Atlantic and dragged colonists and Indians alike into their web. On four occasions in the half-century after 1689, Great Britain, together with its American colonists, went to war with France and its American colonists and numerous Indian allies. Spain joined France against Britain in three of those conflicts. But to many English colonists it must have seemed that these intercolonial wars differed only slightly from the earlier wars, as the most visible enemy— sometimes the only foe that was seen—remained the Native Americans. However, these wars differed in at least one significant way from their predecessors. From the 1690s onward European statesmen, in comfortable offices three thousand miles from America, decided when these wars started, when they ended, and, without consulting the colonists (or the Indians), swapped and grabbed American territories in the peace settlements.

The English colonists received no help from London while waging the Indian wars in the seventeenth century. The Crown first sent soldiers to America in 1676, seventy years after the first permanent colony had been planted, and then not to assist with a war but to suppress a rebellion in Virginia. Nor were large armies dispatched to aid the colonists in their first three wars against the French and Spanish, although a royal fleet was sent in 1711 to participate in a joint operation with colonial armies against the French. The English settlers who crossed the Atlantic in the seventeenth and eighteenth centuries may have prayed for peace, but they emigrated with the knowledge that they were entering a world of dark menace where war was likely. Before sailing, the earliest settlers often listened to farewell sermons that warned them to prepare for war, and not infrequently they brought along artillery, specialists who could build gun carriages and search out the alloys and nitrates needed to make ammunition, and professional soldiers to ready them for hostilities.

Many a colony was no more than established before it organized the militia, for centuries the home defense system in England. All able-bodied men between the ages of sixteen and sixty were required to serve in the militia, or trainband as it was sometimes called, which was used in emergencies to safeguard the settled areas. Volunteer armies were raised to take the war to the enemy. Left on their own to fight the Indians, the Americans adapted to the demands of waging war in an untamed wilderness environment and of contending with Native Americans who did not fight according to European traditions. Colonial soldiers rapidly discarded cumbersome armor and pikes, and learned to avoid fighting in the thick, dark forests, where their advantage in firepower was negated. Although the colonial armies did not abandon martial discipline or the tactical concepts that were commonplace in Europe, they added new wrinkles that were not customary in European warfare. The colonists learned how to minimize the chances of an enemy ambush, sometimes employed a hit-and-run style of fighting, often utilized a mobile strategy, and not infrequently adopted terror tactics that included torture; killing women, children, and the elderly; the destruction of Indian villages and food supplies; and summary executions of prisoners or their sale into slavery in faraway lands. In time, warfare in the colonies came to be associated with a manner of fighting that England's career soldiers variously called "irregular war," "bush war," or simply the "American way of war."[1]

The recurrent warfare did not transform the colonies into a militaristic state. No English colony ever resembled ancient Sparta or eighteenth-century Prussia, but societies emerged that made a virtue of soldiering and devoted considerable energy and enterprise to molding warriors. After all, the English colonists fought their wars with armies of citizen soldiers, men who had to be rapidly refashioned to one degree or another from individualistic civilians into soldiers who could follow orders and carry out harsh measures. Throughout the English colonies military officers were exalted. Those who served for a year or two earned the right to ever after be addressed by their military title and deferential neighbors often turned to them as natural leaders in church and civil life. In New England in particular a literature flowered that praised soldiering and sought to infuse young men with qualities that included boldness, heartiness, fortitude, and sobriety, all essential in a good soldier. Young men were to be strong and bold, to renounce indolence and effeminacy. If they succeeded, and if they willingly sacrificed for the greater good and looked on danger with contempt, they were told that they might become "valiant Heroes."[2]

THE BRITISH first committed large armies of regulars to fight in the colonies only in the final intercolonial war, the Seven Years' War, or French and Indian War as it was often called in America, the conflict in which Evelyn and Glover got their initial taste of soldiering. This was the only instance in all these wars when considerable numbers of colonial citizen-soldiers served alongside Britain's professional army. It was not a happy experience for either the regulars or the provincials. The rub was that the British army and the armies raised in the colonies were as different from one another as night is from day. The eighteenth-century British army resembled most European armies of the time. It was a professional force. Officers, who were drawn largely from the aristocracy, customarily entered the army in their teenage years. Enlisted men were drawn from the lower social orders, often choosing a soldier's life because they lacked any other discernable means of support. They, too, made a commitment to soldiering until they were old men. These men were subjected to exacting training and merciless discipline, the object of which was to make soldiers who would unhesitatingly follow orders in the heat and chaos of battle, standing and fighting when every instinct cried out to run for safety.[3]

The armies raised in the colonies in the French and Indian War, like those fielded during earlier American wars, remained armies of amateurs. Only the highest-ranking officers were likely to have had any prior military experience, and not infrequently the field officers were as callow as their men. George Washington, for instance, first entered an army at age twenty-two in 1754, and was named its commander in chief a month later. Virtually none of the men who entered the provincial armies that were raised in the 1750s had ever spent a day in an army, though some had trained a bit with the militia. They served a one-year hitch. Few reenlisted. Whereas the British regulars often had years of training before they experienced combat, colonial soldiers sometimes spent only a few hours on the training field, and few ever grew into hardened and well-ordered soldiers. A disciplinary system existed, but it was not excessive, desertion rates exceeded those in regular units, and it was not unusual for men to break under fire. The redcoat professionals were spit and polish, but the provincial forces usually had a rag-tag look. Few colonial soldiers wore uniforms, they were equipped with a rich variety of weapons, entire units appeared to be ungainly on the parade ground, and the soldiers often looked slovenly and tousled. All this appalled Britain's regular officers, but what they found particularly troubling was the American habit of insisting that their soldiers agreed to a covenant, or contract, upon enlisting. The colonists insisted that they were guaranteed several things when they joined, including prior knowledge of the company in which they would serve and the identity of the company officers, and precisely how long they were to serve. They were very much citizen-soldiers. They never lost sight of the terms to which they had agreed, including above all their designated length of service. They absolutely refused to serve one day longer than required by the covenant.[4]

Some in high places in the British army admonished their officers to try to understand the provincials and harmonize with them. It was easier said than done. More than a few British officers came to look with brusque impatience on the provincial soldiery, disdaining them as misfits when they complained, especially when they objected to being assigned unglamourous—not to mention hard—duties, such as digging emplacements, felling trees, and building roads. Many officers in the regular army threw up their hands in disgust at the colonials, and the highest-ranking British officers were nearly unanimous in their vilification of America's soldiers. They reproached them as "slothful and languid," totally devoid of martial habits and skills, ruinously individualistic, "Obstinate and Ungovernable" to the core, and good for nothing but the sort of manual labor ordinarily expected of "Peasants." Months of frustration led several senior British officers to bluster that the colonial soldiers were the "lowest dregs" of humanity and "the dirtiest most contemptible cowardly dogs" imaginable. Some believed the American officers were no better than the men, and a few blasted America's civilians, chafing at the "horrible roguery and Rascality in the Country people" and complaining angrily that "no one in this country can be relied on." One British officer raged: "I never saw such a sett of people, obstinate and perverse to the last degree." Nor were British generals the only ones who complained. During the French and Indian War many officials in London grew indignant at the lack of cooperation between the colonies. To them, it often seemed, America consisted largely of small-minded officeholders who were blind to larger imperial interests, profiteering American businessmen, merchants who traded with the enemy, colonies that failed to meet the manpower quotas assigned it by royal officials, and provinces that did not adequately supply the Anglo-American armies.[5]

If the regulars were scandalized by the conduct of the provincials, many Americans—who likewise were meeting British officers and observing the regular army for the first time—were similarly dismayed by what they discovered. Many colonials were shocked by the strutting hauteur of Britain's aristocratic officers. John Campbell, Lord Loudoun, the commander of the British army, debouched in New York City in the summer of 1755 accompanied by seventeen servants, a secretary, his mistress and her maid, and four additional hangers-on. The colonists were also sickened by the sight of the brutalities that the redcoat officers visited on their men. The treatment of the regular soldiery went beyond contempt. It sometimes seemed as if someone was scourged daily and some men were sentenced to such horrific beatings—up to a thousand lashes—that they died. Executions were staged with appalling regularity. Scores of regulars were hanged in the course of the French and Indian War, sometimes as many as ten at one time.[6] But it was the British officers' unconcealed insolence and scorn toward their American counterparts that most angered the provincials. When the American soldiers were held out of combat, or assigned invidious duties, such as digging latrines or hauling supplies, many colonists regarded their treatment as contemptible, and some believed that the colonials had been sullied with a second-class status merely because they were colonials.[7] Colonial officers also bristled at British army regulations that recognized the lowest-ranking regular officers as superior to—and outranking—the highest provincial officers.

It was not just a matter of anger. A string of setbacks in the French and Indian War sowed questions in the minds of many colonists about the abilities of the regulars. In 1755 an army under General Edward Braddock, tasked with taking control of the head of the Ohio River, stumbled into a smaller enemy force on the Monongahela River, deep in the dark and remote Pennsylvania interior. Over 900 of the 1,500 men in Braddock's army—including 120 of the 150 Virginia soldiers—were casualties in the battle that ensued. Braddock's debacle inspired a

rigorous post mortem among some of the more thoughtful in the colonies, leading eventually to the widespread belief—and one largely without merit—that
Britain's generals and their men were unprepared for fighting in America in the
face of the "Novelty of an Invisible Enemy."[8] From this, too, came a rising belief
that the colonists were better at soldiering in the American environment.
Washington, who was with Braddock on that horrible day, came close to reaching such a conclusion. He railed at the "cowardice" and "dastardly behavior of
those they called regulars," while extolling the "Virginia troops [who] showed a
good deal of bravery" when they "behavd like men and died like soldiers."[9]

Three years later, almost to the day, another British force suffered even
more appalling losses. An army of regulars and colonists under General James
Abercromby attempted to capture Fort Carillon, a French fortress on Lake
George that guarded access to Canada. Abercromby ordered that the installation
be taken by a frontal assault. A bloodbath resulted. Men were "Cut . . . Down
Like Grass," according to an American private, as they tried to breach an impenetrable obstruction of felled trees with sharpened branches that protected the
French garrison. Abercromby might have used his artillery to destroy the impedi-
ment, but instead he ordered one doomed attack after another. He lost more
than twice the number killed and wounded under Braddock. Such a flawed
performance raised fresh questions about the dismaying capabilities of Britain's
military leaders, and prompted colonial soldiers to crustily comment on
Abercromby's shameful tactics that had resulted in the "injuditious and wanton
Sacrefise of men."[10]

Rancor aplenty was aroused in the colonies by the practices of the British
army. Frontier inhabitants complained bitterly that Britain's army campaigned in
their vicinity only long enough to stir up the Indians before they departed for
other sectors, leaving the settlers unprotected. Anger swelled in the port towns
when the Crown prohibited all trade with the neutral nations that supplied the
French. Residents almost everywhere were riled by the disquieting practices of
royal recruiting officers, whose stock in trade was bamboozling gullible rustics,
often after they were liberally plied with liquor.[11]

Above all else, American indignation crystallized around two aspects of
the martial relationship with the parent state. By the time of the American
Revolution the impression had hardened—before then it appears to have been
more felt than articulated—that London was repeatedly dragging the colonists
into wars that were only peripherally in the interest of the Americans. Thomas
Paine, in his *Common Sense* published in 1776, spoke for many in his time when he
complained that "Great Britain, tends directly to involve this continent in
European wars and quarrels, and set us at variance with nations who would
otherwise seek our friendship, and against whom we have neither anger nor
complaint." Wars were commonplace events in Europe, he added, as it was
so "thickly planted with kingdoms." When hostilities erupted on the Continent,
the colonists at the very least suffered trade disruptions. Usually it was far worse.

War generally came to America, prompting Paine to write that so long as the colonies were tied to Great Britain, no colonist was safe.[12]

It was not just that the colonists felt they were being dragged into wars. The feeling mushroomed in America that Britain ignored the interests of the provincials when peace was made. Nothing pointed to this aspect of the mother country's behavior so much as London's decision in the Peace of Aix-la-Chapelle, which ended King George's War in 1748, to return Louisbourg to France. The news of the treaty struck New England like a bombshell. A New England army had suffered extraordinary losses—nearly a quarter of the entire force—in winning that vital French post. Louisbourg's capture had been viewed as an epic victory throughout New England, and the news of its conquest had touched off a tumult of celebration. New Englanders saw it as the first step toward the subjugation of New France and the ultimate and long-cherished goal of pacifying their bloody frontiers. But without consulting the colonists, Britain's diplomats relinquished Louisbourg at the bargaining table in order to regain territory that it had lost to France within present Belgium. New Englanders felt betrayed, and it was what was seen as knavery of this sort that prompted Paine to subsequently protest that, "America is only a secondary object in the system of British politics. England consults the good of this country no further than it answers her own purpose."[13]

GREAT BRITAIN won the French and Indian War. Indisputably, the colonists had contributed to the triumph in vital ways. In the course of six years the colonies raised armies that, taken collectively, totaled nearly 75,000 men, roughly the number that ordinarily comprised the armies of the major European powers. In the campaign for Quebec in the summer of 1759, the decisive engagement in the American theater during this war, the troops furnished by six northern colonies far exceeded the number of British regulars. Not only had provincial soldiers bled and died, but colonists at home had supplied the armies, built ships, and paid excessive war taxes. When news of the French surrender of Quebec eddied through the colonies that autumn, ecstatic celebrations erupted, especially in the northern provinces. The rapturous citizenry burned festive candles in their windows and great glowing bonfires outdoors. Bells pealed in the large city churches and rang from the weather-worn steeples of small meetinghouses in countless farming hamlets. Sermons of thanksgiving were preached across the land. Militia units gathered in the streets and village greens to parade and to offer up "Rejoicing Fires" with small arms, while both town artillery and guns on ships at anchor in the busy harbors thundered out elated salutes to victory. Fireworks illuminated city skies and joyous concerts were hastily arranged. Many colonists, caught up in the euphoria, wore their patriotism on their sleeve. "I am a BRITON," Benjamin Franklin proudly exclaimed, and many shared his exuberance. Many conceded the help that London had provided, and some contributed to memorials to fallen British heroes or named new towns after imperial leaders.[14]

France—hated France, despised Roman Catholic France—was finished in North America. In the Treaty of Paris it lost everything that it had once claimed on the North American continent, and Spain, which had joined France late in the war, was stripped of Florida. Great Britain—or Anglo-America as the colonists preferred to think—got everything from the Atlantic to the Mississippi River. But it was not just the end of the war, and the prizes that had been secured, that provoked the rapturous mood throughout much of America. It was the belief that the great Anglo-American victory promised peace for the lifetime of the celebrants, and perhaps for their children and grandchildren as well.

Yet the peace that came in 1763 lasted only an instant. War was on the colonists again by 1775. Fittingly, in this land whose history was so stained with war, the next round of hostilities—what would become the War of Independence —arose in part out of the ashes of the previous conflagration.

Britain faced a budget crisis in 1763. Not only had repeated wars left the nation deeply in debt, but, following the peace, the ministry in London resolved to keep several regiments of infantry—some 8,500 men—in newly won Canada and the trans-Appalachian West. Additional revenue had to be found. Parliament imposed heavy taxes on the citizens at home and for the first time it levied duties on the colonists, hoping to raise in America some of the £220,000 needed to support the regulars who occupied the newly won frontier. While an innovation, most in Parliament thought it only proper. The colonies had been founded with British help, many argued, and besides it was fitting that the colonists pay for the regulars who would defend them and open the West to settlement. Others more stridently maintained that taxation was justified in as much as some provincials had traded with the enemy during the late war and several colonies had failed to meet their assigned troop quotas. The ministry meanwhile had a hidden agenda. It wished to tighten its control over the provinces, commencing a more strenuous enforcement of its nearly century-old trade laws and increasing its influence over the imperial administrative machinery and colonial currency.[15]

The Stamp Act, the first direct tax ever levied by Parliament on the colonists, aroused some opposition in England. Some questioned the ministry's premise that in light of all that London had done for the Americans, the provincials should be happy to pay the levy. Colonel Isaac Barré, a British officer who had suffered disfiguring facial wounds in the French and Indian War and now sat in Parliament, told the House of Commons that it was untrue that the colonies had been planted and nurtured by Britain. The Americans, he insisted, had founded and sustained their settlements in the face of the "Cruelties of a Savage foe" and without the least help from London. It was Britain that had been helped by the colonists, he declared, for without the sacrifices of the American "Sons of Liberty" who had "nobly taken up Arms in your defense" in four intercolonial wars Great Britain could never have subdued France.[16]

Barré's rhetoric won few converts in the Commons, but it inspired many Americans. Antitax protestors organized Sons of Liberty chapters and Franklin took up Barré's argument. In testimony before the Commons in 1766 Franklin pointed out that the "Colonies raised, cloathed and paid during the last war, near 25,000 men [annually], and spent many millions." They had also paid taxes "far beyond their abilities, and beyond their [fair] proportion, [and] they went deeply into debt doing this," he added. Franklin even questioned the need for the presence of the British army in the West. The colonists, he said, had a long history of having coped quite successfully with their domestic enemies. "They defended themselves when they were but an handful, and the Indians much more numerous. They continually gained ground, and have driven the Indians over the mountains, without any troops sent to their assistance from this country. . . . There is not the least occasion" to keep a British army in America. The colonists "are very able to defend themselves." To this, he added ominously that the "military force sent into America . . . will not find a rebellion [but] they may indeed make one."[17]

Widespread protests in America caused Britain to repeal the Stamp Act after a year, although in the Townshend Duties and Tea Act Parliament subsequently attempted to levy other taxes on the provincials. The taxes not only stirred American acrimony, they reawakened and helped to shape the anger sown among many provincials during the two final intercolonial wars. Much of the fury and pulsating distrust of Great Britain that welled up among the colonists after 1765 was focused on the presence of the British army, which increasingly was pulled from the West and deployed in the East, especially in New York City and Boston. It was clear to many Americans that the army had been positioned to force compliance with Parliament's taxes. The most radical American newspapers sounded the tocsin about the danger of a standing army, the time-tested cudgel of would-be tyrants, and one claimed that the troops had been left in America to "dragoon" the colonists into "supine submission." Passions warmed even more when London ordered a regiment to Boston in 1768. Zealots in that city, such as Samuel Adams, talked openly of resisting the landing of the king's soldiers with force, but cooler heads prevailed. Nevertheless, Adams published an essay in which he insisted that the colonists' liberties were "threatened with military troops" whose job was to make Americans "the slaves of dirty tools of arbitrary power."[18]

Boston's radicals treated the presence of the British regulars as an "invasion" and a "military occupation." They insisted, too, that the British soldiers would provoke an incident that could be used by the royal officials as a pretext for crushing American dissent by force, and it was not long before an inflammatory event occurred. In March 1770 British soldiers guarding the Customs House fired into an unruly crowd, killing five and wounding several more. The radicals called the incident the Boston Massacre, and turned the bloody event into a propaganda extravaganza. On each anniversary they held a commemorative service, highlighted by the fiery oratory of a radical activist, occasions that over time contributed to the lethal erosion of good will toward the mother country, at least within New England.[19]

Protests against the Tea Act culminated in the Boston Tea Party in December 1773, bringing Anglo-American relations to a boiling point. Parliament retaliated with the Coercive Acts, punitive measures that among other things voided Massachusetts's charter and set the Royal Navy to blockading Boston harbor until restitution was made for the destroyed tea. Simultaneously, the ministry named General Thomas Gage, the commander of the British army in America, to be the royal governor of Massachusetts.

Frederick North, Lord North, headed the British ministry that formulated the Coercive Acts. Forty-two years of age in 1774, North hailed from a family that was neither prominent nor wealthy, though it had been part of the British aristocracy for more than two centuries. A model student at Eton and Oxford, North had been elected to Parliament at age twenty-two. Fifteen years later George III, the monarch, asked him to head the government. North had serious doubts about his capacity for heading a cabinet, an uneasiness that was not entirely misplaced, but he was unable to refuse the king, then or ever. North was bright and agreeable, pleasantly witty, and charming, courteous, and patient. Though rather sophisticated, he was never pompous, and while enough of a politician to fight back, he disliked, and sought to avoid, contention. There was much to praise in North's character and temperament, and in some things

Frederick Lord North, Second Earl of Guilford. Painting by Nathaniel Dance, before 1775. North lacked the qualities of greatness, but he came closer to winning the war than many, including himself, thought possible.

political he excelled—notably his superb skills as a manager of the House of Commons—but the qualities that are often part of the makeup of truly great leaders escaped him. He was not fiery, enthralling, seductive, or overbearing. Nor was there anything in his physical appearance that captivated others. Of average height, North was obese and awkward, and not infrequently disheveled in dress. His eyes were protuberant and according to one observer North suffered a habitual thickness of speech, the result of his "Tongue being too large for his Mouth." Some castigated him as "blubbery North" and one described him as a "great, heavy booby-looking" man. Horace Walpole cruelly portrayed him in the most unflattering terms. His "large prominent eyes rolled to no purpose (for he was utterly short-sighted), while his wide mouth, thick lips, and inflated visage gave him the air of a blind trumpeter."[20] Much of the press found his appointment as prime minister—a title that he disdained—to be astonishing, but he would have few equals in longevity, holding the post for more than a dozen years.[21]

North, who took office in 1770, was never particularly optimistic about finding a peaceful solution to the imperial troubles. "I wish for harmony" with America, he said shortly after coming to power, "but I see no prospect of obtaining it."[22] During his first four years as prime minister, North dealt with the colonies by ignoring them as much as possible, and when the crisis triggered by the Boston Tea Party descended on him, it took him by surprise, as it did most of England. He suddenly found himself at the head of a government that had to make choices that could result in war, though he thought hostilities unlikely. His cabinet appears to have gone about its business with a shrug of its shoulders, giving precious little thought to what it might be getting into. It acted when England was roused to fury by news of the Boston Tea Party, a destructive act that confirmed in the minds of many "the dark designs" of Boston's radicals. It was a moment, according to one observer, when popular opinion "sets sharply against America."[23]

North's ministry proceeded in a measured manner, taking nearly seventy-five days to prepare its response, but from its initial meeting a huge majority believed the time for appeasing the colonists was over and that "effectual steps" must be taken. There were those in London who cautioned that coercion would lead to war—"New England Men . . . will not tamely receive the Yoke. Blood will be shed," it was said—but North and those about him discounted the possibility.[24] To the end, the cabinet believed that the troublesome Americans would back down, a view cultivated by George III, who advised that General Gage had told him that the colonists would "be lyons whilst we are lambs but if we take the resolute part they will be very meek."[25] In the off chance that the colonists did take up arms, the cabinet, drawing on the army's experiences with the provincials in the French and Indian War, doubted that American resistance would pose a serious threat. Some were persuaded of what one official called the colonists' "want of bravery."[26] More believed that as the Americans lacked a professional army, they were doomed to field a "poor species of fighting man."[27] They heard several of their colleagues assure the House of Commons that the colonists "did not possess any of the qualifications necessary to make a good soldier." One ridiculed provincial soldiers by stating that there "was more military prowess in a [native English] militia drummer."[28] None thought it conceivable that the Americans could stand up to the awesome might of the British armed forces, and some perhaps would have agreed with the general that Benjamin Franklin heard exclaim, "with a Thousand British grenadiers, he would undertake to go from one end of America to the other, and geld all the Males, partly by force and partly by a little Coaxing."[29] The colonists were neither united in 1774 nor had much history of cooperating with another, even in the face of danger. On the eve of the last war every colony had rejected the proposed Albany Plan of Union, a plan conceived by Franklin that urged the creation of an American national government to coordinate the military efforts of the thirteen colonies. No province had wished to relinquish even a shred of its authority. Even so, the ministry did what it could in this crisis to forestall unity among the colonies. Although enforcement of the Tea Act had also been prevented in New York City, Philadelphia, and Charleston, as well as in Boston, the Coercive Acts singled out Massachusetts for punishment. If resistance occurred, North's cabinet believed it would be confined to only one region, New England. But the most likely result was that the Americans, fully aware of their impotence, would peacefully submit to Parliament's measures. As North himself put it: "The good of this act is that four or five frigates will do the business without any military force."[30]

The ministers were wrong. The Coercive Acts unified the provinces as had nothing previously. America responded with a Continental Congress that met in Philadelphia in the fall of 1774, and twelve of the thirteen colonies sent delegates. Some congressmen desperately hoped that a peaceful solution to Anglo-American differences might yet be found, perhaps through a compromise settlement. Others wanted to resist the parent state with a national boycott. Many colonists prayed that the show of American unity would induce London to back down. Still others thought war was inescapable, and for them Congress was an essential first step in preparing for war.

The First Continental Congress spurned capitulation and compromise, agreeing instead to a boycott of British imports. It additionally urged each colony to put its militia "upon a proper footing."[31] Some had wanted Congress to go further by assisting the colonies in readying their militia, or even by creating a national army and navy. Such steps were too radical for this assembly. Congress, said John Adams, a delegate from Massachusetts, was "fixed against Hostilities and Ruptures, except they should become absolutely necessary." He believed that most congressmen prayed that their resolute stand would cause Britain to beat a retreat. But if war came, Adams had some idea of what it might mean. Once begun, he predicted, an Anglo-American war would "light up . . . flames . . . through the whole Continent," sparking a conflict that "might rage for twenty years, and End, in the Subduction of America as likely as in her Liberation."[32]

Following Congress's lead, the colonies prepared for war that fall and winter. Massachusetts, the epicenter of the imperial troubles, had launched its preparations even before the Continental Congress met. In September a convention in Worcester called for reviving and reconstituting the militia, a program that was embraced by the colony's Provincial Congress, an extralegal legislature. It directed each town to organize its militia, urged them to begin training immediately, and stipulated that "one-third of the men of their respective towns, between sixteen and sixty years of age, be ready to act at a minute's warning." These "minutemen," it further recommended, "should be immediately equipped with an effective fire arm, bayonet, pouch, knapsack, thirty rounds of cartridges and balls, and that they be disciplined [trained] three times a week, and oftener, as opportunity may offer."[33] Some units were training before the end of the year, and by early 1775 militiamen were also on muddy drill fields in Rhode Island, New Hampshire, Maryland, South Carolina, and Virginia. In Fairfax County, Virginia, the exercises at times were personally supervised by Colonel Washington, who rode over from nearby Mount Vernon.[34]

The most conservative colonists, many of whom would remain loyal to Britain throughout the coming war, were shocked at what was occurring. Many decried military preparedness, warning that the colonists would be no match for the regulars and that defeat would be followed by a punitive peace. The only hope of success, they cautioned, would be with the assistance of France, but that would be worse than defeat, for America would fall under the shadow of the autocratic Catholic monarch in Versailles. European intervention might also produce a stalemated war, which, they admonished, not infrequently ended in a settlement in which the belligerents divided the spoils. Should an Anglo-American war end in the partitioning of America, they warned, Britain might retain some colonies, but others might pass under the jurisdiction of France and Spain.[35]

These fears were quickly answered in print. Charles Lee, who had served for seventeen years in the British army, rising to the rank of lieutenant colonel before leaving the service and moving to Virginia in 1773, was one of many to publish a rebuttal. He ridiculed much of the redcoats' performance in the late war and disparaged their current crop of general officers as "the refuse of an exhausted nation." In contrast, the Americans, he insisted, had given a good account of themselves in the previous war. They knew how to fight in the American environment. Besides, provincial farm boys "are accustomed from their infancy to fire arms." They were also "skillful in the management of the necessary instruments for all military works; such as spades, pickaxes, hatchets, etc." On top of all else, the American soldiery would be "animated in defence of every thing they hold most dear and sacred."[36] Likewise, John Adams authored a series of essays in which he argued that a Britain "sunk in sloth, luxury and corruption" could never subdue "hardy, robust" colonials who had been shaped by a long tradition of "fire and sword." Thomas Jefferson also played on some of these themes in his first publication, a pamphlet that appeared early in 1775. While Britain had been inattentive "to the necessities of [the] people here" during countless wars, the colonists had learned to defend themselves. He added: "fear . . . is not an American art."37

As some Americans drilled and others wrote, the British government made the fateful decision for war. Learning during the summer that the Continental Congress was to meet, North's cabinet had begun moving toward a decision to use force. It was nudged along by the king's conviction, aired to North, that "blows must decide whether they [the colonies] are to be subject to this country or independent." The attorney general also advised that the rebel leaders in Massachusetts had committed treason.38 By late December, aware at last of the defiant actions taken by Congress, the ministers were prepared to issue war orders, but George III stayed their hand temporarily, asking them to reflect on the matter for a month. During January the cabinet spurned proposals by William Legge, Lord Dartmouth, the American secretary, for softer measures and the recommendation of William Pitt, Lord Chatham, to open negotiations with the Continental Congress. The ministry did adopt a plan—it would be known as the North Peace Plan—that would have abandoned parliamentary taxation of America in return for a pledge that the colonials would appropriate sufficient revenue to meet their defense and other governmental responsibilities. The scheme was hooey. For one thing, London would determine the amount of revenue to be raised, and even assign a quota to each province, while the colonists decided only what kind of tax to impose on themselves. Furthermore, it was never intended for resolving imperial woes. North's plan was designed to divide the Americans, as it would give the most conservative colonists what purported to be a ministerial concession onto which to grasp. While the peace plan was readied for public consumption—it was the only step that was revealed to the public—the cabinet agreed to send an additional 3,500 men, four regiments together with several hundred marines. Finally, on January 27, 1775, Dartmouth, at the behest of the North government, directed General Gage to use "a vigorous Exertion of . . . Force" to seize the ringleaders behind the Massachusetts protest, an action that would constitute "a signal for Hostilities." He added that whatever resistance might be offered by the Massachusetts militia "cannot be very formidable."39

The government's decision to use force was hardly unexpected. Already dissenters in London were openly cautioning that an American war might not be easily won. The use of force, some said, would drive the Americans to confederate, creating a union where none had previously existed. Others wondered how effective the Royal Navy would be in its attempt to blockade an American coastline that extended for one thousand miles. One critic warned that 2,000,000 free colonists could raise an army of 100,000 men, more than double the size of Britain's existing army and probably larger than a British force augmented by mercenaries. Several predicted that the war would bankrupt the nation.40 Then there was General Gage himself, who since late summer had been urging his government not to take the Americans lightly. The "Flames of Sedition" have "spread universally throughout the Country," and in particular all New Englanders were "as furious as they are" in Massachusetts, he cautioned. Furthermore, as the colonists were likely to field an army of about 50,000 men in the event of war, Gage told London that the rebellion could be suppressed only by "a very respectable Force" of regulars, including some who were trained in the American way of war. He requested massive reinforcements. He might need 100,000 men, for whole "Provinces shall [have to] be conquered." The "Crisis is indeed an alarming one," he concluded.[41] North's government responded to Gage's prudent advice by considering his removal. He was viewed as a defeatist.

WAR ERUPTED within days after Dartmouth's orders reached Boston. On April 19 Gage put into operation a plan with twin objectives. He sent out a force of nine hundred men to capture John Hancock and Samuel Adams, two of the principal provocateurs who were thought to be in Lexington, about a dozen miles northwest of Boston. The detachment was then to proceed to Concord, five or six miles further west, and destroy an arsenal that contained stocks of rebel weaponry and powder. Gage had not hit on these targets randomly. Not only had his intelligence network passed along good information, but he understood that speed and surprise were essential to the success of the operation. Gage's plan was to set his troops in motion before midnight, complete the operation in Concord by 8:00 a.m., and have his force safely back in Boston by noon, well before multitudes of minutemen could respond.[42] Unfortunately for Gage and his troops, the popular movement also possessed a good spy network, and it had prior knowledge of the British commander's intentions. The colonists may have divined Gage's design through loose lips, or they may simply have guessed correctly by piecing together numerous shards of intelligence that were being gathered daily. An hour or so before midnight on April 18, while the sleepy British soldiers who were to undertake the mission were pulling on their heavy wool uniforms and gathering their arms, Paul Revere and other dispatch riders set out from Boston to alert Lexington and Concord, and other towns throughout the hinterland.

Fortune smiled on the colonists, for on this night the regulars did not move with haste. The men that Gage had selected—a combination of light infantry and grenadiers, the elite of the redcoat army—set out before midnight, marching to Boston's Back Bay, where the navy was to transport them across the Charles River. But Gage's best-laid plans were bollixed. The navy had brought too few boats, and what should have been a brief operation turned into an interminable wait for the shivering men. Hours were lost. It was two in the morning on this moonlit night before the last man was across the river. Gage's dream of haste and surprise had been fatally compromised. Two hours before the regulars marched, Revere—astride Brown Beauty, the fastest mount that could be found for him— had reached Lexington with his dismaying tidings. As the militiamen gathered, Hancock and Samuel Adams, who were indeed lodging in the hamlet, fled to safety. Even as the bell in the village's tall, white meetinghouse tower vibrantly sounded the alarm, Revere sped off in the brooding darkness to warn Concord, leaving behind a beehive of activity. The tolling of Lexington's bell had not only summoned the town's sleepy citizen-soldiers, it set off local dispatch riders to arouse those in nearby towns so that they could start their minutemen toward Concord.

First light came at 4:00 a.m. on this historic day. Thirty minutes later, with streaks of orange and purple visible in the eastern sky, an advance party—six companies totaling 238 men—reached Lexington Common, where they found about 60 men, a portion of a single company of the Lexington militia. The colonials were citizen-soldiers. Most were dairy farmers. A few were craftsmen. To Major John Pitcairn of the Royal Marines, a fifty-three-year-old Scotsman and no-nonsense veteran officer who commanded the lead element of regulars, they appeared to be nothing so much as a motley collection of troublemakers. Wasting no time, Pitcairn briskly approached the provincial commander, Captain John Parker, a tall, weather-beaten forty-six-year-old farmer who had experienced some combat in the previous war. Pitcairn did not exchange pleasantries. "Lay down your arms, you damned rebels," he curtly demanded. Parker never hesitated. He wanted no part of leading a heavily outnumbered force in the treasonous act of killing the king's soldiers. He commanded his men to step aside, although he did not direct them to surrender their weapons. Not one man laid down his arms.

At this anxious moment, in the half-light of daybreak, someone squeezed off a shot. No one ever knew who fired that first shot. It might have been a nervous soldier or an overly zealous man on either side. Some said later that the shooter might even have been a radical hothead hidden behind a nearby stone wall. Although there is no way to know whether the shot was fired by accident or design, what is apparent is that once the shot rang out, several jittery regulars and white-faced militiamen instinctively fired. Some got off more than one shot. Others never discharged their weapon. That was especially true of the militiamen, most of whom immediately broke and ran for their lives. A few got only a step or two before they were shot down. Some of the wounded were bayoneted where they lay, killed by regulars now caught up in a frenzy of passion. The incident was over within thirty to forty seconds, but within that space eight colonists had been killed and nine others wounded. One regular, a private, had been hit, but not fatally.

When order was at last restored and the regulars had secured Lexington Common, they began the search for Hancock and Adams. It was futile, of course, but it consumed time, prompting several regular officers—who now knew that dispatch riders were alerting the countryside—to urge Lieutenant Colonel Francis Smith, whom Gage had placed in charge of the operation, to call off the march to Concord. Smith refused, although he sent Gage a request for reinforcements. At length—around 9:00 a.m. on that sun-soft spring day—the regulars set off once again for Concord. They met no resistance along the way or when they entered the village. The Concord militia had long since mustered, and minutemen from the surrounding area had joined them, but, like their counterparts in Lexington, they were heavily outnumbered. They took up a position on the field where for the past several weeks Concord's militiamen had assembled for their training exercises, a site across the North Bridge, which spanned the Concord River, and nearly a half-mile from the heart of the village. They neither interfered with the grenadiers who set to work destroying the arsenal in town nor attempted to stop a large party of redcoats that crossed the North Bridge, marching toward a suspected second magazine roughly a mile from the center of town.

The British found little in either supply depot, as most of Concord's stores had been transferred elsewhere following an alert from Boston's radical leaders two weeks earlier, but the regulars destroyed what ordnance they found. As they spiked artillery and tossed powder into the nearby river, ever more militiamen from outlying communities, farmers and artisans for the most part, arrived in Concord not to defend an American union—nothing of the sort really existed— but to defend their province, Massachusetts, against what they believed to be the malevolent intentions of a far-off imperial government. All were under the command of Colonel James Barrett, a sixty-four-year-old miller who was the head of Concord's militia. Barrett took up arms that day wearing an old coat and leather apron, as if it was any other workday. By mid-morning, pressure built on Barrett to do something, but he was no more eager than Captain Parker to order the shooting of British regulars, especially not with a force that throughout the morning remained numerically inferior to that of the regulars. Barrett forestalled the men under him until about 11:00 a.m., when smoke from the center of Concord was seen curling above the bare trees.

Colonel Barrett could wait no longer, for it appeared as if the regulars were torching the village, though in reality they were burning wooden gun carriages found in the arsenal. Barrett ordered the men to load their weapons and marched them toward the North Bridge. There, they found 115 regular infantry posted on the opposite side in order to secure the road into town. These British soldiers were scattered and relaxing, but as the Americans approached they hastily assembled. The Americans were tense and excited as they advanced. The regulars were just as anxious. As the Americans moved forward, a shot rang out, this time unmistakably fired by a regular, either in panic or by accident. No command to fire had been given, but when that gunshot sounded, trigger-happy British soldiers immediately fired their weapons. Then, at last, the British commander gave the order to fire, and the regulars unleashed a volley. Incredibly, not a single shot had been fired by the allegedly undisciplined militiamen, who continued to advance on the bridge. Only when men began to fall did Barrett give the order to return fire, and the militiamen unloosed their own volley. Twelve regulars were hit, three fatally. Outnumbered perhaps five to one, the regulars—like the militiamen at Lexington—broke and ran.

Colonel Smith hurriedly secured his position and took no further casualties in Concord, but he had seen enough. Besides, he had wreaked about all the damage that he could inflict on the arsenal. Precisely at noon he ordered his beleaguered men, who had already marched eighteen miles or more, performed strenuous physical labor in destroying the magazine, and been party to two firefights, to start back to Boston, a trek that in the eyes of many militiamen was "a dishonarebel Retret."[43]

All along the narrow Concord Road—after this day it would be called Battle Road—a steadily growing number of militiamen gathered in the course of the next few hours. By early afternoon more than a thousand provincial soldiers were present, giving the Americans numerical superiority for the first time all day. They included Captain Parker and the Lexington militia, now 120 strong and no longer reluctant to kill the king's soldiers. A large contingent massed at Meriam's Corner, about a mile east of Concord, but down the road other men hid behind unpainted barns and leafless trees, and crouched low behind ragged, brown haystacks and thick stone walls. The provincials waged an American war, repeatedly ambushing the regulars, and with deadly effect, as they laid down a crossfire on their prey. It was all the worse, Gage subsequently explained, because the regulars "were so fatigued with their March" that they could not adequately "keep out their Flanking Parties" that might have flushed out the Americans who lay in wait.[44]

The regulars had sustained heavy casualties by the time they reached Lexington, where they found the reinforcements that Smith had summoned, but worse was to come. At Lexington, what had until then been a largely disjointed, almost vigilante, corps of colonial militia was organized into a martial force with a plan. The men came under the command of General William Heath, an affluent Roxbury farmer, who conceived the idea of sending out skirmishers to envelop the regulars who were seeking to muscle their way home by marching in a square formation. The rebels "knew too well what was proper to do," one British officer later remarked. Captain Evelyn, in the thick of it from Lexington back to Boston, said he was "under one incessant fire" for fourteen miles. Forty of his comrades from the King's Own were casualties. The heaviest fighting all day, and the greatest number of casualties, occurred at Menotomy, about half way between Lexington and Boston. The fighting raged throughout the afternoon, with losses piling up on both sides. Civilians as well as soldiers died, usually when the regulars stormed their homes, believing (often justly) that the inhabitants had acted as partisans, shooting from their windows at the passing British soldiers. One minuteman entered a house to find bodies everywhere. The "Blud was half over [my] Shoes," he said.[45] The carnage ended only when the sun sank and the weary regulars, some of whom had marched nearly forty miles on this harsh day, stumbled into Boston in the starry darkness.[46]

Gage's most hellish nightmare had come true. Ninety-four colonists lay dead, wounded, or missing. The regulars had suffered 65 dead and 207 wounded or missing, one-third the number that had set out from Boston some eighteen hours earlier. With studied understatement, Gage said that his men had been "a good deal pressed" by the Americans, who had descended on them with "Surprizing Expedition."[47] Lord Hugh Percy, the thirty-two-year-old veteran who had commanded the reinforcements and perhaps saved the entirety of Gage's original force, remarked at the close of the long day's fighting that he had never imagined that citizen-soldiers could display "the perseverance" that the New Englanders had exhibited. Like Captain Evelyn, Percy had learned something from the day's events. Anyone who expected a New England army to be "an irregular mob," he said, "will find himself much mistaken."[48]

That night every leader and every soldier, and the civilians along the way who had witnessed the carnage, and sometimes had fallen victim to the fury of the regulars, knew that the day's events had changed their world forever.

2

"A LOSS THAT IS GREATER THAN WE CAN BEAR": GOING TO WAR

Two months had passed since the bloody day along Battle Road. It was June 14, and in sweltering Philadelphia John Adams wished to address the Continental Congress on an urgent matter. Rising from his chair, Adams took the floor in the stuffy Pennsylvania State House and told Congress that he wished to nominate a man to command an American army, a soldier who was "modest and virtuous, . . . generous and brave." He sits "among Us and [is] very well known to all of Us," Adams went on, "a Gentleman whose Skill and Experience as an Officer, whose independent fortune, great Talents and excellent universal Character [will] commend the Approbation of all America and unite . . . all the Colonies better than any other Person in the Union." That man was Colonel Washington of Virginia.[1]

Much had occurred between the day of fighting outside Boston and Adams's speech. The Massachusetts militia had swelled to twelve regiments in the course of that bloody April 19. During the rainy night that followed, militiamen poured steadily into the outskirts of the city, the sense of adventure and importance strong with them. Many came considerable distances in a surprisingly short time, as was the case with the minutemen from Nottingham, New Hampshire, who claimed to have covered fifty-five miles on foot in twenty hours. The next morning, gray and chilly, the redcoats awakened to discover that they were besieged by a vast American army. Over the next few days the siege army, or Grand American Army, as some called it, grew to nearly 16,000 men.[2]

Actually, there was not one siege army, but four separate armies in place, stretching in a serpentine arc from Chelsea, northeast of Boston, through

Cambridge, to the north and west, and on to Roxbury on the southwest side of the city. One army was from Massachusetts, and New Hampshire, Rhode Island, and Connecticut had each sent an army. As each army took its orders from its legislature, it seemed at times as if no one was really in charge. However, General Artemas Ward was the ranking officer in Massachusetts and the armies were on Massachusetts soil. He was supposed to be in command.

A forty-seven-year-old native of Shrewsbury, Ward had earned two degrees from Harvard. He had taught and farmed, and held a variety of offices, including judicial posts in his hometown and for twenty years a seat in the Massachusetts assembly. Ward had soldiered in the French and Indian War, and in 1758 his regiment had been part of Abercromby's misbegotten assault on Fort Carillon. While Ward escaped unhurt in that engagement, his health suffered lasting ill effects from months in the field. Sick and bedfast on April 19, he had missed the action on Battle Road, but the following day he gingerly pulled himself atop his horse and made a painful thirty-mile ride to the environs of Boston to take command of his colony's army, a post to which the Provincial Congress had appointed him in February.[3] He had not been given wide authority. Leery of any army, and any commander of any army, the Provincial Congress, through its Committee of Safety, set up shop in Cambridge and, under the leadership of Dr. Joseph Warren, a young Boston physician and firebrand, ran the siege operation.[4]

Some one thousand Rhode Islanders were in camp, roughly two-thirds the number the colony had promised. Their commander was General Nathanael Greene, a thirty-three-year-old Quaker iron-master who had never experienced combat and, indeed, had never even been part of a military unit before the previous autumn. In the frenzy that gripped New England during the fall of 1774, he had enlisted as a private in a company that called itself the Kentish Guards. Six months later, in the aftermath of Lexington and Concord, the Rhode Island assembly created the Army of Observation and named Greene its commander, jumping him over several veteran officers. His appointment smacked of politics. Greene not only was close to Samuel Ward, a member of Continental Congress and powerful figure in the colony, but he was also a member of the Rhode Island assembly and his brother held seats both in the legislature and on the province's Committee of Safety.[5]

Connecticut, which had mobilized a quarter of its men of military age, sent four thousand of them to Boston. Nearly half went home after a few days. Those who stayed were commanded by Joseph Spencer, a sixty-year-old East Haddam magistrate and former assemblyman who had fought the French in two wars. A second brigadier general in Connecticut's army, Israel Putnam, was better known and more respected as a soldier. "Old Put," as he was called, was a fifty-seven-year-old fireplug of a man, five feet six inches tall, wide, thick, and muscular with a face, according to one writer, that resembled "a cherubic bulldog mounted on a jaw cut like a block of wood." In the French and Indian War he had served with Rogers' Rangers, a unit skilled in bush warfare, and on scores of

General Israel Putnam. Graphite on paper, by Colonel John Trumbull, date unknown. Although an extraordinary leader of men in battle, Washington concluded by late 1776 that Putnam lacked the administrative talent and strategic insights necessary to be a successful general. His role in the war diminished from 1777 onward, and ended entirely following a debilitating stroke several years into the conflict.

occasions Putnam had come under fire. Once the Indians captured him and beat him mercilessly and would have burned him at the stake had he not been saved by the timely arrival of a French officer. Putnam was one of the few English colonists who continued to serve after Canada was taken in 1760, eventually seeing combat in Havana. Accounts of Putnam's many exploits, some more or less true, others noticeably embroidered, circulated widely, making him a folk hero throughout New England. A man with little formal education, Putnam in peacetime farmed in Pomfret, Connecticut. He was sodbusting on April 19 when the alarm reached his village. He literally dropped his plow, mounted his horse, collected his minutemen, and headed for Concord, which he reached at sunrise on the day after the battle. The next day he was present for General Ward's initial council of war in Cambridge.[6]

New Hampshire furnished 1,200 men, half the number it had promised. They were led by John Stark, a forty-seven-year-old veteran of the French and Indian War. Born on the frontier to parents who had emigrated from Londonderry, Stark, like Putnam, was tough and fearless, the sort who caused others to sense that they were in the presence of a dangerous individual. He, too, had served with Rogers' Rangers, rising to the rank of captain and so impressing the British regulars that they offered him a commission if he would stay in the army after Canada was taken. He declined and returned to New Hampshire, where he built a sawmill on the Merrimac River.[7]

The siege army was only hours old when Ward assumed command. He immediately faced daunting problems, though finding adequate amounts of food—a chronic headache for nearly every other American commander in the years that followed—caused Ward little trouble. Each of the four armies had its own supply system, chiefly for importing comestibles from interior farming hamlets. They supplemented their stores by seizing livestock and other goods from Tories who lived nearby.[8] Ward devised ways for apportioning the victuals, and he also managed with a fair degree of success to find tents, utensils, entrenching tools, and medical supplies. Ward had the men swear to an oath that compelled them to serve until late in the year, arranged a swap of prisoners, and quickly sent out reconnoitering parties to determine suitable locations for constructing breastworks.[9]

While the improvised army coped as well as it could, it was beset with insoluble difficulties. The Massachusetts Provincial Congress thought 30,000 men were needed to conduct the siege, but the army never had more than half that number. There was also an appalling shortage of arms, artillery, and ammunition. Nor did anyone know where the revenue would come from to pay the soldiers, especially if this became a lengthy siege. Illness broke out, too, and with so many men living in close proximity it quickly reached epidemic proportions. In no time, half or more of the men in some units were unfit for duty. To a considerable degree the camp disease resulted from a lack of discipline. This was a jerry-built army that literally had come together overnight, and it was composed more of citizens than soldiers. The middle- and lower-grade officers, almost to a man, were devoid of military experience, and the company level officers were in command of neighbors and chums from home. Not a few enlisted men looked on this as the adventure of a lifetime, a chance to play soldier for a while and to escape the tedium of farming or toiling at the workbench. Following orders—especially when given by an old friend—was not a high priority among these men.[10]

In the face of mounting problems, both the leaders of the Massachusetts Provincial Congress and various general officers importuned the Continental Congress for assistance. Some said that the army was shot through with inept officers, particularly at the company and battalion levels, which rendered it "[in]capable of perfect regulation." Some even cautioned that it could not be long before the undisciplined soldiery turned into an armed mob that plundered civilians. Others warned that the siege army could not be kept together indefinitely, either because the yeomen could not afford to be gone from their farms for too long, or because the New England colonies lacked the resources to sustain the army. The solution, several told Congress, was the establishment of "a Continental army of which this will be only a part," and early in May a radical activist from Plymouth urged John Adams to see to the appointment of Colonel Washington and Charles Lee "at the Head of it."[11]

Congress had been moving in that direction, albeit gropingly, since it reconvened a couple of weeks after Lexington and Concord. The congressmen knew the country was committed to war. En route to Philadelphia, many had found that "a good Spirit" prevailed, and newspapers throughout the land were reporting that men "every where [were] learning the use of arms." Virginia and South Carolina, like the four New England colonies during the previous autumn, had gone beyond the mere reorganization of their militia—which was all they had been asked to do by Congress—and created provincial armies. Within days of reassembling in May, Congress recommended that the other seven provinces take similar steps.[12]

Nevertheless, Congress did not act immediately when Virginia's Richard Henry Lee proposed in mid-May that a national army be created. Adams said that such a "vast Multitude of Objects . . . press and crowd Us so fast that we know not what to do first," but in reality much time was consumed in a protracted debate over a proposal—pushed by the most conservative members of Congress—to petition the king, expressing American loyalty and asking him to intervene and resolve the dispute. The more radical delegates not only dismissed the idea that George III would override North's government as wishful thinking, but feared that the supplication would make America look weak and timorous. Yet to maintain unity they reluctantly consented to the Olive Branch Petition, as the peace offering to the monarch was called. But while the contest over the petition played out, military matters kept intruding, and Congress never entirely ignored the war. It responded to Lee's motion by creating a committee to look into securing military supplies and agreed to borrow £6,000 to purchase powder. A few days later, when rumors reached Philadelphia—they were untrue, it turned out—that Gage planned to reinforce the regulars posted in New York City, Congress urged that colony to raise a three-thousand-man army, though it was to act only defensively.[13]

That last step had hardly been taken when Congress learned that Connecticut and Massachusetts not only had acted offensively, the two provinces had, without an invitation, mounted operations on the soil of a neighboring colony. The two New England colonies had authorized a strike at Fort Ticonderoga, where Lake Champlain met Lake George in New York. This was the very installation that General Abercromby, with disastrous results, had tried to take from the French, who had called it Fort Carillon. Connecticut gave the job to Ethan Allen, the leader of a band of frontier vigilantes called the Green Mountain Boys. Massachusetts put Colonel Benedict Arnold in charge of its force. Each commander was surprised to find the other at the target site, but they more or less cooperated in an attack on May 9. As Allen and Arnold and their 250 men burst into the installation, they discovered that the post was defended by only 45 mostly over-age regulars. They took Ticonderoga bloodlessly in "the name of the great Jehovah, and the Continental Congress," or so Allen purportedly exclaimed to the startled British commander. Bristling with energy, Allen followed up by taking the British fort at Crown Point, further north in the Champlain Valley. A bit later Arnold captured the small British fleet at St. Johns, even further north on the Richelieu River. Ticonderoga and Crown Point yielded a treasure trove to the arms-starved Americans: seventy-eight serviceable cannon, six mortars, three howitzers, thousands of cannonballs, eighteen thousand pounds of musket balls, and thirty thousand flints.[14]

Congress was at once delighted and appalled. As happy as it was to get its hands on the weaponry, it understood that nothing could pose a greater threat to the nascent American union than for a colony, on its own initiative, to dispatch an army across its neighbor's border. Just as troubling was word that Colonel Arnold, buoyed by his string of successes, proposed to invade Canada, declaring that he would forfeit his life, if necessary, to take Montreal and Quebec.[15] Congress immediately nixed his proposition. Only a few weeks into the war, most in Congress had come to see that a centralized control over the provinces had to be established, lest the volatile forces that had been unleashed on April 19 spin fatally out of control. Furthermore, Congress, a body drawn almost exclusively from the colonial elite, wanted to wage this war with an army modeled along the lines of Europe's rigidly hierarchical armies, the sort of military organization that would symbolize, and help to sustain, the existing social distinctions that most congressmen thought essential to a well-ordered society.[16]

This motley mix of factors laid the groundwork for the creation of a national army, a step that finally took place on June 14 when Congress agreed to raise troops for "the American Continental army." Once that vote was taken, Adams was immediately on his feet in the stifling chamber to nominate Washington to be its commander. Adams knew that many congressmen were especially eager to put a non-New Englander in charge of the army. Some, such as Connecticut's Eliphalet Dyer, believed they were anxious lest "an Enterprizing eastern New England Genll proving Successful, might with his Victorious Army give law to the Southern & Western Gentry." Adams more correctly suspected that they simply wished to advance their own sectional interests. Whatever, he understood that a recommendation to replace Massachusetts's Artemas Ward as the commander of the siege army would carry more weight if it came from a representative of the Bay Colony.[17]

Washington, a Virginia congressman who had none too subtly been attending Congress in the uniform he had worn during the French and Indian War, excused himself so that his colleagues could discuss the matter fully and frankly. Apparently they did just that, deliberating for the remainder of that day and part of the next. No record has survived of what was said, but there was some opposition to Adams's motion. It likely arose not so much from concern about any shortcomings of Washington as from uneasiness over whether New England's soldiers—who were the only men in the army at the time—would follow a non-New England commander.[18] There may also have been some concern over whether trouble would ensue in Massachusetts should General Ward be displaced. Much time was probably consumed, too, in questioning the Virginia delegation about Washington's background, military record, character, and temperament.

The son of a wealthy planter-businessman, Washington had started life with a promising future, but when barely into adolescence his chances of ascendancy were dealt a serious blow. His father died from one of the virulent fevers that stalked the Chesapeake. Not only was young Washington denied the education provided to his older brothers (he may have had only a year or two of formal schooling), the lion's share of his father's estate went to his senior male siblings. George inherited little more than a few slaves and a spent farm in Fredericksburg, sufficient for local prominence, but without wealth or education he was unlikely to ever be an important figure in Virginia. Young Washington was ambitious, and especially so once he grew close to his older half-brother Lawrence. Educated in London and an officer in an American regiment that served with the British army in the Caribbean and in South America during an intercolonial war in the early 1740s, Lawrence eventually came home to Mount Vernon, which he had inherited, and married into the Fairfax family, the wealthiest clan in Northern Virginia. Starting around 1744, when he was twelve, George visited Mount Vernon at every possible opportunity. There, and at the Fairfax family mansion, George beheld a world he had never before seen, including homes crowded with luxury goods and inhabited by powerful and urbane men and women who were deferred to by their social inferiors. Young Washington wanted that for himself, and he chose the most promising paths toward those ends. At age sixteen he became a surveyor, a career that, with luck, could lead to the slow accumulation of land, and wealth. But young Washington was in a hurry, and soldiering—as Lawrence had demonstrated—could lead to immediate renown.

With another round of British-French warfare on the horizon in 1753, Washington, at age twenty-one, volunteered to carry a message from Virginia's governor, Robert Dinwiddie, to the French deep in Indian territory above the head of the Ohio River. It was an arduous and dangerous mission, one that Washington barely survived, and it won praise from the governor. The next year, when Virginia created an army to send to the Ohio Country, Dinwiddie named Washington to be its second in command, though he was virtually devoid of military experience. When the commander of the Virginia Regiment died in an accident a few weeks later, Washington, at age twenty-two, succeeded him, and he held the post for the better part of five grim and dangerous years. When the Ohio Country was won for Great Britain, Washington, now acclaimed a hero in Virginia, left the army at the end of 1758 and took the one remaining step needed to complete his dizzying arc of ascent within his colony. He married Martha Custis, the wealthiest widow in Virginia. He now possessed Mount Vernon (as Lawrence, tragically, had died of tuberculosis), considerable acreage elsewhere, and scores of slaves. In the fifteen years that followed, he sat in the Virginia assembly and succeeded to a remarkable degree as a planter-businessman. In the late 1760s Washington began to take an active role in the Virginia protest movement against Britain's new colonial policies, and the provincial assembly named him as one of its seven delegates to the Continental Congresses that met in 1774 and again the following May.

At age forty-three in 1775, Washington remained an imposing figure. Twenty years earlier, his aide-de-camp in the Virginia Regiment had described him as powerfully built, with broad-shoulders and a narrow waist. He had filled out as he grew older, but otherwise not much had changed. At a time when the median height of native-born adult males in the colonies was about five feet seven inches, Washington towered over most men, standing about six feet three inches. A few years later, at age fifty, he weighed a trim 209 pounds, suggesting that he was considerably more svelte than he appears to be in numerous wartime paintings. His hair remained light brown and, except for formal occasions, he never powdered it. He combed it straight back without a part, and tied it in a ponytail, a conventional style of the day. His eyes were a striking blue-gray and his skin was fair and sunburned easily. His face was slightly pockmarked as a result of an adolescent bout with smallpox. Some teeth were missing and others were disfigured, likely the result of a gum disease, and to compensate he wore primitive dentures. Many remarked on his agility as an equestrian, a sign of athleticism in that age, and not a few were struck by the supple grace and fluidity of his ordinary movements.[19]

Washington was not an outgoing man, especially when surrounded by the likes of his colleagues in Congress, virtually all of whom were college graduates and many were lawyers. Probably at an early age, he had found it safer to listen and learn, particularly when in the company of better educated, more cosmopolitan sorts. That taciturn manner had become an ingrained habit by middle age. His public demeanor was one of gravitas. Some thought him cold, and to be sure he could be aloof. Abigail Adams, John's wife, who first met Washington later that year, described him as a man of "dignity which forbids familiarity." It was likely a strategy that he adopted early on, a ploy to keep others at arm's length in order to hide what he feared were his weaknesses. Few ever got close to him, and in the real sense of the word Washington may never have had a true friend. Rather, he tended to look on others in terms of their usefulness to him. If Washington sought to hide his liabilities, he carefully exhibited what he saw as his strengths, his astounding physique, incredible physical prowess, sobriety, deliberate habits, and remarkable self-control. He also worked hard to win the assent of others. He could be charming, although he is seldom remembered for that characteristic. For the most part, people tended to see him as hardy, resolute, energetic, fair-minded, prudent, steady, and above all crowned with success. Women, around whom he appears to have felt more comfortable than with most men, often saw another side to him. Abigail Adams, for instance, in the very remark in which she mentioned Washington's redoubtable formality, also noted his "easy affability which creates love and reverence."[20]

Washington was unmistakably tenacious and courageous, and an iron-hard ruggedness shined through the patina of genteel cultivation that he had gradually acquired. It set him apart from most other men. He had soldiered for five years, often facing supreme danger. Much was known about his brave exploits. His euphoric remark, uttered during the French and Indian War, about having "heard . . . Bullets whistle and believe me there was something charming in the sound," had gotten into the newspapers and was remembered. Most observers were probably also aware that two horses had been shot from beneath Washington during Braddock's battle on the Monongahela in 1755, and that his shirt and hat had been riddled with bullets in that engagement. It was commonly known, too, that some British regulars with whom he had served in that war had praised Washington's valor under fire. Years later, the painter Gilbert Stuart put best what many discerned in Washington. With his artist's eye for divining character, Stuart thought Washington's features were "indicative of the strongest and most ungovernable passions." Had Washington been born in nature, Stuart added, "he would have been the fiercest man among the savages."[21]

The congressmen who considered him to lead the Continental army may have sensed, or heard from the Virginia delegates, that Washington had learned much about himself in the course of years of soldiering. He had discovered that he could cope with mortal danger, that he relished adventure, and that he could endure hardship. Washington had additionally found that he was capable of making difficult decisions and of taking charge of other men, including officers who were often older and more experienced soldiers. He had also learned to mold an army. Seeking to model the Virginia Regiment on those in Europe, young Washington had imposed a harsh discipline on his men, and in time he succeeded in transforming civilians into obedient soldiers. Nor was any detail too small for his attention; Washington attended to pay, promotions, provisions, housing, hygiene, and countless other matters that were essential to the smooth operation of an army, and its morale. Washington not only made the Virginia Regiment into a reasonably good provincial force, but in the process, as historian Edward Lengel has observed, he matured "both as a leader and as a man," discovering that more could be accomplished "by working through subordinates or political back channels than . . . through petulance or bluster." When Washington left the Virginia Regiment his officers signed a memorial that praised his fairness, sagacity, sensitivity, personable manner, and courage, and also lauded how he had "train'd us up" to be better leaders.[22]

If the congressmen probed into Washington's performance during the French and Indian War, they would have discovered that he had made mistakes. He had often been absent from his army, visiting friends, looking for land to purchase, taking fencing lessons, and chasing after a commission in the British army. He had been burned by those derelictions when an anonymous Virginia newspaper essayist took him to task as an immature martinet under whose leadership the Old Dominion's army had suffered heavy losses and scored no significant victories. Washington's greatest blunder had been to antagonize Governor Dinwiddie. Washington had hectored him mercilessly about pay, inadequate supplies, too few troops, and the unreliability of the militia, but he crossed the line when he not only questioned Dinwiddie's strategy, but appealed over his head to friends in the Virginia assembly in the hope of forcing the governor to change course. The outraged chief executive, who had been Washington's patron, had berated his young colonel, charging him with ingratitude. Washington, ordinarily not one to acknowledge his errors, had admitted that he had "foibles, and perhaps many of them."[23] But Washington had been young and inexperienced during that earlier war, his colleagues in the Virginia delegation likely told Congress, and they might have added—for it was quite true—that he was introspective and likely had learned from his mistakes.

Some in Congress may have been troubled that Washington had never commanded an army in a conventional European-style engagement against an army of regulars. He had spent the French and Indian War bush fighting against Indians. But Washington had learned from that experience, and he may have said as much to some of his colleagues. He had discovered that five hundred Indians could tie down five thousand English soldiers, he said once, and he had come to admire the Indians' ability to use the environment to great advantage.[24] Washington had also learned much from the time he spent with British regulars in that war. He had served at headquarters on Braddock's staff as an unpaid, unranked volunteer in 1755, and three years later, when the Virginia Regiment was brought under the command of General John Forbes, he once again got a close-up look at the British army. In each instance Washington not only had seen how a large European army was organized and administered, he had met several British officers, including Thomas Gage, at the time a lieutenant colonel who had seen promise in the young provincial officer. Some of the regulars had shared their military manuals with Washington, his introduction to the guidebooks that were essential reading for aspiring European officers.[25] Above all, Washington had discovered that the British army was far from perfect and its soldiers were not supermen.[26]

How much of this was divulged to Congress by Washington's fellow Virginians cannot be known, but they almost certainly stressed how Washington had prospered as a planter and businessman through study and rumination, a willingness to take risks, and the successful management of a considerable body of workers at Mount Vernon. Many congressmen from outside Virginia had already taken the measure of Washington through what amounted to subtle interviews. In conversations over tea and wine, their object had been to divine his character and to determine whether he could be trusted with an army. He passed their test. They found that he was not a social revolutionary. He was the model of virtue, no "harum Starum ranting Swearing fellow," said one congressman, "but Sober, steady, and Calm." It is likely that every member of the Massachusetts delegation had fastened on Washington to lead the American army prior to setting out for Philadelphia a month earlier, and they were the ones who took the lead in finally securing his appointment on June 15 "to command all the continental forces, raised, or to be raised, for the defense of American liberty."[27]

General Thomas Gage. Oil on canvas mounted on masonite, by John Singleton Copley, c. 1768.
Commander of the British army in America, Gage gave the order to march on Concord on April 19,
1775, and to attack the rebels on Bunker Hill two months later.

The following day Washington spoke to Congress. He felt unequal to the
task, he said, but pledged to do his best. He also declined a salary, asking only that
he be compensated at war's end for his expenses. A few days later, in a public statement, Washington acknowledged that civilian authority must always be superior
to the military.[28] What he said was in keeping with the rhetoric of republican
virtue, about which much had been heard from the American protest movement
in recent years. The social character of the American people, many radical activists
had been saying, was simple and sacrificial, and characterized by a willingness to
put the common good above individual interests.[29] Washington understood the
republican ethos, and from his first days as commander sought to embody it. No
leader ever got off on a better footing. Even a London newspaper applauded his
virtue and wished for a few such "disinterested patriots" in the British army.[30]

Washington's selection was the easy part. Congress turned next to the vexing
matter of appointing the other general officers in the Continental army. It set out
to name eight additional officers—two major generals, an adjutant general, and
five brigadier generals. Filling three of the slots was effortless. One of the major
general positions went to Artemas Ward, and Washington went to bat for two

General Charles Lee. Engraving by A. H. Ritchie after a caricature by Barham Rushbrooke.
Lee was the personification of tragedy, a talented general whose flawed personality drove him to
self-destruction.

men, Charles Lee and Horatio Gates. Both were former officers in the British
army whom he had met while serving with Braddock, and both had moved to
Virginia after resigning their commissions. Congress went along without dissent,
in part because the new commander wanted them, but also because each could
bring needed skills to the formation of the new army.

Lee, who was the same age as Washington, had an impressive background.
He had a good education and a first-rate mind, which he had put to use with years
of rigorous study in military theory and tactics. He had served in the British army
for nearly two decades, seeing considerable action, and suffering wounds in the
Fort Carillon disaster. When Britain's army was sharply reduced following the
Peace of Paris, Lee retired on an officer's half-pay pension and headed for eastern
Europe as a soldier of fortune. By the time he returned to England in 1770, he had
come to sympathize with the plight of the colonists. Three years later he revisited
America and never left, living on land that he purchased in western Virginia. As
war clouds gathered in 1774, he paid visits to those who might help him find a

General Horatio Gates. Painting by Charles Willson Peale, from life, 1782. The hero of Saratoga, but a failure later in the southern theater, Gates was neither as good a general as his many New England supporters imagined, nor as bad as he was presented as being by those who had hitched their wagons to Washington's star.

military role should hostilities occur. He was in Philadelphia when the First Congress met and at year's end he spent five days at Mount Vernon. Tall and wafer thin, with a pinched and homely face, Lee was given to quirky behavior. He was habitually unkempt, slovenly even, and voluble. Opinionated and prone to ceaseless monologues, he also never learned to curb his penchant for delivering a searing riposte. Lee had never married and insisted that he preferred dogs to most people. He spoke "the language of doggism," Lee said, adding that he found canines attractive because, unlike many people, they were neither bigoted nor inclined to put their "convenience, pleasure, and dignity" ahead of his. He traveled everywhere with his pack of dogs and seldom hesitated to foist them on others. "He is a queer creature," John Adams said of him, and Lee would have been the first to agree. He once confessed to his sister that in his "cooler candid moments" he understood that "my deportment must disgust and shock." Yet, if Adams thought Lee was given to "Whim and Eccentricity," he also thought him the "best qualified" of all the general officers and certain to "do great service in our army," particularly "at the beginning of things, by forming it to order, skill, and discipline." Adams' colleagues concurred. With Lee's record speaking for itself, Congress named him the second major general.[31]

Gates was appointed adjutant general, with the rank of brigadier general. Whereas Lee's ancestry had been distinguished, Gates came from the ranks of commoners. Wishing a career in the British army, he gained the assistance of well-connected aristocrats who employed his mother and who secured his appointment as an officer. He served for nearly fifteen years, virtually all of them in North America, and often in staff positions. He had risen to the rank of major before leaving the peacetime army that was cutting back after 1763. He embraced political radicalism, longing for sweeping reforms in domestic England and supporting the colonists in the on-going Anglo-American clashes through the 1760s. In 1772 he wrote to Washington about land in Virginia, and with his assistance Gates acquired a modest country estate some fifty miles west of Mount Vernon (and near Lee's tract). Gates was strikingly different from Lee. Less well educated, Gates was married and a devoted father. He was polite, friendly, and mild-mannered. Like Lee, Gates was ambitious and eager to soldier again, and he took pains in 1774 to let influential colonists, including Washington, whom he visited, know that he was available should war erupt. Both Washington and Congress believed that the new army could draw on his administrative experience.[32]

Things got stickier once these appointments were made. Connecticut and New York squawked loudly at not having gotten to name one of their own as a major general, and after two days of wrangling Congress mollified both by creating two more positions of that rank than it had originally intended, commissioning Israel Putnam and Philip Schuyler. The background of the latter was similar in many ways to that of Washington. Essentially the same age, Schuyler came from the New York aristocracy, lived on a large country estate, speculated heavily in frontier land, was a conservative assemblyman, had soldiered for five years in the French and Indian War, and was a member of Congress. The New York delegates spoke admiringly of his courage, prudence, perceptivity, thoughtfulness, and attention to detail. They said that he possessed some engineering skills, and they mentioned that he was habitually well prepared.[33]

Congress also bowed to pressure in choosing the brigadier generals, selecting three more than originally planned, and ultimately agreeing to tie the number of officers allotted to each colony to the number of men to be contributed by the various provinces. Under this arrangement, Massachusetts secured three slots (Seth Pomeroy, William Heath, and John Thomas) and Connecticut two (David Wooster and Joseph Spencer), while Rhode Island, New York, and New Hampshire were given one apiece—Nathanael Greene, Richard Montgomery, and John Sullivan, respectively. It had not been a pretty business, and John Adams remarked that nothing that Congress had undertaken had caused him "more anxiety" or frustration.[34] Although content with some of the appointees, he correctly suspected that many owed their selection to politics rather than to a reasoned and scrupulous attempt to find the best-qualified men. It was not the best start for a congress that was asking the citizenry to make republican sacrifices for the common good.

Some American generals—George McClellan and Fighting Joe Hooker in the Civil War come to mind—have swaggered and filled the air with braggadocio upon assuming command. Washington was cut from different cloth. He was reserved by nature and, if not given to self-effacement, had a habit of dissembling both about his ambition and his suitability for coping with monumental challenges. But when Washington acknowledged that he was "Imbarked on a tempestuous Ocean," and wondered anxiously if he was up to the demands that he would face, he was free of pretense.[35] His successes during five previous years of soldiering had been few and modest. The only thing that he knew for certain in June 1775 was that he faced vexatious uncertainties—about the new union, the new army, and the new officers, of whom he felt confident only about Lee and Gates.

Washington remained in Philadelphia for several days following his selection, doubtless wishing to hear what was said about those being considered as general officers, and perhaps hoping for some input as Congress established several civilian administrative positions relating to the army. During those days, Congress allotted Washington an aide-de-camp and a secretary, and he selected two young Philadelphians for those positions. He named Thomas Mifflin, a successful businessmen and former member of Congress, as his aide and Joseph Reed, a lawyer who had graduated from Princeton, to be his secretary. Congress also created a Northern Department, nationalizing the force it had directed New York to raise three weeks earlier, and named Schuyler its commander. That army was to guard the Canadian frontier while Washington was occupied with the siege of Boston.[36]

A thousand and one matters having been seen to, Washington at last was ready to depart for the front. Just after sunrise on June 23, he and his entourage gathered before the State House. Reed and Mifflin were there, as were Schuyler and Lee, the latter having returned to Philadelphia to lobby yet again, if need be, for an important post. Most of the congressmen were there as well. The ceremony, if that is what it was, was simple. Goodbyes were said and heartfelt wishes of good luck expressed. The soldiers mounted horses and fell in behind the Philadelphia militia and a small martial band. After a handful of congressmen boarded carriages, all set off, the band playing valiantly, though its music could barely be heard above the great clatter the procession made as it moved over the city's cobblestone streets. At the city's edge, the congressmen turned back, while the soldiers shifted from horseback to more comfortable carriages for their long ride northward into an incalculable future.[37]

THE MASSACHUSETTS AUTHORITIES, including General Ward, were unaware of what had transpired in Philadelphia. Likewise, the last news that Washington and Congress had from Boston was more than a week old, the time it took for a dispatch rider to make the run between the two cities. Near dusk on the day prior to Washington's departure, Congress learned of large battles in Boston at Bunker Hill and Dorchester Point on June 17, but it was a sketchy account, and some discounted it, as numerous false reports of bloody encounters had reached Philadelphia during the past six weeks. Yet this one had a ring of authenticity. "God send us a good acco[un]t," the president of Congress wrote to Ward. "We are anxious," he added.[38]

Congress would learn, and Washington would discover in the course of his journey, that a great battle had been fought on June 17 at Bunker Hill near Boston, though not at Dorchester. Early in May, Ward had received intelligence—erroneous it turned out—that British regulars planned to occupy both Charlestown Heights, rolling farmland situated on a narrow peninsula across the Charles River from Boston, and Dorchester Heights, more or less similar terrain south of the city. Both sites were crucial, as each commanded the city's harbor. Ward at once dispatched parties to scout both locations. He received a recommendation to construct breastworks atop the heights at Charlestown immediately. Commanders within the siege army divided on the recommendation. Putnam wanted to act, hoping that it would draw the redcoats out of Boston and into an engagement that he believed the colonists could win. Ward and the Massachusetts Provincial Congress doubted that the siege army could hold the heights, given the state of their organization—some said disorganization—and shortages of arms, artillery, and powder. Putnam, angry and defiant, rashly marched most of Connecticut's men up and down Bunker Hill on May 13 in plain view of the British, vainly trying to provoke action. He failed. Gage was unprepared to act. All that Old Put accomplished was to provoke the Massachusetts authorities to try to rein him in.

A week passed, then two, then a month. But in mid-June fresh intelligence, which was accurate, reported that Gage planned to occupy the Charlestown Heights on the night of June 18. Even so, Ward remained reluctant to fortify the place. He worried that by shifting units to the heights, the center of the American siege lines due west of Boston would be fatally weakened. If Gage only planned a feint at the heights, and instead attacked the center of the American position, his regulars might break through and envelope one wing of the siege army. Ward also worried that if the rebels occupied the Charlestown peninsula, Gage might mount a joint land-sea operation to cut off the Americans' lone exit—the isthmus, or Charlestown Neck—dooming all on the heights. But the decision was out of Ward's hands. The Massachusetts Committee of Safety was calling the shots and it wished to fortify the peninsula. On June 15 it readied the soldiery for marching, ordered the inhabitants of nearby towns to give—actually to sell—their firearms and grubbing tools to the siege army, a step that netted 1,065 muskets and nearly 800 spades and pickaxes, and directed that Bunker Hill be "securely kept and defended." The following day Ward ordered Colonel William Prescott to begin construction of fortifications on Bunker Hill.[39]

Prescott looked like a soldier and was very much a warrior. He had served in armies raised by Massachusetts in the two previous wars, enlisting as a rifleman in King George's War and as a junior-grade officer in the French and Indian War.

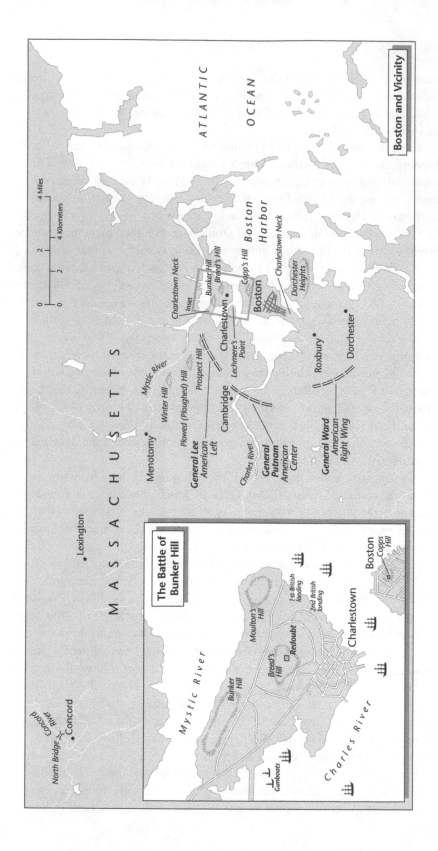

Boston and Vicinity

ATLANTIC

OCEAN

Boston Harbor

MASSACHUSETTS

Mystic River

Winter Hill

Plowed (Ploughed) Hill

Prospect Hill

General Lee
American
Left

Menotomy

Cambridge

Charles River

**General
Putnam
American
Center**

Lechmere's
Point

Charlestown

Roxbury

General Ward
American
Right Wing

Dorchester

Charlestown Neck

Bunker Hill

Breed's Hill

Copp's Hill

Boston

Charlestown Neck

Dorchester
Heights

Inset

0   2   4 Miles

0   2   4 Kilometers

Lexington

North Bridge

Concord

Concord River

**The Battle of
Bunker Hill**

Mystic River

Bunker
Hill

Moulton's
Hill

Breed's
Hill   Redoubt

1st British
landing

2nd British
landing

Charlestown

Charles River

Gunboats

Boston

Copps
Hill

Like John Stark, Prescott had impressed his redcoat superiors, who offered him a commission in the regular army, but he, too, declined and returned home to Pepperel to farm. Though deep into middle age by 1775—he was forty-nine—Prescott remained a trim and muscular six-footer, and in the course of the preparedness campaign he had been appointed a colonel in command of a regiment of minutemen.

When Ward ordered Prescott up Bunker Hill, he gave him nearly 1,200 men. Prescott assembled them on the Common in Cambridge, where they heard a homily and prayer offered by the president of Harvard College. When the long shadows of evening gathered, Prescott started his men on a silent march toward the Charlestown Heights. As the Bay Colony soldiers approached Charlestown Neck, Putnam met them with roughly 250 men from Connecticut's army. Leaving some to guard the water's edge, Prescott took the bulk of his men to the summit of this tall ground on the peninsula. Prescott and Putnam looked over the terrain, and may have argued about where to begin digging. Prescott's orders were to construct a redoubt on Bunker Hill. Putnam preferred Breed's Hill. Though lower—it was seventy-five feet tall, while Bunker Hill rose thirty-five feet higher—it was nearer to Boston and its harbor, could be more readily seen from Boston, and thus was virtually certain to elicit a response from Gage.[40] The latter site was chosen.

It was midnight before work on the redoubt commenced. By the time the sun rose on June 17 the hearty New Englanders had constructed a four-sided, square redoubt—each side was 136 feet long—with a redan, a pointed or angular protrusion, on the southwest side. The ground had been excavated at the base of the rampart, which made the walls tall and steep. The dirt from that excavation was then utilized for the construction of a breastwork, a thick earthen wall six feet high that extended out some fifty yards on the east side of the redoubt.[41]

It was impossible for hundreds of men wielding picks and shovels to work quietly, and in the course of the night a British patrol detected, and reported, their activity. Not long passed before British warships in the Charles began to bombard the hilltop. At roughly the same moment, Gage was awakened and alerted to the work in progress. He summoned several officers for talks. Most urged immediate preparations for a dawn assault. Gage demurred. He preferred to wait for daybreak so that he might better take stock of the colonists' installation. He would then plan accordingly. The British generals presumably returned to a fitful sleep, though sometime after sunrise Gage called them to a formal council of war. It came to a decision after a spirited discussion. General Henry Clinton, who had won acclaim for his soldiering in Germany during the Seven Year's War, and who had just arrived in America, urged what Ward most feared: the immediate dispatch of a naval-land force to seize Charlestown Neck. Clinton argued that taking the neck and mercilessly bombarding the heights would result in a bloodless conquest. General William Howe, who had accompanied Clinton on the ocean crossing to Massachusetts, dissented. He recommended a frontal

The Honorable Sir William Howe. Engraving, London, 1780. From Washington Irving's *Life of Washington*, volume 3, part 1, between pages 82 and 83. Commander of the British army in North America between 1775–1778, Howe proved to be more hazardous than Washington to Great Britain's cause.

assault. Gage chose the course recommended by Howe. According to Clinton's later recollection, Gage not only was cocksure, he was inclined to ignore anyone who was devoid of experience in fighting in America.[42]

Gage's decision speaks volumes about the thinking of the British command at the outset of the war. His decision to assault the rebel installation, which almost surely was supported by a majority in the council of war, reflected the regulars' disdain for America's untrained soldiers. The leadership of the British army simply could not imagine that an army of tatterdemalion farmers and workers would stand and fight against advancing regulars. Many in the officer corps, such as Captain Evelyn, also craved the opportunity to thrash the Yankee troublemakers who had killed their comrades on Battle Road a few weeks earlier. But more than contempt and revenge shaped Gage's decision. He and many of his generals believed that regaining "the respect, and control, and subordination" of the colonials could be achieved by establishing the "idea that trained troops are invincible against any numbers or any position of undisciplined rabble."[43] In other words, the humiliation of the citizen-soldiers on Bunker Hill would demonstrate the folly of making war against the king's professional soldiers and break the resistance movement throughout America. Gage may also have had very personal reasons for choosing this course. He need not have been clairvoyant to know that some in London thought him weak-kneed for repeatedly emphasizing the need for reinforcements, and he must have also presumed that the ministry would not be happy when it learned the outcome of his operation against Concord. Gage may have sought redemption through an assault on Bunker Hill.

The lack of speed with which the British responded to the rebels' takeover of Bunker Hill was an augury of things to come. Whereas Gage was aware of what was afoot well before sunrise, the decision to attack was not made until four hours after dawn. Another five hours passed before the first regulars stepped ashore on the Charlestown peninsula, and yet another ninety minutes elapsed before they marched into action. The Americans capitalized on the nearly twelve-hour reprieve, using the time for additional entrenching. As the morning slowly ebbed away and Ward saw no evidence that Gage was planning a feint, he also brought up two regiments of New Hampshire troops and four additional Massachusetts regiments to augment those already in place on the heights.[44]

Gage gave responsibility for the attack to General Howe, forty-six years old and a veteran with twenty years service. Six feet in height, bulky, burly, and swarthy, with a mouth that had "fallen in" from the loss of numerous teeth, Howe looked and carried himself like a soldier. He maintained an air of inscrutability, though he was widely respected as a man of stout common sense. Howe hailed from a family with such close ties to the crown that he had been raised at court, where he was the companion of young George III. Howe had entered the army at age sixteen and was a lieutenant colonel well before he turned thirty, in part because of his privileged position, but more as a result of his bravery under fire and his skills as a tactician. General James Wolfe had commended Howe for valor in the Louisbourg campaign in 1758 and the next year gave him responsibility for the daring—and successful—landing on the Heights of Abraham during the Quebec campaign. Howe spent the interwar years at home sitting in Parliament, where as a moderate Whig he had opposed the American policies of several ministries, including that of Lord North. When war clouds gathered in 1774, Howe advocated a policy of conciliation toward the colonies, even telling his constituents that he did not believe the British army could conquer the Americans. He had said that he would refuse a command in America, but in the end he agreed to come when the king urged him to do so. He also knew that the unpopular Gage was running on borrowed time, raising the possibility that he might someday gain command of Britain's army in America.[45]

Howe was given 2,300 infantry for the operation on Charlestown Heights. He fed his men lunch before marching them through the streets of Boston to the waterfront, where they boarded barges and rowed across the eight-hundred-yard-wide Charles River. They moved in full view of numerous spectators gathered on Beacon Hill to observe the spectacle, and as they crossed the river the redcoats were onlookers themselves to the navy's shelling of Charlestown. It was an operation that many rebel soldiers believed was carried out so that the enemy could "attack us under the cover of the smoke from the burning houses." Actually, the bombardment was designed to flush out snipers and sow terror.[46] The town, which consisted almost solely of wooden houses and shops, was engulfed by a spectacular blaze, and at day's end one New England soldier raged that the "merciless Dogs" had left Charlestown "a heap of Ruin with nothing standing but a heap of Chimneys."[47]

The British infantrymen, wearing heavy wool uniforms and weighted down with equipment, were wedged into their amphibious craft. Each man carried a canvas knapsack crammed with a three-day supply of food and topped with a rolled grey blanket. Strapped to each man was a canteen, a haversack for personal items, including a cup, tools for cleaning his weapon, a scabbard filled with a two-pound bayonet, and a cartouche, or cartridge, box. So heavy was all this equipment, according to historian Richard Ketchum, that it was akin to having "carried a good-sized deer on their backs." Each man was additionally outfitted with a smoothbore, muzzle-loading musket popularly known as the Brown Bess, after its dark-hued walnut stock. The weapon was four feet, nine inches long, weighed twelve pounds, and fired a ball that was three-quarters of an inch in diameter (.75 caliber). Loading and firing the weapon was such an involved, time-consuming process that a well-trained soldier, who practiced the procedure endlessly, could get off no more than four shots in a minute. Hitting a target was not a sure thing. Muskets were notoriously inaccurate above fifty yards, which doubtless led to the saying among British soldiers at the time that "it took a man's weight in bullets to kill him." That said, muskets were lethal at close range, a fact that led rival infantry units on European battlefields to fight on open ground and at close quarters. Soldiers did not take aim. The muskets were not fitted with a rear sight and the men were simply ordered to "level muskets," whereupon they pointed their weapons in the direction of the enemy. The thinking of the day was that a massed fire might blow a hole in the adversary's lines, or cause him to waver, and that either eventuality could be exploited by a bayonet charge.[48] (That was precisely what Captain Evelyn and his men would attempt at Pell's Point.)

The redcoats landed unopposed near the southeast corner of the somewhat pear-shaped peninsula. The burning village was about two thousand yards down the beach to their left, while directly ahead lay sloping, treeless, farm land that was intersected here and there by rail fences and low stone walls. Up the rise, the grass remained uncut, and in places rose nearly to waist-high levels. The redoubt stood roughly five hundred yards upgrade, situated near the center of the peninsula. The tall earthworks extended to the British right, ending roughly one hundred yards short of the Mystic River. Howe was aware that rebel snipers were posted in and around Charlestown on his left, crouching behind trees or hidden in houses, barns, and farm outbuildings, particularly in the northeastern sector of the village, which remained largely intact. Howe also knew that some entrenched colonial soldiers were posted between the town and the redoubt, and that on his right some American units were in position beyond and above the breastworks. Most of these men, clad in homespun and wearing the same wide, floppy wool hats that they donned to protect them from the sun when they plowed and hoed their fields, lay behind an improvised shield made, according to one witness, from "strong railing taken from the fences and stuffed with hay." Others knelt behind a hastily built stone wall near the water's edge. From intelligence reports, Howe also knew that this sector, the American left, had been the last area to be occupied, from which he surmised that it was the least-well fortified on the field. That, he decided, was where his first blow would fall.

Howe personally took charge of the British right that was to assault the rebels' left flank. He took about 1,100 men and gave the remainder, nearly 1,200, to General Robert Pigot, a veteran officer who was assigned responsibility for attacking the redoubt. Howe expected his men to launch the onslaught, break-through, and get behind the doomed Americans at the very moment that Pigot assailed the American left and center.

Up the hill, Stark with five hundred men and two artillery pieces awaited Howe on the American left. To their right, between them and the breastworks, and ensconced in fleches—two-sided, V-shaped entrenchments—were fifty to seventy men, positioned so that Howe's force would be subjected to a fire from three sides—front, right, and left. Posted at the other end of the rebel lines, between Charlestown and the redoubt, were another seventy-five or so men from Connecticut, who were to pour small arms fire into the advancing red line of enemy soldiers. In the center, under Prescott—though Putnam was present, too—stood most of the American soldiery who would fight on this day. There may have been 1,500 men here, roughly 300 in the redoubt, the remainder behind the breastworks. Most were from Massachusetts, but many were from Connecticut. Eight artillery pieces had been hauled to this sector.

Howe made two crucial decisions before ordering the advance. He might have avoided the assault on the American left altogether. With the luxury of naval superiority, he could have ordered gondolas, or floating batteries, to proceed up the Mystic River and open a point-blank shelling of the lines commanded by Stark. If he ever considered the option, he rejected it, but, noting that the siege army was "pouring in all the strength they could collect," he asked Gage to send over reinforcements, just in case they might be needed later in the day.[49]

Leaders on both sides addressed their men in the last minutes before the battle, a ritual incantation to boost spirits and staunch fears. Earlier in the day, after a man in the area of the redoubt was decapitated in the bombardment, Colonel Prescott had climbed atop the parapet and walked about, pretending to inspect the site. He knew that he was an inviting target, but he hoped that his fearless example would buck up the others. Now, seeing that the enemy was about to move out, he told the men at the summit that the regulars would never reach them if they followed his orders throughout the engagement.

Throughout the war many American soldiers spoke of the terror of the last seconds prior to combat. One soldier exquisitely called it the "awful pause." Many soldiers in many wars have recollected on this gut-wrenching moment, a time when, they feared, death was tapping them on the shoulder. Nearly all remembered the wait for battle as "a seeming eternity . . . of . . . supremely agonizing suspense" when they "broke out in a cold sweat," their "stomach was tied in knots," and they "had a lump in their throat and only swallowed with great difficulty," their "knees nearly buckled," nausea swept over them, and they feared their "bladder would surely empty itself." Above all else, many thought it "seemed unreal" that they found themselves in such perilous circumstances.

Just after 3:00, on what had become an uncomfortably hot afternoon, the redcoats at last stepped off. Trouble surfaced immediately. Not only was it nearly impossible for the grenadiers to move the artillery through the swampy terrain at the foot of the peninsula, but they had been furnished with the wrong size cannon balls. Still, Howe ordered the advance to proceed without artillery. The regulars moved out again, this time in an atmosphere of eerie silence, as the British naval bombardment had been suspended for fear of hitting their own men. The light infantry, advancing across level terrain near the edge of the Mystic River, closed more quickly than the grenadiers to their left. At three hundred yards no one on either side fired. Nor at two hundred yards. Behind the stone wall and rail fence, the colonial officers from New Hampshire and Connecticut reminded their men to aim low, as muskets tended to fire high. "Aim at the handsome coats," one cried out.[50] At one hundred yards the colonials still held their fire. And they did not break and run, as the British high command had expected. Perhaps the New England soldier was correct who noted in his journal, "our Men ant Scart at trifles."[51]

When the regulars were at fifty yards, and near the point where they would deploy and charge, the Americans opened fire. The volley blew apart the redcoats' line. When the back rows stepped into the breach, they, too, were cut down by the salvos that followed. What the British were attempting, wrote historian Christopher Ward, was akin to "pushing a wax candle against a red-hot plane."[52] Lead units disintegrated. Men fell where they had stood. Others were driven backward or were spun around by the force of the shot that struck them, and some toppled mortally wounded into the nearby water. Still, the regulars regrouped and came again, and again, stumbling over their fallen comrades. But they, too, were stopped with heavy losses. Finally seeing the futility of it, the officers ordered a fallback. It was only the beginning of a savage battle, one that many veteran regular officers later characterized as the sharpest they had ever experienced.[53]

Hard on the heels of this bloody rebuff, Howe readied the British lines further to the left for the attack on the redoubt. He resolved to go forward, despite the failure of the flank attack. He took about thirty minutes to regroup, plugging in the remnants of the battered light infantry and grenadiers, men who had just walked into hell and were being ordered to do so again. Finally, all was ready. The scarlet line started forward unhurriedly. Some Americans, accustomed to fighting Indians, were struck by—and in subsequent days commented on—the regulars "very slow march." Burdened with their equipage, the British soldiers plodded through the tall grass and with great effort clambered over fences that they found to be too stout to push down.

As the regulars drew to within three hundred yards, they came under attack from the artillery on the summit, a shelling "which did so much mischief," a British survivor later said.[54] At two hundred yards they walked into crossfire from the snipers and riflemen on their left and, less accurately, from those on their right who had not been taken out in the initial assault. One regular later said that the Americans nearly "picked us all off." When the regulars drew to within one hundred yards of the redoubt, they surmounted the last fence. The rebels in the redoubt had been told not to fire until the redcoats were within twenty-five yards, but now, before the enemy could charge with fixed bayonets, first one, then another, then several nervous and overanxious militiamen fired. The officers screamed at them to hold their fire. This time they prevailed. The small arms fire ceased. The regulars moved closer, and closer. When the redcoats approached to within twenty-five yards the order to fire was given at last. A regular who survived described the volley as having resembled "a continual sheet of lightening," with a deafening roar like "an uninterrupted peal of thunder."[55] The official account of the Royal Marines acknowledged that the blast "staggered the assailants."[56] The regulars made excellent targets. Many Americans aimed at the point where their foe's bright, white shoulder belts crossed in the middle of the men's chests. Some men deliberately picked out officers, and one who fell was Major Pitcairn, who had tried to disarm the militiamen on Lexington Green two months before. Hit with four rounds, he was carried dying from the field by his son, a young officer.[57] Howe was in the midst of it, but emerged unscathed, though all about him men fell, including two on his staff (in the course of day, every man on his staff would be killed or wounded). Howe was startled, and briefly immobilized. Later he confessed that the carnage gave him "*a Moment that I never felt before.*"[58] While he could not have known the toll precisely—it appears that more than two hundred men had fallen in a few murderous minutes at this grim spot—Howe did know that the losses were staggering. He halted the attempt to advance, pulling his men back several hundred yards below the redoubt. They "retreated with a quicker step then they came up," one rebel soldier noted.[59] Not only did Howe have to regroup once again, he summoned yet more reinforcements.

Some of Howe's subordinates pleaded with him not to attack again. He did not listen. More than anyone, save for Gage, he was responsible for the tactics that the regulars had employed, and he held intransigently to what he had recommended earlier in the day in the serene environment of headquarters.

While Howe was making up his mind, Prescott was exhorting his men to make one last stand. If they did so, it would be over, he promised, for if repulsed yet again, the regulars would have no more fight left in them.

A long, uneasy lull set in as the British awaited reinforcements. Men on both sides tried to relax, though with death all around and the knowledge that more was to come, most were overstrung. At length, more redcoats disembarked from barges, this time squarely at the bottom of the peninsula. They grouped and marched to join their comrades on the slope above, seeing—and hearing as they drew nearer—the havoc that had been wreaked. Bodies were everywhere. The tall green grass was streaked with blood. The wounded could be heard crying, pleading, for water, for help, for life. When the fresh men reached their comrades, the officers placed them in the proper order for another assault. At last, Howe was ready. He now had four infantry regiments and a battalion of marines under his command. Deep in the afternoon, Howe for the third time gave the order to move out.

As before, the scarlet-coated line came under attack at three hundred yards, raked again by crossfire and the American artillery ahead and above. The American officers inside the redoubt once again directed the men to hold their fire, and Prescott allegedly shouted in a steady voice: "Men, you are all marksmen; do not any of you fire until you can see the whites of their eyes." That would be when the redcoats were only about twenty-five yards away. Every man was low on powder, and some had only one round left. Prescott and Putnam opened artillery cartridges and distributed that powder to the beleaguered men.[60]

When the advancing regulars drew to within twenty-five yards, the beginning of the end commenced. The Americans opened up. Some fired their last ball and fled, but others, picking up nails or pieces of iron, and ramming those objects into their muskets, stayed and fired again, and yet again. This time the redcoats kept coming. Suddenly they were on the rebels, even around them, as men from one British regiment hurried in a run to flank the west wall of the redoubt. Now it was an unequal fight for the Americans. The regulars still had ammunition, and bayonets. The Americans had neither, but they used their muskets as cudgels, and according to one regular they fought "more like Devils than Men." For many, the redoubt quickly turned into a den of death, as sword-wielding officers cut them down. One young American officer saw many of his comrades "wounded [and] weltering in their Blood." ("I never had such a tremor come over me before," he added.)[61] Some rebels got out, only to be shot before they took more than two or three steps. Others were gunned down further along in their flight. This was the fate of Dr. Warren, the leader of Massachusetts's Provincial Congress, who had spent at least a part of the engagement in the redoubt, and was fatally shot as he raced toward Charlestown Neck. Still others made it to safety in the rear, though some had horrific wounds. A soldier who was ordered to help the wounded from the boats that had carried them away from the hill noted that he and his comrades "were obliged to bail the blood out of them like water."[62] But, aside for those in the redoubt, most rebels who fought that day escaped unharmed. Even a considerable number in the redoubt survived because, as luck would have it, the regulars burst in from three sides at once, causing them to hold their fire for fear of hitting one another. The American soldiers raced down the hill, and, though "Balls flew like Hailstones" about their heads, as one soldier later remembered, most were beyond the range of the redcoats' muskets.[63]

At last, it was over. More than three hours after it began, the shooting stopped. After a momentary breather, the surviving regulars were set to transporting the wounded and burying the dead from their army. General Ward's worst fears had not materialized. Most of his men had escaped. Putnam's most sanguine dreams had been realized. The siege army's occupation of the Charlestown Heights had lured the British out for battle, and as the crusty Connecticut officer had predicted, the redcoats paid dearly to retake these heights. Fully 50 percent of the regulars who saw combat were killed or wounded—226 had died, 928 were casualties. Ninety British officers, nearly 40 percent of the officers in Boston, died or were wounded. In two engagements, on April 19 and now at Bunker Hill, Gage had lost nearly 1,500 men, almost a quarter of the force that occupied Boston. Colonial losses were heavy as well. Counting the dozen or so who died in captivity (of the roughly 40 who were taken prisoner), 160 Americans perished and at least 271 were wounded.[64]

The Battle of Bunker Hill. Oil on canvas by Howard Pyle, 1898. Bunker Hill was one of the turning points of the war, as it led not only to changes in British strategy, but demonstrated to the colonists that their citizen-soldiers could fight successfully against regulars.

The British had won the battle. They had taken their objective and would hold this strategic site for as long as they remained in Boston. But their victory had come at a ghastly price. Some military triumphs exact an oppressive toll, but are deemed pardonable. The U.S. Marines lost one-third of their men at Iwo Jima in World War II, but in the process they destroyed 95 percent of the Japanese defenders, and within six months Japan surrendered. But the British success at Bunker Hill had come at a cost that was immediately seen by the army's leadership as catastrophic. Gage acknowledged that the "loss we have Sustained, is greater than we can bear."[65] Clinton called it a "dear bought victory, another such would have ruined us."[66] Howe admitted that the "success is too dearly bought."[67] A younger officer raged that the British army was "all wrong at the head." Its leadership, he said, had as much as "murdered" the fallen redcoats with an ill-conceived plan that grew from "gross ignorance." Such commanders, he added, "gives us for the future anxious forebodings."[68] The Royal Artillery's official history simply noted that the "plan of attack was faulty, and the defence of the Americans admirable."[69] Many redcoats were badly shaken. A few days after the battle one officer wrote, "the shocking carnage that day never will be out of my mind till the day of my death."[70] Another British officer worried that the engagement would give "the rebels great matter of triumph by showing them what mischief they can do us."[71] Gage knew that the American rebels had already demonstrated the harm they could do, and he wondered what that would mean for the future. Shortly after the Battle of Bunker Hill he remarked: "The [American] People Shew a Spirit and Conduct against us, they never shewed against the French."[72]

3

CHOICES, 1775

I T SEEMED TO SOME in England that every ship arriving from America brought bad tidings. The first account of the staggering losses suffered by the regulars at Lexington and Concord reached London late in May. The disbelieving government rejected the story as an American fabrication, but within a week the nation knew that the news had been painfully accurate. Two months later word arrived of the loss of Ticonderoga and Crown Point, followed the very next day by an account of the battle for Bunker Hill and the stupendous price that the British army had paid to take it. Later in the summer the press reported the arrival in Plymouth of the *Charming Nancy*, a handsome three master, whose passenger list included nearly two hundred soldiers wounded on Charlestown Heights, "some without legs, and others without arms; and their cloaths hanging on them like a loose morning gown," according to one story. Disembarking with them were scores of widows and children of the slain soldiers. It was, wrote one scribe, "a most shocking spectacle."[1]

During the first cruel weeks of this war, Lord North abandoned the ministry's established practice of a long summer hiatus from business. He called his cabinet to three separate meetings in June and July to consider the confounding emergency in America. The last summons came on the day after word arrived of Bunker Hill, causing most members to make hurried journeys from their country homes to London.[2] North's ministry, like many another government stung by dire news from the war front, radiated optimism in public, proclaiming that the engagement in Charlestown had been a British victory. In private, the ministers were more honest, realizing—as an undersecretary of state put it—that if "we have eight more such victories there will be nobody left to bring home the news of them."[3] North himself remarked, "the war is now grown to such a height that it must be treated as a foreign war."[4]

Incredibly, North's government had led Britain into a faraway war without a plan for waging it. All along it had presumed that the Americans would back down when faced with British force. The government also believed if the rebels were so foolish as to resist, their army could not possibly be a match for regulars. It, and the rebellion, would be crushed in short order. Lexington-Concord, and especially Bunker Hill, awakened most ministers from their reverie. At the summer meetings, and subsequently as it prepared for the fall session of Parliament, the cabinet—meeting in felicitous surroundings, often over a pipe and a steaming pot of tea—rapidly came to a decision to fight, then more slowly, and sometimes amid strident division, found a consensus on numerous points about how to wage the war. All but Lord Dartmouth, who was in charge of American affairs, supported hostilities and believed that victory would be achieved, although after Bunker Hill the realization sank in that the war would take longer than previously thought. North, for instance, spoke that summer of "the first year of a war," a tacit admission that a second year of hostilities would follow. Over a period of several weeks the cabinet agreed to send reinforcements to America, increase the size of the army and navy, secure foreign troops, and ask for new taxes with which to finance the war. In some instances the government had a lucid view of what it was likely to be up against. It understood that the greatest danger would occur if France, possibly with Spain in tow, intervened on the side of the Americans. The ministers also concurred that the prospect of that happening would increase the longer the war continued. On the other hand, despite considerable evidence to the contrary, the cabinet myopically held to the view that the great majority of colonists remained loyal to Great Britain and that little support for the rebellion existed below New England.[5]

Drawing on these notions, North's government contrived a formula for success that drew on the old axiom that the beast would die if its head was severed. It envisaged victory by suppressing the rebellion in New England, which was thought to be vulnerable on several counts. Some believed that a naval blockade alone might be sufficient to break the back of the New England rebels. By obstructing the region's commerce, denying mariners access to the fisheries, and shutting off the importation of food—believed to be essential for New England, a poor farming region that was urbanized and crowded—such privation could be sowed that organized resistance might crumble. At the very least, a naval blockade would isolate the region from the Atlantic world, where it might receive succor. New England was also thought to be susceptible to encirclement, and gradually North's government came to think that with its naval prowess and formidable army of regulars the heart of the region could be penetrated simultaneously from the Atlantic coast, Long Island Sound, Canada, and, if need be, the Hudson River. Even after Bunker Hill, North's cabinet remained confident that America's citizen-soldiers were no match for regulars and that the war would be neither long nor difficult. Most ministers concurred with the king, who allowed that, "When once the rebels have felt a smart blow, they will submit." North and his brethren came to one other substantive conclusion. Looking on the Americans as kin, and understanding that this was a civil war the object of which was to reestablish political control and reclaim the affection of the colonists, the ministers were persuaded that the military must disdain the use of terror tactics. Burning towns, plundering civilians, and slaughtering captives were not to be countenanced. Unbridled savagery would only nourish the rebellion and make for daunting problems in the peace that followed Britain's victory.[6]

The ministry came to these conclusions in the face of troubling doubts raised both publicly and privately. Parliament was flooded with addresses and petitions. Most came from mercantile interests who pleaded for a peaceful solution to avert a "ruinous civil war."[7] Members of the Opposition, who had long questioned the government's American policies, also cast suspicions on the notion that this was "an affair with Boston [New England] only." Resistance to Parliament's policies had occurred "from one end of the continent to the other," it was said, and Edmund Burke warned in the House of Commons that this would be "a war with the whole" of America and "not a scuffle with Boston" alone.[8] Several members of the army administration expressed skepticism that the war could be won. They warned that the Americans could replace their losses more easily than the British, and they raised troubling concerns about the difficulty of waging a war so far from home. They pointed especially to the stupendous demands that would be faced in supplying a large army three thousand miles away. Nor could the challenge of attempting to suppress a rebellion that was raging through such a huge region be taken lightly. Any two of the larger colonies were nearly equivalent in size to England, and once they were pacified another eleven provinces would remain to be dealt with. New warnings were aired about America's potential for raising large numbers of men, and no less than General Jeffery Amherst, who had commanded Britain's army in America toward the end of the last war, cautioned that Britain would be stretched to the limit to find sufficient manpower to do the job.[9]

General Gage had been saying the same thing for nearly a year, and after Bunker Hill he baldly informed the American secretary that a British triumph would "not [be] easy" or fast. It could be achieved, he added, only by raising a huge army that could simultaneously strike "in various Quarters," causing the Americans to fatally divide their forces.[10] The Duke of Grafton, North's predecessor, advised that the Americans would have up to a year to prepare their new army before the redcoats would be ready to take the initiative. Considering the brave and capable performance of America's untrained soldiers on Battle Road and at Bunker Hill, Grafton added crustily that the outcome of an American war might "not only . . . be hopeless," it could result in "certain disgrace and ruin" for Great Britain.[11] Some within the army worried that the provincials might eschew conventional warfare in favor of guerrilla tactics. Britain's adjutant general pointed out that should the colonists abandon the coastal towns and deploy in the hinterland, using militia forces to torment the regulars that sallied into the interior after them—as they had done on April 19—Britain would find itself in a war that it could not win. Any "attempt to conquer" them, he added, would be "an ugly job . . . a damned affair indeed," and was likely to result in the destruction of the army by "damned driblets."[12] All the while, the Opposition press was filled with trenchant admonitions against the war. Newspaper essayists frequently declared that hostilities would destroy commerce, leading perhaps to national bankruptcy. War would sap British power, some writers insisted, leaving France to make gains at Britain's expense. Perhaps the most frequently stated warning was that "the Americans, by a lingering contest, will gain an independency."[13]

Dismissing these warnings, the ministry made its choices and prepared a program for war to submit to Parliament. As had long been customary, Parliament was annually opened with an address by the monarch, and on October 26, a sunny, clear day, more than 60,000 lined London's freshly swept streets, festooned with flags and garlands, to see George III ride in his majestic coach from the royal palace to Westminster. A popular king, he alighted to cheers from an adoring throng ready to support whatever he said. The monarch had been saying to his ministers in private since mid-summer that war was unavoidable, and that it must be waged with force and energy. He had also pressured North and Dartmouth into consenting to an unsparing proclamation that he issued late in August. Accusing "divers parts" of the colonies of an "open and avowed rebellion" that included "traitorously . . . levying war against us," he vowed to use the "utmost endeavours to suppress such rebellion and to bring the traitors to justice."[14] What George III told Parliament in October merely elaborated on that earlier proclamation. Facing nobles in their red robes, and mostly admiring commoners, the king read his speech in a vibrant voice. Both he and Parliament, he said, had been patient and forbearing, "anxious to prevent . . . the effusion of blood . . . and the calamities which are inseparable from a state of war." But the colonists, spurred on by perfidious demagogues, had launched a war "for the purpose of establishing an independent empire," a result that would have "fatal effects" for the British nation. No choice existed, he declared, but to fight and "to put a speedy end to these disorders by the most decisive exertions."[15]

The monarch's speech touched off a lively debate in the House of Commons. Although the Opposition members were noticeably reluctant to question publicly whether the war could be won, they excoriated the government for its "piratical" policies that had led "the nation into an unjust, ruinous, felonious, and murderous war" that might be "fatal . . . to our country." Labeling the war "cruel, unnecessary, and unnatural," many urged the repeal of all American legislation passed since 1763 or called on the ministry to pursue reconciliation through peaceful means. Some castigated the government for the spin it had put on the outcome of Bunker Hill, declaring that the outcome "smacked more of defeat than victory." But Colonel Barré alone pointed to the difficulties that lay ahead. As "an army of 22,000 of our forces, with 20,000 provincials, and a fleet of 22 sail of the line . . . were three years in subduing Canada" during the French and Indian War, he wondered aloud what Britain was getting itself into. He ridiculed those who called the Americans cowards and warned that if "this American storm" spread beyond New England, the "whole American continent was lost for ever."[16]

NORTH'S GOVERNMENT had rapidly agreed on its strategy for waging the war, but it took much longer to settle on how to put its design into operation. The voices of dissent may have had something to do with this, but the steady diet of bad news, and a growing realization of the complexities that it faced in this war, led the ministers to repeatedly reassess earlier decisions. Throughout the summer and fall, for instance, word dribbled across the Atlantic of the loss of royal control in one province after another south of New England, including news that Virginia's governor had taken refuge offshore on a naval vessel and North Carolina's inside a British fort, and that the few royal officials who remained in office were figureheads without real authority.[17] The reality of what was occurring throughout America played havoc with the idea of concentrating solely on New England.

The government's conception of how to realize its manpower needs changed as often as London's weather. After learning of Lexington-Concord, the cabinet agreed to have 20,000 regulars in America by the next spring, although Gage had said that he needed at least twice that number. Gage said, too, that he would seek to augment those being sent across the Atlantic by recruiting ample numbers of Indians and African Americans, apparently believing that the latter would serve the king in return for their freedom.[18] North, with the backing of the cabinet, directed General Guy Carleton, the governor of Quebec, to find Indians who would "take up the hatchet against His Majesty's rebellious subjects" and to raise two thousand Canadians to serve under Gage. The government additionally approached Catherine the Great with an offer to hire 20,000 Russian soldiers. All these plans were dashed soon enough. Not only did the Tsarina decline to provide mercenaries, but before the summer ended Carleton reported what he called the "backwardness" of Canada's Indians and "peasantry," virtually none of whom were eager to serve.[19]

These were not the only disappointments that North encountered. Recruiting not only failed dismally that fall, but the government discovered that the existing regiments were not at full strength. They contained only about 60 percent of the manpower that the ministry had initially presumed. From the moment the war erupted, and especially after Bunker Hill, so many officers requested permission to transfer to corps posted outside North America, or to sell their commissions, that the king was compelled to announce in November 1775 that he would no longer listen to such petitions.[20] North was soon compelled to scale back. In early autumn he spoke of sending 10,000 regulars to

America by early 1776. He believed he could find that number by expanding the army from 33,000 to 55,000 men, and by drawing on the numerous regiments posted throughout England, Scotland, and Ireland. Even that step proved more difficult than he had imagined, and the government was driven to improvise. North sent what he could from home, transferred six battalions to America from Gibraltar and Minorca—replacing them with hired soldiers from Hanover— embarked on negotiations to secure still more Germans for the American theater, and advised the royal officials in New York and North Carolina to arm and use the Loyalists. In mid-December the War Office also announced that enlistees could join for three years or the duration of the war, rather than the customary lifetime commitment, and these volunteers were awarded a bounty of a guinea and a half (about the cost of three theater tickets). As Christmas approached, North believed that he had scraped together nearly 10,000 redcoats for deploy- ment across the Atlantic—which would more than double the number already in North America—but they were to be dispersed from Canada to the Caribbean in a desperate attempt to staunch the further erosion of royal authority.[21] One-fifth of the reinforcements were sent to Gage in Boston, his second reinforcement since August, bringing his troop strength to some seven thousand men. During the summer Gage had assured his superiors that he could secure the city with this number, although as he faced a siege army of 15,000 men, there would be no prospect of taking the initiative.[22]

North additionally readied for war by getting rid of Gage. Weary of what he saw as Gage's caviling, North had wished to replace him with Amherst nearly a year earlier, but his hopes were dashed when Amherst declined the king's offer to assume command of Britain's armies in America. North did what he believed was the next best thing. He dispatched Howe, Clinton, and John Burgoyne to serve under the commander and presumably stiffen his backbone, but Bunker Hill finished Gage. Within three days of learning of that costly victory, the monarch asked North to recall him. Howe was named his successor and assumed command on October 10.[23]

Long before then, London had made the decision to abandon Boston, though Howe learned nothing of this until he had been on the job for a month. In August, Gage and his principal generals, including Howe, had recommended transferring most of the army from Boston, leaving behind just enough men to hold the city. New England was so united in carrying on resistance, the generals concurred, that the redcoats in Boston faced insurmountable difficulties.[24] Gage proposed instead a campaign to take New York City and nearby Long Island, where the army could be secured and its supply lines more easily kept open. Gage had expected that a campaign to take New York would require 20,000 men. Howe thought it would take 30,000 men. Without at least that number, he said gloomily, the British army should withdraw entirely from the northern colonies, leaving the colonists to suffer the ravages of anarchy until they invited the redcoats to return. North's ministry told Howe that he would ultimately have the manpower that he needed, but in the meantime he was to take the army to a place of his choosing outside New England, somewhere that it could be safely supplied by the navy throughout the winter.[25]

As 1775 waned, the government's grand strategy slowly came together. Campaign 1776 was to be built around the strangulation of New England. While the navy blockaded New England's eastern and southern coasts, New York City and Rhode Island were to be taken. Once secured, New York was to be the launching pad for a drive up the Hudson River to join hands with regulars coming down from Canada. Encircled, New England at last would be invaded from several points simultaneously. It was well into November before Howe received these orders. Owing to the shortage of available transports, and his reluctance to mount a campaign to establish a base in New York during the harsh winter months, Howe opted to remain in Boston until spring.[26]

North's final step toward preparing for hostilities involved a shakeup in the cabinet. Two ministers who were lukewarm about waging war were dumped and Dartmouth, who had never been keen on using force, was shifted to a less vital post. North named Lord George Germain, a noted hawk, as American secretary. Germain was one of three secretaries of state—one was responsible for northern Europe, another for southern Europe, and a third for America—but in time he came to be the closest thing that existed to a minister of war. North knew what he was getting when he brought Germain aboard. A resolute advocate of the use of force since the Boston Tea Party, Germain had long openly advocated replacing

Lord George Germain. Twentieth-century copy by Dorofield Hardy of the eighteenth-century original painting by George Romney. A poor choice for the vital post of American secretary, Germain's background and temperamental quirks added to his woes.

Gage with Howe and arming the American loyalists. North additionally knew that Germain was "a man with a past," in the words of historian Piers Mackesy.[27] Born in 1716 and raised amid great wealth in Kent, Germain had been a so-so student at England's finest preparatory schools before going on to graduate from Trinity College in Dublin. He chose a military career and within barely fifteen years rose to the rank of major general. His ascent seemed unlimited. When only in his early forties, Germain not only held a seat in the Irish House of Commons, but was second in command of the British army in the European theater during the Seven Years' War, as the French and Indian War was called in Europe. However, in 1759, Germain was accused of having disobeyed orders and performed cravenly under fire during the Battle of Minden. Though cleared of the charges of cowardice, he was dismissed from the service and subjected to mockery and reproof. Many old acquaintances, including some he had thought to be his friends, treated him with a studied incivility. Others stood firmly by him and believed that he had been the victim of personal resentments, and in time his true friends came to power and saw to his rehabilitation, beginning with appointments to minor offices in the mid-1760s.

When North brought him into the cabinet in 1775, Germain, then sixty years of age, was muscular and ruggedly handsome, and his bearing remained that of the soldier he once had been. Many looked askance at his entering the ministry, and especially at his assumption of the colonial secretariat. Some continued to hate him for his war record. Others were cool, put off by his aloof, even haughty, manner and his seeming incapacity for forming warm relationships. Not a few worried that his obsession with personal redemption might color his judgment, particularly as he would have to make weighty military decisions. On the other hand, many were struck by his supreme self-confidence and believed that he possessed extraordinary skills as an administrator, not an inconsiderable asset when faced with managing a distant war.[28]

For his part, North had several reasons for wanting Germain. He, too, regarded Germain as man with administrative prowess, something badly needed in a government not known for its efficiency. As Lord Sandwich, who was responsible for the navy, sat in the House of Lords, some observers believed that North was drawn to Germain for the help he would provide in the inevitable debates over military matters in the House of Commons. North's style of governance was also crucial in leading him to Germain. While North sometimes alluded to the cabinet's collective responsibility in reaching decisions, the reality was that his government was one of nearly autonomous departments. Disdaining the title of "prime minister," North to a considerable degree saw the ministers as a collection of equals. Given this, it was paramount that the American secretary be strong and assertive, for strategic planning and the care of the army would be within his sphere of responsibility. What is more, Germain's well-known toughness, and his belief that force alone could solve the American problem, made North eager to have him.[29]

About the time that Germain took office, Parliament approved the ministry's war measures, including the revenue bill, by lopsided majorities.[30] It had taken North's government roughly six months after it learned of Bunker Hill to complete this work, and even then it was clear to all within the cabinet that several additional months would elapse before the British armed forces in America would be ready to launch a major military offensive. Nevertheless, most were confident that the war could be won, probably in 1776. The colonists might come to their senses following one or two spectacular British successes. If not, the combined might of Britain's land and sea forces would crush New England, and whatever rebellion existed elsewhere would simply collapse.

WHILE NORTH'S GOVERNMENT struggled with its options, the Continental Congress likewise changed its mind at times. Congress, dominated by those who sought reconciliation with the crown, first voted to return Ticonderoga and Crown Point to the British—though it never considered relinquishing the military hardware that had been captured—but after two weeks it reversed itself and late in May asked Connecticut to occupy those posts.[31] Its most significant change of heart was with regard to Canada.

Early on Congress had restrained Benedict Arnold from invading Canada, but before two months passed it authorized an invasion. When the initial decision was made, many in Congress had doggedly clung to the hope that war might be averted. Bunker Hill laid to rest that pipedream and started many congressmen thinking about securing the northern border. After all, should a British army invade New York from Canada, striking through the Champlain Valley, it would threaten either the encirclement of the new Continental army that was besieging Boston or the seizure of the Hudson, isolating New England from the provinces to the south. Furthermore, the time seemed ripe for acting. Existing intelligence —much of it provided by Massachusetts, which in February had sent an agent to Canada to snoop—indicated that Britain's hold on the region was tenuous. Not only were barely seven hundred regulars posted in Canada, it was taken for granted that the Canadian citizenry, which was mostly French, was hostile toward Great Britain and would welcome a rebel army as liberators. Congress additionally wished to "shut the door against [London's] dangerous tampering with the Indians." If the British were driven from Canada, it was assumed, the neutrality of the Native Americans would be ensured for the duration of the war. Late in July, Congress directed General Schuyler to "take possession of . . . the country," so long as such a course of action was not "disagreeable to the Canadians."[32] Congress thus dictated two broad strategic objectives: drive one British army from Canada and, at a minimum, confine the other to Boston.

In the meantime, Congress had vested Washington "with full power and authority to act as you shall think [necessary] for the good and Welfare" of defending "American Liberty and for repelling every hostile invasion." But Congress had also imposed specific demands on him: "[W]e . . . require you" to see that the new army be well disciplined and orderly, and "to regulate your conduct" according to the articles of war that it soon expected to adopt. He was admonished "to observe and follow" all congressional "orders and directions," and to make his most substantive decisions only after "advising with your council of war," that is, after consultation with other general officers.33 Washington was the commander in chief of the Continental army, but he was not a war lord.

Not at all certain that Washington would be favorably received by the New England public or soldiers, or that the decision to demote General Ward would be tolerated, Congress engaged in one of America's first public relations campaigns. One New England delegate after another wrote home touting Washington's qualities. "Our youth [should] look up to This Man as a pattern to form themselves by," advised one. Others said that Washington "Unites the bravery of the Soldier, with the most consummate Modesty & Virtue," or asserted that he was "highly Esteemed for his Military & other Accomplishments" and "Suited to the Temper & Genius of our People." They characterized him as bright, discreet, and trustworthy, and John Hancock called him "a fine man" that "you will all like." Praise aside, the reality was that Washington's appointment was essential. Connecticut's Eliphalet Dyer pointed out that Congress had turned to Washington, who was not from New England, in order "to keep up the Union & more strongly Cement the Southern and Northern Colonies."34

Congress was united on waging war, but underlying this broad consensus lay deep divisions over the object of the war. Congress had barely convened in May 1775 when John Rutledge of South Carolina asked: "do we aim at independency? or do We only ask for a Restoration of Rights . . . on our old footing" as subjects of the Crown?35 Fourteen months would be required to answer his question.

Throughout 1775 moderates who wanted no part of independence dominated Congress. The mid-Atlantic provinces—New York, New Jersey, Pennsylvania, and Delaware—together with South Carolina were especially set against breaking ties with Great Britain. All had long since been drawn into the economic web of the Atlantic world. For decades the products of the backcountry—furs, hides, lumber, meat, and grains—had moved through New York and Philadelphia to markets in the Caribbean and England. Charleston exported many of these same articles, as well as indigo, rice, and sea island cotton. In return, English manufactured goods entered the colonies through these ports. Business had flourished for decades, leaving many thriving merchants and planters unwilling to rock the boat. Many owed their prosperity to credit supplied by English and Scottish bankers, to protection offered by the Royal Navy, or to services rendered by Crown diplomats. Many residents of these provinces would have agreed with the Philadelphia merchants who declared that independence would "assuredly prove unprofitable" and that the "advantages of security and stability lie with America remaining in the empire."36 Many congressmen also believed that a war for limited aims would be brief, but a struggle for independence—which Britain would resist with all its might—would be protracted. Wars that lasted for years sometimes unleashed unsettling changes that could not be foreseen. The colonists also probably lacked the capacity to win a long war, these congressmen asserted. Outnumbered by the mother country by nearly five to one, and lacking the means of producing weapons and munitions on a large-scale basis, a lengthy war almost certainly would drive the colonists to search for foreign assistance. Many found the thought of French or Spanish intervention to be especially menacing. They feared that it would lead to an "independent" America that, in reality, was merely a puppet of an autocratic European power. Others feared that an independent America—an America separated from the aegis of conservative, aristocratic, monarchical Great Britain—would lay open to a revolution of transformative proportions.[37]

There were those in Congress who favored independence from the moment the war began, but they were in the minority throughout 1775 and shrank from openly advocating a radical agenda. Led by John Adams, they feared that if they moved too fast, the frightened moderates would flee back into the arms of Great Britain, dashing the new American solidarity and terminating resistance. "Progress must be slow," Adams told those of his persuasion. Patience was his guiding principle. He likened his strategy to that of "a large Fleet sailing under convoy. The fleetest sailors must wait for the dullest and slowest." His rule was that the word "independence" was never to be uttered in public, and all talk of foreign assistance was to be avoided. Yet from the outset Adams believed that independence was inevitable. War would radicalize the outlook of the populace and force Congress to make decisions that were unthinkable at the outset of the contest. The war itself, he believed, would someday compel Congress to break all ties with Great Britain and create an independent American nation.[38]

The war that Congress embarked on in May 1775 was not a war for independence. Congress was waging war for reconciliation, but on its terms. During the first fifteen months of hostilities, America fought to reconstitute the British empire into a confederation of sovereign states united under a common king, but one in which Parliament's authority, if it existed at all, was severely circumscribed.[39]

Part Two

The War in the North, 1776–1779

4

"HASTENING FAST TO A CRISIS": JUNE 1775–JUNE 1776

WASHINGTON had been to Boston once before. In 1756 he had come to plead with the commander of British forces in America for a commission in the British army. He returned in 1775 hoping to defeat the British army.

After eight hard days on the road from Philadelphia, Washington arrived at Cambridge, across the Charles River from Boston, on July 2. The Continental army had been assembled on a makeshift parade ground for the occasion, but a sudden heavy rainstorm caused a postponement in the festivities. The next day, the new commander met his army amid what one soldier thought was "a great deal of grandor."[1] Washington read a short speech that included the 101st Psalm, a song of mercy and judgment, and a vow to "destroy all the wicked of the land [and] . . . cut off all wicked doers from the city of the Lord." Several soldiers noted his speech in their journals and letters, but none appear to have been especially impressed by its content or delivery. One even remarked: "nothing hapeng extrorderly we preaded [paraded] thre times" and were dismissed.[2]

From what he had heard in Congress, Washington expected to face formidable problems with the new army, and he had only just arrived in Cambridge when the Massachusetts Provincial Congress told him that the siege army was untrained and undisciplined. Neither soldiers nor officers, it added, had the least understanding of the steps necessary for "the preservation of Health and even of Life" within the army. To make matters worse, he was also informed that "it was highly probable *Gage's* Troops would very Shortly attack our Army."[3]

Setting up headquarters in the mansion of a Tory merchant, Washington's first business—he was acting on Congress's orders—was to determine the size of his army and that of the enemy. He had been promised an army of 20,000, but found only 16,000 men, of whom 2,000 were unfit for duty. Intelligence reported that 11,500 redcoats were confined in Boston and posted on the Charlestown Heights, roughly twice their actual number. While gathering the numbers, Washington faced a sticky wrangle among several generals regarding their ranking. The difficulties arose as Congress had appointed Massachusetts's William Heath before—and consequently over—John Thomas and Connecticut's Israel Putnam ahead of Joseph Spencer, reversing the order of rank that had been decided previously in each colony. Congress's decisions were almost certainly made at the behest of New England delegates who hoped to rectify what they believed had been poor choices made earlier by the provincial assemblies, but the new alignment provoked immediate rancor. Thomas nearly resigned, a step that was averted when Seth Pomeroy declined his commission due to age, and Thomas—with Heath's consent—was plugged into that slot. Spencer was no less livid at what he believed was tantamount to a demotion. He went home in a pother, but when he got no help from the Connecticut authorities, he swallowed his pride and returned to camp as Old Put's subordinate. (The general feeling, as noted by one young officer, was that it was "better for us to lose four S[pencers] than half a Putnam.") Washington's first week culminated with his initial council of war, which agreed to redeploy numerous units to shore up vulnerable spots, but recommended against fortifying Dorchester Heights or even fighting to prevent the enemy from occupying that vital position.[4]

At the end of that first week Washington declared that "abuses in this army . . . are considerable . . . and the new modelling of it" was unavoidable. It was precisely what the Massachusetts authorities had in mind when they urged Congress to replace the siege army with a national army, as they believed that the existing army could be rebuilt only if it was first torn down. Washington must have had some inkling of the need for reform before he left Philadelphia, and over the next six months, in consultation with councils of war and a congressional committee that came to camp in the fall, he presided over the reorganization of the army. In the end, the structure of the Continental army continued to resemble the British army, but significant differences emerged. There were fewer companies in each American regiment, but more men bearing arms in a Continental battalion than in its counterpart. This would facilitate the massing of firepower, especially useful when in a defensive posture, as Bunker Hill had demonstrated. There was also a higher ratio of officers to men, the better for leading raw recruits into adversity.[5]

Washington immediately saw a need for far more than organizational change. He found an army without discipline, run by officers who in many instances were unfit for a command position. Many soldiers came and went at will, and some went and never returned. Some were drunk and disorderly, and not a few failed to salute their officers. Sentries were sometimes found asleep at their post, if they were at their post. Men stole from one another and from nearby civilians. Some men, Washington was told, were even consorting with the enemy. He was appalled and in one of his first written orders told the army: "It is required and expected that exact discipline be observed, and due Subordination prevail thro' the whole Army, as a failure in these most essential points must produce extreme Hazard, Disorder and Confusion, and end in shameful disappointment and disgrace." It seemed apparent to him that the shocking lack of discipline was due primarily to the inadequacy of the junior officers, the lieutenants and captains who were directly above the enlisted men in the companies. He also concluded that in many instances the wrong sort of men had been chosen for the task. A social conservative through and through and a southerner who was unfamiliar with the more egalitarian culture of New England, Washington was startled to find that many officers were from "the lower class of these people" and "nearly of the same Kidney with the Privates." He was correct. Often, there were few social, economic, or educational distinctions between the junior officers and their men. Furthermore, as civilians many of these newly appointed officers had been friends and neighbors of the men they now commanded. Washington saw that fatal problems could grow from this situation, as many officers seemed incapable of giving, or enforcing, orders. Discipline could never exist, he believed, unless officers exerted an uncompromising authority over those beneath them. He recoiled in horror at the sight of officers fraternizing with their men, sometimes shaving them or repairing their shoes. As bad as that was, there was worse. Washington learned that some officers had embezzled money or supplies from the army. Some, like the men, were absent without leave. Without authorization, some had given their men furloughs for brief visits home. Incredibly, some men were even sent to work on their officers' farms. Washington railed that New Englanders not only were "the most indifferent kind of People I ever saw," but "an exceeding dirty and nasty" bunch. Yet he believed they could become good soldiers "if properly officered," and he set out to make them the best possible soldiers and officers.[6]

He imposed a harsh disciplinary regimen. Those who disobeyed orders were to be punished, and those officers who hesitated to exercise their authority faced the prospect of a humiliating dismissal from the army. Washington moved quickly to make "a pretty good Slam" against the incompetents, and after two months he boasted that he had rid the army of two colonels, a major, and several junior officers. He also exhorted Congress to recruit deserving officers from outside New England, steadfastly insisting that "merit only" was reason to be an officer. In this vein, he not only elevated several officers, but issued battlefield commissions to some enlisted men who had exhibited "spirited behaviour and good conduct" in the fight at Bunker Hill. A regimental chaplain told the folks at home that a "great overturning in the camp" had occurred. "The strictest government is taking place, and great distinction is made between officers and soldiers. Every one is made to know his place and keep in it."[7]

Washington additionally acted as a teacher. Each day he invited a different junior officer to the officers' mess, wishing to scrutinize the young men and to give them an opportunity to learn from their superiors. Through his daily orders Washington also frequently instructed his callow young officers on what he saw as the qualities of leadership. Officers must set a positive example, be strict but not unreasonable, maintain a respectful distance from their men, demand compliance with their orders, hear the complaints of the soldiery and seek to remedy their grievances if well founded, discourage vice, treat the men fairly and justly, reward the deserving, guard against surprises, read military manuals, and act bravely.[8] Bravery above all else. Those who were brave would "be known to the General Congress and all America," one officer remarked, but those who "dishonor the army . . . shall be held up as an infamous coward and punished as such . . . and no connexions, interest, or intercessions . . . will . . . prevent the strictest execution of justice."[9] Washington also wanted his officers to look like officers, and he devoted considerable attention to their appearance. The commander was to be distinguished "by a light blue Ribband, wore across his breast," he decreed, while the major generals were to wear purple, the brigadiers pink, and the aides-de-camp green. Lower-grade officers were distinguished by various "colour'd Cockades in their Hatts." He additionally sought to fabricate esprit de corps by having each regiment adopt its own distinctive "Colour, Cut and fashion" coat, though he mandated considerable uniformity, even specifying the number of buttons to be sewn on all coats.[10]

From the outset Washington also understood that if a truly national army was to exist, provincial distinctions would have to be overcome. He preached to the men that this war had not grown exclusively from New England's troubles. The imperial problem was an American one, and the purpose of the conflict was to obtain a satisfactory American solution. The thirteen colonies had gone to war to prevent "a diabolical Ministry" from "Inslav[ing] this great Continent," he said. The entire "Country is in danger," he continued, adding that this was a fight for "personal Liberty" for all free Americans.[11]

Understanding that the citizenry was devoted to the militia tradition and suspicious of armies, Washington labored to reassure the populace. He exhorted his officers to prevent their men from "all Invasions and Abuses of private property," and encouraged them always to act with a "ceremonious Civility" toward private citizens. Showing the way, he stressed his civilian background when in the presence of civilians, and said things such as "there is not a Man in America, who more earnestly wishes [the] Termination of the Campaign, as to make the Army no longer necessary."[12] Washington believed, too, that the war was a struggle for the hearts of the American citizenry. He tirelessly discouraged behavior that might bring "shame & Disgrace and Ruin to themselves & Country if they should by their Conduct turn the Hearts of our Brethren." He forbade "profane cursing, swearing & drunkenness" and sought to minimize contact between soldiers and civilians. Just as earnestly, he emphasized the need for cleanliness, hoping at once to protect the army and to prevent an army-spawned epidemic that might be ruinous to the civilian sector.[13]

After three months on the job, Washington relaxed a bit. He had feared an imminent British attack when he had taken command, but by September his defensive lines were completed and he had concluded—correctly—that "the Enemy have no Intention to come out, untill they are re-inforced." He even dared to believe that the British leadership, scarred by the carnage on Bunker Hill, was "afraid of us." How "is the dignity of great Britain fallen," he scornfully observed, and he relished the belief that only a few weeks before London had believed "that the American's were such paltroons & Cowards that they would not fight," but now their generals have "no Inclination to pay us a visit." He exaggerated. One of Howe's generals was more nearly correct. He remarked that the British army was "so small that we cannot afford a victory, if attended with any loss of men."[14]

But in this war, as Washington would learn, the next crisis usually lurked just around the corner, and in the autumn he faced true peril for the first time. The men from Connecticut and Rhode Island who became part of the siege army on April 19, or in the days immediately thereafter, had signed on to serve until December 10, while those from Massachusetts and New Hampshire had enlisted through the end of the year. Unless these men reenlisted, or were replaced, Washington knew that the "Army must absolutely break-up," Starting early in the fall, he set out to line up his officers, believing that the men "will not inlist untill they know" their company and regimental commanders. He had relatively good luck, in some measure because Congress raised the pay of the junior officers. When Washington turned to the men, he appealed to their honor and patriotism, and told them that the "great Cause we are engaged in" transcended saving liberty. It also included protecting "innocent Women & Children," and "our towns." He seized on a devastating mid-October naval raid on Falmouth— now in Maine, but at the time a part of Massachusetts—as confirmation of Britain's "barbarous Designs." He granted furloughs and provided additional supplies to those who reenlisted, promising them two dollars and a blanket that they could keep following their service. Despite his pleas and enticements, reen- listments proceeded slowly. Not even a cash bonus of one month's pay, which Congress offered late in 1775, turned many heads.[15] Farmers could ill afford to be away from home for a second consecutive growing season. Besides, most had wearied of the great adventure. Soldiering, they long since had discovered, was a hard life, filled with danger, loneliness, discomfort, and at times humiliating punishments and constraints.

In private, Washington raged at the "dearth of Publick Spirit, & want of Virtue." (His remark was occasioned by the departure, en masse, of the men from Connecticut, whose officers had informed Washington that they would stick it out.) He lashed out at the "dirty, mercenary Spirit" of those who wanted to return home to save their small farms, blind to the fact that scores of slaves toiled in his absence to keep Mount Vernon intact. Had he foreseen what he would face, Washington said that fall, "no consideration upon Earth should have induced me to accept this Command." With time the recruiting crisis was gradually resolved. In early December, Washington asked the New England governors to raise a total of five thousand militia. All four complied, sending in unhappy men who veterans quickly dubbed the "Long-Faced People." Later, he urged the governors to raise men for the Continental army through conscription. They declined that request, in part because enlistments were slowly increasing. Enlistments had picked up, at least partially, when Congress changed step and permitted men to sign on for six-month tours of duty. Nearly 8,000 men were in camp at Christmas—many were veterans who in the end stayed on—and two months later the army's rolls totaled 12,510 rank and file. Together with the militia on active duty, Washington had more men under arms early in March than had greeted him on his arrival in July.[16] Nevertheless, the ordeal of having "one Army disbanded and another to raise" within sight of an army of British regulars had been taxing, and on many nights, he later remarked, he had laid awake while "all around men [were] wrapped in sleep." That he got through it, he told an aide, was due only to "the finger of Providence." But he knew that he likely would face a similar crisis at the end of 1776 unless Congress agreed to enlist men for the duration of the war.[17] That was not in the cards. Too many delegates, such as Samuel Adams, believed that a standing army was "always dangerous to the liberties of the people," or, such as John Adams, were certain that only "the meanest, idlest, most intemperate and worthless" men in society would enlist for the long haul.[18]

As THE RECRUITING CRISIS unfolded in New England, preparations for the projected invasion of Canada sputtered in New York. Congress had left the matter to General Schuyler, a less decisive and more dilatory individual than most congressmen had realized. When he at last reached Ticonderoga, two weeks after Washington arrived in Cambridge, Schuyler was shocked to find that he had only 2,500 men in his Northern Department, many of whom were ill and unfit for duty. As he tried to make a decision about invading Canada, Schuyler saw problems everywhere. Food and ammunition were lacking. He needed boats for the long trek northward, but he had neither a sawmill nor the pitch and oakum needed for building the vessels. He could not act, he believed, until he knew the disposition of the Six Nations Indian confederation, the neutrality of which was essential if the incursion was to have any chance of success. Nor could he make a decision until he had better intelligence regarding the size of Britain's army in Canada.

Most of Schuyler's experience had been in logistical services, and as August moved toward September, evidence mounted of his success as an army administrator. A navy consisting of a schooner, a sloop, gondolas, bateaux, row-galleys, and pirogues materialized, powder arrived, and so, too, did carriages for the field guns. Men came as well, most of them ordered up from Manhattan by Congress.

General Philip Schuyler. Engraving by T. Kelly, from a painting by John Trumbull, c. 1835. Although an effective administrator, Schuyler suffered health and temperamental problems that foiled his bid for greatness as a leader in the war. Even so, he performed ably when beset by the great crisis produced by Burgoyne's invasion of New York.

While some were incapacitated by illness and others would have to be left behind to hold the chain of forts on the lakes, Schuyler knew that he would have an invasion force in excess of one thousand men, superior to the number which Carleton was believed to possess in Quebec. He was told by intelligence that neither the French Canadians nor the Indians would help the British, aside from perhaps a bit of scouting. Despite that good news and the materials he had secured for his army, Schuyler waffled on ordering an invasion. Benedict Arnold, who met with him in July in the hope of securing an important command position in the invading army, came away doubting that Schuyler was the man to lead an invasion. As one niggling letter after another from Schuyler arrived at Washington's headquarters, doubts gathered in the commander in chief's mind as well. Seven weeks after Congress authorized the invasion, Schuyler told Washington: "I am preparing . . . to . . . move against the Enemy, unless your Excellency or Congress should direct otherwise." With a bite in his tone—"I am glad to relieve you from your Anxiety"—Washington responded by telling Schuyler that no more time could be lost, as the harsh Canadian winter approached and eventually Carleton would be reinforced. His impatience showing, Washington added: "I am sure you will not let Difficulties not insuperable damp your ardour. Perseverance and Spirit have done Wonders in all ages."[19]

General Benedict Arnold. Engraving by Benoit–Louis Prévost, copy after Pierre-Eugène du Simitière, 1780. At once, Arnold was one of America's best generals and worst enemies.

In the meantime, Washington took a step that virtually compelled Schuyler to act. Washington told him of his plan to detach more than a thousand of his men for a force that would proceed through Maine to Quebec City. If Carleton emerged from his citadel to challenge Schuyler upriver, say at Montreal or further south on the Sorel River, the way would be open for the other American army to assail lightly defended Quebec. Should Carleton stay put in Quebec City, the two American armies would link up there and, with a force nearly four times larger than the redcoats in Canada, subdue the British defenders, either by attack or siege. The idea of sending a second force through Maine was not a new idea. The notion had surfaced in New England immediately after Lexington-Concord and, in June, Benedict Arnold sent Congress a plan for such an endeavor. There can be little doubt that it was presented to Washington soon after his arrival, and he heard it again directly from Arnold, who came to Cambridge to meet with him during the second week in August.[20]

Washington was impressed with Arnold, perhaps feeling that he had glimpsed a mirror image of himself. Arnold, who was eight years younger than Washington, had risen from owning an apothecary shop in New Haven to operating a small fleet through which he carried out a profitable trade in Canadian,

Caribbean, and Central American markets. Glib and intelligent, he dressed and acted like a gentleman, but what likely caught Washington's eye above all else were Arnold's resilient, combative, and tenacious qualities. He epitomized the leadership traits that Washington sought to convey to his young officers. The Massachusetts authorities had seen the same things, and in May had put Arnold in charge of taking Ticonderoga. Before the end of August, Washington quietly told Arnold that he was to command the force that was to penetrate Canada through Maine.[21]

Around September 1, Washington at last learned that the invasion from New York would proceed. Schuyler responded to Washington's earlier missive by assuring him that there no longer was "a trace of doubt on my mind as to the propriety of going into Canada And to Do It," though in reality the final decision had been made for him.[22] Schuyler had gone to Albany during the third week in August to parley with Indians. During his absence, fresh intelligence poured into Ticonderoga that Carleton was building a fleet of his own, but that it was far from ready. If the Americans moved quickly, they could control Lake Champlain before Carleton was ready to defend it. Richard Montgomery, the second in command in the Northern Department, thought it would be folly to postpone a final decision until Schuyler returned. Since even before the appointment of the general officers in the Continental army, Montgomery had also fretted over whether Schuyler possessed the *"strong nerves"* needed for high command. He saw little that summer to ease his concerns, especially as Schuyler was complaining almost daily of some new physical malady, first "a bilious Fever," next a "Barbarous Complication of Disorders," and eventually a "violent Flux."[23]

Late in August, without orders, Montgomery acted on his own, launching the campaign. He wrote Schuyler to say simply that if the army waited any longer, " 'tis over with us this summer." He also advised Schuyler to "follow us in a whale boat," adding—perhaps with his tongue planted firmly in his cheek—that, if he did so, it "will give the men great confidence in your spirit and activity."[24] Almost two months to the day since Congress had authorized an invasion, Montgomery, with 1,200 men, set off for Canada. Two weeks later, Arnold, with 1,051 men, moved out.

Montgomery was one of three former British generals that Congress commissioned as general officers. A member of the Irish gentry who had attended college for two years, he, like many of his forebears, chose a career in the British army. Commissioned an ensign at age eighteen, Montgomery launched his military service in 1756, the year the Seven Years' War was declared. He soldiered for sixteen years, six of them in America, in the course of which he was part of Amherst's successful campaigns to take control of the Champlain Valley and Montreal. Passed over for promotion to major in 1771, a resentful Montgomery sold his commission and emigrated to the colonies. He purchased a small farm thirteen miles above Manhattan and a year later married into the powerful Livingston clan, a move that first helped him secure election to the New York

Provincial Congress and later assisted in his gaining appointment in the Continental army. Thirty-seven years old in 1775, Montgomery was tall, slender, and balding, with a heavily pockmarked face. Acquaintances described him as amiable and genteel, but every inch the soldier. It was thought that he would bring experience, professionalism, and youthful vigor to his new assignment. No one was happier than Washington to have him aboard, and he personally awarded the commission to Montgomery when he passed through New York en route to Boston.[25]

Success in the Canadian invasion was predicated on a rapid advance to Quebec, and as the colonists were possessed of considerable numerical superiority, they envisioned little serious opposition. In war few things go as planned, and in the campaign for Canada, virtually nothing went according to design.

Montgomery's first objective was St. Johns, a fort about twenty miles south of Montreal. His expedition shoved off into Lake Champlain under a glorious blue sky just before sunset on August 28, and it seemed as if nothing could go wrong. But during its first night out, the little armada was assailed by such a heavy storm that it was forced to put ashore. The north wind blew a gale the next day. The fleet could go nowhere. Nine long days passed before the expedition reached Isle aux Noix, where for the first time the target was visible. By then, Schuyler had caught up with his army, and had brought along five hundred additional men.

Schuyler now had 1,700 men equipped with five field pieces, three mortars, and several large cannon mounted on the vessels in his little fleet. St. Johns was garrisoned by about five hundred men. Washington later suggested that Schuyler might have fortified the lake, to keep British naval craft from going south and troubling Crown Point and Ticonderoga, and by-passed St. Johns altogether.[26] Schuyler, however, never imagined that the badly outnumbered British could hold out for long. He decided to attack, first sending units forward to probe the defenses of the British post.

The men were untrained and untried, and their performance was ugly. The slightest sound, or no sound whatsoever, spooked them and produced panicky flights. Rumors of ambushes and tattle that hordes of Indians had taken up with the British caused entire units to lose their nerve. On more than one occasion, several hundred overwrought men hightailed it for safety, abandoning their officers, who were forced to flee as well. Some men feigned illness to avoid the front lines. Others simply found other things to do, such as wandering about the countryside plundering terrified civilians. Beginning to wonder what he had gotten himself into, Montgomery declared that this army consisted of "a set of pusillanimous wretches."[27]

A week passed, then a week and a half. The army made no progress, though more reinforcements—Green Mountain Boys and a New York artillery company —arrived, bringing the rebel force up to two thousand men. The British sent in reinforcements as well, and their troop strength rose to about 725. Carleton envisaged forcing the invaders into a lengthy siege, which would forestall the

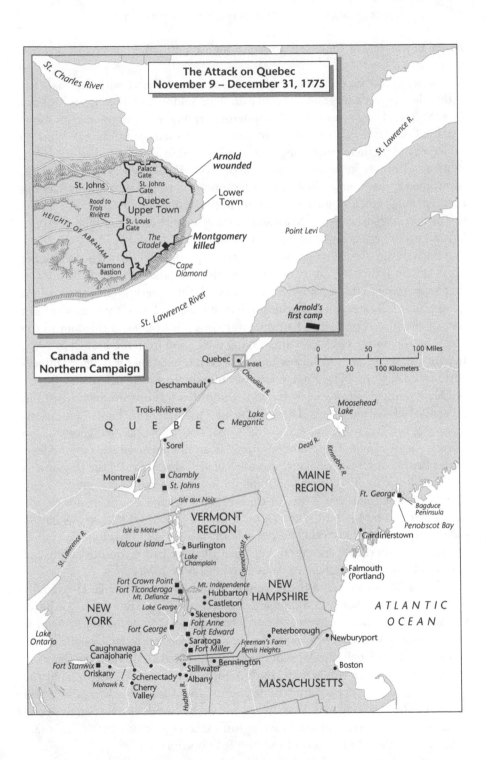

The Attack on Quebec
November 9 – December 31, 1775

St. Charles River

St. Lawrence R.

Arnold
wounded

Palace
Gate

St. Johns

St. Johns
Gate

Road to
Trois
Rivières

Quebec
Upper Town

Lower
Town

Point Levi

HEIGHTS OF ABRAHAM

St. Louis
Gate

The
Citadel

Montgomery
killed

Diamond
Bastion

Cape
Diamond

St. Lawrence River

Arnold's
first camp

Canada and the
Northern Campaign

Quebec ☐ Inset

Chaudière R.

Deschambault

| 0 | 50 | 100 Miles |
| 0 | 50 | 100 Kilometers |

Trois-Rivières

Lake
Megantic

Moosehead
Lake

Q U E B E C

Dead R.

Kennebec R.

Sorel

Montreal

Chambly
St. Johns

MAINE
REGION

Ft. George

Bagduce
Peninsula

Isle aux Noix

Isle la Motte

VERMONT
REGION

Penobscot Bay

Gardinerstown

Valcour Island

Burlington

Lake
Champlain

Connecticut R.

Falmouth
(Portland)

St. Lawrence R.

Fort Crown Point
Fort Ticonderoga
Mt. Defiance

Lake George

Mt. Independence
Hubbarton
Castleton

NEW
HAMPSHIRE

ATLANTIC
OCEAN

NEW
YORK

Skenesboro
Fort Anne

Fort George

Fort Edward

Peterborough

Newburyport

Lake
Ontario

Caughnawaga
Canajoharie

Saratoga
Fort Miller

Freeman's Farm
Bemis Heights

Fort Stanwix

Bennington

Boston

Oriskany

Stillwater

Mohawk R.

Schenectady

Albany

Hudson R.

MASSACHUSETTS

Cherry
Valley

arrival of this ragtag American army at Quebec until after the cruel Canadian winter set in.

Schuyler did not remain with his army for long. Afflicted with new maladies —this time it was a fever and rheumatism—he seldom emerged from his tent. After two weeks he returned to Ticonderoga. It now was Montgomery's show. On his first day in command he brought 1,400 men from Isle aux Noix to St. Johns and set them to building siege works. Within a week two batteries were in place within eight hundred yards of the fort. While supervising the work, Montgomery was nearly killed. A British cannonball ripped through his flapping coat, spinning him around and knocking him over into the breastworks, but he was unhurt. When he displayed a disconcerting inclination to continue to expose himself to danger his reputation grew with the men.

Early in the siege Montgomery dispatched parties that fanned out along the Sorel and St. Lawrence Rivers to gather intelligence and harvest the manpower that supposedly waited breathlessly to join with the American liberators. Little good came of the attempt to recruit soldiers in Canada. Few Canadians wanted a part of this war. The British had prudently extended religious freedom to the Catholic population in Canada after taking the region from the French in 1763. In contrast, the invading Yankees had a deserved reputation for religious illiberality, especially the New Englanders. Bostonians had long celebrated Pope's Night, an annual evening of Catholic-bashing that was observed with gusto in a carnival-like atmosphere. During the previous fall the First Continental Congress had bashed London's liberal Canadian policies as "dangerous in an extreme degree to the Protestant religion." In an ill-conceived and ugly Address to the People of Great Britain, Congress had also characterized the papacy as a malign force that had "dispersed impiety, bigotry, persecution, murder, and rebellion throughout every part of the world." Carleton got his hands on the document and had it posted throughout the province.[28] Thus, it was hardly surprising that rebel recruiting parties beat the bushes in Canada to little avail. A few hundred recruits were raised, but most of them had second thoughts and deserted before they reached the American lines at St. Johns.

Ethan Allen was one of the recruiters turned loose in Canada. He initially rounded up more than 250 volunteers, a success that quickly went to his head. Despite orders to find recruits and hurry back to the siege at St. Johns, Allen— with visions of grandeur swimming in his head—decided to attack lightly held Montreal. It was a debacle. Most of the recruits melted away when the shooting started, leaving Allen vulnerable. His diminutive force was overwhelmed by the small, but better equipped, army of defenders, and Allen was taken captive. He had not delivered a single Canadian recruit to the invading army. If any good came of his egregious failure, Washington exclaimed, it was that Allen's fate might teach others "a Lesson of Prudence & Subordination."[29]

During the third week in September it began to rain at St. Johns. It hardly stopped for three miserable weeks. Life for the soldiers grew miserable. Food shortages not only were evident for the first time, but men complained that for nearly twenty days they were never dry. Predictably, illnesses spiked within the camp. Men also noticed that the foliage was turning. They had departed Ticonderoga in the lush green of summer. The campaign was a month old, Canada's numbing autumn was gathering, and Quebec was far away.

Late in October, two months after the campaign had been launched, and fifty days after the siege commenced, Carleton attempted to rescue the besieged garrison. With the temperature now dropping below freezing every night, he knew that what he had already accomplished was significant. The holding operation at St. Johns had delayed the American invaders, perhaps fatally. But if Carleton could liberate his men from the siege at St. Johns, they could fight again, perhaps at Montreal, and the invaders might never see Quebec. Carleton had gathered a force of nearly 1,000 men, mostly militia, though 80 Caughnawaga Indians and about 150 regulars were also present. It was a promising endeavor, but just south of Montreal a large force of Green Mountain Boys and New York Continentals intercepted the relief force. The Americans set up artillery on the banks of the Sorel and raked Carleton's force with a heavy fire, forcing it to turn back. Two days later, Montgomery erected his last battery at St. Johns, bringing the doomed garrison under a sustained and more accurate barrage. Down to a three-day supply of food, the besieged British knew that they were beaten, and on November 2, the fifty-fifth day of the siege, they surrendered.

Montgomery presided over a lenient surrender. He had learned that Allen was being treated harshly (he was shackled in heavy irons beneath decks of a warship), and it was Montgomery's hope that civility could be restored to the treatment of captives. He permitted no reprisals, though vengeance was a common and lawful practice at the time against garrisons that capitulated following a lengthy siege. Under the terms that were negotiated, the defenders were permitted to surrender with honor and the men were allowed to retain their personal possessions, including their reserves of winter clothing, a gesture that sparked a short-lived mutiny among the shivering New York troops, who wanted the heavy garments for themselves.[30] At last it was over. The Americans swelled with pride, and optimism. Their victory, thought one New York soldier, was "a most fatal stab" that would ultimately doom the British throughout Canada.[31] Taking Quebec now seemed to many to be a certainty.

Montgomery did not linger at St. Johns. Under heavy grey clouds, his men began the march to Montreal less than seventy-two hours after St. Johns fell. Progress was slow. It rained. Then it snowed. Next the road, such as it was, froze. When it thawed, it turned to fetid ooze, a knee-deep quagmire that made each step a labor-intensive ordeal. Nine days were required to cover twenty miles, but it was not a reprieve that Carleton could use to his advantage. He had only 130 soldiers at his disposal, and he never considered making a defense of Montreal. He had to husband his resources. Only Quebec City really mattered. As Montgomery closed in, Carleton and his men fled, leaving the city to the invaders. Montreal was taken on November 11. Montgomery almost took an even bigger prize.

Carleton and his tiny army set out on their retreat to Quebec City aboard three armed vessels, but they did not get far. Below Montreal, at the Sorel River, the fleet came under fire from American shore batteries, manned by the very men that had foiled Carleton's relief expedition to St. Johns two weeks earlier. Convinced that it was impossible to run the gauntlet, the British surrendered their ships, men, and supplies. But Carleton was not part of the cache. He changed into the clothing of a peasant, was rowed ashore, and succeeded in making his way to Quebec, an escape that perhaps subsequently enabled the British to carry out a last-ditch defense of their capital.[32]

Montgomery had taken St. Johns, Montreal, and the overwhelming majority of the British army in Canada, but he was beset with problems. Snow was falling almost daily and he had not reached Quebec, a target he had expected to see weeks earlier. Worse still, many Connecticut men went home in November when their time of service expired. They were joined by the Green Mountain Boys, who felt that they had done enough. Montgomery had never imagined that taking Quebec City would be easy. He had characterized its conquest by the British in 1759 as "a lucky hit," and he reckoned that he too would need a heaping measure of good fortune to succeed even against an emasculated foe.[33] On November 28, he set out aboard the captured British vessels on the last leg of his trek. With him were three hundred men, all that was left and healthy of an army that fifty days before had totaled nearly seven times that number. Five days later he rendezvoused with Arnold's force at Point aux Trembles, eighteen miles up river from Quebec. Montgomery's men had gone through hell to get there, but the torments they had endured paled against those that Arnold's army had suffered.

Arnold, now a colonel in the Continental army, began to scour for supplies for his expedition during the third week in August. Washington helped in a variety of ways, including sending out a notice for volunteers. More men than Washington could afford to lose stepped forward, either from eagerness to escape the monotony of camp life, or from fervor for adventure, or both. Arnold was looking for "active Woodsmen" who were "well acquainted with batteaus," and he and his staff, with the assistance of Washington and Gates, selected the most fit from among the horde that assembled on the bucolic common in Cambridge to be scrutinized.[34] A week later, Arnold's newly minted army of 1,050 men—mostly New Englanders and New Yorkers—stepped off on a sixty-mile march to Newburyport, where they were to be loaded aboard a small flotilla that would transport them the one hundred miles to the Kennebec River in Maine.[35] Once in Newburyport, the men paraded before a large crowd of "much affected" spectators, causing one soldier to wonder if perhaps the townspeople knowingly suspected that "many of us should never return." The army that marched about this little New England village included a surgeon and his mate, a chaplain, a few musicians, twenty artificers and carpenters, two women (the wives of a sergeant and a private from Pennsylvania), and four St. Francis Indians who signed on as guides. Nearly three hundred Pennsylvania and Virginia riflemen were also in the ranks. When Congress created the Continental army, it had voted to raise ten companies of "expert riflemen"—six from Pennsylvania and two each from Maryland and Virginia—to meet the army's need for marksmen.

Rifles were almost unknown in New England. They were a backcountry tool, made mostly in Pennsylvania and used there and in the Chesapeake colonies by men who hunted for much of their fresh meat. Unlike muskets, which were a smooth bore weapon, the long barrel of a rifle was etched, or "rifled," with seven or eight grooves. Rifling made the weapon accurate at a range of about two hundred yards, perhaps even three hundred, several times the reliable reach of a musket. But rifles had never been adopted by the British army, as they were slower than a musket to load and fire, and could not be equipped with a bayonet. Congress believed riflemen could be useful. As the various rifle companies marched north that summer to join the Continental army, many had stopped in villages along the way to put on shows of marksmanship for awed civilians, including even hitting targets held by a death-defying comrade. During some exhibits, the riflemen donned "Indian shirts" or stripped to the waist and "painted [themselves] like savages," according to witnesses. A Philadelphia newspaper was so impressed that it concluded that "Had Lord North been present," he would have immediately called off the war.[36]

Arnold, who also thought the riflemen desirable, incorporated three companies in his army and put Captain Daniel Morgan in command of them. A forty-year-old giant of a man, Morgan stood six feet tall with thick, broad shoulders and arms like tree trunks. A fellow Continental officer said that he was "strong, not too much encumbered with flesh, [and] exactly fitted for the toils and pomp of war." Morgan, who had grown up on the Virginia frontier, had worked as a teamster in the French and Indian War, hauling supplies to the British army. Fast tempered, Morgan once struck a redcoat officer during an altercation. He paid for his act with a flogging of several hundred lashes that left his back permanently scarred. Later in that war, Morgan served as a ranger in Virginia's army. Still later, he soldiered in another Virginia army that fought the Shawnees in the Ohio Valley. When the Continental army was created, Morgan immediately signed on with a rifle company and was elected a captain. Over a span of just twenty-two days he and his hardy men marched the six hundred miles from the Virginia frontier to Boston, arriving just days before the call was issued for the Canadian expedition. Morgan and his men wasted no time volunteering and were among the first selected.[37] They were woodsmen, to be sure, and unlike the run-of-the-mill Continentals they were always attired in long linen hunting shirts with leather leggings and moccasins. In addition to his rifle, each carried a tomahawk and a scalping knife with a twelve-inch blade.

The New England and New York musketmen in Arnold's force had claimed to have had experience in roughing it on the frontier when they volunteered, but more than a few may have been like Private Jeremiah Greenman, a seventeen-year-old city boy from Newport. He had enlisted a few weeks earlier, he said, to make a man of himself. Like Greenman, many men may have been pretending, but quite a few emulated the riflemen by arming themselves with tomahawks and butcher knives, and a number dressed like Morgan and his men.[38]

As darkness gathered on September 22, twenty-four hours after their departure from Newburyport, the last of the eleven vessels in Arnold's armada reached Gardinerstown, Maine, a tiny village with a shipyard some thirty miles up the Kennebec. The army paused there for forty-eight hours while trees were felled and local shipwrights, working around the clock, constructed two hundred narrow, flat-bottomed bateaux from the green wood. Once the men embarked, they were to portage. The men would use their bateaux—each craft was capable of carrying several men and a considerable cargo of supplies—on every available river, stream, pond, and lake, but when falls were encountered, the soldiers would literally have to muscle their way through thick swamps and dense forests, with four men assigned to carry each two-hundred-pound boat during these detours while others coped with the supplies. Once each craft was built, it was loaded with the gear that Arnold had acquired. He believed that he could make the trek in twenty days, though to be safe he had put in provisions for forty-five days, some sixty-five tons of supplies in all. He was bringing along salted beef and pork, flour, bread, and dried vegetables, which he hoped to supplement with fresh fish and

On the Last Portage of the Great Carrying Place. Drawn by Denman Fink, published in 1903. American soldiers toil with portaging and a thousand other woes during the expedition into Canada in the fall of 1775.

game. One hundred rounds of ammunition per man had also been laid in, together with blankets, tents, spare clothing, medical supplies, cooking paraphernalia, shovels, and axes.[39] Arnold understood that he faced a difficult undertaking, but he hardly thought it impossible. Washington was even more optimistic, remarking that the obstacles presented by the Maine wilderness were "too inconsiderable to make an Objection." Arnold's primary concern at this juncture was with the bateaux, which he suspected might be too flimsy, and he ordered the construction of twenty more as a safeguard.[40] Still, Arnold radiated cheer. He looked forward to the cooperation of the *habitants* of Canada, and in his pocket he carried an appeal to them from the commander of the Continental army. Washington asked that they aid the American soldiers. The "Sons of America," Washington declared, had "taken up Arms in Defense of our Liberty, our Property, our Wives, and our Children," and against London's "Tools of Despotism." The American soldiers, he added, had no wish "to plunder." When at last all the preparations were complete on September 25, Arnold shouted the command to shove off: "To Quebec and victory." All along the way, as he encountered men at various portaging points, Arnold would repeat the chant, until his soldiers knew it as his mantra. With Arnold's joyous clarion call ringing in their ears, the men boarded their bateaux and descended into Maine's dark interior.[41]

Little time passed before it was evident that the leadership had grossly underestimated the difficulties that would be confronted in the wilds of Maine. Within the initial three days—over a fifty-mile stretch that drew the army well beyond Maine's last settlement—the soldiery came on a succession of churning rapids and disquieting falls, including some "very bad rips," as one soldier noted, which resulted in far more portaging than had been anticipated. Arnold's concerns about what he had called the "badness" of the bateaux also proved to be dismayingly accurate, as many sprang leaks. The bigger problem, however, was that many were irreparably damaged as they hurtled and scraped over the rocky bottoms of swift, shallow streams, or were ruined when their crew unexpectedly ran upon steep waterfalls. Tended by inexperienced hands, many bateaux overturned, sending their entire cargo to a watery grave. Nearly a quarter of the army's precious food supply was ruined, or lost, in the first seventy-two hours of the trek. The men were wet constantly—"you would have taken" them for "amphibious Animals," Arnold wrote to Washington—and the night temperatures routinely plummeted below freezing. Each morning the men awakened, said one, to find their clothing "frozen a pane of glass thick." Before he had been in the interior of Maine a week, Arnold reported the "great Fatigue" of his men and quietly worried over whether he had brought along a sufficient supply of food and blankets. The men grew concerned as well, and not only about the dwindling supplies. They "most dreaded" the cold, fearing not only disease, but anxious at their fate should they fall on ice and fracture a leg or hip while deep in the wilderness.[42]

Ten days into the expedition, the food was already being carefully rationed, and it consisted solely of salt pork and flour. Everything else had been ruined, or in the case of the beef that had been brought along it had been preserved so recently that, according to one soldier, it "not only [was] very unwholesome, but very unpalatable." On the nineteenth day the first snow fell. Arnold was not ready to panic. He still had 950 effectives, which suggests that whether or not his men were frontiersmen, most were hardy sorts who were accustomed to hard labor and a strenuous lifestyle. Arnold also believed that within another ten or twelve days he would reach the villages of French *habitants* south of Quebec City, where food would be plentiful. Soon, however, his optimism ebbed as worries on other scores piled up. In mid-October, a nor'easter blew through, toppling trees. The rain, driven by the ferocious winds, painfully lashed the men. The rains lingered, making it difficult to build fires. Swollen rivers only added to the difficulty of paddling and poling the bateaux. Compounding the misery, portaging was a nightmare. One portage point was twelve miles across, and traversing it was not easy. "Every step we made sank us knee-deep in a bed of soft turf," one soldier lamented. Another declared that this entire region was so rugged that it "could scarcely be passed by wild beasts." By now, men had also discovered that constantly wet shoes disintegrated. Many soldiers had no choice but to walk barefoot through forests thick with sharp pinecones. Illness overtook a tenth of the men. Most were felled with diarrhea, but some suffered with debilitating rheumatism and arthritis. Before mid-October, Arnold toyed with the idea of turning back.[43]

But he pressed on, not knowing that worse lay ahead. On October 19 more torrential rains and howling winds whipped the men, probably from a late season hurricane that had struck the Maine coast and pressed inland, its fury barely diminished. Already swollen rivers surged out of their banks. The water rose at an incredible rate—eight feet in nine hours. Grabbing everything they could lay their hands on, the men struggled, slipping and sliding, to reach the highest ground. More bateaux were lost and, worse still, more of the food supply was ruined. Arnold and his men were in deep trouble. On the eve of the storm, he had calculated that he had only a two-week supply of food remaining. Now there was even less. Facing the stolid gaze of his officers and trying to conceal his sullen gloom, Arnold nevertheless confided to one of the officers that "we have but a melancholy prospect before us."[44]

Shrouding the rampant misery, and contributing to everyone's wretchedness, was uncertainty. They had been isolated from the outer world for a month. Arnold had no idea what awaited him in Quebec, including whether Montgomery would be there with his army. Nor did he know if Carleton had learned of his expedition. If so, he might fall on Arnold's beleaguered army the minute it reached the St. Lawrence. The men shared the same concerns, and dwelled on others, including the hand-wringing fear, spread by rumor, that they would be made to spend the winter in the menacing Maine wilderness. Arnold walked among them seeking to allay their concerns. If they could make it another thirty miles, he told them, they would reach Lake Megantic and, from it, the Chaudière River, which emptied into the St. Lawrence. The worst would then be behind them, Arnold promised, as once on the Chaudière they could float effortlessly toward their objective.

The men's miseries only multiplied. Three days after the second great storm blew itself out, the ground was covered by two inches of snow. Three days later the snow was six inches deep. At this point, the men had gone without meat for eight days. Food was so scarce that each man was allotted only a pint of flour daily. Hunting for fresh meat was next to useless, as the racket made by the large army drove away the game. Some men supplemented their meager diet with soup concocted from boiled shoes and gruel fashioned out of melted candles, while pet dogs and strays that had joined in the expedition in search of human companion- ship and a scrap of food, wound up in mess pots. Most men soldiered on. But not all. On October 25 an entire battalion of 450 men under Lietenant Colonel Roger Enos defected, stripping the army of more than one-third of its manpower and almost half of its supplies. It was treachery of the worst sort. Enos com- manded the rear division of Arnold's army, the portion that was customarily entrusted with the reserves of food. He possessed a sufficient store of victuals so that, before defecting, he might have sent forward roughly 150 men with a seven- or eight-day supply of provisions. Instead, he absconded with all his men and provender. So bitter were those who persisted that, according to one soldier, they "made a General Prayer" that Enos and his men "might die by the way, or meet some disaster." (Enos survived to face a court martial on his return to Massachusetts, where he was exonerated, in large measure because all who might have testified against him were in Quebec.). Arnold was left with some 550 ill and famished men.[45]

Just as the sun set on October 27, after four snowy days of travail, the army reached Lake Megantic. They were five hundred miles due north of Boston. Arnold was full of fight again. While the men paused, he wrote Washington that if Carleton was "not apprised of our coming, and there is any Prspect of surprsing the City, I shall attempt it."[46] Arnold dispatched parties to search out residents and, hopefully, to purchase food, after which, with renewed vigor, he set the army on the move again, confident that the worst of his tribulations were behind him. Arnold's glee was misplaced. The Chaudière ran too swiftly for these landlub- bers. One bateaux after another overturned. Others hurtled into giant rocks and were smashed apart. Many boats were lost, and with them the last of the food and equipment. Always before, there had been something to eat, however scant. Now the men had only what they could gather. For most, that meant going without. Some shot small game—an owl here, a partridge there. Acting with a few of his buddies, Private Greenman, the tenderfoot from Newport, killed a dog and "boyled [it] up together" with "the head of a Squirll" and "a parcel of Candill wicks." It "made very fine Supe," he declared. On the third day beyond Lake Megantic one famished soldier noted in his diary that he could "scarce stand." On awakening and taking his first step of the day, he said, he had "staggered about like a drunken man." Another, who somehow still had a sense of humor, quipped that cooking lately was "very much out of fashion." But toward the end of that same day one of the lead parties encountered a small band of French settlers who sold them corn meal and tobacco. Though not much, one soldier declared that he and his comrades "blessed our stars and thought it a luxury." The next day the most "Joifulest Sight" came into view—a French village, Sartigan (St. Egan today), a tiny town with thatch-roofed houses. The residents were "very civil" and sold considerable food to the men, though at exorbitant prices. Most soldiers had their first fresh meat in weeks.[47]

In the first days of November, the last man (and the two women) in the invading army emerged from the wilderness to find occasional villages consisting of whitewashed houses and thatched roofs. The French inhabitants were surprisingly friendly, especially given the appearance of the ragged, bearded men who, said one, must have "resembled the animals . . . called the Ourang-outang." Washington had given Arnold strict orders to treat the Canadians and Indians as "Friends and Brethren," and to "avoid all Disrespect or Contempt of the Religion of the Country," and Arnold saw that the directive was enforced. The army scrupulously purchased its supplies, and the residents were anxious to sell for hard currency. Suddenly, food was plentiful. The men dined on oxen, pork, chicken, lamb, beef, beef broth, and an array of vegetables.[48] The Indians in the neighborhood were peaceful and some were helpful. The only sour note to reach the Bostonnais, as the habitants called the American soldiers, was word that Carleton's intelligence network had discovered the advancing army. The element of surprise was lost. Still, the men were exhilarated. They had survived the ordeal posed by Maine's inhospitable hinterland. Perhaps they would get home alive. Soon they were on the St. Lawrence and on November 9, sixty-five days after having fatefully volunteered in Cambridge, the men sighted Quebec City, barely visible through the blowing snow.

Arnold paused again, sending out parties to determine whether the city was defended or if Carleton was up river coping with Montgomery. They were also to seek information on Montgomery's condition and whereabouts. Over several days, the intelligence-gatherers returned with strikingly good information. Some of Carleton's men were elsewhere coping with Montgomery, but some regulars and militia—perhaps eight hundred men, Arnold was told—were inside Quebec's nine-foot-tall walls. Arnold summoned a council of war to consider the options. After a lengthy debate, a majority of the officers voted against assaulting Quebec, preferring to wait and link up with Montgomery, and to gamble that London would not reinforce the enemy in the interim. Arnold, who was scorchingly ambitious, was disappointed by the council's vote, but he listened to his officers.[49]

Another nettlesome matter awaited a decision. Arnold not only had to get his army across the mile and a half wide St. Lawrence, he had to land it on the west side of Quebec City if he was to rendezvous with Montgomery. That meant slipping past the British naval craft that patrolled the river. Arnold did not wish to undertake such a risky enterprise until the weather was right: a windless night with heavy skies that hid the moon. He did not have to wait long. The operation commenced on November 13. His plan was to cross the river, land at Wolfe's Cove about two miles southwest of the city, and climb to the Plains of Abraham. The first contingent set out at 9:00 p.m. on the stygian night, with Arnold in the lead canoe. A second group followed thirty minutes later, then a third. After seven hours, all the men were safely across. None had been spotted by British security.

Once across, Arnold assembled those who were fit to make a show of force. He had them give three cheers, whereupon, noted one soldier, the defenders of Quebec "gave us as many cannon shot" in return. Undeterred, Arnold sent over a messenger with a demand that the British surrender. Lieutenant Colonel Allan Maclean was in command. He had led the relief force Carleton sent to liberate the garrison at St. Johns, but had returned to Quebec City just prior to Arnold's arrival. Maclean acidly spurned the order to surrender. Arnold, his bluster unavailing, directed his ragged men to make their final march in a swirling snow to Point aux Trembles, about twenty miles away, where he said he would await Montgomery with "Impatience." Frustrated, he knew that he had come close to achieving victory; "Had I been ten Days sooner, Quebec must inevitably have fallen into our Hands, as there was not a Man there to oppose us."[50]

Arnold and his men waited anxiously, uncertain whether Montgomery or an enemy force dispatched from Quebec would be the first to reach Point aux Trembles. He need not have worried. Carleton, who had finally reached Quebec about a dozen days after Arnold's arrival, had no plans to emerge from his fortress. A professional soldier who had served as General Wolfe's primary engineer during the campaign for Quebec in 1759, and who had suffered three wounds in the Seven Years' War, Carleton spent his time readying his defenses. Quebec had been through previous sieges, so Carleton worked from experience. He had begun to acquire, and carefully manage, his supplies as early as six months before. If the Americans invaded Quebec, and food from London did not arrive before the St. Lawrence froze at year's end, the besieged garrison would need perhaps a six-month supply of comestibles. He repaired the walls about the city and positioned his artillery. And he tracked down men to defend the post. He had about 150 regulars. To these, he added 37 marines and some 350 sailors from the Royal Navy. He also laid his hands on nearly five hundred militiamen, at least 60 percent of whom were French Canadians. Altogether, Carleton had scraped together more than one thousand defenders.[51]

While he waited, Arnold made contact with Montgomery, who was at Montreal. Telling him that his army was "as ready, as naked men can be," Arnold urged him to come quickly. Montgomery did just that, stepping ashore on December 2 to the lusty cheers of the shaggy men at Point aux Trembles. Montgomery's arrival brought the American troop strength to 1,325, about one-third the number that had comprised the twin invasion forces two months earlier. Montgomery also brought along food, winter clothing, and two hundred pairs of shoes from Montreal, as well as cannon that he had stripped from the captured British vessels.[52]

One of the first tasks facing Montgomery, who assumed command, was to persuade the remaining New England men, whose tour of duty was to end at the end of the day on December 31, to reenlist. There were few takers, even when the general pleaded with them to sign on only until April 15, or until reinforcements arrived, which might be as early as late January. Although he failed, Montgomery was impressed with Arnold's men. They were tough and hearty, and some were battle hardened, having fought on Bunker Hill.[53]

Twenty-four hours after arriving, Montgomery moved the army to the Plains of Abraham, just outside Quebec, and began preparations for what he knew would be a formidable challenge. A siege was out of the question. The army was too small to encircle Quebec and seal off the flow of supplies from rural Canada. Nor did Montgomery ever imagine that Carleton would surrender before year's end, and for that matter he correctly suspected that the British had laid in sufficient supplies to hold out until London could run in reinforcements in the spring. Montgomery also believed that Carleton would not replicate the mistake of the Marquis de Montcalm, who had emerged from the protective womb of Quebec to fight a set-piece battle against the British sixteen years earlier. Quebec, Montgomery said from the outset, would have to be taken by assault, an operation that he took to referring to as the "storming plan." Like Arnold before him, he went through the motions of demanding that the garrison surrender, and when that failed he commenced a bombardment, hoping that his "fire pills," as some of his men labeled the fusillade, would sow dissension within the walls of the citadel. The British responded with a cannonading of their own. With heavier artillery, they were able to pour shells into the rebels' lines. In one instance, Montgomery once again narrowly escaped death when a shell hit a carriage from which he had alighted only seconds earlier, destroying it and decapitating the horse that had pulled it. During another fusillade one of the two women with the army was struck and killed.[54]

Montgomery originally planned his assault for the wee hours of December 28, but it was a clear moonlit night, which frustrated all hope of surprise. He aborted the attack and the next morning revised his battle plan. The prospect of combat had driven one or two men to desert to the enemy, and Montgomery suspected that they had divulged what they knew to Quebec's defenders. The American commander had to know that the odds were against him, as he sat down to draw his final plan of attack. Not only had Quebec always been thought to be impregnable, sitting as it did atop a tall, steep promontory, but it was an axiom of eighteenth-century warfare that those who attacked a heavily defended garrison must have a substantial numerical superiority. Montgomery knew that Carleton had achieved virtual numerical equality and possessed superior artillery. Still, Montgomery was not without hope, or so he said. "Fortune favors the brave," he declared, and he knew that battles often hinged on intangibles such as leadership under fire, heroism, good fortune, blunders, resiliency, planning, tenacity, and surprise.[55] His new plan built in as much surprise as possible, and he was confident that his men, who had exhibited such mettle in getting to Quebec, would be more hard-nosed than the defenders. He knew too that Carleton had to defend an enormous area, and that his troops, of necessity, would be widely scattered, leading Montgomery to plan an attack by a heavy concentration of American fire power. Depending on the weather, the attack would take place in the small hours of the morning on December 30 or 31.

Montgomery's initial plan had been to act during "the first strong north-wester." He would break into the lower town and set it ablaze, hoping the gusty winds might produce a giant conflagration that would consume the palisade and sow confusion, allowing his men to storm into the upper town.[56] Under his new plan Arnold, with about six hundred of his men, was to circle around on the north and northeast side of Quebec, while Montgomery, with three hundred New Yorkers, was to do the same on the southwest side. Each force would have to fight its way through two formidable barricades, made of felled trees, and defended by small British detachments. Montgomery also planned two diversions, attacks by small American forces at St. John's Gate and the Cape Diamond Gate, both on the southwest side of the citadel, designed to deceive Carleton with regard to where the real blow was to fall. All the while, a mortar battery was to pour fire into the city to sow additional confusion. Once Arnold and Montgomery had surmounted the barricades, they would link up at the entrance to the lower town, the site of the business district, and the least fortified portion of Quebec. They would proceed up the steep, nearly mile-long road that connected the lower and upper towns. At the top, they would have to fight their way through Prescott's Gate and into the walled defenses of Quebec. If they managed this much, Montgomery was confident that resistance would break down. But even if they failed to breach Prescott's Gate, he calculated that he could force Carleton's capitulation by threatening to raze the commercial district that would be in his possession. It was a well-conceived and daring plan for a Herculean task.

It began propitiously. A snowstorm commenced after nightfall on December 30. Not only would that limit the visibility of the defenders, preserving the element of surprise, but Carleton might not anticipate an attack under such adverse conditions. Arnold and Montgomery readied their men after midnight, and at 4:00 a.m.—it was now December 31—each moved out. Each man had pinned a piece of white paper to his hat so he could distinguish friend from foe in the dark, and some had scribbled "Liberty or Death" on their scrap of paper.[57] Almost immediately things went wrong. Montgomery had hoped to coordinate the varied activities of his army by launching flares, and while that worked, it also tipped off the British to the pending attack. The pealing of alarm bells inside the citadel announced to Montgomery that the defenders knew that he was coming. His two feints, moreover, were carried out by such small detachments that the British were never for a moment fooled.

The men under Arnold and Montgomery advanced through treacherous conditions. Ice-laden paths, snowdrifts, blinding snow, and (in Montgomery's sector) huge chunks of ice tossed ashore from the storm-lashed St. Lawrence, dogged the soldiers every step. Men who were moving along unfamiliar paths "got bewildered."[58] Conditions aside, Arnold's men reached the first barricade that guarded the lower town, arriving at this first target thirty minutes or more before Montgomery came to his first obstacle. The Americans, with a single field piece, opened fire, hoping to blow apart the obstacle and hurry through. The defenders responded both with artillery of their own and a hail of musket fire. In the first minutes of the engagement, Arnold was hit, taking a ricocheting ball in his lower left leg. It penetrated to the edge of his Achilles tendon, leaving him unable to stand and facing the loss of copious amounts of blood. Daniel Morgan took charge and eliminated the resistance at this barricade. He led his men to the second obstacle three hundred yards away, where he ordered four unsuccessful assaults before discipline broke down.[59] Their leader, Arnold, was gone, having been carried to the rear in the hope of saving his life, and Montgomery was nowhere to be seen. The men's weapons were wet and many were no longer serviceable. Carleton, deducing that Morgan's assault on the second obstacle posed the maximum danger, at least for the moment, had rushed reinforcements to that sector. Faced with a withering fire, the Americans fell back. The British pressed their advance and even recaptured the first barricade.

Montgomery's men, moving along the river, had faced a more difficult trek and were late reaching their first barricade. It was undefended. Wielding axes, the Americans hurriedly cut their way through. They had hardly set out for the second barricade when they ran upon a two-story blockhouse that guarded the path toward the lower town. Montgomery gathered his men and hurried forward, hoping to take it easily with his overwhelming numbers. Fifty yards from the blockhouse he formed his lines for a charge, and gave the order to move. The men took only a step or two before they ran into an artillery salvo and sheets of musket fire. Montgomery was one of the first to be cut down, taking multiple hits that killed him instantly. Others fell all about. The fight raged on for a spell, but the attackers never took the blockhouse, and never reached the second barricade. By around 7:00 a.m., with day breaking under a grey snowy sky, the battle was over and the Americans who could do so were on the retreat back to the Plains of Abraham, leaving their dead and wounded behind.

The American losses were staggering. Not only had the six-month campaign to take Quebec, and Canada, failed, but sixty men had been killed and wounded. Another 426 who had endured unimaginable torments to reach this objective had been taken prisoner. In three hours, more than a third of the American army in Canada was lost. British losses totaled only eighteen men.[60] Not only had the British won a huge military victory, but the triumph provided a monumental emotional lift. The "Yankees were no longer held in a respectable light; our

General Guy Carleton. By A. H. Ritchie, late in the nineteenth century. A British general who served as the chief executive of Canada, Carleton's tenacity led to a great triumph in 1775, but his caution robbed him of crucial victories in 1776.

success at least was equal to a reinforcement of 5000 men," said one of the soldiers who had defended Quebec.[61]

The Americans had bitten off too much. With untrained men, inadequate planning, and a dearth of supplies born of callow optimism, the rebels had attempted an extremely risky undertaking, and failed. What is most amazing is how close they came to success. Victory likely would have been theirs had Arnold reached Quebec a few days earlier, when both Carleton and Maclean were far away dealing with Montgomery, and Quebec was essentially undefended. What is almost as astonishing is that Arnold reached his objective at all, given the colossal adversities his army faced. In the detritus left by this failed campaign, Arnold's leadership and perseverance stood out, and so, too, did the mettle of the citizen-soldiers that he commanded. But Guy Carleton was not to be outshone. Though faced with many of the same tribulations of his adversaries, he deftly kept Montgomery at bay for three crucial months, after which he prepared a masterful defense of Quebec that was too much for the Americans to overcome.

THE NEW YEAR began with a dark crisis for General Washington—the disbanding of one army and the need to recruit another. On January 17 another emergency fell on him when he learned from Schuyler of the "severe Check" suffered at Quebec. Washington immediately convened a council of war to determine whether he could afford to strip any men from his army and send them north to continue the siege of Quebec. The officers decided quickly that they had no men to spare, though they asked Massachusetts, Connecticut, and New Hampshire to immediately raise a Continental regiment of 728 officers and men, and they complied.[62]

Washington was eager to do something with his army. A man of action, he was temperamentally ill suited to inactivity, which he came close to equating with dishonor. Real or imagined, he also felt pressure from Congress and the New England authorities to do something. He had been in command for six months and had been immobile all the while. His predecessor had acted in June, scoring what now was seen by all as a great American victory at Bunker Hill. Moreover, Washington believed that British reinforcements were likely on the way, and when they reached Boston his opportunity for taking the initiative would be gone.

At a council of war in September, Washington had raised the possibility of attacking the regulars in Boston by making a feint on the Cambridge side of the city, then striking across Boston Neck well to the south. His officers rejected the suggestion, prudently arguing that the redcoats were strong and entrenched, the Continentals lacked artillery and ammunition, and the neck was so narrow that it could easily be defended. An attack, they seemed to say, would likely result in a debacle of Bunker Hill proportions, but this time for the Americans. Washington accepted their advice, but he chafed quietly, later saying that had he understood the "backwardness" of most of these officers, he never would have listened to their counsel.[63]

The Continentals and the British remained inactive that fall and winter, and the men on both sides settled in for a long siege operation. Later in the war it was the Americans who would suffer most in winter, almost always facing a dearth of supplies, but during the war's first winter the British soldiers had the worst of it. The Americans faced shortages of men, arms, and munitions, but with nothing to inhibit the flow of supplies from New England's farms, food was plentiful. The men were adequately sheltered as well. Some lived in barracks, though most were in hastily constructed huts made of wood, stone, or brick, or in tents fashioned from sailcloth. Now and then, shortages plagued the Americans, as was the case late in December when a temporary scarcity of wood caused some "to Eat their Provision Raw for want of firing to Cook." Many men implored their wives to send help. Lieutenant Joseph Hodgkins, who had been a cobbler in Ipswich before the war, asked his wife to send thread as "I must make a pr or two of Boots," and he also requested bedding, shirts, stockings, sugar, and coffee. Colonel Loammi Baldwin of nearby Woburn at one time or another appealed to his wife for paper, ink, quills, broadcloth, linen, bread, potatoes, onions, cabbage, rum, brandy, salt, cornmeal, and shoes. On the whole, morale remained high among the American soldiery, who, according to an officer, "express a strong desire to fight."[64]

The British, on the other hand, were "cooped up in a corner . . . without great prospect of supplies," as one of their officers remarked. Trapped in a city that ordinarily depended on the surrounding countryside for its supply of food and was cruelly short of pasturage for the livestock, the redcoats faced alarming shortages. They were never devoid of food, but the army never had more than a twenty-day supply on hand that winter. Much of the time the men had neither fresh meat nor vegetables. Howe often complained to London that he was "in great Pain from the small quantity of Provisions," and he sent convoys to forage for hay and oats in the Bay of Fundy and the Province of Quebec, and to search for rice and other comestibles near Savannah. Otherwise, the British relied on what had been stored prior to April 19 and what arrived from England. Relief ships reached Boston from time to time, but in more than one instance the food they brought had rotted or been severely damaged in the course of the ocean crossing. Like his rebel counterparts, Captain Evelyn asked his family to send him beef, butter, and peas, adding that, "any of them would be extremely acceptable in these hard times." Food was not the only item that the redcoats found wanting. They endured acute deficiencies of coal, wood, and good tents, insufficiencies that caused untold miseries when New England's autumn rains, often accompanied by a "keen wind," beset the city and left many redcoats reminiscing about "the comforts of a chimney corner." Worse followed when winter struck, as many British soldiers had never experienced the likes of the bitterly low temperatures, not to mention the snow and ice, which afflicted Boston for weeks on end. Howe had no choice but to order out parties to tear down fences and abandoned houses and businesses, and to cut down trees for fire wood. Boston's Liberty Tree, an old elm around which the Sons of Liberty had rallied to protest British policies, was one of the casualties. It was good for fourteen cords. Even some of Boston's wharves were torn apart for firewood. Given these deprivations, it was not long before smallpox, scurvy, and other ailments set in. At times as many as thirty British soldiers died daily.[65]

Washington would have liked to increase the redcoats' suffering, but there was little he could do. He ordered an occasional raid or bombardment, but none caused much damage. From the outset, Washington's options were limited by his lack of artillery. When he reorganized the army during the summer, Washington proposed the creation of an artillery regiment, and he happened on a young officer who he believed possessed the skills to organize and lead such a corps. Four days after arriving in Cambridge, Washington had inspected the siege lines laid out in Roxbury under the guidance of Henry Knox. Washington was impressed by what he saw, and even more certain of Knox's talent when General Lee lavishly praised the engineering that had gone into these works. Washington kept an eye on Knox and, when Congress consented to the army's reorganization, he worked quietly to secure the assent of the general officers to leapfrog Knox over Colonel Richard Gridley, a fifty-four-year-old veteran soldier who had previously been responsible for the army's engineering needs. Washington got what he wanted. In mid-November, Knox was commissioned a colonel in the Continental Army and made commander of the army's new artillery regiment.[66]

General Henry Knox. Painting by Charles Willson Peale, from life, c. 1784. With the help of John Adams and other Massachusetts officials, Washington discovered Knox soon after assuming command. Knox proved to be one of the most capable of the Continental Army's general officers.

Knox was just twenty-five. The son of an English immigrant, he had dropped out of school after three years and gone to work for a bookseller at age thirteen. Bright and inquisitive, and drawn toward military history, young Knox read every book on the subject in the shop where he worked. In 1766 he joined a militia company of artillery that the royal authorities organized. From then on he keyed his reading to matters concerning ordnance, especially artillery, and in the early 1770s Knox helped organize the Boston Grenadier Corps, an artillery company under the control of provincials. Just a day or two after Lexington-Concord, he volunteered for service in the siege army. Knox was an imposing figure. Stout and above six feet tall, he dwarfed most men. Boomingly outgoing, Knox exuded boundless energy, a jovial spirit, and a keen mind, and he struck many powerful men—including John Adams, who put in a word with Washington on his behalf —as just the right man to get an artillery regiment up and running.[67]

Two weeks before Congress approved Knox's appointment, Washington ordered his putative artillery commander to undertake a mission to retrieve the artillery taken when Fort Ticonderoga had been captured. Knox was told to act with the "utmost dispatch," and he complied, bringing off one of the most remarkable feats of this war.[68]

Accompanied by a brother and servant, Knox reached snow-shrouded Ticonderoga about two weeks after his departure from Cambridge. He spent three days sorting through the weaponry—some of the artillery was dilapidated —and supervising the disassembling and loading of the useful ordnance onto gondolas. Fifty-five guns weighing about sixty tons, together with incredibly burdensome barrels of flints and boxes of lead, were eventually muscled onto the vessels. These guns included thirty-nine field pieces, two howitzers, and fourteen mortars. The field guns of that day ranged from three-pounders to forty-two-pounders, with the weight referring to the poundage of the solid shot that was fired. Howitzers were weapons with short barrels that could be fired at a greater variety of angles. Mortars were the smallest of these weapons and, as is the case today, were fired at a high angle. Field guns and howitzers fired either solid shot (an iron ball) or grape and canister (antipersonnel devices that flung small iron balls and other shrapnel over a wide area). Mortar shells were iron balls loaded with powder and a fuse. Mortars had a range of up to 1,300 yards. The longest howitzers could reach a target two thousand yards away, and the biggest field guns could hurl a projectile well over a mile. If the Continental army, separated from the besieged British by the wide Charles River, was to inflict real damage, artillery was the weapon of choice.[69]

On December 9, with a party of three hundred soldiers and civilian workers, mostly teamsters, Knox shoved out onto Lake George. At its lower end, with more snow gathering, he collected 160 oxen, several span of horses, more than forty heavy-duty sleds, and numerous cattle. After carefully calculating how much weight each draft animal could manage, Knox ordered his freight transferred to the sleighs, and set out overland. Near Albany, roughly fifty miles below Fort George, Knox's heavily laden sleds made a treacherous crossing of the frozen Hudson. Spacing the sleds two hundred yards apart in order to minimize their weight, he almost got all his cargo to the other side without incident, but one of the larger cannon broke through the ice and sank to the bottom of the Hudson. Fortunately, it went under in shallow water near the shore, and with help from nearby residents, who pitched in without being asked, Knox retrieved that artillery piece. He immediately christened it "The Albany" and resumed his eastward journey. During the second week of January the train entered the Berkshires, forcing the teamsters to grapple with twisting roads and hills so tall, said Knox, that from their summit "We might almost have seen all the kingdoms of the earth." There were also valleys, ponds, rivers, and ever-deeper snow, and above all the special danger of contending with the heavy and unwieldy sleds on steep downhill grades. Using block and tackle, and infinite care and deliberation, they made it without the loss of a single life or weapon. Knox's party exited the mountains near Springfield around January 20, and he rode ahead to Cambridge to notify Washington of his achievement and to oversee the construction of carriages for his artillery. Knox reached headquarters forty-seven days after departing Ticonderoga and the artillery arrived over the next two weeks. At Cambridge, Knox happily discovered that in his absence the *Nancy*, a British ordnance vessel had been captured. Its cargo included thousands of artillery shot and shells, as well as two thousand muskets and two tons of musket balls and powder.[70] Two months earlier Knox had commanded an artillery corps without artillery. He could never have enough weaponry, but the two months since his appointment had brought an amazing transformation.

While Knox was on his mission to Ticonderoga, Washington had pondered what course to pursue should he attain the artillery that he coveted. At the outset of the year he had told Congress that he would do something "the first moment I see a probability of success." Two weeks later he advised a council of war that he could scrape together about 13,000 men—half would be militiamen—and added that he wished to make "a Bold attempt" to drive the redcoats from Boston during the next few weeks. But what, exactly, could he do? Through January and into early February, Washington toyed with three notions: send the army across the frozen Charles to assault the entrenched British army in north and northwest Boston; attack Bunker Hill, hoping to drive off the British who had occupied it since June; or, take control of Dorchester Heights, which overlooked Boston harbor from south of the city, and invite Howe to replicate his fight for Charlestown Heights. Washington eventually embraced the first choice—attacking across the Charles—and in mid-February summoned another council of war. He made it clear that the time for action had arrived. There now were 16,000 men in camp, he said, and intelligence was reporting that Howe had no more than 5,000 fit for duty. He presented the generals with what he saw as the three options, and advocated an assault on the enemy's lines, declaring that a "Stroke well aim'd . . . might put a final end to the War." His generals were stunned by his proposal. Gates remarked straightaway that the commander's duty was to fight a defensive war, not to risk an untried and untrained army in assaults on an enemy that was well dug in. The generals quickly advised against assailing the British in Boston or on Bunker Hill, fastening instead on taking Dorchester. Seizing those heights might draw Howe into an especially bloody undertaking, as Washington would have artillery and ammunition that Prescott could only have dreamed of while defending Bunker Hill. Washington was urged to reconnoiter the region. He did so that evening, and the next, and concluded that it, like Bunker Hill, could be made into a formidable defensive site.[71] From that point forward, Dorchester was the focal point of Washington's planning, but he never entirely abandoned his preference for an assault across the Charles. He laid his hands on four thousand small craft and made ready to use them. If Howe sent an army up Dorchester Heights, Washington would launch an attack in his rear.[72]

Washington was free to occupy Dorchester Heights, as neither Gage nor Howe had bothered to do so. The American high command had expected the British to take possession of the heights during the summer and were perplexed when they failed to do so. Not only should they have wanted to keep the heights out of the hands of the Americans, but the region would have served as good pasture land for their horses and cattle.[73] Several factors stayed the hand of the British. A torpor fell over them in the immediate aftermath of Bunker Hill, and a lassitude also appears to have shrouded Gage once he suspected that his recall was imminent. From the moment that he assumed command, Howe had been given the green light by London to abandon Boston, and for some time he believed he would be gone before New Year's Day. The British also knew that while they could easily occupy the heights, they might have to pay a heavy price to keep it, for the Dorchester peninsula could be attacked simultaneously from three sides, and it could be bombarded mercilessly should Washington secure artillery.

Washington's final plan for taking Dorchester Heights, cobbled together in the course of frequent meetings with his principal officers, called for carrying out a steady bombardment of Boston on the nights of March 2 through 4. On the last of those three nights, while the distracting barrage continued, two thousand men under General Thomas, accompanied by oxen that were to pull wagons loaded with paraphernalia, were to steal up the heights and prepare defensive installations on its two hills. As the earth was frozen to a depth of nearly eighteen inches, it would be impossible to dig out a redoubt and earthworks quickly. Instead, the men were to construct a breastwork made from felled trees and what eighteenth-century armies called chandeliers, wooden frames packed with gabions (cylindrical wicker baskets stuffed with dirt), fascines (bundles of three or four long wooden stakes), and hay. Richard Gridley, who had chosen the site for the redoubt on Bunker Hill, and whom Washington had passed over in selecting Knox, was given responsibility for preparing the entrenchments. When this work was complete, these men were to come off the hills, and be replaced by three thousand fresh troops under the overall command of Artemas Ward. The success of the undertaking hinged on secrecy and speed.[74]

The operation unfolded nearly perfectly. Even the weather cooperated. Although a bright moon hung in the clear winter sky, the night was unseasonably mild and a low-lying fog shrouded Boston, obscuring the British army's view of Dorchester Heights. The shuddering bombardment also drowned out the sounds of the rebels' heavy labor. Abigail Adams in Braintree was three times as far from the American lines as was Howe in Boston, and she spoke of the "amazing" and "incessant Roar" of cannon that literally shook her house some eight miles away.[75] (One aspect of the operation that did not go so well was that the barrels burst on several of the invaluable artillery pieces that Knox had brought from Ticonderoga, the result mainly of inexperienced gunners using too much powder.)[76] When morning arrived the British awakened to find American infantry and artillery staring down at Boston harbor, and guarded by a labyrinth of defensive emplacements. It was "a most astonishing night's work," one British officer marveled.[77] Another was so startled by the speed with which the Americans had occupied the hill that he thought it had been accomplished magically, as if Washington had employed "the Genii belonging to Aladdin's Wonderful Lamp." In the ruddy light of dawn, Howe gaped at the sight through a telescope and allegedly remarked that the "rebels have done more in one night, than my whole army could do in months." Later, he told London that

Washington must have had 10,000 laborers at work to have accomplished the job so swiftly.[78] The chief engineer of the British army in Boston estimated that Washington had employed 20,000 workers.[79]

With the American artillery now commanding his lifeline to Great Britain, Howe had to do something. His first instinct was to attack, and he was urged to do so by some of his generals. James Grant, for instance, had been insisting all along that the British had been "too gentle" with these "Rough Republican Fanatic People." He wished to send the army up the heights, kill every rebel that could be found, then "burn this town" and leave. Sow terror, he advised, and the "American Bubble must soon burst."[80] Howe readied a force of two thousand men, but wet and windy weather knifed into Boston before it could move, forcing a postponement. The williwaw also gave Howe time to reconsider. Howe was a changed man following his dreadful experiences on Charlestown Heights. His unwavering audacity, previously his hallmark, had withered in the aftermath of that bloody day. But it was not entirely a lack of stout-heartedness that led to his reluctance to assault Dorchester Heights. Howe knew that he at last possessed sufficient vessels to exit Boston, an escape of which he had dreamt these past six months. He saw little reason to risk the lives, and morale, of his soldiers by undertaking what could only be a bloody and uncertain attack.

Getting out of Boston unscathed would not be easy. From Dorchester Heights, the American artillery could rake Britain's transports, possibly sending Howe's entire army to the bottom of Boston harbor. To eliminate this threat, Howe played his trump card on March 7, forty-eight hours after discovering that the rebels were on the heights, offering Washington a bargain. If "his Majesty's Troops should not be molested during their Imbarkation or at their Departure," he would not put the torch to Boston. Washington's choice was not an easy one: possibly capture or destroy Howe's entire army versus the utter destruction of Boston. He was immediately pressured by the Massachusetts authorities, many of whom had homes and businesses in the city, to accept Howe's proffer. Washington also feared that the destruction of Boston would have an adverse effect on opinion in other cities, possibly causing the leading lights in Philadelphia, New York, and Charleston to redouble their efforts to pursue a settlement with London. Washington accepted the deal.[81]

Leaving Boston was a time consuming process. The British had much to pack and load aboard ships, while other items that could not be taken were to be destroyed to keep them from the hands of the rebels. Finally, ten days after Washington assented to the agreement, the last British vessel, loaded with regulars, sailed over the horizon and out of sight. London's eight-year military occupation of Boston was over. On March 17, Washington sent in a regiment to take control of the city. He graciously permitted Artemas Ward to ride at its head, with Old Put just behind him. All the men in this party were smallpox survivors, as Washington had received intelligence—erroneous, thankfully—that Howe "had laid several Schemes for communicating the infection of the small-pox, to the Continental Army, when they get into the town." Bostonians welcomed their liberators with "lively joy" on their faces, said one soldier. They cheered from open windows and rushed into the street to hug the soldiers. A Connecticut sergeant, who longed to tell the home folks that he had been in Boston, recalled that "females opened their doors & windows with decanters of wine in their hands to bid us welcome." The Continentals found that much had been destroyed or plundered, and they were particularly outraged to find that the regulars had demolished one church and turned another, the Old South Meeting House, into an exercise site for their horses, tearing out its pews and pulpit, and covering the floor with dirt. To their delight, they also discovered that the redcoats had left behind two brigantines, four schooners, two sloops, more than a hundred horses, eighteen cannon, some mortars and swivel guns, and a variety of equipment. Other American soldiers entered Charlestown on that same sunny day. They walked its gutted streets and climbed to the top of Bunker Hill, where they cheered themselves hoarse at their victory. Washington quietly entered Boston the next day, forgoing the opportunity to lead a victory parade, but in his official report he postured as the originator of the plan to occupy Dorchester Heights— Howe's "flight" from Boston, he said, "was precipitated by the appearance of a Work which I had order'd . . . on an Eminence at Dorcester"—never telling Congress of the alternative operation that he had preferred, or of his generals' opposition to his scheme.[82]

It was a majestic triumph for the Americans. For many in London it was a humbling reversal, something that Lord North's cabinet had never imagined possible when it debated how to respond to the Boston Tea Party thirty months earlier. Critics in Parliament and the press had a field day. They labeled Howe's evacuation a "flight," called it "a blot of dishonor" to be "forced to quit that town which was the first object of the war," and prayed that the loss of the city, as well as the ample and "bloody proofs" of American courage, would lead the government to reassess its American policy.[83] If a sullen mood fell over England, the colonists celebrated, and nowhere more than in New England, which felt vindicated in its resistance and sacrifice. No one was honored more than Washington. Harvard College awarded him an honorary doctorate and Congress ordered a gold medallion struck that showed Lady Liberty, spear in hand and leaning on Washington's shoulder, while in the background the British fleet, "all their Sterns towards the Town," could be seen sailing from Boston.[84]

WASHINGTON had little time to celebrate. Within two weeks he was on his way to New York City, to prepare its defenses for Howe's return, probably during the summer. Nor was America's celebration long lived, as the colonies were shortly overwhelmed with sour news—there could be no other, it seemed—from Canada. Reinforcements from Pennsylvania and New Jersey were added to those being raised in New England, and sent north. American troop strength peaked at about 2,500 during the first grey days of spring, but by late April it had plummeted again to 1,900, and nearly half of those men were unfit for duty. Smallpox was rampant, though influenza and frostbite took a heavy toll and desertion also added to the depletion of the ranks.[85]

After the failed attack on Quebec, the Canadian venture was futile, at least in the short run. The bedraggled rebel army outside Quebec was without artillery and adequate manpower, and it lacked specie for purchasing supplies. Not surprisingly, its siege operation broke down altogether in January and February, allowing Carleton to resupply. Poor leadership additionally bedeviled the rebels. With Montgomery's death, David Wooster became the ranking commander in Canada. Deservedly, Washington had no confidence in Wooster's abilities—in private, he spoke of his lack of "Enterprizing genius"—and sought to replace him with Charles Lee, but Congress sent that veteran officer elsewhere. Washington also hoped that Schuyler might someday go into the field and take command of his army, but he remained at Fort George, complaining now of having been "seized with a copious scorbutic Eruption" as well as "a vile Ague."[86] During the winter Congress dispatched a three-member commission to Canada to look into what was occurring, and it urged Wooster's recall, characterizing him as "unfit, totally unfit, to Command your Army," which it described as "broken and disheartened . . . without discipline . . . without pay . . . and reduced to live from hand to mouth."[87] Congress responded by sending General John Thomas, who had served competently throughout the siege of Boston, and with time he might have gotten the army into better shape. But Thomas had no time. Within a week of his reaching Quebec, Carleton's long-awaited reinforcements began to arrive. A flotilla of twelve ships brought eight regiments—roughly 5,100 men—to Quebec on May 6, and roughly an equal number of redcoats and Hessians trickled in over the next two months. His long contained pugnacity boiling over, Carleton did not even wait for the first batch of regulars to disembark before he made a sortie against the rebel lines. It was his first time out of his lair since Arnold's arrival the previous November.

All too aware of the utter hopelessness of their situation, the Americans buckled in an instant in the face of Carleton's enterprise. In a "panic so violent," according to a British observer, the rebels immediately began a retreat that did not finally end until these ragged men crossed back into New York. It was not a pretty sight. At the sight of an enemy that was ready to fight, and that within in a day or two would have overwhelming numerical strength and absolute naval superiority, the demoralized Americans set off "flying" along the muddy river road with "loaded carts driving full speed," crowed one British official. Haste overshadowed all else. Along the way, some rebel soldiers forsook ill buddies or those who, plagued with frostbitten feet, could not keep up. This army, said an American officer, had "dwindled into a mobb."[88] It fought only when fighting was unavoidable, engaging in rear guard actions to prevent their capture and attacking when the British—thanks to their naval strength—landed marines up river to cut off their lane of retreat. The situation only worsened, if that was

General John Sullivan. Painting by Richard Morrell Staigg, after John Trumbull, 1876. Washington once said that Sullivan's ego tended to get him into trouble. His difficulties also stemmed from having been made a general by Congress despite lacking experience as a soldier.

possible, late in May when General Thomas succumbed to smallpox. While discipline may have existed in some units, the army as a whole was virtually leaderless for days.

Thomas was succeeded by New Hampshire's John Sullivan, who was ordered north with six regiments, totaling nearly six thousand men. Sullivan was thirty-six, a lawyer with no prewar military experience, save for occasionally marching with the militia on the training field. A member of Congress since 1774, Sullivan had pulled the necessary strings to secure a general officer's post, and he rushed to Canada spoiling for a fight. "I now think only of a glorious Death or a Victory," he grandly proclaimed. Not long passed before he faced the fight of his life.[89] When Sullivan reached St. Johns, he found an army in chaos and eviscerated by illness, and he reported to Washington that, "it is a serious truth that our Army is extremely weak." Worse still, "almost Every one [is] Frightened at they know not what," and most of the men wished to "Retreat before an Enemy which no person among them has Seen."[90] Fortunately for Sullivan, Carleton, after his initial burst of fervor, displayed an excessive wariness. Carleton's caution arose largely from his having been isolated from the outer world for six months. He did not know how many reinforcements were on the way and, lacking intelligence, he knew little about the rebel army. At first, he thought Sullivan commanded as many as 25,000 men. Carleton also believed that London expected little of him beyond sweeping the invaders from the St. Lawrence, which once had been true, though Germain now certainly wished the utter eradication of the rebel army. Only as more and more troops from England straggled in through the late spring, did Carleton grasp that the British government anticipated that he would inflict a mortal defeat on the invaders, and then cooperate with General Howe to pacify New York.

Still, Carleton only narrowly failed to destroy Sullivan and his entire army. Sullivan, despite his army's debilitation, wasted no time moving forward, toward, then down, the St. Lawrence. He intended to "keep possession of the Ground we have & keep advancing our posts," he said.[91] Simultaneously, and with great deliberation, Carleton moved his forces to Three Rivers, a sizeable settlement near the mid-point on the St. Lawrence between Quebec and Montreal. Once there, Carleton began the buildup for an advance against Sorel and Montreal. Carleton planned to divide his army. He would lead one division against the rebels in Montreal, while General John Burgoyne, who had arrived early in June, was to pursue Sullivan. But before either he or Burgoyne could move, Sullivan reached Three Rivers and attacked. He, too, was the victim of poor intelligence, though Sullivan was also given to reckless haste and imprudence. Believing that the British force at Three Rivers totaled no more than eight hundred regulars and a few Canadian militiamen—it actually consisted of more than six thousand men, mostly regulars—Sullivan detached two thousand men and launched his attack on June 8.[92]

Those men stepped off into an inferno. Sullivan characterized his blunder as "a Strange Reversal of fortune," and, seemingly anticipating the accusations that would be leveled at his conduct, almost immediately notified his superiors that his "Ill Success never happen'd by my Rashness Imprudence or Cowardice."[93] Sullivan's men were repulsed with heavy losses of men and equipment. Worse yet, they were driven to the north side of the St. Lawrence and cut off from the main American army. Carleton had it within his grasp to wipe out this American force, but he adhered to his preconceived plan, gambling that it offered the best hope of inflicting much greater losses on the rebels.[94] He failed. Not only did Sullivan and his men extricate themselves from what had appeared to be a fatal snare, the small rebel garrison in Montreal, under Arnold, escaped before that trap was sprung. At last, Sullivan saw that the situation was hopeless. Disease was gnawing into the ranks of his men and intelligence was reporting that ever more British replacements were streaming into Quebec. Even the combative Arnold advised Sullivan that there was "more honour in making a safe retreat" than in facing certain defeat by standing "against such superiority."[95] Seeing things in the same light, Sullivan organized an orderly withdrawal. He drew back to Sorel, then pushed on below Montreal and past St. Johns to Isle aux Noix, a relatively secure site where he might regroup and obtain supplies from Ticonderoga. At every step, his army moved too quickly for their pursuers.

But tragedy stalked this woebegone army. At Isle aux Noix, a barren, swampy, mosquito-infested island, smallpox was joined by dysentery and malaria. Dying began in earnest. Up to fifteen men perished each day, and as many as three hundred were dead within a bit more than two weeks. One observer described the scene as "the very acme of human misery," and Sullivan said that men were "Daily Dropping off Like the Israelites before the Destroying Angel." So many died so quickly that there was no choice but to bury the dead in huge common graves.[96] A Continental physician who treated the doomed noted in his log that men were "continually groaning, & calling for relief, but in vain!" Some of the living, he said, had "large maggots, an inch long, Crawl out of their ears" and cover "almost every part of the body. No mortal will ever believe what these suffered unless they were eyewitnesses." To this he added: "Death reigns triumphant—God seems to be greatly angry with us" and "in all probability will sweep away . . . our army to Destruction."[97]

Ten months after it began, the American invasion of Canada was over, a calamity of epic proportions. In the course of nine months more than 12,000 men had been poured into the Canadian venture, of which at least 500 had died and another 500 had been taken captive. Many more had been wounded or were finished as soldiers as a result of debilitations suffered from frostbite, disease, or mental anguish. Two armies had been decimated, two commanders were dead, and tons of precious equipment had been abandoned. The misadventure had culminated in a sorry spectacle in which soldiers refused to fight and leaders failed to lead. One year after the ecstasy inspired by the heroics at Lexington-Concord and Bunker Hill, the American rebels appeared to be on the cusp of defending against simultaneous British invasions of New York, one at Gotham, another through the Champlain Valley. "Our Affairs are hastening fast to a Crisis," the president of the Continental Congress reported, "and the approaching Campaign will in all Probability determine for ever the Fate of America."[98]

5

———————

CHOICES, 1776

THE CANADIAN DEBACLE brought about the Declaration of Independence. To be sure, Congress would have cut all ties with Great Britain sooner or later, but the military disasters at Quebec and along the St. Lawrence led it to make the break in July 1776.

As public opinion polls had not yet come into fashion, it is impossible to know what most colonists thought at any given moment in 1775–1776 about breaking away from Great Britain. Congress was never a precise barometer of public opinion. Its members were chosen by the colonial assemblies, most of which were apportioned in favor of the older, often more urban, eastern sectors of their provinces. This gave Congress a deeply conservative cast, almost certainly leading it to proceed more slowly than most citizens would have preferred. In addition, the war effort required the support of every colony, and especially the backing of large and powerful provinces such as New York, Pennsylvania, and South Carolina, which were dominated by economic interests with deep ties to the mother country. This amplified the clout of the most conservative colonies and compelled those congressmen who had favored declaring independence since early in the war to take a more measured course. Many of those who favored independence privately grumbled that the conservatives, with their expectation that the king would intervene on the side of the colonists to save the empire, were given to dreamy reveries of an "Imbecility" that lent a "silly Cast to our whole Doings." But month after month, the radicals went along, avoiding a congressional battle over independence.[1] They had no choice but to do so if they wished to continue the war.

When the Second Continental Congress convened in the spring of 1775, three weeks after war broke out, every congressman supported hostilities, but the more conservative delegates still hoped that reconciliation was possible. Believing that armed resistance would compel London to negotiate, and that the monarch —the sole official who supposedly looked after the well-being of the entire realm —would intercede to save the empire, they pushed through the Olive Branch Petition that appealed to George III for help. The conservatives' terms included the hope for an Anglo-American union in which the monarch's authority would be recognized, but the American provinces would be nearly fully autonomous and Parliament would have little or no jurisdiction over them. Nothing more would ever be heard of parliamentary taxation.[2]

Many congressmen had bristled at the Olive Branch Petition, and in November 1775 proof arrived of the futility of having petitioned the monarch. Congress learned not only of the king's malice-laden August proclamation in support of the war, but that George III had refused even to receive the Olive Branch Petition, declaring it the product of an illegal body. "[H]is Majesty seemeth to have turned a deaf Ear to all the supplications of his Loyal Colonists," one congressman remarked wryly.[3]

During the month that followed Americans learned that the Royal Navy had shelled, and largely destroyed, Falmouth and that the royal governor of Virginia, Lord Dunmore, had offered freedom to slaves who escaped and helped him fight the rebels. While conservatives had once believed that the king would rescue the colonists, many congressmen, such as Thomas Jefferson, were coming to see the monarch as "the bitterest enemy we have." Jefferson knew that after having "drawn the sword there is but one more step they [the Americans] can take." That was independence. He avoided using the word, but he argued that breaking with the mother country "is now pressed upon us" by the bloody actions of king and Parliament.[4]

In January 1776, hard on the heels of these provocations, Thomas Paine, English born and a recent immigrant, a man with a taste for assertion and a refreshing talent for literary grace, published *Common Sense*. His electrifying polemic captured what most Americans—if not most congressmen—felt. He opened with a nearly unanswerable assault on the folly of hereditary kingship, and indeed on monarchy itself, that drove the last nail in the coffin of monarchical rule for the revolutionary generation. No less significant was the gloomy tableau he painted of reconciliation. To reconcile with the mother country was to bequeath control over North America to a government three thousand miles away in which the colonists were not represented. Reconciliation would inhibit American commerce. It would also guarantee that the colonies would be dragged repeatedly into Britain's many wars. "'TIS TIME TO PART," Paine exhorted, and in three passages that sounded the clarion call for all who dreamt of radical reform, he advised that independence would usher in bounteous change that would be to the benefit of generations yet unborn. Independence, Paine said, promised that "a new era for politics is struck," that the "birthday of a new world is at hand," and that Americans would be vested with the "power to begin the world over again."[5]

Common Sense enjoyed an astounding reception. Paine himself estimated its sales at 150,000 copies. Thousands more who never purchased it read sulfurous excerpts in newspapers or listened as portions were read to them by town criers or, in the case of Continental soldiers, by military officers. In April a congressman who had recently returned to Philadelphia from North Carolina said that all along his route he had "heard nothing praised but Common sense and Independence." It was the talk of Congress as well, for Paine's bold assertions pried open the box in which the discussion of independence had been sequestered.[6] Within days of *Common Sense's* appearance, Congress voted down the plaintive request of its leading reconciliationists to adopt another "humble & dutiful" address to the king, this one disclaiming independence.[7]

Congress had turned a corner, and sentiment for independence increased in the ensuing weeks as word arrived from London that George III was seeking to obtain German mercenaries, perhaps the most feared soldiers in Europe, to help suppress the American rebellion. If he took that step, several congressmen quickly announced, they would be "willing to declare the Colonies in a State of Independent Sovereignty."[8] In March, as the cruel winter of 1776 neared its end, word of the American Prohibitory Act reached America. This measure, sent up by North's government as part of its program for war, aimed at shutting down American commerce, which on the eve of the war had annually exceeded more than £11,000,000 worth of imports and exports. Adams rejoiced at the news. He thought the punitive legislation "a Gift" to those who yearned to declare independence. Virginia's Richard Henry Lee remarked that this latest step by the ministry had "put the two Countries asunder."[9] Congress responded by throwing open its ports to ships from outside the British Empire.

Congress took that step scant weeks after it had been secretly visited by an agent of the French government. During the late summer of 1775, just about the time that the invasion of Canada was launched, France dispatched Julien de Bonvouloir to pursue discussions with Congress. Bonvouloir's mission indicated that not only London and the colonists wrestled with options and choices, but France as well. The French government had kept a wary eye on the Anglo-American situation since the first signs of discord. It had sent over a veteran naval officer, then secret agents, to snoop about, and as early as 1765 they reported that there was much open talk of independence in the colonies. But France prudently avoided the temptation to try to foment an American rebellion. Instead, it undertook to rebuild and modernize its fleet, its Achilles heel in the American theater in the Seven Years' War, and firmed up its alliance with Spain, both necessary precursors to any serious thought of war. Otherwise, it patiently watched and waited.[10]

Charles Gravier, Comte de Vergennes. Engraving published in Paris during the era of the American Revolution. The wily French foreign minister whose assistance helped keep the rebellion afloat in 1776–1777. He presided over the consummation of the Franco-American alliance in 1778 and the orders for a French fleet to sail to North America in 1781.

Charles Gravier, comte de Vergennes, had been France's foreign minister for only a year when the American war started. At fifty-five, hobbled somewhat by rheumatism and given to bouts of depression, Vergennes impressed others with his polished manners, considerable reserve of charm, and legendary industry. Most found him to be staid, diligent, well organized, contemplative, and sensible. Above all, he was cautious, and during the first months of the American war he charily monitored the situation, vacillating frequently over the best course to pursue. Vergennes understood that Great Britain's predicament might offer France an opportunity to reconfigure the European balance of power, secure economic gains at England's expense, and recover the power and prestige it had lost in the late war. But high danger lurked as well. A misstep could plunge France into another potentially ruinous war with Great Britain. Still, if France did nothing, it was likely, he feared, that military adversity would eventually drive the colonists back into London's arms. By late in the summer of 1775, Vergennes was inching toward secretly extending aid to the colonists, a course of action aimed at prolonging the war and preventing reconciliation. He believed that if the Americans displayed adequate muscle and staying power, the day might come when France, in league with Spain, would join America in the war. For the moment, the only thing that Vergennes had decided was that he needed more information.[11]

It was in this frame of mind that he authorized the mission of Bonvouloir, a former French naval officer who was to pose as a merchant from Antwerp. Bonvouloir was to do two things. He was to get a handle on congressional thinking, and in particular the depth of sentiment within that body for independence. He was also to assure the Americans that France had no interest in regaining Canada and that it would welcome the commercial ships of an independent America in French ports.[12] By the time Bonvouloir reached Philadelphia, about a week before Christmas in 1775, American merchantmen were already taking on cargoes in French harbors.

Willing, Morris & Company, a large Philadelphia firm, had for some time prior to the war engaged in illegal trade with the French. The staple of that peacetime commerce had been the exchange of American tobacco for French luxury items, but after the war began American ships returned to Philadelphia with cargoes of gunpowder. The senior partner in the firm, Thomas Willing, joined Congress on September 13. Five days later Congress created the Secret Committee to arrange contracts for importing arms and ammunition. Willing was named to the committee, and his company reputedly made windfall profits in the last months of 1775 from the arms trade alone. Other companies in other cities probably got a piece of the action as well, although exactly what the Secret Committee did is unknown, as it not only vowed to act with "great Circumspection and impenetrable Secrecy," but its account books were subsequently lost in a fire.[13]

Vergennes was aware of this illicit trade when he sent Bonvouloir, and he must have known of the voyage of Pierre Penet and Emmanuel de Pliarne, who docked in Providence at the same moment that the ship that brought Bonvouloir to America reached Philadelphia. Representatives of a firm in Nantes with which Willing, Morris & Company had been doing business, Penet and Pliarne made contact with merchants in Rhode Island. Their pitch was that in return for whale "Oil, Tobacco & all Kinds of Provisions," they would supply "the Continent with Arms & Ammunition." The businessmen in Providence immediately took them to Washington's headquarters, and he in turn just as quickly sent them to Congress with a letter of introduction. Penet and Pliarne opened talks with the Secret Committee early in January 1776, but discussions proceeded slowly until word reached Philadelphia of the disastrous failure at Quebec. Thereafter, contracts were let in record time.[14]

By February Vergennes knew of Bunker Hill, and he was also aware that Howe's army was under siege in Boston and that the Americans had invaded Canada. That month, as well, Vergennes received Bonvouloir's report. It advised that Congress would ultimately declare independence and that the Americans were eager to purchase arms. Vergennes at last was ready for a bigger, riskier step.[15] Late that winter he proposed to the king, Louis XVI, that France secretly furnish arms to America. France must provide "secret favors" and instill "vague hopes," he said, in order to prevent America's reconciliation with Great Britain.[16]

At almost precisely the moment that Vergennes made his recommendation, the Secret Committee decided to send one of its own to France to conclude contracts for military supplies. It chose Silas Deane, a successful businessman and a member of Connecticut's delegation. On May 2, while Deane was crossing the Atlantic, Louis XVI agreed to provide a secret subvention to the Americans for the acquisition of military materials.[17]

In late winter and early spring 1776 Congress was willing to take whatever France was giving away, and it was just as eager to trade for and purchase whatever else it could get. But it was not interested in an alliance with France. Distrust of France was deeply embedded in a Protestant America that had, together with the mother country, fought four wars during the past seventy-five years against French monarchs. Suspicions of Europe in general, and European monarchs in particular, had been heightened among an American people that had loved Great Britain only to have been betrayed—they now believed—by those whom they had trusted. The outlook of John Adams was not unlike most in Congress. A French alliance, he warned in mid-April, raised the specter of "exchang[ing] British for French tyranny. . . . We only Want, commercial Treaties," he said.[18]

The disaster unfolding in Canada—"Defeated most ignominiously," moaned one delegate in mid-May—ultimately led many in Congress to appreciate the corner into which the colonists had been pushed. Canada was lost, and with it substantial portions of two American armies. During May, Congress additionally learned—it first got word from an Irish newspaper—that the Crown had concluded treaties with several German provinces for the use of their soldiers. Supposedly, London was sending 40,000 "foreign mercenaries" to help suppress the American rebellion.[19] New York faced the dismaying prospect of invasions on its Canadian and Atlantic borders. There could now be no doubt that French assistance was imperative. Copious amounts of military supplies were needed, far more than could be had through commercial channels. The rebels knew that only by declaring independence could they hope to see an ample number of French ships plying the Atlantic, their cargo holds bulging with the sinews of war. It was folly to expect France to provide much aid so long as the colonies sought to be reconciled with Great Britain. France stood to gain nothing through the reuniting of the American colonies with the mother country. Congress had to declare independence to get its hands on the materials that would enable it to win this war and, perhaps, to save the lives of those in America, and in Congress, who had waged this war.

By the late spring of 1776 Congress faced difficult choices: reconcile on London's terms; fight on alone, knowing that America lacked the resources to win a protracted war; or, declare independence and seek massive French assist-ance. The choice was clear. Independence was an idea whose time had come.

"It is not choice then, but necessity that calls for Independence, as the only means by which foreign Alliance can be obtained," Richard Henry Lee of Virginia confessed early in June. Sentiment for independence swept the countryside "like a Torrent" that spring, one congressman remarked, and several colonies author-ized their congressmen to vote to sever ties with Great Britain. New England "panted" after independence, John Adams said, and he thought the "great Majority" in the southern colonies also now wished to separate from Britain.[20] Sentiment was more divided in the mid-Atlantic colonies, but by June there no longer was a question of whether Congress would declare independence. Opinion in Congress had caught up with popular opinion. Most, like Adams, had come to believe there was "something very unnatural and odious in a Government 1000 Leagues off" managing American affairs, and a majority now thought that the military situation made declaring independence unavoidable. "We seem at present to be in the Midst of a great Revolution," said one congressman.[21] The only question that remained was whether the vote would be unanimous.

In June, Congress paused for a month to permit sentiment for independence to harden in New York and Pennsylvania. While it waited, it created a committee that included Jefferson, Franklin, and John Adams to draft a declaration of independence. On July 1 Congress at last took up the momentous question: whether to declare independence. Adams anticipated the "greatest Debate of all," and he was not disappointed. When the motion for independence was read in Congress's sweltering chamber, Pennsylvania's John Dickinson, a steadfast foe of a break with Britain, was the first delegate on his feet. Standing before a paneled wall decorated with a British sword, drum, and regimental flag captured at Fort Ticonderoga, he spoke for nearly two hours. He reiterated themes that his col-leagues had often heard: a war for reconciliation would be shorter and less brutal ("Boston might have been burnt" had independence been declared before the troops ascended Dorchester Heights, he said); independence would bring France into the war, a step fraught with danger; and remaining under the protective cloak of Britain assured greater prosperity and security. When Dickinson finished, Adams followed with a lengthy rejoinder. As he spoke, a great thunderstorm swept across Philadelphia. Lightning danced in the sky and rain lashed at the tall windows of the Pennsylvania State House, what shortly would be known as Independence Hall. With thunder rumbling like cannon, Adams also addressed familiar themes: Great Britain was corrupt and its king and ministry were tyran-nical; it was better for Americans to govern themselves than to submit to nabobs in a land across the sea; declaring independence would buttress morale for the long war ahead; and victory hinged on foreign assistance, which in turn required severing ties with Britain.[22]

Virtually every member of Congress wanted to speak on this historic occasion, and the oratory stretched until beyond sunset and into the next day.

As the speechifying continued, urgency mounted. Word arrived confirming that "Genl Howe with near 100 Sail" lay off the New York coast."[23] Britain's invasion of New York was at hand. Sometime on July 2, Congress at last voted on independence. Every colony save for New York—the delegation of which awaited authorization from the provincial assembly—voted for independence. The vote was unanimous. Twelve colonies—which were instantly transformed into states by their decision—voted for independence. None were opposed. Although every delegation was of one mind, nearly one-fifth of the congressmen voted against independence.

Once the vote was taken, Dickinson resigned. He went home, joined a Delaware militia company, and saw combat during the campaign for Pennsylvania in 1777, fighting not for independence, but to compel Great Britain to offer acceptable terms for reconciliation.[24]

Two days later Congress approved the Declaration of Independence, which assailed George III for, among other things, "waging war against us" and for "transporting large armies of foreign mercenaries, to compleat the works of death, desolation & tyranny, already begun with circumstances of cruelty & perfidy scarcely paralleled in the most barbarous ages." Independence was but the latest change brought on by a war that the colonists had entered into to prevent Great Britain from instituting change. "You will think me transported with Enthusiasm," said John Adams once independence was declared, "but I am not. I am well aware of the Toil and Blood and Treasure, that it will cost Us to maintain this Declaration."[25]

6

"KNOCK HIM UP FOR THE CAMPAIGN": THE BATTLE FOR NEW YORK, 1776

WASHINGTON had inherited a difficult assignment in attempting to liberate Boston. He took on a nearly impossible mission in defending New York City against the British invasion.

Washington had never doubted that New York would be Howe's primary objective. In January, while Knox was struggling to bring his artillery through the Berkshires, Washington had dispatched Charles Lee to New York "to put that City in the best posture of Defence." He trusted Lee to determine whether New York could be defended and, if so, how best to plan its defense. Lee, he said, was "zealously attached to the Cause—honest and well meaning," with "an uncommon share of good Sense." He also regarded Lee as "the first Officer in Military knowledge and experience we have in the whole army." Above all, Washington divined rare qualities in Lee: military expertise, cool judgment, unflinching bravery, and above all the will to fight. Like Washington, Lee was convinced that "the consequences of the Enemy's possessing themselves of New York" were "so terrible" as to be nearly unimaginable. If New York and the Hudson River fell to the enemy, the line between New England and all the provinces to the south—"upon which depends the Safety of America," said Washington—would be severed.[1]

Lee set to work when he reached Manhattan. After reconnoitering, he put men to constructing fortifications and batteries, and he ordered the removal and relocation of the artillery from the vulnerable battery at the lower tip of Manhattan. He also proposed taking into custody the entire Tory population in two adjacent counties and incarcerating them in Connecticut, but Congress blanched at such a thought. Instead, those who refused to take a loyalty oath were

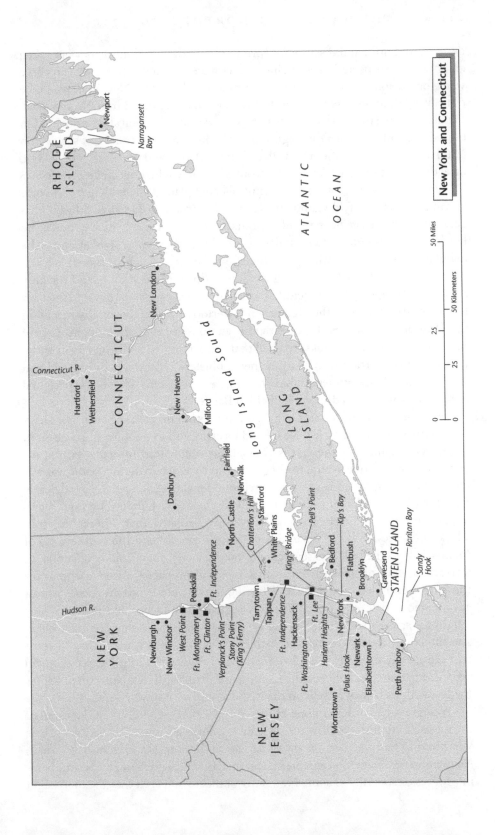

New York and Connecticut

RHODE ISLAND

Newport
Narragansett Bay

ATLANTIC OCEAN

New London

CONNECTICUT

Connecticut R.
Hartford
Wethersfield

New Haven
Milford

Long Island Sound

Fairfield
Norwalk

Danbury

North Castle
Chatterton's Hill
Stamford
White Plains

LONG ISLAND

Pell's Point

King's Bridge

Kip's Bay

Ft. Independence

Peekskill
Ft. Montgomery
Ft. Clinton
Verplanck's Point
Stony Point
(King's Ferry)

Bedford
Flatbush

STATEN ISLAND
Gravesend
Brooklyn

Raritan Bay

Sandy Hook

West Point

Newburgh
New Windsor

Hudson R.

NEW YORK

Tarrytown
Tappan
Ft. Independence
Hackensack
Ft. Washington
Harlem Heights
Ft. Lee
New York

Paulus Hook
Newark
Elizabethtown

Perth Amboy

Morristown

NEW JERSEY

0   25   50 Miles

0   25   50 Kilometers

designated Tories and disarmed. More than one thousand muskets were taken and nineteen suspected loyalist ringleaders were arrested. After less than three weeks on the job, Lee informed Washington that defending New York would be difficult. "[W]homever commands the Sea must command the Town," he reported. He did not have to add that the British possessed absolute naval superiority. On the other hand, he told Washington that the British army could not survive on Manhattan unless it also controlled Long Island, and especially Brooklyn, directly across from New York City, from where it would draw much of its food.[2]

By then, Lee had formulated a multifaceted plan for defending New York: "form a strong fortify'd Camp" to defend the Brooklyn Heights; "throw up a great number of large fleches and Redouts" at King's Bridge, which spanned the Harlem River roughly fifteen miles above the city, linking Manhattan to the mainland; "barrier the principal Streets" in the city, which in the eighteenth century extended northward from the lower tip of Manhattan Island for only about twenty blocks; "erect inclos'd Batteries" to seal off the entrance to the East River; construct forts on the high ground overlooking the Hudson River; and fill the Hudson and the East River with chevaux-de-frieze, obstacles consisting of sunken hulks with tree trunks attached that were designed to prevent navigation. Lee, who was no stranger to boasting, never blustered that the British would find New York's defenses impenetrable. Instead, he said that his scheme was designed to render New York "a disputable Field of Battle."[3]

Lee's strategic conception hinged on the notion that to take New York City the enemy would ultimately have to land its army and to fight for its possession. He never dreamt that the rebels could hold Manhattan forever. Rather, his plan—which was conceived at the beginning of 1776, when the aim of the war was reconciliation on American terms—envisioned making the British pay so dearly for taking New York that London might lose the will to fight on. Lee appears to have believed that the British would seek to take Brooklyn first. Thereafter, from a lack of choices, it would have to land its invasion force at the southern tip of Manhattan. As the redcoats struggled to take the city, they would encounter an intricate system of street defenses that Lee had prepared. Avant garde in his thinking, Lee understood that a well-fortified city would afford the rebels "a most advantageous field of battle." Britain's regulars would be bled white as they fought for street after street. So long as "our people behave with common spirit, and the commanders are men of distinction," Lee was confident that "it must cost the enemy many thousands of men to get possession of it." Once they did take Manhattan, Lee believed the Continental army, still in possession of King's Bridge, with its lane of retreat off the island, could withdraw to safety.[4]

Congress had ordered none of this. Fearful that a Congress in the thrall of the reconciliationists would refuse to sanction defensive measures for New York, Washington had acted on his own.[5] As late as three weeks after he sent Lee to Manhattan, Washington remained concerned that Congress might halt the work in progress, especially as some New York authorities feared that the mere sight of Continentals digging entrenchments would prompt the Royal Navy to shell the city. Not until the end of February did Washington learn that Congress had sanctioned the defensive preparations, and by then the congressmen were acting energetically to prepare for Howe's invasion, even recommending steps to be taken. The New York Provincial Congress fell in step, as well, ordering that all male inhabitants of the city and all black men who dwelled in Gotham and New York County must work on the fortifications.[6]

Washington began redeploying troops from New England to New York even before Howe sailed from Boston, and he arrived in Manhattan, together with the bulk of the army, in mid-April. Over the next several weeks Washington continued the work that Lee had begun. This was not the Olympian Washington of latter years. Unfamiliar with the city, and uncertain of his own authority, he often deferred to the local authorities, making substantive changes to Lee's plans even as he confessed that Lee was the only officer whose engineering skills he trusted. Washington's jaunty, almost cocksure, post-Dorchester demeanor had vanished after he learned the fate of "our shattered, divided & broken Army" in Canada, the first Continentals to be truly tested, and as he got a handle on the scope of the formidable difficulties involved in defending New York. His greatest shock occurred on July 12 when the *Phoenix* and *Rose*, two British frigates, blithely sailed up the Hudson, rudely scudding past the marine obstacles and fortifications that had been painstakingly constructed over the past several months. In a flash, Britain's overarching supremacy was evident. The enemy could attack wherever it pleased. Virtually all the previous planning was rendered meaningless, as was clear even to New York's civil authorities, who pointed out to Washington their concern that the British might "cut off the Communication between the City and Country by landing above Kingsbridge."[7]

The liabilities involved in defending New York—"surrounded . . . by Water & covered with Ships," as Washington put it—were readily apparent, but he remained bent on defending the city. He did not have much choice. Congress had quietly leaned on him to stay and put up a fight, probably making clear its wishes when it summoned him to Philadelphia for consultation late in May. About to declare independence, Congress knew that the epic disaster in Canada would not make a favorable impression in Versailles and it feared that the French authorities might doubt America's resolve if its Continental army fled New York without a fight. For his part, Washington saw no suitable alternative to staying on Manhattan. He recognized that its possession was, as he put it, "of the last importance to us." Should the enemy take Manhattan, New York's harbor would become the portal through which their men and supplies would flow into America. It would also be the base of operations for the Royal Navy's blockade of the Atlantic coastline, and General Howe could use Manhattan as a seat for incursions into New Jersey, Pennsylvania, and southern New England. Despite the obvious difficulties, Washington was not reluctant to face a campaign in New York. He felt confident about his army. It was well trained and well entrenched, leading him to believe that he could make the enemy pay a price for taking New York that was even steeper than they had paid for Bunker Hill. Echoing Lee, Washington that summer remarked that if "the Men . . . will stand by me the place shall not be carried without some loss" to the redcoats. Not that Washington was without problems. As the summer approached its zenith, his anxiety mounted. He had too few troops, he said, and too few general officers, too few arms, too few flints, and too few engineers with "the least skill in . . . laying out any work of the least consequence." He may have wondered, too, if the alterations that had been made to Lee's plans for defending New York would come back to haunt him. Though he was not aware of it, he had managed to add to his growing mountain of troubles by chasing away the entire troop of the Connecticut Light Horse, a cavalry unit consisting of five hundred men, the only large body of horse soldiers in the Continental army, and an invaluable tool for gathering intelligence and coping with infantry attacks. Shortsightedly, Washington thought them expensive "Indulgencies" of little practical value, a way of thinking that appeared to bear out his nearly simultaneous confession to a "want of experience to move upon such a large Scale." As the test of battle loomed, he prayed that "the same Provedence" that had seen him through the French and Indian War would get him through this ordeal safely.[8]

ON JUNE 28 an American sentinel, armed with a spyglass and posted in the tallest building on Broadway, spotted the bright white sails of the British armada bobbing off Long Island. Over the next forty-eight hours, 130 ships were counted. On July 3, the royal fleet—the largest expeditionary force that Great Britain had ever assembled, or would muster again until World Wars I and II, so vast that it looked to one New Yorker like "a forest of masts"—began to drop anchor at Staten Island. Through the night and the next day, while a light rain fell, word reached Washington's headquarters that Howe's force was "continually landing."[9] Howe was arriving from Halifax. He had taken the army from Boston to Nova Scotia in part to recover from the trying winter it had endured, but primarily to await reinforcements and shipments of supplies. He had anticipated a sojourn of perhaps a month, but when provisions were late in arriving—some never arrived—his stay lengthened to nearly ten weeks.[10]

When Howe at last sailed for New York his objective was to carry out the strategic conception that North's ministry had agreed on six months earlier, a plan that he had a hand in shaping through recommendations he had filed from Boston. Taking control of New York and inflicting a decisive defeat on the Continentals was to be Howe's first step. When that was achieved, he hoped to detach forces to seize Rhode Island and eastern New Jersey, while he advanced up the Hudson with the main army and joined with a British army that was to descend from Canada. While General Howe was busy with these endeavors, America—and New England in particular—was to be squeezed by a naval blockade administered by his brother, Admiral Richard Howe. "Black Dick" Howe, as the admiral was nicknamed both for his swarthy complexion and his grave manner, was a veteran of nearly twenty years service, and of two intercolonial wars.

General Howe expected to ultimately have about 32,000 men, nearly five times what he had possessed in Boston. Lord North had scurried and scraped to put together an army of that size. Some men were attained through frenzied recruiting at home. Others were garnered through redeployment and by ignoring Howe's earlier requests to leave an army of five thousand men in possession of Boston. Some ten thousand "Hessians," as the rebels habitually referred to them, comprised the remainder of Howe's force. Howe might have had an even larger force had he tapped into the sizeable, and eager, loyalist population in New York following his arrival on Staten Island, but he hardly took the trouble. Perhaps his professional contempt for untrained soldiers won out, or as he was to have more men than he had ever asked for, he may simply have seen the Loyalists as an unnecessary encumbrance. With an army that appeared to be adequate to the task, and more than two-fifths of the ships and men in the world's greatest navy on hand to help, the Howes envisioned inflicting crumpling blows against the Continental army and encircling New England before the end of 1776. That alone might break the back of the rebellion. If not, the invasion of New England in 1777 would finish the job.

All of General Howe's men were ashore before sunset on July 4, and his brother arrived a week later, but Britain's military forces remained immobile for nearly two months. This was due in part to the Howes' commitment to a carrot-and-stick approach. Both of the Howes had served in Parliament and opposed the American policies that produced the war. Even after hostilities broke out, both continued to believe that it was possible to reach a negotiated settlement of Anglo-American differences, a rapprochement on terms somewhere between the extremes of American independence and absolute parliamentary sovereignty. During the spring of 1776 the Howe brothers were named to a "peace commission" that Lord North dispatched to America. In reality, the commissioners were only empowered to accept the colonies' surrender, which was to be accompanied by the dissolution of all congresses, restoration of royal officials, disbanding of all armed bodies, surrender of all fortifications, and a commitment by the lawful provincial assembly to obey parliamentary laws.[11] The Howes, however, misconstrued, or more likely deliberately contorted, the ministry's intentions. They wanted, and tried, to negotiate. Convinced that London could keep its colonies only through concessions, the Howes planned to use the stick to demonstrate that rebellion came with a terrible price in an uncertain war, while they dangled the carrot to entice the chastened colonists back into the fold. They first extended the carrot. While the army was idle that summer, Lord Howe attempted, without success, to open discussions with Washington.[12]

Other factors were also responsible for General Howe's unhurried summer. He had arrived with nine thousand men, about 60 percent of the number that

Washington possessed, and he knew that the American commander could rapidly augment his numbers by summoning militia. Howe waited for his remaining men, including all the Hessians he had been promised, and for the supply ships that were known to be crossing the Atlantic. Time was also required to gather intelligence and reconnoiter this unfamiliar region. Sickness was rampant in his army as well, not least among the Hessians, who finally arrived in mid-August, an incredible 125 days after their fleet sailed from Bremerlehe. For more than a week, large numbers of the mercenaries were unfit for duty, down with fevers, diarrhea, scurvy, even exhaustion.[13] Their Atlantic crossing, like many the British would experience in this war, had been a nightmare, somewhat along the lines of one described that summer by a British officer: "There was continued destruction in the foretops, the pox above-board, the plague between decks, hell in the forecastle, the devil at the helm."[14] Howe also awaited troops that were to come up from the Lower South, men who had recently been involved in the first major fighting on American soil since Bunker Hill.

THE NOTION of a campaign in the South emerged from the labored discussions in North's cabinet during the previous fall. Amid the sobering dispatches on Lexington-Concord and Bunker Hill, disquieting tidings had also arrived from the Carolinas. The royal governors of both North Carolina and South Carolina, Josiah Martin and Lord William Campbell, had been forced from office, one taking refuge in a British fort, the other establishing a rolling and pitching office aboard a sloop off the coast. Along with word of his expulsion, Martin sent wildly delusive reports about hordes of Tar Heel Loyalists who supposedly waited with impatience to help restore royal authority. In a flood of blather, he claimed that he could raise nine thousand Tories. If London would only furnish the arms, he went on, the British flag would once again fly over North Carolina. Clinging to the rapturous illusion that the rebels were strong only in New England, the idea of a southern campaign germinated in London in the last weeks of 1775.[15]

General Howe had protested immediately, fearing that the southern initiative would cause delays in his operations in New York, but his complaint reached London after the armada carrying the troops to Carolina had already set off across the Atlantic. Nevertheless, Germain responded by sending word to the commander of the invasion force, Sir Henry Clinton, that he was free to scuttle his mission if he saw that it was unpromising.[16]

Clinton had crossed to America on the *Cerberus* in the spring of 1775 in the company of Howe and Burgoyne. Of the three, Clinton had the deepest roots in America. Born into England's aristocracy in 1730, the son of an admiral, young Henry moved with his family to Manhattan in 1743 when his father became the royal governor of New York. Henry, who entered the army in 1745, remained in America for six years before his profession took him to England and Europe. He fought in the Seven Years' War in Germany, where he took a bullet in the leg that caused him difficulty for the remainder of his days. In some respects, Clinton was the most capable of Britain's generals in America in 1776. He was industrious, meditative, and prudent, and his ability to see the big picture was unsurpassed, leading many to regard him as the best strategic planner on the British side. But he was not without limitations. He lacked self-confidence and was never popular with those he commanded. Touchy, suspicious, quarrelsome, and often acerbic, he was utterly incapable of making friendships. Today he would be called a loner—Clinton characterized himself as "a shy bitch," his most memorable, and perplexing, stab at self-analysis—and he seemed happiest when given the solitude to study nature and play the violin. Clinton was alone and lonely when he returned to America at the outset of the war. His wife of five years had died in 1772 delivering her fifth child. It was a catastrophic blow from which he never recovered, and resulted in a grief so deep and prolonged that some of his associates thought it aberrant.[17]

Second in command to Howe, Clinton was awarded command of the southern venture, and in January 1776, with several hundred men detached from the army in Boston, he set off. The plan, put together in London, called for Clinton to rendezvous off Cape Fear with five Irish regiments that were crossing the Atlantic. His troop strength would be awesome: about 3,300 regulars in addition to the horde of eager Loyalists that Governor Martin had promised. Clinton arrived in March "big with expectation," according to his aide. He soon was disappointed. No Loyalists were waiting for him. Carolina rebels had crushed them two weeks earlier in a battle at Moore's Creek Bridge near Wilmington. Nor was he greeted by the invasion armada. Tossed by raging Atlantic storms, it did not arrive until six weeks later. While he waited, Clinton idled away much of the time on shipboard trying to decide what to do. Although he was given leeway to scrap the mission, the decisive events at Moore's Creek Bridge led him to believe that the southern Tories might be lost forever unless he took steps to rally them. Clinton shifted his thinking to Charleston, or more accurately to Sullivan's Island, which lies at the mouth of the city's harbor. Clinton doubted that Charleston could be taken without a protracted siege, and he also knew that even if it miraculously fell into his hands, it could not be held, as he and his men were to join Howe for the New York campaign. On the other hand, the naval squadron that he awaited was laden with 10,000 muskets for the Carolina Loyalists. From a toehold off South Carolina, it might be possible not only to distribute the weaponry, but to impede commerce into and out of Charleston. There was a dreamy quality to Clinton's thinking. It was never clear who would garrison Sullivan's Island or how it could possibly be supplied. Usually the most logical of British generals, Clinton appears to have succumbed to the pulsating passion to do something, anything, and to pray that it worked.

With the Irish regiments and an armada of fifty sails, Clinton arrived off South Carolina early in June, about a week before Howe departed Nova Scotia. Given his resources, including the formidable firepower of his fleet, he foresaw an easy go of it in taking Sullivan's Island.

While Clinton was sailing for the Carolinas, Congress named General Lee to command a newly created Southern Department. He would have preferred to go to Canada—"I am the only general officer on the Continent who can speak and think in French," he said with typical immodesty—and Washington wanted him there, as well, thinking that Lee alone might prevent the rebels' expulsion. But with his new appointment in hand, Lee laid aside the work on fortifying New York and rushed south.[18] He stopped first in Virginia to cope with Lord Dunmore—primarily by ruthlessly suppressing the Tories—then hurried to the Lower South when he learned of Clinton's presence off Cape Fear.[19] With two thousand troops from Virginia and North Carolina in tow, Lee arrived in Charleston early in June, on the same day that Clinton began reconnoitering for a site to land his troops. Lee quickly discovered that South Carolina had already raised 4,700 troops, but he also found that the defenses in Charleston were woefully inadequate. If Clinton attacked quickly, Lee feared, the city would be his. Luck was on Lee's side. Storms and unfavorable winds idled the British fleet for three weeks, allowing time for the Americans to strengthen the city's fortifications. By late June, Lee was convinced that the city could be held, but he was equally certain that Sullivan's Island could not be successfully defended.

On the eve of battle, Lee and the South Carolina authorities wrangled bitterly over which site to defend. Lee predicted that Sullivan's Island was a "slaughter pen" without escape routes. He was equally fearful that the royal fleet might bypass it altogether, cutting off those on the island. General William Moultrie, who was in charge of Sullivan's Island, just as adamantly insisted his installation could be held. He had constructed a fort fashioned from palmetto trunks, with sand and marsh clay packed in between. The installation contained twenty-six guns and nearly three tons of powder. He was convinced that the fort would hold and that it could inflict serious damage on the attackers. Lee eventually conceded, fearful that South Carolina's troops would go home if he overruled the local authorities, and committed men to help with the last stages of Moultrie's construction work, including laying out a bridge that linked the island to the mainland.

Clinton put his army ashore on desolate Long Island, just one hundred yards above Sullivan's Island. While he scouted the harbor and planned the attack, the men spent a miserable month of summer roasting in their heavy uniforms and swatting mosquitoes and sand flies. Finally, on June 28, Clinton was ready. While the fleet bombarded Fort Sullivan, his men were to wade to Sullivan's Island across a ford that he believed to be only eighteen inches deep. Not for the last time in this war, nearly everything went awry. First, the supposedly shallow inlet turned out to be seven feet deep, and Clinton lacked sufficient numbers of small boats to get his men across.[20] The redcoats remained on Long Island, immobile and useless. Next, when the squadron maneuvered to open fire on Fort Sullivan, three of its four frigates, the vessels sporting the most guns in the fleet, ran aground, reducing the attacker's firepower by roughly 25 percent. All the while, Moultrie's men fought back with a deadly fire. The American gunners were "very cool," one of the regulars noted, laying down a "slow, but decisive" fire.[21] The commodore of the British fleet acknowledged 190 casualties.[22] Just as the stolid Moultrie had said, Fort Sullivan bore up splendidly. The British fired nearly seven thousand shells in the day-long engagement, but the fort's soft palmetto walls absorbed what was thrown at it. By early evening, it was over.[23] Clinton spent a few days contemplating his next move, but he eventually decided that any further actions would be fruitless and, early in July, sailed for New York. From start to finish, Britain's southern campaign had been a fiasco. Among other things, it revealed both the liabilities of preparing military plans three thousand miles away in London and the drawbacks to relying on unproven information gathered weeks before and hundreds of miles away. As Clinton turned his back on the South and the Loyalists he had come to save, one of his men wrote home that the account of this failed mission "will not be believed when it is first reported in England."[24]

THE IRISH REGIMENTS under Clinton reached Staten Island on August 1, part of a steady stream of manpower that Howe happily welcomed in a span of three weeks. During the second week in August he pronounced that his numbers were adequate, but he delayed a bit longer waiting for the sickness among the Germans to run its course and for the vessels bringing long-awaited camp equipment. During his nearly fifty days on Staten Island, Howe had gathered information, which ultimately led him to scrap his original campaign plan and substitute another. The choice he made was crucial and may have cost the British whatever chance they had for victory.[25]

Since the Previous Autumn Howe's first object had been to bring the Continental army to a great pitched battle. His initial plan called for landing his forces on Manhattan north of the city, which would force Washington into an epic battle to escape and survive. His new plan envisaged opening with a campaign on Long Island. Howe was abandoning his plan to annihilate the Continentals in favor of a strategy of taking territory. Piece by piece, and at a low cost, he contemplated gobbling up real estate, until, eventually, rebel morale sagged and the reconciliationists regained supremacy in a Congress. When that occurred, Howe was confident the colonists would open negotiations, which he and his brother would conduct for Britain.[26]

Howe's intractable commitment to reconciliation shaped his thinking, but so, too, did sound military thinking. During his weeks on Staten Island, Howe discovered that Washington, contrary to the hoariest of military maxims, had divided his army in the face of a superior foe, placing some of his men on Long Island, others in New York City, and still others in Harlem Heights to the north of Manhattan. After mid-July Howe also knew that he owned the waterways that encircled Washington's troops. This knowledge helped change his outlook. With his naval arm, he possessed a mobility of which Washington could only dream. Howe could move his men and supplies, and move them quickly, affording him a reasonable alternative to a colossal battle at a site of Washington's choosing. Howe believed he could win such a showdown, but he also feared that he would pay dearly for that victory. Such a clash would likely make Bunker Hill appear as a trifle. After all, at Bunker Hill the Americans had only a day to prepare their defenses. The Continentals had spent nearly six months constructing their fortifications in New York. Washington's year-old army was also doubtlessly better organized, trained, and equipped than its counterpart atop Charlestown Heights, and it possessed several times the number of artillery at Prescott's disposal.[27] Slowly, Howe moved away from his initial plan and conceived instead the notion of eradicating the Continentals piecemeal, first on Long Island, next on Manhattan. He would possess numerical superiority in every engagement, his losses would be considerably lower, and in the end the result would be the same: the Continental army would be vanquished.

Washington's thinking also changed during the summer of 1776. Like Lee earlier, though for different reasons, he came to believe that he could not keep his adversary from taking New York. The best he could do was to exact heavy losses and hope to impress France favorably, which, in some respects, was why he was expected to fight for New York in the first place. Washington had come to see just how untenable his position was in New York. He had too little with which to defend too much. Perhaps most soldiers betray uncertainty on the eve of battle; by late August, Washington was way beyond that. He was baffled. So many options were available to Howe that Washington was without hope of discovering "the real designs of the Enemy." The least likely target for an attack, he believed, was Long Island, and over the past eight months that region had barely been reconnoitered. Washington thought it more likely that the enemy's initial blow would fall somewhere on Manhattan. Then again, it might occur to the east of King's Bridge, around Pell's Point, though it was also "very probable" that the British might simultaneously assail several targets.[28]

Part of Washington's problem was that the intelligence he received in New York was quite inferior to that which he had gotten in Cambridge. During the siege of Boston, Washington had drawn on a spy network that the popular protest movement had fashioned years earlier. Nothing that streamlined existed in New York. If anything, the British won the intelligence gathering war in this theater. Although the flourishing committees of safety that the rebels had instituted in every village and county severely impaired the success of British spies, Howe turned to the Loyalists, whose numbers always grew when the British army was in the neighborhood. Many Tories were only too willing to provide assistance.[29]

Washington was not taken by surprise when Howe at last acted. On August 22 he reported to Congress that "all circumstances [are] Indicating an Attack . . . We are making preparations to receive 'em." Later that very morning 15,000 regulars under Earl Cornwallis landed unopposed at Gravesend on the western end of Long Island, roughly six miles below Brooklyn Heights. While Washington saw the attack coming, his intelligence was flawed. He was led to believe that no more than nine thousand of the enemy had landed, and he sent reinforcements to Brooklyn Heights that brought the total of American troops on Long Island to seven thousand. As his men would be protected by a maze of carefully constructed fortifications—since February the Continentals had built six forts, three redoubts, breastworks, and other entrenchments that extended for miles, all protected by ditches, abatis, fraise (pointed stakes driven into ramparts), and twenty-eight cannon—Washington believed his troop strength was adequate.[30]

The landing of what appeared to be a small force, however, only sowed more doubts in Washington's mind. Was this a feint? Did the enemy seek "to draw our Force to that Quarter when their real Design" was Manhattan? Washington's suspicions grew when days passed with no real action. Cornwallis had followed his landing by immediately moving north to Flatbush, but when he sought to advance further north to Brooklyn—with Captain Evelyn and the King's Own in the van—he encountered rebels along a densely wooded ridgeline known as the Heights of Guana.[31] Cornwallis ordered a fallback to Flatbush. While Cornwallis waited, and Howe considered his choices, confusion prevailed in the highest levels of the Continental army.

Some of the entropy in the command structure arose from the misfortune of an untimely illness that felled Nathanael Greene. During the siege of Boston, Washington had come to believe that Greene was his most reliable American-born general, and he had put him in command of the defense of Long Island. But eight days before the British landing, Greene fell seriously ill with "a raging fever," likely typhoid, that left him bedfast for more than two weeks. Two days before Cornwallis came ashore, Washington perplexingly assigned responsibility for Long Island to General John Sullivan, an officer whose talent he had previously questioned. While "active, spirited, and zealously attach'd to the Cause," Washington also knew that Sullivan was troubled by what he called "his foibles," chiefly a "little tincture of vanity" that, when combined with inexperience, led him to act impetuously. Washington's choice was questioned by some of his staff, who recalled that Sullivan's performance in Canada had hardly been exemplary and that Congress had stripped him of responsibility in that theater. Soon enough, Washington also had second thoughts.[32]

During his first hours on Long Island, Sullivan made a crucial decision. With Washington's concurrence, he moved nearly half the men from the intricate defenses in Brooklyn to the Guana ridgeline and set them to digging fresh earthworks on the very cusp of the British invasion. (These were the rebels that Cornwallis had encountered as he moved north.) The ground that Sullivan had chosen would have been an excellent site to make a defensive stand had he possessed a considerably larger force. The terrain was thick with forests, rose steeply to heights ranging from twenty to forty feet, and could only be approached via four narrow and relatively easily defended roads. But the ridgeline ran on for nearly six miles, and could not be adequately defended by his small force. Twenty-four hours later, after Putnam demanded the command on the grounds

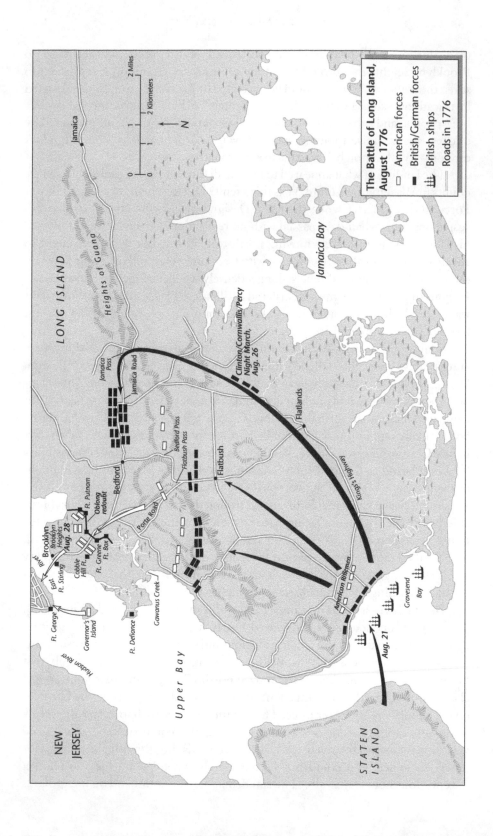

The Battle of Long Island, August 1776

☐ American forces

■ British/German forces

⚓ British ships

— Roads in 1776

LONG ISLAND

Heights of Guana

Jamaica

Jamaica Pass

Jamaica Road

Bedford Pass

Flatbush Pass

Bedford

Clinton/Cornwallis/Percy
Night March,
Aug. 26

Flatlands

Flatbush

King's Highway

Jamaica Bay

American Riflemen

Porte Road

Ft. Putnam

Oblong
redoubt

Brooklyn
Brooklyn
Heights
Aug. 28

Ft. Greene

Ft. Box

Cobble
Hill R.

Ft. Stirling

East
River

Ft. George

Governor's
Island

Ft. Defiance

Gowanus Creek

Hudson River

Upper Bay

NEW
JERSEY

Grovesend
Bay

Aug. 21

STATEN
ISLAND

N

2 Miles

2 Kilometers

1

1

0

0

of seniority, Washington put him in charge and gave Sullivan responsibility for the rebels' left wing between Flatbush Pass and Bedford Pass. Washington was always sensitive to matters of rank, although in this instance his move may have been hastened by his reservations about Sullivan. It is also possible that others, remembering Putnam's heroism on Bunker Hill—he was widely hailed among the officers as "the brave old man"—urged Washington to vest Old Put with command of the defense of these heights.[33] Putnam, the third commander of this army in five days, had hardly taken command before he moved units hither and thither, even though he was not especially familiar with the new sector that was to be defended. Reflecting the apparent, and perhaps real, indecision at head-quarters, some units in this obstreperous army moved indiscriminately on their own. An increasingly worried Washington lectured Putnam on the "distinction between a well-regulated army, & a mob."[34]

While confusion reigned on the American side, Howe gave Cornwallis another five thousand men, mostly Hessians, and plotted his next move. Aware that his army would have a four-to-one numerical advantage on the Guana Heights, and a two-to-one superiority on Long Island itself, Howe appeared to have two choices. Some of his advisors urged a frontal assault against the ridge-line's defenders. It would be bloody, they acknowledged, but the Continentals would be rooted out and utterly destroyed. His second option stemmed from intelligence reports that the Jamaica Pass road, which meandered east of the American lines on the ridge, was undefended. By taking that road, the British might envelope the Guana defenders. Howe was skeptical about the likelihood of marching a large force undetected for several miles, but he was eager to minimize his losses. He opted for the flanking maneuver. On the night of August 26–27 he set the design in motion.[35]

Howe broke his army into three divisions. As the dark stain of night gathered over Long Island, Howe, together with Clinton and guided by three Loyalists, set out with half his army over a maze of back roads leading toward the Jamaica Pass eight miles away. It was slow going, and noisy. A two-mile-long line of 10,000 soldiers, accompanied by a horse-drawn baggage train and eighteen artillery pieces, made what Howe feared was a terrible din. This column was still on the march when, just at sunrise, Howe's two other divisions sprang into action. Redcoats under General James Grant and Hessians under General Philip von Heister opened a bombardment against each end of the American line. This was a diversionary move, designed to preoccupy the rebels as Howe made his way around them. For more than three hours on that luminous morning the Americans under Sullivan on the American left and Alexander Lord Stirling on the right held out. Washington, who had hurried to Brooklyn at the sound of the cannonade, watched the fight through a spyglass. It appeared to be going well. The Americans were giving no ground. Looks were deceiving. Not for the last time, Washington had fallen prey to a feint by his adversary. Just as optimism mounted in the Continentals' ranks, a British signal cannon fired in the rear of the entrenched rebel lines. Howe, finding the Jamaica Pass held by only five militiamen—who quietly surrendered—had turned the American flank.

Regulars suddenly exploded in a scarlet blur from the wooded moraine behind Sullivan's men. Simultaneously, British and Hessians advanced on them from the front. The American line held until the enemy soldiers, their bayonets gleaming in the morning sun, began their ascent up the craggy hillocks. Some Americans immediately dropped their muskets and surrendered, many calling out "Pardon!"—meaning quarter or mercy—to their captors.[36] Many rebels broke and ran, and their flight set off a chain-reaction panic. Not all made it to safety. Large numbers were shot or captured. The attackers next surged to the west, falling on, and behind, Stirling's force. Seeing what was coming, Stirling had reorganized his men and for a time they waged an orderly, and spirited, resistance that one soldier equated with "Roman valor." But the British, with overwhelming strength on their side, sealed off every road leading to Brooklyn and gave "the Rebels a d_ _ d crush," as a redcoat later remarked. Shorn of hope, "the Poltroons ran in the most broken disgraceful and precipitate manner," another regular noted. Some of Stirling's men sought to escape through the thick woods, though many were hunted down and killed or captured by the light infantrymen who gave pursuit. Some rebels even sought out redcoats to whom they might surrender, rather than risk falling into the hands of the Hessians, who allegedly gave no quarter. Some of the fleeing Americans dived into Gowanus Creek, nearly as wide as a football field, and tried to swim to safety. Some who were not good swimmers called "out to their fellows for God's sake to help them out," one survivor recollected, "but every man was intent on his own safety" and no assistance was rendered.[37] Some men drowned and others were shot like fish in a barrel. Although the skirmishing continued until mid-afternoon, the engagement was largely over before noon. The Americans had lost about 300 killed and 1,100 wounded or captured, including both Stirling and Sullivan, who were taken prisoner. Howe's losses approached four hundred.[38]

There was plenty of blame to go round for this debacle, but Washington was the commander in chief. Unsure and indecisive on the very eve of battle, Washington had permitted the plan for defending Brooklyn, around which every preparation had been made for six months, to be altered. Together with Sullivan and Putnam, he was culpable as well for having failed to batten down the Jamaica Pass, which in turn secured his flank, the most elementary responsibility for any commander faced with battle. Washington's decision to spurn a cavalry arm, so useful for preventing surprises, had also come home to roost. His performance shook some of the officers and sowed doubts about his abilities. "[L]ess Generalship never was shown in any Army since the Art of War was understood," fumed a lieutenant colonel who had barely escaped in the disaster.[39] The colonel of one regiment thought, "the Vast Burthen appears too much" for a man of Washington's experience. "Wd to Heaven General Lee were here," he added.[40] Washington survived the debacle, and though Putnam continued on as well,

Washington had lost confidence in him. Putnam's courage was beyond question, but he had betrayed an ignorance regarding both logistical matters and moving about large numbers of men. Furthermore, at age fifty-eight, Putnam was fifteen or twenty years older than most general officers and some, including perhaps Washington, thought him too old for the work at hand. (Putnam would suffer a stroke and some paralysis less than three years later.) Although Washington's views never surfaced, some also thought Putnam lacked the proper bearing for commanding an army. For instance, one rather snobbish junior officer from Pennsylvania, thought Old Put was "much fitter to head a band of sickle-men or ditchers, than musketeers."[41]

Miraculously, four out of five Americans escaped back to Brooklyn Heights. There, 9,500 men—including reinforcements that Washington improbably sent over after the disturbing defeat—awaited Howe's next blow, whether an assault or a siege.[42] Howe rapidly opted to besiege his prey, a decision for which he has been mercilessly pilloried. Howe said later that he could "have carried the redoubt," but as he believed that "the lines must have been ours by a very cheap rate by regular approaches," he opted not to "risk the loss that might have been sustained in the assault."[43] The logic of his thinking was apparent. His quarry was pinioned against the East River, which was in the possession of the world's strongest navy. Seemingly, the Continentals could not be supplied. Nor could they escape. To order a wasting frontal assault was to repeat the terrible experiences of Fort Carillon in 1758 and Bunker Hill in 1775. Victory could be achieved through an assault, but the losses would be stupendous. Victory was also assured by investment, and the casualties would be minimal. Howe chose victory through a siege.

Across the East River, at his Manhattan headquarters, Washington wrestled with his choices, and within forty-eight hours of the ridgeline defeat he had concluded that he must try to remove his men from Long Island. They were doomed if they stayed. Washington brought the matter before a council of war on August 29 and encountered opposition. Some objected that an attempt to move the army across the mile-wide East River would be chancier than remaining in Brooklyn. Others blustered against "giving the enemy a single inch of ground." Still others, notably Putnam, insisted: "Give an American army a wall to fight behind and they will fight forever."[44] In some respects, the generals divided between those who believed victory in this war could be had by denying the British a decisive victory while keeping American losses at a minimum and those who believed that to win the Continentals would have to exact the highest toll possible against the enemy, whatever their own losses might be in the process.

Washington prevailed, thanks perhaps to a nor'easter that had hit the region, dumping rain for two days, ruining everyone's ammunition, and bringing with it strong, gusty winds that inhibited the movements of the Royal Navy. The council of war agreed to use the foul weather to its advantage. An attempt was to be made to extricate the army that very night. Washington had already gathered a small flotilla of crafts of every size and description, and that afternoon he set some of his army on Manhattan on a frantic search to find still more. The rain continued through the afternoon and into the evening. When night tightened over Brooklyn, and the black storm clouds obscured the moon, the boats, manned by two Massachusetts regiments under Colonel Glover, and consisting almost exclusively of experienced mariners, were brought across the East River. The evacuation began at 10:00 p.m. So secret was the operation that even some of the officers believed the army was being shifted elsewhere on Long Island in preparation for launching an attack against the British. Ordered not to talk or to smoke, or even to cough, the men left their campfires burning and trudged toward the shoreline through the muck created by the incessant rain. Some carried stores and tents. Others wrestled with the invaluable artillery, which sank like rocks in the Brooklyn mud, forcing them to abandon the largest and heaviest pieces. Once at the river's edge—under the watchful eye of Washington, who had crossed to take charge of this hazardous undertaking personally—the men climbed into boats and embarked. Those units that were deemed the least reliable were brought off first. The trip that followed must have seemed interminable to these men, as they stared intently into the soot black night praying not to see a British warship. One unit followed another throughout the night, although when day beckoned a considerable portion of the army remained in Brooklyn, the operation having been slowed by the very conditions that made it possible in the first place. But just as day was breaking, the rain stopped and a most welcome fog rolled in. Some thought it Heaven-sent, this fog so thick according to one soldier that he "could scarcely discern a man at six yards distance." In the singular lemon-yellow light made by sun and fog, the Continentals completed the operation, an extraordinary undertaking that succeeded through a mixture of rare decisiveness, careful and shrewd planning, and good fortune. And, as Washington told Congress, it was brought off "without any Loss of Men or Ammunition."[45]

Some at Howe's headquarters were "most agreeably surprized to find, that the Rebels had entirely abandoned Long Island," as it confirmed in their mind that the Americans could be brought to heel and made to negotiate a settlement. Some were relieved that an assault had not been ordered, especially after they inspected the rebels' defenses. The redoubts were so well constructed, according to a German, that "determined troops could have held out against a far stronger enemy than we were." Others on Howe's staff were bitter at the way things had been handled. They instantly understood that the lost opportunity to crush the enemy presaged another year of war. The Howe brothers sought to make the most of their little victory. They sent a compliant Sullivan to Philadelphia to ask that Congress send emissaries to Staten Island to treat with them in an official peace conference. Many in Congress were disgusted with Sullivan's willingness to play the lackey. He was privately ridiculed as a "pidgeon" and a "decoy" sent to stampede the "half Tories and those called moderate men" into a surrender. But ever conscious of mollifying the weak-kneed among them, Congress sent John

Adams, Edward Rutledge, and Benjamin Franklin to parlay. Nothing came of it. The American delegation refused to negotiate unless the Howes first recognized American independence, which they could not do.[46]

Washington had been changed by his success at Dorchester Heights, but the events in Brooklyn produced an especially redemptive transformation in him. Some military commanders can never change. They remain faithful to the earlier lessons they have learned or hold inflexibly to their original choices. But Washington underwent a stormy transit of reexamination that moved him by fits and starts to conceive a new strategy. Since assuming command he had believed that he could fashion an army of adequately trained officers and men, one that would be a match for an army of Europe's regulars. The engagement on Long Island was the first real test for his army, and the troubling realities of what had occurred shook him to the core. Chaos and confusion had prevailed among the officers. Many men had panicked under fire. In the aftermath of the Guana Heights drubbing, a sense of "apprehension and despair" gripped much of the soldiery. Washington himself felt a "want of confidence in the Generality of the Troops." They were too green to undertake offensive operations, he said, and at the same time they lacked a "readiness to defend even strong posts." Washington also decided—though only for a brief time—that Howe had learned from his experience and henceforth would avoid an "Attack upon Lines when [he] can avoid It." Howe, Washington concluded early in September, would henceforth resort to maneuvers at which his army was especially skilled.[47]

Given these realities, Washington told Congress that it was necessary to wage what he called "a War of Posts." The Continentals must remain on the defensive, he said, adding that "we should on all occasions avoid a general Action or put anything to the risque unless compelled by a necessity into which we ought never to be drawn."[48] Washington's remarks pointed toward a Fabian strategy, so named after the Roman general Fabius Cunctator, who had been compelled to fight in this manner against a superior Carthaginian adversary. Washington would now pick when and where to fight, and even then he would hazard but a small portion of his army. The idea of a grand and decisive battle had given way to the notion of a war of attrition. Independence was to be won only by prolonging the war and wrenching from Britain such a heavy toll in time, blood, and treasure that it would at last set America free. Perhaps, too, France, observing America's staying power, would join the fray and its belligerency would force London to end hostilities.

THE NEW STRATEGY led Washington to the logical conclusion that New York City must be abandoned. Not only could the enemy "drive us out," he said, but far worse was in store for his army if it waited for the blow to fall. The British army, he knew full well, was capable of "taking post in our Rear" while the Royal Navy "secure[d] the Front." Should that occur, the Continentals would be "cut [to] peices." Washington, it seems clear, wished to move his army to Harlem Heights,

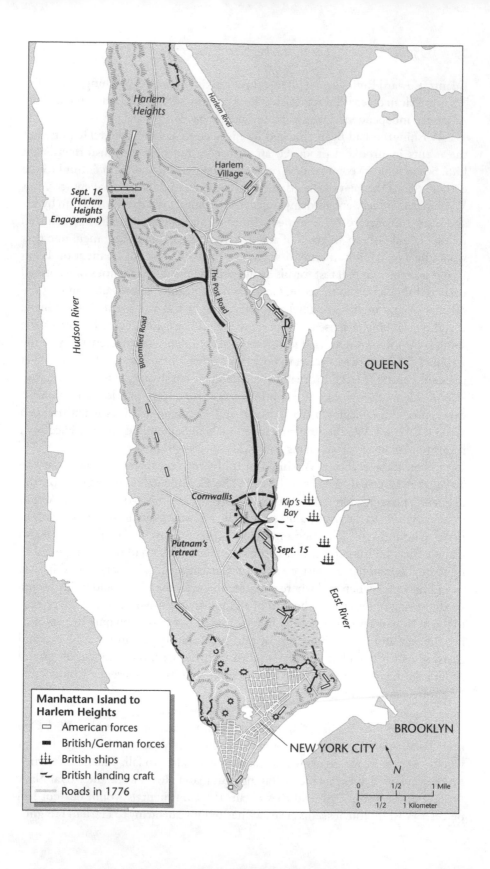

Harlem
Heights

Harlem River

Harlem
Village

Sept. 16
(Harlem
Heights
Engagement)

The Post Road

Hudson River

Bloomfied Road

QUEENS

Cornwallis

Kip's
Bay

Putnam's
retreat

Sept. 15

East River

**Manhattan Island to
Harlem Heights**

☐ American forces
■ British/German forces
⚓ British ships
〜 British landing craft
═ Roads in 1776

BROOKLYN

NEW YORK CITY

N

0   1/2   1 Mile
0   1/2   1 Kilometer

quitting the city and burning it. That would deny Howe its "great conveniences" when he went into winter quarters, obliging his redcoats to endure another raw and vexed winter, one that would make its grim predecessor in Boston pale by comparison. Washington did not feel that much would be lost by laying waste to New York City, as the lion's share of the property was owned by Tories.[49]

Despite his penetrating analysis, Washington refused to abandon the city until his officers signed on. The first council of war that took up the issue was rent with angry divisions, but a majority of officers voted that New York be defended. Washington shrank from defying them. For that matter, he did not wish to take on those congressmen who insisted that, claiming that it was defensible, the city "be maintained at every hazard," and that a retreat would "dispirit the Troops and enfeeble our Cause." Against his better judgment, Washington relented. Even so, he sought to turn Congress his way, and likely spoke in private with the generals, explaining the manifold dangers in defending the city and the many advantages that would accrue from jettisoning it. Abandon it, he said, and "we deprive the Enemy of the Advantage of their Ships." Once out of town, no more than a fraction of the army need ever be put in danger. Get to the mainland, he went on, and the army's stores and artillery can be secured. Pull back and draw the enemy on, and its supply lines would grow longer and more vulnerable. Retreat and the army will survive until winter ends the year's fighting. Washington had his way. He summoned a second council of war on September 12, and it agreed to the evacuation of New York City, but "holding up every Shew and Appearance of defence, till Our sick and All our Stores could be brought away." Washington hastily notified Congress. The legislators in Philadelphia said nothing, save for adopting a resolution that forbade Washington from burning the city. Its silence was interpreted at headquarters as a sign that Congress expected its army to defend New York. Many of the generals buried their fury behind a tight-lipped countenance, although one privately raged about how the congressmen were "unhinging the army by their absurd interference."[50]

Washington once again divided the army. Leaving 3,500 men in the city until Congress authorized its evacuation, he posted others in the lush rolling terrain at Harlem Heights to the north, at King's Bridge further north, and at Forts Washington and Lee on opposite sides of the Hudson. Still others were scattered here and there at a variety of posts. Then he waited for Howe, expecting his landing to come in Harlem or further north at Kingsbridge. At last, on September 14, he learned that Congress had sanctioned the abandonment of New York City, claiming that it had never intended that the city be defended. Relieved, Washington ordered the removal of the stores and the sick, with the last to come out assigned responsibility for removing the heavy artillery.[51] But it was too late. Howe moved first.

Great Britain's last best chance to destroy the Continental army and crush the American rebellion occurred in September 1776, but the opportunity slipped away through a series of monumental mistakes. Howe devised another clever plan—a landing at Kip's Bay, between the two principal divisions of the Continental army, and a site that Washington, once again, had not considered a prime target—but the British commander waited seventeen days before implementing it. Had he moved rapidly following Washington's escape from Long Island, he might have capitalized on the confusion and despair in the ranks of the Continentals. Entire regiments of militia had left for home—three-quarters of Connecticut's militiamen were gone—and Washington acknowledged that a "want of discipline" prevailed in many units. By the time Howe finally moved, a measure of order had been restored and fresh militia were in the lines. Howe was habitually unhurried, and in this instance he had dallied while he micromanaged preparations and awaited the outcome of the never-promising meeting with Congress's envoys.[52]

Howe's blow fell on Sunday, September 15. Five heavy warships, accompanied by seventy-five flatboats, galleys, and bateaux that contained a landing force of about four thousand men, entered Kip's Bay (near present 34th Street) under cover of darkness. At sunrise, from only two hundred yards offshore, the fleet laid down a shuddering bombardment against a coastline that was defended by a single brigade of callow New Englanders who lacked adequate entrenchments. Quaking in nauseated terror, they flattened themselves to the ground in what was little more than a shallow ditch. Few had ever experienced a shelling, and none had previously been subjected to such a dreadful cannonading from such close range. Nor had any previously experienced the churning, miasmic fear that tore at them. The noise was like a thousand simultaneous claps of thunder. Smoke, thick and suffocating, was everywhere. Shrapnel, rocks, and wood shrieked just over the men's heads. One soldier said later that the bombardment was "woeful," and added that he had lain on the hard ground wondering "which part of my carcass would go first." The men stayed in their places, not daring to rise, as the footfalls of the exploding shells crept nearer and nearer. Although Washington later contended that the warships were too close to angle their guns properly in order to score direct hits on the trenches, the men on the American left finally could take no more. Leaping up, they ran as fast as their legs could carry them for safety. Their flight set off a panicky dash for the rear by the entire force.[53]

Following the hour-long shelling, the British landed. They encountered virtually no resistance. Washington, who had heard the fusillade in Harlem some four miles away, rode to the scene, arriving not long after the effortless British landing had begun. The first thing he saw was his soldiers fleeing to safety. In their panic, many had thrown down their weapons. No one was in charge. Officers were running as hard as their men. They often led the flight, trying, one said, "to escape death or captivity" by "all sober means." More than one soldier thought the army's high command regarded him as expendable, someone to fight, and die, and through his sacrifice to buy time so that the remainder of the army might be readied to respond to the enemy action. Others thought they had been posted at Kip's Bay by officers who had failed to concoct "some proper plan of defense." When Washington saw what was unfolding, he was besotted with rage. He rode among the panicked men, screaming and cursing, swinging his sword and waving his pistols, but nothing could arrest their flight. He rode without caution, not noticing at one point that he had galloped upon a party of Hessians. He was saved by an aide, who, seeing the danger, grabbed the bridle of Washington's great grey charger, turning it about with considerable effort, and pulling his commander to safety before the startled enemy could open fire. Among the most vulnerable men on any battlefield are those in a disorganized, blind panic, and it is conceivable that nearly all the fleeing defenders of Kip's Bay might have been captured throughout that day had not reinforcements—chiefly Colonel Glover's New England regiment—arrived and restored a semblance of order, if not resistance.[54]

For a second time in less than three weeks, Howe's men had an opportunity to score a major, perhaps decisive victory. Had they moved quickly to seal off every road that linked the Continentals in the city with their comrades in Harlem Heights, one, and maybe both, divisions of Washington's army could have been eradicated. There can be no question that the Continentals who were still in the process of evacuating New York City—roughly one-quarter of Washington's army—would have been trapped. Perhaps never during the entire war was the Continental army in such mortal danger as at mid-day on September 15, but it was saved by the excessive caution of the British command. Getting men ashore is always a matter of heart-stopping concern for the commander of an amphibious landing. The British had planned this landing around the prospect of vigorous American resistance on the beaches, including even a spirited rebel counterattack. Neither occurred, and as all too often was the case, the British leadership failed to improvise. Some delays were unavoidable. The first wave of regulars came ashore in a green meadow, where they waited interminably for reinforcements and their artillery, both of which required time for unloading and the latter of which was transported with agonizing deliberation. But that was the tip of the iceberg. All through this warm, sunny day, the British proceeded slowly, tentatively. As it turned out, the Continentals in the city did not begin their long march north until well into the afternoon, and did not reach a point that was perpendicular to Kip's Bay until perhaps six hours after the first redcoats landed. Led by young Aaron Burr, Putnam's aide who had lived on Manhattan, they took a country lane along the west side to safety. Astonishingly, in those six hours the British had failed to secure the handful of roads on this island that was barely five miles wide. Legends arose about British units pausing to brew tea or about officers who stopped for a repast with Tory families. There may have been some of that, and the Hessian lieutenant who raged that the British officers "seemed more intent upon looking out for comfortable quarters . . . than preventing the [American] retreat" was perhaps accurate as well, but what most crippled this operation were habits of patience and deliberation, a by-the-book formula that discouraged resolution, audacity, and innovation. The entire force of Continentals in the city managed to reach Harlem Heights, albeit without a single one of their cannon. The British had squandered a golden opportunity.[55]

Less than a week later New York City burned. Before the blaze was brought under control—thanks largely to "a sudden change of the wind," according to one official—about a quarter of the city, roughly one thousand houses and buildings, had been destroyed. Royal authorities arrested thirteen incendiaries, several with "combustibles under their clothes" and one with a torch in his hand. Three other men who were caught starting fires were lynched by mobs of New Yorkers that had gathered to fight the conflagration. The number of arsonists skulking about the city that night deservedly aroused suspicion among the British that Washington had ordered the city's destruction, a belief strengthened by the knowledge that the American commander had recently ordered the removal of all alarm bells, allegedly to be melted down for making artillery. Washington disclaimed any role in New York's destruction, although he never denied wishing to torch the city. He steadfastly insisted that he had abided by Congress's edict that New York City not be razed, a policy that he privately lambasted as "amg the . . . capitol errors" of the legislators. In all likelihood Washington had his way through the time-tested manner of leaders: expressing his hope that New York would be burned before trusted subordinates, knowing that some enterprising take-charge officer would see to organizing the firebugs.[56]

Given his close call on September 15, and his earlier talk of a "war of posts," it is remarkable that Washington did not now abandon Manhattan Island. He remained in his snare for another month, during every minute of which his army faced almost certain destruction should Howe suddenly act purposefully. Washington had been given tacit authorization to take his army off Manhattan. Both a council of war and Congress had authorized a withdrawal from New York City, if not the island, and Greene was urging that the "Island of Newyork" be abandoned. Manhattan was unimportant, he told Washington, adding that strategy should be planned around the "General Interest of America," not merely that of New Yorkers. Washington, he went on, should proceed with the understanding that "Tis our business to . . . avoid any considerable misfortune. And to take post where the Enemy will be Obligd to fight us and not we them." Such a vista did not include making a stand in Harlem Heights, though that was what Washington intended. It was one of the most baffling choices that he made during this long war.[57]

Despite his earlier cant of never again hazarding the entire army in a major engagement, Washington remained fixated on doing just that, and in particular on fighting the British on a Bunker Hill of his own making. It was a shortsighted outlook, and it stemmed from his inexperience, combative nature, and the inner demons that gnawed at him following the army's embarrassing showing on Long Island, driving him to seek redemption through a decisive showdown with the hated enemy. Other factors were in play, too. On the day after Kip's Bay,

Washington sent out 150 New England men to reconnoiter the positions that the British had taken about two miles south of Harlem Heights. A small skirmish broke out, but it grew exponentially until artillery was brought up and nearly three thousand men on each side were engaged. Early in this fray, when the Americans pulled back, the British taunted them with bugle calls reminiscent of signaling the chase in a fox hunt, a sound whose meaning was not lost on Washington, who had often ridden with the hounds at Mount Vernon. Spoiling for a fight, he threw more men into the battle, and with great daring seized the offensive, hoping to envelop and destroy his foe. His reach exceeded his grasp, but the engagement ended with a British withdrawal, a dulcet sight for the beleaguered American commander. He was "greatly inspirited" by what he had seen, he said, taking it as confirmation that his men would "behave with tolerable bravery" if well led.[58]

Washington believed he was in good shape should Howe assault the American lines in Harlem Heights. He had some 10,000 Continentals and militia in that sector, all within intricately connecting entrenchments that ran along the rocky ridge between the Hudson and Harlem Rivers. He also possessed scores of artillery.[59] But Washington was playing a dangerous game. Howe had displayed no proclivity for a frontal assault since Bunker Hill, which Washington, in fact, had acknowledged only three weeks earlier. If he again disdained such an attack, landing instead behind Washington, the entire Continental army in New York might be doomed, trapped on an island by the enemy's land and sea forces. But Washington stayed where he was, and may have done what he could to force Howe's hand, as it was only four nights after the skirmish below Harlem Heights that the attempt was made to burn New York City. Washington likely hoped that by razing the city Howe, without quarters, would be compelled to try to end the war in a decisive battle before the onset of winter.

But Howe remained inactive. He told London that the rebels were "too strongly posted to be attacked in front and innumerable difficulties" lay in the way of turning their flank. Once again, the legacy of Bunker Hill was crucial, though other considerations operated on Howe. From the start he had harbored reservations about Britain's ability to suppress such a widespread rebellion. The best hope of winning the war, he appears to have concluded, was to do just enough damage to bring about a resurgence of the American moderates and the downfall of the radicals. It was a viewpoint best articulated by Howe's chief engineer, who later remarked that he "never had an idea of subduing the Americans—I meant to assist the good Americans to subdue the bad ones."[60] Furthermore, on the eve of the Kip's Bay landing, Howe had learned that a convoy with eight thousand additional men had been about ready to embark from Portsmouth eight weeks earlier. Although his current force was superior to that of Washington, he opted to wait a few days in the hope that those reinforcements might appear.[61] It was a fateful pause. A full year would pass before he had another opportunity to fight Washington's entire army.

Washington found Howe's idleness "perplexing," just as he had a year earlier, but he stayed put. He was "resolved not to be forced from this ground," he said, and he remained confident that an enemy attack could be repulsed, or that Howe would pay for his gains "with sorrow and loss." After three weeks of waiting, intelligence reported activity in the British fleet. Washington was convinced that Howe was readying his "Attack on our present Post." The American commander was dead wrong. On October 12, four weeks to the day since the landing at Kip's Bay, Howe landed men above King's Bridge on the mainland at Throg's Neck.[62]

Howe's strategy was well conceived and had it succeeded, and been followed by a resolute sprint to the Hudson, Washington's entire army could have been trapped. Pinioned on Manhattan Island, Washington would have faced the very dilemma he had feared a month earlier in New York City: "cut off . . . thereby reducing us to the necessity of fighting our way out under every disadvantage— surrendering at discretion—or Starving." Howe, the professional, had once again outmaneuvered Washington, the amateur. But Washington was saved again. Betrayed by inadequate maps and poor intelligence, Howe had chosen a low-lying peninsula for a landing site, an island for all practical purposes, for Throg's Neck was separated from the mainland by marshes and a creek. A bridge and a causeway were the only links to the mainland, and men from a Pennsylvania rifle regiment defended each. Greeted by deadly small arms fire Howe saw immediately that he would take heavy casualties and face an interminable delay should he try to fight through this morass. He rapidly reloaded and set out to find a more suitable landing site.[63]

Washington had made one egregious mistake after another during the New York campaign, but every blunder that he made pales in comparison to his inexplicable response to the manifest dangers posed by Howe's landing above King's Bridge. Howe's action was further confirmation that he had no intention of making a frontal attack on his entrenched adversary. Howe's intent, Washington remarked, was one of "getting in our rear & cutting off" the roads that led to safety—two to Connecticut and one to Albany. But vulnerable as was Washington's position, he did nothing over a period of five long days to extricate his army from the trap that was about to spring. Instead, he manifested an unwarranted confidence, and many around him shared his optimism.[64] They had jousted with the great British army for two months and while they had won nothing, they had avoided a mortal blow. They were certain as well that Howe had accomplished relatively little of real importance. The commander's young aide-de-camp Tench Tilghman reflected their brash self-deception: "If we can foil Gen. Howe again, I think we can knock him up for the Campaign," he said.[65] The British saw things differently. If they landed successfully above King's Bridge, the best prospect facing Washington would be to "attack . . . us on our own terms," as Clinton remarked. The redcoats would have the American army precisely where they wanted it.[66]

Perhaps only the timely arrival of Charles Lee saved Washington and the army. Returning from his adventures in the South, Lee reached Harlem Heights two days after Howe's misbegotten landing at Throg's Neck. In an instant, he saw what Washington could not see. He pleaded with the commander to abandon Manhattan. Lee was fluent and persuasive, a veteran professional soldier who bore listening to, and he appears to have convinced Washington of the wisdom of retreating. Washington immediately convened a council of war. With both the commander and Lee advocating jettisoning Manhattan, the generals—with only one dissenting vote—endorsed their recommendation. The next day Washington not only issued the evacuation order, he put on alert the small contingents of Continentals that he had posted at every conceivable site near where the British might land. One of those was Colonel Glover's Fourteenth Continental infantry regiment, which was to resist a landing on or near Pell's Point. The very next morning, October 18, a British force of four thousand men, which included Captain Evelyn, landed at Pell's Point as the first rays of sunrise spilled over the beach.[67] "We are . . . upon the Eve of something very important," Washington wrote that morning.[68]

The grim fight waged by Glover's men that day at Pell's Point enabled the Continentals—with the exception of those who garrisoned Fort Washington—to retreat off Manhattan to the relative safety of the mainland. The army moved quickly. The men had little to encumber them, some having lost their tents and supplemental clothing in earlier hurried retreats. Those men who still had a spare shirt or stockings, or almost any other possession, were now forced to leave behind nearly everything in the haste to escape. For some, the war had already taken on that grim face that the Continentals would come to know so well in the ensuing years. For weeks, many men had slept without tents on the cold, often wet, ground. Few had a blanket and most were still wearing summer clothing, though the nights had long since turned chilly. When it rained, each man tried to protect his musket, but otherwise, according to one soldier, they simply sought to "weather it out." Service, that soldier added, had boiled down to "hard duty and nakedness." Conditions worsened on the retreat. The army's logistical system was tenuous at best. It was not very adept anytime the army was on the move and grossly inefficient when a move was unplanned. Food was scarce during this retreat. One soldier later recalled that he ate only chestnuts that he found in foraging and a sheep's head, the leavings of a meal the butchers had prepared for some "gentlemen officers." Washington knew of the stark conditions and at every step he implored the authorities in nearby Connecticut to find victuals for his men. If they failed to do so, he warned, they likely would face "the fatal consequences" of "Mutiny and plunder."[69] Connecticut's chief executive, Jonathan Trumbull Sr., the only colonial governor to side with the rebels, responded by asking Washington "to provide blankets and Clothing" for the province's militiamen "who have been so unfortunate as to loose them in retreating from the Enemy." Thirty days later Trumbull finally sent clothing to the Continentals,

noting the "utmost pains" his state was "takeing to furnish . . . the distressed
Troops for whom we most sensibly feel."[70]

Washington's destination was White Plains, roughly twenty miles above
Harlem Heights. The Continentals were just off Manhattan Island when Howe
at last got his entire army ashore at beachheads such as Pell's Point along the
western end of Long Island Sound and set off after them. The Americans stayed
west of the Bronx River, marching past stubbly, shaggy farmland and orchards
heavy with the scent of fallen fruit. The British remained on the other side, about
eight miles away. Approximately 14,000 American soldiers made the trek in five
days. It took ten days for about the same number of British to cover roughly the
same distance. They stopped often to locate badly needed wagons, bring up
supplies, reconnoiter the unfamiliar countryside, and contend with parties of
skirmishers sent out by Washington to slow their advance. The redcoats' lumbering progress had one advantage. In the course of his pursuit, Howe learned
that the long-awaited reinforcements had arrived—roughly equal numbers of
Hessians and British recruits—a portion of which he immediately brought up to
guard his rear.[71]

When Howe reached White Plains late in October he discovered that the
Continentals had occupied several hills and, given a week to prepare, had constructed solid entrenchments that were anchored by a lake on the left and
Chatterton's Hill on the right. Chatterton's Hill was actually a long, steep, heavily wooded ridge. At its base was the fourteen-foot-wide Bronx River. Slightly
more than one thousand rebels were posted on the hill under the command of
General Spencer. Not many were dug in. Most were concealed behind the
ubiquitous stone walls that dotted the landscape in these parts. The American
position appeared to be exceptionally strong, especially as the topography made
any flanking maneuver highly unlikely. Though nothing here was to Howe's
liking, he chose to do what he had previously declined to chance: he opted
for a frontal assault on Chatterton's Hill, hoping to turn the right flank of his
adversary. His decision likely arose from a realization that to do nothing would
crimp morale within his ranks while it swelled the spirits of his adversary.[72] He
may also have chosen this course in response to the grumbling in some quarters
about the scarce achievements of his desultory campaign. Nearly 125 days
had passed since the British landing on Staten Island, and in that time Howe's
formidable force had covered barely thirty-five miles, engaged the rebels in only
one major battle, and failed to score a decisive victory.

On October 28, Howe assigned the Hessians responsibility for assaulting
Spencer's line, though he paraded his entire army of red, green, and blue coated
warriors in a spent and shaggy wheat field, evidently hoping that his adversary
would crumple at the sight of 13,000 regulars poised and ready to move out. But
no one ran. Nor did they buckle under a heavy artillery barrage that preceded the
attack. Howe then sent forward two columns to take Chatterton's Hill. They
marched across the russet farmland and into a murderous fire. But they kept

coming, though for a time the scene was reminiscent of the fray on Bunker Hill. Their assaults continued until the Germans in Colonel Johann Rall's land grenadier regiment found an unguarded hill on Spencer's left. As the Germans moved onward, the American defenders on Chatterton's Hill realized suddenly that they were in danger of being flanked, and they fell back behind another wall, then another, causing some militia units to break and flee. The American position had become tenuous, not just on Chatterton's Hill, but on this entire battlefield. Not only was the entire British army now setting off through the wheat field where the Germans had passed earlier, the sun glinting brightly off bayonets and gun muzzles, but should the Hessians take Chatterton's Hill, they could pour an enfiladed fire into Washington's right wing while the main body of Howe's army attacked. Victory—not a decisive victory, but a victory—seemed to be within Howe's grasp. In the face of these realities, Washington made the proper choice. He withdrew the entire army into a more secure position. Howe, perhaps, did not make the proper choice. Even though the Hessians were completing the conquest of Chatterton's Hill, Howe suddenly stopped the advance of his army. As the slanting shadows of late afternoon gathered, he decided to wait until morning before launching his frontal attack. He wanted more information about the rebel positions before continuing the fight.[73]

Soldiers often exaggerate the importance of battles in which they fight, as did a young Rhode Islander who said, "on this Day's action [at White Plains] seamd almost to Depend the fate of this years Campaine."[74] It actually had been an engagement that involved only small portions of both armies, but even so the fight on Chatterton's Hill had been ferocious, and for the Americans nearly as bloody and desperate as the struggle on Bunker Hill. The British, with roughly a three to one superiority, and with a cavalry arm, had attacked and kept attacking, sometimes not firing their weapons but employing bayonet charges. In some sectors, especially when engaging callow militiamen, the regulars had rapidly overrun the American lines; in other areas, the Americans, at least for a time, had fought their foe to as standstill. In the end, superior firepower won out. The losses on each side were slightly greater than 150 killed and wounded.[75]

Soon dusk gathered over White Plains, followed by what one Continental called the "silent gloom" of night that always descended on a battlefield that, in a few hours, would once again be a killing ground.[76] When morning arrived, Howe decided to wait for reinforcements. That same day Washington's headquarters reported to Congress that it was "distressed" by a situation that no longer was "so advantageous." On October 30 six new regiments of Hessians reached the battlefield, but again it was too late in the day to think of battle. Howe now planned his grand attack for the next morning. But morning brought an end to a long string of golden, dry autumn days. A cold front moved in and rain lashed the area for nearly twenty-four hours. The rains had stopped by late the following morning, October 31, but dark clouds still hovered overhead and the ground was so sodden that equipment could hardly be moved. Howe thought he would at last be able to act the next day, but when he awakened on November 1, a frigid, soggy morning, he discovered that Washington was gone. The rebels had retreated to the heights at North Castle further north. Left to ponder his choices, Howe, mindful of the dangers of being lured deeper into the hinterland, abandoned the pursuit and, unruffled, marched back to Manhattan. He had been foiled by the newfound Fabian strategy that Washington finally had employed. Even more, Howe was thwarted by his own transfixed habits and an utter absence of those daring and enterprising qualities that have distinguished history's great generals from those who were merely mediocre, or failures.[77]

The leafless trees and more frequent days of leaden skies were heralds of winter's rapid approach. Decisions had to be made on both sides. Howe was certain of only one thing. All along, he had been committed to flushing every American soldier from Manhattan Island during 1776, and he had removed all but about four thousand rebels, those posted at King's Bridge and Fort Washington. Howe set to work immediately on getting rid of them. On the day after the engagement at White Plains, he ordered General Wilhelm von Knyphausen, who was posted with six Hessian regiments at New Rochelle, to cross the Bronx River and secure the mainland between Manhattan and White Plains, including King's Bridge. The Hessian commander accomplished his mission even before Howe departed White Plains. On November 4, Knyphausen reached Fort Independence, which guarded the northern approach to King's Bridge, and discovered that the Americans had abandoned and razed that installation on Washington's orders.[78] The British were now confident that every exit from Manhattan, save that across the Hudson, had been closed to the Americans who were garrisoned at Fort Washington.

Howe's plans jelled during the first two weeks in November, partly as a result of discussions with his brother, and partly from events. He contemplated a move to take Rhode Island, an idea that he had first broached back in January. He possessed adequate numbers, he believed, and Admiral Howe championed taking Rhode Island. Newport, he argued, would provide a better-protected port than New York, and one whose climate was more temperate. Newport would also be an excellent base for conducting raids all along the New England coast, and when the time came to invade Massachusetts, one prong of the invasion force could spring out of Rhode Island. Howe additionally mulled the idea of pacifying eastern New Jersey, an idea that had come to him after he landed on Staten Island in July, and one that he had originally embraced as much from political as military considerations. He was enthralled with taking territory, hopeful that every acre he gained and every citizen that he redeemed as a Loyalist would further sap America's resolve, eventually bringing about negotiations leading to reconciliation.[79]

Before Howe's designs were complete, he knew the disposition of the Continentals, and that too shaped his thinking. On the day after the British pulled out of White Plains, Washington summoned a council of war to formulate

American strategy. It voted to break the army into four parts. Washington would take two thousand men into New Jersey and, augmented by militia, stand ready for any move that Howe took in that sector. Lee, at North Castle, was given seven thousand men. He was to guard against an invasion of New England through New York or Connecticut, but if the enemy eschewed an offensive in this region and struck into New Jersey, Lee was to come to Washington's aid. Even so, Washington cautioned Lee that "the appearance of Imbarking Troops for the Jerseys may be intended as a feint." With Washington professing "the most entire confidence in your Judgment," Lee was instructed to use his discretion with regard to coming to New Jersey. The council debated whether to retain Fort Washington, and Lee at least argued against its retention, asserting that it was of "little or no use" and could not be saved if the British attacked it. But the council recommended its retention, and Greene was left with a third portion of the army with which to hold both Fort Washington and Fort Lee. General William Heath got the remainder—about four thousand men—who were to prepare defenses in the highlands along the Hudson above Manhattan. Putnam was left without an independent command.[80]

A week later Washington entered New Jersey with his diminutive force. About the same time Howe finalized his plans. Many options had been available. General Clinton, for instance, had vociferously objected to sending troops to Rhode Island on the grounds that it could be taken at any time and that to possess it straightway would in itself lead to nothing that was decisive. Instead, he proposed cogent alternatives that pulsed with energy and activity, and held a promise of immediate, and pivotal, results. Clinton offered three plans, each of which eyed a concentration of British force that could destroy Washington's minuscule army in New Jersey. His most grandiose design conceived of a three-pronged attack into the region between upper New Jersey and Philadelphia. He proposed that a land-sea force disembark in the northern Chesapeake, after which one division was to advance on Philadelphia from the southwest, while another came up the Delaware River approach to Philadelphia. A third force was to drive simultaneously toward Philadelphia from the north. When Howe rejected that scheme, Clinton scaled back, recommending two variations of his original plan. In both, one force was to advance on Philadelphia from the north while a second force either landed on the Jersey coast and cut off Washington's lane of retreat or it proceeded up the Delaware River to Philadelphia, driving Congress from the city and sowing disorder in the American command structure.[81] Howe spurned those proposals as well.

Clinton's plans appear to have offered real hope for attaining a crucial victory, perhaps even the elusive turn-of-the-tide triumph. Typically, however, Howe chose caution over audacity. He feared that heavy British losses, as at Bunker Hill, would stoke spirits in America while smothering them in Britain, and it might invite foreign intervention before he could undertake his climactic 1777 campaign. Howe was also cheered by intelligence that pointed toward the unraveling

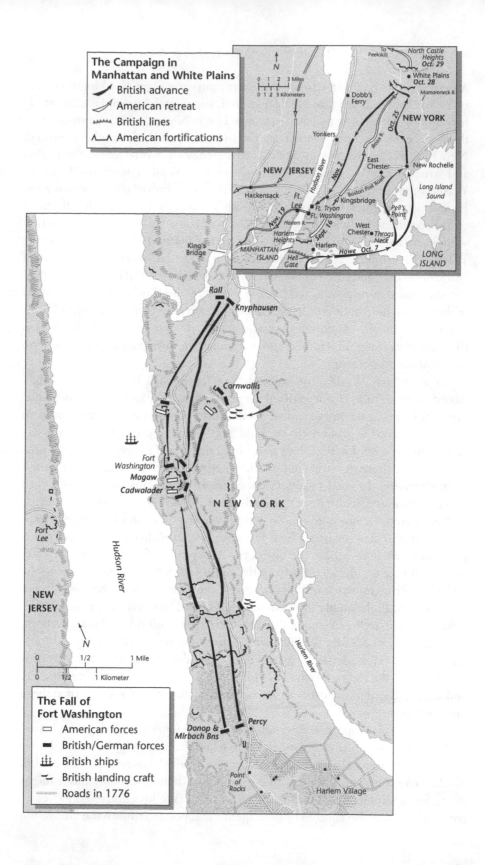

The Campaign in Manhattan and White Plains

- ⌒ British advance
- ⌒ American retreat
- ⌄⌄⌄ British lines
- ⌃⌃⌃ American fortifications

To Peekskill

North Castle Heights Oct. 29

White Plains Oct. 28

Mamaroneck R.

Dobb's Ferry

NEW YORK

Yonkers

Oct. 25

Bronx R.

Nov. 2

East Chester

New Rochelle

NEW JERSEY

Hudson River

Long Island Sound

Hackensack

Ft. Lee

Nov. 19

Boston Post Road

Kingsbridge

Pell's Point

Ft. Tryon

Ft. Washington

Harlem R.

Sept. 16

West Chester

Throgs Neck

King's Bridge

Harlem Heights

MANHATTAN ISLAND

Harlem

Howe Oct. 7

LONG ISLAND

Hell Gate

King's Bridge

Rall

Knyphausen

Cornwallis

Fort Washington

Magaw

Cadwalader

NEW YORK

Fort Lee

NEW JERSEY

Hudson River

Harlem River

Donop & Mirbach Bns

Percy

Point of Rocks

Harlem Village

The Fall of Fort Washington

- ▭ American forces
- ▬ British/German forces
- ⚓ British ships
- ⌒ British landing craft
- Roads in 1776

0   1   2   3 Miles
0   1   2   3 Kilometers

N

0   1/2   1 Mile
0   1/2   1 Kilometer

of the rebellion. He knew that the Continental soldiery was ragged and hungry, and that Continental currency was showing signs of collapse. Well informed, he was also aware that high wartime taxes and the lack of military success were eroding the will to continue among some civilians.[82] On top of everything else, Howe—doubtless to his surprise—learned that the Americans had not abandoned Fort Washington. Desirous of cleansing Manhattan before winter, Howe opted to seize that installation. Once it was taken, he would send Cornwallis after Washington in New Jersey while Clinton—to Sir Henry's utter disgust—was to be given responsibility for subduing Rhode Island. Sometime in December, Howe would put his army in winter quarters and await the campaign season of 1777.

If the rebels' retention of Fort Washington astonished Howe, it has been no less astounding to historians. In June, Washington had authorized the construction of the installation north of Harlem on the highest point on Manhattan. It afforded a superb view of the Hudson some three hundred feet below, and was conceived as ideal for sealing off the river to British warships. Furthermore, as it would sit atop a tall, craggy, steep, granite mound, a fort on this site was thought to be invulnerable. Yet, only a month after construction started the *Phoenix* and *Rose* easily ran past the fort's gunners. That alone should have called into question the value of the facility. Instead, Washington responded by ordering that additional obstructions be sunk in the Hudson to slow future warships and render them more vulnerable. Some advisors questioned the notion—the American general George Clinton, a New Yorker, frankly told his commander that he had "no Faith" in such a scheme—but Fort Washington was retained.[83]

Howe had not moved against Fort Washington when Washington arrived at Fort Lee from White Plains on November 13. Colonel Robert Magaw, a Pennsylvania colonel who had practiced law in Carlisle until shortly before the war, was in command of the garrison, while Greene, who was also at Fort Lee, had responsibility for the army in this sector. Both urged Fort Washington's retention, especially as two weeks earlier artillery from the fort had damaged two British frigates, the *Pearl* and the *Repulse*, that had drawn near. Putnam and the New York Committee of Safety, among others, added their voices to the chorus recommending that the installation be defended. It was Washington's decision to make, and he was sorely tempted to disregard the counsel of those wishing to hold the fort. A week earlier, from White Plains, he had written Greene that he could imagine no "valuable purpose" that could be performed by the fort. But he did not act on his instincts. He said later that he had not done so because he respected Greene's "judgment and candour," and because Congress had recently directed him to seek to "obstruct effectually the navigation" of the Hudson River "by every art, and whatever expense." Other factors shaped his thinking. Like Greene and Magaw, Washington believed the fort to be impregnable if assaulted. He believed that Howe would have to take it by siege craft. Magaw had advised that he could hold out until late in December, which would tie down perhaps as many as 10,000 of Howe's men during the next six weeks, the very time when a new army was being recruited. Magaw also advised that when the time came to abandon the installation, he could get most of his men to safety across the Hudson.[84]

Washington had only forty-eight hours to make a final decision. Making rapid decisions was never his strong suit, and in this instance after weeks of pulsing anxiety, hard travel, and sleepless nights, he was not at his best.[85] In the grip of numbing fatigue, he reflected on his choices, waffled, and thought some more. Then the decision was made—for him. Howe attacked just after dawn on November 16. This was not a siege after all, but a simultaneous assault from three directions, an uncharacteristic act for Howe. It came about when William Demont, Magaw's adjutant, defected and provided valuable information about Fort Washington, including details on its weaknesses (for which he was compensated with a cash stipend roughly the equivalent of the annual income of a skilled artisan and an appointment as commissary of prisoners).[86]

The British attack was carried off with dispatch and skill, perhaps affording a glimpse of what might have been had similarly resolute operations been mounted earlier in this campaign. Howe employed 13,000 men in this operation, giving him a four-fold advantage over the defenders. He sent Hessians under Knyphausen down from the north and British and Germans under Lord Percy and Cornwallis up from Harlem. Each confronted rebels in the fort's outer defenses, where Magaw had deployed most of his men. To get at them, the attackers had to climb steep precipices, moil through tangled thickets, and surmount numerous obstacles (from felled trees to fences) that the defenders had placed in their path. Laboring under their heavy equipment, the British and Hessians struggled, but moved up the rugged terrain sometimes by "grasping the wild boxtree bushes," or in other instances each man simply "held out his hand to help the next man, and this way, the passage was forced." In an area that witnessed particularly heavy fighting, Knyphausen personally led his men and, according to one Hessian soldier, with contemptuous ease "tore down the fences with his own hands to urge the men on."[87] From the beginning, some of the rebels thought their situation was hopeless. A Pennsylvania private later recalled officers with "tears trickling down both their cheeks" not just because of their personal plight, but "as it will be such a terrible stroke to our cause."[88] Nevertheless, as at Bunker Hill, the Americans fought tenaciously and riflemen from Virginia and Maryland, in particular, exacted a heavy toll. A Hessian later remarked that in the thick of the fight he and his comrades "had a hard time of it," and another noted the inordinate number of wounded, men who were "shattered," lying "in their own blood" and "whimpering," looking at their comrades and "pleading that in one way or another we could ease their suffering and unbearable pain."[89] Some rebel units resisted for more than two hours, and the battle might have lasted longer had their weapons not fouled with powder from excessive firing. In the end, the weight of British numbers, and the size of the area that the rebels had been asked to defend, proved to be too much. As on the Guana Heights, the American lines were too extensive for their small force, inhibiting their efforts to marshal an effective concentration of fire and leaving soft pockets that the enemy exploited. Faced finally with bayonet charges, the defenders retreated inside the walls of the fort.

The British surrounded the installation and brought up their artillery. Before they opened fire, Magaw was offered the opportunity to surrender. To refuse was to invite a bombardment that was certain to be catastrophic. Furthermore, to lose after refusing to surrender was to run the risk that the victors, driven to an insane fury by the loss of comrades, would give no quarter. Magaw, who had blustered of fighting to the death and of holding out for weeks, conceded to brutal reality. He surrendered. From start to finish, the operation had consumed only five hours. When the gates of Fort Washington opened, 2,870 men paraded into British captivity. Another 149 Americans had been killed and wounded in the battle, and vast amounts of arms were lost. The British, in turn, had lost 458 killed, wounded, and missing, proportionally but a small fraction of their losses at Bunker Hill. While delighted with their conquest, more than a few British and Hessian officers were upset that Howe had permitted the rebels to surrender. Many would have preferred to storm the fort and kill as many rebels as possible. There would have been "no difficulty" in the operation, said one, and the bloody results would have "struck such a panic through the Continent, and would have prevented the Congress from ever being able to raise another Army."[90]

Some of the American soldiers were drunk when they emerged from the fort and into British captivity, having tipped the rum pot as the desperate afternoon wore on. They were frightened, and had every right to be. More than one British officer loudly exclaimed: "What! Taking prisoners! Kill them, kill every man of them." Hearing such threats "unmanned me," one of the captives later admitted.[91] But none were killed, although some were beaten by the Germans and all were taunted. When one captured officer extended his hand to General Knyphausen, it was rebuffed with a gruff: "Naw, naw, naw, I no shake hands mit a rebel." One of those taken later recalled that plundering commenced immediately. "[S]ide arms, watches, shoe-buckles, and even the clothes on our backs were wrested from us," he said.[92] The prisoners of war were marched through a gauntlet of New York civilians who "treated us with volleys of indecent language," another prisoner later recalled. Several believed that the women in the crowd were the most abusive, and one captured rebel subsequently said that it was in response to the demands of these women—whom he called the German soldiers' "trulls"—that the "Hessian soldiers began to cut the knapsacks off the backs of our men." (That same soldier also said that once the Americans were in captivity they were visited by the wives and mistresses of the Germans, who brought them cake and coffee.)[93]

After having saved his army by fleeing Manhattan and resorting to a Fabian strategy, Washington had once again blundered badly, though in his subsequent reports he endeavored to shift the blame onto Greene for what he called "the unhappy affair." But Washington knew the truth. Cowed with gloom and shaken by his latest monstrous error, he was said to have wept uncontrollably in the presence of other officers. If so, it was a rare loss of composure, probably the result of fatigue and frayed nerves, but also brought on by the unsettling realization that he would be held accountable and that some would lose confidence in his abilities. Indeed, Lee immediately, and indelicately, asked him bluntly: "Oh General why wou'd you be over-perswaded by men of inferior judgment to your own."94

As inexcusable as was the loss of the men and supplies at Fort Washington, another unforgivable calamity followed hard on its heels. Ten days before Fort Washington was taken, Washington realized that the huge stash of supplies at Fort Lee, just across the Hudson, might no longer be safe, and he ordered Greene to see to its removal and relocation in the interior of New Jersey. But after Fort Washington fell, Washington—whether from indecision or because he had been lulled by Howe's languid habits into believing that urgent action was unnecessary —waited nearly seventy-two hours before ordering the evacuation of Fort Lee. For once, Howe moved swiftly. He gave Earl Cornwallis responsibility for taking the fort, and made available twelve battalions of assault troops, about five thousand men, for the job. Led by three Tories, the British force started across the Hudson just before midnight on the rain-black night of November 19. Apprized of the gathering danger, Washington only then issued orders to abandon Fort Lee. Heavily outnumbered, he gave no thought to attempting to stop his adversary's advance, although Cornwallis' landing took place at the foot of unbelievably tall, steep cliffs. Scaling those nearly vertical heights posed a formidable task under any circumstances. Doing so on this rain-slick night only added to the difficulty. Some in the attack force were amazed that the rebels put up no resistance. Fifty men at the summit could have held off Cornwallis' entire force with a few rocks, one Hessian claimed with only slight exaggeration after he completed the daunting climb. Once over the top, Cornwallis' force spotted only a few American stragglers. Most of the rebel garrison had fled quickly, leaving water boiling in pots over open fires and unserved dinners on the tables in the officers' quarters.

Cornwallis found a treasure trove of supplies, left there, Greene later pleaded, because he had lacked the wagons and boats to convey the precious materials to safety.95 The losses would have been serious for any army, but they were nearly catastrophic for a force as ill provisioned as the Continental army. Gone were thirty cannon, 8,000 cannon shot, 4,000 cannonballs, 2,800 muskets, 400,000 cartridges, 500 entrenching tools, 300 tents, 1,000 barrels of flour, and untold amounts of baggage.96

IN EIGHT MONTHS America's fortunes had plummeted from the high that followed the British evacuation of Boston to an enveloping despair brought on by these monumental failures. The army that had celebrated in March was "half naked & greatly dispiritied" in November, and much of it was running for its life.97 "A

Shudder went thro' the Continent," a Rhode Island official remarked that dark autumn.[98] Morale was shredded in some sectors. Samuel Adams thought that the majority of the inhabitants in the mid-Atlantic states were "determined to give it up." Washington despaired at the "want of spirit & fortitude" that seemed to have taken hold of the citizenry, and for the first time recognized that defeat was possible, maybe even imminent. Some in Congress took to looking for a scapegoat. Quietly, some whispered about the "capital Errors" that had been made by those at the head of the army, while others railed at those who had perhaps fatally delayed independence and "poisoned the Minds of the People" by chasing after the chimera of reconciliation, a course that may have deprived the country of massive assistance from France. Despondency gnawed at those on the front lines. Where some had once been fired by noble dreams and expectations, most now— said one soldier—"grow tired" and "count the Days of Service which yet remain" until they could escape for home. Another soldier, probably like many of his comrades, simply prayed that "god will still Presarve us & Carry us through all Defcltyes & Dangers" until the period of his enlistment ended.[99]

7

"THIS HOUR OF ADVERSITY": TO THE END OF 1776

W ASHINGTON'S TATTERED LITTLE ARMY began to run on November 20, the day Cornwallis crossed the Hudson above Fort Lee. It did not stop running for twelve days, until it was in Pennsylvania and the Delaware River lay like a welcome rampart between it and the enemy. Two months earlier neither Washington nor Howe had thought the campaign of 1776 would boil down to this. Both commanders had believed that if the fighting moved beyond Manhattan, it would center around a contest for control of the Hudson River, with Howe attempting to link up with the British army coming south out of Canada. Consequently, throughout the grim struggle for New York, both leaders—but Howe in particular—had impatiently sought word of Carleton's invasion of northern New York.

DURING THE FRANTIC retreat from Canada in the late spring, Benedict Arnold— now a general, having been promoted in January—linked up with Sullivan's main army and fell back to death-infested Isle aux Noix. Once there, Sullivan sent him to break the news to Schuyler of the "sad necessity of Abandoning Canada."[1] Arnold finally located Schuyler late in June at his home in Albany, laid low again by illness. For Arnold, who had endured nearly fifteen months of constant campaigning, it must have been cause for rejoicing to be inside a comfortable dwelling, let alone a mansion. Schuyler welcomed him, providing food and drink, after which he sat up until nearly midnight listening as Arnold, a veritable armory of ideas, discussed the military situation. In the course of that mild summer night the American response to the threat posed by Carleton took shape. Both

Arnold and Schuyler believed that Carleton hoped to capture Crown Point and Ticonderoga, and that if he took them early enough he would move against Albany, some seventy-five miles to the south. Nevertheless, Arnold, who did most of the talking, radiated confidence, certain that the Americans had time to prepare. Carleton would have to build a fleet, and an immense flotilla at that, to transport thousands of regulars and tons of supplies. Moreover, the provender needed by an army engaged in a wilderness campaign would not be available until the harvest was in at the tag end of the summer. While conceding that Carleton was a defensive genius, Arnold doubted that he was accustomed to offensive warfare, and his preparations for the invasion would be more time consuming than for other more experienced leaders. At the earliest, Arnold guessed, Carleton would not be able to move before September. When he did move, Arnold suggested, the Americans must wage a delaying action that would forestall the British invasion of New York until the following year, when the Americans might be better prepared. Arnold proposed two steps. The defenses at Ticonderoga must be strengthened and work should begin on an American squadron of thirty vessels that would challenge Carleton's navy as it sailed up Lake Champlain, a step that would further delay Carleton by compelling him to build an even larger fleet.[2]

Arnold and his host concurred on these points and that same evening, after midnight, Schuyler wrote Washington requesting help in finding ship carpenters and supplies for the construction of the fleet. In the days that followed Schuyler beseeched the authorities in Massachusetts and Connecticut to send workers and equipment to Skenesborough (modern Whitehall, New York), a site with sawmills about a dozen miles below Ticonderoga. Two weeks later a council of war that included Schuyler, Arnold, and Horatio Gates, whom Congress had appointed to replace Sullivan as commander of what was still euphemistically called the Canadian army, agreed to abandon Crown Point—it was in "so perfect a Ruin," said Gates, that "Several Summers" would be needed to rebuild it—and to devote their time and energy to the construction of the fleet and bolstering Fort Ticonderoga. Arnold, the former merchant with marine experience, was given command of the fleet and ordered—as Gates put it—to "give life and spirit to our dockyard."[3]

During July and August, while Howe and Washington were poised on the cusp of battle in New York, the bucolic countryside near the southern end of Lake Champlain hummed with activity. Schuyler, whose greatest talent lay in logistical matters, recruited workers and mariners, and found the cordage, cables, oakum, blocks, sailcloth, axes, crosscut saws, swivel guns and shot, and countless other articles needed for constructing the fleet. He also met with representatives of the Six Nations tribes at German Flats on the Mohawk River. Ten days of exhausting festivities and tedious negotiations resulted in a renewed promise of neutrality from the Native Americans. Gates, meanwhile, took over an army that continued to be ravaged by smallpox. He transferred the ill to Fort George and took enterprising steps to improve sanitation at Ticonderoga. Within a month he not only had reduced the number of sick troops by two-thirds, but he was able to report that "the Small-Pox is now perfectly removed" from his army of 9,157 men posted at, and in the vicinity of, Fort Ticonderoga.4

Arnold wore two hats that summer. He cobbled together scouting parties that set off down the lake to gather intelligence on Carleton's activities and he oversaw the work on his fleet. When completed, his Champlain navy was about half the size he had hoped for, but it was a credible squadron nonetheless. He had seven gondolas, each a fifty-foot-long flat-bottomed craft that could accommodate a crew of forty-five and three guns, one in the bow and two amidships. July and August also witnessed the construction of eight row galleys, each about eighty feet long, large enough for a crew of eighty together with ten guns, and a cutter about the size of the gondolas, but faster, as it was equipped with lateen sails. A sloop and three schooners—something of a cross between the gondolas and a row galley—all of which had been taken from the enemy, were part of the fleet as well.5

Arnold's little navy sailed from Crown Point on September 1. Merely sixty-eight days had elapsed since he had broached the idea to Schuyler, eloquent testimony to American enterprise and can-do spirit, with an assist from wartime exigency. If the construction of the flotilla had been something to behold, the intelligence gathering operations had been largely unproductive. Arnold set out with no knowledge of the size or whereabouts of the enemy fleet. He knew only that Carleton had also spent the summer readying his naval arm.

Carleton had not sailed when Arnold's fleet put out onto Lake Champlain. He had encountered numerous delays, many of which, in his estimation, were attributable to a lack of help from the homeland. North's government had sent 13,000 men, the last of which arrived in late summer just as Arnold sailed, but London had done little to assist in solving the gigantic problem of transporting those men south to invade New York. Howe's campaign was the main show in 1776 and it got the bulk of artificers and materials from home. Carleton had started with only fourteen gunboats—small vessels armed with merely a single gun—and ten landing craft, all of which had been torn down to fit into the cargo hold of the supply ships that crossed the Atlantic. All required reassembly in Canada. Everything else had to be built from scratch. Carleton spent precious time rounding up skilled craftsmen, and it was not until late July that work was underway at sites along the St. Lawrence and at St. Johns, which was refashioned as a dockyard. The flotilla came together slowly, in part because the vessels built in other parts of Canada had to be dismantled for the onerous portage past the ten-mile-long Richelieu rapids above St. Johns then reassembled. Carleton's start was further delayed by his unwanted meddling, including his decision, reached only in September, and against the wishes of some advisors, to build one more ship, the *Inflexible*, a fully rigged sloop equipped with eighteen twelve-pounders. Four long, plodding weeks were required to construct that mammoth vessel, but finally, early in October, work was completed. Carleton's armada was formidable. In addition to the *Inflexible*, it consisted of two schooners that carried twenty-six guns between them, a radeau with fourteen guns (christened the *Thunderer*), twenty-four gunboats, and a gondola containing seven guns. The royal squadron would possess twice the firepower of its rival, and it was packed with much of the British army in Canada, well in excess of 10,000 men, together with 700 seamen and about 400 loyal Indian warriors.[6]

Carleton's navy weighed anchor on October 4 before a scrum of well-wishers. Arnold's fleet awaited it at Valcour Island, a small islet of high bluffs on the western side of Lake Champlain, about halfway between St. Johns and Crown Point. Arnold's orders were to make a "resolute but judicious" effort to inhibit the "progress" of the British invasion force. In other words, victory was unlikely, but he was to do what he could to keep the enemy from the gates until winter ended the northern campaign of 1776.[7]

Arnold's plan was simple. He sequestered his navy in the bay on the south-western side of Valcour Island, hoping the British would be past him before he was spotted. As they could not permit an enemy squadron to remain in their rear, where it could sever their umbilical cord to supply depots in Canada, Carleton's fleet would have to beat about and sail into the bay against the normally strong northern headwinds, an undisputed obstacle to holding a battle line. To assure that Carleton did not simply wait for favorable winds, Arnold planned to initiate the action.

After an anxious and interminable wait, Arnold at last spotted his foe gliding past his cove on the morning of October 11. He immediately emerged for battle. The over-confident British were no less eager for a fight and hurried into action without forming an extended battle line. The two navies began the slugging match shortly before noon. The fight, desperate and vicious, continued until the sable night descended over the lake. Bitter as the action had been, the day-long encounter ended in a stand-off. That was all that Carleton required, for as darkness gathered his fleet formed a battle line across the bay's exit. Arnold's navy was pinioned inside the bay. When the wind turned, whether on the following day or the day after, the American flotilla would be destroyed. But with the chill of night a fog—not uncommon at this time of year—rose up like an opaque cowl over the lake. Arnold saw his chance and seized it. He opted to make a run for safety, using the night and fog as Washington had on Long Island.

With oars muffled, and the wounded from the day's battle carried inside cabins so their groans would not be heard, Arnold's navy set out in single file around 7:00 p.m., moving ever so slowly and noiselessly. Each vessel suspended a lantern on its bow, hooded so that a tiny lenticular beam was visible only to the boat that followed, a beacon to keep the line of rebel boats on course. By shortly after midnight every American vessel had gotten through the British cordon, and by daybreak, when a startled and furious Carleton discovered what had occurred, Arnold was nearly eight miles away. Carleton immediately gave chase. Nagged by unfavorable winds, the British were unable to close the gap substantially during much of that morning. But Arnold was not able to lengthen his lead. He lost precious time when he paused to transfer ordinance from three battle-damaged vessels that were no longer seaworthy.

In the afternoon a favorable wind sprang up. The British began to close on the rebels. The next morning, with the British gaining on him by the minute, Arnold made a bold decision. Determined to save as much of the American fleet as possible, he ordered ten vessels in his navy to continue on toward Crown Point, two days away. He planned to take on the British fleet with two row galleys, *Congress* and *Washington*, and three gondolas, all of which were expendable. His goal was not to gain victory, but to fight a desperate holding action that might save the others. Carleton's navy caught Arnold near Split Rock. This time, predictably, the British got the best of it, even compelling the surrender of *Congress* after it was battered broadsides. After nearly three hours of desperate maneuvering and shelling, Arnold ordered what was left of his little squadron to turn windward and try to outrun the adversary. He succeeded, making it to Buttonmould Bay, ten miles above Crown Point. There, he and his men disembarked, struggling to extricate the wounded. (Desperate and blinded by fury, Arnold killed one of his gunners who had refused to help with the infirm, running him through with a sword.) Next, he spread gunpowder and set fire to his battered vessels. Arnold and his nearly 150 men were far from safe. They faced a long overland hike to reach Crown Point, one made more difficult when Carleton put ashore his Indian allies to search for the beleaguered rebels. Carrying the wounded in makeshift slings fashioned from sailcloth, the hungry, hard-pressed Americans hurried along an overgrown wilderness path, finally reaching tumbledown Crown Point literally one step ahead of their pursuers. They did not linger. Arnold ordered that the fort, along with its docks, barracks, and storehouse, be burned. As flames licked at their backs, the Americans set off on the last leg of their journey—to Ticonderoga.[8]

Rebel losses during the past few days were heavy. They had sustained a 25 percent casualty rate, with 80 killed, numerous wounded, and about 120 taken captive. Two-thirds of the American fleet was destroyed. The Americans had lost this campaign. Carleton had gained an overarching supremacy on Lake Champlain. But lost battles do not always add up to a lost war. Many historians have agreed with the assessment of the early-twentieth-century scholar Claude van Tyne: "the American cause . . . was saved" by the bloody resistance on Lake Champlain. The rebels' preparations and Arnold's fight had delayed Carleton's advance by several weeks, and his triumph on Lake Champlain had come too late for him to launch an invasion of New York in 1776.[9] Some in Carleton's army reached the same conclusion. His displeasure palpable, the Hessian general Baron von Riedesel subsequently charged that had Carleton set out four weeks earlier, the war "would have ended" in 1776.[10] Instead, he spent those four weeks constructing *Inflexible*, an unnecessary luxury, and it frustrated his hopes of taking Ticonderoga in 1776.

Carleton landed his force near the still-smoldering ruins of Crown Point only hours after Arnold and his men departed. But instead of proceeding against Ticonderoga immediately, he sent to Canada for reinforcements. On October 20, as he waited for more men, the first snow of the season fell. A week later Carleton dispatched units across the fresh snow to probe Ticonderoga's outer defenses. His intelligence reported, erroneously, that he was considerably outmanned. Carleton was led to believe Gates had more than 20,000 men, when in actuality he possessed about 15,000. Carleton additionally suspected that Gates, once a veteran British officer, had utilized the summer and early fall to make Fort Ticonderoga nearly impregnable. With winter approaching, a protracted siege was out of the question, and given the Americans' supposedly formidable numerical superiority, an assault was unlikely to succeed. Nevertheless, Carleton's chief of artillery, Major General William Phillips, a veteran of the previous war in America, together with other British officers urged an attack. Some believed the rebels would buckle at the first display of British resolve. Others thought that Gates had extended his men over too great a distance, leaving them vulnerable to a frontal assault. It was Carleton's call, and his decision made clear that Arnold, from the outset, had taken the measure of his foe. Carleton's forte was defensive warfare. Consumed with doubts, he wavered, cleaving to his surmises about the adversary's menacing strength. In the end, Carleton chose to go home, a step that he had hinted at in a letter to Germain just after his initial naval battle with Arnold. Early in November, about two weeks before Howe successfully assaulted Fort Washington, the British force sailed back down Lake Champlain, ending the bloody northern campaign in 1776 and leaving historians to ponder the might-have-beens.[11]

WHEN THE BRITISH landed at Kip's Bay in mid-September, Howe believed that Carleton had already launched his invasion of upper New York, and that he was coming south with 14,000 regulars and Canadian militia, as well as 1,000 Indian warriors. Throughout the ensuing campaign for Manhattan, Howe's plans included the possibility of uniting with the Canadian army, a rendezvous that would restore the Hudson River to British control and isolate New England. It was not until mid-November that he discovered the bitter reality of how Carleton's campaign had ended, compelling Howe to put taking the Hudson on the back burner. He focused instead on crushing Washington's little army in New Jersey and conquering Rhode Island. The latter was accomplished without resistance following Clinton's landing at Newport early in December.[12]

Following the spectacular fall of Forts Washington and Lee, and the capture of the treasure house of Continental army stores, it immediately occurred to some of the younger officers that should Howe rapidly land a second force at Amboy, on the New Jersey coast—using the troops earmarked for the Rhode Island enterprise—the British could "push on to Philadelphia, with very little difficulty."[13] Howe had brushed aside this suggestion when Clinton proposed it, and he did so again. He had other plans. Not only was he fixated on Rhode Island, he could not conceive that Cornwallis's army required assistance in dealing with a fatally debilitated foe. Howe thought it illuminating that the rebels recently taken captive were dirty and inadequately clothed, many were only boys, and not a few were old men. They looked so unlike warriors that, according to a Welsh fusilier, their "appearance . . . excited the laughter of our Soldiers."[14]

Thus, destroying the threadbare rebels in New Jersey was left solely to Charles Cornwallis, a thirty-seven-year-old veteran officer. He hailed from an old and influential aristocratic family that had been nationally prominent for four centuries. After a prep school education at Eton—where he suffered a disfiguring injury playing hockey that left him with a permanently quizzical expression—and a stint at an Italian military academy, Cornwallis entered the British army at age eighteen. Three years later he was a lieutenant colonel and soldiering in Germany during the Seven Years' War, where he won deserved acclaim for valor. Following hostilities, Cornwallis first became an aide-de-camp to George III then entered the House of Commons. There, like General Howe, he steadfastly opposed the government's colonial policies. When he was thirty, Cornwallis courted and married Jemima Jones, the daughter of an army officer. The couple forged a close, loving relationship that was somewhat rare among aristocrats, many of whom were in arranged marriages.

When war with the colonists erupted in 1775, Cornwallis volunteered to serve in America. Promoted to the rank of major general, he crossed with the reinforcements that were to serve under Clinton in the Carolina campaign. Cornwallis fought there and in a variety of engagements in the campaign for New York, including at Pell's Point. Cornwallis was a man of contradictions. Though deeply in love with Jemima, the army was his first love, and the passion above all else that drove him was a quest for military glory. A career soldier, he eschewed the affectation and pretentiousness that so often went hand-in-glove with holding high military rank, acting with honesty, tolerance, justice, and genuine compassion toward the men whom he commanded. More staid than Howe, less cerebral than Clinton, he was a dedicated soldier who could be counted on to get the most from his men and to pursue his objective with resolution, energy, and zeal.[15]

Late on November 20, the day he captured Fort Lee, Cornwallis dispatched dragoons to search out Washington's whereabouts. They found the four thousand Continentals and militia falling back to the south and west, away from the coast, and crossing the Hackensack River into the hamlet of Hackensack, about ten miles from Fort Lee. The forward units were across, but the rear of the American army was vulnerable. Officers of the elite Hessian mounted rifle units, the jägers, pleaded with Cornwallis for authorization to attack. Not only could the rear of the American army be eradicated, they said, but Washington's entire force would be imperiled, as the river at Hackensack was not wide—never more than half a football field in breadth—and it was fordable in numerous places. But Cornwallis demurred. "We do not want to lose any men," he said, adding, "One

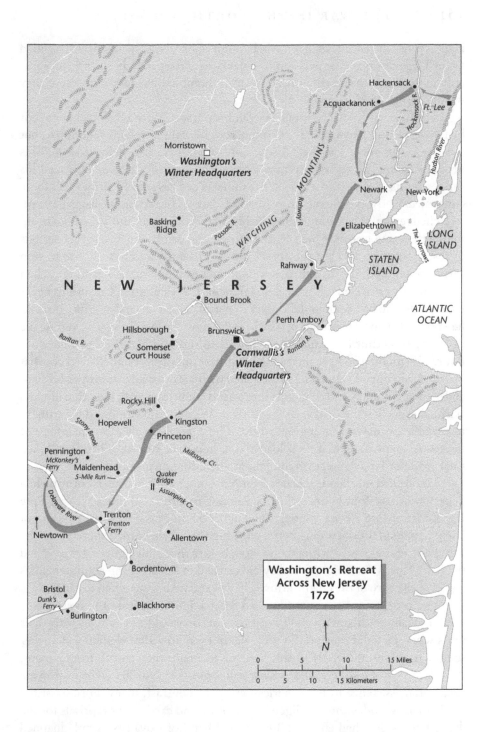

Hackensack

Acquackanonk

Ft. Lee

Hackensack R.

Hudson River

Morristown
*Washington's
Winter Headquarters*

Newark

New York

WATCHUNG

Rahway R.

Basking
Ridge

Passaic R.

Elizabethtown

LONG
ISLAND

N E W   J E R S E Y

Rahway

STATEN
ISLAND

The Narrows

Bound Brook

Perth Amboy

ATLANTIC
OCEAN

Raritan R.

Hillsborough

Brunswick

Raritan R.

Somerset
Court House

*Cornwallis's
Winter
Headquarters*

Rocky Hill

Hopewell

Stony Brook

Kingston

Princeton

Millstone Cr.

Pennington

*McKonkey's
Ferry*

Maidenhead

5-Mile Run

Quaker
Bridge

Delaware River

II

Assunpink Cr.

Trenton

*Trenton
Ferry*

Newtown

Allentown

Bordentown

Bristol

*Dunk's
Ferry*

Blackhorse

Burlington

**Washington's Retreat
Across New Jersey
1776**

N

| 0 | | 5 | | 10 | | 15 Miles |

0   5   10   15 Kilometers

jäger is more important than ten rebels." Subsequently, British officers confided to the Germans that Cornwallis was under order "to spare" the enemy, presumably in the hope that if the Americans were humbled but not humiliated, they would "terminate the war amicably."[16]

The following day Cornwallis began his pursuit. With reinforcements sent by Howe, he now had nearly 10,000 men, roughly a three-to-one superiority, but the size of his force may have been more hindrance than help. It slowed his progress, as he had to be careful not to move so rapidly that he outpaced his support units. Feeding an army on the move is not easy, and Cornwallis's force consumed nearly seventeen tons of food daily. His extensive baggage train stretched several times longer than the line of fighting men, and was drawn by up to one thousand horses, which also had to eat and drink, and be allowed periods of rest during the day, lest they break down. His army additionally had to stop early enough each day to gather wood, its fuel for cooking and heating. When subsequently criticized for his slogging pursuit of Washington, Cornwallis never pleaded that he had been under orders to permit his adversary's escape. Instead, he spoke of being hampered by "bad roads" and "broken bridges," and of the necessity to permit his "quite tired" horses to rest and his men "to bake their flour." He might also have mentioned that the Americans pitched in to do what they could to impede him. The rebels felled trees across roads, destroyed bridges, and sent out infantry and rifle units that waged countless small, but often bloody, skirmishes. When the British crossed a river, Washington employed his artillery to make it a time-consuming operation. The Americans also took painful, but necessary, steps to lighten their load and hasten their retreat. They abandoned their cattle and much precious equipment, including their tents.[17]

The British reached Hackensack on November 22. The American army had departed twenty-four hours earlier, continuing to move to the west, crossing the Passaic River into Acquackanonk Landing (modern Passaic), as the pale sun of late day glinted off the water. In the morning the rebels headed south along the west bank of the river, starting their march before the ruddy light of dawn bathed the landscape. When night fell, they bivouacked in Beeville, still about ten miles ahead of the core of the enemy army. They next day they marched to Newark.

The retreating American army had received no help from the New Jersey militia. Many militiamen would not turn out, or would not remain with their units when they did muster. To no avail, an essay in a Philadelphia newspaper sought to shame them. "If in this hour of adversity they shrink from danger, they deserve to be slaves," the essayist had scolded.[18] Nor did civilians provide substantial assistance to the American army. In contrast, many Tories assisted the British as guides and intelligence gatherers, and carried out reprisals for the depredations they had endured. One armed band of Loyalists even kidnapped Richard Stockton, a signer of the Declaration of Independence, and persuaded him to recant his support for the Revolution. New Jersey's Tories grew by quantum leaps that fall. Late in November, the Howe brothers offered a pardon to all who took an oath of future loyalty. It promised "a speedy remission of past offenses" to those pledged to "remain in a peaceable obedience to his Majesty." Nearly three thousand residents of New Jersey—roughly 15 percent of the free adult male population—accepted the pardon in the first week after it was promulgated.[19] The bulk of the residents, many of whom had supported independence, hid their food and valuables as the American army approached. They feared that the desperate and undisciplined soldiers would plunder or that their property would be confiscated by the Continental army, either for its own use or to keep it from the enemy. Whatever these inhabitants now felt about the American Revolution, their first loyalty was to family, and their overriding concern at the moment was the survival of self and property.

The retreating rebel army did not strike civilians as a spit and polish aggregation, though it included some who later would be among the most illustrious figures in American history, including the first and fifth presidents of the United States (James Monroe was an eighteen-year-old Virginia lieutenant); the future war and treasury secretaries (Knox and Alexander Hamilton, a nineteen-year-old New York artillery officer); Thomas Paine, the unequaled pamphleteer; and the renowned artist Charles Willson Peale. Ragged and unkempt, the soldiers must have looked like a band of violent malefactors. An astounding number were in desperate straits as deep autumn's bitter cold descended on New Jersey. Washington reported that "many of 'em" were "entirely naked" or "so thinly clad as to be unfit for service," a statement corroborated by Colonel Glover, who remarked that he had seen men "Go on Duty without Stockings Breeches or Shoes, nothing to cover their nakedness but a Blankett."[20] They were among the fortunate. Some had no blanket. Virtually none possessed a tent, and during that November and December every common soldier at times experienced the pangs of hunger. One officer said that an alarming number resembled "animated scarecrows."[21] Peale, on temporary duty with the Pennsylvania militia, did not even recognize his own brother, a Continental whom he had last seen only a few weeks before, when the two ran upon one another. "He was in an old dirty blanket-jacket, his beard long and his face full of sores . . . which . . . disfigured him. . . . Only when he spoke did I recognize my brother James," the startled Peale recounted.[22] With precious equipment lost or destroyed in the course of four separate retreats since the first one from Long Island in August, with storehouses such as Fort Lee captured, and with a supply system that was taxed under the best of circumstances, it was a wonder that the soldiers had any provisions. That they did was due in large measure to the administrative skills of General Greene, who beginning nearly two weeks prior to the Fort Washington disaster had, after consultation with Washington, established magazines along a prearranged route of retreat.[23]

On his first day in Newark, Washington appears to have spoken individually with his general officers, eschewing a formal council of war. The hard choices that he presented consisted of proceeding west to Morristown and entering winter quarters in the Watchung Mountains or staying between Cornwallis and

Philadelphia, which he believed was the enemy's objective. Several officers urged the first course, as the safer option. Washington ignored them, opting to continue to the south. His army, though "broken down," in the words of a Delaware captain, had actually grown. On that day it stood at 5,410 men, as units from several states had arrived in the course of the retreat. The enlistments of roughly 40 percent of the men were due to expire on December 1. The remainder would be free to go on January 1. Still, Washington knew that he would possess a substantial force throughout the month, and one that could be augmented by available Continentals from elsewhere. Gates, for instance, had nearly 9,000 men in upper New York, while Lee and Heath, posted on the New York mainland above Manhattan, possessed more than 11,000 men between them. Some of those men would doubtless be discharged on December 1, but some would remain. While still in Hackensack, Washington had directed Lee to bring his army across the Hudson. On his second day in Newark he gingerly—too gingerly —wrote again, advising Lee that his assistance against Cornwallis was "well worthy of Consideration." Two days later Washington unequivocally ordered Lee to bring seven thousand men. He also directed Gates to come south with reinforcements. Washington's plan was to retreat to Brunswick, roughly twenty-five miles below Newark, and if augmented sufficiently, "to make a stand there."[24]

The Continentals had the luxury of five quiet days in Newark. Cornwallis had been stopped in his tracks by a visit from Howe, who wanted a first-hand look at the front. Howe had not previously envisaged moving below Hackensack, but his inspection changed his mind. Seeing no obstacle to a further advance, and startled by the agricultural bounty in New Jersey, he instructed Cornwallis to advance to Brunswick. The British army set out on November 26 and covered the ten or so miles to Newark in the same amount of time that the Continentals had taken to make their march. But Washington was gone when the British arrived. He had put his army in motion the previous day. When the Continental army broke camp, pickets led the march, scouting ahead for trouble. An advance party that would have to hold off ambushers was next in line. Washington usually turned to infantry and rifle units, men who had been raised on the frontier and were among the hardiest and toughest of his troops, for this vital assignment. Infantry regiments came next, with artillery interspersed throughout the train. Washington, together with Greene and Knox, and a bevy of adjutants and aides, followed, riding just ahead of the militia. The support train—wagons that carried kitchen equipment, grubbing tools, the officers' baggage, medical supplies, and liquor—came next. Camp followers, women and civilian entrepreneurs with items to vend, were intermixed in this sector. Experienced infantry units guarded the army's rear.[25]

Marching through a day-long rain, the Continentals crossed the Raritan River and entered Brunswick on November 29. Shortly before Washington rode into this little river town, where he expected to be joined by Lee's army and to establish a defensive line, a dispatch rider reached him with a message from Lee.

What Washington read astonished him. Lee had not even broken camp. He was days away, if he was coming at all. The following day another letter arrived from Lee, this one addressed to Colonel Joseph Reed—the army's adjutant general and Washington's former secretary, and perhaps his closest confidant in the army. Reed was away on a mission, but Washington, desperate to know Lee's whereabouts, tore open the missive. What he read was lacerating. Lee had written unsparingly to Reed, saying that he agreed with him that "fatal indecision" on Washington's part had spelled "eternal defeat" for the American army.[26] In the aftermath of the debacles at Forts Washington and Lee, Washington had to have suspected that powerful men were whispering about his capability. Here was confirmation. Here, too, was the disquieting revelation that Reed, the officer in whom he had placed his greatest trust, had lost confidence in him, while Lee, whom he had regarded as his best general, distrusted and apparently had abandoned him.

The weeks between Fort Washington and year's end reshaped Washington. He crashed to the nadir in the last half of November. He no longer was certain that he could trust anyone. He was convinced that a shortsighted Congress had repeatedly forced him to the abyss of doom. He was persuaded that the states, which he once believed were steadfastly committed to the revolutionary cause, had betrayed him. His letters and conversations were a litany of high voltage despair: his reputation was destroyed; if he had the choice to make again, "a pecuniary rewd of 20,000£s a year would not induce me to undergo what I do;" he received "no assistance from the militia"; "I tremble for Philadelphia"; "I am wearied almost to death with the retrog[r]ade Motions" of the army; he might have to "cross the Allegheny Mountains" and from there carry on "a predatory war"; given the dearth of supplies, his soldiers were "reduced to nothing"; from "want of spirit & fortitude, the Inhabitants instead of resistance, are offering submission"; American "Affairs are in a very bad way"; the "conduct of the [people of New] Jersey, has been most Infamous"; the "game is pretty much up"; and, finally, no one can grasp "the perplexity of my Situation. No Man . . . ever had a greater Choice of difficulties & less means of extricating himself than I have."[27]

But Washington emerged reborn from his tribulations. He came to rely more on his own judgment, his own instincts. If he survived this epic crisis, any future failures of insight, discretion, and choice would be his alone. He ached to fight. He had a reputation to resurrect. He longed to silence his critics and save himself. In Brunswick, at his low ebb, he looked forward to preventing the "Enemy from making much further progress." He believed in himself and the "justice of our Cause," and he additionally believed that his and the nation's "prospect[s] will brighten, although . . . it is, at present hid under a cloud." Even in the slough of despair, he had begun to ruminate on the possibility that he might "face about" and "march back" to attack his pursuers.[28]

This black crisis changed others as it transformed Washington. John Adams, quoting from the biblical Jeremiah, spoke of the desperate times as a "Furnace of Affliction" and likened coping with the awful danger to a "Ride in the Whirlwind." With the enemy bearing down on Philadelphia, the members of Congress suddenly understood that they must act or, as Adams put it, "We are undone. . . . We shall perish in infamy."[29] The "Time is short. Let this be the only Subject of our Thought and Consultation," Samuel Adams exclaimed. "[W]e must stop" them, he added. If the enemy advance was not halted, Rhode Island's William Ellery wrote, they will "carry Fire and Sword into our States, in which Case . . . private Property . . . will be destroyed."[30]

Congress, its dread of a standing army notwithstanding, was driven in this emergency to order that henceforth enlistments were to be for three years or the duration of the war. No less astounding, on December 12 it bestowed on General Washington "full power to order and direct all things relative . . . to the operation of the war" for the ensuing six months.[31] Nothing less than a grant of dictatorial powers, Congress had, as one of its members remarked, given Washington authority "fully equal to the object" at hand, while it had removed from Congress's reach "matters of which it is supremely ignorant."[32] Washington wanted even more and, with Greene serving as his point man, he asked for and received specific authority to appoint and remove all officers beneath the rank of brigadier general, determine promotion procedures, arrest Tories (for trial by the civil judiciary), and to confiscate items from civilians, with the army setting whatever "reasonable Price" it saw fit for remuneration.[33] In this same span, Congress also gave over executive authority to a troika of Philadelphia merchants, charging that they were to "take Care of the public Interest" and find the means of overcoming the "distress of our Soldiers" and "keep[ing] a Sufficient Army in the field." In the meantime, the Secret Committee sent agents to the states to collect clothing for the soldiers. Acting with renewed zeal, it also acquired a fleet of ten ships to pursue trade in the Dutch and French Caribbean islands of St. Eustatius and Martinique, where tobacco and rice could be exchanged for blankets, clothes, shoes, and weaponry. The great crisis, Samuel Adams said, had caused Congress to do "more important Business in three Weeks than we had done . . . in six Months."[34] It prompted a Virginia congressman to remark to a colleague from Philadelphia: "Congress has given up most of their power. . . . [I]f this don't save your City nothing we can do will."[35] Once it had taken these extraordinary steps, Congress, like many civilians who were fleeing Philadelphia to escape "massacre and starvation" at the hands of the British army, packed its bags and moved to Baltimore.[36]

The future held promise, but only if the rebellion survived this enveloping crisis. Overcoming the emergency meant that popular opinion, which was cascading into the valley of despondency, had to be rallied. Fortunately, the writer who had demonstrated the greatest talent for reaching a wide reading audience was embedded with the retreating Continentals. Shortly after July 4, Thomas Paine had joined a militia outfit called the Philadelphia Associators. It was an act of incredible patriotism, idealism, and personal sacrifice for a man who was nearly forty years old and given to feckless bohemian habits. In September, while posted at Fort Lee, Greene chose him to be his aide-de-camp. Following the loss of that installation, Paine marched with the other ragged Continentals across New Jersey. Early in the retreat he was approached by officers in the highest echelons of the army who wanted him to put his pen to use to raise morale. While the army paused at Newark, in all likelihood, Paine began to write, according to legend using a drumhead for a desk and a campfire for illumination. Usually a slow writer—he had a penchant for working only when the mood struck him, which was infrequently—Paine wasted no time on this occasion. Within ten days his tract was largely completed, whereupon Greene sent him to Philadelphia to finish the job and see to its publication. On December 19 his piece appeared in a Philadelphia newspaper, and later in the week it was issued as a pamphlet under the title *The American Crisis*.[37] It was a short tract, only a quarter the length of *Common Sense*.

Not much of the polemic is remembered, save for its first two sentences, a hook that few writers have ever equaled:

> These are the times that try men's souls. The summer soldier and the sunshine patriot will, in this crisis, shrink from the service of their country; but he that stands it *now*, deserves the love and thanks of men and women.[38]

Gracefully written in his uniquely familiar rhythm and cadence, Paine depicted the war as a struggle against tyranny. While he papered over some of the catastrophes suffered by the Continentals, he was amazingly candid about how the British might have crushed the American army that fall, adding that Howe's blunders and "some providential control" had saved it. He could, he said, "see the way" out of the crisis. True patriots must suppress the Tories and must bear arms in "our new army." If both steps were taken, the result would be "a glorious issue." But if "cowardice and submission" was the popular choice, "slavery without hope" awaited the inhabitants of America.[39]

The significance that Paine's tract held for contemporaries remains conjectural. Many historians believe that *American Crisis* rekindled hope during that black December crisis.[40] Legend has it that a draft of Paine's essay was read to the troops in December and revived their spirits, although neither Washington nor Greene alluded to such an event.[41] Disconcertingly, John Adams, who seemed to comment on almost every happening, big and small, never mentioned the pamphlet. Only one congressman, New Hampshire's William Whipple, is known to have praised *American Crisis*, calling it "a most excellent thing."[42] Years later a Philadelphia newspaper publisher, who harbored a visceral dislike for Paine, recollected that *American Crisis* had "rallied and reanimated" sagging morale in December 1776, a remark—considering the source—that was likely on target.[43]

Like Congress, the states promised to do more, and many seemed to move mountains to get troops to General Washington. While still in Brunswick,

Washington drew sustenance from the new mood, but without Lee's army he could not make a stand behind the Raritan, as he had previously hoped. He withdrew from the village on December 1, telling Congress that the "Enemy are fast advancing; some of 'em are now in sight." He had already made the decision to cross the Delaware River into Pennsylvania at Trenton, about thirty-five miles from Philadelphia. Once there, he resolved to "govern myself by circumstances." This last retreat by the Continentals was undertaken free of British pressure, for Cornwallis had stopped, as Howe had ordered, at Brunswick. The rebel soldiery passed through Princeton and on December 2 reached Trenton, where they found boats waiting to convey them across the river. Washington had earlier asked state and local authorities to procure them for his army.[44] The crossing out of New Jersey began immediately and continued through the sullen night under an eerie orange-yellow illumination provided by giant fires built on the shores, making for what a Pennsylvania militiaman thought was "rather the appearance of Hell than any earthly scene."[45]

Once across, Washington organized a defensive line, repeating his oft-made mistake of trying to defend too much, as he posted units along a twenty-five mile stretch of the Delaware River. Much of his time was consumed in a search for additional soldiers, for with the expiration of enlistments on the day prior to his crossing his force had shrunk to less than three thousand men. Militia, especially from Pennsylvania and New Jersey, came in, and Washington put many of them to rounding up every available boat along the Delaware. He also worked with the Pennsylvania navy—a squadron of thirteen black gondolas, each manned by thirty sailors, not counting rowers, who sometimes were captive Tories—to secure total control of the river.[46] Washington knew that Lee's presence would go a long way toward solving his manpower problems, and the commander wrote him six times in twelve days ordering that he "march immediately" to the Delaware.[47] But two weeks after he entered Pennsylvania, Washington still had not seen Lee.

Lee's seemingly audacious behavior has invited speculation among scholars. Some have surmised that he deliberately betrayed Washington, hoping that another American defeat would result in Washington's dismissal and his appointment as commander of the Continental army. Others have concluded that Lee hoped to distance himself from Washington, whom he saw as destined for ruin because of his incurable irresolution. No one can know precisely what was in Lee's heart, but it is unlikely that his motive was treachery or that he plotted to ensure Washington's defeat. Days before he was ordered to come to New Jersey, Lee told a confidant that he was coming south to save Washington. To "confess a truth," he said with his customary bluster, "I really think our Chief will do better with me than without me."[48] Besides, no one had to remind Lee that as a former British officer he might face a traitor's execution should the American rebellion be crushed.

Lee's initial orders had been to remain in New York until Howe's intention was crystal clear, lest the Americans once again be the victims of a British diversion. Washington did not explicitly direct him to bring his army south until November 27, orders that Lee received late at night on November 29, the very day that Washington entered Brunswick harboring the unrealistic expectation that Lee should be only a day or two away. Lee responded to his chief's order by immediately seeking supplies from Connecticut and Massachusetts that his army would require for its long march. In addition, indicating that he had a "positive order" from Washington and that he intended "to take two thousand [men] . . . into the Jerseys," Lee ordered Heath to detach two regiments that were to accompany him. Heath, certain that he had contrary orders from Washington, twice refused to give up any of his men. Lee was also slowed as his own army was about to be depleted when enlistments expired on December 1. He was compelled to await reinforcements and reenlistments before setting off. He did start for New Jersey early in December, but the need to take a circuitous route through hilly western country in order to avoid Cornwallis's superior force slowed his descent. Lee pushed hard and managed to march his men from Peekskill to Morristown in fewer days than it had taken Washington to cover the much shorter distance from Fort Lee to Trenton. Lee reached Morristown on December 8, six days after Washington crossed the Delaware.[49]

If Lee deserves censure for anything other than not making his intentions clear to his commander, it was for his decision to remain in Morristown for seventy-two hours. Even so, there were mitigating circumstances to his tarrying. Instead of hurrying on to join Washington, he paused to consider an attack on Cornwallis's rear at Brunswick, a stab that, if successful, would have alleviated the pressure on Washington and might have induced Howe to abandon much, or all, of New Jersey as a site for winter quarters. There can be no question that once at Morristown, Lee violated Washington's orders, although throughout their eighteen-month relationship Washington had given him broad discretionary powers. From habit, Lee may have believed that his superior continued to want him to exercise an independent judgment. Finally, on December 11, after receiving orders that Washington had dictated the previous day, and in which the commander explicitly disapproved of "your hanging on the Rear of the Enemy," Lee set his army off on the last leg of its journey toward the Delaware. En route Lee, who unwisely chose to stay apart from his army in a tavern at Basking Ridge, was ignobly captured by a British scouting party tipped to his whereabouts by local Tories. In his last moments as a free man, Lee wrote to Gates deploring Washington's "ingenious manoeuvre" at Fort Washington, signing off: "a certain great man is damnably deficient."[50] Washington welcomed the arrival of Lee's men, who marched in on December 20 under Sullivan, but he never lamented having to do without Lee, for whom he now nursed a poisonous distrust.[51]

Lee's two brigades and the soldiers under Gates, who reached the Delaware two days later after a long, difficult march from northern New York, brought Washington's Continentals to 6,104 men fit for duty. Militia were with him as well, including the Pennsylvania Flying Camp, a mobile unit led by Brigadier

General James Ewing, a native of Lancaster whom Washington had met when the two served under Braddock more than twenty years earlier. Paine's old unit, the Philadelphia Associators, were there, too, commanded by thirty-four-year-old Colonel John Cadwalader, thought by some to be Philadelphia's wealthiest merchant. Cadwalader had been active in his colony's protest movement and had quickly taken up arms when hostilities erupted. He had fought in New York and was among those taken captive at Fort Washington, but a British officer who was friendly with his father had released him.[52]

As Christmas approached, the demoralizing fear that Philadelphia was certain to be lost—a prospect that had induced Congress to flee to Baltimore—had abated. Howe had taken command at Brunswick on December 6 and marched his army to Trenton two days later. The Americans expected, and so did some of the Hessians and younger redcoat officers, that the British would seek to cross the inhospitable river, either then or when it froze, and continue on to Philadelphia, merely a day's march away. Joseph Galloway, once a member of Congress and now a leading Tory, found sufficient materials in Trenton for constructing a pontoon bridge, and urged Howe to use it for a rapid crossing. But Howe was finished for the year. Believing that his lines were already overextended, he opted for winter quarters. He broke down Cornwallis's army, posting it in seventeen cantonments across eastern New Jersey. Brunswick was the principal base. The three most forward garrisons, each on the Delaware, were assigned to Hessians. As Cornwallis had asked for a leave to return home, Howe put General James Grant in charge of the occupation army in New Jersey.[53] Grant, like Howe, anticipated few problems. He declared that the "Enemy . . . in fact does not exist in the Jerseys." Even if it did, it was hardly cause for worry, as there was "nothing more despicable than the Continental Troops."[54]

While Howe may have been ready to suspend the fight for the next several months, Washington was not. A proud man, he had chafed miserably under his string of defeats. He thought a retreat—any retreat—was mortifying. As a young soldier in Virginia, he had craved being on the offensive. Now, more than ever, he burned with desire to lash out at an enemy that had acutely humiliated him and brought him to the threshold of ruin. But more than revenge gnawed at him. Washington knew that the war, and American independence, hung in the balance. Flagging spirits must be revivified. Recruitment of another army for 1777 was likely to be linked indissolubly to achieving some immediate success. As Reed advised him: "something must be attempted to revive our expiring Credit [and] give our Cause some Degree of Reputation. . . . [S]ome Enterprize must be undertaken . . . or we must give up the Cause."[55]

Washington needed no prodding. He had begun to contemplate fighting back during the retreat, and long before he read Reed's letter he had spoken of "effect[ing] something of importance" that might "give our Affairs such a turn as to make 'em . . . more promising." At first, he saw no hope of doing more than making a defensive stand, though his options appeared to broaden in December.

Not only had his army more than doubled since he crossed the Delaware, but the inhabitants of the four counties about Trenton, provoked by the countless indignities that accompanied occupation—homes had been appropriated, even razed, property stolen, and residents abused, sometimes violently and criminally —had risen up to reclaim their homeland. Acting independently of Washington —no one was more surprised by their sudden activity than the American commander—the once somnolent New Jersey militia, as well as Pennsylvania's militiamen, sent by authorities eager to keep the enemy on the other side of the river, had begun to lash out like guerrilla bands, attacking small redcoat and Hessian patrols and even harassing the larger garrisons. Their strikes took a toll. Enemy soldiers were unnerved and exhausted by incessant night patrols, their spirit shred by fresh losses atop the already heavy attrition since the campaign began back in August. (Just before Christmas one Hessian brigade commander informed his superior that his men were so worn down by the "miserable weather and continuous service" that they were "in no condition to defend" their post.)[56] But Howe's decision to carve up his army into numerous small units of occupation was a veritable invitation for Washington to act as he had envisioned when he embraced a war of posts strategy. The isolated and potentially vulnerable cantonments opened the likelihood of making the sort of "brilliant stroke" with some "probability of success" of which he had spoken in September when he outlined a Fabian approach. Keeping more and more authority in his own hands, Washington pieced together an intelligence-gathering network that was to report to him alone. If he knew more than any other officer, he must have reasoned, he could more likely bend future councils of war to his way of thinking.[57]

On December 22, the day that Gates's men arrived, Washington convened a council of war to discuss the options. Four enemy cantonments—each isolated and situated about ten miles from the nearest friendly post—lay nearby. About 1,500 Germans occupied Trenton, more or less directly across the Delaware River from the center of the Continental lines. Roughly the same number of Hessians was at Bordentown, about ten miles down river on the rebel right. A small German force—one battalion of grenadiers—held Burlington, ten miles below Bordentown. Princeton, some twelve miles above Trenton, was the least-vulnerable British post, as nearly 2,500 infantry and dragoons were stationed in the little college town. The officers at the council of war discussed whether to attack, and if so, how many targets to strike. They failed to come to a decision, but that evening Washington summoned another council of war, this time attended by fewer officers. After careful deliberation, it agreed to strike the Hessians in Trenton at dawn on December 26. No official record of the two meetings exists, but it is a good bet that Washington conceived the broad outlines of the operation that was finally adopted, with modifications, during the second meeting.[58]

The next day—a day when the army's countersign, or password, was "Victory or Death"—the plan was explained to the mid-level officers.[59] It was a simple scheme, though one fraught with exquisite, and unavoidable, complexities

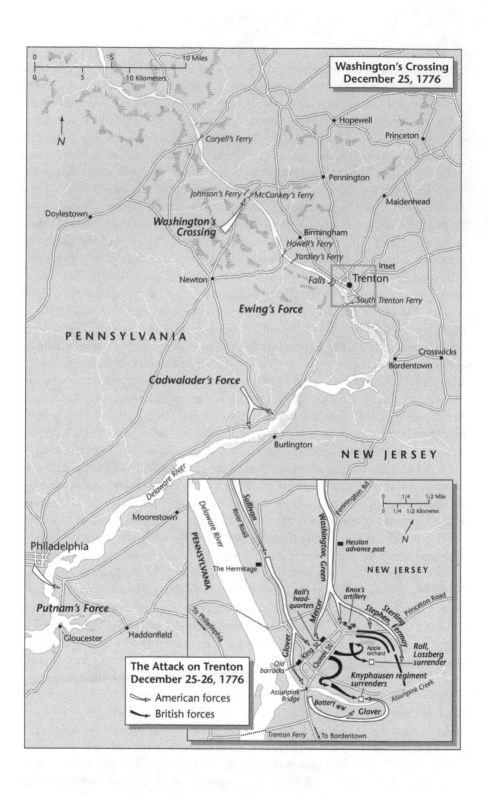

Washington's Crossing
December 25, 1776

0   5   10 Miles
0   5   10 Kilometers

N

Hopewell

Princeton

Coryell's Ferry

Pennington

Maidenhead

Johnson's Ferry   McConkey's Ferry

Washington's Crossing

Doylestown

Birmingham
Howell's Ferry
Yardley's Ferry

Inset

Trenton

Newton

Falls

South Trenton Ferry

Ewing's Force

PENNSYLVANIA

Crosswicks

Bordentown

Cadwalader's Force

Burlington

NEW JERSEY

Delaware River

Moorestown

Philadelphia

Putnam's Force

Gloucester   Haddonfield

The Attack on Trenton
December 25-26, 1776

American forces
British forces

Delaware River

Sullivan

River Road

Rennington Rd.

Washington, Green

0   1/4   1/2 Mile
0   1/4   1/2 Kilometer

N

Hessian
advance post

NEW JERSEY

PENNSYLVANIA

The Hermitage

Rall's head-
quarters

Knox's
artillery

Mercer

Sterling

Stephen, Fermoy

Princeton Road

To Philadelphia

Glover

King St.

Queen St.

Apple
orchard

Rall,
Lossberg
surrender

Old
barracks

Knyphausen regiment
surrenders

Assunpink
Bridge

Battery

Glover

Assunpink Creek

Trenton Ferry   To Bordentown

and impediments, and its success appeared to hang on surprise and carefully implemented timing. Washington, with about 2,400 of the most seasoned Continentals, was to cross the Delaware ten miles above Trenton just after dark on Christmas night, and after a further march of nine miles, approach the town from the west. A second force of eight hundred Pennsylvania militia under Ewing was to cross directly to the south side of Trenton and secure the bridge across the Assunpink Creek, the enemy's only escape route on that side of the village. Simultaneously, Cadwalader was to cross twelve miles below Trenton, near Burlington, with a combined force of 1,800 Continentals and Philadelphia Associators. It was crucial that he succeed, as his mission was to create a diversion that would prevent the Hessians posted at Bordentown from coming to the aid of their comrades in Trenton. The plan called for each of the American divisions to reach its objective approximately an hour before daybreak, or at around 6:00 a.m. Washington expected to attack just before the first light appeared in the eastern sky, taking the Hessians by surprise. If the element of surprise was lost, and the Hessians succeeded in taking up defensive positions, it was presumed that they could repulse the assault. Washington's greatest nightmare was that they might even manage a counterattack. If that occurred, and the rebel force was compelled to retreat, Washington knew there was no hope of getting his army back across the Delaware River while under fire.

The Hessians at Trenton were under the command of Colonel Rall, a fifty-year-old veteran of more than three decades service. He had seen considerable combat in Europe and Turkey, and during the past few weeks he had led key attacks at White Plains and Fort Washington, earning the sobriquet "The Lion" for his aggressiveness under fire. His *Landgrenadiere* was not an elite regiment, but it was regarded as a superior combat unit. Rall did not anticipate facing a large-scale rebel attack. His enemy seemed obsessed with making defensive stands. In the first twenty months of this war the only major offensive action by the Americans had come at Quebec. It also seemed inconceivable to him that the bedraggled Americans—whom he called "clodhoppers," farm boys, not soldiers —could launch an attack. Other considerations, however, gave Rall concern. He not only disliked being posted with only 1,500 men directly across from a much larger force, he rapidly discovered that Trenton, which lacked walls and fortifications, was not an easy site to defend. At times, he appeared frazzled. He admitted his inability to "understand the object" of his enemy and acknowledged that he was distracted and worn down by "constant alarms and troubles." The state of the garrison was "so unsafe," he said, adding that his beleaguered men were spent from sleep deprivation and nerves that had been stretched to the breaking point. Rall took most of the precautions that one would expect of a seasoned officer, and he did not fall victim to self-deception. He was curiuosly fatalistic as well as optimistic. He did not expect an attack, but did not especially fear one either. "Shit on them," he said contemptuously of the Americans. "Let them come," adding that if they did come, "we will simply fall on them and rout them."[60]

The Americans came on Christmas night.[61] Few operations in war go exactly according to plan, and crucial aspects of this operation went awry. To preserve secrecy, the Americans could not stir until darkness gathered, leaving much to be accomplished in a short period before morning light streaked the eastern sky. Once the men began to move, moreover, unforeseen delays occurred, mostly due to the weather. It had been cold and clear throughout Christmas day, but around sunset, just as the American forces were setting out, the temperature rose and, paradoxically, conditions quickly fell apart. It began to rain. Hail followed. Snow came next, driven by keening winds that one soldier equated with "a perfect hurricane."[62] Either a nor'easter or an arctic cold front had struck.

Washington's men were already behind schedule when they began the crossing at McConkey's Ferry. The men went across on small river craft and Durham boats, forty- to sixty-foot-long vessels that were ordinarily used to transport cargoes of iron, grain, wood, and whiskey down river to Philadelphia's docks. The horses, artillery, and ammunition went across on large ferries. Under the overall direction of Knox, mariners from Philadelphia, local river men, and Glover's omnipresent Marblehead regiment, got the army across. The operation was three hours behind schedule when the last man stepped ashore in New Jersey. Unbeknownst to Washington, his men were the only ones who crossed the river that night. The forces under Cadwalader and Ewing were frustrated by swift currents and huge chunks of ice that had broken apart during a spate of unseasonably warm weather earlier in the previous week.

Crossing the Delaware on a night such as this was a remarkable feat. The long march that followed was hardly a cakewalk. The men had already marched several miles to reach McConkey's Ferry. Now they faced a lengthy trek over a road that mostly ran upgrade. Wrestling with balky artillery over squashy, mud-bogged, and unfamiliar roads in the dead of night, all the while lashed by wind and sleet that "cuts like a knife," according to one soldier, was almost worse than a battle itself.[63] Even worse, few men were adequately clothed for this bitter weather, and early on most had been soaked to the skin by the rain. Some were barefoot or had tied rags about their feet. More than one soldier subsequently remembered seeing bloody footprints in the snow. Throughout the night, Washington was up and down the line amid his men, encouraging them "in a deep & Solemn voice," a New Englander remembered.[64]

At times during this bitter night, Washington must have feared the operation was hopeless. His attack would come long after sunrise, likely robbing him of the chance to take his foe by surprise. To make matters worse, his force had barely set off from the Delaware when it ran up on a party of fifty American soldiers. They were Virginians, and they informed a horrified Washington that they had been sent across by General Adam Stephen to conduct a raid, in the course of which they had attacked a Hessian outpost. Washington's oppressive doubts combusted into a white-hot rage. A seething mass of feelings, he reproved Stephen on the spot, certain now that his attack had put the Hessians on alert, ending all hope of surprise.

But Washington, as so often was true, was a lucky man. In this instance, he benefited from what he had presumed were ruinous occurrences. The Germans were not prepared when the American army arrived nearly an hour after sunrise, but their surprise was not, as legend has it, due to sleeping off a liquor-soaked night of Christmas revelry. Instead, the raid that Stephen had ordered proved to be a blessing in disguise. It had resulted in midnight patrols that came away empty handed, after which Rall, expecting no further alarms on this night, relaxed his vigilance. The horrid storm that sowed so much misery among the American soldiers, and provoked exasperating delays in carrying out the operation, also led the Germans to let down their guard. Thinking it inconceivable that any operation could be conducted in such circumstances, Rall cancelled the regular dawn patrols.

Washington had divided his force about three miles west of Trenton. Greene led a division along the northern road to the village. It consisted largely of veterans of the long retreat across New Jersey. Sullivan, who for the most part commanded the men that Lee had brought down from New York, proceeded along a southerly artery near the river, the frozen breath of men and horses visible in the early morning light. When both divisions were at last in place on the edge of town, and with snow still falling from a pewter sky, the anxious silence was broken at 8:00 a.m. when Washington shouted the order: "Advance and charge."

Greene's force moved in three columns, with Washington leading the men in the center, and attacked the north and west side of Trenton. Three minutes later Sullivan opened his assault on the south side. The amazed Hessians realized that they were under attack only when the American guns opened up. By then they were being attacked from three sides. Bugles sounded and shouts rang out: "Der Feind! Der Feind! Heraus! Heraus!" (The Enemy! The Enemy! Turn out! Turn out!). Awakened by the clatter, Rall was still pulling on his blue coat as he mounted his horse and rode into the streets in a desperate attempt to organize his startled and frightened men. What he encountered was utter chaos. Men were falling all about him. Some were in flight. Not only were the Americans pouring a ferocious artillery bombardment into the narrow streets of the village, but unseen rebel soldiers, using the cover of houses to advance, were laying down withering small arms fire. Rall desperately sought to organize his own artillery, but to little avail, as his artillery commander was among those who panicked and fled. The grey-faced artillerymen who remained struggled valiantly, but forlornly, to hitch horses—spooked by the deafening uproar in their midst—to their field pieces so they could be properly positioned and brought into play. One American soldier was close enough to hear Rall "shouting in Dutch, 'My brave soldiers, advance.'"[65]

Misled into believing that the village was surrounded, Rall made no attempt to withdraw. He tried instead to organize a fallback to an apple orchard and open field on the east side of town. If he could get there, his left would be anchored by the Assunpink and he would have a reasonably good chance of forming an effective defensive position. In time, he might counterattack. But the odds were against him. In the noise and confusion, some units never heard his orders, or if they did, a paralyzing terror hamstrung their implementation. Whole chunks of Rall's force were disintegrating or surrendering. Washington weighed in as well, sending some of his units to attack the enemy's right flank. Surprised, caught in a crossfire, and outnumbered by an adversary that had more artillery, the Hessians were doomed, Rall literally. Deep into the engagement, the Hessian commander was cut down by two fatal gunshot wounds to his side. His fall sowed even more disorder among the Germans. Soon, large numbers of men capitulated. Some lowered their standards. Others put their hats atop their swords. Most simply threw down their arms, giving up because they knew that otherwise "they must inevitably be cut to peices," as Washington said later.[66] It was over. The fight, bloody and terrible, had lasted less than an hour.[67]

The Americans knew that they had won a sensational victory. Washington, the least demonstrative of men, grabbed the hand of a young officer and exalted: "This is a glorious day for our country." One of his soldiers, a Massachusetts sergeant, understood instinctively that what had just occurred would raise the "drooping spirits . . . and string anew every nerve for our Liberty and Independence."[68] In the aftermath of the engagement, the American leaders counted heads—and bodies—and the scope of their success came into focus. Although roughly 500 Hessians had escaped—the price paid for Ewing's inability to make it across the Delaware—150 had been killed or wounded, and almost 900 were taken prisoner. The Americans had also taken all the Germans' brass field pieces, six wagons, forty horses, one thousand muskets and bayonets, considerable ammunition, and forty hogsheads of rum (which Washington ordered destroyed, though not before many of his men had repeatedly toasted their triumph). The American losses were small. Washington said that no more than four men had been lost, but the toll was slightly greater, as some died of exhaustion and exposure, and still others perished in the days that followed from illnesses related to the forbidding ordeal in the elements.[69]

A happy public gave Washington credit for the victory. A British traveler in Virginia, who had recently heard his hosts question Washington's "want of skill and experience," said that after Trenton those same individuals, believing the "scale is turned," now extolled "Washington's name . . . to the clouds." Congressmen were lavish with their praise, exalting that the victory "puts new life" into the Revolution, and attributing the turnabout "entirely to your [Washington's] Wisdom and Conduct."[70] Washington deserved the praise. He had wanted to attack, and he had the savvy to see his opportunity and the daring to run the risk.

But one man alone does not win a battle. Many American officers and soldiers, and even civilians, acted heroically that night. They benefited, too, from the enemy's many mistakes. Howe, having grown over confident by his easy successes since August, had sought to occupy too much territory with too few men, in the course of which he dangerously diluted the detachments that were posted in the forward areas on the Delaware. General Grant, who commanded the occupation forces, was as blind to the danger as Howe, telling Hessian commanders, who understood the reality of their predicament, that they were "safe," even advising that they needed little more than "a corporal's guard" to cope with the bedraggled rebels.[71] Rall, at Trenton, had erred egregiously. Despite the abundance of Tories in the neighborhood, he had failed to establish even a primitive intelligence network. What is more, whereas the Americans hardly paused for a smoke without building a redoubt, Rall in three weeks in Trenton never turned a spade of earth in the construction of fortifications. On Christmas night he compounded his negligence by ignoring his officers' entreaties to send patrols to the ferry landings, a simple and customary precaution that might have stopped the Americans in their tracks miles from Trenton.[72]

WASHINGTON WAS A FIGHTER, and a gambler, and his blood was up following his first real victory under fire in this war—in any war, for that matter. It ate at him, too, to think how close he had come to taking the entire Hessian force at Trenton. Had Ewing and Cadwalader gotten their men across the Delaware, he might even have scored more than the one spectacular victory at Trenton. He might have attempted to deliver major blows against the Germans in Bordentown or Burlington, or both. But it was not until Washington heard from Cadwalader on December 27 that he began to consider crossing the Delaware once again. Thinking that Washington was still in New Jersey, Cadwalader had at last gotten his men across the river that very morning. He quickly discovered that the Hessians had abandoned Burlington and Bordentown, and in some disarray were retreating toward South Amboy on the coast. Cadwalader advised that if Washington crossed again, the Americans could conduct a pitiless "pursuit [that] would keep up the Panic." He added: "If we can drive them from West Jersey, the Success will raise an Army by next Spring, & establish the Credit of the Continental Money, to support it." Washington immediately summoned a council of war.[73]

The officers divided over the wisdom of making a second crossing of the Delaware. Some saw it as a chimeric quest that, with a bad turn or two, could reverse the recent magnificent victory. Others argued that crossing back into New Jersey would announce to the world—and above all to France—that the American army was resilient and undefeated. To score another major victory might result in the liberation of much of New Jersey and the suppression of the Jersey Tories. It would, said one, produce a "Shock to the Enemy [that] must be very great." All agreed that if the army was to act, it had to do so immediately. Washington would not only shortly lose the militiamen who had been mustered before Christmas, but in five days the enlistments of many seasoned Continentals were to expire. Triumphant at last, it is probable that Washington acted more authoritatively at this council of war, and he may even have played his generals as a virtuoso. In the aftermath of Trenton, the officers' confidence in his judgment had grown and Washington's self-assurance had swelled. Following a warm debate, the officers voted to do as Washington surely wished: cross the Delaware and "pursue the Enemy in their retreat," striking at vulnerable small detachments before they reached safety. This was what he had envisioned in the war of posts strategy, and it seemed to be a relatively safe operation. It was to be conducted in the extensive region that splayed south of Perth Amboy and Sandy Hook, where Washington would have ample space for maneuver and escape, and where his army could be easily supplied.[74]

But the plan quickly went awry. The weather turned bad again, delaying the recrossing so that the last soldier did not get over until December 31, only hours before the most experienced troops were to be "at Liberty," as Washington put it. If he was to continue with the operation, Washington had to do something to keep the army intact, at least for a time. He first had his general officers beseech their men to stay on for a bit longer "for our country." Their entreaties failed. Next, Washington tried his hand. One of the few things he hated more than public speaking was begging, but he did both, soliciting his men's "service to the cause of liberty, and to your country." His pleas produced a patchy response. Only about two hundred men, less that a tenth of those who could depart, agreed to reenlist. Not even Glover's Marblehead men would stay on. They wanted to return home to fight at sea as privateers. One final ploy remained to Washington. Having procured funds from Robert Morris—one of those merchants left in charge in Philadelphia by Congress before it fled—Washington offered a ten-dollar cash bounty for each man who volunteered for an additional six weeks' service. Money talked. Slightly more than half of those who were about to go home agreed to stay on.[75]

Conditions had changed, however, in the four days since the council of war approved crossing back into New Jersey. For one thing, the Hessians had reunited with their allies. For another, the British, once thought to have no more than six thousand men scattered throughout New Jersey, were now known to have upward of eight thousand, which they had brought together at Princeton, only ten miles away from Trenton. Washington also knew that the redcoats planned to come after him. He had about 5,000 men, three-fifths of them veteran Continentals, while some 1,800 men, mostly militia, were with Cadwalader at Crosswicks, near Bordentown, about seven miles to the east. Late on January 1, Washington called another council of war, which met at his temporary head-quarters in a house on Queen Street in Trenton. He put three options on the table: retreating back across the river to safety; marching east and joining Cadwalader and his men; or, keeping the two American forces divided, with Washington's men making a defensive stand at Trenton, while Cadwalader's force circled around and attacked what was likely to be the lightly defended British storage depot at Brunswick. After considerable wrangling, the council opted for something else. Cadwalader was to march his force to Trenton and link up with Washington. The officers were now thoroughly familiar with the terrain in Trenton, and concluded that it would be a suitable site for making a defensive stand. When the meeting ended, Washington dispatched riders—including Dr. Benjamin Rush, a Philadelphia physician and member of Pennsylvania's delegation in Congress, who had chosen to be with the Continental army while Congress was on the run—to fetch Cadwalader. Washington then posted nearly one thousand men near Maidenhead, about halfway up the road toward Princeton, to lay down a harassing fire that would hopefully delay the enemy's advance until Cadwalader's men arrived and could get into position.[76]

This was not what Washington had envisaged when he crossed into New Jersey. He had stumbled into this situation, though he appears to have welcomed the prospect of entrenching and awaiting the enemy, confident after watching his men fight on the defensive at Throg's Neck and White Plains that they could inflict heavy losses should his adversary dare to attack. He was reverting to the thinking that had dominated his outlook before the New York disasters. His plan was to make a Bunker Hill–type stand in Trenton. For the moment, at any rate, he had jettisoned his Fabian strategy. He was taking an enormous risk. His back would be to the Delaware, and the danger that he and his army might be pinioned there was all too evident. Not for nothing did he later say that his "situation was most critical."

Be that as it may, Washington's situation was far from hopeless. When joined by Cadwalader's force, he would possess about 6,800 men, nearly 1,000 fewer than his adversary, although the manpower difference would be offset somewhat by the fact that his men would be entrenched and fighting defensively. He had at least thirty artillery pieces—several times the number used to defend Bunker Hill, including much larger cannon—and ample firearms, powder, and shot, three-fourths or more of it acquired from France during 1776 and brought to Pennsylvania via Delaware Bay, which Admiral Howe had left unguarded.[77] Washington occupied strong ground, as well. He positioned his army on sloping terrain behind the Assunpink Creek, which flowed east of Trenton before emptying into the Delaware almost due south of town, and thanks to three consecutive days of warm weather—the temperature had climbed above fifty degrees on New Year's Day—the Assunpink was high and running swiftly. It could be crossed in only a few places, and via a bridge in only one place. Washington posted his men and artillery so that a deadly crossfire could be directed at the few crossing points, and especially at that lone stone bridge. He anchored his left wing on the Delaware. The British could not turn that flank. His right wing, three miles up the creek, was more vulnerable, though to attack in that sector the enemy would have to slowly wade through a low, wide swamp before attempting to cross a roiling stream.[78] It is likely, too, that Washington had come to agree with Putnam's oft-repeated axiom that when posted behind adequate defenses, American soldiers would acquit themselves in combat. Above all, Washington believed that in a worst case scenario the odds were good that his army could escape to the east, into a country that his men knew better than the adversary, and in which there was ample room to run from a cumbersome British army whose pursuit was likely to be further hampered by wintry conditions.

On January 2, just as the rising sun struggled to get above the trees, the British force of eight thousand men—just as Washington's intelligence had reported—stepped off from Princeton toward Trenton. Cornwallis was its commander, his leave having been canceled by Howe after word reached New York of the debacle at Trenton. Cornwallis's orders were unequivocal: find the American army and destroy it. Some of his officers urged him to divide his army, marching one column to Crosswicks, which would inhibit Washington's chances of escape to the east. But after what had occurred following Howe's dilution of the occupation army, Cornwallis had no stomach for sundering his force. He marched all his men toward Trenton. They had to cover ten miles, half the distance of the redcoats' march along Battle Road on that fateful day in April 1775, but this trek consumed nearly twice the time of its predecessor. Cornwallis's force was eight times larger than the one that Gage had sent to Concord and his men—and especially his cannon and wagons—were hampered by a road that been turned into a quagmire by the thaw. Worse still was the harassment they faced from the pickets that Washington had dispatched, men led primarily by Colonel Edward Hand of the Pennsylvania Rifle Regiment. Cornwallis's army had hardly left Princeton before it encountered resistance. Utilizing their rifles, justly famous for their long-range accuracy, the rebels repeatedly waylaid their foe with a lethal fire from concealed positions in the untidy dark brown forests, rancid with dank, decayed leaves. Time and again, the Americans ambushed the British, waging time-consuming firefights before melting away to take up new positions further down the road, from which they opened up yet again on their prey. At one juncture, rebel pickets tied down the enemy for two precious hours. When the lead elements in Cornwallis's force finally reached the Assunpink, the long, sloping black shadows of late day swaddled the landscape. Less than an hour of daylight remained.[79]

Given Washington's well-known penchant for wiggling out of traps, Cornwallis would have been wise to have postponed his attack and used the final moments of daylight to seal off the rebels' only possible escape. There were other compelling reasons for delaying until the following morning. As day's end approached, only about half of Cornwallis' men had reached the Assunpink. Some were still straggling in from their hazardous and exhausting march, and the rear units of the British army were merely half way down the Princeton road. With fewer men, Cornwallis would have to string out his army all along the creek in order to protect his flanks. That, in turn, would reduce his chances of mounting an assault with overwhelming power in any one sector. If he chose to fight in the dwindling light of this day, he would be able to deploy only about 1,500 men in the sectors where the creek could be crossed. Still, Cornwallis chose to fight. Like Washington, he ached for a fight, and the Hessians with him, in their zeal to avenge the recent humiliating defeat inflicted on their comrades, urged an immediate attack.[80] In the fading pink light of that pivotal day, Cornwallis disdained a siege. He would not repeat the great mistake that Howe had made in Brooklyn. He sought a quick victory. In the gloom of late day, Cornwallis readied his men. Across the river many Americans swallowed hard at the sight of the massing of the enemy. With their backs pressed to the river and nowhere to go, some men thought their situation "a most awful crisis," even a "momentous crisis."[81] Knox thought the American position was "strong but hazardous." Battles were unpredictable, and he knew that if the British rolled up the American right, the remainder of the rebel army would likely be "thrown into Confusion or push'd into the Delaware."[82] For the rest of his life, Colonel James Wilkinson believed that if ever there was "a crisis in the affairs of the revolution, this was the moment."[83]

Ready at last, Cornwallis ordered assaults at two major crossings on the American left, one at the stone bridge. The British and Germans, slowed to a deadly pace by their heavy equipment and the rank mire created by the unseasonable weather, advanced into a calamitous hail of American musket and rifle fire and a terrifying artillery bombardment. The attackers were forced back. Cornwallis next ordered German grenadiers, trained as shock troops, to storm the bridge. No soldiers ever fought more bravely, or futilely. After ten minutes that seemed to be ten hours, their assault ended in failure. They had gotten no further than halfway across the bridge, and they had taken extraordinary losses to get that far. Now it was about dark, but Cornwallis ordered more assaults, these by the British infantry. Each attack followed an eerily macabre pattern: form, advance, collapse in the face of heavy losses, retreat in failure. What a Delaware soldier called the "great Slaughter" went on and on until the bridge, in the words of a New Englander "looked red as blood, with their killed and wounded, and their red coats."[84] A Pennsylvanian thought it the most "furious Engagement that Ever was."[85] Nightfall, not Cornwallis's good judgment, finally prevented the dispatch of even more men into the meat grinder. As the winter night stole over the Assunpink, 365 of Cornwallis's men had been lost in the hour-long fight for the bridge. Throughout the long bloody day the British had suffered nearly five hundred casualties, almost 8 percent of the force that had marched down from Princeton to wage what some call the Second Battle of Trenton. More than one hundred Americans had perished or been wounded.[86]

During the cold night that followed, Cornwallis planned the next day's action. He would go after Washington's pregnable right wing. He foresaw the annihilation of the rebel army, and possibly the end of the rebellion. Legend has it that he told his officers: "We've got the Old Fox safe now. We'll go over and bag him in the morning."[87] Cornwallis was not to savor the military glory after which he lusted. During that night, his prey stole away, slipping out of his grasp through the door that he had left open on the American right.

While Cornwallis plotted his attack for January 3, Washington had summoned a council of war to consider his options. They were stark: stand and fight, or attempt to retreat. Washington may have hinted that he preferred a withdrawal under the cover of darkness. It offered the best—probably the only—chance to wiggle out of the snare, for as Washington subsequently remarked, "the Enemy were greatly superior in number" and "their design was to surround us." Knox favored attempting to escape, and that appears to have been the prevailing sentiment from the outset. As the discussion proceeded, talk must have turned to the plodding pace with which the enemy had moved both when it chased the rebels in November and on the preceding day as it marched down from Princeton. Gradually, the idea gestated during the meeting that the army should not merely slither from this trap, it should advance on Princeton and strike the small British force that had been left to hold the town. Thanks to his intelligence network, Washington had a good idea where the British were garrisoned in Princeton and the location of their weak spots, and through natives of the area, including Reed, he was familiar with backcountry routes well to the east of the Trenton Road. It was conceivable that the trek could be made, an attack carried out, and a retreat from Princeton conducted long before Cornwallis's army arrived from Trenton. The meeting was brief, and concluded with an agreement to withdraw from the Assunpink and advance on Princeton by skirting the left flank of the enemy.[88]

Washington's phenomenal good fortune persisted. After four consecutive nights during which the temperature had not fallen below freezing, winter miraculously returned. A hard freeze bore down on Trenton, firming up previously squishy roads, and enabling the Americans, who began to move out after midnight, to proceed with greater dispatch. Thick clouds piled high, adding to the darkness, and a cold wind blew from the northwest, carrying sounds away from the British lines. Once again, the rebel soldiers were ordered not to talk and to muffle sneezes and coughs. Heavy cloths were wrapped around wagon wheels to stifle their customary din. All torches were extinguished, but the American campfires on the hillside overlooking the Assunpink were left blazing brightly in the hope that the enemy would not suspect the attempted escape. Deep in the night the British discerned movements on the hillside, but Cornwallis guessed that the rebels were preparing an attack at dawn. He guessed wrong. By the time he realized that his fox was gone, the rebel army was already in Princeton. It had made the dark sixteen-mile march in less time than the British had taken to march ten miles the previous day.[89] One of Washington's young officers, an ensign from Virginia, ever afterward believed that had Cornwallis sealed off the Continentals' sole avenue of escape "the war would have ended."[90]

Not all of Washington's luck was good. As at Trenton on Christmas night, he had hoped to attack in Princeton at daybreak, catching his adversary off guard. But at sunrise the American force was still six miles from its objective. They would not have caught the redcoats by surprise anyway. During the night, orders from Cornwallis for reinforcements reached Princeton, and the local commander, Lieutenant Colonel Charles Mawhood—a clever veteran of twenty-four-years service who was given to eccentricities that included riding into battle on a brown pony with his two spaniels tagging along—had set off before dawn for Trenton with about seven hundred men. Two miles south of Princeton, his force and the lead elements of Washington's army simultaneously spotted one another through a cuff of trees. It was just a bit after 8:00 a.m. Mawhood ordered his heavily outnumbered column to continue to advance, while Greene, commanding one of Washington's two divisions, sent forward a brigade under General Hugh Mercer, a fifty-one-year-old Virginia physician and pharmacist who had learned to soldier while fighting in the Scottish rebellion against Britain in 1745 (for which he had been exiled to America).[91]

The two infantry forces faced off—they were only forty yards apart in an open field—for a classic European-style encounter. The Americans had better than a two-to-one numerical advantage, and some rebels were firing a deadly combination of ball and buckshot. The British took heavy losses, but did not break. After several volleys, Mawhood ordered a bayonet charge. "I never saw men [who] looked so furious as they did," said one American soldier, who, like many of his comrades, broke at the prospect of what one rebel called "pushing bayonets."[92] Mercer was one of the victims of the bayonet attack. Trying to rally his men, he was shot, then clubbed off his horse, and repeatedly, and fatally, stabbed.[93] Seeing what was occurring, Washington personally led reinforcements into the fray, stanching the retreat. Sitting high in the saddle on his large grey horse, Washington continued to direct his men from a point no further from the nearest enemy soldier than a pitcher is from a batter on a baseball diamond. In time, more and more American units arrived. Washington organized them and renewed the attack, and the outnumbered, and now outflanked, redcoats broke and ran, with the Americans in pursuit. "It is a fine fox chase, my boys," one soldier recalled hearing Washington exclaim. Cadwalader remembered shouting to his men: "They fly, the day is our own."[94] The battle had lasted barely fifteen minutes, but the carnage was extensive. The dead and dying lay all about, their blood pooled atop the frozen earth, turning the landscape crimson.

Hearing the shooting, the five hundred or so British troops in Princeton took steps to defend the town, but they were doomed by the heavy odds against them. Fighting raged through the cold, sun-drenched morning, first on the Clark farm, then in Frog Hollow, next on the periphery of the town, then in the village, and finally on the campus of what is now Princeton University. At every step, the British were overwhelmed, although their stout, professional resistance bought time, enabling most of the garrison to flee toward Brunswick, and to take with them extensive supplies and arms. For those who stood and fought, the losses were appalling: roughly 450 British soldiers and officers were killed, wounded, or captured in the Battle of Princeton, nearly 50 percent of those who saw action. The Americans suffered, too. Up to thirty-seven lay dead—including a colonel and a general—and at least that number were wounded.[95]

The last shot at Princeton on January 3 ended a catastrophic ten days for the British. Their losses from Trenton through Princeton exceeded two thousand men. Some two hundred Americans were lost in that period.[96] But the manpower losses were not the entire story. Washington was able to inform Congress that "Genl Howe has left no men either at Trenton or Princeton" and that the New Jersey "Militia are taking spirit."[97] The American army had achieved what Cadwalader had said might be possible. It had flushed the enemy from lower New Jersey.

Its success energized the American rebellion. Four months before, the British high command had expected to inflict one blow after another on the rebels. A month earlier—at a time that General Howe was knighted by the king for his victory in New York—few British officers had believed the Continental army would even exist by the start of 1777. Instead, the new year opened with Carleton long since having been reduced to a long winter of inactivity in the far north, while his counterparts in New Jersey were abandoning posts and thinking only of how to protect their army from attack by the Continentals.[98]

When he departed the Assunpink, Washington's initial intent "was to have pushed on to Brunswick," Howe's largest supply depot in New Jersey and the repository of his "Military Chest containing 70,000£," the capture of which, the American commander rapturously dreamt, would "put an end to the War." But his good judgment resurfaced and overrode his daring. His men were exhausted from ten days of arduous campaigning and Cornwallis was coming after him, retracing his march up the mirthless Trenton Road "in a most infernal Sweat, running[,] puffing & blowing & swearing at being so outwitted," according to the colorful account that Knox provided to his wife.[99] Washington understood fully "the danger of losing the advantage we had gained by aiming at too much," and decided instead to march to Morristown and take up winter quarters, the option that he and his generals had first considered in Newark six long weeks before. At Morristown, he added, his "bear foot & ill clad" soldiery could rest and be resupplied, and a new army recruited.[100]

Late in the morning, only about two hours after arriving at Princeton, Washington marched his men toward Somerset (now Millstone), finally entering the village in the cold red glow of dusk. Cornwallis's army began to enter Princeton shortly after the rebels departed. The redcoats, who had chased the Continentals across New Jersey a few weeks earlier, made no effort to pursue their weary adversary on this occasion. The British, a Hessian soldier remarked contemptuously, looked "like an army that is thoroughly beaten. Everyone was so frightened that it was completely forgotten even to obtain information about where the Americans had gone." Too late, he added, Cornwallis discovered that the rebels were nearby, "completely exhausted, without ammunition and provisions."[101] It was a fitting end to campaign 1776, the year that had offered Great Britain its best chance to destroy the American rebellion.

8

CHOICES, 1777

THE SUMMER and fall of 1776 had been a heady time for Ambrose Serle, secretary to Admiral Howe. The "Raggamuffins"—his term for the American army—"as usual, were defeated," he often noted in his diary. Not long after the Continental army was driven from Manhattan, Serle encountered General Howe and warmly congratulated him on "his repeated Successes." On Christmas Eve Serle expressed confidence that campaign 1776 had brought on the "dying Groans of Rebellion" in America. Two days later he received "very unpleasant News." He learned of "a whole Brigade of Hessians . . . being taken Prisoner at Trenton." Suddenly, he was "exceedingly concerned." A week passed, then "News very important . . . of an Action yesterday." It was more bad news, this time regarding the British setback at Princeton. Serle understood immediately that Washington's bold thrusts were of pivotal importance. The American victories, he said, would "revive the drooping Spirits of the Rebels." The war, which he had believed to be nearly over, was to continue, possibly for a very long time.[1]

General Howe saw what Serle saw. He, too, knew that this would be a longer war than he had previously expected, and he no longer believed it would end with one great engagement. Doubting that he could ever bring Washington to fight that one epic battle, Howe now thought that victory could only be achieved by a series of hammer blows and the relentless application of force.[2]

As 1776 drew to a close, the war remained popular in an England yet unaware of Trenton and Princeton. A quiet confidence existed within North's government. Throughout the year France's assistance to the rebels—secret, but not that secret—had caused worry. Some had expected France to do what was necessary to keep the rebellion alive, including joining the war. So fearful of French belligerency was Sandwich, the head of the Admiralty, that on three occasions he refused Lord Howe's pleas for additional ships and he would not permit warships sent home for repair to return to America. During the autumn, the dark cloud lifted somewhat. The disillusioned French appeared to pull back in the wake of the steady diet of gloomy tidings about the New York campaign, even sending reassurances of their strict neutrality to London. When word of the American debacle at Fort Washington reached London at Christmas, fretting over French intervention largely vanished altogether, although one cynical member of Parliament remarked that "France to us sends most fair words, to America, stores and officers."[3]

Then, in the last two weeks of February 1777, news reached London of Trenton-Princeton and the collapse of the occupation of much of New Jersey. Overnight, a clamor swelled among the foes of ministerial policy, highlighted by the publication of a tract written by Edmund Burke proposing that Britain's only chance for retaining the colonies was to yield to every demand made by the Americans.[4] Although the government continued to possess a commanding majority in Parliament and refused to entertain any thought of concessions, it understood the dreadful price of its shortcomings in 1776. It knew all too well that the Continental army still existed and was dangerous, that the colonists in New Jersey had turned their back on taking the loyalty oath to the king; and that the naval blockade was as porous as a sieve. Worries resurfaced within the ministry about the rebounding of French zeal. Hand in glove with these realizations, the ministry moved to shore up its war effort, knowing that changes had to be made.

Overriding the objections of Sandwich, the cabinet—which was virtually being run by Germain, the American secretary, while North convalesced at his country estate from a fall from a horse—voted to commit six ships of the line, the battleships of the day, to the fleet in America, and to send another six thousand men across the sea. That would make Britain's armies in North America six times larger than had been thought necessary on the eve of hostilities. Germain also instructed Howe to act with less lenity.[5]

This was merely for starters. Heads rolled in Canada. Germain viscerally disliked Carleton. It was an animus that arose in large measure from Carleton's close ties to men who were responsible for Germain's court martial conviction in 1760, and it was nurtured by the governor's churlish refusal to assent to the appointments of men for whom the American secretary pushed. But Germain was roused by more than personal ill will. He saw in Carleton the same qualities that Arnold had seen. Carleton, Germain believed, was ill suited for leading an offensive war. He lacked the daring and aggressiveness, and perhaps the cold ruthlessness, needed for leading a successful invasion of New York. Germain seethed at Carleton's unwillingness to turn loose Britain's Indian allies against civilians on the northern frontier in 1776 and his hesitation to strike hard against the eviscerated enemy. Germain additionally believed that Carleton's tactics had been wanting during the attempted invasion of New York. Had he made a strong diversionary incursion into the Mohawk River Valley, Germain thought, Gates might have detached part of his garrison at Ticonderoga, leaving the fort vulnerable to assault. Fed up with Carleton, the American secretary made it known privately that he wanted Carleton stripped of all authority and recalled, but North and the king protected their man in Canada until Germain leaked to the press several army officers' criticism of Carleton. The officers had carped about the manner in which the attempted invasion of New York had been handled and especially about Carleton's decision not to attack Ticonderoga. But the most damaging blow was one general's charge that Carleton was "totally unfit for such a command, and must ruin his Majesty's affairs." As the new mood dawned in London in the aftermath of Trenton and Princeton, Carleton's displacement was a foregone conclusion.[6]

December 1776 was a busy month for Germain. In addition to his campaign against Carleton, he was preoccupied with planning for the new year and beset with having to cope with Generals Burgoyne and Clinton, both home on leave and seeking interviews. During that same month, Germain received General Howe's plan for campaign 1777, prepared on November 30, nearly a month prior to the Christmas surprise at Trenton. Howe proposed that while a considerable force held New York and harassed Connecticut, eight thousand men were to make a diversion against Philadelphia. That feint would hold in check a substantial portion of the Continental army. The bulk of the British army was to be divided into two equal parts of 10,000 men. One force would advance from Newport and take Providence, then continue on to Boston "and if possible . . . reduce that town." The other would drive up the Hudson to Albany, where it would rendezvous with the British army that invaded New York from Canada. In the autumn, with the Hudson again in British hands, all components of the British army would combine and steamroll through Philadelphia, Virginia, and the Lower South. By Christmas, the British army would be in Georgia.[7]

Burgoyne beat Howe's plan to London by three weeks. Getting wind of Germain's hatred of Carleton, Burgoyne advertised himself in the hope of being appointed commander of the army in Canada. He secured two audiences with the king. In each session, Burgoyne planted the seed that he possessed the enterprise and audacity to lead the invasion of New York. Burgoyne somehow also learned the details of Howe's campaign plan, and, with his keenness for guile, drafted a deft plan of his own that accorded with what he knew of the thinking of the king and Germain regarding American strategy. Not only had Carleton been too restrained, Burgoyne wrote, he should have acted in concert with Indians and Canadian militia to make a feint in the Mohawk River. As for 1777, Burgoyne said that a diversion in the Mohawk Valley was essential, but the brunt of Britain's invasion should come through the Champlain corridor. Once Ticonderoga was taken, the army was to proceed to Albany and unite with Howe's force. Hedging his bets, Burgoyne additionally spoke of two alternative courses. He suggested marching the army eastward from Ticonderoga, through the Green Mountains to the Connecticut River Valley, an expedition that might be facilitated by diversionary actions by the British forces in Rhode Island. He also proposed that the Canadian army might be taken south by the British fleet to act in concert with Howe somewhere south of the Delaware River.[8]

On February 23, just four days before he intended to recommend Burgoyne's plan to the cabinet, Germain received a new campaign plan from Howe. Drafted on December 20, less than a week prior to Trenton, Howe had reconsidered his original proposal in light both of Cornwallis's success in penetrating to the Delaware River and of the surprising number of New Jersey residents that had stepped forward to take the loyalty oath. Having learned from insiders at home that he would not get the reinforcements that he had requested, Howe scaled back in his second plan. Gone entirely was any mention of advancing on Albany or of retaking Boston. He spoke only in the vaguest terms of the need "to facilitate in some degree, the approach of the army from Canada." Instead, Howe proposed an entirely new objective: taking Philadelphia. It was a campaign in which he believed the vast numbers of Loyalists in New Jersey and Pennsylvania would play a vital role. Furthermore, Howe believed that Philadelphia, the home of Congress, had a talismanic significance for Americans. Washington would have to stand and fight to defend it.[9]

Germain was still working on his response to Howe's second plan when on March 3, to his utter astonishment, a third plan from the general arrived. Composed in the aftermath of Trenton and Princeton, Howe renewed his plea for reinforcements, made necessary in part because of his recent heavy losses, but also as his dark doubts about the reliability of the Tories had resurfaced. Otherwise, Howe stuck to what he had proposed in his second plan: the capture of Philadelphia remained his primary objective. As before, he made no mention of cooperating with the army coming south from Canada, save to advise that the invasion army might be assisted by a force of up to 3,500 redcoats, a portion of the army that he planned to leave in New York City.[10]

Since late in 1775 the ministry had held to the strategy of seizing control of the Hudson from Albany to New York. Germain had never wavered from that objective, and Howe had not only endorsed the strategy when he took command, his invasion of New York in campaign 1776 was undertaken in large measure to realize that end. Now, in his final two plans, Howe had proposed a radical departure. Some scholars have wondered if narrow personal ends accounted for his decision: Carleton outranked him, so that if the two British armies united at Albany, Howe would become the second in command. In his second plan, in fact, Howe had recommended that Clinton, whom he outranked, be given command of the Canadian army. Be that as it may, it is more likely that Howe's thinking was altered by events between November and early January, especially as in his last plan he confessed that Trenton had been far more damaging than he had first imagined. Faced now with a protracted war, capturing Philadelphia took on an urgency that had not previously existed. Its possession would close down a major rebel port, add to the supply problems that the Continental army already faced, and—as had been true in New York—the city and its environs were thought to be a bountiful source for supplies and badly needed Loyalist soldiers. Other considerations also riveted Howe's focus on Philadelphia. The sole hope of ending the war in 1777 was to bring Washington to battle, and the only probable means of forcing him into a general action was to compel him to defend Philadelphia. Howe was also confident that the rebels, when simultaneously faced with an invasion of New York from Canada and his strike into Pennsylvania, would have to divide their armies to meet the twin emergencies.[11]

Three proposed strategies had crossed Germain's desk that winter. There were the two distinct courses that Howe had recommended: Britain's two armies might seek to link up on the Hudson and squeeze New England (his first plan) or the invasion force from Canada might be left to its own devices while Howe waged a campaign to take Philadelphia (his two final plans). The third option was to scrap an advance from Canada altogether, as Burgoyne had suggested, and bring the northern army by sea to cooperate in a combined operation with Howe's army, either against New England or Pennsylvania. Germain might embrace any one of these three strategies, or he could intermingle one of Burgoyne's suggestions with a variant of Howe's initial proposal, having the Canadian army drive south unassisted—either toward Albany or the Connecticut River—while Howe's army invaded New England through Rhode Island and Connecticut.

The ministry, with the king's assent, did not finally approve a plan for campaign 1777 until the last week in March, and what it chose was an alloy of Howe's plans. It reflected Germain's influence. Carleton was to be confined to domestic responsibilities. Burgoyne was given command of the Canadian army. He was to create a diversion along the Mohawk as he advanced on Ticonderoga through the Champlain Valley.[12] Tories were to be raised and armed, and, together with allied Indians, turned loose along the Pennsylvania, New York, and Virginia frontiers to wage a campaign to erode morale and draw away men and supplies from the main rebel armies.[13] Howe was to take Philadelphia, but as he was not expected to be "detained long" by that undertaking, London presumed that there would be ample time for him to "cooperate with the Northern Army." It was a plan constructed on shifting sand. The army in Canada was to be increased by four thousand German troops, but even that was unlikely to give it numerical superiority for attacking Ticonderoga or for campaigning to take Albany. As for Howe's end of things, the ministry was betting that he could take Philadelphia within a few weeks, even though in 1776, against a less-experienced foe, several months had been required for him to take New York. Once Philadelphia was captured, moreover, Howe would have to move his army more than one hundred miles northward in order to cooperate with Burgoyne, an operation that was bound to be time-consuming.

To make matters worse, six weeks after the ministry adopted its plan for 1777 it heard from Howe once again. He planned now, he informed the ministry, to take his army from New York to Philadelphia by sea, "and from this arrangement we must probably abandon the Jerseys." Neither matter had been mentioned previously.[14] This exercise of working out plans for the campaign of 1777 gave cogent meaning to Burke's presumption that the empire could no longer be maintained as it had been, if for no other reason than the vast distances that separated colonies from homeland. "Seas roll, and months pass, between the order and execution" of plans, he had observed, "and the want of a speedy explanation of a single point is enough to defeat a whole system."[15]

It was not just the planning that put Britain on an uphill slope in 1777. The choice of Burgoyne to command the Canadian army was shortsighted. Burgoyne was fifty-four that year. He had received a fine education at the Westminster School, the alums of which were something of a who's who within Britain's military, clerical, and political systems. He left school at age fifteen to begin a military career, but until he was in his thirties soldiering was an on again, off again thing in his life. He served two stints in the army that totaled ten years, resigning both times after he had gambled himself into such debt that he could not hope to purchase a promotion. He returned to the army for good during the Seven Years' War. By then his luck had improved at the gaming table, to which he was every bit as addicted as is a junkie to drugs or a dipsomaniac to the bottle. More important, he had entered into a fortuitous marriage to an earl's daughter. He now possessed both the financial resources and the family connections that were crucial for advancement. When Burgoyne resumed his military career, he served with courage and valor, largely as a cavalryman in small-scale coastal raids in France and during a backwater campaign in Spain. He succeeded in getting elected to Parliament in the course of the war, and the resulting political connections that he forged partially explain how an officer with his record—good, but not spectacular—could have risen with such meteoric rapidity. Burgoyne went from captain to brigadier general in the space of half a dozen years. He stayed in the army and in Parliament after the war, once again becoming a connoisseur of the good life. He drank heavily, gambled, chased women, and hung around the theater, acting a bit, but mostly writing plays. He also wrote some revisionist tracts on army discipline and the use of artillery that earned him a reputation as a daring thinker in the field of military science. Of greater importance, he demonstrated savvy abilities as a political networker and was unrivaled in his artful mastery of politics within the military establishment. Almost everyone saw Burgoyne as bright, charming, and energetic, and most acknowledged that he was an excellent leader of men who would make a fine regimental commander.[16] But he had never had an independent command nor been part of a military expedition as large and complex as that which he was expected to lead to Albany. In hindsight, his appointment was testimony to the fatal flaws in the nation's governance system, as no one cabinet official possessed unambiguous responsibility—and authority—over the war as a whole, and in Britain's army, in which merit was often a secondary consideration in the elevation of officers. Burgoyne had "a half-understanding" of things, Horace Walpole once said of him, "which was worse than none." But the appointment was his because Germain was bent on ousting Carleton, no one was too keen on Clinton (though Howe had recommended him), and many—not least George III—had been pulled into Burgoyne's orbit by his captivating manner and crafty intriguing.[17]

THE PREVIOUS YEAR had been a brush with catastrophe for the rebels. Two armies had been mauled in Canada and for weeks the Continentals in New York and New Jersey had walked on the edge of perdition. No single factor accounted for the near disasters and all too real calamities, but Washington thought the malady was a too small army in which men served only a brief tour of duty. From late 1775 onward he told Congress of the difficulty in making soldiers of civilians drawn from America's culture of individualism, adding that to make "Men well acquainted with the Duties of a Soldier, requires time." To "bring them under proper discipline & Subordination, not only requires time, but is a Work of great difficulty," he went on, especially "in this Army, where there is so little distinction between the Officers and Soldiers." Washington also advised Congress that to try to raise an army each year in the face of European regulars was to court ruin.[18]

What Washington said was sound, but until the great crisis in late 1776 most of his countrymen shrank from long-term enlistments, convinced that standing armies—historically the prized weapon of tyrants—were inevitably an "*armed monster*," the arch-enemy of freedom. Only unrelenting military failures, and the presence of the enemy merely eighteen miles from Philadelphia, changed the perspective within Congress.[19]

The choices that Congress made late in 1776 substantively altered the face of the Continental army. Henceforth, men were to enlist for longer periods, up to three years. Longer service necessitated inducements to help with recruiting, chiefly cash and land bounties. In January 1776 Congress had offered its first bounty, a tempting $6.66, to those who enlisted in the army that was to be sent to Canada. But in 1777 the enticement was sweetened. A recruit who signed on for the duration of the war could receive up to a twenty-dollar cash bounty, an allotment of clothing, and a land bounty of one hundred acres that was to be awarded following the successful end of hostilities. For the first time, too, Congress assigned to each state a quota of troops to be raised, ranging from fifteen regiments in the largest states (Virginia and Massachusetts) to a single regiment in the smallest (Georgia and Delaware). Congress also altered the Articles of War. Much of the work was done by John Adams, who was a member of the Committee on Spies that was assigned the task, and he drew heavily on Great Britain's Articles of War. The principal change from the original articles—adopted when the army was created in 1775—was to permit more draconian punishments. The maximum corporal punishment was increased from thirty-nine to one hundred lashes. The number of capital crimes increased from two (abandoning a post and divulging the password to anyone outside the army) to nine. A soldier now could be executed for throwing away his arms, striking an officer, causing false alarms, assaulting anyone bringing supplies to the army, giving supplies to the enemy, protecting the enemy, and plundering civilians.[20]

Longer terms of service created new choices for men of military age. In 1775 and 1776 the composition of the Continental army had been something of a cross-section of American society. Concord, Massachusetts, for example, furnished 190 men to the Continental army in 1775–1776, roughly the same number of men between the ages of eighteen and thirty living in the town.[21] Probably most men who had joined, regardless of the state or colony that they called home, had been property-owning farmers and tradesmen who left home to serve for one year, seeing their sacrifice as a patriotic duty. So strong was the rage to soldier during the first two years of the war that some who failed to take up arms were overcome by guilt at not entering the army. John Adams, for instance, a forty-one-year-old member of Congress in 1776, filled letter after letter with a glorification of soldiering. Soldiers, he said, had a unique opportunity to "refine" the character of the people. The military regimen was "Sublime" and "Beautiful." Confessing a "flow of Spirits" unlike anything he had previously experienced, he said that he yearned to become a soldier. "Oh that I was a Soldier! I will be," he promised, adding that he was reading military manuals in preparation for going to war. But he never soldiered, and it bothered him enormously that two of his fellow congressmen, John Dickinson and Patrick Henry, went home to take up arms.[22]

Patriotism alone did not explain every man's enlistment. Some men saw the war as a means of bringing about seminal changes—especially political and social equality—whether or not independence was achieved. Others doubtless soldiered because of social pressures. Soldiering was the thing to do, and it seemed as if everyone was doing it. Most men hailed from small rural hamlets where everyone knew everyone else, and many feared that the failure to serve would result in a humiliating lifelong disgrace. Many felt pressed to enlist, leaned on by parents, wives, girlfriends, friends, and esteemed and powerful local men. Other men were swept up by the pulsating war rhetoric broadcast in the press and preached from pulpits. Men often heard that it was better to die a hero than to live as a coward, and in New England in particular countless sermons proclaimed war to be a purifying agent. Men often heard their pastors insist that to die in a just war was next to godliness.[23] Not all men required a push to soldier. Some yearned for adventure or dreamt of heroism. And some, as had been true of young George Washington in the previous war, were men on the make who saw military service as the path to bigger and better things. That was the outlook of a young New England officer taken prisoner at Bunker Hill who told his captors, "as to the Dispute between great Britain & the Colonies, I know nothing of it." He fought, he said, because he was ambitious. If "killed in Battle, there would [be] an end of me," he said fatalistically, "but if my Captain was killed, I should rise in Rank, &

should still have a Chance to rise higher. These Sir! were the only Motives of my entering into the Service."[24]

Most who served in 1775 or 1776 chose not to reenlist. Many were farmers who, faced with rapacious creditors and tax collectors, feared losing their farms if they were away for a second consecutive year. Most felt that they had done their duty. "[R]epose should be ours," said one who went home when his enlistment expired.[25] It was someone else's turn to sacrifice. After the debacles of 1776 a few confessed that their "noble spirit of patriotism is in a considerable degree extinguished."[26] A great many spurned reenlistment because they had grown disenchanted with soldiering. Military service was filled with boredom and the loss of one's freedom, not to mention loneliness, discomfort, poor or inadequate food, occasional insults and humiliation, and abundant danger. One man had said that he had taken up arms expecting the "Glorious life of a Soldier." Instead, he had been nearly constantly "ragged, dirty," and hungry.[27] Some raged at what they believed had been their officers' seeming indifference to their plight. One private said that he and his comrades might have been dead "for aught they knew or cared." His officers, he added, "did not feel the hardships which we had to undergo, and of course cared but little, if anything for us."[28] Many soldiers complained of incessant labor and duty, and not a few spoke of frequently experiencing a "fetegue" unlike anything they had known in the civilian world. Much of what they were made to do seemed nonsensical to them. One irritated soldier spoke of being awakened at 4:00 a.m. to prepare for a march that did not finally get under way for hours. On many occasions, he added, he and his buddies were made to march several miles before they could eat breakfast.[29] Another soldier, who was part of the retreat off Manhattan Island carped that "we have Ben all this Summer Digging & Billding of Foorts to Cover our heads and now we have Ben obliged to Leave them" and have "not one shovell full of Durte to Cover us."[30] There was still another factor in their decision to return home. Many knew someone who had been taken prisoner, or who had been wounded and left to face a lifetime of debilitation, or who had been killed in action, not infrequently in a little skirmish that appeared to the participants to serve no useful end, or who died slowly, painfully, and ingloriously from a camp disease.

The growing reality of war had made it more difficult to find volunteers in 1776. It grew steadily more difficult in the years that followed. In Petersborough, New Hampshire, for example, one-third of all males of military age had marched to Boston upon learning of Lexington and Concord, and a large number joined the Continental army that summer. By the end of 1776 more than half the males in the town had served in the army. But only 14 percent of those who were eligible enlisted in 1777 and barely 4 percent were in the army between 1778 and 1780.[31] Beginning in 1777 the civil and military authorities throughout America had to troll as never before to find men willing to make a long-term commitment, and they had to battle the sinister suspicions of many of the poor that they were being manipulated to bear arms by "sagacious polticians" who served the elite.[32] Congress offered fifty acres to Hessians who would desert and join the Continental army, and it gave those taken captive at Trenton the opportunity to serve as Continentals in their own so-called "German volunteers" corps. Neither expedient succeeded. Meanwhile, the army dispatched both officers and enlisted soldiers in search of men to fill the depleted ranks. Recruiters were paid eight dollars for every enlistee they secured. They were supposedly guided by the criteria for soldiering set forth by Congress: each recruit was to be healthy, between sixteen and fifty years of age, a minimum of five feet two inches tall— some states stipulated a minimum height of five feet, four inches—and white. But the money dangled before recruiters, as well as the need to meet a quota quickly, led to abuses. Sometimes children and disabled men were signed up. One soldier, presumably exaggerating, recollected some recruits with "two eyes, some with one, and some, I believe, with none at all."[33]

The introduction of conscription before the end of 1777 somewhat minimized these shortcomings. States utilized the draft only as a last resort when a quota could not be had through volunteerism. Some states conscripted men for only one year's service, but others—such as Virginia—drafted men for three years. The arrival of a draft notice did not necessarily mean that the recipient would become a Continental. In some places one could escape service by paying a fine, which led to the conscription of someone else, until finally a man was found who could not, or would not, pay the levy. Everywhere, too, it was lawful to avoid service by hiring two men as substitutes in one's stead.[34] John Adams claimed, "Persons draughted are commonly the wealthiest," as they had the resources to hire "their poorer Neighbours, to take their Places." If so, the practice was not universal. Virginia consciously singled out the poorest of its citizens for conscription. In 1776 the state assembly passed legislation that permitted the impressment of "rogues and vagabonds," defining the latter as propertyless men who failed to pay their taxes and parish levies.[35]

Recruiters worked hard to find volunteers and avoid conscription. They used a variety of artifices to induce men to enlist, including bringing along an ample supply of liquor to curb uncertainties and ignite ardor. Some recruiters found that a quiet and earnest approach worked best, others were fast and glib, and still others relied on bombast. Some made passionate speeches on the village green. One New Englander remembered a recruiting officer who visited his hamlet as being "a jovial, good-natured fellow, of ready wit and much broad humor. Crowds followed in his wake when he marched the streets; and he occasionally stopped at the corners to harangue the multitude in order to excite their patriotism and zeal for the cause of liberty." The recruiter's eyes lit up, he recollected, "when he espied any large boys among the idle crowd around him." He "would attract their attention by singing in a comical manner . . . [a] doggerel" about escaping the humdrum life of a rustic village.[36] Some recruiters preferred low-key, one-on-one entreaties. Others appealed to their listeners' patriotism or loathing of England, and emphasized—perhaps invented—stories of abusive actions by the king's soldiers or, later in the war, Britain's Indian allies.[37] Many found that they had to emphasize the bounties. Not a few played on the psyche of their quarry, especially emphasizing how proud the recruit's father would be of his patriotic son. Some attempted to reach their callow and impressionable prey with glowing tales of adventure or winsome yarns about army life. More often than not the core of the recruiter's pitch was often aimed at the subject's ego, and more than one recruit subsequently confessed to have been "animated by a hope of applause" from parents and neighbors.[38]

Men chose to soldier for a bit of all the reasons that the recruiters put forth, but for many the bounties were a crucial inducement. Indentured servants and apprentices signed on, but so, too, did free men such as Joseph Plumb Martin of Milford, Connecticut. He enlisted in the summer of 1776 because of the pressure he felt from peers who were signing up, but he reenlisted in 1777 for the money, he later candidly acknowledged.[39] Even so, had financial reward been the only enticement, many of these men likely would have joined the king's army, where monthly wages were guaranteed, and where payment was made in a currency that could be expected to retain its value. However pecuniary the motives of the enlistees, a great many no longer saw themselves as Britons, but as Americans, and many must have chosen the American side from a patriotism borne by the hope that independence would usher in a better world. For them, bounties were the icing on the cake.[40]

Recruiters did not secure all the men that Congress had dreamily anticipated for 1777. Congress had voted to raise eighty-eight battalions, or roughly 75,000 men, but the Continental army peaked that year in October with 39,443 men, almost 20 percent beneath its pinnacle in 1776.[41] It was an army with a new look. Those who soldiered after 1777 tended to be younger than their predecessors. The median age of Virginia's soldiers after 1777 was twenty, and 5 percent were younger than sixteen. Paradoxically, there appears to have been a larger percentage of older men in the ranks than in 1775–1776 or in the colonial wars. But the greatest difference in the composition of the Continental army after 1777 was that the enlistees were more likely than their predecessors to be poor, landless, unskilled, itinerant semi-employed or unemployed, unmarried, and not infrequently foreign born. A study of Maryland soldiers recruited later in the war revealed that the lion's share came from the poorest one-third of the population, many were indentured servants, and some were so poverty-stricken that they would have fallen within the legal definition of pauperism. In the first two years of the war, America had fielded an army composed largely of men drawn from what that class-conscious age defined as the "middling sort." After 1777 the soldiery came overwhelmingly from among what they called the "lower sort."[42]

AMERICAN DIPLOMATIC ACTIVITIES proceeded in earnest through that winter. Benjamin Franklin arrived in Paris five days before Washington's Christmas surprise. The British ministry was aware of Franklin's arrival and it also knew that

Foreign Minister Vergennes received him within the week. According to an insider at Whitehall, Germain and Sandwich were "a little stunned" at Franklin's reception.[43] Britain's officials had good reason for concern. Late in September, while the Continental army sat uneasily in the snare that was Harlem Heights, Congress had appointed Franklin, Silas Deane, and Arthur Lee, a Virginia merchant and former agent for his colony in London, as commissioners to seek recognition of the United States and a commercial treaty with France. Franklin had crossed on the *Reprisal*, an armed sloop loaded with South Carolina indigo, which when sold in France would provide the funds to cover the commissioners' initial expenses.[44]

Congress had hoped that its formal proclamation of American independence would result in more than secret aid. Richard Henry Lee's June 1776 motion calling for independence had also proposed that Congress "prepare a plan of treaties to be proposed to foreign powers."[45] Congress had rapidly created two committees; one that was thought of as Jefferson's committee was to draft a declaration concerning independence, while the other was to prepare a model treaty to guide the envoys who would be dispatched to France. John Adams emerged as the key member of the second committee.

A broad consensus existed in Congress concerning what was hoped for in America's relationship with France. Acting on the assumption that a political and military alliance would be fraught with plentiful dangers—the most obvious of which was that the United States might be dragged into its ally's wars in Europe or elsewhere—Adams drafted a plan that instructed the commissioners to seek only a reciprocal commercial pact. Adams completed his draft two weeks after independence was declared, and late in September Congress adopted the Plan of Treaties without substantive change.[46]

The most popular toasts in Philadelphia that September were those to the French and the money and materials they had secretly extended, and might continue to offer.[47] Congress had rarely been more optimistic. It believed "that France means not to let the United States sink in the present Contest."[48] After Trenton and Princeton, some in Congress clutched at the rosy notion that "the Independence of America hath catched the attention of Europe." Many believed that several nations, "wishing for a Share of our Commerce," would recognize the United States and sign trade treaties. Several congressmen even believed that France and Spain would declare war on Great Britain. "The Hearts of the French are universally for Us, and the Cry is strong for immediate War," said one.[49]

The congressmen were overly optimistic, as Franklin and his fellow commissioners discovered in December and January. France was most cautious. Louis XVI and his finance minister, as well as many powerful merchants, feared that providing extensive economic aid to the American rebels might ruin France's economy. Aiding the Americans might also lead Great Britain to declare war, and the navy cautioned that it was unprepared for hostilities, as its massive rebuilding program was incomplete. Vergennes wanted Spain on his side should France become involved in another war with Britain, but Madrid was ambivalent about the prospect of an antimonarchical, republican nation being created on the doorstep of its American colonies. Nor were the Spanish convinced that Britain would be seriously weakened by the loss of its provinces. On top of everything else, until several weeks into 1777 the last hard news from America had been of the setbacks in the New York theater.[50]

Vergennes remained amiable and forthcoming when he met with the commissioners. He granted the United States a loan twice as large as the gift that France had extended in 1776, and he additionally put the envoys in touch with the Farmers General, a consortium that managed the tobacco monopoly. It agreed to pay two million livres for Chesapeake tobacco. Vergennes also worked behind the scenes to induce French army officers to come to America, where they could share their expertise with the Continental's callow leaders. But he declined the commissioners' entreaties for ships of the line and "an immediate Supply of twenty or thirty Thousand Muskets and Bayonets, and a large Quantity of Ammunition and brass field Pieces." Nor was he prepared to extend diplomatic recognition to the United States or to sign a formal trade treaty. Such steps would almost certainly mean war with Britain. Not even word of Trenton and Princeton, which reached France in mid-February, and resulted in General Washington being "much applauded by the Military People here," budged Vergennes.[51]

Their backs to the wall, and with little to offer in return, the commissioners first chose a heavy-handed response. If their requests were not met, they blustered, Congress might face "unconditional Submission by force of Arms, or an Accommodation" with London. In either case, they went on, Great Britain would emerge as "the most formidable Power . . . that Europe has yet seen," and it would turn its wrath on France—isolated and alone—for the assistance it had already given to America. That crude tack was unavailing, and it soon led Franklin, Deane, and Lee to ignore the Plan of Treaties and hint at America's cheerful willingness to enter into a military alliance with France. They also promised that should a Franco-American alliance result in a Franco-British war, the United States would never make a separate peace with London. Vergennes did not bite. He had gone as far as he was willing to go prior to campaign 1777, a fact that Britain's extraordinarily capable intelligence network reported to the ministry by early March, and which contributed to the choices that Germain made in planning that campaign.[52]

Two DAYS after Christmas in 1775, while Montgomery and Arnold were planning the attack on Quebec, the large British merchant ship *Adamant* docked in London. Its arrival drew numerous spectators anxious for a glimpse of several American prisoners, including Ethan Allen, who had been confined below decks in irons en route to captivity in England. The other passengers, a banker, a few businessmen, four or five army officers, some royal Indian officials, including

Thayendanegea (Joseph Brant). Mezzotint by J. R. Smith, c. 1776. An Iroquois who believed in Great Britain and knew that the best hope for his people lay in crushing the American rebellion, Brant, as he was known among the English, rallied the Iroquois and fought with courage throughout the war.

Britain's superintendent of Indian affairs for the northern colonies, Guy Johnson, and a light skinned Native American named Thayendanegea, "two sticks together" in his native tongue, or Joseph Brant as his British friends called him, disembarked without notice. Brant had come to complain to imperial officials of boundary problems that nettled his Mohawk tribesmen, and to seek a better understanding of the war that he had left behind in America. Among Johnson's reasons for crossing the Atlantic was the wish to inform ministerial officials of what he believed had been General Carleton's poor management of the defense of Canada, especially his reluctance to turn loose the Indians.[53]

Brant, who was thirty-two, had been born in a dark hut in the Ohio Country, near present day Cleveland. His mother and father were Mohawks, but many thought it likely that a grandparent might have been English, perhaps a captive who wed one of his antecedents. For fifteen years or more Brant had benefited from the patronage of Sir William Johnson, Guy's uncle and Britain's first superintendent for Indian affairs. Around 1760, Sir William had taken Brant's sister, Molly, to be his mistress, housekeeper, and surrogate mother to his white children, and he had also taken Brant under his wing, sending him to be formally educated at the Anglican Mohawk mission and Eleazer Wheelock's school for Indians in Lebanon, Connecticut. At Wheelock's, Brant converted to Christianity, was baptized, and learned to read, write, and speak English fluently. By age thirteen he was fighting for the English during the French and Indian War, serving as a Mohawk warrior in the Lake George and Montreal campaigns. A young adult by war's end, Brant was spare and tall—he was nearly six feet in height—and ruggedly handsome, with dark eyes, full lips, and ample jet black hair that he tied in a queue, after the British custom. Usually also dressing in the English fashion, Brant struck observers as grave, dignified, courteous, intelligent, and "manly." He remained in the Mohawk River Valley after the war, working as a translator for royal Indian officials and helping an Anglican clergyman translate the Gospels into the Mohawk language. He settled in Canajoharie, one of two Mohawk villages in the valley, and in 1765 married the daughter of a leading chief in a Christian ceremony. In the decade before the outbreak of the War of Independence, Brant became a substantial property-owning farmer, eventually possessing more than six hundred acres, on which he raised corn, kept livestock, cared for an orchard, and produced maple sugar. He married three times— Anglican priests conducted two of the ceremonies—and fathered nine children. His first two wives, who were Native Americans, died young of tuberculosis. His third wife's mother was a Mohawk and her father a New York Indian trader and land speculator.[54]

Brant's people, the Mohawks, were part of the Iroquoian-speaking peoples that comprised the Iroquois Confederacy of Six Nations, a confederation of tribes (Mohawks, Oneidas, Tuscaroras, Onondagas, Cayugas, and Senecas) that governed territory from the Adirondack Mountains to the western shores of Lake Erie, and from present Ontario southward into Pennsylvania. The Mohawks, a dwindling minority of only some four hundred people, lived at the eastern edge of Iroquoia, placing them closest to the steadily expanding frontier settlements of upper New York. Natives and settlers intermingled uneasily, sometimes fractiously, when forests or hunting and fishing areas were compromised, or when altercations between individuals threatened to widen into raging tempests.[55] The Mohawk and other Iroquois relished European commodities, and for decades they had traded furs for manufactured goods and the services of English craftsmen, particularly blacksmiths and gunsmiths. But the Mohawks sought a recognized boundary between themselves and the English, a cordon of sorts that would keep the persistently encroaching settlers at bay. Boundaries had been set elsewhere in Anglo-America. They seldom lasted long or worked well, primarily because, as General Gage remarked in 1767, the "Frontier People" were "Licentious Ruffians" given to perpetrating "violences . . . upon the Indians" in order to further their insatiable desire for land.[56] Nevertheless, the expedient was tried again in 1768 when Sir William Johnson met with more than three thousand Indians—75 percent of whom were Iroquois—and negotiated the Treaty of Fort

Stanwix. The Indians ceded all of present-day West Virginia and Kentucky, southwestern Pennsylvania, and much of the Mohawk Valley, and they agreed that Brant's Canajoharie, as well as the Mohawk village of Tiononderoge and the Oneida town of Oriske, were to be within New York, though they were to be treated as Indian enclaves. In return, the sachems received presents and cash in excess of £10,000, and a treaty that designated virtually everything north and west of what had been relinquished as Iroquoia.

The ink was hardly dry on the treaty before land speculators resorted to customary chicanery in pressing for deeds to lands in Tiononderoge (Fort Hunter) and Canajoharie. Incidents occurred, including one in 1774 in which Brant and his followers physically assaulted a nemesis. The year 1774 was one of white-hot Anglo-American tensions, and throughout the colonies militias were formed. The patriot militia organized in Tryon County, New York, which included the Mohawk Valley, took charge of the region. The meaning of what was occurring was not lost on the Mohawks. Sensing dispossession, Joseph Brant expressed his people's fears. The American patriots, he charged, had begun "this Rebellion to be sole Masters of this Continent."[57] To most Mohawks, merely 400 people surrounded by some 40,000 New Yorkers who dwelled in Albany and Tryon counties, it seemed evident that their only hope of remaining in their ancestral homeland was through the restoration of imperial authority. The first step had to be the defense of Canada, for if it was lost to the rebels, all was lost. The second was to rally Canadian Mohawks to help them. In 1775 Brant led most of the Mohawks' warriors northward, accompanied by Guy Johnson and other Indian Department personnel. Molly stayed behind and served their cause as an informant.[58] Nearly three thousand Indians and Loyalists met in councils at Oswego and Montreal in July and sang their war songs. However, while Brant aided the defenders of St. Johns against Montgomery's army that fall, he and his warriors were largely stymied at every turn by Carleton, who feared unleashing a bloodbath that would only alienate potential Loyalists in New York and New England. It was Carleton's decision not to use Indian warriors that hastened Johnson's voyage to London late in 1775. That he brought along Brant was no accident.[59]

If Brant was unnoticed when he came ashore in England, he soon was an object of considerable attention. He was presented to the king—Brant later remarked that there was no finer man—met every imaginable dignitary, including James Boswell, who interviewed him for the *London Magazine*; attended parties and masquerade balls (he came attired in Indian war garb); sat for the renowned painter George Romney; was initiated in a Masonic lodge; and received seemingly every conceivable sort of gift, including firearms, a watch, and silk shirts. England was everything that he had imagined it would be, and more. He loved it all, but especially its women, music, and horses, he said. Brant spent nearly four months in the metropolis, lodging at the down-at-the-heels Swan with Two Necks Inn (Johnson and the British Indian officials enjoyed more luxurious surroundings), and in March his stay was capped by an audience with Lord Germain.[60]

Brant entered Germain's plush office wearing Mohawk attire and addressed the American secretary as "Brother." He made a presentation in which he emphasized the Iroquois' traditional loyalty to Great Britain and spoke of the Mohawks' grievances that the New York rebels were ignoring the Fort Stanwix accord, a solemn pact. "We are tired out in making complaints & getting no redress," he added.[61] Germain immediately promised Brant that the Mohawks "might rest assured [that] as soon as the troubles were over, [their] every Grievance and Complaint should be Redressed." In return, Brant avidly reaffirmed the Iroquois' long ties with Britain. The "Six Nations will continue firm to their engagements with the King their father," he said, and Brant assured Germain that on his return to America he would seek to arouse his people to "join with them [the British] in the most prudent measures of assisting to put a stop to those disturbances."[62]

A few weeks later Brant sailed for home aboard the *Lord Hyde*. After weeks of observing Britain's throbbing power, he returned to America utterly convinced that the rebels' ragtag armies could never win this war. Arriving at Staten Island in July 1776, as Howe prepared to open the campaign for New York City, Brant stayed and served with the redcoats through October. He departed after the Battle of White Plains, slipping through Washington's lines in disguise and traveled under cover of darkness back to Iroquoia. Throughout the bitter winter that followed, Brant moved from one Indian village to another in the Six Nations Confederation. At each stop he stridently exhorted his people to take up arms and to make raids into the Mohawk Valley. He advised in a triumphant tone that he had seen Britain's wealth and power, and promised that the American rebellion would be crushed. Feckless neutrality carried greater risks than belligerency, he insisted, and he added that "fighting for the King" would "insure ourselves and our children a good inheritance." Many Iroquois were unconvinced. Some had no wish to challenge Carleton, who still opposed the use of Indians in any fighting in the Mohawk Valley. Others wanted to await the outcome of Britain's invasion of New York before committing, and still others, seeing the Anglo-American war as a family quarrel, believed that neutrality would best serve the Indians' interests. Brant enjoyed greater success with Tories in frontier Tryon County, many of whom responded to him as their deliverer. As the first signs of spring became visible in 1777, Brant's Volunteers, a mix of Mohawks and Loyalists, came into being. Dressing as Indian warriors, these vigilante bands roamed the county, remorselessly taking cattle, horses, and food from little hamlets and isolated farms, and demanding that the settlers declare for Britain or leave the region.[63]

As Germain made his final choices for the invasion of New York from Canada, Indians in upper New York were making fateful choices about the role they would play in the coming fight. Destiny had left them with nothing but bad choices.

9

"THE CAPRICE OF WAR": AMERICA'S PIVOTAL VICTORY AT SARATOGA

THE LAST LONELY STREAKS of daylight slanted through the leafless trees as the Continental army entered Morristown, New Jersey, on January 6, 1777. This was to be the army's quarters for the winter. Twenty-six miles west of New York City, astride both the Whippany River and the post road that linked the Hudson and Delaware Rivers, Morristown was a market center for local farmers and iron miners. Situated in a region of rolling, sometimes lofty hills, the craggy narrow passes leading to the village could be easily defended, and the river that coursed through it was entirely in American hands. The village sat atop a triangular plateau. Hollows fell down two sides of the town and rugged Thimble Mountain stood tall at its back. Morristown was a carefully chosen site. The Continental army would be unassailable in these quarters.[1]

Morristown looked like scores of other hamlets. A church, courthouse, cemetery, two or three shops, a tavern, and perhaps fifty houses, most with lovingly tilled farm land, splayed out from the center of the village. Washington appropriated the tavern, a three-story frame structure, for his headquarters. He occupied two rooms, a bedroom for himself and Martha, who arrived in March, and a parlor. A kitchen and dining room downstairs served the residents and guests, a few rooms were reserved for visiting dignitaries and general officers, and the remainder was allocated to Washington's several aides and his military secretary, Robert Hanson Harrison, a fellow Virginian who had been his principal lawyer prior to the war. Washington had begun the war with one aide-de-camp and a secretary. Soon, the number of his aides swelled. Sixteen men had already served in that capacity, some only briefly, and four who came with the commander to Morristown departed to become regimental commanders in the revamped—and supposedly expanding—Continental army. Washington recruited three new aides while at Morristown, the most important of whom was Alexander Hamilton, who came to headquarters on March 1.[2]

Somewhere between nineteen and twenty-two years old (the date of his birth is uncertain), Hamilton had risen from humble origins in the West Indies, and the stigma of illegitimacy, to attend King's College, which later became Columbia University. Since 1775 he had commanded a New York artillery company. Either during the fight for New York or the desperate retreat across New Jersey, Hamilton's actions had brought him to the attention of his superiors, one of whom (probably Henry Knox) arranged for his interview with Washington for the vacant aide position. Short and slight—Harrison nicknamed him "the little lion"—Hamilton was boundlessly energetic, formidably bright, self-assured, and glib. He wasted no time taking over.[3] Within weeks of becoming an aide, Hamilton, according to a visitor to headquarters, "presided at the General's table" and "acquitted himself with an ease, propriety and vivacity."[4]

Fewer than eight hundred Continentals remained with Washington when he arrived at Morristown. The "Enemy I hope are deceived as to our Numbers, and we must endeavor to keep them so, till we can draw in the new Levies," he remarked. He scattered the men about the vicinity of Morristown, where they shivered in tents until they could construct their own rude log huts. These men had been poorly clad and ill fed for weeks, and now a harsh winter was upon them, prompting Washington to immediately tell Congress that his soldiers needed blankets, shirts, breeches, coats, caps, and "Shoes & Stockings particularly." They "are now absolutely perishing for want" of apparel, he added ominously. Food, however, was more plentiful. Washington dispatched forage parties that were "empower'd to collect all the Beef, Pork, Flour, Spirritous Liquors &c. &c. not necessary for the subsistence of the Inhabitants in all parts of East Jersey." Additional food was purchased by the quartermaster corps, or arrived from France and the Caribbean, and was stored in magazines scattered in Pennsylvania, from which it could be brought to Morristown as needed.[5]

Pressing as was the need for clothing, Washington faced another problem that was at least as serious. The new recruits who arrived in camp at the end of January brought with them a most unwelcome companion: smallpox. Variola, or smallpox, took the lives of roughly 10 percent of those between late adolescence and age thirty who contracted the disease. Those who survived were incapacitated for six weeks or longer. If an epidemic erupted within America's army, little could be done to cope with the redcoats for a dangerously long period.

Two means existed for defending against smallpox. One was quarantining the ill, a step made feasible because a victim was not contagious until the first smallpox sores erupted, about four days after flu-like symptoms had appeared The great drawback to isolation was that the initial symptoms did not surface until at least ten days following the contraction of the illness, a period in which many unknowing victims might flee the gathering outbreak, disseminating the disease over a wider area. Variolation, or inoculation, offered a second defense. The first experiments with vaccination had occurred in Constantinople three quarters of a century earlier and word of the practice quickly reached Europe. Inoculation involved the implantation of live variola in an incision in the hand or arm, after which smallpox ensued. The great advantage to inoculation—for reasons that remain unknown today—was that the resulting infection was less severe than from natural contraction, resulting in a lower fatality rate. As early as 1721, when an epidemic struck Boston, it was discovered that whereas 15 percent of those who naturally contracted smallpox perished, only 2 percent of those inoculated died. Nevertheless, many in early America feared that variolation could trigger an epidemic, and when the War of Independence began only the middle colonies—which included New Jersey—tolerated inoculation.

Dealing with smallpox was nothing new for Washington. Within four days of taking command in 1775 he learned that the disease had erupted in besieged Boston. He chose quarantine rather than inoculation, from fear that the British would attack if they learned that most of his men were disabled. Consequently, he ordered that civilians suspected of carrying smallpox be isolated in nearby Brookline, banned refugees from army camps, and sent soldiers with symptoms to a smallpox hospital in Cambridge. The crisis passed, but the scare was instructive. During the summer of 1776, Artemas Ward, who had been placed in command of the Continentals that remained in liberated Boston, had his men inoculated. Washington demurred, and was fortunate not to face a serious outbreak during the New York campaign. The American army that invaded Canada was not so lucky. It faced a devastating outbreak in the spring of 1776 that killed hundreds.[6]

Shortly after arriving at Morristown, Washington discovered not only that the troops who left the army in December had carried the disease home, the fear of smallpox in the army was hindering recruiting. He responded indecisively. He alternately told the army's physicians to "use every possible Means . . . to prevent the Disease from spreading in the Army," while confessing that he was "much at a loss what Step to take to prevent the spreading of the Smallpox." He also expressed reservations about inoculation, saying that it would surely lead to "a great part of our Army [being] laid down." His hand was eventually forced by the reality that "small pox has made such Head in every Quarter that I find it impossible to keep it from spreading thro' the whole Army." On February 5 he ordered the inoculation of "all the Troops now here, that have not had it," as well as the vaccination of all vulnerable enlistees before they reached the army. The practice persisted through the remaining winters of the war.[7] One soldier who was inoculated that year recalled being confined to a makeshift hospital that was, in reality, a farmer's thatch-roofed barn. His vaccination resulted in "a severe turn of the dysentery, and immediately after . . . I broke out all over with boils . . . each as big as half a hen's egg." But he survived, as did every man in his company.[8]

WHEN THE ARMY limped into Morristown, Washington had no intention of committing it to battle any time soon. Usually combative, he was absorbed with getting a new army ready for the spring campaign season, even advising in a rare moment of candor that "Victory . . . will be certain" if he could field a fresh army, as the enemy was in a distressed condition from its recent hard campaigning.[9]

What ensued in the ten weeks or so after the Continental army entered winter quarters was as surprising to Washington as it was to the leadership of the British army. Jersey militiamen, who had come alive in December to reclaim their occupied state, remained active, waging what Europe's professional soldiers called a *petite guerre*, what today would be variously called partisan or guerrilla warfare. The militia attacked provision trains and engaged in sabotage activities —they "cut the wheels" of grist mills used by the enemy, one British officer railed—but their primary prey was enemy forage parties.[10] While the British and Hessian soldiers who were posted in New Jersey were generally well provisioned, their horses were not. Armies at the time—and even as late as at the start of World War II—relied heavily on horses, and it was customary for the number of horses that accompanied an army to equal up to 25 percent of the number of soldiers. Horses drew artillery and baggage wagons, and furnished mounts for the cavalry. Oats were sent across the Atlantic for them, but not in sufficient quantities to see them through a year of service. To make up the shortfall, horses were pastured or large forage parties were sent to search for fodder, principally hay.[11]

Washington had not believed the Continentals capable of impeding the enemy's gathering of supplies. "Militia must be our dependance," he said, though he doubted that the New Jersey militia was up to the task. He quickly saw that he was wrong. Small parties of Jersey militia attacked British forage parties on three occasions while Washington's army was marching from Princeton to Morristown. Some regulars died or were captured in the attacks, and the foragers went home with precious little fodder. Those successes emboldened the militia, which began to turn out in larger numbers. In short order, the enemy was compelled to commit more men to cover and protect their foragers. By mid-winter the British never sent out fewer than five hundred men, and often up to two thousand men comprised a forage party.[12]

The militia excelled in these battles, as it had in the somewhat similar skirmishes that occurred on the day of Lexington and Concord. They attacked without warning, often laying down a deadly fire from behind fences or deep inside thick forests, then melting away if the adversary pursued. Sometimes only one or two regulars, chiefly the vulnerable rear guard, were cut down, but on occasion scores of regulars were killed, wounded, or captured, and now and then large numbers of horses, wagons, and baggage were seized. Invariably, it seemed, the enemy lost more men than the rebels in these skirmishes. Before January ended the inspired Jersey militia had begun to mount raids against Loyalist units and to harass civilian Tories. Though unsuccessful, two raids were even launched against Amboy, where a redcoat brigade was garrisoned.[13]

Taking note of the surprising success of the militia, Washington exulted at the "daily Skirmishes," and allowed that the already drained enemy "must be distressed greatly before the Winter is over." As his army slowly grew that winter, he used Continentals to augment the militia's efforts to beleaguer enemy foraging parties, at times producing skirmishes between several hundred men on each side.[14]

These harassing tactics were difficult enough to endure, but having to live in poor accommodations in a cold, damp foreign land—"we . . . have to stand under arms for hours in the deepest snow," a Hessian fumed—further eroded the spirits of the British and Germans. Their losses climbed to nearly a thousand in the first ninety days of 1777, and the strain brought on by frequent and dangerous foraging missions—duty that was characterized by one hardened Hessian officer as "very disagreeable"—sapped morale. What is more, among some redcoats opinions were changing about their adversary. Some who had dismissed the rebel soldiers as "contemptible" now praised them as "formidable." Gloom set in at British headquarters, as well. Not only had the army of occupation been withdrawn from the Delaware after Trenton, garrisons from central New Jersey, including those in Elizabethtown and Hackensack, were abandoned. The British were compelled to import supplies from Rhode Island, then ship them from neighboring New York to much of the army that remained in New Jersey. There was no other choice. Otherwise, a Hessian remarked darkly, "the army would have been gradually destroyed through this foraging."[15]

Washington had been pleasantly surprised by the dramatic effectiveness of the militia, though on the whole rebel militiamen in the War of Independence have been dogged by a negative image. Washington did as much as anyone to create that impression. While acknowledging their usefulness on the home front and, early in 1777, even lauding "the Important Services" they had "rendered their Country at this severe, & inclement season," Washington never wavered in his belief that militia were unreliable when summoned to the front to support the Continental army during a major campaign. That they "soon become tired and return Home . . . is but usual with them," he said. He characterized militiamen as habitually "dismayed [and] Intractable," as given to a "want of discipline [and] unwillingness, nay refusal to submit to that order and regularity essential in all Armies." In combat, he charged, they were prone to run "away in the greatest confusion without firing a Single Shot." While adding little by their presence, militiamen not only consumed incredible portions of the army's often scarce supply of food, they often walked off with the Continentals' precious equipment. "To place any dependance upon Militia is, assuredly resting upon a broken staff," he remarked in the fall of 1776, a view that never changed. He added: "The Dependence which the Congress has placed upon the Militia . . . I fear will totally ruin, our Cause."[16]

Most field grade and general officers in the Continental army shared Washington's views, and until recently so, too, did most historians, many of whom disparaged the militia system of that day as a colossal failure. Today, a more nuanced view prevails. As militiamen lacked the training and combat experience of Continental soldiers, most historians believe that Washington's harsh judgment was generally accurate. They were citizen-soldiers fresh from civilian pursuits, and at the company level the men served under officers who were inexperienced and often close acquaintances. In the New England militia companies, and in some others as well, it remained customary throughout the war for company-grade officers to be elected by the men. Perhaps because of these factors, the pre-Revolutionary militia had rarely been used in any colony to carry the brunt of fighting. Traditionally, they had been utilized as a home guard.[17] None of this meant that the militia was absolutely incapable of performing adequately when serving side-by-side with Continentals. Their performance hinged on numerous variables, but above all the militia's effectiveness hung on the quality and character of its leadership.

Washington never disputed that the militia had a vital role to play. Militia units had already played an indispensable part in launching the war. In one colony after another they had disarmed Loyalists, squelched Tory uprisings, enforced Congress's embargo of British trade, kept watch for slave insurrections, and taken possession of military stockpiles, keeping them from the hands of royal authorities. It was militiamen who fought the regulars at Lexington and Concord, and it was militiamen again who defended Bunker Hill. Their actions led historian Don Higginbotham, the scholar who has done the most to create a balanced view of the militia, to write that these civilian-soldiers were "exceedingly important" in what was "quite likely the most crucial period of the Revolution," the very beginning of hostilities.[18]

As THE WINTER OF 1776–1777 ran its course, General Howe had no reason for optimism. The army of 31,000 that he had assembled on Staten Island barely six months before had shrunk to just 14,000 fit for duty. Nearly 4,500 men had been killed, wounded, or captured. Great Britain could cope with such losses in a short war, but Howe now knew that he faced a protracted war. After his experiences in Boston and New Jersey, Howe also realized that the military occupation of America was problematical so long as the Continental army existed and militiamen were willing to fight. Something had to be done. The first sign of change came in March and April when the Howes authorized raids on Peekskill, New York, and Danbury, Connecticut, steps they had refused to countenance in 1776. Both villages sustained devastating damage, and the Continentals lost precious stores. The Danbury raid was particularly costly, with nearly four hundred casualties and the death of General Wooster, the third among the thirteen general officers that Congress had appointed beneath Washington in June 1775 to die in this war. In its wake General Howe, the most languid of commanders in 1776, assembled 18,000 men in New Jersey and in mid-June marched them from New Brunswick to Somerset. His objective was to lure Washington and his Continentals into battle.[19]

Washington had already emerged from winter quarters, having moved his army to Middlebrook, near Brunswick, just days before. Through the winter, the American commander had wondered whether he would ever have the strength to exit Morristown, or even to survive in that enclave. He endured sleepless nights over how he would cope should Howe launch a winter campaign. In mid-February, when the Delaware River froze and the roads firmed up, Washington expected his adversary to seize the opportunity and steal a march on Philadelphia. But to his "very great surprize," Howe did not move. At first, Washington attributed his foe's inaction to his "want of Horses" and ignorance "of our numbers and situation," but by April he was coming to the immeasurably harsh conclusion that perhaps Howe was "unfit for the trust reposed in him."[20]

By the first day of spring, the Continental army at Morristown had ploddingly grown to 2,543 men. Ten weeks later it had swelled to 8,188 men, tenfold the number that entered winter quarters and four times the number Washington had possessed when he started his retreat across New Jersey the previous fall. Getting the men had not been easy. As late as early April most states had raised only about a quarter to half of their assigned quotas. Atop the customary recruiting problems, two new ones had surfaced. Many men refused to enlist until bounties, driven they prayed by the laws of supply and demand, rose even higher. The existence of bounties also created a new phenomenon—"bounty-jumping." Some men enlisted and received a cash bounty, only to desert and enlist again elsewhere to collect another bounty. Some men did it again and again. Washington responded by offering pardons to deserters who returned. He ordered draconian punishments on those who did not come in. The culprits were tarred and feathered, flogged mercilessly, made to run the gauntlet, even sentenced to serve on an American frigate for the duration of the war.[21] Even these measures did not fully stop bounty jumping.

In mid-May, with the days warmer and the verdant countryside bursting toward spring's zenith, Washington emerged from Morristown. Augmented by militia, he had about 12,000 men. He advanced to Middlebrook, secured by the first range of the Watchung Mountains, a site from which the movements of the British army could be observed. His army had been waiting there for more than two weeks when, suddenly, Howe on June 14 marched his regulars to Somerset. Washington never suspected that his foe planned to drive on to Philadelphia, as Howe had left behind his heavy baggage. He surmised instead that Howe's activity was a ruse either to induce him to "draw off our troops" guarding the Hudson in the highlands or, more likely, to lure the Continentals in New Jersey into battle. The latter was precisely what Howe had in mind, but Washington did not take the bait. He adhered to his war of posts strategy, although when Howe began his retreat to the coast, Washington sent forward several brigades to strike at his rear. Howe wheeled about suddenly and attacked, hoping to cut off one or more of the American divisions. "[S]ome pretty smart skirmishing" ensued, but with "very little loss," said Washington, before the endangered Continental units extricated themselves from trouble. Following two weeks of futility in seeking to draw Washington into a full-scale engagement, Howe returned to New York. Washington presumed that the operation had been a "disappointment" to his foe, leaving him "much chagreen[ed]." Whatever Howe's reaction, many at British headquarters were mortified. Hearing a "great Firing . . . in the Jersies," they anticipated word of "an Action of Importance." Instead, they learned that Howe had again been involved in an "Action not so considerable." When the truth was known, Admiral Howe's secretary, Serle, confessed that he was "Much dejected in my Mind at the Appearance of Affairs. . . . All things seem at a Stand." Indeed, half the year was gone and the British had nothing to show for it.[22]

DURING THE LAST WEEK of April the ice on the St. Lawrence River at Quebec began to break up "with a most astonishing noise," according to an observer. Spring had come. A week later, just prior to Washington's emergence from winter quarters, General Burgoyne alighted from the *Apollo* at Quebec's docks, eager for his moment in the spotlight on his grandest stage. The first order of business that he faced—as if an augury of the unpleasantness to come—was the nasty chore of presenting General Carleton with Germain's letter stripping him of command of the invasion army. Germain's letter was filled with low blows (the most preposterous was an insulting imputation that Carleton's failure to take Ticonderoga in November had somehow permitted the debacle at Trenton), but Carleton, the better man of the two, immediately transferred authority to Burgoyne, and hurried to Montreal to assist with preparations for the invasion.[23]

Burgoyne also got down to business. The broad outlines of the plan of invasion had been put together in London late in the winter, and were based largely on Burgoyne's written suggestions and Germain's tinkering. Burgoyne was to leave 3,700 men with Carleton for the defense of Canada and to relinquish 675 regulars—of which 133 were green-coated provincials in the King's Royal Regiment of New York, or the Royal Yorkers as they were popularly known—to Colonel Barry St. Leger for the Mohawk Valley expedition that he had trumpeted. He was to have the rest, about 7,250 regulars, roughly 1,000 fewer men than he had wanted.[24] That was not his only disappointment. Burgoyne had crossed the Atlantic expecting to find upward of two thousand Canadians and Loyalists under arms. Instead, he got three hundred, some clad in smart new green jackets, brown waistcoats, and tan breeches, and sporting hats trimmed with red, green, or blue ribbons. They looked like soldiers, but Burgoyne held the same low opinion of them that Britain's officers had always harbored toward America's citizen-soldiers. The shortfall in Loyalist numbers was disconcerting, but not too alarming, as Burgoyne had been assured that New York teemed with Tories eager to serve in the king's army. He expected to raise three Loyalist battalions below Ticonderoga. Burgoyne had also wanted a thousand workmen, mostly sawyers and axmen for clearing roads and teamsters for driving the wagons that carried the army's provisions. To his dismay, Burgoyne found that virtually none had

General John Burgoyne. Painting by Sir Joshua Reynolds, 1776. A gambler and dramatist, Burgoyne's moment on the stage arrived in 1777. He failed, but only partly as a result of the mistakes that he made.

been recruited. He demanded that Carleton institute a corvée, the raising of forced labor. Carleton complied, but the desertion rate among the dragooned workers was so astounding that Burgoyne's army never came close to having the number of artisans for which he had hoped. Burgoyne was similarly frustrated with arrangements for hauling the copious baggage required by a sizeable army. He had expected 1,500 horses and 1,000 wagons. Instead, he obtained about a third the number of horses that he wanted and five hundred two-wheeled carts, each capable of carrying only about half the load of a conventional four wheel baggage wagon. The only shortfall that did not particularly trouble Burgoyne involved his Indian allies. He had expected one thousand Native American warriors to accompany him, but got less than half that number. Like most British officers, he recognized that Indians were indispensable as scouts, but otherwise Burgoyne thought them more trouble than they were worth, and outrageously expensive. Those with him, and with St. Leger as well, had been offered "Arms, pipehathets, Tomyhawks, Knives, Kettles, Vermillion, Indn Shoes, [and] Flints," and the chance to obtain still more plunder through victory. With some hyperbole, Burgoyne complained that it cost more to secure 1,000 Native American warriors than 20,000 regulars.[25]

Only the most shortsighted observer that chilly spring in Canada could have doubted that the coming invasion would be a stupendous undertaking that was studded with risks. Burgoyne knew that he faced imposing hurdles. His army was smaller even than the force that Howe had left to occupy New Jersey over the winter. His vital transport arm was not what it should have been, and he expected his enemies to make it impossible for him to acquire horses and wagons in New York. He knew that he was invading a region defended by Continentals and from where countless New England and New York militiamen could be raised. Against these drawbacks, Burgoyne believed that he had addressed, and satisfactorily resolved, his most formidable problems, including how to supply his army, which he thought would be his most daunting challenge. He had concocted a plan that called for establishing strategically placed magazines from Crown Point southward. Besides, in a pinch the men could forage, as they had always done. Had Burgoyne been aware of the army's recent troubling experience in attempting to supply itself in New Jersey, his outlook might have been different.

On the eve of the invasion, Burgoyne exuded optimism. There was little sickness in his army, something that one of the Germans attributed to the cold Canadian winter. It had "taken the place of the best physician," he remarked.[26] Burgoyne was confident that St Leger's Mohawk River Valley expedition would divert many of New York's militia units, and he believed that most of the Continentals in his path would be eliminated when he took Ticonderoga. While his adversary's numbers decreased, Burgoyne foresaw his army swelling as New York's Loyalists rushed forward to bear arms. Despite what he had seen at Bunker Hill, Burgoyne remained convinced that the rebels were no match for regulars. Above all, he anticipated that Howe, too, would be moving on Albany, as that had been the plan when he had sailed from England.[27] An addict of gaming, Burgoyne embarked on his greatest gamble, shutting his eyes to the disagreeable and embracing the fanciful, confident as only the compulsive gambler can be that fortune was on his side.

Burgoyne's army proceeded south in stages. An advance force of soldiers and woodsmen under Brigadier General Simon Fraser, a forty-eight-year-old Scot who had been wounded twice in the previous war, once while fighting in North America, set out late in May under a golden, strengthening sun to scout the region. It was followed within a few days by the left wing of the invasion force, commanded by Major General William Phillips, a corpulent and terrible-tempered artilleryman who had won laurels in the last war, and who had been Carleton's loudest critic in 1776. Phillips oversaw a huge artillery train of 138 guns. Burgoyne had no intention of repeating Abercrombie's horrid blunder of assaulting Fort Ticonderoga with small arms. The German wing, on the right, followed in its wake. These hired troops were commanded by Major General Friedrich Adolf Baron von Riedesel, a thirty-nine-year-old veteran with an enviable, and deserved, reputation for courage and coolness under fire. Burgoyne was nearly the last to sail, on June 13. On the eve of his departure from St. Johns, a courier arrived with a letter from Howe to Carleton. Dated April 2—the day that Burgoyne had left England—Howe indicated that the invasion army could expect "little assistance" from him. This was news to Burgoyne, but he blithely discounted its importance. Aware that the king believed "the force from Canada must join" the main British army at Albany, he was confident that Germain would order Howe north to complete the capture of the Hudson River.[28]

During the third week in June, the entire invasion army rendezvoused at Cumberland Point (now Plattsburgh, New York). With the curtain rising on the drama, Burgoyne seized the moment to deliver two speeches and issue a proclamation. Addressing his men who were about to put their lives on the line, Burgoyne swore off theatrics and simply tried to build their confidence.[29] In contrast, his written proclamation was bloated and strident. Aimed at the residents of New York and New England, he pledged "to strike where necessary, and . . . to save where possible." But he warned that if the rebels did not abandon "the Phrenzy of Hostility," his army would sow "Devastation, Famine, and every concomitant Horror."[30] His second speech was delivered to four hundred Indian allies gathered "in Congress" at the falls on the River Bouquet. His audience, scantily clad, adorned in various patterns of red, black, and green war paint, and—according to one regular—looking "uncivilized and . . . fierce as Satan," listened first to Burgoyne, who spoke in French, then to translators. Swept away by the intoxicating approach of battle, the general succumbed not only to his theatrical nature but to his baser instincts. "Warriors, you are free—go forth and . . . strike at the common enemies of Great Britain and America, disturber of public order, peace and happiness." The frenzied braves responded "Etow! Etow!" (Yes! Yes!). Sensing that he was unleashing unspeakable horrors with his unguarded remarks, Burgoyne caught himself. "I positively forbid bloodshed, when you are not opposed in arms," he said, adding that he countenanced scalping only those who were already dead. If Burgoyne did not know that the restraint he urged would go unheeded, he got a hint when a sachem responded that his warriors "had sharpened their affections upon their hatchets" and the braves broke into a war dance. Without much conviction, one of the Germans noted in his journal that day that he hoped "All the Savages" would "follow the noble sentiments of the Royal troops."[31]

Burgoyne's proclamation quickly found its way into American and English newspapers, as did portions of the speech to the Indians. His theatrics inspired laughter in London and led to a new nickname for Gentleman Johnny— "General Swagger." The response in America was different. His speech and proclamation resounded like claps of thunder. A torrid anger and boundless fury swelled in New York and New England, particularly at Burgoyne's willingness to turn loose the previously neutral Indians. The outrage was spectacularly stoked by an often-reprinted poem—written anonymously by Francis Hopkinson, a member of Congress—that purported to flesh out Burgoyne's bloodcurdling speeches, with, among other passages, the following:

> *I will let loose the dogs of Hell*
> *Ten Thousand Indians, who shall Yell*
> *And foam and tear, and grin and roar,*
> *And drench their mocassins in gore . . .*
> *I swear by George and St. Paul,*
> *I will exterminate you all.*[32]

Major General Arthur St. Clair arrived at Fort Ticonderoga to assume command only hours before Burgoyne sailed from St. Johns. Tall and handsome, St. Clair (pronounced Sinclair) was a forty-year-old Scotsman who had come to America as a subaltern in the British army during the French and Indian War, and had fought at Quebec, where his commander had been William Howe. Later, he married a wealthy woman from Boston, left the army, and remained in the colonies, moving to the Pennsylvania backcountry. When this war erupted, he served first in the militia, then in the Continental army, fighting in Canada and at Trenton and Princeton.

Fort Ticonderoga sat at the gateway connecting upper and lower Lake Champlain, and above a gorge through which Lake George emptied into Lake Champlain. The fort itself, consisting of barracks, blockhouses, breastworks, and small redoubts, was situated on a promontory that rose about seventy feet above the water. It, in turn, was connected by a quarter mile long pontoon bridge to a tall and rugged bluff—recently christened Mount Independence—on the east side of the lake. Entrenchments extending nearly two thousand yards had been dug into that fifty-foot-tall rise, and a redoubt had been constructed at its summit. Two miles northwest of the fort, rising like a cone and commanding the road to Lake George, stood Mount Hope. Only a rebel barbette battery—which is elevated to fire above the crest of a parapet, and consequently has a wider range of fire—guarded that summit. A mile to the southwest loomed Mount Defiance, an unguarded promontory that rose some 750 feet above the fort and the lakes. Although Fort Ticonderoga enjoyed a widespread reputation of mythic impregnability, and some even referred to it as America's Gibraltar, St. Clair quickly saw that the installation was not in good condition, something noted a year earlier by the congressional team sent north to learn the reasons for the Canadian debacle. The British had permitted the facility to decay, and from a dearth of time, men, and money, the United States had done little to rehabilitate it. St. Clair was troubled by Ticonderoga's woebegone state and doubly so in as much as Mount Defiance, towering over the fort within firing range, was undefended. Gates and Anthony Wayne, his predecessors, had known that, of course, but both had doubted that the British could ever drag their artillery to the summit of such a steep hill. St. Clair was not so sure. Worse still, he knew that he could not withstand a siege. He possessed only a thirty-nine day supply of food and merely 2,500 poorly equipped men were with him.33

St. Clair was a newcomer. It was General Schuyler who had exercised responsibility for Ticonderoga since the creation of the Northern Department two years before. Schuyler had almost been disappointed when Carleton elected not to attack Ticonderoga in November, as he believed that the enemy surely would have failed. But he expected the British to come back, and after Washington pulled away Gates and most of his men to help him in New Jersey, Schuyler was filled with foreboding that the British would attack when the lake froze. When that did not happen, he advised that the British, probably in April, would attempt an invasion from Canada. He predicted a Mohawk River Valley diversion as well.

A tireless administrator, Schuyler's strengths were those that one might hope for today from a capable middle manager, and some at the time believed that he held a rank one or two notches above the level that he should have attained. That winter Schuyler worked diligently to secure men and supplies not just for Ticonderoga, but for the several posts and magazines along the Lake George and Lake Champlain corridors, and for Fort Stanwix (or Fort Schuyler, as it had been renamed) on the Mohawk River. He oversaw a system that utilized nearly fifty bateaux and more than one hundred wagons to funnel supplies from Albany to Ticonderoga, an arduous trek that required seven transshipments of goods from boats to wagons.34 Aware too that some Iroquois and Mohawks were agitating to end the Six Nations' neutrality, Schuyler devoted many hours to finding gifts for the tribes and in establishing fair prices for their trade commodities, though he also promised retribution should the tribes choose to side with the British. His initiatives with the Indians were largely successful, though he had not—and could not have—kept all the Mohawks in line. On the other hand, Schuyler came up nearly empty-handed with regard to his other preparedness steps, though it would be unfair to lay all, or even much, of the blame on him. For instance, Congress had urged New Hampshire, Massachusetts, and Connecticut to furnish 4,500 men and twenty field pieces for Ticonderoga. None of the states had fully complied. Congress' orders to the commissary general to lay in an eight-month supply of food at both Fort Anne (on Wood Creek) and Albany had not been carried out. Nor had much progress been made in overhauling Fort Ticonderoga's defenses. Schuyler had especially wished to improve defenses on the southeast side of the fort, which the British would have to control in order to conduct a successful siege, and to construct a large log boom—a formidable obstacle held together by heavy iron chains—to hamper the enemy flotilla. By late June 1776 none of his preparations had been completed.35

Many of the failings were due to manpower shortages, chronic illness that sapped the available labor pool, and weather-related delays. But at bottom much of the problem stemmed from a lack of revenue, which arose in part from the near fatal degree of political decentralization that existed. The colonies had brought the Continental Congress into being eight months before the war erupted, but they had never relinquished their sovereignty. (The Declaration of Independence proclaimed the colonies to be "free and independent states" having "full power . . . to do all . . . things which independent states may do.") Thus, Congress could request actions by the states, but it had no means of making them comply. Nor was Congress inclined to push very hard. After all, the American rebellion was a protest against a far-away imperial government that had sought to strip the colonies of much their autonomy. State officials doubtless wished to do the right thing, but many saw Congress as a threat to state powers while others were myopically preoccupied by local concerns. Virtually all found it difficult to ask the citizenry (whose tax burden had skyrocketed since the war began) to accept still another tax hike. The shortcomings of the political system were exacerbated by problems arising from America's primitive economic state. In this era before large corporations had come into being, small businesses produced iron and lumber, flour and tools, and the myriad other items that an army required. Those who were situated near an army with its insatiable appetite for the commodity they produced could seldom resist the temptation to charge exorbitant prices. New York's revolutionary government contemplated laws that would set prices or allow the seizure of supplies, but it shrank from taking steps that would rankle thousands of farmers and artisans, and raise divisive concerns about the safety of private property.[36] Many farmers and businessmen flourished through war profiteering, while the army, and its soldiery, often suffered.

Washington also contributed to the 1777 crisis in the Northern Department. Believing from the outset that Philadelphia would be Britain's primary objective in 1777, he was convinced that Howe "will bring round all the Troops from Canada, to reinforce" him in the New Jersey–Pennsylvania theater. Even if he was wrong about the army being transferred from Canada, Washington was convinced that the Canadian army would "dare not Attempt to penetrate" New York unless Howe brought his army north to assist. In either case, men posted for the defense of Albany would be "a useless Body of Troops" while the fight for Philadelphia raged. He took as many of those troops as he could get his hands on, arguing that the Northern Department was safe so long as Howe was "held in Bay, curbed & confined" in his campaign to take Philadelphia.[37]

By March, Schuyler had begun to suspect that a disaster was in the making and that he would be the one to take the fall. Two years into the war, he had many foes. His problems were deeply rooted, and some at least were of his own making. Not a few congressmen were rankled by his failure to take the field with his army. To many, he appeared to be affixed to Albany, his home and headquarters. In 1775, he had never gone further north than St. Johns, and he had lingered there for barely twenty-four hours. Schuyler further harmed himself with his injudicious remarks about Connecticut's soldiers during the failed invasion of Canada, and in 1776 he had roused the ire of New Englanders by relinquishing Crown Point. New England officers at that installation had responded with a remonstrance declaring that the abandonment of the post opened the door to a British invasion of their states. Had Schuyler possessed a scintilla of political savvy, he would have gone to New England—which furnished much of his manpower—to mend fences, but he never stepped foot in the region. In addition to his own missteps, there were ideological overtones to New England's antipathy toward Schuyler. Haughty, aristocratic, and socially conservative, he and his kind were viewed as barriers to the new, more egalitarian, world that Thomas Paine had promised, a republican world that offered enhanced opportunities for social and economic ascendancy.[38]

On top of everything else, Schuyler could feel the hot breath of General Gates on his neck. In June 1776, after Sullivan was recalled, Congress had put Gates in charge in Canada. But before he could take command, the American army had retreated back into New York. Undeterred, Gates insisted that Congress had meant for him to command the army in New York and Canada, and that he was not subordinate to Schuyler. At Schuyler's behest, Congress clarified matters that summer: Schuyler remained in command of the Northern Department, while Gates, under Schuyler's jurisdiction, was made responsible for Ticonderoga. Gates remained at that post until Washington ordered him and most of his army to the Delaware River late in 1776. Many of Gatess' men fought at Trenton and Princeton, but Gates himself had not lingered for the campaign. Wan and exhausted from a lingering battle with dysentery, he thought he must get away from the front in order to recuperate. Congress had just fled to Baltimore from beleaguered Philadelphia and, not coincidentally, Gates chose Baltimore as his site for rest and relaxation. He did as much politicking as recuperating that winter. Ambitious and prideful, Gates, a former British regular, must have chafed at taking orders from many of America's amateur generals. He lusted as well for an independent command. That alone, he must have reasoned, offered hope for glory, and fame in turn would provide his the best chance for securing a lofty position in his adopted land in the postwar years. Highly political and aggressive, Gates feverishly intrigued that winter with some of New England's congressmen, including John and Samuel Adams, for Schuyler's removal and his own elevation to head the Northern Department. Gates's reach exceeded his grasp, but he did succeed in being named to command the army in upper New York. Schuyler's authority appeared to be sharply undercut.[39]

Schuyler responded by threatening to resign. John Hancock, the president of Congress, convinced him not to quit the army, although intriguingly Washington—who was without peer at divining the character and talents of those about him—made no effort to dissuade him. "You are the best judge," he said coldly, when he learned of Schuyler's bluster about leaving the army. Washington offered not a single positive word about his prior service.[40] He appeared to have lost confidence in Schuyler and probably hoped for Gates's appointment as his successor, although Greene unblushingly declared that he could "plainly see" that Washington "wants me to go but is unwilling to part with me."[41] Whomever he desired, Washington held to his habit of remaining aloof from the political minefield of promotions and appointments. Schuyler, who had never resigned his seat in Congress, hurried to Philadelphia (where Congress had returned) to seek to undo Gates's handiwork. Despite the looming threat of a British invasion, Schuyler remained at his seat in Congress for ten weeks, and he secured much that he wanted, especially Congress's reaffirmation that he was the commander in the Northern Department. He finally returned to Albany on June 3. Twenty days later a patrol sent out by St. Clair at Ticonderoga spotted Burgoyne's invasion armada.[42]

TIME HAD RUN OUT FOR ST. CLAIR. Nothing more could be done to obtain reinforcements or to complete the defensive preparations at Ticonderoga that should long since have been made. If Burgoyne made good use of time, quickly destroying the rebel army at Ticonderoga and not dragging his feet in moving south, he might take Albany before the enemy could raise a massive force against him.

Congress, like Washington, had anticipated that the enemy would send its Canadian army to help Howe take Philadelphia, and it told St. Clair that any British force that appeared at Ticonderoga would likely be diversionary. Schuyler had come to the same conclusion, and he still clung to that notion when he made a rare visit to Ticonderoga on June 20, eight days after St. Clair's arrival. Schuyler had known for weeks that a force was gathering in Canada, and he knew that in the near future a British force of unknown size would arrive at Ticonderoga. He summoned a council of war to determine how best to deal with whatever size force arrived. Virtually everyone who attended agreed that Fort Ticonderoga was in wretched shape and that there were too few troops to defend both it and Mount Independence. It was agreed to withdraw from Ticonderoga when the British appeared, but to attempt to hold out on Mount Independence for as long as possible, delaying the British advance. No one thought it likely that the garrison could withstand a lengthy siege, if for no other reason than it would be difficult to get water to those on Mount Independence.[43]

By late June, St. Clair possessed remarkably accurate intelligence about the size of Burgoyne's army and he knew that he faced more than a British diversion. Reinforcements came into Ticonderoga, but in a trickle, not a stream. Ultimately, St. Clair possessed 3,800 men, of whom nearly a quarter were unfit for duty, leaving him with a fighting force about one-third the size of his adversary. St. Clair had roughly eight thousand fewer men than Gates had commanded when Carleton called in October 1776, and nearly six thousand fewer men than Schuyler had earlier said was necessary for defending the post against a formidable adversary. St. Clair had counted on obtaining roughly two thousand men from Peekskill, a promise that Washington had made to Schuyler in the event of an emergency, but in the end the commander in chief took those men for himself.[44] St. Clair had also hoped for legions of militiamen, but when he discovered the small supply of food that had been laid in at Ticonderoga, he had not pleaded for them.[45] St. Clair did not have long to wait before the hopelessness of his situation became apparent. Burgoyne easily took Mount Hope on July 2, forty-eight hours after his arrival. That closed all possibility of a rebel escape via Lake George. The following day Hessians moved on St. Clair's right flank at Mount Independence, threatening to cut off his lane of retreat south toward Woods Creek. On July 4 the British succeeded in getting artillery to the top of Mount Defiance, the feat that Gates and Wayne had thought impossible. St. Clair immediately summoned a council of war. Its options were stark: stay, gain a few meaningless days, and lose the entire army; or, flee and hope to fight another day. The council quickly, and unanimously, agreed that retreat was the best choice. St. Clair accepted its recommendation, knowing that more than likely he would be censured for abandoning what many believed was an unconquerable post. (He told an aide at the time: "if I evacuate the place, my character will be ruined; if I remain here, the army will be lost.")[46] He ordered the withdrawal to begin in the wee hours of the morning, when the landscape, under a new moon, would be shrouded in sooty darkness.

Colonel Pierce Long, a forty-eight-year-old former assemblyman in New Hampshire, was given what remained of Arnold's navy and nearly two hundred bateaux to transport all but a few field pieces, the precious stores, and the sick as far as Fort Anne. The healthy were to march with St. Clair. The artillery that was to be abandoned opened up on the enemy around midnight and continued through the night, in a desperate effort to hide the on-going flight. Dawn was just breaking when the last American came off Mount Independence.[47] They left behind more than fifty field pieces, "extraordinarily large supplies of ammunition," muskets, tents, rice, coffee, sugar, and even "a new flag," said one flabbergasted Hessian. What was even more incredible, said the German, the Americans had left almost everything inside Ticonderoga intact, from barracks and weapons, to bakeries and breweries.[48]

The rebels were fortunate to escape Mount Independence. Hessians on St. Clair's right had earlier reached the foot bridge that led to the road south, but they not only left that span intact, during the night they had been inexplicably pulled out of that sector. In the first ruddy light of dawn, Burgoyne saw that he was the latest in a succession of British generals to have permitted a seemingly trapped enemy army to escape. He immediately ordered a pursuit. Fraser moved out with a battalion of grenadiers, the storm troops of the British army; another of light infantry, elite troops famed for their daring and endurance; and two companies of regular infantry. Later, Burgoyne sent a support force of Hessian jägers (riflemen) and infantry under General Riedesel. The Americans had a two-hour head start, but their pursuers had a bit of good fortune. Once the rebels exited Mount Independence, they had tried, but failed, to burn the bridge leading off hill.[49] Fraser pushed his men at a grueling pace, but St. Clair, knowing the enemy would come after him, drove his men as well. It was a hard day for everyone, but worse for the British and Germans. This July day was hot and still, and these men, who were hardly acclimated to an American summer, were outfitted in wool uniforms. Adding to their woes, the men had been up all night and, as a young British officer complained, were "without any sort of provisions" throughout the long day.[50] The sun was low in the sky when St. Clair's exhausted men reached Hubbardton, twenty-four miles from Mount Independence, but he ordered most to press on to Castle Town, six miles further away. He left 150 Green Mountain Boys under Seth Warner in Hubbardton and posted two militia regiments at Ransomvale, about a third of the way between the two divisions of his army. Warner's orders were to wait for the rear elements of the American army—the men who had remained on Mount Independence throughout the nighttime retreat—and to link up with St. Clair by sunrise the next day. Warner was experienced in this sort of thing, having protected those retreating at Bunker Hill.[51]

Three regiments drifted into Hubbardton during that black night, but once they were there Warner ignored the order to join St. Clair. Why he did so is a mystery. He was prone to march to his own beat, but in this instance it may have been that the last of the rebels to arrive from Mount Independence were so bone-tired that he believed them unable to take another step before sunrise. Given his head start, Warner may also have been lulled into a sense of false security, a conclusion pointed to by his failure to post sentries. Whatever the reason, Warner blundered egregiously.

Fraser had managed to keep pace with his prey during the previous day's difficult march. Riedesel's Germans, who were frequently criticized by the British for their alleged languor, had made even better time, catching up with Fraser around sunset. The next morning Fraser set out at 3:00 a.m., taking his men and a few select German units noted for their ability to move with considerable speed. Riedesel would start later. After a two-hour march the British force ran up on the American camp at Hubbardton. Fraser had 850 men, but had no idea how many men were with Warner. He guessed that his foe might have up to two thousand, overestimating his enemy by half. Fraser opted to attack anyway, hoping to catch his foe off guard and gambling that the element of surprise would shift the odds in his favor.

Fearing that Warner would be alerted to his presence, Fraser had not reconnoitered. He was attacking blindly, unaware of how the rebels were deployed and uncertain of the topography. His men immediately ran into trouble. Whatever other errors Warner had made, he had at least put his men on high ground and behind stone walls and cordons of felled trees. Even before the Americans could form their lines, the attackers had lost heavily and were in danger of having their right flank turned. Fraser sent word to Riedesel to come at once. The attackers had "mounted the hill" into "showers of balls mingled with buck shot, which they plentifully bestowed among us," exclaimed a young grenadier.[52] As the leaders on both sides gained control and sized up the situation, the engagement turned into a three-hour slugfest in which neither force gained the upper hand. The British were more experienced, but the Americans enjoyed favorable terrain and made good use of every conceivable screen when forced to retreat. Though a small engagement, it was one of this war's most ferocious fights, with total losses proportionally equal to those of the Battle of Waterloo. The Americans had come close to dealing the adversary a sharp repulse. Had St. Clair not advanced so far beyond his rear guard, he might have joined with Warner and overwhelmed his foe. The rebels were betrayed, too, by the militia regiments posted at Ransomvale. They ignored St. Clair's commands to advance and join the fray. Fraser, on the other hand, might have scored a decisive victory had his Indian allies accompanied him, but they opted out in favor of plundering at Ticonderoga. Fraser did get relief, however, when Riedesel's reinforcements at last arrived, and the sound of their approach—their martial band was heard before they were seen—signaled the beginning of the end.

Once the Germans were plugged into the British line, Fraser and Riedesel ordered a bayonet charge. Americans who were well entrenched had a good record of standing firm against an advancing adversary, but on numerous occasions in this war they blinked in the face of gleaming steel bayonets. On this day, unnerved first by the arrival of fresh enemy troops, then by the sight of the bayonets, they took flight. The British had won the Battle of Hubbardton. The field was theirs. But their losses were heavy—nearly 200 killed and wounded (the Americans had lost 330 men, nearly two-thirds of whom were taken prisoner). Beaten up, needing to care for their wounded and prisoners, and fearful of running into a massive counterattack by St. Clair, neither Fraser nor Riedesel gave any thought to a further pursuit of the fleeing, disorganized Americans. This tough little fight was significant. It stopped the British pursuit and allowed St. Clair to make his getaway to the east, away from the environs of Lake Champlain, over tall hills and through thick forests to Manchester (in what would subsequently become Vermont), where he was eventually reunited with the survivors of Hubbardton.[53]

Colonel Long, with the army's supplies and its invalids, was also running for his life. British artillerymen had required only thirty minutes to blast apart the uncompleted boom that the Americans had sought to construct, enabling Burgoyne's flotilla to sail up the lake. Burgoyne hoped to overtake Long's fleet or to land men who might cut off the rebel's access to Fort Anne. Long made his escape, thanks largely to a twelve-hour head start. He also left a wake of devastation in his path. He burned what he could at Skenesborough when the British closed in, and repeated the process at Fort Anne, finally falling back to Fort Edward, sixteen miles further south. On the final leg of his retreat Long left felled trees across the road behind him, obstacles that "cost the Army much labour and time" to clear the way, a German noted with despair.[54] Long reached the safety of Fort Edward, but he arrived virtually empty handed. All the provisions that had been rescued from Ticonderoga—meat, flour, salt, and rum—had been abandoned and had fallen into the hands of the enemy, as had more than twenty field pieces and two score barrels of powder, together with more than three thousand shot and shells. Altogether—at Ticonderora, Hubbardton, and along the path of Long's flight—the British had captured 128 artillery pieces.[55]

In the space of two weeks, Burgoyne had taken Crown Point, Ticonderoga, and Fort Anne, stripped his foe of precious supplies, scattered the American army in the Northern Department, leaving it in tatters, and was running his own supplies up Lake Champlain from Ticonderoga. He was just seventy-five miles from Albany and it was not at all clear whether the Americans could reconstitute their army in time to stop him. Burgoyne was heady with optimism. George III was even more ecstatic when word of Burgoyne's opening triumphs reached London. He purportedly burst into the queen's boudoir and exalted: "I have beat them! I have beat all the Americans!"[56]

Schuyler was at Albany, about ninety miles from Ticonderoga, when he learned on July 7 that the installation had been abandoned without a fight. The news activated him. That same day he rode forty-five miles on horseback to Fort Edward. During stops to water and oat his horse, Schuyler wrote Washington and various civil authorities for help. He justly painted a dark picture: the "prospect of preventing them from penetrating [to Albany] is not much. . . . Our Army, if it should once more collect [itself] is weak in Numbers, dispirited, naked . . . destitute of provisions . . . with little Ammunition, and not a single piece of Cannon. . . . [T]he Continental Troops have lost every Thing." Chillingly, Schuyler had no idea where St. Clair had gone or whether his army was intact. He knew only that he had about 700 Continentals and perhaps 1,500 militia with which to oppose a large enemy army that was "flushed with Victory" and "plentifully provided."[57]

Help was on the way. Three days before Ticonderoga fell, Washington had ordered a six-hundred-man brigade under General John Nixon to march northward from Peekskill. After hearing from Schuyler, he also sent Colonel Glover with 1,300 men. Seth Warner arrived next with eight hundred Green Mountain Boys and, on July 12, St. Clair finally reached Fort Edward. He had 1,500 of the roughly 2,800 men that had been with him at the outset of his retreat. Within eleven days of dispatching his urgent appeals, Schuyler's force had grown to 6,359, but he remained uneasy. Nearly a quarter of the men were militiamen who, "being extremely uneasy at being detained here in the very Time of Harvest," were deserting in droves, he said. Another quarter of the men were ill and unfit for duty. Many of Nixon's Massachusetts men "are Negroes and many of them young small and feeble boys," he added disparagingly.[58]

Through it all, Schuyler was a whirling dervish of activity. Always gifted at finding supplies, he diligently searched for replacements for what had been lost at Ticonderoga, especially the tools, and got the equipment out of Fort George before it had to be relinquished. Schuyler put his soldiers to work felling trees across roads, destroying bridges (more than forty were laid waste), constructing interlaced timber barriers (they were so intricate that British army engineers had to be called in to dismantle them), driving away livestock and burning crops, damming Wood Creek so that it would be too shallow for the use of bateaux, plugging up other streams in order to create bogs where roads had once been, and harassing Burgoyne's work parties. His object was to retard Burgoyne's progress, buying time during which he might restock his army, but also to add to his enemy's logistical woes.[59] For the moment, Schuyler had chosen "to let the forest fight for him," as Washington had once advised.[60] Time was everything. "If the Enemy will permit us to pass unmolested" a few days longer, Schuyler said that July, there might be sufficient time to regroup and stop his advance.[61] The regrouping took place at Stillwater, to which he finally withdrew, falling back in stages from Fort George, Fort Edward, Moses Kill, and Saratoga. By retreating, Schuyler had postponed the inevitable clash with Burgoyne for as long as possible.

Many times in this war a decisive victory was seemingly within reach of the British, only to slip away for one reason or another. During the second week in July, Burgoyne stared at a possible opportunity for a dazzling triumph. In the space of seven days he had taken Ticonderoga and advanced thirty-six miles below it. Although Albany was more than fifty miles away, Burgoyne knew that the rebels, in flight in two separate directions, had lost vast quantities of precious supplies. He could have attempted a hurried drive toward Albany. Some at the time, including Gates, thought that had Burgoyne acted with alacrity, he would have concluded his campaign triumphantly in July. Resolute action had been the crux of his previous successes as a commander, and it was what he had offered when he lobbied in London for an independent command. But now Burgoyne, taking a page from Howe, went nowhere for three long weeks that month, and it took him three additional weeks to get as far as Saratoga, some thirty miles above Albany.

Burgoyne might have sent Fraser forward with a large contingent of light infantry. Unimpeded by cumbrous artillery and baggage trains, light infantry forces were adept at living off the land and moving rapidly. Unopposed, as the British were for a spell in July, they might have moved with lightening speed. But Burgoyne, who was famed as an innovator, chose to conduct his campaign in the most orthodox manner. He paused at Skenesboro to wait for supplies, and especially for his huge artillery train, before moving south. He remained committed to proceeding with artillery, though that would slow his progress immeasurably. To "convey artillery . . . would be attended with difficulties," he had written in his invasion plan back in February, but field guns would be "worthy" against callow soldiers dedicated to entrenching, and they would be useful for blowing away the "obvious impediments" that the rebels would use "to block up the road." Burgoyne additionally anticipated finding that the rebel installations would be nearly inviolable against any army without an artillery arm.[62] He ordered that fifty-two field pieces be brought south, together with tons of powder, shells, and shot, all to be conveyed by hundreds of horses and fifty teams of oxen. Deep in the enemy's lair, and about to go deeper, and enveloped by an inhospitable environment that on occasions in the past had eroded many of the customary advantages that Europe's regular soldiers and armies had enjoyed, Burgoyne the risk-taker became Burgoyne the cautious. In the plan that he drafted while in London, Burgoyne had allowed that victory could be had by "an officer of a sanguine temper" given to "timely" action, by which he apparently meant someone who was the diametric opposite of a Gage, Howe, or Carleton. Burgoyne now acted like those other British generals. He paused, and in doing so he gave his enemy the reprieve for which Schuyler had prayed.[63]

Burgoyne made another crucial decision at this juncture. All along, he had envisaged moving his men and equipment up Lake George, then making a short and fairly easy march to Fort Edward. Once at Skenesboro, he opted for the Lake Champlain–South Bay–Wood Creek route to Fort Edward, though it was nearly one-third longer and certain to be rife with every adversity that his enemy could devise for him. (In his February plan for the invasion, Burgoyne had written that "considerable difficulties may be expected" along this route, "as the narrow parts of the river may be easily choked up" and "there will be necessity for a great deal of land-carriage.")[64] His choice stemmed from concern that to retreat to Ticonderoga, in order to alight on Lake George, would add two weeks to the length of the campaign, and he feared that a retrograde movement might prove harmful to morale.[65] But choosing the Lake Champlain route meant taking a longer road that had to be cleared before his artillery train and baggage wagons could be moved.

Burgoyne set his men to work, though removing the obstructions that the rebels had made for him and building bridges (and at one point the redcoats constructed a two-mile-long causeway) proceeded at a snail's pace. The army advanced about one mile each day. Burgoyne convinced himself that his time-consuming advance might be for the best. Howe was not coming north anytime soon. Help might be more readily available in August than in July, in September than in August.

The additional time that Burgoyne bestowed on Schulyer was both a friend and foe. Schuyler needed time in order to regroup for the looming showdown with Burgoyne. On the other hand, the extra time gave his many political enemies the opportunity to coalesce and push for his removal. Officials everywhere had been shocked at learning of the loss of Ticonderoga—Washington called it "altogether unaccountable"—and while the decision had been St. Clair's, it was the latest in a string of disasters that had occurred in Schuyler's department. For many it was the final straw.[66] Samuel Adams raged that the debacle was what he had come to expect from Schuyler. He added: "It is indeed droll . . . to see a General not knowing where to find the main Body of his Army. Gates is the Man of my choice. He . . . has the Art of *gaining the love of his Soldiers.*" John Adams said that with Schuyler in charge he had "expected this Catastrophe."[67] New England had long been the epicenter of anti-Schuyler sentiment in Congress, but several congressmen from the mid-Atlantic states, convinced of his daunting insufficiencies, now joined in to demand his ouster. The crux of their case was that not only New Englanders, but now northerners in general would refuse to serve under Schuyler. The popular perception was that he lacked the ability to "retrieve our affairs in that Quarter." Gates, on the other hand, emanated vigor and had "shewn what he can do" when he "Collected [the] shattered remains of [the American] army last year under every disadvantg. Reduced it to order. Repulsed the enemy."[68] The New York delegation and many southerners stood with Schuyler, but for some it was only from fear that his dismissal would set off a political earthquake in New York. Schuyler's support in New York eroded late in July as the desertion rate escalated. No one thought he could find militia replacements in New England. (Schuyler himself acknowledged, "the Spirit of Malevolence" toward him "knows no Bounds" in New England.) Before the month ended, the New York Council of Safety admitted that many New Yorkers were "disgusted" by Schuyler's record. In this climate, Schuyler's foes in Congress secured a vote for an inquiry and packed the investigating panel with his enemies. On August 4, Congress voted to recall St. Clair and to replace Schuyler with Gates. The vote was by an eleven-to-one margin.[69]

DECISIVE EVENTS occurred during the fifteen days between Congress's appointment of Gates and his arrival in Albany on August 19 to relieve Schuyler of command. At the end of July, three weeks after reaching Skenesboro, Burgoyne at last moved his army to Fort Edward. Clearing road and stream, amid seemingly incessant rainstorms and in the airless, humid forest, was grueling work. Nor was the army's actual move a bed of roses. The road rapidly turned into one long glutinous mud hole that nearly swallowed whole the horses and wagons. That difficulty was exacerbated by Burgoyne's decision to have permitted what must have seemed to be half the population of Canada to accompany the army. Wives, girlfriends, and mistresses, together with their copious wardrobes, came along, as did children, pets, and sutlers with goods to sell to those with cash. Nor had Burgoyne neglected his own needs. He commandeered thirty wagons to convey his personal creature comforts. This army's baggage train stretched over the horizon. It might have been worse. Burgoyne had to leave behind 1,400 men to garrison Ticonderoga and the other posts that were his lifeline to Canada. But knowing that he would eventually need these men in the fighting that lay ahead, he appealed to Carleton for reinforcements. None ever arrived.[70]

Burgoyne's troubles grew exponentially when, three days before his army occupied Fort Edward, his Indian allies brought to camp the scalp of a young woman named Jane McCrae. She had lived in the area and was engaged to a Loyalist officer serving with Burgoyne's army. She was one of eleven luckless frontier inhabitants who had been killed by the Indians on that day, but her death "caused quite an uproar in the army," a German remarked. That same outraged Hessian fumed that the "Savages" resembled "a tiger that is only moved by blood and prey."[71] Burgoyne, who already believed that the Indians were next to useless as an ally, as they had to be treated with "all the caprices and humours of spoiled children," reacted with horror to McCrae's death. He was disgusted by its hideousness. He was also fearful that the atrocity would inflame the residents of the frontier. Hoping to mitigate the outrage of frontiersmen, he sought to have the murderer executed for his crime, but the Indians would not hear of such a thing. Burgoyne backed off, and simply worked more diligently to control his allies. But the abomination could not be undone. Within days the story of Jane McCrae's killing was in New York and New England newspapers, where it was often luridly embellished. A Boston newspaper reported that she was one of sixty women and children who allegedly had been murdered in the course of the Indians' reign of terror, while a New Hampshire newspaper provided gruesome details of the Indians' murder of two children who had been sent by their parents to pick berries. Gates proved to be an even better propagandist. After taking command, he drafted for publication a letter portraying Burgoyne as a terrorist who was ultimately responsible for the death of "Miss McCrae, a young lady lovely to the sight, of virtuous character, and amiable disposition" who had been "scalped, and mangled in a most shocking manner."[72] By mid-August Burgoyne's worst fears were realized. Frontiersmen were arming and rushing to the defense of their homes and loved ones.

The British army spent ten days at Fort Edward gathering supplies and loading them onto bateaux. While there, Burgoyne negotiated with his Indians, who were disappointed with the restraints imposed on their conduct and threatening to go home. He mollified them with liquor, but declined to sanction their "cruelties against the enemy." He tried, he said later, to impress on them the standards of "European humanity."[73] On August 3 he heard again from Howe, this time in a letter written two weeks earlier. With unmistakable clarity, Howe let Burgoyne know that he was on his own.[74] This was Burgoyne's opportunity—his last good chance, it turned out—to scuttle his campaign. But he plunged on, starting his army south once again during the second week in August. It was one of several crucial decisions that he made at this juncture of the campaign. Burgoyne had always known that to reach Albany he would at some point have to cross to the west side of the Hudson River, a move that would sever his ties to his supply line. He had two choices. He could remain tethered to his tenuous supply line until the very end, not crossing the Hudson until he was on the opposite shore from Albany. The problem with that alternative was that the river was exceedingly wide at Albany, and getting an army across in the face of determined resistance would be difficult. He could more easily cross at Fort Miller, forty-seven miles above Albany, but there were problems with that choice as well. It would afford the rebels the opportunity to entrench south of Fort Miller at a site of their choosing, leaving Burgoyne to fight his way through stout defenses in order to reach Albany. The choice to cut his umbilical cord to Ticonderoga while still some distance from Albany would also necessitate finding an alternative source of supplies, and quickly. Neither choice was a good one, but Burgoyne concluded that crossing at Fort Miller offered the best hope of success. He took that step and, simultaneously, detached 750 men under Lieutenant Colonel Friedrich Baum to seize the large rebel supply depot at Bennington, some twenty miles east of the Hudson.[75]

The Bennington expedition was Burgoyne's Lexington-Concord. Like Gage in 1775, he believed that secrecy was crucial to the success of the venture, but three weeks earlier Schuyler had already foreseen that Burgoyne would "attempt to march . . . [to] Bennington, in order to procure Cattle & Carriages." He had sent out warnings to the New Hampshire militia.[76] Baum set out for Bennington on August 9, and he appears not to have been terribly worried, as he would face no Continentals, but only what he called "uncouth militia." Those militia—General John Stark and his New Hampshire trainbandsmen—were waiting for him when he marched into Bennington on August 16. As he waited for the Germans to arrive, Stark's numbers had been augmented by the arrival of Massachusetts militiamen, Stockbridge Indians from New England, and Seth Warner's Green Mountain Boys. The rebels possessed nearly a three-to-one numerical advantage, and Baum had no cavalry arm (due to the shortage of horses) to offset the odds. As one Hessian subsequently remarked: "there was a fatality attending all our measures." When the rebels surrounded their foe early in the battle that ensued, the Indians, who according to a German soldier, "had hitherto acted with spirit and something like order, lost all confidence and fled." The battle came down to bitter hand-to-hand combat between professionals and hardened frontiersmen. The fight, one of Baum's men later remarked, "defies all powers of language to describe. The bayonet, the butt of the rifles, the sabre, the pike, were in full play, and men fell, as they rarely fall in modern war." Baum was one who fell, mortally wounded. The frontiersmen, tough and tenacious, won out. The regulars, "Outnumbered, broken and somewhat disheartened," in the words of a survivor, "wavered and fell back, or . . . were . . . cut down at their post."[77] Triumphant in this desperate engagement, the frontier militiamen also routed a relief expedition that Burgoyne sent. Altogether, Burgoyne lost nine hundred men. When that number was added to those who had been lost at Hubbardton, as well as those who had been detached to guard the supply line, the army that Burgoyne had set out with in May had shrunk by almost a quarter, and Albany was more than thirty miles away.[78]

After Bennington, an oppressive sense of doom prevailed at British head-quarters. A dismayed Burgoyne now believed not only that the Indians were undependable, but that he had been deceived with regard to the number, and zeal, of the Loyalists in the upper Hudson Valley. He also knew that no assistance could be expected from Howe, and he had come to see just how wrong the North government had been to insist that the rebels were a small minority that somehow had seized power. He poured out his bitter feelings to Germain in a trenchant letter written on August 20. "The bulk of the country is undoubtedly with the Congress," he declared, adding that upper New York and Vermont "abounds in the most active and rebellious" of peoples. Awaiting him was an American army that was well supplied by France and not only "superior to mine in [Continental] troops," but its commander could have "as many militia as he pleases." His afflictions, he said, "hang like a gathering storm."[79]

With a victorious militia on his left and a large and growing army to his south, Burgoyne knew that a successful retreat was highly uncertain. Still, he contemplated falling back to Fort Edward, only eight miles away, where he might remain until reinforced, even if that did not occur until the following year. In the end, he spurned such a move. Rumors buzzed through the army that Burgoyne had declared: "Britons never retreat."[80] If he did say that, he also said that he expected the arrival of a victorious St. Leger, who would bring reinforcements and whose mere presence would draw away some of the rebel militia. He additionally expected relief from General Clinton, whom Howe had left in command in New York City. At the very least, he expected Clinton to make a show of force in the highlands, a step that would contain rebel forces in that area and likely compel Gates to dispatch some of his units to help out.[81] Burgoyne may have suspected that he was clutching at straws. More likely, he was driven to advance into the face of probable devastation by equal parts of vanity and desperation. After all, he was linked indissolubly to the plan for an invasion from Canada, and to withdraw was to draw down on himself a ruinous crescendo of calumny, worse even than had been levied at Carleton. To retreat was also to risk the loss of his independent command in 1778, for he might be recalled as a failure, or the invasion might be scrapped altogether, or Howe—who outranked him—might come north in the next campaign and take charge. Burgoyne also had to know that his survival at Fort Edward for months on end could not be guaranteed. With the countryside rising up, it was unlikely that he could maintain his supply line. Like most professional soldiers, Burgoyne thought, "Fortune is often fickle, but especially in war."[82] Burgoyne preferred to hazard all in a fight rather than to lose all in an ignominious retreat or while idling in winter quarters.

AROUND THIS SAME TIME Burgoyne learned that his hope of help from Colonel St. Leger was misplaced. St. Leger, a thirty-eight-year-old Irishman who had soldiered for two decades, had not set out until he learned of Ticonderoga's fall, but in mid-July his force of two thousand men—British and German regulars, Canadian militia, provincial units composed of Loyalist volunteers, and roughly eight hundred Indians, nearly a third of which had been secured by Joseph Brant, who was part of the operation—entered the Mohawk Valley after a grueling march that included "cutting a Road thro the Woods for 25 Miles to bring up Artillery."[83] Their objectives were to take Fort Schuyler before proceeding eastward toward Albany.[84] St. Leger's intelligence had reported that only 60 rebels were holding the fort, but when the British arrived at Fort Schuyler on August 3 they found that 750 men with six weeks' provisions garrisoned the installation. In short order, St. Leger learned from Brant's sister, Molly, that more rebels were on the way.[85] Some eight hundred Tryon County militiamen under Brigadier

General Nicholas Herkimer, the fifty-year-old son of a German immigrant, were marching toward the fort.

St. Leger marched his men about for a while, hoping to impress the militiamen inside the fort, after which he surrounded Fort Schuyler and offered the garrison protection from the Indians if it surrendered immediately. His offer was "Rejected with disdain." Seeing that he faced "a respectable fortress strongly garrisoned" and in possession of a large train of artillery "we were not masters of"—the British had brought along only four field pieces and four mortars—St. Leger wisely decided to deal with Herkimer first.[86] On August 5, while Burgoyne's army languished at Fort Edward, St. Leger sent out a blocking party of more than six hundred men to ambush Herkimer's militiamen. Slightly more than fifty of the men were regulars or Loyalists. The preponderance were Indians, some three hundred warriors from assorted tribes and three hundred of Brant's Oneidas and Canajoharie Mohawks. Brant selected a site for the ambush at Oriskany, planning to fall on the enemy at a spot where the road ran between two ravines, then climbed steeply upward. Regulars were set at the top of the rise. Once they opened fire, the Indians were to leap out of the thick forests, seal off the route of retreat, and overwhelm the militiamen.[87]

It was hot and humid that August morning as the rebel detachment, stretching out more than half a mile and including sixty Oneida warriors, marched toward the trap that awaited them. They were tense. As always, rumors had swirled throughout their march that they might be ambushed, a staple of Indian warfare. These citizen-soldiers were even more concerned over another story that had made the rounds: in reprisal for their having taken up arms, the Indians would strike the militiamen's farms and families while they were away.[88]

Despite their awareness of the possibility of an ambush, and irrespective of having taken every conceivable precaution, the Tryon County militiamen walked into the maw of disaster. The regulars, peering down the dark forest, waited breathlessly as their prey marched ever closer. But before the New Yorkers were within musket range, and before Herkimer's force was in place to be enveloped, impulsive Indians fired into the train of the startled rebels. The first volley took a heavy toll, including Herkimer, who was badly wounded (he died a few days later from his wounds). In an instant, the militiamen broke for the woods. A British soldier remembered hearing a rebel shout in German: "O Lord God Almighty, run, boys or we will all be gone!" Some could not outrun the Indians. They were dead or disabled within moments of the start of the battle. A few succeeded in reaching the nearby Mohawk River, where they swam to safety. The majority stood and fought. For nearly forty terrible minutes the fighting was one on one. The soldiers got off one shot, after which they used their muskets as cudgels, swung bayonets as knives, wielded hatchets that they had brought along, clutched at heavy fallen limbs and used them as clubs. If all else failed, they tried to kill their attackers with their bare hands. The Indians fought in the same fashion. They bobbed from one tree to another, suddenly, terrifyingly, materializing before—

sometimes behind—an unsuspecting soldier. The braves wielded knives, axes, clubs, and spears, and in time they were joined by the Scottish regulars, who waded into the woods and fought at close quarters with their bayonets. The fight was savage and primordial, as civil wars tend to be, for in this desperate engagement Loyalists fought rebels who once had been their neighbors, and Indians fought Indians with whom they had once joined hands in the Six Nations Confederation. Every man knew that the vanquished would never leave this forest. No quarter was given. None was asked. It was brutal, elemental, kill or be killed. In time, some order was established and the militia formed defensive circles that enabled them to use their muskets once again and to lay down a concentrated fire that kept most of the enemy some distance away. The fighting went on past midday, but now more on terms to which the rebels were accustomed. Early in the afternoon, a great summer storm blew up, unleashing gales of rain. The fighting stopped for nearly an hour, though during the tempest the Indians slaughtered many men who had surrendered or who lay wounded in their presence. When the deluge ended and the sun reappeared, the battle resumed full bore. It was a standoff now. The militiamen had taken cover in two-man parties. One man fired, then reloaded while his comrade fired. Within a few minutes, the fighting began to wind down. As the contest grew more even, the Indians began to melt away. Not even the arrival of British reinforcements—some seventy men from the King's Royal Regiment of New York, often called the Royal Yorkers, approached from Fort Schuyler—stanched the withdrawal of the Indian warriors, who cried out: "Oonah! Oonah!" (Retreat! Retreat!) After six gruesome hours this bloody fight was over. It had been ghastly. More than half of the Tryon County militiamen, 465 in all, had been killed, wounded, or captured.[89]

Learning what had occurred, Schuyler sent forward reinforcements, nine hundred Continentals under General Arnold. Although he longed for a fight, Arnold found no battle. He sent ahead Hon Yost Schuyler, a mysterious man who has been depicted by some as mentally deficient and by others as a captive Tory who agreed to cooperate with the rebels in return for a pardon from a death sentence. Whatever he was, Hon Yost Schuyler posed as a Loyalist and broadcast the story that Arnold's force contained more than three thousand men. St. Leger's Indians fell for the ruse and for a second time abandoned their British leader. By August 23, when Arnold reached Fort Schuyler, St. Leger was gone, having retreating to Canada. He would not be joining Burgoyne at Albany. As was true of the origin of the tactics that hindered Burgoyne's advance and the actions that led to the rout at Bennington, St. Leger had been undone on Schuyler's watch and prior to Gate's arrival to take command.[90]

UNAWARE OF THE OCCURRENCES IN THE WEST, Burgoyne pushed ahead. He hoped to move forward rapidly, getting in position to fight the enemy before many more rebel militiamen arrived. But he could not move quickly. His men were tired, worn down from weeks of campaigning, as well as from the heat, which British veterans of campaigns in East India claimed was worse than they had faced in Madras.[91] Burgoyne was slowed as well by his inability to obtain adequate intelligence. Few Indians remained with him, and if Burgoyne is to be believed, their scouting was ineffectual, as they were terrified of the rebel riflemen. Likewise, those same riflemen exacted a heavy toll on the patrols that Burgoyne dispatched to gather information and supplies. The American "riflemen and other irregulars," according to the British commander, fired from the "darkness of the surrounding woods," repeatedly ambushing his men and frustrating one mission after another.[92] ("We have seen . . . how the enemy attacks," said a German. Either "lying on the ground or standing behind trees, they load their guns and shoot. They run from one tree to another . . . as . . . the Savages do.")[93] Uncertain of Gates's whereabouts, Burgoyne moved cautiously, advancing merely six miles in four days after his departure from Fort Miller, a trek that took him to the west side of the Hudson and on to Saratoga. It was mid-September. Seventy long days had passed since the fall of Ticonderoga.

If Burgoyne was in the dark about his enemy, Gates was aware of his foe's every step. In almost every conceivable way, Gates was the opposite of Burgoyne, and of many other American generals. He was not the charismatic sort. Short, a bit on the stout side, and given to wearing spectacles when he read, Gates looked as if he belonged in the pulpit or the countinghouse rather than in command of an army. His appearance led his troops to refer to him as "Granny Gates," though they did not mean it in a derogatory sense. Gates was genuinely popular with the soldiers, but not because of dash or flamboyance. His was a parsimonious style. His men liked him for his open manner, and for never having forgotten his roots. He was what he was: a commoner, like almost all those who served under him. He disliked monarchs and hated aristocracies. He believed fervently in republicanism and meritocracy. He believed, too, in a careful, well-crafted, common sense approach to things, the manner that had led to his success in an elitist-based institution such as the British amy. Above all, his men trusted him. They did not think that he would throw away their lives in vain and irrational pursuits. They believed that like a kindly guardian, an altruistic grandfather, Gates would take care of them.

As Gates plotted his strategy, New England militia drifted into camp in extraordinary numbers, the result of a furious campaign by regional leaders eager to demonstrate that men who had refused to serve under Schuyler would bear arms for Gates. Other factors were important, too. The victory at Bennington helped, and so did clever propaganda and a deep-seated faith in Gates among the militiamen. Above all, these militiamen, such as Jonathan Brigham of Marlborough, Massachusetts, were convinced that unless Burgoyne was stopped, "a total dismemberment of the states" would be the result.[94] Continentals also came in. Washington was compelled by Congress to send some units, especially the Eleventh Virginia Regiment of riflemen under Daniel Morgan. "Oh for some Virginia riflemen," New Yorkers had been heard to say, and Congress got the message. Gates and Congress also leaned on the New England states to furnish

Continentals.[95] On the eve of Gates's arrival in Albany the entire American army on the Hudson totaled 5,900 men. Two weeks later there were more Continentals than that in camp. At the beginning of September, Gates had two thousand militiamen under his command, and their number nearly tripled in the next three weeks.[96]

At the end of the first week in September, Gates moved north to a position at Bemis Heights selected by his engineer, Thaddeus Kosciuszko, a volunteer from Poland. It was anchored on the right by the Hudson and on the left by heavy woods and craggy, sometimes steep, bluffs. Gates installed the rebel lines in the hillocks in between, with many men ensconced behind a U-shaped breastwork that stretched for three-quarters of a mile. The site was infinitely superior to Bunker Hill, Brooklyn Heights, and the escarpment that Washington had utilized on the Assunpink. Gates additionally posted a large force east of the Hudson. Just as Burgoyne had long expected would be the case, he would have to slug his way through an entrenched rebel army in order to reach Albany. Considering the terrain, and the numbers against him, Burgoyne had to know that a breakthrough was well nigh impossible.[97]

Burgoyne made his move on the foggy morning of September 19. He hoped to get his army onto the heights on the rebel left. To get there, his men had to cross what the locals called Freeman's Farm, a pastoral twelve-acre spread once owned by John Freeman, a Loyalist who ironically was serving with Burgoyne. If Burgoyne's army reached the precipice, it would command a ridgeline above the rebel lines, and it might succeed in flanking the American left, the breakthrough of which Burgoyne dreamed. Fighting began in the early afternoon in the fertile fields and green meadowlands of the farm, giving the encounter its name in history: the Battle of Freeman's Farm. At first, Gates believed that Burgoyne was only making a probe. Once he understood the danger, Gates pulled units from their entrenchments and detached them to block the enemy's advance. After two hours of savage fighting, the action died down as Burgoyne regrouped. But around 3:30 p.m. the battle resumed with unbridled fury. Alexander Scammell, a Harvard graduate, schoolteacher, surveyor, and New Hampshire colonel who served throughout the war, later called this engagement "the hottest Fire . . . that ever I heard."[98] Another American thought, "Few battles have been more obstinate and unyielding."[99] A British officer with twenty years' experience said that the fighting included an "explosion of fire [such as] I never had any idea of before." He added that the artillery's "great peals of thunder," enhanced by "echoes of the woods," had "almost deafened us."[100] One of Burgoyne's senior officers, a veteran of many battles, remarked, that "the fire was much heavier than ever I saw it any where."[101] This was a brutal slugging match, and though Burgoyne remained on the battlefield throughout, issuing "orders with . . . coolness in the heart of danger, and fury of the fight," as one of his men put it, the outcome hinged on willpower, not canny generalship. The Americans exhibited ample will, fighting well outside their entrenchments, repeatedly standing up to

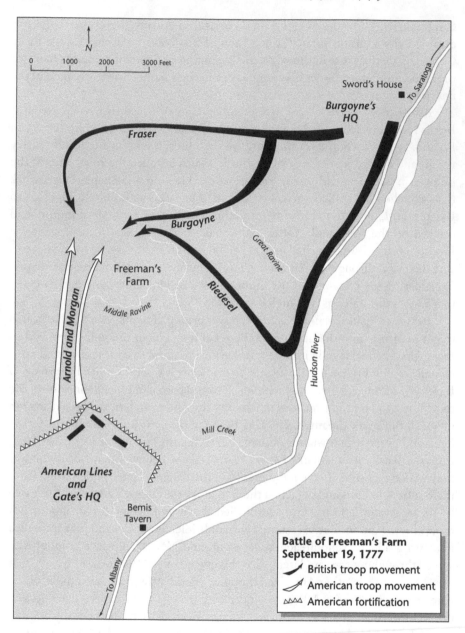

Battle of Freeman's Farm
September 19, 1777
British troop movement
American troop movement
American fortification

the regulars' bayonet charges. Typically, too, the rebels fought unconventionally. Many men, especially the backcountry riflemen under Morgan—who were moved about by their leader sounding his turkey-call as the ebb and flow of the battle dictated—fought as snipers and sharpshooters, picking off numerous regulars, especially the officers, who were easily distinguished from the enlisted men.[102]

Twice on that warm afternoon the British center was nearly crushed. Once it was saved when Burgoyne ordered Riedesel, on the river road, to attack the rebels' right flank, forcing Gates to plug men into that sector. Later in the day, with the British in deep trouble, General Phillips brought his Twentieth Regiment into the battle in a cornfield on the eastern edge of the farm and prevented a rout. The fight went on for three desperate hours until darkness enveloped the blood-soaked corn rows and fields of grain. The British held the battlefield. Usually, that is a sign of triumph. But the Battle of Freeman's Farm was an American victory. The rebels not only had prevented their foe from breaking through, but Britain's losses—nearly six hundred killed and wounded—were about twice those of the Americans.[103]

The next morning, September 20, was eerily quiet. The fields that had been filled with terror only hours before were calm and bucolic, and empty, save for the mangled bodies that lay motionless and a few riderless horses that ambled about aimlessly. Burgoyne chose not to fight that day. Overnight, he had received a missive from Clinton written eight days earlier. Clinton had said that around September 22—now just two days hence—he would "make a push" to get past the Americans' highland forts and bring two thousand men to Burgoyne. But, Clinton added, if he could not reach Burgoyne quickly, he would return to Manhattan "to save this important post." Burgoyne wasted no time in responding. He urged his comrade to come: "Do it, my dear Friend, directly."[104] With help perhaps on the way, Burgoyne abandoned all thoughts of another immediate attempt to break through. He ordered his men to dig in, hoping to lure Gates into an attack, but even more hopeful of seeing the tall masts of Clinton's flotilla bobbing up the blue-green Hudson.

Gates neither intended to attack nor to comply with a just received request from Washington. The commander had asked him to detach Morgan's corps, if "circumstances will admit," and send it to join him in Pennsylvania. "Your Excellency," Gates responded, "would not wish me to part with the Corps of the Army of [which] Burgoyne are most Afraid of."[105] Morgan stayed. Holding the upper hand, Gates wished to do nothing that would diminish his strength. His lines were impregnable and his foe's available supply of food was dwindling daily. Sooner or later, Gates believed, Burgoyne would have to attack again. With a knowing take on his adversary, Gates allowed that Burgoyne would in the end likely "risque all upon one Throw."[106] Days passed as Burgoyne waited for Clinton to appear and Gates waited for Burgoyne to reemerge. More days passed. Burgoyne called a council of war and proposed another attack. His senior officers objected. It was too soon. Two more days went by. The nights were growing colder and the hillside forests were taking on autumn hues of red and yellow. Burgoyne's forage parties were returning nearly empty-handed. He cut his army's daily rations by a third on October 3.[107] No word from Clinton.

On October 5, seventeen days after the fray at Freeman's Farm, Burgoyne called a second council of war. With Fraser's support, Riedesel proposed a retreat

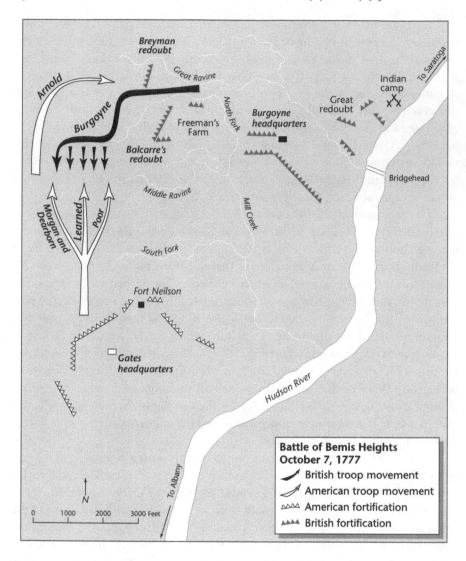

Battle of Bemis Heights
October 7, 1777

to the Batten Kill, the tributary of the Hudson above Saratoga where the army had crossed the great river. From there, he argued, the army could seek to reopen its line to Fort George. If successful, and if Clinton never came, the army might retreat to Ticonderoga. Burgoyne was opposed, and after what must have been a heated discussion—Riedesel later charged that Burgoyne was "Incited by Zeal," not reason—the commander had his way. Burgoyne proposed a second attack, following a plan not unlike its predecessor, except that a larger force would be committed to battle and the army would advance below Freeman's Farm. He called it a "reconnaissance in force," but the object was the same: gain the bluffs and bombard Gates's army with his mighty artillery train, eventually securing the coveted breakthrough on the American left.[108]

Burgoyne readied his army, but waited another forty-eight hours, hoping against hope to hear something in the meantime from Clinton. Where was he? Clinton had said that he would move up the Hudson around September 22. That was fifteen days earlier. Clinton had not departed Manhattan for the highlands by September 22. He had not received Burgoyne's letter pleading for him to act until September 29, and on October 3, the day of Burgoyne's initial council of war, Clinton finally moved out from New York City with three thousand men. He left in the belief—or so he said later—that Burgoyne's army was still advancing on Albany. Clinton landed his men on October 5 in the highlands, and during the next seventy-two hours took Forts Montgomery and Clinton, and forced Putnam to abandon Peekskill. In the course of the operation, a messenger from Burgoyne caught up with Clinton at Verplanck's Point on the east side of the Hudson. The courier brought alarming tidings: he not only described the slow erosion of Burgoyne's army, but reported that it was cut off from its supply base. Burgoyne, he added, was outnumbered by nearly three to one, a good estimate, as the British commander possessed 6,617 men while Gates had 11,469 with him and an additional 8,000 under arms in the sector.[109] The messenger also brought a letter from Burgoyne. Incredibly, the beleaguered general asked Clinton for orders. To Clinton, this seemed—rightly—like an attempt to make him responsible for the defeat that Burgoyne now anticipated. Clinton declined to be the fall guy. "Sir Henry Clinton cannot presume to give any Orders to General Burgoyne," he stiffly responded. Making ready to return to Manhattan, Clinton ended his reply to Burgoyne cruelly: "I sincerely hope this little Success of ours may facilitate your Operation."[110] He sent his response with three messengers, hoping that one could get through the American lines. None succeeded, and one was captured and executed by the Americans.[111] A cautious man, Clinton had done all that he had promised and all that he cared to do, although in the fallout that subsequently raged in London, he disingenuously claimed that he had "entertain[ed] hopes that I should even be able to support General Burgoyne should he incline to force his way to Albany."[112]

At last, early on the bright, chilly afternoon of October 7, Burgoyne's army moved out, initiating the Battle of Bemis Heights. Once again, Gates—who was at headquarters dining on ox heart when word arrived of the enemy's advance—initially misunderstood the seriousness of the threat. Within thirty minutes, Arnold, among others, pleaded with him to commit a larger force to the gathering battle. Gates was reluctant to send his men from their entrenchments—like Washington, he did not wish to permit his adversary to dictate his course of action—and he sent only limited reinforcements. Arnold was furious. "That is nothing," he raged to his commander, and again urged Gates to send more men.[113] Until recently, Gates and Arnold had gotten on well enough, though inevitable dust-ups had occurred between these two men of such dissimilar temperaments. Arnold was impulsive and offensive-minded. Gates was patient, tentative, and had a better understanding of the virtues of defensive tactics against an army of European regulars. Gates may have taken umbrage at Arnold's unabashed support of Schuyler, adding an edge to their relationships. But it was the fight at Freeman's Farm, and its aftermath, that opened deep wounds. Arnold was furious when Gates had not listened to his pleas for reinforcements during that earlier engagement, but his fury boiled over when he learned that Gates had not acknowledged his role in his report on the battle to Congress. Nearly a week before the Battle of Bemis Heights, Arnold, no wallflower, had written three rude and strongly worded letters to Gates, in one even suggesting that the officers disapproved of their leader's tactics.[114] In a cold fury, Gates responded by relieving Arnold of his command. When fighting resumed on October 7 and Arnold appeared at headquarters, Gates told him curtly: "You have no business here."[115]

Most of the fighting was occurring in a farmer's wheat field that was bounded by heavy woods on two sides. Gradually seeing what was occurring, Gates committed reinforcements, sending many into the woods that looked onto the British left. A forest was an ideal site for the American soldiers, offering shelter from Burgoyne's ten field pieces and concealment from the enemy infantry. From this position, the rebels—including riflemen who acted as snipers, frequently taking to perches in trees—laid down a deadly enfiladed fire. An hour into the fight, the British right began to fall back. As it did, a blue-coated American general rode on to the battlefield, gathering up regiments and leading them in an attack. It was Benedict Arnold. Filled with rage—and strong drink, according to some—and to be sure acting without orders, he led his men in an attack on a German redoubt that anchored the right wing of Burgoyne's army, flushing out its inhabitants (who, according to some of the British, had offered "a most shameful resistance") and sowing chaos and confusion among the remaining British units. Men ran for safety, exposing others, who then also instinctively fled "with great Precipitation & Confusion," said one rebel, leaving behind their cannon and "a Conciderable Number of Waggons with Ammunition & other stores."[116] "Each man for himself, they made for the bushes," a German captain remembered.[117]

The Battle of Bemis Heights—sometimes called the Second Battle of Saratoga—was over. The British army had again suffered heavy losses—894 men killed and wounded, of which more than two score were officers, including two generals, one of whom was Fraser, gut shot by a Virginia rifleman astride a limb high in a tree. A bullet through the abdomen was almost always lethal, and Fraser died the next morning, in his final breath bemoaning the "fatal ambition" that had brought about his early demise.[118] A horse had been shot from under Burgoyne, and his hat and waistcoat were filled with bullet holes, but miraculously he was unscathed. Arnold was shot in the same leg that had taken a ball at Quebec, and the leg was broken when his horse fell on him. Gates never came close to the battlefield. Like Washington in some engagements, he had remained at headquarters two miles away, where he could sift through the inevitably confusing, often contradictory, reports from the field and try to make reasonably well-educated responses. Among the Americans who fought, 130 had been killed or wounded.[119]

The following day, parties on both sides gathered the limp bodies of the wounded and buried the dead that they could reach. Those they could not get to were prey for wolves that "came down from the mountains to devour" their remains.[120] While the burial details went about their business, Burgoyne huddled with his officers. To a man, the Germans wished to make a stab at retreating. They were joined by many British officers. Rather than losing every man, it was better to "return at least one corps of soldiers to the King, even if we had to abandon all our baggage," some argued.[121] Burgoyne was not swayed, but on October 9—in the dead of night, leaving tents standing and fires burning to deceive the rebels—he pulled back from Bemis Heights. The advance on Albany was over. "What a great alteration in affairs!" a young British soldier exclaimed.[122] Rain, followed by a piercing autumn wind, lashed at Burgoyne's army over the next two days, adding to the misery of tired, hungry, and defeated men and their camp followers. By October 11 all hope of escaping to Ticonderoga, or even Fort Edward, had vanished. The rebels had sealed off their enemy, or in the lexicon of the New Englanders, they had *"yarded Burgoyne."*[123] The British camp spiraled into a squalid hell. Men were entrenched in foul mud holes. Starving cattle were dying, causing a "stench . . . very prejudicial," according to one soldier. Many of the wounded were suffering horribly. Some had lost an arm, others a leg or both legs, some their eyesight. A British major, an aide to Phillips, had been shot through the mouth. The bullet had torn through both cheeks, taken teeth out, and sliced through his tongue, and now he was choking on the pus in his mouth. Off and on, day and night, the Americans lobbed artillery shells into their midst. Every "little while a ball wold come crashing down among the trees," Riedesel said later, and to that nightmare, daring rebel snipers from time to time crept close enough to squeeze off a shot, often killing or maiming an unsuspecting regular. The "state and situation of our army was truly calamitous!" a young redcoat allowed. Presently, deserters poured from the camp like water through a sieve. Within a couple of days, nearly three hundred regulars streamed into the American lines or were captured.[124]

On October 12, and again the next day, Burgoyne called councils of war. He invited all officers down through the rank of captain to the second council. In a tempestuous atmosphere, the officers discussed their options, including a proposal by Burgoyne for an every-man-for-himself flight toward Ticonderoga. Presumably, men in small parties would hike through the dark forests in search of their destination, fifty-five miles away. The majority wanted no part of that. The mortality rate would be extraordinary. "Want, misery and hunger would . . . soon gain ground and a lot of people, not able to endure such kind of difficulties, would be lost," a German general argued. The discussion then turned to surrender, and after deciding that it would not be dishonorable to surrender given the fatal debilitation of the army, it was agreed that Burgoyne should draft the terms of a capitulation proposal and send it to Gates. Overnight he worked on the document, which was delivered to American headquarters by a deputy adjutant general under a white flag the following morning, October 14. Without glancing at his opponent's document, Gates produced his own written terms: unconditional surrender.[125]

At sunset, Burgoyne countered with another proposal. The British would surrender immediately, but the regulars were to be permitted to sail to Great Britain and the Loyalists and Canadians were to be guaranteed safe passage to Canada. To Burgoyne's astonishment, Gates accepted his foe's terms on the following day and consented to an immediate ceasefire. Gates's precipitate response aroused Burgoyne's suspicions. Did Gates know that Clinton was coming up the Hudson? Were Gates's militiamen beginning to abandon him? Burgoyne was on the right track. Intelligence had reported to Gates—correctly—that forty-eight hours earlier Clinton had sent out another relief force, this one a twenty sail flotilla loaded with two thousand newly arrived reinforcements. Burgoyne was in the dark, but he tried to stall. He pleaded the necessity to carefully consider the fine print of the tentative agreement, of which in fact he was the author. Foolishly, Gates on October 16 permitted two representatives from each army to meet to hammer out the details. They came to an agreement early that evening (among other things, the word "capitulation" was dropped and replaced by "convention"), but Burgoyne, still dragging his feet, refused to sign, niggling over the meaning of certain words. Gates allowed the charade to continue overnight, but early the next morning he presented Burgoyne with an ultimatum: sign within an hour or firing will resume. Burgoyne signed at 9:00 a. m., seventy-two hours after he had first broached surrender terms.[126]

The surrender was to begin one hour later. For once, the British and Germans assembled on time. Many officers, overcome with despair, wept openly as company after company, brigade after brigade, marched down a muddy road lined on both sides with rebel soldiers. When they reached the appointed place, the gray-faced soldiers stacked their arms and parked their cannon. Nearly 12,000 Americans watched the unfolding spectacle in stony silence, and some, according to one redcoat, "dare scarce lift up their eyes to view the British Troops in such a situation." A German remembered that the rebels displayed no sign of "hatred, mockery, malicious pleasure or pride for our miserable fate." Only the commands barked out in English and German, and the heavy thud of British and Hessian drums—which, according to one sad English officer, "seemed to have lost their former inspiriting sounds"—could be heard.[127] The American onlookers may have been quiet, but they were filled with a hushed rapture. Jeduthan Baldwin, a colonel from Massachusetts, called the capitulation ceremony "the most agreeable sight that ever my eyes beheld."[128] Another rebel exalted quietly that this was "the greatest Conquest Ever known."[129] The surrender of 5,895 men took time, more than four hours. When the last man had departed the field of surrender, Gates hosted an outdoor dinner on this sun-soft autumn afternoon for Burgoyne and his brigade and regimental commanders. When Riedesel's wife came as well, Schuyler, who had shown up but apparently had not been invited to Gates's repast, graciously served her a warm and welcome meal in his tent. Burgoyne, a large man wearing his best scarlet coat festooned with gold epaulettes, greeted Gates cordially: "General, the caprice of war has made me your prisoner."[130] Then these officers, who only hours earlier had been trying to kill one another, sat down together to a dinner of ham, goose, beef, mutton, and assorted side dishes, all washed down with cider mixed with rum. When the meal was done, and the shadows of late day stretched over the idyllic fields that recently had witnessed untold agony, the British and German officers stood, stiffly said their goodbyes, mounted their horses, and rode off to join their men in the march to Boston and an uncertain future.[131]

10

"WE RALLIED AND BROKE": THE CAMPAIGN FOR PHILADELPHIA, SEPTEMBER–DECEMBER 1777

W HEN WASHINGTON learned in June that Burgoyne's army was advancing on Ticonderoga, he thought "there can be little room to doubt" that Howe would "cooperate with [Burgoyne's] Northern army." But he could not be certain, and for a spell Washington even suspected that Burgoyne's expedition up Lake Champlain was "a feint—calculated to amuse & distract." Word of the loss of Ticonderoga disabused him of that notion. Convinced now that Burgoyne and Howe would seek "to form a Junction up" the Hudson, Washington immediately moved his Continentals northward, well above Manhattan.[1]

But Howe never intended to link up with Burgoyne. For months his focus had been on Philadelphia. When Washington's Continentals started north in mid-July, Howe told Burgoyne that he would provide relief should Washington proceed toward Albany. Otherwise, he never wavered in hoping to take Philadelphia. In the seven months since he drafted his first plan for campaign 1777, Howe's thinking changed only with regard to how to get to Philadelphia. Initially, he had envisioned an overland march from New York. In April he called for taking his army south by sea, then approaching Philadelphia via the Delaware River. In July he opted to come up the Chesapeake Bay instead, changing his plan once again because intelligence reported that the army could be landed more safely in Maryland than on the Delaware River.[2]

During much of July, Washington and Howe warily eyed one another. Washington's army was at the Clove, a craggy gorge in the highlands on the west side of the Hudson. Aware that Howe was gathering a huge flotilla, Washington knew that from the Clove he could march to Albany or back into Pennsylvania as circumstances dictated.[3] Howe delayed his departure for Philadelphia until he received word of Burgoyne's progress, but when he learned of the fall of Ticonderoga, the British commander surmised that the invasion army could fend for itself. Not everyone at British headquarters concurred, and some warned that if Burgoyne was abandoned, he would be "cut up alive."[4] Howe brushed aside the naysayers, and on July 23 his fleet of 267 ships, packed with 16,000 men, sailed for Philadelphia. When it stood out to sea, Washington ordered his army back into New Jersey, but when Howe's armada dropped over the horizon, Washington was left to lament that he was in "a State of constant perplexity" as to his opponent's destination. Only on July 31 did the American commander receive word that Howe's fleet had been spotted off the Delaware capes, and he concluded that there "could be no doubt" that Howe's objective was Philadelphia.[5]

Burgoyne had based his undertaking on orders from London, but Howe had his hands on the controls throughout campaign 1777. He called the shots, and the choices that he made marked him as unfit for the responsibilities that he undertook, just as Washington had begun to suspect several months earlier. Scholars have been sharply critical of Howe's decision to proceed to Philadelphia by sea, though there were arguments to be made on behalf of the course that he chose. To come by land was to march up to one hundred miles through unfriendly territory—ten times the distance that Cornwallis had marched from Princeton to Trenton at the beginning of the year, and his tribulations had been immense— and to leave many of his men behind to guard the supply line. Howe has also been criticized for coming to Philadelphia via the Chesapeake Bay rather than the Delaware Bay, as it added considerably to the length of his voyage, but the rebels had spent two years fortifying the Delaware River. The only obstacle that Howe would face after landing at the head of the Chesapeake was the Continental army, and bringing Washington to battle was one of his cardinal aims. But Howe did make two egregious blunders. One was in failing to act in concert with Burgoyne, an error that almost everyone but Howe divined as that pivotal summer unfolded. (In mid-July even Washington said that Howe "certainly ought now, in good policy, to endeavor to cooperate with Genl Burgoine.")[6] Howe's second mistake was even more inexcusable. He should have opened his campaign months earlier. He might have struck when the Delaware River froze during the inhospitable winter, crossing the river with relative ease and capitalizing on the woes of the depleted and sickly Continental army at Morristown. At the latest, he should have launched his campaign in early April when Pennsylvania was bathed by a kindly sun. Had he sailed from New York in early spring, the Philadelphia campaign might have been concluded by mid-June, the very time that Burgoyne's army departed Canada. Instead, inexplicably and unpardonably, Howe did not move on Philadelphia until the year's seventh month had nearly run its course.

Howe's voyage was a nightmare. It consumed thirty-two days, four times what had been anticipated, and twice as long as an overland march would have

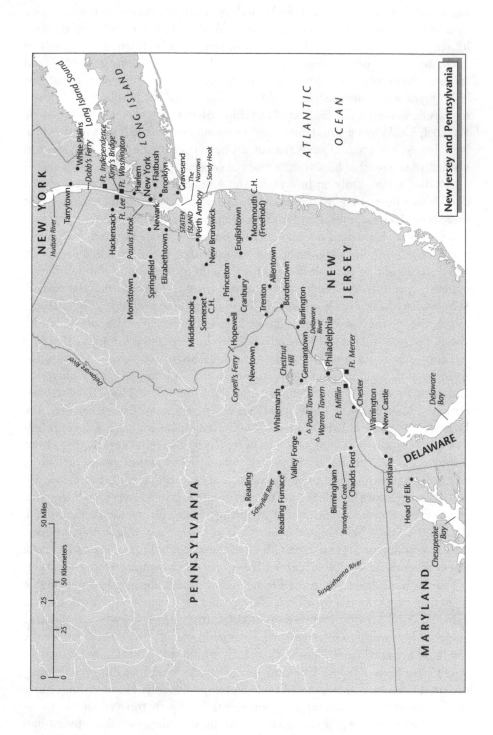

New Jersey and Pennsylvania

required. Day after day, the luckless British had been unable to draw favorable winds. Men and horses alike suffered terribly from the stifling heat in their fetid, noisy, airless compartments. The soldiers endured a steady diet of bread "which is spoiled or full of worms" and "Stinking water with all the impurities mixed in." Twenty-seven men and 170 horses perished in the course of the voyage, and many of the mounts of the sole cavalry unit that Howe had brought along went lame. Another 150 horses, weak and emaciated—and useless for their military duties—were heartlessly destroyed. Several intense squalls and terrible summer thunderstorms blew up, with a "frightful lightening . . . such as is never seen in Germany," according to a Hessian. During one ugly tempest, lightning struck the masts of two vessels, killing three horses and paralyzing two men.[7]

When Washington at last determined Howe's objective, he moved his Continentals south within thirty-six hours of his discovery. He hurried to Philadelphia ahead of his army. On August 23, while dining at Stenton House, the residence of a wealthy Quaker merchant, one observer found Washington to be "extremely grave and thoughtful," while the officers with him were "very quiet."[8] The next morning—the day before Howe's men splashed ashore—the rebel army marched through Philadelphia. Washington, who sent the baggage and camp followers around the city, issued strict orders against straggling, lest the men be victimized by "an inundation of bad women from Philadelphia." The commander tried to spruce up the appearance of his army by ordering that each man wear green sprigs in his hat, and the soldiers stepped to the sprightly music of drum and fife.[9] Washington rode his great grey mount at the head of the army. Beside him rode the Marquis de Lafayette, a French volunteer who had recently arrived in America. Thousands of residents turned out to see their army. Opinion ran the gamut. Some congressmen were pleased by the men's "lively smart Step" and "fine appearance," but John Adams, while conceding that the soldiers were "tolerably disciplined," wrung his hands over their lack of precision and absence of jauntiness. "[O]ur soldiers have not yet quite the Air of Soldiers," he anguished, and once the pass-by ended, Adams, whose head was on the line in the event that the rebellion was crushed, hurried to pray at a nearby church.[10]

Washington never planned to attempt to prevent the British from coming ashore. He had no idea where Howe intended to make landfall. He marched his army to Wilmington, arriving on August 25 at about the same time that the British and Hessians were landing at Head of Elk, Maryland. Howe was fifty-seven miles from Philadelphia, twice the distance he had been the previous December when his army had come to Trenton, and about the same distance that he would have been had he begun his march from Amboy. Many of his men were sick and exhausted, and all faced a monotonous diet during the march ahead, for rebel militia had been sent to the top of the Chesapeake to burn grain fields in the path of the regulars. Howe being Howe, he permitted almost three weeks to elapse after the landing before he went into battle. Washington used the time to prepare for the looming encounter. His army was in reasonably good shape, but he would not have as many advantages as Gates had enjoyed in the north. Washington never possessed a numerical superiority. He had roughly 14,000 men, about 2,000 fewer than his adversary. And as Greene observed, the "face of the country is favorable to the Enemy, being very flat and leavel."[11] On the other hand, Howe did not have the advantages that he had possessed the previous summer and fall. His numerical superiority was scant, the Continentals had gained experience, and the British navy would not be a factor in the fighting to take Philadelphia.[12]

Sometime in August or September, Washington decided to cast aside his war of posts strategy and slug it out with the British in a formal battle. No single factor can explain his decision, but one of his young officers put his finger on a prime ingredient when he grumbled, "our great and good Washington made a sacrifice of his own excellent judgment upon the altar of public opinion."[13] If Howe took Philadelphia, Congress would take flight. Many congressmen would be unhappy, and they would be unhappier still if they had to flee because Washington had not fought to defend the city. Washington also had to know that some congressmen had never approved of his Fabian tactics, thinking of them as "Inactivity," or simply an "execrable defensive Plan," as John Adams complained. By early September, Washington was also aware of the rebel victory at Bennington and had begun to anticipate what eventually occurred at Saratoga. He was not alone. Some in Congress had caught the scent of a triumphant end to the war in 1777, if only Washington, like Gates, could score a major victory. The purge of Schuyler, moreover, may have added to Washington's uneasiness. If Congress removed Schuyler in favor of Gates, would it wish to replace him with Gates? But Washington's temperament was also a factor in his wish to fight. From time to time he turned to a war of posts strategy, but he had never done so with glee. He was a fighter who was eager to have a go at Howe, and his army had swelled to 16,000 men, virtual parity with Howe's force.[14]

Washington moved forward a bit and prepared a system of breastworks behind Red Clay Creek, but Howe had no intention of assailing a well-entrenched foe.[15] Keeping to the west of the Continentals, Howe moved to cross the Brandywine Creek and drive on toward Philadelphia, hoping that Washington would try to stop him somewhere along the way. He did not have long to wait. On September 8, Washington emerged from his defenses and, under cover of darkness, fell back to the Brandywine. He deployed his army at Chadd's Ford, the first crossing place on the road from Head of Elk to Philadelphia.[16] The Continentals had only a bit more than twenty-four hours to prepare for battle. Washington did not make good use of that time to reconnoiter the area properly. Howe arrived at Kennett Square, seven miles west of the creek, at about the same time that Washington began to take up positions on the opposite side. Aided by Loyalists and his professional staff, he quickly gained an excellent understanding of the lay of the land.

Washington posted two brigades of Pennsylvania militia on his left, an area anchored by steep knolls that made an attempted crossing unlikely. Thinking that

Chadd's Ford, which lay across the road to Philadelphia, was the most likely place for Howe to mount his principal assault, Washington entrusted Greene's division to secure this point, augmented by Anthony Wayne's division and abundant artillery strung along the rolling heights to Greene's immediate right. Washington ordered a light corps of riflemen under Brigadier General William Maxwell, a hard-living New Jersey bachelor who had soldiered in the French and Indian War, to take up positions west of the Brandywine and harass the enemy as it advanced, much as Hand's men had done prior to the desperate fight before the Assunpink. Based on his ineffectual reconnaissance, Washington concluded that there were no fords "within Twelve miles to cross" above Buffington's Ford, and it was a "Long Circuit through a very Bad Road" to reach that ford.[17] Thus, he posted three divisions under Sullivan to guard his right wing at Buffington's Ford.

It was an excellent plan, save for one thing. Howe not only was aware of Jeffries Ford, only two miles above Buffington's Ford, he knew that the rebels had left it undefended. (Howe got some of his information from local farmers, who had been paid by the Philadelphia Loyalist, Joseph Galloway, to reconnoiter the likely battle site.)[18] The British commander devised a plan that replicated the one that had succeeded on the Heights of Guana below Brooklyn. Howe divided his army—a sign that he held Washington's battlefield acumen in low esteem—and ordered General Knyphausen, with about 6,800 British and Germans, to assault the rebels' center at Chadd's Ford. That was a diversion. Howe was to march with 8,500 men to Jeffries Ford, where he would cross. If all went well, Sullivan would be taken by surprise and the British would turn Washington's right flank. That would set the stage for the rebel center to be squeezed, and destroyed, in a pincer movement.

September 11 dawned foggy, shrouding Howe's movements. He started his men on their seventeen-mile march at 5:00 a.m. Led by a Tory, they kept to wooded regions, hoping to avoid detection. Knyphausen moved out an hour later. His lead units, mostly green clad Loyalists, had not gotten far before they encountered Maxwell's pickets. "All the woods were full of enemy troops," a Hessian exclaimed, and what followed was all too familiar.[19] Fighting in their customary irregular way, the Americans hid in the woods and behind ridges, fences, and rocks. They laid down a "running fire," as a British soldier characterized it, that left nearly 50 percent of Knyphausen's advance units casualties. Over a span of five miles, the rebels fired, then vanished in the forests or across the nearest knoll, only to resurface down the road and do it all over again.[20] It took Knyphausen nearly five hours to drive the last rebel back across the Brandywine. Once there, he paused, settling into an inconsequential artillery duel as he awaited word of Howe's flanking maneuver.

Howe rode at the head of his men, sitting astride a mount that one eyewitness described as nothing but skin and bones. For all his precautions, Howe's advance did not go undetected. On more than one occasion, he was spotted by an American patrol, which reported to headquarters on what it had seen, and portions of his force even fought small skirmishes on a couple of occasions. Other rebel patrols saw nothing, and that too was reported to Washington. As is always the case in battle, intelligence sometimes is good and sometimes it is wildly incorrect. It falls to the commander, working quickly and under enormous pressure, to sift through the contradictory reports and put the pieces together, hoping against hope that his decisions will be the proper ones. Until late in the afternoon, Washington's responses were flawed. He laughed openly at an early report that Howe was attempting a flanking maneuver, and for too long—an almost fatal length of time—he held to the belief that Knyphausen's "sham attack," as a Hessian called it, was the enemy's principal assault. As morning turned to afternoon, Washington not only continued to plug more units into the center of his line, but ordered Sullivan toward the center in preparation for a counterattack against Knyphausen.[21]

Howe's columns emerged from the thick woods and crossed Jeffries Ford in the midday heat. They had made extraordinarily good time, having covered nearly twelve miles of thick and tangled terrain in a bit more than seven hours. His men were hot and tired, and Howe paused to give them a well-deserved rest and to reconnoiter, but by about 1:30 p.m. the redcoats were on the move again. As they advanced, the British were amazed to find that a narrow defile that they had to traverse had been left undefended. They knew, however, that they could not go undetected much longer, and indeed at about this very moment word reached both Sullivan and Washington of an enemy column so large that it caused "Dust [to] Rise back in the Country for above an hour."[22] Though still not convinced that Howe's force constituted a real threat, Washington called off the planned counterattack in the center and sent limited reinforcements to his right wing. Ninety minutes later, at 4:00 p. m., the engagement on the American right began in earnest, commencing with a ferocious bombardment that could be heard twenty-five miles away in Philadelphia, followed by the advance of ranks of British infantry, marching to martial music played by their military bands. Serious fighting began along Osborne Hill and Birmingham Hill, where a Quaker meetinghouse stood. It was grim and bloody, and crucial. One soldier described it as "Excessive severe."[23] Another characterized the armies as "obstinate on both sides."[24] This was one of those moments when a truly decisive victory lay within the grasp of the British. In the past, they had often squandered these opportunities by not fighting. This time Howe's army fought, and fought hard and capably, to achieve what all knew could be a pivotal moment in this tough war.

The fighting was savage. One redcoat was amazed by the "most infernal fire" on this field, as balls whistled and set "trees crackling over one's head" and "leaves falling as in autumn."[25] Much of the combat was at close quarters, "almost Muzzle to Muzzle," according to one rebel. A French volunteer with the Continentals, who had fought in many battles in Europe, declared that he had never witnessed "So Close & Severe a fire." A Delaware soldier thought the "small arms roared like the rolling of a drum."[26] A Marylander, who had been in the army for only three days, somehow lost his gun in the midst of the battle, "but made my escape."[27] Another rebel was not so fortunate. "I was wounded," a New Jersey soldier said, "having a Ball with the Wad shot through my left forearm & the fuse set my coat and shirt on fire."[28] A private in the Bucks County, Pennsylvania, militia remembered "bombshells and shot fell round me like hail, cutting down my comrades on every side, and tearing off the limbs of the trees like a whirlwind."[29] Battles are confusing to participants, a collage of noise, frantic movement, and blinding terror. Private Elisha Stevens, who fought at Brandywine, left a description that in its breathlessly unhinged way captures the disorder that he had just experienced: "The Battel was . . . Cannons Roaring muskets Cracking Drums Beating Bumbs Flying all Round, men a dying woundeds Horred Grones which would Greave the Heardist of Hearts to See Such a manner as this."[30]

The British had almost twice as many men in this sector as the Americans, at least at the outset, but they could not overwhelm the rebels. Some Americans—one wing of Sullivan's force—broke and fled, but most fought well. The rebels were driven from Birmingham Hill five times. They retook it four times. "We broke and Rallied and Rallied & broke," was how one American soldier described it.[31] But after ninety minutes of desperate fighting the British prevailed, due primarily to sheer numbers and a spirited bayonet charge. The Americans reeled back in some disarray. It was the moment of maximum danger for the rebels. But Washington, fully aware at last of the shape of affairs, had ordered Greene's division to his imperiled flank, directing him to "Quick march to the right." Those men covered four miles in forty-five minutes, though encumbered with equipment weighing twenty pounds or more.[32] They fought stoutly, taking cover behind buildings, trees, and fences, retreating, taking up new shelter, and fighting again. Washington had arrived as well—he sprang on his powerful charger and rode like the wind from the center of the field, his horse leaping "all the fences without difficulty," a civilian guide marveled—and took command.[33] At great peril he rode about the battlefield restoring order by his presence and obvious courage, but also beginning to organize his army's withdrawal from the field as Greene's men fought desperately to hold the enemy at bay. Howe's plan had called for Knyphausen to advance at the appropriate time to complete the envelopment of the rebel right wing. Waiting at the Brandywine until he saw Greene's men moving to their right, Knyphausen assumed that Howe's flanking maneuver had begun and at last began to cross. It was slow going, less from rebel resistance than from the difficulty of getting men through waist deep water and past the logs and other debris that the rebels had placed in the creek as impediments. Finally across, the British, with overwhelming numbers, moved swiftly in the face of rapidly collapsing American resistance. But at Dilworthtown, with the sun low in the sky at 6:00 p.m., the English and German grenadiers encountered stubborn resistance and took heavy casualties. The fighting there raged for nearly an hour, until the sun pitched over the horizon, bringing the bloody fray to an end, and

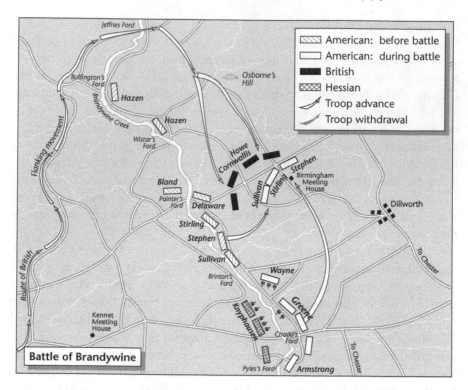

Battle of Brandywine

enabling Washington to safely retreat from this battlefield.[34] One American soldier remembered that the retreat was nearly as ghastly as the battle itself. "Our way was over the dead and dying," he recalled, "and I saw many bodies crushed to pieces beneath the wagons, and we were bespattered with blood."[35]

The Battle of Brandywine was a British victory. One redcoat sergeant insisted, perhaps correctly, that the rebels had "escaped a total overthrow, that must have been the consequence of an hours more daylight."[36] A rebel concurred, confessing that by nightfall "our army was something broke."[37] Not only did Howe possess the field, but the Americans had taken the heaviest casualties, losing about 1,100 men. The British lost about half that number. Howe once again had outgeneraled his rival, prompting a Hessian on the day of the engagement to conclude that "Howe is not a middling man but indeed a good general."[38] Nevertheless, Howe gained little from his victory. To achieve a truly pivotal triumph, he had to destroy Washington's army. Howe had performed ably, while Washington had again been indecisive, but at day's end the Continental army remained intact. Brandywine might have ended differently had Howe started his flanking operation earlier. He would have been wise to have done as Washington had done in his march on Trenton: commence his march in the scorching red light of sunset on the previous evening. By waiting until nearly sunrise to start his march, he squandered hours of daylight; only about three hours of daylight remained when he began his furious bombardment on the American right. Howe was also virtually devoid of cavalry, having brought few horse units with him and having lost so many horses during the voyage. But the Continental army had something to do with Howe's failure to score a knockout punch. It fought well, in part because it now was composed mostly of long-term soldiers, but also because its officers at every level now had one or two years experience under their belts.

Washington had withdrawn at day's end, but he remained full of fight, and hopeful of getting another shot at his nemesis. He appears not to have considered setting up behind the Schuylkill, as he had done on the Delaware River ten months earlier, wary of being trapped between the Schuylkill and Delaware Rivers. Instead, Washington hoped to engage Howe either as the redcoats, who were devoid of amphibious equipment, moved toward one of the Schuylkill's shallow upper fords, well to the northwest of the city, or to fall on the regulars as they attempted their crossing. Howe was no less eager to fight, and when he learned that Washington's army was at Warren Tavern, on the Lancaster Road in Chester County, he marched there rapidly. But the battle that each leader wanted never occurred. In what some called the Battle of the Clouds, an all-day soaking rain system moved into the area just as the two armies prepared to square off. ("I wish I could give a description of the downpour," a German said. "It came so hard that in a few minutes we were drenched and sank in mud up to our calves.") For men equipped with powder and flints, fighting was impossible. Nor could fighting begin when the squall finally ended, as the Americans discovered that incessant rain had ruined their ammunition supply—nearly 400,000 cartridges. Washington slipped away, withdrawing to an ammunition dump at Reading Furnace to resupply. Howe pushed on toward Philadelphia.[39]

Washington rushed fresh ammunition to Wayne's division of 1,500 men, and ordered it to tag along after the British army and to strike at the enemy's rear guard and baggage train, if possible. Prudently, too, he warned Wayne to "take care of Ambuscades." Wayne failed to take that advice. He shadowed Howe's army, looking for the opportunity to harass it, but when the regulars paused, Wayne halted as well, setting up camp about four miles away at Paoli Tavern. Wayne's mistake was to stay at Paoli for three successive nights. When his whereabouts were reported by local Loyalists, Howe on September 20 sent a force of two thousand men under Colonel Charles Grey, a forty-eight-year-old veteran of two wars, to deal with the rebels. What followed was not an ambush, as Wayne had nearly an hour's notice that a large British force was in the vicinity. However, that Grey chose to attack in the dead of night, an uncommon practice among European armies, came as a terrible surprise. Grey refused to permit his men to carry loaded muskets, for fear they would shoot one another in the darkness. He ordered a bayonet assault. The regulars, one said later, "took a circuit in Dead silence," and when Grey screamed the order to attack—"Dash on, light infantry!"—they burst from the dark forest with "such a cheer as made the wood echo." Most wielded bayonets, but some carried sabers, and the fighting took place in the orange half-light of low burning campfires. It was, said a British officer, a "dreadful scene of Havock." Another redcoat laconically noted in his journal that the regulars "stabbed great numbers" of Americans. Rebel losses were staggering. Nearly four hundred men were lost and almost all the division's equipment was abandoned and fell into enemy hands.[40]

Thereafter, Howe moved quickly. Seemingly always capable of outmaneuvering Washington, he did so once again on September 22. Washington himself said that the "Enemy, by a variety of perplexing Maneuvers," succeeded in crossing the Schuylkill without opposition at both Gordon's and Fatland Ford. That was not the half of it. Washington was a full twenty miles out of position.[41] The way to Philadelphia was clear. Congress had been warned of the imminent threat nearly sixty hours earlier. The congressmen had packed previously, in preparation for a hasty exit. Some, like John Adams, bloviated about staying and fighting, but that was a charade. When the alert was sounded—a party sent by Alexander Hamilton arrived and began knocking on doors in the wee hours of the morning —the members of Congress rolled from their beds, dressed hurriedly, gathered their transportable belongings, and set off on horseback. They "decamped with the utmost precipitation and in the greatest confusion," a Philadelphia Tory laughed, so much so that Nathaniel Folsom of New Hampshire even forgot to saddle his horse. The congressmen, from whom the residents of Philadelphia "still expected protection," left the city's dwellers in the lurch, the exultant Loyalist added wryly.[42] Desperate to avoid capture, they remained east of Philadelphia as they rode away, praying that they did not run up on a British patrol as they hurried on in the stygian night. Their ultimate destination was Lancaster, about fifty miles to the west, a previously agreed upon site for reassembling. In the meantime, most scurried into New Jersey. They were frightened and some were angry that the British army had not been stopped. "Ruin . . . seems to await" this great cause, Adams railed. "We have as good a Cause, as ever was fought for. We have great Resources. The People are well tempered." Given these assets, he wondered why one military disaster after another befell the American army.[43]

Units of the British army, with Cornwallis at their head, accompanied by several Pennsylvania Loyalists, including Joseph Galloway, who had headed the colony's delegation at the First Continental Congress three years earlier, marched into Philadelphia on September 26 to what the soldiers and Tories said was a tumult of celebration. Some rebel residents described the scene differently. The conquerors were met with stony silence, they said.[44] If they are to be believed, all that could be heard that sunny day was the British military band, playing among other things "God save great George our King"—described by an observer as "a solemn tune"—and the resounding, rhythmic thudding of boots and the clatter of horses' hooves on cobblestones. The triumphant soldiers were grave, displaying "no wanton levity, or indecent mirth," said a resident, but the victory parade had hardly ended before the pillaging began.[45] The soldiers searched especially for "salt and good bread," but some looted shops and homes of whatever pleased them. Soldiers in the occupation force encountered a hostile, resentful population, none more so than the German-Americans who lived in Philadelphia. They "were against us" and "could hardly conceal their anger and hostile sentiments" at the Hessian presence, said a puzzled German soldier. Speaking in fluent German, one perplexed resident asked him: "What harm have we people done to you, that you Germans come over here to suck us dry and drive us out of house and home?"[46]

The British had their prize, though Washington hoped for an action that might take the luster off Howe's September successes and that, like Trenton, might deal the enemy a heavy blow before winter. He asked for, and received, reinforcements—New Jersey and Maryland militia came in, as did Continentals called down from the highlands (it was at this point, in between the two Battles of Saratoga, that Washington asked Gates to detach Morgan's riflemen to the south)—bringing his troop level up to 11,000. On September 28, Washington summoned a council of war at Pennypacker's Mill (present-day Schwenksville) and told his generals that Howe had divided his army, posting half in the city and the remainder, some eight thousand men, at Germantown. Washington itched to make "a general & vigorous attack" on those at Germantown. The rebels not only would have numerical superiority, Washington was personally familiar with Germantown, having been there twice within the past forty days. He was confident, too, that he could achieve another stunning surprise, but the council of war rebuffed the notion of an attack, at least until additional reinforcements were garnered.[47]

The next day Washington moved the army to Skippack, a step closer to Germantown. Combing through the intelligence that came in, he learned that Howe had transferred some units out of Germantown. Washington may have discovered as well that the British commander, like Rall at Trenton, had not fortified the little village. During his first seventy-two hours at Skippack more Continentals from the highlands arrived, as did units of green Virginia militiamen. More eager than ever to act, Washington did not summon another potentially balky council of war. He spoke separately and privately with each general officer then announced his decision. He would attack.[48]

Washington prepared a complicated plan that required intricate synchronization. Under the best of circumstances, the odds were long against its success. For an army led by amateurs, and operating at night in a strange environment, it was a plan that was destined for trouble. The army was to proceed in four columns from Skippack, sixteen miles from Germantown, and attack the British from four directions simultaneously. While Maryland and New Jersey militia came in below Howe's right wing and Pennsylvania militiamen did the same below his left wing (forming the jaws of a pincer), the cream of the army—some under Sullivan, others under Greene—were to strike the left and right of the enemy line.

The units faced with the longest march were to set out just before nightfall on October 3; the others would follow at staggered intervals. All were to be in place to launch what Washington hoped would be a coordinated attack at 5:00 a.m. Little time elapsed before his plan began to go awry. A dense fog settled over the landscape during the wee hours of that morning—it was the "thickest fog known in the memory of man," declared one soldier—causing monumental problems for officers who were unfamiliar with the roads.[49] The march, already slowed because many soldiers were wearing threadbare shoes, or no shoes, was further drawn out by the occluded conditions. Only Sullivan's column had reached its appointed place by 5:00 a.m., perhaps because Washington rode with it and brooked no languor. "[W]hat with the thickness of the air . . . we could see but a little way before us," said one of Sullivan's men, but in spite of the dense fog, and unaware of the status of his three other columns, Washington ordered Sullivan to launch the attack, sending the men forward with orders "not to fire till . . . the buttons upon their Clothes" were visible.[50] Some men charged ahead screaming "Have at the bloodhounds! Revenge Wayne's affair!!"[51]

The British were not taken totally by surprise, as had been the case with the Germans at Trenton. Local Tories had tipped them off to preparations in the rebel camp at Skippack, and some Continentals who had been taken captive while on patrol during the preceding thirty-six hours had talked when interrogated. But the regulars did not know precisely when or where the blow would fall and, besides, Sullivan's force heavily outnumbered the light infantry stationed on the British left where the opening assault came. The redcoats fought hard, but fell back, carrying out their retreat after the American fashion, taking cover behind walls and buildings, and, according to one rebel, even dragging their cannon into brick buildings, from which they wailed away.[52] Sullivan came close to turning the British flank in the early going, an event that might have produced a victory that approximated those at Trenton-Princeton. "We . . . fell upon them and by a vigorous attack . . . putting them to flight [succeeded in] capturing their tents, baggage, provisions, artillery, &c. In short, they were entirely routed," crowed Henry Miller, the captain of a Pennsylvania rifle company composed of men from the vicinity of Gettysburg.[53]

Victory was elusive. Several things went wrong. The Maryland and New Jersey militia never found Germantown. The Pennsylvania militia at least reached the village, but quickly got pinned down by a small unit of Hessians in a remote southern sector of the hamlet. Greene, who had two-thirds of the army with him, arrived thirty minutes late. This combination of misfortunes negated the rebels' magnificent beginning. Other factors were also crucial in undoing Washington's plan. Early in the engagement, Lieutenant Colonel Thomas Musgrave took about 120 of his redcoats from the Fortieth Foot into the capacious two-story stone Chew House (owned by the chief justice of Pennsylvania), converting it in effect into a fort. The rebels, as many officers at the time urged, should have passed the house by and fought elsewhere. Instead, Washington,

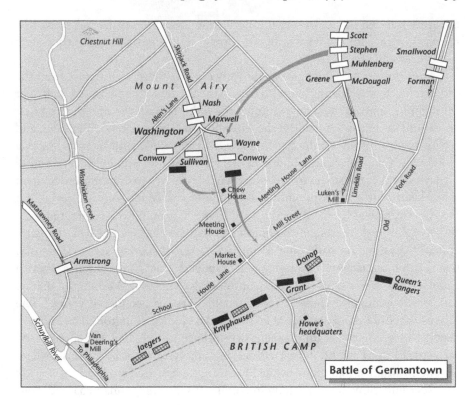

Battle of Germantown

who was swayed by Knox, wasted an entire brigade, precious firepower, and a full hour in an unsuccessful, and entirely unnecessary, siege of the property. One disgusted rebel officer said later that his men's "ardor abated" as a result of the ill-advised, and unsuccessful, siege.[54] Another American raged that "a glorious victory fought for and eight tenths won, was shamefully . . . lost" by poor leadership.[55] Even some of the enemy, who had come to respect their adversary, later expressed amazement that the usually "Clever Washington" would commit such an egregious blunder.[56] Nor was that the only failing. General Adam Stephen, who had nearly wrecked the Christmas surprise a year earlier, blundered at the outset of the contest by taking his Virginians in the wrong direction, playing havoc with the commander's intricate plan. Later, without authorization, he ordered a withdrawal that unhinged adjacent units. In the confusion of battle, other adversities cropped up. In this instance, some leaders became confused in the fog and smoke. General George Weedon, a Virginian who had soldiered for nearly ten years in two wars, subsequently remarked that it was "impossible to Distinguish our men from the Enemy at a greater Distance than Sixty yards, and many favourable Advantages were lost."[57] In the most appalling case— Washington maintained later that it was the single most important reason why the army was denied victory—two American units crossed paths and each, mistaking the other for the enemy, opened fire.[58] The ghastly error touched off a panic in several units.

After three hours, the fighting abruptly ceased. Neither entreaties from the officers, nor from Washington, who was on the battlefield and exposed to danger throughout, spurred the men to resume the fight. It was over, and the best that now could be done was to collect the wounded and the precious field pieces, and retreat before British reinforcements arrived from Philadelphia. It had been a bloody day. One American soldier said that all across the battlefield "dead bodies . . . lay as thick as the stones in a stony plowfield."[59] For Washington and his men it had been a bitterly disappointing day. One Pennsylvania soldier grieved that the Americans had been "obliged . . . to leave the ground to a conquered foe," and to relinquish the enemy's equipment that had been seized in the early going.[60] Washington had come within a whisker of scoring a crucial victory. Instead, he came away empty-handed. General Louis Duportail, a French engineer who was serving with the Continentals, later told Washington that he had "really conquer'd General How, but his Troops conquered yours." The Americans could claim nothing from the battle, save Washington's lame remark that it had been "rather unfortunate than injurious." He had lost about 1,200 men—nearly 35 percent of the fatalities, incredibly, at the Chew House, where the enemy lost just four men—while Howe's losses reached around 500.[61]

Recriminations were not long in coming. One congressman charged, "our miscarriage sprung from the usual source—want of abilities in our superior officers."[62] In the face of such allegations, some in the army's leadership searched for a scapegoat. General Stephen was made the fall guy. A full week after the battle he was accused for the first time of having gone into combat in an inebriated state, a charge that was never proven. The focus for having failed to gain an important victory came to center on his unauthorized retreat at a pivotal moment of the battle. It was a sordid episode. Many appear to have pointed fingers at Stephen to save their own skin and some realized that by laying the blame on him the spotlight would be removed from the Chew House fiasco. Other army politics were involved as well. Stephen's disgrace not only would clear the way for the ascent of others, but through his removal a command position for Lafayette would be opened. Stephen was court-martialed, convicted, and dismissed from the service.[63]

AFTER GERMANTOWN, Washington could not get at Howe, who shortly pulled his entire army into Philadelphia. Nor could Howe get at Washington, as his logistical needs required that he first clear the Delaware River approach to Philadelphia of three American forts, multiple chevaux-de-frieze, and an American flotilla consisting of a frigate, brig, schooner, row galleys, floating batteries, and numerous fire ships and fire rafts. It was the beginning of what Congressman John Adams had forecast: once Howe "had Philadelphia . . . he could not get away."[64] Like Gage in Boston, Howe was going nowhere. His was a hollow victory. British casualties continued to mount as forty laborious and dangerous days were required to clear out the rebels along the Delaware. In an attack on Fort Mifflin, for instance, Howe suffered losses equal to half the number that he had lost at Brandywine and Germantown combined.[65]

Before the British destroyed the last rebel fort on the Delaware, Washington's thoughts had turned to winter quarters. He envisaged scattering his army throughout multiple winter camps running in a line from about sixty miles northwest of Philadelphia to roughly the same distance due west of the city. He reasoned that both supply and health issues could be more easily managed through such an arrangement. Pennsylvania's officials and many congressmen had other ideas. Some did not want Washington to go into winter quarters at all, but to mount "one vigorous Effort" whose object would be to see that "Mr Howe . . . [met] with the fate of his brother officer G Burgoyne." What they had in mind was an attack on the British army lodged in Philadelphia, and Congress sent delegates to Washington's headquarters to discuss such an enterprise.[66] Washington, who had repeatedly urged an attack on the British in Boston in 1775–1776, and who was always a fighter, was intrigued. But he was ultimately dissuaded by General Greene. A year earlier, Greene's advice regarding Fort Washington had been horribly flawed. This time he saw things in a sober light. Greene understood that to attack Philadelphia was to walk into a death trap, a Bunker Hill in reverse. Howe not only had put his army behind fourteen redoubts that guarded the approaches to the city on the north and west, he had summoned four thousand reinforcements from New York.[67] Greene also fathomed his commander, and he knew that following Gates's success at Saratoga, Washington felt the need to act, believing that many in Congress and throughout the countryside would be satisfied with nothing less. (By late autumn people in some parts of the country were dancing a step known as the "Burgoyne surrender" and a popular song also celebrated the victory at Saratoga, a line in it proclaiming that "Brave Gates will clear America before another year.")[68] Greene applied the proper emollient, urging Washington to put aside all thoughts of a "hassardous attempt" that might "disgrace . . . the Army." He urged such a course for "your Sake . . . & for my Country's Sake." The "Cause is too important to be trifled with to shew our Courage, and your Character [is] too deeply interested to sport away."[69] It was the best advice that Washington ever received. To his credit, he took it.

Washington's discussions with the state officials and the congressional committee were polite, but tense, and in the end the commander convinced them that a winter campaign was fraught with potentially ruinous difficulties. He added that the time could be put to better use by recruiting, inoculating, and training new recruits, who would go into action in the spring or summer of 1778. While Washington deflected the pressure to attack, he was less successful with regard to his plan for quartering the army in numerous camps. Congressmen from

Pennsylvania, New Jersey, Delaware, and Maryland, backed by remonstrances from the legislatures in some of those states, insisted that the Continental army take up winter quarters near Philadelphia in order to assure that Howe could not emerge to cause mischief. Some grumbled, too, that Washington's notion of scattered cantonments for the winter bore an uncomfortable resemblance to what Howe, with "pernicious Consequences," had tried the previous year in New Jersey."[70]

Washington caved in, though he seethed at civilian intrusiveness and feared that the meddling might produce a disaster. For the most part, he kept his emotions in check, but just before Christmas his deep-seated bitterness seeped into a letter that he wrote to Congress. His army, he said, could not provide "protection to every Individual and to every Spot of Ground in the whole of the United States." In all wars, he went on, some are "exposed . . . to ravage and depredation." His first responsibility was "the preservation" of the army, that it might live on as an effectual force and someday secure the ultimate triumph. Then he boiled over. It "is time to speak plain." It "is a much easier and less distressing thing, to draw Remonstrances in a comfortable room by a good fire side" than to face a soldier's life and "to occupy a cold, bleak hill, and sleep under frost & snow without Cloaths or Blankets."[71]

With that, Washington marched his army into winter quarters near Philadelphia. The site that was chosen was a place called Valley Forge.

11

CHOICES, 1778

WINTER HAD A WAY of bringing bad tidings to London. The city had learned of the Boston Tea Party, the boycott adopted by the First Continental Congress, and the military disasters at Trenton and Princeton during earlier dark winters, but the worst news yet arrived in December 1777. Londoners learned of the loss of Burgoyne's army at Saratoga.

London had long been awash with gloomy rumors about the military situation in America, but until December 2 the hearsay was unsubstantiated.[1] To the last minute, Germain held out hope. "Burgoyne's situation is bad," he confessed to the king on December 1, "but it is hoped not so very bad as reported by the rebels."[2] The very next day a dispatch arrived from Carleton that confirmed the ministry's worst fears. Verification had not been required for Opposition members in the House of Commons to wale away at the government and to savage Germain. As early as October, Charles James Fox had blasted the idea of placing "the two armies in such a position as from their distance made it absolutely impossible that the one should receive any assistance from the other." Burgoyne's "army was not equal to the task," Fox had said all along, and in November he stridently maintained that Germain's policies had driven "the Americans to a declaration of independence," caused "the continuance of the war," and now had led a "gallant general [to be] sent like a victim to be slaughtered."[3]

After December 3, when Lord North first publicly expressed his "sorrow at the unhappy news," the fury of the Opposition knew no bounds.[4] "Ignorance had stamped every step taken during the course of the expedition," one raged. Another "condemned the whole of the expedition," but especially the licensing of

"a diabolical system of blood and carnage" that was to be carried out by the ravening hordes of "savages." Fox reiterated that Germain was "solely responsible"
for Britain's "disgrace" through his "obstinate, wilful ignorance." Burke thought
there had never been a greater disaster in British history, but he absolved
Burgoyne. The government alone bore responsibility for this "crime," he said.
Burke also challenged the government's representation of the "Americans . . . as
cowards," a recurring theme during the past three years. Gates and Arnold not
only had been brave, Burke retorted, they had been "generous to the last degree"
in paroling a British army that had availed itself of "the savages to butcher them,
their wives, their aged parents, and their children." Temple Luttrell, radiating
cold fury, went further than any member of the Opposition. He drew a parallel
between the "timid" conduct of Germain at Minden and the weak-kneed advice
that he had given the king about military affairs in America. Luttrell's intemperate remarks provoked an altercation on the floor of the Commons, but they also
spurred his brother James, a member from Stockbridge, to assail the very heart of
the government's American policies. "[W]hilst unconditional submission is the
language of the ministers and parliament, all efforts to conquer America must
prove in vain," he insisted.[5]

The North ministry's survival past December was due in some measure to
George III, who remained persuaded that the war with America must continue.
He steadied North, who had been battling depression since his accident the
year before, and who was ready—eager even—to resign upon receiving word of
Burgoyne's fate. Bolstered, the government easily beat back attempts by the
Opposition to end hostilities and force the repeal of some of its American measures. Its position stabilized, the government secured a month's adjournment of
Parliament, a time when North began to formulate a strategy for dealing with the
war crisis. In reality, North had already begun to grope toward a new American
policy. One of his first steps, taken two days after he learned of Burgoyne's surrender, was to send a secret agent—Paul Wentworth, a New Hampshire Loyalist who
was living in London—to Paris to open talks with the American commissioners.[6]

THE AMERICAN COMMISSIONERS—Franklin, Lee, and Deane—learned of Burgoyne's
surrender two days after North received the news. They immediately informed
Foreign Minister Vergennes of the "total Reduction of the Force under General
Burgoyne," and added that Gates had sent reinforcements to Washington for use
against Howe, who "it was hoped . . . would soon be reduced to the same Terms
with Burgoyne." When that did not pan out, Franklin told all who would listen,
including Vergennes, who met with the commissioners in mid-December, that
"instead of *Howe* taking *Philada.—Philada* has taken *Howe*," for the British army
was "shut up in Philadelphia, scarce of provisions, and surrounded by conquering
troops."[7] Even if Franklin's claim was somewhat overblown, word of Saratoga
and of Howe's less than completely successful campaign, touched off frenzied
activity in Paris and London.

It is conceivable that Saratoga was not absolutely essential for France's entry into the war. Vergennes had long considered the spring of 1778 as the earliest moment for his country to become a belligerent, as the rebuilding of the French navy—begun nearly fifteen years before—would by then be far enough advanced for hostilities to be considered. The previous spring, when Burgoyne's army was still preparing for its invasion of New York, Vergennes held discussions with Spain aimed at securing Madrid's agreement to a joint war with Great Britain that might begin early in 1778. The Spanish had not been interested. Throughout 1777, Vergennes had walked a tightrope. He knew that it was not in France's interest to go to war alone against Great Britain, but it was also not in France's interest to permit an Anglo-American reconciliation, a step that might occur if the rebels were not properly assisted. Vergennes had funneled money and equipment to the rebels, and he had even promised to assume the cost of completing two American frigates under construction in Amsterdam. His largess was undertaken in such secrecy that the American commissioners complained to Congress that they were "scarce allowed to know that they give us any Aids at all," adding that they were "left to imagine, if we please, that the Cannon, Arms, &c. . . . are the Efforts of private Benevolence."[8]

All the while, Franklin, who had landed in France one year and one day prior to the arrival of the news of Saratoga, had spent 1777 actively courting French opinion. All governments, he believed, were swayed by public opinion, even an autocracy such as France. Franklin had long been well known in France for his electrical experiments, and a considerable portion of his public writings had been translated and published in France, some of it twenty years earlier. America also enjoyed a favorable reputation among the French. In some enlightened circles America had long been proclaimed as unspoiled and uncorrupted, a land inhabited by simple rustics who enjoyed social equality and religious freedoms to a degree unknown in the Old World. Some Parisian reformers portrayed Franklin as the very symbol of the New World, and he shrewdly plugged into what one historian has labeled the "radical chic" of the moment. With his sure hand for public relations, Franklin put away his powdered wig and velvet suits, and assumed the role of the primitive American by donning a fur hat and unpretentious clothing (while living in a mansion with a cellar stocked with more than one thousand bottles of wine). Parisian society embraced him and his image appeared on medallions, prints, clocks, vases, dishes, handkerchiefs, candy boxes, and pocketknives. His avuncular face even peered up from the bottom of porcelain chamber pots.[9] But Franklin's public relations successes had little to do with France's calculated decision to ally with the United States, at least according to John Adams, who came to Paris that spring. Burgoyne's defeat and Washington's daring attacks at Trenton, Princeton, and Germantown, Adams insisted, had achieved "more in Europe, than all our Ambassadors." Comte d'Estaing, more or less echoing Adams, noted that Washington's "talent and great actions" had led him to be seen in France as the "deliverer of America."[10]

If battlefield actions had helped bring around the French king, his conversion was finally sealed by the commissioners' open and disquieting reception of North's envoy, Wentworth. The Wentworth mission was yet another blunder by the British government, as it simply played into the rebels' hands. Unwilling to consider American independence, North's ministry merely empowered Wentworth to explore whether there was a possibility of reconciliation with the colonists, perhaps involving concessions by London along the lines that had been demanded by the First Continental Congress before the outbreak of hostilities. The commissioners were eager to see what Wentworth would offer—at one point, Franklin raised the prospect of London's recognition of American independence, followed in turn by a formal Anglo-American alliance—but for the most part the American envoys used him for their own guileful ends. They made sure that Vergennes knew they were meeting with a British official—Franklin was also simultaneously meeting openly with two British acquaintances from his years in London—and the foreign minister in turn seized on the activities of the American diplomats to help sway Louis XVI and those ministers who had opposed an alliance with the Americans. For his part, Wentworth reported to London that only Britain's recognition of American independence would prevent a Franco-American alliance and hostilities with France.[11]

Free at last to open serious talks with the commissioners, Vergennes sent Conrad-Alexandre Gérard as his representative, and negotiations commenced during the second week in January 1778. Within the first hour of discussions the Americans proposed a treaty of commerce and Gérard agreed in principle. The commissioners then asked for France's immediate entrance into the war. Gérard demurred, but countered with a proposal for a treaty of military alliance that would leave France to decide on the timing of its belligerency.[12] This was far afield from the instructions that Congress had given its envoys in the summer of 1776, but much had occurred during the intervening eighteen months: majestic victories and chastening defeats, staggering logistical problems, financial adversities, recruiting woes, and the capture of three major American cities, New York, Philadelphia, and Newport. Canada had also slipped from the rebels' tenuous grasp and the war had widened. The Indians were in it now and the frontier was certain to be an expanding battleground in the future. If the commissioners spurned France's offer, America faced a choice of fighting alone in a protracted war or of reassuming its colonial status, albeit on more favorable terms than London had been willing to offer before the war. Choosing a French alliance, on the other hand, was a good bet. If Britain had been unable to suppress the rebellion while unhindered by war with a European power, it seemed unimaginable that it could defeat both the United States and France.

Franklin, Lee, and Deane huddled for three days before responding to Gérard. Ultimately, they accepted his offer, though they complained about France's inability to bring Spain on board. Gérard softened their disappointment with the hint that France might assist the Americans in conquering Canada.

From start to finish, things proceeded quickly and smoothly. On January 18, Gérard provided the Americans with drafts of a treaty of commerce and a treaty of military alliance. Nine days later—much of the intervening time was consumed in translating the drafts and with discussions among the commissioners—the two parties came to terms. In the course of the negotiations, the Americans had proposed only two substantive changes to Gérard's drafts. One called for a guarantee that the war was not to end until Britain recognized the United States' possession of the Mississippi valley. The second called for the insertion of a stipulation that should France not formally enter the war, it was to provide the United States with an "annual Subsidy in Money" and warships. Gérard refused both proposals. Unruffled, the Americans, almost panting after an alliance, dropped both matters and asked instead for some face-saving stylistic alterations, "if not thought absolutely improper." Nonetheless, the Americans hardly came away empty-handed. They, too, were protected by the French-inspired clause stipulating that neither side would make a separate truce or peace with Great Britain, and they were delighted by the provision that the partners "mutually engage not to lay down their arms until the independence of the United States shall have been formally . . . assured by the Treaty or Treaties that shall terminate the War." They were also happy that France renounced all claims to Canada. The accords were signed on the cold, starry evening of February 6 at the Paris office of the French Foreign Ministry in the Hôtel de Lautrec.[13] A few days later Louis XVI received the commissioners at Versailles. Abjuring ceremony, the monarch wore his dressing gown to the ceremony. Franklin, in keeping with his carefully crafted image as the uncorrupted American republican, wore a simple brown suit, eschewed a sword (a standard prop for diplomats of the time), and left his hair hanging loose. Some observers said that he looked like a Quaker.[14]

THROUGH SPIES who were confidants of one or more of the unwary commissioners, the North ministry knew at every turn what was afoot in Paris. What was readily apparent, a member of the Commons remarked, was that Britain and France, the world's two greatest powers, were "fairly running a race for the favour of America."[15] Races are won by the swiftest, which put the measured British, with their parliamentary system, at a disadvantage. Autocratic France, which was bidding to sustain the embryonic American republic, faced no such obstacles. Its parliament had not met for a century and a half.

North later claimed that he had toyed with offering major concessions to the Americans even before Saratoga, but hard evidence is lacking that he contemplated genuine conciliation until after he learned of Burgoyne's epic capitulation. William Eden, a close friend and a former undersecretary of state, approached North early in December "with the feelings of a man who has just seen some dreadful Calamity."[16] Eden pleaded with the prime minister to seek peace and reconciliation with America through bold measures of imperial reform, including perhaps the renunciation of all Parliamentary authority over the colonies. That alone, he suggested, could save the empire and prevent war with France. Over a period of seven weeks—beginning nearly a month prior to Gérard's first meeting with the commissioners and continuing through, and beyond, the melancholy Parliamentary recess—North consulted with Eden, the king, and several under-secretaries and subministers (but with no one in his cabinet) in conceiving and drafting a plan of conciliation. Racing to provide the colonists with an alternative to the French alliance, and harried by dread that the Opposition would beat him to the punch, North worked so hard that he pushed himself to the brink of a physical collapse. When at last the legislation was ready, North divulged it to the cabinet. This was five days after the treaties had been signed in Paris (though North was unaware that the pact had been signed). Six additional days passed before he introduced the bills in the Commons in a long, somber address that Walpole characterized as North's "confession and humiliation."[17]

North proposed a sweeping reconsideration of the rights of the colonies and the powers of the imperial authority. His was an enormous about-face, as he embraced the federal principle and took a long step toward what ultimately would become Britain's commonwealth system. North did not dwell on the specifics of his plan. He spoke in vague terms because he was recommending that peace commissioners, who would receive secret instructions to guide them in their negotiations, be sent to America, but also because he had not made up his mind on every last particular that might be negotiated. Still, it was evident that he was prepared to renounce Parliament's long-standing claim to possess the authority to legislate for America in all cases whatsoever, including the power to tax the colonists. North was also ready to restore the charter of Massachusetts, which had been ripped away in the Coercive Acts in 1774.[18]

The House listened in what the *Annual Register* described as "a dull melancholy silence," and no fireworks followed the address, as the Opposition found North's retreat to be "in the main, so ample and satisfactory." Only Fox had his say, and he could not resist pointing out in a taunting riposte that the prime minister's new position was virtually identical to the imperial reforms that the Opposition had recommended in preference to war three years before. If the House was calm, somber even, on the day of North's address, it was consumed with repeated firefights over proposed amendments to the legislation in the weeks ahead. Every alteration that the Opposition urged—recognition of American independence, preventing the dispatch of further troops to North America, condemnation of the use of Indians, and agreeing to the removal of any cabinet official to whom the colonists objected—was quashed.[19]

It was only in the preparation of the instructions to the peace commissioners that North at last was compelled to decide what specific concessions he was prepared to make. The magnitude of his retreat was breathtaking. In addition to the repudiation of taxation, the envoys were authorized to treat with Congress, "as if it were a legal body," and to conclude a "treaty" in which Britain, if need be, would agree to:

suspend all legislation pertaining to America that had been enacted since 1763;
never again keep a standing army in America in peacetime;
never again change a colonial charter without the assent of the colonial legislature;
assist the colonies in reducing their war debt;
give Americans preference when filling colonial offices;
make all colonial offices elective;
eliminate Crown officers to which the colonists objected;
staff the American customs service solely with Americans;
consider American representation in the House of Commons.

Under North's plan, an armistice was to begin when the treaty was signed, but the British army would continue to occupy Manhattan, Long Island, and Rhode Island until Parliament ratified the treaty. Nor were any of the concessions to apply to Canada, East Florida, or West Florida. Under North's conciliatory plan, all that would remain of the old imperial system in the thirteen American colonies was the authority of the king and the commercial regulations that dated back a century or more, neither of which had been objected to by Congress before the war.[20]

The peace commissioners were named in April. The commission was to be headed by the Earl of Carlisle, who was young and inexperienced, and whom Eden—who was also named to the commission that he had been the first to envisage—described as a "Bepowdered Fop."[21] Carlisle was chosen, as best anyone could tell, because he had been a schoolmate and chum of Fox. The third member (after his predecessor quit in protest because the recognition of American independence was not permitted) was William Johnstone, formerly the colonial governor of West Florida, a man whom Walpole described as "brutal, rash, overbearing, litigious, and rather clever."[22] (True to those qualities, Johnstone had already publicly questioned Carlisle's fitness to be part of the diplomatic effort.) The members of the Carlisle Commission sailed for America on the *Trident* in mid-April, 136 days after word of Saratoga reached London and 69 days after the American commissioners signed the treaties with France.

Two huge choices remained for North and the king. One involved whether or not to leave Germain and the Howes in power. The other concerned how, or even whether, to wage the war. From the moment that Burgoyne's fate was known, Germain and Howe were mercilessly flayed in the press and Parliament, but the American secretary by far got the worst of it. An essayist in the *Public Ledger* wrote that on Germain's watch "Fifty thousand veteran troops, have not, in three years, been able to obtain secure possession of fifty miles of ground in America!"[23] In the legislature, in one malice laden speech after another, Germain was blasted for having authored "an inconsistent scheme, an impractical one, unworthy of a British minister." Not even "an Indian chief" would have been so derelict as to have failed to order Howe to assist Burgoyne, said one Opposition speaker. An entire army, said another, had been destroyed "through the ignorance . . . and incapacity of the noble lord." More than any other individual, Fox charged, Germain was responsible for "the calamity of his country."[24] Even some within the ministry signaled that they had lost confidence in Germain. Few who remained in his camp defended him publicly. North did so, however, maintaining that Germain had "acted on the soundest principles of ardour and deliberation," and insisting that he had been betrayed by the "want of information" from distant America.[25] Actually, North would have been overjoyed to have been free of Germain, but it was politically untenable to dump a secretary whose plan had been approved by the cabinet. In the feeding frenzy that would follow Germain's dismissal, the ministry likely would be consumed. Germain survived, though North agreed to a Parliamentary inquiry into the campaign of 1777, which he imagined could be managed by his majority and that would end—as was the case—in a whitewash of Germain and the government.[26]

The Howes were also savagely assailed—the general for the "ill success of the Canada expedition," the admiral for having failed to institute an effective blockade—but the monarch refused to permit their recall until more information filtered in on the recent campaign. The delay afforded the Admiralty the time it needed to flex its muscles against any inquiry into Lord Howe or naval affairs. Sir William was not so fortunate. Someone had to pay for the disaster in 1777 and late in January the king instructed North to choose between Germain and General Howe. For purely political reasons, North tabbed Howe as the one to go. He recalled him in mid-February—by accepting Howe's resignation, which he had offered in November—and simultaneously gave Admiral Howe leave to resign and come home as soon as his successor was named.[27] On the same day that the Howes were dumped, Clinton was named the commander of Britain's armies in America. His appointment was by default. North preferred Amherst, but he once again refused the assignment, Burgoyne was in captivity, Cornwallis was in London and tainted by what had occurred at Trenton and Princeton, and Carleton, who had also resigned, was unacceptable to Germain. (The latest strain between the two had come when the general, in his blustering letter of resignation, had charged that the American secretary had "insult[ed] the authority of the king" by permitting his policy decisions to be dictated by "private enmity.")[28]

Not all the clamor in London had been directed at those who had planned and waged the war. Biting criticism of the war itself was heard. The tone was set early on by the *Evening Post*, which attacked the "absurdity, folly, and wickedness of continuing to fight." More than one M.P., such as the Tory Edward Gibbon, faced a crisis of conscience at continuing to support "a war whence no reasonable man entertains any hope of success."[29] There were still supporters of the war, and some mounted a vigorous defense of staying the course. In a press campaign that was in equal parts accurate and steeped in hooey, they insisted that the Americans were in deep trouble: Congress was without money; the army was without provisions; Washington was without men; the soldiery was undisciplined and insolent; the citizenry was war-weary; many foreign volunteers were about to quit and return home; so many in Congress favored elevating Gates over Washington that paralyzing political troubles might be on the horizon. Atop all this, they advanced the consoling thought that the rebel's one great victory, Saratoga, had hung on the slenderest of threads. Had Burgoyne possessed only a few days more food, he "might well" have been saved by Clinton.[30]

During that winter the war's supporters appeared to be a minority. In the dark aftermath of Saratoga, some thought that "there seems to be an universal desire for peace." Had a vote been taken that December, Gibbon said, no more than twenty members of the House of Commons would have balloted to continue hostilities.[31] Walpole believed that "the King alone" wished to continue the war.[32] But the war was to continue. Powerful forces were unwilling to let go of America. Militant nationalists, as is often their habit, deluded themselves as to the truth of the military situation. Bureaucrats protected themselves. The Opposition was divided, rent between those who wished an end to the war and those who sought conciliatory measures backed by force. Many in the Opposition also feared being steamrolled by a surging patriotic fervor brought on by the likelihood of war with France. (A French observer in London reported to Vergennes that the English people were "shamelessly eager" for war with France.)[33] Undeterred, the king used his clout to keep the war on track, and North, though terribly conflicted, summoned his skills to please his monarch, maintain his majority, and simultaneously pursue war and appeasement.

While the war would continue, the bleak outcome of campaign 1777, and the virtual certainty of Anglo-French hostilities, necessitated a strategic reappraisal. By mid-February, North's government expected the worst. Its minister to France had reported strong circumstantial evidence that "France has . . . thrown down the die" through treaties with the Americans, and by early March the prime minister had been forced to publicly acknowledge that "it was possible, nay too probable" that France was on the verge of entering the war.[34] Long before things reached that juncture—before Christmas even—the king had demanded a review of strategy. Both the monarch and North would have been delighted had Germain stepped down in the wake of the American debacle, enabling them to bring in a fresh face to participate in the military review, and when the American secretary's wife died in mid-January from the measles, their hopes soared that, in his despair, he might return to private life. Alas, Germain stayed on, and he was to wield a heavy hand in the deliberations. But he did not act alone. Sandwich, among others, was involved, and the monarch directed North to consult General Amherst as well.[35]

The review was lengthy and fretfully complicated. It was undertaken in two stages. The first was spread over several weeks between December and February, and was ushered in by Saratoga and the realities of Howe's campaign for Philadelphia. The second occurred late in the winter, when it was presumed that war with France—and conceivably Spain as well—was unavoidable. By January, the review had led to a profound conclusion: America could not be conquered militarily, but American independence might be prevented. The army and navy together might even succeed in reclaiming and securing some of the colonies, though it was agreed that an army of upward of 80,000 men would be necessary to retake all thirteen colonies, and that was out of the question. Even so, a large army would be needed to cope with both France and America, and men had to be found to replace those that were lost in campaign 1777. Beginning in 1778 the army might draft men for a period of five years or the duration of the war, the physical standards for entering the army were lessened and the age requirements broadened (and would be further altered in 1779), and a greater cash bounty was offered for voluntary enlistment.[36] The consensus was that the navy's coopera- tion with the army in 1776-1777 had enfeebled the blockade. Henceforth, the navy was largely to restrict its activities to impeding the flow of goods into and out of America. The construction of heavy warships was also to be accelerated. Budget cuts during the long peace after 1763, together with unfortunate acci- dents (including a fire in the Portsmouth shipyard in 1770 that had laid waste to twenty-five ships of the line that were under construction) had left Great Britain with only two-thirds as many ships of the line as France and Spain were capable of putting under sail. This stage of the review culminated with orders to Clinton to attempt to bring Washington to battle, but if that was impossible, to focus on coastal raids in New England. If need be, he was authorized to abandon Philadelphia.

As evidence mounted that French belligerency was inevitable, the review careened toward other, radically different conclusions. It was assumed— correctly, it turned out—that France would have little interest in regaining Canada, and that its focal point would be Britain's sugar islands in the Caribbean. Possession of those lucrative islands was crucial to Britain's economy, but also essential for the long-term coercion of America, as throughout the eighteenth century the colonies had conducted a substantial percentage of their commerce through the Caribbean. These presumptions resulted in the decision to transfer most of Britain's ships of the line, and some of its frigates, from North America to the Leeward Islands, and to redeploy upward of 10,000 of Clinton's men, with half or more going to the West Indies and the remainder scattered between East and West Florida, Halifax, and Newfoundland.[37] This strategic change was profound. Though unarticulated, it was tantamount to a conclusion that the thirteen colonies were no longer to be the main effort of the war, and, as the third anniversary of Lexington and Concord approached, that New England was to be relinquished. London's gaze was turning south.[38]

Commercial considerations were as important as harsh military realities in the evolution of the reappraisal, and what came of them was a new strategy. This phase of the rethinking may have originated with Charles Jenkinson. At least he was the first to put his ruminations on paper. A veteran undersecretary in the Treasury—nearly fifteen years before, he had prepared some of the Grenville ministry's new colonial policies that stoked the American rebellion—Jenkinson had always been a hardliner and had always had the ear of the king. North, too, held him in such awe that Burke, with considerable hyperbole, concluded in 1775 that "Jenkinson governs everything" and was the man most responsible for the government's drive toward war.[39]

After Saratoga, Jenkinson was a proponent of giving up New England. He believed that with peace New England once again would be an excellent market for Britain's goods, but as the region largely turned out what was produced in England, its exports were immaterial. The South was a different matter altogether. Its retention was crucial, as it produced such vital cash crops as tobacco, rice, indigo, and sea island cotton, and naval stores that were crucial to the ship construction and maritime industries. The mid-Atlantic colonies were not as economically important as those below the Potomac River, but they were of more consequence than New England. As Manhattan and Long Island were already in British hands, Jenkinson concluded that Britain should henceforth concentrate its energies on securing all the provinces from New York City southward.[40]

Jenkinson's striking conclusions were without precedent, and they caught the eye of those seeking to devise a viable military strategy. Making the South the military pivot appeared to many to be a prudent choice, not least because armies that had been considerably larger than the one Clinton would have at his disposal had failed to conquer New England and the mid-Atlantic region. It was also believed—accurately, in fact, and it soon would be anchored in Germain's mind—that the South was the region with the greatest percentage of Loyalists. Many southerners were drawn to Toryism as a result of their economic ties to the mother country, their fear of the African Americans that they kept in bondage, and their membership in the Anglican Church, the established church in every southern colony. Georgia, new and thinly populated, had special problems. A frontier province, its residents yearned for help against Indians that could only be provided by a strong central government, and the only one around was the imperial government.

Looking at matters in this fashion led some to conclude that Saratoga did not mean that all was lost. Britain held Canada and several precious islands in the Caribbean. If their Indian allies could secure the trans-Appalachian West, and Britain's armed forces could regain the region below the Potomac, there was quickening hope that Britain's American empire would remain huge and lucrative. Britain still might emerge from this war with a crescent-shaped realm that extended from Canada through the American frontier, and downward to encompass several lucrative provinces between the Potomac and the Floridas, and finally on into the indispensable Caribbean. Though reduced in size, Britain's sturdy and strapping American empire would encircle the tiny, feeble United States, making its survival problematic. Shortly after the ministry chose this course, an upbeat Germain announced that he saw nothing "but good in the King's affairs."[41]

By the time the new strategy, the "Southern Strategy," was fully conceived and accepted by the ministry, the Franco-American treaties were known and it was generally presumed that America would choose those accords over the conciliatory measures that the Carlisle Commission would tender. Without exaggeration, Walpole remarked that the uninitiated Earl of Carlisle was "very fit" to "make a treaty [with America] that will not be made."[42]

Confronting war with France also brought the cabinet to a pivotal showdown in April and May over how to utilize the Royal Navy against its looming adversary. Intelligence reckoned the French navy at between thirty-three and forty-three ships of the line, divided more or less equally between an Atlantic squadron at Brest and a Mediterranean fleet at Toulon. Against this, Britain had forty ships of the line ready for service, half of which had been designated for the defense of the homeland, a so-called Channel fleet that was commanded by Admiral Augustus Keppel. By early spring, London was aware that France had signed a treaty of alliance with the United States, though the pact had not been made public. North's government also knew that the Toulon fleet was readying to sail, but remained in the dark as to its destination. The fleet had been ordered to the American theater. It was nearly ready to sail when the American treaties were signed in February, but Vergennes had kept the squadron in port for two months, a decision that would have an enormous impact on the war in America that year. Vergennes chose this course because he was eager to have Britain fire the shot that opened hostilities. It was not an ethical issue with him. Aware that Britain and the Netherlands had signed a defensive pact that obligated the Dutch to join hostilities only if its ally was attacked, Vergennes was driven by a longing to keep the Dutch neutral. Knowing that the Toulon fleet would see action against British forces once it arrived in America, Vergennes delayed its departure, hopeful that the British navy would, in the interim, open hostilities against the French somewhere off the European coast.[43]

The North ministry concluded that the Toulon fleet might be preparing for any one of four possibilities: it might be about to sail to India; it might intend to join the Spanish fleet at Cadiz, signaling Madrid's entrance into the war; it might be shipping out to the American theater; or it might hope to link with France's Brest squadron and assail England itself. The last two eventualities could be prevented entirely if Keppel's superior fleet stopped it before it passed through the Straits of Gibraltar. The risk in that, of course, was that should Keppel's fleet be sent to Gibraltar, England would be vulnerable to the Brest squadron. In the cabinet discussions that ensued, Sandwich argued vehemently that it would be "a very dangerous measure" to order Keppel's Channel fleet away from England. Germain, in contrast, asserted that if the Toulon fleet reached America, it would be vastly superior to Britain's American fleet (which consisted of five ships and numerous frigates), enabling it to "possess either of Halifax, Philadelphia, or Quebec." The stakes were high and there was no clear-cut choice. Had there been a minister of war or a strong prime minister, the matter might have been rapidly resolved. In the absence of either, an intense struggle embroiled the cabinet for six weeks, causing a delay in reaching a final decision that would have ominous consequences in campaign 1778. Sandwich at first appeared to be the victor in the ministerial imbroglio, as it was initially decided to keep the Channel fleet at home. But once the Toulon fleet sailed into the Atlantic and it became clear that its destination was America, Germain renewed the battle, waging a rearguard action. He appealed to the king, writing that in "all military operations of importance some risk must be run," and that if the nation remained "inactive and tamely submit[ed]"—that is, if it did not detach ships from the Channel fleet to America to contest the French squadron—"the absolute ruin of Great Britain would ensue." Germain asked the monarch to strip thirteen ships of the line from Keppel and send them across the Atlantic. His argument swayed George III, and a squadron under Vice Admiral John ("Foul Weather Jack") Byron was readied for departure to America. It was early June before it set out, two long months after the Toulon fleet had sailed. Vergennes could not have been happier with London's muddled response to this frightful crisis.[44]

ACROSS THE ATLANTIC, Congress faced two crucial choices. One involved the fate of Burgoyne's army. No one liked the convention that Gates had agreed to at Saratoga, a pact that paroled the soldiers who had laid down their arms and permitted their return to England. According to the sense of honor that prevailed in the eighteenth century, the parolees could never again serve in America during this war. However, once back in England, they could be sent anywhere to take the place of equal numbers of British regulars who, in turn, could then be shipped to America. Carping about the convention began at once. Washington said simply, "we should not be anxious for their early departure." A Connecticut congressman amplified on that thought: should the United States "suffer Genll Burgoyne to Embark with his Troops," they will "be more dangerous to us than if we never had accepted of his Surrendry." Others trained their fire on Gates, suggesting that he had been flimflammed by Burgoyne.[45]

Congress eventually resolved the matter by breaking the agreement that Gates had signed. One congressman, John Witherspoon of New Jersey, uncomfortable with reneging on a solemn agreement, consoled himself with the happy thought, "History affords us many examples of evasive and artful conduct in some of the greatest men and most respected nations, when hard pressed by necessity." Feeling hard pressed on this matter, Congress announced that the Convention Army, as it was being called, would not be permitted to depart for London until the British government ratified the accord. Congress knew full well that North's government would never consider such a step, as to do so was tantamount to recognizing the sovereignty of the United States. Thus, while Burgoyne was allowed to go home in mid-April 1778, his men were confined to America, where many remained until the end of the war.[46]

Congress had one other issue to deal with: the choice between the French treaties and North's conciliatory terms. Immediately after the Franco-American pacts were signed, Franklin and Deane wrote Congress to prepare it for the unauthorized military alliance. In letters drafted in every shade of rose, they insisted that France had treated the commissioners with the "greatest Cordiality" and that it had not attempted to take advantage of "our present Difficulties, to obtain hard Terms from us." They also assured Congress that the "Hearts of the French are universally for war, and the Cry is strong for Immediate War with Britain." Do not be fooled if you hear that the "Court still gives Assurance of Peace to the British Ambassador." In truth, a French fleet "is preparing with all Diligence." Its destination: the United States.[47]

As it took weeks for letters to cross the Atlantic, Congress was in the dark through the winter and early spring about the diplomacy transpiring in Europe. Some despaired that "the Americans are doomed to stand another Campaign unaided by any Force." Even in late April some were convinced that France "will not yet a while engage in a war with G.B. unless . . . drawn into in by some unforeseen accident." Some in Congress cynically asked why France should take up arms to help America, as it was "Ingrossing the whole Trade" of the United States "without entering into a War." France has not "done one act of kindness towards us but what has been plumply for the promotion of her own Interest," one raged, and another concluded that France's real policy was "to see both parties [America and Britain] well beaten." Some observers saw a ray of hope. The great victory at Saratoga, many believed, would "Operate powerfully in our favour," and some were hopeful that London's talk of reconciliation would "draw France in to open War."[48]

All the while, the treaties were ever so slowly making their journey across the Atlantic. Almost three weeks passed after they were signed before a suitable ship was ready to sail for Philadelphia. That vessel crossed in March and April, and during its last two weeks at sea the *Trident*, which carried the members of the Carlisle Commission, was also rocking and pitching its way toward America. During the last week in April rumors swirled in Philadelphia that a treaty with France had been signed. "Imagine how solicitous we are to know the truth of this," the members of Congress' Committee for Foreign Affairs sighed.

They did not have long to wait to learn the truth. On Saturday night, May 2, the treaties reached Philadelphia. France had been "magnanimous," swooned several congressmen who only recently had bashed America's benefactor. Congress did not dally. It ratified the treaties in its third session following their arrival, and the very next day it sent word of what it had done to Paris by packet ship. Many, such as Virginia's Richard Henry Lee, jubilantly predicted that "Great Britain has its choice now of madness, or meanness. She will not war with the house of Bourbon and N. America at the same time."[49]

The members of the Carlisle Commission disembarked in Philadelphia thirty-one days after the treaties were ratified. They were told curtly that Congress would only enter into discussions to end the war, and it would do so only after Britain's envoys had recognized the independence of the United States.

Having authority to do neither, the Carlisle Commission's work was done before it began.[50]

Congressman Lee and his colleagues did not know it, but the choices that had been made since December in Versailles, London, and Philadelphia did not mean that peace was at hand. They meant that a world war was about to begin.

12

"A RESPECTABLE ARMY":
THE GRIM YEAR, 1778

THE CONTINENTALS marched down Gulph Road toward their winter quarters, tramping past trees with scruffy brown leaves and over small patches of old snow that once had been white. On December 19 they entered the place that was to be their encampment, a site that one soldier called a "wooded wilderness."[1] These men were not in high spirits. Had they known of the diplomacy under way in Paris, they would have been happier, but as it was they were hungry and exhausted after weeks of campaigning, and their thin and tattered clothing offered no defense against the bite of early winter. The army's supply system, at its best never particularly distinguished, had begun to crumble around the end of October. Some men had not savored a good meal, or known a full stomach, for longer than they cared to remember. The officers were troubled by the plight of their soldiers and incensed that the civilian authorities seemed unable to get a handle on the army's logistical needs. Many of the senior officers were angry with the choice of Valley Forge for winter quarters, and angrier still that such a substantive decision had resulted from the meddling of state and national officials. One was vexed that Washington had bowed to the demands of Congress. "It is unfortunate," he said, "that Washington is so easily led." Another fumed that it was "unparalleled in the History of Mankind to establish Winter Quarters in a Country wasted and without a single Magazine."[2]

Washington and most of his generals would have preferred to scatter the army in a series of small camps on a line from Reading to Lancaster. A few general officers, including Greene, to whom the commander usually listened, preferred an encampment at Wilmington, below Philadelphia on the Delaware

River. The army would be closer to Philadelphia if posted at Wilmington, they reasoned, better situated for harassing the British, and might be more easily supplied. Some claimed, too, that by taking up quarters at Wilmington, the army would not convey the "complexion" of a force in retreat, which would only add to the difficulty of recruiting. There were disadvantages to both sites. Reading-Lancaster was now home to many refugees from Philadelphia. To situate the army in that sector would mean that the soldiers would have to compete for food with both the displaced Philadelphians and the residents of the thickly settled backcountry. Wilmington, on the other hand, was so close to Philadelphia that it might be susceptible to attack. Little support existed for any other option. Only one general recommended spending the winter at Valley Forge, and one other advocated "a Winter's campaign."[3]

In the end, neither most of the officers nor those in Congress who had wanted the Continentals to stay in the field throughout the winter had their way. The officers thought it of far-reaching importance that Washington had stuck to his guns and entered winter quarters. Encampment, and a cessation of campaigning, was essential for rehabilitating, training, and preserving the soldiery. As there would be another campaign in 1778, it was "of much greater Utility," Brigadier General Peter Muhlenberg said, to prepare the army for the serious fighting ahead than to focus on "any small Advantages" that might accrue from tormenting Howe over the winter.[4] Ultimately, the politicians and Washington compromised: the army would go into winter quarters, but at Valley Forge, just twenty miles from Philadelphia, closer by half than Washington had wished.

Valley Forge has usually been portrayed as a bleak, barren, and remote site.[5] In fact, it lay at the juncture of the Valley Creek and Schuylkill River (the camp was just west of the river) in populous Chester County, home to 30,000 people. Although the area about Valley Forge was dotted with furnaces, forges, and gristmills that were vital to the Continentals' successful conduct of the war, most of the residents were commercial farmers. Some were garden and dairy farmers who sent their goods to nearby Philadelphia, but the lion's share worked some of America's most fertile land, farms that averaged 130 acres, on which they produced wheat and flour for the Atlantic market. They kept just enough livestock for their own needs. Philadelphia County was immediately east of the Schuylkill. Nearly half of its 55,000 inhabitants—most of whom were also farmers—lived north of the city and within twenty-five miles of Valley Forge. West of the Schuylkill, in a long fan-shaped arc, lay numerous vibrant market centers—including Lancaster, York, Wilmington, and Reading—none more than fifty miles away. Valley Forge was an excellent choice for a winter encampment. It not only was a secure site, as the Schuylkill served as a rampart against an enemy attack, but it was situated within a cornucopia of provisions.[6]

While Washington took the bulk of the army into Valley Forge, security concerns and other considerations led him to post some men nearby at sundry sites in Chester County. Leaving the Pennsylvania militia east of the Schuylkill,

Washington sent detachments of his Continentals to guard important hamlets and the nine roads into and out of Philadelphia, or placed them so that they might harass enemy foragers. Once the construction of the encampment at Valley Forge was completed, Washington sent other contingents to Trenton and Wilmington.[7]

Everyone at Valley Forge, including Washington, initially slept in a tent. When not asleep, the men worked frantically to bring the "log city," as one called it, into being. While army engineers surveyed the site, assigning each brigade an area, work parties were formed to cut trees and haul timber. Once wood was available, the soldiers were divided into squads of a dozen men each to built fourteen-by-sixteen-foot huts that would be their homes for the season. To speed the work before the weather grew nasty, Washington made a contest of it, offering prize money to the team in each sector that completed its hut first. (Some men cheated, tearing down the fences and barns of nearby farmers, to obtain their building materials.) The scene, Thomas Paine said memorably, was akin to that of "a family of Beavers; every one busy . . . and . . . in a few days . . . a Curious Collection of Buildings in the true rustic order" sprang up. Paine notwithstanding, it actually took nearly forty days to get the last man into a hut. Within the first week Washington abandoned his tent and took a two-story stone house for his headquarters, appropriating a bedroom upstairs and another room downstairs for his office. Most of the general officers secured housing in private residences well away from the center of camp. Not atypically, Brigadier General William Maxwell lodged in a fourteen-room stone house with a cellar well stocked with hard cider and Brigadier General Charles Scott lived in a capacious Georgian house that for a time had served as General Howe's headquarters. The field grade and lower-ranking officers, like the men, lived in jerry-built log huts, but while the men dwelled twelve to a one room cabin the officers enjoyed less cramped quarters. At most, officers from two companies—there were usually three to five officers per company—shared a facility, which usually consisted of two rooms and two fireplaces. Common soldiers occupied places "to *stay* (not to *live*) in," as one soldier put it. Lafayette accurately characterized the enlisted men's abodes as "scarcely gayer than dungeon cells," while another foreign volunteer said that the common soldiers "lie in shanties." Every cabin appeared to be leaky and drafty, and few of the inexpertly constructed chimneys drew properly. But the men were in their huts only when sleeping or if ill. Otherwise they were kept busy. Some men were put to work constructing redoubts. Others, who knew something of carpentry, built a bake house, several infirmaries, and a dining room add-on to Washington's headquarters. Still others served as "bullock guards" when livestock were present. The great majority soldiered—standing guard, pulling patrol duty, foraging, or contesting British forage parties.[8]

Four days after entering Valley Forge, Washington told Congress that the army was without meat and down to its last twenty-five barrels of flour. It had no soap or vinegar, and there were shortages of clothing, shoes, and blankets. Nearly three thousand men were "barefoot and otherwise naked," he reported. "I much doubt the practicability of holding the Army together much longer," he added, and he issued a dire warning: "[U]nless some great and capital change suddenly takes place . . . this Army must inevitably be reduced to one or other of these three things: Starve—dissolve—or disperse. . . . [R]est assured, Sir, this is not an exaggerated picture."9 While there probably was some hyperbole in his sharp note, Washington did not overstate the army's woes by much. That is borne out by the diary of Albigence Waldo, a surgeon's mate in the Connecticut Line. Waldo noted food shortages eleven days before the army entered Valley Forge, adding ominously that the "Army which has been surprisingly healthy hitherto, now begins to grow sickly." On the final day of the march to Valley Forge he said that the army was "poorly supplied." Three days after entering the camp, Waldo heard men complain of having no comestibles save for "Fire Cake & Water." That night the men chanted: "'No Meat! No Meat' Imitating the noise of Crows and Owls." Their taunting cries sounded like "confused Musick," he added. One soldier spoke of his diet as consisting of "a leg of nothing." Many soldiers grew gaunt, and some claimed, only half jokingly, that they had consumed so much fire cake (a mixture of flour and water that was roasted on coals or baked on a stick or in a pan) that their "glutted Gutts are turned to Pasteboard." A visitor to the camp subsequently recollected that the soldiers tunefully—and menacingly—sang: "No bread, no soldier." Not even the men in "Burgoins Army . . . when in their Greatest Distress" had suffered more than the soldiers at Valley Forge, one soldier raged. Scarce food was not the only complaint. At least initially, New England's soldiers, sent south after Burgoyne's surrender, were adequately fed— one of them complained of the lack of salt for his "fresh beef & flour"—which caused rancor in other units at the army's "unequal distribution" system. But if the Yankees had full stomachs, their supply of clothing was inadequate for the brutal winter conditions that descended on Valley Forge early in January. This was "as cold weather as I almost ever knew at home," said a Massachusetts colonel, who saw his "poor brave fellows . . . bare-footed, bare legged, bare breeched . . . in snow, in rain." By the end of that month, only one-third of the men were fit for duty in one brigade.10

A dear price was paid for what one private described as the "truly forlorn condition" in the camp. Late in December, according to a physician, five thousand men were hospitalized.11 Lafayette remembered soldiers whose "feet and legs turned black with frostbite, and often had to be amputated."12 Many fell to typhus and an assortment of fevers.13 The suffering appears to have been borne almost exclusively by the enlisted men. Washington and the highest-ranking officers did not enjoy a sumptuous lifestyle, but they lived comfortably, enjoying daily repasts that included meat, vegetables, hard bread, deserts, and wine.14 (On Christmas Day, in the midst of the initial subsistence crisis, Washington enjoyed a dinner consisting of mutton, veal, potatoes, and cabbage.)15 The lower-ranking officers did not share the comforts of their superiors, but they enjoyed amenities—and, to be sure, the basic necessities—that were sometimes unavailable to the men. Their chief "murmurs and complaints," at least according to General Greene, were over a "want of spirits." They had to rub along with "nothing but bread and beef to eat morning, noon, and night, without vegetables or anything to drink but cold water." For "people that have been accustomed to live tolerable," Greene added with incredible insensitivity, this was "hard fare."[16] But not all complained. Lieutenant James McMichael, a young Pennsylvanian, kept a journal throughout the Valley Forge months that is devoid of grievances. He spoke instead of passing "many hours in recreation."[17]

For most, however, the winter in Valley Forge was a hard time, a sustained period of poor nutrition, spent "naked"—as Washington put it—in a squalid environment of low, choking smoke and the stench of death.[18] How did the gathering calamity of near starvation occur? The army had previously experienced episodic supply shortages, but nothing akin to the long grim weeks at Valley Forge had occurred during the first two winters of this war. What is more, crops had been abundant in 1777, approximately 75,000 farmers lived within a fifty-mile radius of Valley Forge, and New Jersey, Maryland, and Virginia—unoccupied and unthreatened by the enemy—lay only short distances away. This crisis arose from bad planning, no planning, inexperience, ineptitude, criminality, villainy, the structure of governance in America, and a large dose of bad luck.

Over the years Congress had established a host of committees and boards to cope with the procurement of supplies abroad and at home, and it issued contracts to civilian suppliers. When it founded the Continental army, moreover, Congress told Washington to appoint a quartermaster general—in August 1775 he named his aide-de-camp, Thomas Mifflin, who had been a Philadelphia merchant—to oversee the army's needs, and two months later it created two offices of Commissary General of Stores and Purchases, one for the Northern Department and one for Washington's army. Congress subsequently created the posts of clothier general and wagonmaster, as well as a medical department. Mifflin and the commissaries general, Joseph Trumbull and Walter Livingston, administered armies the combined manpower of which usually hovered around 20,000. They were either incredibly capable or extremely fortunate, for great crises never occurred on their watch. But all three were gone as the Valley Forge winter approached. Livingston left after about a year and Trumbull stepped down in the summer of 1777 in a huff over congressional regulations, and once they departed, Congress was unable to find talented men who would stay on for any length of time. A few months before Valley Forge, warnings were heard that the commissary general for Washington's army did not know "how to act or what to do." Some cautioned that "shifting Hands in the Midst of a Campaign" might come back to haunt the army.[19] Mifflin, who hated his job, resigned early in October. Roughly seventy-five days later, when the army entered Valley Forge, his office still had not been filled, and another seventy-five days passed before General Greene reluctantly consented to become the quartermaster general. A congressional investigatory committee subsequently laid much of the blame for the supply crisis on the "Want of Genius & Activity" in the Commissary Department and the failure to promptly replace Mifflin, for it likened the quartermaster general's responsibilities to a "great Wheel in the Machine" that was "diffusive thru every Part of your military System."[20]

Nonetheless, almost everyone appeared to recognize that the logistical mess was the result of numerous factors. The army itself was part of the problem. Washington worked long and hard on the army's administrative structure, but, as historian Edward Lengel has observed, at Valley Forge it continued to be "plagued by incompetent staff, poorly defined departmental responsibilities, and intersecting chains of command."[21] In addition, unlike the two previous winters, the army in 1777–1778 was quartered in a region that had recently been the site of a lengthy campaign. Both armies had picked over eastern Pennsylvania in search of food, and the British had confiscated the goods stored in more than one American magazine, including one at Valley Forge in mid-September (from which it had garnered four thousand barrels of flour). Clinton's destructive raids along the Hudson in October and Admiral Howe's earlier assault at Danbury destroyed priceless stores, and armed Loyalist raiders struck convoys laden with supplies earmarked for Valley Forge. The weather was also to blame. Legend aside, the winter of 1778 was milder than normal, which was unfortunate for the army, as it rained more than it snowed, rendering America's unpaved roads impassable. Hard freezes occurred from time to time, and they shut down river traffic. Even in good weather the Wagonmaster Department, which transported provisions to the army, sometimes faced insurmountable problems. It frequently experienced shortages of wagons, teamsters, and horses, or at least horses that were sufficiently fed and could work. Its teamsters were civilians who contracted to drive for the army, but they were often difficult to find, as they were enticed to work for better paying private businessmen. Chicanery was also rife. Some crooked drivers embezzled their cargoes. Others lightened their load by draining the brine from the salt pork they were carrying, which spoiled the meat they were delivering to the unsuspecting soldiers.

It was often difficult for the army's supply service to get its hands on provisions. Many farmers were reluctant to sell to the army, some because they were Quaker pacifists, some because they were disaffected and "toriestically Inclined," as General Wayne put it.[22] Most were simply small businessmen who sought a better deal. Some states had imposed price controls that were inevitably below market value, prompting Washington to immediately complain to Congress that such limitations had "a disagreeable effect upon our supplies of meat," as it drove many farmers to reduce their acreage in production or to sell their surplus to the British army.[23] The redcoats not only paid more, they paid in specie, while the Continentals offered a depreciated paper currency. But even when farmers sold their produce to the army there was no guarantee that the food would reach Valley Forge. Goods shipped over long distances—from New England, say, to Pennsylvania—were sometimes seized by armed bands of Loyalists or commandeered along the way by state officials, including local militia officers. Commodities that had become especially precious due to wartime shortages also had a way of disappearing. This was not the only malfeasance that dogged the army. Contractors and suppliers swindled the military, knowingly supplying it with shoddy equipment and ruined food, and even with casks supposedly packed with flour or meat, but which actually contained inedible substances, including dirt and rocks.[24]

The Valley Forge supply crisis had peaks and valleys. The worst food shortages commenced before the army entered Valley Forge and lasted roughly until the end of the first week in January, resurfaced thirty days later in the gloom of deep winter and persisted for about two weeks—one soldier termed it the "second Rupture" and Washington labeled it the "fatal crisis"—and recurred a third time at the end of February ("seven days without meat and several days without bread," one general noted on February 26). If the food crises occurred episodically, the shortages of clothing, blankets, shoes, stockings and much invaluable equipment was habitual and accompanied with no less dangerous consequences. For instance, an inveterate dearth of kettles hindered the production of soap, a crucial ally in the battle against disease. "Our men are . . . infected with the itch," one general said early on, adding that he had "seen the poor fellows covered over with scab." (Without success, army physicians prescribed an ointment comprised of sulfur mixed with hog's lard.) The supply crisis might have been tempered had Congress appealed to civilians to conduct drives to secure needed items, but Washington, who faced a nightmarish dilemma, opposed such a course, lest the enemy learn the truth about the state of affairs in his army. Upward of 2,500 of Washington's men perished that winter, very nearly one man in seven of the Continentals that were with him late in December. (In contrast, about one American in thirty who were involved in operations in the Battle of the Bulge, one of the deadliest American engagements in World War II, died *in battle*). More than seven hundred of the army's horses perished as well.[25]

That the death toll was not more appalling was due in part to Congress's speedy response to Washington's trenchant warnings. Congress called on the states to aid the Continentals, and Governors William Livingston and George Clinton, of New Jersey and New York respectively, outpaced their counterparts in finding meat for the army.[26] General Washington also quietly appealed to the states and individual provincial leaders to rally them to action. "I fear I shall wound your feelings" by divulging the woes of the army, he told Governor Patrick Henry in Virginia, but with crystal clarity Washington related the army's plight, urging the chief executive to turn his "attention to this indispensably essential Object" in order to halt the "sufferings and loss of Men." From necessity, Washington micromanaged the procurement of supplies. He ordered one officer to Boston in search of boots and saddles, another to the environs of Philadelphia to barter hides for shoes, sent still others to designated hamlets in

Pennsylvania, Maryland, and Virginia to find clothing, flour, and horses, and dispatched yet others to search for lost wagons laden with goods. He assigned some officers responsibility for seeing to the repair of tents and weapons, organized parties that were sent into New Jersey to guard cattle that were being driven to Valley Forge, and sent out units to find provender for the horses. His attention to detail shows through in his correspondence: "I made enquiry" about production at a tannery, "I have consulted" regarding how best to pack certain commodities for shipment, and "I observe" in an inventory that five thousand damaged muskets are gathering dust in Albany.[27]

Necessity also nudged Washington toward a substantive change. Even as a young officer in the French and Indian War, he had hesitated to seize the property of civilians. During that conflict Washington once had nearly been shot by an irate farmer whose grain he was about to confiscate.[28] The incident seared in his mind the fine line between patriotism and hatred of armies that often existed among civilians. In this war he lectured his men that the American Revolution was a struggle for "Rights, Liberty and Property." If the army came to be seen as "plunderers instead of protectors," he cautioned, the war would be lost.[29] At Valley Forge he faced an especially prickly dilemma. Pennsylvania not only stipulated that the Continental army must secure the state's permission to seize civilian possessions, but many in the population that surrounded Valley Forge, at best, had been only lukewarm supporters of independence and the war. Confiscation of their goods might push them into the arms of the enemy. Yet to fail to impress their commodities might result in disaster for the army. Washington responded by persuading Congress to lean heavily on the authorities in Pennsylvania to find provisions for the army, and he often used strong-arm tactics, though he hid beneath the fiction that he was seizing property so that it would not fall into the hands of the enemy. His officers did not have to be coaxed into taking harsh steps. "[L]ike Pharoh I harden my heart . . . I am determine to forage the country very bare," General Greene declared. Coercion succeeded. It helped keep the army intact and even won the praise of the congressional committee at Valley Forge, which defended the necessity of having the "Soldiery . . . disperse in the Neighborhood & take indiscriminately the Provisions laid in by the Inhabitants for the Winters Support of themselves & Families."[30]

John McCasland, a twenty-seven-year-old western Pennsylvanian who had been conscripted in January, served on one such mission. His company was ordered into Bucks County, north of Philadelphia, on a foraging operation, and in the course of the mission McCasland and fifteen comrades were sent on a patrol to search out Hessians who were suspected of being in the area. They found them occupying "a large and handsome mansion house," and discovered, too, that the Germans had posted only a single "large Hessian" outside as a sentinel. The guard had to be disposed of before the others could be taken, but no one wanted "to shoot a man down in cold blood." After some debate, those who were thought to be the best shots drew lots to determine whose job it would be to take out the sentry. McCasland won (or perhaps lost) the draw. While he readied himself, the others surrounded the house. Finally set, McCasland decided that he would not shoot to kill, but instead fire "to break his thigh. I shot the rifle and aimed at his hip," he remembered. The shot struck a tobacco box in the soldier's pants pocket, ricocheted and entered his leg "and scaled the bone of the thigh to the outside." Hearing the shot, the other Hessians immediately decided that they were heavily outnumbered and must surrender. As none spoke English, one "came out of the cellar with a large bottle of rum and advanced with it at arm's length as a flag of truce." The sixteen Americans took twelve Germans prisoner "and delivered them up to General Washington."[31]

THE PLIGHT of the soldiers and the army was not all that troubled Washington that winter. In the wake of Gates's spectacular victory at Saratoga, and his own less-successful campaign to defend Philadelphia, Washington feared that malcontents might gin up recollections of his past failures as they conspired to remove him as commander. His worst fears soon materialized. In November, Lord Sterling notified him of scuttlebutt concerning Brigadier General Thomas Conway. An Irish-born French volunteer who had come to America to fight in 1777, and who had seen combat at Brandywine, Conway purportedly had written to Gates that "Heaven has been determined to save your Country; or a weak General and bad Councellors would have ruind it."[32] Thin-skinned and insecure, Washington appears to have already had those in his fabled intelligence network listening closely for any murmurings against him. Without much effort, he was persuaded that a cabal of army officers and congressmen had hatched a plot to replace him with Gates. Those scholars who shared Washington's belief, by and large nineteenth-century historians, dubbed the alleged conspiracy the "Conway Cabal." (Even Washington soon enough acknowledged that he had been "well informed that no whisper of the kind was ever heard in Congress.")[33]

In all likelihood, the supposed intrigue never amounted to more than a hand-ful of disgruntled individuals who grumbled to one another about Washington's shortcomings. It is almost certain that Conway never belonged to any cabal, although he doubtless said harsh things about Washington. (Nor was he alone among the European professional soldiers in so doing. Major General Johann de Kalb, a German-born career soldier with more than twenty years experience, thought Washington "the weakest general" under whom he had ever served. De Kalb added that if Washington ever "does anything sensational he will owe it more to his good luck or to his adversary's mistakes than to his own ability.")[34] Conway had written Gates earlier that he preferred to serve under him rather than Washington, which was hardly surprising, as both were veteran professional soldiers. Conway was also known to have lamented: "What a pity there is but one Gates!"[35] Sundry informants led Washington to believe that numerous officials, including Conway and Mifflin, were "holding up General G[ate]s to the people" as a successful leader while "making them believe that you have done nothing [and that] Philadelphia was given up by your Mismanagement." The aim of the plotters, Washington was advised, was to "throw Such obstecles and difficulties in your way as to force you to Resign." Conveying such tattle gave Washington's spies the opportunity to pledge their loyalty. "[M]y Freindship is so Sincere that every Hint which has a tendency to hurt your Honour Wounds me most Sensibly," one told the commander. Another prattled that he had "too high a Sense of the obligations America has to you to abet or countenance so unworthy a proceeding." Yet another advised Washington, "no Friend of America can be an Enemy to you, for by God . . . there is not nor ever was in the world A man who Acted from more Laudable and disinterested motive than you do."36

Washington may have welcomed, or even fostered, the impression of a conspiracy, as it afforded an opportunity to at least plant seeds of malice against Gates, his latest antagonist. From the outset, he had kept the one general whom he had believed to be a real rival, Artemas Ward, relegated to the sidelines. Now Gates loomed as a potential rival. On more than one occasion he spoke of "a faction" that plotted for "Gates . . . to be exalted, on the ruin of my reputation and influence." He told others that Gates was involved in the alleged plot.37 But, despite what had occurred in campaign 1777, Washington had to know that he was in a strong position. Most in Congress understood that he had faced a stronger British force—the cream of the enemy army—and few had expected him to be as successful as Gates. The president of Congress, Henry Laurens, father of John Laurens, one of his most devoted aides, supported him, and he had the solid backing of Virginia, one of the largest and most powerful states. Any concerted attempt to remove Washington would have touched off a ruinous political firestorm. Besides, with the army in desperate straits at Valley Forge, this was hardly a propitious moment for Congress to risk a crisis over changing its commander.

Washington had few peers in the art of political infighting, having honed his talents in bitter wrangles involving his Virginia regiment during the French and Indian War. He was also surrounded by ambitious and talented aides and officers who had hitched their wagon to his star. Some possessed an aptitude for tearing down rivals. Hamilton, who had now been at headquarters for a year and was coming to be something of a chief of staff to the commander, was Washington's point man in this battle. He branded the conspirators as "vermin" and "villainous" incendiaries whose scheming threatened to ruin America's efforts to bring France into the war. Others wrote to friends in Congress urging that they close ranks behind Washington. "I am fully convinced," said Lafayette, "that if any dissension take place in Congress . . . or between the militar and the civil power of this niew feeble country, America is lost." While at it, they smeared Gates and defended Washington. "It was almost impossible for him [Gates] not to conquer" Burgoyne, said one, given the vast turnout of militiamen. He added that Washington, though "defeated by a superior number," had waged a campaign that was superior to "the finest" ever conducted by Caesar or other military immortals. Likewise, Mifflin was pilloried with accusations that he had deliberately brought on the supply crisis at Valley Forge in order "to wound the general's [Washington's] reputation." Washington also did his part, letting Congress and other correspondents know of his loathing for Conway, "the man I deem my Enemy," and that he regarded certain unnamed "concealed enemies"— Gates, presumably, though he was careful not to say so—as "secret traitors."[38]

It was a virtuoso performance. When the dust settled, Washington had emerged as a leader literally above questioning. (He would not again face open criticism until the second term of his presidency, nearly twenty years in the future.)[39] To many in public life the episode demonstrated that the consequences of criticizing the commander were simply too great to be undertaken. Many of those who had allegedly carped about Washington's leadership or plotted against him were left in shambles. Within three months Conway was out of the army, and both he and Mifflin faced repeated challenges to duel from among Washington's madly vindictive satraps who were also eager to demonstrate their devotion. (Conway was seriously wounded in a duel with Cadwalader, while Mifflin's craven contrition spared him a fight, but made him a laughingstock.) Gates, who was innocent save for having done nothing to rein in the plotting of others, learned that being seen as a threat to Washington was decidedly different from being Schuyler's enemy.[40]

Washington faced an additional threat that winter. This, too, came from disgruntled officers, though their disaffection had nothing to do with his leadership. Virtually all his field officers were drawn from society's upper crust, and most had served since early 1776, though some went back to the army's creation. They had come to see themselves as a brotherhood, socially and through their shared experiences of having confronted mortal danger and endured callous deprivation. Many seethed with anger at the civil authorities for having often been oblivious to the army's plight, leaving it habitually ill provisioned and undermanned. Although they were supposedly republican officers in a republican army fighting to establish an American republic, they now demanded what existed for their counterparts in the king's army: an annual pension for life for themselves and their beneficiaries in the amount of half their pay when they voluntarily left the army at war's end, and the right to sell their commissions (which they had not purchased) upon their retirement. As one put it: every officer "Desarves a Penshon During Life." It was not their finest moment. Their effrontery at urging such reforms was matched only by their threats to resign—upward of three hundred officers did quit that winter—if they did not get their way. Washington went to bat for his officers, whether because he agreed with their position (he said that he did) or from fear that the army would be emasculated if his experienced officers abandoned him (he said that as well), or from his conviction (which was tangible) that the army's officers must be drawn almost exclusively from among the elite. The argument that he made on their behalf did him little honor. The officers, he told Congress, had "no sufficient ties" to induce them to serve unless they were awarded the pension, this from the commander who had repeatedly exhorted the enlisted men to make incredible sacrifices for their country and their liberty. Congress was not happy with the threats, but the army's officers had the congressmen by the throat. During the spring Congress passed legislation that provided for a half-pay pension for seven years at war's end and an immediate bounty of eighty dollars—in 1778 worth roughly one-quarter of its value back in 1775—for enlisted men who signed on for the duration. Congress spurned the proposal to permit officers to sell their commissions.[41]

The officers additionally made a great pother over questions of rank and seniority. Washington had encountered rancor on this score during his first hours in Cambridge in 1775 and he continued to endure "infinite anxiety" over these issues until nearly the last day of the war. Rank was a matter of crucial importance to the officers. To a man, they were scorchingly ambitious, and many were driven by truly monumental egos. Washington once said that these men "would sacrafice every thing to promote their own personal glory." At stake were honor, prestige, and the potential for everlasting glory. John Adams, who had to deal with the "Jealousies, Envy, and Distrust" that surrounded promotions and rank while chairing Congress' Board of War, eventually threw up his hands and exclaimed: "I am wearied to Death with the Warfare between military officers, high and low. They quarrel like Cats and Dogs. They worry one another like Mastiffs. Snarling for Rank and Pay like Apes for Nutts." The problem of rank arose from two sources. While Congress appointed and removed the general officers, it gave governors and the generals blank commissions for the naming of the lower-ranking officers. Not uncommonly, more than one colonel—or lieutenant colonel or major—was appointed on the same day, one, say, by the governor of Massachusetts and another by the chief executive of Virginia. Resolving the order in which these men ranked, in terms of seniority, was next to impossible. Problems also arose from the numerous commissions that had been granted to European volunteers by America's envoys in Paris, especially Silas Deane. The practice sparked wrangles over whether a foreign volunteer whose commission was dated earlier than that of an American officer of similar rank actually outranked the native son. At Valley Forge, the officers came unglued over two recent appointments. In November, Congress elevated twenty-year-old Lieutenant Colonel James Wilkinson to brevet brigadier general, and in the following month it bumped up Conway to the rank of major general. Eight colonels filed a protest with Congress in the former case and nine brigadier generals signed a remonstrance complaining of Conway's elevation. Congress tabled both complaints, but it eventually resolved the imbroglio over Wilkinson by naming him to be the secretary of its Board of War. Conway's resignation in April ended the other tempest. Washington had to leave to Congress matters pertaining to the general officers, although while at Valley Forge, and at the behest of Congress's Committee at Camp, he appointed a board of general officers to resolve a bitter dispute over the order of rank of brigadier generals

Friedrich William Augustus, Baron Von Steuben. Painting by Charles Willson Peale, after Charles William Peale, 1781–1782. Arriving in America during the Valley Forge winter, he won Washington's admiration for his training of the Continentals, and later for his service in Virginia during the desperate days of 1780–1781.

from Virginia. For the lesser officers he appealed to brigade commanders to resolve disputes, urged men to drop their complaints "for the good of the service," sought congressional intervention (even asking it to consider "vacating [some] Commissions" and to start from scratch), and implored state officials to resolve sticky cases. Few disputes were ever resolved to everyone's satisfaction and ultimately many officers quit the service over issues of rank during the Valley Forge winter.[42]

PERHAPS THE MOST ENDURING MYTH of Valley Forge is that Friedrich Steuben— self-styled as Baron von Steuben—emerged to transform single-handedly the ragtag Continentals into an effective fighting force. The truth is more complicated. The army at Valley Forge consisted mostly of men who were about to begin their second year of service. They had undergone some training at Morristown during the previous winter and a tough campaign that summer and fall, but Washington was eager to resume their drilling. One of the cardinal objects of any winter quarters encampment, he insisted, was "training the Men, and endeavouring to bring them into the Feild in a more regular manner." Two months before the army entered Valley Forge, he and his generals discussed

"Establishing one uniform Sett of Manoeuvres and Manual Exercise" and teaching "the Tricks of parade [to] a Single company" that might serve as a model for others. Their aim was to "Teach their men to move in Large Bodies" and to "gain some knowledge of the System form'd by the most essential Manoeuvres" so that they would be more efficient, and manageable, on the battlefield. Ten days after the army marched into Valley Forge, General Conway tipped Washington to an accelerated training method utilized by the French army, and several others throughout Europe, and which was so efficient that upward of 200,000 men could be adequately trained within three months. Conway proposed doing just that for the Continentals, pledging that in short order he could convert "a raw, confused, unwieldy flock" into soldiers capable of standing up to "old Disciplin'd troops." Had Conway not been ruined by his alleged participation in the putative cabal, Washington probably would have set him to drilling the soldiery. Instead, it fell to Steuben.[43]

Steuben arrived at camp late in February, nearly seven weeks after the decision to institute a uniform training regimen had been made, though due to bad weather, supply shortages, and the need to construct and secure the cantonment, drilling had not yet begun in earnest. Steuben was not the Prussian aristocrat that he claimed to be. Raised in humble surroundings, he had served in the Prussian army, although the precise nature of his service remains shrouded in mystery. What is known is that he was given to prevarication, a talent that he used with Franklin and Deane to secure their recommendation that Congress permit him to serve the Continental army as a volunteer. They told Congress what he had told them: Steuben was a nobleman who had served as Frederick the Great's aide-de-camp and quartermaster general. He told others that he was a baron of the Holy Roman Empire. Congress bought into his story and wasted no time getting him to Valley Forge, where he was to improve the camp's fortifications. Observant and savvy, Steuben rapidly determined that the hurried retraining of the American soldiery was high on Washington's priority list; he claimed to know how it could be done, which was true, for almost anyone with experience in a European army would, as Conway had said, have known the secret. Washington probably deduced that Steuben was not all that he claimed to be. Despite the jeweled star that he wore, which he claimed was a gift from Frederick the Great, Steuben shortly confessed that he lacked the financial resources to stay with the army if he was denied a paycheck. If not a European aristocrat, Washington thought him a gentleman and a zealous and experienced soldier who could be useful.[44] Washington vested him with responsibility for "establishing regulations for manoeuvres." Steuben put into effect a training system that was more or less similar to that suggested long before by Conway, save for one difference. In Europe, the men were simply told what to do, and they did it. In America, Steuben quickly discovered, it was necessary to tell the men *why* they were to do something. He started with Washington's Corps of Guards of Virginia, a hundred carefully chosen men, drilling them in the blinding light of a snow covered muster field. They in turn individually fanned out into various units to "spread the instruction." Soon those men "repair[ed] to their respective Regiments" to teach others. It was a classic case of snowballing.[45]

Watching Steuben at work—or more accurately, listening to him—was an endless source of merriment among the officers. As he spoke little English (he had only "Goddamn" and a few other expletives down pat), he communicated with those whom he drilled in sharp guttural German and harsh French, with a bit of body language thrown in. His system worked, as Conway had insisted it would, and after six weeks Washington praised Steuben's "intelligence, zeal and indefatigable industry, from which we experienced very happy effects." Convinced that he had instilled a new "spirit of discipline" in the men, Washington urged Congress to appoint Steuben to succeed Conway as the inspector general. Congress assented.[46]

Steuben's efforts to make better soldiers was but part of a broader program of "new modelling the Army" that Washington wished to undertake during the winter.[47] In the course of the first grim month at Valley Forge, Washington dictated a lengthy paper—it ran eighty pages in Hamilton's handwriting—calling for the restructuring of the army in order to correct "numerous defects" and eliminate the "sufferings of the army, and the discontents reigning among the officers." When Congress, partially at Washington's behest, sent a camp committee to Valley Forge late in January, Washington was ready with his recommendations. They were extensive: fuse ninety-seven regiments into eighty, institute conscription, improve the pay of soldiers and officers, provide pensions for the officers, create a military police, and reform the method of promoting officers, an "indispensably necessary" step for eradicating "a pregnant source of uneasiness, discord and perplexity."[48] The camp committee spent weeks fine-tuning the proposals, most of which were adopted—some with modifications— by Congress in May. It was, in the words of Edward Lengel, a Washington scholar, a "masterpiece of military administration" that "influenced the form of administration of the modern American army."[49]

BELIEVING THAT Howe was well informed about the plight of the Continental army at Valley Forge, Washington expected him to attack, and was perplexed when he failed to act. Washington was correct about Howe's knowledge of conditions in the American cantonment. Galloway, the Pennsylvania Tory who had been appointed the police commissioner of occupied Philadelphia, had cobbled together an intelligence network that funneled extraordinarily accurate information to British officials throughout the bitter first months of 1778. He reported that more than 1,100 of Washington's troops had deserted to Philadelphia alone by late March, another 2,500 had perished, few of the Continental army's horses had survived, and that the rebels soldiers were "sickly and destitute of Cloathing, without Medicine, without Salt or Salt Meat," living in "very uncomfortable Lodgings," and "in a manner naked."[50] But to the chagrin of Galloway and a

growing legion of disenchanted Loyalists, Howe did nothing. One outraged
Tory finally published a doggerel that played on the well-known fact that Howe
lived with a mistress in Philadelphia:

> *Awake, arouse Sir Billy,*
> *There's forage in the plain,*
> *Ah, leave your little Filly,*
> *And open the campaign.*[51]

One can only wonder what would have occurred had Howe attacked the
Continentals at Valley Forge. Galloway never doubted that he would have
destroyed Washington's army, but he was a Philadelphia lawyer, not a soldier.
Some American generals conceded that an attack would cause major problems,
including perhaps the loss of most of the army's artillery, as there were
insufficient horses to draw away the cannon should a retreat be necessary. But it
was a moot point. Howe, his cautious self to the end, never seriously considered
attacking. Early in December, two months after Germantown and three weeks
before the Continentals went into winter quarters, the British commander
marched his army twelve miles northwest of Philadelphia, to Whitemarsh, where
he made one last melancholy stab at luring Washington into battle. Howe paused
for forty-eight hours, hopeful that Washington's impulsive side would win out
over discretion, but the rebel commander declined the invitation to come out for
a fight. Howe returned to Philadelphia and spent six additional months as the
commander of Britain's army in America, but psychologically he was finished.[52]

ANTICIPATING THAT the ministry would accept the resignation he had submitted
in October, Howe occupied his time preparing his defense for the almost certain
parliamentary inquiry into his failure to suppress the American rebellion. He also
labored tirelessly to secure the release of the Convention Army. Campaigning
was hardly on his mind. He had few concerns about an American attack on
Philadelphia. From the reports of Galloway, and others, he knew that the piteous
condition of the Continentals precluded such an action. He knew, too, that many
blamed him for Burgoyne's fate, and for some that would have served as a catalyst
for action that might bring redemption. Not so for Howe.[53] He had nearly
17,000 regulars with him in Philadelphia, at least twice the number that
Washington could put under arms to defend Valley Forge. Howe might also
have conducted a winter campaign in the South, which he had once promised.
He had access to a fleet and London's authorization to take the war further south.
But Howe had come to the end of his tether. He offered up the now customary
excuses: he had too few men and the Loyalists were untrustworthy.[54] In reality,
Howe's problem with attacking Valley Forge lay in Bunker Hill's ineradicable
hold on him. With the one exception of Brandywine, since June 1775 he simply
had been unable to conceive of an attack on a well-entrenched American force
of any size.

Thus, the British army languished in Philadelphia throughout the winter and spring. It was the regulars' most comfortable winter yet. Once the Delaware River was opened, provisions flowed in from New York and across the sea, and from nearby farmers who succeeded in getting their goods through the rebels' cordon. Not only were the soldiers well fed, many residents of Philadelphia —about 20,000 of the city's 30,000 inhabitants remained throughout the occupation—welcomed them with open arms. Parties for the officers were common. There were young women to date, and the citizenry formed clubs for the soldiers' entertainment, gave concerts, and welcomed them to their churches and theaters. The officers put on their own plays, relaxed in taverns, played chess among themselves and with the Philadelphians, and even held fun-filled parades, such as on Saint Patrick's Day. Philadelphia's red light district grew, too, and many soldiers devoted their energies to drinking and gambling (up to $50,000 on occasion changed hands in these high stakes games). It was the polar opposite of gloomy Valley Forge, and more than 1,100 of Washington's soldiers defected to the British in Philadelphia.[55]

As it became clear to Washington that an attack on Valley Forge was unlikely, his thoughts in the spring turned increasingly to developing a plan for the campaign of 1778. In mid-April he envisaged three possible courses: an attempt to recover Philadelphia, a campaign to retake New York City, or simply to remain "quiet in a secure, fortified Camp . . . arranging the army" until the British acted, then to "govern ourselves accordingly."[56] Actually, a fourth option existed. Some in the army and Congress hoped for a second American invasion of Canada. With Burgoyne's army in captivity and Canada only lightly defended, it was natural that some would once again see promise in such a course. Before Washington's men entered Valley Forge, many congressmen from New York and New England urged such an enterprise, and Congress turned the matter over to its Board of War for consideration. After a few days study it recommended an "irruption . . . in Canada." Congress approved another Canadian campaign in mid-January, and agreed that Lafayette would command the invasion army, hopeful that Canada's French denizens would warmly greet an army led by the young French officer.[57] Had the congressmen known that Carleton and his successor were reporting to London "the defenceless state of every post" and the "entirely rotten" fortifications at Quebec, not to mention that the "province cannot be preserved" should the rebels mount an invasion, they would have demanded such a campaign.[58]

Washington, however, saw no allure in the prospect of another Canadian campaign. He pronounced the notion a "child of folly" that was likely to be "productive of capital Ills," and worked covertly to smash the endeavor before preparations could proceed. Washington had good, and ample, reasons for opposing such a campaign: the failed invasion of 1775–1776 demonstrated the monumental obstacles to success in such an enterprise; another invasion would siphon off provisions from the army that he was struggling to supply at Valley

Marquis de Lafayette. Painting by Charles Willson Peale, 1779. Despite his lack of military experience, Lafayette won Washington's heart with his verve, daring, and sycophancy, and in time he justified his commander's belief in him.

Forge; it would also diminish the strength of his army, reducing his ability "to crush . . . the army under General Howe's immediate command," the lone "decisive" triumph, in his estimation, that could secure independence and end the war.[59]

Each point was a compelling reason for resisting another foray into Canada, and it is likely that Washington entertained additional concerns as well. While he doted on Lafayette, Washington may have questioned his ability to lead such a campaign. Only twenty years old and virtually devoid of command experience, it was natural to wonder whether Lafayette could succeed where Montgomery, Arnold, Schuyler, Thomas, and Sullivan had failed. Washington was not alone in his skepticism. The president of Congress "feared the Marquis being a Young man full of fire would [rush] . . . our Soldiers into too much danger."[60] Washington also saw the scheme as yet another instance of congressional infringement on his authority. Worse still, the plan for the invasion was the handiwork of the Board of War, and Gates and Conway occupied two of the panel's three seats. Not only did virtually everyone identify Gates as the author of the plan, but when Congress approved the invasion, it named Conway as the second in command under Lafayette. Arising as it did in January, in the very midst of his obsessive brooding over the supposed Conway Cabal, Washington saw the proposed campaign not as a sound military initiative, but part and parcel of a conspiracy that aimed at Gates's elevation and his own ouster.

Washington's troubled appraisal was off base. The Canadian venture was hardly the work of a small cabal. The president of Congress said that all but three congressmen supported an attempted invasion. Many proponents had championed such a course throughout the war, finding as many sound reasons for the undertaking as Washington could list against it. The plan's adherents believed that lessons had been learned from the mistakes of 1775–1776, and evidence now existed of "a general disaffection . . . among the Canadians," arousing hope that this time they would assist the invaders.[61] Proponents pointed out that only Lake Champlain and St. Johns had to be taken to close America's back door, the portal through which Carleton and Burgoyne had sought to invade the United States, and they insisted that taking Canada almost certainly would compel the northern Indians to make peace. The loss of Canada might also lead London to end the war. To be sure, the acquisition of Canada would assure that the postwar United States would be huge and more powerful, for with Canada would likely come the Ohio Country, the sprawling frontier region bounded by the Appalachians, the Ohio River, the Great Lakes, and the Mississippi River.[62]

Time was of the essence if Gates's plan was to succeed. His scheme called for gathering a force of 2,500 men in Bennington and in February setting off over the frozen Lake Champlain for St. Johns. If Canada's civilian population was inhospitable, the invaders were to destroy every vessel and raze the shipyards in St. Johns, and return to New York. If the Canadians were helpful, or even just neutral, Lafayette's army was to advance on Montreal and take that city. But Lafayette, the prince of sycophants among the many who surrounded the commander in chief, hurried not to northern New York, as he had been ordered, but to York, Pennsylvania, where Congress was meeting, and he went to do Washington's bidding. In conferences with Congress and the Board of War, he asserted that unless Conway was dropped from the command structure, he would resign and return to France. Lafayette was in a bind. He lusted after the opportunity to command, but he hardly wished to antagonize Washington, and he wrote his commander often to assure him that he was trying to protect him from Congress's "worse scheme against yourself and your army." Lafayette's demands also put Congress in a bind, as it was desperately anxious not to offend France, which might occur if Conway, a French officer, was dumped. Nevertheless, Congress buckled and reassigned Conway with Henry Laurens, assuring Lafayette that Congress understood that his comrade "is *deceitful*" and had been "paid in his own Coin." That little triumph cost Lafayette several days and he squandered still more when he stopped at Valley Forge to report his success to Washington. (He did not wish "your excellency [to] forget a little absent friend," he said.) Lafayette finally got as far north as Albany when February was nearly gone, and he immediately pronounced that if it was still "the month of January I would be certain of carrying the business." Unfortunately, he claimed, he believed that he "could not do any thing in our present situation." Congress suspended the invasion.[63]

All in all, the Valley Forge winter was a time of triumph for Washington. The war had begun without him and during its first three years he had, in effect, been responsible for only half of America's military effort. But at Valley Forge he gained supreme control over the army's waging of the war. For better or worse, this was now General Washington's war. With the Canadian invasion scrapped, Washington once again struggled to decide between attacking New York City or Philadelphia, or simply responding to the actions of the British army. Retaking New York, he thought, would be the "most desirable" outcome, but it would be the most difficult to achieve. Each alternative was attended by what he called a "baneful influence." The campaigns for New York and Philadelphia would result in "great waste of Military Stores" and would require "great supplies of Provisions; which, probably, was not within reach." On the other hand, to fall back on the Fabian strategy would "be a means of disgusting our own People by our apparent inactivity." Washington was still mulling his options on May 1 when the news of the Franco-American treaties reached Valley Forge. He was ecstatic, but those who might have hoped for some memorable remark from him were disappointed. As always, he concealed his ebullience beneath an impregnable formality. The news "affords me the most sensible pleasure," he said in his usual parsimonious manner. (A month later he privately allowed that the treaties "chalk out a plain and easy road to independence.")[64]

Certain that the war was nearly over, many in Congress were euphoric. "America has now taken her rank among the Nations," said one, adding that with open French assistance it "has it in her power to [soon] secure her Liberty & Independence." Others went on in a similar vein: the alliance "puts our Independence beyond a doubt;" if the nation "will but step forth this campaign" of 1778, London "will acknowledge our Independence" before year's end; if a "respectable Army [takes] the Field this campaign, the War will be our own." From the moment that word of the alliance arrived, the consensus in Congress was to reject whatever Britain offered in the way of conciliatory proposals. The overriding sentiment was that "Congress will abide by their Independency at all events." A majority in Congress had coalesced for independence two years earlier. Now, with victory seemingly at hand, independence alone was alluring. Having grown accustomed to autonomy, no mood existed in Congress to contemplate a semi-autonomous status, which of course was as far as the king and Lord North's government were willing to go. North's appeasement—often called the North Peace Plan of 1778—was never considered.[65]

Washington was no less ecstatic when Congress approved the French treaties, and he told his soldiers that "it becomes us to set apart a day of . . .

General Joy" on which to celebrate the French alliance and the army's deliverance through the long difficult winter. He designated May 6 for the observation, and planned a ceremony that was to include a *feu de joie*, a fire of joy. Winter had slipped over the horizon, and in stark contrast to what had been Valley Forge's chronic dreariness through much of the army's stay, the day was warm and the grand parade ground a vernal green. The men gathered early under a soft linen-blue sky and marched smartly to their designated spots, where they stood in the delectable sunshine listening first as summaries of the treaties were read, then to an hour-long sermon delivered to each brigade by its chaplain. At 10:30 a single cannon blast rumbled low across the rolling terrain, and Washington, on his large gray mount, trailed by aides and the other general officers, rode out to a low knoll. When they were in place, the review began. Company after company marched past, more spit and polish than ever before, each taking the salute of the general officers. When the last company had passed in front of Washington, cannon roared, one after the other, thirteen in all. Following the first thundering artillery blast, the men in each company from right to left, then left to right, fired their muskets. After each successive cannonade, they cheered, beginning with "Long Live the King of France," then "God Save the Friendly Powers of Europe," and, after the last thump of artillery, "To the American States." At the conclusion of the fire of joy, the men were marched back to their huts, but the senior officers marched arm in arm to the shade of canopies that had been erected at the end of the trodden grounds. They were joined there by all the army's officers and several young women from nearby hamlets who had been invited to the celebration. They feasted on cold meats and a wide assortment of liquors and wines, "enjoying all desirable mirth and jolity," one soldier noted somewhat sourly. The officers' party did not end until long shadows lay over Valley Forge.[66]

The Franco-American treaties abruptly terminated debate on whether to attack New York or Philadelphia. Two days after the *feu de joie*, a council of war voted unanimously to sit tight.[67] A new mood was gathering. Do nothing risky. See what unfolds. See if France sends open assistance. See if British strategy changed. Wait and see.

TWO DAYS AFTER THE FESTIVITIES at Valley Forge, General Clinton arrived in Philadelphia to relieve Howe. He brought along a ministerial dispatch that minced no words: war with France was imminent and, henceforth, Britain's principal energies were to be directed toward defeating its old European adversary. Clinton's orders were to prepare for a campaign in the lower South in the autumn, and to accompany it with diversionary raids in the Chesapeake. As upward of a third of his army was to be redeployed to other theaters, the continued occupation of Philadelphia was out of the question. "It is a joke to think of keeping Pennsylvania," George III had declared to North in March, and Clinton had no more than disembarked at the city's riverfront before he broke

Sir Henry Clinton. Britain's commander in America from 1778–1781, Clinton might have presided over a better fate for his country had his orders been followed, or had he had been more unyielding with Cornwallis.

the news to his general officers.[68] They were not happy, but their despondency paled next to the "Horror & melancholy" of Pennsylvania's Loyalists. Until recently they had believed that victory was within their grasp, as the woeful American army at Valley Forge was vulnerable and could be "crushed by spirited Exertions." Instead, they were to be "deserted" by London, abandoned to the "Rage of [their] bitter Enemies," and "left to wander like Cain upon the Earth without Home, & without Property." Mortified, Howe's civilian secretary wondered, "where will all the Villainy end," and he declared: "I now look upon the Contest as at an End."[69]

With Howe about to close his three fateful years in America, his officers organized a surreal farewell extravaganza, a Meschianza (from the Italian word for "medley"). Held on May 18, as disconsolate Philadelphia Tories packed what belongings they could for their doleful journey into what many feared would be a permanent exile, the fete opened late in the afternoon. As a band on shore played lively martial music, several colorfully festooned vessels, each bearing the highest-ranking officers, glided down the Delaware River. When the Howes and others alighted, processing under a "triumphal arch" at the Market Street wharf, trumpets sounded, signaling the beginning of a mock medieval jousting tournament. Two teams of officers—the Knights of the Blended Rose versus the

Knights of the Burning Mountain—vied for the hands of young maidens dressed in extravagant Turkish gowns. Tea and dancing followed until nightfall, when fireworks lit the sky. At 10:30, while another band played, dinner was served for nearly 750 guests in a specially built "salon . . . decorated with mirrors and candelabra and chandeliers," a gluttonous repast served by "Many Negroes and other servants." Toasts were given and huzzas shouted to the king, the army and navy, the Howe brothers, and every rank of officers. Every conceivable object save one—a British victory—was toasted. The festivities, which cost in excess of £12,000 (the equivalent of the combined annual wages of hundreds of skilled artisans), ended only when the sun was visible in the eastern sky.[70]

General Howe left America forever during the last week of May, almost three years to the day after his arrival with Clinton and Burgoyne on the *Cerberus*, though his brother, the admiral, was compelled to await the arrival of his successor. Two weeks later the members of the Carlisle Commission landed in Philadelphia, only to discover that the British army, on orders from London, was preparing to abandon the city. The commissioners were "greatly astonished," livid even, that Clinton's orders had "been kept a secret from us." At some hazard, and much personal sacrifice, the three had made a journey that they now believed to have been a fool's errand, for with the British army in apparent retreat, they were without leverage to conduct negotiations. They hung around Philadelphia only long enough to attempt to bribe a few officials into turning coat. One of their targets, Joseph Reed, now a congressman, made their folly public. He spurned their money with the tart comment that he "was not worth purchasing, but such as he was, the king of Great Britain was not rich enough to do it." In the autumn, the commissioners sailed home, ending what had been Britain's first real attempt to reconcile with America.[71]

Clinton, meanwhile, carried out his orders, including preparations for withdrawing from Philadelphia. His original plan was to load his army aboard transports and sail for New York City. That went awry when he consented to give passage to as many Loyalists as wished to ship away with the army. His fleet was swamped. There simply was inadequate space for soldiers, civilians, horses, and tons of baggage and equipment. Clinton was compelled to rethink his plans. He could abandon the Loyalists to their often-vulturine enemies or he could make a one-hundred-mile march overland from Philadelphia to New York. He not only was too much the humanitarian to betray the Loyalists, he knew that if he was unfaithful to them the Southern Strategy would be undercut before it was attempted. Clinton opted to march. Such a course was not without risks. The redeployment ordered by the ministry had already reduced his army to about 10,000 men, fewer, his intelligence service accurately reported, than Washington possessed. Clinton also knew that the Continentals would shadow his army at every step, and attack its rear if the opportunity arose. Clinton felt that he had no choice. After ordering the force on Manhattan to make a feint into Connecticut (to distract the American troops in the highlands and New England), he put his army in motion on June 18. The first men stepped off in Philadelphia's ebony streets at 3:00 a.m., marching south to a site four miles below the city where a fleet of flatboats waited to convey them across the Delaware River and into New Jersey. Long before the sun reached its zenith, the last regular had departed Philadelphia.[72]

Washington had been watching carefully. Since the second week in May, his spies had been reporting that the British planned to leave the city. The signs were readily apparent, not least the army's sudden destruction of river craft and lame horses, and eventually the demolition of fortifications, bridges, and excess munitions. What Washington could not know until nearly the last minute was whether his adversary would travel by land or sea, although all along he believed they would "march the flower of their army, unencumbered with baggage through the Jerseys."[73] He was anxious to get at it. The warrior spirit quickened within him as seldom before, for after the events of the past autumn he hungered for redemption. He was cocksure, too, believing that Steuben had fashioned a better army, an excellent army, one that he was eager to use. General Lee was also back, to Washington's delight. The commander was "most cordially, and sincerely" happy at Lee's "restoration . . . to the Army," he said, and he meant it. It was as if Washington drew sustenance from having Lee at his side.[74]

Captured in December 1776, Lee had spent nearly sixteen months in British custody. For the most part he had been treated well, although during the early stages of his captivity he faced the menacing reality that Germain wanted him sent to London to face a court martial for desertion. It was a ludicrous charge, given that Lee, formerly a British officer, not only had resigned from the king's army years before this war, he had publicly repudiated his half-pay pension when he joined the Continental army. Yet Lee was savvy enough to know that a court martial was not always a scrupulous search for the truth. He also knew that if tried and convicted, he could be executed, especially if Britain won this war. His predicament likely drove him down a tortured path. A few weeks after falling captive, Lee not only openly urged Congress to negotiate with the Howes for peace, but he secretly offered his captors military advice on how to suppress the American rebellion. Early in 1777, he advised Howe to take Philadelphia, Annapolis, Alexandria, and either Baltimore or the lower Susquehanna River, steps that would supposedly seal off Virginia from the northern provinces and ignite Loyalist uprisings that would cause the "whole system of defense" to come "unhinge[d] and dissolve" in Pennsylvania, Maryland, and Delaware. Some scholars believe that Lee's obliging forthrightness was treasonous. Others, probably more accurately, feel that he sought to hoodwink the British by offering wrongheaded advice. Lee subsequently claimed that he had attempted to deceive Howe, which the British appear to have always suspected was the case. They distrusted him and, save for the previously planned campaign to take Philadelphia, wisely ignored his counsel, which, had it been successfully implemented, would hardly have helped the British cause.[75]

The Damoclean threat under which Lee had lived was lifted in the spring of 1777, thanks largely to the tenacity of Congress. Against Washington's wishes, Congress threatened retaliation against a half dozen Hessian and British lieutenant colonels and majors in American captivity should Lee be harmed. Washington, who was no less concerned than the congressmen for Lee's safety, objected to their "impolicy." He cautioned that as Britain held six Americans for every prisoner of war in U.S. custody, American retaliation might spark British reprisals that would result in a bloodbath for the rebels. But Congress was right. Its tough stance forced the British to back off their threat to prosecute Lee, and following the capture of a British general of equivalent rank, a deal was struck in December 1777 to parole both general officers. Neither was set free, but neither was any longer incarcerated. While he waited to be formally exchanged, Lee was permitted to move about Manhattan at will, and to once again be attended by a former servant and enjoy the company of one of his dogs. ("I never stood in greater need of their Company," he had pleaded soon after his capture.) Early in the spring of 1778, just prior to his release, Howe brought Lee to Philadelphia and treated him as a brother officer. The two talked at length. Supposedly, Howe confessed that he had erred in ever accepting a command in America. Lee, who was moved by the experience, subsequently expressed his affection for the British general in his customarily askance fashion, characterizing Howe as corrupt and lazy, but a good soldier, and a man whom he memorably described as having repeatedly "shut his eyes, fought his battles, had his little whore." Two days later, on April 5, Howe released Lee from captivity, though he was ineligible to soldier until he was formally exchanged. That occurred later in the month.[76]

Washington was extravagantly gracious toward Lee. Reacting with "much Eagerness" to the news of his imminent release, Washington sent one of Lee's former aides and a small mounted party from his own "Horse guards" to escort him to Valley Forge on April 5. Washington even rode four miles down the road from Valley Forge to greet and warmly embrace Lee "as if he had been his Brother." The army was drawn up to receive him and a military band played as Lee rode into the encampment. That evening the general and Martha Washington hosted a festive dinner in Lee's behalf, with "Music playing the whole time," an observer noted. Lee retired after dinner and according to his enemies—whose allegations are not always to be believed—spent the night with a strumpet he had fetched along from Philadelphia. The next morning, when Lee overslept, Washington, who ordinarily waited for no man, delayed his breakfast until Lee emerged, disheveled and looking "as dirty as if he had been in the street all night."[77] When Lee, still awaiting his exchange, departed for home a couple of days later, Washington wrote him a letter that abounded in good natured humor, perhaps the only waggish missive that he ever wrote to another general. Washington was delighted to have Lee back again. He had once valued Lee's counsel, and it is possible that he had come to feel that he suffered for having been denied it during the past campaign.[78]

Late in May, about two weeks prior to Clinton's evacuation of Philadelphia, Lee—at last having been formally exchanged—returned to Valley Forge and resumed his old position as second in command beneath Washington. Disagreeing with several fellow officers, he encouraged Washington to remain on the defensive and advised that the British were likely to open a campaign in the Chesapeake. Washington thanked Lee for his candor, but there were signs that the commander's earlier effervescence toward his mercurial subordinate had given way to rising wedges of doubt. Lee's taste for assertion had gotten him in trouble again. He had quarreled with Lafayette, assailed conditions at Valley Forge, and carped indiscreetly about Washington's allegedly injudicious generalship in the campaign for Philadelphia, supposedly even telling Elias Boudinot, the commissary general of prisoners who had negotiated his release, that "Washington was not fit to command a Sergeant's Guard." Some of this doubtless got back to Washington. What Washington did know to be sure was that Lee, in his customarily undaunted manner, had criticized the new-modeled Continental army, Washington's pride and joy. He told Washington straight away that it was impossible to fashion an army from America's individualistic citizenry that could match up to British regulars. The best bet, he said, was to go with the militia, short-term soldiers who had proven their worth in the Bunker Hill and Saratoga campaigns. Nothing could have been more inexpedient than to broadcast such an idea. Some who had the commander's ear, and who were truculently suspicious of Lee, or were jealous of his position, almost certainly whispered their misgivings to Washington. All that can be known for sure is that sadly for Lee, and perhaps for the American cause, his myopia blinded him to the realities of the politics of Washington's headquarters.[79]

During Lee's first weeks back with the army, Washington's energies were consumed with attempting to learn where Clinton's army was going and how it would get there. He sent Lafayette with 2,200 men across the Schuylkill to gather intelligence, ordering him to keep moving at all times. It was a bizarre and useless mission, and one that nearly ended disastrously. Lafayette disregarded his orders by taking up a stationary position on Barren Hill, a few miles from Philadelphia. Learning of this at once, Howe, in his final major action, set a trap for the rebels and marched nearly half his army toward Barren Hill to spring the snare. Howe even invited friends to "meet the Marquis de La Fayette" at a dinner party set for the next evening, so confident was he of capturing his novice foe. He likely would have succeeded, too, had not a rebel army surgeon stumbled on the advancing British and alerted the unsuspecting Frenchman, who barely escaped. Playing the diplomat once again, Washington lauded his young truckler for having "handsomely" conducted himself and "disgraced" the enemy.[80]

Three days before the British evacuation of Philadelphia, Washington learned through a tip—provided by a laundress for the Carlisle Commission—that the regulars' departure was imminent. On the day that the British finally departed, spies along the Delaware alerted headquarters of what was occurring.

Washington immediately detached a small force to reclaim the city after the nine-month occupation, and with the bulk of his army he set off for New Jersey in pursuit of his adversary. By now, summer in all its miasmic oppressiveness was descending on the mid-Atlantic. High humidity, linked with temperatures that soared to near one hundred degrees, blanketed the region. Men in both armies were miserable, but especially the British, weighed down with heavy backpacks and wool uniforms. Heat strokes were commonplace, for these men were marching and working, struggling to cross swollen streams and grappling with wagons that bogged down in roads turned to a putrid sludge by violent thunderstorms nearly every afternoon. To add to their miseries, the Continentals' advance units acted as Schuyler's men had earlier, felling trees across roads and destroying bridges and wells.[81]

Washington had dared to hope for an army of 40,000 men for the 1778 campaign, about half the number that Congress had proposed fielding. Instead, he had only 13,000 men, though his army slightly outnumbered that of Clinton, and it was reasonably well supplied, thanks largely to the end of winter's inclemency. The rebel army, as usual, moved more quickly than the lumbering British, who managed to advance less than fifty miles in six days. The Continentals crossed the Delaware at Coryell's Ferry and by the sixth steamy day of their trek, June 24, they had reached Hopewell, northwest of Princeton, and were situated near the presumed path of their foe.[82] During that day, Washington summoned a council of war to discuss options, the first gathering of its kind since the officers had met a week earlier at Valley Forge. At that previous meeting only two of the fifteen generals present had favored bringing on a full-scale engagement. Cadwalader had argued that with Clinton's army inferior in numbers and unable to sustain itself in the middle of New Jersey, the "present, appears to me to be as good an opportunity to as we shall probably have during this Contest to strike a decisive Blow." Even if a "Defeat of our Army" resulted, he went on, it "will be no essential disadvantage to us & cannot in the least serve their Cause." Wayne maintained that an attack, however it turned out, would lead the public to believe that the enemy had been forced to retreat and that the Continentals had succeeded in "*Burgoyning* Clinton."[83]

A dozen general officers attended the June 24 council of war. The majority opposed "putting the Enemy in a situation which might bring on a general engagement," though they favored harassing activities to be carried out by a force of some 1,500 men. Several, including Lee, held to the view that they had articulated a week earlier. It was best, they said, to avoid taking great risks, as France was coming into the war and a French fleet, which might be sailing to the United States, was known to have put to sea. Wait, they counseled, and act in concert with the new ally. These officers advocated marching the army to the Hudson or White Plains, from which it could confine the British in New York until the French arrived. Lee, in his usually inflammable language, said that "to risk an action . . . wou'd be to the last degree criminal."[84]

Possessed of an army that he was eager to test, Washington had wanted to do more than merely harass his adversary. So, too, did a handful of his officers. Wayne was so enraged that he refused to sign the council of war's recommendation. Colonel Hamilton, Washington's aide, sneered to a friend that the majority of the generals "would have done honor" to a "society of midwives." Lafayette did what no American general could do. He reproached Washington for having called a council of war. Formulating tactics in such a manner, he caviled, "will never be a mean of doing what is consistent with the good of the service." Together with Wayne and Greene, he submitted a written proposal that urged Washington to commit a larger force, though none were "for Risquing a General Action with them—unless Ciurcumstances should Render Success Certain." Greene, who always had Washington's ear, advised that should the rebel army get "near the Enemy" and make no attempt "to do the . . . least injury," the public would assume that "our courage failed us."[85]

What followed remains woolly today, as it was at the time. It can only be explained if Washington once again was seized with irresolution. He pondered matters for two days before coming to a determination, to the degree that he ever settled on a plan. It appears that Washington, accepting the council of war's recommendation, initially offered command of a 1,500-man force to Lee, the ranking general. Lee declined on the grounds that it was beneath someone of his rank to command such a small detachment. Unaccountably, Washington passed over Greene and Stirling, and gave the command to Lafayette. Either before Lafayette accepted, or soon thereafter, Washington—moved by the arguments of the dissenters—decided to quadruple the size of the force that he was about to send out. It now was to consist of three divisions with a combined strength of 5,340 men. One was to operate on Clinton's right flank, another on his left flank, and the third was to move against his rear. What Washington anticipated in the looming encounter had evolved as well. Two days earlier, he had issued orders about "harassing the enemy," but ever the fighter and risk-taker, Washington now gave the impression of looking forward to a sizeable engagement in which he could use the army that he believed Steuben had shaped for him. On the eve of battle, Washington appears to have hoped to destroy the enemy's rear guard of two thousand men, the elite of Clinton's army.[86] If successful, he would have scored another victory on the order of Trenton-Princeton.

Once the nature of the operation was rethought, Lee reconsidered his previous objection to assuming command. He may even have been urged to take command by nervous comrades who had little confidence in Lafayette's abilities. Lee told Washington simply that he now "viewed it in a very different light"— his refusal to accept the command, he said candidly, "would of course have an odd appearance"—and he offered "a thousand apologies for the trouble my rash" behavior occasioned.[87] Washington consented, but concocted a peculiar arrangement that was designed to avoid "wounding the feelings of the Marquis de la Fayette," a rare display of empathy by the commander. Lafayette was to be in

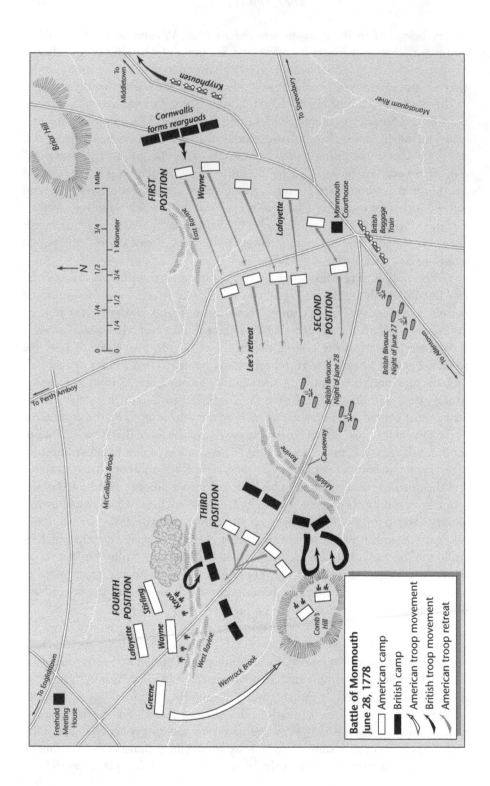

Battle of Monmouth
June 28, 1778

American camp
British camp
American troop movement
British troop movement
American troop retreat

To Middletown
To Knyphausen
Cornwallis forms rearguads
Briar Hill
FIRST POSITION
Wayne
Lafayette
Monmouth Courthouse
British Baggage Train
To Shrewsbury
Monosquom River
East Ravine
1 Mile
3/4
N
1 Kilometer
3/4
1/2
1/4
1/2
3/4
1/4
0
Lee's retreat
SECOND POSITION
British Bivouac Night of June 27
To Allentown
To Perth Amboy
British Bivouac Night of June 28
Ravine
Causeway
Middle
McClellan's Brook
THIRD POSITION
Knox
FOURTH POSITION
Stirling
Lafayette
Wayne
Greene
West Ravine
Comb's Hill
Wemrock Brook
To Englishtown
Freehold Meeting House

charge of the detachment that would threaten Clinton's left flank and to be in overall command until contact was made with the enemy. At that point, Lee would assume command. The two armies were now headed for a major clash. Each moved only slightly over the next three sultry days. In the gathering darkness of June 27, Clinton took up a good defensive position at Monmouth Court House, indisputably inviting an attack. The main force of Continentals lay nearby at Englishtown, where Washington met with Lee and the three division commanders—Maxwell, Wayne, and Lafayette—to plan for the next day's engagement. With little understanding of the enemy's disposition, and no knowledge whatsoever of the terrain, it was impossible to prepare a set plan of battle. What was most unusual was that Washington did not give Lee written orders concerning what he was to seek to accomplish. Washington merely told Lee to attack. Lee's behavior, or so it seemed, was to be dictated by what happened when the armies collided.[88]

Lee moved out at 7:00 a.m. on June 28 against a British army that had resumed its march four hours earlier. The vanguard of redcoats was already several miles down the road to Sandy Hook. Behind it came the baggage train, stretching out for twelve miles.[89] The second division, about six thousand men under Clinton and Cornwallis, followed, and they, too, had set out two hours prior to Lee's advance. Lastly came the rear guard, which Lee intended to strike. As Lee moved forward over terrain that had not been reconnoitered, he discovered to his horror that three deep ravines sluiced through the landscape. They would weigh heavily on his mind throughout that fateful morning. These defiles were yawning morasses that could be crossed only slowly, and with difficulty. They could delay, even trap, an army that faced the need to retreat, and they could forestall the speedy arrival of reinforcements, should they be needed. (Clinton subsequently remarked that he "could not entertain so bad an opinion of Mr. Washington's military abilities as to suppose that he would risk" a large part of his army "over these difficult passes.")[90] Despite what he saw, Lee proceeded, and in time he gained considerable confidence. His intelligence reported that the British rear guard under Cornwallis lay ahead with just two thousand men. Possessing a numerical advantage that neared three-to-one, Lee exalted. He and one of his aides told those nearby—and Washington, in a message that Lee sent to headquarters—that the "rear guard of the enemy is ours." But Lee faced a fluid and muddled situation. He was going after an opponent that was in motion. This was not an attack on a stationary target, as Washington had led at Trenton. Lee had known that he would have to throw together a plan as events unfolded, and it became clear that victory in this battle would go to the side that was best at improvisation.

Skirmishing broke out as various detachments made contact. Seeing what was happening, Clinton, no less eager than Washington for a fight, brought up his force of four thousand men to protect Cornwallis. In the heat and confusion of the battle, Lee knew that his adversary's numbers were growing while his

remained stationary. Although he did not know the precise size of his enemy—
the two forces were now about evenly matched—Lee was aware that his considerable numerical advantage had vanished just as he faced the prospect of fighting
the flower of the enemy force. He knew, too, that his lane of retreat—if it came to
that—was obstructed by those three ravines. Still, Lee fought, seeking to cut off
the enemy's rear guard in a complicated pincer movement. What ensued was
extraordinarily confusing. As units moved about frenetically in the stultifying
heat and choking dust, the battlefield in the words of one historian took on the
look of "a great anthill" that seethed with activity.[91] Much of what unfolded was
disorderly, due in no small measure to the conduct of the officers. Indeed, the
men who fought at Monmouth appeared to be far better trained than those who
commanded them. Lee issued orders that were often ignored or overridden by
the commanders of the three detachments. On several occasions, those officers
took substantive actions without orders from Lee, sometimes producing delete-
rious ripple effects. The most crucial action occurred when Lafayette withdrew
his force to another position, a fallback that in the estimation of some—notably
Wayne—was unwarranted. Observing the movement, General Scott concluded
erroneously that Lafayette was retreating. He drew back his men, and kept
retreating until he was entirely off the field of battle. His precipitous withdrawal
set other units to falling back. In short order, Lee saw that there was no hope of
destroying the enemy's rear guard. Scott had disappeared. Other units were
retreating. Due to a mix-up in orders, Morgan's riflemen had never arrived. The
rebels were now outnumbered. To this point, Lee had not ordered any retreat,
but he found himself in a swelling predicament, and concluded that a withdrawal
was prudent. The odds were running against him, and he feared that if the retreat
turned into a frenzied flight—always a danger in a perilous situation—disaster
could be the result, especially given the presence of those menacing ravines in his
rear. Better, he thought, to order a retreat and endeavor to bring it off in an orderly
fashion. Lee covered the withdrawal with rear guard actions, and extricated his
force safely. (Clinton subsequently praised Lee for having withdrawn just in the
nick of time to avoid having his right wing rolled up by a British cavalry sweep.)[92]

Lee fell back across the east ravine to the middle ravine, only to find that the
position his French engineer chose for him was flawed. He ordered yet another
pullback. His plan now was to take up a defensive position behind the last, or west,
ravine. Given his situation, Lee acted properly in all respects save one.
Distracted, he failed to keep Washington informed about what was occurring,
and the commander learned of the retreat from soldiers who were drifting to the
rear. The last that Washington had heard was that Lee was about to destroy the
enemy's rear guard. Suddenly, he discovered that the whole army was in flight.
Washington, seven miles to the rear, hurried forward to see for himself. En route
to the front, Washington spotted a fifer walking from the direction of the fight.
He rode to the boy to ask what was occurring, and was informed that Lee's force
was retreating. The commander, a witness recalled, was "exceedingly surprized,

and rather exasperated." He rode further, until he ran upon an entire division in retreat. They told him that Lee had ordered the withdrawal, that he was "flying from a shadow," even that he had called for the fallback after his forward units had fired merely a single volley, which was palpably untrue.[93] In an instant, Washington's mounting suspicions combusted in a firestorm of rage. According to a private who witnessed the exchange, Washington was now "in a great passion." Some soldiers said they heard him mutter "D—n him," referring to Lee, and Scott subsequently remarked that Washington "swore that day till the leaves shook on the trees."[94] Washington spurred his mount and sped forward again. Washington's aggressive distrust of his subordinate led him to conclude that only the rankest treachery could explain what was happening. When he reached Lee, Washington's legendary volcanic temper erupted. In a confrontation that lasted only a few seconds, Washington allegedly cursed Lee, calling him "a damned poltroon," and demanding: "What is all this?" What is this "unaccountable retreat?" According to the varied accounts of some observers, the normally voluble Lee was so ruffled that for once in his life—perhaps the single most important moment in his life—he was either speechless or he could only stammer "Sir, Sir?" Other witnesses remembered Lee claiming that his men had taken flight following a British bayonet charge. Still others recalled that Lee, his face hot from Washington's insult, lividly retorted: "You know that all this was against my advice."[95] Whatever was said, it is probable that Washington had already decided on a course of action before he reached Lee. He abruptly relieved Lee of command and took charge himself.

As "shot from the British artillery were rending up the earth all around him," one soldier remembered, Washington rode among the men, gathering the remnants of two brigades, which he posted behind a fence. Their job was to fight off the enemy advance. In riding about, the commander ran upon Lee, who was still on the battlefield. Incredibly, given what had transpired only minutes earlier, Washington, calmer now, vested him with responsibility for this defensive position while he hurried about rounding up the units in retreat. In time, Washington returned and organized a new line of battle. He established it where Lee had planned to make his stand, behind the west ravine.[96] Subsequently, Lafayette and Hamilton gushed that Washington had saved the day. His "fine appearance on horseback, his calm courage . . . gave him the air best calculated to excite enthusiasm," said the Frenchman. In the same vein, Hamilton said that Washington's "coolness and firmness were admirable," and both said that the men drew sustenance from their commander's bravery.[97] Washington's courage and incredible instinct for leadership are beyond dispute, but the success that ensued on this day owed much to the terrain where the stand was made, to the reinforcements that Washington summoned (their presence afforded him better odds than Lee had faced shortly before), and to the numerous errors that Clinton made in the course of the engagement. Clinton had less experience than either Washington or Lee in leading armies in battle, and he had never taken this army into combat. On this day, the British commander failed to use some of the available troops, watched his grenadiers fall into disarray after he ordered them to ignore their customary fighting formation, and at one point lost control of his light infantry.[98]

The Battle of Monmouth raged through what remained of this broiling summer day. It was so hot, said one officer, that the battlefield was "untenable." The "heat was so intense," Lafayette remembered, "that soldiers fell dead without having been touched."[99] In this furnace-like atmosphere, the British, as at Bunker Hill, made three assaults. Rebel soldiers concealed by hedgerows repulsed each assault. Fiercely, desperately, they fired volleys into the British ranks, sometimes from a distance of only forty yards, and raked the enemy with deadly artillery barrages. After fighting for three hours or more in "weather . . . almost too hot to live in," as one American soldier put it, the British abandoned their bloody charges, and for two final hours, until 6:00 p.m., when the evening's cooling shadows swathed the bloody landscape, the battle morphed into an artillery duel. (Some of the American rounds were supposedly fired by "Molly Pitcher"—perhaps Mary Ludwig Hays of Carlisle, Pennsylvania—who allegedly took up a rammer and helped fire the field gun previously operated by her mortally wounded husband, if the doubtful story is true.)[100] As dusk gathered, Clinton was finished. Washington was not. Although he subsequently acknowledged that his men were "fainting with faticgue, heat, and want of water," he did his best to organize an American attack on both British flanks.[101] Perhaps it was his good fortune that darkness tightened about the field before the attacks could be launched. Washington eagerly planned to renew the fight the following morning, and that night he and his men slept on the open ground in air that was sour with smoke and death. But at sunrise Washington discovered that Clinton was gone, having slipped away as he himself had done so often. The Battle of Monmouth was over. It had been bloody and desperate. Including scores of heat-stroke victims, the Americans lost 360 men and the British about 500.[102]

Monmouth was not a pivotal engagement. It is remembered now largely because of the Lee-Washington confrontation, but also because it was the longest one-day battle of the War of Independence and it featured the war's largest artillery exchange. It was also the last major battle fought in the northern states in this conflict.[103] Neither side gained anything by this fight, although Clinton could assert that he had beaten back an attack, enabling him to complete his objective of getting his army back to New York successfully. Washington stressed that the enemy's losses were "considerable" and emphasized his role in the battle. "I determined . . . I found . . . I marched . . . I gave directions," until at last the Continentals "recovered the field of Battle" after getting off to a "bad beginning" and "hence our affairs took a favorable turn."[104] Washington did not pursue Clinton. The British had a headstart of several hours on him and not far to go before they reached the well fortified Jersey shore near New York.

Washington still had Lee to deal with. He did nothing for two days. As he learned more details of the early portion of the battle, evidence mounted that

Lee's behavior under fire had been credible. Washington may even have grown remorseful over his conduct toward Lee, although he said nothing. Whether he intended to set things right with Lee can never be known, for within those two fateful days Lee self-destructed. Lee had initially complained loudly about his mistreatment to all who would listen—some of which doubtless got back to Washington—and in due time he wrote Washington three unsparing and ill-advised letters. Not only did he object to the "very singular expressions" that Washington had uttered in their showdown, he insisted that the commander had been in no position at the time to fairly judge "the merits or demerits of our manoeuvres." Predictably, Lee crossed the line. He baldly declared that Washington had been misled into acting with "cruel injustice" by the "very stupid, or . . . very wicked . . . dirty earwigs" who surrounded him. He demanded a court martial in order to clear his name.[105]

Hamilton, John Laurens, and Lafayette were among the "dirty earwigs" to whom Lee referred. They may have egged on Washington, sensing the opportunity to destroy another potential rival to their commander, one whom they found to be venomous and distasteful. Lafayette, overlooking the fact that it was his withdrawal that had set in motion the initial American retreat, blathered on that Lee's conduct had grown from his inclination "in favor of his english nation." Hamilton claimed that Lee had "lost his senses" on the battlefield and acted with a "certain indecision . . . and hurry of spirits." Not requiring much of a push, Washington appointed a court martial panel and the trial began six days after the battle. In recent years, most scholars who have examined the transcript of the trial have concluded that the evidence exonerated Lee on the two most serious charges: a "breach of orders" and having ordered an "unnecessary, disorderly, and shameful retreat." But Lee was doomed. He could not win a fight with Washington in the midst of the war, and he most assuredly faced ruin from judges who served under Washington and in many cases viewed the defendant as an acrid rival who had been a constant irritant. In mid-August, Lee was convicted on both charges, as well as on a third count of having been disrespectful to the commander in chief. He was suspended from command for one year. During that year Lee repeatedly insisted—including, unforgivably, in published newspaper essays—that he had been the victim of judicial lynching, the result of a "hellish plan" concocted by those about Washington. There "is something rotten betwixt him [Washington] and his People," he told some members of Congress. In a lengthy newspaper polemic, Lee additionally dredged up the treatment of General Conway to illustrate that no criticism of Washington would be brooked. His actions were intolerable, leading Congress to dismiss him from the Continental army forever. Too late, Lee learned that "No attack it seems can be made on Gen. Washington, but it must recoil on the assailant," for, as he remarked, the commander in chief, more for political than military reasons, had become indispensable and was to be "indulged in the sacrifice of any officer whom from jealousy pique or caprice He may have devoted to destruction." (Lee died of a fever in Philadelphia late in 1782. In his last letter, he congratulated Nathanael Greene on his meritorious service, so unlike some generals who had acquired "the infatuation of the People" by "employing puffers"—idolatrous writers—"to scoop out the brains of the People and then fill their skulls with mundungus.")[106]

WASHINGTON'S HOPES of inflicting a heavy blow against his enemy had not materialized at Monmouth, but in the days that followed he narrowly missed the opportunity to score a greater victory than he had ever dreamt of, a conquest that likely would have been the decisive blow in this war. Mere days after Clinton's army had been carried away from New Jersey to New York, the Toulon fleet of sixteen sail—twelve ships of the line and four frigates—together with four thousand marines, glided majestically up to Sandy Hook. Its commander was Vice Admiral Count d'Estaing, a forty-eight-year-old soldier who had earned a reputation under fire in India. Strikingly handsome, d'Estaing was given to a "Reserved affability" that led many to describe him as "a most agreeable Man, Sedate, polite."[107] His orders were to fight, and had his squadron reached the New Jersey coast earlier—which it would have had Vergennes not fatally delayed its departure for two critical months—d'Estaing and Washington might have

Comte d'Estaing. Engraving by an unknown artist, first published in 1782. Bad luck repeatedly frustrated d'Estaing. With good fortune, he might have smashed the British army in July 1778, the British navy the following month, or the defenders of Savannah a year later.

pinioned, and destroyed, Clinton's army. Even with the delay in sailing, d'Estaing might have arrived in time to wipe out Clinton had he made a faster crossing from Toulon, but unfavorable winds made his an interminable voyage. As it was, his voyage was longer than it need have been as he had made for Philadelphia, only to discover when he reached the Delaware Capes that the enemy had abandoned the city. With a bit of luck, d'Estaing might have destroyed Admiral Howe's overmatched fleet before it escaped Philadelphia on June 28, the day of the Battle of Monmouth, a close call that subsequently prompted Charles James Fox in the Commons to remark that had "the French fleet arrived but six days sooner," it would have eradicated "the naval power and glory of Great Britain."[108] Fox knew that nothing could have saved Clinton. Howe's fleet was by then scattered all along the Atlantic coast, and Vice Admiral Byron's squadron, which the ministry, after much indecision, had sent as protection against d'Estaing, was nowhere to be seen. It had not sailed until almost two months after the Toulon fleet weighed anchor, and it chanced upon a storm-tossed Atlantic summer. The first ship in Byron's fleet, the flagship, finally reached America only on August 8, a month after d'Estaing arrived at Sandy Hook. Just a few days difference in d'Estaing's time of arrival, gasped an English supporter in Manhattan, and "our cause would have been totally ruined."[109]

Washington's disappointment was palpable, but he quickly saw the "most interesting advantages" that might accrue from the presence of the French squadron. All along, he had looked on retaking New York as the biggest prize to be had, and on being apprised that d'Estaing was en route, Washington, prior to Monmouth, had contemplated how to wage a campaign for winning back the city. Ultimately, he conceived of a two-part operation: d'Estaing would take possession of Sandy Hook, a four-mile-long island that commanded New York's harbor; when every British vessel was driven from its anchorage, the French fleet would assist the Continentals as they made simultaneous strikes in several sectors of Manhattan. It was "at least probable" that such a scheme could work, Washington thought.[110] But it was not to be. Keen to the value of Sandy Hook, Clinton—displaying an enterprise that Gage and Howe had never evinced toward the similarly vital Bunker Hill and Dorchester Heights—sent 1,800 men to occupy the site on July 19. Of greater significance, d'Estaing's pilots ascertained that New York's channel was too shallow for France's heavy warships, which drew twenty-seven feet to the twenty-two of their British counterparts. Washington's burning vision of recovering New York City, which he believed "would have reduced to a moral certainty, the ruin of Great Britain," melted away in a moment during that cruel July.[111]

D'Estaing was disappointed as well, but he and Washington rapidly identified another inviting target—Newport, garrisoned by 6,700 men under the command of Robert Pigot. D'Estaing's formidable fleet swept away all British shipping within its vicinity, and within a month those enemy soldiers appeared to be trapped. Radiating confidence, Washington spoke of the "certainty of success" as he detached troops to join the one thousand Continentals near Newport.[112] The one apparent fly in the ointment was that the Rhode Island Continentals were commanded by General Sullivan. His performance in Canada in 1776 had been so poor that Congress had replaced him, and following the Battle of Brandywine several congressmen clamored for his removal from the army, charging him with a series of battlefield errors that nearly brought on disaster. A Maryland congressman, driven by a suffocating rage, had fought to prevent men from his state from ever again having to serve under Sullivan. Even some of Sullivan's officers vilified him in letters to Congress. Sullivan immediately confessed that he "never . . . pretended that my Disposition in the Late Battle [of Brandywine] was perfect. I know it was very far from it," but he pleaded with Washington for his backing against the charges. Washington demurred. A court of inquiry eventually vindicated Sullivan, but he was embittered and during the winter of 1778 threatened to leave the army. It might have been better had Washington let him go. Oddly, he encouraged Sullivan to stay on, though Washington long before had concluded that Sullivan was given to making bad choices. Ultimately, Washington saw to it that Sullivan remained in the army by vesting him with the Rhode Island command. As Washington's actions occurred in the midst of his scare over the Conway Cabal, it may be that he wished to keep Sullivan around because, despite his flaws, he was loyal. But there were other reasons as well. Washington liked generals who were fighters, and there was no doubt that Sullivan was combative. Washington may also have feared that if Sullivan was cut loose, it would arouse the furor of New England's congressmen, who largely backed the New Hampshire general against all charges, most of which had been brought by southerners.[113]

When Washington had given Sullivan his post Rhode Island had been in the backwater of things. Now America faced a crucial campaign under Sullivan's command. That Washington was uneasy was obvious, but according to Greene he left Sullivan in place rather than to give "a doubtful friend" the opportunity to win further laurels. What Greene was alluding to was that had Sullivan been passed over, it would have been difficult for Washington to avoid naming Gates to command the enterprise. Gates was popular everywhere, but a hero in New England, and he wanted the post. Whatever his reasons, Washington's uneasiness shone through. He ordered that the Continental troops and militia be amalgamated into two divisions, one commanded by Lafayette, the other by Greene, each of whom was to ride herd on Sullivan. (Even before setting out for Rhode Island, Greene cautioned Sullivan that "Every thing depends almost upon the success" of the campaign to retake Newport. "Your friends are anxious, your Enemies are watching. *I charge you to be Victorious*.") Washington exhorted Sullivan to do nothing rash. "[W]eigh every desperate matter well before it is carried into execution," Washington counseled, and he added that Sullivan was to heed "the good advice of those about you," meaning Lafayette and Greene, of course. Often prefacing his remarks with the comment that "this will be an object well worth your attention," Washington poured out advice and raised questions in letter after letter. He even provided Sullivan with the most elementary advice: "The most certain way of calculating the Enemy's strength, is first to ascertain the number of Regiments, and then endeavor to find out the number of Men in them by examining deserters and others."[114]

Timing was crucial in this enterprise. D'Estaing's fleet arrived at Point Judith near Newport on July 29, prompting Pigot, who sensed an enveloping hopelessness, to scuttle his four frigates so they would not fall into the hands of the French. Unfortunately for the allies, the rebel force—which would eventually total 10,127 men, 60 percent of them New England militia, including a large contingent from Massachusetts under the command of John Hancock, who had little military experience, and none in combat—was still gathering.[115] To d'Estaing's considerable annoyance, the Americans would not finally be ready for nearly two weeks. In the interim, Sullivan and d'Estaing met and concocted a plan. The French fleet was to proceed up the Middle Passage in Narragansett Bay and land its marines on the west side of Aquidneck Island, on which Newport was situated. Sullivan was to bring his force south from Providence and, after crossing the Seaconnet Passage at Tiverton, put his men ashore on the isle's east side. The two landings were to take place simultaneously on August 9, and were to be followed by a siege operation.[116]

Things quickly went awry. Problems began with a rash act by Sullivan. He put his men ashore twenty-four hours early, infuriating d'Estaing, who had not been consulted. Not only did he feel that Sullivan had acted recklessly—the plan of attack had been predicated on the assumption that the outnumbered enemy would be less able to cope with simultaneous landings—but he also raged that French national honor made it "militarily inadmissable" for the Americans to land first or for a mere major general, as was Sullivan, to establish his beachhead before a lieutenant general, as he was, had the opportunity to act. Affairs took a much worse turn the next day, August 9, when a British fleet was spotted on the horizon. Admiral Howe had gathered a powerful squadron from up and down the coast, including the one ship in Byron's fleet to have reached America and a man of war from the West Indies. Howe's fleet was the larger of the two—twenty fighting ships to sixteen—and it carried more guns, 914 to 834. D'Estaing rapidly recalled the marines that he had landed only that morning and prepared for a naval battle. Like two wary heavyweight boxers, the massive fleets maneuvered for two days, each seeking an advantageous position. However, before a shot was fired, a vast and destructive storm (perhaps a nor'easter, but possibly a hurricane) lashed out of the Atlantic. Both fleets were scattered and severely damaged, and Howe quickly bore away to New York for refitting.[117]

While the navies had maneuvered for an edge, Sullivan kept his men moving. By August 15 his large force was digging parallels on the east side of Newport. The French, he figured, would do the same on the opposite side of the city when they returned. As the warm and sultry days dragged by in the wake of the violent tempest, desertion in the unseasoned militia units grew to alarming proportions. The storm was especially ghastly for the militiamen, few of whom had tents. Their spirits shredded, many men headed home. Others left in despair at the sight of tons of powder and cartridges ruined by the gale, and still others, fed up with rank mud everywhere and putrid knee-deep water in every trench, departed as well. Finally, on August 20, the French fleet returned, but with discouraging words. As Sullivan listened with a dark, tightened face, d'Estaing announced that he, too, needed to make repairs and was heading for Boston. Sullivan, knowing that the expedition was ruined if d'Estaing could not be dissuaded, sent Lafayette and Greene to plead with him to continue the campaign. It was useless. The French fleet had been badly mauled by the storm, though Greene also thought that d'Estaing was eager to be refitted and get back at sea before Howe returned and shut him up in Boston harbor.[118] At midnight on August 21, under a gorgeous summer moon, the French warships sailed away from Newport.

Sullivan and his officers were astounded by the actions of America's new ally. Without d'Estaing's fleet, "our expedition is now at an end" and "will terminate with disgrace," one whimpered. In a fury, Greene privately charged that the French had "desert[ed] us." Before d'Estaing sailed, the rebel officers had made a last, desperate attempt to dissuade him. They drafted a "Protest" that was signed by nine generals, including Sullivan, Greene, and Hancock, but not Lafayette, who knew that taking part could jeopardize his career in the French army. A firestorm of passion, the remonstrance was audacious and undiplomatic, the very sort of impetuous undertaking for which Sullivan was noted. It charged d'Estaing with failing to follow orders (though no American had seen his orders) and with abandoning the rebels to "ruinous consequences." It additionally questioned his motives and, implicitly, his courage, and alleged that he had "injur'd" the "honor of the french nation." As with everything else in this campaign, the officers' timing was off. The document was not ready until after d'Estaing had sailed. Given that it was by then a moot point, the protest should have been abandoned. Instead, in keeping with his customary bad judgment, Sullivan ordered that it be delivered to d'Estaing in Boston. The French commander, needless to say, was indignant, though he said nothing, for, as young John Laurens reported to Washington, diplomacy imposed "the painful but necessary law of profound silence." But d'Estaing privately complained to Greene of Sullivan's "abuse," and warned that such intemperate actions could "create ill blame between the . . . two nations." Washington, who was one of America's better diplomats, quickly interceded to mollify d'Estaing, writing dulcetly that he and "the thinking part of Mankind" understood his actions.[119]

When the French fleet sailed, Sullivan's militiamen "desert[ed] by shoals," as Greene put it. Sullivan and his generals agreed to abandon the siege, which all now saw as "folly," instead launching a "storm," an assault on the rear of the enemy's defenses. The plan was never put into operation. The desertions (which reduced Sullivan's army by half) rendered an attack unthinkable, and on August

24 Sullivan learned from Washington that Clinton was gathering scores of craft, possibly with the intent of falling on the rebel force in Rhode Island. Sullivan immediately convened a council of war, which recommended a retreat to the defenses on the north end of the island. As was usually the case, the council had not come to a unanimous decision. Some wanted to hold on, forlornly hoping that d'Estaing might return. Sullivan was wracked with indecision. Four long dangerous days passed before he finally ordered the retreat. Under cover of darkness on August 28, the American army pulled away from Newport. It was a perilous undertaking. Pigot emerged to pursue his fleeing opponent. The fighting that ensued was often desperate and seesawed back and forth, with the issue very much in doubt for a considerable period. Initially, the rebel rear guard beat back the British pursuit, but later they were driven back themselves. In the end, the Continentals, fighting valorously, repulsed three Hessian charges, and Sullivan was able to take his army back into the redoubts on Quaker Hill near the northern end of Aquidneck Island. His army did not remain there long. The next day, August 30, further word arrived from Washington: Clinton had sailed with reinforcements for Rhode Island and Admiral Howe was back at sea with a patched-up fleet. Washington strongly suggested that Sullivan should quit Aquidneck Island altogether. Sullivan took the hint and on that same day moved his army by the Howlands Ferry across to Tiverton, and seemingly to safety.[120]

In reality, Sullivan's force remained in grave danger. Clinton was bringing three thousand men, giving the redcoats a considerable numerical advantage. If he could persuade Admiral Howe to help out, it was conceivable that Sullivan's army could be bottled up below Providence, and the very sort of attack that the rebels had so recently dreamed of making against Pigot could be inflicted on them. Alas, for the last time in this war one of the Howes foiled a good chance at a major victory. Admiral Howe refused to cooperate, setting off instead on a fruitless search for d'Estaing. Left empty-handed, Clinton pulled the plug on the Newport campaign.[121] The Americans had lost slighly more than two hundred men, the enemy nearly three hundred, and the British still held Newport.[122]

WHILE THE NEWPORT CAMPAIGN flamed out, Washington moved his army to the highlands, the better to watch the activity of the British armed forces in New York. He discovered that there was little to see. It was perplexing and left him "in an awkward, and disagreeable state of suspence."[123] By late October, Washington did know that d'Estaing's fleet was about to sail to the Caribbean (it departed Boston for Martinique on November 4). Washington looked forward to acting in concert with the French fleet in the future, he told d'Estaing. Privately, he prayed that Spain would enter the war, an event that would enable the allied fleets to administer "a decisive blow to the haughty dominion, which Britain has so long affected to maintain over the Sea." As November played out, Washington knew that campaign 1778 was over. With the trees once again bare and leaden skies hinting that the season's first snow was imminent, Washington abandoned "all Idea, this fourth Winter" of further action. Once again, he began "to throw the Troops into Cantonments for their Winter Quarters."[124] What Washington could not know was that the War of Independence was changing before his eyes, and that what was to follow the autumn of 1778 was to be very different from what had gone before. Nor could he know how much he, too, was about to change.

13

CHOICES, 1779

IN THE SWELTERING SUMMER OF 1778, *La Chimère*, a French frigate, docked at Chester, below Philadelphia, and Conrad-Alexandre Gérard came ashore. Three congressmen were there to greet him and escort him to the city, where that same afternoon he was the guest at a dinner party at the residence of Benedict Arnold. Although still recovering from the wound he had sustained at Saratoga, General Arnold had returned to active duty just before the Continental army departed Valley Forge, and Washington had asked him to become the military governor of Philadelphia, eastern Pennsylvania, and southern New Jersey until he was physically able to take the field again. Arnold consented and entered Philadelphia with the detachment that Washington sent to reclaim the city when the British abandoned it. He took up residence in the Penn mansion, the house that had been Howe's headquarters only days before, and it was in that capacious dwelling that Arnold and several congressmen entertained Gérard, who was a very special guest. He was France's minister plenipotentiary to the United States.

Gérard, who hailed from an upper-middle-class family of Alsatian public servants, had been trained in the law before turning to diplomacy. Close to Vergennes—he had been his first secretary—Gérard had been the foreign minister's choice to negotiate the Franco-American treaties. His every move that summer in Philadelphia was something of a spectacle to the callow Americans, most of whom had never met anything quite so exotic as a Frenchman, not to mention the House of Bourbon's first emissary to the United States. Many Philadelphians, and not least the members of Congress, gaped at Gérard as if he was a newly discovered species, noting that he was "a pretty Large Man [though] not very fat" who dressed "Richly but Decently" and comported himself with "Ease & Dignity without any of the foppish airs of your low bred" sort. All found him a "man of Politeness, Good Breeding and affability without troublesome ceremony" who was quick witted, well-read, and cannily perceptive. He was "as grave as a Frenchman can be," spoke "pretty good English for a foreigner," and endeared himself to his hosts with his fervor "to Humble the Haughty pride & Insolence of Brittain."[1] For his part, Gérard, who had been a diplomat for twenty years, was bowled over by the exaggerated good will that he discovered in Philadelphia. He was grateful, and frankly startled, at the zeal of the republican populace for the alliance and the French king, and he sent Vergennes a clipping from a Connecticut newspaper that marveled at America's affection for France, a turn of events that "Four years ago . . . was not in the view even of imagination."[2]

Not that the relationship was devoid of problems. The Newport campaign occurred barely a month after Gérard's arrival, and for a time the press in New England brimmed with vindictive essays blaming d'Estaing for having ruined the rebels' chances of scoring a decisive victory. To make matters worse, d'Estaing's fleet had barely anchored in Boston for refitting before a riot broke out between French sailors and American workers. Three additional melees ensued over the next six weeks, in the course of which a French naval officer was killed. The street brawls sprang from Boston's entrenched anti-Catholicism and Francophobia, nourished by considerable amounts of liquor. Fortunately for the rebels, there were those in Boston and Philadelphia who understood the danger that these outbursts posed to the new alliance, and they acted to mollify the French. Great pressure was exerted to persuade newspaper editors to forego further attacks on d'Estaing, and in a short while the inflammatory stories faded from sight. The authorities in Boston, moreover, portrayed the disturbances in a fashion that would have done honor to a modern spin doctor. With a wink and a nod, they attributed the riots to bread shortages. While they prevaricated, prominent residents of the city rolled out the red carpet for the French officers, wining and dining them, and giving dances and recitals in their honor. Congress also did what it could to undo the damage, adopting a resolution that lauded d'Estaing and dispatching Steuben to Boston to serve as something of an emissary to the French. Washington, who was quite familiar with the temperament of Bostonians, had very nearly predicted the riots. If things are not "prudently managed," he had cautioned, "popular prejudices and resentments" of the French would boil over. After the riots, he joined the campaign to smooth ruffled feathers by ladling treacle on d'Estaing and Lafayette in long, soothing letters.[3]

Washington had no more than put that nasty episode behind him when he received another plan from Congress calling for a joint Franco-American invasion of Canada. He was not surprised that the notion had resurfaced. Early in September, Lafayette had predicted to him that "your occupation of next winter and spring" would be Canada, and he added that he wished to "fight along with you, and I much desire to see your excellency in Quebec next Summer."[4] Lafayette had tried to keep the idea of a Canadian campaign before Congress throughout 1778, and during operations at Newport he had written d'Estaing proposing a Franco-American invasion. (He had suggested that Washington might send armies into Canada through the Lake Champlain and Mohawk Valley corridors while d'Estaing's fleet took Newfoundland and Nova Scotia.) Support for a Canadian invasion had never waned in New York and New England, and Gates, who had been restored to his command in the Northern Department in April, had continued to champion such an undertaking. During his first days in Philadelphia in July, Gérard sent word home that fervor abounded to conquer Canada, and in mid-September a congressional committee spoke with him about a joint campaign to take the region. Gérard's response was reserved. Vergennes had instructed him—and d'Estaing—that France was not interested in a Canadian campaign. When France had renounced "forever its possession" of Canada in the Treaty of Alliance, it had meant it. Gérard notified Lafayette of French policy. When a congressional committee spoke with Lafayette in mid-October he was suddenly guarded, more or less telling the congressmen what Washington had told him a couple of weeks earlier: "Many circumstances, & events must conspire to render an enterprize of this kind practicable & advisable."[5]

All the same, the hope of invading Canada flowered again that autumn, driven by the diminution of Clinton's army and a report by an Indian agent at Fort Schuyler that pro-American sentiment remained strong in Canada and among the Caughnawaga Indians. Congress rapidly considered a detailed plan for a joint invasion and not only directed its envoys in Paris to open discussions with France on the subject, but asked Lafayette—who had been given leave to return home—to consult with his government.[6] Next, it solicited Washington's opinion. He responded with two letters, one for the members of Congress in which he addressed only the military issues, and one for Henry Laurens, the president of Congress, in which he candidly expanded on sensitive issues of foreign policy. To the members of Congress, Washington raised the same objections to an invasion that he had brought up nearly a year earlier. He hinted to Laurens that he believed the plan to invade Canada had originated in France and that Lafayette had dutifully served as its conduit. He found the notion of France's participation in an invasion of Canada to be deeply disturbing, and made it clear that he saw a joint invasion as the first step toward France's reacquisition of Canada. That would not be in the best interest of the postwar United States. "In our circumstances," he went on, "we ought to be particularly cautious; for we have not yet attained our sufficient vigor and maturity to recover from the shock of any false step into which we may unwarily fall."[7]

Washington's geopolitical conclusions were sound. Understanding that if France possessed Canada, including the Ohio Country—today's Midwest, which Washington had fought to wrest from France in the French and Indian War, and where he still owned thousands of acres—and if Spain, France's long-time ally, held everything west of the Mississippi River, those European powers would surround the United States. All hope of America's westward expansion beyond the Appalachians would be lost. But if Washington saw that palpable danger, he seemed oblivious to the danger of doing nothing more to win Canada. Unless the United States won Canada on the battlefield, it—and perhaps the entire trans-Appalachian West—would remain in Britain's control following the war. It was no more acceptable to the interests of the United States for Britain to possess Canada and the West than for France to control those regions. But Washington, for reasons at once wise and self-serving, refused to consider a Canadian invasion. Congress, unwilling to cross Washington, went along, and once again "deferred" a Canadian invasion. "Prudence," it said, "dictates the arms of America should be employed in expelling the Enemy from her own shores, before the Liberation of a Neighbouring Province is undertaken."[8]

WHILE WASHINGTON ACTED with dispatch to head off those who clamored for a joint campaign to defeat the British in Canada, the American commissioners in Paris were seeking to expand France's role in the naval war. John Adams, who had arrived in Paris in the spring of 1778 as Silas Deane's replacement, was the driving force behind this effort. Adams had been an ecstatic supporter of the French alliance when he arrived in Paris. For centuries to come, he had predicted, France would be America's rod and staff against "the rapacious Spirit of Great Britain." But Adams had been in France only a brief time before he grew wary of America's ally. He saw indisputable evidence that France no longer treated the United States as an equal partner, but as a client state. Though the ties with France were indispensable for gaining independence, Adams came to fear that the alliance was a "delicate and dangerous Connection" with a potential for adversely affecting the long-term interests of the United States. Cautioning that Gérard might seek to influence American foreign policy, Adams also warned Congress that the longer the war continued, the more the United States would grow dependent on France. If the war was not rapidly brought to a successful conclusion, he worried, the postwar United States might find itself reduced to nothing more than a mere satellite of this great world power.[9]

Adams also grew impatient with Franklin. He acknowledged that Franklin was adored by the French—streams of Parisians, many among them attractive women and illuminati, flocked daily to the residence that the two commissioners shared in the hope of meeting Franklin—and that he was honest and devoted to the American cause. But Adams questioned his effectiveness as a diplomat. With more than a bit of exaggeration and jealousy, Adams contended that Franklin lived a life of such debauchery that he was unable to tend to his diplomatic responsibilities. Worse still was Franklin's style of diplomacy. He "hates to offend," said Adams. Franklin hesitated to push Vergennes, fearful that the French foreign minister would take umbrage and retaliate by denying America desperately needed loans. However well meaning, Franklin's wastrel habits, as well as his excessive caution, could prolong the war, with frightful consequences for the United States, Adams feared.[10]

Adams responded to what he saw in two ways. He urged his countrymen to fight as they had at the outset of hostilities, when they had stood alone. Americans must abandon their "Foppery . . . Avarice . . . Ambition . . . [and] Vanity," and rekindle what would later become known as the "Spirit of '76." He also wanted the American commissioners to push France, and push hard, to make greater military commitments. In the fall of 1778, Adams induced his fellow envoys to beseech Vergennes to commit a part of the French navy to the protection of allied merchant ships and to attacking the British whaling fleet. Vergennes declined. Undeterred, Adams exhorted his colleagues to once again approach Vergennes, this time asserting that the war was to be won in American waters and inveighing the French to send more heavy warships across the Atlantic. Franklin shrank from such a step, thinking it too risky, as it might offend Vergennes. But this was a three-member commission, and Adams and Arthur Lee outvoted their partner. With Franklin reluctantly going along, the three American diplomats pressed their case to Vergennes shortly before Christmas. The French foreign minister immediately rebuffed their request, mostly with sardonic silence, though at year's end France quietly sent seven ships of the line to America, four under the command of Commodore François de Grasse, and a few months later it committed five additional heavy warships under Commodore la Motte-Picquet.[11]

In his discussions with the commissioners, Vergennes had indicated that France was eager to join Spain in an invasion of England, and that the navy must be kept at home for that eventuality. What he had said was both true and false. Madrid and Versailles had been discussing a joint invasion of England, though it was not an undertaking that the French foreign minister savored. All the same, it was a venture that he was coming to believe was unavoidable. Vergennes badly wanted Spain to enter the war. He, in fact, now saw Spanish belligerency as imperative to France's success. But he also knew that an attempted conquest of England was the price to be paid for Spanish belligerency. Vergennes had gambled on a quick victory when he took France to war early in 1778. D'Estaing's fleet was to be the instrument of the triumph. Much that had occurred before July 1778 made Vergennes appear to be a diplomat without peer. The Toulon fleet had successfully slipped into the Atlantic, Dutch neutrality had been preserved, and Britain's forces were ominously vulnerable when d'Estaing reached America. Yet, as Charles James Fox had said in his scathing attack on the "grossest and dullest ignorance" displayed by North's ministry in permitting the enemy to position itself to inflict a mortal blow, "fortune" alone—sheer good luck—"had fairly declared" on Britain's side. By the thinnest of margins, d'Estaing had arrived too late to crush Howe's fleet or Clinton's army, and the British garrison at Newport had been fortunate to survive. In the sobering light of hindsight, Vergennes could see that his earlier successes were for naught. D'Estaing had failed in 1778 to destroy even one British ship of the line. France now faced a protracted war against a foe that was indisputably its naval superior. France had sixty-four ships of the line that it could put under sail in 1779, but Great Britain could put ninety to sea. The United States did not have a single heavy warship. Unless the French could bring Spain into the war, France and its American ally at best faced a long, grim war of attrition. At worst, they faced defeat.[12]

The Spanish were conflicted with regard to entering a war that might lead to American independence. According to France's minister in Madrid, "Spain regards the United States as destined to become her enemy in no remote future."[13] On the other hand, several of Spain's possessions in the Caribbean had recently been devastated by a series of El Niño and La Niña induced hurricanes and droughts, prompting Madrid to open commercial connections with the Continental Congress. In exchange for American flour, Spain had secretly provided the rebels with arms, munitions, and almost 1,000,000 pesos in the first thirty months after independence.[14] As 1778 drew to a close, Spain suddenly found itself in a unique diplomatic position. France wanted it in the war and Britain hoped to keep it neutral. Madrid responded by choosing "to blackmail both sides," as historian Richard B. Morris wrote.[15] Spain's foreign minister, the Conde de Floridablanca, offered to mediate the war between France and Britain, a thinly veiled ploy to see what each side would offer for its assistance. What Spain chiefly wanted from Britain was the return of Gibraltar, lost in a war nearly seventy-five years earlier, but it started the bargaining by also demanding the recovery of Minorca, East and West Florida, and Jamaica, all taken by Britain as prizes in earlier wars. Madrid wanted French help in regaining Gibraltar, but it also demanded a joint invasion of England, as it offered Spain the best hope for a rapid victory before Britain could attack its vulnerable colonial outposts. Vergennes was not keen to invade England. He knew that it would be defended by a sure-to-be augmented Channel fleet, some 40,000 redcoats—those currently posted at home and others brought in from garrisons in Ireland—and English militiamen. Vergennes saw it as a no-win course for France. Success was unlikely. However, should the invasion proceed better than anticipated, Vergennes worried that other nations in Europe—some who feared a radical alteration in the balance of power and others who wished to exploit the change—would be drawn into hostilities. That was not an outcome that Vergennes welcomed, as an increase in the number of belligerents would only increase the uncertainties of the postwar period. But Vergennes was backed into a corner. As campaign 1779 loomed, he found himself somewhat in the position of the proverbial man riding the back of a tiger. He was compelled to meet Spain's demands. The North ministry, on the other hand, could not concede everything that Madrid demanded. It was unwilling to yield Florida and Jamaica, and it knew that public opinion would never permit the surrender of Gibraltar and Minorca.

It was Floridablanca's choice: war with Britain, or minor concessions from London, and peace. He chose war. Belligerency had grown more attractive. An allied victory, he believed, was nearly a foregone conclusion. With misplaced optimism, Floridablanca assumed that France and America would win the war, whether or not Spain entered the fray. Spanish belligerency, he concluded, made a likely bet a virtual certainty. With Spain's entry, the allies would possess a huge naval superiority, 121 ships of the line to Britain's 90 in 1779. Fate had conspired, Floridablanca believed, to present Madrid with an unprecedented opportunity for regaining Gibraltar and securing other spoils. Furthermore, entering the contest would also afford Madrid the opportunity to avail itself of French leverage to limit the territorial ambitions of the United States. It seemed a prudent choice. If the United States was certain to be both independent and an emerging menace to Spain, Madrid's belligerency seemed the best means of holding the American threat in abeyance. On April 12, 1779, France and Spain secretly signed a treaty of alliance at Charles III's summer palace at Aranjuez. While Spain pledged not to make peace without France's consent, France promised not to make peace until Gibraltar was returned to Spain, to help with the recovery of East and West Florida, and to participate in the joint invasion of England.[16]

With a naval debt alone that was expected to exceed 40 million livres in 1779, the French government was driven to secure a loan immediately. It was but one legacy of d'Estaing's spectacular lack of success in campaign 1778. His failures also shattered America's dream that the French alliance portended a speedy end to the war. It now was painfully apparent that substantive changes in the war were overtaking Americans. An American victory was unimaginable without French help, while for France, victory was unlikely without Spain's assistance. Each European power had important ends that it hoped to accomplish before it agreed to peace, a reality that might mean an interminable war for an America that had pledged never to make a separate peace while France remained at war. An American rebellion that had begun for the purpose of securing greater autonomy from Great Britain had morphed into a war in which the United States was in the grasp of the faraway powers in Europe.

WHILE SPANISH MEDIATION was on the table, Minister Gérard had a talk with the leaders of Congress. Although war's end lay in the remote future, Vergennes wanted his ally to be ready to come to the bargaining table when, and if, Britain signaled a willingness to parley. Gérard asked Congress to determine its peace terms and appoint a minister plenipotentiary to conduct the peace negotiations, whenever they occurred. At first blush, it seems odd that Congress had waged war for thirty months without having decided what, aside from independence, it hoped to gain from the conflict. But there were good reasons why Congress had kept the matter at bay. Before Saratoga, peace talks were not within sight. Even more, divisions between states and sections were sure to arise in the bargaining over the peace aims. Why sow domestic discord when unity was essential for winning the war? Over and above that, some American territorial demands might anger France or Spain, jeopardizing the quest for a European ally. But, by the winter of 1779, when Gérard urged Congress to act, this thorny business could no longer be postponed. What few in Congress appear to have understood was that Vergennes had a hidden agenda. He was committed to protecting Spain's interests in North America against the cravings of the United States and to advancing French ends. Vergennes wished to safeguard the bounteous fishing rights off Newfoundland that France had enjoyed for two centuries. Although he had no interest in recovering Canada—Washington's fears on that score were misplaced—Vergennes had no desire to see the United States acquire the region. Guilefully, he preferred that Canada remain in Britain's hands. Should that be the outcome, and should Spain retake the Floridas, the United States, surrounded by adversaries, would be compelled to remain reliant on France.[17]

In February 1779, Congress stitched together two committees, one to make recommendations on America's peace demands—what would be known as the peace ultimata—the other to choose three envoys: the minister to negotiate peace, the minister to France, and a diplomat to be sent to Madrid to beseech help. The battles that ensued were the most bruising since the fight to declare independence.

Gérard, who was sent to do Vergennes's work, was delighted to find numerous conflicting interests in Congress. New England saw the fishing industry as vital to its economy and it relished the acquisition of neighboring Canada, for reasons of security as well as for its abundant farmland. It had little or no interest in the trans-Appalachian frontier that splayed westward to the Mississippi River. But the southern states coveted that region. Virginia had legitimate claims to much of the West through charters that dated back 150 years. Many affluent southerners (Washington and Jefferson among them) held title to western lands or were eager to speculate in that region, and many poorer southerners believed that this war, at least in part, was being fought to unlatch the door to the fertile West, a portal that London had kept bolted shut since 1763. Southerners cared little for Canada and even less about fishing rights. The mid-Atlantic states were dominated by Philadelphia and New York merchants, whose interests at times were similar to those of New Englanders, and at other times to those of the southerners, and every once in a while to both, or neither.

As John Adams grew more circumspect about the French alliance throughout 1778, he cautioned that the day might come when "French . . . Emmissaries . . . may have too much Influence in our Deliberations" and may seek to limit those American interests that conflicted with theirs "by Attaching themselves to Persons, Parties, or Measures in America."[18] That day arrived during the scuffle over the peace ultimata. Gérard not only astutely played congressmen off of one another, he hired polemicists to write newspaper essays that advanced some peace objectives while disparaging others. In the end, France got everything it wanted. Congress set as its goals a claim to all territory westward to the Mississippi River, a southern boundary at the thirty-first parallel (roughly today's Florida-Georgia border, but running to the Mississippi), and a northern border set on a line well below Montreal. It thus claimed little of Canada or Florida. Nor did it insist on the right to navigate the Mississippi River. It merely agreed to request navigation rights from Spain. Congress also failed to demand fishing rights, lamely agreeing to seek access to the fisheries in postwar commercial negotiations with Great Britain. No section got everything that it wished, but New England, where the war had begun, got nothing.

Gérard was less successful—barely—in the choice of America's diplomats. Franklin was named minister to France, a choice welcomed by Vergennes, who found the veteran envoy to be pliable, and therefore useful. Adams was Congress's choice to be the peace commissioner. Vergennes was not amenable to Adams's selection, viewing him as assertive, independent, and intractable, but Gérard lost this battle. After New England lost on Canada and fishing rights, it fought relentlessly to secure the appointment of a New Englander to negotiate the peace treaty, hopeful that a native son might secure at the peace table that which Congress had omitted from the peace ultimata. Gérard was more successful in the choice of the emissary to be sent to Madrid. Many southern delegates favored Virginia's Richard Henry Lee, but after Arthur Lee had joined with Adams to question France's conduct of the war, Vergennes had no wish to see another Lee in Europe. In the end, Congress chose New York's John Jay, whom Gérard had backed.[19]

THE SOUTH had lost the battle over Lee's appointment, but as 1779 dawned it faced a more immediate, and far more dangerous, matter. In the last days of the old year, Britain had unleashed its Southern Strategy, confronting the southern states with terrible new realities about the War of Independence. Late in November a formidable British force—3,500 men drawn from the Seventy-first Highlanders, two Hessian regiments, four Loyalist battalions, and a detachment of artillery—sailed south from New York. Its commander was Lieutenant Colonel Archibald Campbell, a flinty, forty-year-old Scotsman who had spent two years as an American prisoner of war (he had been with a contingent of Highlanders that were captured in the spring of 1776 when the ship bringing them to America unsuspectingly sailed into Boston, which General Howe had abandoned a few days earlier). Campbell's orders were to "attempt the reduction of Georgia." Two days before Christmas, he and the men in his task force spotted the Georgia coast, lush and verdant even in winter. Under a warm December sun, Campbell sent his troop transports, guarded by a single ship of the line, past sandy Tybee Island and up the Savannah River toward Savannah, Georgia's capital. Campbell put his men ashore at a plantation that was linked to the river by an eight-hundred-yard causeway through boggy rice fields. From there, the colorful army—the Highlanders wore green-plaid trousers and red-plaid bonnets, while most of the Germans were attired in blue—advanced overland.[20]

Campbell's counterpart was Brigadier General Robert Howe. A wealthy North Carolinian who had been educated in Europe, Howe had so impressed Congress with his service in defense of Newport, Virginia, in 1776 that he had been made a brigadier general in the Continental line. A year later, he was promoted and named commander of the Southern Department. Much of his two years in Georgia had been spent in combating border raids staged primarily by Tory outfits, such as the King's Rangers, a guerrilla war in which Howe had little success. In the summer of 1778, seeking to crush the Loyalist raiders in their nest, Howe had attempted an invasion of Florida, but the expedition was badly mismanaged and the American army got no further than the Georgia-Florida border. The fiasco destroyed what was left of Howe's reputation, already badly sullied through his impolitic and undiplomatic manner. In September, Congress replaced him, but at Christmas the lame-duck Howe remained on the job, awaiting the arrival of his successor.

Howe had little with which to defend Savannah. Altogether, only 854 men were under arms, more than a third of them Georgia militiamen, and the rebel artillery regiment consisted of merely forty men equipped with nine four-pounders. Howe was partially to blame for his predicament, as he had neglected Savannah's decrepit fortifications, constructed twenty years earlier to defend against the Spanish threat in the French and Indian War. Unable to force his adversary to undertake a siege operation, Howe faced three choices. He could establish a line at Brewton's Hill, a bluff that overlooked Campbell's landing site. He might establish a defensive position outside Savannah and invite a frontal assault. Or, he could abandon Savannah without a fight. He made the wrong choice. Had he chosen Brewton's Hill, he might have raked the invaders with a deadly fire, as Glover had done at Pell's Point. With nine artillery pieces—Glover had not had a single field gun—Howe might even have stopped the enemy in its tracks, and he certainly could have made it pay a terrible price for taking possession of Savannah. Campbell believed that Howe had erred in not making this choice. With five hundred men and four cannon, the British commander subsequently remarked, the rebels could have "destroyed the greatest part of this Division of our little Army in their progress to the Bluff."[21]

After a council of war rejected abandoning Savannah, Howe deployed his men in a line "in the Stile of an Half Moon," according to Campbell, across a road leading to the town. It was a strong position, anchored by woods on one side and a swamp on the other. Campbell, who reconnoitered the site by climbing high into a tall oak tree that overlooked the American defenders, later intimated that he had anticipated a bloody trial when his men launched their frontal assault. But such an assault never took place. At the last minute, a slave, most likely Quamino Dolly, who was owned by Georgia's last royal governor, showed the British a "private way" around the swamp on the American right. It was to be the key to British victory on this day, especially as Howe had failed to post pickets in this area. As the bulk of the Highlanders and Germans hurried through the swamp, Campbell opened with a feint against the rebel left. Distracted, Howe was none the wiser to his enemy's plans until Britain's principal blow fell in his rear. Enveloped, the Americans were quickly routed. The rebels lost eighty-three killed, some thirty of whom drowned trying to escape across Yamacraw Creek. Nearly three quarters of the Americans in the battle were captured, including George Walton, who had signed the Declaration of Independence, a fact that the British never discovered. Howe's force additionally lost enormous quantities of arms and munitions. The British suffered just seven killed and seventeen wounded. Within hours, Savannah, a low-lying village festooned with palm trees and Spanish moss, was in British hands. Soon, too, numerous homes had been pillaged and several of the residents had been arrested, most of whom faced incarceration aboard prison ships.[22]

The British army had entered Georgia offering freedom to slaves who deserted their rebel masters. Within a short period extraordinary numbers of African Americans, some runaways, some who had been abandoned by owners in flight from the invaders, were behind British lines. Within six months of the British landing, up to 1,500 former slaves were working as cooks, laundresses, nurses, and butchers for the British army.[23]

General Washington, betraying a blind spot toward the significance of the war in the South that would not soon vanish, pooh-poohed these events, dismissing the loss of Savannah, and perhaps even all of Georgia, as certain to "contribute very little" to the British war effort. Southerners in Congress knew better. "The Enemy have at length discovered our weak part," said one. Not only would Britain's logistical woes be alleviated by the capture "of every grain" of rice and corn, and all the "Cattle, Horses, and other live Stock" throughout Georgia, but "the Auxiliary forces of Savages and disaffected Persons" would aid the enemy in too many ways to contemplate. "But the greatest source of Danger," said a Maryland congressman, "is the accession of strength they will peacefully receive from the black inhabitants."[24]

The choices that had been made for 1779 were revolutionizing this war.

14

"A BAND OF BROTHERHOOD": THE SOLDIERS, THE ARMY, AND THE FORGOTTEN WAR IN 1779

CONGRESS no longer attempted to dictate to Washington and it said nothing when, following the departure of the French fleet in November 1778, he divided and dispersed the army for the winter. He posted some infantrymen at Danbury, Connecticut, others at West Point in the Hudson Highlands, and the remainder in Middlebrook, New Jersey, where he established his headquarters. The cavalry, which was to locate forage, was spread from New England to the Shenandoah Valley.[1]

The men were quickly put to work building their huts, so that at the outset each encampment took on the same feverish air that had characterized the startup at Valley Forge. But this winter was to be considerably different. The wisdom of scattering the army in several camps was quickly borne out. Supplies flowed relatively smoothly into each post, though that was due to more than Washington's good judgment. The winter was mild—"scarcely a . . . fall of snow, or a frost" for three months, reported an officer posted in New Jersey—and Clinton, with an army only about half the size that Howe had possessed the previous winter, was in no position to harass the Continentals' supply system. Substantive French aid had also poured in during the autumn, one of the first rewards of the alliance and commercial pact. The army especially welcomed the vast shipments of French clothes and uniforms (some coats were blue, others brown, and the states drew lots to determine which received the coveted blue). So much arrived that ill-clad soldiers were no longer seen—for a time, anyway— and Washington had to take the deliciously unaccustomed step of establishing proper storage facilities for the surplus.[2]

On a personal level, this was Washington's most comfortable winter thus far. He sat for a portrait painter and ordered silver and china for his table, to replace his metal dishes that—in his words—had become "little better than rusty iron." Martha was at his side again, a practice that had begun in Boston during the first winter of the war. She ordinarily arrived a few days after the army entered winter quarters and remained until the next campaign season beckoned, when she "marched home," as Washington remarked. While he lived snugly, Washington was careful to avoid the ostentatious habits that had invited public criticism when he commanded the Virginia regiment. Critics in the 1750s had portrayed him as a rakish nabob who lived lavishly and often was not even with his army.[3] During the War of Independence, in contrast, Washington left the army only when he was called away by Congress. When he took the army into winter quarters at the end of 1778, he had not been separated from the army for approximately thirty months, and he had not seen Mount Vernon for three and a half years. When choosing a site for headquarters, he ordinarily shunned pretentious dwellings in favor of large farmhouses that could accommodate his staff and numerous visitors, usually taking a room or two for Martha and himself, and another for his office. He also abandoned the pastimes that he had relished as a civilian. There is no record of him fox hunting, fishing, or playing table games during the war, although on rare occasions he picnicked with those with whom he worked closely. He put in a long workday, seven days a week. As had been his habit on the farm, Washington rose before dawn and worked in seclusion for up to three hours, tending to his correspondence and reading reports, savoring this sole period of solitude each day. He emerged at about 7:30 a.m. and with his entourage rode about the camp on horseback, inspecting the varied activities of the men and speaking with officers along the way. An hour or so later he returned to headquarters for a light breakfast. From roughly 9:00 a.m. until 3:00 p.m. he worked in his office, meeting with officers and visiting dignitaries, dictating letters, and issuing orders. Work paused in mid-afternoon for the day's principal meal, a substantial repast that lasted for about two hours and was customarily attended by around twenty persons, principally other general officers and important visitors to camp. Afterward, he occasionally rode again, this time mostly for exercise, and he routinely put in another couple of hours of work, calling it a day about 7:00 p.m. When Martha was in camp, she and her "Old Man," as she referred to her husband, spent their evenings together, sometimes attending social events hosted by the officers, including plays that they staged.[4] Otherwise, he often relaxed with his young aides over a glass of Madeira, mellow times given over to frank conversations with men who were blindly loyal and whom he trusted explicitly. He usually retired early in the evening.

Washington enjoyed phenomenally good health throughout the war. He experienced three minor illnesses in eight years, each a one- or two-day bout with what might have been a virus. The numerous portraits painted of him during the war show a man aging as one would expect for an individual who passed from age forty-three to fifty-one. His hair grayed, lines and wrinkles grew more pronounced, and he was forced into reading glasses, though only those at head-quarters were aware that he used spectacles. He remained robust and vigorous, and trim as well. Shortly after celebrating his fiftieth birthday, Washington weighed 209 pounds.[5]

Lady Washington, as many called Martha, was not the only woman in camp. The wives of several senior officers, and sometimes their daughters, wintered with the army. Like Martha, most devoted considerable time to knitting and sewing for the soldiers, and occasionally they visited the troops. But this was also something of a cheery social season for these women. In many ways the atmo-sphere at camp was akin to that of a normal community cleaved by impenetrable social divisions and barriers. However, there was a surreal quality to a wartime army camp in which the enlisted men retreated after dark to their cold, over-crowded huts while only a few hundred yards away officers reveled in ebullient society, attending parties, enjoying formal dinners at which bands of musicians played, and delighting in balls that lasted into the night. "[W]e live by Eating, Drinking and Danceing," one general officer remarked that winter. At one bash in March, Washington and Catherine Greene, General Greene's wife, "danced upwards of three hours without once sitting down. Upon the whole we had a pretty little frisk," said Greene himself, ever one to oblige his commander. Some soirées were arranged as matchmaking affairs at which young single officers would have the opportunity to meet the young daughters of senior officers and public figures who were visiting camp. On one occasion at the Middlebrook cantonment, Royal Flint, an assistant commissary of purchases, "had the pleasure of gazing upon the agreeable" Gracia Cox, the daughter of Colonel John Cox of Pennsylvania, one general reported, adding that his "looks and such squeezes as he gave her hand, plainly indicated his wishes." On another occasion Greene personally looked after the daughters of friends, hoping to find escorts for them to "a little hop" that was planned. The most memorable spark to come from these affairs occurred when Colonel Hamilton became engaged to Elizabeth Schuyler, the general's daughter, one month after he renewed her acquaintance at the winter encampment in 1780.[6]

The general officers' wives were but a small fragment of the women who lived for a part of the year with the Continental army. It was illegal for a woman to enlist, but many wives of enlisted men accompanied their husbands while the army was in winter quarters, and a few remained with the Continentals through-out the year. The best estimate is that these women—who were called "camp followers" in the eighteenth century—ordinarily totaled about 3 percent of the number of soldiers. As the average soldier in the standing army was young and single, an extraordinary percentage of the married men must have had their mate at their side.[7]

The presence of females had long been commonplace in the British army, in which men signed on for what was expected to be almost a lifelong commitment.

During the War of Independence, camp women totaled 8 to 10 percent of the number of redcoats. So routine was the practice that the British supply services factored in women when calculating rations, allowing provisions for six women per company. In the provinces, however, where soldiering had been a short-term proposition, it had been uncommon—though not unheard of—for women to keep company with an army. Perhaps that explains Washington's crusty surprise at finding such a large number of females in his camp early in this war, though he also feared that their presence would create the impression that the Continental army was a standing army.[8] In addition, Washington feared the women would divert the men or impede operations, though he mostly worried that the women would deplete the army's always meagerly stocked pantry. When a battle loomed, Washington often ordered that "No Woman under any pretense whatever" may "go with the army," and when the Continentals marched he was vexed by what he called "the pernicious practice of suffering the women to encumber [ride in] the Waggons," as it resulted in "a much greater proportion of men [being] with the baggage than could possibly be necessary." On one occasion, in August 1777, he attempted to prohibit additional women followers from entering camp, railing that the "multitude" already present was "a clog upon every movement." Failing egregiously in this effort, he subsequently—and with some distaste—suffered their company, particularly in the winter cantonments, knowing that any attempt to banish the camp women would provoke widespread desertion and result in the loss of "some of the oldest and best Soldiers."[9] Some four hundred women are believed to have marched into Valley Forge with the men in December 1777, one woman for every forty-four men. During 1780–1781 the ratio in some brigades was one female for every thirty to forty men, though by that time it was one to eleven in Washington's private guard and in some artillery units. Yet another inconsistency in Washington's thinking was that while he welcomed the wives of officers, whose stay was financed by the taxpayers, he objected to public assistance for the enlisted men's wives who were left alone at home. Such a practice he declared, "Would be robbing the public and encouraging idleness."[10]

If Washington could not get rid of the camp women, he sought to certify that those who came to camp were married to a soldier and, as far as possible, he subjected them to the army's rules and regulations. In a sense, therefore, the camp followers were treated as if they were in the Continental army. Like the soldiers, their mobility was restricted, fraternization with the enemy was prohibited, they were immunized against smallpox, and they were quartered in tents, huts, and barracks. At times, the army hired these women for essential tasks, including making soap, herding cattle, and working as nurses, laundresses, and milk maidens. Not infrequently, high-ranking officers—including Washington—employed them to wash, cook, and serve as their housekeepers. In time, too, the army's logistical service adopted the British practice and set aside rations for the women, at a ratio of one woman for every fifteen men. Those women who were with the army when it entered battle often helped out by lugging water to thirsty soldiers and to artillerymen who had to swab the barrels of their cannon between rounds. Like the fictitious "Molly Pitcher," some may have briefly fought. As in many early wars, women sometimes successfully passed as men and enlisted, not the most difficult feat in an army that took in countless beardless young boys. Most of the imposters were quickly discovered, and some were punished, though some may have served for extended periods. The most famous of the female soldiers was Deborah Sampson, a twenty-one-year-old woman from rural Massachusetts who had been a teacher and weaver in civilian life. She entered the army as "Robert Shurtliff" early in 1782 and served for seventeen months, fighting in two engagements in the Hudson Highlands. She was wounded twice though, incredibly, her gender went undetected by the physicians who treated her. When she was finally discovered in the summer of 1783 while being treated for camp disease, the army treated her leniently, probably because the war was nearly over and she had served with valor. She remained in the army until the Fourth Massachusetts Regiment was mustered out, and she received an honorable discharge.[11]

The wives of soldiers were not the only followers of the Continental army. Winter encampments took on something of the air of a market town. Sutlers—merchants who would have been called peddlers by civilians in the eighteenth century—hung on the army like white lint on a dark coat. They carried items for which there was a market among soldiers—food, tobacco, tea, coffee, soap, clothing, and especially liquor. Knowing that the presence of sutlers was inevitable, Congress from the start subjected these small businessmen to the control of the army. Washington had not been on the job ten days before he first restricted their trafficking, acting, he said, because they had been "so daring as to supply the Soldiers with immoderate Quantities of Rum." The army sought to set the prices that sutlers could charge, designated where they could set up shop on the periphery of the army's camps, and forbade the sale of alcohol to enlisted men without a pass from an officer. The army also permitted only those sutlers that it licensed to do business, and in turn it ordered soldiers to purchase items only from an approved provisioner.[12]

Prostitutes were another sort of entrepreneur with wares to sell to the soldiers, and they inexorably gathered near the army. From the first days of the siege army's existence, "lewd women" had been warned away from the encampments outside Boston. When the army moved to Manhattan in the spring of 1776 venereal disease not only became a serious problem, but two soldiers were murdered and a third castrated while visiting a slatternly New York City district commonly called the Holy Ground. The "kippen," the soldiers' slang for prostitutes, were more easily controlled by the army in rural cantonments, and tarts who were seized inside a cantonment were liable to have their heads shaved before being ceremonially driven from camp to the slow cadence of what was known as the "whore's march."[13]

It was hypocritical of Washington to permit his wife to be at his side while he endeavored to deny that luxury to his married soldiers, or for him to accept consorting between his unmarried officers and female visitors while forbidding the men to have girlfriends in camp. But armies are seldom bastions of egalitarianism, and the Continental army most assuredly was home to incredible distinctions between officers and enlisted men. In many ways the army reflected the society that had given it birth: each was hierarchic and mirrored the commonplace notion of the time that there was a place for everyone, and each person was expected to know his place. Neither many congressmen nor many officers, least among them General Washington, saw the American Revolution as a movement to bring about social leveling, and to some degree the Continental army had been designed by Congress to be an institution that would help sustain established ways. But what most drove the army's leaders was the desire to instill in the men an ironclad discipline. In the hour of peril, amid terror and confusion, it was hoped that the men would unthinkingly follow the orders of their officers. This meant that the men had to be stripped of their civilian, or individualistic, sensibilities, but the officers who were to lead during the din of battle also had to be assured of their power and made confident of their superiority. The learning process began by fostering the conviction that officers were gentlemen and enlisted men were of a lower order, for this was an age that had always recognized that "men of character"—gentlemen—were the natural leaders and the lower sort were the followers.[14] In innumerable practices—many borrowed from the British army, which reflected the English society that so many Americans yearned to escape—the daily routine of life in the Continental army was structured so as to engender respect for rank and privilege. In countless belittling ways, those practices were also calculated to diminish the self-esteem of the men.[15]

The distinction between enlisted men and officers included a wide gulf in pay. In the first years of the war the lowest-ranking officer, an ensign, was paid nearly twice what a private earned. The gap broadened to a fivefold difference by 1778. Officers enjoyed more comfortable housing and a more bountiful and nutritious diet—for one thing, they were more likely than the men to have the financial means to purchase additional supplies from sutlers—and the needs of many officers were tended by servants and slaves. (Washington's so-called body servant—that is, his personal slave, William Lee—was at his side throughout the war.) Most officers dressed in a genteel manner, wearing tailored uniforms, shirts made from expensive fabric and well-crafted shoes or boots. Few enlisted men wore a true military uniform. Most wore work clothes or what at the time was called the hunting shirt, a long, loose-fitting garment made from deerskin, wool, or linen. When the army was on the move, the men marched, but officers—at least field grade officers—rode on horseback. The men were always expected to show deference. They were to salute their officers and step aside when they passed on foot. Hand labor and heavy, dirty work were thought to demean officers. Constructing quarters, gathering firewood, digging and maintaining latrines, and policing—or cleaning—the camp fell exclusively to the enlisted men. With slight variations, countless days began with incantatory orders for the men to see that "all offal, putrid flesh and bones are buried."[16]

Officers and men alike fell victim to an array of dangerous illnesses. One young officer from Massachusetts mentioned having suffered in the space of three years from severe colds, stomachaches, rheumatism, boils, influenza, and lameness. But the men may have been more apt to suffer illnesses than their officers, as they faced a harder regimen while suffering poorer nutrition, inade-quate clothing, unclean cooking conditions, and overcrowded living facilities. Typhus and typhoid (called "putrid fevers" at the time), dysentery (the "bloody flux"), viruses ("fevers") that produced severe pulmonary and respiratory disor-ders, and smallpox created the greatest havoc. Smallpox and typhus, in that order, were the leading killers among rebel troops. Rheumatism, severe dermatological disorders—which everyone apparently simply called "the itch"—and venereal diseases stalked every camp, as well. With gallows humor, the soldiers also spoke of falling ill with the "Meases," maladies attributed to James Mease, the clothier general, who was blamed for woes believed to have been caused by a lack of warm clothing and shoes. One observer, who saw no humor in it, said it was sheer "black murder" for soldiers to face potentially fatal diseases from want of provisions. Exposure to the elements also added to the soldiers' plight. Michael Teter, a Pennsylvania soldier, was not alone in suffering frostbite while on guard duty. In Teter's tragic case, all his fingers had to be amputated.

The seriously ill were likely to fall into the clutches of the army's medical department, or "hospital," as many referred to the branch. Even though soldiers in America's colonial wars had been about four times more likely to perish of dis-ease than battlefield wounds, Congress had not considered a medical department when it created the Continental army. During his first month on the job, Washington asked that a medical service be created, and Congress obliged. It went through two reorganizations during the next six years, but for the most part it was administered by a director general and included a commissary of hospitals, who was responsible for feeding the patients, and an apothecary general, who supplied them with drugs. To fall into the hands of the medical service was to increase one's chances of dying. There were administrative problems (the first director general, Dr. Benjamin Church of Massachusetts, turned out to be a British spy, and was exiled once his treachery was established), but the nub of the problem was that this was the premodern period of medicine. Anesthesia was unknown, knowledge of germs was a century down the road, and antibiotics would not come into being for more than 150 years. Physicians bled and purged patients, and administered medicines that frequently did little good and sometimes resulted in considerable harm. A concoction that included spring water, sumac roots, and gunpowder was often prescribed for venereal disease, while olive oil mixed with mercury was used for snake bite. (Once when an officer died suddenly after taking a laxative, it fell to General Knox to write a comforting letter to the grieving widow. He told her that her husband had perished due to the

General Anthony Wayne. Lithograph made from the original painting, drawn by Jas. Herring, engraved by E. Prudhomme, from a sketch by Colonel John Trumbull. After the war, Washington said that Wayne was vain and injudicious, with a tendency to make wrong moves that led to trouble. An excellent judge of men, Washington was correct about Wayne.

"afflictive dispensation of providence.") An army hospital was often an unsanitary and uninviting "house of carnage," as General Wayne characterized one facility. A visitor to another hospital described having seen "one man lying dead at the door; . . . inside two more laying dead, two living lying between them; the living with the dead had so laid for four-and-twenty hours." When Private Joseph Plumb Martin fell ill with yellow fever he believed, not without good reason, that he had survived only because the regimental physician was away on furlough. For every soldier killed in combat, more than two died of disease, a better ratio than had existed previously and superior to that of many of Europe's professional armies. Several factors probably accounted for this. The rebel soldiery was reasonably well fed for much of the first thirty months of the war, and in the years that followed it foraged in its home territory, giving it access to substantial amounts of fresh food. The army was also on the move much of the time, enabling the men to escape unsanitary camp conditions. What is more, once the army went over to long-term enlistments in 1777, veteran soldiers and seasoned officers knew from experience what to do and what not to do in order to safeguard their health. Still, many men died, and when death occurred, the army typically distinguished between officers and enlisted men. Officers were likely to be given a ceremonial interment that included a parade and an honor guard. Moreover, only deceased officers were named in the official returns. The enlisted men were committed to unmarked graves, and at times to mass burial pits.[17]

Officers and men were worlds apart when it came to punishment. Two punishments sufficed for officers. Some indiscretions—a first offense of fraternizing with the men or of performing the duty of a subordinate, for instance—were likely to result in a private or public reprimand. More serious transgressions, such as cowardice, sodomy, desertion, perjury, and thievery, were liable to result in the officer being drummed out of camp in a ceremony designed to produce shame and disgrace. The men were humiliated at times, too. Some were berated by their officers as the "worst of all creatures," while others were made to wear signs that advertised their offense. Some were tied naked to a tree in full view of their comrades, were forced to wear women's clothing, or were shackled to a heavy log that had to be dragged about wherever the soldier went. But corporal punishment, which was never inflicted on an officer (nor administered by an officer), was the most common penalty meted out to the men. There appears to have been little uniformity in sentences. One court martial might sentence a man to ten lashes while another might order many times that number for another soldier for the same offense. Stealing, falling asleep on duty, failing to obey orders, plundering civilians, and numerous other infractions could result in a flogging. Repeat offenses were punished more severely, and sentences of one hundred lashes—a gory and ghastly beating, usually with a cat-o'-nine-tails—were not uncommon. Pitiless as were such floggings, Washington asked permission to inflict sentences of up to five hundred lashes, but Congress, some of whose members came from states that had adopted constitutions that prohibited cruel and unusual punishments, denied his request. The men were also punished by being made to ride the wooden horse (to sit on a pointed wood frame while restrained and unable to move), run the gauntlet (to be made to walk slowly between two long lines of men wielding sticks or strips of hide), and to endure the piquet (to be suspended off the ground by one arm for a protracted period). At times, men were punched or clubbed by a gun-wielding officer. For some behavior—including homosexual acts—men were "drummed out of camp." Capital punishment was legitimate under the Articles of War. Up to one hundred men—all enlisted men—are believed to have been executed during the war, sometimes by firing squad, more often by the hangman, and primarily for desertion or plundering. A Massachusetts lieutenant recorded in his journal during the Rhode Island campaign that a deserter had been recaptured. He added laconically: "We shot him in about an hour after we took him prisoner." (It was the fourth execution he had witnessed in two years of soldiering, and he would watch his fifth a few weeks later.) In the summer of 1779, Major Henry Lee (the father of Robert E. Lee) requested authority to carry out the decapitation of a deserter. Washington disapproved, fearing that "the appearance of inhumanity" might "give disgust."

All the same, one of Lee's officers had the deserter shot, then beheaded, and ghoulishly displayed the remains on the camp's gallows. Horrified, Washington ordered that the body be taken down immediately and buried secretly, "lest it fall into the enemy's hands" and be used to inflame American popular opinion. No one was punished for this gruesome action.[18]

Civilians often segmented the lives of the Continental soldiery into the time spent campaigning and the remainder of the year when they occupied winter quarters. The soldiers did not see such a neat dichotomy. There "was no cessation of duty," one soldier remarked, adding that "it was one constant drill" year round. As with "an old horse in a mill," said another, "it was a continual routine." Campaigning ordinarily consumed less than half of each year and combat was rare. Few soldiers experienced more than one or two major battles a year, each a single day encounter. But one need not be in a large, formal battle to be in harm's way. One veteran of several years service later recalled that serving in foraging parties and on routine patrols—usually to gather intelligence, canvass for provisions, or disrupt enemy foraging parties—were nearly as dangerous as being in a large-scale engagement, and in some ways was even more stressful. "No one who has never been upon such duty . . . can form any adequate idea of the . . . ten thousand . . . causes [that] . . . harass, fatigue and perplex" soldiers in such parties, he said. This war included hundreds, perhaps thousands, of clashes between small parties of men, each with the risk of death, injury, or capture. In all likelihood, none of the soldiers who were involved believed, even for a minute, that these risky skirmishes would have the slightest impact on the outcome of the war. Even so, some men welcomed foraging duty. Although it often involved "travel far and near, in cold and in storms," and posed "the *risk* of abuse . . . from the inhabitants" whose property was being seized and the hazard of battle, it was "not altogether unpleasant," admitted one soldier. It provided a welcome absence from camp and, most importantly, it afforded access to food. The soldiers' motto, said one, was "Rub and go." Take what could be gathered for the army, with a bit on the side for one's self, and scat. "Devil now and then tell us, that it was no harm sometimes to pull a few potatoes and cabbages, and pluck, once in a while, an ear of corn," said another soldier. With little remorse, Private Martin confessed after the war that he had taken food, soap, and clothing for his own use. It was an act of self-preservation, he said. After foraging almost daily during the first three months of 1778—the same lean months that stalked those at Valley Forge—Martin encountered one of his former officers who inquired: "Where have you been this winter? Why you are as fat as a pig." Martin subsequently acknowledged that his diet was substantially better that winter than in any other three-month period during the nearly eight years that he soldiered.[19]

Those soldiers who never left camp to patrol or forage did not see their months in winter quarters as a time of inactivity. Like most officers, Washington believed that idleness among the men was tantamount to "leisure for cherishing their discontents." When "men are employed and have the incitements of military honor to engage their ambition and pride, they will cheerfully submit to inconveniences," he said with equal parts moxie and self-delusion. Kept busy throughout the year, army life for most men was a mixture of boredom, unbearable loneliness, fatigue, and harsh conditions, including what at times seemed to be senseless make-work endeavors. It was not just the seeming absurdities of army life that bothered many soldiers. Military life was strikingly different from what every soldier had known as a civilian. It introduced soldiers to much that was new, some of which was nearly overwhelming for some men. Not a few concluded that they were encompassed by depravity. "Wickedness Prevales Verry much," lamented one man who found himself living with comrades given to salty language and shady habits. For men who mostly hailed from rural areas, and were unlikely ever to have been more than a few miles from home, the most troubling aspect of military service was the need to live with others who exhibited new and strange habits. Some expressed shock at the "odd and disgusting" practices they saw, when in truth most of it simply involved encountering soldiers from different cultural backgrounds. On first meeting Pennsylvanians, Private Martin, who was from Connecticut, remarked that "it would puzzle a philosopher to tell whether they belonged to this world or some 'undiscovered country.'"[20] For most, perhaps, the great discovery about the army was the dark reality that a soldier never controlled his own life.

While in a winter cantonment, the soldiers were awakened by the beating of reveille. As clocks and watches were uncommon, sentries were usually instructed to sound reveille when there was sufficient light to see a thousand yards. After dressing and eating, the men assembled in their companies for roll call and inspection—among other things, this ascertained who was unhealthy and whether anyone had deserted overnight—and to receive the orders of the day and the day's password and countersign (essential for getting past the sentries who guarded the entrances and exits to the camp). The men were also assigned specific tasks for the day. Some might be posted on a construction detail—"like the wild animals," said one private, the men built a new home for themselves each year—others were sent on patrol (for security purposes, but also to search for escaped prisoners and to police nearby "tippling houses"), and still others drove cattle, blasted stone, cleared paths, repaired arms, made cartridges, reconnoitered the area, policed the camp, or were sent to fetch equipment stored elsewhere. Each day several men were assigned duties as picketmen or outguards. These sentinels and guards were principally to defend against surprise attacks, keep an eye out for deserters, and protect civilians from plunder. One soldier recollected being assigned to walk ten miles to relieve a guard along a key road, and to remain there on guard duty until he himself was relieved forty-eight hours later, after which he faced the long trek back to camp. He pulled that duty repeatedly in the space of six months. For most, the camp workday was long and hard. The "fall business in Flaxseed time"—that is, the taxing labor at harvest, the most demanding work faced by farmers—"is nothing to be compared to the fatigues I undergo Daily," one soldier remarked. There was a pause for an hour or more in mid-afternoon for the second, and final, meal of the day. Like breakfast, it was prepared by the men themselves, and not always under the strictest of sanitary conditions. Pots and utensils might be filthy and the water contaminated. One soldier remembered a cantonment where "the warter we had to Drink and to mix our flower with was out of a brook that ran by the Camps, and so many a dippin and washin [in] it which maid it Very Dirty and muddy." Work ended at sundown, whereupon the men reassembled in their companies for another roll call. Those not assigned some sort of night duty, such as standing sentry or patrolling roads that led to the camp, were free for a couple of hours until tattoo, the signal for lights-out.[21]

Few men were assigned duty on Sunday, though roll call was conducted. On occasion, prayers were intermingled with the reading of the daily orders on the Sabbath, and the men were encouraged to attend a worship service. Many men idled away their free day, playing cards or various games with balls, or they fished, skated, swam, read, made music, and now and then gathered nuts or fruit in nearby forests and orchards. At times, the men organized competitive events, such as foot races, marksmanship, and wrestling and boxing matches. Annual celebrations were held to commemorate Independence Day, St. Patrick's Day, May Day, Burgoyne's surrender at Saratoga, and the King's Damnation Day on September 22, a date that had been celebrated before the war as the King's Coronation Day. From time to time, Congress proclaimed a day of thanksgiving.[22]

The army was generous with furloughs during the winter. Washington wished to limit those on leave to twenty men per regiment (about 3 percent of the total) at any one time—he was willing to permit a far greater proportion of the officer corps to be gone—but his subordinates appear to have paid relatively little heed to his orders. During the winters of 1777 and 1778 nearly half of the men in General Heath's brigade in New England were on furlough. In January 1779, 15 percent of the men in the army were away on leave. The field officers' generosity in granting leaves was due to several factors: an enemy attack in winter was unlikely, furloughs helped sustain morale, and each soldier who was absent was one less mouth to feed. Private Martin secured a two-week pass to visit loved ones early in 1779 and another, longer furlough two years later. Martin enjoyed his initial leave, but he found himself out of place at home during his second furlough. He had grown contemptuous of civilians, save for Quakers, whom he praised for their unflagging compassion. Most civilians, he thought, not only refused to make sacrifices, they were indifferent to the plight of soldiers. On more than one occasion he had experienced the studied disrespect of civilians. Once, a civilian bluntly told him: "I do not like you soldiers." In another instance, while on an assignment on a warm summer day, Martin stopped at a house and asked for a drink of water, but the owner "refused, saying that he would not let a soldier have a cup to drink from if it were to save his life." While at home on his second leave, Private Martin discovered that he missed "my companions" in the army, and he returned to camp thirty days before the expiration of his furlough.[23] He realized that he and his fellow soldiers

> had lived together as a family of brothers for several years, setting aside some little family squabbles, like most other families, had shared with each other the hardships, dangers, and sufferings incident to a soldier's life; had sympathized with each other in trouble and sickness; had assisted in bearing each other's burdens or strove to make them lighter by council and advice; had endeavored to conceal each other's faults or make them appear in as good a light as they would bear. In short, the soldiers, each in his particular circle of acquaintance, were as strict a band of brotherhood as Masons and, I believe, as faithful to each other.[24]

In the depths of despair at the many tribulations of soldiering, Private Martin sometimes raged at his "imbecility in staying" in the army. Not everyone did stay. Accurate statistics do not exist, but desertion was widespread, with the rate of deserters appearing to spike at about 20 percent during the devastating New York campaign and the cruel autumn of 1776. At the height of the distress at Valley Forge, the army's official reports indicated a desertion rate that ranged between 5 and 7 percent among those fit for duty. Civilians sometimes sheltered deserters and Washington reported instances of captured fugitives having been "rescued by the People." A worried Congress in 1777 urged the public to report deserters, and it simultaneously strengthened the Articles of War to provide for harsher punishments for those who absconded. Those steps might have helped reduce the incidence of desertion. Enemy intelligence reports suggested that the rebel desertion rate declined after the spring of 1778, an assessment borne out by the Continental army reports, which for the months of January in 1779, 1780, and 1781 show a desertion rate at between 1 and 3 percent. The British attributed the decline in desertion to the French alliance, but the establishment of a standing army composed of soldiers who joined for the long haul likely was more the cause.[25]

While Private Martin at times fumed that doing time in a "state prison would be preferable" to serving in the army, he and most of his buddies never deserted. The comradely bond that had been forged within the "brotherhood" of soldiers was a powerful glue that held the army together. So, too, was what Martin alluded to as the soldiers' "truly patriotic" spirit. An officer, who was somewhat astonished at the soldiers' staying power in the face of baleful conditions, likewise attributed the steady service of the men to "the principles of patriotism: they glory in the noble cause of their country."[26] Many among the rank and file appear to have believed with Thomas Paine that the American Revolution was about creating a new world, a place in which liberties and opportunities would surpass those that had existed in the Anglo-American world they had known before this war.

SOLDIERS IN 1779 belonged to a Continental army that had changed in substantive ways since its inception. The men served under a more draconian Articles of

War, one that bore distinct similarities to that which had long governed Britain's standing army. Many wore uniforms made in France and carried firearms of French origin (early in 1779 France shipped 100,000 Charleville muskets to its ally). Knox's artillery, moreover, now included more than two hundred field pieces that France had given the United States. The Continental army also now included troops of light horse. Congress had taken the lead late in 1776 by requesting that Virginia incorporate its horse units into the national army. When Virginia complied, Washington came on board and Congress ultimately adopted the regimental organization that he recommended. After much tinkering, a troop (the cavalry equivalent of an infantry company) contained sixty-eight troopers (a cavalryman was a trooper, an infantryman a soldier), fifty-four of which were dragoons (the counterpart to the infantry's private). One man was a trumpeter and another a farrier who shod the horses and had veterinary responsibilities. Washington ordered the troops to use dark horses, which would be less prominent, and to recruit only native-born Americans, whom he regarded as more trustworthy than immigrants.

The army of 1779 included numerous French, Prussian, and Polish officers. Some had been commissioned by America's envoys in France without adequate background checks on their character and talents. Others crossed the sea on their own and deluded the gullible—and, at times, desperate—congressmen with vivid, though illusory, accounts of their experience and skills. Some foreign officers proved to be beyond their ken and failed miserably. One was Philip Tronson du Coudray, a military theorist with the rank of major in the French army, whom Deane had made a major general of artillery in the Continental army. Happily for all but du Coudray, he drowned when his horse fell off a ferry during the Philadelphia campaign. Some turned out to be imposters. Several could not speak English and were useless to line units. But many were useful. Washington embraced Steuben and Lafayette, and he additionally valued the four military engineers that France loaned to the United States, which was devoid of trained engineers. Congress vested Colonel Louis de Presle Duportail with authority over all the army's engineers and it gave Colonel Andrew Thaddeus Kosciuszko, a Polish captain who had been trained in France, command of a corps of engineers that it created two days after the Christmas surprise at Trenton. The engineers built pontoon and more permanent bridges—two spanned the Schuylkill at Valley Forge, one made of floating rafts and the other of thirty-six wagons sunk in shallow waters at a ford—and constructed forts, including the original fortress at West Point, an extensive compound of integrated works strikingly unlike the simple installation that Fort Washington had been.

Many new components within the army had come into being since 1775. Washington, a surveyor in his youth and a general who suffered from a lack of maps at Brandywine and Monmouth, persuaded Congress to permit him to appoint a geographer and surveyor of roads, who with a topographical staff could make sketches of the war zones. He named Robert Erskine, a Scottish civil engineer who had immigrated to New Jersey shortly before the war, to this post. Late in 1777, Casimir Pulaski, a Pole, was appointed commander of horse with the rank of brigadier general, making him the cavalry's counterpart to Knox. Congress additionally created a corps of two hundred Frenchmen—it consisted of riflemen and chasseurs, or light infantry—that was designed to carry out raids behind enemy lines. Command was given to Charles Armand Tuffin, or Colonel Armand as the Americans knew him. Two other partisan corps—as they were called—existed by the time the army went into winter quarters in 1779, one of which was entirely mounted and commanded by Virginia's Henry Lee, or "Light Horse Harry," as he came to be known. By that winter the Marechaussee Corps— the name came from the *maréchaussee*, the provincial cavalry in the French army—a mounted police corps that consisted of sixty-three men (four of whom served as executioners), had come into being as well. It was a police force for the encampments and during marches. When the army went into combat, it was stationed so as to secure the rear and prevent desertion. A Prussian veteran, Captain Bartholomew Von Heer was its commander, and he recruited his men from among the Pennsylvania-German citizenry. (Washington preferred to have the foreign born as his chief enforcers, thinking they would be more detached in pursuing their grim duties.) Another corps with constabulatory duties, the Corps of Invalids, had been established in 1777 under Colonel Lewis Nicola. Consisting of men who had been wounded, injured, or were recovering from severe illnesses and were unfit for field duty, this unit guarded prisoners of war and was assigned garrison duties. Before the winter of 1779, Congress had also authorized an Artillery Artificer Regiment with responsibility for repairing equipment and maintaining ordnance and munitions. Colonel Benjamin Flower was its commander. In 1778 a seventy-five-man company of bakers was established to keep the army supplied with fresh bread. While at Middlebrook, Washington organized special companies of sappers and miners. The former dug what Europeans called "saps" (entrenchments) for use in sieges and the latter constructed subterranean tunnels. Finally, under Steuben the post of inspector general became the Continental army's supreme administrator and, in effect, Washington's chief of staff.[27]

Many of these changes were far removed from the day-to-day activities of the average soldier. What chiefly struck the old-timers whose service went back to 1776 or earlier must have been the changed demographics of the army. Few property-owning farmers and successful tradesmen with a family at home remained in the army. By 1779 most soldiers were young, single, and propertyless. What had begun as an army exclusively of New Englanders had become an army of men from throughout the nation, though nearly half of all soldiers were now drawn from the mid-Atlantic states and many were immigrants. The army boasted a "German Battalion" and almost 50 percent of the men in some Pennsylvania regiments were Irish immigrants. In 1779, Joseph Galloway told Parliament, "about one-half of the Rebel Army was Irish."[28] While he exaggerated, he correctly discerned that many Continental soldiers were what Private Martin derisively called "lowbred Europeans, especially Irishmen."[29]

A growing number of soldiers by 1779 were also African Americans. Congress had prohibited their enlistment after the fall of 1775, but each of the New England states, having difficulty meeting its manpower quota, quietly ignored the law. Some blacks who entered the army were slaves who served as substitutes for their owners, with the promise of emancipation at war's end. Some states permitted slaves to enlist with the consent of their owners. Rhode Island compensated owners for the loss of those slaves who enlisted at the rate of "£120 for the most valuable Slave, and in proportion for those of less Value," and it stipulated that those who volunteered would be "absolutely made free, and entitled to all the Wages, Bounties and Encouragement given by Congress to any Soldier inlisting into their Service."[30] Free blacks, like whites, were lured into the army either by bounties or the Revolutionary ideology. Confronted with indomitable recruiting woes, proposals for allowing blacks to serve began to surface in 1776. Benedict Arnold, for instance, urged that as many as six hundred slaves be recruited as mariners, with manumission promised following the war. There was talk in New Jersey of recruiting a black unit to serve as a home guard in the state. Neither proposal was adopted, and the number of African Americans serving before 1778 remained small, likely no more than a few score. But dramatic changes occurred soon thereafter.

Sketch of American Uniforms. By Baron Ludwig von Closen, 1781. This sketch was made after the French and American armies rendezvoused in New York in the summer of 1781. The rifleman wears the typical backwoods dress, and the African American is a Massachusetts soldier.

In the gloom of Valley Forge, with recruiting suffering and desertions abounding, General James Varnum of Rhode Island approached Washington with a proposal. He suggested that his state's two woefully depleted regiments be combined, and that officers be sent home to recruit a new regiment in which all enlisted men would be African Americans. Varnum added that "a Battalion of Negroes can be easily raised there."[31] Washington, who three years earlier had wished to see all blacks removed from the army, may have welcomed the suggestion, if only from desperation, although at the time one of his aides said that the commander thought African Americans were "a resource to us that should not be neglected."[32] Washington forwarded Varnum's proposal to the governor of Rhode Island with the comment: "I have nothing to say . . . on this important subject, but to desire that you will give the Officers employed in this business all the assistance in your power." Although he did not explicitly endorse Varnum's proposal, Washington's action in sending it was taken as an unmistakable goad to act. Rhode Island quickly enacted legislation enabling slaves to serve and in no time about 250 blacks enlisted for the duration of the war in the First Rhode Island Regiment (which six months later fought valorously in Sullivan's retreat from Newport). Before that summer ended, Massachusetts and Connecticut had raised black companies (the Bay State's was called the Bucks of America and marched under a flag given it by John Hancock). In August 1778, some 755 African Americans were serving in the Continental army, about 5 percent of the soldiery at that time.[33] Some served in the same companies as whites, the last of America's integrated military units for nearly 175 years. More than a dozen blacks are known to have become noncommissioned officers.[34]

Exhilarated by Rhode Island's success, Washington's aide Colonel John Laurens of South Carolina, approached his father, the president of Congress, with a plan to raise a light infantry force composed of five thousand southern slaves who would be freed at war's end. Young Laurens, who had been educated in England and Geneva, was an abolitionist with advanced views on racial matters. That was not true of Henry Laurens, who gave his son's plan short shrift, leading to its quiet death in March 1778. But, following Britain's capture of Savannah at year's end, Colonel Laurens revived his plan and left for Charleston, where he hoped to persuade authorities to raise as many as four black battalions, arguing that they would be the state's last hope of avoiding "Calamity." With the enemy just a step away in Georgia, his worried father now endorsed the notion of enlisting black soldiers, as did young Laurens's dear friend and fellow aide Alexander Hamilton. While Laurens was riding south in March, Hamilton brought up the matter with new president of Congress, John Jay, in a letter that pulsed with avant-garde thoughts on race.[35]

"I have not the least doubt," Hamilton wrote, "that the negroes will make very excellent soldiers." Some contend that "negroes . . . are too stupid to make soldiers," but he insisted that "their natural faculties are probably as good as

Colonel John Laurens. Watercolor on ivory, by Charles Willson Peale in 1780. An aide to Washington, Laurens hoped to raise—and liberate—South Carolina's slaves. He died fighting not far from Charleston near the end of the war.

ours." Americans must not only overcome the "contempt we have been taught to entertain for the blacks," they must put the national interest above "prejudices and self-interest." Hamilton closed with two pragmatic reasons for raising black regiments. Without African American soldiers, the Continental army would be unable to put a "sufficient force . . . in that quarter [South Carolina]." He added, "if we do not make use of them in this way, the enemy probably will."[36]

An apprehensive Henry Laurens, who estimated that five thousand slaves in Georgia had fled to the enemy when Savannah fell, now sought to shepherd his son's plan through Congress. He induced his delegation to bring up proposals urging that units from the Continental army and the militias of nearby states be detached to South Carolina and that Congress help in raising "Battalions . . . of able bodied Negroes." The key to their plan was that Congress provide severance pay to the black soldiers when they left the army at war's end and compensation to slave owners who would lose their labor supply to the military. Congress created a committee—three of its five members were southerners—that responded favorably, but recommended congressional action only if the "State of South Carolina . . . Shall Judge it expedient."[37] Predictably, the proposal to raise black battalions ran into immediate trouble in South Carolina. Many were "much disgusted at Congress," it was reported. Many in Congress believed that

Washington alone—a southern slave owner and already the most esteemed American—could save the proposal. Both Laurens and Thomas Burke, a North Carolinian who had served on the congressional committee that had endorsed raising black units, appealed to the commander for his support. Both were confident that he would give it, given his tacit endorsement of the Rhode Island experiment. But Washington refused. Disingenuously, Washington claimed that "this is a subject that has never employed much of my thoughts," and he went on to counsel that if South Carolina armed its slaves, the British would respond in kind, initiating a race to see who can recruit the African American population the fastest. It was a contest, he warned, that the United States could not win.[38] Virtually everything he said was absurd, and puzzling as well. The historian who has most thoroughly studied the subject of Washington and slavery believes that the general refused to support raising and liberating slaves "because he feared the consequences for his own slave property."[39] According to Henry Wiencek, Washington was apprehensive that the example set by freeing some slaves would stimulate unrest and rebellion among the remainder, until all bondsmen were freed. According to this view, Washington had fallen into the trap of which Hamilton had warned: his self-interest overrode his sense of the national interest. However, other more charitable explanations exist for the stance that he took. Washington had legitimate reasons to fear that taking such a step would cause South Carolina to quit the war, an act that might also lead Georgia and perhaps North Carolina to withdraw from the contest. It is possible, too, that Washington wished to hold off arming slaves until Britain had first taken that step in the Lower South, hoping that by so doing the British would bear the opprobrium among Southern slave owners for having initiated the practice of arming slave-soldiers.

Without a commitment from Washington, only twelve South Carolina legislators supported raising black regiments, and the Laurenses' plan died. Rubbing salt in young Laurens's wounds, the legislature decreed that it would seek to meet its manpower crisis by offering slaves as bounties to whites who enlisted. Elsewhere, however, African Americans continued to enlist, and scholars now believe that altogether some five thousand blacks served in the Continental army in the course of the war. As about 100,000 men are believed to have been in the army during this conflict, blacks would have comprised 5 percent of the Continentals who served. As most blacks enlisted in 1778 or later, and as they joined for the duration and served longer than many white soldiers, it is possible that during the final crucial years of the war as many as one Continental army soldier in ten was an African American.[40]

SHORTLY BEFORE CHRISTMAS in 1778 Congress summoned Washington to Philadelphia to discuss campaign 1779. In the six weeks since d'Estaing's fleet had sailed for the Caribbean, Washington had not offered the least hint of his plans for the coming months. Since adopting Fabian tactics, his moves had largely been dictated by the enemy's actions, but he now admitted that Britain's designs were a "mistiry," save that they were "upon the eve . . . of some capital move." Through spies, he knew that the British in New York were loading transports. For a brief time he grasped at the sunbeam of hope that Britain was pulling its forces out of the United States in order to fight the French elsewhere, though he was never sanguine about such a possibility. Congress feared that the enemy's preparations pointed toward an attack on Charleston, but Washington made light of that notion. The British "long ere this, are perfectly well satisfied that the possession of our Towns, while we have an Army in the field, will avail them little." The redcoats know "that it is our Arms, not defenseless Towns, they have to Subdue." As it turned out, both Congress and Washington were wrong. The invasion fleet that the British were readying was aimed at Savannah. A bit later, Washington also learned that the enemy had "made a considerable detachment (about five or 6000 Men) for . . . the West Indies."[41]

With Britain's forces in North America shrinking, Clinton was left with few options for conducting offensive warfare. The war was changing, and many in Congress wanted to talk over the various military options with Washington. As Clinton's hands were tied, some thought the time propitious for the Continentals to seize the initiative. Some were uncomfortable with Washington's cautious approach. A few had never liked his Fabian strategy and there may have been ragged murmurs from those who no longer saw much need to adhere to it. Many southerners, fearing that the war was heading in their direction, wanted assurances that adequate steps would be taken to safeguard their region. Many New Yorkers and New Englanders remained interested in Canada. Some spoke of yet another campaign to take Newport, and some Yankees yearned to seize Nova Scotia. Washington was no less eager to meet with the legislators. His cautious side had taken control and he wanted to head off the adventurism of many congressmen. Washington's correspondence between October and December 1778 betrays no hint of the audacious commander who had twice crossed the Delaware for battle in late 1776 or who had been so zealous for a showdown at Monmouth only a few weeks before. Speaking of making "every prudent and practicable exertion, to put ourselves in a good posture of defense," Washington said that his object was to demonstrate to the enemy that America was "prepared for War." This, he added, would convince "Britain [to] relinquish her ideas of conquest and withdraw her Armies" from America. He had arrived in his thinking at precisely the point where Charles Lee's had been on the eve of Monmouth six months earlier: with France an ally and victory seemingly within grasp, it would be folly to engage in grand and risky unilateral actions.[42] Something else may also have drained Washington of his avidity for action. Perhaps his own lack of success, coupled with Gates's stunning triumph, had left him hesitant to engage the enemy. As never before, Washington appeared to lack confidence; uncertain of his own judgment after innumerable mistakes; somewhat adrift without Lee, who had often provided him with the most reliable advice; and wary of the general officers who surrounded him and who were sure to offer every shade of counsel, much of which he had learned to listen to with circumspection. He seemed to hunger for the guidance that could only be offered by an experienced professional soldier. Never again in this war would Washington act daringly unless he did so in league with his ally and his action enjoyed the sanction of a French general.

The one exception to Washington's defensive posture was his contemplation of a campaign against the Iroquois Confederation. Shortly after the bloody ambush at Oriskany, Brant's Volunteers burned the Oneida town of Oriske in the Mohawk Valley, an act of retaliation for the help those Iroquois had given the rebels. Patriots responded in kind, plundering the two Mohawk enclaves, Tiononderoge and Canajoharie, ransacking the home of Molly Brant, and launching wholesale attacks on Loyalist residents, looting their homes and sometimes brutally beating, even horsewhipping, the men. Ferocious acts bequeathed brutal retribution, and by 1778 parts of the frontier in New York and Pennsylvania were in flames. The rebels gave Joseph Brant credit—or blame— for causing the most damage, though in reality he was merely one of many who carried the war into frontier settlements, razing houses, rustling cattle, killing, and maiming. A raid on the Wyoming Valley in Pennsylvania on July 3, carried out by eight hundred Indian, Loyalist, and British regulars, resulted in the death of scores, almost all soldiers, although the rebel press broadcast false reports that the "infernals"—the Indians and Tories—had locked women and children in houses and "set fire to them, and they were all consumed together." The rebels struck back hard in the autumn, carrying the war to the Iroquois and Tories by razing Unandilla, about fifty miles below the Mohawk Valley, and Onoquaga, down the Susquehanna in Pennsylvania. Not long passed before Tories, Iroquois, and British Rangers retaliated, first laying waste to German Flats—"they burnt all the Houses and Barns of consequence," destroyed three grist mills and the sawmill, and "drove off with them" more than seven hundred livestock, said a patriot officer—before they ravaged the hamlet of Cherry Valley, fifty miles west of Albany, the seventh New York frontier settlement to be laid waste. In Cherry Valley nearly seventy-five residents were slaughtered or taken captive and every building was burned after being plundered. According to rebels in the area, the Loyalists—the "Tory rabble," as one put it—"prove themselves worse than the heathens" in wreaking "immortal infamy." Be that as it may, Washington insisted that "the only certain way of preventing Indian ravages is to carry the war vigorously into their own country," and he hinted at "a personal conference" with Congress to discuss that and other matters. He was immediately invited to Philadelphia. Washington's visit was to have a momentous impact on him.[43]

Washington arrived in Philadelphia in the final days of 1778 and remained for five weeks, lodging at the residence of Henry Laurens, where Martha joined him. Although he was the guest at a festive dinner nearly every night, it was hardly a vacation for the commander, as he met with congressmen and other public officials almost daily. At the conclusion of his stay, Washington—if not every congressman—came away happy with the military decisions that were reached. Talk of another invasion of Canada was laid to rest. Congress approved the offensive against the Iroquois Confederation that Washington favored and it also urged him to make a strike against Staten Island. D'Estaing was the wild card in all the planning. Washington spoke with Minister Gérard and expressed his hope that the French fleet would come north. If it returned to New York, he pledged to "relinquish all the present projects of the Campaign and collect our whole force in this quarter . . . for the reduction of the enemy's Fleet and Army" in New York and Rhode Island.[44] Before he left town, word arrived of the British invasion of Georgia and the loss of Savannah. Washington assured the legislators that they were not to worry. Although Congress, back in September, had appointed General Benjamin Lincoln as commander of the Southern Department and sent him to Charleston to prepare for its defense, Washington turned a blind eye toward the South. At first he was convinced that the British had no plans to fight for the region. After Savannah fell, he concluded that the redcoats' activities in Georgia were merely a sideshow.[45]

It was only in mid-March, weeks after he departed Philadelphia, that Washington first seemed to take the southern theater seriously. By then the press was filled with statements by the king and his ministers indicating London's intention of continuing the war and their plans, as Washington put it, for "another desperate effort" somewhere. At last, he suspected that the enemy intended to conquer and hold Georgia, and probably South Carolina as well. Still, he announced, "no part of the army can be spared" for the South. The men were to be kept in the North so that they might cooperate with the French fleet, provided it ever returned. Besides, Washington added unconvincingly, it would take three months for the troops to get from New Jersey to South Carolina and the force "would be dissipated by sickness" when it arrived. It was at this desperate moment that young Laurens and his father, with Hamilton's help, launched their campaign to raise a black regiment.[46]

HAPPY AS WASHINGTON may have been with the plans for campaign 1779, he returned to bleak and cold Middlebrook early in February deeply shaken by what he had found in Philadelphia. For one thing, he came away convinced that the capabilities of perhaps most of those who sat in Congress had declined significantly since May 1776, when he last had been in their company for any significant time. The composition of Congress had changed markedly over the years. Only twelve of the forty-seven delegates with whom Washington had met three years earlier remained. Franklin and Adams were abroad on diplomatic missions, some, such as Jefferson, had left for state offices, and from economic necessity—or simple avarice—more than a few had abandoned public life altogether. Homesickness had taken others away, and a few had dropped out because they opposed independence. Many talented veteran congressmen still remained—including Roger Sherman, Thomas McKean, Samuel Adams,

Elbridge Gerry, James Duane, and Richard Henry Lee—and such conspicuously able men as John Jay, Philip Schuyler, and Henry Laurens had joined them. The overriding problem was not a diminution of talent, but Congress's lack of power. The states were sovereign and each state marched to its own drummer. Many no longer met their manpower quotas. Connecticut, for instance, raised only a third of the number it had been assigned for 1779 and Virginia, North Carolina, and New Hampshire also lagged badly.[47] In South Carolina, where only a quarter of the white population owned slaves, the slave-owning minority that controlled the state refused to send white soldiers north to fight, lest they be needed at home to subdue slave insurrections, and it rebuffed the appeals of those who wished to raise black soldiers from fear that it would cost them their fortunes.

Washington's assessment of the congressmen may have been off the mark, but it was not entirely incorrect. The talents of many who once had served in Congress were now monopolized by their states. This was madness, Washington declared. If the national cause failed, the states would cease to be states. He wished that the states would "absolutely compel their ablest Men to attend Congress." He was even more disturbed that many men of merit were no longer serving in any capacity, whether because they mistakenly believed that "the contest is at an end" and that further service was unnecessary, or as they were consumed with aspirations "to make money, and get places," or that from a "want of public virtue" they lived idly, heedless of the war. His anger palpable, Washington pointedly asked a fellow Virginian: "where are our Men of abilities? Why do they not come forth to save their Country?" Where, he added, are "Jefferson and others?"[48]

Washington was disappointed with Congress, but he was mortified by the seething indifference toward the war and the plight of the soldiers that he had discovered among the most affluent in Philadelphia. While his army barely rubbed by only fifty miles away, the elite in Philadelphia lived sumptuously, dining on every conceivable delicacy and hosting lavish dinner parties at which scores of dishes were served. Concern with fashion proceeded as if peace had already come, and indeed Washington lamented that "little virtue and patriotism" had been in evidence. Joseph Reed told him of hearing "public Frugality, Spirits, and Patriotism laugh'd at." Samuel Adams said that extravagance and luxury had caused "Foppery" to become the "ruling Taste of the Great," a penchant that he feared would erode martial qualities.[49] As if these concerns were insufficient, Washington's stay in Philadelphia awakened him to a new worry. He had discovered the magnitude of the new nation's economic problems that were just setting in.

Like every American, Washington had known for some time of the depreciation of the paper currency. Within less than a year of declaring independence, Congress was aware that too much paper money had been issued without adequate provision for its redemption. By April 1777, Continental money was worth half of its original value, which in turn doubled the cost of goods and services.

During that year, Congress had set out to reduce the over-supply by urging the states, which had issued nearly half the money in circulation (approximately $34,000,000), to forego further issues and to withdraw what it had previously issued through loans and taxation. Congress pitched in, too, by requisitioning $5,000,000 from the states. Its actions might have solved the gathering problem, but when word arrived in the spring of 1778 that d'Estaing's task force was en route to North America, Congress made a fateful choice. It abandoned its prudent economic measures. It needed money immediately if it was to cooperate with its new ally. In short, Congress gambled that joint Franco-American operations in 1778 would bring the war to a victorious conclusion. Congress lost its gamble. Instead of victory, Congress and the American people faced a rapidly deteriorating currency, hyperinflation, state and national indebtedness that had already skyrocketed to around $140,000,000 (nearly what Great Britain had faced in 1763), and the threat of national bankruptcy. To make matters worse, now that France was in the war, it could no longer be counted on for a loan. Continental money had held more or less steady at about five to one of specie through 1778. Then the dam burst. By the spring of 1779 it was at twenty to one and worsening, as prices rose to about eight times what they had been when the war began. Congress began to have serious problems managing the war, and Washington grew especially anxious that his officers could not afford to remain in the service in the face of runaway inflation and that his men could not be provisioned. Soon, he raged that the army could ill afford to purchase a "Rat, in the shape of a Horse." A disgruntled Connecticut Yankee was more pithy. The Continental dollar, he said, was "no Better than oak leaves & fit for nothing But Bum Fodder [toilet paper]." Washington was aware of the problem—if not its magnitude—before he went to Philadelphia, but he was confident the problem could be fixed, and fixed quickly.[50]

Washington's stay in Philadelphia produced a sea change in his outlook. While he soured on the abilities of Congress to overcome the nation's economic woes, he was truly appalled by the luxurious habits of Philadelphia's elite and their unwillingness to make the sacrifices that might put America's economic house in order. Worse still, he saw that the biggest businessmen were "preying upon the vitals of this great Country." Through their hoarding, trading, and speculative practices, many merchants had a hand in driving up prices, and they did so for their personal gain while soldiers suffered and the war effort teetered on the brink of doom. "[L]ittle else but making money is attended to," he said after watching the riot of excess in Philadelphia. He concluded that businessmen and the Philadelphia gentry, often one and the same, had come to be "infamous harpies, who to acquire a little pelf, would involve this great continent in inextricable ruin." To this point, Washington had believed that the common people were the weak link in the successful prosecution of the war. By the time he left Philadelphia, Washington had come to believe that the self-serving greed of the most affluent Americans posed an even greater threat to the cause.[51]

Washington's troubled brooding was not misplaced. A mercenary spirit had taken hold among many of the most powerful, and it was as much of a menace to the war effort as were Britain's army and navy. But whereas Washington feared that venality threatened the Continental army with doom, others were haunted by different worries. Some of the more socially conservative congressmen fretted that economic desperation would lead workers to the principle of "let us take our Neighbor's Property and convert it to our Use." Then there was the worry that arose from the realization that it was impossible for the high rollers to sustain their sumptuous habits. What would happen, some wondered, when the economic woes finally overtook the affluent? Would the rich and powerful who had opposed independence—and who had dominated Pennsylvania's congressional delegation down to the very day of the vote for independence in July 1776— regain control? Would Pennsylvania swing toward reconciliation with Great Britain, as well? Would others follow? These fears led Washington to conclude that time was running short. If this war lasted much longer, the American Revolution, and all the dreams that went with it, might be lost. Never in the darkest days of 1776 had Washington believed that the Revolution was "in such eminent danger as at present," he said in March 1779. Unless the "thirst for gain" was brought under control, he cautioned, "it must plunge every thing" into "one common Ruin." To save the day, Washington believed that men of extraordinary talent must be restored to Congress. "[U]nless the bodies politick will exert themselves to bring things back to first principles [and] correct abuses, . . . inevitable ruin must follow. Indeed we seem to be verging so fast to destruction." Do not "let our . . . noble struggle end in ignominy," he pleaded.[52]

Washington's remarks notwithstanding, Congress attempted in a variety of ways to find sound money and provide therapy for the nation's financial ills. Resorting to the modern practice of putting the burden for paying for the war on future generations, Congress in 1779 borrowed by selling loan certificates at interest rates ranging from 4 to 7.5 percent. It raised about $60,000,000 before year's end. It also sought some $90,000,000 through three separate requisitions from the states and it instructed Franklin to seek another French loan while it dispatched Jay to Madrid and Henry Laurens to The Hague in pursuit of loans. By 1780 it had secured nearly 11,000,000 livres (roughly $2,200,000 in specie) in loans and gifts from abroad. Congress's motives in granting Lafayette leave to return to France early in 1779 remain a mystery, but circumstantial evidence suggests that it wanted him to go home to persuade his government to commit troops to North America—once home, he requested that 1,700 troops, including additional artillery be sent—and to smooth the way for the loan that Franklin would request. Congress also prosecuted corrupt officials, reformed the army's supply system once again, and voted simply to stop issuing currency when the amount in circulation reached $200,000,000. Despite its commendable efforts, nothing worked. The American Revolution, which had begun as a protest against British taxation, had come almost full circle. Not only did a tax riot erupt in

Norwich, Connecticut, in February 1779, but during that year the states were involved in what was tantamount to a rebellion against Continental taxation. Here and there—notably in Philadelphia and Boston, but in backcountry hamlets as well—committees sprang up to regulate prices, a covert means of fighting taxation, for economic regulation virtually brought internal commerce to a halt, stymieing Congress's efforts to raise tax dollars. The most rapid currency depreciation in United States history occurred that year, a faster free fall than followed the stock market crash in 1929. In January 1779, eight dollars in Continental currency had been needed to purchase one dollar in specie. By October, thirty dollars were required. By December, forty-two dollars were needed. Toward year's end, one of the army's principal supply agents observed that "People are running or rather flying thro the Country getting rid of their Cash at any rate." As the value of paper money plummeted, the power of Congress—which in 1775–1776 had been sufficient to take the states to war, create an army, conduct diplomacy, and declare independence—dwindled as well.[53]

Washington's letters to Congress portray an army so emasculated by the economic collapse that his ability to wage war was adversely affected. By mid-1779 the number of Continental soldiers was down by some three thousand since the previous autumn, yet Washington was not immobilized by the sudden financial crisis. He entered the campaign season in 1779 with some 12,000 Continentals under his command, a force that could have been augmented—as it would be in future campaigns—by the militia.[54] His warnings, bathed as they were in despondency, were remarkably similar to the alarming remonstrances that had poured from his headquarters at Valley Forge a year earlier. The Valley Forge exhortations had jolted Congress, galvanizing it to make reforms and comply with the army's wishes, and it may be that Washington, having learned how to get results, resorted to the same tactics a year later. He may also have seized on the growing economic distress as a means of defending his Fabian tactics, or even more as vindication for his apparent decision to remain inactive until the French fleet returned. The collapse of the currency "oblige[s] me to a more defensive plan," he told Congress. With the "strength and resources of the Country" crippled by the raging inflation, he asserted, the army could not "compleat *our Battalions*," rendering him unable "to pursue such measures as the public good may seem to require, and the public expectation to demand."[55] Nor is it inconceivable that he seized on the economic problems as a means of silencing those congressmen who were pushing him to take actions that he thought imprudent. Washington now abjured unnecessary hazards, especially as he believed that the chances were good of receiving news of "great and important events" from the European theater or from on the high seas.[56] But there were contradictions in Washington's stance. On the one hand, he had intimated to Congress that the economic collapse meant that time was of the essence, that victory must be won quickly, or the war would be lost. But as the campaign season for 1779 approached, he implied that there was ample time to defer all other substantive actions while awaiting the indefinite return of the French fleet. What shines through most clearly about the Washington of 1779 is that he had begun to obsess over acting only in concert with the French navy and to fixate intransigently on New York. It was a pattern filled with dangers, though the magnitude of the hazards would not be fully understood for some time.

IMMEDIATELY upon returning to Middlebrook, Washington began to conceptualize the expedition against the Iroquois. His most immediate objective was to provide relief to the frontier inhabitants in New York and Pennsylvania. He operated on the premise that—as another general remarked—"Nothing can so Effectively draw the indians out of your Country, as Carrying the War into theirs."[57] The campaign might also close off those regions as a source of supply for the enemy and, he hoped, compel the British to commit more of their forces to the defense of Canada and the protection of their Indian allies, depleting their strength elsewhere. In his wildest dreams, Washington hoped that the enterprise would force the Iroquois into neutrality. He had a free hand in planning the scope of the campaign. It could be as grandiose or as modest as he desired. He chose to think small. He might have linked this initiative to the much discussed notion of taking Lake Champlain and St. Johns, and perhaps even Montreal, but he had long since spurned such thoughts. Or, he might have included the objectives of seizing either the British fort at Detroit or their installation at Niagara, or both. Taking the former would have pacified much of the trans-Appalachian West above the Ohio River. Possession of the latter would almost assuredly have driven the Iroquois from the war. That Washington shrank from the larger ends was part and parcel of his growing caution, but it also reflected his increasing fixation on New York City. If d'Estaing's fleet returned, he wished to cooperate with it in a campaign to defeat Clinton in New York, an epic victory—like that of Wolfe over Montcalm at Quebec—that would end the war. But a battle for New York might not be possible if the preponderance of his army was scattered over the remote frontier.[58]

Drawing on questionnaires that he sent to experts on Indian affairs, Washington devised a well-conceived plan.[59] He wanted a multipronged invasion of the Iroquois Confederation to begin in late spring. The main body of American troops was to advance on Seneca territory via the Susquehanna-Chemung Rivers approach. Other forces would enter Iroquoia from New York and eastern Pennsylvania, and a small detachment from Fort Pitt was to move up the Allegheny River into far western New York below Lake Erie. Altogether, these troops would total in excess of four thousand men, about a third of the Continental army. But, in some respects, the heart of Washington's design was to have units under Colonel Moses Hazen, one of the most vocal proponents of a Canadian invasion, begin unmistakable preparations for what would appear to be a campaign to take Canada by driving up through the Connecticut Valley. Washington planned Hazen's activity as a diversion to tie down as many regulars in Canada as possible. The plan was so secret that not even Hazen was aware that he would be going nowhere. In the meantime, Washington had to select some-one to command the invasion of Iroquoia. He would have preferred Schuyler, but he was back in Congress. Although the prevailing sentiment within the army was that "old Country men," those raised in the British Isles were "totally unac-quainted with that kind of fighting" and "by no means Equal" to the challenges of an Indian campaign, Washington had no choice but to offer the assignment to Gates, as he ranked first in seniority. However, Gates, who was fifty-four years old and practically unschooled in bush warfare, declined. With candor and insight, he told Washington that the "Man who undertakes the Indian Service, should enjoy Youth and Strength; requisites I do not possess." Washington turned next to Sullivan, who accepted with little enthusiasm. (It took him a week to make up his mind.)[60]

The ruse of a Canadian invasion was to be the key to success for the Sullivan Expedition, as it would come to be known. The British governor and commander in chief in Canada, Sir Frederick Haldimand, who had succeeded Guy Carleton, fell for the feint that Washington had devised. He pried loose 1,500 men from Clinton in New York and dug in his heels to await the blow. That left the Tories and Indians largely to fend for themselves in New York and Pennsylvania, and they were no match for a European-style army that consisted of fifteen regiments of infantry and one of artillery. John Butler, a native of Connecticut and a tough woodsman who had long served Britain's Indian Department as an interpreter, was the principal Loyalist leader. He had about six hundred men under his command. Brant led the largest Iroquois force, a mere three hundred warriors. Unable to resist the invaders, Butler and Brant responded as had the Indians in similarly forlorn circumstances going back to encounters with the first Englishmen in America 150 years earlier. Together with the inhabitants of the Indian towns, they withdrew steadily into the interior. (Sullivan characterized their tactics as a case of "the enemy . . . flying like armed women before us.")[61]

Sullivan's force was virtually unopposed. Only two skirmishes and one small battle were fought. Nothing stood in the way of the army carrying out Washington's orders: "lay waste all the settlements around . . . that the country may not be merely *overrun* but *destroyed*."[62] Between early August and mid-September—typically, the campaign was launched months behind schedule—Sullivan's men entered one empty town after another and put to the torch everything in sight, causing corn cribs, fields of grain, and "all their Gardens which were replete with Herbage to be destroy'd," as Sullivan reported.[63] The night sky over parts of Iroquoia glowed an eerie orange, lit by raging fires that consumed the Indians' possessions and their autumn food supply, including the utter destruction of forty hamlets and at least 160,000 bushels of corn. Some four thousand refugees of the Six Nations straggled into Canada, many nearly naked against the piercing winds and swirling snows of the approaching winter, and all hungry and homeless. Few perished in the invasion, though many failed to survive the horrid winter of 1779–1780. But they were not vanquished. "[W]e do not look upon ourselves as defeated for we have never fought," a sachem told the British, and promised revenge in 1780.[64] It was a promise that would be kept. For all the terror sown by the American army, it had been a nearly useless operation, made futile by the limited objectives with which it was saddled. Blood continued to flow in retaliatory raids in 1780. Meanwhile, frontiersmen and others, their appetites sharpened by the published descriptions of the abundance that had been found in the Indian towns, were more eager than ever to dispossess the natives in Iroquoia following hostilities. What is more, the rebel army, not by happenstance, had been accompanied by survey parties that mapped out the terrain in preparation for the postwar westward stampede and land bonanza.[65]

BEFORE 1779, the War of Independence had spread to other frontiers. At the outset of hostilities, commissioners from Virginia and Congress had negotiated a pact of neutrality with the Cherokees, but it had been tenuous and short-lived. Younger tribesmen, anxious to seize the advantage offered by the war between the whites, had taken up their weapons in the backcountry from Georgia to Virginia in 1776. The four states below the Potomac raised soldiers and, in a precursor to Sullivan's tactics, crushed the rebellion largely by destroying countless Indian towns. The Cherokees paid for their belligerence. In July 1777, just as Burgoyne took Ticonderoga, they ceded all their lands east of the Blue Ridge, as far south as the Nolichucky River in present eastern Tennessee and western North Carolina.[66]

   That lucrative victory whetted the appetite of speculative and land-hungry Virginians who had long coveted Kentucky and the Ohio Country, the fertile western prairies bounded roughly by the Ohio River and the Great Lakes, the Appalachians, and the Mississippi River. Virginia's interest in the Ohio Country was hardly new. Claiming title to those lands through its earliest charter, the colony had first sent an army—under young Colonel Washington—to fight for the Ohio Country in 1754. The region had been won for Great Britain in the Peace of Paris, but London failed to open the territory speedily for settlement, a factor of no small importance in the decision of some Virginians—including Washington, who owned 60,000 acres in the area—to consider American independence. Even as the Cherokee subjugation was being negotiated in the spring of 1777, some Virginians, acting privately, sent spies as far west as present-day Illinois to gather intelligence. Finding that the British had largely withdrawn from present-day Kentucky, Ohio, Indiana, and Illinois to reinforce Fort Detroit, George Rogers Clark—a twenty-eight-year-old Virginian who had spent a considerable portion of his adult life living and fighting in Kentucky—became the principal lobbyist for a campaign to vanquish the Native Americans in the Ohio Country and, perhaps, to take Detroit. The Virginia assembly quickly approved military action, asserting—as aggressors invariably do—that their soldiers were being sent for defensive purposes, in this instance to safeguard Kentucky.[67]

While the Continental army shivered and starved at Valley Forge, Clark with a force of 350 jumped off from near present-day Cincinnati in June 1778. His mission succeeded beyond all expectations. That summer, Clark's little army conquered outposts at Vincennes and Kaskasia, and early in 1779 it repulsed a British counterattack, capturing the governor of Detroit, Colonel Henry Hamilton, in the process. Washington had said nothing during Clark's operations, but following Hamilton's capture he hinted that it would be desirable if "by any means" a Virginia force could seize Detroit.[68]

WASHINGTON'S MOOD had sunk steadily since the *feu de joie* at Valley Forge. A year later, in May 1779, he despaired that neither America's "first Statesmen" nor the French navy were anywhere to be seen. He feared, too, that in the "unhappy train" of a collapsing currency, "G. Britain is ready to pour forth her utmost vengeance" in the pending summer campaign. Washington might have felt better had he been capable of reading the mind of his counterpart, General Clinton, for the American commander's oscillating moods mimicked those of his rival. When Washington had exalted at the army's festivities at Valley Forge, Clinton, who was just assuming command of the British army, had found himself heartbroken, as he had put it, at the dismemberment of his army on London's orders. Clinton had grown so melancholy in the late summer of 1778 that he asked to be recalled. Germain denied his request, placating him with a promise to send 6,600 men to New York by early summer 1779, and urging that he raise provincial units composed of Loyalists. Thereafter, Clinton's mood brightened and Washington's darkened. Early in 1779, the British commander began planning a series of coastal raids that were designed to destroy rebel supplies, erode American morale, and force the states to keep troops at home, leaving the Continentals more shorthanded than ever.[69]

Clinton's first blow fell on Virginia in May 1779. A flotilla of twenty-eight sail under Commodore Sir George Collier arrived off Newport, taking the Virginia authorities by surprise. Over a span of two weeks, 1,800 redcoats under Major General Edward Mathew repeatedly landed along the coast, destroying forts, the entire town of Suffolk, and 137 merchant ships, privateers, and vessels under construction in shipyards. Collier seized so much booty that seventeen ships were needed to cart it all back to New York. Among his cargo were 518 slaves that had fled behind British lines.[70]

On the day after the armada returned to New York, Clinton dispatched it above Manhattan to seize Stony Point, on the west side of the Hudson, a dozen or so miles below West Point, and Fort Lafayette at Verplanck's Point, almost directly across the river. The two rebel posts fell quickly. Exultant, Clinton crowed that Washington must be "distressed."[71] He was correct. The rebel commander sighed that the loss of the installations gave the enemy "a new source of supplies . . . and a new door to distress and disaffect the country." But in Clinton's mind there was an even greater advantage to taking the two posts.

Their possession laid the groundwork for an advance on West Point, the campaign that he envisaged for summer 1779, an enterprise that he believed would compel Washington either to surrender a post that he could ill afford to relinquish or to fight. Clinton believed he found the means to bring on the grand showdown.[72] He was correct. Washington would fight. He gathered the Continental army in the Hudson Highlands and waited.[73]

Gates, who was watching closely, believed that had Clinton struck immediately, he might have taken West Point. But the British commander, like Howe so often before him, had decided that he could not act until the promised reinforcements arrived. They were due any day. Clinton waited, and waited. In mid-June, Gates speculated that Clinton had already waited too long. His "delay has ruined him"; Clinton "will be beat" if he now tried to take West Point, Gates pronounced.[74] Without the additional troops—they did not arrive until nearly the end of the summer, and for weeks thereafter they were too sick to soldier—Clinton was forced to scale back, turning instead to raids that he regarded as invidious even as he ordered them. This time New Haven, Norwalk, and Fairfield in Connecticut absorbed the blows, and each sustained severe damage. All told, nearly four hundred structures were destroyed, nearly half of them dwellings; cattle were taken; and farmers were distracted from their harvests. Better than anyone, Clinton knew that these raids were mere pinpricks. Like Washington at the same moment, he slid into an enveloping despair. Campaign 1779 had been for naught, Clinton seethed. "Another year's expense of this destructive war was now going to be added to the four which had so unprofitably preceded, without a probability of its producing a single event to better our condition or brighten our prospects."[75]

Clinton's despair was made more palpable by an action that Washington ordered in July. The American commander had at first presumed that nothing could be done in response to the loss of the forts on the Hudson, but when intelligence reported that Stony Point might be vulnerable, Washington tasked Anthony Wayne, commander of the light infantry at West Point, to investigate further. Wayne reported that while the installation could not be successfully stormed, a surprise assault might work. After personally reconnoitering the Stony Point area, Washington and his staff, with Wayne in daily attendance, planned an operation. No one ever thought it would be an easy undertaking. The fort sat on a point that rose 150 feet above the Hudson and was surrounded by water on three sides. A swamp, passable by foot only during low tide, lay on the fourth side. It was garrisoned by nearly seven hundred enemy soldiers and its fortifications were daunting—two abatis, three redoubts, and cannon trained on every approach. The plan that Washington and Wayne finally agreed on was so risky that the advance parties were labeled the "forlorn hope" in the planning documents, "suicide squads" in today's lexicon. Wayne was to lead two hundred carefully chosen volunteers, daredevils who were to strike after midnight on July

15. Each man was to wear a piece of white paper in his hat to signify that he was a comrade to other rebels.

The attack came off nearly flawlessly. After a sun-seared march of fourteen miles along a ragged woodland path (past craggy places with names such as Degaffles Rugh), Wayne's force arrived undetected in the blackness of a moon-less night. Shortly after midnight, right on schedule, Hardy Murfree's North Carolinians opened the engagement by laying down a heavy barrage of musket fire—the only American shots that were fired in the battle—at the surprised British sentries. While the redcoats fought without success to hold off the attackers, the ax-wielding men in the forlorn hope broke up the abatis, clearing the way for two columns of comrades to penetrate the installation at separate points. They dashed inside screaming: "The fort's our own!" Once inside, the fighting was hand-to-hand, with the rebels wielding bayonets, swords, and spontoons (a half-pike), swinging their muskets as cudgels, and flailing with their fists. The vicious fight did not last long. Seeing the futility of further resistance, the overwhelmed redcoat defenders, according to one rebel, cried out: "Mercy! mercy! Dear Americans, mercy! Quarter! Brave American, quarter! Quarter!" In a few minutes of furious brawling the Americans had suffered nearly 100 casualties—17 of 20 in one party of forlorn hope were killed or wounded, and Wayne sustained "a flesh wound in the head"—but the British lost 676 killed, wounded, and captured. At 2:00 a.m. Wayne notified Washington that Stony Point had been taken. "The fort & Garrison . . . are our's," he said. "Our Officers & Men behaved like men who are determined to be free."[76]

Over the next two days, Washington took the fifteen cannon and sumptuous stores at Stony Point, then razed the installation that he knew he could not long hold. Unlike his counterpart, Washington did not crow at his triumph and, as was his habit, he did not describe it in memorable terms. It had been "a pretty impor-tant stroke," he said simply. Others were more effusive. Gérard lavishly praised the daring assault, and it was even lauded in the British press. The *New Hampshire Gazette*, in a comment that was typical of the exaltation in American newspapers, exclaimed, "No action during the war has equaled this *coup de main*."[77]

For Clinton, more bad news followed. In August, Colonel Henry Lee led a daring raid on the British post at Paulus Hook, a sandy spit of land that jutted into the Hudson directly across from Manhattan. After taking New York, the British had fortified the position, building redoubts, bringing in artillery to guard the river, and garrisoning it with some 250 men. Lee had persuaded Washington to authorize an assault by roughly a hundred men. Neither thought the installation could be held, if taken, but its capture could unhinge and embarrass the enemy, while building morale among the Continentals. There was something to be said for taking prisoners as well. The operation took place on August 19. It was less successful than Wayne's storming of Stony Point, but with a loss of only five Americans, Lee's men nearly captured or killed the entire British garrison.[78]

Immediately after the raid on Paulus Hook, Clinton learned that Spain had entered the war. For the first time in the war, the allies possessed naval superiority. Clinton thought it prudent to relinquish Rhode Island, and he seethed at his inability to undertake a monumental operation and his setbacks. Cranky, and so overwrought that he sometimes wept openly, Clinton venomously blustered to trusted underlings that these latest British calamities, like so many before them, were due to Germain's treachery in failing to provide adequate manpower. Without success, he once again asked to be recalled.[79] Clinton's despondency infected many in his army, but for some it was their commander, not London, that was to blame for the woes visited on Britain's war efforts. With stunning unfairness, one officer who arrived in October, when Manhattan was draped in its vibrant autumn splendor, stormed that Britain's army was led by an "ignorant, capricious, irresolute commander" who displayed "no abilities to plan [and] no firmness to execute."[80]

Whoever was at fault, Washington concurred that the "enemy have wasted another Campaign," but he seemed not to know what it signified. "We are now," he said oppressively that October, "launching into a wide and boundless field, puzzled with mazes and o'er spread with difficulties."[81]

15

"WE HAVE OCCASIONED A GOOD DEAL OF TERROR": THE WAR AT SEA

T HE NEW American-built *Alliance*, a thirty-six-gun frigate, eased out of Boston harbor early in January 1779. France was its destination. The *Alliance* made the Atlantic crossing in the uncommonly rapid time of twenty-six days, but its voyage was not uneventful. Near Newfoundland it almost foundered in a merciless storm that tore off the main topmost. Later, the English among its mixed crew mutinied. Their hope was to take the commandeered vessel and its most famous passenger, General Lafayette, to England, where they hoped to find a hero's welcome and a monetary reward. But the uprising was suppressed, with the help of the sword-wielding Lafayette, and thirty-eight mutineers were clasped in irons. Not a day too soon the lookout spotted Brittany on the western coast of France, and *Alliance* limped into port at Brest.[1]

Lafayette had come home in the hope of securing a French army to lead into Canada. Congress had sanctioned his plan, then changed its mind after Washington objected, but its urgent communiqué disapproving another Canadian venture arrived in Boston after the *Alliance* sailed. It made no difference. Once in France, Lafayette discovered that his government was not interested in participating in an invasion of Canada. Undeterred, he requested a force to lead in retaking Newport, something he and Congress had probably discussed as a fallback to a Canadian venture. France's leaders were not interested in another Rhode Island campaign either. Plans were taking shape at Versailles for an invasion of England. Thirsting for glory, Lafayette, with his sure instinct for adapting, jumped on that bandwagon. He asked for "a corps of 1,500 of the best possible men, that is to say, all Frenchmen," that he might lead in "attacks on the coast of England." A precursor to the invasion, his coastal raids not only would serve as "reprisals for what the Americans themselves have experienced," Lafayette said, but would divert the enemy, leading London to spread its defenses thin and enhancing the chances for success by the Franco-Spanish invasion armada. Lafayette added that it would be an "exquisite pleasure" to avenge Britain's attacks on America's coastal towns by striking at one or more of the following: Bristol, Cork, Liverpool, Lancaster, Whitehaven, or Bath. The latter was especially "tempting," he went on, as the "best of London's society" would be there and it "would furnish some well-qualified hostages." His scheme was to hold both individuals and entire towns for ransom, and he predicted that the "terror that we would spread would be felt . . . intensely."[2]

Lafayette spoke with Franklin, just named the American minister to France, and he heartily approved the plan. Lafayette remembered that Franklin had been feverishly "excited" at the kidnapping scheme, which he thought would "exact from them [the British] a heavy Contribution" in extortion. But to succeed, Franklin added, the enterprise required "a prudent & brave Sea Commander who knows the Coasts of England." He knew just the right man, an American naval officer named John Paul Jones. Once Louis XVI and Antoine de Sartine, France's minister of marine, signed off on the plan, Lafayette was in business. In the early spring of 1779, he met with Jones, whom Sartine shortly provided with a flagship for the enterprise. It was named the *Le Duc de Duras*, but Jones immediately rechristened it the *Bonhomme Richard*, which seemed fitting. After all, Franklin, "Poor Richard" himself, not only was involved in helping to organize the mission, but he had told Jones that the planned raids were "understood to be an American Expedition."[3] Like Jones, Franklin was all too aware that the war for American independence was being waged on the sea as well as on land.

THE NAVAL WAR had begun at almost the same time as hostilities ashore. Three weeks after Lexington-Concord, activists from Dartmouth on Buzzards Bay, on the south side of Cape Cod, retook a small American merchant vessel that had been seized by a royal sloop and overpowered the tender escort that was taking the prize to port, capturing fourteen British seamen in the process. A month later, a Royal Navy vessel—the *Margaretta*, an armed schooner that Gage had sent to fetch precious materials for his besieged army in Boston—was fired on and captured by local Whigs at Machias, three hundred miles to the north in the district of Maine.[4]

Before the end of the war's first summer, Washington began outfitting schooners to prey on British supply ships en route to Boston. He hoped to tighten the noose around Gage's beleaguered army and to secure desperately needed supplies for his own force. He called the vessels privateers, though technically that was inaccurate, as Congress had not issued commissions, or letters of marque, for such undertakings. Under international law the rebel raiders were more nearly pirates, but the corsairs were embraced by the American public, which dubbed the little fleet "Washington's Navy." Most of the crews, as Washington said, were "Soldiers (who have been bred to the Sea)," mariners from along New England's jagged coast. Before 1775 ended, Washington's Navy consisted of seven vessels, all sent out from ports in Massachusetts, which had created its own admiralty court to hear prize cases. During its first six months, the little fleet enjoyed some success. Fifty-five prizes were taken, including one vessel whose cargo consisted of nearly two thousand barrels of flour. The most sensational prize was the ordnance brig *Nancy*, taken in November off Cape Ann by the *Lee* out of Beverly. From its crowded hold, the Continentals harvested 11 mortars and 31 tons of shot—which were immediately used to shell the British army in Boston—as well as 2,000 muskets and 100,000 flints. The hard-pressed Washington characterized what fell into his hands as a bounty of "divine favour."[5]

Washington had acted boldly without consulting Congress. He feared Congress would rebuff his entreaties, and he was doubtless correct, as Congress did not legalize privateering until March 1776. Long before then some colonies had already issued their own commissions, but congressional action touched off a bonanza of privateering. With scant exaggeration, a Bostonian claimed that every dockside vessel in the city that could obtain arms had sailed as a privateer in the summer of 1776. Privateering was a long-established American practice in wartime, and the *Lee's* lucrative voyage late in 1775 quickened the appetite of entrepreneurs and seamen eager to cash in on the prizes to be had. For the most part, the earliest privateers sailed on small vessels that carried no more than six guns and a crew of around twenty-five, though in time larger vessels that mounted up to a dozen guns went out with larger crews. Armed they might be, but unlike warships that went to sea with the expectation of fighting, privateers wished to avoid combat. They dodged vessels of larger, or even comparable, size, searching instead for smaller ships that would capitulate without a fight. Perhaps as many as three thousand rebel privateers ultimately went to sea in the course of the war, and they took thousands of prizes. It has been estimated that Massachusetts privateers alone took 1,200 prizes and that the combined catch of raiders from the states north of the Potomac exceeded 2,100 British merchantmen. As U.S. war vessels were additionally taking prizes, the Americans had a weapon that disrupted the enemy's trade and economy and added to the woes of Britain's army.[6]

In the meantime, some in Congress were working to create an American navy that would consist of larger, more powerful vessels that might be used in a variety of endeavors. John Adams, who had emerged as the leader of those seeking independence, was also the chief figure among the pronavy congressmen. He faced an uphill battle. Enemies of independence feared that a navy would be another step leading to separation from Britain. Others protested that it was "the maddest Idea in the World" to contemplate constructing a fleet to fight the world's greatest navy. But the tide was running against the navy's foes. It was transparently evident that the sea was crucial to the war on land. Word reached Philadelphia almost every week of the sailing, or the arrival, of British transports or supply ships, or that a royal vessel had seized yet another American merchantman. Many also glimpsed a pot of gold at the end of the naval rainbow. Some hoped to profit through government contracts for building ships or purchasing and outfitting existing vessels. Others stood to gain through the navy's protection of commerce. Seamen and dock jockeys, without jobs since the Coercive Acts or the outbreak of war, hoped the founding of a navy would put them back to work.

Before 1775 ended, Congress appropriated $100,000 for the acquisition of four existing vessels that were to be converted into war craft, with the largest mounting up to thirty-six guns. It also created the "first and second battalions of American Marines," named Esek Hopkins, a veteran sea captain who, perhaps more importantly, happened to be the brother of a Rhode Island congressman, as commander in chief of the navy, and adopted a naval Articles of War. This was just the beginning. Congress voted $866,666—$66,666 per ship—for the construction of thirteen frigates. To spread the wealth, they were to be built in seven different provinces. Congress created a thirteen-member Marine Committee to oversee the new American navy, and by mid-1777 it had authorized the building of five additional frigates and, incredibly, three ships of the line, each carrying seventy-four guns. But Congress's reach exceeded its grasp. None of the behemoths and only about half of the frigates were ever finished.[7]

Shipbuilding know-how was present in abundance in early America. One in three ships flying the British flag on the eve of the American Revolution had been built in an American shipyard, and by 1770 ships ranked fifth in value among the colonists' exports.[8] The raw materials for ship construction were also readily available, from naval stores—tar, pitch, resin, and turpentine—to timber for the masts, spars, hulls, and planks to hemp and flax for the cordage and canvas sails. The warships of the day ranged from ships of the line, the huge battleships of the age, down to an infinite variety of smaller vessels that included frigates, brigs, corvettes, scows, cutters, sloops, pinks, schooners, brigantines, and barks. Eighteenth-century navies consisted of three classes of vessels, each determined by the number of guns that a vessel carried. Ships of the line, the two or three deck monsters that Congress dreamt of but never realized, ranged from sixty-fours— vessels that mounted sixty-four guns—to what the British navy labeled "first-rates," titans that carried one hundred or more guns and were nearly the length of a football field. The seventy-four was the workhorse of the royal battle fleet, comprising 45 percent of the British navy's men-of-war by war's end. Frigates, the first thirteen ships that Congress ordered built, comprised the next class, and usually carried between twenty-four and forty-four guns on a single gun deck. They were mostly used for commerce raiding, scouting, convoying, and hunting down privateers. Vessels that mounted fewer than twenty-four guns were collectively called "post ships" in the Royal Navy, and were used for many of the same purposes as frigates. Because the War of Independence, unlike Europe's

Raleigh. Model of Continental frigate, made by August L. Delin from Admiralty Plans. One of thirteen frigates ordered by Congress, *Raleigh* was launched in 1776 and captured by the British two years later. Only three of the Continental Navy's frigates survived to the end of the war.

conflicts, was fought on lakes and rivers, as well as the high seas, other small vessels, including gondolas, xebecs, and bateaux, were important.[9]

Exclusive of Washington's navy and Arnold's Champlain fleet, the United States navy consisted of fifty-seven vessels in the course of the War of Independence. Fewer than 40 percent of those vessels were built in American shipyards. A slightly larger percentage of the fleet was purchased in the United States or abroad, while some 20 percent were loaned to the United States by France or were captured British craft.[10] The construction levels anticipated by Congress fell short for numerous reasons. Progress was hampered by war-related labor shortages, an economy that went to rack and ruin, and the wartime scarcity of iron. Congress's slapdash approach to the construction of its navy was also an important factor. Sealed bids were never utilized and the Marine Committee never adopted a common design for the frigates. Worse yet, the member of the Marine Committee from each state selected to build a ship was authorized to choose an agent who was to be responsible for bringing the vessel into being. Invariably, these congressmen chose a friend, relative, or well-connected political ally who might—or, then again, might not—have any knowledge of building ships. The agents, in turn, selected a shipbuilder, who also more often than not turned out to be a close acquaintance or political confeder-ate. It was an excellent system for assuring that the rich got richer, but not a very sensible means for building a superb fleet. Among other things, it often resulted in the concentration of building contracts in one town and even one terribly overburdened shipyard. Security was compromised as well. The contracts for New York's two frigates were given to one builder, who sought to construct both vessels in the same shipyard in Poughkeepsie, but both the yard and the two vessels under construction were destroyed in a British raid.[11] The incentive that Congress provided for getting the job done was to award the agent a 5 percent commission, a whopping $3,300 for each frigate that finally slid safely into the nearby cold water, this at a time when a skilled artisan might earn $200 annually and a private in the Continental army made $82 a year. That carrot notwithstand-ing, a negligible proportion of vessels under contract ever made that pleasing slide down the shipyard stocks.

It may not have especially mattered, for had all the projected vessels been built, a lack of crewmen probably would have prevented some boats from going to sea. Congress had little difficulty finding marine officers, commissioning 340 during the war, mostly idled officers from the merchant marine. Finding men for the fleet was another matter. A congressional survey made when the navy was created estimated that 30,000 seamen were unemployed and available, but according to the best estimate fewer than 3,000 sailors served in the U.S. navy during this long war. A few eligible men with a maritime past were Tories, but the bigger problem to finding sailors was that many veteran seamen were on duty in the Continental army or had enlisted on a privateer. Privateering was especially alluring, as it required an enlistment for only a few weeks at a time, in contrast to the standard one year hitch in the Continental Navy, and the pay was 50 to 100 percent better than the $6.66 to $8.00 per month offered by the navy.[12] Many men were also enticed by the hope of striking it rich on a privateer. The money realized from the sale of prizes was divided, with the biggest share going to the ship's owner, the next largest to the captain, and finally down through the officers, petty officers, and seamen, to the lowly cabin boys. The seamen's odds of realizing a financial windfall were about as poor as those today for a lottery player, and to boot one could get killed by taking this gamble. To be competitive, the U.S. navy also distributed prize money—though, unlike the army, it refused to offer bounties—and to aid in recruiting it eventually set the crew's share of prize money at 50 percent, a far better deal than one could find on any privateer. (It could be quite lucrative, at least for the officers. John Paul Jones collected more than three thousand dollars in prize money during his initial eighteen months of duty, a period prior to the collapse of the dollar, and this was atop his monthly salary of thirty-two dollars.)[13] Not many were enticed and Congress ultimately resorted to conscription to find sailors, using the hated British practice of sending press gangs along the waterfront to dragoon the unlucky into the service.

Sailors faced a hard and dangerous life. There was no respite from the danger of the heartless sea. Moreover, the enemy, the Royal Navy, was the world's most powerful naval force. Seamen worked hard and the topmen, those who toiled aloft in the masts, especially faced hazards aplenty. Discipline had to be maintained, as in the army, but strictness depended on a ship's officers. While it is unclear whether sailors on the whole faced a more stringent regimen than soldiers, there is no evidence that any seamen were ever executed during the War of Independence.[14] Sailors enjoyed some advantages over their counterparts in the army. They usually had a roof over their head, a hammock, if not a bed, to sleep on, and rarely experienced severe food and clothing shortages. Before the American Revolution the British navy had demonstrated that through scrupulous cleanliness, proper ventilation, and a diet that included fresh fruit and vegetables it could keep at bay the diseases that ravaged armies of that age. The death rate in the British fleet had been reduced to a mere 1 percent annually, prompting the historian N. A. M. Rodger to conclude that royal sailors were "the healthiest body of British subjects in the world."[15] Unfortunately, the lessons learned in the royal navy had not been assimilated by all American naval commanders. As was true for soldiers in the Continental army, about two sailors in the Continental navy died from illness for every one that was lost in combat. The worst killers were ship fever, or typhus, which was transmitted by lice; dysentery, commonly contracted from foul water or spoiled food; and scurvy, a malady caused by an insufficiency of vitamin C. But sailors who escaped disease had a better chance of surviving the war than did those in the army. Whereas one Continental soldier in four died in this war, about one in eight Continental sailors perished.[16]

The rallying cry in Congress for creating a navy had been that it could provide the rebels with an offensive punch at sea. Much of that turned out to be wishful thinking, especially with regard to American waters, although in the first months of its existence the navy enjoyed a couple of successes. Shortly before Howe abandoned Boston, the Marine Committee directed Commodore Hopkins to clear the coast of British raiders around the mouth of the Chesapeake and below. Disregarding his orders, Hopkins instead sailed with an eight-vessel squadron—and with seven hundred sailors and more than two hundred marines —to the Bahamas. Late in March, his little fleet entered Nassau Harbor on New Providence Island and the marines were sent on their first amphibious landing. In short order, the island's two forts surrendered, yielding seventy-eight cannon, fifteen mortars, sixteen thousand shells and balls, and twenty barrels of powder. Congress praised the "Spirit and Bravery" of the sailors and said that it looked forward to "similar Exertions of Courage on every future Occasion." With the Continental army at Boston having recently been blessed with the artillery that Knox transported from Ticonderoga, Hopkins was ordered to send his pieces to Philadelphia, where they were used in the outfitting of ships in the growing navy.[17]

Later in 1776, with autumn's sting already evident on frosty mornings, Commodore Hopkins turned to one of his young captains for a mission into the

John Paul Jones. Mezzotint portrait by J. M. Moreau, from a bust by Jean-Antoine Houdon, about 1781. Bold, daring, and rash, Jones's achievements were not fully recognized until more than a century after his death.

forbiddingly cold waters north of New England. Like Franklin later on, Hopkins saw John Paul Jones as the right man for a demanding undertaking. Born John Paul in Scotland twenty-nine years before, Jones—he added his new last name in the 1770s—had turned to the sea like many another restless, ambitious young British lad of his time. John Paul was the son of a gardener, but he wanted none of that. Longing for adventure and seeking to escape from afflicting obscurity, he was drawn by the lure of the sea. At age thirteen he sailed out of Whitehaven on a commercial brig, the beginning of a life at sea. At age twenty-one, with numerous Atlantic crossings and one middle passage on a slaver under his belt, he became the captain of his own ship. By 1773, after five years as a ship's commander, he had accumulated substantial assets, but at Christmas of that year he killed a crewman in what he later claimed was an act of self-defense during a portside mutiny in Tobago. He did not wait to stand trial. Leaving behind his ship and much of his savings, he fled to Fredericksburg, Virginia, the home of his immigrant brother. People embraced the American Revolution for all sorts of reasons, but for John Paul Jones—who had risen steadily to a comfortable middling respectability only to suddenly find himself adrift in the mid-1770s without much prospect of ascent —the war that went with the rebellion was a godsend. Once it erupted, about a year after his arrival in Virginia, he scraped together what money he could find and hurried to Philadelphia to offer his service should Congress create a naval counterpart to the Continental army. When Congress at last acted near the end of 1775, Jones—he had adopted his new name as part of his disguise while on the run from the law—was commissioned a first lieutenant. He immediately became part of Hopkins's flotilla that sailed to Nassau, after which he raided British shipping from Nova Scotia to below the Delaware Capes.[18]

The mission that Hopkins gave to Jones in the fall of 1776 was to return to Nova Scotia and liberate scores of American prisoners of war who were thought to be toiling in Britain's coal pits as virtual slave laborers. It was into November before Jones's two-vessel squadron pushed out of Narragansett Bay under a sad grey sky. By the time the *Alfred* and *Providence* reached their destination, ice was encrusted in the rigging of the vessels. Jones found no American captives—they had joined the British navy as an escape from the mines—but he discovered other things to do. He captured the *Mellish*, a British transport laden with thousands of winter uniforms for Carleton's redcoats in Canada, seized coal ships bearing fuel for the British soldiery in burned out New York City, took 140 prisoners, and razed an oil warehouse in Canso.[19]

Numerous other ambitious plans were conceived in 1776 and 1777, some by Jones, whose imagination knew no bounds, and some by others who seemed to always consider him the best man for carrying out a bold and grandiose scheme. Jones proposed an attack on British colonies in Africa. He also suggested waylaying Britain's East India fleet as it headed home with exotic treasures or perhaps destroying the British fishing fleet off Newfoundland. Robert Morris, the rich and powerful Philadelphia merchant who sat on the Marine Committee, wanted Jones to lead a force to plunder British-held Saint Kitts and Pensacola. Nothing came of any of these dreams, and for the most part the navy, created for offensive actions, remained on the defensive, at least in American waters. It protected commerce, convoying merchant ships from port to port, including Caribbean anchorages. It additionally searched for Loyalist raiders and served as a quasi-merchant fleet itself, transporting mostly military items that were shipped by still neutral France to the United States via the Dutch island of Saint Eustatius in the Leeward Islands.[20]

The Continental navy, like the army, had its share of command problems, none bigger than that involving Commodore Hopkins. Less than a year after being named commander in chief, Hopkins was censured by Congress for a variety of indiscretions. Six months later he was stripped of his command and still later dismissed from the navy. Congress never appointed a successor. It left overall command responsibility in the hands of its own Marine Committee.[21] Taking this step at about the same moment that doubts first surfaced about Washington's capabilities, it may be that many congressmen, perhaps feeling that they were stuck with the commander of the army, seized the opportunity to avoid a similar situation in the navy.

Britain's royal navy was more capable of taking the offensive in American waters, although it, too, faced enormous problems at the outset of hostilities. The royal navy, which had gained command of the seas in the Seven Years' War, had been permitted to decline alarmingly in the years of peace after 1763. No one factor accounted for the navy's woes, though much of the blame could be laid at the feet of North who, given to pinching pennies to balance budgets and reduce the national debt, had taken an ax to expenditures, including naval appropriations. Not only did little peacetime construction occur, but the preservation of the existing fleet was slighted. A war crisis with Spain in 1770 served as a wake-up call. North brought Sandwich into his government for his third stint as first lord of the admiralty, and he labored to reverse course during the last years before the American war. He faced formidable obstacles, none more than bad luck. It was Sandwich's ill fortune that obsolescence set in all at once in the early 1770s. Part of the problem arose from dry rot, the great enemy of wooden vessels. Frost curtails dry rot, but England had recently experienced a spate of mild winters. In addition, during the last war many ships had been hurriedly built with green wood. It was an unsound practice, and it caught up with the royal navy ten to fifteen years later. Many vessels prematurely reached the end of the line. By 1775 the navy was far from ready for war. As always, it had been demobilized in peacetime, and most officers and men had drifted into the merchant marine or other pursuits. Naval mobilization was not immediately ordered when the war with the colonies erupted. Convinced that the rebellion was confined to New England, and that the army could suppress it, two years of war passed before mobilization occurred.[22]

When the war broke out, Vice-Admiral Samuel Graves, Britain's naval commander in North America, possessed only thirty warships. As they had been sent to the colonies for the most part to enforce imperial trade laws, Graves's squadron was scattered from Nova Scotia to Florida. Within a couple of months of Lexington-Concord, he had set roughly half his fleet to blockading the seemingly measureless coast from Rhode Island southward. Half of the remainder was given the task of safeguarding Nova Scotia. What was left was put to suppressing the rebels' trade into and out of Massachusetts, gathering fuel and forage for the British army in Boston, and keeping open the army's lines of communication with the homeland. Much of the Bay Colony's maritime commerce was shut down, but southward American ships slipped in and out almost at will. Merely one ship patrolled the entrance to Delaware Bay and two warships and a tender tried to control rebel traffic on Chesapeake Bay. Graves proposed that his fleet turn to the destruction of every seaport in New England, and he started by razing Falmouth in October 1775. But the campaign of terror went no further. British officials recoiled, fearing that such tactics would only create more rebels.

London sent over reinforcements during that first year of the war— one-third of the Royal Navy, fifty-one warships (all frigate class or smaller), sailed

American waters by early 1776—but at the same time a steadily larger percentage of royal sail were shifted from an offensive to a defensive role. Many vessels were pressed into escorting British ships, protecting them from the growing number of rebel privateers. Some British warships hunted for American merchantmen sailing from European and African ports, although the most crucial theater outside North America was the Caribbean, where merely ten warships were tasked with impeding the rebels' flagrantly open trade in munitions in the Dutch, Danish, and French West Indies. During the first vital year of hostilities, the royal navy enjoyed some success. It seized more than 120 rebel ships off the coasts of the thirteen mainland colonies alone. What was most striking, however, was how effectively America's stupendous size diluted the effectiveness of the world's greatest navy.

In 1776 the Royal Navy played a critical role in three offensive enterprises. Ships were sent to Quebec to lift the rebel siege. About the same time, the navy took part in the endeavor to take Charleston. But the big show that year was the campaign to retake New York. Two of the three enterprises succeeded, but at the expense of the ongoing effort to tighten the blockade. Lord Howe simply had too few ships to do it all. When he arrived to take command of the navy in mid-1776, Howe had about seventy warships, nearly half of which were involved in the New York and Canadian operations. He was left with a fleet of forty-two ships—some of which at any given time were in port for repairs or refitting—with which to blockade a coastline that stretched nearly three thousand miles. Although his fleet of warships grew to exceed eighty-five sail by mid-1777, the state of Britain's blockade did not significantly improve. Now and then an American ship was taken, but there is every reason to believe that more than 75 percent of the rebel vessels got through the British net. After late 1776, when the Royal Navy was first pressed into supplying the beleaguered redcoats and Germans who occupied New Jersey, then into transporting General Howe's Philadelphia-bound army to the Chesapeake, Britain's blockade fleet at times dwindled to as few as twenty ships. Materials poured into the hands of the rebels, not only helping to bolster morale on the homefront, but providing Washington and Gates with much needed provisions for conducting their respective campaigns. Faced with an impotent blockade, Germain in 1777 resurrected Graves's proposed strategy of decimating numerous coastal towns. The secretary's thinking was that if American privateers and merchantmen had no port from which to come and go, the burden placed on the royal fleet would be reduced. But the Howe brothers objected. The raids, they thought, would be invidious. Besides, they said, the vessels were needed for other purposes. But the Howes said they would consent to the coastal raids if London sent naval reinforcements. London declined. With war against France on the horizon, it could spare no further ships for the American theater.[23]

Long before the Franco-American alliance, the Admiralty's gaze fell on French harbors, which were invitingly open to American cruisers. London blustered and threatened, seeking to compel France to maintain strict neutrality, but the French continued to admit and aid rebel vessels. The Americans of course were delighted that the French government "winks at the supplies we obtain here," said a Continental navy captain, and for the opportunity to make repairs, take on supplies and replacement crewmen, and especially to be outfitted with arms that were all but nonexistent in the United States. These were "very essential aids" that permitted the rebels to operate far from home, he added. The Continentals had been receiving assistance in French ports since late in 1776 when the *Reprisal*, which had taken Franklin to France, refitted in Nantes, sailed into the English Channel and took five prizes, concluding its mission by unabashedly cruising into L'Orient to sell what it had seized. The *Reprisal's* captain, Lambert Wickes, a Marylander, was not about to stop there. When he reemerged, he joined the cutter *Dolphin* and brig *Lexington*, and headed for the Irish Sea in search of additional prizes. His little rebel fleet enjoyed eye-catching success, taking about a score of prizes carrying cargoes of wheat, coal, sugar, rum, tobacco, and hides before it barely escaped after being chased along the French coast by a British man-of-war. The raids drove up British insurance rates and compelled Sandwich not only to transfer four frigates to the Irish Sea, but to dispatch sloops of war and cutters to patrol the Shetland Islands; St. George's Channel; the Dutch, Portuguese, and Spanish coasts; and to guard major ports. The Admiralty was also driven to convoying commercial shipments from India, West Africa, the Baltic, Caribbean, and the fisheries. Captain Wickes, still hot under the collar after nearly being captured in French waters, displayed bedazzling chutzpah by carping publicly that the British "pay very little regard to the Laws of Newtrality."[24]

Wickes's headline-grabbing exploits lured Gustavus Conyngham to meet with the American commissioners in Paris. An Irish-born immigrant to Philadelphia, Conyngham had sailed for years for a trading company, but when hostilities erupted he volunteered his services, declaring that "from the first day of the revolution my Motive was to Injure & distress the Enemy." Congress's Secret Committee sent him to France to obtain "every thing necessary for War," as he put it.[25] He and his ship were taken by the British on the homeward voyage, but Conyngham escaped to Dunkirk, where he languished until he heard of Wickes's exploits. In mid-1777 he visited Franklin, who commissioned him a captain in the Continental navy and may have pulled the necessary strings to find him a cutter, the *Surprize*. In no time, Conyngham seized two British vessels with full cargoes, but acting "imprudently" (as Franklin put it), stupidly (according to Vergennes), he attempted to sell what he had taken in Dunkirk. Britain's response was so menacing that the French foreign minister, fearing that a British declaration of war was imminent, impounded and returned the prizes, and ordered all French ports closed to American privateers. Unruffled, Conyngham, with Franklin's help, was quickly back at sea in a new cutter that he christened with the madly vindictive name *Revenge*. He rampaged through the Channel and into the North Sea, above and around Scotland and into the Irish Sea (even landing briefly in Ireland), before finally putting into port in Spain. He had taken, or destroyed, twenty ships. He came out again late in the summer of 1777 and marauded for months in the Mediterranean, and between Spain and the Canary Islands, before Madrid closed its ports to him. But he had been enormously successful. In eighteen months, Conyngham had taken at least twenty-seven additional prizes and destroyed another thirty-three British vessels.[26]

Not long after Conyngham's heroics, France learned of Saratoga and entered into the American alliance and the war. French belligerence changed the war at sea as it altered the land war. In America, the Royal Navy was forced into an almost entirely defensive posture. Nearly half of its ninety-two ships guarded New York, Philadelphia, and Rhode Island, while the remainder continued their futile efforts at blockading the extensive coast. The exception to its defensiveness that year consisted of a devastating September raid on New Bedford, Massachusetts; Germain had once again ordered the burning of seaports, but his policy was visited only on this one star-crossed village, and the invasion of Georgia at the end of the year.[27] France, on the other hand, went to war with the expectation of seizing the offensive on the high seas and of gaining a rapid and majestic triumph through its naval prowess. Not only did it send d'Estaing's Toulon fleet to North America, France's Brest fleet had achieved parity with Britain's home fleet.[28]

The French were disappointed in campaign 1778. The British and French navies fought in July off Ushant, an engagement that is best remembered as having formally started the war between the two great powers. The fleets were evenly matched, thirty-two French ships of the line to Keppel's thirty. More than one thousand men died or were wounded in bloody fighting that ended indecisively after three days. D'Estaing meanwhile accomplished nothing in six months across the sea, including two months in the West Indies that witnessed Britain's capture of Saint Lucia. By January 1779 the Royal Navy had established numerical supremacy in the warm southern waters.[29]

The dismaying fruitlessness of d'Estaing's mission meant that war's end was nowhere in sight, and led ultimately to France's commitment to a joint invasion of England. Under the Convention of Aranjuez, sixty-six French and Spanish ships of the line were to sail the moment that word was received—probably toward mid-May 1779—that Britain had rejected Spanish mediation. The two navies were to rendezvous at the end of the month at Corunna, on the northwest coast of Spain, and sail for the English Channel to pulverize the overmatched enemy fleet. Once command of the Channel had been established, a French invasion force of 37,376 men—roughly the same size force was at Howe's disposal when he invaded New York three years earlier—would cross for England. Its primary target was Portsmouth. Cork, home of the Royal Navy's primary supply depot, was to be an important secondary objective. Beyond those ends, the ultimate goal of the invasion was left undetermined. At the very least it was hoped that the destruction of the royal fleet and the occupation of Portsmouth would compel Britain to recognize American independence and relinquish Gibraltar to Spain. Romantics, adventurers, and the vengeful, wanted far more. They dreamed of using Portsmouth as a staging area for a campaign to take London.

Giant operations of this sort usually include diversionary actions. This was the role that Lafayette had come to envision for himself early in 1779 after his Canadian and Newport proposals were rebuffed. He hoped to lead an enterprise to raid and take captives along the English coast. There was an antecedent upon which he could draw—the daring actions of John Paul Jones during the preceding year. Jones had sailed for France in command of the black and yellow frigate *Ranger* two weeks after Burgoyne's surrender. Before he departed America, Captain Jones had spoken to his backers in Congress, notably Robert Morris, about a campaign to raid ports on Britain's coast, kidnapping inhabitants to trade for American seamen in British prisons and generally spreading terror. He had other designs, too, he said. He hoped to erode morale on Britain's homefront and at the same time to force the Royal Navy to detach ships to guard its coasts that might otherwise be used in blockading rebel ports. Congress never formally ordered such a mission, but Jones's congressional friends smiled approvingly as he expanded on his scheme, and he sailed with a letter from the Marine Committee that directed the commissioners to purchase a frigate for him, the beginning of what would be a Lilliputian squadron with which to conduct a menacing sortie. Jones never got his other frigate. It was to be acquired in the Netherlands, but Britain got wind of the American plans and forced the Dutch to back off. Undeterred, Jones put his audacious scheme into operation in the spring of 1778, sailing from Brest on *Ranger* with an American crew of 140 men. The frigate looped around Ireland and into the Irish Sea. Jones's target was Whitehaven, a small Scottish port on Solway Firth directly across from Belfast, the very port from which he had first gone to sea in 1760 as a thirteen-year-old. With forty volunteers, Jones carried out a dangerous cut-and-run raid on Whitehaven on the cold night of April 22, 1778, taking three captives, but shedding no blood. He was the first enemy sailor to conduct a wartime raid on Britain since a Dutch party had put ashore and razed Sheerness, a town on England's coast, 111 years before. Nor was Jones quite finished. With daylight, he landed again, this time on nearby St. Mary's Isle in Kirkcudbright Bay. His hope was to seize the Earl of Selkirk, the great nobleman of the region, the embodiment of the bitter social deprivation that Jones's Paul family ancestry had faced.

Jones failed to nab the Earl—he was away in England taking the baths— but he confiscated the household silver and a few bottles of wine, and in twenty minutes he was gone. Again, no one was injured. Back at sea, *Ranger* engaged in a slugfest with HMS *Drake*, and bested it. It was the first instance in this war that an American navy ship had defeated a British warship of similar size and power. Twenty-three of the *Drake's* crew were killed or wounded, and scores were captured, together with the vessel itself. In less than thirty days, Captain Jones

John Paul Jones' Cruises
in The British Isles
1778 – 79

←— Ranger,
April 1778

←— Bonhomme Richard,
August – September, 1779

SHETLAND
ISLANDS

ORKNEY
ISLANDS

North Minch

SCOTLAND

Inchcape
Rock

NORTH

SEA

Dundee

Leith

Edinburgh

HOLY
ISLE

Bamburgh

Kirkcudbright   New Castle

Flamborough
Head

Londonderry

Belfast

Whitehaven

X

Bonhomme
Richard
vs.
Serapis

ISLE
OF
MAN

Scarborough

Lancaster

Hull

IRELAND

IRISH

Liverpool

Dublin

SEA

WALES

ENGLAND

Cork

Bristol

London

Bath

Mizen
Head

Plymouth

Land's End

ATLANTIC
OCEAN

English Channel

USHANT

Brest

FRANCE

N

Lorient

0   50   100   150 Miles

0   50   100   150 Kilometers

had captured a British frigate and two merchantmen, taken captive two hundred enemy sailors, destroyed several smaller prizes, landed in a British town, and spread fear through every port in Great Britain.[30]

The cyclonic impact of Jones's voyage made his name a household word throughout England and led the French to toast his dauntless exploits. Those intrepid feats inspired Lafayette in the cold winter of 1779 to conceive of similar, though larger, raids on bigger British port cities, and, with Franklin's help, eagerly to hook up with Jones. Great planning went into their projected enterprise, which was to be launched about seventy-five days before the Franco-Spanish invasion armada sailed up the English Channel, just far enough ahead of the invasion to induce London to scatter its forces, leaving Portsmouth more vulnerable. But, Lafayette's hope for glory in coastal raids was dashed. At the last minute, the French government yanked him from the endeavor and assigned him to the command staff of the invasion army.[31] The French, however, still wanted Jones.

Few men liked Jones, but when a daunting assignment was under consideration, his name seemed to leap to mind. Rugged, resolute, and hard in appearance rather than handsome—one biographer aptly wrote of his "hawkish face"—Jones's features were dominated by such intensely burning eyes that John Adams thought he saw a "Wildness" in them. Some described Jones as small ("a little fellow," said one observer), but that was due to his slight frame, not his height. He stood five feet six inches tall, only an inch below that of the average American-born man of the time, with light brown hair that was flecked with grey before his thirtieth birthday. Jones was moderate in his habits, neither drinking nor eating to excess. He could be polite and gracious, though he tended to be aloof, abrasive, brooding, and fast-tempered, and to many his undisguised and burning ambition—he "aspires very high," said Adams—was off-putting, and never more so than when it drove him by turns to manifest intrigues or transparent sycophancy. He struck some as the sort who habitually used others for his own ends, and he impressed almost everyone as being a perfectionist, a quality that annoyed some, but which many seamen liked in a ship's master, feeling that a meticulous skipper improved their odds against the hazards of the sea. Like General Washington, who often provoked quite dissimilar responses from his male and female observers, Jones, too, showed a different side to women. Expecting to find him a "Rough Stout warlike Roman," Abigail Adams instead discovered a man "soft in his Speech[,] easy in his address[,] polite in his manners, vastly civil." Rather than sending him into harm's way, she poignantly dreamed of "wrapping [him] in cotton wool and putting him into my pocket." But she, too, understood that "under all this appearance of softness he is bold[,] enterprizing[,] ambitious and active." Those qualities were what Franklin and Hopkins saw in him as well. The historian Samuel Eliot Morison sagely concluded that Jones was "not at peace even with himself," much less his world or the people who inhabited it, and perhaps it was the sullen edginess that burgeoned from his unfulfilled wants and needs that left him nearly friendless. He hungered after glory—Adams once characterized him as "leprous with vanity"—and indeed his entire life was a struggle to escape what he saw as the mire of his humble cottager background and to gain the love, admiration, and above all the deference of those at the apex of society. He was one of those revolutionaries who appears not to have fought for ideological reasons. He risked life and limb not to change the world into which he had been born, but to win the approval and homage of those who ran that world.[32]

What Marine Minister Sartine saw in Jones was an intrepid naval officer who was anxious to "astonish the world," a man whose temperament and keen understanding of the psychological dimensions of warfare made him the proper choice for a mission whose purpose was to spread terror, constraining the British Admiralty to redirect some of its fleet from the English Channel to hunt him down.[33] Sartine ordered him on a diversionary operation toward northern England or Scotland. His exact orders have not survived, but for a very long time Jones had envisaged far more than privateering, and it is likely that he and Sartine were in synch on that score, as on this mission Jones brought along "combustibles" with which to raze a port town.

France had invested heavily in Commodore Jones's undertaking, putting a quarter as many livres into it as it had given or loaned to the United States over the past four years. Jones had a small squadron, including vessels that Lafayette had procured or that Sartine provided. Its flagship, *Bonhomme Richard*, was old and slow, a vessel of about nine hundred tons that was outfitted with forty guns. Of its officers 17 out of 20 were Americans, as were 62 of its 187 men. Although nearly 40 percent of its officers and crew were British, they were men who were loyal to Jones, if not to their homeland. The ship also carried 137 French marines, garbed in red coats and white breeches, and thirty-six motley French "landsmen," mostly workers and peasants, some of whom had recently been sprung from English jails, and all of whom were eager for work or revenge, or both. Two other frigates (including *Alliance*, the largest vessel in the squadron), a corvette, and a cutter—with a grand total of 1,071 men—comprised his little fleet, and so, too, did two large armed privateers (one, the *Monsieur*, was virtually the same size as the *Bonhomme Richard*) were to accompany him. The American officers in this task force wore the naval uniforms that Congress had adopted in 1777—blue coats with white lapels, flat yellow buttons adorned with an anchor, slash cuffs, and a stand-up collar, blue waistcoats (Jones, who marched to his own drummer, wore a buff waistcoat), and blue breeches. Jones wore gold lace on his waistcoat, two gilt epaulets, and a sword. There was no uniformity in the dress of seamen, save that they wore somewhat short, baggy trousers and, in colder weather, a jacket. Many also tied a handkerchief about their necks, while for headgear some wore round wool hats, but others donned stocking caps, flat straw or cotton hats, or even another handkerchief. Jones preferred that his men wear a brown jacket and round hat.[34]

Commodore Jones had been given a minor part in the invasion plan, but among Americans what he accomplished is not only the best-remembered aspect of the projected invasion, but of the War of Independence at sea. Jones's task force put to sea from L'Orient in mid-August, moving slowly in the sultry days of high summer, its speed curtailed by the need for the faster vessels to wait on the plodding *Bonhomme Richard*. Jones followed largely the same course past the west coast of Ireland that he had taken with *Ranger*, but this time, instead of cruising into the North Channel, he sailed on above Scotland, between the Shetland and the Orkney Islands, and into the North Sea on the east side of Great Britain. A month to the day after weighing anchor, the squadron reached the Firth of Forth, gateway to Edinburgh's port of Leith. Jones had set out with a coastal raid in mind, and he believed that conditions were right to assail this inviting target. He even drafted an ultimatum to present to the city authorities: unless Leith paid protection money that would serve as "your contribution towards the reimbursement which Britain owes to the much injured citizens of America," he would "lay it in ashes."[35] Under cover of darkness, Jones approached the city with three ships, planning a 4:00 a.m. landing, but only minutes before zero hour a frightful williwaw blew up, lashing and scattering his ships, and causing some damage. By the time he could act, his presence was known. Reluctantly, he cancelled his planned raid and moved on.

From Leith, the squadron sailed south, down the English coast. Little had been achieved during the four weeks of the voyage. Seven prizes had been taken, but two had been lost—*Monsieur* absconded with one and another sank in a storm—and most of what remained was of scant importance.[36] Jones's aborted plans at Leith had alerted eastern England to his presence. Naval craft now patrolled the North Sea looking for him. Ten anxious days passed as he sailed and watched uneasily for the Royal Navy. Although his spirits were in shreds at the prospect that his grand dream would go unfulfilled, Jones—as always—had another scheme up his sleeve. He intended to raid Newcastle upon Tyne, the source of London's coal supply. He sailed toward it, but never got there. Instead, just after noon on September 23, off the chalk cliffs of Flamborough Head on the Yorkshire coast, his lookout spotted a large commercial fleet, forty-four merchantmen returning from Scandinavia. Obviously a convoy, it was under the watchful eye of a small royal sloop, the *Countess of Scarborough*, and a new copper-bottomed frigate, the *Serapis*, armed with fifty guns and captained by Richard Pearson, for thirty years a sailor, the past six as a captain in the Royal Navy. Though he knew the *Bonhomme Richard* was slow and assailable, Jones never hesitated. He was a fighter. He immediately ordered out studding sails to increase his speed, and as the afternoon wore on, and the distance between his ship and *Serapis* slowly narrowed, Jones readied for action. Axes, pikes, pistols, heavier firearms, grenades, and cutlasses were broken out for distribution. The yards were braced in the hope that they would not fall to the decks if hit. The ship's physician prepared his equipment to care for the wounded.

At 5:00 p.m. Jones, who according to one observer carried a cutlass and wore twelve pistols on his waist belt, ordered the men to their action stations. The gun crews required time to unlash the guns, which always were securely fastened to the ship when not in use, as otherwise in a tempest or a rough sea they might careen perilously about the deck, or even be lost by crashing through the ship's side, endangering the vessel. As the men removed the wooden tampions, plugs that kept moisture from the muzzle, the "powder monkeys" brought cartridges from the magazine below to each gun crew. A bit after 6:00 p.m. the ruddy sun sank behind the tall grey cliffs on shore, casting dark shadows over the water. Slowly the light faded and night crept over the sky, though a huge harvest moon laid a bright ochre glint on the dark sea. Within an hour the two ships had drawn so close that men on the *Bonhomme Richard* could hear the orders that were being barked on the opposing vessel. At 7:15 a trigger-happy sailor on *Bonhomme Richard* fired the first shot. Then all hell broke loose. Up to twenty cannon on each ship erupted simultaneously, leveling a salvo at its adversary a mere twenty-five yards away.

Naval ordinance, like the muskets carried by soldiers in every army, were smooth bore weapons and, hence, not accurate. Given that a ship's guns were aimed from a rolling and pitching vessel at a moving target, after being sighted through dense powder smoke, naval cannon were notoriously inaccurate. But when fired at such a short range as separated *Bonhomme Richard* and *Serapis*, they could not miss. The heavier guns—the largest on both vessels were eighteen-pounders—were enormously powerful, capable of hurling eighteen-pound cast iron balls well over a mile. Some were loaded not with balls but with bar shot and case shot. Bar shot were heavy round iron objects separated by a short bar or chain, and were designed to tear down the spars and rigging. Case shot— essentially grapeshot—consisted of bags filled with clusters of various size iron balls that flew apart like shrapnel, and was designed to kill and maim men. Both ships were also equipped with coehorns, small mortars that lobbed bombs, and swivel guns, light mounted cannon.

It seemed miraculous that anyone could live through such a bombardment. Many did not. Those on the top deck, where Commodore Jones remained throughout the battle, were in the greatest danger. Many were decapitated or cut to pieces, dying instantly. They were the lucky ones. Other men suffered horrible burns or grotesque injuries that resulted, inevitably, in slow, agonizing deaths. The men below deck, shielded somewhat by the thick, heavy hull, stood a better chance. Incredibly, it was rare for a ship to be sunk in such a battle. A vessel had to take a hit at, or below, the waterline to face the likelihood of going down, an uncommon occurrence given the difficulty of depressing the guns and reliably honing in on a jouncing target. The object in such battles was less to sink one's rival than to kill so many of the enemy that too few would be left to keep up the fight, or to disable the vessel by knocking down its masts and rigging, leaving it a sitting duck, or to set afire the adversary, impelling its captain to ask for quarter before his powder and ammunition ignited, blowing all aboard into eternity.[37]

In an instant after this fierce struggle began, the placid decks turned into a scene of devastation. Men lay here and there among cordage and shattered yards and booms, crying and groaning, making piteous, unintelligible noises. The planking on each vessel, like that on most ships of that day, was probably painted red to hide the blood that sloshed about freely. If so, the camouflage was unavailing. After the initial broadside, the two vessels drifted apart, and the maneuvering began for the next fusillade. Pearson grabbed the windward, giving him more maneuverability, and fifteen minutes after the opening barrage he crossed the *Richard's* undefended stern, or aft, raking Jones's momentarily helpless vessel. The *Serapis* got off three broadsides, wreaking more butchery aboard the already wounded *Bonhomme Richard*. Bodies, and parts of bodies, were scattered everywhere, and the ship, badly punctured beneath the waterline, was taking on water dangerously fast. As Pearson maneuvered to get off what likely would be the final, fatal broadside, the wind miraculously died. Jones saw hope, and seized it. He tried to ram *Serapis*, as a prelude to boarding the ship. He saw hand-to-hand combat as his only hope against this faster, more nimble, foe. But Jones's desperate ploy failed. Seventy-five minutes into the battle, catching a puff of a breeze, Jones had another chance at success, and tried to cross Pearson's bow, and rake him. Again he failed, and this time *Serapis* rammed the *Bonhomme Richard*, leaving the two ships entangled. Neither could break free. Each fired at the other from point-blank range with swivel guns, while crewmen on both ships opened fire with handguns, muskets, and heavy blunderbusses. Both ships were now burning. Just then, at 9:15, *Alliance* arrived and opened fire, hitting the *Richard* (and it would do so a few minutes later). The hits that it took from its sister ship, seemed to be the final straw for the *Bonhomme Richard*. Thinking that Jones might have to capitulate, Pearson shouted over the din: "Have you struck? Do you call for quarters?" To which Jones, according to conflicting contemporary accounts, may have answered with one or the other of the following scarcely catchy responses: "I may sink, but I'll be damned if I strike," or "I haven't as yet thought of surrendering," or "No sir, I will not—we have had but a small fight as yet." Many years later his remark was retooled: "I have not yet begun to fight." It was lyrical and defiant, and while historically inaccurate, it became immortal.[38]

Hearing that Jones would not quit, Pearson tried to get a boarding party onto *Bonhomme Richard* to win this fight through hand-to-hand combat. His men were beaten back. But just when it must have seemed that this engagement would never end, it came to a sudden finish. A crewman on the *Bonhomme Richard* succeeded in lobbing a baseball-sized grenade through an open hatch on the *Serapis*. It detonated, setting off a series of devastating explosions. The grenade had touched off powder cartridges that littered the areas where the soot-faced gun crews worked. Cannon were blown apart and in an instant fire danced the length of the British vessel. Almost immediately, Pearson called for quarter. "Cease firing," Jones ordered. This bloody fight that had continued into its fourth hour was at last over.

The carnage was incredible. Fully half of the nearly six hundred men who had been in the battle were dead or wounded, and the victor, the *Bonhomme Richard*, was fatally damaged—"mangled beyond my power of description," Jones subsequently remarked. Two days after the battle it was reluctantly abandoned. But *Serapis* was afloat, and Jones gathered it and the *Countess of Scarborough*, which had been seized by other vessels in his task force, together with 504 British prisoners and several captured merchantmen. All were taken to a safe haven in the Netherlands. When the prizes were sold, the crewmen in Jones's squadron each received thirty-two dollars in prize money. Jones's share came to $2,658.[39] He was touted everywhere, even by some in Britain, though most of the English press labeled him a pirate. No one was happier to receive the news of Jones's victory than his benefactor Franklin. "Few Actions at Sea have demonstrated such steady cool determined Bravery," he said of Jones's heroics. The mission, Franklin said without exaggeration, had "alarm'd those [British] Coasts exceedingly, occasion'd a good deal of internal Expence, done great damage to their Trade." And relishing the turnabout of an American sowing fear in port towns all along the British coast, Franklin crowed that "tho' we have burnt none of their Towns, we have occasioned a good deal of Terror & Bustle in them."[40]

Aside from Jones's one legendary night, the long-planned invasion of England was forgettable, save as a muddled or misguided venture. From the outset, the allies agreed that the operation had to be completed by the end of August, when treacherous winds characteristically reappeared that made the Channel untenable for an invasion fleet. Had Las Vegas existed at the time, its odds makers surely would have favored the Franco-Spanish side. The royal fleet was heavily outnumbered: sixty-six to thirty-nine ships of the line.[41] North's ministry found 21,000 regulars and mobilized 30,000 militiamen to resist the force that would bear down on the homeland, but as the invasion site was unknown, Britain's soldiers were scattered from pillar to post, deployed in pretty much equal numbers in Plymouth, Chatham near London, and at Portsmouth in between.

The only predictable thing about this war was the unpredictability of every campaign. Problems arose at once for the allies. The French fleet, troubled with recruitment problems and having difficulty securing materials needed for maintaining its ships—getting its wood from the Baltic Sea region, for instance became infinitely more complicated once France entered the war—was tardy in sailing. It reached Corunna three weeks late, only to discover that the Spanish fleet was nowhere to be seen, and was not fully present for another six weeks, until near the end of July, more than sixty days past the planned target date for sailing for the Channel. In the interim, the French sailors not only consumed half the comestibles that they had brought from Brest, but the French ships, living up to their reputation for squalor, were swept with debilitating illnesses, mostly typhus and smallpox. The armada did not appear off Portsmouth until mid-August, a scant two weeks before the previously agreed on termination date. The British home fleet was not there to greet them. Now under Admiral Sir Charles Hardy, it had pulled back to Spithead, hoping to frustrate the enemy and buy time, and perhaps lure the allied armada into more enclosed waters.

As that troubled summer dragged past, the Spanish had begun to talk of reducing the objectives of the campaign. They proposed taking lightly held Falmouth at the far western end of the Channel and garrisoning it through the winter, a toehold from which to resume operations in the spring of 1780. That was unpalatable to Vergennes, who was not keen about spending a second summer attempting to invade England. He believed there were better ways to win the war, notably through victories in the American theater that would, not coincidentally, enhance French interests in that part of the world. What little fervor he had mustered for the invasion of England had long since waned. It collapsed altogether when intelligence reported that the British fleet, through reinforcements that consisted largely of warships deemed unseaworthy in the event of a bad storm, had uncomfortably narrowed the gap between the rival navies. By then, too, disease had reached pandemic proportions in the French fleet. Half of the 1,100 men aboard the flagship were sick or dead. On September 3, France ordered its fleet home. The projected invasion of England was over. No attempt had been made to land the French army. The enterprise had been doomed by poor planning, unavoidable bogs and snares, an artful British naval strategy, and a fatal lack of will on one side together with a steely resolve on the other.[42] After squandering resources that might have been put to better use, the allied fleets went back to their respective ports "without having effected anything," as Franklin sneered. There was another outcome to the fiasco, which Adams noted with equal distaste. The egregious allied failure had given a disheartened Britain "a Flash of Spirits" such as it had not experienced since the first heady days of Howe's invasion of New York three long years before.[43]

WITH THE EXCEPTION of Wayne's bold assault on Stony Point and Commodore Jones's epic voyage on *Bonhomme Richard*, Americans had little to cheer about in 1779. By the time they learned of the failed attempt to invade England, they were aware of two additional failures, both in the North American theater of operations. In early June, ten weeks before the *Bonhomme Richard* sailed, a British armada suddenly appeared off the Maine coast at the mouth of the Penobscot River. Sent from Nova Scotia on orders from Germain, it carried 650 redcoats, who debouched and set to work building a fort—christened Fort George—at present-day Castine on Bagduce Peninsula, a carefully chosen site atop a steep, one-hundred-foot bank overlooking the glistening blue waters of the river and Penobscot Bay. The little installation was guarded by artillery that the British army positioned on nearby Nautilus Island and by three Royal Navy sloops of war carrying a combined forty-four guns. Erected roughly 175 miles above Boston, the British saw their little outpost as an eventual settlement for displaced Loyalists, but for the immediate future it was to serve as a base of operations for raids against the New England coast and a post from which to intercept rebel privateers. The existence of Fort George was intolerable to Massachusetts, which readied a response without consulting Congress, Washington, or Gates, the commander of the Northern Department. In a throwback to military expeditions that it had raised against foreign adversaries going back to 1690, Massachusetts fielded a thousand-man army and furnished its entire state navy, consisting of three cruisers. New Hampshire pitched in with a brig and the Continental navy— once Congress was consulted—contributed a few marines and three vessels, including the thirty-two gun frigate *Warren*. Troop transports and supply vessels brought the number of naval craft involved to thirty-four. The fleet was under the command of Dudley Saltonstall, a captious and contrary individual who, many believed, owed his appointment as a ship's captain in the Continental navy less to his long career at sea than to the fact that he was Silas Deane's brother-in-law. Not without skill, Saltonstall had no experience in coping with the rigors of a land-based campaign. Solomon Lovell and Peleg Wadsworth shared command of the army. Both were talented and Wadsworth had considerable experience, though neither had commanded in battle. But the major flaw in this endeavor was that no one was given overall responsibility. Late in July, the flotilla—the rebels' largest amphibious operation of the war—arrived in Penobscot Bay.

Given their overwhelming superiority in manpower and firepower, the New Englanders should have swiftly overpowered the defenders. Instead, after the marines took Nautilus Island and the Yankee army, following an amphibious landing, overran the British redoubt on the high banks, about six hundred yards beyond the unfinished fort, the operation turned into a siege. Lovell and Wadsworth refused to order their men to storm the fort so long as the three British sloops stood nearby. They demanded that Saltonstall use his surpassing edge to destroy the tiny British squadron. But Saltonstall was not a risk-taker. He knew that the loss of some ships and men was inevitable if he acted, and he refused to move. Not even orders from the Eastern Navy Board—"attack and take or destroy them at once"—stirred him to action. The useless and ill-advised siege dragged on for three weeks until, predictably, a British relief force of seven vessels, including the sixty-four-gun giant, *Raisonable*, arrived from New York under Vice Admiral Collier. The rebels were doomed. Saltonstall retreated up the bay without a fight, and when he realized that there was no way out, he scuttled what he could of his squadron, including the *Warren* (the tenth of the thirteen frigates built since 1776 to be lost). All the intact vessels fell into British hands. Most of the soldiery escaped, but faced a long, arduous wilderness trek to safety at Portsmouth, a march that in many ways was dreadfully similar to the awful tramp that Arnold's men had endured en route to Canada four years earlier. Saltonstall and many of the officers, including Paul Revere, who commanded the artillery force, were court-martialed. Most, including Revere, were acquitted, but Saltonstall was convicted and dismissed from the service. This inexcusable failure produced great outrage, and it nearly bankrupted Massachusetts (it cost the state

£1,739,000). It had been misguided, it was said, to attempt such a large enterprise under the leadership of mostly militia officers, and some blustered that "somebody ought to be hanged" for the debacle. General Greene came closer to the truth in his assessment. The campaign, he said, was "a child of vanity, nourished by folly, and destroyed by temerity."44 It was, in truth, a sorry and troubling episode, a black mark against the Continental navy and a blow to American morale already weighed down by an economy in shambles and a war that seemed to have no end.45

D'ESTAING'S FLEET had not been seen in North America since it sailed from Boston nine months earlier, but it had been busy, and provided with reinforcements early in 1779, it had at last accomplished something. In July, d'Estaing had taken Grenada and fought off an attempt to regain it, inflicting heavy losses on Britain's West Indian fleet. Washington had been waiting anxiously since the spring for d'Estaing's return north, careful to make Minister Gérard aware of his smoldering hopes for a joint campaign to retake New York, which he often alluded to as certain to be the "decisive blow." Even so, Washington had finally come to understand the dangers that were gathering down south, especially should Clinton, as intelligence suggested, launch a major campaign to take South Carolina. Washington knew—as had the far-seeing architects of the Southern Strategy in London back in late 1777—that the South, to a degree unrivaled in the United States, coped with what he acknowledged was "internal weakness, disaffection, the want of energy, [and] the general languor that has seized the people." Washington now understood that Britain's hand would be alarmingly strengthened—and America's immeasurably weakened, perhaps fatally so—if the redcoats retook Georgia and the Carolinas. Washington let Gérard know that if d'Estaing could not come to New York, he hoped he might sail for Savannah and be part of a joint endeavor to recapture the city. Retrieving Savannah, he believed, was the best antidote against Clinton having "a further career" in the South. Remarkably, Washington sent only scant reinforcements southward and refused to consider transferring the bulk of his army to the southern theater. Claiming to be filled with "infinite anxiety" at the thought of his army campaigning in that miasmic sector, he curiously maintained that the southern climate would be "more adverse to our troops than to theirs."46

Savannah it was to be, but not because of Washington. Congress, with daily access to Gérard, had made clear its interest in driving the British from Georgia, which it believed would save South Carolina. The governor of South Carolina, John Rutledge, the French consul in Charleston, and General Moultrie also urged d'Estaing to come to Savannah, but the most influential petition came from the Marquis de Brétigny, a French volunteer in the Continental army. He informed d'Estaing that the British had neglected their defenses in Savannah and were vulnerable. In June, d'Estaing notified officials in Charleston that he would

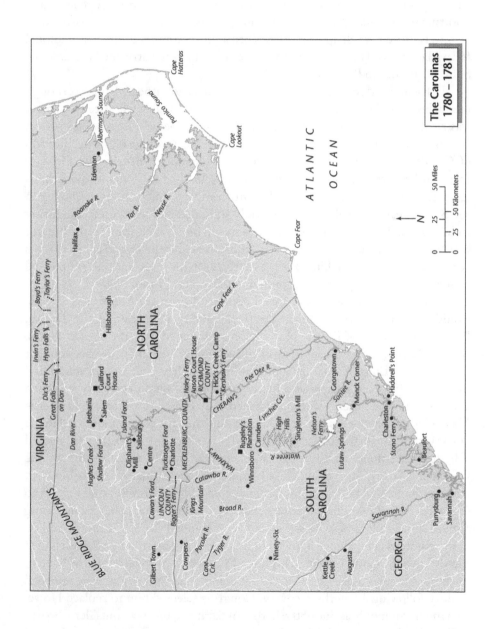

The Carolinas
1780 – 1781

VIRGINIA

NORTH
CAROLINA

SOUTH
CAROLINA

GEORGIA

BLUE RIDGE MOUNTAINS

ATLANTIC
OCEAN

Cape Hatteras

Cape Lookout

Cape Fear

Albemarle Sound

Pamlico Sound

Edenton

Roanoke R.

Halifax

Tar R.

Neuse R.

Dan River

Irwin's Ferry
Boyd's Ferry
Taylor's Ferry
Dix's Ferry
Hyco Falls
Great Falls
on Dan

Hughes Creek
Shallow Ford

Oliphant's
Mill
Centre
Salisbury

Bethania
Salem

Guilford
Court
House

Island Ford

Tuckasegee Ford
Charlotte

Hillsborough

Cowan's Ford
LINCOLN
COUNTY
Bigger's Ferry

Kings
Mountain

MECKLENBURG COUNTY

Haley's Ferry
Anson Court House
RICHMOND
COUNTY
Hick's Creek Camp
Kershaw's Ferry

Cape Fear R.

CHERAWS

Pee Dee R.

Catawba R.

Broad R.

Gilbert Town

Cowpens

Cane
Crk.
Tyger R.
Pacolet R.

Ninety-Six

Kettle
Creek

Augusta

Savannah R.

Purrysburg

Savannah

WAXHAWS

Winnsboro

Camden

Rugeley's
Plantation

Lynches Crk.

High
Hills

Wateree R.

Singleton's Mill

Nelson's
Ferry

Eutaw Springs

Georgetown

Santee R.

Monck Corner

Charleston
Stono Ferry

Haddrell's Point

Beaufort

N

0   25   50 Miles

0   25   50 Kilometers

come. Late in the summer, despite having received orders to return to France with his squadron before the hurricane season set in, d'Estaing sailed north. By early September his huge fleet—it included twenty-two ships of the line and eleven frigates—bobbed in the warm, blue-green waters off Tybee Island. Spotting the armada, Britain's commander in Savannah dispatched a swift royal brig to retrieve naval help from New York and to summon Lieutenant Colonel John Maitland and his eight hundred redcoats who were garrisoned in Beaufort, South Carolina, on Port Royal Island.

D'Estaing had come to a southern theater that had witnessed intense, though inconclusive, fighting in the nine months since Savannah's fall. After Savannah was retaken in December 1778, the British had put General Augustine Prevost, who had served in Florida for the past sixteen years, in charge of the pacification of Georgia. The son of a Swede who had soldiered for Britain, the fifty-six-year-old Prevost—of Swiss background himself—had followed in his father's footsteps. This was his third war in the British army. While fighting at Quebec in the Seven Years' War, he had been badly wounded and left with a disfiguring facial scar that led some of his men to secretly call him "Old Bullet Head." Prevost was "brave as Caesar," according to an aide, but he was the first to admit that his years were wearing on him. He was afflicted with gout and enervated—he believed—from long years in the bush in semitropical Florida.[47]

The Americans had also changed commanders in the South, but as time would demonstrate their choice was less salutary than that of the British. Following its recall of Robert Howe, Congress passed over the likes of Gates, Arnold, Greene, and Putnam in favor of Benjamin Lincoln. Ten years younger than Prevost, Lincoln's background could hardly have been more dissimilar. Born in Hingham, Massachusetts, he had soldiered as a militiaman in the French and Indian War, after which he farmed and played a leading role in the Massachusetts protest against British policies. When the colony mobilized in the fall of 1774, Lincoln took up arms again. After Lexington-Concord he was named a lieutenant colonel in the siege army at Boston. He rose steadily in the Continental army, in some measure because he caught the eye of Washington, who was impressed both with his leadership and administrative skills.[48] In 1776 Congress named him a major general, passing over numerous officers, including Arnold. Lincoln fought in New York and commanded the New England militia in the Saratoga campaign, where his right ankle was shattered by a British ball at Bemis Heights. Gates lamented his loss of Lincoln, whom he lauded as "one of the best officers as well as Men" under his command.[49] Shortly after he returned to duty following a lengthy recovery, Congress selected him to replace Howe, viewing him not only as one of the heroes of Saratoga, but as an outsider who was disinterested in southern political battles. He also enjoyed a reputation for tact and diplomacy, qualities that might have brought his predecessor some success. Corpulent and moon faced, Lincoln was still troubled by his year-old wound in the autumn of 1778, and since his youth he had been afflicted with narcolepsy,

General Benjamin Lincoln. Painting by Charles Willson Peale, from life, c. 1781–1783. Lincoln led his troops to America's worst defeat in the war. He was betrayed by many in the defense of Charleston, but a better general would have escaped to fight another day.

which caused him to abruptly fall asleep (though one of his officers remarked that Lincoln "was never asleep when it was necessary for him to be awake").[50]

When Prevost and Lincoln arrived in Savannah and Charleston respectively —on very nearly the same day near the end of 1778—the British held only Savannah. To keep the redcoats out of South Carolina, Lincoln rapidly cobbled together a force of about 1,700 men and, acting much as Washington had on the Delaware before Christmas 1776, posted it at Purrysburg, twenty miles from Savannah on the east side of the Savannah River. But Prevost, at least for the moment, was less interested in South Carolina than in rousing Georgia's back-country Loyalists and, if successful, in stirring the Creeks and Cherokees to once again take up arms against Britain's enemy. Prevost shared Germain's deep-seated conviction that the Loyalists would offer abundant assistance. Like the American secretary, Provost also thought Georgia's pacification would lead inevitably to the reestablishment of British rule in South Carolina.[51]

Prevost got to work in January by sending Colonel Campbell, who had taken Savannah less than a month earlier, to seize Augusta, about 120 miles up the Savannah River. Taking Augusta was easy. Maintaining it hinged on a sizeable turnout by the Loyalists, who not only would have to become the city's civil officials, but to defend it against the insurgents. The Loyalists failed to material-ize. Intimidated by a sizeable Georgia and South Carolina militia force that hov-ered nearby, most Georgia Loyalists—aware of how their brethren in New Jersey and Philadelphia had been abandoned by their protectors—were not about to openly rally around the British flag until the redcoats had thoroughly suppressed and disarmed the rebels. For every Georgia Tory who stepped forward to fight for the Crown, roughly three Georgians took up arms against the king.[52]

Campbell's only hope, it became evident, lay in raising Tories elsewhere. He sent recruiters into the rugged North Carolina backcountry and overnight a Tory force that may have numbered eight hundred was gathered, procured largely from among Scottish immigrants who lived along the state's southern border. They marched for Augusta, but never made it. They crossed the north-west corner of South Carolina, plundering and terrorizing—and, not coinciden-tally, arousing—the inhabitants. Shortly after crossing into Georgia early in February the Tory force ran into a surprise attack launched by a smaller force of South Carolina partisans at Kettle Creek, a tributary of the Savannah River. What ensued was a Tory disaster. More than 150 Loyalists were killed or captured, and some captives were executed. It was a crushing blow, dooming Britain's hold on Augusta. More important, it radically diminished whatever little zeal lingered among the Loyalists. Prevost notified Germain that the Tories could no longer be relied on. Faced with "laws formed by the rebellious provinces [that] are so severe and awful in execution," and rebel neighbors given to "barbarity," the "most zealous amongst them to the King's cause are deterred" from aiding Britain's war effort. "Our success," he added, "must depend on the exertions of the King's troops." And, like Gage, Howe, and Clinton before him, Prevost wanted more of the king's troops.[53]

Having discovered the awful truth about the Loyalists, Prevost abandoned Augusta and turned his gaze on South Carolina. His new course was made possi-ble when Lincoln unwisely moved most of his army to Augusta, leaving Moultrie at Purrysburg with an emasculated force. Prevost also saw an opportunity because the American authorities had deployed so few men to the southern theater. South Carolina's authorities had tried their best to secure more Continentals. Governor Rutledge had written to the state's delegation in Philadelphia decrying both Washington's and Congress's "scarcely credible" tactics in withholding men from the immediate danger in the South in order to have them ready for an unlikely opportunity to act in the North. South Carolina's lieutenant governor, Thomas Bee, minced no words: "the people begin to think that the Southern States are meant to be sacrificed." If that was the case, he added, let South Carolina know so it could surrender on favorable terms.[54]

Seeing his chance to secure much needed supplies in South Carolina, and perhaps to destroy Moultrie's inferior force while he was at it, Prevost crossed into South Carolina late in April. Moultrie retreated, destroying bridges and felling trees in the path of his pursuer, as the rebels had done during their retreat from Ticonderoga. Moultrie, watching in horror as his army shrank from mass desertions, waited breathlessly for Lincoln to come to his aid. He waited in vain. Lincoln, new to the South and to an independent command, discounted Prevost's threat. He did not budge from Augusta. Yet the threat was all too real. In only eight days Prevost's army dashed all the way to Charleston, leaving in its wake a swath of destruction and terror-stricken inhabitants. Still Lincoln refused to come, asserting that Prevost lacked the strength to seriously threaten Charleston. He was half right. Prevost, with barely 2,100 men and no artillery to speak of, was outnumbered by the city's defenders. Taking Charleston was beyond his reach. Or so it seemed. There was a possibility that the city might be gained by bluffing, and that was precisely what Prevost attempted. He went through the motions of preparing to assault the American lines, prefacing his action by issuing a demand for the unconditional surrender of the defenders.[55]

The prospect of Charleston's destruction prompted one of the most dishonorable actions of the war. Governor Rutledge, who had been given near dictatorial powers in the emergency, drafted a proposed settlement that would prevent an attack. His terms were that in return for the city being spared, South Carolina was to remain neutral for the duration of the war, with the final decision regarding "whether the state shall belong to Great Britain, or remain one of the United States [to] be determined by the treaty of peace."[56] Moultrie opposed Rutledge's terms and Colonel Laurens, who had been in the action all along, archly refused the governor's request to deliver the faint-hearted message to Prevost. Rutledge found a messenger, but Prevost, perhaps unwisely, rejected the governor's proffer. He said that he had not come in a legislative capacity. It is more likely that he doubted that Congress would honor Rutledge's offer, as it had refused to abide by the terms that Gates had extended to Burgoyne at Saratoga. Prevost once again demanded instead the surrender of the city and its defenders.

Those with more backbone—and more zeal for independence—than South Carolina's governor, rejoiced in Prevost's rejection of Rutledge's craven offer. "Thank God! We are on our legs again," young Laurens exalted, as the defenders again prepared to fight. Then, to everyone's surprise the threat to the city immediately ended. Prevost, his bluff having been dashed paradoxically by his own hand, dropped his pretensions and withdrew. But he did not immediately abandon South Carolina. His army plundered along the coast for a month, seizing food and valuables from farms and plantations, making little effort to determine whether the victims were Whigs or Tories. Only after Lincoln finally arrived from Augusta—he did not reach Charleston until twelve days after Prevost departed, and did not catch up with the invaders for another five days—did Prevost return to Georgia, leaving behind eight hundred men under Maitland on Johns Island, eighteen miles from Charleston. On June 20, Lincoln, with a three-to-one numerical superiority, attacked Maitland, his only real action in the campaign. The encounter, the Battle of Stono Ferry, resulted in roughly equal losses of about 150 men on each side, and the withdrawal of Maitland's force to

Beaufort on Port Royal Island. After six months, the war in Georgia and South Carolina, like the war as a whole, was stalemated. But the arrival of d'Estaing off the coast in September held the promise of breaking the impasse.[57]

Once D'Estaing landed he discovered to his dismay that only a small force of Continentals was posted in the South. Learning that Lincoln possessed barely one thousand American regulars, d'Estaing briefly considered scrapping the operation. He had agreed to remain in Georgia for only eight days, and he now knew that it would be impossible to raise a suitable force within that time. Ultimately, he stayed on, largely from fear that he would be disgraced at home if he did nothing to liberate Savannah, and that if he should abandon this enterprise—as he had done at Newport a year earlier—the alliance would be gravely threatened. Having decided to remain, he beseeched Lincoln to come at once. D'Estaing had arrived in Georgia with 3,500 troops, a force that included French regulars; some 600 Volunteers of San Domingo, the first free black soldiers to serve in the French army; and more than 150 West Indian volunteers. Over several days, they were joined by what d'Estaing called the "*américains de la georgie.*" Lincoln came from Charleston with his infantry and three hundred light horse under Pulaski. Another three hundred men arrived from Augusta, brought down by General Lachlan McIntosh, a native Georgian who had requested a transfer to the South after Savannah's fall left his family in British custody. Unaccountably, Lincoln's force required twelve days to cover the fifty miles to Savannah, finally arriving on September 16, five days after the previously agreed on date for the armies to rendezvous. Though happy to see the reinforcements, not every French soldier was impressed by the Americans. "[W]hat a disappointment . . . when you see them firsthand," an artillerist remarked. The "troops from the north[ern states] are better," he added.[58] For better or worse, the allied armies were together, and they numbered 7,722 men.

Until the third week in September, when Maitland arrived with his eight hundred men, Prevost had roughly 4,100 men—regulars, Loyalists, even a few armed slaves. Not only were the British heavily outnumbered, Prevost had been complacent about preparing the city's defenses. Only four redoubts had been constructed during the nine months that the British occupied Savannah. But the instant that he spotted the tall spires of the enemy armada, Prevost set men to work in earnest. Entrenching tools were distributed to more than five hundred slaves and many of the regulars. Digging began on an intricate labyrinth of épaulements and traverses, screened by a menacing abatis that surrounded the town. It was the design of the redcoats' chief engineer, James Moncrief, whom Henry Clinton once commended simply as an "engineer who understood his business."[59]

Success in battle often results from seizing the moment. D'Estaing's moment came in the days before Prevost's reinforcements arrived and the city's defenses were strengthened. He let it slip through his fingers. He spent much of this crucial period trying to bluff Prevost into surrendering without a fight, offering liberal terms should he lay down his arms. That was like manna from heaven for the British commander. He agreed to discussions, and he talked and talked, buying time for Maitland to march in from Beaufort and to continue work on his defenses. Maitland finally arrived, following another of those epic journeys of this war, a trek in wilting heat through marshes and swamps abounding in "Sandfliegen . . . Schlangen und Crocodillen [sand flies, snakes and alligators]," according to a wide-eyed German soldier.

A week after rebuffing rebel entreaties to launch an attack immediately, d'Estaing put his men to work digging parallels for a siege operation. Wielding picks and spades in Savannah's oppressive summer heat, which clings tenaciously to coastal Georgia into the autumn, was hard labor, though no more difficult than it had been to move the heavy guns from the ships to the siege lines. Ten days were required to get the artillery—thirty-seven cannon and nine large mortars—in place.

On October 4—a month and two days after work had begun on Moncrief's formidable defensive system—d'Estaing opened a shuddering bombardment of Savannah. For the regulars in their entrenchments, it sounded worse than it was. They took virtually no casualties. But the shelling was a nightmare for civilians. Numerous residents, including untold numbers of slaves, perished. Everyone sought refuge. Some, like Prevost's wife and General McIntosh's family, fled to cellars, where they crawled under heavy mattresses while the shells burst nearby. One citizen was awakened in his bed by a cannonball that crashed into his house "and drove the plastering all about." He feared seeking shelter in his basement, as it was well stocked with highly flammable rum, but he saw no other option. He survived that night, though a few days later his house was set ablaze in another shelling. Fortunately, he said, "my negro . . . drew out of the flames" many of his most valued possessions. Many other residents of the city hurried to the waterfront, where they huddled beneath the tall riverbanks, safe from all but an unlikely direct hit. They had to share their sanctuary with huge wharf rats, and for days they alternately endured a blistering sun or were lashed by rain and howling winds during ferocious afternoon thunderstorms. Not every soldier in the siege army was comfortable with the havoc wrought by the cannonading. "I feel most sincerely for the poor women and children," a Georgia militiaman wrote at the time. "God knows what will become of them." He learned a few days later when a deserter brought word that many civilians had been "killed in their beds" and "mangled" in their basements."[60]

After a week's bombardment, d'Estaing summoned a council of war and proposed an assault on Prevost's lines. The American officers changed step. An attack was premature, they now said, arguing that the odds against success were far too long. But d'Estaing overruled them. His fleet had been anchored off the Georgia coast for forty days and intelligence was warning that the royal squadron in the Caribbean, and maybe even a task force from New York, was coming after him. Even if they never appeared, he knew that each day he remained he ran the risk of being hit with an awful Atlantic tempest, worse perhaps than the one that had battered his fleet off Newport. He consulted his engineers regarding how much longer it would take to secure the approaches to the enemy's lines. Ten days! He did not have that long. D'Estaing ordered an assault for 4:00 in the morning on October 9.

D'Estaing, like Prevost, knew that the emplacements on the British right flank were the weakest link of Moncrief's resplendent system of fortifications. That was where d'Estaing planned to attack. After feints had been made elsewhere along the line to divert the redcoats, his main force was to spring out of the tall, thick underbrush in the predawn darkness and overwhelm the British right, setting in motion their envelopment. It was a good plan, but inevitably things went awry.[61]

The attack started ninety minutes late. The feints were carried off in darkness, but the first streaks of light could be seen in the eastern sky before the main attack was launched. Nor were all the units in place when the lead forces moved out. The main attack commenced with ranks of men wading out of rice swamps and advancing on the redcoats' Spring Hill redoubt. They were led personally by d'Estaing, who was in the thick of the fighting throughout (he was later characterized by one of his officers as "a true grenadier," though a "poor general"). The attackers ran into a hail of fire, including a murderous artillery shelling. They were driven back, reformed and came on again, and again. (They "obstinately persevered," Prevost said later in his report.)[62] Both the French and the Americans, including militiamen, displayed great courage, scrambling up a bluff and surmounting the formidable abatis, but they could not scale the tall parapet. Little help came from the horse unit, which was mauled by a murderous crossfire that brought down Pulaski, fatally shot in the leg and chest. At every point of attack, the allies were repulsed and suffered staggering casualties. Savannah was another Bunker Hill, only this time the British were the victors, and they retained what they had defended. The allies suffered 117 killed and 707 wounded, including d'Estaing, who took shrapnel in his arm and a bullet in his right calf. The British losses totaled some seventy-five men. Almost all the allied losses were at the Spring Hill redoubt, where about 4,000 men had been repulsed by the 110 redcoats within the fortification, with some help from another 165 redcoats in the nearby Carolina redoubt, and immeasurable support from the artillerymen. Thus, 20 percent of the attackers at this key site were casualties (nearly 40 percent of Virginia's Continentals were cut down). Later, some of the British defenders marveled at the carnage on this battlefield, having never seen anything that compared with it. Bodies were literally stacked high in the ditch before the redoubt and corpses littered the open field beyond to a distance of more than fifty yards.[63]

Acrid smoke still curled above the bloody battlefield when d'Estaing called off the siege and marched his men back to their ships. Some of the rebel soldiers, including South Carolina's Charles Cotesworth Pinckney, who one day would nearly be elected president—in the election of 1800—believed that a siege could still win out, as the British were short of ammunition and provisions. But it was over. When Washington learned what had occurred, he put a rosy face on the defeat, a skill that he had perfected. The loss was "by no means as disagreeable as represented," he stated, as "we met with no opposition afterwards in removing our stores and baggage." In his more candid moments he acknowledged that Savannah had been a "disaster" that "puts matters . . . on a delicate footing in the South." He confessed too that he did "not know what we can do more" in that theater.[64]

THE YEAR 1779 had been filled with disappointment and a notable lack of significant achievement for the Americans and their ally. Hostilities persisted and though it is clearer in retrospect than it was to contemporaries, Britain's staying power and its Southern Strategy were beginning to weigh heavily on an increasingly war-weary American public.

No one knew better than Washington the dangers that potentially lay ahead in campaign 1780. He shuddered to think of the turns the war might have taken in 1779, he said, had not Clinton been kept by "providential" occurrences from "pursuing [more] vigorous measures."[65]

Gone was the glowing optimism that had prevailed eighteen months earlier when word of the French alliance reached America. As 1779 faded into a new year, victory seemed more elusive than at any time in the war, more remote even than it had appeared to be in the darkest days of 1776. At that time there had been reason for hope, as foreign help was on the way. But as 1780 approached, concern was growing over how long France would remain in a war from which its gains were so negligible.

16

CHOICES, 1780

A MONTH after d'Estaing's failure in Savannah, John Adams, America's
minister plenipotentiary for peace, sailed for France on the frigate *La
Sensible*. Adams learned of his appointment only about six weeks after he
returned from a fifteen-month assignment in France. Accepting Congress's call
meant a second hazardous wartime crossing of the Atlantic and still another long
separation from his family. (Between his service in Congress and abroad, he had
already been apart from Abigail and his children during fifty-five of the past sixty
months.) Many men—perhaps most—would not have accepted the appointment,
but Adams never hesitated to accept. He thirsted after glory, and hoped for
accolades once he negotiated the peace settlement. Despite Abigail's pleas that
she be permitted to accompany him, he refused. He feared what might happen to
her should *La Sensible* be captured, but he also wanted her at home to manage the
farm, their security for latter years. When he accepted Congress's appointment,
Adams told Abigail that she was "all that is dear to me in this World." He also
reminded her that if the Revolution was to succeed, the revolutionaries must
make personal sacrifices. "We shall be happy, whenever our Country is so,"
he said.[1]

Adams's outlook mingled optimism with profound concern, as he looked
toward 1780. The European diplomatic situation appeared favorable for the
United States, as Britain was isolated, the scope of its imperial power having led
Europe to be nearly "universally and Sincerely united in the Desire of reducing
her." Furthermore, he remained confident that France continued to see "the
great Importance of our Independence to their Interests," and he was optimistic

that the United States might open trade with some of the neutral nations in Europe, and possibly even secure loans from Holland and Prussia.[2] On the other hand, Adams feared that France and Spain failed to understand how to win this war. It could only be won in America, he believed. While those European powers lacked the strength to score breakthrough victories in Europe, they possessed naval superiority in America. If the Franco-Spanish navies destroyed Britain's Caribbean trade or seized some of Britain's prized sugar islands, or if the Franco-American forces scored a decisive victory in a joint operation, London would be driven to the bargaining table. That, Adams was convinced, was how to win the war. But that raised another matter. Adams remained convinced that Franklin would never push France to make greater military exertions in the American theater. "He may be a Philosopher, for what I know, but he is not a sufficient Statesman," Adams declared, and he added that Franklin was "too old, too infirm, too indolent and dissipated" to spend the time learning what he should know. Adams urged Congress to "give positive Instructions to their Minister." That is, he wanted Congress to lean hard on Franklin.[3]

Before Adams sailed he had already decided to petition Vergennes to commit a larger fleet to American waters and to consider sending over a large French army. Neither was a new idea. Almost a year earlier Adams and his fellow commissioners had beseeched the French foreign minister to commit a greater navy to American waters. He had also shared his ideas with Lafayette, whom he had met in Paris early in 1779, and exhorted him to seek to convince Vergennes that the "Ennemy . . . are weak in Canada—weak in Hallifax—weak in Rhode Island—weak at New York [,] weak in the Floridas, and weak in every one of the West India Islands." Britain's possession of each of its holdings depended on the retention of the others "for reciprocal support," he told Lafayette. Lose one or two and it would be "impossible for the others to subsist." By itself, Adams had said, the Continental army could never retake New York or Rhode Island, but it could succeed with the help of a sizeable allied fleet. An operation "by a sea force cooperating with [French and American] land forces" held the prospect "for conducting this War to a Speedy, successfull and glorious Conclusion."[4] Like Charles Jenkinson, the royal official who in the dark days after Saratoga had seen hope for Britain through a Southern Strategy, Adams glimpsed a way for the allies to shake off their inertia and reverse the present alarming course of the war.

Adams bade goodbye to his loved ones and boarded the French frigate on a grey November day, exhilarated at the prospect of someday negotiating an historic peace treaty. In no time, he and his sons (he had brought along twelve-year-old John Quincy and Charles, who was nine) found themselves on a vexed journey. Early on, *La Sensible* was badly damaged by a dreadful storm that tossed the vessel about like a rag doll for three terrifying days. During the two weeks after the tempest, Adams took his turn on four-hour shifts operating manual pumps in a desperate effort to keep the maimed ship afloat. The distraught vessel barely limped into port in Spain, from which Adams and his sons—accompanied by four other New Englanders, two servants, and two Spanish guides—traveled overland in a little mule caravan from Ferrol to the French border. At almost every step, they coped with poor and dangerous mountain roads and ever-present cold and fog, winding their way from one remote village to another, and to a steady succession of flea and lice-infested beds. It took more than fifteen days to reach French soil, where they traded their mules for a chaise, ending what Adams subsequently called the most severe trial of his life.[5]

A mixed bag awaited Adams when he finally reached Paris in February 1780, ninety days after leaving home. He was delighted to discover that France was sending naval reinforcements to the Caribbean under Comte de Guichen, a force that was readying to sail just as he reached Paris. Soon, too, Adams ascertained that a French army of 5,500 men under Donatien de Vimeur, Comte de Rochambeau, was also preparing for departure, though Vergennes kept its destination a secret from his ally for five months. Gathering what information he could from newspapers, Adams clutched at the hope that it was headed for America, and he was cheered by the belief that "whatever its destination it cannot fail of being beneficial to my Country by making a Diversion at least." Privately, however, he raged at Vergennes's unwillingness to share the information, or any intelligence. "We get nothing. They communicate nothing . . . to any body, not to me nor to Dr. Franklin," he fumed. Finally, in July, Vergennes confided that Rochambeau was being sent to Rhode Island. Adams's hopes soared. "The English proud and porr . . . Still think themselves a Match for France and Spain, and America if not for all the World, but [its] delirium cannot last long."[6]

Adams's joy rapidly evaporated. He wished to make public his mission, hoping that an awareness of the presence of America's peace envoy would strengthen Britain's antiwar faction. Vergennes objected strenuously, and sensibly, to any such announcement. It would only strengthen Lord North, he told Adams, as the prime minister could claim that his policies had driven the Americans to hunger for peace. Adams next proposed a trip to The Hague, hoping to secure a Dutch loan. Once again, Vergennes demurred, this time from fear that it would provoke Britain into declaring war on the Dutch, with potentially ruinous consequences for French commerce. To Adams, the episode underscored America's quandary. The United States was part of an alliance that it could not do without, but the affiliation was filled with potential hazards. France was the dominant partner and its interests dictated its—and increasingly America's—behavior. As never before, Adams fretted that American interests might be neglected, or even lost. Within weeks of reaching Europe, he told Congress that America had no choice but to wage war as if it had no ally: "Americans must be Soldiers, they must war by Sea and Land: they have no other Security."[7]

IF FRANCE KEPT ITS INTENTIONS about Rochambeau's army from its American ally, it most certainly concealed the truth of its troubled relationship with Spain. Adams would have been startled, and distraught, had he known how strained the friendship had become between Madrid and Versailles. Following the aborted invasion of England, Spain had sought to persuade the French to gather together another armada and try again, but Vergennes stood firm. As Britain would have adequate time to prepare, Vergennes doubted that any French army could mount a successful invasion of England. He repeatedly told Floridablanca that their objective must be to humiliate Great Britain, not destroy it. Any attempt at its destruction, he argued, would sow alarm among neutral nations that feared the overturning of the existing balance of power, driving them into Britain's camp. But Spain was obsessed by Gibraltar, the great prize that had lured it into the war. Immediately upon entering the conflict, Spain had imposed a blockade on the British garrison at Gibraltar, and Floridablanca now argued that a threatened invasion of England would tie down the Royal Navy's home fleet, impeding it from supplying the hungry redcoats. The threat to invade England, he said, was the easiest means of forcing the garrison on Gibraltar to succumb.

Vergennes first tried to win his battle with Floridablanca by claiming that the French navy was spread too thin to contemplate another invasion. It faced urgent needs in America, the Caribbean, Indian Ocean, North Sea, and Mediterranean, he insisted. Floridablanca greeted that argument with unconcealed skepticism, which only further strained their relationship. Vergennes finally found a way to win this diplomatic contest. As Spain had not paid its share of the 1779 campaign, Vergennes indicated his willingness to try another invasion, but on the condition that Madrid begin paying its portion in advance. Spain quickly abandoned its insistence on an invasion, leaving France free to augment its fleet in the West Indies and to dispatch Rochambeau.[8]

In the meantime Spain strengthened its Gibraltar squadron, bringing it to eighteen ships of the line. What neither the Spanish nor the French knew, or expected, was that London would act with uncharacteristic audacity. During more than two months of anxious deliberation, North's government made several difficult choices in the winter of 1779–1780, each forced on it by Britain's perilous situation. For the first time in a string of wars Great Britain stood without an ally against the combined might of France and Spain, facing the still lingering possibility of an invasion, peril at Gibraltar, danger in the Caribbean, and the all-too-real likelihood—or so the ministers believed—of an American invasion of Canada. After weeks of deliberation, the cabinet took two steps. It sent reinforcements to Jamaica. Simultaneously, it launched two intriguing diplomatic initiatives. On the one hand, the ministry sought to either draw Russia into an alliance or, failing that, to persuade St. Petersburg to act to mediate the American war in Britain's favor. On the other hand, London explored making peace with Spain. As the latter was an especially delicate matter, the Spanish were approached at low levels. Private citizens—including George Johnstone, one of the Carlisle commissioners—spoke with various Spanish envoys, some in London, some elsewhere. But the principal channel of contact was through an Irish priest, Father Thomas Hussey, who, before the war, had first studied in Seville, then served as a chaplain at the Spanish embassy in London. Late in 1779, Hussey traveled to Madrid. As the feeling out process got under way, North's government debated what it might be willing to surrender to secure Spain's withdrawal from the war. These hard-nosed discussions produced a division between one faction that was willing to yield Gibraltar and another that preferred surrendering some of Britain's West Indian possessions.

In due time, a compromise was reached. While the ministers leaned toward relinquishing West Florida and the Mosquito Coast (the east coast of present-day Nicaragua), they agreed late in October to attempt to relieve the garrison at Gibraltar and to send further reinforcements to the Caribbean. Those decisions had hardly been reached before news poured in that affected matters. Between mid-November and late December, London learned not only that France had disbanded its invasion army, and that a small British naval force—dispatched when Spain had entered the war six months earlier—had conquered Spanish Omoa on the Bay of Honduras. North's government was still assimilating those tidings when the news of d'Estaing's defeat in Savannah reached London. The dramatic turn of events left Britain freer to act than before. Meeting on Christmas Eve, the cabinet made its final plans. It opted for a generous commitment of force not just to save Jamaica, Britain's most important Caribbean possession—it produced 40 percent of the sugar and 90 percent of the rum in Britain's empire— but to permit offensive operations in those warm tropical waters. It also agreed to a greater expedition to assure the relief of Gibraltar. Admiral George Rodney, with eighteen ships of the line, was to shepherd a convoy laden with stores for the beleaguered men at Gibraltar and troop transports crammed with three battalions, one for Gibraltar and two for the West Indies. In all, five thousand men were being deployed. The cabinet had made some exacting choices. To vest Rodney with such a large squadron was to reduce the Channel fleet substantially. To deploy so many men was also to gamble—it was a conscious roll of the dice, made after considerable discussion—that the Americans would not try anytime soon to invade Canada, which had been left weak and vulnerable.[9]

Rodney—who was sixty-two years old that winter—hailed from a family that had furnished soldiers since the Crusades. This was his third British war. Through December, as London employed one ruse after another to make its adversaries believe that the fleet was sailing directly for America, Rodney slowly outfitted his squadron. In the last hours of 1779, he put to sea. Despite Britain's subterfuge, the French not only guessed Rodney's destination, they knew his strength. Ten days before Christmas, Vergennes advised Madrid that a large squadron was being readied at Portsmouth, and around New Year's Day he told the Spanish that Rodney would sail with possibly as many as two dozen ships of the line. Remarkably, in one of the worst blunders of the war, neither the French nor the Spanish were terribly alarmed. Both believed the Spanish fleet that guarded the Straits of Gibraltar could cope with Rodney.

A bit more than a week into his mission, Rodney seized a Spanish ship of the line and twenty-one merchant vessels in a convoy overflowing with valuable naval materials. Eight days later he surprised the Spanish fleet off Cape St. Vincent. The Spanish commander, Don Juan de Lángara, knew that the enemy was coming, but he had failed to send out his frigates to scout for the British fleet. The Spanish were also undermanned, as many of their ships were in port for repairs. Giving orders from his bed, where he had been confined with the gout, Rodney attacked in what became known as the Moonlight Battle. It was a rout. The Spanish lost six ships of the line. Madrid's hopes of retaking Gibraltar had vanished. Rodney, with a swagger, notified London that "Great Britain was again Mistress of the Straits." Two days later he replenished Gibraltar.[10]

When Rodney completed the Gibraltar operation and sailed for the Caribbean in late January, the French squadron under de Guichen—the fillip of delight for Adams upon his arrival in Paris—was about to ease out of Brest on its voyage to the tropics. Even as de Guichen prepared to depart, intelligence reached London that yet another French squadron was outfitting, though its destination was unknown. The initial reports convinced the Admiralty that it was to be a small task force, perhaps no more than three or four vessels, leading London to conclude that its destination must be India. In time, intelligence reported that the task force was growing rapidly. It was, of course, the fleet that was to carry Rochambeau's expeditionary force to Rhode Island. Naval command had been given to Commodore the Chevalier de Ternay, a forty-year veteran with a reputation as a diplomat—thought to be essential for dealing with the rude and bumptious Americans—and he had been given seven ships of the line, three frigates, a cutter, a hospital ship, and some three thousand marines with which to escort the troop transports. A squadron of such size, London concluded, could mean only one thing. It must be headed for America. Germain reckoned almost immediately that its destination was Canada. He came to that conclusion in part because he believed that the Continental army was too weak, even with French assistance, to contemplate retaking New York. Germain knew that Lafayette had returned to America and, after the fashion of Pavlov's dogs, when the secretary heard the name "Lafayette," he thought "Canada." The expectation that Canada would be attacked forced another difficult choice on the ministry. There were no more troops to be sent to America, but there were ships, and their potential availability led to the final great battle within the ministry over strategy for campaign 1780. Arguing that France's actions meant unequivocally that the allies had no plans for invading England, Germain proposed stripping away eleven ships from the Channel fleet and sending them to North America. That was far too risky for the Admiralty's taste. In the end, it was agreed to detach five ships, a decision made in some measure because of the king's backing—prodding would be more accurate—for meeting the presumed threat to Canada. Admiral Thomas Graves was vested with command and feverish work began to see that he could get away at least concurrently with Ternay's departure. London failed in that hope. Although unfavorable weather delayed the sailing of the French fleet for three weeks, Graves's squadron was unable to depart until two weeks later.[11]

London's decision to send Graves's fleet to America was not reached easily. France's decision to commit an army to America came no easier. Since 1777 many French officers in America had implored their government to consider sending an army to do what they believed the ragged Continentals were incapable of doing. No one argued more earnestly than Lafayette that Washington needed the assistance of French regulars, but Franklin also told Vergennes as early as February 1779 that "4 or 5000" French troops could be "advantageously used" by his countrymen. For quite some time Vergennes remained unmoved. Before campaign 1779 he saw little reason for panic with regard to the rebels' conduct of the war. He not only had committed d'Estaing's fleet in 1778, but France kept considerable quantities of clothing, arms, and munitions flowing across the Atlantic. However, as 1780 beckoned, America's financial woes and Washington's newfound caution caused the French to reconsider. Vergennes postponed a decision until he knew the outcome of his navy's action in Savannah, but when d'Estaing came home on crutches in December bearing word of the sad fate of the joint operation to liberate Georgia's capital, the foreign minister decided that something must be done to restore the rebels' confidence in France. He was additionally alarmed by the accounts of conditions in America brought back by French volunteers. Some portrayed a war-weary ally the plight of which resembled that of a seriously ill patient struggling to remain alive. (According to one French volunteer, there now was more enthusiasm for the American Revolution in Parisian coffeehouses than in the American states.) Almost as importantly, Vergennes learned about the same time—through Lafayette—that both Washington and Hamilton had requested a French army. Washington did so in a sideways manner, making his request in a letter to Lafayette written without congressional concurrence. It may have been the most cloying letter that Washington ever wrote. Maundering about his "esteem and attachment[,] . . . warmth of affection[,] . . . [and] perfect love and attachment" for Lafayette, Washington promised that should his young French friend return "at the head of a Corps of gallant French (if circumstances should require this) . . . I shall welcome you in all the warmth of friendship to Columbia's shore." Hamilton did not beat around the bush. "It would be good if 2,000 troops could be sent over," he told Lafayette, adding that should the French regulars join with the Continentals, it "would ensure" victory over Clinton's "considerably diminish[ed]" army.[12]

In the end, Vergennes committed an army to America because he believed French interests would best be served by doing so. With the second anniversary of the Franco-American alliance looming, the foreign minister could hardly point to a single success from the war. Worse, the nightmare of a protracted war with Great Britain now appeared to be all too likely, a prospect made the more unsettling for Vergennes by his foreboding that both of France's allies lacked staying power. If something was not done immediately, France could find itself in the unpalatable position of having to fight alone against Great Britain. Only the presence of a French army could break the stalemate in America, and it was in America, Vergennes now understood, that the war had to be won. In January, he recommended the plan code-named *Expédition Particulière*: the dispatch of an army across the Atlantic. Louis XVI's council gave its approval on February 2, and not long thereafter it authorized a subsidy of 6,000,000 livres for the United States, this atop the 8,000,000 livres that would be needed to provide for Rochambeau's army. These expenditures pushed the French deficit above 46,000,000 livres, a harsh and menacing danger that increased the need for France to find a way to speedily bring the war to a successful conclusion.[13]

The Americans faced hard economic choices of their own. Prices had risen dramatically two years earlier. By late 1779, they had reached such staggering levels that increasing numbers of people were forced to do without essential items. Salt which had sold for a dollar a barrel before the war, had skyrocketed to thirty-six dollars, and in many places it could be found only on the black market. "A waggon load of money will scarcely purchase a waggon load of provision," said Washington at a time when it cost $20,000 to purchase a horse and $400 to acquire a hat. Ordinary citizens often saw the problem as one of an "excessive scarcity of money," for from their vantage point they lacked the funds with which to purchase commodities whose prices had soared into the stratosphere.[14] Something had to be done. "[W]e are Pretty near the End of the tether," one congressman sighed early in 1780. New York's delegation collectively proclaimed that the United States faced a choice between "some firm and decided measure, or public bankruptcy and ruin."[15] Short of resorting to widespread confiscation of grain and livestock, Congress had almost no hope of supplying the army. But confiscation might destroy morale, already buckling from war weariness, according both to several French officers and British intelligence. Besides, there often was little to confiscate. Many yeomen, despairing of getting good money for their crops on the open market, or fearful that the army would seize their produce, had stopped growing surpluses, virtually becoming subsistence farmers. This was especially true in Pennsylvania, New York, and New Jersey, where farmers were already owed nearly $60,000,000 for crops and cattle that they had earlier sold to the army, a payback that perhaps most had abandoned hope of ever seeing.[16]

Congress acted in March 1780. After much "Labour and Deliberation," its president informed the states, Congress had taken "the happiest Expedient that could be adopted." To this point, Congress had fought the economic malaise by attempting to appreciate the currency back to its 1775 value. Now it took a different tack. It issued a new paper currency and virtually repudiated the old paper money. It also revalued—or devalued—old Continentals at 40:1 specie, and, as one congressman explained, it hoped "to call in all the [old] money in about one year and by taxes [to] destroy it." Congress additionally relinquished to the states some of the responsibilities that it had previously tried to meet, including paying the army, and rather than resorting to requisitions of money, it called for itemized supplies from each state, leaving it to the states to determine how to pay for those commodities.[17]

This confronted the states with difficult choices, as the leaders in every province feared that the citizenry had been pushed to the limit on taxation. Rather than impose additional taxes, every state took a step that virtually all had previously refused to consider, even after Congress had urged the action—the seizure and sale of Loyalist property. Massachusetts took the lead by seizing the property of "Certain Notorious Conspirators" that it designated (such as the last royal governor and lieutenant governor) as well as that of "absconders," Tories who had fled the state and could be deemed "open avowed enemies." Most states not only adopted legislation that followed the pattern set by the Bay State, they also jettisoned price regulation, an initiative that they hoped would keep prices high as the dollar was made more sound, thus encouraging farmers to produce a surplus once again.[18]

At Continental army headquarters a cautious optimism prevailed. Washington greeted the news warily, hoping against hope that the new measures would "have a salutary operation, and give to our affairs in general a more agreeable countenance."[19] James Madison, who had entered Congress only days before, was equally cautious, predicting only that the new scheme would "probably create great perplexity and complaints" in some quarters.[20]

PRIVATE CITIZENS, like government officials, were faced with an endless array of decisions. None was reached with greater difficulty than the decision of Joseph Galloway, the Pennsylvania Tory, to sail for England in 1778. His choice was made the more burdensome as it meant leaving behind his wife, Grace. She refused to leave, preferring to remain in Philadelphia and fight to retain the family's property. Earlier, in peaceful times, Galloway had been a successful lawyer and politician. Together with Benjamin Franklin, he had formed one of America's earliest political parties, the Quaker Party, which dominated Pennsylvania politics during much of the twenty years prior to the Revolution, a period in which Galloway served several terms as speaker of the provincial assembly. He led Pennsylvania's delegation to the First Continental Congress in 1774, where he labored to find a compromise solution to the imperial crisis. Although reelected to Congress in 1775, he had refused to serve in a body that waged war with the mother country. Choosing neutrality, he retired to "Trevose" in Bucks County, one of the family's five homes, but in November 1776, as Cornwallis pursued Washington across New Jersey, Galloway opportunistically proclaimed his loyalty to Great Britain. He sailed with the British armada that invaded Pennsylvania in 1777, located supplies for the British army during the campaign for Philadelphia, and provided intelligence that Cornwallis subsequently characterized as "very material" to the redcoats' success. During the occupation, Galloway served as Philadelphia's superintendent general of the police, recruited Loyalists for the army, and dipped into his own wealth to raise a troop of Loyalist cavalry. Easily the most visible civilian in the service of Great Britain in Pennsylvania, Galloway was the most hated Tory in his province. Facing certain arrest if he lingered after Philadelphia was abandoned, Galloway, with his eighteen-year-old daughter Elizabeth in tow, accompanied the British to New York City, from where they sailed for England. He was drawn to London in hopes of introducing his daughter into society—a strategy that succeeded, as she shortly married an English aristocrat—and to campaign to alter Britain's conduct of the war.[21]

Galloway almost immediately had an opportunity to speak out. His chance came when the Howe brothers demanded, and received, a Parliamentary inquiry to clear their names. Conducted in May and June 1779, the Howes fought to transfer blame for Britain's military failures to Germain. The secretary, in turn, conducted a rebuttal, in the course of which Galloway was summoned to testify. Whatever Galloway may have thought of Germain, he was anxious to denigrate General Howe, to show that the war could have been won—and was yet winnable —through aggressive leadership. With his judgment fed by reverie, Galloway claimed that although four-fifths of Americans opposed independence—a preposterous allegation to all but the true believers—Howe had failed to make proper use of the vast legions of Loyalists. Through excessive caution, he went on, Howe had repeatedly, and shamefully, squandered his incredible numerical superiority. He also invidiously charged that Howe had erred egregiously by sailing up the Chesapeake to invade Pennsylvania. He might have landed anywhere on the New Jersey coast and successfully taken Philadelphia in a brief campaign, leaving him ample time to rescue Burgoyne.[22]

Outraged by Galloway's claims, the Howes alleged that he had been bribed to make false statements. Taking a line from Shakespeare's *Romeo and Juliet*, Lord Howe remarked that Galloway's "poverty but not his will consented" to a payoff, a charge reiterated by Burke and others in the peace faction. The Howes demanded an opportunity to question their accuser, but North was eager for Galloway's indictment of General Howe, and implicit defense of ministerial policy, to be the final word. On the day set for the cross-examination of Galloway, General Howe arrived several minutes late—what could have been more in character?—and North, seizing his chance, suspended the inquiry.[23]

Throughout the inquiry, backers of the Howes and the peace faction joined forces, the one anxious to defend policies that they had supported, the other eager to demonstrate the folly of continuing the war. Toward the end of the hearings, the advocates of peace introduced a resolution designed to end the war. It went further than the motion they had backed unsuccessfully following Saratoga. At that time, they had advocated a cease-fire, repeal of all parliamentary acts respecting America, and the opening of peace talks. Now they called for a new ministry that would explore avenues to peace. Their campaign for peace could not have come at a less propitious moment. The French and Spanish fleets were readying their attempted invasion of England, a threat that restored national pride in an instant. North's majority rebuffed the motion without a division.[24]

Although the foes of the war had been rebuffed, Galloway grew more apprehensive that the peace advocates would ultimately win out. On reaching England, he had been startled to discover the number of newspapers that treated the war as lost, a theme that rose to a crescendo in a bewildering stream of pamphlets that appeared in the wake of Parliament's inquiry. Galloway believed that the war could still be won, but he knew that Britain would not fight endlessly in a stalemated war. Displaying an almost legendary energy, Galloway took up his pen in the summer of 1779 to do what he could to secure a British victory before time ran out. He became the Loyalists' principal polemicist, churning out thirteen pamphlets before the war ended, nine in the thirty months following the Howe inquiry. In one tract after another, each written in a bristly style, he asserted that Britain faced ruin if it lost America. Conversely, if the Anglo-American union could be preserved, the two peoples, in their combined might, could sweep across North America and through South America, erecting the richest, most powerful empire in history. But Britain must first win the war. Adopting a confident tone, Galloway asserted that victory was possible if only London would make three changes in its conduct of the war: its army must "be *ordered into the field*" to wage a relentless offensive war against Washington's army; it must shed its "romantic sentiments" and employ terror tactics by turning the redcoats into the "soldier-executioner"; finally, it must tap into the vast legion of American Loyalists.[25]

The peace faction had long regarded Galloway and his ilk as "eminently outrageous," and they now dismissed his cant as a formula for prolonging a war that could not be won. Burke responded that "we might have kept [America] very easily, but when the natural Bonds of dominion are so broken, it is better . . . to look for a friendship that will hold, than an Authority that will not."[26] But the peace faction was not Galloway's only foe. He burned his bridges with the ministry through his continued sniping at Britain's misguided military strategy. Ultimately, he was left with an audience that included few save other desperate Tories.

IN THIS SEASON of recrimination, friends of the government rebutted Galloway's charges, and so, too, did John Adams from Paris. Answering Galloway was in some respects a difficult choice for Adams, as he knew that Vergennes wished him to remain silent. But Adams had already traduced his ally's wishes, making it easier to do so in this instance. For six weeks after his arrival in France, Adams had stewed over Vergennes's opposition to an announcement that he was commissioned to negotiate the peace settlement. The more he thought about it, the more Adams became convinced that while it might be in France's interest for him to remain silent, it was not in America's best interest, and he was the representative of the United States. Driven by his swiftly mounting agitation, Adams chose to defy Vergennes. Acting through Edmund Jenings, an American-born inter-mediary in London, who in all likelihood was an American agent or a double agent, Adams in April 1780 placed an anonymous notice of his mission in London's *General Advertiser*. In the months that followed it was as if a conveyor belt ran from his desk in Paris to Jenings's London residence. The voluble Adams dashed off essays that countered speeches by Germain and others, and even authored an account of his wintertime odyssey through Spain. In the spring, he learned of the first of Galloway's pamphlets. Adams was not fond of Galloway. He had clashed with him at the First Continental Congress six years earlier. Now, in light of the Pennsylvanian's wartime activities, Adams sneered privately that "a meaner, falser, heart, never circulated Blood" in any man. Adams answered Galloway in twelve brief essays. He said little about the conduct of the war. Instead, he wished to demonstrate that American independence would not harm Britain, but also to convince the British that the war could not be settled short of total American independence. Curiously, Jenings, who said the essays were "of such Importance, that I shall be careful to whom, they are Trusted," appears to have sat on them for two years before seeing them into print.[27]

Adams's choice to defy Vergennes cost him dearly. While he acted in secret, he also acted clumsily—who else might have submitted an account of his Spanish travels—and Vergennes knew what the American envoy was doing. Since December 1778, when Adams had mobilized the other commissioners to pressure France for a greater naval commitment, Vergennes had concluded that he was a man with an indomitable will. What the French foreign minister most wanted was a compliant American peace negotiator, one who would not get in the way of France's realization of its territorial and economic objectives. In June 1780, in light of Adams's most recent provocations, Vergennes moved to rid himself of a troublesome envoy who was regarded in the foreign ministry as "*Bien Scandaleux*." Spinning his web perfectly, Vergennes summoned Adams to discuss Congress's recent attempt to revalue America's currency, a matter that he should have taken up with Franklin. Vergennes expected Adams to balk at the French position on the issue, and when he did the foreign minister instructed his minister in Philadelphia to seek Adams's recall on the ground that he found it impossible to work with the rebel envoy.[28]

SOME IN THIS WAR made good choices. Others, such as Adams and Galloway, injured themselves through their choices. But no one suffered a greater injury from another's choice than Grace Galloway, who bore the heavy burden of her husband's decisions. Staying on in Philadelphia, she felt the hatred and contempt of many revolutionaries, was spurned by old friends, feared for her safety, and eventually lost her homes and nearly all of her possessions. The Pennsylvania General Assembly, forced from Philadelphia to York when Howe came in 1777, thirsted for revenge against those who had aided the British. While Philadelphia was still occupied by the British army, it passed legislation permitting the seizure of Tory-owned items useful to the Continental army. Subsequently, additional legislation allowed the confiscation of Loyalist property, an act passed almost two years before other states resorted to expropriation. Immediately after the British army abandoned Philadelphia, a newly created Committee of Safety in the city swooped down on the Tories. Grace Galloway, the wife of a man who was viewed by every patriot as the archtraitor, was one of the first to face eviction. For two months, she fought successfully in the courts to keep from being turned out, but on August 20, 1778, a party of glowering agents led by Charles Willson Peale, the soldier-artist, broke into her mansion at Sixth and Market, and removed her.[29] She was permitted to take her clothing, but not her furniture, a penalty imposed, Peale declared, both because her husband "had treated people Cruely" and had acted with "Generosity" toward British officers. "I was drove out of my house distitute," Grace said that evening, as she moved into modest rental quarters.

"[F]riendless and alone," she felt as if she was "an Outcast." The worst acts of "cruilty," she lamented, came from those who had once "pretended to be My friends." Now they "come not to see me," she sighed. She cried out that "all we had [is] gone," including her carriage, seized and sold to a patriot who one day clattered past her as she walked along a Philadelphia street in a cold rain. Although Grace continued to fight in the courts to regain her property, she was never optimistic. "I know all is lost," she admitted confidentially. She was also "vexed About My Mony" in the face of the runaway inflation, not to mention the pernicious wartime taxes, which she feared "will eat up ye whole income & I shall have Nothing." Some Tory acquaintances held out hope for a British victory, but she no longer thought that was likely. As 1780 loomed, she mourned: "I fear it is over with ye english[.] I am undone." At the nadir of despondency, she sobbed that she was "wrap[p]ed in impenetrable Darkness," faced with the loss of everything. But worse than all the slights and deprivation was the separation from her daughter. It was, she said, "a Dagger to My Mind." Initially, she turned her wrath on the Howes for her misfortune, but in time Grace blamed her husband. His "baseness had pulled down me & my child with him," she raged, adding that she "cou'd Not forgive" him for what she called his "ill conduct" during the war. Mostly, she was bitter that he had not taken better care to see that she would be adequately provided for in his absence. He "has left every thing in Confusion." He has "hurt me." His "ungenerous conduct" was the denouement of their relationship, and in time she grew to believe that all along she had been trapped in an unhappy marriage. She came to see that living alone, not subject to her husband's wishes, she was happier than she had ever been. Though admitting that "some affection" for her spouse lingered, Grace added: "Ye Liberty of doing as I please Makes even poverty more agreeable than any time I ever spent since I married." She was, she said, "easey Nay happy not to be with him."[30]

GRACE GALLOWAY and Abigail Adams were hardly the only women whose world was torn asunder by the war. The outlook of Sarah Hodgkins, mother of seven (including three very young children) and wife of an Ipswich shoemaker who enlisted, reenlisted, and reenlisted yet again, eddied over the years from that of a zealous patriot who did what she could to sustain her husband while he was in harm's way, to that of a lonely, dejected woman overwhelmed by her solitary efforts to meet her family's remorseless needs. Joseph Hodgkins, a thirty-one-year-old minuteman, marched on the day of Lexington and Concord, took his place in the ranks of the Boston siege army, and saw action on Bunker Hill. When his tour of duty neared its end late in 1775, Hodgkins signed on for another year of service. He spoke of his need to do "my Duty" to "sarve my Contery" until "our Enemy are gone." He said that he wanted to serve until "peas"—peace—came, but the closest he came to expressing what the American Revolution meant to him was to simply refer to the struggle for independence as "this glories [glorious] Cause." When Sarah, who was twenty-four when the war erupted, learned that he would serve a second year, she told him that she was "something disapoined" by his decision, adding that alone at home she faced a life of "troble & disppoint-ments." She advised that "there Seems to be Something wanting[.] I wanted you at home." "I want to See you very much but I darest not think about it," she admitted, as it made her all the more lonely. She continued by telling him how she wished he was with her in their bed, signing her missives as "your Loving wife till Death." Repeatedly, she told him that she would "waite patiently" for him to come home. Sarah added to her already considerable workload by mending her husband's shirts and by making new clothing both for him and assorted relatives in the army. She gathered and sent him paper, candles, and materials that he needed for repairing his shoes and those of others. Sarah also regularly consoled her husband with letters in which she poured out her love for him, and she sought to comfort him with prayers and assurances drawn from her faith. The year 1776 was especially anguishing. While Joseph was in the thick of the fighting in New York and the cold, disconsolate retreat across New Jersey, the couple lost their eighteen-month-old son to smallpox. As Joseph's second year of service neared an end, Sarah begged him not to reenlist, something she had not done the previous year, at least not so boldly. "I dont know what you think about Staying [home] but it cant be inconsistent with your duty to come home to your family." He had given "time enough" to the service of his country, she added. But Joseph signed on once again, this time for a three-year hitch. As he moved into the last year of his third tour of duty, Sarah ever more stridently urged him to leave the army. She could "write a vollum" and not satisfactorily "express what I feel" about the "dis-appointments [that] are alotted for me." "I due really want to see you very much," she said, adding that she no longer understood why she "must be contented to Live a widow. . . . Let Some body else take your Place." She played on his emotions, never more so than when she spoke of their "Sweet Babe," a young daughter who "have got no farther." It is "your Duty to come to your family," she finally asserted, for without him "my troble will be grate surely it will be atroble indeed." For reasons that are not entirely clear, Joseph's zeal for the war abated in the wake of the Newport campaign, in which he served, and during 1779, after more than four years of soldiering, he resigned his commission and came home.[31]

Few, if any, affluent women had faced the rigors that this war imposed on Sarah Hodgkins or the torments and deprivation it caused Grace Galloway. In Philadelphia, in the very midst of Galloway's cyclonic distress, many elite women had enjoyed—as Washington had been mortified to discover—lives of sumptuous excess. But the advent of 1780 confronted Americans as never before with the prospect that this war might not be won, a new reality that produced in some women a rebirth of the spirit of republican sacrifice. Esther Reed, the wife of Washington's first secretary, Joseph Reed, now the president of Pennsylvania, organized a campaign that year to aid the wretched Continental soldiery. Beginning with a broadside, *The Sentiments of an American Woman*, she urged that women renounce expenditures on luxuries and instead donate that money to the relief of the troops. Next, she orchestrated a fund-raising drive that sent female volunteers to every house in the city—Franklin's daughter, Sarah Bache, likely knocked on Grace Galloway's door, resulting in a conversation that unfortunately for the nosey in future generations was not preserved—and collected $7,500 in the new currency. The Philadelphia plan sparked similar campaigns by women in other Pennsylvania towns, as well as in Virginia, Maryland, and New Jersey. Ultimately, something on the order of $10,000 was raised. Reed's hope, which betrayed a less than realistic understanding of the army's needs, was that General Washington would divide the money among the men. He wanted no part of that. Fearful that a giveaway of hard money would lead those with an "inclination to drink" into "irregularities and disorders," he preferred a "benevolent donation" of shirts for the poorly clad men. Reed complied, using the funds to acquire linen and mobilizing additional volunteers to sew more than two thousand shirts, each bearing the name of its seamstress, for the soldiers. Moved deeply by the women's sacrificial spirit, little of which had been visible of late, Washington said that those in Reed's Ladies Association deserved "an equal place" with patriots who through "love of country" had sacrificed in quest of victory.[32]

Washington told others that every sign of popular sacrifice and support for the war would only help to convince London that it was in their "interest to bring [the war] to a conclusion." Rather ominously, as it had not previously been a concern, he also remarked at the dawn of 1780 that every step that could be taken for the "appearance of preparation and vigor" would convince France and Spain to stay the course.[33]

Part Three

The War in the South, 1780–1781

17

"A YEAR FILLED WITH OUR DISGRACES": DEFEAT IN THE SOUTH, 1780

NEW YORK CITY could hardly have been more bleak as 1779 drew to a close. Winter, cold and gray, had turned streets into slush and deposited a blanket of snow on homes and shops. Residents faced a scarcity of fuel and spot food shortages. For the rebel inhabitants, Gotham was a city occupied by a foreign invader. For its Tory residents, mostly refugees from other colonies, the city was a safe haven, but not home. Yet, as seldom during the long years since Saratoga, the hopes of the Loyalists soared in December. As snow swirled and sidewalks iced over, the Tories noticed feverish activity along the waterfront. Troop transports, ordnance vessels, and hospital ships were being outfitted. The British were unmistakably preparing for a campaign. Just before Christmas, company after company of soldiers—some 8,700 men in all—marched through the unkempt streets to board the transports. On Christmas Day, General Clinton and his staff rode to the harbor and boarded a ship of the line. Something big was up. The city buzzed with word that the gathering armada was bound for Charleston, but not even the ships' captains knew the destination of the task force. For security reasons, each of them had been given a sealed envelope revealing where the armada was headed, but they were instructed not to open the packets until the ships were at sea.[1]

Charleston had long been on the minds of Britain's war planners. Clinton had gone there in 1776 to restore royal rule and Howe, in one of the many plans that he concocted for campaign 1777, had proposed marching through the Chesapeake provinces and on to South Carolina and Georgia following his conquest of Philadelphia. Once Britain's Southern Strategy crystallized in the wake of Saratoga, Germain had often spoken of taking Charleston, and never more ardently than after Prevost's unopposed march from Savannah through South Carolina in the spring of 1779. Though Prevost raised cautionary flags about the timidity of the Loyalists, Germain preferred to believe that the success of the redcoats in South Carolina was "indubitable proof of the indisposition of the inhabitants to support the rebel government." Regain Charleston, the American secretary predicted from his neat, uncluttered world in London, and "I flatter myself . . . the recovery of the whole of the province and probably North Carolina would soon follow."[2]

Clinton was one of the few British leaders who was skeptical of the notion that the war could be won in the South. When Germain broached the idea of an invasion of South Carolina in 1779, Clinton had bristled, firing off the angriest letter that he ever wrote to his superior. "[H]ow mortified . . . must I be" at being directed to do things that Howe, with an army twice the size and no need to worry about the French navy, had never been asked to do. He savagely accused Germain of having "adopt[ed] the ill-digested or interested suggestions of people who cannot be competent judges," an obvious reference to Tories such as Galloway. The best course was to "leave me to myself . . . I am on the spot," he said in an unintended double entendre. Clinton, like his predecessors, was absorbed with the hope of bringing Washington to battle, knowing—as historian John Shy wrote—that "destroying the Continental army might do in a day what would take a year or more to do in a methodical southern campaign of . . . pacification." Clinton's most insightful proposal was that one commander be appointed who would be responsible for all British operations in America. Much as the British and American allies in World War II would vest authority in a supreme commander, Clinton believed that a single British commander in this war could annually prepare comprehensive and realistic plans for the two American theaters, concentrating power in the Caribbean in the winter and in North America after April. Though a well-founded suggestion, Germain brushed it aside.[3]

Despite his initial reservations, Clinton in time—and after considerable deliberation and vacillation—embraced the Southern Strategy. He was won over by Collier's naval raid on the Virginia coast in May, which produced tantalizing confirmation that a considerable Tory population did indeed inhabit the South, and by Prevost's ability to move about almost at will in South Carolina. He was never as sanguine as Germain about the Loyalists, though like Prevost he believed the "king's friends" would come forward with a helping hand once the British, through smashing successes, had minimized the likelihood of patriot reprisals. He dared to hope that Prevost's experience demonstrated that support for the rebellion might be withering, at least in the low country. Above all, Clinton was loath to act until he could enter the South in strength and with the intention of remaining. The last thing he wished was to have to abandon the Tories who surfaced, as had occurred in New Jersey and Pennsylvania. Clinton finally set the date for an October invasion of South Carolina—he feared that campaigning in the heat and draining humidity in the summertime South would be a deathtrap for the British and German soldiers—though unavoidable delays pushed back the start into 1780. His objectives were to retake South Carolina and complete the pacification of Georgia, and in the process to have at last the chance to bring to battle, and destroy, a large rebel army. "This is the most important hour Britain ever knew" in this war, he declared on the eve of sailing. "If we lose it, we shall never see such another."[4]

FROM THE OUTSET, Washington's spies in New York—he referred to them as his confidential correspondents—apprised him of the enemy's preparations to dispatch a large army. But Washington was in the dark as to the enemy's destination. For a time, he thought its target was Virginia, although intelligence steadfastly reported that the task force was en route to South Carolina or the Caribbean. It was not until late February, sixty days after the British fleet sailed, that Washington knew where it finally landed.[5] Nearly a month before Clinton sailed, General Lincoln, the rebel commander in the South, told Washington that he was seriously undermanned. He was perplexed as well by the "aversion the people have for service here" and miffed when South Carolina's legislature spurned Laurens's proposal to raise African American soldiers.[6] By then, Congress had already ordered roughly 3,400 men from the North Carolina and Virginia lines to march to South Carolina, sent three Continental frigates to Charleston, and rushed down powder, flints, kettles, and assorted equipment, including two "traveling forges" for making cannonballs.[7]

With overall responsibility, Washington had the authority to intrude in the operations of the Northern and Southern Departments. While he never micromanaged business in the Northern Department, he had never ignored it. He had conceived and helped organize Arnold's invasion of Canada in 1775 and during the crises in 1776 and 1777 he had shuffled troops northward from the Hudson Highlands. Washington devoted far less attention to the southern theater, so little that for a very long time he appears to have underestimated the importance of hostilities in the South, viewing the region as an inconsequential backwater of the war. However, there were additional explanations for his behavior. Before December 1779, he was preoccupied with the ever-present possibility that Clinton might come after West Point. Furthermore, so long as Prevost's little force in Savannah was Britain's sole army in the South, Washington was confident that Lincoln possessed the means for coping. Nevertheless, Washington's inactivity following Clinton's departure for Charleston is difficult to explain. Clinton was so worried about the safety of New York in his absence that he abandoned Newport, plugging those troops into Manhattan's defenses. Even then only 11,000 men held the city, and many were unseasoned Tories, leaving the British commander apprehensive at what might occur should the rivers freeze, immobilizing the royal fleet and affording the Continentals the opportunity to attack across the ice. The rivers did freeze ten days after Clinton sailed, but aside from a small, mismanaged raid on Staten Island that failed egregiously, Washington did nothing. In January, Washington possessed 12,356 Continentals and he might easily have secured nearly that many militia. Washington could not have retaken New York, but with his decided numerical advantage, he might have struck a damaging blow, and virtually any daring action on his part probably would have forced Clinton to abandon his plans for South Carolina and return to defend the city. Instead, it was the British who acted boldly that winter, attempting raids at four sites in New Jersey and another at White Plains. The latter resulted in the nearly total destruction of five companies of Continentals, an episode that Washington characterized simply as "very unlucky."[8] No less strangely, Washington clung to the army that he was not using. Despite Lincoln's pleas for help, Washington sent him only the Maryland Line and Delaware's regiment, and he did not order them south until almost fifty days after he had become aware of Clinton's destination.[9]

This was a burdensome time for Washington. When he learned in November that d'Estaing was not coming north, he quickly put his men in winter quarters. Most were posted at or near Morristown, where the army had spent the winter three years earlier. The winter of 1779-1780 almost made the experience at Valley Forge seem like a frolic. It was a singularly bitter winter, one that was always remembered by veterans as "the hard winter." Snow began falling in December, and just after Christmas a blizzard struck that raged for nearly thirty-six hours. Fresh snow fell every few days throughout January and February, piling atop the old snow. With temperatures seemly stuck below freezing, snowdrifts rose to six feet in January. In February they were twelve feet tall. With but a single blanket apiece, the men often slept huddled together in search of warmth, and those in tents at times awakened to find that they were "buried like sheep under the snow," according to one soldier.[10]

As at Valley Forge, fresh meat was in short supply and deficiencies of flour, which had first grown scarce during the army's last weeks in the field, occurred now and again throughout the winter. The men were forced toward comestibles that were not part of their routine diet, prompting Washington to remark that they had been reduced to "eat every kind of horse food but hay." Some of what they consumed has a modern ring about it—rye bread, brown bread, cornbread, buckwheat, and rice. There were times when there was no food. Private Martin once went four days with nothing to eat, and he later remembered seeing men "roast their old shoes," gnaw on tree bark, and consume luckless dogs. Early in January, General Greene anguished for the "Poor Fellows," half of whom were "naked, and above two thirds starved." A month later he reported that the army was on "the point of disbanding for want of provisions." In March he acknowledged that the men had only corn to eat, and little of that. Late in April he said that the soldiers had been placed on half-rations in order to spread out the meager supplies. "A Country, once overflowing with plenty, are now suffering an Army employed for the defense of every thing that is dear and valuable, to perish for want of food," he raged.[11]

The causes of the army's miseries were more complex than Greene suggested. Many farmers once again deliberately curtailed production rather than sell their crops and livestock for worthless money. The enduring bad weather made it impossible for long stretches to move stores. Snow and ice closed down road and river traffic, as well as water-powered mills. Later, when the inevitable thaw set in, the roads turned to impermeable mud. In addition to these customary impediments, new problems surfaced. Some parts of the country had experienced a ruinous drought during the preceding summer and fall, reducing agricultural yields. The supply service was emasculated when numerous staff employees left in 1779 for better paying jobs in the private sector. Congress's decision to relinquish to the states the job of supplying the army also haunted the cold, hungry soldiers at Jockey Hollow. Most states were not up to the challenge. More than at any other moment in the war it was in this winter of deprivation and despondency that the seeds sprouted for what later would be called the "nationalist" or "consolidation" movement, the drive to create a strong and sovereign national government, a quest that culminated in the Constitutional Convention in 1787. It was while the miseries of Morristown were fresh on his mind that Washington first despaired that "our measures are not under the influence and direction of one council, but thirteen." He added that unless Congress possessed "absolute powers in all matters relative to the great purposes of War, and of general concern," and that the states were restricted to "matters of local and internal polity," the United States was "attempting an impossibility, and shall very soon become (if it is not already the case) a many headed Monster . . . that never will or can, steer to the same point."[12]

Washington's letters that winter resonated with new warnings. At no "stage of the War," he declared, had "disatisfaction . . . been so general or alarming" among the soldiery. As never before he worried about mutinies—an uprising did occur within a Connecticut brigade in the spring—and over what might happen should the enemy take the offensive. Clinton could take West Point if he tried, Washington seemed to say, and he added that should the British drive him from Morristown "at this inclement season," it "would be a most serious calamity." Preoccupied as he was by what he called a "crisis . . . perplexing beyond description," Washington was drowning under too many worries of his own to deal adequately with Clinton's threat to South Carolina.[13]

CONGRESS WAS NOT as debilitated as Washington imagined, having reacted immediately to the disaster at Savannah by sending men, ships, and supplies to the Southern Department. Some in Congress who voted to do so acted despite their towering anger toward South Carolina, furious that the state had furnished little help to the northern states in their hour of trial, and that they had even "neglected themselves. They will not *draught* to fill their Battalions, they will not raise *black Regiments*, they will not put their militia . . . under Continental Rules," a Yankee congressman bristled. But Charleston was too crucial to the American cause to be ignored, a fact that General Lincoln never permitted Congress to forget. Lose Charleston, Lincoln said, and all of South Carolina and Georgia will be gone, with North Carolina next in Clinton's cross hairs. Lose those three states, he added, and the massive indebtedness of the United States, as well as the cost for caring for hordes of Southern refugees, would have to be borne by the remaining ten states. Lose South Carolina and Georgia, he went on, and the Creeks and Cherokees would likely take to the warpath in North Carolina and Virginia, threatening the ability of those states to remain in the war.[14]

Lincoln made Washington and Congress, as well as the governors of North Carolina and Virginia, aware that he had little with which to defend Charleston. Like every general, he fudged considerably, reporting that he possessed merely 2,400 men, nearly half of whom were militiamen. In reality, he believed that he might have nearly four times that number. He could redeploy the men he had left at Augusta, and he was virtually assured of the services of the nearly nine hundred men in Charleston's militia. In addition, Lincoln hoped for more than 1,500 militiamen from the South Carolina backcountry and an equal number from both North Carolina and Virginia, and he was aware that Congress had ordered Continentals from the Upper South to South Carolina. Before the British armada reached its destination, Lincoln in his wildest dreams anticipated having in excess of eight thousand men, a force about the size of the invasion army. Lincoln additionally knew early on that he had a squadron with some muscle—six frigates (three from the Continental navy and three others left by d'Estaing for his ally), a sloop of war, two brigs, two galleys and a few other smaller vessels that belonged to the South Carolina state navy, 260 guns afloat and another 40 or so artillery pieces in Fort Moultrie and on Sullivan's Island.[15]

Lincoln's expectations were to be dashed from nearly every quarter, but by none so cruelly as South Carolina. As the enemy task force approached the state, Lincoln requested that Governor Rutledge, the commander of the state's militia, summon two thousand men to arms. Never more than three hundred militiamen from outside Charleston answered the governor's call, a mere fraction of the number furnished by neighboring North Carolina and possibly less than those sent by tiny Georgia. The poor turnout was not due to lack of effort by Rutledge, who, when faced with the loss of Charleston, worked tirelessly and twice issued proclamations threatening the confiscation of the property of those who refused to serve. Backcountry militiamen had fought in Georgia and would subsequently serve valiantly when their region was threatened, but they had no love for Charleston, home to wealthy planters and merchants who had long controlled the colony and state, and steadfastly discriminated against the backcountry when it came to taxes and services. Now the chickens came home to roost. Backcountry militiamen were unwilling to risk their lives to save those who had victimized them.[16] In this emergency, Lincoln renewed Laurens's request that slaves be armed, but his appeal was dismissed out of hand, prompting David Ramsay, a Charleston physician and one of the first historians of the American Revolution, to remark that the "patriotism of many is . . . a voice and nothing more. . . .

A spirit of money-making has eaten up our patriotism. Our morals are more depreciated than our currency."[17]

LINCOLN KNEW WEEKS in advance that the British might come, and they arrived during the second week in February after an appalling voyage. The storms that lashed the American army at Morristown churned in the Atlantic as well, hammering the armada "with unbelievable fury," one soldier remarked. During nearly half its days at sea the fleet was bedeviled by "Snow, rain, hail, storm, foaming waves, and bitter cold," a German soldier noted. Bolts of lightening danced close by. Incredible gales lashed the ships, tossing them about as if they were toys. Many men were seasick and most were wet much of the time, as waves washed over the ships, sending water into the holds where the men trembled with cold and fear. The temperatures grew so unbearable that some dared to build fires in their cramped holds, enduring choking smoke for a few minutes warmth. Even on calm days, the soldiers—landlubbers all—complained that there was "no end of rolling, creaking," and wrung their hands at the incessantly "fearful . . . noise." Nearly all the army's 1,400 horses and much of the siege artillery were lost at sea, the latter going to the bottom with the ordnance ship *Russia Merchant*, although miraculously that was the only vessel that sank. When the lookout in the tall mast at last spotted land, a Hessian noted in his journal, "Every face brightened" instantly. Soon, he marveled that though it was the dead of winter, South Carolina's coastal "air was as warm as it is in Germany in the summer."[18]

On the dark, rainy night of February 11, nearly forty days after sailing from New York, the first of Clinton's shaken men went ashore on sandy Simmons Island, about twenty miles below Charleston.[19] As usual, the men in the landing boats were a heterogeneous lot, including English, Scots, Irish, Welsh, Germans, and Americans. Only the presence of a large number of Americans was something of a novelty. They were Tories, and for one of the first times in the war the British were making substantial use of them, just as the North government's Southern Strategy had envisioned.

During the first years of the war the British military had largely ignored the Loyalists. Neither Gage nor Howe had made any attempt to raise a Loyalist force while in Boston, as both knew that the city was to be abandoned. Howe also displayed no interest in a Loyalist corps when he invaded New York. He expected a brief campaign and like most senior British officers, he had come out of the intercolonial wars with a jaundiced view of American soldiers. Early on, Howe was under no pressure from London to raise Loyalists. North's government understood that while Tory soldiers might be raised quickly, they could not be trained rapidly, and expecting a short war, the ministry had not believed that troubling with Tory soldiers was worth the expense. Only a few provincial regiments were raised before 1778. Influential Loyalists handled the recruiting and shouldered much of the expense, but the Tory outfits went largely unnoticed and were treated as despised stepchildren by the regular army. No provision was made for many features that were standard in the British army, such as regimental hospitals or nursing care, and the officers not only were ranked below regular army officers of comparable station, they were not eligible for half pay following their service. These forces were utilized almost solely in a support capacity. The major exception occurred in St. Leger's invasion of New York during campaign 1777.[20]

As it struggled to regroup after Saratoga and France's expected entrance into the war, Britain began to envision a truly significant role for its provincial corps. It moved to incorporate the Loyalist regiments more fully into the army, for the first time furnished arms for each man, and offered cash and bounties to those that enlisted. Whereas previously "rank and wealth," and success as a recruiter, had determined who was commissioned, merit was henceforth to be a key criteria in the appointment of officers. The number of Loyalists under arms swelled dramatically. Only about one thousand Tories—almost all Canadians—had borne arms in 1775, and by the end of 1776 no more than three thousand Loyalists had been under arms in Canada and the mainland colonies. But by the end of 1778 nearly 7,500 provincials were with the British army in units such as the King's American Regiment, the King's Orange Rangers, the Loyal Americans, the Royal Guides and Pioneers, the Prince of Wales Americans, the Royal Highland Emigrants, the Royal Fensible Americans, and the Queen's Rangers. A year later, when Clinton sailed for South Carolina, nearly nine thousand Tories were serving with the British army. At the same moment, 18,700 men were on the rolls of the Continental army, but the Continentals had been actively recruiting for several years longer and the rebels had the luxury of recruiting from the entire continent, while to this point the British had been able to secure enlistees almost solely from just three mainland colonies, New York, New Jersey, and Pennsylvania. The British had additionally formed militia units in the occupied areas. Nearly six thousand militiamen could be mustered in greater New York by 1780. They served with foraging parties, helped with Britain's coastal raids, and were part of forays into New Jersey and Connecticut to kidnap local patriots. Many more Loyalists, perhaps thousands, served in the Royal Navy or on board Tory privateers.[21]

When the British invaded Georgia late in 1778, four Loyalist battalions had been part of Campbell's force. Given their alleged "resentment at the ignominious treatment they have received," British leaders had eagerly anticipated that as many as six thousand madly vindictive Tories might emerge to help take up Savannah. The results were disappointing, leading Clinton to tell Germain that the Loyalists' "numbers were so few" that the money spent on them "exceeded the advantages." During 1779 rays of hope appeared. Campbell had organized 1,100 Georgians into twenty militia companies, upward of eight hundred South Carolina Tories had surfaced when Prevost invaded the state, and a Loyalist legislature was elected in Georgia that disenfranchised 151 leading patriots and nullified all legislation enacted in the state since 1776. Several Tory units had served in the defense of Savannah in September 1779—including Brown's Rangers (mostly Georgia, Florida, and Carolina Tories)—which were in the thick of the action at the Spring Hill redoubt. When Clinton came south, he left behind most of his Loyalist units to defend New York, but he brought along— or soon added—numerous Tory units, including a company of seventy black pioneers (laborers, axmen, and road builders) from New York and another of two hundred men that had been organized in Georgia. Roughly one man in five in his army in South Carolina—2,135 men altogether—was a provincial soldier.[22]

When the British soldiery splashed ashore below Charleston, Clinton found himself in strange circumstances. Frustrated by his lack of manpower, and exhausted and homesick—seven years had passed since he had seen what he called his "motherless babes," his four young children—Clinton had asked the previous summer to be permitted to resign. He was still awaiting London's answer even as he stepped onto South Carolina soil, leaving him in limbo and exacerbating an already awkward situation with his second in command, and possible successor, Earl Cornwallis. Cornwallis had come to America in 1776 to serve under Clinton in the initial foray against Charleston. He subsequently had fought in New York, New Jersey, and Pennsylvania before going home in 1778 to be with his ailing wife. He had not planned to return to America, but Jemima's death early in 1779 had left him lonely and disconsolate, and he recrossed the Atlantic hoping to find solace amid the pressures of war.

Cornwallis and Clinton had never been close. Reserved and contentious, Clinton drew near to few people, but he harbored an especially deep resentment toward Cornwallis. Howe had divulged to him that during the engagement at White Plains in 1776, Cornwallis had pleaded not to be placed under Clinton. "I cannot bear to serve under him," he had allegedly said. Outraged, Clinton subsequently confronted Cornwallis about his remark. Clinton later said that Cornwallis apologized; for his part, Cornwallis denied ever having made any such comment about Clinton. Regardless of who was correct, rancor and suspicion divided the two men, and when Clinton finally learned—a month after the landing in South Carolina—that the king had denied his request to resign, his uneasy relationship with Cornwallis collapsed totally. In a bizarre move, Cornwallis asked not to be consulted further on any plans during the operation to take Charleston. Outlandishly, Clinton was left without the counsel of his most experienced general for the duration of this crucial campaign.[23]

Clinton's invasion force advanced slowly. Two weeks were consumed in moving merely six miles to barren James Island. Bad weather was a factor, and so, too, was the need to search for food to replace what had been consumed or lost at sea. The rebels had not resisted the landing, but thereafter their cavalry repeatedly and effectively harassed the redcoats, whose light horse had been put out of commission by the loss of their mounts during the voyage. The British advance may also have been slowed by the realization, noted by an edgy German soldier, that they were passing through tall marsh grass inhabited by "crocodiles

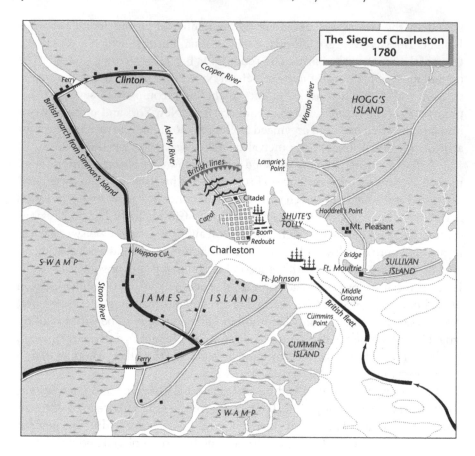

The Siege of Charleston
1780

sixteen feet long...wolves and several species of venomous snakes." On March 10, a month after the landing, an advance force crossed the Stono River at Wappoo Cut and pushed forward to the Ashley River, which flowed along the west side of the narrow neck of land that Charleston occupied. On a distant horizon, Charleston was visible for the first time, and to a British dragoon it looked "not a little like New York." The British quickly erected their initial battery at Fenwick's Point, using guns removed from Royal Navy vessels.[24]

Lincoln knew of the enemy's arrival even before the first grenadiers came ashore, and with the cavalry serving as his eyes—not to mention ongoing intelligence reports provided by lookouts posted in Charleston's tallest church steeples—the American commander was always aware of the whereabouts of his foe. Charleston's defenses had been planned by a French military engineer sent south by Congress immediately after Savannah's fall late in 1778, and in March work proceeded in earnest under the watchful eye of another French engineer, Colonel Jean-Baptiste-Joseph, Chevalier de Laumoy. Scores of Continentals were impressed into working on the emplacements, but the heaviest work was done by six hundred slaves furnished by the state. "[L]ike mushrooms," installations "sprang from the soil," said an observer, and before long Lincoln was confident that his army was protected by a highly sophisticated defensive system. It was not an overstatement. The hornwork, a fortification with two-foot-thick walls made of tabby (lime and sea shells) stood at the entrance to the city. It was surrounded by a ditch. On its north side, looking toward Charleston Neck, stood a line of redans and redoubts that stretched across the nearly mile-wide stretch of land from the Ashley River on the west to the Cooper River on the east. A ditch six feet deep and nearly twelve feet wide lay at the foot of this parapet. Two lines of abatis and numerous "wolf traps"—deep, masked holes—guarded the ditch, and in front of them the Americans had dug a canal. It was ten feet wide and eight feet deep, and also spanned the terrain between the rivers. Beyond the canal the landscape had been cleared of trees and houses for nearly one hundred yards. Within these formidable defenses, Lincoln possessed eighty pieces of artillery and numerous mortars.[25]

From the outset, Clinton had thought in terms of a siege operation. One look at the daunting American defensive works convinced him that he had no alternative. Four years earlier, Clinton had favored using joint operations of the army and navy to fence in Washington on Manhattan. He now fancied the same fate for Lincoln.[26] Lincoln's thinking is more difficult to reconstruct, and the likelihood is that it was all along a work in progress. Congress had not ordered him to defend Charleston at all costs. Although many congressmen grumbled about Washington's Fabian strategy, nearly all had learned the wisdom of not repeating the mistakes that had been made in New York in 1776. Washington's actions in the campaign for Philadelphia seemed to offer the best template for the defense of Charleston: make the enemy pay a price for gaining the city, but in the end get the American army out so that it might fight another day.

Lincoln's situation was not identical to that of Washington during the Philadelphia campaign. Washington's army had been roughly comparable in size to the force that Howe landed in Pennsylvania, but Clinton possessed nearly a two-to-one numerical superiority over Lincoln's army. There had been no reason in 1777 for Washington to worry about the royal navy. Lincoln could never forget it. Facing a superior army and a huge navy, Lincoln could have hardly entrenched and fought on the sea islands where the British had landed. His only feasible opportunity for making a Brandywine-like stand would have been when the enemy tried to cross the Ashley, but at that juncture, with Clinton's army having been augmented by the arrival of the Savannah garrison, Britain's manpower superiority had climbed to almost three to one, as there were some 11,000 redcoats faced by just 4,300 rebels.[27]

Lincoln's expectations for the American fleet proved to be his Achilles' heel. At first blush the small American squadron was hardly a match for a mighty British task force that included five ships of the line, three other large vessels with nearly fifty guns apiece, and four frigates.[28] But Lincoln was convinced that the quirks of Charleston harbor leveled the playing field. The Charleston Bar, a long sandbar, lay at the harbor's entrance, and was nearly an impenetrable obstacle to large warships. However, a few narrow channels sliced through it, although even the best seaman would have to proceed slowly and cautiously when attempting to navigate those hazardous passages. Lincoln believed that the Continental frigates could make a stand at the bar. Posted just inside the bar with broadsides to any approaching heavy warship, the Americans would have "crossed the T." That is, the Continental vessels would be positioned to hammer the behemoths, which could return only light fire from their small front-mounted guns. Many of Lincoln's advisors believed the Royal Navy would never attempt such a chancy undertaking, but if it did, few believed their ships could fight their way past the rebel frigates. Even if they succeeded, the men of war would not yet be in the harbor. They still must run past Fort Moultrie, the forty-gun installation that had stopped Britain's ships in 1776. Lincoln, who had been in command in and about Charleston for fifteen months before the British landing, had studied the vagaries of this harbor and was confident that the Royal Navy could never penetrate the American defenses. He believed, too, that if Clinton's naval arm could be nullified, the British commander would be forced to choose between storming the rebels' seemingly impregnable lines on Charleston Neck or abandoning the operation. Finally, should the royal fleet somehow succeed in sailing into the harbor—Lincoln's worst-case scenario—he remained confident that the little rebel fleet could keep the enemy navy from the Cooper River, at least for awhile, leaving open the escape hatch for the American army.

At numerous times between February and April changing circumstances cried out for Lincoln to rethink matters. The first instance came before the British landing. America's naval commander, Abraham Whipple, a Rhode Island mariner and prewar activist, balked at making a stand at the Charleston Bar, offering a variety of excuses. Though startled by what he heard, Lincoln had not panicked, confident that under sufficient pressure Whipple would relent. He was wrong. Late in February, three weeks before the British moved forward to the Ashley, Lincoln learned beyond the shadow of doubt that Whipple would not make a defense at the bar. However, Whipple agreed to build a chain of obstructions in Rebellion Road, the narrow channel on the city side of Fort Moultrie, to slow, and maybe stop, any British ship that got through the bar. He further promised to post his little fleet near Fort Moultrie and join with it in battling the enemy vessels that attempted to enter the harbor. Lincoln was faced with his most crucial decision yet. If Whipple's defensive scheme failed, the chance that the beleaguered rebel army could escape would be dramatically reduced. Lincoln deliberated and finally consented to the revised plan for defending the harbor. Three weeks later, in mid-March, Lincoln learned from Whipple that the chain of obstructions would never be completed. The channel was deeper and wider than previously thought, and the current was swifter.[29] This presented Lincoln with his best opportunity to abandon Charleston, especially as the Virginia Continentals had not reached the city. Instead, he opted to stay on, beguiling himself with the belief that if the British got into the harbor, they could never get into the Cooper River. With no place left to hide, Lincoln reasoned, Whipple would have to station his frigates broadside at the narrow entrance to the Cooper. While the frigates kept the men of war at bay, Lincoln's army could slip across the river to their escape hatch, the road leading toward North Carolina. All along, Lincoln had clutched at straws. This was the shortest straw in the batch.

The noose about Charleston was steadily tightening, although there was still ample time for Lincoln to get out. The British fleet safely crossed the bar on March 20, but during the next eighteen days it did nothing. On March 29 advance parties of redcoats crossed the Ashley, and the entire British army was on Charleston Neck within two days. They wasted no time constructing siege works. Under the direction of James Moncrief, the engineer who had designed Prevost's defenses at Savannah, work on the first parallel was completed by April 5, and that same day the bombardment of Charleston commenced. Three days later the royal fleet successfully ran past Fort Moultrie, losing only one transport in the action. If Lincoln was to retreat, he had to act, and quickly.

Two days after the first shells fell on Charleston, the long-awaited Virginia Continentals—1,400 men in all—finally reached the city. They had been ordered south nearly 125 days earlier, but were remarkably slow in departing. Once they marched, they moved at a whirlwind pace, covering 505 miles in only thirty days. They arrived in good shape, too, calling into question Washington's earlier assertion that it would be fatal for his Continentals to slog into the southland. The Virginians arrived just as the trap slammed shut.

Less than a week after they reached the city, and to a degree because they had arrived, Clinton stepped up his plans to get across the Cooper River. He sent 1,500 men under Colonel James Webster to establish a foothold. Two British infantry regiments and two provincial contingents were with Webster. One of the Loyalist outfits, the American Volunteers, was comprised largely of Tory regulars from New York and New Jersey, and commanded by Major Patrick Ferguson, a thirty-six-year-old Scotsman who had served in America for three years. At one point earlier in the war Ferguson had held in his hands the possibility of dramatically altering the course of the war. While out with a forward scouting party on the day of the Battle of Brandywine, Ferguson, an expert marksman, had seen an American officer ride slowly by, not more than one hundred yards away. The officer, astride a large gray mount, had presented an inviting target, but Ferguson had declined to shoot, saying later, "it was not pleasant for me to fire at the back of an unoffending individual who was acquitting himself very cooly of his duty."[30] The following day Ferguson learned that the officer had been General Washington. Later in that battle, Ferguson's right elbow had been shattered by a rifle ball, and he permanently lost the use of that arm. During the next couple of

Colonel Banastre Tarleton. Painting by Sir Joshua Reynolds, 1782. An intrepid and daring cavalry officer, his merciless qualities were an important factor in rallying southerners to resist the British invaders after mid-1780.

years he served primarily in intelligence work until, just before sailing for South Carolina, he was promoted and given command of the Tory unit. The other Loyalist unit with Webster was the green-coated British Legion, a regiment of infantry and cavalry under Lieutenant Colonel Banastre Tarleton. The twenty-six-year-old scion of a well-to-do Liverpool merchant, Tarleton had entered the army only in 1775 after brief stints at Oxford and the Middle Temple, England's law school. He came to America with the force that tried to take Charleston in 1776. His daring and flash in the campaign for New York, including his participation in the capture of Charles Lee, contributed to his spectacular ascent. Within barely three years he rose from the lowest commissioned rank in the British army to lieutenant colonel. Stocky and powerful, with sandy red hair and a rugged visage that disclosed a hard and unsparing nature, Tarleton had the reputation of one who was "anxious of every opportunity of distinguishing himself."[31]

Colonel Webster's force had been ordered to attack an American force of approximately five hundred rebel cavalry and militia under Brigadier General Isaac Huger, a South Carolinian who had fought in nearly every major battle in the southern theater since 1776. Huger's charge was to hold the forks of the Cooper near Monck's Corner, thirty-two miles above the city. On April 12,

Webster crossed the tawny and quiet Cooper in the dead of night. Once across, he detached Tarleton with the cavalry, a force that had been replenished with new mounts acquired between Savannah and Charleston. These were farm horses, and some were ponies, clearly inferior to the horses lost at sea, and to those that carried the rebel dragoons. His only chance of success, Tarleton believed, was to surprise his adversary. Learning the precise location of his foe from a slave, Tarleton's force approached in the wee hours of a pitch black spring morning. Luck was with him. Huger had failed to post pickets or send out patrols. The British struck just as the distracted Americans were making preparations to move out. Caught off guard, the rebels were cut to pieces. Those who resisted, mostly enlisted men, were killed or wounded. The lion's share of the officers, who were already mounted, escaped into the surrounding swamps, but Tarleton took 184 horses, nearly all that Huger had possessed, as well as fifty wagons laden with arms and ammunition, and about sixty-five prisoners. In a flash, Lincoln's army had been stripped of its cavalry east of the Cooper. Webster's infantry and grenadiers rendezvoused with Tarleton at Cainhoy, well up the Wando River, a tributary of the Cooper, and began to move east, beginning the conquest of the last area with a road remaining open toward the Carolina backcountry. If Lincoln was to extricate his army, it now could only be via Lampriers Point, a tongue of land that crept into the Cooper near its junction with the Wando, and directly across from Charleston Neck. As soon as he learned of the disaster at Monck's Corner, Lincoln rushed men and six eighteen-pound cannon, taken from now useless Fort Moultrie, to secure his sole link to the road to safety.[32]

The investment of Charleston had not occurred overnight. Two months elapsed between Clinton's landing and the debacle at Monck's Corner. Thirty days had passed between the nearly simultaneous time that Cornwallis reached the Ashley and the royal fleet crossed the Charleston Bar and Tarleton's routing of Huger. Many factors contributed to the looming disaster. Commodore Whipple's inexcusable conduct had repeatedly drawn the rebels ever deeper into the vortex. Neither Congress nor Washington had provided Lincoln with ample troops, and to be sure South Carolina failed egregiously in its promises to raise adequate militia. Lincoln subsequently pleaded that Congress expected him to defend the city to the last, and as proof he pointed to the fact that between February and April it never told him that "attempting ye defence of it were improper."[33] But Congress not only never dictated how he should conduct his campaign to save the city, it was absurd for Lincoln to suggest that a body that had accepted Fabian tactics for four years would suddenly, and without explicit orders, expect him to risk the entire southern army in a siege.

The conclusion is inescapable that Lincoln's shortcomings produced this extraordinary crisis. It was his responsibility to see the big picture, to wage a campaign with the interest of all South Carolina, and all the Southern Department, in mind. Instead, Lincoln permitted himself to be cowed repeatedly by Charlestonians who heatedly demanded that their city be defended. Like others,

Governor Rutledge told Lincoln that an acceptable justification for abandoning Charleston "will never exist." Reading between the lines of the chief executive's threat, and fully aware of the tepid support for the American Revolution within powerful circles in the state, Lincoln convinced himself that if he withdrew from the city, South Carolina and Georgia would withdraw from the war. Lincoln did not want to bear the burden for having brought on such a cataclysmic turn of events. Another consideration must have also haunted Lincoln. The harsh reality of this war was that only Washington could walk away from a fight and win praise. Lee had been ruined after his retreat at Monmouth and St. Clair, though exonerated, had suffered irrevocable harm to his reputation for having abandoned Ticonderoga (as Lincoln knew all too well, having presided at the court martial). But the single greatest factor leading to this gathering disaster was that Lincoln lacked the qualities of a great commander. He had never held an independent command before he was sent south, and he had not shined during his fifteen months in the theater prior to Clinton's landing. No one understood Lincoln's deficiencies better than Lincoln himself, for he confessed to Washington his "insufficiency" from "want of experience" a month before the British arrived. Lincoln made many of the same mistakes at Charleston that Washington had made in New York, but Washington had been saved by acting on the counsel of a highly respected officer, Charles Lee, who urged that Manhattan be sacrificed. Lincoln was served by lesser lights, although some of them, such as General McIntosh, advised at a council of war on April 13 that "we should not lose an hour longer in attempting to get . . . out." Lincoln chose not to listen. Washington's counsel might also have been helpful—the moment he learned that Whipple refused to defend the bar, the commander, at headquarters in New Jersey, remarked that "the Town . . . ought to have been relinquished"—but he provided no instruction, despite Lincoln's pleas for advice.[34]

By the time Lincoln learned of the disaster at Monck's Corner, he was largely out of options. Clinton immediately put Cornwallis, with 2,300 men, in charge of securing the area east of the Cooper. Lincoln did not have the resources to deal with that threat, and each day, with the precision of a well-oiled machine, more and more of that region—with its cattle, until now the American army's sole source of fresh meat—fell to the British. By mid-April, moreover, the last of Moncrief's three planned parallels had been constructed. It was a half-mile forward of the first parallel and barely 275 yards from the main American line. For two weeks already the British had bombarded the city and rebel defenses, killing soldiers and civilians, and damaging stores and houses (including that of Governor Rutledge). From their new parallel, their aim only improved. As terrified residents of Charleston huddled beneath any shelter they could find, the bloated corpses of horses littered streets and yards, and a pall of gray-black smoke wafted menacingly above the town. (Clinton rapidly forbad the use of incendiaries, calling it "absurd, impolitick, and inhuman to burn a town you mean to occupy.") All the while, depredations were occurring beyond the city in the region that Cornwallis was subduing. Looting and plundering were rampant. Civilians who had a relative soldiering for America got the worst of it. The Loyalist troops, less well disciplined than the regulars, and often churning with vitriol, were responsible for most of the atrocious incidents. Homes were stripped clean—in one instance, a family with a new-born child watched helplessly as the pillagers even took the baby's clothes—and residents were physically assaulted, with some rapes reported.[35]

Faced with disaster, Lincoln summoned three councils of war within a thirty-six-hour span on April 20–21. Each was attended by his highest ranking officers and the principal civilian authorities who had not already fled the city. If the army was to attempt a crossing of the Cooper River—not unlike Washington's crossing of the East River to escape Brooklyn in 1776—it had to be done now. Getting the army across the river would be dicey, but possible, as the royal fleet had never attempted to secure the Cooper. Its commander, Vice Admiral Marriot Arbuthnot, Whipple's clone when it came to a disinclination to act with vigor and audacity, had been deterred by the American frigates in the lower Cooper, the rebel fortifications at Lampriers Point, and the obstructions (several sunken ships) that Lincoln had put in the channel leading from the harbor to the river. Yet, if the army got across the Cooper, it was far from safe. Cornwallis's force would lie in wait. To reach safety, the Americans would have to fight their way through what was certain to be a well-entrenched enemy force, much as Burgoyne had tried, and failed, to do at Saratoga. The alternatives to retreat were not good: hold out for as long as possible and hope for a miracle—perhaps a ruinous storm or the arrival of a French fleet—or capitulation. The councils of war were acrimonious, and in the final meeting the civilian officials verbally abused the army's officers. Despite South Carolina's wretched record in providing militia, one Privy Council member accused the officers, and Lincoln in particular, of having failed to protect the city, while another treacherously declared that if the army abandoned Charleston, he would open the city gates to the invaders and aid them in attacking the American army.[36] General Pinckney demanded that the besieged army hold out to the "last extremity," adding with high drama that to die for one's country was "the greatest felicity a patriotic soldier can hope for."[37] All along Lincoln had been overawed by the civilian leaders, and he flinched again, permitting them to dictate the final decision. There would be no attempt to escape. It was agreed instead to draft terms for ending the siege, but the rebels proposed fanciful conditions: a thirty-six-hour cease-fire, during which all Continentals, militiamen, and rebel navy vessels would be permitted to depart. Clinton responded that such ludicrous stipulations "could not be listened to." He demanded an unconditional surrender to save Charleston from "havock and destruction." When Lincoln spurned that demand, the cannonading resumed.

Thereafter, day after day, night after night, the city's residents and the American soldiers were subjected to a shuddering bombardment. The troops lived a miserable existence. Seven or eight soldiers were killed or wounded daily by artillery fire or enemy snipers. These men not only coped with ever-present fear, many lived in mire, occupying ditches filled with brackish water, and all suffered from both the high sun and the remorseless attacks from mosquitoes and sand flies. Hunger was their relentless companion as well, as rations were steadily reduced until nothing but a handful of rice remained in their diet. One officer claimed that "for want of sleep, many faces were so swelled they could scarcely see out of their eyes."[38] Life was not much better for civilians. Some were plundered by famished soldiers who skulked about at night in search of food. Nor was anyone safe from the enemy. At any moment a cannonball might crash through the house, setting it ablaze or knocking it down. Over everything hung the terrible reality that if there was life after the siege, it would be filled with the hand-wringing uncertainty that always accompanies surrender and military occupation.

By early May, Clinton knew that he could not permit the siege to continue much longer. Intelligence from New York had reported that a fleet was being prepared in France for sailing, though its destination was unknown (it was the task force that would bring Rochambeau's army to Rhode Island). On May 6, Clinton sighed that he was beginning to believe that the rebels "will be Blockheads enough to wait the assault."[39] As he prepared plans for storming the rebel defenses, Clinton once again demanded an unconditional surrender, advising that if it was spurned, he could not be responsible for "whatever vindictive Severity exasperated Soldiers may inflict on the unhappy people" in the city.[40]

After a council of war at which forty-nine of the sixty-one who attended favored capitulation, Lincoln on May 9—a day of "murderous fire" by the besiegers, said one soldier—once again sought to bargain. Although his conditions had been scaled back in the seventeen days since he first proposed terms, Lincoln still asked that his rebel militiamen be permitted to return home. Anxious to get the bulk of his army, and the fleet, back to New York, Clinton consented, but on the condition that the militiamen be "prisoners upon parole," meaning that they could not again serve until they had been formally exchanged. Incredibly, Lincoln balked. Clinton scorned further bargaining. He reopened the bombardment, returning now to the "red-hot shot, which set fire to several houses," one of his soldiers noted. The Americans answered with "a tremendous cannonade" of their own that night. It was "a glorious sight," but a "dreadful night," Moultrie said, with the shells "like meteors crossing each other and bursting in the air; it appeared as if the stars were tumbling down." But every American knew that "it availed us nothing," and perhaps most knew while it was in progress that it was "our last great effort," as one said. What eventually assured that this was the final shelling came in the midst of the bombardment. The South Carolina militiamen petitioned Lincoln to accept Britain's terms.[41] Faced with the makings of a mutiny, Lincoln at 2:00 p.m. on May 11 raised a white flag. Sensing that the Americans had decided to end their resistance, some of the British and

German officers broke out bottles of wine and quietly began their celebration even as Lincoln's letter was being carried to Clinton. Lincoln had agreed to the terms set forth by Clinton two days earlier. Utterly vanquished, Lincoln had suffered the worst American defeat during the War of Independence.[42]

Early the next afternoon under a buttermilk sky, British and Hessian soldiers entered Charleston's gate and took possession of the hornwork. A few minutes later, two regiments marched in, together with a military band. With music wafting over the still smoking ruins of the city, Clinton and his highest officers rode into Charleston and were received by a weary Lincoln astride his horse. After they chatted momentarily, the British artillery fired a twenty-gun salute, the last enemy rounds that Charleston would hear until the Civil War. When the field pieces were quiet, the American soldiers marched out and surrendered. One observer thought their faces were etched with "chagrin and anger," but most were struck by their "miserable condition." The "rebels appeared . . . ragged and very dirty," said a German, and another noted that few wore shoes, their clothing was threadbare, and all "looked greatly starved." One thought them "the most ragged rabble I ever behold," while another simply dismissed the Americans as "a ragged dirty looking set of People as usual," though he added that they have "more appearance of discipline than we have seen formerly." The officers, each in a "different colored uniform and with different facings," struck one of the conquerors as "comedians about to commence a show, which together with their troops, without shoes, made a very comical scene." Mostly, the victors were exuberant. "[T]his victory will within a short time make the Crown of England dominant again from Pensacola to the James River," a Hessian jubilantly remarked.[43] The ebullience in Charleston would soon spread to London, where Germain dared to hope that this victory was a harbinger of "a speedy and happy termination of the American war," especially as intelligence was reporting that morale in the colonies was sinking beneath the weight of "general distress and sufferings."[44]

The long campaign for Charleston was over. Casualties were strikingly low, considering that nearly a million rounds of artillery had pummeled the city and the rebel defenses. The Americans lost 225 men (4 percent of those who had served), the British 265 (2 percent of their soldiery). Some 5,700 American soldiers and 1,000 sailors were taken prisoner. Approximately 2,500 of those captured were Continental soldiers and perhaps 200 were French troops that d'Estaing had left with his ally. The Americans additionally surrendered five thousand muskets and nearly four hundred pieces of irreplaceable artillery, and all three Continental navy frigates, as well as South Carolina's *L'Adventure*. Two signers of the Declaration of Independence, Thomas Heyward and Arthur Middleton, were among the civilians taken captive, and both were sent to confinement in Florida. A host of military officers—including seven generals— were captured. The highest-ranking officers were paroled—Lincoln departed the city soon after surrendering and was in Philadelphia within a month—but the enlisted men lost every scrap of freedom on May 11. They had become prisoners of war and faced an uncertain future.[45]

CHARLESTON yielded the largest collection of prisoners taken by Britain in a single engagement, a number that exceeded the combined total captured at Quebec and Fort Washington, the two other battles in which record numbers of Americans surrendered. Each man who was led away into captivity entered a world that was perhaps more dangerous than anything he had previously experienced as a soldier. Scholars believe that at least 8,500 of the 18,154 Continental soldiers and sailors who were captured in this war died while in captivity. In contrast, the best estimate is that about 6,800 Continentals died in battle and 10,000 perished in camp of disease. Put another way, whereas one Continental soldier in eighteen was killed in action and one in ten died of a camp disease, an astonishing 47 percent of those who became prisoners of war perished in captivity, roughly the same percentage of U.S. soldiers who died in Japanese internment camps during World War II but greater than the percentage of Union troops that succumbed in the infamous Andersonville prison during the Civil War. In addition to the Continentals, thousands of militiamen and privateers were also made prisoners of war. Exact figures can never be known, but when they, too, are included in the toll, it is possible that as many as 11,000 Americans may have died in captivity between 1775 and 1783.[46]

At one time or another, American prisoners languished in Barbados, St. Lucia, the Leeward Islands, Portugal, Senegal, Ireland, Scotland, Wales, Canada, Savannah, Philadelphia, and Florida, but the largest numbers were confined in four places—England, New York, on prison ships, or at Haddrell's Point, about six miles from Charleston. The Haddrell's Point facility was something of an anomaly, a prison camp that was quickly erected near the site of a surrender. Previously, the British had sent most of their prisoners to New York, where at one time thirteen separate prisons had been utilized. Late in 1776, when Britain held four thousand prisoners, warehouses, abandoned buildings, churches, King's College, the City Hall, and the city's two jails—Provost and New Bridewell—had served as lockups. Though some installations were spacious (the Liberty Street Prison, formerly a sugar warehouse, was a five-story building), overcrowding was a common problem. The British resolved the matter by converting obsolete naval and merchant vessels into prison ships, the most loathsome, and dangerous, facility that any prisoner could face. Ultimately, at least twenty-eight prison ships were put to use, mostly in the bays and rivers around New York, although one lay outside Charleston harbor and took on many of the sailors that surrendered when the city fell.

Under the best of circumstances, prisoners hardly faced felicitous conditions. Provided with rations that were two-thirds those allotted British soldiers, a prisoner's diet was inadequate in quantity and nutrition, and sometimes the food was spoiled or chock-a-block with maggots or worms. One prisoner reported a

Interior of the Jersey *Prison Ship.* Wood engraving, first published by H. Howe in 1855. This anonymous sketch shows the deplorable conditions faced by American prisoners of war aboard British prison ships. Confinement on a prison ship was nearly tantamount to a death sentence.

daily ration of bread laced with "yellow and green streaks of mold." Others recalled "beef like oakum," and remembered allocations of "heads of sheep with the horns and wool thereon." Clothing and bedding were provided irregularly. But when America's commissary of prisoners visited the Provost facility in February 1778, the loudest complaints that he heard concerned the "shocking barbarity" of the warden, who allegedly punished refractory prisoners with beatings, inadequate water in hot weather, and incarceration in "Dark, damp Dungeons." A captive confined elsewhere in Manhattan told of a jailer who liked to brandish a noose and rail that he "had already hung several, and . . . he imagined he would hang some more." Others said they were "severely flogged for imaginary faults." These unhappy conditions were magnified aboard the prison ships, where the same rebel official reported that the men "suffer greatly and die daily."[47] Those held captive on ships were confined below deck in lethally squalid surroundings. Little sunshine or fresh air penetrated the murky hold, home and latrine to the prisoners for sixteen hours or more each day, and round the clock for days on end when inclement weather inhibited their being brought on deck. The captives lived amid the unspeakable stench of illness and human waste. They tried to eat in this environment, too, cooking their food in a large kettle filled with water gathered from alongside the vessel, the very site where the previous day's excrement was dumped each morning.[48]

On land and sea, but especially the latter, Britain's prisons were incubators for a myriad of diseases that carried off the prisoners in appalling numbers. One American officer confined in New York estimated that 1,100 of the 2,800 men taken prisoner at Fort Washington died within sixty days of entering captivity. Survivors later recalled that each morning the guards on the prison ship *Jersey* called out: "Rebels, bring out your dead." Seldom a day passed that a corpse or two was not hoisted to the hatch, though the captors sometimes left the dead lying in a pile until a sufficient quantity of bodies accumulated to make a cartload.[49] Philip Freneau, later a renowned journalist in the partisan press war in the early Republic, wrote a poem about these horrid vessels in which he drew on his two months captivity aboard a prison ship off Brooklyn in 1778. A "quick ruin" was the fate of most who were left to "perish in this dismal den / Starved and insulted by the worst of men" until every prisoner grew "Meagre and sad and scorch'd with heat below / They look like ghosts ere death had made them so."[50]

The acute class-consciousness of that day was evident in the treatment of prisoners. Virtually all officers were paroled and lived in what was tantamount to an indulgent house arrest. General Pinckney, who had insisted on dying in a last ditch defense of Charleston, survived the siege and spent his captivity on his cousin's plantation near the city, where his needs were attended by one of his slaves and his family and friends, who were permitted unlimited visits.[51] Captive officers in New York were allowed to reside in private homes, paying room and board to the owner, to move about freely within the city, though they could not leave Manhattan, and even to marry, as Abner Everett, a young Georgian, chose to do. Lieutenant Jabez Fitch, a thirty-nine-year-old farmer from Norwich, Connecticut, was captured on the first day of fighting on Long Island and spent fifteen months in captivity, all but the first five weeks following his capture on parole. He first resided with several other officers in a large house kept by a landlady on Broadway (near today's City Hall), but in January 1777 most of the captive officers were transferred to Long Island and Fitch thereafter resided on a three-hundred-acre farm in what today is Brooklyn. Fitch endured few real hardships in captivity, save for missing his wife and eight children. He occasionally sank into a funk at his "Tedious & useless" life, but he was upbeat most of the time. He was treated with the "greatest humanity & Tenderness," he said, and always "dwelt in Affluent Circumstances." After six months as a prisoner he admitted that he was "in such happy Circumstances, as to stand in Necessity of Nothing but Liberty itself." His diet was always adequate, and on occasions he enjoyed what he called "a noble dinner." On Christmas Day 1776—a day that he might have spent marching in a snowstorm to fight in Trenton had he not been captured—he enjoyed what he acknowledged was a feast with all the trimmings, including baked goose, pork pie, cider, and coffee. He worked now and again— he took jobs such as unloading firewood and barrels of apples—to earn money for purchasing necessities. He visited the barber regularly, bought a wig, and was never short of tobacco (he took up smoking while a prisoner). Kindly neighbors, widows of soldiers, and even Manhattan's prostitutes furnished him and other captives with tea, sugar, bread, clothing, and money. Fitch hunted, read voluminously, worshiped regularly, and attended the funerals of his company and regimental commanders who died in New York in captivity. Fitch was confined to his residence after dark, but during the day he strolled about and visited with a wide circle of friends among the city's residents, some of whom frequently invited him to stay for dinner so that he enjoyed an incredibly varied culinary experience. Friends and other soldiers visited him as well, including even the British sergeant who had taken him prisoner. Each week Fitch called on the enlisted men from his regiment who were held prisoner, once finding "4 of em dead in the Yard, & several others Dieing in House." When he moved to Long Island, Fitch shared a room with another paroled officer, Captain Ozias Bissell, a forty-eight-year-old fellow New Englander who made the most of his time as a prisoner. Bissell spent some nights drinking at a nearby tavern and other evenings, as Fitch put it, visiting the "Bedstead" of a woman who had been his landlady while he was confined on Manhattan. Late in 1777 Fitch was exchanged for a British commissary of forage who had been captured six months before. He arrived home just before Christmas, eighteen months after having left to enter the army.[52]

Most American sailors were held prisoner in England. They were scattered about the countryside, but the primary detention centers were Forton prison, near Portsmouth, and Mill (or Old Mill) prison, near Plymouth, which between them held nearly 2,500 rebel prisoners by 1780. Like their counterparts in New York City, these men faced an inadequate diet, though their needs were better tended with regard to clothing and bedding. The most striking difference between captivity in England and America was that naval officers were not paroled. They, too, were held in Forton and Mill prisons, though at their request they were segregated from the enlisted men. At least two officers who had won public acclaim for their exploits did time in these prisons, Captain John Manley, who had gained note by capturing the ordnance brig *Nancy* in 1775, and daring Gustavus Conyngham.[53]

The United States also took prisoners. Early in the war, responsibility for captives was left to the state in which each prisoner was taken. With independence, however, Congress took control. It scattered the prisoners about, usually confining them in remote locations well removed from the coast. Some men were housed in jails, but the most fortunate wound up in newly constructed barracks. Captive British and German officers were paroled and rented rooms in private residences. The enlisted men held captive by the Americans, like their rebel equivalents, faced a difficult life. Often unable to adequately provision their armies, it was usually beyond the capability of the Americans to provide for their prisoners. Food allocations sometimes fell short of the two-thirds of the daily rations of a British soldier that was the announced standard, and not infrequently the captors appear to have made little attempt to provide clothing and blankets. Instead, they appealed to the British army to tend to the needs of their own. Like the British, the Americans permitted their prisoners to work to earn money with which to supplant their food rations and procure other necessities. Numerous captives labored on farms, at forges, in shipyards, and even in mines. Although many prisoners faced deprivation, and many died in captivity, the Americans —with one glaring exception—did not set out to deliberately mistreat their prisoners. The black stain on America's record was its treatment of captive Loyalist soldiers, who often were consciously subjected to inhuman treatment. Left to the states, some Loyalists were housed with the mentally ill and others were thrown into loathsome makeshift prisons in mines or aboard barges, where they faced despicable conditions that rivaled those on Britain's prison ships.[54]

The most famous of America's prisoners were the men in the Convention Army, the force surrendered by Burgoyne in October 1777. The Saratoga Convention had promised that the 5,900 men taken captive were to be paroled— on condition of agreeing never again to serve in America during this war—and returned to England. Congress immediately reneged on the agreement. The captives were marched to Cambridge, Massachusetts, where most spent their first year in captivity. While the officers rented rooms—Burgoyne first lodged at a tavern just off Harvard Square, then occupied a house where he entertained lavishly—the enlisted men lived in tumbledown barracks that had been hastily constructed during the siege of Boston. Over the next twelve months more than 1,300 prisoners escaped, including all the musicians in the Sixty-second Regiment. Many were working on farms in the Boston area and fled captivity (and the British army) after marrying local girls. One year after Burgoyne's surrender, Congress ordered what was left of the Convention Army to be marched to Charlottesville, Virginia. Nearly six hundred men escaped during the long trek south, which ended in January 1779. While the officers crowded into rooms in the dozen houses in the tiny village, or in farmhouses in the vicinity, the men built log huts that resembled the accommodations at Valley Forge. When spring came they built a church and theater as well. Many men worked on local farms, but the officers idled away their time, and the highest ranking were entertained at Monticello now and again by Charlottesville's most esteemed resident, Thomas Jefferson. After nearly two years in Virginia, a turn in the war compelled Congress to move the army again, this time to Maryland. Still later it was marched to Connecticut. By late 1781 only 2,650 men remained, and fewer still were left in captivity at war's end when the Convention Army finally went home.[55]

Each side appointed a commissary general of prisoners and the commander in chief of each army devoted countless hours to prisoner-related matters. Washington had been on the job for only six weeks when he wrote his first letter to his British counterpart complaining about the conditions faced by American captives. Washington bristled that officers were not being given preferential treatment. But what was uppermost on his mind was to secure for the American captives the status of prisoners of war.[56] If declared rebels in a colonial uprising, the prisoners might face execution. The British never formerly complied with

Washington's wishes, as to do so might be interpreted as a tacit recognition of American sovereignty. From fear of retaliation, however, Britain's leaders never prosecuted their captives as insurrectionists. Only two American prisoners were executed in the course of the war. Late in the conflict Captain Joshua Huddy of the New Jersey militia fell into the hands of a group known as the Associated Loyalists, who hanged him in reprisal after a Tory refugee died in mysterious circumstances while in the custody of the New Jersey militia. The second victim was Private Isaac Hayne, a South Carolina militiaman who had been paroled in the surrender of the Charleston garrison. A year later Hayne signed a British loyalty oath and served briefly in a Loyalist militia unit before defecting to the American side. He was subsequently recaptured by the British and after a short incarceration was tried on a charge of treason. Following his conviction, Hayne was hanged in Charleston in August 1781. Both executions sparked vehement demands for retaliation. Following Huddy's death, Washington threatened the execution of a British captive—Captain Charles Asgill drew the short straw—if Clinton did not turn over the leader of the Associated Loyalists for prosecution by the American authorities. Upon reflection, Washington and Congress decided that putting Asgill to death would set in motion a blood bath. Vergennes, who likewise feared for Frenchmen held captive, got the Americans off the hook by appealing for clemency for Asgill, which Congress granted.[57]

The American commissioners in Paris and Congress expended considerable effort toward improving conditions for the prisoners in England. The commissioners—and later Minister Franklin—corresponded with the prisoners and also sent an emissary, John Thornton, to visit Forton and Mill. His eventual report excoriated the prison authorities for their callousness, leading Franklin to complain of the "cajoling & menacing" practices within those facilities. Although North's government did not respond, the publicity aroused caring people in England. Fund-raising drives followed for the relief of prisoners—at least one of the commissioners, John Adams, contributed—and residents who lived near the prisons solicited donations of money and supplies, or simply took items of their own to the inmates. The collective endeavors by the English to aid the American prisoners appear to have outpaced similar undertakings in America.[58] From time to time Congress appropriated money for distribution among the American prisoners, though it approved far greater expenditures to assist the officers who had to pay for their accommodations. Once the American currency began to collapse, Congress increasingly sent food and clothing rather than money, and beginning in 1777 it shipped flour to be sold in New York City, with the proceeds used to compensate local businessmen who supplied prisoners with essentials. Some states pitched in as well, notably Virginia and Maryland, whose men comprised the bulk of those held at Haddrell's Point. The American public provided next to no benevolence for the enemy prisoners in their midst.[59]

Late in 1779 Franklin remarked to an English friend that "we have now more English Prisoners than you have Americans."[60] While true at the time, that had not always been the case, nor would it be following the siege of Charleston. Scholars now believe that during this eight-year war roughly the same number of prisoners were taken by both sides, though until Saratoga the great majority of those in detention were American. The British held 4,430 prisoners at the end of 1776, the Americans about a quarter of that number. A year later, the United States had in custody approximately twice the number confined by the British.[61]

While many men endured an excruciatingly lengthy captivity, others were freed following a relatively brief incarceration. Escape aside, there were three principal ways in which a prisoner might gain his freedom. Both sides offered captives freedom in return for defecting and joining their armed forces, and both sides carped about their adversary offering such enticements.[62] The Americans were the least successful in getting prisoners to switch sides, leading Congress to self-righteously forbid the practice in March 1778.[63] Far greater numbers were released from confinement through paroles. Set free, a parolee pledged not to soldier again before he had been formally exchanged. It was both a humane and cost-cutting expedient, and one that Britain first used in mid-1776 when it paroled the roughly three hundred surviving captives from Arnold and Montgomery's failed attempt to take Quebec. Prisoner exchanges were the third method of liberating captives. Swapping prisoners held real advantages for the British, whose soldiers always served for the duration. If they got back a soldier, he immediately added to their manpower total. If the British delayed a prospective exchange until after their rebel captive's terms of enlistment had expired, they reduced the number of Continentals during that campaign season.[64] Despite these drawbacks, Washington favored exchanges, fearing that if the American captives were left in British hands for years, the public would be persuaded that military "service [was] odious." Such a conclusion, he warned, "will injure drafting and recruiting, discourage the militia & increase the discontents of the army."[65] But Congress saw anything that strengthened the British army as "bad policy." On several occasions it thwarted negotiations toward a so-called cartel, the rules that designated exchange procedures, especially how many men of lower rank were to be relinquished for a man of higher rank, as well as the settling of accounts with regard to the expenses incurred in housing and feeding captives. Although several partial exchanges were arranged, sometimes involving as few as only one or two men, no major exchange occurred until late in the war. At one point in 1778, Washington, frustrated and seething, virtually accused Congress of ruining morale and risking the loss of life among the captives. He told Congress that "the Wish of the Army . . . demands an Exchange." But Congress did not budge until the horrific surrender at Charleston, when thousands of Americans were once again in British hands. Thereafter, some limited exchanges occurred. Congress did not intrude in the negotiations concerning seamen confined in England and a greater traffic in exchanges occurred. The commissioners in Paris secured three exchanges of naval captives and in 1779 and 1780

Charles Cornwallis, First Marquess Cornwallis. Painting by Thomas Gainsborough. A sound general, Cornwallis fought with vigor and daring, but his decision to take his army into Virginia in April 1781 completed Britain's ruin.

Franklin arranged for the release of nearly 275 American prisoners by swapping some of the captives taken by John Paul Jones.[66]

FOLLOWING THE AMERICAN SURRENDER at Charleston, Clinton remained in South Carolina only long enough to launch operations to pacify the backcountry. He faced a novel opportunity. The British had lacked the manpower to stray beyond Boston, and when their forces had taken New York and Philadelphia, the defeated American armies had survived largely intact. But for a time after Lincoln's capitulation, there was no American army in South Carolina. Putting Cornwallis in charge of subjugating the interior, Clinton told London straight-away that this would be a test—the "fairest opening," he called it—of "those loyal dispositions which are believed to inspire so great a number." Cornwallis quickly sent out three columns to secure a huge arc of the countryside around and above Charleston. The operation proceeded spectacularly. Before the end of May, forces consisting largely of Tories had occupied Augusta and Ninety-Six, a trading post nearly 175 miles beyond Charleston, as well as Georgetown, sixty miles above the capital on the coast.[67] The most crucial portion of the campaign occurred in the green, undulating sector known as the Waxhaws above the Santee River, along the road leading from Camden to Charlotte. Cornwallis had been aware from the outset that scattered remnants of Lincoln's army, including the forty cavalrymen who had escaped at Monck's Corner, were in that region. So, too, were some 340 Virginia Continentals, who had marched into the state after the trap had been sprung on Charleston, and nearly 800 North Carolina militiamen, who likewise had arrived too late to be of help to Lincoln. Cornwallis took 2,500 men and set out to find these rebels. He had not gotten far before intelligence reported that the North Carolinians had gone home and that the Continentals, under Colonel Abraham Buford, were retreating toward North Carolina. Aware that the cavalry alone might overtake the rebels, Cornwallis detached his British Legion. Tarleton responded with alacrity. Madly driving his 270 men—the bodies of horses that had been ridden to death in the wilting heat and humidity soon littered the dusty roadside—Tarleton's Legion covered an incredible 160 miles in two days. On May 29 the British cavalry force caught the Americans.

The startled Buford was without artillery, having sent it ahead to hasten his retreat, but he outnumbered his green-clad enemy by nearly two-to-one. Given little time to prepare, Buford hastily formed a single defensive line. If he hoped that Tarleton might be deterred, Buford was wrong. Tarleton was full of fight. He ordered a cavalry charge at the very center of the American line. The legion had only about three hundred yards to cover, a span that a horse at full gallop could cover in a few seconds. Each defender could squeeze off only a single shot. Buford had two choices. He could order his men to "fire by platoons," so that rebel fire was spaced out incrementally, or he could attempt to stop the attackers by one thunderous massed volley. He chose the latter tactic, giving the order to fire when the enemy was barely ten yards away. Buford's choice failed. Some cavalrymen were brought down, but the blast failed to stop most of Tarleton's men. The momentum of those who were unscathed carried them into the enemy's lair, or like Tarleton, whose horse was killed beneath him, they simply cleared their fallen mount and sprinted the few final yards toward their foe. Whether on horseback or foot, the attackers swung their sabers, cutting men to pieces, overwhelming their stunned adversaries. Battlefields are horrid places, but this one was especially ghastly. Here were men with severed hands and limbs, crushed skulls, and breached arteries. Some men were decapitated by the slashing cavalrymen. Others were trampled by maddened horses. The bellies of many were laid open by bayonets. Although resistance ended within seconds, the carnage continued. Tarleton did not order the slaughter that ensued, but he did not stop it either. As the Virginians screamed for "quarter," for mercy, Tarleton's men waded among the helpless rebels hacking and bayoneting in a saturnalia of bloodshed. It was a massacre. ("I have cut 170 Off'rs and Men to pieces," Tarleton said straightforwardly in his report.) In a war in which rarely more than 6 or 7 percent of combatants fell on a battlefield, nearly 75 percent of the Virginians fell victim on this day of horror in the Waxhaws.[68] As the British Legion was a Loyalist outfit, scholars have sometimes attributed the slaughter to a frenzy of retribution by neighbor against neighbor, but Tarleton's men consisted almost entirely of fairly recent Scottish immigrants who had been recruited in Northern provinces. Other historians have depicted Tarleton as a bloodthirsty ogre. That, too, seems not to have been true, but he was relatively new to command responsibilities and he had previously exhibited a habit, for which Cornwallis had reprimanded him, of not controlling his men in the immediate aftermath of battle, when churning passions, including bloodlust, drove men to act in unspeakable ways. From this day forward, southern rebels called him Bloody Tarleton and spoke of "Tarleton's quarter" in the same vituperative manner in which they uttered an expletive.[69]

THE RESPONSE IN THE NORTH to the southern defeats at Charleston and through the South Carolina backcountry was varied, and curious. Joseph Reed thought they might be a blessing in disguise, just what was needed to refocus the energies of the country.[70] Washington echoed that sentiment, hoping it would lead the states to vest Congress with the powers it required to act decisively. He also predicted that it would compel the British to "dissipate their force" in order "to hold conquests so remote" from what he considered the epicenter of the war, New York. Many in Congress saw things differently. With Georgia already lost, they feared the "loss of the whole State" of South Carolina and likely North Carolina as well. Some wondered if Virginia could survive. Not only had its Continental line been decimated, but thanks to what a Pennsylvania congressman called the greed of its "Land-Jobbers & Speculators," Virginia was spread thin, having committed some of its manpower to the West to fight to secure its land claims. Unlike Washington, few congressmen saw anything besides a "Catastrophe" in the South, the "worst disaster" that "has befallen us," a "fatal blow . . . to the common Interest of the Union." Some worried about French opinion. As "disgraceful" as the huge surrender at Charleston had been to the United States, it must be "disgustful to our Allies."[71] A Massachusetts congressman who feared that the pacification of South Carolina would further erode support for the war among the wealthy planter class in the South, forecast that "this Year will be filled with our Disgraces."[72]

What Congress did know in June was that the army at Charleston was lost and that Tarleton had "cut to pieces" what was left of the remaining Continentals in South Carolina. It quickly made the "Expulsion of the Enemy from the several Posts" in the South its first priority. Washington responded that if precious resources were taken from him, his army would be "condemned to a disgraceful and fatal inactivity," an argument that must have perplexed many congressmen, given the dearth of action that had taken place in the North over the past two years.[73]

Following a lengthy debate, Congress gave General Gates command of the Southern Department. Washington, who had hated and feared Gates since the days of the alleged Conway Cabal, would have preferred Greene or one of Virginia's brigadier generals, but as was his custom he did not intrude in

Congress's deliberations. Gates had a sizeable following in Congress. He was after all a professional soldier and the hero of Saratoga. What is more, as the militia had rallied behind him in the fight against Burgoyne, many hoped that Gates could arouse the militiamen in South Carolina. He was also cunning and highly political. He not only had carefully cultivated some congressmen over the years, but when he learned that Charleston was doomed, Gates had rushed to Philadelphia to lobby to be Lincoln's successor. Thus, Gates, who incongruously had been shuffled off to the backwater of the war during the three years since Saratoga—the single field post that Washington had offered him, to lead a campaign against the Iroquois in 1779, was "the only command to which I am entirely unequal," Gates had complained—finally had an independent command once again. He soon discovered that he was given little with which to work. He would have the 1,400 Delaware and Maryland Continentals under General Johann de Kalb that Washington had ordered south in April to reinforce Lincoln (and who had gotten no further than North Carolina before learning that Charleston had surrendered) and some North Carolina and Virginia militia. Usually upbeat, Gates immediately exclaimed that he had "an army without strength, a Military Chest, without money, a Department [devoid of] . . . Public Spirit."[74]

His little army was saddled with "increasing wants," he told the governors of North Carolina and Virginia, and he urged them to send tents, wagons, horses, arms, powder, bayonets, medicine, and food. Virginia's governor, Jefferson, had done little to help Lincoln in the spring, but immediately upon learning of the fall of Charleston, the state assembly—realizing that Gates alone stood between Cornwallis and Virginia's southern border—ordered 2,500 militia to Carolina. Jefferson followed by feverishly scraping together prodigious amounts of materials, including 10,000 stand of arms and, oddly, hundreds of tomahawks, and hurried them to Gates. There was little food to be sent, and for that Jefferson felt Gates's scorching wrath. The general railed at the governor for his "unpardonable Neglect" of "your Starved Fellow Citizens."[75] When Gates arrived in North Carolina and assumed command, he found a force of about four thousand men waiting for him. When Gates had won at Saratoga, 70 percent of his force had consisted of Continentals. Now, three quarters of Gates's men were militiamen, and he had next to no artillery and only about fifty cavalrymen.[76] His army was also so short of food that the men were on half rations. With the exception of Washington's bedraggled force that retreated across New Jersey in 1776, no American army had faced a major campaign in such a woeful state. The straits in which Gates found himself were worse even than Washington had confronted during that dark November and December four years earlier, for the commander in chief had possessed a strong artillery arm and a good intelligence network, and his adversary in 1776 had been almost devoid of cavalry.

Facing bad odds, Washington in 1776 had resorted to a Fabian strategy, falling back over one river after another, staying just beyond the reach of Cornwallis. Gates should have learned from his commander's example. He might have attempted to draw his adversary deep into the interior. In time, perhaps, Cornwallis might have acted injudiciously, affording Gates the opportunity to pounce, as Washington had done at Trenton. Instead, Gates, who took command on July 25, set out two days later to find the enemy, even though his army—as one soldier noted—was "so miserably poor that scarce any mortal could make use of it."[77] It was a decision, according to Colonel Otho Williams of the Maryland line, that caused "great astonishment." Williams, and perhaps others, had urged Gates to remain in North Carolina, where the army could be supplied by staunch patriot settlements and by "convoys of stores from the northward," and from which he could draw on the sizeable militias of Rowan and Mecklenburg counties.[78]

Several factors prompted Gates's to turn a deaf ear to such advice. As intelligence sources—mostly South Carolina backcountry militia—reported (correctly) that Cornwallis had divided his force to pacify the countryside, Gates believed that a rapid advance might permit him to pick off his adversary by stages. Gates had also been advised (less accurately) that large numbers of militiamen awaited his arrival in South Carolina; he knew that he would not have their services if he waited and campaigned in North Carolina. Gates was also driven by his demons. Despite his victory at Saratoga, some—especially those closest to Washington—had belittled his generalship in that campaign. Gates, they had whispered, had displaying little daring. He "hug himself" on the defensive, they said.[79] It was the actions of Schuyler and Arnold, they insisted, that had led to Burgoyne's undoing. The disparaging comments, part of a campaign to deny him credit for America's greatest victory in the war, had gnawed at Gates for three years. Frenetically ambitious and impulsive for glory, Gates now must have also hated Washington, who he believed had treated him meanly and unfairly, and he doubtless longed to once again score a more decisive victory than his commander in chief had ever won. Washington, as insecure as any man who ever reached a high station, had, like Gates, heard taunts about his record and had ached savagely for triumphs and glory. But Washington had better control of his passions, and for years he adhered to a strategy that he viscerally detested, doing so because he believed it was the best course for the cause. Gates should have exceeded Washington as a military leader. He had long experience in a professional army and was more loved by his men. But Washington's character was superior to that of his rival, and it made him a great man, whereas Gates was merely a good soldier.

On July 27 Gates put his men in motion. He had two immediate targets in mind: Lieutenant Colonel Francis Rawdon's small British force, consisting mostly of Loyalist regulars, that was conducting operations near Camden, and Camden itself, the site of a storage depot that Cornwallis had established to facilitate his eventual invasion of North Carolina. Gates hurriedly set out, moving before the main force of his cavalry, which had scattered after twice being shredded in recent weeks by Tarleton's Legion, could join with the army. Gates also ignored the advice of de Kalb, and others, and advanced toward Camden by the most direct route, though it took him through a region that had been picked clean of food and forage. Most of the residents had fled in fear, and their abandoned farmhouses were empty of victuals, either because they had taken everything with them or because their ravening neighbors, who had left later, had helped themselves to every last scrap of food. For several days Gates's men marched under a blinding sun, stirring up smothering clouds of dust as they tramped past unpainted houses on forlorn knolls. The only creatures to be seen, aside from mosquitoes and fat, green flies, were dogs that stayed warily off the road and barked excitedly at the intruders. The men subsisted on green corn boiled with lean beef, molasses, and unripened peaches. It was "not unpalatable," said one soldier, but it caused stomach cramps and diarrhea (which some officers tried without success to fend off by concocting what they hoped would be an antidiarrheal mixture of hair powder and water).[80] As Gates neared the unhurried hamlet of Camden on August 14, he possessed about three thousand able-bodied men, sufficient, he believed, to give him a considerable numerical advantage over Rawdon.

What Gates did not know was that Cornwallis had arrived the day before with reinforcements. The British commander, tending to administrative duties in Charleston, had learned on August 9 that a rebel army was advancing on Camden. Gathering a force, he set out to find the enemy, pushing his sunburned men hard through ragged fringes of the backcountry. Cornwallis and his redcoats, together with four companies of light infantry summoned from Ninety-Six, reached Camden after dark on August 13, just ahead of the rebel army. Gates's force remained the slightly larger of the two—by about a three-to-two majority

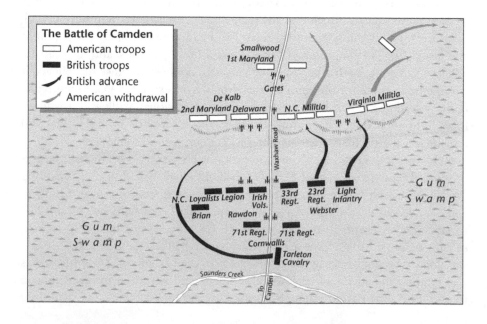

—but the British had more regulars, more artillery, and a nearly five-to-one edge in cavalry. Gates's haste for battle had led him into a deadly predicament, a snare that he only began to comprehend on August 15. In the wee dark hours of that day, he marched his men toward Camden. But the British were on the move, too, and advance units of the two armies collided in the stygian night. After a bit of inconsequential shooting, the two sides fell back, neither side wishing a night fight, a nearly unheard of occurrence in eighteenth-century warfare. Gates had taken prisoners in the little firefight, and they divulged the "unwelcome news" of Cornwallis's arrival. His "astonishment could not be concealed," one of his officers subsequently remarked. Gates must have known, too, that he was out of options. The British cavalry could probably seal off the roads, making an orderly retreat difficult, perhaps impossible. Even if he withdrew successfully, the dragoons would badly cut up his force. After a hurriedly assembled council of war, Gates concluded that his best hope was to take up the strongest possible defensive position, the stratagem that had served him well at Saratoga. In this instance, however, he had no time to select a desirable site or to adequately entrench. He knew that the fight would be on him not long after the sun rose.[81]

As he hastily prepared for combat in the first moments after the pink streaks of dawn broke through the southern pines and began to further heat the already steamy South Carolina countryside, Gates compounded his earlier series of blunders with another gaffe, one that historian Don Higginbotham aptly characterized as "the biggest mistake of his military career." Although he was aware of how Cornwallis was posting his attack force, Gates positioned his army so that his Continentals were to face the attack by the Loyalists and his militiamen would have to cope with the British and German regulars (who were to be led by Colonel Webster, whom Clinton had entrusted with getting the first redcoats across the Cooper River during the siege of Charleston). Worse still, misinterpreting his enemy's maneuvers, Gates ordered his militia to move from their primitive defensive positions and charge the enemy regulars. Disaster followed.

Once in the open, the militiamen panicked at the sight of the British marching resolutely toward them, bayonets and gun barrels gleaming in the bright sun, the redcoats ferociously chanting their traditional battle huzzas. Garret Watts, a North Carolina militiaman, thought he fired the first shot of the battle "without thinking except that I might prevent the man opposite from killing me." But if Watts got off a shot, he was one of the few militiamen rebels to do so. Men and officers began to break and flee, often throwing down their loaded muskets as they raced for what they thought was safety in the rear (Watts threw his gun down, too, but later fearing that he might be punished for being without a weapon, he retrieved an abandoned drum and pretended to be a drummer boy as he sped off).[82] The panic was contagious, and was later described by an officer as having acted "Like electricity" in that it "operate[d] instantaneously" and was "irresistible where it touche[d]." Untrained and poorly led, the militiamen had broken under fire, but once off the battlefield their panic only accelerated, as all feared capture or, worse, falling into the hands of Tarleton's men, who might reenact the Waxhaws slaughter. Seeing what was occurring, Gates momentarily rode about the area, a visible target atop his horse, desperately seeking to stanch the flight and restore a defensive line. It was hopeless. Many men no longer had muskets, and virtually none any longer had the will to fight. Only the Maryland and Delaware regulars under de Kalb, and a North Carolina militia regiment next to them, put up a fight, in some measure perhaps because they were unaware of the stampede occurring on the other side of the battlefield. Their view was obscured by the morning fog and the dense grey smoke from thousands of firearms that was contained at ground level by the heavy, humid air. These few American regulars not only continued to battle, they were even winning their fight before Cornwallis poured reinforcements into that sector and simply overwhelmed them. Before their fight ended, these Continentals had been abandoned not only by their comrades, but by their commander. Gates was later accused of cowardice, but that was not the case. According to one of his officers, Gates made a valiant effort to halt the retreat and regroup. Another characterized what happened as a case of Gates having been "bore away in the croud," swept back and ever further away from the battlefield as he rode about trying to stop the militiamen's flight, until it was all but impossible for him to fight his way through to those who were still on the front lines. Ultimately seeing the impossibility of continuing the battle, Gates, too, rode for safety, and did not stop riding until he reached Charlotte, sixty miles away.[83] Once the panic took hold, it was every man for himself, a ragged, leaderless mob that hurried in all directions "as their hopes led, and their fears drove them," according to one officer.[84] Not all escaped. Tarleton's cavalry gave chase, tracking down tired and thirsty, and defenseless, soldiers as far as twenty-two miles north of the battlefield. There is no record of how many militiamen perished at the hands of the British dragoons, but Tarleton himself described what occurred as a "rout and slaughter."[85]

The Battle of Camden, fought ninety days after the fall of Charleston, was an outrageous and unmitigated disaster. More than six hundred Americans were lost, more than a fifth of those who went into the fight, including de Kalb, who died after suffering eleven wounds. For the second time in three months—the third time in twenty months—the British had destroyed America's southern army. The debacle also finished Gates as a trusted general, ruined as much by his flight—which began while some of his men remained on the battlefield, an indefensible act—as by his inexplicable tactical errors. Washington's huggermuggers of character assassination saw to Gates's final destruction, orchestrating a campaign to complete his ruin. (One, Hamilton, was married to Elizabeth Schuyler, whose father had been removed from command as a result of Gates's conniving.) Gates was flayed unsparingly for his "military absurdity" and mocked for "running away . . . from his whole army" and "leaving all his troops to take care of themselves."[86]

The British had their fun as well. A Loyalist newspaper in New York rushed the following satire into print:

REWARD

Strayed, Deserted, or Stolen, from the subscriber . . . a whole ARMY . . . with all their baggage, artillery, wagons and camp equipage. The subscriber has very strong suspicions from information received from his aid de camp, that a certain CHARLES, EARL CORNWALLIS, was principally concerned in carrying off the said ARMY. . . . Any person or persons, civil or military, who will give information, whether to the subscriber, or to . . . the Continental Congress, where the said ARMY is so that they may be rallied again, shall be entitled to demand from the Treasury of the United States the sum of THREE MILLION of PAPER DOLLARS as soon as they can be spared from the public funds. [Signed:] HORATIO GATES[87]

The American cause was in free fall toward its nadir in this terrible war. Yet, as in the gloom that followed the disasters on Long Island and Manhattan, Washington glimpsed a new strategy that offered hope. The aim of the war in the South must no longer be to "expel them [the British] from the Country intirely," he counseled, for by "attempting too much, instead of going forward, we shall go backward." He now advised that the Americans must settle for a more modest objective: to "oblige them to . . . relinquish a part of what they now hold."[88]

In the meantime, Washington candidly acknowledged that the way was open for Cornwallis to invade Virginia. America's situation was grave. It "absolutely require[d] activity" by the French and Americans, he wrote to the newly arrived Rochambeau in September 1780.[89] A few days later, Washington, with forty staff and bodyguards accompanying him, rode from headquarters in New Jersey toward Hartford, where for the first time he was to meet with the French general. Along the way, he crossed the Hudson at Peekskill, where he dined with Benedict Arnold, now the commander of America's most important Hudson Highlands post, the installation at West Point. It was a delightful dinner and a pleasant evening. Washington liked the younger general and, with all the uncertainties in this war, he knew that Benedict Arnold was a man upon whom he could depend.

18

"SOUTHERN MEANS AND SOUTHERN EXERTIONS": HOPE AND DESPAIR, JUNE–DECEMBER 1780

THE FRENCH ARMY OF 6,500 MEN under General Rochambeau had been expected to make landfall in Rhode Island early in June. Like almost everything else in this war, it arrived late. The French soldiers, resplendent in their distinctive formfitting white uniforms and black hats, did not come ashore until July 15. The huge French task force had slipped undetected through the Royal Navy's Atlantic cordon, and the entire French army was unloaded and its defenses nearly completed before Admiral Arbuthnot was aware of its arrival. Clinton's hopes of assailing the French while they were vulnerable, perhaps driving them away before they established a toehold in America, were dashed. An angry Clinton did nothing that summer, save to ask London to recall Arbuthnot.[1]

Washington had learned that the French were on the way nearly seventy-five days before they finally arrived. From Lafayette, who had returned to America in April after a sixteen-month absence, Washington had also discovered that Rochambeau had been ordered to permit the American commander to establish the armies' course of action. For Washington, that meant one thing: a joint campaign to retake New York. Since the arrival of the first French fleet under d'Estaing two years earlier, Washington had fixated on New York, intransigently refusing to move his army from its shadow, lest he lose the opportunity to attempt its conquest should another French squadron happen by. Washington now feared that the last chance to win the war might be at hand. With American morale crumbling and its economy shot, by mid-1780 he had come to believe that time was running out. "This is the time for America by one great exertion to put

Jean-Baptiste-Donatien de Vimeur, Comte de Rochambeau. Painting by Charles Willson Peale, from life, c. 1782. Commander of the French army in America in 1780–1782, Rochambeau worked well with Washington. He was the mastermind behind the decisive campaign that resulted in victory at Yorktown.

an end to the war," he remarked. The only question in Washington's mind was how to go about taking New York. Should it be done by assault or by siege? Lafayette, his impetuous streak intact, favored the former. Knox recommended the latter. Washington came down on the side of Knox. Before the French could catch their breath after debouching onto American soil, Washington sent Lafayette to communicate his thoughts to his ally.[2] It was Washington's hope that Ternay would move by August 5 to establish naval superiority in New York, after which the allied armies, through what he called a "nervous and rapid" action, would open the siege. Incredibly, after having insisted for the better part of two years that he lacked the manpower to undertake a major campaign, Washington told the French that the rebels could furnish 35,000 men.[3]

Ternay and Rochambeau reacted coolly to Washington's proposal. They were awaiting reinforcements, both additional ships of the line and another 2,500 men, that the British navy had bottled up in Brest. It was folly, Ternay said, to think of establishing naval dominance in New York before those ships—or others from the Caribbean—arrived, and even then, like d'Estaing earlier, he doubted that his heaviest warships could enter New York harbor. For his part, Rochambeau cast a jaundiced eye on the manpower numbers that Washington had mentioned. He thought it more likely that the allies could muster only about 14,000 regulars between them, roughly the same number of men that Clinton possessed. In Europe, he said, it was a rule of thumb that the besieging army required up to a three-to-one numerical superiority in order to succeed. He also noted that siege operations took time, sometimes three months, more often up to six months, occasionally a full year. Rochambeau granted that the militia would turn out, but he observed that militiamen customarily served for only ninety days, insufficient time to bring on capitulation in New York, where the British had stockpiled supplies for four years. The objections made by the French were sound, but behind them lay an uneasiness with what they had found during their first days in America. The loss of Charleston, which they discovered upon landing, had filled Ternay and Rochambeau with foreboding about their ally's will and savvy. Ternay rapidly concluded that the American rebellion was in "desperate straits." The American people "want peace," he wrote home, a view strengthened by Lafayette's revelation that America's "exhaustion" was such that he "did not count on seeing them ... in another campaign" after 1780. Rochambeau swiftly discovered that the Continental army's supply system was far more primitive than he had been led to believe and both Frenchmen were appalled by Lafayette. It was bad enough that he acted like an American rather than a French nobleman, but they were alarmed that such an imprudent and inexperienced young officer—Rochambeau thought him a "hotheaded" individual who "proposes extravagant things"—would have gained Washington's confidence. It made him eager to size up the American commander, and he and Ternay asked for a meeting. Washington was no less anxious to meet his counterparts, and a conference was scheduled for Hartford in September.[4]

Washington's hopes for swift action in August were dashed. His spirits sagged, but he understood the reluctance of the French to act before naval reinforcements arrived. He admitted, too, that it would be irresponsible to pressure his ally into doing something it did not wish to do. Any major failure could irredeemably harm the alliance. Washington drew some comfort from Lafayette's reassurances that the French ministry was resolved to keep Rochambeau's army in America "till a peace is concluded and to support it with all theyr power." Still, as the date for the Hartford meeting approached, Washington received more bad news. The French naval reinforcements had been unable to get past the British blockade. They likely would not be coming at all in 1780.[5]

When Washington left New Jersey for Hartford, he had several plans in mind. Taking New York remained at the top of the list, and at the very least he wished to convince his ally that its fleet should move to the periphery of Manhattan in order to prevent Clinton from sending assistance to Cornwallis. If the French balked at these notions, he was prepared to propose a joint expedition to the South, which would draw down Clinton to assist Cornwallis and might lead to a climactic battle. He was even ready to urge a joint invasion of Canada, a course of action that he had steadfastly opposed during the past two years, supposedly because he did not trust the French. That he would contemplate a Franco-American invasion at this juncture suggests his desperation, his fear that little time was left with which to save the American Revolution.[6]

Washington met with the French for two days during the third week in September. While they were "delighted" with Washington—whom they characterized as sober, thoughtful, meticulous, and methodical—the French were not so taken with his plans. They reiterated their objections to a siege operation in New York, and maintained that the French fleet was too small to contemplate either a Canadian or a southern campaign. Rochambeau and Ternay concurred that "the most important and the most decisive" object was "the reduction of New York," which would be attempted should France achieve "a constant naval superiority" and the allies—meaning Washington primarily—could field a "land army of 30,000 men." Though not surprised, Washington was disappointed. Likely at his behest, Lafayette almost immediately wrote to Vergennes to solicit naval reinforcements. Had an adequate fleet been present in the spring, he told the foreign minister, "New York could have been ours." On the other hand, if "the British remain in command of the sea, we shall have to restrict ourselves to awaiting attacks."[7]

ON THE MORNING following the final meeting at Hartford, as a low-lying fog hugged the ground, a portent of the approaching autumn, Washington and his party set out on horseback for West Point. Washington never stopped worrying about a British attack on the installation and, scrupulous as always, he wished to inspect the fort that he had not seen for ten months. He had also learned from a spy that an American officer "high up" had turned coat. Although intelligence of this sort was almost always unreliable, Washington wished to be sure that every conceivable step was being taken at West Point to maintain security.[8] After all, its commander, Benedict Arnold, was new to the job, having assumed command there barely a month earlier.

After suffering a horrid wound in the fighting at Bemis Heights—his right thighbone had been shattered—Arnold had faced a slow and painful recovery. When he visited Washington at Valley Forge nine months after suffering that combat injury, Arnold was still walking with a cane and unable to ride a horse. With a field command clearly out of the question, Washington asked him to be the military commander of Philadelphia. It was supposed to be a comfortable post that would see him through until he was well again. Instead, it was the worst assignment that Arnold could have been given. In many ways, Arnold resembled an individual of the variety described by Max Hastings, the military historian. The "sort of people you need to win your wars are seldom if ever going to be the ones you would call normal human beings," Hastings has said. Often they "possessed an uncongenial personality" and were "somewhat unhinged," and not infrequently they "terrified" or at least aroused the "deepest suspicion by other soldiers around them."[9] From the outset, some in politics had thought Arnold was "hot and impetuous," and some of his fellow army officers described him as an "evil genius." There had been issues with Arnold from the outset, but a deep-seated disgruntlement took hold of him early in 1777—not long after his heroics on Lake Champlain—when Congress promoted five junior officers over him. It was "a very civil way of requesting my resignation," Arnold thought, perhaps correctly, and he did resign. Whatever others thought of him, Washington found qualities in Arnold that he admired, especially his lion-heartedness, utter lack of fear, and his indomitable will, and the commander likely worked behind the scenes to persuade congressmen to get Arnold back into the army. With Burgoyne's invasion looming, Congress relented and promoted Arnold early in 1777. He reentered the Continental army and fought under Schuyler and Gates in the Saratoga campaign. Although in his official report Gates failed to mention Arnold's role in Burgoyne's defeat, Washington decorated him.

Though furious at what he regarded as his reprehensible treatment, Arnold had probably given no thought to defecting before he took over as military governor in Philadelphia in June 1778. Even then, he did not hastily settle on his perfidious course. It was a decision made in the course of a year, perhaps even two. Philadelphia was a cauldron of hate and greed in 1778–1779, a time when scores were settled against Loyalists such as Joseph and Grace Galloway. It was a time, too, when rapacious businessmen were suspected, with good reason, of preying on a hapless public. In this strained and venomous atmosphere, allegations of misconduct were bruited against many. Arnold, with his headstrong habits and flair for making enemies, quickly rose to the top of the list of those suspected of misconduct. He closed shops to check inventories, ostensibly for the purpose of confiscating Tory property, and some believed he pocketed some of the booty that was seized. Others thought he sold on the black market some of what he stole. Before the end of 1778 Philadelphia's newspapers were filled with complaints of his alleged peculation, including imputations that he had used Continental army wagons to haul what he looted. Arnold's expensive habits fed the rumors of his misdeeds, and his proclivity for hobnobbing with known or suspected Loyalists only further provoked many in the city. His open courtship of Peggy Shippen, half his age and the daughter of a reputed Tory, was the final straw for many. While countless Philadelphians were furious at Arnold, he was outraged by the invective that they directed against him. Few of his countrymen had risked more, or suffered more, in this war. Most of his critics had never faced danger, never spent weeks in a bleak, cold wilderness, never endured combat, never been wounded, never been wounded twice. But it was not just the sancti-monious Philadelphians who aroused his ire. He sullenly resented Congress. It had earlier passed him over for promotion. Now, it shabbily refused to award him the back pay that was he was due.

Not long after marrying Shippen, Arnold, through intermediaries, opened negotiations with General Clinton. The initial discussions occurred in the summer of 1779, a time when he also approached Congress about a naval command in the Caribbean. It is conceivable that had his request been granted he might never have reached his infamous agreement with the enemy. Arnold's price for turning coat was £20,000—a figure that today would be equivalent to winning a very large jackpot in the lottery—and the command of a Loyalist corps. Clinton did not think the British would get much for their money, aside from drawing away what many redcoats believed was "the boldest and most enterprising of the rebel Generals." and a final agreement required nearly sixteen months of bargaining. In the end, it was agreed that Arnold was to seek command of West Point, which he would relinquish to the British, and that Clinton was to pay him the amount that Arnold had demanded if West Point was handed over. Otherwise, Arnold would receive £6,000. In either case, he was to be given command of a Loyalist force.

In June 1780, less than a month after learning of Charleston's fall, Arnold put the wheels of treason in motion. He called on Washington at Morristown and requested appointment as commander in the Hudson Highlands, which included West Point. Washington, who was eagerly awaiting Rochambeau's arrival and already planning the siege of New York, instead offered Arnold the command of the Continental's left wing in that operation. Arnold pleaded that he was yet convalescing. Washington did not make a final decision regarding Arnold until August, when he learned from Lafayette that the French would not agree to besiege New York any time soon. Only then did the unsuspecting Washington put Arnold in command of West Point. Arnold immediately sealed his shameful pact with Clinton. The first pay off for the British came in September when Arnold divulged that Washington was traveling to Hartford to meet with Rochambeau and Ternay, and that on September 18 he would cross the Hudson by ferry to Peekskill and be his guest for dinner. As Washington approached, Arnold set in operation a scheme through which the American commander, like General Lee earlier, might be seized—or killed—by a party of the king's dragoons. Arnold sent word of Washington's presence to the *Vulture*, a British sloop of war anchored not far away. The commander of that vessel, in turn, was to notify the horsemen to swing into action. None the wiser, the American commander crossed safely, and that evening he and his party, which included not only Lafayette but three men who would later serve in President Washington's cabinet—Knox, Hamilton, and James McHenry—enjoyed a delightful, and uneventful, meal with Arnold at the home of a hospitable resident of Peekskill. Arnold's diabolical plan for Washington's capture went awry because his message reached the *Vulture* too late to be acted on successfully.

Washington continued his journey the following morning. A week later, on September 23, having completed his talks with the French, Washington began the return trip, with plans to stop at West Point. That same day, Major John André of the British army crossed behind American lines out of uniform to meet with Arnold and arrange the final plans for the delivery of West Point. Three militiamen stopped him near Tarrytown. Somehow thinking the militiamen were Loyalists, the rattled André blurted out that he was a British officer. Taken into custody and searched, papers were discovered in his stocking. André was detained and Arnold was notified of what had transpired, but the crucial papers were kept for Washington to see upon his arrival. On September 25, Washington reached West Point, where he discovered that Arnold was gone and his wife was hysterical. When Washington finally saw the papers that André had been carrying, he immediately understood the reason for Peggy Shippen Arnold's overwrought behavior—her husband had defected. Washington knew, too, that had Arnold's conspiracy worked to perfection, West Point not only would have been lost, Washington and his aides likely would have been taken with it. Turning to Knox, Washington, in a voice that trembled with rage, said: "Arnold has betrayed me. Whom can we trust now?"[10]

Washington had felt betrayed previously, by Lee and Gates for instance, whom he had helped to become general officers in the Continental army. But he had never before felt so personally violated. Nor had America's cause ever before been put in such peril by the actions of a single person. This was close to the lowest point that Washington experienced in the war. Defeat had followed defeat in the South, where within the past one hundred or so days two entire armies had been lost. Georgia was for all practical purposes out of the war and, for all he knew, South Carolina might soon be lost to the Union. Now, one of the Continental army's highest ranking officers, and a soldier that he had admired above almost all others, had done the unthinkable. Washington's anguish was surpassed only by his wrath. He literally wished to kill Arnold. He tried to swap André for him, but Clinton refused, and the young British officer was hanged as a spy on October 2. Washington also arranged to have a Virginia volunteer, John Champe, a strapping young man with combat experience, travel to Manhattan, posing as a deserter from Lee's cavalry. Once in New York, Champe was to attempt to search out Arnold. Champe was given his orders by Colonel Lee, who took his instructions from Washington. While it is not entirely clear what Washington intended—he wanted it to appear that he wished only to have Arnold kidnapped and returned to West Point to stand trial—most of the evidence strongly suggests that Champe was instructed to shoot Arnold if necessary. In the end, Champe's mission failed. (He succeeded in enlisting in Arnold's Loyalist unit, but was transferred from New York before he could act.) Relentless in his outrage, Washington, for the duration of the war, never stopped dreaming of "seeing Arnold in Gibbets." That alone would satiate his fury.[11]

The nation was shaken by Arnold's treachery nearly to the same degree as Washington. "Be! astonished! o friends of american freedom," one patriot exclaimed.[12] America's lack of success since Saratoga, and its egregious setbacks at Charleston and Camden, had spawned chatter in newspapers about what had gone wrong in the war. For many, the answer was that America's fortunes had soured when many of its citizens had fallen prey to luxury and greed, the habits that Washington had been so shocked to discover during his stay in Philadelphia early in 1779. Now, according to many essayists, Arnold—who had taken filthy pelf for his false-hearted act—was the exemplar of the deadly corruption that was eating at the national soul, threatening military defeat and the ruination of the hopes of the American Revolution. Arnold was "mammon's sordid slave," it was said, and, for many, his sellout was seen not just in military terms, but as a fatal betrayal of the supposed republican virtue that had inspired them to become revolutionaries in 1776. Like Washington, most Americans wished to see Arnold swing. They, like Washington, were filled with rage and vengeance, and for many only the traitor's blood could cleanse the nation of its impurity.[13]

JUDGING BY HIS CORRESPONDENCE, Washington was only dimly aware of what was occurring in the South Carolina backcountry in the second half of 1780. He understood that the British were prosecuting that war with a "severity" not previously witnessed, and he knew that success in the South "must rely on Southern means and Southern exertions," but Washington did not fully understand the venomous struggle that was underway. Despairing at Washington's blindness, Governor Rutledge wrote Congress to urge that it ask the commander to come south and "see with his own Eyes" what was occurring. The South Carolinians were standing alone. National assistance "has been trifling," Rutledge added with dismay.[14]

The inhabitants of South Carolina's backcountry had remained largely inactive during the campaign for Charleston, the Tories warily awaiting the outcome before committing, the patriots unmoved by the plight of the low country "rice kings." The almost effortless ease with which Cornwallis in May and early June occupied important interior sites from Augusta eastward through Camden and over to Cheraw, not far from the North Carolina border, hinted at the rapid subjugation of all South Carolina. Almost swooning, Clinton remarked that the success of his siege operation meant, "both the Carolinas are conquered in Charles Town." Early in June, he departed for New York, confident that pacification was proceeding satisfactorily, even allowing on the eve of his departure that through "all the country in general" the resistance of the rebels had been broken, save for "a few scattering militia."[15] Cornwallis was on the same wavelength. Within days of Clinton's departure, he noted with confidence that "everything [is] wearing the face of tranquility and submission."[16] It must have seemed so. In the first blush of British success the Loyalists, as London had long anticipated, flocked to enter militia units created by the British army. Before the end of May hundreds showed up in Charleston with their muskets, and the outpouring of Tories in Ninety-Six District, the region east of Augusta lying between the Savannah and Saluda Rivers, was equally gratifying. Within six months of the fall of Charleston seven regiments containing nearly 1,500 men had been established. Although Cornwallis had longed for even more, hopeful signs abounded. In coastal Georgetown, for instance, the leading lights of the town signed an address announcing their willingness to abide by peace terms proffered by Lord North in 1778. "We are therefore desirous of becoming British Subjects" once again, they proclaimed, "in which capacity we promise to behave ourselves with all becoming fidelity and loyalty."[17] Nor was it only Tories who took up arms for the British. Several months before he invaded South Carolina, Clinton—on June 30, 1779—issued a proclamation promising freedom to slaves who deserted their rebel owners. Within forty-five days of Charleston's fall, more than one thousand slaves from the environs of the city had fled behind British lines. By July, Cornwallis had enrolled hundreds of exslaves in his army.[18]

Tories and slaves were not the only ones stirring that summer. Backcountry patriots also reached for their weapons. Some acted to defend their homeland against what they believed was a foreign invasion. Others believed that an American victory offered hope of bringing political change, not least of ending the stranglehold that the low country had long held on the upcountry. Some rebels—as was true of many Tories—chose activism for crassly self-serving reasons, including the opportunity to plunder the land and slaves owned by those on the other side. (At least one partisan band lured recruits by offering African American slaves as pay—one slave for a private who signed on for ten months, three for an officer who agreed to serve for a year.) Not a few who might have sat out the war were infuriated by Clinton's deceit immediately following the fall of Charleston. After agreeing to generous terms, at least as far as the militia was concerned, Clinton in essence countermanded the surrender pact by proclaiming that the paroled militiamen must take an oath of allegiance to the king—which made them liable for military service under the royal banner—or be looked on as "rebels and enemies to their country." For many, this was simply further evidence that Britain could never be trusted. Some were stirred by intensely personal reasons. Boys sometimes fought because their fathers were fighting. Fifteen-year-old Thomas Young took up his musket after Tories killed his older brother. "I . . . swore that I would never rest till I avenged his death," he later wrote, adding that eventually "a hundred tories felt the weight of my arm for the deed." Others, like thirteen-year-old Andrew Jackson had been taught by their parents how the English has plundered their homeland and its inhabitants. Most back-country rebels were Scotch-Irish who had seen America—and then American independence—as deliverance from a Great Britain that they detested. Most also were Presbyterians who had always bridled at the requirement that they pay tithes to the Church of England, the established church in South Carolina. Like the Tories, who took heart from the British invasion of South Carolina, patriots were encouraged in mid-summer to learn that a general of Gates's caliber had been given command of the Southern Department. And to be sure, many fought because they were appalled by the enemy's ruthlessness, of which Tarleton's massacre in the Waxhaws was but one incident among many. For most who became partisan fighters it was not one outrage but many, great and small, that drove them to go to war. Young Andy Jackson joined a partisan unit after helping his mother care for the mangled survivors of a Tory massacre, and observing that many survivors had three or four, or more, wounds. Jane Black Thomas, who lived in the Catawba River Valley, was so outraged when Tories jailed her ailing and elderly husband that she served as an intelligence conduit to partisans. On one occasion, having learned that the Tories planned a raid on guerrillas, Thomas rode fifty miles through Loyalist controlled territory to sound the alarm, a feat that probably was more dangerous than the more celebrated ride of Paul Revere.[19]

Residents of the New Acquisition District, just west and above the Waxhaws (and slightly below Charlotte), formed a militia regiment after Tarleton's nearby outrage against Buford's men, choosing William Hill as its colonel. Hill, who had immigrated from Northern Ireland in 1762, had opened an iron ore mine on his property and eventually, like Washington's father, an iron furnace. (By 1775 Hill was turning out cast-iron firebacks inscribed with the words "Liberty or Death.") When the British learned of the formation of Hill's force, they dispatched a detachment of the British Legion under Captain Christian Huck, a Philadelphia Tory, to suppress the defiant settlers. Huck and his men were heavy-handed, prompting local rebels to dub him Lord Hook. They murdered an unarmed boy (who at the time was reading the Bible, according to the story that the rebels disseminated); burned a Presbyterian church and its parsonage; pillaged several residences; destroyed Hill's ironworks, including its sawmill and gristmill, which were vital to the neighborhood; and took away the ninety slaves that toiled for Hill. They also incarcerated rebels in unspeakably squalid conditions. (In one instance, 250 men were confined in a jail built for a tenth that number.) In the wake of such occurrences, the New Acquisition's rebel regiment grew as never before, attracting volunteers from nearby North Carolina and faraway Georgia.[20]

There are always those who wish to sanitize war by portraying its grand and noble deeds—which sometimes occur—while drawing a veil over its shameless side. By its nature, war is harsh, brutal, and pitiless, and while it can call out the best in humankind, it can also awaken the darkest side of human nature, arousing in many participants a coldhearted callousness. For most, danger begets fear. For some, fear sires ferocity, and ferocity spawns a ruthlessness that subsumes compassion. For still other men, more than is gratifying to acknowledge, soldiering is a license to unleash iniquitous qualities that they had struggled to suppress in peacetime. Alongside the honorable—Ferguson's refusal to shoot Washington at Brandywine, for instance—indescribably wanton behavior occurred on every battlefield in this war. But what South Carolina was about to experience was what at the time was called a partisan or irregular war, what today would more commonly be referred to as guerrilla war. Guerrilla warfare is often more barbaric than conventional warfare. Guerrillas lack the means of coping with prisoners, they are usually less well disciplined than those in a conventional army, and, whatever their ideological ardor, many guerrillas are drawn to fight from an inveterate hatred of their foe and an engrossing eagerness to settle old scores.

Three partisan leaders—Thomas Sumter, Francis Marion, and Andrew Pickens—overshadowed others in South Carolina at the time, and today remain the best known of the many that emerged to lead irregular bands. Each of the three was more or less Washington's age. Sumter and Pickens were the children of immigrants, Marion the grandchild of French Huguenots who had migrated to South Carolina. All three first soldiered in the Cherokee War in 1760–1761, a brutal struggle that provided a grim education in guerrilla warfare. When peace returned, Sumter became a merchant and miller at Eutaw Springs and Marion a plantation owner just four miles away. Pickens was a farmer and justice of the peace in Ninety-Six District. All three took up arms against the Tories when the war erupted in 1775 and each was active in the campaign in Georgia in 1779. Like most from the backcountry, Sumter did not fight for Charleston in 1780, but immediately after it fell he offered to raise militia and wage partisan war. In May the rebel government of South Carolina appointed Sumter brigadier general and commander of the state's militia, prompting Tarleton's men to loot and burn his home, while his wife, who was partially paralyzed, was made to sit on the lawn and watch the carnage. Sumter was aloof and overbearing, not good at taking orders, and obsessed with being in control. He had a facility for selling himself, but it was his pugnacity—an almost pathological combativeness—that attracted like-minded men to follow the "Carolina Gamecock," as they took to calling him.

Marion served during the siege of Charleston, though halfway through the ordeal he dislocated his ankle in a freak accident and left the doomed city. In June, having recuperated, he gathered a small partisan force, which he led to North Carolina and made available to de Kalb. It was sent to the Pee Dee River area to scout for the enemy and locate supplies. When they returned, Gates had taken command. The story goes that Gates was neither impressed with Marion, who was nearly fifty, frail and short, and hampered with malformed knees and ankles, nor with his shaggy men, who had literally just emerged from a swamp. Supposedly Gates, having concluded that Marion's hirsute little band was useless, detached it elsewhere simply to be rid of it. It is more likely that Gates, like de Kalb, thought these partisan fighters could do more good behind the enemy's lines. He sent the unit south to harass the British, so that Marion missed the Battle of Camden, launching instead his career as a guerrilla warrior. Soon known by the sobriquet "Swamp Fox," Marion was in most ways the opposite of Sumter. Described by another soldier as being "of the smallest size, thin as well as low," and with "a visage . . . not pleasing," Marion was a quiet sort who had long lived a Spartan existence, eating little and habitually drinking a concoction of vinegar and water. His passion for order and cleanliness antagonized many, including one of his officers who ranted that Marion was an "ugly, cross, knock kneed, hook-nosed son of a bitch." Yet men flocked to serve under him, not because he was endearing, but as he tended to succeed.[21]

Pickens, a militia officer who was captured and paroled in the spring of 1780, remained neutral until Loyalists plundered his home late in the year. A dour

Calvinist with a reputation for seldom smiling and never laughing, Pickens was a taciturn individual. When he did say something, it was his habit to speak with painstaking deliberation. He "would first take the words out of his mouth, between his fingers, and examine them before he uttered them," said one exasperated listener.[22]

Others, like William Hill, the iron entrepreneur, also emerged to lead militia and guerrilla bands in the backcountry. South Carolina's Elijah Clarke, Virginia's William Campbell, and Isaac Shelby and John Sevier, who came from what today is eastern Tennessee, bore striking similarities to the better-known partisan leaders. Each was a first- or second-generation American, none had any formal education to speak of, all had taken up arms to fight the Indians at the first possible opportunity, and with the exception of Marion and Clarke, who were nearly fifty, most were young men under age thirty-five. Only William Richardson Davie of North Carolina was strikingly different. A Princeton graduate and lawyer in Salisbury, North Carolina, Davie had not soldiered before the American Revolution, but he laid aside his law books to fight on four separate occasions after 1777, when he turned twenty-one; his final hitch began in the summer of 1780, after nearly a year's recuperation from a serious wound suffered at Stono. Davie and Campbell led conventional militia forces in the unconventional war that ensued, but the remainder organized partisan bands (though they were sometimes designated as militia). Shelby and Sevier, for instance, were leaders of what they called Over Mountain Men, frontiersmen from across the Blue Ridge who were the southern counterparts of the Green Mountain Boys. They and their men—whom Light Horse Harry Lee described as "stout, active, patient under privation, . . . brave," and "delight[ing] in the fury of action"— carried hunting knives and Kentucky rifles, a weapon on which these men had honed their skills as sharpshooters while hunting Appalachian squirrels. Shelby answered the call when North Carolina's authorities summoned him to raise militia following the fall of Charleston, and by early July he was at Cherokee Ford, five miles inside South Carolina, with two hundred mounted riflemen.[23]

At the outset of the summer, Cornwallis was calling the shots. Left with 6,369 men in fifteen regiments, six of which were Loyalist contingents, he had sent large detachments across the state to begin the pacification of South Carolina. Within forty days nearly four thousand of his men garrisoned installations through the backcountry, including four outposts along the border with North Carolina. Cornwallis's plan was simple. The presence of these regulars would encourage local Loyalists to step forward, and they in turn would complete the process of mopping up the few remaining rebels. In addition, the British would use their economic leverage to further break the back of resistance, purchasing supplies only from Loyalists while confiscating the property of the openly disaffected. As that work proceeded through the summer, Cornwallis prepared for the invasion of North Carolina, which he set for the fall, when the South's forbidding summertime heat finally abated. He was confident that by then pacification would be complete, and that he could open the campaign for North Carolina assured that behind him Georgia, Florida, and South Carolina were loyal provinces.[24]

But by mid-summer Cornwallis no longer called the shots. Even before Camden, he had reported to New York that the "whole country" along the border and in northeast South Carolina was "in an absolute state of rebellion."[25] Rebels were pouring out of the woodwork to take up arms under one leader or another. Six engagements were fought in the last two weeks of July, more or less the inaugural salvo of partisan resistance. Sixteen more battles of varying size were fought in the seventy-five days that followed. For many, the catalyst to activism came from abominations committed by Captain Huck when he was sent again into the New Acquisition District, this time to root out resistance once and for all. Gathering about four hundred men, some of whom were Loyalists from that district, Huck rode about the area in July, pausing now and then to deliver speeches that struck the Presbyterians as blasphemous. If the rebels were as thick as weeds and Jesus Christ himself was their commander, Huck thundered that he could still whip them. He did more than talk. His men plundered many homes; roughed up several civilians, including a few women; and at the Williamson farm seized two men in the act of melting pewter to make bullets. Huck decreed that his two prisoners would be executed the next morning, but during the night rebel militia under Sumter were notified of the Tory's plans. By dawn, nearly 250 patriots who had ridden hard through the black night, ringed the Williamson property. They attacked immediately after the fierce red sun crept above the horizon. Caught by surprise, sixty-five Loyalists were killed or wounded in the brief fight, including Huck, who suffered two head wounds, allegedly while the battle was in progress. Many of his men fled, only to be hunted down and summarily killed, one of the first reprisals for Tarleton's Waxhaws massacre. One of the rebels said that 85 percent of the Tories were casualties, and another remembered that their bodies littered the farm "like dead hogs." In contrast to Bunker Hill or Quebec, it was a small encounter, yet the Battle of Huck's Defeat, as it came to be called, was big with importance for South Carolina. News of this first British setback in the state spread rapidly through the backcountry, setting it ablaze. Sumter's force swelled to six hundred men within a few days. The first signs also appeared of a deceleration in the Loyalists' willingness to volunteer.[26]

Many of the engagements that followed throughout the summer were small affairs between a few score men on each side. Some involved Loyalist attempts to track down rebel bands, but more often the Tories were the hunted, and the victims. Some skirmishes occurred when one side or the other sought to liberate prisoners or reclaim lost supplies, or, in the case of the threadbare partisans, to secure stores, horses, and arms. Not a few guerrilla attacks were ambushes of the enemy's supply line. To provision their far-flung outposts, the British were compelled to ship goods by river or, more often, to organize wagon trains that groaned with powder, rum, salt, and comestibles and were often accompanied by herds of livestock. Cornwallis procured the necessities for his army in three ways: some goods were purchased from Loyalists, more were confiscated from rebels, and still other essentials were raised on—or impounded from—one hundred or so confiscated plantations in the low country, giant farms worked by upward of four thousand slaves and managed by the Commissary of Sequestered Estates. (Having been abandoned by their fleeing owners, rather than having deserted their rebel masters, these African Americans did not qualify for freedom under the terms of Clinton's proclamation. The British kept them in servitude, working them on the appropriated plantations under the watchful eyes of more than a hundred overseers employed by the commissary.) The problems involved in shipping materials from the coastal region to remote interior posts would have vexed the most capable supply officer in peacetime. With partisan bands on the loose, the British faced a logistical nightmare. These guerrilla fighters were almost entirely horse soldiers. They sallied from their lairs in dark swamps and thick forests, swiftly covered considerable distances, struck their adversary, and just as quickly were back in their sanctuary. Their intelligence was superb. From friendly farmers, captured enemy soldiers, and their own discoveries while on mounted patrols, the partisans often knew precisely when and where to expect a British supply convoy. The British never knew when, or if, the guerrillas were coming. Some raids were spectacular. In August, for instance, Sumter's men knocked over a supply convoy en route from Ninety-Six to the Waxhaws, capturing fifty wagons filled with booty and 250 prisoners. Merely the knowledge of the guerrillas' existence hamstrung the enemy, as it was forced to draw away units from other endeavors to protect the supply line.[27]

The partisans additionally targeted mills used by Loyalists and redcoats, destroyed river craft to keep them from Cornwallis, plundered Tory farms, and sought to thwart the enemy's mobility by menacing fords on the inland waterways. Combat action was sporadic and usually brief. William Gipson later recalled that the only memorable thing about his two weeks with Marion's band was they "caught one Tory." Moses Hall, a twenty-year-old serving under Davie, spent three months occasionally sniping at redcoat forage parties, largely hoping "to impress them with our intention to resist them to the last." After the war he worked in the lead mines, which he considered a more dangerous pursuit than his partisan activities.[28] When the partisans surfaced, they often spread such terror that one British general declared that they were given to a wantonness "unheard of before," and he added that the guerrillas were a species "beyond every curb of religion, & Humanity."[29]

When their objective was to take one of the British frontier strongholds, the partisans habitually resorted to more conventional tactics, with a noticeable lack of success. Despite repeated attempts, they failed to seize the most important installations in Britain's outpost system in northern South Carolina. Otherwise, through their punishing attacks, great and small, the guerrillas subjected the enemy to a wasting attrition. While the exact losses suffered by the British and Loyalists will never be known, at least 650 men are known to have been killed, wounded, or captured, and one entire Loyalist regiment was nearly annihilated, in a stretch of sixty days after the Battle of Huck's Defeat. Those losses were roughly twice the number sustained by the rebels, who were also more capable of replacing those who were lost. When Cornwallis added his losses at Camden to the toll exacted by the partisans, he knew that the British force in South Carolina had been reduced by about 10 percent before the summer of 1780 was spent. He also knew that Loyalist recruitment had slowed to a snail's pace.[30]

Cornwallis fought back as best he could, and in a variety of ways, throughout that cloying summer. His actions were a hybrid of the velvet glove and iron fist. Fearing that brutality would only turn neutralists into rebels, he counseled his field commanders to treat captive partisans with the "gentlest methods which the nature of that business will admit of," and he threatened to "severely punish" those British soldiers who abused civilians. But Cornwallis never fooled himself into believing that South Carolina could be pacified without using force, and he feared too that any appearance of weakness on his part would harm whatever chance existed of rousing the Loyalists to take up arms. He threatened to hang two captives for every Tory executed by the partisans. He also ordered that parole violators who were caught fighting were to be "immediately hanged," directed that "the most vigorous measures" be taken "to extinguish the rebellion," and pledged that partisans were to be "punished with the greatest rigouor." Cornwallis kept his three hundred or so cavalrymen active in the search for guerrillas, and allowed them to destroy the abandoned farms of known partisans.[31] He additionally dispatched Major James Wemyss with a Tory regiment called the South Carolina Rangers—a unit that Wemyss acknowledged was filled with "banditti" and "plunderers"—to restore order to the Pee Dee region in the east, and he put Major Ferguson in charge of crushing resistance in the northwestern region of the state, knowing that his subordinate believed that only a "war of desolation" that was "shocking to Humanity" could bring the rebels to heel.[32] After carefully studying the brutal backcountry war, historian Walter Edgar concluded that had an international court existed in that day, "Cornwallis and his subordinates . . . would have been hauled before [it] . . . as war criminals."[33]

The log kept by Lieutenant Anthony Allaire, who served under Ferguson, shows that he marched 184 miles in pursuit of partisan bands between early June and mid-August, with little to show for it. Time and again he recorded that his unit was "on our way to meet a party of Rebels," only to arrive and find "no Rebels here." Once learning that the prey "had moved seven miles" away, his unit marched on the new rebel camp only to find that the partisans had "sneaked from their ground about half an hour before we arrived." On the one occasion that they did catch up with the rebels, Allaire and his comrades walked into an ambush near present Spartanburg, losing thirty-six men.[34] On the other side of the state Wemyss was spreading terror. He plundered and burned the homes of those who served with Marion; hanged several parole violators; torched the property of those who tried to save the condemned; razed loom houses, mills, and blacksmith shops that might be of help to the guerrillas; and destroyed a Presbyterian church, which he called a "sedition shop." All the while, his primary objective was to find Marion and his 150 followers. Ultimately, Wemyss confessed: "I never could come up with them." Failing in that, he told Cornwallis, he "push'd them . . . hard . . . to break them up." He failed in that as well. According to historian John Buchanan, Wemyss succeeded in only two things. By summer's end he had become, after Tarleton, "the second most hated man in the Carolinas" and he was the hands-down winner as "Francis Marion's most successful recruiting officer."[35]

Cornwallis had originally thought that he could invade North Carolina in the autumn, as by then there would be nothing left for him to do in South Carolina, but as fall approached he concluded that the rebellion in South Carolina could be brought under control only through the conquest of North Carolina. Some may doubt the prudence of such a course, he told Clinton, but "I am convinced it is a necessary one." If North Carolina was not pacified, he said, "we must give up both South Carolina and Georgia, and retire within the walls of Charlestown."[36] Cornwallis was on an escalator to nowhere. Fifteen months earlier, the solution to Prevost's inability to pacify the backcountry in Georgia had been to subdue South Carolina. Now incapable of extinguishing the blaze in South Carolina's interior, the remedy was to be the subjugation of North Carolina.

THROUGHOUT THE SUMMER Cornwallis laid his plans for taking the war into North Carolina. He established magazines in the backcountry, made contact with Tory leaders above the border, readying them for a fall campaign, and exhorted Clinton to make another raid on Virginia to draw away some rebel forces from North Carolina. Finally ready to move in September, Cornwallis took 2,200 men, leaving behind nearly three-fifths of his Anglo-American army to hold Charleston and their backcountry posts and to cope with the guerrillas. He planned to march from Camden to Charlotte, pausing there until reinforcements from Charleston arrived and Loyalists from North Carolina joined him. Ultimately, too, Cornwallis expected to rendezvous with Major Ferguson, his inspector of militia, whom he had detached with a force of roughly 350 Tory militiamen to the region west of Charlotte to raise Loyalists. When Ferguson joined forces with him, Cornwallis intended to advance to Hillsborough, where the remnants of Gates's army were posted. Unlike so many before him, Cornwallis was a leader who was willing—anxious even—to act, a general who believed that the rebellion could be suppressed only through relentless offensive action.[37]

Cornwallis's plan began smoothly. He occupied Charlotte without great difficulty late in September, three weeks after Ferguson established his headquarters at Gilbert Town, fifty-five miles to the west. Ferguson was heartened by the arrival of numerous Georgia Loyalists and an outpouring of North

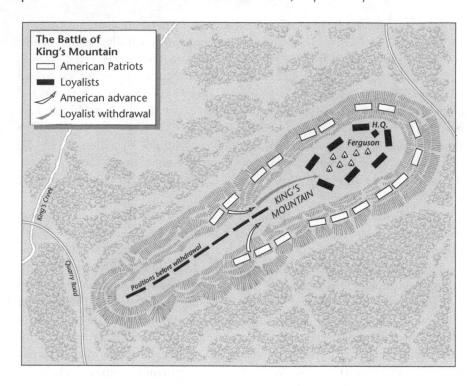

Carolina's frontier Tories, who according to Lieutenant Allaire, had begun to "come in very fast." Many men who stepped forward had never wavered in their loyalty to Great Britain, but others may have been swayed by Ferguson, who glowingly promised: "We come not to make war on women and children, but to relieve their distresses."38 In less than two weeks, Ferguson's force nearly tripled, finally reaching about 1,200 men. Swept away by his auspicious beginning, Ferguson sent a defiant edict to the backcountry rebels: the Tennessee men must "desist from their opposition to British arms" or he would "march over the mountains, hang their leader, and lay their country waste with fire and sword." If Ferguson thought his ultimatum would cow the frontiersmen, he was mistaken. His menacing words were more akin to lighting the fuse to a powder keg. Shelby responded by engaging Sevier, and the two used Ferguson's decree as a recruiting tool. All the while, other patriot bands were surfacing in North Carolina, just as they had in South Carolina, and many South Carolinians—including Sumter with four hundred men—crossed the border, eager for a fight with Ferguson. Many of the partisans brought their ministers and families along, and the wives cooked, sewed, drove cattle, and helped with the army's equipment.

The various components of this force, what some called a "posse," rendezvoused at Sycamore Shoals on the Watauga River in today's Tennessee. Thinking the force needed a commander, the assorted leaders chose Virginia's Colonel William Campbell, a red-haired, six-foot six-inch giant who was married to Patrick Henry's sister, then set out for Gilbert Town in search of Ferguson. Even before he was entirely aware of what was occurring across the Blue Ridge, Ferguson had begun to worry. Aware that a force "of some consequence" was gathering, he ordered a retreat to Charlotte, where he could link up with Cornwallis. Three days into his withdrawal, Ferguson discovered that the enemy gathering against him probably would outnumber his men. He beseeched Cornwallis for reinforcements. He also appealed to the men of North Carolina to join his force. Those who stood by idly, Ferguson cautioned, would be prey for what he called the "Back Water Men," whom he styled as undisciplined "barbarians," the "dregs of mankind," and a "set of mongrels" who would rob, ravish, and murder at every farmstead they visited.[39]

Ferguson never made it to Charlotte. Instead, on October 6, he decided to make a stand atop King's Mountain, twenty or so miles from Cornwallis's army. What went into his thinking is not clear. He may have feared that his force would be cut off before it reached Cornwallis, leaving him to fight in an uninviting place of the enemy's choosing. Perhaps his longing to fight overrode his better judgment. (Given his unslakeable thirst for action, Ferguson's officers had long before nicknamed him the "Bull Dog.")[40] He may have sold his enemy short. Or, he may have believed that the natural defenses offered by King's Mountain would see him through. Most likely, he concluded that King's Mountain's features would sustain him for a couple of days until the reinforcements sent by Cornwallis arrived. He would be outnumbered—he reckoned by about a three-to-two margin, though it turned out to be closer to two-to-one—but he knew that his men were better trained and disciplined. He may have anticipated inflicting a blow of Bunker Hill proportions on the rude farmers who were after him.

The rebel pursuers arrived on the day after the Loyalists took up their position, but a cold rain delayed the battle until October 8, giving Ferguson nearly sixty hours with which to throw up fortifications. Strangely, he did not erect a single abatis or dig one line of earthworks, a curious lapse for a professional soldier. Evidently, he concluded that the rugged, tree-lined hillsides afforded impediments enough. Some 1,800 rebels gathered at the foot of the hill and just a notch above 1,000 Loyalists prepared for battle on the summit. Save for Ferguson, every man about to go into combat was an American. Most were dressed alike, too, wearing long hunting shirts and wide brimmed hats, though to distinguish friend from foe the Tories affixed pine twigs and the rebels pieces of white paper in their hats. At the base of King's Mountain the men gathered around their immediate leaders for last minute instructions and a final prayer. The battle plan was hardly intricate. "The orders," one soldier later recalled, "were at the firing of the first gun, for every man to raise a whoop, rush forward, and fight his way as best he could."[41] Those immediately under Campbell heard their leader not only order them to move out, but to "Shout like hell and fight like devils." Most did just that, setting off with a hair-raising war cry learned from Indian braves, the precursor of the "Rebel yell" in the Civil War. They did not march up the hill in the fashion of European armies. They charged up the slopes, taking cover now and then to reload and fire, then pressing forward once more, another lesson they had learned from fighting Indians. A sixteen-year-old soldier, coming under fire for the first time, remembered that he feared being thought a coward more than he feared the Tories. He fired six shots during the battle. The first time he drew a bead on another man, he recollected, "I really had a shake on me." Killing became progressively easier with each shot he squeezed off.[42] It was a surprisingly short fight, though reaching the top of the hill was not easy. The rebels struggled up a steep slope, ragged with rocks and unsure footing. In some sectors, the Loyalists came down to meet them, firing on them at close range, even attacking with bayonet charges. Some units were driven back, regrouped, and started up again, only to be driven back and forced to once more scuffle up the hillside. Many were never driven back. Most found the hillside boulders and trees to be a godsend, a temporary haven rather than the encumbrance that Ferguson had imagined. (One rebel later claimed to have fired off several shots through a knothole in a hollow chestnut tree, as a soldier might have done from behind a parapet.) The rebels came up three sides of the hill. When at last they reached the top they laid down a deadly crossfire at their foe, bringing an abrupt end to the engagement. Its last act came when Ferguson attempted to lead a charge down the hill, an act that Shelby ever after believed was a suicidal step by a man who had sworn to "never . . . yield to such a d_ _ d banditti." If he did not want to survive the battle, Ferguson got his wish. An inviting target astride a white horse, and instantly recognizable in his traditional plaid hunting shirt worn over his British uniform, Ferguson got no more than twenty yards before he was riddled with at least seven gunshots.

When Ferguson fell, the Tories immediately began to throw down their arms and plead for mercy. Little compassion was shown them. Crying "Buford! Buford! Tarleton's quarter!," the rebels again exacted retribution for the Waxhaws massacre. Men—a great many men, some waving white flags—were shot down before the patriot officers, their blood lust at last satiated, restored order. Even then, a bevy of rebels took turns urinating on Ferguson's lifeless body while scores of wounded Loyalists, many pleading for help, were indifferently left to die agonizing deaths. In some instances the end did not come until hours later when ravening packs of wolves and wild dogs were drawn to the hill. Few of the Tory dead were buried, though rebel leaders permitted several enemy officers to give Ferguson a decent burial, lowering his body, and that of Virginia Sal, his mistress who was killed early in the engagement, into the same grave. The war was over for every Tory who fought at King's Mountain. While the rebels lost 90 men, the Tories suffered 319 killed and wounded. Another seven hundred Tories were taken prisoner, and they were not safe just yet. Most were plundered of their shirts and jackets, and it was a rare captive who was left with his shoes. Without food or adequate water, and devoid of ample clothing to fend off the first chilly nights of autumn, the prisoners were marched to Gilbert Town nearly forty miles away. It was a nightmarish trek filled with unsurpassed malice and terror. The captives were abused, even killed, along the way. At one point Colonel Campbell tried to halt the spasms of violence by issuing a stunning order in which he asked his officers "to restrain the disorderly manner of slaughtering . . . the prisoners." Once they reached their destination, the rebels established what Lieutenant Allaire called "an infamous mock jury" to try the supposed leaders among the Loyalist captives, some of whom were accused of having incited the Indians to take up arms. Thirty-six men were sentenced to death and that night, in the eerie orange glow provided by torches held by rebel soldiers, the ogreish job of executing the victims was carried out. The condemned were brought out in groups of three and hanged on a large oak tree. All "died like Romans," Allaire declared. Many rebels were unmoved by the ghastly spectacle, feeling like the partisan who wished "to God every tree in the wilderness bore fruit such as this!" But Shelby stopped the ghastly carnival after nine men had been dispatched, partly because he was appalled by the massacre, and partly because he had received information that Tarleton's Legion was coming.[43]

King's Mountain was the icing on the cake that had been fashioned by the partisan war. All British hopes of a great outpouring of Southern Loyalists—a major part of the thinking that had nourished the Southern Strategy—were dashed. Within a mere eighteen days of reaching Charlotte, Cornwallis, learning of the loss of nearly a third of his force, departed North Carolina, retreating back to Winnsboro, South Carolina.

CONGRESS DITHERED over Gates's future for more than a month after it learned of Camden, but early in October, with criticism of his behavior mounting, it suspended him pending an inquiry. His fate was sealed when it became clear that he had lost the support of many southerners, and especially the governor of North Carolina, though Benjamin Rush's assessment was true as well. "Gates," he remarked, "is now suffering not for his defeat at Camden, but for *taking General Burgoyne*," as Washington's backers moved to scuttle the commander's last remaining threat among the army's general officers.[44] Congress turned to Washington to name a successor. It had done so before, and he had always declined to be drawn into what he feared was a political minefield, but on this occasion Washington overcame his reluctance and named General Greene to replace Gates. The perilous military situation in the South drove him to act, as did his belief that after the utter failure of three successive Continental generals— Howe, Lincoln, and Gates—someone with considerable savvy had to be appointed. The Southern Department, Washington believed, needed a commander who

General Nathanael Greene. Painting by Charles Willson Peale, from life, 1783. Greene rose to the challenge when he was given an independent command in the southern theater. Always thoughtful and prudent, he proved to be surprisingly daring once he had an independent command.

understood the wisdom of Fabian tactics and possessed sufficient backbone to stand up to the South's civilian leaders. Greene was tough enough, and he was skilled in diplomacy, as he had exhibited following the debacle at Newport two years earlier. At Fort Washington, moreover, he had learned the painful lesson that came with making a stand against bad odds.

Greene did not reach Hillsborough to relieve Gates until the end of November. He stopped in Philadelphia to beseech Congress for more of everything, and pitched similar arguments to the governors of Maryland and Virginia. He faced disappointment in Annapolis and Richmond, where he discovered that those states had "neither money or credit, and the temper of the people are afraid to push matters to extremities." After visiting with Governor Jefferson, Greene told Washington that unless the commander could light a fire under Virginia's authorities, "the affairs in the Southern Department will and must go to ruin." Without your support, Greene candidly told Jefferson, the army likely faced "fatal Consequences" in North Carolina, after which Cornwallis's gaze would fall on Virginia. In the meantime, Greene's thoughts jelled with regard to how he would prosecute the war. His army must be highly mobile, he determined, and it must coordinate its efforts with the "Partizan Corps." Greene had barely stepped foot in North Carolina before he met with Sumter, who recommended an attack on Cornwallis's army. "I am not altogether of [that] opinion," Greene said politely. In demurring, Greene understood that the "Impatience of the People to drive off the Enemy" could lead him into a "Thousand Misfortunes." He resolved not to permit that to occur. He wished, as much as possible, to be his own master. If his army fought the regulars, Greene wanted it to be because he had seen an advantageous opportunity to strike.[45]

Greene quickly took a momentous step. He divided his army. Conventional wisdom said that it was folly to divide an army in the face of a superior foe, and indeed it often was, as Washington had discovered in New York in 1776 and Cornwallis had recently learned during his foray into North Carolina. But Greene opted to detach almost half of his army, putting Daniel Morgan in command of six hundred men, who were to be joined by Sumter's partisans, west of Charlotte. Greene explained that Morgan's presence was essential to "spirit up" the inhabitants in that sector. With the remainder of the army, about eight hundred men, Greene was to move south toward the Pee Dee, 120 miles away on the opposite side of the Carolinas, where the Swamp Fox was to assist by "keep[ing] up a Partizan War." It was a step taken "partly from choice and partly from necessity," he said. The dearth of supplies around Charlotte dictated the

General Daniel Morgan. Painting by Charles Willson Peale, from life, c. 1794. He fought in numerous engagements, for a time was confined as a prisoner of war, and was looked upon by Washington, Gates, and Greene as indispensable. Rising from captain to general, Morgan achieved his greatest fame at Cowpens in January 1781.

necessity of splitting the army. He also took that step because it "compels my adversary to divide his, and holds him in doubt as to his own line of conduct." Should Cornwallis ignore Morgan and come after Greene, Augusta and Ninety-Six would be left unprotected. Should the British go after Morgan, Greene said that he would have "the whole country open before me," all the way to Charleston.[46] It was a bold and daring plan, and one that was filled with colossal risks. It was also the first evidence of imaginative thinking from headquarters in the Southern Department since the war had descended on this region two years before.

As the last short days of 1780 passed, Washington's spirits continued to sink. He had not only presided over what he called yet another "inactive Campaign," but every ray of hope that had flickered during the year—help from the French navy, joint operations by France and Spain in the Caribbean, upheavals in England, the expectation that Europe's neutrals might act against Britain to force it to sue for peace—had "prov'd delusory," he sighed. The crowning denouement had been Arnold's treason, and he feared there might be others whose villainy could be purchased by the British. The "great revolution" hung in the balance, he brooded late that year. "We have no Magazines, nor money . . . and in a little time we shall have no Men," for at year's end the enlistments of many would expire. Once again, too, as at Valley Forge, Washington's officers were "mouldering away by daily resignations." He feared that the public's will to keep up the fight was waning, and for the first time he wondered if "we mean to continue our struggles." By late November he worried that the war could not be continued without another French loan. The "public calamity," he said in mid-December, had reached its nadir, and he trembled at the prospects for 1781, when "the Enemy . . . push[ed] us in our enfeebled state."[47]

Conditions could not get worse. But they did. On New Years' Day 1781 men in the Pennsylvania Line, in winter quarters near Morristown, mutinied. The conditions in which the men lived were deplorable, and they had not been paid for twelve months, although new recruits had received handsome bounties. But what caused their simmering rancor and resentments to ignite was that at the expiration of their term of service, or what the soldiers believed to be the end of their commitment, the army refused to discharge them. They had served for three years. They understood that the covenant they had entered into required them to soldier for a maximum of three years. But Congress understood that these men had enlisted for three years or the duration of the war. As the war had not ended, Congress believed that these soldiers remained soldiers. Nearly one thousand men—15 percent of Washington's army—rebelled. Killing one officer and wounding several others, the mutineers took control of their camp, seized half a dozen field pieces, and marched on Congress in Philadelphia. They wanted their back pay and they wanted out of the army, or they wanted another cash bounty for reenlisting for another three years.[48]

This was the event that Washington had feared above all others throughout this war, and for several sleepless nights he anguished that the Pennsylvanians' mutiny might trigger a calamitous epidemic of insurrections, imploding the army. The continuance of the war and the success of the American Revolution were in greater peril than ever before. Washington, who was at West Point, could not even go to New Jersey to deal with the crisis. He dared not leave West Point, for fear that in his absence the men there would mutiny, hazarding that crucial post and, with it, the outcome of the war.

America was plummeting to the black bottom of its long war. As never before—never in 1776, never while at Valley Forge, never in the dark despair that accompanied the economic crash in 1779—had Washington wondered so openly if the war could be saved. The Americans were "a commercial and free people, little accustomed to heavy burthens," Washington said as campaign 1780 closed, and he feared that such a people, now weary and disheartened, might lack the will to continue the fight.[49]

19

CHOICES, 1781

[W] E ARE BANKRUPT with a mutinous army," Congressman James Lovell reported on the second day of 1781.[1] At that very moment British naval and land forces—the help that Cornwallis had requested from Clinton to facilitate his planned invasion of North Carolina —were launching a raid on Virginia. Far away in France, Foreign Minister Vergennes, frustrated with a war that was going nowhere, was willing to consider a way out, some means of quitting the war on honorable and satisfactory terms for his nation, if not for his American ally. An uncharacteristically exuberant mood prevailed in Great Britain, which only recently had learned of Camden. Hope was widespread that the guerrillas in Georgia and South Carolina could not hold out forever, especially if North Carolina and Virginia were reconquered. Not every-one in England was sanguine, but North's ministry had retained its majority in elections during the autumn, the first contest for Parliament since before the war. Perhaps most observers, like Samuel Johnson, read into the outcome that "As to the American war, the *sense* of the nation is *with* the ministry."[2] The foreboding that had gripped England in 1777 as Burgoyne plunged south of Ticonderoga was not present as Cornwallis prepared to move into North Carolina. Not every-one expected that he would succeed, but hardly anyone feared a calamity.[3]

If the mood in Britain had grown more positive, morale in America had sunk to its lowest ebb. Arthur Lee, returning home in mid-1780 for the first time since before the war, could scarcely believe what he found. Many Americans had come to believe that an accommodation short of independence might become an "inevitable necessity." More than a few feared that it was only a matter of time before the reconciliationists—whom General Sullivan, who had left the army and now sat in Congress, called the "Timid & the neutral," and Samuel Adams labeled "our most dangerous Enemies"—regained control of Congress.4 The belief was gathering that campaign 1781 was the last chance to salvage victory, and that only a decisive victory in that campaign could break the stalemate and save the American Revolution.

The first order of business at the outset of 1781was to deal with the mutiny in the Continental army. Two choices existed: suppress the uprising in the Pennsylvania Line with force or resolve the crisis through negotiation. Washington favored using force, but shrank from that choice. He was not sure that soldiers would fire on their comrades from Pennsylvania and he feared that coercion and bloodshed might cause the mutiny to spread through the army with the speed of a wildfire. He ordered General Wayne, who was in command on the scene, to use force only if the mutineers attempted to join with the British army. Otherwise, Washington urged "a reasonable compromise," a course that effectively dumped the burden of finding a solution into the lap of Congress. While Congress sent a committee to New Jersey to conduct talks with the sergeants who led Pennsylvania's rebellious soldiery, Washington took steps to prevent a similar uprising by the soldiers at West Point, where the troops, like those elsewhere, had not been paid for up to eighteen months. He appealed to the governors of the neighboring states to find money to provide three months back pay and sent Knox though the four New England provinces to round up food and clothing. Within a few days the crisis passed. There was no explosion at West Point and an accord was reached with the mutinous Pennsylvanians. It came at a heavy price. Charges were dropped against all the rebellious soldiers. Those who had enlisted three years before were given the choice of leaving the army or of reenlisting for "three years or the war." If they reenlisted, they were to receive another cash bounty and a ninety-day furlough before beginning their new hitch. Half the mutineers chose to leave the army.5

Almost immediately a second mutiny flared. Smaller than its predecessor, it involved about two hundred men in the New Jersey Line. Washington immediately resolved to suppress this mutiny brutally. Convinced that only the use of force could prevent future rebellions, he dispatched General Howe with orders to crush the uprising and "instantly execute a few of the most active and most incendiary leaders."6 Howe followed orders explicitly. He surrounded the rebellious soldiers, disarmed them, set up a drumhead court-martial that within minutes returned guilty verdicts and death sentences. Howe instantly carried out the verdict. Two ringleaders were shot by a firing squad composed of their fellow mutineers.7

DURING THAT GRIM WINTER America's civil leaders continued their unabated efforts to find a remedy for the new nation's tumble-down economy. The expedient of foisting greater responsibility onto the states, set in motion early the previous year, had been no more successful than Congress's previous choices. Many states resorted to perilous levels of taxation—the citizenry collectively groaned under £85,000,000 in taxes by 1781—yet, aside from the disquieting erosion in morale, little came of it. Runaway inflation consumed most of the new revenue and several states verged on bankruptcy. One choice seemed unavoidable as 1780 drew to a close—to beg France for still another loan. At about the very moment that General Greene took command in North Carolina, Congress resolved to seek 25,000,000 livres from the king, an amount more than twice that which France had loaned the United States since 1776.[8]

In the sober light of a crumbling war effort, that decision came easily. The difficult choice was whether to have Franklin, the American minister, seek the loan or to appoint a special envoy. A large number of congressmen distrusted Franklin. Some believed he lacked the will to act forcefully and decisively. Others thought Franklin lacked the energy to do so. They saw him as old and feeble, a figurehead who once had been useful in Paris, but whose time, in this crisis-laden atmosphere, had passed. "How long," asked a Virginia congressman, "must the dignity, honor, and interest of these United States be sacrificed to the bad passions of that old man under the idea of his being a philosopher?"[9] There may even have been a secret vote taken on whether to recall Franklin.[10] If so, Franklin survived the vote of confidence, but Congress named young Colonel Laurens as its envoy extraordinary to cross the Atlantic and plead for the life-saving loan.[11] Laurens sailed in January 1781, his pockets bulging with letters from Congress and Washington. The commander candidly told Laurens that his mission was crucial. The "patience of the army . . . is nearly exhausted" he said, and the "people are discontented" from relentless taxation and a war that—or so he claimed—had become a stalemate because America's financial woes prevented it from being aggressively waged. Washington also added an item to Laurens's list of objectives. He implored his former aide to urge the French to send a powerful fleet to the United States. At the very least, allied naval superiority would force Britain onto the defensive, taking away their "motives for prosecuting the war" and bringing them to the bargaining table. Even better, it would permit the Franco-American armies "to convert the war into a vigorous offensive."[12]

That winter also witnessed the application of intense pressure on Maryland, the lone holdout in ratifying the Articles of Confederation. Richard Henry Lee's June 1776 motion to declare independence had also called for a foreign alliance and a constitution for the United States. Only the approval of the constitution remained. Congress had created a committee to write a constitution at the same time that Jefferson's committee drafted the Declaration of Independence, but the framers quickly encountered dangerous shoals. Issues such as state versus national sovereignty, taxation, and commercial regulation were rife with divisive choices that could jeopardize the war effort. Congress largely suspended work on the constitution until the great victory at Saratoga created the illusion that the war was nearly over. It then rushed to complete the Articles of Confederation, which in effect created an alliance of equal and independent states, with a national government that was to be so weak it would lack the authority to levy taxes and regulate commerce. Thirty months later, early in 1781, twelve states had ratified the proposed constitution, but unanimity was required. Maryland had refused to act so long as Virginia intransigently held its royal titles to western lands beyond the Appalachians. The damaging British raid on Virginia in January, and the all too likely possibility that Cornwallis might invade the state, finally prompted Virginia to announce that it would relinquish its western land claims if all private claims to land in the West were also waived. Many powerful individuals in Maryland had invested heavily in private land companies that had purchased land "titles" from the Indians. Maryland refused to budge until it was bullied into doing so, especially by the French minister, who hinted that his country might not stay the course if the Articles of Confederation was not ratified. Maryland voted for ratification. The constitution took effect on March 1, 1781.[13]

Ratifying the articles hardly seemed worth the fuss, as Congress under it possessed no more power than had the old Continental Congress. But some saw ratification as a necessary first step in strengthening the national government and resolving America's economic plight. These men—later they were called Nationalists and still later Federalists—yearned for a strong national government capable of waging war, gaining victory, and securing the interests of the United States. Some among them also looked on "consolidation"—their term for the centralization of authority in a powerful and sovereign U.S. government—as the means of arresting what they saw as threatening democratic and social changes within the states that had been unleashed by the American Revolution. But many, possibly most, Nationalists in 1780–1781 were angry and humiliated by the sight of ragged, poorly fed, unpaid soldiers, and mortified that the Continental army had been forced by a powerless government into what Washington called a "feeble and oppressive mode of conducting the war." The inactivity of the Continental army in the north, and the disasters at Charleston and Camden, made them more fearful than at any time during the war—and certainly since Saratoga—that independence might slip away.

In literally the first hours after the new Articles of Confederation took effect, one Nationalist-dominated congressional committee proposed that Congress request emergency powers for the duration of the war, while another insisted that Congress, through its "implied powers," already possessed the authority to coerce the states into compliance with national laws, a legal sleight of hand through which the United States might immediately enact and enforce revenue-raising measures. The Nationalists, however, lacked a majority in Congress —and perhaps the will—to attempt such draconian remedies. Instead, they supported a constitutional amendment that would permit Congress to levy an impost, a 5 percent duty on imports. Helped along by hyperbolic rhetoric— Rhode Island's congressman Ezekiel Cornell urged a dictator for the United States and Colonel Hamilton published *The Continentalist*, six essays in which he dilated on how the "WANT OF POWER IN CONGRESS" had crippled the war effort, making it likely that Americans would be a "CONQUERED PEOPLE" and not a "HAPPY PEOPLE"—Congress passed the amendment and sent it to the states for ratification. But all knew that ratification, if secured at all, would be a slow process. The war crisis was immediate. Everything now hung on a loan by France or the dispatch of a French fleet to North America. Winning the war, even continuing the war much longer, Washington privately wrote in January 1781, "exceeded the national abilities of this country." French assistance was "indispensable" to prevent the war from being lost, he said.[14]

OFFICIALLY, France was unwavering in its commitment to its American ally, but few any longer saw the French through rose-colored glasses. John Adams, in letters from Paris in 1779, had been the first to caution that France acted in pursuit of its own interests. While Adams was circumspect—the danger that his correspondence would be captured while crossing the Atlantic was too great to permit candor—the implication of his warnings was that Vergennes would support the American war only so long as it was useful to do so. While Adams did not know what was occurring behind closed doors in the French foreign ministry, the steady diet of bad tidings throughout 1780 led him to worry as never before about the steadfastness of his ally. Evidence was growing that the peace faction was ascendant in the French ministry. When the naval minister, Sartine, was forced out in the autumn of 1780, it was universally, and correctly, taken as a sign that those who feared that this interminable war was driving France to bankruptcy had engineered his ouster. America's military and economic woes also had a disturbing effect beyond France. Adams, for instance, learned at Christmas that the "friends of America" in Europe "tremble[d]" at the new nation's "current abasement." At the same time he told Congress that the defeats at Charleston and Camden, as well as Arnold's treason had caused Dutch "professions of Friendship" to dry up. Now, said Adams, there was "no Disposition [in the Netherlands] to afford any Assistance" to the United States.[15]

America's crisis fed on itself, inexorably spinning out new emergencies, culminating in the spring of 1781 in perhaps the war's gravest threat of all to independence. As winter slipped over the horizon, Russia and Austria proposed a conference of Europe's principal powers to end the American war through mediation. This was not the first call for reaching peace through the intercession of Europe's neutral powers. Three similar proposals had been broached during the previous thirty months, but nothing had come of them. Sometimes Britain had not been interested. On other occasions the French and Spanish had not been ready to make peace. However, in the spring of 1781, Vergennes summoned Adams from Amsterdam to discuss the proposal, something he had never done before. Knowingly, Adams feared this meant that Vergennes was ready to leave the war and that he was about to seize on a European mediation conference as an honorable means for France's exit.

Adams was faced with what he most feared. He suspected that Europe's great powers—none of them republican states and all exasperated by the economic dislocations that the American war was causing—would propose peace terms that were prejudicial to America. As this was a deadlocked war, a mediation conference would most likely propose a peace based on what the diplomats called *uti possidetis*: each belligerent would keep what it possessed at the moment the armistice that preceded the conference took effect. Should that be the case in 1781, it was a good bet that the fragile United States would be encircled by a mighty Great Britain that retained Canada, the West beyond the mountains, Penobscot, northern Vermont, New York City and Long Island, portions of upper New York, South Carolina, Georgia, Florida, and virtually all its prewar Caribbean possessions. Britain would also have North Carolina, if Cornwallis succeeded there against Greene prior to the armistice. As always, when bargaining occurred, other possibilities existed as well. When the archives were opened generations later it was learned that Prussia favored the partition of America, with France regaining Canada, Britain retaining the southern colonies, and independence accorded to only the eight New England and mid-Atlantic states. If Britain and France accepted any such terms, the United States would face a terrible choice: agree to unpalatable peace terms or attempt to fight on without an ally. Its decision, as Adams knew, would never be in doubt. The United States could not continue the war alone. Adams also believed that after a suitable period Britain would declare war on the isolated and enervated United States and seek to regain more, perhaps all, of its former colonies. For the past 150 years, Adams raged, "America has been the Sport of European Wars and Politicks." Now, despite having fought for six brutal years, America might be forced to accept a European-dictated peace settlement.[16] From the outset of the war, Adams had been brightly optimistic. But with the prospects for victory dissolving, he fell into a black despair. Mediation, he fumed, was a "most insidious and Dangerous Plot . . . to . . . deprive us of our Independence."[17]

Until he reached Paris, Adams could only speculate on what the mediators had proposed and what Vergennes's response might be. As he hurried by coach from Amsterdam, Adams was haunted by the suspicion that the French had lost hope of gaining anything in this war. Fretfully, Adams expected to find Vergennes anxious for an immediate end to the war. Adams's guess was only partially correct. Six months before, with a French army having only recently arrived in Rhode Island and hope abounding that the allied forces could quickly score a knockout blow, Vergennes had prevailed on his king not to listen to those ministers who urged peace. But when word of Camden and Arnold's treachery dribbled across the Atlantic, and when Rochambeau advised that the United States—"this unhappy land," he called it—was destitute and could not remain at war much longer, Vergennes found mediation more attractive. He knew full well that the longer the stalemated war continued, the greater the danger that America would negotiate a return to the British Empire, the outcome that France had sought from the beginning to prevent. Washington's torpid conduct of the war in 1779 and 1780 had eroded Vergennes's patience. The "American army . . . before the alliance had distinguished themselves by their spirit and enterprise," Vergennes reflected, but since France entered the war it had been the picture of "inactivity." Despite doing so little, he added, Washington's army had devoured more livres than a French army four times its size. By early 1781 Vergennes privately confessed that he had only "feeble confidence" in Washington.

Although Vergennes called Adams to Paris to discuss their response to the Russian-Austrian peace proposal, the foreign minister was not ready to immediately accept mediation. Over that winter Vergennes came to the conclusion that war could not continue beyond 1781. His thinking led him along two paths. He would wage war during one last season in the desperate hope of gaining a decisive victory. Another year of campaigning, furthermore, would lay the groundwork for France's honorable exit should that decisive victory not be attained. Vergennes used his influence to persuade Louis XVI to give—and to loan—the United States nearly 6,000,000 livres in silver and three cargoes of military hardware for the coming campaign. Franklin secured two-thirds of the funds in a loan just days before John Laurens arrived in Paris, and the American minister was told that the king wished the money to go directly to General Washington "for the Supply of the Army." The remainder was awarded to Laurens as an outright gift to the United States.

During that same month of March, Vergennes had also instructed his new minister in Philadelphia, Chevalier de Luzerne, to inform Congress that ominous European developments made it likely that France might be compelled to leave the war at any moment and that the United States should be prepared for a sudden mediation conference. Vergennes affirmed that in the event of mediation the issue of independence was not negotiable. On the other hand, there was much that Vergennes did not divulge. He did not tell Congress that in the absence of a decisive allied victory he would ask his ally to relinquish South Carolina and Georgia in return for regaining New York City and Long Island. Nor did Vergennes mention that he favored leaving Canada and the trans-Appalachian West in British hands, a settlement that would compel the vulnerable United States to remain dependent on France.

In March, moreover, Vergennes also instructed Luzerne to seek to have Congress remove Adams—toward whom he harbored a poisonous enmity—as the sole American envoy at any peace conference. Vergennes got what he wanted, but in a roundabout way. Rather than recalling Adams, Congress created a five-member commission to negotiate peace. Franklin, Jefferson, John Jay, and Henry Laurens were to join Adams as peace commissioners. In as shameful an act as any witnessed in this war, Congress directed the commissioners "to govern yourselves by [Vergennes'] advice and opinion" on all matters except independence. The United States, as Adams had warned might someday occur, had become a French client state. The feckless Congress, whose most important voice now seemed to belong to Luzerne, was without the resources, and increasingly the will, to go on. As campaign 1781 beckoned, it chose to pray that France would look out for the interests of its supine ally and to hope that somehow it emerged from the war with some measure of independence.[18]

Adams was not privy to Vergennes's thinking, but as he hurried to Paris he recognized that perhaps the great crisis of the war had arrived. Adams suspected "Chicanery" everywhere. America's ally wanted out. Guileful Britain was intriguing to make a separate peace with France, after which it would turn again on America. The antirepublican monarchies that talked up mediation were set on "chicaning the United States out of their independence." Ominously, Adams told Congress that while it must do its best to prevent mediation, it should consider "treating with the English separately."[19] This was a choice that Congress had refused to consider three years before when the Carlisle Commission had come calling after Saratoga. Now, in a war gone sour, it was a very real possibility.

When Adams at last reached Paris, he discovered that the Russian-Austrian mediation offer proposed an armistice followed by Anglo-American negotiations to determine America's fate. It did not stipulate a prior recognition of American independence. Adams was appalled. To accept this, he said would place "our liberties at a greater hazard, than they can be in a continuance of the war." Adams told Vergennes that America's independence must be recognized before the United States would consent to mediation. Vergennes did not balk. He stalled, anxious to see what 1781 brought militarily before France entered into mediation.[20]

It was not only Adams and Vergennes that blocked mediation in the spring of 1781. The British were unenthusiastic about a European conference at this juncture. The mood in London was that the war effort was looking up. From America, Benedict Arnold reported—and who should know better—that Washington's army had shrunk to merely six thousand "illy clad, badly fed, and worse paid men" who were commanded by officers of poor quality, as "the best" had been pushed aside or "have resigned . . . through disgust, necessity, and a conviction that the provinces will not be able to establish their independence." He added that Congress and the army hated one another, the people were "heartily tired of the war," men refused to enlist, the navy had ceased to exist, and "the treasury is entirely empty." The time was rapidly approaching, he advised, when peace could be concluded on almost any "terms which Great Britain . . . wishes . . . to offer." Germain radiated optimism, buoyed by Cornwallis's harsh measures in South Carolina, which he saw as the only "sure means of subduing rebellion." The war news that reached London was contradictory, but even more it was deceptive. North's government knew that the southern Loyalists left much to be desired and that the backcountry in South Carolina had not been pacified, but the ministers were also aware that their army had won two great victories in 1780. Perhaps inevitably, the clanging headlines about the spectacular triumphs at Charleston and Camden dwarfed all other news about the war. Throughout the land, according to one Briton, hope sprang of "a sure reduction of all the Southern Colonies," leading to "a death blow to rebellion."[21]

In this climate of opinion, North's cabinet reacted coolly to the thought of mediation. The ministers were fixed on the premise that the war was winnable and would shortly be won. At the outset of 1781 the only concessions Britain considered were to show clemency for the rebels and to permit the American colonists to tax themselves. The despondency that had set in following Saratoga was gone. North's government now "have no sort of idea of Peace or accomodation," said an informed insider. "[T]hey mean to . . . push another Campaign for the subjugation of the Southern colonies," he added. Another who was in the know reported that "All Prospect of Peace is vanished, and War in its Extreme will now be carried on."[22]

"[T]HE TIMES ARE PREGNANT," John Adams remarked at the outset of 1781.[23] In every quarter it was brutally apparent that this was to be the last year of the war, "the last struggle of expiring patriotism," as Rochambeau put it.[24] Seven years had passed since Lexington and Concord, and campaign 1781, all knew, would at last determine whether there was to be a United States and, if so, whether it would include thirteen states.

20

"BLOODY AND SEVERE": THE PIVOTAL SOUTHERN WAR, EARLY 1781

No YEAR SINCE 1777 had dawned with the flurry of activity that ushered in 1781. On January 2, Benedict Arnold arrived suddenly at Jamestown, Virginia, with a large British invasion force. At about the same moment, Cornwallis's army at Winnsboro, South Carolina, set out to find the rebels under Morgan and Greene.

Arnold's army was the second to raid Virginia within seventy days. In October, at Cornwallis's behest, Clinton had sent off a 2,200-man force under Major General Alexander Leslie to provide a "diversion" for the redcoats fighting farther south. Leslie's presence, it was thought, would prevent Virginia from dispatching reinforcements to the Carolinas and it might lead it to recall some units. Leslie's mission was a work in progress. While sowing destruction, he was also to interdict rebel supply lines, inhibiting the shipment of much-needed supplies to the Carolinas. According to what occurred in North Carolina, he might even move there to join with Cornwallis. Leslie arrived in Virginia just as autumn's splendorous colors garnished the landscape. After he put his men ashore at Portsmouth, Newport News, and Hampton, the cavalry and light infantry swept the peninsula between the James and York Rivers nearly as far inland as Yorktown, then marauded and pillaged across the extreme eastern end of Virginia below Cape Henry, resettling several families of Loyalists that had sailed with them. The redcoats had no chance to move further inland, as Leslie, in the aftermath of the debacle at King's Mountain, was ordered to join Cornwallis. He sailed in November, only about twenty days after his invasion began, taking with him the recently repatriated Tory families, who would face a bleak future if left behind.[1]

Virginia had been lucky. It was not so fortunate when Arnold arrived. Inheriting Leslie's mission, Arnold's expedition was hurriedly put together in New York so that it would arrive in January, just as Cornwallis was expected to reenter North Carolina and at the very moment that Virginia would face another year-end recruiting crisis. Arnold, upon whom Clinton had bestowed the rank of brigadier general, commanded a force of 1,600 men that included a few regulars and Hessians, but which consisted mostly of provincial units, including his own green-clad outfit that was popularly called Arnold's American Legion. It had been raised in New York during the autumn, although after six weeks of recruiting only forty men had stepped forward to serve under Arnold. Existing Tory companies had to be incorporated into the legion to bring it up to strength. (One of the forty who volunteered was John Champe, who joined in the hope of kidnapping or killing Arnold, and who now feared that if he was captured in Virginia he might be executed as a deserter from the Continental army before anyone could be found who would believe his story.) Arnold's army sailed just before Christmas. Long before then Washington had been keeping Governor Jefferson abreast of the expedition's preparations, and while he did not know its destination, the commander cautioned that Arnold's target might be Virginia and he might arrive at year's end.[2] Jefferson, awaiting a possible blow, faced a tough decision. He had called out six thousand militiamen in October when Leslie arrived, but for most it had been a false alarm, as the British departed before the great majority of militiamen reached the front. To summon the militia so soon again would provoke discontent, needlessly should Arnold's destination be the Carolinas, which Jefferson guessed would be the case. He decided to act only if it was confirmed that the armada's target was Virginia.

On the last day of 1780 Jefferson was informed that a British armada had been spotted in the Chesapeake. For more than twenty-four crucial hours he inexplicably did nothing. When he at last issued the call for the militia, it was too late. On that same day Arnold's fleet reached Jamestown, about fifty miles up the James River. He put half his men ashore to plunder plantations and seize property, including as many slaves as they could get their hands on. Three days later, in the pale sunshine of winter, the bulk of the British invasion force entered Richmond unopposed. Only the city's diminutive militia was on hand, and those men promptly ran away. Those residents who could get out did so, including Jefferson, who crossed the river and watched through a spyglass—while hiding in an old tobacco barn, his enemies ever after alleged—as the invaders looted and burned portions of the town. Arnold's men not only destroyed a foundry, two large tobacco warehouses, and a shipyard, they seized or torched military stores, wagons, tools, salt, wine, printing presses, clothing, and food. Some men, one of the officers later confessed, also "got into private houses and there obtained rum." The devastation was appalling, but it might have been worse. Arnold's orders were to venture into the interior only if it could be done "without the smallest danger." Aggressive as always, he penetrated some 125 miles into the interior in targeting Richmond, and yearned to go even deeper into the hinterland, but while in the capital Arnold received intelligence reports that both militia and Continentals posted in Virginia were gathering to come after him. He lingered for only two days, after which he fell back to Portsmouth, where he went into winter quarters and awaited word of Cornwallis's progress. Arnold's attack, coming so close on the heels of that of Leslie, was conceived more for its diversionary and psychological value. The hope was that it would further shatter what was thought to be Virginia's already wobbly will to fight on. It did not knock the state from the war—no one expected that it would—but it once again demonstrated Virginia's vulnerability to an enemy with naval superiority. The devastating raid also nearly ended Jefferson's public career, as he was assailed by local critics and congressmen for his deplorable response to the emergency.[3]

Cornwallis's army had spent a miserable late autumn at Winnsboro. Many men were ill and recuperating, and Cornwallis himself convalesced during much of that time after being felled in October, probably by a virus. He was not totally inactive, however. Fearing that King's Mountain had "dispirited" the back-country Tories to the point that they were "determined to submit as soon as the rebels should enter it," Cornwallis sought to regain the initiative from the guerrillas in South Carolina. During November and December he kept the cavalry under Wemyss and Tarleton in the field searching for Marion and Sumter. Neither partisan was taken, although the Gamecock was seriously wounded in a skirmish and put out of commission for two months. All the while, Cornwallis planned another invasion of North Carolina. He faced abundant problems. Even with Leslie's expected reinforcements, Cornwallis's army would not be as large as it had been prior to King's Mountain. His men's uniforms and shoes were worn thin from months of hard campaigning—even Cornwallis, who had lost his heavy overcoat, faced the coming winter with only a light coat; he had not succeeded on laying his hands on an adequate number of wagons and horses, and wear and tear had reduced his stockpile of serviceable weapons to a worrisome level. But when he learned that Greene had divided his army, taking his portion to the Cheraws just before Christmas while Morgan moved southwest of Charlotte, Cornwallis prepared to move out after them. Early in January he ordered Tarleton to go after Morgan and "push him to the utmost," staying west of the Broad River and taking care to see that the rebel force was confined in that area as well.[4] Cornwallis sent cavalry and light infantry under Lord Rawdon to deal with any rebel units that might attempt to descend south of Cheraw, just below the North Carolina border, and he marched his army—it would contain 3,200 men when it was joined by Leslie—north to begin the search for Greene. Cornwallis remained on the east side of the Broad River, hoping to stay between Morgan and Greene so they could not hook up. If need be, Cornwallis wished to be able to wheel about and help Tarleton finish off Morgan. Once Morgan had been destroyed and the two British divisions were reunited, Cornwallis would seek out Greene.[5]

Tarleton set off with about 1,200 men, including regulars, provincial units, and some local Tories who served as guides. Morgan's Flying Army, as it was being called, had started from Charlotte with only about three hundred men, two companies of Maryland Continentals and scores of Virginia militia, many with prior Continental service and a sizeable number with combat experience. Day after day militia units caught up with him. About 60 South Carolina militiamen under Colonel Andrew Pickens arrived on Christmas Day, nearly 125 North Carolinians reached Morgan's camp before New Year's, and small bands of battle-hardened Georgians showed up in the days that followed. Eventually, Morgan's army grew to somewhere between eight hundred and one thousand men, including eighty-two light dragoons under Lieutenant Colonel William Washington, a stout and powerful Virginian who was a distant relative of the commander in chief. Like Morgan, Washington never shrank from a fight, and during his first week with the Flying Army his cavalrymen not only chased down and defeated a force of two hundred Loyalist raiders, it overwhelmed a small British stockade in Ninety-Six.[6]

With good intelligence, Morgan knew immediately when Tarleton set out after him. Marching over primitive roads lined with tall, green loblolly pines, Morgan fell back toward the North Carolina border. He was not seeking to escape. Morgan was looking for a fight, and Greene notified him that he would not have long to wait. Tarleton was "on his way to pay you a visit," he advised, adding that he hoped the Flying Army would give him "a decent reception and a proper dismission." Morgan required no exhortations to fight. He was a fighter. Besides, he was convinced that to run would be ruinous. Not only would it destroy the "Spirit which now begins to pervade the People and call them into the Field," it would result in mass desertions among the militiamen, some of whom, rather than going home, would "Join the Enemy."[7] Morgan was falling back to buy time until more militiamen arrived, but he also wished to draw Tarleton deeper and deeper into the interior, hoping to wear him down, and to some extent he succeeded. Tarleton's men faced an unforgiving trek that included endless crossings of bitterly cold streams and days and nights of exposure to the harsh elements. Morgan may additionally have sought to lure his foe into what historian Lawrence Babits called a "logistical trap," a situation in which Tarleton would have to divide his force into forage parties, increasing the legion's exposure to attack.[8] Above all else, Morgan was searching for the right place to make a stand. As he moved, Morgan's greatest fear was that he might be surprised. Every campaigner remembered how Tarleton had burst in on Huger at Monck's Corner and his astonishingly rapid advance to overtake Buford's force in the Waxhaws was legendary. Morgan posted small parties at fords along the rivers that Tarleton had to cross, both to harass and slow his advance, but also to keep a close eye on his progress.

After taking every precaution, Morgan, at daybreak on January 15, was nonetheless startled to learn that Tarleton was only six miles away. As usual,

Tarleton had driven his men, awakening them at 2:00 every morning and pushing them mile after weary mile throughout each long day. He had moved with astonishing speed, "like a thunder storm," a private in Morgan's army later recalled.[9] Morgan's hand was forced. He cut short his men's breakfast that morning and put them on the road again. Little time now remained to find a suitable place for the pending fight, and the next day Morgan settled on a site. He chose a place that the locals called Cowpens, picking it after listening to the recommendations of his scouts and carefully reconnoitering the area himself.

Situated about twenty-five miles west of King's Mountain, Cowpens sat across a road junction. It was an open meadow that had been utilized as a stopping point on cattle drives to the coast. Some five hundred yards long and wide, the unremarkable landscape was dotted with trees, though not thickly forested. While the terrain was predominantly level, it sloped slightly upward toward a modest crest at the north end (the end that Morgan's men would defend), dipped briefly, then rose gently to what would best be described as a low ridge rather than a hill. The sides were devoid of dense forests and black swamps, though streams meandered by a few miles to the northeast and west. Morgan thought it satisfactory, if for no other reason than, unlike Camden, there was no place for panicked militiamen to run for safety. The absence of such natural boundaries on each side meant that the rebel flanks would be "in the air," as soldiers like to say, for there were no natural impediments on which to ground the two sides of the army, or to help prevent the enemy from turning its flanks. Tarleton was delighted when he saw Cowpens, remarking that it offered him wonderful advantages for launching an attack, although he observed that he, too, would have selected this site had he been in Morgan's shoes.[10]

During that busy January 16 Morgan prepared a plan of battle, discussed it with his officers, who in turn went over it to the lower-grade officers, who then explained it to the men. Throughout the night that followed, Morgan—though hobbled with acute rheumatism and "a ciatick pain in my hip" that made it excruciatingly painful to walk—circulated through the camp using his manipulative talents to buck up spirits. He talked with the militiamen, explaining how the plan was to work and disclosing the thinking that went into it, telling jokes, some off-color, throwing in some treacle about their sweethearts back home, and giving deft little pep talks. "Keep in good spirits, and the day [will] be ours," he said with confidence, adding: "Just hold up your heads, boys, three fires, and you are free, and then when you return to Your homes, how the old folks will bless, and the girls kiss you, for your gallant conduct."[11]

The plan that he had concocted was unorthodox. The forward units were to consist of skirmishers, riflemen from the Carolinas and Georgia. These shock troops were to hide behind trees, holding their fire until the enemy drew within a few yards, then open up with a surprising blast that was calculated to jolt the enemy in the first moment of battle, sowing confusion and hopefully thinning their ranks. After getting off a few volleys, the skirmishers were to retreat in an

Lieutenant Colonel John Eager Howard. Painting by Charles Willson Peale, from life, c. 1781–1784. An officer under Greene's command, this dedicated Maryland officer fought in nearly every major engagement in the South from Cowpens onward.

orderly manner to the second rebel line about 150 yards further back. This was the militia line under the command of Pickens. These men were instructed to fire three times, always making an effort to zero in on an officer. After their last shot, they, too, were to retreat and reform behind Morgan's third line. That last line was under the command of Lieutenant Colonel John Eager Howard, a twenty-nine-year-old Maryland aristocrat who had fought in most of the big engagements up north as well as at Camden, and whom a comrade later described as "Placid . . . and reserved," never given to "arrogance or ostentation . . . garrulity or self-conceit."[12] His men were primarily Continentals. Washington's cavalry was to be posted behind this last line, screened from view by the slight knoll, ready to be plugged in wherever Morgan—or Washington—thought it could do the most good. It was a simple plan. Success in large measure would hinge on the militia standing and fighting, then making an orderly fallback while under fire, one of war's most difficult undertakings, even for veteran soldiers. If that element of Morgan's plan broke down, Cowpens would deteriorate into a replay of Camden. Morgan did not expect that to occur. The confidence that he exuded was genuine. He was a rarity, a Continental general who believed that militiamen could be good soldiers. He had been a militiaman once himself. He knew, too, that many of them were good marksmen, and that around 70 percent had come under fire previously. But he took some safeguards. Each man was given twenty-four rounds. No one should feel unarmed, a feeling that added to the already overwhelming terror of the battlefield. Each man also knew the general battle plan. That was essential, Morgan thought. He not only believed that most men would be reassured, seeing that the scheme was well-conceived, but that the men's knowledge of what to expect would offer protection against panicky behavior when they saw their comrades falling back.[13]

Morgan put his men to sleep on the night before Tarleton's expected arrival and awakened them in time for a very early breakfast. Well rested and fed, they moved through the inky darkness to their assigned positions. Tarleton's army, on the other hand, had been on the move for ten days, first securing Ninety-Six, then pursuing Morgan. On the day of the fast-approaching battle, Tarleton awakened his men in the wee hours of the morning, after which they covered several miles of rugged terrain in three hours. His men were not given a good meal that day, and their diet during their days in the field had left much to be desired. Many were exhausted from their physical labors, and especially from sleep deprivation. Now they were about to be hurled into battle. At about 5:30 a.m., in the last throes of the dark starry night, they splashed across muddy Macedonia Creek to the cusp of Cowpens. As they began to organize in the still, cold darkness—the temperature was in the low to mid-twenties—the first low purple of day glazed the eastern sky.[14]

Tarleton may have been surprised that Morgan intended to fight. If so, the British cavalryman never considered not fighting. He did not have much choice. He was in a box that in part went with backcountry campaigning and partially arose from Morgan's cleverness. Tarleton's pantry was empty and he had to know that he would face great difficulties foraging in the face of such a large enemy force. Tarleton also had no prospects of reinforcements, but for all he knew the rebel army might grow substantially if additional militia drifted in. Mostly, though, Tarleton was the type who never backed away from a fight, and after the rebels' showing at Camden, he was not about to turn his back on this one. He was like Morgan in that respect. To this point, Morgan had done everything right during the ten days since Tarleton had set out on his trail. Now all he had to do was win the imminent battle against a slightly larger force.

The battle began about an hour after the British reached Cowpens. Tarleton sent out fifty dragoons to drive off Morgan's skirmishers. The cavalrymen moved quickly, expecting rebel resistance to falter before it began. Instead, they rode into a sheet of gunfire. In an instant, fifteen legion horsemen fell wounded from their saddles. The unit of cavalry buckled, then hurried back to their army. Knowing that he had to dislodge the skirmishers in order to get close enough to see how his adversary was deployed, Tarleton next sent out the light infantry. They did the job, although the advance line of red, blue, and green clad attackers also took casualties from what Morgan later called the "galling fire" of his skirmishers.[15]

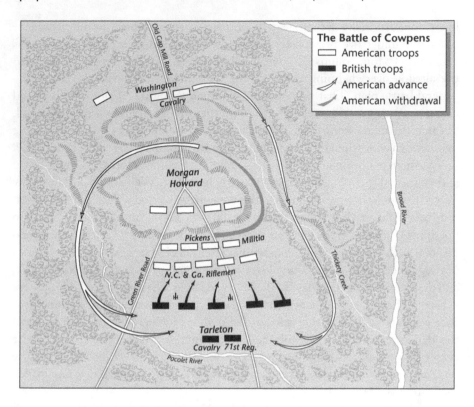

To this point the British had not fired a shot. The real battle for the Americans was about to begin. It would be fought where Morgan had posted his militia. Tarleton kept his troops moving after the skirmishers fell back, even though the Seventh Regiment, which was to be part of the assault, had not arrived in the advancing line. He need not have acted so impetuously, as the rebel line was not going to get any stronger. But doubtless anticipating that there was shock value to be gained from the relentless, piston-like advance of his army, Tarleton kept the infantry in motion, and one American soldier, James Collins, a sixteen-year-old South Carolina private, recalled later that he had been intimidated as he watched the enemy inexorably coming on "as if certain of victory."[16] The British infantry moved rapidly, advancing nearly the length of two football fields in three minutes, huzzaing as they came, drums beating, and fifes sounding. They came "Running at us as if they Intended to eat us up," Morgan thought.[17] But he also understood the psychology of the battlefield, and he had his men answer the approaching foe with the blood-curdling "Indian halloo," as he called the backcountry yell. When the advancing British came within thirty-five yards, Pickens shouted the order to fire. With a thunderous roar, one soldier recalled, "a sheet of flame from right to left" leapt toward the enemy.[18] The volley cut up the British line. It sagged for an instant. But the officers regrouped the men, who

Cavalry Clash in the Battle of Cowpens. Halftone reproduction of drawing from Henry Cabot Lodge, *The Story of the Revolution* (1898). Colonel William Washington, on the white charger, duels with Colonel Banastre Tarleton in the climatic moments of the Battle of Cowpens.

got off their first volley of the day, a hurried uphill effort that largely overshot their target. The militia poured several volleys into the nearby line of British, and with devastating effectiveness. Two-thirds of the British infantry officers were killed or wounded; four companies suffered more than 90 percent casualties.

After getting off their three assigned volleys, the militiamen retreated in a more or less orderly manner. Seeing the withdrawal, the British believed they had won the battle, but to this point neither side had won. The outcome of the battle hung on the performance of Morgan's main line, his Continentals. Their fight lasted no more than ten minutes, but it was as furious as any fighting in the war. Men on both sides got off multiple shots. During this phase of the battle, Tarleton threw his cavalry and the Seventy-first Regiment, the proud Highlanders, at the American right flank. This was the critical moment for the rebels. The Americans retreated, but the withdrawal was ordered by Howard—a pullback designed to better defend his exposed flank—and it was orchestrated in an orderly fashion. The British misjudged when they saw the rebels withdrawing. Sensing a rout, they stormed the American line. They charged into hell.

Howard's men turned and fired on the surprised British. Then, with bayonets fixed, they launched a charge of their own. The skirmishers and militia from Morgan's first two lines reentered the melee at this juncture, both opening up with a deadly enfiladed fire into the British ranks. At this very moment Morgan unleashed Washington's cavalry, which emerged like an apparition from behind the ridge, the horsemen slashing with their sabers and madly shouting "Buford's play" and "Tarleton's quarter." In the blink of an eye, the British began to retreat. Many redcoats, like Gates's callow militiamen at Camden, threw down their weapons as they ran. Washington's horsemen showed no mercy. They set upon armed and unarmed men. They attacked soldiers who were standing and those sitting. Young Private Collins thought this was the turning point of the battle, and he may have been correct. The American dragoons swept about like a "whirl-wind," he said, and "the shock was so sudden and violent" that "the British could not stand it." Taking "themselves to flight," the harried British, he thought, "appeared to be as hard to stop as a drove of wild Choctaw steers."[19] One teenaged South Carolina private reveled in the sight of the enemy's flight. It was "the prettiest sort of running," he declared.[20] Not all escaped, and in a macabre scene many of those who were trapped fell on their knees and pleaded for their lives. According to one rebel soldier, they cried out: "dear, good Americans, have mercy on us! It has not been our fault, that we have SKIVERED [skewered] so many" American soldiers.[21] The entreaties of many went unheeded, though some were saved by rebels whose compassion overcame their crazed predatory ferocity. One young British captain survived because Colonel Howard swooped down and hoisted him onto his horse. (In later years, that British officer wrote Howard often to thank him for his kindness in that feral moment.)[22]

Tarleton's line was falling apart across the battlefield. With great bravery, he rode about Cowpens in a vain attempt to rally his men. He turned next to the cavalry that he had left in reserve—some two hundred horsemen who should have been capable of repulsing Washington's outnumbered dragoons—but there was no fight in them. They ignored their commander's orders and fled the field. With no options remaining, Tarleton ordered a retreat, though first he and about sixty men daringly, and with a valor that lies almost beyond comprehension, attempted to save their artillery. They failed. Washington's cavalry was on them in a flash and the last bloody act of the battle was played out, close quarters fight-ing that included a confrontation between Tarleton and Washington. Tarleton nearly got the best of it. He slashed at Washington, who deflected the blow with the hilt of his sword, which had been broken earlier in the engagement. Tarleton next fired at Washington from close range with his pistol, but somehow missed. With that, Tarleton wheeled about his mount and sped off, perhaps the last British soldier to quit this blood-soaked battlefield. Every green-clad man under him "took to His heels for security—helter Skelter," Morgan subsequently reported.[23] Some did not get away, but Tarleton vanished. Washington's men gave chase "like Blood Hounds," Morgan said, but after riding twenty-four miles they lost the scent. Tarleton had escaped.[24] After forty minutes, one of the fiercest and most crucial battles of the war was over. Morgan, ecstatic with his magnificent victory, picked up his nine-year-old drummer and kissed him on both cheeks. In a tumult of euphoria he rode about shouting: "Old Morgan never was beaten."[25] It was a great victory, "a great thing Indeed," Morgan exalted, for as he put it he had given Tarleton "a devil of a whipping."[26]

For the second time in ninety days the rebels had scored "a compleat Victory," as Morgan reported. This one, said the victor, had come about through the "Justice of our Cause & the Bravery of our Troops." The Americans lost seventy-three men, of which twelve were killed. Tarleton lost nearly everything. Only he and about 250 of his men—mostly the dragoons who at the decisive moment had refused to fight—escaped. More than one hundred British corpses littered the battlefield, many having been killed after they laid down their arms. (Morgan, who knew better, reported to Greene that it was to the "Honour of the American Arms" that "not a man was killed [,] wounded or even insulted after he surrendered.) More than eight hundred, of whom some two hundred were wounded, were taken prisoner. Their arms, artillery, a stockpile of ammunition, a traveling forge, horses, thirty-five baggage wagons, "plenty of hard cash"— carried by the British for foraging purposes—and "all their Music are ours," Morgan crowed.[27] The victors also took the clothing off the losers, leaving the defeated enemy to shiver in the January cold. "Our poor fellows who were almost naked before, have now several changes of clothes," remarked a rebel who was unmoved by the plight of the enemy soldiers.[28]

CORNWALLIS had started north two days after sending Tarleton on his errand, though many of his men were still recuperating from what an army physician labeled a "sickness . . . of the bilious kind mostly tending to a putrescency." (In short, they had been felled by fevers brought on by months of campaigning in what one disconsolate redcoat called a "country full of marshes and small rivers, woods and insects, and a sun so powerful in heat.")[29] Cornwallis's last information was that Morgan was on the Pacolet River perhaps twenty-five miles southeast of Cowpens and about thirty miles above his headquarters at Winnsboro. Remaining east of the Broad River, while Tarleton stayed to the west, Cornwallis moved in the direction that Morgan had last been sighted. For a dozen days Cornwallis's primary objective was to see that Morgan did not cross the Broad and make a dash to link up with Greene. But on January 16 he received intelligence indicating that Morgan was pulling back to the northwest. The British commander no longer had to worry about Morgan reuniting with Greene. Concluding that Tarleton was unlikely ever to catch his prey, given Morgan's considerable head start, Cornwallis turned to an alternative plan. He now focused on finding Greene. Cornwallis summoned Leslie, who had arrived from Virginia and was bivouacking at Camden. Once they rendezvoused, Cornwallis planned to set off toward the northeast. His new design lasted no more than twenty-four hours. Late on January 17, the day of Cowpens, the first sketchy and disquieting reports of the disaster reached headquarters. The following day Tarleton arrived and confirmed Cornwallis's worst fears. A rebel witness, a prisoner of the British, later recounted that a solemn Cornwallis greeted Tarleton as he dismounted from his sweaty horse, and stood leaning "forward on his sword as he listened to his subordinate. Furious at what he heard, Cornwallis pressed so hard that the sword snapped in two, and he swore loudly."[30]

What Cornwallis heard dealt a savage blow to his aspirations and caused another change in his plans. From the outset he had hoped that Morgan's army would be destroyed, leaving him—when joined by Leslie and Tarleton—with a three-to-one superiority over Greene. Instead, he now knew that he had lost a quarter of his army. He also believed that if Morgan united with Greene, the rebel army would be nearly equal in size to his own. Cornwallis made a hurried decision, but one that would have been the choice of most military commanders. He chose to go after Morgan. He would try to prevent him from joining with Greene, destroy him, and liberate the prisoners that the rebels had taken. Then he would hunt down Greene. To turn back and do nothing, he feared, would further demoralize the Carolina Tories, and it would open the door to infinite sapping strikes all through the South Carolina backcountry by partisans who were aided and abetted by Continentals.

Cornwallis, who believed that Morgan's army numbered about two thousand men, was joined by Leslie, but only after a thirty-six-hour-long wait that he could ill afford. When he at last set off, Cornwallis could only guess the direction that Morgan would move, and he guessed wrong. He assumed that Morgan would remain west of the Broad River, possibly choosing to campaign in undefended Ninety-Six, and he moved off in a northwestwardly direction. But Morgan not only knew the peril he was in, he was desperately anxious to reunite with Greene. He moved to the northeast, in the general direction of Hillsborough. For two long days Cornwallis marched the wrong way. He never recovered from his erroneous choice. He finally got back on track, but after five days of marching, when his army reached Ramsour's Mill in North Carolina, Cornwallis learned that Morgan was twenty miles ahead of him, a nearly insurmountable lead. Cornwallis responded audaciously. Vowing to strip his army of all impediments to speed, he ordered a giant bonfire. Anything in the cumbersome baggage train that might slow his army—from tents and wagons to every conceivable luxury item, including wine, rum, china, silver, surplus clothing, and beds—went into the pyre. It was unimaginable that any other British commander in this war would have taken such a step, and indeed it was not long before Clinton scorned it as "something too like a Tartar move." But Cornwallis was a fighter, and he was driven now by an incandescent urge to destroy those who had caused him so much grief.[31]

Morgan soon knew what Cornwallis had done. "I know thay intend to bring me to an action, which I [intend] carefully to avoid," he told Greene, as he was "too weak to fight them." That was quite true. With Leslie and the remnants of Tarleton's shattered force, Cornwallis's army numbered some 2,500 men, almost three times the size of Morgan's little force. At first, Morgan was unconcerned. He had a considerable head start on his foe, and he put even more distance between himself and his pursuer when Cornwallis stopped to make his bonfire. Morgan crossed the Catawba River on January 23, five days before Cornwallis reached it. Morgan paused there. He wrote asking that Greene join him, also telling his commander that he would remain at the Catawba while awaiting word of Greene's plans. When he learned that Cornwallis's army had covered thirty miles on January 24, Morgan began to worry. "Cornwallis will push on," he edgily notified Greene. The only thing that would stop him was "a force . . . to check him." On January 28, still at the Catawba and with the enemy now only ten miles away, Morgan anxiously wrote Greene that he might not be able to outrun his pursuer when the chase resumed, though he was over the Catawba and his men were at work "filling up all the Private fords" with "every obstruction imaginable" to delay Cornwallis's crossing. Later that same day Cornwallis's army reached the Catawba. Now only a river separated the two armies. But the gods of war were with Morgan. Dark clouds piled overhead and it began to rain. Hour after hour it rained, turning the river into a maelstrom, a raging and impassible barrier, beyond anything that Morgan's men could ever have fashioned. Cornwallis was stopped in his tracks for nearly sixty hours.[32]

Greene had not arrived. He had not learned of Cowpens until six days after the battle, the day that Morgan's army reached, and crossed, the Catawba. (Greene had immediately ordered a celebration in his camp, during which, in his elation, he imbibed a bit too much cherry bounce, a concoction variously made from rum or cider.)[33] Two additional days passed before Greene learned that Morgan was waiting at the river for orders. At last aware of the plight of the remainder of his army, Greene responded quickly. Ordering the bulk of his men to march from the Pee Dee toward Salisbury, some forty miles east of Catawba, Greene—accompanied only by a guide, an aide, and a small guard of cavalry—boldly rode a hundred mud-splattered miles through Tory-infested territory to join with Morgan. He wished to assess the situation personally, to determine whether to bring on an action on the Catawba or to continue the retreat. Everything hinged on the militia, which Greene had asked the civil authorities to turn out. If North Carolina's militia responded in large numbers, Cornwallis "must be certainly ruined" in a showdown, he said. Greene was disappointed. Like the New Jersey militia in the early fall of 1776, it failed to appear in significant numbers. Only two hundred or so men drifted into his army, and they arrived over a period of several days. Chagrined, but not surprised, Greene knew that the ravages of war over the past eight months had rendered southerners' "domestick matters . . . in such distress that they will not leave home."[34]

"I see the least prospect of opposing [Cornwallis] with the little force we have, naked and distressed," Greene concluded, and he ordered the resumption of the retreat that Morgan had started on the very day of Cowpens. Morgan urged that the army turn northwest and pull back into the welcoming embrace of the mountains, as Washington had done following Trenton-Princeton. Without calling a council of war, Greene overruled him. He preferred to fall back to the east, to Guilford Courthouse. From there, if need be, he would retreat straight north toward the Dan River, which meandered along the North Carolina-Virginia border. Greene believed that Cornwallis would stubbornly continue the pursuit, and that was fine with him. Greene hoped to lure his foe ever deeper into the interior, ever more drained by the hard rigors of living without tents and proper clothing in the winter elements, ever more fatigued from long, hurried daily marches over roads—cart paths would be a more apt description—that the steady cold rain had turned into viscid snares. As the rebels fell back, both Morgan and Greene called on Virginia to commit more troops—"Great god what is the reason we cant Have more men," Morgan demanded of Jefferson—and Greene additionally sought to reactivate the Over Mountain Men. Greene felt that if his army swelled appreciably, he would turn on Cornwallis at the first good opportunity. If not, he would retreat until he crossed into Virginia, where he believed ample reinforcements could be gathered. Unstintingly meticulous, Greene sent word ahead to gather sufficient boats to get him across the rivers in his path.[35]

Late on January 31, Morgan's army, which had last marched eight days earlier, set out once again. Its immediate destination was Island Ford on the Yadkin River, seven miles beyond Salisbury, where boats were supposedly waiting to convey the men across. These men were accustomed to covering thirty miles or more each day, but the sludge-like roads slowed their progress. Three full days of marching were required to cover the forty miles to the Yadkin. Walking was an ordeal, "every step being up to our Knees in mud," one soldier groaned. Cornwallis began to move his army across the Catawba about a dozen hours after Morgan departed. It was not an easy task. Greene not only had posted small forces at various fords to harass the enemy, the current was running swiftly. The river at the principal ford the British utilized was five hundred yards across and the numbingly cold water was up to four feet deep. Led by a Tory guide, the army moved out at 1:00 a.m., crossing the churning stream in a long, straight line. It was a nightmare. Moving in the black and windy darkness, the men wearily held their heavy muskets aloft. Many slipped on the slick rocky river bottom and every man was drenched by the piercingly frigid water that lapped up to their shoulders. All the while, the rebels ashore fired on them, occasionally hitting a man or taking down a horse that bore an officer. By the time the last man, and the final wagon, reached the other side and Cornwallis's army could start out again, Morgan's division was thirty miles away.[36]

Cornwallis pressed on, grasping at one nub of hope. Perhaps the rain, his enemy at the Catawba, would be his ally at the Yadkin River. Greene and Morgan had to cross the Yadkin before they rendezvoused with the remainder of the rebel army at Salisbury. Cornwallis reckoned that if he could stay close, and if the relentless rains continued, the rebels might find that they could not immediately cross the river. If that came to pass, he would pounce and destroy his adversary. Cornwallis moved with great energy, a far cry from the languid rhythm of his pursuit of Washington across New Jersey more than four years earlier. He drove his men, often covering in a day what had required three days to traverse in 1776. He had no baggage to encumber him, but he had hundreds of horses which ordinarily would have been pulling wagons. Cornwallis put two men on each horse and his entire force moved through the gluey muck with the speed of light infantry. He almost caught the rebels near the Yadkin. Greene found the boats that he had ordered to transport him across the river, but he also discovered that the Yadkin was wild, swollen and seething with heavy wind-lashed waves. To attempt a crossing would be hazardous. But to stand with his back to the river and fight Cornwallis would be madness. Greene pushed his army across the dreadful, rushing river, barely making it, as his rear guard exchanged shots with the van of Cornwallis's force. But Greene's force, with their boats, were across. Cornwallis had no boats. For the second time in a week the British were stopped by a rampaging river. The Americans did not linger once they crossed this river. Retreating under the scudding rain clouds, they hurried to Guilford Courthouse, forty-seven miles away. Once there, Greene's army, divided since before Christmas, was at last reunited. For the first time, Greene summoned a council of war to decide whether to stand and fight or to continue the retreat into Virginia. Greene painted a dark picture for his officers. He no longer expected an increase in the size of his army. He had hoped to find militia gathering at Guilford Courthouse, but once again he had been disappointed. He estimated that he had about 1,400 men, at least 1,000 fewer than the enemy. If Arnold's force sailed south from Portsmouth and landed at the Cape Fear River, as Greene thought likely, Cornwallis's army not only would suddenly double in size, the rebels would face overwhelmingly superior enemy armies to their east and west. The American officers listened uneasily, then voted unanimously "to avoid a general Action at all Events" and continue the retreat.[37]

Cornwallis had been delayed for nearly five days by the impassable Yadkin. With increasing irritation he waited for the turbulent river to fall, until finally, he took his army forty miles to the north and crossed at Shallow Ford. Then, unflappable as always, he was off. Cornwallis's men were bone-tired, worn down from arduous labor, scant provisions, the ever-present and inescapable moisture and cold winter weather, and a march that already exceeded two hundred miles since they had set out from Winnsboro a month earlier. But Cornwallis would not give up. He was obsessed with catching Greene before he slithered out of North Carolina, and with good reason. If he could destroy Greene, not a single Continental soldier would remain below Virginia. If he could accomplish that, and if he could get into Virginia and combine with Arnold, Cornwallis believed he could take, and hold, Richmond as well as every coastal village of consequence.

Operating from those bases, Cornwallis intended to cut the supply lines that sluiced through Virginia to the guerrillas in the Carolinas. Denied the stores that were their lifeblood, the backcountry partisans could not last long. The consummation of Britain's Southern Strategy, conceived three years before, was within Cornwallis' grasp—if only he could catch Greene.

The final leg of the chase began on February 9 when Cornwallis gathered his wet, shivering men on the east side of the Yadkin and doggedly moved out once again. That same day the remainder of Greene's men, long ago summoned from the Pee Dee, joined their comrades at Guilford Courthouse. Twenty-four hours later Greene put his equally weary army in motion. He set off without Morgan, whose sciatica and rheumatism had become unbearable. For six excruciating weeks Morgan had campaigned in incredible pain. Now he could go no further. While his comrades headed almost due north toward the Dan, Morgan departed for home in Virginia by a separate, more direct, route.[38]

For the last desperate flight to safety, Greene once again divided his army. He ordered Colonel Otho Williams to take seven hundred light troops and follow a westward course as if he planned to cross the Dan at its upper fords. Greene, with the larger division, was to stay to the east and head directly for the downstream crossings of the Dan. As the two rebel divisions were to travel

Colonel Otho Holland Williams. Painting by Charles Willson Peale, after Charles William Peale, 1782–1784. Although he fought in campaigns in the North and South, Williams is best remembered for his actions under Morgan and Greene in the grueling fighting in the southern theater in 1781.

parallel roads, Williams's force would be the closest to that of Cornwallis, and for this reason he was given all the army's 250 dragoons, some under Colonel Washington, the others under Light Horse Harry Lee. The horsemen were to be Williams's rear guard, a mobile unit that was to fend off the enemy's cavalry, if it threatened. Williams, whom another officer once described as "elegant in form, made for activity rather than strength," moved out on the same day that Cornwallis crossed the Yadkin.[39] Twenty miles separated the two armies at this juncture. Williams's job was to act as a shield for Greene's larger force, to harass the enemy, to impede its progress by destroying bridges, to draw Cornwallis toward the upper fords on the Dan, giving Greene the breathing space to get to, and across, at the lower fords. Williams and Greene had some forty miles to cover to reach the Dan. They started one day later than Cornwallis. The men were tired before they started. Those who had been with Morgan had already marched more than three hundred miles during the past fifty or so days. Be that as it may, Williams awakened his men at 3:00 a.m. each morning and marched them for four hours or more, when they paused briefly to cook their day's food over pungent, low fires and to eat a hurried breakfast. Whatever else they ate each day was consumed as they marched, or when they stopped in the evening. They took no breaks, marching daily until after nightfall. The men were allotted but six hours for sleeping each night, and not every man squeezed in that much, as some were assigned picket or guard duty. (Greene himself claimed to have slept only four hours in four days in the course of the chase.)[40] The rebels moved quickly. Cornwallis moved more quickly. By February 13, after five days on the road, he had cut the gap between his force and that of Williams to merely four miles. He was within twenty-two miles of Greene's division. Cornwallis knew now that he could not catch Greene before he reached the Dan, but intelligence was reporting that the rebels would have insufficient boats to cross at the upper fords. If true, he might pinion Williams's division to the river and destroy it.

But on that very day, Williams suddenly veered to the right and moved in Greene's direction. The next day, though Cornwallis did not know this, Greene notified Williams by an express that he had reached the Dan in the first hours of darkness on the previous evening. A few hours later another express rider hurried to Williams with another note from Greene: "½ past 5 o'clock. All our troops are over and the stage is clear. . . . I am ready to receive you and give you a hearty welcome." Williams, too, was ready to get his men across. He was fourteen miles from the Dan and Cornwallis was hard on his heels. This time Williams was the faster of the two. He reached the Dan about two hours after nightfall and started putting his men across. Cornwallis arrived the following morning at daybreak, and, in the tilting light of sunrise watched the last rebel soldier—a dragoon—step ashore north of the Dan.[41]

Shortly before Cornwallis arrived, Greene wrote to Governor Jefferson that he was "fatigued to death," but prepared to run further if Cornwallis continued his tenacious pursuit. But the chase was over. Greene not only had won the race to the river, but without boats the British could not cross the Dan immediately. Days would pass before the pursuit could be taken up again, and by then Steuben, whom Cornwallis knew to be in Virginia recruiting Continentals, would have delivered those new, fresh faces to Greene. Virginia's militia would likely have assembled by then as well. Besides, Cornwallis knew that his men were drained from their punishing exertions and privations. Over six long weeks, through skirmishes, dangerous river crossings, sickness, and desertion, the British force had shrunk by 250 men, one-tenth of those that had started out from west of Charlotte. Cornwallis ordered an end to the chase. He issued a proclamation claiming victory (the rebel army had been driven from the Carolinas, he boasted unconvincingly), and after a day of rest during which the rebel soldiers, according to one of Greene's aides, stood "laughing at the enemy who are on the opposite bank," Cornwallis began a retreat of his own to Hillsborough, sixty miles to the south.[42]

GREENE'S ACTIONS had replicated those of Washington in the autumn of 1776. Like the commander in chief, Greene had divided his army, pursued a Fabian strategy, and sought an opportunity to make a sudden strike. Greene had been with Washington in those days and was intimately familiar with his campaign. After learning of his appointment as the southern commander, Greene had visited Washington at his headquarters in Totawa, New Jersey, and the two spent hours discussing the war in the South. No record of their conversation exists, but Washington must have emphasized that Greene's primary objective was to avoid the loss of still another southern army and to keep the South in the war throughout 1781, during which time he and Rochambeau would attempt something decisive. Greene had avoided defeat in January and February, but like Washington after his escape across the Delaware, he sensed the opportunity to do more. Washington, in an enormous gamble, had gone back across the Delaware to Trenton to fight again. Likewise, Greene decided to reenter North Carolina, hazarding his little army in a daring attempt to achieve something that, if not decisive, would have a profound impact on the war in the South.

On the day after Cornwallis began his retreat, Greene sent Lee's cavalry to harass him. Within the week he also sent Williams back across the Dan with light infantry. Three days later Greene returned to North Carolina with the remainder of his army, now reinforced by six hundred Virginia militiamen. In part, Greene believed that his presence was essential to prevent Tories, who might have been bamboozled by Cornwallis's proclamation, from turning out to fight for the king. But Greene hoped for more. Though Cornwallis's army remained "greatly our superior," it was far from its supply base and attempting to provide for itself in an area whose bounty had been picked over by the rebel armies under de Kalb and Gates from the preceding June through the autumn harvest. Even a small rebel force might play havoc with British foraging activities, much as Washington's men had done in New Jersey early in 1777. Greene hoped to slowly bleed Cornwallis as well, accomplishing "by finesse which I dare not attempt by force," he said. Should further reinforcements arrive—Greene was ever hopeful on this score—or should Cornwallis be driven to an ill-conceived act, Greene might even have the opportunity to accomplish more.[43]

Greene's dauntless risk-taking quickly paid dividends. Although Cornwallis rapidly recruited seven companies of Tories in the Hillsborough area, he was not swamped with Loyalist volunteers from elsewhere, a consequence in large measure of a devastating blow inflicted by Lee's cavalry. Late in February, Cornwallis dispatched Tarleton to protect the Loyalist militiamen who were assembling and to escort them safely to Hillsborough. Through scouts and various intelligence sources, Lee learned of the enemy's activities. He set out in the hope of overtaking and surprising Tarleton. He never found his prey, but, on February 25, Lee's dragoons learned that a four-hundred-man Loyalist force under Colonel John Pyle was nearby awaiting the British Legion. Lee fell on the Tories, taking them by surprise—the Loyalists mistook Lee's green-jacketed men for Tarleton's Legion—and cutting them to pieces in an action that was disturbingly similar to the Waxhaws massacre. During the brief encounter that came to be known as "Pyles' Massacre," Lee's men killed ninety and wounded most of the remaining Tories, many of whom, totally unaware of the mortal danger they were in, were

Colonel Henry Lee. Painting by Charles Willson Peale, from life, c. 1782. A Continental cavalry commander, Light Horse Harry Lee fought in the North and South, always with daring and ruthlessness. His greatest contributions came in the liberation of the South.

unarmed. (Evidence, perhaps, of the Tories unreadiness for battle lies in the fact that Lee did not lose a single man.) The rebel leaders, men grown hard by the war's malevolence, were not given to bothersome meditation over the ethics of Lee's action. The "Affair . . . has been of infinite Service," Pickens remarked, speaking for many. "It has knocked up Toryism altogether in this part" of North Carolina. Greene said simply that Lee's men had "made a most dreadful carnage of them," but he lost no sleep over it, as the Tories' debacle had "put a total stop to their recruiting."[44]

Frustrated and angry, believing that he must turn around the steady flow of reversals since October, Cornwallis emerged from Hillsborough following the massacre, though he acknowledged that bringing Greene to battle was probably a forlorn hope. For nearly two weeks in the gloom of late winter the two armies shadowed one another, never more than twenty miles apart. Small skirmishes occurred almost daily, though Greene resolutely refused to be hurried "into a Measure that is not Suggested by prudence." At the outset, the armies were about equal size, but Cornwallis's force was dramatically superior with regard to the number of regulars. Over time the numbers changed. Cornwallis's army stopped growing after Pyles' Massacre. Greene's "little force," as he often referred to it, grew steadily. As militia came in, Greene came to believe that he might "approach the enemy with greater confidence, and eventually . . . harrass their rear." When some Over Mountain Men and North Carolina state troops arrived, Greene grew "determined . . . to move nearer the Enemy," though he continued to believe that to "risque a general action may perhaps be impolitic." When Virginian Continentals came into camp, Greene thought his army "was much more respectable." By the second week in March it had swelled to between 4,500 and 5,000 men, more than twice the number he had possessed when he recrossed the Dan, and more than twice that of his adversary. More importantly, about 40 percent of Greene's men now were Continentals, and a fair number of the Virginia militiamen were battle hardened former Continentals. Greene was ready to fight. Despite the odds, so, too, was Cornwallis.[45]

Greene reconnoitered carefully and chose a site at Guilford Courthouse. It was considerably larger than Cowpens, nearly ten times as long and wide, and it was heavily forested, which Greene liked, hoping that would make it difficult for the British to keep their formations intact and mount bayonet charges, the prospect of which had led more than one militiaman to run in fear. Greene knew the formula that Morgan had successfully employed at Cowpens, and Morgan had written recently exhorting him to use the Cowpens blueprint when arranging his army for battle. If the rebel militia will fight, Morgan predicted, "you'l beat Cornwallis [,] if not, he will beat you." Greene, like Washington, had little to say that was favorable about the militia. "Ten of the militia . . . are not worth one" partisan fighter, he exclaimed that winter. He also thought militiamen were little better than a band of thieves. Their rampant pillaging, he once railed in private, had "corrupted the Principles of the People." To place much trust in them would be "the greatest folly in the world," he remarked.[46] Still and all, Greene had little choice but to use them at Guilford Courthouse, although in his heart of hearts he may have agreed with his adversary, Cornwallis, who said: "I will not say much in praise of the [rebel] militia . . . but the list of British officers and soldiers killed and wounded by them . . . proves . . . that they are not wholly contemptible."[47]

Greene was his own man. He had gotten this far by trusting his instincts and experience. But in this instance he appears to have followed the example provided by Morgan at Cowpens, modifying it only slightly. Like Morgan, he deployed three lines, and he, too, placed militia in the front line, asking them to fire two rounds, then to retreat to the rear. Militia and state troops were posted about 350 yards further back in a second line. Continentals, positioned nearly five hundred yards further back, comprised the final line. Greene flanked his front line with cavalry and riflemen, some in the bare woods redolent with the musty scent of last year's decaying leaves. Breaking with convention, and with Morgan's plan, he kept no units in reserve. As the hour of battle approached, Greene rode from unit to unit, stopping and talking with the men, drawing on his reserve of charm and eloquence to stoke the grit of the lionhearted and instill an ounce of bravado in the fainthearted.[48]

Cornwallis was twelve miles away when he learned that Greene was drawing up for battle. He wasted no time, gathering his force that same day and marching on his enemy the next morning without permitting the men to eat breakfast. Around noon on March 15, a gloriously cool day, the rebels heard, then spotted, the first column of red-clad soldiers as it emerged through a cuff of leafless trees and marched grandly up New Garden Road, awash with the soft, spring sun, and finally onto the bucolic site that Greene had selected for a battlefield. For thirty minutes or more, while Cornwallis formed his lines, each side ineffectually banged away at the other with limited artillery, four rebel six-pounders and three British field pieces of similar size. Cornwallis placed light infantry, grenadiers, and jägers under the redoubtable Colonel Webster on his left, and Highlanders and blue-coated Hessians on the right under Leslie. Tarleton's Legion was posted in the rear, ready to move into action as needed. Two hours of mayhem began when the British stepped off toward their uncommonly immobile foe, marching steadfastly across muddy farmlands.[49]

To the defenders it seemed an eternity before the gaudily colored enemy drew close, but actually only a minute or two passed during the British army's march. When the enemy was much more than one hundred yards away, shots rang out from among the North Carolina militiamen, many of whom were anxious to get off their two rounds and get out. To fire from such a distance was useless. What is more, many militiamen, according to Greene, "left the ground without firing at all."[50] Their conduct struck one mortified militia officer as akin to "a flock of sheep frightened by dogs."[51] But most of the rebels held their fire and remained in place until the long, grimy line of regulars came nearer, present-ing an inviting target as they marched exposed across a broad opening. When they drew to within fifty yards, nearly one thousand rebel muskets and rifles opened almost simultaneously. Many enemy soldiers fell. Those unharmed kept coming for another dozen yards before they stopped and fired their initial volley. Then they charged, hoping to reach the first American line before its members could reload. They did not make it, perhaps because they had stopped first to fire. When the rebel militia got off their second volley, more gaps were blown in the British line. Quickly, very quickly, Webster and Leslie regrouped and moved forward again, only to discover that the American line was gone. The militiamen had hurried back into the craggy woods after firing their second volley. Some were finished for this fight. Some continued to fight.

As the British closed on the rebels' second line, the melee became amorphous. The men now were fighting in wooded areas, and the lines could not be kept wholly intact. Much of the fighting now boiled down to fierce, bloody struggles between small units. The British strived to adhere to their familiar tactics. The rebels, in contrast, fired, withdrew and dropped behind fallen logs or crouched behind trees to reload, and after several seconds peeped out and fired again. The fighting differed from sector to sector, from unit to unit. It was shaped by terrain and environment, by the horror and confusion of battle, by officers good and poor, and of course by the men themselves. Redcoats advanced in some places, and in some places were driven back. In other corners of the field, the king's men mounted bayonet charges. Officers sought desperately to rally their men. Colonel Webster led a charge by shouting: "Come on, my brave Fuzileers." One of his men said later that the timbre of his voice had been "inspiring." Cornwallis's great grey horse was shot from under him, but he commandeered another mount and rode about the field "evidently unconscious of his danger," one of his men thought.[52] After ninety minutes or more of intense struggle in the smoky chaos, the British right was still advancing tenaciously, but the left under Webster—who had taken a ball in his knee, though he stubbornly, valiantly, continued to lead—was fraying dangerously. An American attack in this sector— an assault reminiscent of the tide-turning charge by Washington's cavalry and Howard's light infantry at Cowpens—might have turned Guilford Courthouse into a rout. As never before, the entire British army in the South was perhaps only an instant away from annihilation. Miraculously, the Americans may have been on the cusp of scoring the decisive victory that could have broken the stalemate in this war. But the rebel attack was never ordered. Greene chose to play it safe, perhaps justifiably so. For one thing, in the heat of battle he was unable to see things as clearly as they appeared in retrospect. It is also impossible to know what would have occurred had Greene ordered an all-out attack. Battles are filled with surprises: men, and even entire units, do not always perform as expected; reserve forces sometimes appear unexpectedly; sudden turnabouts can occur when a key officer is struck down. The one thing that Greene did know for certain was that uncertainty surrounded the actions of his militiamen, who had been asked to fire two shots, then leave the field. They had long since fired their two rounds, and he could not know whether there was any fight left in them. Greene also knew of course that he had no units in reserve. If things went awry, his force would be in great peril. He played it cautiously. Had Washington been in command, he likely would have risked everything. But Greene was usually more circumspect than Washington. He also probably felt that he was not as lucky as his commander in chief. Indeed, no man was as lucky as Washington.

In the end it was Cornwallis who took the boldest step. With his army buckling in the close quarters fight with the rebels, Cornwallis cruelly—but necessarily—ordered his artillery to fire into the brawling mass of friend and foe alike. Grapeshot tore down men from both sides. The British commander took his brutal, ghastly step to stop the fighting and the retreating, and with it the ominous likelihood of being overwhelmed. His pitiless gambit worked. The cannonade broke up the fight, enabling the British officers to regroup the unscathed survivors. Having reformed, Cornwallis was ready to resume the fight, but Greene called it off. He believed that what he had accomplished was sufficient, and he was unwilling to put what he had already achieved to further hazard, or to put to additional risk the loss of the entire American army in the South. What Greene later called the "long, bloody, and severe" Battle of Guilford Courthouse was over.[53]

Technically, Cornwallis was the victor, as he held the field, but Greene provided an accurate assessment of the outcome. The "Enemy got the ground . . . but we the victory," he said a few days later.[54] The British had captured all the American artillery—"all the horses being killed," the field pieces had to be abandoned, Greene later explained—and 1,300 stand of the rebels' arms. But Cornwallis had lost nearly 550 men, about twice the number of his adversary.[55] Everyone on the American side, and not a few British, thought the battle a rebel victory. Lewis Morris, Greene's aide, immediately sensed that "one more such action, and they [Corwallis' army] are ruined," while Charles James Fox later told Parliament: "Another such victory would ruin the British army."[56] Guilford Courthouse was fought nearly ten months to the day since Charleston's surrender. In that time the attrition suffered by Cornwallis's army had been appalling. In four major pitched battles the British had lost almost three thousand men. At a minimum, another 750 had been lost in skirmishes and small actions with partisan bands.

Greene was physically and emotionally spent by what he described as his "extreme severe" service during the past three months. He collapsed the day after the battle, the result of sleep deprivation and poor nutrition, but chiefly from excessive burdens too long borne. He recovered rapidly, though for a time he appeared feckless and his private correspondence took on the tone of one broken by unendurable stress and the brutal realities of which he had been a part. He spoke as if he was too weary to persevere, as if he wished nothing more than to return home and resume life "with my little family about me."[57]

Cornwallis, who confessed that he was "quite tired of marching about the country in quest of adventures," took his army to Wilmington on the coast. It would be safe there, and it could rest and refit. More quickly than Greene, he bounced back, looking toward the future, and eager for more action. He decided that it would be futile to remain in the Carolinas, a view that he had groped toward since the previous August. To stay in the Carolinas was to fight on the defensive, which would achieve nothing, or to resume offensive operations that promised only further "desultory expeditions" such as he had endured to no good end for the past two fruitless months. Britain's only hope of salvaging something from this war, he had concluded, was to wage a "war of conquest" in the upper South. Only through taking the upper South, he had come to believe, could the rebellion in the lower South be suffocated. Cornwallis decided to carry the war to Virginia, and he appealed to Clinton to quit New York and join him there. United, they might gain the elusive decisive victory.[58]

21

"WE ARE SUSPENDED IN THE BALANCE": SPRING AND SUMMER 1781

W ASHINGTON remained at headquarters in New Windsor, New York, through the dark winter of 1781, anxiously awaiting word of Greene's fate. He had supported Greene's daring strategy of dividing his army, saying that such a tack could be "supported upon just Military Principles." He continued to caution him "to avoid a general action," predicting that the defeat of the southern army would be "the most probable consequence of such an event."[1] Washington was fully aware of the "miserable situation" that Greene faced: an army consisting mostly of "raw troops" who were "literally naked," while the "southern states have not the resources" to supply its needs. France alone could alleviate that problem, Washington sadly acknowledged. France also held the key, he added, to relieving the pressure on the southern army, which was "pressed in all sides," with Cornwallis menacing it from the south and west, Arnold from the north. From early on, Washington solicited help for the South from Rochambeau and Ternay, pointing to the deficiencies that had resulted from the capture of Lincoln's army and its stores in Charleston, and explaining that it was crucial for the well-being of the postwar United States that it retain Georgia and South Carolina. Clutching at straws, he proposed in December that Ternay seek to persuade the Spanish in Havana to link their Caribbean fleet with his in Newport and, together with the Franco-American armies, the allies could retake Georgia and South Carolina, and liberate Florida.[2]

Rochambeau and Ternay wanted no part of a scheme laden with diplomatic snares—Spain, they gently reminded Washington, was not an ally of the United States—but their thinking took an unexpected turn when they discovered that a monstrous January storm had caused great damage to the British fleet in New York. The French navy in Rhode Island, which consisted of seven ships of the line, had been spared, and for the moment was superior to its adversary. Rochambeau hurriedly notified Washington that a naval force comprised of four vessels was being readied for dispatch to Virginia to deal with Arnold's force at Portsmouth. Though delighted that his ally was doing something, Washington was unhappy with the limited scope of the French response, and he told those around him that such a small fleet had "little prospect of success." He dashed off a tactful note to the French commanders urging that their "whole fleet" and a one-thousand-man army be sent to Virginia, and he told them that he was dispatching a brigade of Continentals under Lafayette. The French would not budge, and in the end merely three vessels comprised the Virginia-bound squadron that sailed south under Arnaud de Tilly. As Washington had foreseen, Tilly presented no problems for Arnold, and he quickly returned to Newport. But Tilly had no more than returned north when the French military commanders, perhaps somewhat sheepish at having muffed such a good opportunity, changed their minds once again. On March 1, an express rider from Rhode Island alighted at Washington's door with word that the French would try again, this time sending their entire fleet and 1,100 men to Virginia. Washington was jubilant, but wished to leave nothing to chance. He decided to hurry to Newport for consultations.[3]

Washington sped to French headquarters through the gloom of late winter, blazing across more than two hundred miles in barely more than three days. There was not a moment to spare. If the mission was to succeed, the French fleet had to establish a defensible position at Portsmouth before a British armada arrived and attacked. Amid great pomp—Washington was feted with military reviews, martial bands, a torchlight procession, lavish dinners, and a formal ball—the American commander met with Rochambeau and Chevalier Charles René Destouches, who had ascended to the naval command in December following Ternay's sudden demise. Washington got everything that he wanted, and at sunset on March 8, as he and Rochambeau stood shoulder to shoulder on the cold wind-swept shore watching, the squadron sailed off into the gathering darkness. Washington was excited, more so by the swelling possibilities of this endeavor than by any enterprise during the past three years. It was "bold and precarious," he rejoiced, and it offered hope, however slim, of a decisive victory.[4]

Washington's cautious expectations had often been dashed in this war, but he felt few disappointments as keenly as those that accompanied the failure of Destouches's mission. Hoping to avoid detection by the Royal Navy, Destouches sailed east for one hundred miles before turning south. When he finally approached Cape Henry on March 16, Destouches discovered a British squadron awaiting his arrival. It had departed New York thirty-six hours after he left Rhode Island, but it had sailed directly south to Virginia. The two evenly matched fleets clashed immediately. The French got the worst of it, losing nearly two hundred men and suffering heavy damage to three ships. Destouches shrank from risking more. He broke off the fight and returned to Rhode Island. Washington was bitter and despairing. Had the French acted three weeks earlier, when he had proposed a joint land-sea venture, he believed they would have succeeded. Instead, the "favourable moment . . . was suffered to pass away" needlessly by an over-cautious ally, he raged in private. The fruitful possibility of gaining "a deci-sive turn to our Affairs in all the Southern States" had been lost, as had a golden chance to score a victory that would "keep us a float"—that is, bolster sagging morale. Washington's anger was tempered somewhat by word of Cornwallis's heavy losses at Guilford Courthouse, a battle fought one day before Destouches's naval engagement. Still, Greene's worthy performance only underscored how much had been lost by the failure of the French maritime operation. Imagine, Washington seemed to say, what might have been garnered had Arnold's army been smashed at the very moment that Cornwallis's force was battered. Instead, Clinton strengthened the redcoat force in Virginia in the wake of the French fail-ure, sending General William Phillips with 1,600 men to reinforce and supplant Arnold. In this season of despair, Washington also learned in April that Mount Vernon had lately been the target of a raid by the sloop of war, HMS *Savage*. In an act that bore similarities to John Paul Jones's sally into Kirkcudbright Bay three years before almost to the day, *Savage* had sailed up the Potomac to the commander's mansion. His house had been spared, but a large boat was seized and seventeen of Washington's slaves fled to the British.[5]

THE GRASS was greening and fruit trees were bursting into color, telltale signs that winter had passed and campaign 1781, the do-or-die campaign, loomed. "[W]e are at this hour, suspended in the Ball[anc]e," Washington wrote in April, and he added: "now or never our deliverance must come." Yet, for the moment, he saw "no prospect of an operation." On edge, he watched restlessly as April slipped into May, then May ebbed away. But in mid-month important tidings arrived from Rochambeau in Newport. The previous September, his twenty-six-year-old son, who was also a career soldier, had been sent to France following the Hartford Conference to seek men and materials for campaign 1781. He had just returned with important dispatches from Versailles, the contents of which Rochambeau did not divulge. But the French general requested a conference, and Washington immediately consented. The two leaders agreed to meet in Wethersfield, Connecticut, during the third week in May.[6]

Washington must have held his breath as he rode to the meeting, guessing at "the expectations from Europe" that the younger Rochambeau had brought across the Atlantic. The French commander had shared nothing with him in his letter, doubtless fearing that his communiqué might miscarry. (Only a few weeks before a letter written by Washington—one laden with unkind remarks about the French—had been intercepted and its contents gleefully published in a Tory newspaper in New York.) From the dispatches that his son carried, Rochambeau had learned of his government's 6,000,000-livre gift to the Continental army. He was also made aware that the ministry had declined to reinforce substantially France's military forces in North America (it was sending over merely an additional six hundred men). While disappointed by that news, Rochambeau was ecstatic to discover that France not only was augmenting its West Indian fleet that spring, the Comte de Grasse had been ordered to bring that fleet from the Caribbean to North America in mid- to late summer. Officials in Versailles had mentioned a joint campaign against Nova Scotia, but left it to Rochambeau and Washington, who were on the scene, to determine how best to use their forces.[7]

As Washington arrived in Wethersfield, the sunny spring weather abruptly turned cold and dark.[8] In contrast, the two generals greeted one another warmly. Washington was also introduced to Comte de Barras, who had been sent to take command of the French squadron in Rhode Island. Following the customary, and wearisome, ceremonial formalities, Washington, Rochambeau, and Barras got down to business. Rochambeau informed Washington of France's monetary gift, although perhaps for security reasons—but more likely as he did not wish his counterpart to intrude—he chose not to divulge that de Grasse would be coming north. Next came the difficult part: what course to pursue in 1781? The three leaders clashed at times, and vehemently, over strategy, especially when Washington intransigently insisted on a campaign to retake New York. He argued now that Clinton's army around Manhattan had been reduced by half since September, what with the detachments he had sent to Virginia and the reinforcements ladled out to Cornwallis in North Carolina. Rochambeau was unmoved, convinced that Washington was filled with rapturous illusions. Bristling, he reiterated what he had said at Hartford eight months earlier: neither a siege nor an attack against New York could succeed. Rochambeau pressed instead for a campaign against the British army in Virginia, as it would be "less expected by the enemy." He even said that he was prepared to take his army south, whether or not a French navy participated. Washington countered that the war in the South must be a secondary alternative, and a distant one at that. (Rochambeau later remarked that Washington "did not conceive the affairs of the south to be such urgency.") There were times, according to a French observer, when Rochambeau treated Washington with "all the ungraciousness and all the unpleasantness possible."[9] Nevertheless, he remained under orders to allow Washington to decide allied strategy, and in the end, the allies agreed "to make an attempt upon New York . . . in preference to a southern operation, as we had not the decided command of the Water" needed to transport the armies by sea to the South. Rochambeau agreed to move his army to New York as soon as possible. Washington made a concession of his own. He consented that should a French fleet "arrive upon the Coast," joint operations should be conducted "as circumstances should dictate." Three days after he arrived, Washington was on his way again. As soon as he was gone, Rochambeau sent de Grasse a record of the conference, to which he appended a note: bring the fleet to the Chesapeake, not to New York.[10]

Rochambeau was not alone in questioning Washington's judgment, not to mention his strategic acumen, given his intractable obsession with New York. Some of his countrymen, including Jefferson, privately expressed doubts about Washington's strategic vision. "The Northern States are safe: their independence has been established," an exasperated Jefferson said in April, adding while "our Enemies have transferred every expectation from that Quarter" to the South, Washington remained mesmerized with New York. Jefferson equated Washington's fixation with that of Spain toward Gibraltar, and remarked that if the allies attempted to retake New York, they would be no more successful than Madrid had been in regaining its former territory.[11] Washington offered abundant justifications for a campaign to retake New York, foremost among which was his conviction that a siege operation would succeed because Clinton's force had dwindled markedly. At other times Washington said that even should a campaign for New York fail, it likely would produce success elsewhere, as Clinton would be compelled to strip Cornwallis of needed manpower in order to beef up his defenses in Manhattan. Washington hinted at political pressures to campaign for New York, unconvincingly contending that such an endeavor had always been the northern states' "favourite operation." He claimed, too, that it would be disastrous to march the French army southward in the midst of the miasmic southern summer. More likely, Washington was wary of fighting in the South, having seen so many American armies come to grief in that theater. He feared a logistical nightmare. A native of the region, he knew there would be formidable problems in supplying the huge Franco-American armies in a region that had been picked over, was sparsely settled, and lacked decent roads. Still and all, it was Washington's obsession with New York that guided his thinking. He was captivated by the presumption that wars usually ended with one side scoring a great climactic victory over its adversary. Sometimes that did occur, as when Britain had sealed its majestic victory in the French and Indian War with a winner-take-all showdown at Quebec in 1759. In 1776 Washington had imagined that his own transcendent victory at New York would drive the former mother country from America. He failed egregiously, suffering one mortifying defeat after another and provoking criticism of his generalship. Retaking New York was out of the question until France entered the war, but from 1778 onward Washington unwaveringly held to a dream of victory gained through the reconquest—his reconquest—of New York.

WHEN ROCHAMBEAU urged a southern campaign and secretly called on de Grasse to sail for the Chesapeake, his objective was not the destruction of Cornwallis's army. He focused on Phillips's army, a force that, together with those under Arnold, totaled some 3,500 men. It was nearly two weeks after the Wethersfield conference before the allied commanders became aware that Cornwallis was marching to Virginia. Until then, Washington knew only that Cornwallis was regrouping at Wilmington, North Carolina, in the wake of having been "baffled" by Greene, as he was now putting it. Washington was perplexed as to the intentions of the enemy. At times he thought Clinton would personally lead a sizeable force south to join with Cornwallis. At other times he suspected that Clinton would recall some of or all the men in Virginia for the defense of New York. On still other occasions he guessed that the British forces already in the South would unite for a campaign either in Virginia or the Carolinas. There were moments, too, when Washington was convinced that the enemy would play divide and conquer, with Phillips on the move in Virginia and Cornwallis active in the lower South.[12]

Virginia had received little attention in the upper echelons of the Continental army before Leslie's raid in October 1780. The following month, when Greene passed though the state en route to take command in the South, he was horrified at "the greatest state of confusion" that prevailed. He left Steuben behind "to put things in the most proper Train" for defending against Leslie, but also to streamline the process for funneling men and supplies further south. But when Cornwallis summoned Leslie, Greene directed Steuben to "send on all the men you can equip" to the Carolinas. Future British raids might be disagreeable to Virginians, but in the larger scheme of things, Greene believed, they were "of no consequence" so long as the main British army operated elsewhere.[13] Washington shared Greene's views, and, despite relentless pressure by officials in his home state to provide greater assistance, he had agreed to send substantial help only when he learned that the French might send Tilly's small squadron to the Chesapeake. He had ordered Lafayette south with 1,200 men, directing him to destroy Arnold's army. If Arnold was captured, Washington added, Lafayette was to "execute in the most summary way" his punishment for "treason and desertion." In other words, Lafayette was to hang him![14]

Lafayette reached Virginia just as Guilford Courthouse was fought. He immediately learned from Steuben that Tilly's little navy had come and gone, and that Destouches's more formidable squadron had also come and been turned away.[15] The glimmering hope that had led Washington to send Lafayette south had vanished before his arrival. Even so, Steuben quickly concocted another plan, one that envisaged a role for Lafayette's Continentals in a daring scheme to destroy Cornwallis's army. Steuben proposed that Virginia send two thousand militiamen to join with Greene, while Lafayette, together with other Virginia trainband, blocked Phillips from marching to Cornwallis's assistance. Once augmented by the Virginia militiamen, Greene could inflict additional damage on Cornwallis's battered force, possibly even finishing him off. The plan was popular in many circles in Virginia, not least because it promised to keep Cornwallis out of the state. But there were good military reasons for supporting the plan. General George Weedon, commander of a Continental brigade at Williamsburg, endorsed it by calling it "a Manoeuver the least suspected," one that might surprise and trap Cornwallis, and "terminate the War." Richard

Henry Lee, now the speaker of the state assembly, thought it had the potential to be "one of those Master strokes" that could be "productive of great effects." Lafayette was enthusiastic as well, largely because he preferred offensive operations. To adopt a defensive strategy, he said, would mean that "we . . . will make very little resistance."[16]

But the plan would go forward only if Governor Jefferson and the council consented. As feared, neither acquiesced. Sending off the militia—with half the state's armament—was too perilous to contemplate, they concluded. Should Phillips go on the offensive, there would be virtually nothing left with which to defend against him. Virginia's decision was the final straw for Steuben, who raged that he was "tired of this State" and its governor, who habitually inflicted "difficulties & disappointmts" on every sound initiative. Weedon, too, was outraged, and charged that Jefferson had "not an Idea beyond Local Security." That was how Greene saw it as well, and he fumed that the war could not be "prosecuted upon a grand Scale" when state officials with "partial views"—that is, a parochial outlook—"have an undue influence." Jefferson, he appeared to believe, was the least cooperative of the southern governors on whom he relied for support.[17]

Whether or not Steuben's plan might have succeeded can never be known, but it is clear that Virginia was not secured by the militia that its governor and council kept at home. Only hours after Steuben's plan was rejected, Phillips emerged from Portsmouth with a fleet of a dozen vessels and marauded at will along the Potomac River, burning houses, seizing and destroying tobacco, and freeing or carrying away slaves, including, as noted earlier, some at Mount Vernon. Phillips did not stop there. During the second half of April the British came up the James and Chickahominy, pillaging along those wide, blue-green rivers. In what Jefferson labeled a "Circle of Depradation," they moved up to Petersburg and Chesterfield County Courthouse, destroying more tobacco, vessels, barracks that had been built for Continentals, and numerous military stores. At month's end Arnold sailed up the James, capturing and destroying nearly twenty-five vessels and burning mills and tobacco warehouses in Manchester and Warwick, near Richmond.[18]

STEUBEN had presumed that someday Virginia would have to deal with Cornwallis's army and when that day arrived Virginia would be "sadly pressed." The day of Cornwallis's coming arrived sooner than most ever imagined. Following Guilford Courthouse, Cornwallis had issued another soaring proclamation, a few sentences of fallacious boilerplate in which he announced the total defeat of the rebels, yet called on the Loyalists for help and promised amnesty to any revolutionary who surrendered his arms. Thereafter, Cornwallis retreated to Wilmington, a ghastly march made by an army that was tired, hungry, and caring for nearly four hundred sick and wounded. Five officers, including the invaluable Colonel Webster, perished along the way, as did numerous enlisted men.[19]

Cornwallis's army was battered from its nearly year-long campaigning in the backcountry, and especially by the grueling ninety days between its departure from Winnsboro and its arrival in Wilmington. But he lingered only eighteen days in the little village on the Cape Fear River. He was eager for more action, and anxious to set off before his army was overtaken by the heat and languor of another southern summer. Cornwallis had considered taking his army to Virginia during that awful preceding summer of relentless struggle against South Carolina's partisans. Nothing had occurred since then to change his mind, and in fact the presence of Phillips's army in Virginia acted as a magnet pulling Cornwallis in that direction. Three days after he reached Wilmington, Cornwallis wrote Clinton that he was "very anxious to receive your Excellency's commands." But he did not wait for orders. On April 25, six weeks after Guilford Courthouse, he set off with 1,435 men, a fateful trek that would take him across the Roanoke River and into Virginia.[20]

Greene did not pursue his adversary. He had remained on Cornwallis's tail for a week after Guilford Courthouse, but even before the enemy reached Wilmington, Greene made a pivotal choice. Regardless of what Cornwallis chose to do, Greene decided to take his force into South Carolina. It was a decision taken against the wishes of many of his senior officers, but Greene reasoned that the enemy "will be obliged to follow us or give up their posts" in South Carolina. Greene was aware that the course he was choosing was "critical and dangerous"— he also called it "bold and . . . unexpected"—especially should Cornwallis let him go and concentrate his energies on Virginia. If Cornwallis went north, he would combine his army with the British forces in the Chesapeake, thereby achieving an overarching supremacy in Virginia. But Greene reasoned that if he, too, went to Virginia, it would mean playing cat and mouse once again with Cornwallis, a course that probably would not lead to a decisive victory. He contemplated trying to confine Cornwallis in Wilmington. If successful, Cornwallis would be impeded from joining other redcoats up north, but in the process Greene would have done nothing to liberate South Carolina and Georgia from British rule. He also hinted that political considerations were no less crucial than military factors in determining the course he chose. Staying in the South, he believed, offered the only hope of keeping South Carolina and Georgia in the war, as well as of retaining both provinces for the postwar American Union. "I am much afraid these States must fall never to rise again" should no American army be present to stoke the rebellion, he said. Greene's choice was a gamble, and one that did not "correspond with . . . Ideas of militiary propriety," as he put it. But, he added, "War is an intricate business, and people are often saved by ways and means they least look for or expect."[21]

Greene set out for South Carolina two days before Cornwallis reached Wilmington. He had about 1,300 men. There were nearly eight thousand redcoats in South Carolina and Georgia, but they were spread from the coast to deep in the backcountry, and from the Pee Dee to the Savannah River.

Cornwallis learned immediately of Greene's movement, and he knew full well what it meant for the British in South Carolina. Greene, he said, would be joined by "Mountaineers and Militia," giving him the capability to "beat in detail" small contingents of the widely scattered British army. Thus, Cornwallis knew full well that by his going north he was at least temporarily sacrificing much of the South Carolina backcountry to the rebels. He was also aware that he was acting in blatant disregard of his commander's wishes. Clinton had never wavered in his conviction that Cornwallis's primary objective must be to pacify the Carolinas. His first orders on giving Cornwallis command of the southern theater in June 1780 had been "to secure the South and recover North Carolina," to which Clinton had added that his subordinate might "assist in operations" in Virginia only when the Carolinas "are safe from any attack." Clinton's subsequent directives never departed from those original orders. Yet Cornwallis wrote Clinton from Wilmington that while "it is very disagreeable to me to decide upon measures so very important, and of such consequence to the general conduct of the war," he was taking his army to Virginia. To do so, he said, was based on a "most solid plan," one that alone offered hope that it might be "attended with important consequences." For the moment, nothing further could be accomplished in the Carolinas: "little assistance" could be expected from the Tories; given "the immense extent of the Country," there was little prospect of bringing to battle an adversary that did not wish to fight; and the British faced enormous logistical trials in the Lower South while "the enemy could draw their supplies from North Carolina and Virginia." But Cornwallis was redolent with hope of success in Virginia. He thought there was a greater expectation that the rebels would have to fight in Virginia, lest they see their link to the Carolinas severed, and that in turn increased his hope of "a successful battle," the long-awaited decisive engagement. Even if he failed to score that elusive decisive victory, Cornwallis believed he could shut off the flow of supplies that coursed through Virginia to the Lower South. Virginia's many rivers also intrigued Cornwallis. The redcoats could use those rivers. By drawing on Britain's naval superiority—what Washington called the enemy's "canvas wings"—the British army would be a highly mobile force that could strike at will, moving faster than the fastest rebel army.[22]

Cornwallis had suggested—by implication—that Clinton's conduct of the war had been a failure, unless Britain was willing to settle at war's end for retaining only South Carolina, Georgia, and Florida from among its mainland colonies. He was not incorrect, and he may also have been accurate in assuming that Virginia held the best promise in the southern theater, if not in America, as a place to win the elusive decisive victory. But it was not Cornwallis's responsibility to make grand strategy, and it was especially imprudent of him to launch such a vital undertaking without having heard from his superior, from whom he had received no word since before he left Winnsboro, well over one hundred days earlier. Cornwallis appeared to be driven to act, moved by a year of frustration, a desire to recoup a reputation that was certain to be blackened by setbacks and empty-handed enterprises, and by his enmity—or at least contempt—for Clinton.[23] Cornwallis's vanity and his aspirations drove him to insubordination, and to a destiny that included a rendezvous with ruination.

When Cornwallis made his choice, Clinton was focused on a battle for New York. Intelligence reports that reached British headquarters pointed toward the likelihood of an epic showdown against Washington and Rochambeau for New York. According to his subsequent remarks, Clinton relished the impending battle. He had long hoped to pull the enemy from its lair and into the field. At last, the great clash was about to occur. The "dark and gloomy" prospects that had dogged him from the moment he had taken command suddenly receded, as he anticipated "every hope of the fullest success" in the battle for New York. Not only did he foresee inflicting a decisive defeat on Rochambeau and Washington, but with the "rebellion in America . . . at its last gasp," he believed his triumph would result in bringing the war to a successful end.[24] Clinton was already speaking of recalling portions of the armies under Phillips and Cornwallis when he learned of Cornwallis's plans to take his army to Virginia. Indeed, Cornwallis was already in Virginia when Clinton learned of his subordinate's plans. "[H]ow great was my disappointment and astonishment," Clinton exclaimed. He was not just stunned; he was furious. He had come to believe that as America's "exigencies . . . put it out of her power to continue . . . the war . . . much longer," it behooved the British to adopt "the policy of avoiding all risks." Instead, Cornwallis was putting his army at hazard. Worse still, his exit from the Lower South would lead to disaster in South Carolina while his presence in Virginia was unlikely to yield seminal results. Clinton might have done something about it. He might have gone to Virginia—a speedy voyage would have taken him there by early June— and relieved Cornwallis of command on grounds of insubordination, or sent him back to South Carolina, or after assessing the situation simply have given him detailed and specific orders. But Clinton did none of these things. With an unbecoming weakness, Britain's commander in chief acquiesced to what had transpired and left Cornwallis, and Britain's hopes in this war, to fate.[25]

CORNWALLIS'S ARMY crossed into Virginia during the second week in May and linked up with Phillips's army at Petersburg during the following week. Together with 1,800 reinforcements already en route from New York to Phillips, the British force in Virginia soon exceeded 7,000 men. Finding on his arrival that Phillips, an old comrade in arms, had died of a fever only days before, Cornwallis immediately perused the orders that Clinton had been sending to Virginia since March. They were straightforward. Clinton had directed Phillips to find, and maintain, a good site for a naval base and to seek "in earnest" to bring to battle the little force of Continentals in Virginia.[26] Cornwallis, who had just ignored Clinton's obvious wishes for the Carolinas, now chose to follow his orders. He found a suitable naval base. Discovering that Phillips had not been enamored with Portsmouth, which Leslie had chosen seven months earlier, Cornwallis latched onto Yorktown, on the peninsula between the James and York Rivers below Richmond, as a preferable site for a base. Situated on a bluff above the green, normally placid, York River, Yorktown looked across toward Gloucester Point, where the river narrowed to a width of only a half-mile. These features, Cornwallis decreed, made it a "safe defensive" site.[27]

While the hunt for a naval base proceeded, Cornwallis searched for Lafayette's Continentals. Sent in February on what had initially been a temporary errand to destroy Arnold, Lafayette had subsequently been ordered to remain in Virginia so that he might join with Greene. After it was learned that Greene had gone south, and that Phillips's detachment had come to Virginia, Lafayette had been directed in March to "confound Phillip's [sic] calculations" and to see that he was "held in check" and unable to join Cornwallis against Greene in the Carolinas. Lafayette found a bittersweet quality to his orders, as Phillips in 1760 had commanded the unit at whose hands his father had died in the Seven Years' War. But despite whatever wish for revenge might have lingered, Lafayette was more interested in being with Washington for what was shaping up as the war's climactic battle, the fight for New York. He asked to be replaced in Virginia. Wanting someone in Virginia that he found dependable, Washington declined his entreaties but he placated Lafayette with word that nearly one thousand Pennsylvania Continentals under General Wayne were being sent to help him. He also sugarcoated his orders to the vain young Frenchman with bromides about his "generosity & zeal for the Service," and assurances of the "successes & glory" that were to be won in Virginia. Lafayette's first success was not long in coming. When Phillips rampaged up the James late in April, Lafayette hurried with his army to defend Richmond. The British sowed destruction in nearby Warwick and Manchester, but opted not to challenge the Continentals, and Richmond was spared another pillaging. Lafayette puffed with pride when a spy reported that Phillips had supposedly flown into "a Violent passion" at his inability to wreak havoc in the capital and "Swore Vengeance Against Me."[28]

But Lafayette was disappointed to learn that he could not take the offensive that he dreamt of, for Cornwallis arrived three weeks after Phillips's last raid. The British army in Virginia was now more than twice the size of the rebel force. Lafayette's temperament pushed him to fight, but he confessed to Washington that he was "Guarding Against My Own Warmth. . . . Was I to fight a Battle I'll be Cut to pieces." On the other hand, if he only ran, Lafayette feared that "the Country would think Herself given up." He was left with one choice. "I am therefore determined to Skarmish. But not to engage too far, and particularly to take Care against their [cavalry] . . . whom the Militia fear like they would So Many wild Beasts." To this he added poetically: "I am not Strong enough even to get Beaten."[29]

From the outset, Cornwallis knew that he would have to track down his adversary. Shortly after arriving in Virginia, he told Clinton that he planned to "proceed to dislodge Lafayette from Richmond" and give chase. With his canvas wings, Cornwallis radiated optimism. "The Boy cannot escape me," he allegedly remarked. Cornwallis's task proved to be more difficult than he imagined, as Lafayette withdrew deeper into the interior, crossing over the South Anna River northwest of Richmond. After flailing about to no avail for a week, Cornwallis changed course. He sent off Colonel John Graves Simcoe with light infantry to find Steuben, who was known to be hiding behind the Fluvanna River, about forty-five miles northwest of Richmond, and Tarleton with 250 of his feared dragoons to raid Charlottesville, where Virginia's assembly had fled and was meeting, and where Jefferson had returned to his hilltop home. Neither accomplished much. Lacking the small craft to get his army quickly across the backcountry's endless streams, Simcoe was without hope of catching up to his prey. Tarleton reached his objective, but Jack Jouett, an alert patriot who was imbibing at the Cuckoo Tavern about forty miles from Charlottesville, saw the green-clad cavalrymen pass and made like Paul Revere, hurrying along back roads familiar only to a native to alert Jefferson and the legislators. Jouett won the race. Most of the assemblymen escaped, as did Jefferson, who rode down one side of the hill atop which Monticello sits as Tarleton rode up the other side. Amazingly, Tarleton did not raze the mansion, though the raiders looted much that Jefferson had lacked time to hide.[30]

After three weeks of largely fruitless marches through the tangled backcountry, Cornwallis was convinced of the futility of his course, and he withdrew down the James River to Williamsburg. With him were about three thousand African Americans, a third of whom had accompanied his army north from the Carolinas, while the remainder were runaway slaves from Virginia who, like those at Mount Vernon, had fled to the British during the winter and spring. He had not done so well with the Tories. One Virginian claimed that only a Loyalist "lawyer and his son: A Barber and his wife [,] a Tailor, a Doctr, a Master Grinder, and two Irish lads" had joined with the redcoats.[31] As he pulled back, Cornwallis advised Clinton that "to reduce the Province & keep possession of the Country, a considerable Army would be necessary." Ominously, he added that "with a small force, the business would probably terminate unfavorably." He called on Clinton to abandon New York and join him in Virginia. If "offensive War is intended," he wrote, "Virginia appears to me, to be the only Province, in which it can be carried on." Cornwallis chose to take up a position far down the peninsula and there await Clinton's decision. If Clinton stuck to his plan to defend New York, Cornwallis would be in a convenient location for a Royal fleet to fetch his army back to Manhattan. If Clinton chose to take the offensive in Virginia, he would rendezvous with Cornwallis's army low down on the peninsula and together they would proceed with the subjugation of the state, after which they could destroy Greene in the Carolinas.[32]

As Cornwallis slowly made his way east, Lafayette emerged for the skirmishing he had promised. At first there was little that he could do. Cornwallis had no interest in a battle, or in trifling with his bothersome opponent. He was low on supplies and his men had been in motion during almost all the sixty days since their departure from Wilmington. Besides, Cornwallis now appeared to be eager to have Clinton make the decision of what was to be done, and in the interim he no longer seemed to be particularly interested in fighting. Little firefights occurred with Lafayette's trailing army, and one sizeable skirmish occurred, a fray with Simcoe's Queen's Rangers at Spencer's Ordinary, in which about thirty-five casualties were suffered on both sides.[33]

By month's end, Cornwallis's army was in Williamsburg, suffering in the oppressive heat and humidity of the low-lying peninsula, but with ample supplies. He had been there only a couple of days when he heard from Clinton. The commander in chief would not yield New York without orders from London. Furthermore, he believed that the best chance to score a decisive victory lay in a battle for New York. For almost five years the British had prepared its defenses, which he did not believe Rochambeau and Washington could pierce without a naval arm. London had notified him that de Grasse might come north from the West Indies later in the summer, but Clinton was confident that he would have no more success getting into New York harbor than had d'Estaing in 1778. Clinton not only expressed skepticism about a major operation in Virginia, a note of foreboding punctuated his thoughts about fighting in the Chesapeake. In each of the past four years a French fleet had shown up on the coast—d'Estaing off New Jersey in 1778 and at Savannah the following year, Ternay with Rochambeau's army in Rhode Island in 1780, and both Ternay and Destouches in the Chesapeake already in 1781. If a superior French fleet got control of the Chesapeake, it would foreshadow ignominy for the British in Virginia. To this Clinton added a keen insight. He had at last learned "that there is no possibility of re-establishing order in any rebellious province on this continent without the hearty assistance of numerous friends," but either the Tories did not exist in great numbers or they were by now too jaded to step forward. What Clinton appeared to say was that the best chance of scoring a decisive victory—probably the sole chance—lay in making a grand defense of New York. Looking ahead and realizing that he would be heavily outnumbered by the allied armies in the campaign for New York, while Cornwallis was vastly superior to Lafayette's little force in Virginia, Clinton ordered his subordinate to send him three thousand men "with all possible dispatch." Cornwallis was to stay in Virginia with what remained, deploying at the site he had selected as a naval base, Yorktown.[34]

Faced with an apparent showdown in New York, it is puzzling that Clinton conceived of leaving any troops in Virginia. He could have safely transferred Cornwallis's entire force back to New York in July, easily completing the operation before the allies were prepared to launch their campaign to retake Manhattan. Clinton subsequently offered two explanations for keeping an army in Virginia. For one thing, he said, Germain had ordered him to mount and adequately support operations in Virginia. In addition, Cornwallis's entrance into Virginia compelled him to leave troops there, for a withdrawal not only

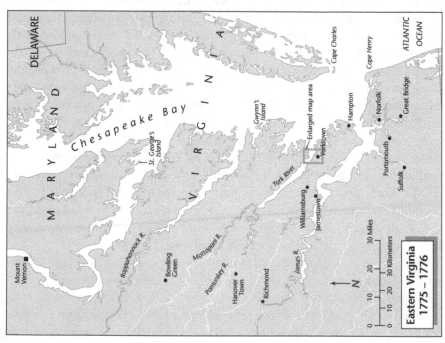

Seige of Yorktown
September to October, 1781

- British
- American
- French

Gloucester Point

York River

Sunken vessels

Cornwallis's quarters

British redoubts taken Oct. 14, 1781

SECOND PARALLEL

American battery

Moore's house

Wormley Creek

FIRST PARALLEL

Virginia Militia

Lafayette's quarters

Light Infantry

N.J.

R.I.

American hospital

Sappers and miners

New York

French hospital

Va. & Pa.

Maryland

Artificers

Laboratory

Magazine

American artillery park

Fusiliers

French battery

Ravine

British outworks abandoned

Surrender Field Oct. 17, 1781

Warwick River

French batteries

French artillery park

Rochambeau's quarters

Washington's quarters

French forces

French forces

0   500   1,000   1,500 Yards

N

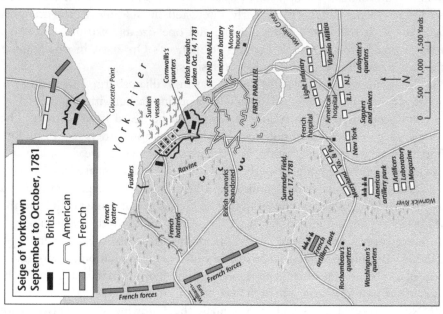

DELAWARE

MARYLAND

Chesapeake Bay

VIRGINIA

Mount Vernon

Rappahannock R.

St. George's Island

Mattaponi R.

Bowling Green

Pamunkey R.

Hanover Town

James R.

Richmond

Gwynn's Island

York River

Enlarged map area

Yorktown

Williamsburg

Jamestown

Hampton

Norfolk

Great Bridge

Portsmouth

Suffolk

Cape Charles

Cape Henry

ATLANTIC OCEAN

N

0   10   20   30 Miles

0   10   20   30 Kilometers

Eastern Virginia
1775 – 1776

would have been disgraceful, but another abandonment of Virginia's Loyalists would have ruined all future chances of British success in the Chesapeake. The problem with Clinton's artful defense of his action is that his letters and orders hint that neither factor dictated his ultimate choice.[35]

Clinton was in the grasp of brooding vacillation that spring and summer, and his indecision was perceptible in orders that were so contradictory that Cornwallis thought them nearly incoherent. Clinton reversed himself in nearly every letter he sent to Cornwallis between May and July, though his turnabouts occurred in part because the situation around New York was shifting. In mid-June, for instance, after he had already written Cornwallis on three occasions, Clinton learned that Rochambeau had abandoned Newport and was marching to link up with Washington's army outside New York. The first clear-cut orders that Cornwallis received were those directing him to detach three thousand men—nearly half his army—to New York. Although Cornwallis complained that he could not spare that many men, he immediately complied. He put his men in motion toward Portsmouth, where transports were to be sent to gather them for the trip to New York. As Lafayette's force had swelled to about 3,600 effectives, and as it was expected to shadow and harass the British march, Cornwallis took along his entire army.[36] Early in July, he moved across the Williamsburg Neck toward Jamestown, where he expected to cross the James River and continue his descent toward Portsmouth. Lafayette trailed him. On the night on July 5, Cornwallis posted his army at Green Spring Farm, a carefully chosen spot just northwest of Jamestown. Between him and his pursuers lay swampy forestland; the only connecting ground between the two armies was a narrow causeway.

Cornwallis hoped the Americans might be foolish enough to attack, and he did what he could to entice them, including sending out several slaves who were accompanying his army to tell the rebels that the bulk of the British army had already crossed the James. Only a small detachment, they related, was at Green Spring Farm. Impetuous General Wayne, who was commanding the van of Lafayette's force, took the bait and near dusk on July 6 ordered his five hundred men to proceed down the slender causeway. With the rebels drawn into his web, Cornwallis attacked from both sides, hoping to outflank Wayne, who lacked room to maneuver. Lafayette, seeing what had occurred, rushed forward and a desperate fight ensued. Wayne was saved from his ill-considered action as much by the sloping black shadows of approaching nightfall as by Lafayette, but the Americans lost 139 men—twice the losses suffered by Cornwallis—and two irreplaceable cannon. Lafayette, who if possible was more imprudent than Wayne, praised "the Glory of Genl. Wayne" for having "attacked the whole British Army" with "a reconnoitring Party only."[37] A Yankee lieutenant, who might have died because of Wayne's folly, saw it differently, and carped in his journal that the near disaster had occurred because the general was "anxious to perform miracles."[38]

The following day, Cornwallis crossed the wide, quiet James. As he pressed on toward Portsmouth in the distressing swelter of the July days that followed, more of Clinton's letters trickled in. The first that Cornwallis received, written late in June, ordered him to take his entire army to Philadelphia, where he was to conduct raids before proceeding on to New York.[39] Clinton's logic was that American supply depots might be destroyed. Four days later Cornwallis received three additional letters from his commander. In these, Clinton directed Cornwallis to send another two thousand men to New York. With his remaining force, Cornwallis was to complete the defenses at Yorktown.[40] A week later, after some of his men had already started for Philadelphia, Cornwallis received another directive from Clinton: remain in Virginia with his entire army.[41] This was the order with which Cornwallis chose to comply, grandly and cunningly telling Clinton that as "a subordinate officer I think it my duty to obey positive orders."[42] At the same time, in a darkly revelatory note he also told Clinton that using the army to defend Yorktown "cannot have the smallest influence on the War." It only "gives us some Acres of an unhealthy swamp" that was "ever liable to become a prey to a foreign" navy.[43]

Clinton's final choice—to leave Cornwallis and his entire army in Virginia—is a mystery for which there is no entirely satisfactory explanation. The twists and turns in his orders that spring and summer lend an air of incoherence to his thinking, but it is possible that in the end Clinton simply decided that Cornwallis's army was not needed in New York. Clinton believed that the city's fortifications, augmented by the formidable Royal Navy, were adequate, and he anticipated receiving reinforcements from the West Indies. (He did receive about six thousand troops from the Caribbean before the summer ended.) He may have reasoned that Cornwallis's presence in Virginia would confine up to two thousand Continentals in the Chesapeake who otherwise would join Washington and Rochambeau for the effort to take New York. There is some evidence that Clinton envisaged emerging from New York after the allies' attack had been repulsed in an attempt to pinion Washington and Rochambeau between his army and that of Cornwallis, which would be brought up from the South to close the deadly jaws of the pincer. But it may be that Clinton's ultimate decision was the result of a fundamental flaw in his makeup. He shrank from confrontation—he was, after all, the man who had characterized himself as a "shy bitch"—and especially from discord with Cornwallis, who was held in high esteem by Germain.[44]

WHEN GENERAL GREENE chose to take the war back to South Carolina, he knew that if Cornwallis came after him, he would run again. He was convinced, too, that he could again outrun his pursuer. "I fear no bad consequences," he declared, so long as he could keep his men supplied. While Greene said that he was trying to force Cornwallis back into South Carolina, he knew that should his adversary choose instead to go north, he faced an opportunity rich with promise in the Carolinas and Georgia. Britain's forces would then be divided between the Lower and Upper South, and the former were spread thin, occupying areas in North Carolina, South Carolina, and Georgia. With his army—now including many officers who were drawn back into the service by Greene's beguiling successes—the militia, and the partisan fighters, Greene might pick apart his scattered enemy.[45]

Finding that Cornwallis opted to go to Virginia, Greene adopted a simple plan of operations. As large British garrisons held Charleston and Savannah, there was little he could do to liberate those cities. But the enemy occupied several backcountry outposts and strategic sites from the coast of South Carolina to the Georgia border. Georgetown anchored the coastal end in the east, Augusta the western periphery. Scattered in between were Ninety-Six, Fort Granby, Fort Motte, Fort Watson, Camden, and Orangeburg. Garrisoned by forces that ranged from about 125 up to 900 men, these installations had been established at strategic sites to secure lines of communication between the backcountry and Charleston.[46] Greene planned piecemeal attacks on each site, and he had about 1,400 Continental and ever changing numbers of militia with which to achieve his ends.

Greene's adversary was Lord Rawdon, whom Cornwallis had left in charge of defending the broad frontier. Though only twenty-seven, Rawdon was an exceptional soldier and an experienced hand. Reputed to be "the ugliest man in England," he had left Oxford to take up a military career in 1774. If he wanted action, he did not have long to wait. Only weeks after putting on the uniform, Rawdon was posted in Boston, where he got his first taste of combat at Bunker Hill, where two bullets pierced his hat, though he emerged unscathed. In the years that followed, he saw considerable combat—always performing capably, often valorously—and he rose rapidly. Clinton also took him under his wing, which did not hinder his ascent.[47] Rawdon faced insuperable obstacles in defending South Carolina. Compelled not only to defend isolated posts, but to keep open the umbilical cords that linked each to supply depots and, eventually, to Charleston, he simply lacked the manpower for his job. That was readily apparent to Clinton, whose alleged first words on receiving the news that Cornwallis was in Virginia were that Rawdon was doomed.[48] Greene suspected that might be the case as well, but it is doubtful that he ever imagined that he would succeed so rapidly.

Within ninety days after Greene entered South Carolina, every major British installation in the backcountry was in rebel hands. Some had been taken in operations by the bulk of Greene's army, others through joint actions by his cavalry and partisan units. Some garrisons surrendered after brief investments, while Camden, Georgetown, and Ninety-Six were abandoned by the British, the latter even though it had successfully withstood a month-long siege. Greene's men faced hard campaigning in these endeavors. Although poorly clad and at times inadequately fed, many men were on the march almost daily, tramping mile after dusty mile down sun-seared roads and under moons that were low and bright, all the while toting their heavy weapons, ammunition, and cumbersome cooking equipment. The leader of one light infantry unit estimated that his men marched 323 miles in a stretch of twenty-two days. Other men were part of a trying foray that became known as the "Dog Days expedition."[49] As ever in South Carolina, this, too, was often war at its worst. When the post at Fort Motte was taken, Colonel Lee executed several Loyalist prisoners, a massacre cut short when Francis Marion intervened to stop the bloody sport. That battlefield incident was hardly a lone occurrence. Nor were Loyalist soldiers alone as victims. Depredations were also visited on Tory civilians, or on those who might have been Loyalists. Sometimes civilians who simply angered soldiers paid a heavy price. General Greene, to his credit, sought to stop the malice-laden carnage, if only because he thought it counterproductive to the war effort. "[W]e have great reason to hate them, and vengeance would dictate universal slaughter," he said of the reprisals against the Tories, but to do so would be a "fatal practice." The rebels' objective must be to "detach the disaffected from the british interest . . . and this can be done by gentle means only." Some civilian leaders understood this, as well. The governor of North Carolina sought to bring to trial militiamen who had been "principals in one of these Murders which have been [fre]quently committed upon prisoners."[50]

Greene fought only one major battle during the spring. In April he paused at Hobkirk's Hill, about a mile outside Camden, to await reinforcements before attacking that post. Seeing the danger, Rawdon, who was outnumbered, vowed to strike first, hoping to take his adversary by surprise. Arming even his musicians and drummer—"in short everything that could carry a firelock," he said— Rawdon fell on Greene's startled pickets in a sudden attack. Rawdon's surprise failed. The rebel sentries fought well, delaying the enemy until the heart of the American army could take up strong positions on the high ground. The fight that followed was fierce and confused, and before it ended Greene was in the thick of it, helping even with the moving of artillery. (One of his officers remarked later that Greene's "conduct during the action resembled more that of a captain of grenadiers, than that of a major general.")[51] Greene might have remained on the defensive, seeking a victory along the lines of Bunker Hill. Given his numerical superiority, he might even have had the opportunity to wreak great damage on the battered British once their attack was repulsed and they were compelled to pull back. Instead, gambling that he might totally annihilate the redcoats, Greene went over to the offensive. The fighting ebbed and flowed for a time, but just when the rebels appeared to have victory in their grasp—Greene later said that he was three minutes away from a triumph—things went awry. Greene, "frantic with vexation," as he later put it, blamed the near miss on an underling's unwise attempt to reposition his Maryland regiment in the heat of battle, a movement that sowed confusion, then terror, among the men. Others believed that the fatal disorder within the Maryland line was sparked by the death of a company commander involved in the drive against Rawdon's center.[52] Whatever the cause, once large numbers of rebels broke and ran, the British won the day, and they might have gained an even greater victory had not Colonel Washington's dragoons belatedly entered the fray and prevented Rawdon from pursuing his scattering foe. While Greene lost the fight, the British losses in the engagement were nearly twice those of the rebels. The outcome left Greene conflicted. He was sore at having missed the opportunity to score a big victory, and he found the "disgrace" caused by the flight of so many of his men "more vexatious than anything else." On the other hand, he knew that he had inflicted damaging losses on his foe. Not long after the battle, he proclaimed that the "little repulse will make no alteration in our general plan of operation." To this he added one of the more memorable comments to survive this war: "We fight [,] get beat [,] rise and fight again."[53] A German officer discerned the same dynamic, remarking of Greene: "the more he is beaten, the farther he advances in the end."[54]

Five months passed before Greene fought a second major battle. It occurred when the British emerged from Charleston, their only remaining possession of any size in South Carolina, and Greene hurried from the High Hills of the Santee to take them on. Though he had already achieved much, Greene was driven to battle in this instance, at least in part, by the open chatter about a war-ending mediation by Europe's neutral nations. The governor of North Carolina had recently informed him that peace might be on the horizon, with the belligerents likely retaining what they possessed at the moment of the cease-fire. Lafayette also hinted to Greene that it was desirable that he should secure as much territory as possible and score dramatic victories. Although it was "Still a profound Secret," said Lafayette, Congress "was debating the Matter."[55]

On September 7, Greene with 2,400 men found his prey, a British force of some 2,000 at Eutaw Springs, about fifty miles above Charleston. General Alexander Stewart now commanded the redcoats, as Rawdon, beaten down by months in the field in the worst of conditions, had gone home. As the Americans approached through the shimmering heat, Stewart, a forty-two-year-old veteran soldier, formed his men in a single line and awaited the assault. When it came, it triggered a four-hour slugfest, one of the longer engagements of the war, a battle that Greene (who had a horse shot from beneath him during the fighting) called the "most Obstinate fight" and "by far the hottest action I ever saw," as well as "the most bloody for the numbers engaged." Greene had put his militia in the front row. It performed well, firing several volleys, but when the British counter-attacked, the militia units broke apart in flight. Greene plugged North Carolina Continentals from his second line into their place. Their line stopped the redcoat advance and drove back the enemy line, although in time they, too, sagged. Greene then rushed forward his entire second line, Maryland, Delaware, and Virginia Continentals. At the same moment the rebel cavalry fell on the enemy flanks. (In the course of that fray, Colonel Washington was first wounded, then captured, when he jumped his horse "into the midst of the enemy," as one of his men later recollected.) Hammered from three sides, the British retreated, and appeared on the verge of flight, until they saw the valiant fight being waged by their Nineteenth Regiment, under Major John Marjoribanks. With a bit of time, the redcoats regrouped, fought heroically, and stanched the rebels' progress. Stopped in their tracks, confusion, then disorder, spread in the American ranks. The rebels were finished for the day, but so, too, were the British, exhausted from an interminable battle under a blazing sun. It had been a case of "one of those little incidents which frequently happen in the progress of War," Greene subsequently remarked, alluding to how Marjoribanks and his 300 men had determined the outcome of a contest in which more than 4,500 men had fought. At the end, as at Guilford Courthouse and Hobkirk's Hill, the British held the field, but as in those earlier engagements, the redcoats had paid dearly for their victory. Two-fifths of the British force—866 men in all—was lost. The Americans suffered heavy losses, as well. Nearly a fifth of the rebel soldiery was lost, and 139 men—one in twenty who came under fire—perished in this seldom-remembered encounter.[56]

In the days that followed the British army retreated to "the gates of Charles Town," as Greene put it. What Greene had achieved since the previous December, and especially after Cornwallis's misguided abandonment of the Carolinas, was nothing less than breathtaking. The British, who only sixteen months before had believed that Georgia and South Carolina had been subdued and pacified, were confined to Charleston and Savannah. No "further ravages upon the Country" were expected, Greene exalted. It must have been with inordinate satisfaction that he could inform Governor Rutledge, who two years before had wished for South Carolina to quit the war and proclaim its neutrality, that the state's frontiers were secure. Most delicious of all, given the surprising occurrences that were just beginning to unfold in Virginia at the same moment as Eutaw Springs, was that Greene saw a sunbeam of hope. He now dared to dream not only that "this cruel war" might be near "an end," but that it might "end gloriously."[57]

Part Four
American Victory, 1781–1783

22

"AMERICA IS OURS":
VICTORY AT YORKTOWN, 1781

H IGH SUMMER bore down in the northern states as the French army began its trek from Rhode Island to New York to link up with Washington's Continentals. Moving along under a merciless sun, and in great swirling clouds of dust, the French soldiers found New England's climate so hot that Rochambeau for the most part terminated each day's march at noon, though some of the afternoon hours were spent in finding food. "The Americans supplied us with nothing," said one disgusted soldier, and he added that the French "were obliged to purchase everything and to provide ourselves with the most trifling things." Near White Plains on July 6—eighteen days after starting out, and eleven months after their arrival in America, the French army joined with the Continental army. The Americans spontaneously cheered and applauded the sight of their allies in their white uniforms. The next day, the French passed in review before Washington and Rochambeau, and the following day, under a pale blue sky, the Continentals reciprocated with a parade of their own. One French officer thought the rebels looked "rather good," though another observed that many American soldiers were barefoot and an alarming number were either barely adolescents or somewhat old for the rigors of military service. He thought it hopeful that "a quarter of them were negroes, merry confident, and sturdy."[1]

The allies' objective, agreed to at the Wethersfield Conference six weeks earlier, was to besiege or attack the British in New York. But on the eve of his departure from Rhode Island, Rochambeau had at last notified Washington that he knew de Grasse was to come north before summer's end, and he asked the American commander where he should be asked to sail. Washington's response indicated that he had grown more flexible, doubtless because he now knew that Cornwallis was in Virginia with a considerable army. Washington told Rochambeau that the Chesapeake might be a "more practicable and equally advisable" place for their campaign, and to this he added that it would "be best to leave . . . to [de Grasse] to judge, from the information he may . . . receive . . . of the *enemy's Fleet* upon this *Coast*, which will be the most advantageous quarter for him to make his *appearance* in." Rochambeau passed along Washington's letter to de Grasse, and to it he attached a missive of his own, once again quietly urging that the squadron be brought to Virginia.[2]

The two armies set off for Dobbs Ferry, near the northern end of Manhattan Island, marching through a war-scarred region of burned and abandoned houses. Washington's ardor to retake New York appeared to swell as he passed through the area. At a July 19 conference with Rochambeau he reverted to his old self. The conquest of New York "should be our primary Object," he again insisted, and the two commanders commenced work on a "definitive plan" for liberating the city. The final strategy would hinge on what was discovered about the enemy's defenses. Daily reconnoitering found few, if any, weaknesses. Other crucial intelligence trickled in as July swiftly passed. The allies learned that Cornwallis, with Lafayette at his heels, was withdrawing toward the Chesapeake, where he might be pinioned by an allied land and sea operation. They also knew that while Clinton was being reinforced, only about 5 percent of the troops and stores promised them by the northern states had arrived by the end of the month. In 1776 Washington had been blind to reality and fatally indecisive. That was not the case in 1781. Faced with mounting evidence that any attempt to take New York was likely to fail, Washington boldly decided that the allies' best bet was "an operation to the Southward," the course that Rochambeau had steadfastly championed.[3]

From that point forward, the allies made plans for moving their armies to Virginia. But given everything that had gone awry in this war, it was all too possible that de Grasse would never come north, or that he would arrive with an inferior fleet. It was conceivable, too, that Clinton might order Cornwallis's entire army to New York, eliminating the reason for a Chesapeake campaign. Should any of these things occur, the French and the Continentals would have to do something in New York. With so much left unresolved, reconnoitering continued and Washington summoned more militia to the periphery of Manhattan. Days passed slowly, anxiously, as both Washington and Rochambeau knew that the outcome of the war hung uncertainly in the balance. Then, suddenly, on August 14, a day when summer's humid air hung heavily, a packet for Rochambeau arrived from Barras in Rhode Island. It brought the long-awaited word. De Grasse had sailed from Haiti eleven days earlier with a squadron of twenty-nine ships of the line, four frigates, and 3,200 men. His destination: Virginia.[4]

Five days later the allies marched. Some seven thousand men, three thousand of them Continentals, set off, marching northward initially, as they were to cross the Hudson upriver at King's Ferry. Now, the great worry was how Clinton might react if he immediately learned their destination. Would he hurriedly recall Cornwallis? Would he also go south to join the fight? Would he cross into New Jersey and try to block the advance of the allies, buying time for Cornwallis's escape? The one hope to which Washington and Rochambeau clung was that Clinton would not know their objective until it was too late for him to act. There was good reason to believe that he would be fooled. Their route during the first ten or eleven days from King's Ferry would be the same as if their plans were to rendezvous with de Grasse at Sandy Hook for a campaign against New York. Just to be sure, the French built ovens—a tell-tale sign of an army preparing for a siege—and Washington made sure that some of his letters outlining a coming siege of New York were intercepted by the British.[5]

All along, Clinton had known almost everything that his adversaries were doing. Since the previous autumn, he had known almost immediately when Washington and Rochambeau met, and he knew, too, that their conference in February in Newport had been followed by a major action, the dispatch of Destouches to the Chesapeake. After the allied leaders met in Wethersfield in May, Clinton expected something big, a surmise that seemed borne out in June when he learned that French supply ships and transports had arrived in Boston with reinforcements, the six hundred men that Versailles had promised. Clinton even knew that de Grasse was expected to come north, likely in July or August, given the late summer and fall hurricane season. But the British commander was in the dark about some things. He neither knew the goal of the Franco-American armies when they began their march on August 19 nor the destination of de Grasse's voyage. Clinton also had no idea how many ships would comprise the French fleet that came north. Throughout that summer Clinton and Royal Navy officials in New York assumed that de Grasse would leave some ships in the Caribbean and send others to France. They made an educated guess that if de Grasse succeeded in joining with Barras's squadron of eight ships in Rhode Island, his fleet would top out at about twenty ships of the line. Against this, the British had seven ships of the line in New York, but late in June Clinton had requested naval reinforcements from the West Indies. Confident that a fleet would be sent, Clinton and Admiral Thomas Graves, who succeeded Arbuthnot that summer, believed the Royal Navy would be superior to de Grasse.[6]

Clinton could not know in July or August what he would know in September. Like any military commander, he pulled together the disparate strands of intelligence that reached headquarters, some of it accurate, much of it erroneous, nearly all of it inexact, and tried to make sense of the jumble, making judgments and guesses as he proceeded. What now is clear is that, with one exception, Clinton largely made the proper choices during the summer of 1781. The exception, of course, was his decision to leave Cornwallis in Virginia. Even as late as the third week in August, when the allies marched, Clinton still had time to issue the orders that would have safely extracted Cornwallis from Virginia. That order was never given.

The allied armies marched quickly to King's Ferry, but crossing the Hudson was exceedingly slow business. Six days were required to get the last man, and the final wagon groaning with equipment, into New Jersey. With spies lurking everywhere, secrecy was the order of the day. Only the highest officers were aware of their destination. The men were simply ordered to march in two columns a few miles apart. Those in the left column, the one closest to the Hudson and most susceptible to British attack, were to be "good men engaged either for the war or for three years." All the while, Washington remained busy with the details of the march and the coming campaign. He sent word ahead to have boats ready at the head of the Chesapeake and directed Lafayette to do all in his power to assure that "the British Army may not be able to escape you."[7]

Over several torrid days the armies headed in the direction of Newark, moving steadily, but slowly, reflecting Washington's long-standing fear that his force would be eviscerated by summer-spawned diseases. Other Continentals, detached from various posts, from time to time rendezvoused with the army, swelling its numbers. Clusters of curious, and hopeful, spectators gathered along the roads for a glimpse, almost as if this was "some theatrical exhibition," one soldier remarked. From these onlookers the soldiers learned of the hard currency that the French had provided to their hard-pressed ally, and at one point in their march the Continentals vowed not to take another step unless they were paid a month's wages. The American authorities paid them.

On August 30, the van of the army was situated about a dozen miles west of Staten Island. When it moved south from there, passing over the Raritan and heading toward Princeton and Trenton, Washington knew that "our intentions could [no longer] be concealed" from Clinton. That same day, it turned out, brought important news. First, Washington learned that a British squadron of only fourteen ships had arrived at Sandy Hook from the Caribbean. When joined with the British fleet in New York, the Royal Navy's optimum strength would be twenty-two ships of the line. De Grasse's squadron would be superior, and if he succeeded in joining with Barras the French fleet would be surpassingly larger. Secondly, Washington heard that day from Lafayette, who wrote that the "Ennemy Have ... Went Round to York[town]."[8] Until that moment, the destination of the allied armies had simply been Virginia. Now, they were headed for Yorktown.

In the days that followed, the armies crossed the Delaware River and descended on Philadelphia, passing over the Schuylkill by ferry. On September 2 the Continental army marched to fife and drum through the city streets in a two-mile-long line that "raised a dust like a smothering snow-storm," according to one soldier. The next day the French, resplendent in their striking white coats faced with green, marched through to the accompaniment of music provided by "a complete band." Their parade was nearly as long as that of the rebels, and concluded with shiny horses carrying dragoons colorfully garbed in light blue jackets, yellow trousers, tall black boots, and high black fezzes. The armies paused the next day to rest and to permit the men to wash their clothing. The following day, while passing through Wilmington, Delaware, a dispatch rider from Virginia found Washington and delivered important news. De Grasse not only had arrived safely in the Chesapeake, he had landed his marines to help Lafayette with the job of impounding Cornwallis at Yorktown. The commander was so excited that he insisted on personally breaking the news to Rochambeau, who had opted to dismount and sail as far as possible down the Delaware River. As the French general and his staff approached Chester, they spotted "General Washington, standing on the shore and waving his hat and white handkerchief joyfully." When Rochambeau came ashore to learn what was up, Washington, normally the most reserved of men, embraced him "*warmly*" and with "deep satisfaction" passed on the glad tidings.

The allied armies immediately stepped up their pace. De Grasse had notified Rochambeau back in August that he could not remain off Virginia beyond mid-October. The first week of September was nearly gone and a lengthy trip down the Chesapeake lay ahead. One day's march brought the armies to Head of Elk, where Howe had landed when he invaded Pennsylvania in 1777. That site now was the allies' embarkation point for Yorktown. But when the men arrived, they discovered a shortage of boats. Many men had to march to Baltimore or Annapolis, where every conceivable sort of vessel was pressed into service. Sixteen days elapsed before the last man finally embarked and another ten days followed before the last allied soldier landed at Jamestown on the Williamsburg Neck. That occurred on September 26, thirty-eight days after the allied armies started out from Dobbs Ferry. Washington had not sailed with his army. During this war he had been separated from his army only when Congress called him away, but in this instance the temptation to visit nearby Mount Vernon, which he had not seen for more than six long years, was too great. He remained with the army at Head of Elk for three days, then rode home, spending four welcome days at his estate, inspecting every inch of the place and entertaining Rochambeau and his staff, as well as men from his own staff. Just before Washington departed for the front, on September 12, he wrote to Lafayette: "I hope you will keep Lord Cornwallis safe, without Provisions or Forage, untill we arrive." Unbeknownst to Washington, the key event in the Yorktown campaign had already occurred.[9]

DE GRASSE had sailed north from the Caribbean early in August. Nearly a week later a fourteen ship British squadron under Admiral Samuel Hood was sent to find him. Hood's orders were to first search for the French in the Chesapeake, then in Delaware Bay. The smaller royal fleet, with its speedier copper bottomed vessels, made better time. On August 25 it reached the Chesapeake, where it saw only British vessels bobbing on the blue-grey water. Nor was there any sign of de Grasse on Delaware Bay. On August 28 Hood reached New York. The next day, de Grasse arrived at the entrance to Chesapeake Bay. When Hood docked in New York, he relinquished command to Admiral Graves, a man who had obtained his flag through persistence rather than distinguished service. Slow and cautious, he was in no hurry to go to sea even at this grave moment, not even when he learned—on the very day that Hood arrived—that Barras had sailed, obviously hoping to rendezvous with de Grasse. Seventy-two hours passed before Graves, in a nineteen-ship squadron, stood off for Virginia. He arrived on September 5, beating Barras to the Chesapeake. However, de Grasse, with twenty-eight warships—he had sent one to Yorktown to help with the containment of Cornwallis—was waiting for him. De Grasse had brought his entire fleet from the Caribbean, something the British never imagined that he would dare to do, giving him command of the largest fleet to sail on North American waters since Howe's invasion force arrived off New York in 1776.[10]

With his overarching numerical advantage, de Grasse might have frustrated his adversary by remaining in the bay and simply blocking its entrance. But had he chosen that option, Barras, whose small squadron was bringing siege guns and other supplies, could not have gotten past the royal fleet. Thus, de Grasse emerged to fight. The French fleet faced the moment of maximum danger when it sailed from the bay, as it was impossible to maintain an orderly battle line while passing through the narrow exit. Had Graves fallen on his foe at this juncture, he might have scored a spectacular victory and altered the course of history. But to have done so would have been out of character for him. The risks were considerable, and Graves was not a risk-taker. If things went awry and his fleet was destroyed, Cornwallis would be lost with it and probably Clinton's army and New York, as well. Graves waited for de Grasse to emerge, then fought a by-the-book naval engagement. It raged for more than four hours, until the huge late summer sun lay low in the western sky. As almost always occurred in such engagements, numerous ships in both squadrons suffered heavy damage, and the carnage among the men on both sides was horrific. About 200 French sailors were casualties, while nearly 350 British seamen were killed or wounded, a number that in an afternoon of fighting totaled more than half what Cornwallis would lose during the next several weeks. Roughly an equal number of ships on both sides were badly damaged. That left de Grasse with the superior fleet, a superiority that increased as the battle progressed, for Barras arrived in the midst of the encounter and slipped into Chesapeake Bay unnoticed and unmolested. The French now had thirty-six ships of the line. During the next few days, while repairs were made, Graves and his highest-ranking officers fought among themselves over what to do next. In the end, almost a week after the battle, the British weighed anchor and returned to New York. Technically, the battle had been a standoff, but as historian William Willcox observed, the British "needed to win and the French did not," making the Battle of the Virginia Capes the most important "naval engagement of the eighteenth century."[11]

ON SEPTEMBER 14, the same day that Graves sailed for New York, Washington rode into Williamsburg. He was greeted as if he was already a conqueror. A twenty-one-gun salute welcomed him, after which Lafayette, who had not seen Washington for the better part of a year, rushed forward and "embraced him with an ardor not easily described," according to one astonished American onlooker, who added that the young Frenchman "absolutely kissed him from ear to ear."[12] That evening, while a French band played softly in the background, Washington was the guest of honor at a lavish banquet hosted by the French.

While Washington was beginning to savor the heavenly taste of seemingly inevitable—and decisive—victory, Cornwallis was coming to understand his desperate plight. On August 31, the day the allied armies began crossing the Delaware, a messenger brought him the shocking news that a large squadron flying the Bourbon flag was at the mouth of the Chesapeake. The next day he discovered that de Grasse had blocked the entrance to the York River and that transports laden with French troops were sailing up the James River, on the other side of the peninsula, obviously to join forces with Lafayette. Cornwallis knew instantly that he was in trouble, though several days would elapse before he was aware of the full extent of his dilemma. As September dawned, he did not know how many reinforcements had reached Lafayette, nor was he aware that Rochambeau and Washington were on their way to Yorktown. He also remained hopeful that a superior British fleet would arrive and drive away de Grasse. It later was apparent that if Cornwallis was to escape, this was the time. Had he attacked Lafayette within three or four days of learning of de Grasse's arrival, before the French marines arrived and were in place, he might easily have broken out. Even during the several days that followed, until about the third week in September, he would have enjoyed favorable odds had he tried to fight his way out. He possessed numerical superiority and he had more regulars than Lafayette. All along, more-over, Cornwallis could have chosen an alternative to fighting his way clear of the peninsula. With ample naval craft at his disposal, he might simply have trans-ferred his army across the York to Gloucester and marched inland, fighting his way past whatever allied forces Lafayette succeeded in putting in his way. But there were problems with that option. A flight would have required Cornwallis to abandon his ill troops, sacrifice the Loyalists who had gathered about him, scuttle his artillery, and turn his back on his tiny fleet, as well as its officers and sailors. War is filled with bad choices, as Cornwallis, who had fired on his own men in order to save the bulk of his army at Guilford Courthouse, knew all too well. Escaping to Gloucester was an option that remained open to him through much of September, but he never exercised that choice.[13]

Cornwallis fatalistically stayed on at Yorktown, ignoring the entreaties to act that came from many of his officers. Early in September, Tarleton implored him to attack and, at about the same moment, Simcoe advised that escape was still possible.[14] Cornwallis remained behind his entrenchments. Later, he explained his conduct by asserting that he had lacked the discretionary authority to act, a plea that stretches credulity to the breaking point. Actually, several good reasons existed for the choice that he made. All along he hoped for help from Clinton, and in mid-September he learned from his commander that assistance was going to be sent. In a letter that reached Cornwallis on September 14, Clinton wrote that "As . . . I can have no Doubt that Washington is moving with, at least, 6,000 French & Rebel Troops against you, I think the best way to relieve you, is to join you . . . with all the Force that can be spared from [New York], which is about 4000 Men." Within three days of receiving Clinton's communiqué, Cornwallis learned the outcome of the Battle of the Virginia Capes, which shut the lid on all hope of imminent aid from New York. Even so, in mid-September Cornwallis believed that he possessed sufficient supplies to see him through until nearly November 1. Forty-five days can be a lifetime in warfare, especially when few other good options exist. Perhaps another, superior, British fleet would be dispatched to Virginia. Perhaps de Grasse could not stay until November. Perhaps a storm would damage and disperse the enemy fleet. Why not hold out as long as possible? No less important, Cornwallis understood that a great turning point in this war was at hand. If a worst-case scenario materialized, he did not wish to be saddled with blame for Britain's failure. As matters stood, he believed that he would not be condemned. After all, he was where he was because Clinton had ordered him to a coastal base. Clinton had also refused his request to bring the army in New York south and seek a decisive victory in Virginia. The daring, dashing Cornwallis who had chased Greene across North Carolina and who, despite inferior numbers, had rushed to fight at Guilford Courthouse in March, was nowhere to be seen in September. He chose to remain within his defenses. As he told Clinton in a letter that month: "I do not think myself justifiable in putting the fate of the War on so desperate an Attempt" as an attack on Lafayette's forces.[15]

WASHINGTON spent his first two weeks on the peninsula awaiting the arrival of the allied armies. During that period he and Rochambeau met with de Grasse. They sailed down the James and out into the Chesapeake aboard a captured British brig, then transferred to a small runabout that took them to the *Ville de Paris*, the flag-ship of the French squadron. Ten years older than Washington, and even taller, de Grasse allegedly greeted the American commander: "*Mon cher petit général!*" It is doubtful that Washington, who was vain and thin-skinned, found the salutation amusing, though everyone within earshot cracked up. But given the military situation, Washington was ebullient and the meeting went off well enough, with the American commander getting what he wanted with regard to the campaign at hand. De Grasse promised to stay on until the end of October, giving the allied armies about six weeks to get the job done, and he consented to run vessels up the York, above Yorktown, shutting off the enemy's only source for additional supplies. De Grasse disappointed Washington only by refusing to commit to an attempt to liberate Charleston following Cornwallis's capitulation.[16]

In a sense, the siege of Yorktown finally began on September 20. On that day the allied commanders dispatched more than one thousand Virginia militia, together with French cavalry and marines, to Gloucester to prevent further

British foraging and to check any attempted breakout in that sector. A week later, the vise was tightened further when the two armies marched the approximately fifteen miles from Williamsburg to Yorktown. They found the enemy in defenses that Cornwallis had ordered prepared around August 1. From the outset, he had found the terrain inhospitable for making a stand, and with considerable truth said that the only virtue of the place was as a naval base.[17] Work on the defenses had proceeded slowly until de Grasse was spotted, after which entrenching began in earnest. Toiling in the summer heat, the redcoats had established outworks up to one thousand yards south of the village, but their main line of defense consisted of a line of earthworks that enclosed the town on all but the river side, with seven redoubts and six artillery batteries linked to the works. Three additional redoubts had been built beyond that formidable line. Fusilier's Redoubt was situated several hundred yards west of the town and Number 9 and Number 10 were positioned about a quarter mile apart some five hundred yards east of the breastworks. Sixty-five cannon had been installed within these defenses, and two frigates lay off the town with a total of eighty-eight guns.[18] With roughly the same amount of time to prepare, Prevost had foiled the allied siege, and attack, at Savannah in 1779, but Washington and Rochambeau possessed several advantages that d'Estaing had not enjoyed. From the outset, the allies at Yorktown knew that their siege could be maintained for roughly three weeks longer than had been allotted the Franco-American armies in Georgia. The British at Yorktown had only some six weeks in which to stock their pantry, whereas Prevost had nearly a year in which to gather comestibles. The allies held numerical and weaponry advantages in both sieges, but at Yorktown their superiority was daunting. The allied armies at Yorktown were more than twice the size of the besieged force. Washington and Rochambeau commanded more than 19,000 men, all but 3,000 of them regulars, while Cornwallis had fewer than 9,000 men. The allies also possessed one-third more cannon than the British.[19]

Their advantages notwithstanding, the allied commanders—which is to say Rochambeau, the only one with experience in siege warfare—concluded that Cornwallis could neither be starved into submission nor overwhelmed through an immediate assault. He had to be taken through traditional siege craft. This meant digging parallels and moving slowly, but inexorably, nearer the target. As the allies closed in, their artillery fire would grow steadily more accurate. Given time, they would be firing heavy cannon from nearly point-blank range. It was all "reducible to calculation," Rochambeau assured Washington. The situation prompted one rebel to rejoice, "Cornwallis may now tremble for his fate." Optimism prevailed. "We had holed him and nothing remained but to dig him out," one rebel soldier remarked, while another, who exalted that he had been set "All on Fire" by "the Great God of War," exclaimed that "we have got [Cornwallis] in a pudding bag."[20] General Wayne exalted that the allies had "the most glorious certainty" of victory.[21] The French took up positions southwest of the hamlet, the Americans due south and southeast of Yorktown.[22] Washington and Rochambeau established separate headquarters in tents erected about 250 yards apart in the region between the two armies. Washington lived and dined in his tent, although on heavy, late summer nights he sometimes slept outdoors under the stars, the moonlight muted by the full trees.[23]

On the second night after the allies had moved up to Yorktown, Cornwallis withdrew from his outlying defenses. It was a sound move undertaken to tighten his lines, though it reduced the obstacles facing the allies, and the time they would require to achieve their ends. A week later, as a gentle rain fell on the dark night of October 5, work began on the first allied parallel. It was situated on the American side, perhaps one thousand yards from the British earthworks and some five hundred yards from Number 9 and Number 10, and it was an excavation project of considerable proportions. Eventually, this parallel would be ten feet wide and four feet deep, and extend for more than two miles. American sappers under the direction of skilled French engineers carried out the digging. While French infantry made a diversionary attack against Fusilier's Redoubt on the other side of town, the allies held a little ceremony to launch the dig. As the sappers leaned idly on their picks and shovels awaiting the signal to begin, Private Martin later reminisced that a "stranger" appeared and "talked familiarly with us for a few minutes." Only when some French engineers approached and addressed the man as "Your Excellency" did Martin—who had served in the Continental army for more than five years—realize that the officer was General Washington. The commander "struck a few blows with a pickax," Martin added, "that it might be said 'General Washington with his own hands first broke ground at the siege of Yorktown.'"[24]

The sappers took over thereafter. Positioned three yards apart, they began to dig out Virginia's sun-baked soil. It was hard work, performed as quietly as possible so as not to alert the enemy. "Not a word or a whisper was uttered— nothing but silent work," was how one sapper put it.[25] All work was done at night. Otherwise, the sappers would have made excellent targets for the British and German sharpshooters in Number 9 and Number 10. Four nights of digging were needed to get all the allied gun batteries in place. Only then, on the fortieth day after de Grasse's fleet arrived, were the allies ready to launch their bombardment. In mid-afternoon on October 9, again following a little ceremony, "General Washington put the match to the first gun . . . and Earl Cornwallis . . . received his first salutation," a rebel soldier noted in his journal. According to the scuttlebutt that swirled through the American lines, that first ball tore through a house in town in which several officers had gathered for mess, killing the man seated at the head of the table and wounding several others. After that initial round, a thunderous barrage followed as scores of American siege guns opened up nearly simultaneously. The next day the French batteries opened fire, the gunners shouting "Huzza for the Americans!" after the first round was discharged. Now nearly a hundred guns hammered away. The bombardment continued day after day, each a ghostly foretaste of the morrow. During the daylight hours, a rebel soldier said, the projectiles were "clearly visible in the form of a black ball." At night, he added, the shelling—at least to those doing the firing—was spellbinding, as the rounds looked "like a fiery meteor with a blazing tail" and were "most beautifully brilliant." With approximately 3,600 rounds slamming into tiny Yorktown every day, the village was quickly reduced to a bombed and burned out shell of its former self, a scene of horror thick with dust and rubble, and the mangled bodies of men and horses. Those in the British army who were not in their trenches—where perhaps the greatest safety could be found—sought whatever shelter was available. Some huddled in wet, debris-filled basements. Others crouched in terror beneath natural overhangs at the river's edge. Some were driven to a troglodytic life. Cornwallis, for instance, was flushed from the smoking ruins of his original headquarters, the home of Thomas Nelson, who had been elected governor of Virginia in June, and into an underground bunker that had been prepared for him. Conditions worsened daily for the besieged, as the trenches, dug in a zigzag pattern, crept steadily closer to their lines. By October 11 allied batteries were within 350 yards of the nearest British post. Three days later the second parallel was under construction and allied guns had moved to within just 150 yards of the nearest British soldiers.[26]

By then only one objective remained. In order to extend the second parallel to the river and make it fully efficient, redoubts Number 9 and Number 10 had to be taken. Each had to be conquered by direct assault. It was agreed that the French with 400 men were to subdue Number 9 on the left, a pentagonal structure occupied by 120 defenders. The Americans drew the easier task, clearing the square-shaped Number 10, held by forty-five enemy soldiers. After listening for days to his endless entreaties for a chance at glory, Washington selected twenty-four-year-old Alexander Hamilton, who had no previous command experience under fire, to lead the American operation. Like his French counterparts, Hamilton was given four hundred men. His were all hardened New England Continentals, and some were African Americans. The men took up their arms that night in the knowledge that they were risking life and limb in what was likely to be the last great fight of this siege, and perhaps even of this long war. On the eve of battle, Hamilton wrote to his wife: "Five days more the enemy must capitulate . . . and then I fly home to you. Prepare to receive me in your bosom."[27]

At 6:30, with the ebony night already shrouding the battlefield, the French launched a covering raid against Fusilier's Redoubt. Thirty minutes later the two allied forces moved out. Their weapons were not loaded, lest they shoot one another in the close quarters fighting. But their bayonets were mounted. As the men advanced, allied signal rockets lit the sable sky, casting an eerie reddish-orange light over the gnarled landscape. The French soldiers stormed their redoubt, wrestling with the abatis that guarded its periphery, then charged through what they had destroyed and into the enemy's position, where hand-to-hand fighting settled the issue. Sappers led the American attack force and destroyed the abatis, after which Hamilton's men, who had surrounded the redoubt, let loose a blood-curdling yell and with bravura charged from every side. Attackers and defenders fought desperately, thrusting with bayonets, slugging with fists, wielding muskets as clubs, hacking with axes. It did not last long, ten minutes at most, but it was unsparing, akin to savage beasts in nature locked in a death struggle. When it ended, the allies held both redoubts. The French had paid the heaviest price for their victory. Coping with an enemy force three times larger than that facing the Americans, the French lost ninety-two men, a quarter of their force. Forty-one of the men under Hamilton, a tenth of those who fought, were lost. Barely a quarter of the British defenders survived unscathed.[28] Once these redoubts fell, there was no question but that the second parallel would creep steadily closer to the town, leaving the British defenders to see their unhappy destiny with crystal clarity.

The following night Cornwallis ordered an assault by 350 men on the rebel lines, his first, and only, sortie against an allied parallel. It was an act known in European warfare as the *baroud d'honneur*, a face-saving action by a doomed commander (and one for which eight redcoats paid with their lives). Much the same followed on the ensuing evening. Under a cover of darkness, Cornwallis made an apparent attempt to escape his trap by getting his army across to Gloucester, from which it ostensibly could make a run for safety. This act, like that of the previous night, bore the earmarks of a commander who knew that he was beaten and was already preparing his defense for the inevitable inquiry that would follow in England. The attempt to escape did not get very far. After roughly a third of the men had been put ashore at Gloucester Point, a heavy rumbling storm with strong winds blew up, making it impossible to get any more men across. The storm was not decisive. Some who made it across reported that the allied defenses were so strong that it would not be possible to break through.[29] As Cornwallis had long known, he was beaten. He was ready to capitulate.

The next morning, October 17, under a clearing autumn sky, the allies opened with a heavier than normal barrage, a deadly, deafening cacophony of terror that, according to one rebel soldier, caused the "whole peninsula" to quake "under the . . . thundering of our infernal machines."[30] The deadly battering had gone on for about three hours when, at 10:00 a.m., a white flag of truce was seen fluttering above the British earthworks. The allied batteries began to halt their firing. From left to right, like a rolling echo, the thunderous artillery blasts ceased, until only the guns on the peripheries, the last to get the word that the enemy wished to parley, ceased firing. Suddenly, an unaccustomed and "solemn silence," in the words of a militiaman, gathered over the tattered landscape.[31] A British officer appeared carrying a white flag and accompanied by a drummer boy beating *en chamade*, the signal that the besieged wishes to negotiate.[32] Immaculate in their red coats and clean white trousers, the two British soldiers walked slowly, but proudly, toward the allied lines. An American officer emerged to meet them. A brief discussion ensued. The drummer boy was sent back to his lines, but the officer was blindfolded and escorted toward Washington's headquarters, nearly a mile away. Once there, his blindfold removed, the British officer produced a letter from Cornwallis:

> Sir, I propose a cessation of hostilities for twenty-four hours, and that two officers be appointed by each side, to meet at Mr. Moore's house, to settle terms for the surrender of the posts at York and Gloucester.[33]

Washington had no experience in such matters. In eleven years, and two wars, no enemy army had ever formally surrendered to him. While the British envoy waited, Washington spoke with his staff, then with Rochambeau. Finally, at 2:00 p.m., Washington gave his written response. He wished to see Cornwallis's proposed terms of surrender before he agreed to talks. As soon as Cornwallis's envoy was escorted back to the British lines, the siege guns erupted once again. The barrage was brief, for Cornwallis did not dally. Within two hours he submitted terms. Washington read what Cornwallis had proposed and spoke again with his staff. Rochambeau perused the document as well. All agreed that what Cornwallis proposed would not be acceptable in the final accord, but his terms were suitable for beginning talks. As the long shadows of late day stretched over the battlefield, Washington sent the latest British envoy back with word that surrender talks would begin the following morning, and in the meantime the guns would remain silent.[34]

Soldiers on both sides had held their breath while these life and death preliminaries transpired, hoping that what was afoot meant they had survived this engagement, maybe even the war itself. As word spread that the cease-fire would last at least a bit longer, men emerged from the trenches, dirty and unshaven, haggard even, and walked about the shell-pocked fields without fear, relaxed under the late day's sun, played games, and listened to the haunting sounds made by a distant redcoat bagpiper, music soon answered by the lively, joyful tunes that one might hear in a Parisian club. That night, for the first time in a month, men slept soundly, without worry of a surprise attack.[35]

In the morning, a bright but chilly day, the four designated representatives gathered at the Moore house near the river and behind the rebel's first parallel. John Laurens and Lafayette's brother-in-law, Vicomte de Noailles, both colonels, sat down with a British colonel and major, one of whom was Cornwallis's aide-de-camp. It turned into a marathon session lasting nearly twelve hours. Each side budged here and there, but each was uncompromising on some points. When they finished, long after night had swaddled the nearby battlefield, the four men returned to their respective headquarters and reported to their commanders. Washington, like Gates at Saratoga, wanted to reach a prompt settlement. The long fancied decisive victory was at his fingertips. Calamities could occur if he permitted the negotiations to spin on indefinitely. He had received intelligence that Clinton was preparing a relief expedition. There was always the possibility that a superior British fleet might arrive. Disease could break out in a rush and emasculate the allied armies. In this season, and in this locale, a hurricane was always possible, perhaps like the great storm that had nearly wrecked d'Estaing's fleet off Rhode Island in 1778. Not wishing victory to slip through his fingers for having dallied over what would be seen by posterity as trivial issues, Washington prudently instructed Laurens to be more flexible. Serendipitously, Cornwallis felt that he had put his army through enough. He was without hope and nearly two thousand of his men were sick or wounded. With one side eager to conclude the surrender and the other resigned to closing this long bloody encounter, the talks on the second day were concluded quickly, within only an hour. By mid-morning the Articles of Capitulation were ready for the respective commanders to study, and perhaps to sign.[36]

The articles called for the surrender of the British army, with its members becoming prisoners of war. Cornwallis had wanted his men to be paroled, but Washington exacted nearly the same terms that Clinton had demanded of the vanquished rebel garrison at Charleston seventeen months before. One officer for every fifty men was paroled, but these men were to remain near the captives and keep watch on their treatment. Washington caved in on two matters. He had wanted the document to stipulate that all slaves who were with the British were to be returned to their owners and that the Tories and American deserters with the British were to be relinquished to the American army. As for chattel, the pact merely stated that those who had been body slaves to British officers could be kept in that capacity. It was silent with regard to Loyalists and deserters, but the agreement permitted Cornwallis to send to New York a vessel carrying "dispatches . . . and such soldiers as [he] may think proper." Washington knew the ship would be laden with those whom he wished to get his hands on.[37]

The document was delivered first to Cornwallis, who read and signed it. Then it was brought to Washington, Rochambeau, and de Grasse, who had gathered in one of the captured redoubts where considerable blood had flowed just five days before. Without ceremony each man signed the surrender papers at eleven o'clock on that bright morning.[38]

Word of the surrender instantly coursed through the lines. It was over. The guns would fire no more. Allied detachments immediately entered Yorktown and took possession of the British entrenchments.

That same afternoon, October 19, at two o'clock, six and one-half years to the day since this war had begun at Lexington and Concord, the British surrender formally began. The British army marched from the tottering ruins of their lockup in Yorktown, accompanied by a band whose "drums [were] covered with black handkerchiefs and their fifes with black ribbons." The defeated British pro-cessed between a long row of French soldiers in their dress whites on their left and the American soldiery, few in uniforms and a considerable number without shoes, on their right. The redcoats appeared surly, one rebel thought, but the Germans seemed to him to be indifferent. A French officer was struck by the appearance of the British, who "seemed . . . much more tired and much less heroic" than the

Surrender at Yorktown. Painting by John Trumbull, c. 1787–1828. The British army under Cornwallis surrendered to the allies at Yorktown on October 19, 1781. Cornwall pleaded illness and asked General Charles O'Hara, shown in the Trumbull painting, to represent him at the ceremony.

Germans. Slowly, dolefully, the vanquished marched toward the designated field of surrender, a prosaic plain midway between the quarters of the victorious allied commanders and the hitherto obscure village whose name was about to be catapulted into history. It was a gorgeous day, bright and sunny, and the leaves were just beginning to show their autumn colors. Throngs of spectators from the Williamsburg Neck had come to watch, nearly as many, thought one soldier, as the numbers that comprised the rebel army. The principal officers rode at the head of the defeated army, save for Cornwallis, who pleaded illness and did not appear. Brigadier General Charles O'Hara was given responsibility for surrendering. About forty, O'Hara had been a soldier since he was a teenager, fighting in Europe and Africa before being sent to America in October 1780, where he always served with Cornwallis. He chased after Greene, fought him at Guilford Courthouse, where he was wounded in the chest and thigh, then fought on in Virginia.[39] O'Hara rode forward to a row of allied officers mounted on horseback and asked which officer was Rochambeau. He was curtly told that he was to surrender to General Washington. But when O'Hara drew up in front of the American commander and offered his sword, Washington disdainfully refused to accept a token from a subordinate of Cornwallis. He directed O'Hara to surrender to General Lincoln, the second in command of the Continental army. Once his distasteful duty was done, O'Hara turned and rode away. According to an eyewitness, "tears rolled down his cheeks." When the little ceremony was concluded, the British soldiers came forward to ground their weapons. It was a lengthy process, and at times the redcoat band played mournful tunes, though contrary to legend it likely never played "The World Turned Upside Down," a popular song of the day. At other times during the ceremony the French band played more upbeat melodies.[40]

More than 8,000 prisoners were taken—of which about 1,300 were Germans and nearly 1,000 were seamen—together with 214 pieces of field artillery, thousands of muskets, numerous wagons and horses, and roughly three score British vessels of assorted size. Cornwallis may have managed to squeeze up to five hundred Tories and American deserters aboard the New York–bound vessel.[41] Neither of the men that Washington perhaps most wanted to see among the captives were part of the surrender. Benedict Arnold had been recalled to New York in June and, in fact, during the siege at Yorktown he had led a damaging raid on New London, Connecticut. Nor was John Champe among those who surrendered. The man who had volunteered to kidnap or kill Arnold had deserted from Arnold's Legion earlier in the year and somehow made his way inside Light Horse Harry Lee's lines. Lee gave him an honorable discharge and sent him home, where he lived out the war.[42]

Cornwallis had been setting free the African Americans with him since early in the siege, partly to conserve his food supply, partly to rid himself of those who exhibited signs of smallpox. Some believe that he hoped they would spread the disease in the enemy's ranks. In the last hours before the surrender, he told many of the blacks who were still with him to leave Yorktown. In the hope of escaping to freedom, many tried to get across the York River or took to the thick woods that covered the peninsula. Some succeeded and fled northward. Most appear to have failed in their quest. Many, alone and abandoned, died awful deaths from smallpox or deprivation. Most were apprehended by their owners who descended on Yorktown in search of their property, or by soldiers who served as bounty hunters, fanning out into the woods to help with the roundup. Some French officers joined in as well, hoping to latch on to a slave or two for their own benefit. Washington appears to have joined in the dragnet and apprehended two of the chattel who had fled Mount Vernon in the British raid the previous spring. They were sent back to captivity.[43]

The losses in the siege were typical of such an operation. The British suffered 556 casualties, the allies about 700, of which 299 were Americans.[44]

That night, after a stilted and somber dinner for the defeated enemy officers, Washington, surely weary, sat at his desk and by candlelight wrote to notify Congress of the long-awaited decisive victory. Not given to grandiloquence, Washington did not pen a letter that would ring for the ages. In a tone of almost unctuous humility, he noted simply that "a Reduction of the British Army under the Command of Lord Cornwallis, is most happily effected." The following day, in a similarly pedestrian manner, he congratulated the Continental army "upon the glorious event" that had brought "general Joy" to "every Breast."[45] Not all were so reserved, and that night many of the soldiers let their ebullience show, "laughing . . . jumping and dancing and singing as they went about," according to an American officer.[46] That spirit of relief and revelry quickly spread beyond the battlefield. A fifteen-year-old Virginia militiaman, who was guarding British prisoners near the Appomattox River on the day after Cornwallis's surrender, remembered that a dispatch rider brought the news of the great allied victory. When the militiamen heard the tidings, he later recalled, "every American present" threw "his cocked hat up in the air" and shouted "America is ours."[47]

23

CHOICES, 1782

PHILADELPHIA was dark and quiet, its residents asleep. Almost no one heard the horse as it clattered spectrally over the empty cobblestone streets just before three o'clock. The rider sought out the home of the president of Congress, Thomas McKean, and awakened him with a start by pounding loudly on his door. Once the rider was shown in, the two men spoke quietly. Visibly moved, McKean immediately sent a servant to deliver word to the town watchman, who patrolled the streets looking for signs of fire or other troubles and on the hour bawling out the correct time. On this night, October 22, 1781, the watchman changed his routine after receiving the urgent message. As he walked the glum streets he cried out his essential news in a happy mixture of his native and newfound tongue: "Basht dree o'clock, und Gorn-wal-lis isht da-ken."[1]

Across the city people awakened and listened. None needed a translation, or an explanation, of what they had heard. Some, perhaps, realized that what they had just heard was the rarest of rare things. They had just learned of a great turning point in history, something that some people never experience in the course of a very long lifetime. For all but a handful, such as Grace Galloway in her cheerless apartment, the news was exhilarating. It was what they had longed to hear through all the anxious years of this seemingly endless war.

As soon as Congress received official word of Cornwallis's surrender, it ordered a day of celebration followed by a night of illumination. During that festive day, the members of Congress walked as a body to the Lutheran Church, chosen because it was the largest in the city, and with almost a thousand others worshiped, giving thanks for the victory and praying that it would "prepare the way for . . . an honorable Peace." That night, nearly every Philadelphian put a candle in at least one window, a light of joy and thanksgiving.[2]

The reaction in Manhattan was different. Most residents had hoped against hope for Cornwallis's deliverance. Their expectations had been raised when Clinton sent twenty-five warships and more than seven thousand troops to attempt the rescue of the beleaguered army at Yorktown. A council of war had authorized the mission in September, though it had urged Clinton to await expected naval reinforcements from England. Nearly a month passed before the ships from England arrived. On October 17 the powerful armada finally set sail for the Chesapeake, but that was the very day that Cornwallis had asked for surrender talks. Given the history of Britain's conduct of this war, it seemed only fitting that its last great military act was played out in such a measured fashion.

Clinton, whose reputation was certain to be in ruins, may have been the man who was most embittered by the catastrophic turn of events in Virginia. In the wake of what he called the "melancholy damp" brought on by Yorktown, he turned reflective. The decisive moment in the war, he concluded, had been King's Mountain. Thereafter, no realistic hope existed of raising substantial numbers of Loyalists. More than any other military action, he believed, it had set in motion a chain of events that led directly to Cornwallis's fateful decision to bring his army into Virginia. The navy also bore a heavy responsibility for Britain's defeat, he thought, but it was Germain who was the real architect of the disaster. The American secretary not only had never sent him sufficient troops, he had never adequately understood the war because he habitually listened to the wrong people. Clinton did not say that to Germain, of course. In his letter breaking the news of Cornwallis's surrender, written aboard the *London* while he returned from having personally led the doomed relief expedition to the Chesapeake, Clinton said simply that Yorktown "is a blow . . . whose loss it will be now impossible I fear to repair."[3]

GERMAIN received dependable word of the Yorktown disaster on November 25. He immediately ordered a coach and made an anxious ride to 10 Downing Street. Once he was shown into the prime minister's study, Germain broke the bad news. North, he said later, received the tidings "as he would have taken a ball in the breast." Agitated beyond description, North paced the floor, repeatedly exclaiming, "Oh God, it is all over!"[4]

When Parliament opened two days later, all London knew of Yorktown—of the "Burgoynishing" of Cornwallis, as some put it—but not everyone was certain of its meaning. To be sure, many in the Commons were furious when the king, in his speech opening the session, urged that the war "to restore my deluded subjects in America" be continued despite the "late misfortune" at Yorktown. When the Commons, as was customary, considered how to answer the monarch, Fox—after fulminating in his usual choleric fashion—introduced an amendment to strike all language in defense of the American war from the government's proposed response. That touched off a fierce debate, one that prompted North's biographer to wryly suggest, "the war was being fought more energetically in London than in America."⁵ Actually, the Opposition was in disarray when word of Yorktown arrived, and had been since the first glad tidings of victories in South Carolina had seemed to suggest that the government's Southern Strategy was working. Caught off guard, the Opposition responded to the king's address with truculent speeches against the war, and sprays of venom at both North and the monarch. These sulky cries aside, the long-time foes of the war were initially unprepared to wage a well-organized campaign for terminating hostilities.⁶ That would take time, though not that much time, as events would demonstrate.

During the intense debate over how to answer the king, some members of the Opposition took the position that as the war was lost it was folly to continue with the killing and the expense of the thing. Burke lampooned the war's history as nothing but "a continued series of marching and countermarching, of taking and evacuating; indeed . . . places in America seemed to undergo an excrementitious evacuation, analogous to that of the human body." North and Germain defended the war, the former in his usual parsimonious manner, the latter more zealously, even clinging to his oft-repeated claim that victory was still possible through the efforts of the "numerous" Loyalists in the colonies. He exhorted those in Parliament not to consider America lost, for if ever America was given up "we shall sink into perfect insignificance." North's majority held, but it was shrinking. His government had once enjoyed a nearly two-hundred-vote majority. Fox's amendment was defeated by eighty-nine votes.⁷

When the cabinet met for the first time after learning of Yorktown, a session that came on the heels of the king's speech, it was nearly as divided as the Commons. Some ministers were ready to end the war. The majority, however, rejected such defeatism. Like North and Germain—who spoke plaintively of the "fatal issue of the Virginia expedition and the loss of so fine a body of men"—they were not ready to instantly make peace. Germain led a faction that wished to continue vigorously prosecuting the war. North spoke for a larger group that wanted to continue hostilities, though most were not immediately certain how to go about it. North's views in fact coalesced only over time, perhaps requiring a month to take shape. At the outset, he appears to have defended the war largely because that was the king's position. To take any other stance was to bring down the ministry and to have in its place one bent on an immediate termination of hostilities. But as Christmas approached, North had come to link war and diplomacy, and he had begun to pursue a cunningly multifaceted design. He envisaged quietly—and separately—approaching both the rebels and the French about making peace. If one nibbled, North would make some sort of peace with that belligerent and continue the war against the other.⁸

If any success was to be had, North knew that it must be attained quickly. Yorktown had touched off a rising clamor against the war. Each day his majority crumpled a bit more. London's papers bulged with denunciations of the war, satires directed against the king and North, and calls for a change in the ministry. Many newspapers acted as if both the North ministry and the "contest for independency" were already over, whether or not the Commons understood that to be the case. Broadsides appeared that attacked the war and both Parliament and the monarch were awash in antiwar petitions and remonstrances. The first really serious threat to North's government came when Sir James Lowther, a former supporter who had come to see that the war "has proved ineffectual," introduced a resolution in the Commons in mid-December which stated that "all further attempts to reduce the revolted colonies to obedience are contrary to the true interests of this kingdom." In the acrimonious debate that followed, North responded that the motion was "the height of impolicy," as it informed the enemy of our "future plan." Without quite saying so, he was asking for time so that his diplomacy might play out. North won again, but this time his majority slipped to only thirty-nine votes."9

In the meantime, George III moved to take some of the heat off North's ministry. At his instigation, Clinton was recalled and General Carleton, whom Germain hated, was named commander of Britain's forces in North America. It was expected that this would be too much for the American secretary to swallow, and it was. After the king elevated him to the peerage as Viscount Sackville, Germain resigned.¹⁰ The most visible, and most hated, champion of the war against America was gone from the cabinet. While that played out, North, through David Hartley—an old friend of Franklin who had been introducing antiwar resolutions in Parliament since 1775—set out to play divide and conquer. For this, Hartley did not mind being used. He wrote Franklin, one of America's commissioners for peace, during the first week of 1782. Hartley began by saying that as a result of Yorktown, it seemed "a very fair opening" for exploring whether "America was disposed to enter into a separate [peace] treaty with Great Britain." Otherwise, he told Franklin, the war would go indefinitely, as Britain would fight "to the last man, and the last shilling, rather than be dictated to by France." But North, he added in the customary cloaked language of diplomacy, was ready for an immediate "*general . . . negociation towards peace, under liberal constructions.*" Hartley appeared to be saying that although the recognition of American independence would be "a bitter trial of humility" for England, North's government would take that step under the proper set of circumstances.¹¹

Within a fortnight, North had his answer from Paris. Franklin responded that gaining immediate peace through the betrayal of its ally would be a poor choice. No American patriot, he said, could abide "deserting a noble and generous Friend for the sake of [peace] with an unjust and cruel Enemy." Though he did not divulge it at the time, Franklin knew that "Lord North had an Emissary here . . . to make [the French] very advantageous Propositions, in case they would abandon us."¹² North's envoy had offered to let France keep what it had won in the Caribbean, while Britain relinquished its rights in Dunkirk and offered concessions in India. Franklin shared with Vergennes what North was up to and the French foreign minister reciprocated. The allies hung together, Vergennes telling London's envoy that France would parley only if Britain was "disposed to treat on equal terms with the allies of France."[13] Franklin's choice was never in doubt. He knew that the United States would require French friendship in the dangerous postwar period. Like Vergennes, he also knew that the allies held the upper hand so long as they remained tied to one another. As Franklin put it to Hartley a bit later, if London "do not chuse" to pursue peace, it must be that "they doubtless flatter themselves that War may still produce success . . . that have hitherto been witheld."[14]

North had Franklin's response by the time Parliament reassembled from its holiday break on January 21. His diplomatic effort at finding a way to gain something from this war had failed. Friends said that he was "in very low spirits," as it was now brutally apparent that his time as prime minister was short. The Opposition had used the six weeks since word of Yorktown burst on London to organize. Bent on bringing down the government, it tested its strength with a peripheral parry to censure Sandwich for the navy's failures. Its foray was beaten back, but it was clear that North's majority had dwindled further. Emboldened, the Opposition made six separate attempts to censure North's government. Each failed, but with each vote the government's majority dwindled.[15]

On February 22—Washington's birthday, though the day was chosen by accident—the opposition shifted gears, introducing a motion condemning the war rather than calling for an end to North's government. Henry Seymour Conway, a former soldier and secretary of state, moved "that the war on the continent of North America may no longer be pursued." After a lengthy debate, the motion failed by a single vote.[16]

That same week North proposed new taxes, some to pay for the war. Inevitably, the discussion turned back to the wisdom of continuing hostilities. Five days after the defeat of his earlier motion, Conway, who prayed that "this mad war" would stop, moved an address to the monarch stating that

> this House will consider as enemies to his Majesty and this country, all those who shall endeavor . . . the farther prosecution of the offensive war on the continent of North America, for the purpose of reducing the revolted colonies to obedience by force.[17]

North was on his feet quickly, but he radiated defeat. He wanted peace, he said, adding that "all parties looked to" end the war. The end could come in one of two ways, he went on. The Commons had to choose between an immediate withdrawal from America and a negotiated peace. Britain's national interest, he thought, would best be served by the second choice. Passing this motion would undercut that option. But time had run out on North. A majority now wanted to end the war in America, and if there were to be negotiations to bring about peace, the majority preferred that another government conduct them. North's majority, which had held since 1770, vanished as a paltry winter sun hung over London on the last day of February 1782. Conway's motion carried by nineteen votes.[18]

North immediately wrote the monarch offering to resign, as he had often done before during the darkest moments of Britain's travail with America. George III declined the offer, but he quietly began to consider a new government, though he held back to see if some of the independents in the Commons who had turned against the American war, came back to support the North government on other issues. They did not. The end for North came on March 20, as the opposition prepared to call for a vote of confidence that seemed certain to carry. North, who wished to avoid being "forever stigmatized" for having been voted out of office, headed off such a fate by first meeting privately with the monarch and resigning, then taking the floor in the House of Commons and announcing: "His Majesty's ministers [are] no more."[19] In no time the virulent rumor swirled about London that despite all North had done, "the King parted with him rudely without thanking him."[20]

The king had vowed not to put together a ministry from among those who had brought down North, but necessity forced his hand. In the end he chose the Marquis of Rockingham, who had urged conciliation toward the colonies since the first weeks of the war, and who had long favored making peace, to head the new government. The Earl of Shelburne was named secretary of state with responsibility for the colonies, the office of American secretary having been abolished. Although a foe of the taxes that had brought on the troubles with the colonies, he nevertheless had steadfastly opposed American independence. He would be responsible for whatever negotiations with the Americans took place.[21]

MANY MIXED SIGNALS were sent by the selection of the new cabinet, sowing perplexity among American observers. Some thought Britain would attempt to negotiate separately with each of the thirteen states. Others believed that London would resume the war full bore after a half-hearted "campaign of negociation." Many believed that Shelburne's appointment—he was described as a master of "Duplicity (or even Triplicity")—signaled that London had no idea of negotiating seriously and no intention of recognizing American independence.[22] But two of America's peace commissioners, Adams and Franklin, saw things differently, and with greater clarity. Adams believed that Shelburne was a thoughtful and reasonable man, and he thought the actions of the Commons in terminating the war in America left him with no choice but to make peace.[23] With what he called the "unclean Spirits . . . cast out" of the government, Franklin, too, believed that peace was on the horizon, but he advised caution: "We cannot be safe while they keep Armies in our Country."[24]

24

"MAY WE HAVE PEACE IN OUR TIME": PEACE AND DEMOBILIZATION, 1782–1783

THOUGH no one could be certain, most thought Yorktown was so decisive that it would lead to peace negotiations. Even so, some 14,000 redcoats still occupied New York and another 10,000 were divided between Charleston, Wilmington, and Savannah. Until peace was made, defenses had to be maintained and opportunities exploited. Washington, for instance, would have liked to follow Yorktown with a siege of Charleston—its seizure "wd infallibly terminate the war at one Stroke," he said—but de Grasse sailed away at the end of October. Left in limbo, Washington emphasized that by standing on a "most respectable Footing . . . for War," the United States could avoid "disgracefull Disasters" and, simultaneously push London toward the peace table. Washington's only concrete move immediately after Yorktown was to order Lafayette, with two thousand men, to join with Greene in South Carolina, but that was frustrated when the young Frenchman requested leave to return home.[1] It was a portent that this war was truly winding down.

Washington quickly fell in step with the more relaxed climate that followed Cornwallis's defeat. Already beginning to look toward his personal affairs in the postwar world, he returned to Mount Vernon after Yorktown, where he spent several days tending his business interests. When at last he rode north his destination was not one of the several sites where the Continental army had entered winter quarters, but Philadelphia, where he remained for several weeks. He did not rejoin his army until March, nearly five months after it had departed Yorktown.[2]

During 1782 it became clear that the British had no intention of actively pursuing the war in the American theater. The House of Commons resolution on the American war had made that apparent, and at the beginning of the year Wilmington was abandoned. The evacuation of Savannah followed in the summer and the redcoats sailed from Charleston just before Christmas. When the British army left those sites, they took with them Loyalists and former slaves, at least nine thousand "unhappy men and their families, white and black," as one official put it.[3] Bitter fighting continued in the South that year, though Britain's regulars were seldom part of it. While vastly superior forces of redcoats were "closely pent up" in Savannah and Charleston by rebel "ragamuffins," a disgusted Loyalist asserted, the last remnants of Tories in Georgia and South Carolina were mopped up in countless bloody, small-scale operations.[4] General Wayne also successfully crushed an uprising among the pro-British Creek Indians in Georgia. The principal actions waged by the regulars occurred during forage operations around Charleston, as they continued to be harassed by the rebels. Young Colonel Laurens died late in August in one of those numerous engagements. Many men never liked serving under him, regarding him as what they called "a widow maker," an officer who took unnecessary risks. That trait cost Laurens his life. Although outnumbered by nearly five to one, Laurens attacked a British foraging party near the Cambahee River west of Charleston. Laurens died in the initial volley and twenty-three other Americans were also killed and wounded in the firefight that need not have occurred. One of his shaken fellow officers said later that Laurens had hoped "to gain a laurel for his brow previous to a cessation of arms." He "wanted to do all himself, and have all the honor," he added.[5]

The worst news for America came from a far away theater of the war. It involved de Grasse, who early in the year had put to sea again to help France's other ally, Spain, which had set its sights on Jamaica. The threat to Jamaica set off the last great struggle in North's cabinet, waged during Germain's final weeks as American secretary. He fought to strip away ships earmarked for operations in the Indian Ocean and utilize them in bottling up a French squadron being readied in Brest to reinforce de Grasse. Germain won the clash and his strategy succeeded. A British fleet under Rodney sailed for the Caribbean in the first week of 1782, finally finding de Grasse off Martinique about fifteen weeks later. Rodney, with considerable superiority both in ships and guns—he had thirty-six ships of the line, de Grass thirty, the first time in this war that a British admiral possessed such superior firepower when confronted by a main enemy fleet—hurried to do battle. At the end of the Battle of the Saints, the French had lost five ships—within the week they lost three others—and de Grasse was a prisoner of the British. The allies abandoned their planned operation against Jamaica, and before long the new British government was contemplating offensive operations in the West Indies.[6]

On receiving the news of de Grasse's defeat, Washington's immediate reaction was that "no Man . . . can foretell all the consequences" of the "disastrous event." It could play out many ways. Britain's victory could be to America's advantage if it persuaded France and Spain to terminate the war, clearing the way for the Franco-American allies to jointly conclude peace with London. But it could lead Britain to spurn all peace overtures and fight on in the hope of gaining additional spoils. Washington correctly guessed that the Battle of the Saints meant that no French fleet would be coming to North America in 1782, but he erroneously predicted that Britain would keep its army in the South and abandon its "mode of defensive War" by attempting some bold initiative.[7]

While trying to digest the meaning of de Grasse's defeat, Washington learned of the failure of still another Franco-Spanish attempt to retake Gibraltar. In September 1782 the allies collected nearly four hundred pieces of artillery—four times the number available to Rochambeau and Washington at Yorktown—and attacked the installation. Their assault failed, and the allies returned to their ongoing siege operation. It also proved hopeless. In October a storm scattered the allied fleet, enabling a royal squadron under Admiral Howe to slip in with essential supplies. When Washington learned what had occurred, he was again perplexed as to whether it "will tend to hasten or retard a general Pacification."[8]

Throughout 1782 Washington confessed that he was "totally in the Dark" respecting the enemy's intentions and what actions the allies should take. At the outset of the year, and especially after he read the king's November 1781 speech to Parliament, Washington remained convinced that Britain would continue to fight, Yorktown notwithstanding. In July he sat down with Rochambeau in Philadelphia, their first meeting since Yorktown, to discuss what they should do that year. Washington proposed a campaign to take Canada, a step he had once bitterly assailed. (Jettisoning his earlier concerns about a French presence in the region in the postwar era, Washington privately had told his generals that the conquest of Canada would subjugate the Indians, bring wealth through the fur trade, and head off "British . . . intrieguing after Peace.") France stood to gain nothing from a Canadian venture and, as Rochambeau observed, it could "recoil upon ourselves, and terminate in disgrace, perhaps in ruin." With a foray into Canada off the table, there was little else that could be done. Without the French navy, trying to take New York—or Charleston, prior to the British withdrawal late in the year—was out of the question.[9]

Washington could not shake the notion that the "haughty Pride of the [British] Nation" would keep it at war. He was even more certain that this was the case when Rockingham died in the summer of 1782 and Lord Shelburne succeeded him as prime minister. "[N]o man had ever heard him give an assent" to the idea of "American Independency," Washington remarked. Ten months into the year, Washington was still saying that he "never was among the sanguine ones" who expected Yorktown and North's fall to bring on peace. True to his "wild career," Washington added, truculent George III could be expected to continue the war in the vain hope that Britain would gain something from this long conflict. It was an unsettling thought, and all the more disturbing when Washington learned early in the autumn that the French army was leaving the

United States, having been ordered to the Caribbean. In October, Rochambeau's army made one last march in America, to Boston. From there, on a cold and bleak Christmas Eve, the French sailed away, leaving the Americans to themselves for the first time in thirty months. Amidst his gloom, Washington saw a positive side to his ally's departure. Britain, almost surely, would have to detach forces from New York to defend their Caribbean holdings, and that would reduce the likelihood of its taking aggressive steps within the United States. Otherwise, Washington groped to understand what Britain might do, all the while agreeing with what Franklin had told him: Britain was "unable to carry on the War and too proud to make peace."[10]

LORD NORTH had initiated the peace process in January with his diplomatic overtures, although real negotiations began in April. During the third week in March Franklin had written Shelburne, an old acquaintance, to express his hope that North's fall would "produce a general Peace." Shelburne responded immediately by sending Richard Oswald, a Scotsman, to Paris to meet with Franklin, setting in motion discussions in which each man initially probed to see what the other was willing to concede. While it may not have been readily apparent to Franklin, Shelburne was willing to recognize American independence, though his primary goal was a close postwar relationship with America, either through some arrangement in which the American provinces remained colonies within the empire or through an all-inclusive treaty with the United States, a pact that would be the first step toward a renewal of Anglo-American economic ties. From what Franklin made clear to Oswald, Shelburne soon enough knew that only the second option was viable.[11]

Although Franklin single-handedly conducted the talks with Oswald from April through July, he was not America's only peace commissioner. He was simply the only one in Paris. John Adams, who was at The Hague negotiating a commercial treaty with Holland, preferred to focus on that important task until the talks in Paris grew serious. John Jay, America's envoy to Madrid, hurried to Paris when he learned that talks were beginning, but he had no more than arrived late in June when he fell seriously ill, leaving him unable to participate before August. Henry Laurens had been captured in September 1780 while crossing the Atlantic. Confined to the Tower of London for more than a year, Laurens was released and permitted to leave England only when Oswald was dispatched to Paris, but his health was so poor that he did not play a substantive role in the negotiations. Jefferson, the fifth commissioner, never left the United States.

To Washington, three thousand miles away, it seemed that the peace talks were going nowhere. In reality, they moved along rapidly, in some measure because of the cordial relationship that developed between Franklin and Oswald. The two had much in common. They were the same age and both had extensive backgrounds in business, Oswald having been a merchant who was active in the slave trade and had furnished supplies to Britain's military in America. Like his counterpart, Oswald owned considerable property in America and had relatives living there. While Franklin and Oswald hit it off, what was even more important was that Shelburne and Vergennes were ready for peace. Shelburne saw that meeting America's terms might make the French more malleable, as it would confront Vergennes with the possibility that his ally might accept independence and quit the war, leaving France to fight on alone. As for Vergennes, after the Battle of the Saints and the latest disappointment at Gibraltar, he was convinced that nothing more could be gained from this war. A recent alliance between Austria and Russia also threatened French interests in eastern Europe, leaving him anxious to wrap up the American war and turn his attention to hot spots on the Continent.

Such progress was made in the talks that, in September, Jay wrote Adams to "come soon—very soon," a signal that the climactic stage of negotiations was about to begin. By the last week in October, when Adams joined his colleagues, agreement had already been reached on several crucial points. The great breakthrough had come in September. From the outset, Franklin and Jay had ignored Congress's infamous order of June 1781 directing them to conduct negotiations according to the "advice and opinion" of France. The two commissioners kept the French informed, but proceeded on their own. In September, with Franklin suffering from a kidney stone and temporarily unable to participate, Jay went even further. He informed Shelburne that America was ready to make a separate peace—a violation of the Franco-American alliance—in return for London's recognition of American independence and other meaningful concessions. Britain yielded immediately. Oswald was permitted to acknowledge American independence. The biggest obstacle to a final deal had been removed.[12]

With Adams on board, the final negotiations played out over the course of a month. Adams insisted on renegotiating some points concerning New England, but the principal sticking point that remained involved the Loyalists. Britain demanded that the United States compensate them for their economic losses. Jay and Adams were agreeable, but Franklin, whose son William had suffered terribly for his Loyalist convictions, was perplexingly intransigent. The British eventually capitulated on this point, clearing the way for finalizing the Preliminary Terms of Peace (preliminary because the accord was to go into effect only if Britain and France, in their separate negotiations, came to terms).

The Anglo-American negotiations concluded on November 29. The next afternoon, under gloomy gray clouds that pelted Paris with a wet snow, the Americans met at Jay's lodging and rode together to Oswald's apartment in the Grand Hotel Muscovite to sign the treaty. The signing took place without pomp or ritual. No crowds gathered to cheer the diplomats, no journalists were present to record the event, no artist was invited to render the historic moment on canvas. As if the war had witnessed sufficient ceremony, the five envoys quietly read over the document, which had been put into final form overnight by their respective aides, and without fanfare each signed. It was over within minutes. When it was done, the diplomats and their staffs rode to Franklin's residence in Passy, a suburb of Paris, where they enjoyed a convivial dinner. That evening Franklin rode to Versailles and broke the news to the disgruntled French foreign minister that the United States had concluded a separate peace with Great Britain. Afterward, with incredible chutzpah, he asked for yet another loan for the United States, which amazingly was granted. Adams, meanwhile, relaxed at his hotel and tried to digest the meaning of the great events of which he had so often played a significant role. He thought it a "mighty Tragedy" that the Anglo-American differences had not been settled peacefully before Lexington-Concord, but breathed a sigh of relief that the war had been won, acknowledging that when campaign 1781 began all hope of victory had "hung upon a Thread." Yet with this magnificent treaty, Adams was certain that the bloodshed and sacrifice brought on by the American Revolution had been worthwhile, for the treaty confirmed that the war "has unraveled itself happily for Us."[13]

It was an extraordinary treaty for the United States, so good that the infant nation realized even more than Congress had stipulated in its peace ultimata of early 1779. American independence was recognized and the territories that Congress wished—the trans-Appalachian West to the Mississippi River and the prospect of a satisfactory southern boundary—were attained. South Carolina and Georgia, whose fate had been very much in doubt through 1780 and 1781, were to be part of the United States. The American republic was to enjoy the right of navigation on the Mississippi River and it was to "continue to enjoy unmolested the Right" to the fisheries, a provision that Congress had not included in its wish list. Britain was to withdraw its troops from U.S. soil. It also agreed not to carry away "any Negroes or other Property of the American Inhabitants." The pact called for the exchange of all prisoners of war, the only clause in the accord that had required no negotiation. With regard to the Loyalists, the treaty said that Congress was to "earnestly recommend" that the states "provide for the Restitution of all Estates, Rights, & Properties which have been confiscated." Both sides knew this clause was meaningless. Congress would make the recommendation, but no state would comply. Because of Carleton's valiant defense of Quebec in 1775–1776, and as the United States never again tried to take the region, Britain kept Canada. Otherwise, all that London achieved from seven terrible years of war was a clause requiring that Americans honor their prewar debts to British citizens and another that forbade future persecution of the Loyalists.

To THE VERY END, Washington remained skeptical that peace was at hand, and in the depths of his heart he continued to expect that Parliament would "provide vigorously for the prosecution of the war." Spring was breaking over the land in 1783 when Washington learned that he had been wrong, and he further discovered that France and Spain in January had also come to terms with Great Britain. (Spain reacquired Florida and Minorca, but not Gibraltar, while France obtained Tobago, two fishing islands, and Senegal, as well as improved fishing rights off Newfoundland.) Hostilities were over. At last, Washington radiated happiness. The news, fittingly brought across the Atlantic by a French frigate named *Triumph*, filled the American commander with "inexpressible satisfaction." This "happy Event," he added, "diffused a General Joy thro' every Class of People and to none more than to the Army."[14] The news unleashed a tumult of celebration across the land and an expectant hope, as a congressman put it, that with the "Jarring and discordant Nations once more brought to shake hands" it would mean "peace in our time." Most congressmen breathed sighs of relief at their deliverance and one gloated at America's promising future, noting that "the Sun riases bright in this our Western world."[15]

The exultation among American officials was more than justified. All thirteen states were free of Great Britain. The United States had come through the war and, given the large domain now under its jurisdiction, its chances of surviving in the face of hostile superpowers were excellent. The United States was the great winner in this war. France was on the winning side, but it had achieved little in the war. It had seen to the weakening of Great Britain by helping to strip it of its American colonies, but the British were hardly eviscerated. Arguably, French power on the Continent was no greater after the war than it had been before hostilities. France's exiguous gains were a ghostly foretaste of the calamities to come for those who ruled the nation. The warpath taken by the Ancient Regime led unswervingly to its destruction. The war plunged France deeper into an inextricable debt that became the mainspring for unleashing the French Revolution before the decade of the 1780s closed, a violent upheaval that devoured thousands, including Louis XVI and Comte d'Estaing, both of whom died on the guillotine in the blood-soaked streets of Paris. Although Spain had failed to obtain its big prize, Gibraltar, it had done surprisingly well with regard to territorial acquisitions. But much of its American empire was nestled on the doorstep of the potentially mighty United States. Had the American Revolution never occurred, France and Spain might have joined hands to prevent, or at least to slow, the further expansion of Anglo-America. After 1783, however, the Spanish were left without a European ally that was willing to risk much to help them retain their New World possessions. Before the next century was a quarter old, and the children who had been born during the era of the American Revolution had grown to middle age, Spain had lost everything in North America that it had gained through the War of Independence, and far more.

Britain was a loser in this war, but the greater losers were the Loyalists and the Native Americans. Tories lost their homes, livelihoods, and in some instances the exalted power they had possessed in prewar America. Up to 80,000 Loyalists fled into exile, almost all to lives of diminished circumstances, and to places where they were utterly detached from the placid world they had known and loved before the war.[16] Likewise, the Indians gained nothing but heartbreak from the war, even suffering the indignity of having an ally that dishonorably betrayed them at the peace table. When Britain ceded all lands to the Mississippi River to the United States, it gave away the territories that the Indians had inhabited for centuries, including what remained of Iroquoia in the Mohawk Valley. At war's end, Joseph Brant dwelled in Canada and a within a few years of the peace the British gave his people land in Ontario. In the fifty years that followed the Treaty of Paris, the United States would destroy, subjugate, or banish, all Indian tribes that dwelled within the territories it had won in the War of Independence.

For the overwhelming majority of the 500,000 African American slaves living in the colonies in 1775, the war may as well have been fought on the moon for all the impact it had on their lives. Some five thousand blacks served in the Continental army. Most were probably slaves when the war erupted and they were liberated at war's end. It has been estimated that approximately 20,000 slaves owned by Revolutionaries fled to the British during the war. Disease claimed many and not a few were recaptured by their owners, but up to 10,000 lived to the end of the war, gaining their freedom and leaving America with the British sometime in 1783.[17]

ON APRIL 9, 1783, Washington issued the orders that he had long hungered to give: "all Acts of Hostility" were to be immediately suspended.[18] By prior arrangement, General Carleton issued a similar order that same day. The war was over, though the army could not disband until all prisoners of war were exchanged and the British army had departed. More than seven long months elapsed before those ends were realized. Washington spent much of that period at the army's cantonment at Newburgh, on the Hudson above New York, living and working in a two-story stone farmhouse that sat atop a leafy, green knoll overlooking the river.

Much of his time was devoted to the final prisoner exchanges. Negotiations concerning prisoners had taken place throughout much of the war with little to show for it. Even when a formula for swapping captives was agreed to in 1780— after eighteen months of on-again, off-again discussions—it was not immediately put into practice. Under the ratio that was established a lieutenant general was to be exchanged for 1,044 privates or corporals, and so on, with one British officer or soldier to be exchanged for rebel corporals and privates according to the following formula:

Major General		372
Brigadier General	—	200
Colonel	—	100
Lt. Colonel	—	72
Major	—	28
Captain	—	16
1st Lieutenant	—	8
Regimental Surgeon	—	6
2d Lieutenant and Ensign	—	4
Sergeant	—	2
Corporals and Privates	—	1

Various combinations were of course possible. A colonel could be swapped for a lieutenant colonel and a major. Yet despite the existence of this blueprint, few prisoners were released before 1782. The roadblock remained the same as earlier in the war: a reluctance on the part of the Americans to exchange prisoners, as the liberated British soldiers would return to their army, whereas most freed Americans, their terms of service having expired, would probably go home. Yorktown ushered in change. During the ensuing months Parliament bestowed the status of prisoner of war on all rebel captives, and in the summer of 1782, without asking for a swap, Britain set free those captives languishing in Forton and Mill prisons in England. Though at the time the peace treaty lay months down the road, London's gesture sent a strong signal that the war was really over, and thereafter prisoner exchanges occurred more frequently. By the time that Washington and Carleton suspended hostilities in the spring of 1783, the United States still held some 4,500 prisoners. During the next couple of months those last remaining captives were exchanged or released, enabling Washington to announce in July 1783 that the United States no longer held any prisoners.[19]

While the number of captives shrank in 1783, the ranks of the Continental army also diminished. There had been nearly 17,000 Continentals at the time of Yorktown, a number that dwindled only slightly before June 1782, when the army was reduced by a third. In the year that followed the army's rolls remained relatively stable at about 11,000 men, but during that year the nation's fiscal woes necessitated painful decisions.[20] Two years had passed since the Articles of Confederation had been ratified and the nation's economic crisis had not abated. With peace on the horizon, many worried that the United States would be unable to repay the staggering foreign debt that it had accumulated since 1777. Domestic creditors were anxious that the states and national government might not have the capability to remunerate them for goods and services they had provided to the army. Others were alarmed about the security of the postwar United States in a world of dangerous superpowers. Some fretted that the United States lacked the power to open the recently won West. Still others, angry at the long national humiliation of soldiers without shoes or pay and a nearly fatally enervated army, swore to never again tolerate such indignities. But the national government required a revenue to resolve these problems, and for that it had to be vested with the power to tax. In 1781 Congress had proposed amending the Articles of Confederation to give Congress authority to levy an impost—a tax on imports—but the amendment fell just short of the unanimity required for ratification. The proponents of national taxation powers mounted another campaign early in 1783, but when it became clear that Congress was unlikely to adopt another impost amendment, some disgruntled champions of strengthening the hand of the national government joined in a conspiracy with a few dissatisfied army officers.

The disaffection among the army's officers arose over the pension issue. Congress had earlier agreed to a lifetime half-pay pension for the officers, but, in 1783, with the states verging on bankruptcy and the national government impotent, it appeared unlikely that the officers' retirement benefits would materialize. If they were to attain anything, some thought, immediate action was necessary while they still possessed some leverage with Congress. Scheming officers and artful congressmen became political bedfellows. There can be little doubt that Hamilton, now a congressman, and General Knox and Benjamin Lincoln, now the secretary of war, were among the plotters, but others were involved in the shadowy business as well. The intrigue, which likely had a full head of steam by January, flowered in March, about two weeks before the *Triumph* arrived with word that the war was over. It is known to history as the Newburgh Conspiracy, as the conniving officers were posted in that Hudson River cantonment. The scheme that the conspirators hatched called for the officers to first agree to accept the commutation of the lifetime half pay to a full-pay pension for a period of five years, after which they were to issue a dire threat: if their modified pension was not funded, the army would disband should the war continue and it would refuse to demobilize should peace come. What they were threatening could not have been more menacing. On one hand, the United States might be deprived of an army while thousands of British troops remained in North America. On the other hand, the army might seize civil authority, anni-hilating the dream of republicanism and establishing tyranny. The plotters hoped that their bullying threat would stampede Congress into passing the impost amendment and sending it to the states for ratification.

Behind the curtain, Hamilton withheld a key part of the scheme from at least some of his fellow conspirators. He tipped off Washington to what was coming. At the appropriate moment, Hamilton advised, Washington could thwart the vile plan to misuse the army, winning even greater accolades from an adoring public for having preserved order, prevented despotism, and perhaps saved the infant Republic. A shaken Congress, having been saved by Washington from a lawless army that was seemingly about to either throw away victory or to act despotically, would take the steps to strengthen the national government. Forewarned, Washington might have acted to frustrate the officers' plot before it came to fruition. Instead, he followed Hamilton's script, acting only after their threats had been made public in a menacing ultimatum known as the Newburgh Address and the entire officer corps at Newburgh had been summoned to meet and endorse the declaration.

At noon on March 15, a clear, cold Saturday, the officers gathered in the Temple of Honor in the encampment at Newburgh. Just as the meeting was being called to order, Washington burst through a side door and took the podium and launched into a prepared speech denouncing the address. His speech bombed. Not only was Washington not an orator of note, his carefully crafted remarks—a collection of circumspect platitudes—swayed no one. But if Washington was wanting as a public speaker, he was without peer as an actor. Intuitively sensing that his speech was failing, he shifted gears. Abandoning his text, he told the assemblage that he wished to read a relevant letter that he had received. An air of breathless anticipation gripped the hall. What could the letter say? Washington unfolded the missive very slowly, allowing the tension to build. The letter, it turned out, was meaningless, a mere prop. As he began to read, he stumbled over the first line or two. He paused again, this time to retrieve something else from his coat pocket. It was a pair of spectacles. The officers were astounded. None but those at headquarters had ever seen their hardy commander in chief wearing glasses. With great care and deliberation he removed the glasses from their case and he as was about to don them, he looked up apologetically toward his officers and said in a low tone: "Gentlemen, you will permit me to put on my spectacles, for I have not only grown gray but almost blind in the service of my country." It was great theater, and it worked. The mood in the Temple of Honor shifted immediately. Many officers, tough men who had been made even tougher by the harsh demands of war, broke down and wept openly. The Newburgh Address was cast aside once Washington left the hall. The threat of a dictatorial standing army was no more. As foreseen by Hamilton, one of the most daring, cunning, and devious figures who ever played on the American political stage, a relieved Congress voted for commutation, threw in three months back pay for the soldiery, and adopted the impost amendment.[21]

Three weeks after his theatrics in the temple, Washington issued his end-to-hostilities order, eliminating the need for a large army. In June, Washington furloughed most of the men, sending them home with the three months pay that Congress had allocated. Called "final settlement certificates," the notes constituted partial back pay for years' worth of wages that the men had never received. It was the last dime that Congress—which would be compensating the officers for the next five years—intended to pay the enlisted men who had honorably served their nation, often for a long stretch of years. It was a despicable end to what for many had been a hard and austere life of soldiering. The tawdriness of Congress's action was compounded by the fact that the certificates, as the soldiers discovered en route home, were next to worthless. Some men, like mendicants, had to sponge off benevolent civilians to pay for their long trek home. Joseph Plumb Martin, the Connecticut private who had borne arms since 1776, and had received only one month's pay between 1777 and June 1783, sold his settlement certificates to a speculator and worked for weeks on a New York farm to find the money to cover the expense of his journey home.[22] A "very great number," according to one soldier, hurried to the windswept docks in New York City in the hope of getting a manual labor job helping out the British army.[23]

Once the furloughed men departed, the army shrank to about 2,500 men, and likely continued to dwindle as the summer waned.[24] There now was little to do but wait for the British army to depart. Washington spent a portion of the time making a 750-mile trip through upstate New York, vacationing and searching for land to purchase. Fittingly, some might say, he acquired a lush tract in the Mohawk Valley.[25] In August, he moved his headquarters to Princeton, where Congress was meeting. The officers who remained at Newburgh created the

Society of Cincinnati, an elite fraternity whose membership was restricted to Continental army officers and their descendants. Washington would eventually become its head, but many, including Jefferson and John and Samuel Adams, were aghast, viewing the society as a backdoor attempt to create a hereditary nobility in America.[26]

The British army remained in New York until it received word of the signing of the definitive peace treaty, the comprehensive accord that had to await agreements between Britain and all its enemies. That treaty, the Treaty of Paris of 1783, signed on September 3, did not alter the preliminary articles that the American commissioners had negotiated. Word of the treaty reached Washington in Princeton early in November. Shortly thereafter General Carleton notified him that the British would leave York Island, as he called it, on November 23. Washington hurried to West Point to take care of the last remaining business facing the army. (His final order from that post discharged all soldiers with at least three years service.) On November 20 he and his skeleton army of a few hundred mostly New York and Massachusetts men, set off on their last march. The soldiers came down the Hudson, across the brown and barren landscape, passing where the Franco-American armies had stayed in 1781 as they prepared to besiege the city, and on past Pell's Point, where Glover's Marblehead men had resisted the British landing seven autumns before, and where brave Captain Eveyln had been mortally wounded. Here and there the little army was joined by additional Continentals, men who had been posted on New York's periphery. In time, this swelling band—it would eventually grow to some eight hundred men—crossed King's Bridge onto Manhattan, where no free Continental soldier had set foot since November 1776. The march continued though the wooded countryside, skirting forests with leafless trees and dark houses that had stood empty since early in the war. The men passed Fort Washington, where folly and vacillation had prevailed, and into rolling Harlem Heights, where Washington had once dreamt in vain of a second Bunker Hill.

There the men stopped and waited. The British army was running behind schedule in its plans to evacuate the city. November 23 passed. Then another day. At last, forty-eight hours late—what could have been a more fitting way for Britain's army to end its stay in the United States—the last German and British soldiers marched toward the troop transports in New York harbor. It was the morning of November 25, a clear and crisp autumn day with a sharp breeze from the northwest that stung the men's ears and made their eyes water. A messenger brought word to Washington that the British were on the move. He in turn moved his army to the very edge of the city, where the men sat and waited until noon, when word came that the last redcoats were either on board or in a small boat and rowing out to the transports. Just in the forenoon, with much creaking and groaning, the giant vessels began to pull away. On board and leaving America forever were some 20,000 British soldiers—including 5,818 white and black men who had borne arms in provincial units—and thousands of civilians.[27] When the voyage of the huge British fleet commenced, the Continental army resumed its march, coming down the Boston Road and into New York City under the flawless blue sky. With drums beating and fifes playing, with banners unfurled and horses prancing, the army marched down Manhattan's east side. Knox, with a select corps, rode at the head of the army. Officers, eight abreast, followed on horseback. Behind them, walking eight abreast, were civilian dignitaries. General Washington and Governor Clinton followed, leading the remainder of the army through streets lined with thousands of residents.[28] Some spectators were sullen and quiet Tories, come to see the army that had vanquished the British. Most were patriots—or people who now styled themselves supporters of the American Revolution—and they cheered the ragged soldiers and their leader, immaculate in his buff and blue uniform. On and on the army marched toward the lower end of the island, down Pearl Street, then west on Wall Street, and ultimately to Cape's Tavern on Broadway, where the commander in chief alighted from his great horse and entered the inn to enjoy the first of a week-long spree of dinners and ceremonies.[29]

THE WAR WAS TRULY OVER. It had lasted well over eight years, 104 blood-drenched months to be exact. As is often the habit of wars, it had gone on far longer than its architects of either side had foreseen in 1775. More than 100,000 American men had borne arms in the Continental army. Countless thousands more had seen active service in militia units, some for only a few days, some for a few weeks, some repeatedly, if their outfit was called to duty time and again.

The war exacted a ghastly toll. The estimate accepted by most scholars is that 25,000 American soldiers perished, although nearly all historians regard that figure as too low. Not only were the casualty figures reported by American leaders, like those set forth by British generals, almost always inaccurately low, but one is left to guess the fate of the 9,871 men—once again, likely a figure that is wanting—who were listed as wounded or missing in action.[30] No one can know with precision the number of militiamen who were lost in the war, as record keeping in militia units was neither as good as that in the Continental army nor as likely to survive. While something of a handle may be had on the number of soldiers that died in battle, or of camp disease, or while in captivity, the totals for those who died from other causes can only be a matter of conjecture. In all wars, things happen. In this war, men were struck by lightning or hit by falling trees in storms. Men were crushed beneath heavy wagons and field pieces that overturned. Men accidentally shot themselves and their comrades. Men were killed in falls from horses and drowned while crossing rivers. Sailors fell from the rigging and slipped overboard. As in every war, some soldiers and sailors committed suicide. If it is assumed that 30,000 Americans died while bearing arms—and that is a very conservative estimate—then about one man in sixteen of military age died during the Revolutionary War. In contrast, one man in ten of military age died in the Civil War and one American male in seventy-five in World War II. Of those who served in the Continental army, one in four died during the war. In the Civil War, one regular in five died and in World War II one in forty American servicemen perished.

Unlike subsequent wars when numerous soldiers came home with disabilities, relatively few impaired veterans lived in post-Revolutionary America. Those who were seriously wounded in the War of Independence seldom came home. They died, usually of shock, blood loss, or infection. Some survived, of course, and for the remainder of their lives coped with a partial, or total, loss of vision, a gimpy leg, a handless or footless extremity, or emotional scars that never healed.

It was not only soldiers that died or were wounded. Civilians perished from diseases that were spread unwittingly by soldiers and not a few on the homefront died violent deaths in the course of coastal raids, Indian attacks, partisan warfare, and siege operations. There is no way to know how many civilians died as a direct result of this war, but it was well into the thousands.

The British also paid a steep price in blood in this war, one that was proportionately equal to the losses among the American forces. The British sent about 42,000 men to North America, of which some 25 percent, or roughly 10,000 men, are believed to have died. About 7,500 Germans, from a total of some 29,000 sent to Canada and the United States, also died in this war in the North American theater. From a paucity of surviving records, casualties among the Loyalists who served with the British army have never been established. However, 21,000 men are believed to have served in those provincial units. The most complete surviving records are those for the New Jersey Volunteers, which suffered a 20 percent death toll. If its death toll, which was below that of regulars and Germans, is typical, some four thousand provincials who fought for Great Britain would have died of all causes. Thus, it seems likely that about 85,000 men served the British in North America in the course of this war, of which approximately 21,000 perished. As was true of American soldiers, the great majority—roughly 65 percent—died of diseases. A bit over 2 percent of men in the British army succumbed to disease annually, while somewhat over 3 percent of German soldiers died each year of disease. Up to eight thousand additional redcoats are believed to have died in the West Indies, and another two thousand may have died in transit to the Caribbean. Through 1780, the Royal Navy reported losses of 1,243 men killed in action and 18,541 to disease. Serious fighting raged on the high seas for another two years, making it likely that well over 50,000 men who bore arms for Great Britain perished in this war.[31]

The French army lost several hundred men during its nearly two years in the United States, mostly to disease, but the French navy suffered losses of nearly 20,000 men in battle, captivity, and from illnesses. Spanish losses pushed the total death toll among those who fought in this war to in excess of 100,000 men.[32]

WASHINGTON WAS ANXIOUS to get home, it now having been more than two years since he had last seen Mount Vernon. It must at times have seemed that New

York would not let him go. He remained for ten days after the British sailed away, looking after the final business of his command, but mostly attending a seemingly endless cycle of dinners and ceremonies. At last, on December 4, he was ready to depart. Only one thing remained. At noon that day Washington hosted a dinner at Fraunces Tavern for the officers. Not many were still with the army. Of seventy-three generals yet on the Continental army rolls, only four were present, and three of those were from New York or planned to live there. Not much should be made of the paltry turnout. Men had been going home since June. Like the enlisted men, the officers were anxious to see their families and put their lives together for the long years that lay ahead. All who attended the dinner knew that the function was less for dining than for saying farewell, and it soon became an emotional meeting. At some level, each man knew that the great epoch of his life was ending. Each knew that he would never again savor the warm pleasures of camaraderie, the pulsating thrill of danger, the rare exhilaration of military victory that had come from serving the infant nation in its quest for independence. Each knew that he was leaving all this for an uncertain future. No man was more moved than Washington, who, if he had planned to give a speech, discarded the idea. He merely asked each man to come forward to say goodbye. With tears steaming down his face, he embraced every man, and they in turn clasped him. Henry Knox grabbed his commander in chief and kissed him.[33] When the last man had bidden him farewell, Washington, too moved to talk, hurried to the door and to his horse that awaited him on the street. He swung into the saddle and sped away for Virginia, and home.

Once off Manhattan Island, Washington traveled the now familiar road to Philadelphia, making most of the journey in a wagon, a concession to middle age that had come upon him in the course of the long war. He stopped in Philadelphia to say goodbye to old friends and, now that he was practically a civilian again, to shop (he purchased a rifle, among other things).[34]

Then he was off to Annapolis, where Congress was meeting. Two items were on his agenda. Soon after arriving, a long month after he had left West Point for Manhattan, Washington submitted his wartime expense account. When he had accepted appointment as commander in chief, he had agreed to serve without a salary, asking only that his expenses be paid. (Congress would eventually rule that Washington had shortchanged himself by one dollar, and it paid him $64,355.30 in paper securities, a windfall, it turned out, once the value of America's currency was reestablished during his presidency.) On his third day in town, Congress gave a dinner for its departing commander, an occasion so formal and stately, said one legislator, that "not a soul got drunk." The following day, December 23, 1783, was Washington's last as commander of the Continental army. At noon he appeared before Congress to resign his commission. Only one man, Thomas Mifflin, who had sat in Congress on the day that Washington was chosen to command the army remained in that body. Striding purposefully and, as always, gracefully, Washington walked before the legislators and slowly read a brief final address. Overcome with emotion, his hand trembled so badly that he could barely see the paper. His voice was so choked that few in the chamber could hear as he said in a low tone that it was fitting that he resign and go home, as the United States had become independent and sovereign, "a respectable nation." When he came to the end of his remarks, he said in a more audible voice: "I retire from the great theater of Action." With that, he drew his commission from his coat pocket and delivered it to Mifflin, now the president of Congress. Washington immediately left the chamber to compose himself, then returned and said goodbye to each man.[35]

While congressmen and spectators wept openly, Washington donned his greatcoat to return to the cold outdoors. Then he was gone.

He rode through the afternoon and most of the following day, one of the last soldiers yet on the road home from this war. At last, as the sun hung red and low in the sky on Christmas Eve, George Washington, private citizen, emerged through the bare trees and onto the path that led to the front door of Mount Vernon. The War of Independence was truly at an end.

25

"LITTLE SHORT OF A MIRACLE": ACCOUNTING FOR AMERICA'S VICTORY

THREE YEARS into the war a scribbler in a London newspaper remarked that any "other General in the world than General Howe would have beaten General Washington, and any other General in the world than General Washington would have beaten General Howe."[1] Study the War of Independence long enough and you might be tempted to bend the wag's observation into the following: any major power other than Great Britain could have suppressed the American rebellion, and any nation other than the United States would have gained victory over Great Britain in a much briefer time.

Contemporaries on both sides of the Atlantic were the first to ponder the mysteries of the war's outcome. In Britain, the tendency was to blame the generals and admirals or to lay responsibility for the defeat either on the king, North, Germain, or Sandwich, or all four. For a great many, including some failed generals and members of the Opposition who had never favored using force against America, it was convenient to argue that the war had been unwinnable and should never have been fought. Americans attributed their near failure to a flawed constitutional structure or self-serving habits that ravaged the republican spirit of sacrifice. That victory was attained, it often was said, was due to the French alliance, the hand of providence, or the magnificent leadership of Washington, but especially the latter. For his part, Washington expressed "astonishment" at the American triumph, calling it "little short of a standing miracle."[2]

How bewildering! Major figures on the losing side concluded that their country could never have won the war while the principal general on the winning side was astonished to have won.

Little is inevitable in history, and even less in warfare. God may be thought to be on the side with the largest battalions, and quite often it works out in that manner, but wars often turn on an untold number of factors, including strategic and tactical decisions, good or bad leadership, the experience of the soldiery, the availability of resources, success in getting supplies when and where they are needed, the conduct of foreign policy, ideological zeal, willpower, and a fair measure of good luck.

DESPITE WHAT NORTH'S GOVERNMENT thought at the outset, Great Britain faced an uphill fight in the War of Independence. In the twentieth century, it became axiomatic in military circles that an imperial state required a numerical superiority on the order of three to one, or greater, to suppress a colonial rebellion. Given America's vast spatial dimensions, Great Britain may have required even more surpassing numbers to have won this war. Britain dramatically expanded its army during the war. When the war erupted the British army totaled 27,000 men. More than 75,000 additional soldiers were raised in subsequent years, and to those numbers were added Germans and provincials, until six years into the war more than 150,000 men were bearing arms for Great Britain. But many of those men were not sent to America, and some who were in North America were sent elsewhere after 1778, so that at the time of Yorktown only 35,000 men were stationed in North America. Proportionately, Britain's forces in North America declined as the war progressed. When the war broke out, a quarter of all British soldiers were in North America. By 1781, a fifth of Britain's soldiers were posted in North America. Between 1776 and 1778 British regulars usually outnumbered those in the Continental army by close to—and often better than—a two-to-one margin, though when a campaign commenced and the American militia was summoned, Britain's numerical advantage declined and sometimes vanished altogether.[3] Britain might have significantly increased its manpower totals in two ways. It might have armed the Loyalists early on, but London dragged its feet on this score until the war was nearly four years old. Had Howe possessed six or eight thousand armed Loyalists in the New York campaign in 1776, or had Burgoyne's army been augmented by considerable numbers of provincial troops the following year, each campaign might have ended differently. Britain might also have done more with African American slaves. When the British could get their hands on slaves owned by Revolutionaries, they set them to work, often in ways designed to further the war effort. But the British ignored calls from some quarters to recruit and arm large numbers of slaves, and in the end only a few hundred African Americans were incorporated into provincial units.[4]

After 1775, Britain's army in North America was spread thin, always divided between Canada and New York, with other sizeable detachments elsewhere, including Rhode Island, the mid-Atlantic states, and the southern theater. The army was also often tied down by what it had taken. When Howe occupied Philadelphia in 1777, John Adams predicted that the city would conquer the

British army. It "will take all their Force to maintain it," he said, adding that they will surely be "cooped up there." He was correct. Charles, First Earl Grey, who soldiered in America for six years, subsequently estimated that 14,000 men were needed to hold New York and upwards of 6,000 to maintain a toehold in Newport, while during the crucial campaign in the Carolinas in 1780–1781, nearly half of the British army in the South was confined to Charleston.[5]

Britain's problems were greatly magnified by France's entry into the war in 1778. The British army had to be scattered even more widely, as it guarded against an invasion of the homeland and was pressed into defending widespread imperial possessions in the Caribbean, India, Africa, and the Mediterranean. The Royal Navy's absolute superiority was instantly jeopardized. A year later, when Spain joined the war, the allies achieved naval superiority. With naval preeminence, the British had come close to scoring a decisive victory in New York in 1776. Without it, they were driven to a nearly fatal wariness, and eventually to cataclysmic defeat at Yorktown. French help was the single most important factor in determining the outcome of the War of Independence. Secret French assistance sustained the drive to declare independence in 1776 and further—and greater—aid from Versailles in 1777 was a key factor in the rebel victory at Saratoga. With the American economy in ruins after 1778, it is inconceivable that the rebels could have waged war for three additional campaigns without a French ally, unless they had shifted almost entirely to guerrilla warfare.

Much has been made of Britain's unswerving devotion to its traditional manner of warfare. The British remained "hidebound by their European background . . . and never improvised sufficiently," wrote one historian (among many). Howe's leadership in particular, it has been said, was characterized by "a timid adherence to accepted practices," including a fixation on taking possession of posts and cities, and fighting few battles in order to keep casualties to a minimum, as it was especially difficult to replace one trained veteran soldier with another.[6] Sometimes the British had little choice but to adhere to convention. Both logistical considerations and the fact that their foe was frequently unassailable dictated how the war was to be waged. To have come after the well-entrenched Continentals in the rugged hills at Morristown or West Point would have been an invitation to disaster. To have chased Washington about the northern backcountry, as Cornwallis pursued Greene across North Carolina, would likely have resulted in the ruinous attrition of British manpower. The British often fought conventionally because it appeared to offer the best hope of success. While the rebels' fabled Fabian warfare has become the stuff of legend, the Americans actually remained amazingly—perhaps injudiciously—faithful to the European manner of war. At Bunker Hill and Dorchester Heights, in New York through 1776, at Saratoga and Brandywine, and at Charleston, Cowpens, Camden, and Guilford Courthouse, American leaders chose (and in each instance it was their choice) to fight a fixed piece European-style engagement. In all of these actions, save at Charleston, the British failed to secure a pivotal victory when presented with a golden opportunity to fight in the manner in which they excelled.

Despite compelling evidence offered by the decade-long colonial protest, including the signs of American unity displayed by the First Continental Congress in 1774, the British for far too long discounted the widespread scope of the rebellion, preferring to believe that disaffection barely existed outside New England. More dangerously, and more absurdly, the British persisted in refusing to take rebel soldiers seriously, blithely dismissing them as callow and craven. They made that mistake at Bunker Hill and, incredibly, five years later they repeated the error at King's Mountain and Cowpens. The British mishandled the Loyalists from start to finish, as well. British officials were too trusting of the Loyalists' counsel, expected too much of them long after their reliability had become questionable, waited too long to arm them, and too often betrayed them by promising protection that proved to be fleeting. Logistical torments added to Britain's woes. The necessity to act within the heart of an uncooperative and largely hostile country left the redcoats unavoidably fettered by a cumbersome supply system. From the early days of the war many believed that a large army that detached itself from supply lines and entered the backcountry would be devastated, and Burgoyne's experience, as well as that of the redcoats in the interior of South Carolina, appeared to confirm the logic of such thinking. Logistical considerations, therefore, moored the redcoats to the coast, or to rivers, in the same fashion that a ship was tethered to the docks. Waging war against a hostile citizenry compelled the British army to rely to a striking degree on provisions sent from overseas. Six years into the war the British were still sending out approximately four hundred ships a year laden with supplies for their military forces in America.[7] Year in and year out many supply ships arrived too late for the summer campaign. Others never arrived, as many fell prey to storms and privateers, or after 1778–1779 to the French and Spanish.

It has been argued that if Britain had acted with greater ruthlessness, especially in the initial phase of the war, the back of the rebellion might have been broken. Early on, many British soldiers urged "harsh, absolute and severe measures," including reducing the countryside to "desolation," trying captives for treason, and even sowing disease within the enemy's ranks.[8] One scholar has maintained that after the rebels rejected the initial offer to surrender at Fort Washington, Howe should perhaps have given the German attackers free reign—which would have been in accordance with the conventional custom of war in that day—to refuse quarter. A bloodbath among the vanquished, he suggested, would have added immeasurably to Washington's difficulties to recruit an army in 1777.[9] In the years that followed many officers insisted, "Nothing will secure these People but Fire & Sword," or asserted that victory could be attained only by "Carry[ing] devastation and terror on the Point of your Sword."[10] But before the unsparing southern war commenced, the British refrained from such pitiless behavior. Some agreed with General Phillips that "when we strike we wound a brother." Some thought terror tactics impolitic, as they would make it more difficult to refashion revolutionaries into loyal British subjects following the colonists' eventual defeat. For some, resorting to terror was simply not the way that war was waged. That apparently was the view of General Clinton. He was mortified by what he saw as the unavoidable necessity to order attacks on civilians in coastal towns. He also refused a Loyalist proposal to infiltrate rebel lines and capture Washington if possible, kill him if need be.[11] Both Howe and Clinton believed, as the latter once put it, that to win the war it was necessary "to gain the hearts and subdue the minds of America."[12] They were convinced that unnecessary brutality would be counterproductive, and the galvanic southern reaction to Tarleton's invidious behavior in the Waxhaws lends credence to that viewpoint.

One of Great Britain's most profound problems was a fatal flaw in the DNA of the British system of governance. Although Germain sought to micromanage British military policy in North American, it was impossible under the best of circumstances for any American secretary who was an ocean away, and weeks removed from the latest news, to adroitly direct the war effort. The situation cried out for the commander in chief in America to be given a freer hand, or for North, on the advice of Clinton, to have appointed a supreme commander of all British forces in North America, and to have given him considerable latitude in making strategy. But with the army drawn in one direction and the navy in another, with the American interest colliding with those in other parts of the empire, and with homeland considerations atop all, a chieftain was needed to ride herd on this toxic mix of weltering causes and concerns, and to fashion a military strategy for a world-wide war. Yet a long winding road had to be traversed before Britain would finally curtail the sweeping authority of individual ministers and vest a prime minister with responsibility for establishing policies that were consistent with the national well-being.

There was rot as well in a structure that permitted professional army officers, such as Amherst, to refuse to serve in America; that enabled a general, such as Burgoyne, to gain a field command through connivance; that facilitated the dismissal of a capable general such as Carleton because of a clash of personalities with a minister; or that allowed officers to rise by purchasing promotions. A military that selected its highest officers on anything but experience and professional competence was markedly defective. So, too, was a structure that tolerated an arrangement in which the same individuals—the Howe brothers—were vested with authority to crush and to conciliate, to find both a military solution and a peaceful solution to Britain's American problem.

Britain also faced several lesser hindrances to success. The British lacked good maps and often found reliable intelligence difficult to come by. British soldiers, unlike their enemy, also reached the war zone only after a lengthy ocean crossing that not infrequently left a large percentage of the voyagers ill and incapacitated for weeks. Widespread sickness among the first Hessians sent to

America forced Howe to delay operations on Long Island for nearly a month in the summer of 1776, which in turn may have wrecked his chances for attempting to take Philadelphia at the end of the campaign. Similarly, the replacements that Clinton received in 1779 arrived in such wretched shape that he was compelled to cancel a foray into the Hudson Highlands, including possibly an attack on West Point. The British and Germans also faced the need to acclimate to America's differing climates. The English found northern winters more severe than those to which they were accustomed, and few Europeans were fully prepared for southern summers.[13]

But despite its many problems, and contrary to the gloomy predictions of the naysayers, Britain possessed the capability to score a knockout punch during the war's early years. Its army of regulars was superior in virtually every way to America's inexperienced and wretchedly equipped Continentals and militiamen, and it enjoyed absolute maritime supremacy. The mere use of its readily available naval prowess might have turned Bunker Hill into a nearly bloodless triumph, with numbing effects on American morale. That the rebels were not crushed in 1776 was due largely to General Howe. Because of his excessive caution, Howe failed to destroy his trapped adversary on Long Island. Later, through appalling languor and wariness he permitted the Americans to escape the coffin that was Manhattan Island. Finally, through torpor and a seemingly astonishing indifference, he let Washington's ragtag army flee across New Jersey and subsist unmolested south of the Delaware. Scoring a decisive victory in 1777 was more problematical, yet any possible chance of doing so was lost when Howe failed to act in concert with Burgoyne's invasion army. With his choice, he ignored not only the wishes of London, but conventional military wisdom, scuttling both his manpower superiority and his maritime arm.

In the face of Saratoga, Britain turned to the Southern Strategy. From the outset there were critics, including some in the army who believed that New England might yet be subdued through simultaneous attacks on Rhode Island, the Hudson, and Long Island Sound, together with mauling naval raids all along the coast. Good on paper, such a plan would have broken down from a lack of troops. With d'Estaing's arrival that summer and the next, a British invasion of New England might well have resulted in a Yankee Yorktown three or four years before Virginia's Yorktown. Numerous historians have disparaged the Southern Strategy, largely because it did not succeed, but it should not be presumed that it could not have succeeded, at least to some degree. The Southern Strategy was never designed to crush the American rebellion in its entirety. As Jefferson subsequently remarked, with Saratoga and the evacuation of Philadelphia, the states north of the Potomac had won independence. If Jefferson understood that, so did Britain's officials in London. The Southern Strategy was set in motion to reclaim those colonies that had held the greatest economic importance to British interests, the four provinces below the Potomac, and to leave postwar Britain with several provinces in North America.

The successful partisan war waged by rebels in the Carolinas and Georgia has convinced many that the Southern Strategy was inevitably doomed. That may not be true. The outcome might have been different had the British launched their attempt to subjugate the South in the Chesapeake rather than in Georgia and South Carolina. That was the conclusion that Cornwallis reached in 1781. He came to feel that the British, with their naval superiority, could exploit the network of rivers in Virginia to enhance their mobility and reduce the backcountry in that state. Once Virginia was subdued, the rebels' supply routes linking the mid-Atlantic states to the Lower South might have been severed. As it was, Clinton's plan, which started in the Lower South, began well enough. In the twenty months after December 1778 Savannah and Charleston were taken, three Continental armies were destroyed, and a fourth allied force under d'Estaing was left in tatters after it failed to retake Savannah. To be sure, once partisan war erupted in South Carolina, the British faced monumental difficulties, but hardly inescapable defeat. To be especially successful, and to survive over the long haul, the guerrillas required the assistance of a regular army. That was one reason why Cornwallis was so anxious to destroy Gates's army, then that of Greene. Had the British recognized that the northern provinces were lost and sent the army that occupied Manhattan to join with Cornwallis, the war would have taken a decidedly different course. Or, had Clinton sent Arnold and Phillips to land behind the rebel army on the North Carolina coast—the nightmare that haunted Greene—instead of employing them in damaging, but essentially meaningless raids in Virginia, the outcome of the contest in the Carolinas might have been strikingly different.

None of what was visited on the British in 1781, or in the eventual peace treaty, need have occurred. Had Britain submitted its fate to a European mediation conference in 1780 or early 1781, it almost certainly would have retained New York City, Georgia, South Carolina, Florida, and a considerable chunk of the West beyond the mountains, all of which it lost in the Treaty of Paris. The disaster at Yorktown would have been avoided had Cornwallis remained in the Lower South, as Clinton intended. In that case, Washington, Rochambeau, and de Grasse might have come after him in the Carolinas, and who can know what the outcome would have been. Had Cornwallis never entered Virginia, it is more likely that the last great battle of the war would have been an allied attack on New York. Once again, no one can know how such a battle would have turned out, but while Washington thought victory possible, the two professional soldiers, Rochambeau and Clinton, expected such a Franco-American campaign to meet with defeat. One thing is clear. Virtually everyone on the allied side believed that campaign 1781 was their last hope. Most also believed that if a decisive victory was not won that year, the war's outcome would be decided at the peace table, with much of the settlement dictated to the rebels. Had the conflict ended in a stalemate, followed by a negotiated peace, Britain would have lost much, but it would still probably have retained most of what it might have gotten two years earlier through a European mediation conference. Together with Canada and its Caribbean possessions, Britain would yet have had a flourishing empire in the Western Hemisphere. The United States would have been far smaller than it was after the Treaty of Paris, and far less secure, as it would have been largely surrounded by areas under the control of Great Britain and Native Americans who were in league with the British.

BRITAIN DID NOT FIGHT this war in a vacuum. It had an adversary, and like the British, the Americans made their share of mistakes. None were greater, or more nearly fatal, than their hard and fast aversion to creating a standing army or the establishment of a sovereign national government with the authority to plan, organize, and finance a concerted war effort.

Several additional problems of their own making also afflicted America's war effort. The selection of the initial general officers was, as John Adams remarked, "so much of accident." Even more, it was a political carnival that inevitably resulted in several poor choices. Politics never disappeared from the process of promoting general officers. Officers fought among themselves to gain titles and get ahead, and they intrigued endlessly with state and Continental officials.[14] It was less surprising that so many generals were mediocre, or unsatisfactory, than that a few good general officers emerged from the muck of state and regional interests and the elitist predilections that drove the process. The rebels' supply system was shamefully tainted with corruption and profiteering from one end to the other, and Congress was unable, or unwilling, to do much about it. Congress was no less capable of coping with America's economic tribulations, which in the second half of the war nearly eviscerated the army and gave the British, who were stretched to the breaking point, a better opportunity to salvage something meaningful from this war. The forlorn conditions under which America's soldiers were made to live and campaign was a national disgrace. That the army did not implode in a frenzy of mutinies long before 1781 was little short of miraculous. It was no less remarkable that morale on the war-weary homefront was never hopelessly shattered. Popular zeal and determination bent, but never broke, thanks in considerable measure to the French alliance and to French steadfastness, which kept alive hope in America that victory might be attained. But the will to continue arose, too, from a dogged commitment to the idea of independence and the conviction that the American Revolution would usher in a new and better world. It was also crucial that after 1776 Britain won few battles, and none that were of a backbreaking nature. The British took Philadelphia in 1777, but Washington's army escaped intact. Britain's capture of Charleston, with its large garrison, was the closest that it came to scoring a decisive victory, but with surprising ease the Americans shrugged it off as merely the loss of another unfortunate city, not something that was likely to have a substantial impact on the course of the war.

In the last years of the war the notion developed in some circles that Washington and the American Revolution were one, that the commander in chief embodied the Revolution and that an American triumph was dependent on him. He was portrayed as the "guardian spirit of America," and Lafayette gushed to him about "the Revolution You Have Made."[15] A few years ago a leading Washington biographer reached a similar conclusion, declaring him to have been the "indispensable man" in America's victory in the War of Independence.[16] More recently, David McCullough, in his best-selling history of 1776, argued, "in the last analysis it was Washington and the army that won the war for American Independence."[17]

Mature and with some command experience, Washington brought many attributes to his position as commander in chief. With seasoning and confidence, and the assurance that came in time from knowing that he had Congress's support, Washington's performance improved as the years passed. That cannot be said of any British commander, and among America's other generals only Greene, and possibly Lafayette, grew better with time. Washington outgrew the anxious impulsiveness that he sometimes displayed during the siege of Boston, leading in the years that followed with a judicious and restrained hand. Virtually every step that he took from early 1776 onward was the result of meticulous planning. Even when he acted boldly, and with a rude audacity that astounded his adversaries—as was true with his first strike across the Delaware into New Jersey at Christmas in 1776 and his attack at Germantown in 1777—he set his army in motion only after preparing a carefully conceived course of action. In all the years that followed the Battle of New York, the only action that Washington took that had an edge of recklessness about it was his second crossing of the Delaware just before the end of 1776, and that enterprise ended brilliantly at Princeton, in part perhaps because its spontaneity caught the enemy flatfooted. Washington was also a meticulous administrator who kept the army intact and in running order. One cannot read his papers without discovering, with some amazement, how much of Washington's time was devoted to logistics, health and hygiene, securing the army and its equipment, preparing reports for Congress and state officials, lobbying those same politicians, and coping with a thousand and one personnel issues, not least of which was his successful management of a motley collection of frenetically ambitious, impetuous, and irascible officers.

Washington's undisputed courage, gravitas, and cool deliberative habits won the admiration of his officers. His deft feel for politics, often overlooked by subsequent generations, resulted in splendid relationships with Congress and state officials. He was an incredibly good judge of others, a talent that led him to divine the inconspicuous attributes of Greene, to discern Knox's potential, and to see through the bluff and swagger of a host of lesser men. He was an excellent diplomat who worked well with his French counterparts. He listened to advice. Better than most, he understood the crucial importance of civilian morale and sought to lighten the potentially heavy hand of those sent to find supplies. He did not abuse his office. He deferred to civilian leadership and made no attempt to exercise powers that he did not possess. There was no hint of scandal in his behavior. He grew to be the very symbol of the selfless, dedicated patriot, remaining at his post year in and year out, never returning home before late 1781, and disdaining a bountiful and ostentatious lifestyle. In so doing, he came to embody—and, for many, to define—the meaning of the American Revolution. Finally, early on Washington demonstrated that he was big enough to acknowledge that his initial conceit for waging the war—that it was possible to train an American army capable of standing toe to toe with British regulars—was faulty. Seeing his error, Washington conceived a war of posts strategy.

For all his virtues, there were flaws in Washington's performance, though it should be remembered that he was neither a professional soldier nor the product of a military academy. Three fourths of his adult years were spent in nonmilitary pursuits, mostly in farming and commercial endeavors, and his only prior experience in soldiering had been to command a small provincial army that was engaged almost exclusively in a bush war. But he never grew appreciably as a tactician, and his limitations were exhibited at Brooklyn, Germantown, and Monmouth. Evidence is lacking that he had learned much thereafter. In 1791, during his presidency, Washington visited the battlefield at Guilford Courthouse. Following his tour, he criticized General Greene's tactics, though that commander had been spectacularly successful. Washington's remarks suggest that had he commanded against Cornwallis that day ten years earlier, there is little reason to believe that he would have fared as well as Greene.[18] Washington's greatest liability was his indecisiveness. It has often been said that he exhibited this failing only in the early going, as if he overcame the shortcoming. In fact, he was dogged by indecision throughout 1776, again at Brandywine in 1777, and yet again as fighting loomed at Monmouth in 1778, where ambivalence so clouded his judgment that he committed men to battle without a clear idea of what he was seeking to achieve. During the three years that followed Monmouth his ability to make rapid decisions went untested, as he never committed his army to a campaign, and at Yorktown, Rochambeau called the principal shots. Many contemporary critics, and even a steadfast admirer and truckler such as Lafayette, who knew unctuousness when he saw it, privately believed that Washington surrounded himself with sycophants. The quality of the advice that Washington received as the war progressed—all too often peddled by yes-men—was at the very least one-sided and devoid of the illuminating breadth on which a good leader should insist.

Washington's insecurities also led him to see enemies where none existed, and to seek the demolition of those whom he regarded as dangerous rivals. Arousing Washington's ire proved ruinous for Lee and Gates, who were among the few truly talented generals in the army. While Lee played no small part in his own undoing, his fall took from headquarters the man who in 1775–1776, and again during the preparations leading to Monmouth in 1778, had provided Washington with the best counsel that he received. Suspected by Washington of having played a leading role in the nonexistent Conway Cabal, Gates was assured of never again receiving his commander's support for an independent command.

Due largely to Washington, the victor of Saratoga, America's greatest victory before Yorktown, was sidelined for three years without a substantive role to play.

Washington was extremely fortunate that his years of largely self-imposed inactivity between 1778 and Yorktown were not disastrous to the American cause. After the New York debacle, and until France entered the war, Washington embraced a strategy of outlasting his foe. His goal was to preserve his force and permit time to bleed the life out of his adversary. He hoped that London, faced with a protracted war, would someday come to see its cause as hopeless, or at least not worth the price it was costing. Once France entered the war, Washington further decided to act only in concert with the French navy, a choice that risked an even longer war. He was convinced that time was on his side, but the long war that ensued came closer than did Britain's armed forces to devouring the American Revolution. In fairness, when Washington chose such a course, he could not have foreseen the collapse of the American economy, and when the economic crash set in, there was no way for him to know that the nation's economic maladies would not be corrected relatively quickly. However, during 1779 it not only became apparent that the fiscal woes were beyond prompt repair, but signs were plentiful that the war was stalemated and civilian morale was cracking. Yet Washington's Continentals remained inactive throughout 1779 and the next year as well. All the while, Washington waited in vain for the arrival of a French fleet and dreamt of— and only of—a grand campaign against New York.

Washington had few choices between 1778–1781. Without a naval arm, an attack on New York was out of the question. That left him with two possible courses of action. He might have taken his army to the South, hoping to score a decisive victory against Cornwallis, or Clinton, should he be lured back to the region. Or, he might have invaded Canada, hoping to draw on the residue of pro-French sentiment among the Canadian populace for help in conquering the enemy in that cold and lonely place. A decisive victory in Canada in 1778 or 1779 would in all likelihood have brought the war to an end. There can be little doubt that such an American invasion would have halted Britain's Southern Strategy in its tracks, forcing Clinton's attention northward and removing pressure from several states in the United States. An invasion conducted in the summer or fall of 1780 would have prevented Clinton from sending additional help to Cornwallis in the South. There would have been risks involved in committing the Continental army to the South or to Canada, but there was a hazard in doing nothing. Had Cornwallis not come north in 1781, or had France and Spain, in the swirl of European mediation offers, opted to end their participation in the war against Britain in 1780 or 1781, the war would have a very different ending, and one that was far less satisfactory for the United States. Had a United States continued in existence, it would have been small, weak, indigent, and surrounded on all sides by mighty Great Britain. It would have faced the bleakest of bleak futures. Enervated and with few prospects of wealth, it is easy to see how the new nation might have disintegrated within a few years, with some or all of it returning to the British fold. Had that been the outcome of the American Revolution,

Washington's generalship after 1778, and Washington himself, would today be seen in a decidedly different light.

In the end, of course, Washington's watchful, cautious course succeeded. He was the happy beneficiary of a series of occurrences in 1781 which he neither foresaw nor over which he exercised the least control: Cornwallis's egregious blunder in advancing into Virginia, Clinton's misguided decision to leave a large, and vulnerable, British force on the Williamsburg peninsula, France's determination to send de Grasse north from the Caribbean, and Rochambeau's covert decision to ask de Grasse to sail not to New York but to the Chesapeake. It was with good reason, and no small wonder, that Washington believed that the American victory, with its magnificent peace, was almost a miracle.

Washington had attained a monumental stature by war's end, esteemed by his countrymen as was no other Continental soldier or Revolutionary figure. His shortcomings were soon forgotten by all but historians, and over the years not a few of them ignored his flaws and exaggerated his contribution to America's victory. Yet, while Washington was not free of failings, it must be asked whether there was anyone else who might have done a better job as commander of the Continental army. Suppose a cabal had succeeded in dumping him in favor of Gates after Saratoga. Gates had many good qualities, though some that were dreadful, and given a choice between him and Washington as the person on which the American Revolution was to hang, Washington wins hands down. Had Washington been killed relatively early in the war—perhaps when he stumbled into the enemy patrol at Kip's Bay or in leading his troops at Princeton or when Ferguson might have shot him at Brandywine—would the country have been better off had command of the Continental army been given to Ward, Schuyler, Heath, Sullivan, Lincoln, or Putnam? No one can know with perfect assurance how an individual will respond to the pressures and challenges of awesome authority and responsibility—Abraham Lincoln and Harry Truman leap to mind as men with unremarkable pasts who went on to exceed all expectations—though it is likely that all these men would have been out of their depth. At the beginning of the war many believed Charles Lee was America's best soldier. But he was perilously unsound and untrustworthy, and would have been a disaster as the army's commander. Greene ultimately responded to the burdensome demands of leadership in a manner that was close to that exhibited by Washington, but not until deep into the war. He was not ready for such awesome responsibility in the early years of hostilities. Of all the important general officers, Washington alone had the preparation for the office of commander in chief at the outset of the war and the intelligence, temper, and character necessary to grow in the office. His defects notwithstanding, fortune smiled on the infant nation when Washington was selected to lead it into this war.

NOTHING WAS FOREORDAINED about the outcome of this war, and indeed had other choices been made during the six months that preceded Yorktown, the issue might have been strikingly different. It was a war without a turning point, although there were numerous pivotal moments. The bloody day at Bunker Hill instilled the colonists with confidence that they could stand up to, and even defeat, Britain's regulars and shaped American strategic thinking—nearly disastrously so—for the next eighteen months. The repeated failings in New York in 1776 convinced Washington to jettison one strategy in favor of another. Cornwallis's feckless pursuit of Washington across New Jersey late that same year—undertaken with Howe looking over his shoulder, and pulling some of the strings in the chase—was a blunder of epic proportions. Washington's brilliant Trenton-Princeton campaign restored American morale, captured the imagination of Versailles, and facilitated the recruitment of another army for campaign 1777. France's decision in 1776 to surreptitiously provide assistance was central to America's war effort, and essential to the victory at Saratoga in 1777, which in itself was instrumental in drawing France into an alliance that added enormously to Great Britain's difficulties. Spain's belligerency in 1780 compounded Britain's problems. Yorktown was decisive, as it turned Britain away from continuing to wage war in North America. But in a great many ways the partisan war in the Carolinas and Georgia in 1780–1781 was where the war was won. It saved South Carolina and Georgia from British conquest and may have prevented the loss of the entire South. It also led directly to King's Mountain, Guilford Courthouse, and Cowpens, which sharply diminished British power in the South, and set Cornwallis, who found himself surrounded in the Carolinas by the sepulchral ruins of his pacification campaign, on the road to Virginia, and perdition.

In the end, Washington became the symbol of virtue, courage, steadfastness, accomplishment, and endurance. His lofty stature was earned to be sure, but it was also carefully crafted by Congress, by those about Washington who saw him as their aegis to success, and by Washington himself. His eminence was crucial for holding together the army and a war-weary nation until, at last, the decisive victory was secured. But victory was not due to Washington alone. Several general officers—notably Ward in 1775; Schuyler, Gates, and Arnold in 1777; Greene and Lafayette in 1780–1781; and Morgan and Knox all through the war —performed with commendable merit in their great hours of trial. Numerous junior officers, such as John Glover, William Washington, and Henry Lee, excelled, outshining their counterparts in the enemy army. Largely devoid of military experience, civilians through and through, they emerged from the pack through their innate talents, drawing on lessons they had learned before the war, but honing their skills as leaders in the course of their cruel experiences under fire in this war. But no commander played a greater role than Nathanael Greene in securing American independence, for it was his daring campaign in 1781 that thwarted Cornwallis and sent him on his fateful errand into Virginia, and it was rebel forces under Greene that liberated South Carolina and Georgia while the allies gathered at Yorktown. John Adams understood that, and nearly his first words on learning of Yorktown were: "General Greenes last Action . . . is quite as glorious for the American Arms as the Capture of Cornwallis."[19]

The militia has often been belittled, but without it the war could not have been won. It secured the homefront in nearly every state by suppressing and disarming the Loyalists in the crucial early stage of the war. Time and again militiamen augmented the Continental army, and, despite some egregious failures, sometimes fought extremely well. At Bunker Hill, Princeton, Saratoga, and Cowpens, militiamen served with valor. "Men are brave only when they are well led," a Hessian officer opined early in the war, and that was doubtless a factor when the militia did stand and fight.[20] In addition, as historian Robert Middlekauff has observed, militiamen usually knew one another and sometimes fought hard to save not only themselves, but their friends and neighbors. Nor was that all. These men had to live the rest of their lives in the same small town with many of their comrades; if they broke down while their fellow soldiers were fighting hard, they would bear the stigma of cowardice throughout their lives.[21]

The common soldiers in the Continental army "had hardships enough to endure," as Private Martin put it, though "the thousandth part of their suffering has not, nor ever will be told."[22] In the depths of their suffering, many felt abandoned. The "poor, little, modest soldier [is put] out of countenance" by civilians and public officials at home, said one, doubtless speaking for many. He and many of his comrades grew contemptuous of those at home who never served and sacrificed, and of politicians who wore their patriotism on their sleeve, described by one soldier as the "blustering hero" who fought "his battles over a glass of Madeira."[23] Their suffering and anger notwithstanding, these soldiers demonstrated repeatedly that when properly led they would fight, and fight well, and from 1777 onward these battle-hardened veterans were the heart of a determined and sound army. America's triumph was also inconceivable without the varied and countless contributions made by thousands of common militiamen and the unnerving challenges faced by dauntless partisans, ordinary men, women, and young boys who looked mortal danger in the face in order to thwart the enemy in their midst.

IN THE FINAL ANALYSIS, Britain's suppression of the American rebellion was foiled in the fighting in the North between 1775 and 1778, but the American victory was won at last in the South in 1780–1781. Many were responsible for that American victory. In the famous first installment of the *American Crisis*, Thomas Paine, seeking desperately to rally the nation in the last dark days of 1776, had with a burning vision promised that through "perseverance and fortitude we have the prospect of a glorious issue." After Yorktown, with peace on the horizon, Paine in the tenth *American Crisis* ruminated that America's victory had been won because this war had been "the country's war, the public's war . . . the war of the people in their own behalf."[24] He was correct on all counts. The American people and their soldiers, and not just General Washington, had endured to gain a victory that, they prayed, would usher in a world filled with greater promise than would have been their lot under aristocratic, monarchical Great Britain.

ABBREVIATIONS

The following abbreviations are used in the notes to designate frequently cited publications, libraries, and individuals.

AA   Abigail Adams
AFC   L. H. Butterfield, et al., eds. *Adams Family Correspondence*. 4 vols. Cambridge, Mass.: Harvard University Press, 1963–???.
AH   Alexander Hamilton
AHR   *American Historical Review*
BF   Benjamin Franklin
CC   Charles Ross, ed. *Correspondence of Charles, First Marquis Cornwallis*. 3 vols. London: J. Murray, 1859.
DAJA   L. H. Butterfield, et al., eds. *The Diary and Autobiography of John Adams*. 4 vols. Cambridge, Mass.: Harvard University Press, 1961.
DAR   K. G. Davies, ed., *Documents of the American Revolution, 1770–1783*. 21 vols. Dublin, Ireland: Irish University Press, 1972–1981.
DGW   Donald Jackson, et al., eds. *The Diaries of George Washington*. 6 vols. Charlottesville: University Press of Virginia, 1976–1979.
GP   *Horatio Gates Papers, 1726–1828*. Sanford, N.C.: Microfilming Corporation of America, 1978.
GW   George Washington
JA   John Adams
JCC   Worthington C. Ford, et al., eds. *The Journals of the Continental Congress*. 34 vols. Washington, D.C.: Library of Congress, 1904–1937.
LC   Library of Congress
LDC   Paul H. Smith, ed. *Letters of Delegates to Congress, 1774–1789*. 26 vols. Washington, D.C.: Library of Congress, 1976–2000.
LP   *Lee Papers, Collections of the New-York Historical Society for the Year 1871, . . . 1872, . . . 1873, . . . 1874*. New York: New York Historical Society, 1872–1875.

LLP	Stanley J. Idzerda, et al., eds. *Lafayette in the Age of the American Revolution: Selected Letters and Papers, 1776–1790*. 5 vols. Ithaca, N.Y.: Cornell University Press, 1976–1983.
MHS	Massachusetts Historical Society
NG	Nathanael Greene
PAH	Harold C. Syrett and Jacob E. Cooke, eds. *Papers of Alexander Hamilton*. 26 vols. New York: Columbia University Press, 1961–1979.
PBF	Leonard W. Lararee, et al., eds. *The Papers of Benjamin Franklin*. New Haven, Conn.: Yale University Press, 1959–???.
PC	President of Congress
PGW:Col.Ser.	W. W. Abbot, et al., eds. *The Papers of George Washington: Colonial Series*. 10 vols. Charlottesville: University Press of Virginia, 1983–1995.
PGW:RWS	Philander Chase, et al., eds. *The Papers of George Washington: Revolutionary War Series*. Charlottesville: University Press of Virginia, 1985–???.
PH	*The Parliamentary History of England, from the Earliest Period to the Year 1803*. 36 vols. New York: AMS Press, 1966.
PJA	Robert J. Taylor, et al., eds. *Papers of John Adams*. Cambridge, Mass.: Harvard University Press, 1977–???.
PMHB	*Pennsylvania Magazine of History and Biography*
PNG	Richard K. Showman, ed. *The Papers of Nathanael Greene*. 13 vols. Chapel Hill: University of North Carolina Press, 1976–2005.
PTJ	Julian P. Boyd, et al., eds. *The Papers of Thomas Jefferson*. Princeton, N.J.: Princeton University Press, 1950–???.
SOS	Henry Steele Commager and Richard B. Morris, eds. *The Spirit of '76: The Story of the American Revolution as Told by Participants*. 2 vols. Indianapolis: Bobbs-Merrill, 1958.
SP	Otis G. Hammond, ed. *Letters and Papers of Major-General John Sullivan, Continental Army*. 3 vols. Concord: New Hampshire Historical Society, 1930–1939.
TJ	Thomas Jefferson
WMQ	*William and Mary Quarterly*
WW	John C. Fitzpatrick, ed. *The Writings of Washington*. 39 vols. Washington, D.C.: United States Government Printing Office, 1931–1944.

NOTES

Introduction. "My Country, My Honor, My Life": Bravery and Death in War

1. John Haslet to Caesar Rodney, Oct. 13, 1776, in George Herbert Ryder, ed., *Letters to and from Caesar Rodney, 1756–1784* (Philadelphia, 1933), 139.

2. Council of War, Oct. 16, 1776, *PGW:RWS* 6:576, 576n.

3. Extract of a letter from Colonel Glover, Oct. 22, 1776, in Peter Force, ed., *American Archives: Fifth Series, Containing a Documentary History of the United States* . . . (Washington, D.C., 1848–1853) 2:1, 188–89.

4. Loammi Baldwin to Mary Fowle Baldwin, Oct. 13–23, 1776, Loammi Baldwin Papers, Houghton Library, Harvard University.

5. Extract of letter of Colonel Glover, Oct. 22, 1776, Force, *American Archives*, 5th Ser., 2:1, 188–89.

6. Evelyn to Frances Leveson-Gower, Aug. 26, 1774, in G. D. Scull, ed., *Memoir and Letters of Captain W. Glenville Evelyn, of the 4th Regiment ("King's Own") from North America, 1774–1776* (Oxford, England, 1879), 30.

7. L. I. Cowper, *The King's Own: The Story of a Royal Regiment* (Oxford, England, 1939), 6–134, 154–55. To compare the uniforms of the King's Own with those of other regiments, see, Henry M Chichester, *Records and Badges of the British Army* (London, 1902) and Edward E. Curtis, *The Organization of the British Army in the American Revolution* (Yorkshire, England, 1972), 154–57.

8. Evelyn to Leveson-Gower, Aug. 26, Oct. 31, 1774, Scull, *Memoir and Letters of Captain Evelyn*, 27, 34, 36; Evelyn to William Evelyn, Oct. 31, 1774, April 23, 1775, ibid., 34, 53; Cowper, *King's Own*, 234.

9. Evelyn to William Evelyn, Feb. 18, 1775, Scull, *Memoir and Letters of Captain Evelyn*, 46, 47, 50; Evelyn to Leveson-Gower, Aug. 26, Dec. 6, 1774, ibid., 29, 42–43.

10. David Hackett Fischer, *Paul Revere's Ride* (New York, 1994), 44–45, 308; Cowper, *King's Own*, 236–38; Evelyn to William Evelyn, April 23, 1775, Scull, *Memoir and Letters of Captain Evelyn*, 54. Evelyn's will is in ibid., 90–91.

11. Fischer, *Paul Revere's Ride*, 126, 309; Cowper, *King's Own*, 245; Evelyn to Leveson-Gower, June 6, Aug. 19, 1775, Scull, *Memoir and Letters of Captain Evelyn*, 59, 60, 64–65.

12. Evelyn to William Evelyn, Oct. 7, 1775, Scull, *Memoir and Letters of Captain Evelyn*, 69; Evelyn to Leveson-Gower, Dec. 4, 1775, ibid., 75; Evelyn to Frances Boscawen, Sept. 24, 1776, ibid., 85; Cowper, *King's Own*, 249.

13. George A. Billias, *John Glover and His Marblehead Men* (New York, 1960), 17–67, 73–74.

14. Ibid., 69–70.

15. Glover to Jonathan Glover and Azar Orne, June 17, July 25, Aug. 31, Sept. 7, 23, 1777, in Russell W. Knight, ed., *General John Glover's Letterbook, 1776–1777* (Salem, Mass., 1977), 13, 38, 39, 42, 43.

16. The best accounts of the engagement at Pell's Point, and the source for the description of the battle, are Billias, *John Glover and His Marblehead Men*, 110–19, and Christopher Ward, *The War of the American Revolution* (New York, 1952), 1:256–59. A brief useful account can also be found in *PGW:RWS* 6:593n.

17. Colonel Glover acknowledged the plundering of Evelyn, whom he thought dead. He wrote later that during the lull one of his men "took a hat and canteen off a captain that lay dead on the ground they retreated from." Extract of a letter of Colonel Glover, Force, *American Archives*, 5th Ser., 2:1, 188–89.

18. David Hackett Fischer, *Washington's Crossing* (New York, 2004), 110.

19. GW, General Orders, October 21, 1776, *PGW:RWS* 7:1; GW to Glover, April 26, 1777, ibid., 9:274.

Chapter 1. "Fear Is Not an American Art": The Coming of the War

1. On warfare in colonial America, including the militia system and especially the French and Indian War, see Douglas E. Leach, *Arms for Empire: A Military History of the British Colonies in North America, 1607–1763* (New York, 1973); John Ferling, *A Wilderness of Miseries: War and Warriors in Early America* (Westport, Conn., 1981); John Ferling, *Struggle for a Continent: The Wars of Early America* (Arlington Heights, Ill., 1993); Jack S. Rodabaugh, "The Militia of Colonial Massachusetts," *Military Affairs* 28 (1954): 1–18; Douglas Leach, "The Military System of Plymouth Colony," *New England Quarterly* 24 (1951): 242–64; William L. Shea, *The Virginia Militia in the Seventeenth Century* (Baton Rouge, 1983); Don Higginbotham, *War and Society in Revolutionary America: The Wider Dimensions of the Conflict* (Columbia, S.C., 1988), 19–41, 106–31; Fred Anderson, *The Crucible of War: The Seven Years' War and the Fate of Empire in North America, 1754–1766* (New York, 2000); William M. Fowler Jr., *Empires at War: The French and Indian War and the Struggle for North America, 1754–1763* (New York, 2005); Harold E. Selesky, *War and Society in Colonial Connecticut* (New Haven, Conn., 1990); Don Higginbotham, "The Early American Way of War: Reconnaissance and Appraisal," *WMQ* 44 (1987): 23073; Howard Peckham, *The Colonial Wars, 1689–1762* (Chicago, 1964); I. K. Steele, *Guerrillas and Grenadiers: The Struggle for Canada, 1689–1760* (New York, 1969). On America's irregular warfare, and the British army's response to it, see Peter E. Russell, "Redcoats in the Wilderness: British Officers and Irregular Warfare in Europe and America, 1740 to 1760," *WMQ* 25 (1978): 629–52. An important recent work minimizes the colonists' military innovations and emphasizes that European tactics were not ineffective in the American wilderness: see Guy Chet, *Conquering the American Wilderness: The Triumph of European Warfare in the Colonial Northeast* (Amherst, Mass., 2003), 30–31, 50.

2. John Ferling, "The New England Soldier: A Study in Changing Perceptions," *American Quarterly* 33 (1981): 26–45; Ferling, *A Wilderness of Miseries*, 57–92; Selesky, *War and Society in Colonial Connecticut*, 145–46.

3. Stephen Brumwell, *Redcoats: The British Soldier and War in the Americas, 1755–1763* (Cambridge, England, 2002), 57–98; Sylvia R. Frey, *The British Soldier in America: A Social History of Military Life in the Revolutionary Period* (Austin, Tex., 1981), 3–21.

4. Douglas Edward Leach, *Roots of Conflict: British Armed Forces and Colonial Americans, 1677–1763* (Chapel Hill, N.C., 1986), 107–10; Fred Anderson, *A People's Army: Massachusetts Soldiers and Society in the Seven Years' War* (Chapel Hill, N.C., 1984), 167–95.

5. The quotations are from Leach, *Roots of Conflict*, 78–79, 86, 103, 94 130–32; Alan Rogers, *Empire and Liberty: American Resistance to British Authority, 1755–1763* (Berkeley, Calif., 1974), 55, 63; Anderson, *Crucible of War*, 147, 149, 166.

6. Brumwell, *Redcoats*, 91, 99–112; Anderson, *Crucible of War*, 143, 287–89.

7. JA to Mercy Otis Warren, July 20, 27, 1807, "Correspondence between John Adams and Mercy Warren Relating to Her History of the American Revolution," *Massachusetts Historical Society Collections*, 5th Ser., 4 (1878): 339–40, 355.

8. Quoted in Brumwell, *Redcoats*, 199. Brumwell demonstrates that the British army learned from Braddock's debacle and took steps that resulted in its gradual transformation into a more effective machine for waging irregular warfare. The colonists, nevertheless, appeared to be largely heedless; see pages 194–263. On Braddock's debacle, see also Paul E. Kopperman, *Braddock at the Monongahela* (Pittsburgh, 1977), Fowler, *Empires at War*, 49–73, and Anderson, *Crucible of War*, 94–107.

9. GW to Robert Dinwiddie: July 18, 1755, *PGW: Col. Ser.* 1:339; GW to Mary Ball Washington, July 18, 1755, ibid., 1:336; GW to John Augustine Washington, July 18, 1755, ibid., 1:343.

10. Anderson, *Crucible of War*, 240–49, 286. The quotations are from pages 244 and 247. See also Ferling, *Struggle for a Continent*, 178–81, and Fowler, *Empires at War*, 130–51.

11. Leach, *Roots of Conflict*, 82–97; Rogers, *Empire and Liberty*, 94–95.

12. Thomas Paine, *Common Sense* (1776), in Philip S. Foner, ed., *The Complete Writings of Thomas Paine* (New York, 1945), 1:20–21.

13. Ibid., 1:26.

14. Anderson, *Crucible of War*, 220, 373–76; Leach, *Arms for Empire*, 449; Francis Parkman, *Montcalm and Wolfe*, reprint (New York, 1984), 348, 526–27; Franklin to Lord Kames, January 3, 1760, *PBF* 9:6–7.

15. Edmund S. and Helen M. Morgan, *The Stamp Act Crisis: Prologue to Revolution* (Chapel Hill, N.C., 1953), 21–22; Anderson, *Crucible of War*, 158–59, 615.

16. Quoted in Morgan, *Stamp Act Crisis*, 68–69.

17. "The Examination of Doctor Benjamin Franklin" (Feb. 13, 1766), *PBF* 13:134, 142, 149, 152.

18. Merrill Jensen, *The Founding of a Nation: A History of the American Revolution* (New York, 1968), 212, 289; Anderson, *Crucible of War*, 720; *Boston Gazette*, Aug. 8, 1768, in Harry A. Cushing, ed., *The Writings of Samuel Adams* (New York, 1904–1908), 1:240; William Fowler, *Samuel Adams: Radical Puritan*, (New York, 1997), 86–87.

19. Hiller B. Zobel, *The Boston Massacre* (New York, 1970), 110–11, 164–205.

20. The quotations are from Alan Valentine, *Lord North* (Norman, Okla., 1967), 1:158, 189.

21. The literature on North is considerable. The foregoing portrayal of North draws largely on Valentine, *Lord North*; Peter Whiteley, *Lord North: The Prime Minister Who Lost America* (London, 1996); and Peter D. G. Thomas, *Lord North* (London, 1976). See also C. D. Smith, *The Early Career of Lord North the Prime Minister* (London, 1979); John Cannon, *Lord North: The Noble Lord in the Blue Ribbon* (London, 1970); Herbert Butterfield, *George III, Lord North and the People* (London, 1949); and W. Baring Pemberton, *Lord North* (London, 1938).

22. Quoted in Whiteley, *Lord North*, 94.

23. Edmund Burke to the New York Assembly, April 6, 1774, in Lucy S. Sutherland, ed., *The Correspondence of Edmund Burke* (Chicago, 1960), 2:527–28.

24. Quoted in Julie Flavell, "British Perceptions of New England and the Decision for a Coercive Colonial Policy, 1774–1775," in Julie Flavell and Stephen Conway, eds., *Britain and America Go to War: The Impact of War and Warfare in Anglo-America, 1754–1815* (Gainesville, Fla., 2004), 97.

25. Quoted in Stanley Ayling, *George the Third* (New York, 1972), 243.

26. Quoted in Valentine, *Lord North*, 1:310.

27. Quoted in John Shy, *A People Numerous and Armed: Reflections on the Military Struggle for American Independence* (New York, 1976), 40.

28. The quotes are taken from Troyer Steele Anderson, *The Command of the Howe Brothers during the American Revolution* (New York, 1936), 30.

29. Quoted in Verner W. Crane, *Benjamin Franklin's Letters to the Press, 1758–1775* (Chapel Hill, N.C., 1950), 263n.

30. Quoted in Valentine, *Lord North*, 1:319.

31. Jerrilyn G. Marston, *King and Congress: The Transfer of Political Legitimacy, 1774–1776* (Princeton, N.J., 1987), 108–10, 137; David Ammerman, *In the Common Cause: America's Response to the Coercive Acts of 1774* (Charlottesville, Va., 1974), 109; *JCC* 1:54.

32. JA to William Tudor, Oct. 7, 1774, *PJA* 2:188; *DAJA* 2:145.

33. John R. Galvin, *The Minute Men: The First Fight* (Washington, D.C., 1989), 52, 57.

34. "Report of the Braintree Committee Respecting Minute Men" (March 15, 1775), *PJA* 2:402–3; David Hackett Fischer, *Paul Revere's Ride* (New York, 1994), 151–53; Jensen, *Founding of a Nation*, 538–41; *DGW* 3:303–21.

35. John Ferling, *The Loyalist Mind: Joseph Galloway and the American Revolution* (University Park, Pa., 1977), 33; Joseph Galloway, *A Candid Examination of the Mutual Claims of Great Britain and the Colonies* (New York, 1775), 46, 62.

36. [Charles Lee], "Strictures on a 'Friendly Address to All Reasonable Americans'" (Philadelphia, 1774), [Early American Imprint Series, No. 13372], 6, 11, 12.

37. [John Adams], "The Letters of Novanglus," III (February 6, 1775), *PJA* 2:251–54; Thomas Jefferson, "Manuscript Text of *A Summary View of the Rights Of British Colonies*" *PTJ* 1:130, 134.

38. Quoted in Peter D. G. Thomas, *Tea Party to Independence: The Third Phase of the American Revolution, 1773–1776* (Oxford, England, 1991), 160.

39. Dartmouth to Gage, Jan. 27, 1775, in Clarence E. Carter, ed., *The Correspondence of General Thomas Gage with the Secretaries of State, 1763–1775*, reprint (New York, 1969), 2:179–83; Dartmouth's circular letter to the American governors, March 3, 1775, *DAR* 9:60–62; Thomas, *Tea Party to Independence*, 143–80.

40. Thomas, *Tea Party to Independence*, 74; William H. Hallahan, *The Day the American Revolution Began: April 19, 1775* (New York, 2000), 272.

41. Gage to Dartmouth, Sept. 2, 1774, Carter, *Correspondence of Gage*, 1:370, 371; Gage to Lord Barrington, Sept. 25, Oct. 3, Nov. 2, 1774, 2:654, 656, 659.

42. Louis Birnbaum, *Red Dawn at Lexington* (Boston, 1986), 148.

43. William Greenleaf to Jonathan Buck, April 29, 1775, in Dennis P. Ryan, ed., *A Salute to Courage: The American Revolution as Seen through Wartime Writings of Officers of the Continental Army and Navy* (New York, 1979), 3.

44. Gage to Barrington, April 22, 1775, Carter, *Correspondence of Gage*, 2:674.

45. Diary of Amos Farnsworth, MHS, *Proceedings*, 2d Series, 12 (1897–1899):78.

46. The account of this epic day is based on Fischer, *Paul Revere's Ride*, in which Pitcairn's order can be found on page 191. For this paragraph, also see Hugh Percy to General Harvey, April 20, 1775, in Charles K. Bolton, ed., *Letters of Hugh Earl Percy from Boston and New York,*

1774–1776 (Boston, 1902), 52; Evelyn to William Evelyn, April 23, 1775, G. D. Scull, ed., *Memoir and Letters of Captain W. Glenville Evelyn, of the 4ᵗʰ Regiment ("King's Own") from North America, 1774–1776* (Oxford, England, 1879), 54; L. I. Cowper, *The King's Own: The Story of a Royal Regiment* (Oxford, England, 1939), 240.

47. Gage to Dartmouth, April 22, 1775, Carter, *Correspondence of Gage,* 1:396.

48. Percy to General Harvey, April 20, 1775, Bolton, ed., *Letters of Hugh Earl Percy,* 52–53.

Chapter 2. "A Loss That Is Greater Than We Can Bear": Going to War

1. *DAJA* 3:322–23; JA to AA, June 17, 1775, *AFC* 1:215.

2. Richard Frothingham, *History of the Siege of Boston* (Boston, 1849), 101; Allen French, *The Siege of Boston* (New York, 1911), 217.

3. On Ward's career, see Charles Martyn, *The Life of Artemas Ward* (New York, 1921).

4. Don Higginbotham, *The War of American Independence: Military Attitudes, Policies, and Practices, 1763–1789* (New York, 1971), 65–66.

5. Theodore Thayer, *Nathanael Greene: Strategist of the American Revolution* (New York, 1960), 15–51; *PNG* 1:xix. The editors of the *PNG* believe that recently discovered evidence "strongly suggests" that NG was a member of the Rhode Island assembly. See ibid., 13:707–8.

6. Richard Buel Jr., *Dear Liberty: Connecticut's Mobilization for the Revolutionary War* (Middletown, Conn., 1980), 36–37; Harold E. Selesky, *War and Society in Colonial Connecticut* (New Haven, Conn., 1990), 204, 229; Jonathan G. Rossie, *The Politics of Command in the American Revolution* (Syracuse, 1975), 15; Louis Birbaum, *Red Dawn at Lexington* (Boston, 1986), 71–74; Richard M. Ketchum, *Decisive Day: The Battle for Bunker Hill* (New York, 1974), 71. The quote on Putnam is from Richard M. Ketchum, "Men of the Revolution: Israel Putnam," *American Heritage,* 24 (June 1973): 26.

7. Birnbaum, *Red Dawn at Lexington,* 76; *Dictionary of American Biography* (New York, 1928–1937), 17:530–31.

8. Frothingham, *History of the Siege of Boston,* 110.

9. Ketchum, *Decisive Day,* 64, 75; Birnbaum, *Red Dawn at Lexington,* 210–15; David Hackett Fischer, *Paul Revere's Ride* (New York, 1994), 269; Selesky, *War and Society in Colonial Connecticut,* 229; Frothingham, *History of the Siege of Boston,* 111–12.

10. Ketchum, *Decisive Day,* 61–62; Frothingham, *History of the Siege of Boston,* 98–101; Fischer, *Paul Revere's Ride,* 269.

11. Jerrilyn Greene Marsten, *King and Congress: The Transfer of Political Legitimacy, 1774–1776* (Princeton, N.J., 1987), 144; James Warren to JA, May 7, June 11, 1775, *PJA* 3:3–4, 24; ibid., 3:6n; *DAJA* 3:321.

12. JA to AA, May 29, 1775, *AFC* 1:207; Jensen, *Founding of a Nation,* 609; Marsten, *King and Congress* 141; *JCC* 2:53.

13. JA to Warren, May 21, July 6, 1775, *PJA* 3:11, 61; Higginbotham, *War of American Independence,* 84; Jack Rakove, *The Beginnings of National Politics: An Interpretive History of the Continental Congress* (Baltimore, 1979), 72–73; Marsten, *King and Congress,* 145; *JCC* 2:49, 59–61.

14. Michael A. Bellesiles, *Revolutionary Outlaws: Ethan Allen and the Struggle for Independence on the Early American Frontier* (Charlottesville, Va., 1993), 115–21; James Kirby Martin, *Benedict Arnold, Revolutionary Hero: An American Warrior Reconsidered* (New York, 1997), 64–79; Willard Sterne Randall, *Benedict Arnold* (New York, 1990), 92–108; Christopher Ward, *The War of the Revolution,* 2 vols. (New York, 1952), 1:63–72.

15. Quoted in Ward, *War of the Revolution,* 1:70.

16. Marsten, *King and Congress,* 151–52.

17. *JCC* 2:89–93, 96–97; Dyer to Joseph Trumbull, *LDC* 1:499; *DAJA* 3:321–23.

18. *DAJA* 3:323.

19. On Washington prior to his selection to command the Continental army, see volumes one and two of Douglas Southall Freeman, *George Washington* (New York, 1948–1957); James Thomas Flexner, *George Washington: The Forge of Experience, 1732–1775* (Boston, 1965) and *George Washington in the American Revolution* (Boston, 1967); John Ferling, *The First of Men: A Life of George Washington* (Knoxville, 1988) and *Setting the World Ablaze: Washington, Adams, Jefferson, and the American Revolution* (New York, 2000); Joseph Ellis, *His Excellency: George Washington* (New York, 2004); Peter R. Henriques, *Realistic Visionary: A Portrait of George Washington* (Charlottesville, Va., 2006); Willard Sterne Randall, *George Washington: A Life* (New York, 1997); Robert F. Jones, *George Washington* (Boston, 1979); Edward G. Lengel, *General George Washington* (New York, 2005); Marcus Cunliffe, *George Washington: Man and Monument* (London, 1959); William S. Baker, *Early Sketches of George Washington* (Philadelphia, 1893); Charles Longmore, *The Invention of George Washington* (Berkeley, 1988); Bernard Knollenberg, *George Washington: The Virginia Period, 1732–1775* (Durham, N.C., 1964); Paul L. Ford, *The True George Washington* (Philadelphia, 1898); Francis R. Bellamy, *The Private Life of George Washington* (New York, 1951).

20. Quoted in Richard M. Ketchum, *Victory at Yorktown: The Campaign That Won the Revolution* (New York, 2004), 3.

21. Ferling, *First of Men*, 84–85; GW to John Augustine Washington, May 31, 1754, July 18, 1755, *PGW: Col Ser* 1:118, 343.

22. Lengel, *General George Washington*, 64–65; "Address from the Officers of the Virginia Regiment," Dec. 31, 1758, *PGW: Col. Ser.* 6:178–81.

23. *Virginia Gazette*, Sept. 3, 1756, in ibid., 3:411–12n; GW to Dinwiddie, Sept. 17, 1757, ibid., 4:412; Dinwiddie to GW, Nov. 16, 24, Dec. 10, 19, 1756, Sept. 24, 1757, in Robert A. Brock, ed., *The Official Records of Robert Dinwiddie, Lieutenant Governor of Virginia, 1751–1758* (Richmond, 1883–1884), 2:507, 523–24, 553, 559–60, 703.

24. GW to John Robinson, April 7, 1756, *PGW: Col. Ser.* 2:337–38.

25. Oliver Spaulding, "The Military Studies of George Washington," *American Historical Review* 29 (1924): 677.

26. For an elaboration of the foregoing, see John Ferling, "School for Command: George Washington in the French and Indian War," in Warren Hofstra, ed., *George Washington and the Virginia Backcountry* (Madison, Wisc., 1998), 195–222.

27. *JCC* 2:91.

28. GW, Address to Congress, June 16, 1775, *PGW:RWS* 1:1; GW, to the New York Provincial Congress, June 26, 1775, ibid., 1:41.

29. Gordon Wood, *The Creation of the American Republic, 1776–1787* (Chapel Hill, N.C., 1969), 53–93.

30. Quoted in Longmore, *Invention of George Washington*, 177.

31. John Alden, *General Charles Lee: Traitor or Patriot?* (Baton Rouge, 1951), 1–75; John W. Shy, "Charles Lee: The Soldier As Radical," in George A. Billias, ed., *George Washington's Generals* (New York, 1964), 22–53; *PGW: Col. Ser.* 10:353; *DGW* 3:298, 302; Lee to JA, Oct. 5, 1775, *PJA* 3:185; JA to Lee, Oct. 13, 1775, ibid., 3:202; JA to James Warren, June 20, 1775, ibid., 3:34; JA to Josiah Quincy, July 29, 1775, ibid., 3:106. Some of Lee's quotes can be found in Alden, *General Charles Lee*, 45, 77.

32. George A. Billias, "Horatio Gates: Professional Soldier," in Billias, *George Washington's Generals*, 79–84. The chief responsibility of the adjutant general was to know how many men were under arms and where they were posted. See Harry M. Ward, *George Washington's Enforcers: Policing the Continental Army* (Carbondale, Ill., 2006), 50.

33. John H. G. Pell, "Philip Schuyler: The General as Aristocrat," in ibid., 54–58.

34. JA to Elbridge Gerry, June 18, 1775, *PJA* 3:26.

35. GW to Martha Washington, June 18, 1775, *PGW:RWS* 1: xx; GW to Burwell Bassett, June 19, 1775, ibid., 1:13.

36. *JCC* 2:93–94, 97, 99, 102–4, 106, 111–22; Robert K. Wright Jr., *The Continental Army* (Washington, D.C., 1983), 22, 26.

37. JA to AA, June 23, 1775, *AFC* 1:226; Freeman, *George Washington*, 3:458–59; Flexner, *George Washington*, 2:23.

38. JA to AA, June 23, 1775, *AFC* 1:226; President of Congress to Ward, June 22, 1775, *LDC* xxx.

39. Frothingham, *History of the Siege of Boston*, 116, 119; Ketchum, *Decisive Day*, 64, 77–79, 81, 82; Birnbaum, *Red Dawn at Lexington*, 231; Higginbotham, *War of American Independence*, 70.

40. French, *Siege of Boston*, 257.

41. Birnbaum, *Red Dawn at Lexington*, 77, 225; Frothingham, *History of the Siege of Boston*, 123; Ketchum, *Decisive Day*, 111.

42. Sir Henry Clinton, *The American Rebellion*, ed., William Willcox (New Haven, Conn., 1954), 19.

43. John Shy, "Thomas Gage: Weak Link of Empire," in George A. Billias, ed., *George Washington's Opponents* (New York, 1969), 25–31. The Burgoyne quote is on page 30. See also John R. Alden, *General Gage in America: Being Principally a History of His Role in the American Revolution* (Baton Rouge, 1948).

44. Birnbaum, *Red Dawn at Lexington*, 231–32, 235.

45. John Buchanan, *The Road to Valley Forge: How Washington Built the Army That Won the Revolution* (Hoboken, N.J., 2004), 2; Troyer Steele Anderson, *The Command of the Howe Brothers during the American Revolution* (New York, 1936), 44; Ira D. Gruber, *The Howe Brothers and the American Revolution* (New York, 1972), 45–48, 56–58; David Hackett Fischer, *Washington's Crossing* (New York, 2004), 67–71; Maldwyn A. Jones, "Sir William Howe: Conventional Strategist," in Billias, *George Washington's Opponents*, 43–46.

46. Amos Farnsworth, "Diary," in *SOS* 1:122.

47. Samuel Blachley Webb to Joseph Webb, June 19, 1775, Dennis P. Ryan, ed., *A Salute to Courage: The American Revolution as Seen through Wartime Writings of Officers of the Continental Army and Navy* (New York, 1979), 7.

48. Succinct accounts of the furnishings of British soldiers, and their muskets, can be found in Ketchum, *Decisive Day*, 125–26, 154; Edward E. Curtis, *The Organization of the British Army in the American Revolution* (New Haven, Conn., 1926), 15–16, 20; Douglas E. Leach, *Arms for Empire: A Military History of the British Colonies in North America, 1607–1763* (New York, 1973), 199; Hal T. Shelton, *General Richard Montgomery and the American Revolution* (New York, 1994), 20–21. For greater detail on eighteenth-century muskets, see Torston Link, *The Flintlock: Its Origin and Development*, ed. John E. Haywood (London, 1965), and Harold L. Peterson, *Arms and Armor in Colonial America, 1526–1783* (Harrisburg, Pa., 1956). See also Harold L. Peterson, *The Book of the Continental Soldier: Being a Compleat Account of the Uniforms, Weapons, and Equipment with Which He Lived and Fought* (Harrisburg, Pa., 1968), 23–140, for a good account of various weapons of the day. George C. Neumann, *The History of the Weapons of the American Revolution* (New York, 1967), contains extensive essays as well as numerous photographs and drawings of the weapons, firearms and other arms, carried by individual soldiers.

49. Howe to the British Adjutant General, June 22 and 24, 1775, *SOS*, 1:131–32; French, *Siege of Boston*, 261, 267–68.

50. The quotations are from Gregory T. Knouff, *The Soldiers' Revolution: Pennsylvanians in Arms and the Forging of Early American Identity* (University Park, Pa., 2004), 123, and E. B. Sledge, *With the Old Breed at Pelelin and Okinawa* (New York, 1990), 55–56. For the "aim at the handsome coats" quotation see Frothingham, *History of the Siege of Boston*, 126, 140.

51. Diary of Amos Farnsworth, MHS, *Proceedings*, 2d Ser., 12:87.

52. Ward, *War of the Revolution*, 1:91.

53. Higginbotham, *War of American Independence*, 75.

54. Account of Adjutant Waller, June 23, 1775, in Samuel Adams Drake, ed., *Bunker Hill: The Story Told in Letters from the Battle Field by British Officers Engaged* (Boston, 1875), 28, 29.

55. Quoted in Ketchum, *Decisive Day*, 163.

56. "Historical Record of the Royal Marines," in Drake, *Bunker Hill*, 32.

57. George H. Scheer and Hugh F. Rankin, *Rebels and Redcoats* (Cleveland, 1957), 63.

58. Howe to British Adjutant General, June 22, 24, 1775, *SOS* 1:132.

59. Recollection of Robert Steele, in Scheer and Rankin, *Rebels and Redcoats*, 59.

60. French, *Siege of Boston*, 275, 278.

61. Samuel Blachley Webb to Joseph Webb, June 19, 1775, in Worthington C. Ford, ed., *The Correspondence and Journals of Samuel Blachley Webb* (New York, 1893), 1:64.

62. John Greenwood, *The Revolutionary War Service of John Greenwood of Boston and New York, 1775–1783*, ed. Isaac J. Greenwood (New York, 1922), 14.

63. Peter Brown to his mother, June 28, 1775, *SOS* 1:124; French, *Siege of Boston*, 279.

64. Aside from the original sources that are cited throughout, this account of the engagement draws on Ketchum, *Decisive Day*, 135–80, 193; Forthingham, *History of the Siege of Boston*, 133–206; Birnbaum, *Red Dawn at Lexington*, 226–54.

65. Gage to Barrington, June 25, 1775, Clarence E. Carter, ed., *The Correspondence of General Thomas Gage with the Secretaries of State, 1763–1775*, reprint (New York, 1969), 2:685–86.

66. Quoted in Ketchum, *Decisive Day*, 183.

67. Howe to Adjutant General, June 28, 24, 1775, *SOS* 1:132.

68. "A British Officer to a Friend in England," n.d., *Massachusetts Historical Society Proceedings*, 44 (1910–1911), 102–3.

69. History Royal Artillery, Drake, *Bunker Hill*, 36.

70. Quoted in Sarah J. Purcell, *Sealed with Blood: War, Sacrifice, and Memory in Revolutionary America* (Philadelphia, 2002), 19.

71. Letter of a British Officer, July 5, 1775, *SOS* 1:136.

72. Gage to Barrington, June 26, 1775, Carter, *Correspondence of Gage*, 2:686.

Chapter 3. Choices, 1775

1. Quoted in Allen French, *The First Year of the American Revolution* (Boston, 1934), 323–24. See also David H. Murdoch, ed., *Rebellion in America: A Contemporary British Viewpoint, 1765–1783* (Santa Barbara, Calif., 1979), 180–81; Peter D. G. Thomas, *Tea Party to Independence: The Third Phase of the American Revolution, 1773–1776* (Oxford, England, 1991), 254.

2. Alan Valentine, *Lord North* (Norman, Okla., 1967), 1:369.

3. Quoted in Charles R. Ritcheson, *British Politics and the American Revolution* (Norman, Okla., 1954), 194.

4. Quoted in Peter D. G. Thomas, *Lord North* (London, 1976), 87.

5. Valentine, *Lord North*, 1:382, 383, 385. The North quotation is on page 377.

6. Julie Flavell, "British Perceptions of New England," in Julie Flavell and Stephan Conway, *Britain and America Go to War: The Impact of War and Warfare in Anglo-America, 1754–1815* (Gainesville, Fla., 2004), 96–109; Piers Mackesy, *The War for America, 1775–1783* (Cambridge, Mass., 1965), 32–36; Ira D. Gruber, *The Howe Brothers and the American Revolution* (Chapel Hill, N.C., 1972), 22.

7. Quoted in Eliga H. Gould, *The Persistence of Empire: British Political Culture in the Age of the American Revolution* (Chapel Hill, N.C., 2000), 151.

8. *PH* 18:263–64.

9. Valentine, *Lord North*, 376.

10. Gage to Dartmouth, June 25, 1775, Clarence E. Carter, ed., *The Correspondence of General Thomas Gage with the Secretaries of State, 1763–1775*, reprint (New York, 1969), 1:407.

11. Sir William Anson, ed., *Autobiography of Augustus Henry, Third Duke of Grafton* (London, 1898), 272.

12. The quotations are from J. W. Fortescue, *A History of the British Army* (London, 1910–1930), 3:169, 171.

13. Anson, *Autobiography of Grafton*, 277; Solomon Lutnick, *The American War and the British Press, 1775–1783* (Columbia, Mo., 1967), 61; Stanley Weintraub, *Iron Tears: America's Battle for Freedom, Britain's Quagmire, 1775–1783* (New York, 2005), 15–18; Catherine Macaulay, "Address to the People of England, Scotland and Ireland on the Present Important Crisis of Affairs," 1775, *SOS* 1:250–51.

14. "The King's Proclamation for Suppressing Rebellion," Aug. 23, 1775, in Merrill Jensen, ed., *English Historical Documents: American Colonial Documents to 1776* (London, 1964), 9:850–51.

15. David McCullough, *1776* (New York, 2005), 3–10; Valentine, *Lord North*, 373; "The King's Speech to Parliament," Oct. 26, 1775, Jensen, *English Historical Documents*, 9:851–52.

16. *PH* 18:769, 734, 761, 766–68; Thomas, *Tea Party to Independence*, 277.

17. William Franklin to Dartmouth, May 6, 1775, *DAR* 9:126; Josiah Martin to Dartmouth, May 18, June 30, Aug. 28, 1775, ibid., 9:139, 210; 11:89; James Wright to Dartmouth, May 25, June 9, 17, Aug. 7, 1775, ibid., 9:144, 168, 175; 11:67; William Tryon to Dartmouth, July 4, 1775, ibid., 11:35.

18. Gage to Dartmouth, June 12, 1775, Carter, *Correspondence of Gage*, 1:404.

19. The two quotations are from Thomas, *Tea Party to Independence*, 241, 256.

20. Stephen Conway, "British Army Officers and the American War for Independence," *WMQ* 41 (1984):267.

21. Edward E. Curtis, *The Organization of the British Army in the American Revolution* (New Haven, Conn., 1926), 55; Fortescue, *History of the British Army*, 3:172; North to Grafton, Oct. 20, 1775, Anson, *Autobiography of Grafton*, 273; Dartmouth to Governor Martin, Oct. 27, 1775, *DAR* 11:168; Mackesy, *War for America*, 525.

22. Fortescue, *History of the British Army*, 3:175.

23. Peter Whiteley, *Lord North: The Prime Minister Who Lost America* (London, 1996), 157–58; Thomas, *Tea Party to Independence*, 180–81; John R. Alden, *General Gage in America: Being Principally a History of his Role in the American Revolution* (Baton Rouge, 1948), 279–83; Dartmouth to Howe, Sept. 5, 1775, *DAR* 11:99–100. On Gage and his views, see John Shy, "The Empire Militant: Thomas Gage and the Coming of War," in John Shy, *A People Numerous and Armed: Reflections on the Military Struggle for American Independence* (New York, 1976), 73–107.

24. Gage to Dartmouth, Aug. 20, 1775, Carter, *Correspondence of Gage*, 1:413–14.

25. Gruber, *Howe Brothers*, 26, 31, 37; Howe to Dartmouth, Nov. 26, 1775, *DAR* 11:193.

26. Howe to Dartmouth, Nov. 26, 1775, *DAR* 11:191.

27. Mackesy, *War for America*, 50.

28. Alan Valentine, *Lord George Germain* (Oxford, England, 1962), 17–18, 21, 398, 411–13; Mackesy, *War for America*, 50–54; Gruber, *Howe Brothers*, 23, 37.

29. Thomas, *Lord North*, 39–41, 89, 106–7.

30. *PH* 18:942, 1,065.

31. *JCC* 2:55–56, 73–75.

32. Jerrilyn G. Marston, *King and Congress: The Transfer of Political Legitimacy, 1774–1776* (Princeton, N.J., 1987), 146, 153–54; Douglas Southall Freeman, *George Washington* (New York, 1948–1957), 3:530; *JCC* 2:109–10; Richard Henry Lee to GW, June 29, 1775, *PGW:RWS* 1:45; JA to James Warren, June 7, 1775, *PJA* 3:17.

33. Commission from the Congress to GW, June 19, 1775, *PGW:RWS* 1:7; Instructions from the Continental Congress to GW, June 22, 1775, ibid., 1:22.

34. Silas Deane to Elizabeth Deane, June 16, 1775, *LDC* 1:494; Eliphalet Dyer to Jonathan Trumbull Sr., June 16, 1775, ibid., 1:495–96; Dyer to Joseph Trumbull, June 20, 1775, ibid.,

1:521; Hancock to Elbridge Gerry, June 18, 1775, ibid., 1:507; Hancock to James Warren, June 18, 1775, ibid., 1:507.

35. Diary of Silas Deane, May 16, 1775, ibid., 1:351.

36. Thomas Doerflinger, *A Vigorous Spirit of Enterprise: Merchants and Economic Development in Revolutionary Philadelphia* (Chapel Hill, N.C., 1986), 167–96. The quotations are on pages 194 and 195.

37. For an elaboration, see John Ferling, *A Leap in the Dark: The Struggle to Create the American Republic* (New York, 2003), 135–48.

38. JA to AA, June 11, 1775, *AFC* 1:216. See also John Ferling, "The Rocky Road to Revolution," *Smithsonian* (July 2004): 96–106.

39. For an excellent discussion, and synthesis, of views on both sides of the Atlantic, see Gould, *Persistence of Empire*, 106–47.

Chapter 4. "Hastening Fast to a Crisis": June 1775–June 1776

1. Joseph Hodgkins to Sarah Hodgkins, July 3, 1775, in Herbert T. Wade and Robert A. Lively, eds., *This Glorious Cause: The Adventures of Two Company Officers in Washington's Army* (Princeton, N.J., 1958), 171.

2. *PGW:RWS* 1:50n; Edward G. Lengel, *General George Washington* (New York, 2005), 105–6.

3. Address from the Massachusetts Provincial Congress to GW, July 3, 1775, *PGW:RWS* 1:52–53; Joseph Hawley to GW, July 5, 1775, ibid., 1:65.

4. Council of War, July 9, 1775, ibid., 1:79–80, 81n; GW to John Thomas, July 23, 1775, ibid., 1:159–62, 61–62n, 94–96n; GW to Richard Henry Lee, July 10, 1775, ibid., 1:99; Lengel, *General George Washington*, 106. The "half a Putnam" quote is from Webb to Silas Deane, July 11, 1775, Worthington C. Ford, ed., *The Correspondence and Journals of Samuel Blachley Webb*, (New York, 1893), 1:80–81.

5. Robert K. Wright Jr., *The Continental Army* (Washington, D.C., 1983), 45–50.

6. GW to Lee, July 10, Aug. 29, 1775, *PGW:RWS* 1:99, 372–73; GW to Samuel Washington, July 20, 1775, ibid., 1:135; GW to Lund Washington, Aug. 20, 1775, ibid., 1:335; GW to John Hancock, July 10 [–11], 1775, ibid., 1:90; GW, General Orders, July 4, 7, Aug. 1, 7, 8, 9, 10, 22, Oct. 7, 9, ibid., 1:71, 73, 119, 128, 207, 260–61, 268, 277–78, 281, 347; 2:121, 255; George Scheer and Hugh Rankin, *Rebels and Redcoats* (Cleveland, 1957), 82.

7. GW to Lewis Morris, Aug. 4, 1775, ibid., 1:241; GW to Spencer, Sept. 26, 1775, ibid., 2:55; GW to Daniel Morgan, Oct. 4, 1775, ibid., 2:93; Jared Sparks, ed., *The Writings of George Washington; Being his Correspondence, Addresses, Messages. . . .* (Boston, 1837), 3:491.

8. GW, General Orders, Aug. 22, 1775, ibid., 1:347; GW to William Woodford, Nov. 10, 1775, ibid., 2:346–47.

9. Sparks, *Writings of Washington*, 3:490.

10. GW, General Orders, July 14, 23, 24, Nov. 13, 1775, ibid., 1:115, 158, 163; 2:357.

11. GW to John Augustine Washington, Oct. 13, 1775, ibid., 2:161; GW, General Orders, Oct. 26, 31, Nov. 14, 20; 2:235, 269, 369, 443; GW to Spencer, Sept. 26, 1775, ibid., 2:55; Don Higginbotham, *George Washington and the American Military Tradition* (Athens, Ga., 1985), 47–48.

12. GW, General Orders, July 4, 5, *PGW:RWS* 1:55, 63; GW to John Hancock, Sept. 21, 1775, ibid., 2:29; GW to Jonathan Trumbull, Sept. 21, 1775, ibid., 2:33; GW to Reed, Dec. 15, 1775, ibid., 2:552; Higginbotham, *Washington and the American Military Tradition*, 49–51.

13. GW to Benedict Arnold, Sept. 14, 1775, *PGW:RWS* 1:456; Mercy Otis Warren to JA, Oct. [?], 1775, *PJA* 3:269; AA to JA, July 16, 1775, *AFC* 1:246–47; Higginbotham, *Washington and the American Military Tradition*, 53–54.

14. GW to John Hancock, Sept. 21, *PGW:RWS* 2:28; GW to John A. Washington, Oct. 13, 1775, ibid., 2:161; GW to Samuel Washington, Sept. 30, 1775, ibid., 2:73; Percy to Harvey,

July 28, 1775, Charles K. Bolton, *Letters of Percy from Boston and New York: 1774–1776* (New York, 1972), 58.

15. GW to Hancock, Sept. 11, Nov. 11, 1775, ibid., 2:25, 29, 350; GW to Philip Schuyler, Nov. 5, 1775, ibid., 2:303; GW, General Orders, Oct. 26, 31, Nov. 14, 17, 1775, ibid., 2:235, 269, 270, 369, 389; *JCC* 3:393–94.

16. GW to Reed, Nov. 28, 1775, *PGW:RWS* 2:449; GW to Hancock, Dec. 4, 18, 25, 31, 1775, ibid., 2:484–85, 574, 602, 625; GW to Massachusetts Council, Jan. 10, 1776, ibid., 3:61, 63n; *JCC* 4:410–13. Richard Buel Jr., *Dear Liberty: Connecticut's Mobilization for the Revolutionary War* (Middletown, Conn., 1980), 55, 69; Douglas Southall Freeman, *George Washington* (New York, 1948–1957), 3:579; Wright, *Continental Army*, 56.

17. GW to Reed, Jan. 4, 14, 1776, *PGW:RWS* 3:24, 89.

18. Quoted respectively in James Thomas Flexner, *George Washington: The Forge of Experience, 1732–1775* (Boston, 1965), 2:67, and Don Higginbotham, *The War of American Independence: Military Attitudes, Policies, and Practice, 1763–1789* (New York, 1971), 390.

19. Christopher Ward, *The War of the Revolution*, 2 vols. (New York, 1952), 1:143–49; James Kirby Martin, *Benedict Arnold, Revolutionary Hero: An American Warrior Reconsidered* (New York, 1997), 100–1; Schuyler to GW, Aug. 6, 1775, *PGW:RWS* 1:256; GW to Schuyler, Aug. 14, 20, 1775, ibid., 1:306, 331–33; Don R. Gerlach, *Proud Patriot: Philip Schuyler and the War of Independence, 1775–1783* (Syracuse, 1987), 35–49; Martin H. Bush, *Revolutionary Enigma: A Re-appraisal of General Philip Schuyler of New York* (Port Washington, N.Y., 1969), 3–39.

20. GW to Schuyler, Aug. 20, 1775, *PGW:RWS* 1:332; Martin, *Benedict Arnold*, 106–8; James A. Huston, "Logistics of Arnold's March to Quebec," *Military Affairs*, 32 (1969), 111; Thomas A. Desjardin, *Through a Howling Wilderness: Benedict's Arnold's March to Quebec, 1775* (New York, 2006), 10.

21. On Arnold's background, see Martin, *Benedict Arnold*, 11–84; Willard Sterne Randall, *Benedict Arnold* (New York, 1990), 18–97; and Willard M. Wallace, *Traitorous Hero: The Life and Fortunes of Benedict Arnold* (Freeport, N.Y., 1964) 1–41.

22. Schuyler to GW, Aug. 27, 1775, *PGW:RWS* 1:368.

23. Schuyler to GW, Sept. 20, 26, Oct. 14, 1775, ibid., 2:17, 54, 166.

24. The quotations are from Hal T. Shelton, *General Richard Montgomery and the American Revolution* (New York, 1994), 68, 87.

25. Copy of Journal of Captain John Topham, 103, in Benedict Arnold's expedition against Quebec, in Charles Edward Banks research materials, MHS; John Joseph Henry, *Campaign against Quebec* (1812), in Kenneth Roberts, ed., *March to Quebec: Journals of the Members of Arnold's Expedition* (New York, 1946), 363; Journal of George Morison, ibid., 535; Shelton, *General Richard Montgomery and the American Revolution*, 8–71, 127.

26. GW to Schuyler, Oct. 26, 1775, *PGW:RWS* 2:238–40.

27. Quoted in Shelton, *General Richard Montgomery and the American Revolution*, 94. See also Gerlach, *Proud Patriot*, 59–65.

28. *JCC* 1:72, 76; Martin, *Benedict Arnold*, 110; Randall, *Benedict Arnold*, 144.

29. Michael A. Bellesiles, *Revolutionary Outlaws: Ethan Allen and the Struggle for Independence on the Early American Frontier* (Charlottesville, Va., 1993), 125–26; GW to Schuyler, Oct. 26, 1775, *PGW:RWS* 2:239.

30. This account of the siege campaign draws on Ward, *War of the Revolution*, 1:150–61, and Shelton, *General Richard Montgomery and the American Revolution*, 79–115.

31. Letter of an officer of New York troops, Nov. 3, 1775, in *SOS* 1:189.

32. Ward, *War of the Revolution*, 1:161–62; Shelton, *General Richard Montgomery and the American Revolution*, 117–23.

33. Quoted in Shelton, *General Richard Montgomery and the American Revolution*, 126.

34. GW, General Orders, Sept. 5, 1775, *PGW:RWS* 1:415.

35. Desjardin, *Through a Howling Wilderness*, 16–19.

36. Robert G. Parkinson, "From Indian Killer to Worthy Citizen: The Revolutionary Transformation of Michael Cresap," *WMQ* 63 (2006): 107, 109.

37. Don Higginbotham, *Daniel Morgan: Revolutionary Rifleman* (Chapel Hill, N.C., 1961), 1–26; Don Higginbotham, "Daniel Morgan: Guerrilla Fighter," in George A. Billias, ed., *George Washington's Generals* (New York, 1964), 291–95. The description of Morgan was offered by Colonel Henry Lee.: see Robert E. Lee, ed., *The Revolutionary War Memoirs of General Henry Lee*, reprint (New York, 1998), 583.

38. Journal of Abner Stocking, in Roberts, *March to Quebec*, 546; Henry, *Campaign against Quebec*, ibid., 337; Jeremiah Greenman, *Diary of a Common Soldier in the American Revolution, 1775–1783*, eds. Robert C. Bray and Paul E. Bushnell (DeKalb, Ill., 1978), xv; Ward, *War of the Revolution*, 1:165; Higginbotham, *Daniel Morgan*, 1–26.

39. Ward, *War of the Revolution*, 1:170; Martin, *Benedict Arnold*, 124.

40. Huston, "Logistics of Arnold's March," *Military Affairs*, 32:112–13.

41. Journal of Stocking, in Roberts, *March to Quebec*, 550; GW to Schuyler, Aug. 20, 1775, *PGW:RWS* 1:332; Arnold to GW, Sept. 25 [–27], 1775, ibid., 2:40–41, 155; GW, Address to the Inhabitants of Canada, Sept. 14, 1775, ibid., 1:461.

42. Journal of Stocking, in Roberts, *March to Quebec*, 549, 555; Arnold to GW, Oct. 13, 1775, *PGW:RWS* 2:155; Greenman, *Diary of a Common Soldier*, 14; Wallace, *Traitorous Hero*, 66.

43. Copy of Journal of Captain Tapham, 77, 79, Benedict Arnold's expedition against Quebec, in Charles Edward Banks research materials, MHS; Henry, *Campaign against Quebec*, in Roberts, *March to Quebec*, 310, 316; Journal of Dr. Isaac Senter, ibid., 203, 206–7, 209; Journal of Simeon Thayer, ibid., 253, 267; Journal of Return J. Meigs, ibid., 178; William Hendricks, *A Journal of the March of a Party of Provincials from Carlisle to Boston and from thence to Quebec* (Glasgow, 1877), 19; Greenman, *Diary of a Common Soldier*, 15; Martin, *Benedict Arnold*, 123–26.

44. Journal of Benedict Arnold, in Roberts, *March to Quebec*, 54; Arnold to Roger Enos, Oct. 24, 1775, ibid., 75; Huston, "Logistics of Arnold's March," *Military Affairs*, 32:114, 116; Martin, *Benedict Arnold*, 127.

45. Henry, *Campaign*, in Roberts, *March to Quebec*, 324, 341; Journal of Henry Dearborn, ibid., 137, 139; Journal of Senter, ibid., 210; Martin, *Benedict Arnold*, 133; Randall, *Benedict Arnold*, 176–81, 184; Ward, *War of the Revolution*, 1:177; Huston, "Logistics of Arnold's March," *Military Affairs*, 116–17.

46. Arnold to GW, Oct. 27 [–28], 1775, *PGW:RWS* 2:244–45.

47. Greenman, *Diary of a Common Soldier*, 18–19; Journal of Senter, in Roberts, *March to Quebec*, 216; Journal of Thayer, ibid., 259; Hendricks, *Journal of the March*, 22; 5 Nov. 1775, copy of Journal of Captain Tapham, Benedict Arnold's expedition against Quebec, in Charles Edward Banks research materials, MHS; Higginbotham, *Daniel Morgan*, 34–35.

48. GW to Arnold, Sept. 14, 1775, *PGW:RWS* 1:456; Journal of Senter, Roberts, *March to Quebec*, 219; Desjardin, *Through a Howling Wilderness*, 110.

49. Arnold to GW, Nov. 13, 1775, *PGW:RWS* 2:358; Martin, *Benedict Arnold*, 143–45.

50. Journal of Senter, Roberts, *March to Quebec*, 226; Journal of Dearborn, ibid., 142; Arnold to GW, Nov. 13, 20, 1775, *PGW:RWS* 2:358, 403.

51. George M. Wrong, *Canada and the American Revolution* (New York, 1968), 297–99; Gustave Lanctot, *Canada and the American Revolution, 1774–1783* (Cambridge, Mass., 1967), 92–123; Desjardin, *Through a Howling Wilderness*, 6; Ward, *War of the Revolution*, 1:183.

52. Arnold to Montgomery, Nov. 25, 1775, Roberts, *March to Quebec*, 96; Martin, *Benedict Arnold*, 155; Shelton, *General Richard Montgomery and the American Revolution*, 122.

53. Shelton, *General Richard Montgomery and the American Revolution*, 122–23, 128.

54. Ibid., 134–38; Martin, *Benedict Arnold*, 157–58, 160, 162–63, 165; Roberts, *March to Quebec*, 483n.

55. Quoted in Shelton, *General Richard Montgomery and the American Revolution*, 143.

56. Jared Sparks, ed., *Correspondence of the American Revolution; Being Letters of Eminent Men to George Washington* (Boston, 1853), 1:496.

57. 31 Dec. 1775, copy of journal of Patrick Daly, Benedict Arnold's expedition against Quebec, in Charles Edward Banks research materials, MHS.

58. Journal of Dearborn, Roberts, *March to Quebec*, 149; Journal of Senter, ibid., 234.

59. Higginbotham, *Daniel Morgan*, 46–48.

60. Martin, *Benedict Arnold*, 167–74; Shelton, *General Richard Montgomery and the American Revolution*, 138–50; Ward, *War of the Revolution*, 1:190–95.

61. 30 Nov. 1775, copy of journal of Colonel Henry Caldwell, Benedict Arnold's expedition against Quebec, in Charles Edward Banks research materials, MHS.

62. Schuyler to GW, Jan. 13, 1776, *PGW:RWS* 3:78; GW to JA, Jan. 15, 1776, ibid., 3:93; Council of War, Jan. 16, 18, 1776, ibid., 3:103–4, 132–34; Circular to the governments of Massachusetts, Connecticut, and New Hampshire, Jan. 19, 1776, ibid., 3:145; Trumbull to GW, Jan. 18, 1776, ibid., 3:144; New Hampshire General Court to GW, Jan. 21, 1776, ibid., 3:162; GW to Charles Lee, Jan. 23, 1776, ibid., 3:170.

63. GW, Circular to the General Officers, Sept. 8, 1775, ibid., 1:432–34; Council of War, Sept. 11, 1775, ibid., 1:450–51; GW to Reed, Jan. 14, 1776, ibid., 3:89–90.

64. McCullough, *1776*, 28; NG to Samuel Ward Sr., Dec. 31, 1775, *PNG* 1:173; NG to Nicholas Cooke, June 18, 1775, ibid., 1:58; Joseph Hodgkins to Sarah Hodgkins, June 20, July 3, Oct. 6, 1775, Jan. 8, 1776, Wade and Lively, *This Glorious Cause*, 169, 171, 178, 189; Loammi Baldwin to Mary Fowle Baldwin, May 3, 4, Oct. 3, 6, 25, Nov. 14, 1775, Jan. 12, 28, Feb. 3, 1776, Loammi Baldwin Papers, Houghton Library, Harvard University; "Diary of Amos Farnsworth," *MHS Proceedings*, 2d Ser. (1897–1899), 12:87.

65. *PGW:RWS* 3:21n; Birnbaum, *Red Dawn at Lexington*, 323–24, 330; Edward E. Curtis, *The Organization of the British Army in the American Revolution* (New Haven, Conn., 1926), 100, 116, 118; Scheer and Rankin, *Rebels and Redcoats*, 96; Piers Mackesy, *The War for America, 1775–1783* (Cambridge, Mass., 1965), 80; Evelyn to William Evelyn, G. D. Scully, ed., *Memoirs and Letters of Captain W. Glenville Evelyn of the 4th Regiment ("King's Own") from North America, 1774–1776* (Oxford, England, 1879), 76; McCullough, *1776*, 73; Neil Cantlie, *A History of the Army Medical Department* (Edinburgh, 1974), 140; Grant to Harvey, Aug. 10, 1775, Papers of James Grant of Bellindaloch, reel 29, LC.

66. North Callahan, *Henry Knox: George Washington's General* (New York, 1958), 32; GW to Hancock, Nov. 8, 1775, *PGW:RWS* 2:331; *JCC* 3:358–59.

67. Callahan, *Henry Knox*, 16–31; North Callahan, "Henry Knox: American Artillerist," in Billlias, *George Washington's Generals*, 240.

68. GW, Instructions to Colonel Henry Knox, Nov. 16, 1775, *PGW:RWS* 2:384–85.

69. B. P. Hughes, *British Smooth-Bore Artillery: The Muzzle Loading Artillery of the 18th and 19th Centuries* (Harrisburg, 1969); Harold L. Peterson, *Round Shot and Rammers* (Harrisburg, 1969). For a wonderful synopsis, see Carl P. Borick, *A Gallant Defense: The Siege of Charleston, 1780* (Columbia, S.C., 2003), 111–13.

70. Knox to GW, Nov. 27, Dec. 5, 17, 1775, Jan. 5, 1776, ibid., 2:434, 495–96, 563–66; 3:29; Callahan, *Henry Knox*, 38–56; Ebenezer David to Nicholas Brown, Jan. 29, 1776, in Jeanette D. Black and William G. Roelker, eds., *A Rhode Island Chaplain in the Revolution: Letters of Ebenezer David to Nicholas Brown, 1775–1776* (Port Washington, N.Y., 1949), 10; Birnbaum, *Red Dawn at Lexington*, 337–38; Journal of Henry Knox, *SOS* 1:176.

71. GW to Hancock, Jan. 4, Feb. 18 [–21], 1776, *PGW:RWS* 3:19, 335; Council of War, Jan. 16, Feb. 16, 1776, ibid., 3:103, 320–24; GW to Reed, ibid., Jan. 23, Feb. 10, 1776, ibid., 3:174, 287–90; GW to Trumbull, Feb. 19, 1776, ibid., 3:345; Freeman, *Washington*, 4:20–21; Ward, *War of the Revolution*, 1:125; Flexner, *Washington*, 2:69.

72. Council of War, Feb. 16, 1776, *PGW:RWS* 3:320–22, 323–24n; GW to Reed, Feb. 26 [–March 9], 1776, ibid., 3:373; Lengel, *General George Washington*, 120; Ward, *War of the Revolution*, 1:126–28.

73. Council of War, July 9, 1775, *PGW:RWS* 1:80; Ward to GW, Aug. 25, 1775, ibid., 1:363.

74. Freeman, *Washington*, 4:27–30; Birnbaum, *Red Dawn at Lexington*, 351; James Thacher, *Military Journal of the American Revolution* (Reprint, New York, 1969), 38–39.

75. AA to JA, March 2, 1776, *AFC* 1:353.

76. Lengel, *General George Washington*, 123.

77. Archibald Robinson, *His Diaries and Sketches in America, August 1775 to April 1776*, in Harry M. Lyndenberg, ed., *New York Public Library Bulletin* (New York, 1933), 286.

78. The quotations are in Ward, *War of the Revolution*, 1:128.

79. Robinson, *His Diaries and Sketches in America*, 73–74.

80. Grant to Richard Rigby, Oct. 5, 1775, Papers of James Grant of Bellindaloch, reel 29, LC; Grant to Harvey, Oct. 5, 1775, March 26, 1776, ibid.

81. *PGW:RWS* 3:377–78n; GW to Reed, Feb. 26 [–March 9], 1776, ibid., 3:376.

82. GW, General Orders, March 14 [–17], 1776, ibid., 3:466; Inventory of Ordnance and Ordnance Stores Found in Boston, April 14, 1776, ibid., 4:63–64; GW to Hancock, March 19, 1776, ibid., 3:490; Birnbaum, *Red Dawn at Lexington*, 361, 367–68; Freeman, *Washington*, 4:53; Thacher, *Military Journal*, 41–42; William S. Powell, ed., "A Connecticut Soldier Writing Home: Elisha Bostwick's Memoirs of the First Years of the Revolution," *WMQ* 6 (1949): 100; Scheer and Rankin, *Rebels and Redcoats*, 108; Lengel, *General George Washington*, 126.

83. Birnbaum, *Red Dawn at Lexington*, 369; *PH* 18:1345; Solomon Lutnick, *The American War and the British Press, 1775–1783* (Columbia, Mo., 1967), 70.

84. *PGW:RWS* 4:2n.

85. Martin, *Benedict Arnold*, 186–89; Ward, *War of the Revolution*, 1:196.

86. GW to Reed, Jan. 23, 1776, *PGW:RWS* 3:173; Schuyler to GW, April 12, 27, 1776, ibid., 4:56, 148.

87. Lanctot, *Canada and the American Revolution*, 126, 139; Commissioners to Canada to Hancock, May 27, 1776, *LDC* 4:81–82.

88. Journal of Thomas Ainslie, May 6, 1776, *SOS* 1:211; John Sullivan to Hancock, June 1, 1776, ibid., 1:215. For Carleton's account, see Carleton to Germain, May 14, 1776, *DAR* 12:137–38.

89. Charles P. Whittemore, *A General of the Revolution: John Sullivan of New Hampshire* (New York, 1961), 1–30. The Sullivan quotation is on page 28.

90. Sullivan to GW, June 8, 1776, *SP* 1:228; Sullivan to Hancock, June 1, 1776, ibid., 1:212.

91. Sullivan to GW, June 7, 1776, ibid., 1:226.

92. Ward, *War of the Revolution*, 1:199.

93. Sullivan to Schuyler, June 19, July 6, 1776, *SP* 1:250, 280.

94. Carleton claimed to have captured twenty-two rebel cannon. See Carleton to Germain, June 20, 1776, *DAR* 12:153. On Carleton's flawed leadership, see Paul H. Smith, "Sir Guy Carleton: Soldier-Statesman," in George A. Billias, ed., *George Washington's Opponents: British Generals and Admirals in the American Revolution* (New York, 1969), 120–23.

95. Arnold to Sullivan, June 13, 1776, *SOS* 1:220.

96. Sullivan to Schuyler, June 22, 1776, *SP* 1:258; Richard Ketchum, *Saratoga: Turning Point of America's Revolutionary War* (New York, 1997), 36.

97. [Lewis Beebe], "Journal of a Physician on the Expedition against Canada, 1776," *Pennsylvania Magazine of History and Biography* 59 (1935): 336, 338.

98. Hancock to Certain Colonies, June 4, 1776, *LDC* 4:136.

Chapter 5. Choices, 1776

1. *DAJA* 3:321; JA to Warren, July 24, 1775, *PJA* 3:89.

2. Jerrilyn G. Marston, *King and Congress: The Transfer of Political Legitimacy, 1774–1776* (Princeton, N.J., 1987), 58–59, 210–14; *JCC* 2:157–58.

3. John DeHart to the New Jersey Assembly, Nov. 13, 1775, *LDC* 2:334.

4. TJ to John Randolph, Nov. 29, 1775, *PTJ* 1:269.

5. Paine, *Common Sense* (1776), in Philip S. Foner, ed., *The Complete Writings of Thomas Paine*, 2 vols. (New York, 1945), 1:17–31, 45. The quotations are on pages 17 and 45.

6. Pauline Maier, *American Scripture: Making the Declaration of Independence* (New York, 1997), 33; JA to Warren, April 20, 1776, *PJA* 4:131; JA to Samuel Chase, July 1, 1776, ibid., 4:353.

7. John Dickinson, "Draft Address to the Inhabitants of North America," Jan. 24 [?], 1776, *LDC* 3:139–44; Diary of Richard Smith, ibid., 3:252; *DAJA* 2:229–30; Milton E. Flower, *John Dickinson: Conservative Revolutionary* (Charlottesville, Va., 1983), 144.

8. Diary of Smith, Jan. 9, 1776, *LDC* 3:72.

9. JA to Gates, March 23, 1776, *PJA* 4:59; Lee to Landon Carter, April 1, 1776, *LDC* 3:470. On colonial commerce, see Merrill Jensen, *The Founding of a Nation: A History of the American Revolution, 1763–1776* (New York, 1968), 15–19; Colin Bonwick, *The American Revolution* (Charlottesville, Va., 1991), 23–24.

10. Richard W. Van Alstyne, *Empire and Independence: The International History of the American Revolution* (New York, 1967), 51–53; Charles H. Van Tyne, "French Aid before the Alliance of 1778," *AHR* 31 (1925–1926), 20–40.

11. Van Alstyne, *Empire and Independence*, 89; Weldon A. Brown, *Empire or Independence: A Study in the Failure of Reconciliation, 1774–1783* (Baton Rouge, 1941), 169; Samuel Flagg Bemis, *The Diplomacy of the American Revolution* (New York, 1935), 20; Orville T. Murphy, *Charles Gravier, Comte de Vergennes: French Diplomacy in the Age of Revolution, 1719–1787* (Albany, 1982), 23, 49, 56, 95, 166, 345; Richard B. Morris, *The Peacemakers: The Great Powers and American Independence* (New York, 1965), 112–13; Jonathan Dull, *A Diplomatic History of the American Revolution* (New Haven, Conn., 1985), 48.

12. Brown, *Empire or Independence*, 175–76.

13. Van Alstyne, *Empire and Independence*, 79–82; Committee of Secret Correspondence to Arthur Lee, Dec. 12, 1775, *LDC* 2:476.

14. *PGW:RWS* 2:532n; Nicholas Cooke to GW, Dec. 11, 14, 1775, ibid., 2:532, 546; GW to John Hancock, Dec. 14, 1775, ibid., 2:548; Diary of Smith, *LDC* 2:538; 3:14; Hancock to GW, Jan. 6, 1776, ibid., 3:42; Minutes, Secret Committee, Feb. 14, 1776, ibid., 3:256; Samuel Ward to Henry Ward, Feb. 19, 1776, ibid., 3:286; Richard W. Van Alstyne, *The Rising American Empire* (Oxford, England, 1960), 29–30.

15. Bemis, *Diplomacy of the American Revolution*, 21–26; Committee of Secret Correspondence to Bonvouloir, Dec. [?], 1775, *LDC* 2:541.

16. Quoted in Van Alstyne, *Empire and Independence*, 89.

17. Ibid., 90.

18. JA to Warren, April 16, 1776, *PJA* 4:122; *DAJA* 2:236.

19. JA to Warren, May 18, 1776, *PJA* 4:192.

20. Lee to Carter, June 2, 1776, *LDC* 4:117; JA to Benjamin Hichborn, May 29, 1776, *PJA* 4:217–18; JA to Warren, May 20, 1776, ibid., 4:195–96.

21. JA to AA, May 17, 1776, *AFC* 1:411; Oliver Wolcott to Laura Wolcott, June 15, 1776, *LDC* 4:226.

22. JA to Archibald Bulloch, July 1, 1776, *PJA* 4:352; John Dickinson, "Notes for a Speech in Congress," [July 1, 1776], *LDC* 4:351–57. Neither notes nor a text for JA's speech have survived. He almost surely said what he had said in countless letters written during the preceding twelve months. See John Ferling, *Setting the World Ablaze: Washington, Adams, Jefferson, and the American Revolution* (New York, 2000), xxii–xxiii.

23. Josiah Bartlett to John Langdon, July 1, 1776, ibid., 4:351. On the long struggle in Congress to declare independence, see John Ferling, "The Rocky Road to Revolution," *Smithsonian* 35 (July 2004): 96–106.

24. Flower, *John Dickinson*, 168–86.

25. JA to AA, July 3, 1776, *AFC* 2:30–31.

Chapter 6. "Knock Him Up for the Campaign": The Battle for New York, 1776

1. GW to Read, Jan. 4, 1776, *PGW:RWS* 3:25; GW to Trumbull, Jan. 7, 1776, ibid., 3:51; GW, Instructions to Major General Charles Lee, Jan. 8, 1776, ibid., 3:53–54; GW to John A. Washington, March 31, 1776, ibid., 3:570; GW to Lord Stirling, March 14, 1776, ibid., 3:470; Lee to GW, Jan. 5, 1776, ibid., 3:30.

2. Lee to Samuel Purviance Jr., April 6, 1776, ibid., 4:259–60n; Lee to GW, Feb. 19, 1776, ibid., 3:339–40; Lee to Isaac Sears, March 5, 1776, *LP* 1:346; Eric Manders, *The Battle of Long Island* (Monmouth, N.J., 1978), 12. (Hereafter General Lee's works are cited as *Lee Papers*.)

3. Barnet Schecter, *The Battle for New York: The City at the Heart of the American Revolution* (New York, 2002), 76–80; Lee to GW, Feb. 5 [–6], 9, 29, 1776, *PGW:RWS* 3:250–51, 291, 390–91; Lee to Benjamin Rush, Feb. 25, 1776, *LP* 1:326.

4. Charles Lee, "Report on the Defence of New York," March 1776, *LP* 1:354–57.

5. Lee to GW, Jan. 5, 1776, *PGW:RWS* 3:30; JA to GW, Jan. 6, 1776, ibid., 3:36–38.

6. GW to Read, Jan. 31, 1776, ibid., 3:228; Hancock to GW, Feb. 12, 1776, ibid., 3:300; *JCC* 4:44–45; Schecter, *Battle for New York*, 69, 76; Judith Livan Buskirk, *Generous Enemies: Patriots and Loyalists in Revolutionary New York* (Philadelphia, 2002), 16.

7. GW to Hancock, March 13, June 23, 1776, *PGW:RWS* 3:462; 5:79; GW to John A. Washington, May 31 [–June 4], 1776, ibid., 4:413; GW to Adam Stephen, July 20, 1776, ibid., 5:408–9; New York Convention to GW, July 16, 1776, ibid., 5:348; David Hackett Fischer, *Washington's Crossing* (New York, 2004), 83–84.

8. GW to John A. Washington, July 22, 1776, *PGW:RWS* 5:428–29; GW to Hancock, June 17, July 17, 1776, ibid., 5:21, 356; GW to Trumbull, June 10, 1776, ibid., 4:496; GW to Stephen, July 20, 5:408–9; GW to George Clymer, June 17, 1776, ibid., 5:19; GW to Ward, July 1, 1776, ibid., 5:179; Edward G. Lengel, *General George Washington* (New York, 2005), 128–29; Fischer, *Washington's Crossing*, 85–86.

9. GW to William Livingston, June 28, 1776, *PGW:RWS* 5:136; Ephraim Manning to GW, July 3, 1776, ibid., 5:194; Bruce Bliven, *Under the Guns: New York, 1775–1776* (New York, 1972), 318; Schecter, *Battle for New York*, 100; John J. Gallagher, *The Battle of Brooklyn, 1776* (Edison, N.J., 2002), 67.

10. Piers Mackesy, *The War for America, 1775–1783* (Cambridge, Mass., 1965), 82–83.

11. Ibid., 81. See also Ira D. Gruber, "Richard Lord Howe: Admiral as Peacemaker," in George A. Billias, ed., *George Washington's Opponents* (New York, 1969), 233–59.

12. See the narrative in John Ferling, *The First of Men: A Life of George Washington* (Knoxville, 1988), 162–63.

13. GW to John A. Washington, July 22, 1776, *PGW:RWS* 5:428; Rodney Atwood, *The Hessians: Mercenaries from Hessen-Kassel in the American Revolution* (Cambridge, England, 1980), 52–57.

14. Quoted in Edward E. Curtis, *The Organization of the British Army in the American Revolution* (New Haven, Conn., 1926), 125.

15. John W. Gordon, *South Carolina and the American Revolution: A Battlefield History* (Columbia, S.C., 2003), 15–36; Hugh T. Lefler and William S. Powell, *Colonial North Carolina: A History* (New York, 1973), 269–77; Don Higginbotham, *The War of American Independence: Military Attitudes, Policies, and Practice, 1763–1789* (New York, 1971), 135.

16. Mackesy, *War for America*, 63–64.

17. William B. Willcox, *Portrait of a General: Sir Henry Clinton in the War of Independence* (New York, 1962), 3–39; William B. Willcox, "Sir Henry Clinton: Paralysis of Command," in Billias, *George Washington's Opponents*, 73–102.

18. Lee to GW, March 3, 1776, *PGW:RWS* 3:404.

19. Proceedings of the Committee of Safety at Williamsburg, April 10, 1776, *Lee Papers*, 1:406–8; Lee to Lieutenant Colonel Eppes, April 11, 1776, ibid., 1:411; Lee to General James Moore, April 23, 1776, ibid., 1:445; John Selby, *The Revolution in Virginia, 1775–1783* (Williamsburg, Va., 1988), 89–94.

20. Clinton to Germain, July 8, 1776, *DAR* 12:163.

21. Letter from a surgeon with the British fleet, July 9, 1776, *SOS* 2:1067.

22. Commodore Sir Peter Parker to Philip Stephens, July 9, 1776, *DAR* 12:170.

23. The narrative draws on the accounts in Willcox, *Portrait of a General*, 78–93; John Alden, *General Charles Lee: Traitor or Patriot?* (Baton Rouge, 1951), 119–31; Gordon, *South Carolina and the American Revolution*, 37–44; John Buchanan, *The Road to Guilford Courthouse: The American Revolution in the Carolinas* (New York, 1997), 11–16.

24. Letter from a surgeon with the British fleet, July 9, 1776, *SOS* 2:1067.

25. Howe to Germain, Aug. 6, 1776, *DAR* 12:178; Ira D. Gruber, *The Howe Brothers and the American Revolution* (Chapel Hill, N.C., 1972)s, 101, 104–7.

26. Ira D. Gruber, "America's First Battle: Long Island, 27 August 1776," in Charles E. Heller and William A. Stofft, eds., *America's First Battles, 1776–1965* (Lawrence, Kans., 1986), 15–17.

27. Lengel, *General George Washington*, 134.

28. GW to Trumbull, Aug. 24, 1776, *PGW:RWS* 6:123; Lengel, *General George Washington*, 141.

29. Fischer, *Washington's Crossing*, 88. While Howe drew on local Loyalists for useful information and guidance, the British army's intelligence-gathering apparatus, like that of most European armies of the day, was primitive. Only when Clinton was commander of the British army, and then not until nearly 1781, did the British develop a spy network with a staff of officers to analyze the data that was collected. See Roger Kaplan, "The Hidden War: British Intelligence Operations during the American Revolution," *WMQ* 47 (1990): 115–38.

30. GW to Hancock, Aug. 22, 23, 1776, *PGW:RWS* 6:102, 111; GW to Trumbull, Aug. 24, 1776, ibid., 6:123; Gruber, "America's First Battle," in Heller and Stofft, *America's First Battles*, 18.

31. GW to William Heath, Aug. 23, 1776, *PGW:RWS* 6:113; GW to Trumbull, Aug. 24, 1776, ibid, 6:123.

32. NG to GW, Aug. 15, 1776, ibid., 6:30; GW to Hancock, June 17, 1776, ibid., 5:21; GW, General Orders, Aug. 20, 1776, 6:89; Terry Golway, *Washington's General: Nathanael Greene and the Triumph of the American Revolution* (New York, 2005), 90–91.

33. Quoted in John Buchanan, *The Road to Valley Forge: How Washington Built the Army That Won the Revolution* (Hoboken, N.J., 2004), 47.

34. *PGW:RWS* 6:128n; GW to Putnam, Aug. 25, 1776, ibid., 6:127; Fischer, *Washington's Crossing*, 92–93.

35. Gruber, "America's First Battle," in Heller and Stofft, *America's First Battles*, 22.

36. Diary of Lieutenant von Bardeleben, in Bruce E. Burgoyne, ed., *Enemy Views: The American War as Recorded by the Hessian Participants* (Bowie, Md., 1996), 69.

37. Account of Michael Graham, in John C. Dann, ed., *Revolution Remembered: Eyewitness Accounts of the War of Independence* (Chicago, 1980), 50.

38. Edward J. Tatum, ed., *The American Journal of Ambrose Serle* (New York, 1969), 78; Christopher Ward, *The War of the Revolution*, 2 vols. (New York, 1952), 1:211–37; Douglas Southall Freeman, *George Washington* (New York, 1948–1957), 4:153–75; Gallagher, *Battle of Brooklyn*, 101–34; Gruber, "America's First Battle," in Heller and Stofft, *America's First Battles*, 20–29; *PGW:RWS* 6:142–43n; *SOS* 1:439, 442, 443.

39. Daniel Brodhead to unknown, Sept. 5, 1776, Dennis P. Ryan, ed., *A Salute to Courage: The American Revolution as Seen through Wartime Writings of Officers of the Continental Army and Navy* (New York, 1979), 41.

40. Haslet to Rodney, Sept. 4, 1776, Ryden, *Letters to and from Caesar Rodney*, 112.

41. Richard M. Ketchum, "Men of the Revolution: Israel Putnam," *American Heritage*, 24 (June 1973), 27; Alexander Graydon, *Memoirs of His Own Time, with Reminisces of the Men and Event of the Revolution*, ed, John S. Littell (Philadelphia, 1846), 179.

42. Gruber, "America's First Battle," in Heller and Stofft, *America's First Battles*, 28–29.

43. Howe to Germaine, Sept. 3, 1776, *DAR* 12:217.

44. Henry P. Johnston, *The Campaign of 1776 around New York and Brooklyn* (Brooklyn, 1878), part 2, 36–39; Fischer, *Washington's Crossing*, 100.

45. Council of War, Aug. 29, 1776, *PGW:RWS* 6:153; GW to Hancock, Aug. 31, 1776, ibid., 6:177; James Chambers to Kitty Chambers, Sept. 3, 1776, Ryan, *A Salute to Courage*, 39; Ward, *War of the Revolution*, 1:233; Gruber, "America's First Battle," in Heller and Stofft, *America's First Battles*, 29; Benjamin Tallmadge, *Memoir of Colonel Benjamin Tallmadge* (New York, 1968), 13; Billias, *General John Glover*, 101–3.

46. Viscount Howe to Germain, Sept. 20, 1776, *DAR* 12:226–27; Tatum, *American Journal of Ambrose Serle*, 82–83; Mackesy, *War for America*, 88; Gruber, *Howe Brothers and the American Revolution*, 115, 117–20; Josiah Bartlett to John Langdon, Sept. 1, 1776, *LDC* 5:89; JA to William Tudor, Sept. 2, 1776, *PJA* 5:3; John Ferling, *John Adams: A Life* (Knoxville, 1992), 162–63.

47. GW to Hancock, Sept. 2, 8, 1776, *PGW:RWS* 6:199–200, 248–52.

48. Ibid., Sept. 8, 1776, ibid., 6:249.

49. Ibid., Sept. 2, 8, 1776, ibid., 6:200, 248–52; Greene to GW, Sept. 5, 1776, ibid., 6:223.

50. Certain general officers to GW, Sept. 11, 1776, ibid., 6:279; Council of War, Sept. 12, 1776, ibid., 6:288–89; Hancock to GW, Sept. 3, 1776, ibid., 6:207; Lee to Gates, Oct. 14, 1776, ibid., 6:443n; GW to Hancock, Sept. 8, 1776, ibid., 6:249.

51. *JCC* 5:749; Hancock to GW, Sept. 10, *PGW:RWS* 6:273; GW to Hancock, Sept. 14, 1776, ibid., 6:308; Council of War, Sept. 12, 1776, ibid., 6: 288–89, 289n; GW to John A. Washington, Sept. 22, 1776, ibid., 6:372–73; Lengel, *General George Washington*, 152.

52. GW to Hancock, Sept. 2, 1776, *PGW:RWS* 6:199; Ward, *War of the Revolution*, 1:239.

53. George Scheer, ed., *Private Yankee Doodle: Being a Narrative of Some of the Adventures, Dangers and Sufferings of a Revolutionary Soldier* (Boston, 1962), 34; Schecter, *Battle for New York*, 183; Ward, *War of the Revolution*, 1:242; *PGW:RWS* 6:315n.

54. Ferling, *First of Men*, 170; Fischer, *Washington's Crossing*, 104; Schecter, *Battle for New York*, 186; Sheer, *Private Yankee Doodle*, 41; Journal of Benjamin Trumbull, *SOS* 1:466; George A. Billias, *General John Glover and His Marblehead Men* (New York, 1960), 108.

55. Schecter, *Battle for New York*, 185–90; Frederick Mackenzie, *Diary of Frederick Mackenzie* (Cambridge, Mass., 1930), 1:49; Diary of Lieutenant von Bardeleben, Burgoyne, *Enemy Views*, 80.

56. Hans Huth, "Letters from a Hessian Mercenary," *PMHB* 62 (1938): 494–95; Mackenzie, *Diary of Mackenzie*, 1:59; Governor William Tryon to Germain, Sept. 24, 1776, *DAR* 12:230–31; GW to Hancock, Sept. 22, 1776, *PGW:RWS* 6:369; GW to Lund Washington, Oct. 6, 1776, ibid., 6:494.

57. Greene to GW, Sept. 5, 1776, *PGW:RWS* 6:222–23.

58. GW to Hancock, Sept. 16, 18, 1776, *PGW:RWS* 6:314, 333; Reed to his wife, Sept. 17, 1776, *SOS* 1:466; Ward, *War of the Revolution*, 1:247–51; Lengel, *General George Washington*, 156.

59. Ward, *War of the Revolution*, 1:246.

60. Quoted in Troyer Steele Anderson, *The Command of the Howe Brothers during the American Revolution* (New York, 1936), 145.

61. Howe to Germain, Sept. 25, 1776, *DAR* 12:232; Gruber, *Howe Brothers and the American Revolution*, 127.

62. GW to Abraham Yates, Sept. 23, 1776, *PGW:RWS* 6:383; GW to Trumbull, Sept. 23, 1776, ibid., 6:382; GW to Lund Washington, Sept. 30, Oct. 6, 1776, ibid., 6:442, 493; GW to Hancock, Oct. 11 [–13], 1776, ibid., 6:534.

63. GW to Samuel Washington, Oct. 5, 1776, ibid., 6:487; GW to Ward, Oct. 13, 1776, ibid., 6:562.

64. GW to Nicholas Cooke, Oct. 12 [–13], 1776, ibid., 6:546; GW to Ward, Oct. 13, 1776, ibid., 6:562; GW to Hancock, Oct. 11 [–13], 1776, ibid., 6:535; GW to Trumbull, Oct. 15, 1776, ibid., 6:574.

65. Quoted in Johnston, *Campaign of 1776 around New York and Brooklyn*, 1:270–71.

66. Henry Clinton, *The American Rebellion: Sir Henry Clinton's Narrative of His Campaigns, 1775–1782*, ed. William B. Willcox (New Haven, Conn., 1954), 48.

67. Alden, *General Charles Lee*, 142–44; Council of War, Oct. 16, 1776, *PGW:RWS* 6:576; Robert Hanson Harrison to Hancock, Oct. 14 [–17], 1776, ibid., 6:565; Schecter, *Battle for New York*, 221–25.

68. GW to Samuel Washington, Oct. 18, 1776, *PGW:RWS* 6:589. See also the editor's note in ibid., 6:576.

69. Scheer, *Private Yankee Doodle*, 47–48, 50; GW to Robert Livingston, Oct. 20, 1776, *PGW:RWS* 6:594; GW to Trumbull, Oct. 20, 1776, ibid., 6:596.

70. Trumbull to GW, Oct. 31, Nov. 30, 1776, *PGW:RWS* 7:73, 242; ibid., 1:113n.

71. Ibid., 7:8n, 52n, 69–70n; Ward, *War of the Revolution*, 1:261.

72. Ward, *War of the Revolution*, 1:260; Gruber, *Howe Brothers and the American Revolution*, 132.

73. The account of the engagement at White Plains draws on Lengel, *General George Washington*, 161–63, and Ward, *War of the Revolution*, 1:262–66.

74. Louise Rau, ed., "Sergeant John Smith's Diary of 1776," *Mississippi Valley Historical Review*, 20 (1933–1934): 259.

75. Ward, *War of the Revolution*, 1:266; *PGW:RWS* 7:52–54n.

76. Deposition of Michael Smith, in Dann, *Revolution Remembered*, 114.

77. Harrison to Hancock, Oct. 29, 1776, *PGW:RWS* 7:51; Gruber, *Howe Brothers and the American Revolution*, 133; Mackesy, *War for America*, 91.

78. *PGW:RWS* 7:69n, 39n; Schecter, *Battle for New York*, 243.

79. Fischer, *Washington's Crossing*, 116; Gruber, *Howe Brothers and the American Revolution*, 83, 104.

80. Council of War, Nov. 6, 1776, *PGW:RWS* 7:92; GW to Lee, Nov. 10, 1776, ibid., 7:133–34; Lengel, *General George Washington*, 164; Richard M. Ketchum, *The Winter Soldiers* (Garden City, N.Y., 1973), 99; Ferling, *First of Men*, 251. For Lee on Fort Washington, see Lee to Reed, Nov. 16, 1776, *LP* 2:283; Lee to Rush, Nov. 20, 1776, ibid., 2:288.

81. Clinton, *American Rebellion*, 54–56; Willcox, *Portrait of a General*, 115–16.

82. Gruber, *Howe Brothers and the American Revolution*, 143–44.

83. *PGW:RSW* 5:184n; GW to Captain Patrick Dennis, July 13, 1776, ibid., 5:294; GW to Rufus Putnam, Aug. 11, 1776, ibid., 5:669; GW to Hancock, Sept. 8, Nov.16, 1776, ibid., 6:291, 7:163; Council of War, Oct. 16, 1776, ibid., 6:576; Ketchum, *Winter Soldiers*, 108–9.

84. GW to Reed, Aug. 22, 1779, *WW* 16:150–52; *JCC* 6:866; GW to John A. Washington, Nov. 6 [–19], 1776, *PGW:RWS* 7:103; GW to NG, Nov. 8, 1776, ibid., 7:115; NG to GW, Nov. 9, 1776, ibid., 7:120; Magaw to NG, Nov. 15, 1776, ibid., 162n; *NPG* 1:354–55n; Ketchum, *Winter Soldiers*, 98. Ferling, *First of Men*, 175. On Greene's role in the disaster, see Golway, *Washington's General*, 98–103.

85. John Adams and Thomas Jefferson, independent of one another, reached the similar conclusion that when it came to making decisions Washington was "slow, but sure." See John Ferling, *Setting the World Ablaze: Washington, Adams, Jefferson and the American Revolution* (New York, 2000), 173.

86. Mackenzie, *Diary of Mackenzie*, 1:94; Ketchum, *Winter Soldiers*, 111–12.

87. "The Capture of Fort Washington, New York, Described by Captain Andreas Wiederhold, of the Hessian 'Regiment Knyphausen,'" *PMHB*, 23 (1899):95.

88. Howard H. Peckham, ed., *Memoirs of the Life of John Adlum in the Revolutionary War* (Chicago, 1968), 71.

89. Accounts of Chaplain Waldeck, Chaplain Assistant Asteroth, and Corporal Philip Steuernagel, Burgoyne, *Enemy Views*, 97, 104, 94; Journal of John Reubner, *SOS* 1:494.

90. GW to Hancock, Nov. 16, 1776, *PGW:RWS* 7:165; ibid., 7:166–69n; *NGP* 1:358–59n; Ward, *War of the Revolution*, 1:267–74; Mackenzie, *Diary of Mackenzie*, 1:109, 111.

91. Alexander Graydon, *Memoirs of His Own Time, with Reminiscences of the Men and Events of the Revolution* (Philadelphia, 1846), 205, 206–7.

92. Isaac Van Horne, *Memoirs*, in Ryan, *A Salute to Courage*, 52.

93. Account of Chaplain Waldeck, Burgoyne, *Enemy Views*, 97; William M. Dwyer, *The Day Is Ours!: An Inside View of the Battles of Trenton and Princeton* (New York, 1983), 7–8; Peckham, *Life of John Adlum*, 74, 75, 78.

94. GW to Hancock, Nov. 16, 19 [–21], 1776, *PGW:RWS* 7:163, 180; Lee to GW, Nov. 19, 1776, ibid., 7:187; Fischer, *Washington's Crossing*, 114.

95. NG to GW, Nov. 18, 1776, *PNG* 1:359–60.

96. GW to Hancock, Nov. 19 [–21], 1776, *PGW:RWS* 7:18–82; GW to Livingston, Nov. 21, 1776, ibid., 7:195; Greene to Cooke, Dec. 4, 1776, *PNG* 1:360–61, 363–64n; Fischer, *Washington's Crossing*, 121–23; Golway, *Washington's General*, 1035; Dwyer, *The Day Is Ours!*, 27.

97. William Hooper to Joseph Hewes, Dec. 1, 1776, *LDC* 5:561.

98. Quoted in Charles Royster, *A Revolutionary People at War: The Continental Army nad American Character, 1775–1783* (Chapel Hill, N.C., 1979) 111.

99. Adams to Elizabeth Adams, Dec. 9, 1776, *LDC* 5:590–91; Adams to Joseph Warren, Dec. 12, 1776, ibid., 5:600–1; Elbridge Gerry to unknown, Dec. 12, 1776, ibid., 5:602; GW to Samuel Washington, Dec. 10 [–17], 1776, *PGW:RWS* 7:291; Robert G. Albion and Leonidas Dodson, eds., *Philip Vickers Fithian's Journal, 1775–1776* (Princeton, N.J., 1934), 241; Joseph Hodgkins to Sarah Hodgkins, Dec. 31, 1776, Herbert T. Wade and Robert A. Lively, eds., *This Glorious Cause: The Adventures of Two Company Officers in Washington's Army* (Princeton, N.J., 1958), 228–29.

Chapter 7. "This Hour of Adversity": To the End of 1776

1. Willard M. Wallace, *Traitorous Hero: The Life and Fortunes of Benedict Arnold* (Freeport, N.Y., 1964), 98; James Kirby Martin, *Benedict Arnold, Revolutionary Hero: An American Warrior Reconsidered* (New York, 1997), 21922; *PGW:RWS* 5:105n.

2. Martin, *Benedict Arnold*, 225–27. The source of Lake Champlain is at the southern end of that body of water, leading locals to say that to come south was to "sail up" the lake.

3. Arnold to GW, June 25, 1776, *PGW:RWS* 5:96–97; Schuyler to GW, June 25, 1776, ibid., 5:104–5; GW to Hancock, June, 20, 1776, ibid., 5:56; Gates to Hancock, July 16, 1776, ibid., 5:339–40n; Gates to GW, July 29, 1776, ibid., 5:499; ibid., 5:288–89n; *JCC* 5:448; Don R. Gerlach, *Proud Patriot: Philip Schuyler and the War of Independence, 1775–1783* (Syracuse, 1987), 158; Martin, *Benedict Arnold*, 234, 237.

4. Gerlach, *Proud Patriot*, 182–87; Schuyler to GW, July 20, 1776, *PGW:RWS* 5:406; Gates to GW, Aug. 28, 1776, ibid., 146, 147–48n; Paul David Nelson, *General Horatio Gates: A Biography* (Baton Rouge, 1976), 64–65; Christopher Ward, *The War of the Revolution*, 2 vols. (New York, 1952), 1:387.

5. Martin, *Benedict Arnold*, 235–36, 247.

6. Paul H. Smith, "Sir Guy Carleton: Soldier-Statesman," in George A. Billias, ed., *George Washington's Opponents* (New York, 1969), 123–24; Piers Mackesy, *The War for America, 1775–1783* (Cambridge, Mass., 1965), 94–96; Ward, *War of the Revolution*, 1:389–90, 393; Martin, *Benedict Arnold*, 272–74; Willard Sterne Randall, *Benedict Arnold* (New York, 1990), 296–97.

7. Martin, *Benedict Arnold*, 261.

8. Ibid., 269–71, 274–84; Ward, *War of the Revolution*, 1:393–97; Randall, *Benedict Arnold*, 290–317.

9. Claude van Tyne, *The War of Independence: American Phase* (Boston, 1929), 373–74.

10. Quoted in Mackesy, *War for America*, 96.

11. Carleton to Germain, Oct. 14, 1776, *DAR* 12:237; Nelson, *General Horatio Gates*, 70–71; Mackesy, *War for America*, 96; Smith, "General Guy Carleton," in Billias *George Washington's Opponents*, 121; Richard Ketchum, *Saratoga: Turning Point of America's Revolutionary War* (New York, 1997), 42; Friedrich A. von Riedesel, *Memoirs and Letters and Journals of Major General Riedesel During His Residence in America*, ed. Max von Eelking (Albany, 1868), 1:79.

12. Edward J. Tatum, ed., *The American Journal of Ambrose Serle* (New York, 1969), 98, 131, 133, 140; Frederick Mackenzie, *Diary of Frederick Mackenzie* (Cambridge, Mass., 1930), 1:45; Ira D. Gruber, *The Howe Brothers and the American Revolution* (Chapel Hill, N.C., 1972), 96, 118; William B. Willcox, *Portrait of a General: Sir Henry Clinton in the War of Independence* (New York, 1962), 121–22; Henry Clinton, *The American Rebellion: Sir Henry Clinton's Narrative of His Campaigns, 1775–1782*, ed. William B. Willcox (New Haven, Conn., 1954), 54–56.

13. Mackenzie, *Diary of Mackenzie*, 1:113.

14. Ibid., 1:111–12.

15. Franklin and Mary Wickwire, *Cornwallis and the War of Independence* (London, 1971), 7–92.

16. *PGW:RWS* 7:185n; Johann Ewald, *Diary of the American War: A Hessian Journal*, ed. Joseph P. Tustin (New Haven, Conn., 1979), 18; William M. Dwyer, *The Day Is Ours!: An Inside View of the Battles of Trenton and Princeton* (New York, 1983), 30.

17. R. Arthur Bowler, *Logistics and the Failure of the British Army in America* (Princeton, N.J., 1975), 5557; William S. Stryker, *The Battles of Trenton and Princeton* (Boston, 1898), 20–21; David Hackett Fischer, *Washington's Crossing* (New York, 2004), 126, 130–31; Enoch Anderson, *Personal Recollections of Enoch Anderson* (New York, 1971), 27; Dwyer, *The Day Is Ours*, 35. For an excellent analysis of the British army's struggle to prevent abuse of provincials by both redcoats and Germans, especially during campaigns such as Cornwallis conducted in the autumn of 1776, see Stephen Conway, " 'The Great Mischief Complain'd of': Reflections on the Misconduct of British Soldiers in the Revolutionary War," *WMQ* 47 (1990): 370–90.

18. Quoted in Dwyer, *The Day Is Ours*, 40.

19. Ibid., 76–77, 84–85; Stryker, *Battles of Trenton and Princeton*, 23, 315.

20. GW to Hancock, Dec. 16, 1776, *PGW:RWS* 7:352; Glover to Jonathan Glover, June 11, 1776, in Russell W. Knight, ed., *General John Glover's Letterbook, 1776–1777* (Salem, Mass., 1977), 11.

21. Quoted in Richard Ketchum, *The Winter Soldiers* (Garden City, N.J., 1973), 279.

22. Quoted in Dwyer, *The Day Is Ours*, 105.

23. Greene to GW, Oct. 29, 1776, *PGW:RWS* 7:46–47; GW to Greene, Nov. 7, 1776, ibid., 7:107; Arthur F. Lefkowitz, *Long Retreat: The Calamitous American Defense of New Jersey, 1776* (Metuchen, N.J., 1998), 57–58.

24. Ibid., 70, 74; Enoch Anderson, *Personal Recollections of Captain Enoch Anderson, an Officer of the Delaware Regiment in the Revolutionary War*, ed. Henry Hobart Bellas (New York, 1968), 26; Fischer, *Washington's Crossing*, 146; William Grayson to Lee, Nov. 20, 1776, *PGW:RWS* 7:186n; GW to Lee, Nov. 21, 24, 1776, ibid., 7:194, 208; Harrison to Schuyler, Nov. 26, 1776, ibid., 7:223–24n.

25. Lefkowitz, *Long Retreat*, 99–103.

26. Ibid., 79–80; Fischer, *Washington's Crossing*, 128; *PGW:RWS* 7:228n; Lee to Reed, Nov. 24, 1776, *LP*, 2:305–6; Reed to Lee, Nov. 21, 1776, ibid., 2:293–94. In an earlier letter to Gates, Lee went even further, calling Washington "damnably deficient." See Lee to Gates, Dec. 1, 1776, ibid., 2:348.

27. GW to John A. Washington, Nov. 6 [–19], 1776, *PGW:RWS* 7:105; GW to Lund Washington, Dec. 10 [–17], ibid., 7:289–91; GW to Samuel Washington, Dec. 18, 1776, ibid., 7:370–71; William Gordon, *The History of the Rise, Progress, and Establishment of the Independence of the United States of America. . . .* (London, 1788), 2:354. Gordon was relating a conversation in his presence between Washington and Reed.

28. GW to Livingston, Nov. 30, 1776, *PGW:RWS* 7:236; GW to Samuel Washington, Dec. 18, 1776, ibid., 7:371; GW to Hancock, Dec. 5, 1776, ibid., 7:262.

29. JA to AA, April 28, 1776, *AFC* 1:399–400; JA to General Samuel Parsons, Aug. 19, 1776, *DAJA* 3:449.

30. Samuel Adams to James Warren, Nov. 29, Dec. 25, 1776, *LDC* 5:552, 661; Ellery to Cooke, Dec. 4, 1776, ibid., 5:571.

31. *JCC* 6:1,024–27.

32. William Hooper to Morris, Dec. 28, 1776, *LDC* 5:688–89.

33. GW to Hancock, Dec. 20, 1776, *PGW:RWS* 7:381–86; NG to Hancock, Dec. 21, 1776, *PNG* 1:370–74; *JCC* 6:1,043–46; Edward G. Lengel, *General George Washington* (New York, 2005), 189.

34. Fischer, *Washington's Crossing*, 145–46, 155–57; Hancock to Robert Morris, Dec. 23, 1776, *LDC* 5:642–43; Secret Committee Minutes, Nov. 23, 1776, ibid., 5:533; Secret Committee to Massachusetts Assembly, Dec. 4, 1776, ibid., 5:576; George Ross to James Wilson, Nov. 26, 1776, ibid., 5:547; William Whipple to Meshech Ware, Nov. 28, 1776, ibid., 5:550; Morris to GW, Dec. 21, 23 [–24], 1776, *PGW:RWS* 7:403, 420–21; Executive Committee of Continental Congress to GW, Dec. 31, 1776, ibid., 7:495; Samuel Adams to JA, Jan. 9, 1776, *PJA* 5:68.

35. Board of War to Morris, Dec. 29, 1776, *LDC* 5:691. Virginia's Benjamin Harrison wrote the letter.

36. Journal of Sergeant of William Young, *PMHB* 8 (1884): 255n.

37. David F. Hawke, *Paine* (New York, 1974), 52–62.

38. Thomas Paine, *The American Crisis*, in Philip S. Foner, ed., *The Complete Writings of Thomas Paine* (New York, 1945), 1:50.

39. The quotations can be found in ibid., 1:52, 54, 57. The entire pamphlet is in ibid., 1:50–57.

40. Fischer, *Washington's Crossing*, 142.

41. Alfred Owen Aldridge, *Man of Reason: The Life of Thomas Paine* (Philadelphia, 1959), 49.

42. Whipple to John Langdon, Jan. 15, 1777, *LDC* 6:111.

43. Hawke, *Paine*, 61.

44. GW to Hancock, Dec. 1, 5, 1776, *PGW:RWS* 7:244, 262.

45. Quoted in Fischer, *Washington's Crossing*, 133.

46. Douglas Southall Freeman, *George Washington* (New York, 1948–1957), 4:302–4; GW to Lund Washington, Dec. 10 [–17], 1776, *PGW:RWS* 7:289.

47. GW to Lee, Dec. 1, 3, 10, 11, 14, 1776, *PGW:RWS* 7:249–51, 257, 288–89, 301, 335–36; GW to Samuel Washington, Dec. 18, 1776, ibid., 7:370. See also ibid., 7:254n.

48. Lee to Reed, Nov. 24, 1776, ibid., 7:238n.

49. GW to Lee, Nov. 21, 24, 1776, ibid., 7:194, 208; Lee to GW, Nov. 30, Dec. 8, 1776, ibid., 7:235, 276; Lee to Heath, Nov. 21, 23, 1776, ibid., 7:206–7n: Heath to Lee, Nov. 21, 23, 1776, ibid., 7:206–7n; Lee to James Bowdoin, Nov. 30, 1776, *Lee Papers*, 2:323; Alden, *General Charles Lee*, 147–55.

50. GW to Lee, Dec. 10, 1776, *PGW:RWS* 7:288; Alden, *General Charles Lee*, 156–57; Lee to Gates, Dec. 13, 1776, *LP* 2:348.

51. GW to Samuel Washington, Dec. 18, 1776, *PGW:RWS* 7:371; GW to Morris, Dec. 22, 1776, ibid., 7:412.

52. Nelson, *General Horatio Gates*, 72, 75; GW to Morris, Dec. 22, 1776, *PGW:RWS* 7:412; Charles H. Lesser, *The Sinews of Independence: Monthly Strength Reports of the Continental Army* (Chicago, 1976), 43; Stryker, *Battles of Trenton and Princeton*, 82; Dwyer, *The Day Is Ours*, 16–17.

53. Fischer, *Washington's Crossing*, 131, 135–37; Dwyer, *The Day Is Ours*, 114; Ewald, *Diary of the American War*, 27; Wickwires, *Cornwallis and the American Revolution*, 95.

54. Grant to General Harvey, Dec. 26, 1776, Papers of James Grant of Bellindaloch, Reel 29, LC.

55. Reed to GW, Dec. 22, 1776, *PGW:RWS* 7:415.

56. Quoted in Fischer, *Washington's Crossing*, 205.

57. GW to Heath, Dec. 14, 1776, *PGW:RWS* 7:334; GW to Hancock, Sept. 8, 1776, ibid., 6:251; Fischer, *Washington's Crossing*, 160–81, 192–95, 201, 202–3, 279–80, 375; Dwyer, *The Day Is Ours*, 185.

58. GW to Reed, Dec. 23, 1776, *PGW:RWS* 7:423.

59. George F. Scheer and Hugh F. Rankin, *Rebels and Redcoats* (Cleveland, 1957), 211.

60. Rall to Colonel von Donop, Dec. 17, 20, 21, Stryker, *Battles of Trenton and Princeton*, 324, 329, 331, 332. The "clodhoppers" quote and Rall's expletive are taken from Fischer, *Washington's Crossing*, 189, 205. The latter has been rendered in the American vernacular. For Rall's sobriquet "Lion," see Dwyer, *The Day Is Ours*, 166.

61. Detailed orders were given to each brigade. See General Orders, Dec. 25, 1776, *PGW:RWS* 7:434–36.

62. John Greenwood, *The Revolutionary War Service of John Greenwood of Boston and New York, 1775–1783*, ed., Isaac J. Greenwood (New York, 1922), 39.

63. Scheer and Rankin, *Rebels and Redcoats*, 212.

64. William S. Powell, "A Connecticut Soldier Writing Home," *WMQ* 6:102.

65. Scheer and Rankin, *Rebels and Redcoats*, 213.

66. GW to Hancock, Dec. 27, 1776, *PGW:RWS* 7:454.

67. This account of the operation and engagement draws on Fischer, *Washington's Crossing*, 206–54; Ketchum, *Winter Soldiers*, 239–68; Ward, *War of the Revolution*, 1:292–302; Rodney Atwood, *The Hessians: Mercenaries from Hessen-Kassel in the American Revolution* (Cambridge, England, 1980), 92–93.

68. Stryker, *Battles of Trenton and Princeton*, 185; "The Good Soldier [Joseph] White," *American Heritage*, 7 (June 1956): 77.

69. GW to Hancock, Dec. 27, 1776, *PGW:RWS* 7:454, 459–60n; Fischer, *Washington's Crossing*, 254–55.

70. *The Journal of Nicholas Cresswell, 1774–1777* (Port Washington, N.Y., 1968), 179–81; Whipple to Josiah Bartlett, Dec. 31, 1776, *LDC* 5:715; Hancock to GW, Jan. 1, 1777, ibid., 6:6.

71. Quoted in Atwood, *Hessians*, 92.

72. Fischer, *Washington's Crossing*, 189; Ketchum, *Winter Soldiers*, 237; Atwood, *Hessians*, 88.

73. GW to Reed [?], Dec. 27, 1776, *PGW:RWS* 7:463; GW to Hancock, Dec. 29, 1776, ibid., 7:477; Cadwalader to GW, Dec. 27, 1776, ibid., 7:451–52; Stirling to William Livingston, Dec. 28, 1776, ibid., 7:488n; "General Joseph Reed's Narrative of the Movements of the American Army in the Neighborhood of Trenton in the Winter of 1776–1777," *PMHB* 8 (1884):391.

74. "Reed's Narrative," *PMHB* 8:395; GW to Hancock, Dec. 29, 1776, *PGW:RWS* 7:477; GW to Morris, Dec. 31, 1776, ibid., 7:497.

75. GW to the commanding officer at Morristown, Dec. 30, 1776, *PGW:RWS* 7:490–91; GW to Morris, Dec. 31, 1776, ibid., 7:497; GW to Hancock, Jan. 1, 1777, ibid., 7:504; Morris to GW, Dec. 30, 1776, ibid., 7:490; Sergeant R, "The Battle of Princeton," reprinted from the Wellsborough, Pa., *Phoenix*, March 24, 1832, *PMHB* 20 (1896): 515–16; Fischer, *Washington's Crossing*, 270; Freeman, *George Washington*, 4:338.

76. GW to Hancock, Jan. 1, 5, 1777, *PGW:RWS* 7:504, 519; Cadwalader to GW, Dec. 31, 1776, ibid., 7:511n; Fischer, *Washington's Crossing*, 277, 283, 291, 295–96; Reed, "Narrative," *PMHB* 8:400; Freeman, *George Washington*, 4:338.

77. Mackesy, *War for America*, 98–102.

78. Gruber, *Howe Brothers and the American Revolution*, 140; Orlando W. Stephenson, "The Supply of Gunpowder in 1776," *AHR* 30 (1924–1925): 272–81; Fischer, *Washington's Crossing*, 155, 303, 401.

79. Wickwires, *Cornwallis and the War of Independence*, 95; Fischer, *Washington's Crossing*, 290–99; Ketchum, *Winter Soldiers*, 289.

80. GW to Hancock, Jan. 5, 1777, *PGW:RWS* 7:521; ibid., 7:525n; Ewald, *Diary*, 50; Fischer, *Washington's Crossing*, 293; Ketchum, *Winter Soldiers*, 290.

81. Dwyer, *The Day Is Ours*, 320; Robert Beale, *Memoirs*, in Dennis P. Ryan, ed., *A Salute to Courage: The American Revolution as Seen through Wartime Writings of Officers of the Continental Army and Navy* (New York, 1979), 57.

82. *PGW:RWS* 7:526n.

83. Quoted in Dwyer, *The Day Is Ours*, 320.

84. Diary of Captain Thomas Rodney, Jan. 2, 1777, Rodney Family Papers, LC; "Good Soldier White," *American Heritage*, 7:77.

85. Journal of Sergeant Young, *PMHB* 8:263.

86. Fischer, *Washington's Crossing*, 304–7, 412, 529.

87. Ketchum, *Winter Soldiers*, 291.

88. GW to Hancock, Jan. 5, 1777, *PGW:RWS* 7:521; ibid., 7: 526–27n; Freeman, *George Washington*, 4:344–46; Lengel, *General George Washington*, 197; Fischer, *Washington's Crossing*, 280–81, 313–15.

89. *PGW:RWS* 7:526–27n; Stryker, *Battles of Trenton and Princeton*, 446–48; Fischer, *Washington's Crossing*, 316–18, 340–41, 401; Lengel, *General George Washington*, 202; Ketchum, *Winter Soldiers*, 294.

90. Beale, *Memoirs*, Ryan, *A Salute to Courage*, 57.

91. Fischer, *Washington's Crossing*, 326–29; John E. Selby, *The Revolution in Virginia, 1775–1776* (Williamsburg, Va., 1988), 50.

92. Diary of Lieutenant James McMichael, of the Pennsylvania Line, 1776–1778, *PMHB* 16 (1892):141; Scheer and Rankin, *Rebels and Redcoats*, 218; "Good Soldier White," *American Heritage*, 7:78.

93. There are numerous conflicting accounts of Mercer's fatal wounding. For varied accounts, see Stryker, *Battles of Trenton and Princeton*, 282; Dwyer, *This Day Is Ours*, 342; Ketchum, *Winter Soldiers*, 303; Fischer, *Washington's Crossing*, 332–33.

94. [Robert Lawrence], *A Brief Narrative of the Ravages of the British and Hessians at Princeton in 1776–1777*, ed. Varnum L. Collins (New York, 1968), 38; *PGW:RWS* 7:528n.

95. Ward, *War of the Revolution*, 1:310–18; *PGW:RWS* 7:528–29n; Fischer, *Washington's Crossing*, 323–40, 413–15; Ketchum, *Winter Soldiers*, 292, 313.

96. Fischer, *Washington's Crossing*, 528–29.

97. GW to Hancock, Jan. 5, 1777, *PGW:RWS* 7:523.

98. Gruber, *Howe Brothers in the American Revolution*, 144, 148; Fischer, *Washington's Crossing*, 343.

99. *PGW:RWS* 7:529.

100. GW to Hancock, Jan. 5, 1777, *PGW:RWS* 7:523.

101. Ibid., 7:529n; Ewald, *Diary*, 50.

Chapter 8. Choices, 1777

1. Edward J. Tatum, ed., *The American Journal of Ambrose Serle* (New York, 1969), 154, 158, 161, 162, 163, 168.

2. Ira D. Gruber, *The Howe Brothers and the American Revolution* (Chapel Hill, N.C., 1972), 156–57.

3. Quoted in Gavin K. Watt, *Rebellion in the Mohawk Valley: The St. Leger Expedition of 1777* (Toronto, 2002), 315.

4. Carl B. Cone, *Burke and the Nature of Politics: The Age of the American Revolution* (Lexington, Ky., 1957), 294–95.

5. Ibid., 158–88; Alan Valentine, *Lord North* (Norman, Okla., 1967), 421–27; Solomon Lutnick, *The American Revolution and the British Press, 1775–1783* (Columbia, Mo., 1967), 9399; Charles R. Ritcheson, *British Politics and the American Revolution* (Norman, Okla., 1954), 210–13; Alan Valentine, *Lord George Germain* (Oxford, England, 1962), 148.

6. Valentine, *Lord George Germain*, 149–61; Richard J. Hargrove Jr., *General John Burgoyne* (Newark, Del., 1983), 92; Max Mintz, *The Generals of Saratoga* (New Haven, Conn., 1990), 113; Piers Mackesy, *The War for America, 1775–1783* (Cambridge, Mass., 1965), 114.

7. Howe to Germain, Nov. 30, 1778, *DAR* 12:264–66.

8. [John Burgoyne], "Thoughts for Conducting the War from the Side of Canada by Lieut.-General John Burgoyne," Feb. 28, 1777, *DAR* 14:41–46. See also Hargrove, *General John Burgoyne*, 102, 104; Gerald S. Brown, *American Secretary: The Colonial Policies of Lord George Germain* (Ann Arbor, Mich., 1963), 88–90; Mintz, *Generals of Saratoga*, 115–16.

9. Howe to Germain, Dec. 20, 1776, *DAR* 12:268–69.

10. Howe to Germain, Jan. 20, 1777, ibid., 14:33; Brown, *American Secretary*, 96.

11. Valentine, *Lord George Germain*, 151; Gruber, *Howe Brothers and the American Revolution*, 192.

12. Quoted in Mackesy, *War for America*, 115.

13. Glenn F. Williams, *Year of the Hangman: George Washington's Campaign against the Iroquois* (Yardley, Pa., 2005), 1–2.

14. Mintz, *Generals of Saratoga*, 117–18.

15. Quoted in Ralph Ketchum, *Saratoga: Turning Point of America's Revolutionary War* (New York, 1997), 70.

16. Mintz, *Generals of Saratoga*, 3–11, 1928; Hargrove, *General John Burgoyne*, 17–68; George A. Billias, "John Burgoyne: Ambitious General," in Billias, *George Washington's Opponents* (New York, 1969), 142–64; John S. Pancake, *1777: The Year of the Hangman* (University, Ala., 1977), 88–94.

17. Quoted in Mackesy, *War for America*, 108. Mackesy argues that Burgoyne's appointment to command the Canadian army was "the worst ministerial error" made early in 1777, and the "only avoidable one." See ibid., 113.

18. Charles Royster, *A Revolutionary People at War: The Continental Army and American Character, 1775–1783* (Chapel Hill, N.C., 1979), 35; GW to Hancock, Feb. 9, Sept. 2, 1776, *PGW:RWS* 3:275–76; 6:199; James Kirby Martin and Mark Edward Lender, *A Respectable Army: The Military Origins of the Republic, 1763–1789* (Arlington Heights, Ill., 1982), 73.

19. Francis Lightfoot Lee to Walter Jones, Dec. 11, 1776, *LDC* 5:598; Morris to Deane, Dec. 20, 1776, ibid., 5:620–21; Oliver Wolcott to Laura Wolcott, Dec. 13, 1776, ibid., 5:606; Richard Henry Lee to Patrick Henry, Dec. 18, 1776, ibid., 5:615; *DAJA* 3:434–35; JA to Knox, Aug. 25, 1776, *PJA* 4:498; JA to Gerry, Dec. 31, 1776, ibid., 4:498; JA to AA, Sept. 22, 1776, *AFC* 2:131.

20. *JCC* 2:11–22; 3:331–34; 5:729, 747, 749, 751, 756–57, 762–63, 788–807; *PJA* 5:38–40n; *DAJA* 3:409–10, 434–35; Richard Buel Jr., *Dear Liberty: Connecticut's Mobilization for the Revolutionary War* (Middletown, Conn., 1980), 53, 68–70, 101–2, 117–18. See also Royster, *Revolutionary People at War*, 64–65. The original Articles of War can be found in *JCC* 2:111–22.

21. Robert A. Gross, *The Minutemen and their World* (New York, 1976), 135.

22. JA to Gen. Lee, Oct. 13, 1775, *PJA* 3:202; JA to AA May 29, 1775, Feb. 13, 1776, *AFC* 1:207, 347; John Ferling, "'Oh That I Was a Soldier': John Adams and the Anguish of War," *American Quarterly* 36 (1984): 258–75.

23. Gregory T. Knouff, *The Soldiers' Revolution: Pennsylvanians in Arms and the Forging of Early American Identity* (University Park, Pa., 2004). See also John Ferling, *A Wilderness of Miseries: War and Warriors in Early America* (Westport, Conn., 1981), 57–92.

24. Peter Oliver, *Origin and Progress of the American Rebellion*, ed. Douglass Adair and John A. Schutz (San Marino, Calif., 1961), 129–30.

25. Quoted in Paul David Nelson, "The American Soldier and the American Victory," in John Ferling, ed., *The World Turned Upside Down: The American Victory in the War of Independence* (Westport, Conn., 1988), 36.

26. James Thacher, *Military Journal of the American Revolution. . . .* , reprint (New York, 1969), 60.

27. Quoted in Nelson, "American Soldier," in Ferling, *World Turned Upside Down*, 45.

28. George Scheer, ed., *Private Yankee Doodle: Being a Narrative of Some of the Adventures, Dangers and Sufferings of a Revolutionary Soldier* (Boston, 1962).

29. Nelson, "American Soldier," in Ferling, *World Turned Upside Down*, 45; "Journal of Ebenezer Wild," MHS *Proceedings*, 2d Ser., 6 (1890–1891): 80–81, 83.

30. Joseph Hodgkins to Sarah Hodgkins, Sept. 5, 1776, in Herbert T. Wade and Robert A. Lively, eds., *This Glorious Cause: The Adventures of Two Company Officers in Washington's Army* (Princeton, N.J., 1958), 219.

31. John Resch, *Suffering Soldiers: Revolutionary War Veterans, Moral Sentiment, and Political Culture in the Early Republic* (Amherst, Mass., 1999), 19–25, 34.

32. Knouff, *Soldiers' Revolution*, 35–36.

33. Scheer, *Private Yankee Doodle*, 197. On the physical and age requirements, see Harry M. Ward, *George Washington's Enforcers: Policing the Continental Army* (Carbondale, Ill., 2006), 16–19.

34. Don Higginbotham, *The War of American Independence: Military Attitudes, Policies, and Practices, 1763–1789* (New York, 1971), 391–93; Ferling, *A Wilderness of Miseries*, 122; Charles P. Neimeyer, *America Goes to War: A Social History of the Continental Army* (New York, 1996), 52–53, 56–57; John R. Sellers, "The Common Soldier in the American Revolution," in S. J. Underdal, *Military History of the American Revolution: Proceedings of the Sixth Military History Symposium, USAF Academy* (Washington, D.C., 1976), 155; James Kirby Martin and Mark Edward Lender, *A Respectable Army: The Military Origins of the Republic, 1763–1789* (Arlington Heights, Ill., 1982), 88.

35. JA to TJ, May 26, 1777, *PJA* 5:203; Michael A. McDonnell, "Class War? Class Struggles during the American Revolution in Virginia," *WMQ* 63 (2006): 321–22.

36. Quoted in Ray Raphael, *A People's History of the American Revolution: How the Common People Shaped the Fight for Independence* (New York, 2001), 77.

37. Knouff, *Soldiers' Revolution*, 56, 68.

38. Quoted in Ferling, *A Wilderness of Miseries*, 122–23.

39. Knouff, *Soldiers' Revolution*, 47–48; Scheer, *Private Yankee Doodle*, 16, 6061.

40. Royster, *A Revolutionary People at War*, 377.

41. Charles H. Lesser, *The Sinews of Independence: Monthly Strength Reports of the Continental Army* (Chicago, 1976), 38, 50.

42. Neimeyer, *America Goes to War*, 15–25; Edward C. Papenfuse and Gregory A. Stiverson, "General Smallwood's Recruits: The Peacetime Career of the Revolutionary War Private," *WMQ* 30 (1973): 120, 123, 125; Sellers, "The Common Soldier in the American Revolution," in Underdal, *Military History of the American Revolution*, 151–61; Royster, *Revolutionary People At War*, 268; Mark E. Lender, "The Mind of the Rank and File: Patriotism and Motivation in the Continental Line," in William C. Wright, ed., *New Jersey in the American Revolution, III, Papers Presented at the Seventh Annual New Jersey History Symposium* (Trenton, 1976), 21–38; Mark Lender, "The Social Structure of the New Jersey Brigade," in Peter Karsten, ed., *The Military in America: From the Colonial Era to the Present* (New York, 1986),

27–44; Martin and Lender, *A Respectable Army*, 89–91; Nelson, "The American Soldier," Ferling, *World Turned Upside Down*, 35–52; Harold E. Selesky, *A Demographic Survey of the Continental Army That Wintered at Valley Forge, Pennsylvania, 1777–1778* (Washington, D.C., 1987), 1–37.

43. Quoted in Gruber, *Howe Brothers and the American Revolution*, 170.

44. Carl Van Doren, *Benjamin Franklin* (New York, 1938), 569.

45. *JCC* 5:428–33.

46. Ibid., 5:576–89. Adams's draft, as well as that of the committee, and the final Plan of Treaties, can be found in *PJA* 4:265–302. A helpful editorial note is in ibid., 4:260–65n.

47. Rush to Jacques Barbeu-Dubourg, Sept. 16, 1776, *LDC* 5:183.

48. Quoted in Alexander DeConde, "The French Alliance in Historical Speculation," in Ronald Hoffman and Peter J. Albert, eds., *Diplomacy and Revolution: The Franco-American Alliance of 1778* (Charlottesville, Va., 1981), 6.

49. Abraham Clark to James Caldwell, Feb. 4, 1777, *LDC* 6:209; Whipple to John Langdon, Feb. 15, 1777, ibid., 6:296; JA to AA, April 2, 1777, *AFC* 2:195–96.

50. Edward Corwin, *French Policy and the American Alliance of 1778* (New York, 1916), 87–88; William Stinchcombe, *The American Revolution and the French Alliance* (Syracuse, 1969), 10–11.

51. Samuel Flagg Bemis, *The Diplomacy of the American Revolution* (New York, 1935), 51, 53, 92; Jonathan R. Dull, *A Diplomatic History of the American Revolution* (New Haven, Conn., 1983), 78; American Commissioners to Vergennes, Jan. 5, 1777, *PBF* 23:122; American Commissioners to the Committee of Secret Correspondence, Feb. 6, 1777, ibid., 23:287; ibid., 23:121n.

52. American Commissioners: Memorandum to Vergennes, Feb. 1, March 1, 18, 1777, *PBF* 23:262, 409–12, 503–5.

53. Isabel T. Kelsay, *Joseph Brant, 1743–1807: Man of Two Worlds* (Syracuse, 1984), 160–62; Williams, *Year of the Hangman*, 18; Barbara Graymont, *The Iroquois in the American Revolution* (Syracuse, 1972), 81.

54. Kelsay, *Joseph Brant*, 43, 66–67, 109, 113, 115, 134, 279, 528; Max M. Mintz, *Seeds of Empire: The American Revolutionary Conquest of the Iroquois* (New York, 1999), 7; Milton Hamilton, *Sir William Johnson: Colonial America, 1715–1764* (Port Washington, N.Y., 1976), 242, 304–5; James T. Flexner, *Lord of the Mohawks: A Biography of Sir William Johnson* (Boston, 1959), 99, 112, 185–86, 233–34.

55. Graymont, *Iroquois in the American Revolution*, 25–85; Kelsay, *Joseph Brant*, 155; Williams, *Year of the Hangman*, 19.

56. Gage to Lord Shelburne, June 13, 1767, Clarence E. Carter, ed., *The Correspondence of General Thomas Gage with the Secretaries of State, 1763–1775*, reprint (New York, 1969), 1:142–43.

57. Quoted in Colin G. Calloway, *The American Revolution in Indian Country* (Cambridge, England, 1995), 122.

58. The foregoing account of the Mohawks and Tryon County residents draws principally on Alan Taylor, *The Divided Ground: Indians, Settlers, and the Northern Borderland of the American Revolution* (New York, 2006), 3–87. See also Calloway, *American Revolution in Indian Country*, 122; Williams, *Year of the Hangman*, 32; and David Preston, "George Klock, the Canajoharie Mohawks, and the Good Ship Sir William Johnson: Land, Legitimacy, and Community in the 18th Century Mohawk Valley," *New York History*, 86 (2005): 473–79. Useful background material can be found in a series of books by historian Francis Jennings: see *The Creation of America: Through Revolution to Empire* (Cambridge, England, 2000); *The Ambiguous Iroquois Empire* (New York, 1984); and *The Empire of Fortune* (New York, 1988).

59. Kelsay, *Joseph Brant*, 155; Mintz, *Seeds of Empire*, 7–8; Raphael, *A People's History of the American Revolution*, 249; Calloway, *American Revolution in Indian Country*, 59–60.

60. Kelsay, *Joseph Brant*, 155; Mintz, *Seeds of Empire*, 14–15; Allan Eckert, *The Wilderness War: A Narrative* (Boston, 1978), 78.

61. Quoted in Taylor, *The Divided Ground*, 88. See also Williams, *Year of the Hangman*, 34.

62. The quotations are in Kelsay, *Joseph Brant*, 167, 173, and Mintz, *Seeds of Empire*, 14.

63. Kelsay, *Joseph Brant*, 181–82, 200; Taylor, *The Divided Ground*, 89–91; Mintz, *Seeds of Empire*, 17–20; Graymont, *Iroquois in the American Revolution*, 104–28; Calloway, *American Revolution in Indian Country*, 122–23; Dale Van Every, *A Company of Heroes: The American Frontier, 1775–1783* (New York, 1962), 88–92. On the divisions within Iroquoia, see Karim Tiro, "A 'Civil' War? Rethinking Iroquois Participation in the American Revolution," *Explorations in Early American Culture*, 4 (2000):148–65; David Levinson, "An Explanation for the Oneida-Colonist Alliance in the American Revolution," *Ethnohistory*, 23 (1976):265–89; Anthony Wonderley, "1777: The Revolutionary War Comes to Oneida Country," *Mohawk Valley History*, 1 (2004):15–48.

Chapter 9. "The Caprice of War": America's Pivotal Victory at Saratoga

1. *PGW: RWS* 8:6n; John Ferling, *The First of Men: A Life of George Washington* (Knoxville, 1988), 144; Christopher Ward, *The War of the Revolution*, 2 vols. (New York, 1952), 1:319.

2. Arthur Lefkowitz, *George Washington's Indispensable Men: The 32 Aides-de-Camp Who Helped Win American Independence* (Mechanicsburg, Pa., 2003), 15, 34, 98, 110; *PGW:RWS* 8:117n.

3. Lefkowitz, *George Washington's Indispensable Men*, 110; John Ferling, *A Leap in the Dark: The Struggle to Create the American Republic* (New York, 2003), 242–46; John Ferling, *Adams vs. Jefferson: The Tumultuous Election of 1800* (New York, 2004), 36–42; Ron Chernow, *Alexander Hamilton* (New York, 2004), 7–106; Richard Brookhiser, *Alexander Hamilton* (New York, 1999), 13–30.

4. Quoted in Lefkowitz, *George Washington's Indispensable Men*, 108.

5. GW to George Clinton, Jan. 19, 1777, *PGW:RWS* 8:102; GW to William Duer, Jan. 14, 1777, ibid., 8:63; GW to Hancock, Jan. 26, 1777, ibid., 8:160; GW to James Mease, Jan. 10, 1777, ibid., 8:36; GW to Francis Wade, Jan. 11, 1777, ibid., 8:41; George F. Scheer and Hugh F. Rankin, *Rebels and Redcoats* (Cleveland, 1957), 222.

6. Elizabeth A. Fenn, *Pox Americana: The Great Smallpox Epidemic of 1775–1782* (New York, 2001), 14–79.

7. Bartholomew Dandridge to GW, Jan. 16, 1777, *PGW:RWS* 8:80; GW to John Cochran, Jan. 20, 1777, ibid., 8:112; GW to Gates, Feb. 5 [–6], 1777, ibid., 8:248; GW to William Shippen, Jan. 28, 1777, ibid., 8:174; GW to Hancock, Feb. 5, 1777, ibid., 8:251; GW to George Baylor, March 28, 1777, ibid., 9:1; Fenn, *Pox Americana*, 87–92.

8. George Scheer, ed., *Private Yankee Doodle: Being a Narrative of Some of the Adventures, Dangers and Sufferings of a Revolutionary Soldier* (Boston, 1962), 65, 67.

9. GW to Hancock, Jan. 22, 1777, *PGW:RWS* 8:126; GW to George Clinton, Jan. 24, 1777, ibid., 8:143–44.

10. Ira D. Gruber, ed., *John Peebles' American War: The Diary of a Scottish Grenadier, 1776–1782* (Mechanicsburg, Pa., 1998), 164.

11. R. Arthur Bowler, *Logistics and the Failure of the British Army in America, 1775–1783* (Princeton, N.J., 1975), 24.

12. GW to Hancock, Jan. 19, 1777, *PGW:RWS*, 8:103; GW to Reed, Jan. 15, 1777, ibid., 8:76; Bowler, *Logistics*, 24.

13. *PGW:RWS* 8:128n; GW to Trumbull, Jan. 24, 1777, ibid., 8:151; GW to Livingston, Feb. 3, 1777, ibid., 8:234; David Hackett Fischer, *Washington's Crossing* (New York, 2004), 347.

14. GW to Hancock, Jan. 17, 1777, *PGW:RWS* 8:89; Tilghman to Philemon Dickenson, March 12, 1777, ibid., 8:564n;

15. Johann Ewald, *Diary of the American War: A Hessian Journal*, ed. Joseph P. Tustin, ed. (New Haven, Conn., 1979), 53, 55; Col. William Harcourt to Earl Harcourt, March 17, 1777,

SOS 1:524; Fischer, *Washington's Crossing*, 349, 359; Bowler, *Logistics*, 69; Ira D. Gruber, *The Howe Brothers and the American Revolution* (Chapel Hill, N.C., 1972), 191–92.

16. GW to Hancock, Aug. 18, Sept. 2, 16, 25, 1776, *PGW:RWS* 6:62, 198, 313–14, 396; GW to Cadwalader, Jan. 23, 1777, ibid., 8:135–36; GW to Abraham Yates, Aug. 30, 1776, ibid., 6:170; GW to Trumbull Sr., Sept. 9, 1776, ibid., 267; GW to John Augustine Washington, Sept. 22, 1776, ibid., 6:374.

17. John Shy, "A New Look at the Colonial Militia," in John Shy, *A People Numerous and Armed: Reflections on the Military Struggle for American Independence* (New York, 1976), 21–33.

18. Don Higginbotham, "The American Militia: A Traditional Institution with Revolutionary Responsibilities," in Don Higginbotham, ed., *Reconsiderations of the Revolutionary War* (Westport, Conn., 1978), 83. 103. See also Don Higginbotham, *The War of American Independence: Military Attitudes, Policies, and Practices, 1763–1789* (New York, 1971), 273–75.

19. Fischer, *Washington's Crossing*, 359; Gruber, *Howe Brothers and the American Revolution*, 202–3, 205–6; *PGW:RWS* 9:19n, 241n; Ward, *War of the Revolution*, 1:323; 2:492–95; Richard Ketchum, *Saratoga: Turning Point of America's Revolutionary War* (New York, 1997), 60.

20. GW to Gates, Feb. 20, 1777, *PGW:RWS* 8:377; GW to Morris, Feb. 22, 1777, ibid., 8:416; GW to the Continental Congress' Executive Committee, Feb. 27, 1777, ibid., 8:452–53; GW to Trumbull, March 6, May 11, 1777, ibid., 8:531; 9:392; GW to Samuel Washington, April 5, 1777, ibid., 9:72; GW to John A. Washington, April 12, 1777, ibid., 9:144; Council of War, May 2, 1777, ibid., 9:324; ibid., 9:516–17n.

21. Return of the American Forces in New Jersey, March 15, 1777, ibid., 8:576; GW to Samuel Washington, April 5, 1777, ibid., 9:72; GW to Cooke, April 3, 1777, ibid., 9:52; GW to Hancock, Jan. 31, April 12[–13], May 21, 1777, ibid., 8:202; 9:128–29, 492–93; GW to John A. Washington, Feb. 24, 1777, ibid., 8:439; GW to a Committee of the Continental Congress, April 12, 1777, ibid., 9:127; Douglas Southall Freeman, *George Washington* (New York, 1948–1957), 4:406.

22. Piers Mackesy, *The War for America, 1775–1783* (Cambridge, Mass., 1965), 125; GW to Putnam, June 20, 1777, *PGW:RWS* 10:88; GW to John A. Washington, June 29, 1777, ibid., 10:150.

23. Germain to Carleton, March 26, 1777, *DAR* 14:53–56; Ward, *War of the Revolution*, 1:400.

24. Burgoyne, Thoughts for Conducting the War, *DAR* 14:41; Glenn F. Williams, *Year of the Hangman: George Washington's Campaign against the Iroquois* (Yardley, Pa., 2005), 40. For details on the allocation of the troops, especially the Germans, see the Mary C. Lynn, ed., *The Specht Journal: A Military Journal of the Burgoyne Campaign* (Westport, Conn., 1995), 42–43, and Lieutenant James Hadden, *A Journal Kept in Canada and Upon Burgoyne's Campaigns in 1776 and 1777* (Albany, 1884), 44–46.

25. Burgoyne to Germain, June 22, 26, 1777, *DAR* 14:119, 121; Carleton to Burgoyne, May 29, 1777, ibid., 14:101; Carleton to Germain, July 10, 1777, ibid., 14:131; Daniel Claus to William Knox, Oct. 11, 1777, New York State Library (Albany), Call No. 11084. See also Mackesy, *War for America*, 115, 131; Richard J. Hargrove Jr., *General John Burgoyne* (Newark, Del., 1983), 117–23; Ward, *War of the Revolution*, 1:402–3; Ketchum, *Saratoga*, 107–11. Burgoyne subsequently claimed to have gotten only 150 Canadian and Loyalist troops, but he appears to have been wrong by half. See John Burgoyne, *A State of the Expedition from Canada as Laid before the House of Commons by Lieutenant-General Burgoyne* (London, 1780), 10.

26. Lynn, *Specht Journal*, 41.

27. Hargrove, *General John Burgoyne*, 122, 123, 125.

28. Lynn, *Specht Journal*, 43–44; *The British Invasion from the North: The Campaigns of Generals Carleton and Burgoyne from Canada, 1776–1777, with the Journal of Lieut. William Digby* (Albany, 1887), 192–97; Ketchum, *Saratoga*, 132–38; Ward, *War of the Revolution*, 1:403; Hargrove, *General John Burgoyne*, 125; Max Mintz, *The Generals of Saratoga* (New Haven,

Conn., 1990), 136. For both George III's comment and Howe's letter, see *SOS* 1:543–44. Hereafter citations from Lieutenant Digby's account are listed as Digby, *Journal*.

29. Hargrove, *General John Burgoyne*, 125–26.

30. Proclamation, June 23, 1777, *SOS* 1:547–48.

31. Burgoyne's speech is in ibid., 1:545–47. The description of the Native American audience is in William L. Stone, translator, *Letters of Brunswick and Hessian Officers during the American Revolution* (Albany, 1891), 92. See also Ketchum, *Saratoga*, 266, and Lynn, *Specht Journal*, 48–49.

32. "A New Jerseyman," Sept. 8, 1777, *SOS* 1:549.

33. Ward, *War of the Revolution*, 1:405–7; Ketchum, *Saratoga*, 116, 160; Mintz, *Generals of Saratoga*, 107.

34. James A. Huston, *Logistics of Liberty: American Services of Supply in the Revolutionary War and After* (Newark, Del., 1991), 86.

35. Don R. Gerlach, *Proud Patriot: Philip Schuyler and the War of Independence, 1775–1783* (Syracuse, 1987), 170, 211–16; Mintz, *Generals of Saratoga*, 142; Ward, *War of the Revolution*, 1:406–7.

36. Gerlach, *Proud Patriot*, 203–19.

37. GW to Morris, Jan. 19, 1777, *PGW:RWS* 8:107; GW to Schuyler, March 12, 1777, ibid., 8:560–62.

38. John H. G. Pell, "Philip Schuyler: The General As Aristocrat," George A. Billias, ed., *George Washington's Generals* (New York, 1964), 64; Jonathan Rossie, *The Politics of Command in the American Revolution* (Syracuse, N.Y., 1975), 38, 98–99.

39. Paul David Nelson, *General Horatio Gates: A Biography* (Baton Rouge, 1976), 76, 80; Gerlach, *Proud Patriot*, 220–22, 229; JCC 7:202; JA to AA, Feb. 21, July 20, Aug. 4, 17, 1777, *AFC* 2:165, 285, 299, 317; JA to Benjamin Rush, Feb. 8, 1778, *PJA* 5:403. For an excellent discussion of the Schuyler-Gates imbroglio, see Rossie, *Politics of Command*, 135–65.

40. Schuyler to GW, April 30, 1777, *PGW:RWS* 9:311; GW to Schuyler, May 3, 1777, ibid., 9:339.

41. Greene to Catherine Greene, July 17, 1777, *PNG* 2:121.

42. Gerlach, *Proud Patriot*, 223–29.

43. Mintz, *Generals of Saratoga*, 140, 142; Ward, *War of the Revolution*, 1:408; *Proceedings of a Court Martial Held at White Plains . . . for the Trial of Major General Arthur St. Clair, August 25, 1778* (Philadelphia, 1778), 14, 20. (Hereafter the transcript of St. Clair's hearing is referred to as *Court Martial of St. Clair*.)

44. Parsons to GW, June 12, 1777, *PGW:RWS* 10:15; GW to Schuyler, June 16, 1777, ibid., 10:54; *Court Martial of St. Clair*, 33. Mintz sets the final manpower total at Ticonderoga on July 4, 1777, at approximately three thousand men. See Mintz, *Generals of Saratoga*, 146.

45. Hoffman Nickerson, *Turning Point of the Revolution, or Burgoyne in America* (Boston, 1928), 1:134.

46. *Court Martial of St. Clair*, 27.

47. Ketchum, *Saratoga*, 167–84; Ward, *War of the Revolution*, 1:410–11.

48. Lynn, *Specht Journal*, 53.

49. Digby, *Journal*, 208.

50. Ibid., 209.

51. Hargrove, *General John Burgoyne*, 138; Ketchum, *Saratoga*, 186–89.

52. Digby, *Journal*, 209.

53. Ketchum, *Saratoga*, 191–206; Mintz, *Generals of Saratoga*, 148–52; Ward, *War of the Revolution*, 1:412–14; Nickerson, *Turning Point of the Revolution*, 1:148–49.

54. Hadden, *Journal*, 94.

55. On Long's flight and the loss of American supplies, see Ketchum, *Saratoga*, 223–30; Mintz, *Generals of Saratoga*, 152–54; Nickerson, *Turning Point of the Revolution*, 1:154–57; Hargrove, *General John Burgoyne*, 140; Ward, *War of the Revolution*, 1:414–15.

56. Quoted in Hargrove, *General John Burgoyne*, 141.

57. Schuyler to GW, July 7, 1777, *PGW:RWS* 10:219–21. This citation draws from two letters that Schuyler wrote to GW on July 7.

58. GW to Putnam, July 1, 22, 1777, ibid., 10:166, 362; Schuyler to GW, July 14, 21, 26[–27], Aug. 1, 1777, ibid., 10:280, 348, 430, 482; Mintz, *Generals of Saratoga*, 160; Gerlach, *Proud Patriot*, 259.

59. Schuyler to GW, July 10, 17, 1777, *PGW:RWS* 10:245, 312; Hargrove, *General John Burgoyne*, 147; Ketchum, *Saratoga*, 246–48; Pell, "Philip Schuyler," Billias, *George Washington's Generals*, 67.

60. Quoted in Gerlach, *Proud Patriot*, 217.

61. Schuyler to GW, July 14, 1777, *PGW:RWS* 10:281.

62. Burgoyne, Thoughts for Conducting the War, *DAR* 14:41, 44.

63. Ibid., 14:42–44. Good accounts of Burgoyne's thinking and crucial decisions can be found in Nickerson, *Turning Point of the Revolution*, 1:163–67, and Hargrove, *General John Burgoyne*, 148–54. On the Indians, see Hadden, *Journal*, 83.

64. Burgoyne, Thoughts for Conducting the War, *DAR* 14:44.

65. Burgoyne to Germain, July 30, 1777, ibid., 14:153; Burgoyne, *A State of the Expedition from Canada*, 54–55. Burgoyne had first proposed the Lake George route in his Thoughts for Conducting the War: see *DAR* 14:41–42. See also Hargrove, *General John Burgoyne*, 147, and Ketchum, *Saratoga*, 240–41.

66. GW to Schuyler, July 12, 1777, *PGW:RWS* 10:261.

67. Samuel Adams to Samuel Cooper, July 15, 1777, *LDC* 7:343; Samuel Adams to Richard Henry Lee, July 15, 1777, ibid., 7:344; JA to AA, July 18, 1777, *AFC* 2:284.

68. Charles Thomson's Notes of Debates, July 26, 28, 1777, *LDC* 7:382–83, 388–89.

69. Schuyler to GW, July 28, 1777, *PGW:RWS* 10:450; Nelson, *General Horatio Gates*, 94–103; Rossie, *Politics of Command*, 159–65.

70. Ketchum, *Saratoga*, 242, 332; Hargrove, *General John Burgoyne*, 153; Higginbotham, *War of American Independence*, 188.

71. J. F. Wasmus, *An Eyewitness Account of the American Revolution and New England Life: The Journal of J. F. Wasmus, German Company Surgeon, 1776–1783* (Westport, Conn., 1990), 66, 64. Hereafter cited as Wasmus, *Journal*.

72. Burgoyne to Germain, July 11, 1777, in Burgoyne, *A State of the Expedition from Canada*, Appendix, xxxviii; Gates to Burgoyne, Sept 2, 1777, *SOS* 1:560; Mintz, *Generals of Saratoga*, 162, 182; Ketchum, *Saratoga*, 274–77; Nelson, *General Horatio Gates*, 110–11.

73. Burgoyne, *A State of the Expedition from Canada*, 11, 21; Lynn, *Specht Journal*, 62.

74. Howe to Burgoyne, July 17, 1777, Nickerson, *Turning Point of the Revolution*, 1:189.

75. Lynn, *Specht Journal*, 60; A German Soldier's Account, Aug. 16, 1777, *SOS* 1:570; Ketchum, *Saratoga*, 341.

76. Schuyler to GW, July 17, 1777, *PGW:RWS* 10:312.

77. The quotes from the Hessian soldier can be found in A German Soldier's Account, Aug. 16, 1777, *SOS* 1:571, 575–76.

78. Good accounts of the battle and the fate of the relief expedition can be found in Ward, *War of the Revolution*, 1:417–31, and Ketchum. *Saratoga*, 291–328. See also Herbert D. Foster and Thomas W. Streeter, "Stark's Independent Command at Bennington," *Proceedings of the New York State Historical Association*, 5 (1904): 24–57.

79. Burgoyne to Germain, Aug. 20, 1777, *DAR* 14:165–67.

80. Baroness von Riedesel, *Baroness von Riedesel and the American Revolution: Journal and Correspondence of a Tour of Duty, 1776–1783* (Chapel Hill, 1965), 47. Hereafter cited as Baroness von Riedesel, *Journal and Correspondence*.

81. Burgoyne to Germain, Aug. 20, 1777, *DAR* 14:166; Howe to Germain, July 7, 1777, ibid., 14:130; Howe to Burgoyne, July 17, 1777, in Nickerson, *Turning Point of the Revolution*, 1:189.

82. Quoted in Ketchum, *Saratoga*, 329. The quote is actually that of Riedesel, though the sentiment was shared by Burgoyne.

83. Claus to Knox, Oct. 11, 1777, John Campbell Papers, New York State Library, Call No. 11084.

84. Gavin K. Watt, *Rebellion in the Mohawk Valley: The St. Leger Expedition of 1777* (Toronto, 2002), 69–70; William J. Wood, *Battles of the Revolutionary War 1775–1781* (Chapel Hill, N.C., 1990), 118.

85. Claus to Knox, Oct. 11, 1777, John Campbell Papers, New York State Library, Call No. 11084.

86. The quotes are from Watt, *Rebellion in the Mohawk Valley*, 130–31. See also page 73 for St. Leger's equipment.

87. Williams, *Year of the Hangman*, 54–55.

88. Ibid., 54.

89. Watt, *Rebellion in the Mohawk Valley*, 154–95, 317. The quotation is on page 164. See also Williams, *Year of the Hangman*, 56–57.

90. On the St. Leger campaign, see Ward, *War of the Revolution*, 1:477–91; Watt, *Rebellion in the Mohawk Valley*, 195–261; Gerlach, *Proud Patriot*, 280, 288–89, 292–93, 298–99, 302–3; Nelson, *General Horatio Gates*, 104; Isabel T. Kelsay, *Joseph Brant, 1743–1807: Man of Two Worlds* (Syracuse, 1984), 194–208.

91. Lynn, *Specht Journal*, 70, 74.

92. Burgoyne, *A State of the Expedition from Canada*, 25.

93. Wasmus, *Journal*, 70.

94. Intelligence Report, ca. Aug. 1777, GP, reel 5; Gates to Trumbull, Aug. 6, 1777, ibid., reel 5; Account of Jonathan Brigham, in John C. Dann, ed., *Revolution Remembered: Eyewitness Accounts of the War of Independence* (Chicago, 1980), 6.

95. The quote is from Don Higginbotham, *Daniel Morgan: Revolutionary Rifleman* (Chapel Hill, N.C., 1961), 61. See also Higginbotham, *War of American Independence*, 194; Mintz, *Generals of Saratoga*, 180, 182; Ketchum, *Saratoga*, 345–46.

96. Mintz, *Generals of Saratoga*, 204.

97. Ward, *War of the Revolution*, 1:502; Ketchum, *Saratoga*, 354.

98. Quoted in Ketcham, *Saratoga*, 363.

99. James Thacher, *Military Journal of the American Revolution* reprint (New York, 1969), 98.

100. Digby, *Journal*, 273.

101. Burgoyne, *A State of the Expedition from Canada*, 57.

102. Higginbotham, *Daniel Morgan*, 67.

103. Good accounts of the Battle of Freeman's Farm can be found in Ketchum, *Saratoga*, 355–72; Ward, *War of the Revolution*, 2:504–12; Mintz, *Generals of Saratoga*, 190–99; Nickerson, *Turning Point of the Revolution*, 309–19; Nelson, *General Horatio Gates*, 115–21; Hargrove, *General John Burgoyne*, 180–84.

104. The two quotes can be found in Ketchum, *Saratoga*, 375, and Hargrove, *General John Burgoyne*, 185.

105. GW to Gates, Sept. 24, 1777, *PGW:RWS* 11:310; Gates to GW, Oct. 5, 1777, ibid., 11:392–93.

106. Quoted in Nelson, *General Horatio Gates*, 134.

107. Lynn, *Specht Journal*, 86.

108. Friedrich A. von Riedesel, *Memoirs and Letters and Journals of Major General Riedesel During His Residence in America*, ed. Max von Eelking (Albany, 1868), 1:205; Hargrove, *General John Burgoyne*, 191–94; Mintz, *Generals of Saratoga*, 206.

109. Mintz, *Generals of Saratoga*, 204–5; Nelson, *General Horatio Gates*, 142.

110. Burgoyne to Clinton, Sept. 27, 1777, *DAR* 14:190–91; Correspondence between Burgoyne and Clinton, Sept. 28–Oct. 5, 1777, ibid., 14:191–92; Clinton to Burgoyne, Oct. 8,

1777, *SOS* 1:588; Henry Clinton, *The American Rebellion: Sir Henry Clinton's Narrative of His Campaigns, 1775–1782*, ed. William B. Willcox (New Haven, Conn., 1954), 74, 378–80.

111. Thacher, *Journal*, 106; William B. Willcox, *Portrait of a General: Sir Henry Clinton in the War of Independence* (New York, 1962), 179–84.

112. Clinton, *American Rebellion*, 79.

113. Ebenezer Mattoon to Schuyler, Oct. 7, 1777, *SOS* 1:594.

114. Arnold to Gates, Sept. 22, 23, Oct. 1, 1777, GP, reel 5. A good account of their relationship can be found in Nelson, *General Horatio Gates*, 122–34.

115. Quoted in Ketchum, *Saratoga*, 394.

116. Lloyd Brown and Howard Peckham, eds., *Revolutionary War Journals of Henry Dearborn, 1775–1783* (New York, 1971), 108.

117. Digby, *Journal*, 288; Georg Pausch, Journal, *SOS* 1:595–96. Good accounts of the Battle of Bemis Heights can be found in Ward, *War of the Revolution*, 2:521–31; Nickerson, *Turning Point of the Revolution*, 358–64; Ketchum, *Saratoga*, 394–404; Mintz, *Generals of Saratoga*, 206–13. Information on the rebel snipers appears in Digby, *Journal*, 286–87, and Account of Samuel Woodruff, *SOS* 1:593.

118. Baroness von Riedesel, *Journal and Correspondence*, 51–52.

119. Thacher, *Journal*, 103; Ketchum, *Saratoga*, 399–400, 403, 405; Mintz, *Generals of Saratoga*, 213; Higginbotham, *Daniel Morgan*, 73–74.

120. Digby, *Journal*, 246. Digby's comment about wolves actually was made about the bodies left at Hubbardton, but it was applicable for all the engagements in this sector.

121. Lynn, *Specht Journal*, 93.

122. Baroness von Riedesel, *Journal and Correspondence*, 54; Digby, *Journal*, 295–96.

123. Account of Josiah Sabin, Dann, *Revolution Remembered*, 21.

124. Baroness von Riedesel, *Journal and Correspondence*, 61; Account of Thomas Anburey, *SOS* 1:599; Digby, Journal, 304; Ketchum, *Saratoga*, 415–17; Riedesel, *Memoirs and Letters*, 1:174.

125. Minutes of the Council of War, Oct. 12–15, 1777, *DAR* 14:212–15; Burgoyne to Germain, Oct. 20, 1777, ibid., 14:233–34; "Record of the Council of War," Oct. 12, 1777, Riedesel, *Memoirs*, 1:175–79; Minutes of the Council of War, Oct. 13, 1777, ibid., 1:179–84; Lynn, *Specht Journal*, 97; Ketchum, *Saratoga*, 418, 420.

126. Mintz, *Generals of Saratoga*, 204, 220–23; Nickerson, *Turning Point of the Revolution*, 387–95; Ketchum, *Saratoga*, 420–25; Nelson, *General Horatio Gates*, 138–41; Hargrove, *General John Burgoyne*, 200–1. The terms of the convention can be found in Digby, *Journal*, 312–17. For Burgoyne's lengthy account of his failed campaign, see Burgoyne to Germain, Oct. 20, 1777, *DAR* 14:228–36. In a second, and private, letter to Germain written on the same day, Burgoyne added: "The British have persevered in a strenuous and bloody process. Had the force been *all* British, perhaps the perseverance had been longer." See *DAR* 14:236–37.

127. Digby, *Journal*, 319–21; Lynn, *Specht Journal*, 101–2.

128. Jeduthan Baldwin, *The Revolutionary Journal of Col. Jeduthan Baldwin, 1775–1778* (Bangor, Maine, 1906), 125.

129. Brown and Peckham, *Revolutionary War Journals of Henry Dearborn*, 111.

130. Riedesel, *Memoirs and Letters*, 1:190.

131. Baroness von Riedesel, *Journal and Correspondence*, 64; Ketchum, *Saratoga*, 426–33.

Chapter 10. "We Rallied and Broke": The Campaign for Philadelphia, September–December 1777

1. GW to Clinton, July 1, 1777, *PGW:RWS* 10:163; GW to Hancock, July 2, 1777, ibid., 10:169; GW to Livingston, July 12, 1777, ibid., 10:256.

2. Stephen R. Taaffe, *The Philadelphia Campaign, 1777–1778* (Lawrence, Kans., 2003), 30–31.

3. Howe to Burgoyne, July 17, 1777, Hoffman Nickerson, *Turning Point of the Revolution, or Burgoyne in America* (Boston, 1928), 1:189; James Thomas Flexner, *George Washington: The Forge of Experience, 1732–1775* (Boston, 1965), 211; GW to Hancock, July 16, 1777, *PGW:RWS* 10:294; GW to Heath, July 13, 1777, ibid., 10:271.

4. Quoted in Ira D. Gruber, *The Howe Brothers and the American Revolution* (Chapel Hill, N.C., 1972), 233.

5. GW to Hancock, July 25, 1777, *PGW:RWS* 10:410: GW to Trumbull, July 31, 1777, ibid., 10:472; Taaffe, *Philadelphia Campaign*, 45.

6. GW to Heath, July 19, 1777, *PGW:RWS*, 10:339.

7. Bruce E. Burgoyne, ed., *Enemy Views: The American Revolutionary War as Recorded by the Hessian Participants* (Bowie, Md., 1996), 164–65; Baron Karl: Leopold Baurmeister, *Revolution in America: Confidential Letters and Journals, 1776–1784* (Westport, Conn., 1973), 93, 98; Taafe, *Philadelphia Campaign*, 53; "Before and after the Battle of Brandywine. Extracts from the Journal of Sergeant Thomas Sullivan of H. M. Forty-Ninth Regiment of Foot," *PMHB* 31 (1907):408. (Hereafter cited as Sullivan, "Journal.")

8. Sarah Fisher, " 'A Diary of Trifling Occurrences': Philadelphia, 1776–1778," *PMHB* 82 (1958): 443.

9. GW, General Orders, Aug. 23, 24, 1777, *PGW:RWS* 11:49, 55; Taaffe, *Philadelphia Campaign*, 58.

10. Marchant to Cooke, Aug. 24, 1777, *LDC* 7:541; Richard Henry Lee to TJ, Aug. 25, 1777, ibid., 7:551; JA to AA, Aug. 24, 1777, *AFC* 2:327–28.

11. Taaffe, *Philadelphia Campaign*, 61; Don Higginbotham, *The War of American Independence: Military Attitudes, Policies, and Practices, 1763–1789* (New York, 1971), 185; Greene to Jacob Greene, Aug. 31, 1777, *PNG* 2:149.

12. Piers Mackesy, *The War for America, 1775–1783* (Cambridge, Mass., 1965), 127–28.

13. Enoch Anderson, *Personal Recollections of Enoch Anderson* (New York, 1971), 38.

14. Samuel Adams to NG, May 12, 1777, *LDC* 7:70–71; Richard Henry Lee to Mann Page, Sept. 15, 1777, ibid., 7:667; JA to NG, April 13, 1777, *PJA* 5:151; Schuyler to GW, Aug. 19, 1777, *PGW:RWS* 11:7–8; Edward G. Lengel, *General George Washington* (New York, 2005), 224.

15. Taaffe, *Philadelphia Campaign*, 62.

16. Lengel, *General George Washington*, 229.

17. *PGW:RWS* 11:187n; Charles P. Whittemore, *A General of the Revolution: John Sullivan of New Hampshire* (New York, 1961), 57.

18. Gregory T. Knouff, *The Soldiers' Revolution: Pennsylvanians in Arms and the Forging of Early American Identity* (University Park, Pa., 2004), 59.

19. Baurmeister, *Letters and Journals*, 107; Lengel, *General George Washington*, 231.

20. Sullivan, "Journal," *PMHB*, 31:413.

21. Johann Ewald, *Diary of the American War: A Hessian Journal*, ed., Joseph P. Tustin (New Haven, Conn., 1979), 83; Whittemore, *A General of the Revolution*, 54, 59; Higginbotham, *War of American Independence*, 128.

22. Quoted in Whittemore, *A General of the Revolution*, 60.

23. "Journal of Surgeon Ebenezer Elmer," *PMHB* 35 (1911):105.

24. Benjamin Tallmadge, *Memoir of Benjamin Tallmadge*, reprint (New York, 1968), 21.

25. Quoted in Taaffe, *Philadelphia Campaign*, 73.

26. Quoted in Christopher Ward, *The War of the Revolution*, 2 vols. (New York, 1952), 1:352.

27. John C. Dann, ed., *Revolution Remembered: Eyewitness Accounts of the War of Independence* (Chicago, 1980), 171.

28. Mark E. Lender and James Kirby Martin, eds., *Citizen Soldier: The Revolutionary War Journal of Joseph Bloomfield* (Newark, 1982), 127.

29. Quoted in Knouff, *Soldiers' Revolution*, 123.

30. Quoted in Charles Royster, *A Revolutionary People at War: The Continental Army and American Character, 1775–1783* (Chapel Hill, N.C., 1979), 225.

31. Lender and Martin, *Citizen Soldier*, 127.

32. Anderson, *Personal Recollections*, 36.

33. Account of William Darlington, *SOS* 1:616.

34. Good accounts of the engagement can be found in Lengel, *General George Washington*, 229–41; Taaffe, *Philadelphia Campaign*, 63–78; Ward, *War of the Revolution*, 342–54; *PGW:RWS* 11:187–93n; *PNG* 2:157–62n.

35. Quoted in Knouff, *Soldiers' Revolution*, 128.

36. Sullivan, "Journal," *PMHB*, 31:416.

37. Diary of Joseph Clark, *SOS* 1:615.

38. Ewald, *Diary*, 87. For Washington's comments on the battle, see GW to Hancock, Sept. 11, 1777, *PGW:RWS* 11:200; GW to Thomas Nelson, Sept. 27, 1777, ibid., 11:332.

39. Baurmeister, *Letters and Journals*, 114; *PGW:RWS* 11:243n; GW to Hancock, Sept. 19, 1777, ibid., 11:269; "Diary of Lt. James McMichael, of the Pennsylvania Line, 1776–1778," *PMHB* 16 (1892): 151.

40. GW to Wayne, Sept. 18, 1777, ibid., 11:266; [Anon.], "The Actions at Brandywine and Paoli, Described by a British Officer," *PMHB* 29 (1905): 368; "Papers Relating to the Paoli Massacre," ibid., 1 (1877): 311, 312; Journal of Major John André, *SOS* 1:622; Paul David Nelson, *Anthony Wayne: Soldier of the Early Republic* (Bloomington, 1985), 52–57; Taaffe, *Philadelphia Campaign*, 84–86.

41. GW to Hancock, Sept. 23, 1777, *PGW:RWS* 11:301; Mackesy, *War for America*, 129.

42. "The Diary of Robert Morton," *PMHB* 1 (1877):3–4.

43. JA to AA, Aug. 19, Sept. 30, 1777, *AFC* 2:318–19, 349; *DAJA* 2:117, 118n, 256n, 262, 265. For a contemporary account of frightened civilians who also fled Philadelphia, see "Journal of Sally Wister," *PMHB* 9 (1885): 319–20.

44. "Diary of Robert Morton," *PMHB* 1:7. A British officer said the streets were "crowded with Inhabitants who seem to rejoice." See Ira D. Gruber, ed., *John Peebles' American War: The Diary of a Scottish Grenadier, 1776–1782* (Mechanicsburg, Pa., 1998), 138.

45. Fisher, "Diary," *PMHB* 82:450.

46. Gruber, *Howe Brothers in the American Revolution*, 241; Ewald, *Diary*, 91–92.

47. Council of War, Sept. 28, 1777, *PGW:RWS* 11:338–39; GW, General Orders, Sept. 28, 1777, ibid., 11:337.

48. GW to Hancock, Oct. 5, 1777, ibid., 11:393; Taaffe, *Philadelphia Campaign*, 98.

49. Quoted in *PGW:RWS* 11:400n.

50. Anderson, *Personal Recollections*, 45; George Scheer, ed., *Private Yankee Doodle: Being a Narrative of Some of the Adventures, Dangers and Sufferings of a Revolutionary Soldier* (Boston, 1962), 72–73.

51. Diary of Lieutenant Sir Martin Hunter, *SOS* 1:625.

52. "Contemporary Accounts of the Battle of Germantown," *PMHB* 11 (1887): 330.

53. "A Memoir of General Henry Miller," ibid., 12 (1888):426–27.

54. Benjamin Tallmadge, *Memoir of Colonel Benjamin Tallmadge* (New York, 1968), 23.

55. General John Armstrong, Oct. 9, 1777, *SOS* 1:628.

56. Ewald, *Diary*, 93.

57. Quoted in Harry M. Ward, *Duty, Honor or Country: General George Weedon and the American Revolution* (Philadelphia, 1979), 106.

58. GW to Hancock, Oct. 5, 1777, *PGW:RWS* 11:394.

59. Quoted in Hugh F. Rankin, *The North Carolina Continentals* (Chapel Hill, N.C., 1971), 115.

60. Memoir of Henry Miller, *PMHB* 12:427.

61. GW to Carter, Oct. 27, 1777, *PGW:RWS* 12:26; Duportail to GW, Dec. 3, 1777, ibid., 12:516. Good accounts of the Battle of Germantown can be found in Taaffe, *Philadelphia Campaign*, 93–107; Ward, *War of the Revolution*, 1:362–71; *PGW:RWS* 11:395–400n. Also see GW to Hancock, Oct. 5, 1777, ibid., 11:394, and John Ferling, *The First of Men: A Life of George Washington* (Knoxville, 1988), 216.

62. Quoted in Rankin, *North Carolina Continentals*, 115.

63. Harry M. Ward, *Major General Adam Stephen and the Cause of American Liberty* (Charlottesville, Va., 1989), 184–212.

64. JA to AA, Aug. 29, 1777, *AFC* 2:332; Ward, *War of the Revolution*, 1:373.

65. Higginbotham, *War of American Independence*, 187.

66. Gerry to JA, Dec. 3, 1777, *LDC* 8:374; Gerry to James Warren, Dec. 12, 1777, ibid., 8:404; Committee at Headquarters to Henry Laurens, Dec. 6, 1777, ibid., 8:380, 381n.

67. Gruber, *Howe Brothers in the American Revolution*, 249.

68. Quoted in Royster, *A Revolutionary People at War*, 177, and Charles Royster, " 'The Nature of Treason': Revolutionary Virtue and American Reactions to Benedict Arnold," *WMQ* 36 (1979):171.

69. Cadwalader's Plan for Attacking Philadelphia, Nov. 24, 1777, *PGW:RWS* 12:371; Greene to GW, Nov. 24, 1777, ibid., 12:378.

70. Committee at Headquarters to Laurens, Dec. 10, 1777, *LDC* 8:399–400; Ellery to Cooke, Dec. 17, 1777, ibid., 8:430; Jonathan Bayard Smith to George Bryan, Dec. 19, ibid., 8:442, 444; James Lovell to Samuel Adams, Dec. 20, 1777, ibid., 8:451. The most detailed analysis of this complex struggle can be found in Wayne Bodle, *The Valley Forge Winter: Civilians and Soldiers in War* (University Park, Pa., 2002), 57–71.

71. GW to Laurens, Dec. 22, 23, 1777, *PGW:RWS* 12:669–70, 685.

Chapter 11. Choices, 1778

1. Stanley Weintraub, *Iron Tears: America's Battle for Freedom, Britain's Quagmire, 1775–1783* (New York, 2005), 119–24.

2. Quoted in Alan Valentine, *Lord North* (Norman, Okla., 1967), 1:473.

3. The quotations are from Alan Valentine, *Lord George Germain* (Oxford, England, 1962), 261, 263, 265, and *PH* 19:540.

4. Quoted in Valentine, *Lord George Germain*, 266.

5. *PH* 19:525, 538, 540, 1200.

6. Valentine, *Lord North*, 1:473–82; Charles Ritcheson, *British Politics and the American Revolution* (Norman, Okla., 1954), 126, 234, 244, 249–52.

7. American commissioners to Vergennes, Dec. 4, 1777, *PBF* 25:236; George Walton to BF, Dec. 20, 1777, ibid., 25:328.

8. American commissioners: Memorandum for Vergennes and Aranda, Sept. 25, 1777, *PBF* 24:555–63; American commissioners to Committee of Foreign Affairs, Oct. 7, Nov. 30, 1777, ibid., 25:40, 212; Editor's note, ibid., 25:207n; H. W. Brands, *The First American: The Life and Times of Benjamin Franklin* (New York, 2000), 538–39; Jonathan Dull, *A Diplomatic History of the American Revolution* (New Haven, Conn., 1983), 88, 91.

9. Gordon S. Wood, *The Americanization of Benjamin Franklin* (New York, 2004), 171–79. The quotation is on page 174. See also Stacy Schiff, *A Great Improvisation: Franklin, France, and the Birth of America* (New York, 2005), 13–93; Esmond Wright, *Franklin of Philadelphia* (Cambridge, Mass., 1984), 26–64, and Edmund S. Morgan, *Benjamin Franklin* (New Haven, Conn., 2002), 260–61.

10. JA to Knox, Sept. 19, 1779, *PJA* 8:152; D'Estaing to GW, July 8, 1778, *PGW: RWS* 16:38. The literature is extensive on the question of whether Saratoga and Washington's actions led France to ally with the United States or whether the alliance came about for

other reasons. For the former position, see: Orville T. Murphy, "The Battle of Germantown and the Franco-American Alliance of 1778," *PMHB* 82 (1958):55–64; Samuel Flagg Bemis, *The Diplomacy of the American Revolution* (New York, 1935), 61; Claude H. Van Tyne, "French Aid before the Alliance of 1778," *AHR* 21:40; Edward Corwin, *French Policy and the American Alliance of 1778* (New York, 1916), 358; William Stinchcombe, *The American Revolution and the French Alliance* (Syracuse, 1969), 152. For those who discount Saratoga and Washington, see: Richard W. Van Alstyne, *Empire and Independence: The International History of the American Revolution* (New York, 1967), 132–33; J. H. Plumb, "The French Connection: The Alliance that Won the Revolution," *American Heritage*, 26 (1974):4; Dull, *Diplomatic History of the American Revolution*, 90–91.

11. Dull, *Diplomatic History of the American Revolution*, 91; Ritcheson, *British Politics and the American Revolution*, 235–41.

12. Dull, *Diplomatic History of the American Revolution*, 92–93; Gérard's Report of the Interview, 9 Janvier 1778, *PBF* 25:441–52; Editor's note, ibid., 25:521–22.

13. Editor's note, *PBF* 25:521–22n; "2nd Act separate and Secret," [on or before Jan. 27, 1778], ibid., 25:522; American commissioners to [Gérard], Jan. 30, 1778, ibid., 25:523; Wright, *Franklin of Philadelphia*, 298; Dull, *Diplomatic History of the American Revolution*, 92–93; Carl Van Doren, *Benjamin Franklin* (New York, 1938), 594. The treaties can be found in *PBF* 25:585–626.

14. Van Doren, *Benjamin Franklin*, 595.

15. Quoted in ibid., 594.

16. Quoted in Ritcheson, *British Politics and the American Revolution*, 258.

17. Quoted in Valentine, *Lord North*, 1:509.

18. *PH* 19:762–67.

19. Weldon A. Brown, *Empire or Independence: A Study in the Failure of Reconciliation, 1774–1783* (Baton Rouge, 1941), 225–26; Peter D. G. Thomas, *Lord North* (London, 1976), 116.

20. Ritcheson, *British Politics and the American Revolution*, 268–69.

21. Quoted in Brown, *Empire or Independence*, 245.

22. Quoted in Valentine, *Lord North*, 1:532.

23. Quoted in Solomon Lutnick, *The American Revolution and the British Press, 1775–1783* (Columbia, Mo., 1967), 110.

24. *PH* 19:534, 540, 645.

25. Quoted in Ritcheson, *British Politics and the American Revolution*, 242.

26. Valentine, *Lord North*, 1:470, 493; *PH* 19:541, 645, 647; Brown, *American Secretary*, 135.

27. Ira D. Gruber, *The Howe Brothers and the American Revolution* (Chapel Hill, N.C., 1972), 252–56, 260–61, 268–76; Valentine, *Lord North*, 1:493; Maldwyn A. Jones, "Sir William Howe," in George A. Billias, ed., *George Washington's Opponents* (New York, 1969), 61–62; Ira D. Gruber, "Richard Lord Howe," in ibid., 244–46. The quotation is in Lutnick, *American Revolution and the British Press*, 107.

28. Quoted in Piers Mackesy, *The War for America, 1775–1783* (Cambridge, Mass., 1965), 147. See also William B. Willcox, *Portrait of a General: Sir Henry Clinton in the War of Independence* (New York, 1962), 207–8.

29. The quotations are from Lutnick, *American Revolution and the British Press*, 115, 108.

30. See ibid., 109–18. The quotations are on page 112.

31. Quoted in Valentine, *Lord North*, 1:473, and Lutnick, *American Revolution and the British Press*, 108.

32. Quoted in Valentine, *Lord North*, 1:449.

33. Quoted in ibid., 1:521. See also Ritcheson, *British Politics and the American Revolution*, 249.

34. Quoted in Valentine, *Lord North*, 1:511. See also *PH* 19:871.

35. Mackesy, *War for America*, 153.

36. Edward S. Curtis, *The Organization of the British Army in the American Revolution* (New Haven, Conn., 1926), 56–60.

37. Willcox, *Portrait of a General*, 222–23.

38. Mackesy, *War for America*, 154–61, 165–70, 181–86.

39. Burke to Lord Rockingham, Jan. 5, 1775, in Thomas W. Copeland, et al., eds., *The Correspondence of Edmund Burke*, 10 vols. (Cambridge, England, 1958–1978), 3:89.

40. Mackesy, *War for America*, 158–59.

41. Germain to Clinton, Sept. 25, 1778, *DAR* 15:208.

42. Quoted in Mackesy, *War for America*, 159.

43. Dull, *Diplomatic History of the American Revolution*, 97–98; Jonathan Dull, *The French Navy and American Independence: A Study of Arms and Diplomacy, 1774–1787* (Princeton, N.J., 1975), 112–20.

44. Brown, *American Secretary*, 149–73; Mackesy, *War for America*, 190–207. The quotations are from *American Secretary*, 157, 161, 163.

45. GW to Jeremiah Dummer Powell, Nov. 5, 1777, *PGW:RWS* 12:138; Eliphalet Dyer to Jonathan Trumbull Sr., Jan. 5, 1778, *LDC* 8:527; Nelson, *General Horatio Gates*, 148–49.

46. John Witherspoon's speech in Congress, Jan. 8, 1778, *LDC* 8:553; *JCC* 9:1064; Richard J. Hargrove, *General John Burgoyne* (Newark, Del., 1983), 216.

47. BF and Deane to President of Congress, Feb. 8, 1778, *PBF* 25:634–35; American commissioners to the Committee of Secret Correspondence, Jan. 17 [–22], March 12 [–April 9], April 28, 1778, ibid., 25:196, 475, 621.

48. John Harvie to TJ, Dec. 29, 1777, *LDC* 8:494; William Ellery to Whipple, Dec. 21, 1777, ibid., 8:453; John Banister to St. George Tucker, April 15, 1778, ibid., 9:416; Charles Carroll of Carrollton to Charles Carroll Sr., April 20, 1778, ibid., 9:448; Henry Laurens to GW, Dec. 24, 1777, ibid., 8:471; Cornelius Harnott to Richard Caswell, Jan. 31, 1778, ibid., 9:696; Laurens to Livingston, Jan. 27, 1778, ibid., 8:664; James Lovell to Samuel Adams, Dec. 15, 1777, ibid., 8:418–19; Lovell to AA, March 21, 1778, ibid., 9:322.

49. Ibid., 9:505n, 561n; Committee for Foreign Affairs to commissioners, April 30, 1778, ibid., 9:547; Ellery to William Vernon, May 6, 1778, ibid., 9:611; Lee to GW, May 6, 1778, ibid., 9:61.

50. Laurens to Carlisle Commission, June 17, 1778, ibid., 10:122–23; Commissioners for Quieting Disorders to Germain, June 15, 1778, *DAR* 15:140–42.

Chapter 12. "A Respectable Army": The Grim Year, 1778

1. Major General Johann de Kalb, Dec. 25, 1777, *SOS* 1:646.

2. James Varnum to NG, Feb. 12, 1778, *PNG* 2:280; de Kalb, Dec. 25, 1777, *SOS* 1:646.

3. GW to Reed, Dec. 2, 1777, *PGW:RWS* 12:500 and editor's note. The quotations are from Greene to GW, Dec. 1, 1777, ibid., 12:459–63; James Irvine to GW, Dec. 1, 1777, ibid., 12:463–64. See also Stephen R. Taaffe, *The Philadelphia Campaign, 1777–1778* (Lawrence, Kan., 2003), 149.

4. The generals' advice on this issue, and on the site for winter quarters, can be found in the preceding note and the following: de Kalb to GW, 1st Xber [Dec. 1], 1777, *PGW:RWS* 12:46465; Knox to GW, Dec. 1, 1777, ibid., 12:465–66; Lafayette to GW, Dec. 1, 1777, ibid., 12:466–68; Muhlenberg to GW, Dec. 1, 1777, ibid., 12:474–75; William Smallwood to GW, Dec. 1, 1777, ibid., 12:482–83; Lord Stirling to GW, Dec. 1, 1777, ibid., 12:483–85; Sullivan to GW, Dec. 1, 1777, ibid., 12:485–87; James Varnum to GW, Dec. 1, 1777, ibid., 12:488–89; Wayne to GW, Dec. 1, 1777, ibid., 12:489–90; George Weedon to GW, Dec. 1, 1777, ibid., 12:491–93; William Woodford to GW, Dec. 1, 1777, ibid., 12:493–94.

5. A veritable treasure trove of information on Valley Forge can be found in the National Park Service's three-volume "Valley Forge Historical Research Project," issued in 1979–1980. Volume one, written by Wayne Bodle, is *The Vortex of Small Fortunes: The Continental Army at Valley Forge, 1777–1778* (1980). Volume two, authored by Jacqueline Thibaut, is *The Fatal Crisis: Logistics, Supply, and the Continental Army at Valley Forge, 1777–1778* (1979). Volume three, also written by Jacqueline Thibaut, is *In the True Rustic Order: Material Aspects of the Valley Forge Encampment, 1777–1778* (1980).

6. Wayne K. Bodle, *Valley Forge Winter: Civilians and Soldiers in War* (University Park, Pa., 2002), 5–10.

7. Ibid., 103–4, 116.

8. GW, General Orders, Dec. 20, 1777, *PGW:RWS* 12:641, 644n; GW to Robert Howe, Jan. 13, 1778, ibid., 13:222; Paine to BF, May 16, 1778, *PBF* 26:487; Elnathan Jennings, in John C. Dann, ed., *Revolution Remembered: Eyewitness Accounts of the War of Independence* (Chicago, 1980), 326; George Scheer, ed., *Private Yankee Doodle: Being a Narrative of Some of the Adventures, Dangers and Sufferings of a Revolutionary Soldier* (Boston, 1962), 102; Charles Royster, *A Revolutionary People at War: The Continental Army and American Character, 1775–1783* (Chapel Hill, N.C., 1979), 190; Robert Wright, *The Continental Army* (Washington, D.C., 1983), 47, 73; Edward G. Lengel, *General George Washington* (New York, 2005), 270; James T. Flexner, *George Washington in the American Revolution* (Boston, 1967), 260; John Ferling, *The First of Men: A Life of George Washington* (Knoxville, 1988), 221–22; Noel F. Busch, *Winter Quarters: George Washington and the Continental Army at Valley Forge* (New York, 1974), 49–53; John B. B. Trussell Jr., *Birthplace of an Army: A Study of the Valley Forge Encampment* (Harrisburg, Pa., 1976), 21; de Kalb, Dec. 25, 1777, *SOS* 1:646; Bodle, *Valley Forge Winter*, 126; *Valley Forge Orderly Book of General George Weedon*, reprint (New York, 1971), 160–62, 182; Harry M. Ward, *Charles Scott and the "Spirit of '76"* (Charlottesville, Va., 1988), 42–43; Harry M. Ward, *General William Maxwell and the New Jersey Continentals* (Westport, Conn., 1997), 88–89.

9. GW to Laurens, Dec. 23, 1777, *PGW:RWS* 12:683–87.

10. Henry Livingston to Robert Livingston, Dec. 24, 1777, in Dennis P. Ryan, ed., *A Salute to Courage: The American Revolution As Seen through Wartime Writings of Officers of the Continental Army and Navy* (New York, 1979), 112; The journal of Ebenezer Wild, in MHS, *Proceedings*, 2d Series, 6 (1890–1891):106; "Diary of Albigence Waldo, of the Connecticut Line," *PMHB* 21 (1897): 304, 306, 308, 309, 310; Pierre Stephen duPonceau, "Autobiography," ibid., 63 (1939): 208; Colonel John Brooks, *SOS* 1:649; Royster, *A Revolutionary People at War*, 191, 193; Ward, *Charles Scott and the "Spirit of '76,"* 45, Scheer, *Private Yankee Doodle*, 101.

11. Rush to GW, Dec. 26, 1777, *PGW:RWS* 13:7.

12. Scheer, *Private Yankee Doodle*, 102; Marquis de Lafayette, "Memoirs of 1779," *LLP* 1:170.

13. Lengel, *General George Washington*, 270n1.

14. Ward, *Charles Scott and the "Spirit of '76,"* 42–43.

15. Thomas Fleming, *Washington's Secret War: The Hidden History of Valley Forge* (New York, 2005), 33.

16. *PGW:RWS* 13:436–37n; NG to GW, Jan. 1, 1778, *PNG* 2:241.

17. James McMichael, "Diary of Lt. James McMichael, of the Pennsylvania Line, 1776–1778," *PMHB* 16 (1892): 157.

18. GW to William Livingston, Dec. 31, 1777, *PGW:RWS* 13:86.

19. James A. Huston, *Logistics of Liberty: American Services of Supply in the Revolutionary War and After* (Newark, Del., 1991), 67–68, 75; *PGW:RWS* 1:266n. The quotations are from E. Wayne Carp, *To Starve the Army at Pleasure: Continental Army Administration and American Political Culture, 1775–1783* (Chapel Hill, N.C., 1984), 44.

20. Committee at Camp to Laurens, Feb. 12, [Feb. 12–25], 1778, *LDC* 9:83, 79.

21. Lengel, *General George Washington*, 272.

22. Wayne to GW, Feb. 26, 1778, *PGW:RWS* 13:678.

23. GW to Laurens, March 12, 1778, ibid., 14:161.

24. The two preceding paragraphs draw on Carp, *To Starve an Army at Pleasure*, 55–73, and Huston, *Logistics of Liberty*, 82. See also, Committee at Camp to Laurens, Feb. 11, 12, [12–25?], 14, 20, 24, 25, March 3, 5, 1778, *LDC* 9:73–75, 79–82, 95, 143–45, 163–64, 168–75, 206, 219–21; Committee at Camp to William Livingston, Feb. 13, 1778, ibid., 9:87–88; Lengel, *General George Washington*, 272.

25. NG to Christopher Greene, Jan. 5, 1778, *PNG* 2:247; de Kalb, Dec. 25, 1777, *SOS* 1:647; Bodle, *Valley Forge Winter*, 167; GW to William Buchanan, Feb. 7, 1778, *PGW:RWS* 13:465; GW to Henry, Dec. 27, 1777, ibid., 13:17; GW, Circular to the States, Dec. 29, 1777, ibid., 13:37; GW to George Gibson, Feb. 21, 1777, ibid., 13:619; GW to James Mease, April 17, 1777, ibid., 14:540; Royster, *A Revolutionary People at War*, 192; Taaffe, *Philadelphia Campaign*, 151, 154, Charles H. Lesser, *The Sinews of Independence: Monthly Strength Reports of the Continental Army* (Chicago, 1976), 55; Thomas Fleming, *Washington's Secret War: The Hidden History of Valley Forge* (New York, 2005), 135, 180.

26. Bodle, *Valley Forge Winter*, 123; Taaffe, *Philadelphia Campaign*, 154.

27. GW to Henry, Dec. 27, 1777, *PGW:RWS* 13:17–18; GW to Samuel Blackden, Dec. 30, 1777, ibid., 13:58–59; GW to Benjamin Flower, Dec. 30, 1777, ibid., 13:67; GW to Officers of Light Dragoons, Dec. 30, 1777, ibid., 13:72; GW to Board of War, Jan. 2 [–3], 1778, ibid., 13:111; GW to Smallwood, Jan. 3, 7, 1778, ibid., 13:131, 168; GW to Thomas Wharton, Jan. 19, 1778, ibid., 13:285; GW to Livingston, Jan. 20, 1778, ibid., 13:296; GW to Putnam, Jan. 22, 1778, ibid., 13:316; GW to Richard Peters, Jan. 24 [–25], 1778, ibid., 13:333; GW to Mease, Jan. 27, 1778, ibid., 13:367; GW to Philip Van Rensselaer, Feb. 8, 1778, ibid., 13:483.

28. GW to Robert Dinwiddie, Oct. 11, 1755, *PGW:Col. Ser.* 2:102; Ferling, *First of Men*, 42.

29. GW, General Orders, July 5, 1775, *PGW:RWS* 1:63; GW, Circular to the States, Aug. 27, 1780, *WW* 19:450.

30. GW to Board of War, Jan. 2 [–3], 1778, *PGW:RWS* 13:112; GW to Greene, Feb. 12, 1778, ibid., 13:514; Committee at Camp to Laurens, Feb. 6, 1778, *LDC* 9:36; NG to GW, Feb. 15, 1777, *PNG* 2:285; Bodle, *Valley Forge Winter*, 165–220; Carp, *To Starve the Army at Pleasure*, 81–85.

31. John McCasland in Dann, *Revolution Remembered*, 156–57.

32. GW to Conway, Nov. 5, 1777, *PGW:RWS* 12:129. See also Ferling, *First of Men*, 158–59, and Taaffe, *Philadelphia Campaign*, 158–59.

33. GW to Landon Carter, May 30, 1778, *PGW: RWS* 15:268. For the two sides of the argument concerning whether the Conway Cabal actually existed, see Bernhard Knollenberg, *Washington and the Revolution, a Reappraisal: Gates, Conway, and the Continental Congress* (New York, 1940), and Flexner, *George Washington in the American Revolution*, 253–59, 262–77.

34. Quoted in Jonathan G. Rossie, *The Politics of Command in the American Revolution* (Syracuse, 1975), 192.

35. *PGW:RWS* 13:556n.

36. James Craig to GW, Jan. 6, 1778, ibid., 13:160–61; Henry to GW, Feb. 20, 1778, ibid., 13:609; Lund Washington to GW, Feb. 18, 1778, ibid., 13:587.

37. GW to Henry, March 28, 1778, ibid., 14:336; GW to Landon Carter, May 30, 1778, *WW* 11:493.

38. AH to Clinton, Feb. 13, 1778, *PAH* 1:427–28; Lafayette to Laurens, Jan. 5, 1778, *LLP* 1:213, 215; NG to Jacob Greene, Jan. 3, 1778, *PNG* 2:243; GW to Laurens, Jan. 2, 1778, *PGW:RWS* 13:119; GW to Livingston, Feb. 2, 1778, ibid., 13:442; Ron Chernow, *Alexander Hamilton* (New York, 2004), 139.

39. John Ferling, *A Leap in the Dark: The Struggle to Create the American Republic* (New York, 2003), 394.

40. Flexner, *George Washington in the American Revolution*, 268–69.

41. GW to Continental Congress Committee, Jan. 29, 1778, *PGW:RWS* 13:377; GW to Laurens, March 24, 1778, ibid., 14:293; Ferling, *First of Men*, 223; Wright, *Continental Army*, 124–25. The "Desarves a Penshon" quote is from Herbert T. Wade and Robert A. Lively, eds., *This Glorious Cause: The Adventures of Two Company Officers in Washington's Army* (Princeton, N.J., 1958), 235. For an excellent essay on the officers at Valley Forge, and their outlook and behavior in general, see Royster, *A Revolutionary People at War*, 200–13.

42. GW to Colonel John Green, Oct. 28, 1777, *PGW:RWS* 12:38; GW to G. Morris, July 24, 1778, ibid., 16:154; GW to Laurens, Nov. 10, 1777, March 24, 1778, ibid., 12:200–1; 14:293; GW to Livingston, Dec. 27, 1777, ibid., 13:19; JA to AA, June 3, 1776, May 22, 1777, *AFC* 2:5, 245; Ward, *General William Maxwell*, 91; *JCC* 10:269; 11:807. See also the discussion in Royster, *A Revolutionary People at War*, 197–213.

43. GW to Glover and Ebenezer Learned, Jan. 8, 1778, *PGW:RWS* 13:172; Sullivan's Opinion, Oct. 29, 1777, ibid., 12:56; Pulaski to GW, Nov. 23, 1777, ibid., 12:367; Conway to GW, Dec. 29, 31, 1777, ibid., 13:40–41, 77–78; St. Clair to GW, Jan. 5, 1778, ibid., 13:154; Knox to GW, Jan. 3, 1778, ibid., 13:129.

44. GW to Henry Laurens, April 30, 1778, ibid., 14:682; Fleming, *Washington's Secret War*, 207, 210.

45. *PGW:RWS* 14:224n; Conway to GW, Dec. 29, 1777, ibid., 13:40; Wright, *Continental Army*, 141; Royster, *A Revolutionary People at War*, 217, 219; Bodle, *Valley Forge Winter*, 199–200.

46. GW to Laurens, April 30, June 18, 1778, *PGW:RWS* 14:682; 15:448; GW to David Mason, April 4, 1778, ibid., 14:407; Flexner, *George Washington in the American Revolution*, 288–89; Ward, *War of the Revolution*, 2:553. For an excellent extended discussion on Steuben and the meaning of his presence, see Royster, *A Revolutionary People at War*, 213–38.

47. GW to Robert Livingston, Dec. 27, 1777, *PGW:RWS* 13:19.

48. GW to Continental Congress Camp Committee, Jan. 29, 1778, ibid., 13:376–404; ibid., 13:20n, 404–9n. GW's quotes are can be found in ibid., 13:376, 403.

49. Lengel, *General George Washington*, 275.

50. GW to Cadwalader, March 20, 1778, *PGW:RWS* 14:235; GW to Laurens, March 24, 1778, ibid., 14:292; JG to Dartmouth, March 24, 1778, in Benjamin Stevens, ed., *Facsimilies of Manuscripts in European Archives Relating to America, 1773–1783* (London, 1889–1898), 24, No. 2090; Fleming, *Washington's Secret War*, 263; John Ferling, "Joseph Galloway's Military Advice: A Loyalist's View of the Revolution," *PMHB* 98 (1974):174–76.

51. William H. Nelson, *The American Tory* (Oxford, England, 1961), 141.

52. GW to Henry, Dec. 10, 1777, *PGW:RWS* 12:590; Taaffe, *Campaign for Philadelphia*, 145–46.

53. Ira D. Gruber, *The Howe Brothers and the American Revolution* (New York, 1972), 255–56, 298.

54. Taaffe, *Campaign for Philadelphia*, 147; Gruber, *Howe Brothers and the American Revolution*, 294.

55. Taaffe, *Campaign for Philadelphia*, 169–71.

56. GW to General Officers, April 20, 1778, *PGW:RWS* 14:567; Washington's Thoughts upon a Plan of Operations for Campaign 1778, [April 26–29, 1778], ibid., 14:641–48.

57. Duane to Gates, Dec. 16, 1777, *LDC* 8:421; Duane to Stark, Dec. 16, 1777, ibid., 8:423; Laurens to Augustin de La Balme, Jan. 11, 1778, ibid., 8:559–60; Laurens to Lafayette, Jan. 22, 1778, ibid., 8:634–35; *JCC* 10:84, 87.

58. Carleton to Germain, June 10, 1778, *DAR* 15:137; Governor Frederick Haldimand, "Sketch of the Military State of the Province of Quebec," July 25, 1778, ibid., 15:169–70; Frederick Haldimand to Germain, Oct. 15, 1778, ibid., 15:224.

59. GW to Nelson, Feb. 8, 1778, *PGW:RWS* 13:481; Paul David Nelson, *General Horatio Gates: A Biography* (Baton Rouge, 1976), 172.

60. Laurens to Lafayette, March 6, 1778, *LDC* 9:229.

61. Laurens to John Rutledge, March 11, 1778, ibid., 9:270; John Thaxton to JA, Jan. 20, 1778, *AFC* 2:386.

62. John Penn to Theodorick Bland, Feb. 6, 1778, *LDC* 9:42; James Lovell to JA, Feb. 8, 1778, ibid., 9:54; Dyer to William Williams, Feb. 17, 1778, ibid., 9:115.

63. Lafayette to GW, Jan. 20, Feb. 9, 1778, *PGW:RWS* 13:291, 489; Lafayette to Gates, Feb. 23, 1778, *LLP* 2:316; Laurens to Lafayette, March 24, 1778, *LDC* 9:330; *JCC* 10:217; Nelson, *General Horatio Gates*, 169–77.

64. Washington's Thoughts upon a Plan of Operations for Campaign 1778, [April 26–29, 1778], *PGW:RWS* 14:641; ibid., 14:579n; GW to Alexander McDougall, May 1, 1778, ibid., 15:5–6; GW to Laurens, May 3, 1778, ibid., 15:20–21; GW to Richard Henry Lee, May 25, 1778, ibid., 15:216–17.

65. Samuel Chase to Thomas Johnson, May 3, 1778, *LDC* 9:572; Charles Carroll of Carrollton to Charles Carroll Sr., May 4, 1778, ibid., 9:595; Gouverneur Morris to Livingston, May 3, 1778, ibid., 9:590; William Ellery to William Vernon, May 6, 1778, ibid., 9:611; Ellery to Cooke, May 3, 1778, ibid., 9:573; *JCC* 11:457–58, 462–63.

66. GW, General Orders, May 5, 7, 1778, *PGW:RWS* 15:38–40, 68–70; ibid., 15:40–41n; Royster, *A Revolutionary People at War*, 250–54; *The Army Correspondence of Colonel John Laurens in the Years 1777–1778* (New York, 1969), 169–70; McMichael, Diary of Lt. James McMichael, *PMHB* 16:159; Ward, *General William Maxwell*, 94–95.

67. GW to Richard Henry Lee, May 25, 1778, *PGW:RWS* 15:216–17; Council of War, May 8, 1778, ibid., 15:79–81; From a Council of War, May 9, 1778, ibid., 15:83–87.

68. Quoted in William B. Willcox, *Portrait of a General: Sir Henry Clinton in the War of Independence* (New York, 1962), 223. See ibid., 223–25, and Gruber, *Howe Brothers and the American Revolution*, 297.

69. Edward J. Tatum, ed., *The American Journal of Ambrose Serle* (New York, 1969), 295–96.

70. Bernard A. Uhlendorf, *Revolution in America: Confidential Letters and Journals 1776–1784 of Adjutant General Major Baurmeister of the Hessian Forces* (New Brunswick, N.J., 1957), 177–78; Taaffe, *Campaign for Philadelphia*, 187; Ira D. Gruber, ed., *John Peebles' American War: The Diary of a Scottish Grenadier, 1776–1782* (Mechanicsburg, Pa., 1998), 181–83; Gruber, *Howe Brothers and the American Revolution*, 299.

71. Weldon A. Brown, *Empire or Independence: A Study in the Failure of Reconciliation, 1774–1783* (Baton Rouge, 1941), 260–92; *JCC* 11:615, 678. The quotations are from Richard W. Van Alstyne, *Empire and Independence: The International History of the American Revolution* (New York, 1967), 260–61, 264, 277.

72. Willcox, *Portrait of a General*, 227–29, 232–33; Christopher Ward *The War of the Revolution*, 2 vols. (New York, 1952), 2:571.

73. GW to Laurens, May 18, 24, 28, 1778, *PGW:RWS* 15:155, 210, 246; GW to Lafayette, May 18, 1778, ibid., 15:152; GW to G. Morris, May 29, 1778, ibid., 15:260–61; Taaffe, *Campaign for Philadelphia*, 194–95.

74. GW to Lee, April 22, 1778, *PGW:RWS* 14:585.

75. Ibid., 8:289–90n; GW to Hancock, March 6, 1777, ibid., 8:522–23; *LP* 2:361–66; Charles Lee, "Scheme for Putting an End to the War, Submitted to the Royal Commissioners," March 29, 1777, *LP* 2:361–66. See also Charles H. Moore, *The Treason of Charles Lee* (New York, 1860); John Alden, *General Charles Lee, Traitor or Patriot?* (Baton Rouge, 1951), 170–71, 174–77, 336n; John Shy, "Charles Lee," in George A. Billias, ed., *George Washington's Generals* (New York, 1964), 40–41.

76. *PNG* 2:32–33n; Lee to GW, Feb. 9, 1777, *PGW:RWS* 8:289; Lee to Rush, June 4, 1778, *LP* 2:398; Alden, *General Charles Lee*, 151–93. For Lee's parole, see *LP* 2:382.

77. Quoted in Alden, *General Charles Lee*, 190. The stories of Lee's appearance and of his consorting with a harlot were offered up by Elias Boudinot, who admitted his hatred for Lee.

78. Elias Boudinot, "Exchange of Major-General Charles Lee," *PMHB* 15 (1891):31–32; *PNG* 2:232n; GW to Lee, April 22, 1778, *PGW:RWS* 14:585.

79. Boudinot, "Exchange of Lee," *PMHB* 15:32, 33; NG to Governor William Greene, May 25, 1778, *PNG* 2:408; NG to Griffin Greene, May 25, 1778, ibid., 2:406; GW to Lee, June 15, 1778, *PGW:RWS* 15:406–7; Lee to Rush, June 4, 1778, *LP* 2:398–99; Lee, "Plan of an Army, &c.," ibid., 2:383–87; Alden, *General Charles Lee*, 200.

80. Ward, *War of the Revolution*, 2:562–68; GW to G. Morris, May 29, 1778, *PGW:RWS* 15:261.

81. Piel, in Bruce E. Burgoyne, *Enemy Views: The American Revolutionary War As Recorded by the Hessian Participants* (Bowie, Md., 1996), 223–26; Taaffe, *Campaign for Philadelphia*, 195, 208; Ward, *War of the Revolution*, 2:573; Ferling, *First of Men*, 244.

82. Ward, *War of the Revolution*, 2:574.

83. Council of War, June 17, 1778, *PGW:RWS* 15:414–17; Cadwalader to GW, June 18, 1778, ibid., 15:435–36; Wayne to GW, June 18, 1778, ibid., 468–69. The responses of the other officers, all written on June 18, can be found in ibid., 15:431–70.

84. Council of War, June 24, 1778, ibid., 15:520–21; ibid., 15:522n; Lee to GW, June 18, 1778, ibid., 15:457–58; Ward, *General William Maxwell*, 99; Alden, *General Charles Lee*, 205–6, 208–10.

85. AH to Boudinot, July 5, 1778, *PAH* 1:510; NG to GW, June 24, *PNG* 2:446–47; Lafayette to GW, June 24, *PGW:RWS* 15:528–29; Wayne to GW, June 24, 1778, ibid., 15:534–35.

86. GW to Lafayette, June 25, 26, 1778, *PGW:RWS* 15:539, 552–53, 554, 555; GW to Lee, June 26, 1778, ibid., 15:556; GW to Dickinson, June 24, 25, 1778, ibid., 15:522–23, 536–37; GW to William Maxwell, June 24, 1778, ibid., 15:531; GW to Charles Scott, June 24, 1778, ibid., 15:534; GW to Morgan, June 24, 1778, ibid., 15:532; Ward, *War of the Revolution*, 2:575; Benson Bobrick, *Angel in the Whirlwind: The Triumph of the American Revolution* (New York, 1997), 344.

87. Lee to GW, June 25, 1778, *PGW:RWS* 15:541–42.

88. GW to Lee, June 26, 1778, ibid., 15:556; Paul David Nelson, *Anthony Wayne: Soldier of the Early Republic* (Bloomington, Ind., 1985), 77–78; Ward, *General William Maxwell*, 103.

89. *PGW:RWS* 15:573n; Piers Mackesy, *The War for America, 1775–1783* (Cambridge, Mass., 1965), 215.

90. *PGW:RWS* 15:573–75n; Henry Clinton, *The American Rebellion: Sir Henry Clinton's Narrative of His Campaigns, 1775–1782*, ed. William B. Willcox (New Haven, Conn., 1954), 91.

91. *PGW:RWS* 15:575n; Ward, *War of the Revolution*, 2:579. See also Nelson, *Anthony Wayne*, 80.

92. Clinton, *American Rebellion*, 91–92, 96.

93. Quoted in Lengel, *General George Washington*, 300.

94. GW to PC, July 1, 1778, *WW* 12:142–43; Testimony of Colonel Richard Harrison, *SOS* 2:712; Scheer, *Private Yankee Doodle*, 127; George F. Scheer and Hugh F. Rankin, *Rebels and Redcoats* (Cleveland, 1957), 331; Ward, *Charles Scott and the "Spirit of '76"*, 50–51.

95. Alden, *General Charles Lee*, 222; Theodore Thayer, *Washington and Lee: The Making of a Scapegoat* (Port Washington, N.Y., 1976), 52; Lafayette, "Memoirs of 1779," *LLP* 2:11.

96. Scheer, *Private Yankee Doodle*, 127.

97. Lafayette, "Memoirs of 1779," *LLP* 2:11; AH to Boudinot, July 5, *PAH* 1:512; *LP* 3:156–57, 159.

98. Taaffe, *Campaign for Philadelphia*, 218–19.

99. Lafayette, "Memoirs of 1779," *LLP* 2:11.

100. Scheer, *Private Yankee Doodle*, 123–33. On legendary Molly Pitcher, see Linda Grant DePauw and Conover Hunt, *Remember the Ladies: Women of America, 1750–1815* (New York, 1976), 90; Martin, *Private Yankee Doodle*, 132–33; Ray Raphael, *A People's History of the American Revolution: How Common People Shaped the Fight for Independence* (New York, 2001), 126.

101. GW to John Augustine Washington, July 4, 1778, *WW* 12:157.

102. This account of the battle draws on Taaffe, *Campaign for Philadelphia*, 212–24; Ward, *War of the Revolution*, 2:576–85; Alden, *General Charles Lee*, 212–27; Willcox, *Portrait of a General*, 233–36; Ward, *General William Maxwell*, 102–5; Ward, *Charles Scott and the "Spirit of '76,"* 49–51; Lengel, *General George Washington*, 297–304; William S. Stryker and William S. Myers, *The Battle of Monmouth* (Princeton, N.J., 1927); Thayer, *Washington and Lee*, 36–58.

103. Taaffe, *Campaign for Philadelphia*, 219.

104. GW to Gates, July 3, 1778, *WW* 12:149; GW to John Augustine Washington, July 4, 1778, ibid., 12:156, 157; GW to PC, July 1, 1778, ibid., 12:143; Ward, *War of the Revolution*, 2:586.

105. All three of Lee's letters were misdated, but they were probably written on June 29 and/or 30. See *PGW:RWS* 15:594–95, 596–97.

106. GW wrote two letters to Lee. See GW to Lee, June 30, 1778, ibid., 15:595–96, 597. AH's Testimony, Proceedings of a General Court-Martial for the Trial of Major General Charles Lee, July 4, 13, 1778, *PAH* 1:509, 517–21; AH to Stirling, July 14, 1778, ibid., 1:522; Lafayette to Laurens, July 6, 1778, *LLP* 2:99; Greene to Jacob Greene, July 2, 1778, *PNG* 2:451; Lee to G. Morris, July 3, 1778, *LP* 2:457; Lee to Reed, July 22, 1778, ibid., 2:479; Lee to the president of Congress, April 22, 1780, ibid., 3:424; Lee to NG, Sept. 12, 1782, ibid., 4:35; "General Lee's Vindication to the Public," *Pennsylvania Packet*, Dec. 3, 1778, ibid., 3:255–65; [Charles Lee], "A Short History of the Treatment of Major General Conway....," *Pennsylvania Packet*, Dec. 3, 1778, ibid., 3:265–69; [Charles Lee], "Some Queries, Political and Military, Humbly Offered to the Consideration of the Public," *Maryland Journal and Baltimore Advertiser*, July 6, 1779, ibid., 3:341–45; Jared Sparks, *Life of Charles Lee* (Boston, 1846), in ibid., 4:330; Alden, *General Charles Lee*, 234, 296–98; Shy, "Charles Lee," Billias, *George Washington's Generals*, 45; Thayer, *Washington and Lee*, 70–104; Boudinot, "Exchange of Lee," *PMHB* 15:32. The proceedings of the court martial can be found in *LP* 3:1–208. For an excellent account of the tainted court martial testimony by one of the so-called "dirty earwigs," see Gregory D. Massey, *John Laurens and the American Revolution* (Columbia, S.C., 2000), 113.

107. AA to JA, Oct. 21, 1778, *AFC* 3:109; Mercy Warren to JA, Oct. 15, 1778, *PJA* 7:142.

108. GW to Gates, July 14, 1778, *WW* 12:176; Ward, *War of the Revolution*, 2:587; *PH* 20:212–14.

109. Quoted in Willcox, *Portrait of a General*, 237. On Byron's crossing, see Gerald S. Brown, *American Secretary: The Colonial Policies of Lord George Germain* (Ann Arbor, Mich., 1963), 170.

110. GW, "A Plan of Attack on New York," June ?, 1778, *WW* 12:135–38; GW to PC, July 12, 1778, ibid., 12:174.

111. Willcox, *Portrait of a General*, 238; Flexner, *George Washington in the American Revolution*, 324; GW to Trumbull, July 22, 1778, *WW* 12:207; GW to John Parke Custis, [July], 1778, ibid., 12:255.

112. Flexner, *George Washington in the American Revolution*, 324; Ward, *War of the Revolution*, 2:588; GW to John Augustine Washington, Sept. 23, 1778, *WW* 12:488.

113. Sullivan to Hancock, Sept. 27, 1777, *SP* 1:462, 469; Charles P. Whittemore, *General of the Revolution: John Sullivan of New Hampshire* (New York, 1961), 64–68, 75; Dyer to Sullivan, Oct. 11, 1777, *LDC* 8:105; Aedanus Burke to Sullivan, Oct. 12, 1777, ibid., 8:108–10.

114. NG to Sullivan, July 23, 1778, *PNG* 2:466–67; GW to Sullivan, July 28, Aug. 4, 10, 1778, *SP* 2:135, 179, 196; GW to Sullivan, July 27, 31, 1778, *WW* 12:238, 250–51.

115. Paul F. Dearden, *The Rhode Island Campaign of 1778: Inauspicious Dawn of Alliance* (Providence, 1980), 93.

116. Mackesy, *War for America*, 218.

117. Gruber, *Howe Brothers in the American Revolution*, 316–17; Mackesy, *War for America*, 218.

118. NG to Charles Pettit, Aug. 22, 1778, *PNG* 2:491; ibid., 2:485n; Sullivan to GW, Aug. 13, 1778, *SOS* 2:718.

119. *PNG* 2:490–91n; NG to Pettit, Aug. 22, 1778, ibid., 2:491–92; "A Protest of the General Officers on Rhode Island to Count d'Estaing," Aug. 22, 1778, ibid., 2:487–90; Laurens

to GW, Sept. 2, 1778, ibid., 2:490n; d'Estaing to NG, ibid., 2:530–31; GW to d'Estaing, Sept. 11, 1778, *WW* 12:423.

120. *PNG* 2:485n; NG to Sullivan, Aug. 23, 1778, ibid., 2:493; GW to Sullivan, Aug. 22, 28, 1778, *WW* 12:350, 368–69; Ward, *War of the Revolution*, 2:591–92.

121. Willcox, *Portrait of a General*, 250–51.

122. Dearden, *Rhode Island Campaign of 1778*, 126; Gruber, *Howe Brothers in the American Revolution*, 319–20; NG to GW, Sept. 1, 1778, *PNG* 2:505.

123. GW to John Augustine Washington, Oct. 26, 1778, *WW* 13:156.

127. GW to d'Estaing, Oct. 27, 1778, ibid., 13:169; GW to John Augustine Washington, Nov. 26, 1778, ibid., 13:336.

Chapter 13. Choices, 1779

1. Bartlett to Mary Bartlett, July 14, Aug. 3, 1778, *LDC* 10:275–76, 384; Laurens to Rawlins Lowndes, July 15, 1778, ibid., 10:285; Richard Henry Lee to Francis Lightfoot Lee, July 12, 1778, ibid., 10:266; Richard B. Morris, *The Peacemakers: The Great Powers and American Independence* (New York, 1965), 1–2.

2. William Stinchcombe, *The American Revolution and the French Alliance* (Syracuse, 1969), 32–34.

3. AH to Boudinot, Sept. 8, 1778, *PAH* 1:545; Lee Kennett, *The French Forces in America, 1780–1783* (Westport, Conn., 1977), 7; AA to JA, Oct. 25, 1778, *AFC* 3:110–11; Samuel Adams to James Warren, Oct. 20, 1778, *LDC* 11:80, 81n; Laurens to d'Estaing, Oct. 20, 1778, ibid., 11:83–84; *JCC* 121:1021; Stinchcombe, *American Revolution and the French Alliance*, 54–61; Douglas Southall Freeman, *George Washington* (New York, 1948–1957), 5:76; GW to Heath, Aug. 28, Sept. 22, 1778, *WW* 12:364, 476; GW to Lafayette, Sept. 1, 1778, ibid., 12:382–83; GW to d'Estaing, Sept. 2, 11, 1778, ibid., 12:389–90, 423–28.

4. Committee for Foreign Affairs to GW, Oct. 27, 1778, *LDC* 11:130; Lafayette to GW, Sept. 3, 1778, *LLP* 2:185n.

5. Lafayette to Laurens, June 4, 1778, *LLP* 2:67; Lafayette to d'Estaing, Aug. 24, 1778, ibid., 2:145–46; ibid., 2:192n; GW to Lafayette, Sept. 25, 1778, *WW* 12:502.

6. *LDC* 11:83n; *JCC* 12:1042–48, 1052–53; President of Congress to Lafayette, Oct. 24, 1778, *LLP* 2:193. The "Plan of Attack" can be found in *PBF* 27:637–42.

7. GW to Laurens, Nov. 14, 1778, *WW* 13:254–57.

8. Laurens to GW, Nov. 20, 1778, *LDC* 11:229; John Jay to Lafayette, Jan. 3, 1779, ibid., 11:408–9. For a more glowing assessment of GW and Canada, see Edmund S. Morgan, *The Genius of George Washington* (New York, 1980), 14–16, 60–63.

9. JA to President of Congress, Dec. 3, 1778, *PJA* 7:247.

10. JA to Samuel Adams, Dec. 7, 1778, ibid., 7:256; JA to Lovell, Jan. 3, Feb. 20, 1779, ibid., 7. 336, 420; JA to Thomas McKean, Sept. 20, 1778, ibid., 7:162; *DAJA* 2:302, 347, 351–52, 367, 391–92; 4:118–20; JA to Samuel Adams, May 21, 1778, ibid., 4:106–8; *Boston Patriot*, May 15, 1811, in Charles Francis Adams, ed., *The Works of John Adams, Second President of the United States* (Boston, 1850–1856), 1:655. See also Jonathan R. Dull, "Franklin the Diplomat: The French Mission," *Proceedings*, American Philosophical Society, 72 (1982):10–17; Robert Middlekauf, *Franklin and His Enemies* (Berkeley, Calif., 1996); John Ferling, "John Adams, Diplomat," *WMQ* 51 (1994): 227–52; Stacy Schiff, *A Great Improvisation: Franklin, France, and the Birth of America* (New York, 2005), 182–95, 197.

11. JA to Samuel Adams, July 28, Nov. 27, 1778, Feb. 14, 1779, *PJA* 6:326; 7:234; 8:413; JA to Warren, Aug. 4, 1778, ibid., 6:347–48; JA to President of Congress, Aug. 4, 1779, ibid., 8:109, 111; JA to Elbridge Gerry, Dec. 5, 1778, Sept. 11, 1779, ibid., 7:248; 8:141–42; Commissioners to Vergennes, [Dec. 20–Jan. 9], 1778–1779, ibid., 7:294–309; Schiff, *A Great Improvisation*, 185–86; Piers Mackesy, *The War for America, 1775–1783* (Cambridge, Mass.,

1965), 261; Jonathan Dull, *The French Navy and American Independence: A Study of Arms and Diplomacy, 1774–1787* (Princeton, N.J., 1975), 125, 159–60, 188.

12. *PH* 20:211–13; Jonathan Dull, *A Diplomatic History of the American Revolution* (New Haven, Conn., 1983), 107, 110.

13. Quoted in Edward Corwin, *French Policy and the American Alliance of 1778* (New York, 1916), 177.

14. Sherry Johnson, "El Niño, Environmental Crisis, and the Emergence of Alternative Markets in the Hispanic Caribbean, 1760s–70s," *WMQ* 62 (2005):365–410; Robert Claxton, "The Record of Drought and Its Impact in Colonial Spanish America," in Richard Heer, ed., *Themes in Rural History of the Western World* (Ames, Iowa, 1993), 194–226.

15. Morris, *Peacemakers*, 14.

16. Dull, *French Navy and American Independence*, 125–43; Dull, *Diplomatic History of the American Revolution*, 108–10; Corwin, *French Policy and the American Alliance*, 173–217; Samuel Flagg Bemis, *The Diplomacy of the American Revolution* (New York, 1935), 70–93; Mackesy, *War for America*, 190.

17. W. J. Eccles, "The French Alliance and the American Victory," in John Ferling, ed., *The World Turned Upside Down: The American Victory in the War of Independence* (Westport, Conn., 1988), 161–62.

18. JA to Roger Sherman, Dec. 6, 1778, *PJA* 7:254.

19. Stinchcombe, *American Revolution and the French Alliance*, 62–76; John Ferling, *A Leap in the Dark: The Struggle to Create the American Republic* (New York, 2003), 210–16.

20. In his initial orders to Clinton, Germain had directed him to seize Georgia. See Germain to Clinton, March 8, 1778, *DAR* 15:60. For Campbell's directions, see Commissioners for Quieting Disorders to Germain, Nov. 16, 1778, ibid., 15:258–59. Clinton told Germain that should Washington send reinforcements to Georgia, the British force would either fail or be compelled to surrender what it had taken. See Clinton to Germain, Oct. 25, 1778, ibid., 15:232.

21. Archibald Campbell, *Journal of Lieut. Colonel Archibald Campbell*, ed. Colin Campbell (Darien, Ga., 1981), 24.

22. Ibid., 25–29. The best account of the campaign for Savannah can be found in David K. Wilson, *The Southern Strategy: Britain's Conquest of South Carolina and Georgia, 1775–1780* (Columbia, S.C., 2005), 65–80, which, with Campbell's journal, is the principal source for my account. See also Christopher Ward *The War of the Revolution*, 2 vols. (New York, 1952), 2:679–83.

23. Cassandra Pybus, "Jefferson's Faulty Math: The Question of Slave Defections in the American Revolution," *WMQ* 62 (2005): 253.

24. GW to Lafayette, March 8 [–10], 1779, *WW* 14:219; John Henry to Thomas Johnson, Jan. 30, 1779, *LDC* 11:538; Laurens to Reed, Feb. 9, 1779, ibid., 12:39.

Chapter 14. "A Band of Brotherhood": The Soldiers, the Army, and the Forgotten War in 1779

1. GW to Greene, Oct. 29, 1778, *WW* 13:179; Douglas Southall Freeman, *George Washington: A Biography*. 7 vols. (New York, 1948–1957), 5:87.

2. James Thacher, *Military Journal of the American Revolution* reprint (reprint, New York, 1969), 161; GW to Jedidiah Huntington, Jan. 14, 1779, *WW* 14:14; GW to Daniel Kemper, March 3, 1779, ibid., 14:184; GW to George Measam, March 10, 1779, ibid., 14:217; James A. Huston, *Logistics of Liberty: American Services of Supply in the Revolutionary War and After* (Newark, Del., 1991), 121, 123, 194.

3. GW to William Gordon, Aug. 2, 1779, *WW* 16:39; See John Ferling, "School for Command: Young George Washington and the Virginia Regiment," in Warren R. Hofstra, ed., *George Washington and the Virginia Backcountry* (Madison, Wisc., 1998), 195–222.

4. Martha Bland, quoted in George F. Scheer and Hugh F. Rankin, *Rebels and Redcoats: The American Revolution through the Eyes of Those Who Fought and Lived It* (Cleveland, 1957), 224.

5. For an elaboration, see John Ferling, *The First of Men: A Life of George Washington* (Knoxville, 1988), 239, 258–60.

6. GW to John Mitchell, Feb. 17, 1779, *WW* 14:127–28; Holly A. Mayer, *Belonging to the Army: Camp Followers and Community during the American Revolution* (Columbia, S.C., 1996), 15, 147–49; NG to Jeremiah Wadsworth, March 19, 25, 29, 1779, *PNG* 3:354, 366, 373; Ron Chernow, *Alexander Hamilton* (New York, 2004), 129–30.

7. Charles H. Lesser, *The Sinews of Independence: Monthly Strength Reports of the Continental Army* (Chicago, 1976), 54–55, 100–2; Mayer, *Belonging to the Army*, 133; Harry M. Ward, *The War of Independence and the Transformation of American Society* (London, 1999), 117–18.

8. For this insight I wish to thank Holly Mayer, who has generously permitted me to borrow from her presentation "Continental Camp Followers: Spouses, Sutlers, & Servants," George Washington Teachers Institute, Mount Vernon, June 28, 2006.

9. Walter A. Blumenthal, *Women Camp Followers of the American Revolution*, reprint (New York, 1974), 15–54; Peter Way, "Venus and Mars: Women and the British-American Army in the Seven Years' War," in Julie Flavell and Stephen Conway, *Britain and America Go to War: The Impact of War and Warfare* (Gainesville, Fla., 2004), 41–68; Mayer, *Belonging to the Army*, 125–26; GW, General Orders, Sept. 13, 1777, *PGW:RWS* 11:212; GW, General Orders, June 7, 1779, *WW* 15:240; GW to Superintendent of Finance, Jan. 29, 1783, ibid., 26:78–80; Ward, *War of Independence*, 117.

10. John Rees, " 'The Multitude of Women': An Examination of the Number of Female Camp Followers with the Continental Army," *Minerva* 14 (1996):3, 19, 30; GW to John Stark, Aug. 5, 1778, *PGW: RWS* 16:256.

11. GW, General Orders, Aug. 4, 1777, *PGW:RWS* 10:496, John C. Dann, ed., *Revolution Remembered: Eyewitness Accounts of the War of Independence* (Chicago, 1980), 242, 247; Mayer, *Belonging to the Army*, 129–30, 130, 134, 136–39, 143; Blumenthal, *Women Camp Followers*, 63, 74; Ward, *War of Independence*, 118; 121–22. On Deborah Sampson, see Alfred F. Young, *Masquerade: The Life and Times of Deborah Sampson* (New York, 2004). Young's *Masquerade* is the source for women camp followers being vaccinated and the quote concerning good artillery soldiers leaving the army if provisions were not made available for women. See page 96 for both.

12. GW, General Orders, July 11, 1776, *PGW:RWS* 1:106; Mayer, *Belonging to the Army*, 86–96.

13. GW, General Orders, April 27, 1776, *PGW:RWS* 4:141, 142n; Christopher Ward *The War of the Revolution*. 2 vols. (New York, 1952), 123–25.

14. See the illuminating essay on society and social hierarchy in Gordon Wood, *The Radicalism of the American Revolution* (New York, 1992), 11–92.

15. A good starting point in the literature of officers and enlisted men is the essay by Holly A. Mayer, "Soldierly Subordination: The Issue of Deference in the Continental Army," in Peter Karsten, ed., *The Training and Socializing of Military Personnel* (New York, 1988), 293–307.

16. Caroline Cox, *A Proper Sense of Honor: Service and Sacrifice in George Washington's Army* (Chapel Hill, N.C., 2004), 46–47, 54, 58–59, 66–67, Charles Bolton, *The Private Soldier under Washington* (London, 1902), 91; General Orders, July 29, 1778, *PGW: RWS* 16:195.

17. Cox, *A Proper Sense of Honor*, 119–62, 164–65; Gregory T. Knouff, *The Soldiers' Revolution: Pennsylvania in Arms and the Forging of Early American Identity* (University Park, Pa., 2004), 88; Robert Middlekauff, *The Glorious Cause: The American Revolution, 1763–1789*, rev. ed. (New York, 2005), 523; Wayne to Gates, Dec. 1, 1776, *SOS* 2:828; Bolton, *Private Soldier under Washington*, 52; Knox to Mrs. Baxter Howe, Oct. 2, 1781, in Dennis P. Ryan, ed., *A Salute to Courage: The American Revolution as Seen through Wartime Writings of Officers of the Continental Army and Navy* (New York, 1979), 248; Harold L. Peterson, *The Book of the Continental Soldier: Being a Compleat Account of the Uniforms, Weapons, and Equipment with Which He Lived and Fought*

(Harrisburg, Pa., 1968), 170; Oscar Reiss, *Medicine and the American Revolution: How Diseases and Their Treatment Affected the Colonial Army* (Jefferson, N.C., 1998). Reiss asserts that smallpox and typhus were the leading killers among diseases that befell the rebel soldiers; see page 186. An excellent account of the army's medical department can be found in Mary C. Gillet, *The Army Medical Department, 1775–1818* (Washington, D.C., 1990).

18. Journal of Wild, MHS, *Proceedings*, 2d Ser., 6:107, 116, 119; Cox, *A Proper Sense of Honor*, 76–117; Harry M. Ward, *George Washington's Enforcers: Policing the Continental Army* (Carbondale, Ill., 2006), 156–57, 163, 175, 183–84, 186. See also Huston, *Logistics of Liberty*, 150–62; GW to President of Congress, Feb. 3, 1781, *WW* 21:178–79; GW to Henry Lee, July 9, 10, 1779, ibid., 15:388, 399; Charles Royster, *A Revolutionary People at War: The Continental Army and American Character, 1775–1783* (Chapel Hill, N.C., 1979), 81; George Scheer, ed., *Private Yankee Doodle: Being a Narrative of Some of the Adventures, Dangers and Sufferings of a Revolutionary Soldier* (Boston, 1962), 255–56.

19. Scheer, *Private Yankee Doodle*, 68–69, 107, 111–12, 198, 285; Daniel Barber, *The History of My Own Times* (Washington, D.C., 1827), 16.

20. GW to the Committee of Conference, Jan. 20, 1779, *WW* 14:28; Herbert T. Wade and Robert A. Lively, eds., *This Glorious Cause: The Adventures of Two Company Officers in Washington's Army* (Princeton, N.J., 1958), 174; Scheer, *Private Yankee Doodle*, 198.

21. "Itinerary of the Pennsylvania Line from Pennsylvania to South Carolina, 1781–1782," *PMHB* 36 (1912):273–92; James McMichael, "Diary of Lt. James McMichael, of the Pennsylvania Line, 1776–1778," ibid., 16:153; John Ferling, *A Wilderness of Miseries: War and Warriors in Early America* (Westport, Conn., 1980), 100–1; Scheer, *Private Yankee Doodle*, 115, 166, 174, 267, 275; Ward, *George Washington's Enforcers*, 92–98, 102–5; Bolton, *Private Soldier under Washington*, 77, 143, 145, 151.

22. Bolton, *Private Soldier under Washington*, 158–76; Wade and Lively, *This Glorious Cause*, 32.

23. GW to Putnam, Nov. 27, 1778, *WW* 13:342; Lesser, *Sinews of Independence*, 100–1; Allen Bowman, *The Morale of the American Revolutionary Army*, reprint (Port Washington, N.Y., 1964), 63, 65; Martin, *Private Yankee Doodle*, 112–14, 153, 159, 202, 210–12.

24. Scheer, *Private Yankee Doodle*, 280.

25. Ibid., 186; Don Higginbotham, *The War of American Independence: Military Attitudes, Policies, and Practice, 1763–1789* (New York, 1971), 399–401; Royster, *Continental Army in the American Mind*, 71; Lesser, *Sinews of Independence*, 59–61, 101, 149, 194; Benjamin F. Stevens, ed., *Facsimiles of Manuscripts in European Archives Relating to America, 1773–1783*. 25 vols. (London, 1889–1898), 24:2,094; GW to Reed, April 28, 1780, *WW* 18:310–11; *JCC* 7:115, 154–55; Wayne K. Bodle, *Valley Forge Winter: Civilians and Soldiers in War* (University Park, Pa., 2002), 304n; For a good discussion of desertion in the Continental Army, see Allen Bowman, *The Morale of the American Revolutionary Army* (Washington, D.C., 1943), 63–92.

26. Scheer, *Private Yankee Doodle*, 182, 194; Thacher, *Military Journal of the American Revolution*, 188.

27. The foregoing paragraphs draw on Ward, *George Washington's Enforcers*, 140, 143, and Robert Wright, *The Continental Army* (Washington, D.C., 1983), 105–7, 128–46.

28. Charles P. Niemeyer, *America Goes to War: A Social History of the Continental Army* (New York, 1996), 27–64. The Galloway quotation is on page 42.

29. Martin, *Private Yankee Doodle*, 145.

30. Nicholas Cooke to GW, Feb. 23, 1778, *PGW:RWS* 13:646.

31. Varnum to GW, Jan. 2, 1778, ibid., 13:125;

32. The aide was Colonel Laurens. See ibid., 13:285n.

33. Henry Wiencek, *An Imperfect God: George Washington, His Slaves, and the Creation of America* (New York, 2003), 191, 215, 218; Edward G. Lengel, *General George Washington* (New York, 2005), 317; John Ferling, *Setting the World Ablaze: Washington, Adams, Jefferson and the*

American Revolution (New York, 2000), 189; GW to Cooke, Jan. 2, 1778, *PGW: RWS* 13:114; Alexander Seammell, "Return of the Negroes in the Army," Aug. 24, 1778, ibid., 16:336n; Niemeyer, *America Goes to War*, 75, 83; Ray Raphael, *A People's History of the American Revolution: How Common People Shaped the Fight for Independence* (New York, 2001), 287–88; Ward, *War of Independence and the Transformation of American Society*, 180–81.

34. Benjamin Quarles, *The Negro in the American Revolution* (Chapel Hill, N.C., 1961), 52–57; Herbert Aptheker, *The Negro in the American Revolution* (New York, 1940), 49; William Cooper Nell, *Services of the Colored Americans in the Wars of 1776 and 1812* (Boston, 1852), 9, 11–12.

35. Wiencek, *An Imperfect God*, 223–25; Philip S. Foner, *Blacks in the American Revolution* (Westport, Conn., 1975), 61; Gregory D. Massey, *John Laurens and the American Revolution* (Columbia, S.C., 2000), 93–97, 130–31.

36. AH to Jay, March 14, 1779, *PAH* 2:17–19.

37. Raphael, *People's History of the American Revolution*, 261–62; Thomas Burke's Draft Committee Report [ante March 25, 1779], *LDC* 12:242–44, 244n; Henry Laurens's Draft Committee Report [ante March 25, 1779], ibid., 12:247.

38. Niemeyer, *America Goes to War*, 77; Burke to GW, March 24, 1779, *LDC* 12:238–39; H. Laurens to GW, March 16, 1779, ibid., 12:200; GW to H. Laurens, March 20, 1779, *WW* 14:267.

39. Wiencek, *An Imperfect God*, 227–32. The quotation is on page 229.

40. Niemeyer, *America Goes to War*, 82; Raphael, *People's History of the American Revolution*, 290; Quarles, *Negro in the American Revolution*, ix.

41. GW to Edward Rutledge, Oct. 5, 1778, *WW* 13:36; GW to Henry, Oct. 7, 1778, ibid., 13:46; GW to John A. Washington, Oct. 26, Nov. 26, 1778, ibid., 13:156, 335; GW to Samuel Washington, Oct. 22, 1778, ibid., 13:129; GW to John Parke Custis, Oct. 30, 1778, ibid., 13:183; GW to H. Laurens, Oct. 3, 1778, ibid., 13:15.

42. H. Laurens to Lowndes, Jan. 31, 1779, *LDC* 11:545; James Lovell to Gates, Nov. 3, 1778, April 5, 1779, ibid., 11:167; 12:299; ibid., 12:306n; GW to Henry, Oct. 7, 1778, *WW* 13:46. GW to PC, Dec. 13, 1778, ibid., 13:389, 390; *JCC* 12:1230.

43. Colonel Peter Bellinger to Henry Glen, Sept. 20, 1778, Peter Bellinger Papers, New York State Library, Call No. 11147; John Henry Livingston to his brother, Nov. 23, 1778, Jacob A. Lansing Papers, New York State Library, Call No. 40; Glenn F. Williams, *Year of the Hangman: George Washington's Campaign against the Iroquois* (Yardley, Pa., 2005), 185, 298; Joseph R. Fischer, *A Well-Executed Failure: The Sullivan Campaign against the Iroquois, July–September 1779* (Columbia, S.C., 1997), 9–33; Alan Taylor, *Divided Ground: Indians, Settlers, and Northern Borderland of the American Revolution* (New York, 2006), 91–94; Ward, *War of the Revolution*, 2:633–37; GW to PC, Nov. 16, 23 [–24], 1779, *WW* 13:264, 315.

44. *LDC* 12:455n; GW to Gérard, May 1, 1779, *WW* 14:471.

45. Freeman, *George Washington*, 5.93; GW to the Committee of Conference, Jan. 8, 1779, *WW* 13:485–91; GW to Lafayette, March 8 [–10], 1779, ibid., 14:219; GW to Lincoln, Oct. 3, 1778, ibid., 13:17, 17n.

46. GW to President of Congress, March 15, 1779, ibid., 14:243; GW to H. Laurens and Burke, March 18, 1779, ibid., 14:257.

47. Ferling, *Leap in the Dark*, 217.

48. GW to Benjamin Harrison, Dec. 18 [–30], 1778, *WW* 13:467–68; GW to George Mason, March 27, 1779, ibid., 14:299–301.

49. James T. Flexner, *George Washington in the American Revolution* (Boston, 1967), 235–39; GW to Harrison, Dec. 18 [–30], 1778, *WW* 13:467; John C. Miller, *The Triumph of Freedom, 1775–1783* (Boston, 1948), 436, 474–76; Kate Haulman, "Fashion and the Culture Wars of Revolutionary Philadelphia," *WMQ* 62 (2005): 625–62. The Samuel Adams quotation can be found on page 660 of the latter article.

50. GW to Gouverneur Morris, Oct. 4, 1778, *WW* 13:21; GW to John A. Washington, Nov. 26, 1778, ibid., 13:335; Albert Bolles, *The Financial History of the United States* (New York, 1879), 1:159–60; Richard Buel, *Dear Liberty: Connecticut's Mobilization for the Revolutionary War* (Middletown, Conn., 1980), 140–49, 166. The "Bum Fodder" quote can be found in Buel, page 199.

51. GW to Mason, March 27, 1779, *WW* 14:299–300; GW to Burwell Bassett, April 22, 1779, ibid., 14:432; GW to G. Morris, May 8, 1779, ibid., 15:25; GW to John A. Washington, Nov. 26, 1778, ibid., 13:335; GW to William Fitzhugh, April 10, 1779, ibid., 14:365; GW to Lund Washington, May 29, 1779, ibid., 15:180; GW to Reed, Dec. 12, 1778, ibid., 13:383.

52. G. Morris to Robert Livingston, Aug. 24, 1779, *LDC* 13:411; Whipple to Bartlett, Aug. 24, 1779, ibid., 13:415; GW to Harrison, Dec. 18 [–30], 1778, *WW* 13:467–68; GW to Mason, March 27, 1779, ibid., 14:299–300; Richard Buel Jr., *In Irons: Britain's Naval Supremacy and the American Revolutionary Economy* (New Haven, Conn., 1998), 122–28; E. James Ferguson, *The Power of the Purse* (Chapel Hill, N.C., 1961), 25–44.

53. Buel, *In Irons*, 129–32; Buel, *Dear Liberty*, 103, 171; Ferguson, *Power of the Purse*, 32, 35–39, 44–47, 126; Lafayette to Vergennes, March 26, 1779, *LLP* 2:247–50; Lafayette to Comte de Maurepas, March 14, 1779, ibid., 2:238–41. The quotation is from Buel, *In Irons*, 132.

54. Freeman, *George Washington*, 5:110, 110n.

55. GW to PC, July 9, 1779, *WW* 15:391–92; GW to John Armstrong, May 18, 1779, ibid., 15:98.

56. GW to Lafayette, Sept. 30, 1779, *WW* 16:372.

57. Sullivan to Colonel Samuel Hunter, July 30, 1779, *SP* 3:89.

58. Joseph R. Fischer, *A Well-Executed Failure: The Sullivan Campaign against the Iroquois, July-September 1779* (Columbia, S.C., 1997), 36–41.

59. For instance, see GW to Lachlan McIntosh, Feb. 15, 1779, *WW* 14:114–18; GW to General James Potter, March 2, 1779, ibid., 14:175–76.

60. Fischer, *A Well-Executed Failure*, 1–2, 43–52; GW to Jay, April 14, 1779, *WW* 14:384; GW to Gates, March 6, 1779, ibid., 14:198–200; Gates to GW, March 16, 1779, 14:200n; GW to Sullivan, March 6, 1779, ibid., 14:201–2. The quote regarding "old country men" is in Sullivan to GW, April 16, 1779, *SP* 3:8.

61. General Sullivan's Address to the Oneida Indians, 1779, *SP* 3:118.

62. GW, Instructions to Sullivan, May 31, 1779, *WW* 15:190.

63. Sullivan to the President of Congress, Aug. 15, 1779, *SP* 3:97.

64. Quoted in Fischer, *A Well-Executed Failure*, 192.

65. The account of Sullivan's Expedition draws on ibid., 53–80; Isabel T. Kelsay, *Joseph Brant, 1743–1807: Man of Two Worlds* (Syracuse, 1984), 120–21, 254–71; Taylor, *Divided Ground*, 97–108; Williams, *Year of the Hangman*, 294; and Ward, *War of the Revolution*, 2:638–45.

66. John E. Selby, *The Revolution in Virginia, 1775–1783* (Williamsburg, Va., 1988), 184–88.

67. Ibid., 189–91. On the West as a motive for breaking with Great Britain, see Ferling, *Setting the World Ablaze*, 66–67, and Woody Holton, *Forced Founders: Indians, Debtors, Slaves, and the Making of the Revolution in Virginia* (Chapel Hill, N.C., 1999), 3–38.

68. Selby, *Revolution in Virginia*, 192–97; Ward, *War of the Revolution*, 2:850–60; GW to TJ, July 10, 1779, *WW* 15:401.

69. GW to John A. Washington, May 12, 1779, *WW* 15:58–59; Willcox, *Portrait of a General*, 260–75.

70. Selby, *Revolution in Virginia*, 204–8.

71. Quoted in Willcox, *Portrait of a General*, 276.

72. GW to Schuyler, June 9, 1779, *WW* 15:243; Willcox, *Portrait of a General*, 276.

73. GW to Sullivan, June 4, 1779, *WW* 15:226; GW to Brodhead, June 23, 1779, ibid., 15:304.

74. Quoted in Freeman, *George Washington*, 5:109.

75. Henry Clinton, *The American Rebellion: Sir Henry Clinton's Narrative of His Campaigns, 1775–1782*, ed. William B. Willcox (New Haven, Conn., 1954), 277; Willcox, *Portrait of a General*, 276–83; Buel, *Dear Liberty*, 190–94.

76. Wayne's message is in Freeman, *George Washington*, 5:113. The account of the engagement draws on Ward, *War of the Revolution*, 2:596–603; Paul David Nelson, *Anthony Wayne: Soldier of the Early Republic* (Bloomington, Ind., 1985), 94–100; Scheer and Rankin, *Rebels and Redcoats*, 361–63; GW to PC, July 21, 1779, *WW* 15:447–53; GW to Gates, July 25, 1779, ibid., 477.

77. GW to Gates, July 25, 1779, *WW* 15:477–78; GW to George Clinton, July 19, 1779, ibid., 15:439; GW to Lincoln, July 30, 1779, ibid., 16:17; *SOS* 363; Freeman, *George Washington*, 5:121.

78. Ward, *War of the Revolution*, 2:604–10.

79. Clinton to Germain, Oct. 8, 1778, *DAR* 15:209; Germain to Clinton, Dec. 3, 1778, ibid., 15:278; Willcox, *Portrait of a General*, 279, 291.

80. Quoted in Mackesy, *War for America*, 271.

81. GW to Harrison, Oct. 25, 1779, *WW* 17:20, 21–22.

Chapter 15. "We Have Occasioned a Good Deal of Terror": The War at Sea

1. Lafayette, "Memoir of 1779," *LLP* 2:18, 225–26; Harlow Giles Unger, *Lafayette* (Hoboken, N.J., 2002), 92–94.

2. President of Congress to Lafayette, Jan. 3, 1779, *LLP* 2:217; Lafayette to Vergennes, Feb. 14, March 26, 1779, ibid., 2:229–30, 247–50; Lafayette to Maurepas, March 14, 23, 1779, ibid., 2:238–41, 244–47; JA to Lafayette, Feb. 21, 1779, ibid., 2:234–36; H. W. Brands, *The First American: The Life and Times of Benjamin Franklin* (New York, 2000), 576.

3. Lafayette to Maurepas, March 23, 1779, *LLP* 2:244; BF to Lafayette, March 22, 1779, *PBF* 29:186–87; Lafayette to BF, March 31, 1779, ibid., 29:240; BF to Jones, April 27, 1779, ibid., 29:384; Brand, *The First American*, 579.

4. William M. Fowler Jr., *Rebels under Sail: The American Navy during the American Revolution* (New York, 1976), 17–19.

5. GW to Hancock, Oct. 5, 1775, *PGW:RWS* 2:100; GW to John A. Washington, Oct. 13, 1775, ibid., 2:161; GW to Reed, Nov. 20, 30, 1775, ibid., 2:409, 463; George A. Billias, *General John Glover and His Marblehead Mariners* (New York, 1960), 73; John Ferling, *The First of Men: A Life of George Washington* (Knoxville, 1988), 135; Fowler, *Rebels under Sail*, 16–38; James Morgan, "American Privateering in America's War for Independence, 1775–1783," *The American Neptune*, 36 (April 1976): 80; Nathan Miller, *Sea of Glory: The Continental Navy Fights for Independence, 1775–1783* (New York, 1974), 71.

6. Miller, *Sea of Glory*, 81–84; Morgan, "American Privateering," *American Neptune*, 36:84–85; Jack Coggins, *Ships and Seamen of the American Revolution: Vessels, Crews, Weapons, Gear, Naval Tactics, and Actions of the War of Independence* (Harrisburg, Pa., 1969), 65–78.

7. Fowler, *Rebels under Sail*, 42–72; Miller, *Sea of Glory*, 52–55, 61–75; Jack Coggins, *Ships and Seamen of the American Revolution*, 26. On Congress's activities in creating the navy, including notes on its debates, see *DAJA* 2:198–99, 201–2, 205, 220, 229–30; Silas Deane's Proposals for Establishing a Navy, [Oct. 16?, 1775], *LDC* 2:182–87; Secret Committee Minutes of Proceedings, Dec. 14, 1775, ibid., 2:485–86. On JA's role in the battle, see *DAJA* 3:342–51, and John Ferling, *John Adams: A Life* (Knoxville, 1992), 137–38. For the navy's Articles of War, see: "Rules for the Regulation of the Navy of the United Colonies," [Nov. 23–Dec. 1775], *PJA* 3:147–53, and the useful editorial commentary that accompanies the document.

8. John J. McCusker and Russell R. Menard, *The Economy of British America, 1607–1789* (Chapel Hill, N.C., 1985), 320.

9. Coggins, *Ships and Seamen of the American Revolution*, 33–42; Howard Chapelle, *The History of American Sailing Ships* (New York, 1945), 44–75.

10. Coggins, *Ships and Seamen of the American Revolution*, 203–5.

11. Howard Chapelle, *The History of the American Sailing Navy: The Ships and Their Development* (New York, 1949), 56, 60.

12. Ibid., 66.

13. Samuel Eliot Morison, *John Paul Jones: A Sailor's Biography* (Boston, 1959), 69–70.

14. Coggins, *Ships and Seamen of the American Revolution*, 175–79; Fowler, *Rebels under Sail*, 275.

15. N. A. M. Rodger, *The Command of the Ocean: A Naval History of Britain, 1649–1815* (New York, 2005), 399.

16. Fowler, *Rebels under Sail*, 291–94.

17. Hancock to Hopkins, April 17, May 7, 1776, *LDC* 3:548, 637–38; Fowler, *Rebels under Sail*, 72–73, 96–99.

18. Morison, *John Paul Jones*, 3–76; Evan Thomas, *John Paul Jones: Sailor, Hero, Father of the American Navy* (New York, 2003), 13–66.

19. Morison, *John Paul Jones*, 76–86; Thomas, *John Paul Jones*, 67–75.

20. Morison, *John Paul Jones*, 76; Fowler, *Rebels under Sail*, 91–94, 100.

21. Fowler, *Rebels under Sail*, 261, 275–77.

22. Rodger, *Command of the Ocean*, 329, 332, 368–71; Robson, *War for America*, 166–70.

23. The foregoing draws on David Syrett, *The Royal Navy in American Waters, 1775–1783* (Aldershot, England, 1989), 1–91.

24. Wickes to the American Commissioners, June 28, 1777, *PBF* 24:233; Syrett, *Royal Navy in American Waters*, 65, 67–68; Fowler, *Rebels under Sail*, 128–34.

25. "Attestation of Gustavus Conyngham," [ND], in Robert Wilder Neeser, ed., *Letters and Papers Relating to the Cruises of Gustavus Conyngham, a Captain of the Continental Navy, 1777–1779* (Port Washington, N.Y., 1970), 158–59.

26. BF to Richard Bache, May 22, 1777, *PBF* 24:64; Fowler, *Rebels under Sail*, 135–42; Jonathan Dull, *The French Navy and American Independence: A Study of Arms and Diplomacy, 1774–1787* (Princeton, N.J., 1975), 78–79.

27. Syrett, *Royal Navy in American Waters*, 110, 113.

28. Dull, *French Navy and American Independence*, 109–20.

29. John A. Tilley, *The British Navy and the American Revolution* (Columbia, S.C., 1987), 129; Dull, *French Navy and American Independence*, 121–24.

30. Morison, *John Paul Jones*, 103–63; Thomas, *John Paul Jones*, 87–136.

31. Harlow Giles Unger, *Lafayette* (Hoboken, N.J., 2002), 102; Thomas, *John Paul Jones*, 160, 172; Lafayette to Jones, May 22, 1779, LLP 2:267.

32. *DAJA* 2:370–71; AA to Elizabeth Cranch, Dec. 3, 1784, *AFC* 6:5. Thomas, *John Paul Jones*, includes a detailed analysis of Jones's temperament. The "hawkish face" quotation is his biography, page 72. The "little fellow" and "not at peace" quotations are from Morison, *John Paul Jones*, pages 155 and 202 respectively. Jones campaigned for Congress to rethink Continental navy uniforms and instead prescribe a uniform that would be virtually identical to that of the royal navy, an act that a psycho-historian would doubtless find intriguing. See Morison, *John Paul Jones*, 70–72.

33. Quoted in Thomas, *John Paul Jones*, 144. These were Jones's words, not Sartine's.

34. Morison, *John Paul Jones*, 71, 186–99, 201, 203–6; E. James Ferguson, *The Power of the Purse* (Chapel Hill, N.C., 1961), 40–41; Coggins, *Ships and Seamen of the American Revolution*, 182–84.

35. Quoted in Thomas, *John Paul Jones*, 174.

36. Morison, *John Paul Jones*, 207–19.

37. Coggins, *Ships and Seamen of the American Revolution*, 147–62.

38. For a survey of what Jones was alleged to have said, see Morison, *John Paul Jones*, 240–42.

39. This account of the epic battle draws on Thomas, *John Paul Jones*, 168–205, and Morison, *John Paul Jones*, 200–40. The prize money figures are from Morison's biography, pages 266–68. Franklin put the number of prisoners at four hundred. See BF to Eastern Navy Board, Oct. 17, 1779, *PBF* 30:546.

40. BF to Samuel Cooper, Oct. 27, 1779, *PBF* 30:598; BF to Jane Mecom, Oct. 25, 1779, ibid., 30:583.

41. Rodger, *Command of the Ocean*, 341.

42. These paragraphs on the projected invasion draw from Dull, *French Navy and American Independence*, 142–58, and Piers Mackesy, *The War for America, 1775–1783* (Cambridge, Mass., 1965), 278–97. The statistics on disease in the French fleet are in Morison, *John Paul Jones*, 192.

43. BF to Jay, Oct. 4 [–28], 1779, *PBF* 30:467; JA to PC, Feb. 19, 1780, *PJA* 8:336.

44. Jacob Greene to NG, Aug. 27, 1779, *PNG* 4:339; Samuel Otis to NG, Aug. 30, 1779, ibid., 4:347; NG to Colonel William Finnie, Sept. 3, 1779, ibid., 4:356.

45. Coggins, *Ships and Seamen of the American Revolution*, 163–68; Fowler, *Rebels under Sail*, 111–18; William B. Willcox, *Portrait of a General: Sir Henry Clinton in the War of Independence* (New York, 1964), 280–81; Walter E. Hayward, "The Penobscot Expedition," in *Essays in Modern English History in Honor of William Cortez Abbott* (Cambridge, Mass., 1941), 221–53; Henry I. Shavo, "The Penobscot Assault—1779," *Military Affairs* 17 (1953):83–94.

46. GW to G. Morris, May 8, 1779, *WW* 15:24–25.

47. On Prevost, see David K. Wilson, *The Southern Strategy: Britain's Conquest of South Carolina and Georgia, 1775–1780* (Columbia, S.C., 2005), 83, and Alexander A. Lawrence, *Storm over Savannah: The Story of Count d"Estaing and the Siege of the Town in 1779* (Athens, Ga., 1951), 38–45. (The quotations on Prevost are from Lawrence, page 41). See also Prevost to Germain, *DAR* 17:176.

48. GW to Lincoln, Dec. 18, 1776, *PGW:RWS* 7:368; GW to Hancock, Dec. 20, 1776, Jan. 22, 1777, ibid., 7:386; 8:128.

49. Quoted in David B. Mattern, *Benjamin Lincoln and the American Revolution* (Columbia, S.C., 1995), 49.

50. On Lincoln, see ibid., 6–59. The quotation on Lincoln's sleeping habits is on page 13.

51. Germain to Archibald Campbell, Jan. 16, 1779, *DAR* 17:32; Prevost to Germain, Jan. 18, Nov. 1, 1779, ibid., 17:43, 241.

52. Wilson, *Southern Strategy*, 86.

53. Prevost to Germain, March 5, June 10, 1779, *DAR* 17:143; Wilson, *Southern Strategy*, 84–89.

54. All quotes are taken from James Haw, *John and Edward Rutledge of South Carolina* (Athens, Ga., 1997), 123–24.

55. Prevost to Clinton, March 1, May 21, 1779, *DAR* 17:69 70, 127 29.

56. Rutledge's draft has disappeared. Through interviews with the participants, it was reconstructed by a contemporary historian. See David Ramsay, *The History of the American Revolution*, reprint (Indianapolis, 1990), 2:27.

57. The best account of this phase of the war in Georgia and South Carolina can be found in Wilson, *Southern Strategy*, 81–131, upon which my account draws. Prevost's account of his campaign is in Prevost to Germain, June 10, 1779, *DAR* 17:141–43.

58. Account of Phillip Séguier de Terson, in Benjamin Kennedy, ed., *Muskets, Cannon Balls & Bombs: Nine Narratives of the Siege of Savannah in 1779* (Savannah, 1974), 30.

59. Quoted in Wilson, *Southern Strategy*, 158.

60. Account of Anthony Stokes, in Kennedy, *Muskets, Cannon Balls & Bombs*, 110–11; Account of Major John Jones, ibid., 131–32.

61. Lawrence, *Storm over Savannah*, 46–53, 76–84.

62. Prevost to Germain, Nov. 1, 1779, *DAR* 17:247.

63. The above account of the battle draws on Wilson, *Southern Strategy*, 133–77. Prevost's account can be found in Prevost to Germain, Nov. 1, 1779, *DAR* 17:241–50. For other good assessments of the battle, see Christopher Ward *The War of the Revolution*. 2 vols. (New York, 1952), 2:688–94; Lawrence, *Storm over Savannah*, 100–12; Harvey H. Jackson, *Lachlan McIntosh and the Politics of Revolutionary Georgia* (Athens, Ga., 1979), 91, 96–97. For an excellent brief account, see Henry Lumpkin, *From Savannah to Yorktown: The American Revolution in the South* (Columbia, S.C., 1981), 27–40. The quotation about d'Estaing is from Lawrence, *Storm over Savannah*, 109.

64. GW to Wayne, Nov. 17, 1779, *WW* 17:120; GW to Schuyler, Nov. 24, 1779, ibid., 17:176; Lawrence, *Storm over Savannah*, 127.

65. GW to PC, Nov. 18, 1779, *WW* 17:131.

Chapter 16. Choices, 1780

1. JA to AA, Dec. 2, 1778, Jan. 1, 1779, *AFC* 3:124, 145; John Ferling, *A Leap in the Dark: The Struggle to Create the American Republic* (New York, 2003), 214–16; John Ferling, *Setting the World Ablaze: Washington, Adams, Jefferson and the American Revolution* (New York, 2000), 202–3.

2. JA to President of Congress, Aug. 4, 1779, *PJA* 8:109, 111–14; JA to Gerry, Sept. 10, 1779, ibid., 8:131.

3. JA to Rush, Sept. 19, 1779, ibid., 8:153; JA to Thomas McKean, Sept. 20, 1779, ibid., 8:161. On JA and BF as diplomats, see John Ferling, "John Adams, Diplomat," *WMQ* 51 (1994):227–52.

4. JA to Lafayette, Feb. 21, 1779, *PJA* 7:421–23; JA to Leray de Chaumont, Oct. 5, 1779, ibid., 8:191.

5. *DAJA* 2:403–4; 4:191–203; John Thaxter to AA, Dec. 15, 1779, *AFC* 3:251; JA to AA, Feb. 12, 1780, ibid., 3:271.

6. JA to Samuel Adams, Feb. 23, 1780, *PJA* 8:353–54; JA to Warren, Feb. 23, 1780, ibid., 8:359; JA to Joseph Gardoqui & Sons, March 1, 1780, ibid., 9:1; JA to Vergennes, July 2 [3], 1780, ibid., 10:17; JA to Edmé Jacques Genet, April 29, 1780, ibid., 9:249–50; JA to Gerry, May 23, 1780, ibid., 9:333; Jonathan Dull, *The French Navy and American Independence: A Study of Arms and Diplomacy, 1774–1787* (Princeton, N.J., 1975), 187–88.

7. JA to Vergennes, Feb. 12, 19, 1780, *DAJA* 4:243–454, 250–51; Vergennes to JA Feb.15, 1780, ibid., 4:245; JA to PC, Feb. 20, 27, 1780, *PJA* 8:346, 371; JA to Lovell, March 16, 29, ibid., 9:55, 92.

8. Dull, *French Navy and American Independence*, 163–67.

9. The preceding paragraphs draw on Piers Mackesy, *The War for America, 1775–1783* (Cambridge, Mass., 1965), 225, 275, 306–18. On Rodney, see N. A. M. Rodger, *The Command of the Ocean: A Naval History of Britain, 1649–1815* (New York, 2005), 344. On the diplomatic initiative with Spain, see Samuel Flagg Bemis, *The Hussey-Cumberland Mission and the American Revolution* (Princeton, N.J., 1931).

10. Dull, *French Navy and American Independence*, 171–74, 178; Mackesy, *War for America*, 322–23; Christopher Lloyd, "Sir George Rodney: Lucky Admiral," in George A. Billias, ed., *George Washington's Opponents* (New York, 1969), 327–54.

11. Lee Kennett, *The French Forces in America, 1780–1783* (Westport, Conn., 1977), 12; Arnold Whitridge, *Rochambeau* (New York, 1965), 85; Mackesy, *War for America*, 324–29.

12. BF to Vergennes, Feb. 25, 1779, *PBF* 28:604; BF to Committee of Foreign Affairs, May 26, 1779, ibid., 29:553; GW to Lafayette, Sept. 30, 1779, *WW* 16:369; Lafayette to Maurepas, Jan. 25, 1780, *LLP* 2:344–45; AH to Lafayette, ibid., 2:349n; Thomas Fleming, *Washington's Secret War: The Hidden History of Valley Forge* (New York, 2005), 6; Kennett, *French Forces in America*, 7–10; Dull, *Diplomatic History of the American Revolution*, 115.

13. Kennett, *French Forces in America*, 10; Jonathan Dull, *A Diplomatic History of the American Revolution* (New Haven, Conn., 1983), 168; William Stinchcombe, *The American Revolution and the French Alliance* (Syracuse, 1969), 88.

14. GW to Jay, April 23, 1779, *WW* 14:437; Ferling, *Leap in the Dark*, 222; Edward G. Lengel, *General George Washington* (New York, 2005), 319.

15. John Fell to Robert Morris, March 12, 1780, *LDC* 14:489; New York Delegates to George Clinton, March 21, 1780, ibid., 14:529.

16. *DAR* 17:52; Richard Buel Jr., *In Iron's: Britain's Naval Supremacy and the American Revolutionary Economy* (New Haven, Conn., 1998), 137–41; E. James Ferguson, *The Power of the Purse* (Chapel Hill, N.C., 1961), 58–60.

17. Samuel Huntington to the States, March 20, 1780, *LDC* 14:521; Ezra L'Hommedicu to Clinton, March 15, 1780, ibid., 14:506; Buel, *In Irons*, 130, 142–45; Ferguson, *Power of the Purse*, 48–52; Jackson Turner Main, *The Sovereign States, 1775–1783* (New York, 1973), 251.

18. Richard D. Brown, "The Confiscation and Disposition of Loyalists' Estates in Suffolk County, Massachusetts," *WMQ* 21 (1964):534–50; Staughton Lynd, "Who Shall Rule? Duchess County, New York, in the American Revolution," *WMQ* 18 (1961):352–53.

19. GW to Trumbull, March 25, 1780, *WW* 18:151.

20. Madison to James Madison Sr., March 20, 1780, *LDC* 14:524.

21. John Ferling, *The Loyalist Mind: Joseph Galloway and the American Revolution* (University Park, Pa., 1977), 7–46.

22. *PH* 20:805–6; *The Examination of Joseph Galloway, Esq., Late Speaker of the House of Assembly of Pennsylvania, before the House of Commons, in a Committee on the American Papers, with Explanatory Notes* (London, 1779); Ira D. Gruber, *The Howe Brothers and the American Revolution* (Chapel Hill, N.C., 1972), 325–50; Ferling, *Loyalist Mind*, 57–60.

23. The quotation can be found in Gruber, *Howe Brothers and the American Revolution*, 348. See also *PH* 22:338–57; 23: 374–412, 439–517, and *Examination of Joseph Galloway*, 47–64, 79.

24. *PH* 19:549–60; 20:836–53, 905, 915; Charles Ritcheson, *British Politics and the American Revolution* (Norman, Okla., 1954), 244.

25. Galloway to Grace Galloway, March 21, 1777, Galloway Papers, LC; Galloway to Burgoyne, ca. 1780, ibid., Joseph Galloway, *Fabricius, or Letters to the People of Great Britain on the Absurdity and Mischiefs of Defensive Operations Only in the American War* (London, 1782), 7–8.

26. Burke to Rockingham, May [3], 1776, Thomas W. Copeland, at al., eds., *The Correspondence of Edmund Burke*, 10 vols. (Cambridge, England, 1978), 3:265; Burke to John Erskine, June 12, 1779, ibid., 4:87.

27. JA to Jenings, July 18, 1780, *PJA* 10:10; Jenings to JA, July 27, 1780, ibid., 10:52. On this episode, see the editor's extended essay in ibid., 9:53–41. JA's twelve essays follow in ibid., 9:541–87. On Jenings, see James H. Hutson, ed., *Letters from a Distinguished American* (Washington, D.C., 1978), ix–xx. This source also prints JA's twelve essays.

28. See the editor's extended essay, "The Revaluation Controversy," *PJA* 9:427–30; James H. Hutson, *John Adams and the Diplomacy of the American Revolution* (Lexington, Ky., 1980), 57, 60–66, 98–99.

29. Wilbur H. Siebert, *The Loyalists of Pennsylvania* (Boston, 1972), 56–57; Lillian B. Miller, ed., *The Selected Papers of Charles Willson Peale and His Family* (New Haven, Conn., 1983), 1:290–91n.

30. Raymond C. Werner, ed., *Diary of Grace Growden Galloway* (New York, 1971), 54, 60, 80, 85, 87, 158, 167, 168, 172, 177, 178, 180, 189.

31. Sarah Hodgkins to Joseph Hodgkins, Oct. 9, Nov. 19, Dec. 10, 1775, Feb. 1, 11, May 23, Oct. 19, 1776, April 26, 1778, in Herbert T. Wade and Robert A. Lively, eds., *This Glorious Cause: The Adventures of Two Company Officers in Washington's Army* (Princeton, N.J., 1958), 179, 184, 186, 191, 192, 203, 224, 239–40; Joseph Hodgkins to Sarah Hodgkins, Nov. 30, 1775,

March 20, Nov. 15, 1776, April 17, Aug. 18, Oct. 13, 1778, ibid., 186, 195, 226, 238, 241. See, too, the lengthy narrative provided by Wade and Lively, 3–164.

32. GW to Esther Reed, Aug. 10, 1780, *WW* 19:350–51; GW to Mrs. Anne Francis, Henrietta Hillegas, Mary Clarkson, Sarah Bache, and Susan Blair, Feb. 13, 1781, ibid., 21:221; Mary Beth Norton, *Liberty's Daughters: The Revolutionary Experience of American Women, 1750–1800* (Boston, 1980), 177–86; Ray Raphael, *A People's History of the American Revolution: How Common People Shaped the Fight for Independence* (New York, 2001), 116.

33. GW to Gerry, Robert Livingston, and John Mathews, Jan. 23, 1780, *WW* 17:435; GW to Gerry, Jan. 29, 1780, ibid., 17:463.

Chapter 17. "A Year Filled With Our Disgraces": Defeat in the South, 1780

1. Bruce E. Burgoyne, ed., *Enemy Views: The American Revolutionary War As Recorded by the Hessian Participants* (Bowie, Md., 1996), 363. On the weather in New York City, see Ira D. Gruber, ed., *John Peebles' American War: The Diary of a Scottish Grenadier, 1776–1782* (Mechanicsburg, Pa., 1998), 315–16.

2. Germain to Clinton, Sept. 27, 1779, *DAR* 17:224.

3. Germain to Clinton, Jan. 23, June 25, 1779, ibid., 17:44, 150; Clinton to Germain, April 4, May 22, 1779, ibid., 17:97, 129; William B. Willcox, *Portrait of a General: Sir Henry Clinton in the War of Independence* (New York, 1962), 272–73. The John Shy quote can be found in Shy, "British Policy for Pacifying the Southern Colonies," in Jeffrey J. Crow and Larry E. Tise, *The Southern Experience in the American Revolution* (Chapel Hill, N.C., 1978), 161.

4. Clinton to Germain, April 4, May 22, Dec. 15, 1779, *DAR* 17:97, 129–30, 259–60; Clinton to Eden, Dec. 11, 1779, Benjamin F. Stevens, ed., *Facsimiles of Manuscripts in European Archives Relating to America, 1773–1783.* 25 vols. (London, 1889–1898), 10:1034; Willcox, *Portrait of a General,* 289–99; Shy, "British Policy for Pacifying the Southern Colonies," in Crow and Tise, *Southern Experience in the American Revolution,* 157, 163–64; Gruber, "Britain's Southern Strategy," in Robert W. Higgins, ed., *The Revolutionary War in the South: Power, Conflict, and Leadership* (Durham, N.C., 1979), 220–26.

5. GW to PC, Nov. 29, 1779, Jan. 18, 1780, *WW* 17:206–7, 406; GW to Heath, Dec. 21, 1779, ibid., 17:295; GW to TJ, Dec. 11, 1779, ibid., 17:246; GW to Lincoln, Feb. 27, 1780, ibid., 18:55.

6. Quoted in David K. Wilson, *The Southern Strategy: Britain's Conquest of South Carolina and Georgia, 1775–1780* (Columbia, S.C., 2005), 195.

7. Samuel Huntington to GW, Nov. 10, 1779, *LDC* 14:173; Carl P. Borick, *A Gallant Defense: The Siege of Charleston, 1780* (Columbia, S.C., 2003), 34, 35. Washington took credit for having dispatched the North Carolina and Virginia troops. See GW to Brigadier General James Hogun, Nov. 19, 1779, *WW* 17:133–34; GW to PC, Nov. 29, 1779, ibid., 17:206; Wilson, *Southern Strategy,* 196.

8. James T. Flexner, *George Washington in the American Revolution* (Boston, 1967), 359; Willcox, *Portrait of a General,* 301; Charles H. Lesser, *The Sinews of Independence: Monthly Strength Reports of the Continental Army* (Chicago, 1976), 148–49; Douglas Southall Freeman, *George Washington: A Biography.* 7 vols. (New York, 1948–1957), 5:147–48; GW to Heath, Feb. 16, 1780, *WW* 18:18.

9. GW to PC, April 2, 1780, *WW* 18:197–99; Freeman, *George Washington,* 5:155; David Mattern, *Benjamin Lincoln and the American Revolution* (Columbia, S.C., 1995), 88.

10. GW to Lafayette, March 18, 1780, *WW* 18:125; George F. Scheer, ed., *Private Yankee Doodle: Being a Narrative of Some of the Adventures, Dangers and Sufferings of a Revolutionary Soldier* (Boston, 1962), 169–70; Flexner, *George Washington in the American Revolution,* 354–56; Freeman, *George Washington,* 5:143–52; James Thacher, *Military Journal of the American Revolution* reprint (New York, 1969), 184–85; Edward G. Lengel, *General George Washington* (New York, 2005), 319.

11. GW to Schuyler, Jan. 30, 1780, *WW* 17:467; Freeman, *George Washington*, 5:143; Scheer, *Private Yankee Doodle*, 172; NG to Moore Freeman, Jan. 4, 1780, *PNG* 5:230; NG to Christopher Greene, Feb. 10, 1780, ibid., 5:363; NG to Jeremiah Wadsworth, March 17, 1780, ibid., 5:460; NG to Griffin Greene, April 25, 1780, ibid., 5:531–32.

12. E. Wayne Carp, *To Starve the Army at Pleasure: Continental Army Administration and American Political Culture, 1775–1783* (Chapel Hill, N.C., 1984), 171–73; GW to Fielding Lewis, May 5 [–July 6], 1780, *WW* 19:132; Ferling, *A Leap in the Dark*, 226–80.

13. GW to PC, April 3, 1780, *WW* 18:209; GW to Henry Champion, May 26, 1780, ibid., 18:424; GW to Heath, Dec. 21, 1779, ibid., 295; GW to Livingston, Dec. 21, 1779, ibid., 17:293; GW to Steuben, April 2, 1780, ibid., 18:203; Lengel, *General George Washington*, 320–21.

14. Lovell to Gates, Nov. 11, 1779, *LDC* 14:179.

15. Carl P. Borick, *A Gallant Defense: The Siege of Charleston, 1780* (Columbia, S.C., 2003), 36, 39–40; Wilson, *Southern Strategy*, 208; Lincoln to TJ, Jan. 7, 1780, *PTJ* 3:260–61.

16. Wilson, *Southern Strategy*, 203–5; Borick, *A Gallant Defense*, 67; Mattern, *Benjamin Lincoln*, 91–92.

17. Quoted in Wilson, *Southern Strategy*, 194–95.

18. Johann Ewald, *Diary of the American War: A Hessian Journal*, ed. Joseph P. Tustin (New Haven, Conn., 1979), 193–95; Henry Clinton, *The American Rebellion: Sir Henry Clinton's Narrative of His Campaigns, 1775–1782*, ed. William B. Willcox (New Haven, Conn., 1954), 159; Bernard A. Uhlendorf, ed., *The Siege of Charleston: With . . . Diaries and Letters of Hessian Officers. . . .* (Ann Arbor, Mich., 1938), 111, 113, 117, 119, 121, 125, 127–45, 179–81; Burgoyne, *Enemy Views*, 366–68; Clinton to Germain, March 9, 1780, *DAR* 18:53; Germain to Clinton, March 15, 1780, ibid., 18:60.

19. Gruber, *John Peebles' American War*, 338.

20. Claude H. Van Tyne, *The Loyalists of the American Revolution*, reprint (New York, 1970), 165–89.

21. Germain to Clinton, Jan. 23, 1779, *DAR* 17:46–47; Lesser, *Sinews of Independence*, 144–45. The foregoing on Britain and the Loyalists is drawn from Paul H. Smith, *Loyalists and Redcoats: A Study in British Revolutionary Policy* (Chapel Hill, N.C., 1964), 13–78. On the Loyalist militia and their activities, see Van Tyne, *Loyalists of the American Revolution*, 165–89.

22. Clinton to Germain, Dec. 15, 1779, *DAR* 17:260; Clyde R. Ferguson, "Carolina and Georgia Patriot and Loyalist Militia in Action, 1778–1783," in Crow and Tise, *Southern Experience in the American Revolution*, 176–83; Edward J. Cashin, *The King's Ranger: Thomas Brown and the American Revolution on the Southern Frontier* (Athens, Ga., 1989), 100; Robert S. Lambert, *South Carolina Loyalists in the American Revolution* (Columbia, S.C., 1987), 82; Robert Calhoon, *The Loyalists in the Revolutionary America, 1760–1781* (New York, 1965), 477; Cassandra Pybus, "Jefferson's Faulty Math," *WMQ*, 62:254.

23. Willcox, *Portrait of a General*, 27, 29, 282, 316; Clinton, *American Rebellion*, 53–54, 65.

24. Peter Russell, "The Siege of Charleston: Journal of Peter Russell, December 25, 1779, to May 2, 1780," *AHR* 4 (1899):484; Uhlendorf, *Siege of Charleston*, 29; Borick, *A Gallant Defense*, 49–65; Anthony Allaire, *Diary of Lieut. Anthony Allaire*, reprint (New York, 1968), 10.

25. Clinton, *American Rebellion*, 163; Uhlendorf, *Siege of Charleston*, 55, 91–95, 201, 211, 415; Borick, *A Gallant Defense*, 115–18; Mattern, *Benjamin Lincoln*, 93, 96.

26. Willcox, *Portrait of a General*, 303.

27. Borick, *A Gallant Defense*, 66; Wilson, *Southern Strategy*, 205.

28. Borick, *A Gallant Defense*, 23.

29. For Whipple's correspondence with Lincoln, see, *Original Papers Relating to the Siege of Charleston, 1780* (Charleston, 1898), 27–33.

30. James Ferguson, *Two Scottish Soldiers, A Soldier of 1688 and Blenheim, A Soldier of the American Revolution, and a Jacobite Laird and His Forebears* (Aberdeen, Scotland, 1888), 68.

31. Robert D. Bass, *The Green Dragoon: The Lives of Banastre Tarleton and Mary Robinson*, reprint (Orangeburg, S.C., 1973), 11–31; John Buchanan, *The Road to Guilford Court House: The American Revolution in the Carolinas* (New York, 1997), 58–60, 196–98, 202; Hugh F. Rankin, "An Officer Out of His Time: Correspondence of Major Patrick Ferguson, 1779–1780," in Howard H. Peckham, ed., *Sources of American Independence: Selected Manuscripts from the Collections of the William L. Clements Library* (Chicago, 1978), 2:287–90.

32. The above account of the tightening of the noose about Charleston draws on Borick, *A Gallant Defense*, 71–73, 96–108, 121–26, 130–34, 145–60. On Tarleton's victory, see Wilson, *Southern Strategy*, 246–47; Allaire, *Diary of Lieut. Anthony Allaire*, 11–12; Tarleton's account in *SOS* 2:1103–4. See also Clinton to Germain, May 13, 1780, *DAR* 18:87.

33. Lincoln to GW, July 17, 1780, *Original Papers Relating to the Siege of Charleston*, 14–17.

34. Lachlan McIntosh, "Journal of the Siege of Charleston, 1780," Lilla Hawes, ed., *University of Georgia Libraries Miscellanea Publications*, No. 7 (Athens, Ga., 1968), 101. GW to Colonel John Laurens, April 26, 1780, WW 18:299. A good analysis of Lincoln's thinking can be found in Mattern, *Benjamin Lincoln*, 88–89. The Rutledge and Lincoln quotations are in ibid., 93, 95.

35. Allaire, *Diary of Anthony Allaire*, 12; Borick, *A Gallant Defense*, 152–54.

36. McIntosh, "Journal," *University of Georgia Libraries Miscellanea*, No. 7, 104–5, 107.

37. Quoted in Marvin R. Zahniser, *Charles Cotesworth Pinckney: Founding Father* (Chapel Hill, N.C., 1967), 63–64.

38. Quoted in Hugh F. Rankin, *The North Carolina Continentals* (Chapel Hill, N.C., 1971), 228–29.

39. Quoted in Borick, *A Gallant Defense*, 204.

40. Clinton to Lincoln, May 8, 1780, *Original Papers Relating to the Siege of Charleston*, 39.

41. "Humble Petition of the Country Militia Now in Charleston," ND, ibid., 62–70.

42. Borick, *A Gallant Defense*, 126, 137, 139–41, 159–76, 197, 201, 207, 209, 211–19; Ewald, *Diary of the American War*, 237; Uhlendorf, *Siege of Charleston*, 287, 395; Moultrie, in *SOS* 2:1109. The surrender negotiations and the final terms of capitulation can be found in *Original Papers Relating to the Siege of Charleston*, 43–55.

43. Bruce E. Burgoyne, ed., *Diaries of Two Ansbach Jaegers* (Bowie, Md., 1997), 145; Ewald, *Diary of the American War*, 238; Gruber, *John Peebles' American War*, 372; Uhlendorf, *Siege of Charleston*, 415; Burgoyne, *Enemy Views*, 389.

44. Germain to Clinton, May 3, Aug. 3, 1780, *DAR* 18:83, 131, 134. The quotes about a "ragged rabble" and the American's customary raggedness are from Rankin, *North Carolina Continentals*, 231.

45. Clinton to Germain, May 13, 1780, ibid., 18:88–89; Wilson, *Southern Strategy*, 234–35, 241, 315–16n; Borick, *A Gallant Defense*, 222.

46. Howard H. Peckham, *The Toll of Independence: Engagements and Battle Casualties of the American Revolution* (Chicago, 1974), 11, 28, 46, 56, 66, 78, 93, 98, 99, 108, 113, 117, 120, 123, 125–27, 130–32. Peckham indicates that 15,427 soldiers in the Continental army became prisoners and that 2,727 Continental sailors were held captive. On death rates for American prisoners in other wars, see, Robert C. Doyle, "Prisoners of War," in John W. Chambers, ed., *The Oxford Companion to American Military History* (New York, 1999), 561, and William Marvel, *Andersonville: The Last Depot* (Chapel Hill, N.C., 1994), 238–39. Roughly 35 percent of Union captives at Andersonville perished.

47. David Sterling, ed., "American Prisoners of War in New York: A Report by Elias Boudinot," *WMQ* 13 (1956):380–81, 385; Robert Troup, Affidavit, Jan. 17, 1777, in Dennis P. Ryan, ed., *A Salute to Courage: The American Revolution as Seen through Wartime Writings of Officers of the Continental Army and Navy* (New York, 1979), 67; Gregory T. Knouff, *The Soldiers' Revolution: Pennsylvania in Arms and the Forging of Early American Identity* (University Park, Pa., 2004), 132; Howard H. Peckham, *Memiors of the Life of John Adlum in the Revolutionary War* (Chicago, 1978), 80.

48. The quotes can be found in Robert E. Cray Jr., "Commemorating the Prison Ship Dead: Revolutionary Memory and the Politics of Sepulture in the Early Republic, 1776–1808," *WMQ* 56 (1999): 570.

49. The foregoing draws largely on Larry G. Bowman, *Captive Americans: Prisoners during the American Revolution* (Athens, Ohio, 1976), 7–61. See also Arthur B. Tourtellot, "'Rebels, Turn Out Your Dead!'" *American Heritage* 21 (Aug. 1970):16–17, 90–93, and Robert E. Cray Jr., "Commemorating the Prison Ship Dead," *WMQ* 56:570. For conditions in prisons in Quebec, see the various journals in Kenneth Roberts, ed., *March to Quebec: Journals of the Members of Arnold's Expedition* (New York, 1946). The quote is from Caroline Cox, *A Proper Sense of Honor: Service and Sacrifice in George Washington's Army* (Chapel Hill, N.C., 2004), 200. The figure for the death rate among the Fort Washington captives is from Judith L Van Buskirk, *Generous Enemies: Patriots and Loyalists in Revolutionary New York* (Philadelphia, 2002), 86.

50. [Philip Freneau], *The British Prison-Ship: A Poem* (Philadelphia, 1781), Early American Imprint Series, No. 17159, pages 8, 10, 11.

51. Zahniser, *Charles Cotesworth Pinckney*, 65–67.

52. Jabez Fitch, *The New York Diary of Lieutenant Jabez Fitch of the 17th (Connecticut) Regiment from August 22, 1776, to December 15, 1777*, ed. W. H. W. Sabine, reprint (New York, 1971). The quotations can be found on pages 60, 89, 92, 121–22, 125, 152. On Abner Everett's marriage see Van Buskirk, *Generous Enemies*, 84.

53. Sheldon W. Cohen, *Yankee Sailors in British Gaols: Prisoners of War at Forton and Mill, 1777–1783* (Newark, Del., 1995). See especially pages 30–89.

54. *LDC* 9:298–99n; Rodney Atwood, *The Hessians: Mercenaries from Hessen-Kassel in the American Revolution* (Cambridge, England, 1980), 98, 198; John Wesley Moody, "British Prisoners of War in the American Revolution," M.A. Thesis, University of West Georgia (2002), 10–11, 16–17, 22–23, 25–28, 53–59. Though he focuses more on the treatment of civilians than soldiers, see also Van Tyne, *Loyalists in the American Revolution*, 213–42.

55. See Thomas Fleming, "Gentleman Johnny's Wandering Army," *American Heritage* 24 (December 1972):10–15, 89–93; William M. Dabney, *After Saratoga: The Story of the Convention Army* (Albuquerque, 1954); Richard Sampson *Escape in America: The British Convention Prisoners, 177??–1783* (Chippenham, England, 1995).

56. GW to Gage, Aug. 11, 1775, *PGW:RWS* 1:289–90.

57. Bowman, *Captive Americans*, 81, 85–87, 101–3.

58. Cohen, *Yankee Sailors in British Gaols*, 84–85, 102–3; Bowman, *Captive Americans*, 54; JA to Silas Talbot, June 26, 1781, *PJA* 11:398; Catherine M. Prelinger, "Benjaimin Franklin and American Prisoners of War in England during the American Revolution," *WMQ* 32 (1975): 261–94; BF to Hartley, March 21, 1779, *PBF* 29:176. Beginning in 1778, the *PBF* are filled with correspondence from prisoners in England recounting their tribulations. A good example is Two Hundred and Eighty American Prisoners to BF, Feb. 3, 1780, ibid., 31:442–44.

59. Bowman, *Captive Americans*, 68–81.

60. BF to Hartley, Oct. 19, 1779, *PBF* 30:559.

61. Cox, *Proper Sense of Honor*, 215; Bowman, *Captive Americans*, 12, 29.

62. As an example, see GW to Howe, Nov. 14, 1777, *PGW:RWS* 12:255–56.

63. Prelinger, "Benjamin Franklin and American Prisoners of War in England," *WMQ* 32:275.

64. Cox, *Proper Sense of Honor*, 214.

65. The quote is taken from a letter written by GW's aide, Colonel Hamilton. See AH to G. Clinton, March 12, 1778, *PAH* 1:440–41.

66. Bowman, *Captive Americans*, 93–112; GW to H. Laurens, March 7 [–8], 1778, *PGW:RWS* 14:84–85; *PNG* 9:98n; Betsy Knight, "Prisoner Exchange and Parole in the American Revolution," *WMQ* 48 (1991): 201–22; Prelinger, "Benjamin Franklin and American Prisoners of War," ibid., 32:276–77, 281.

67. Ward, *War of the Revolution*, 2:704–5.

68. Bass, *Green Dragoon*, 79–83; Wilson, *Southern Strategy*, 242–61.

69. For an especially good assessment of the composition of the Legion, see Wilson, *Southern Strategy*, 243.

70. Quoted in Freeman, *George Washington*, 5:168.

71. GW to Joseph Jones, May 31, 1780, *WW* 18:453; GW to Trumbull, June 11, 1780, ibid., 18:509–10; Thomas McKean to William Atlee, June 12, 1780, *LDC* 15:304; William Houston to William Livingston, June 4, 5, 1780, ibid., 15:245, 251; James Madison to TJ, June 23, 1780, *PTJ* 3:461.

72. Lovell to AA, June 13, 1780, *LDC* 15:314. For the rumor, see ibid., 15:371n.

73. Schuyler to GW, June 18, 1780, ibid., 15:345; Robert Livingston to Schuyler, June 16, 1780, ibid., 15:336; Samuel Huntington to GW, Aug. 5, 1780, ibid., 15:545; GW to PC, Aug. 20, 1780, *WW* 18:403.

74. The two quotations are in Paul David Nelson, *General Horatio Gates: A Biography* (Baton Rouge, 1976), 209, 219.

75. Gates to TJ, July 19, 22, Aug. 3, 1780, *PTJ* 3:495–96, 501, 524–25; TJ to Gates, Aug. 4, 15, 1780, ibid., 3:526–27, 550.

76. John S. Pancake, *The Destructive War: The British Campaign in the Carolinas, 1780–1782* (University, Ala., 1985), 103.

77. William Seymour, "A Journal of the Southern Expedition, 1780–1783," *PMHB*, 7 (1883):287.

78. "A Narrative of the Campaign of 1780, by Colonel Otho Holland Williams, Adjutant General," in William Johnson, *Sketches of the Life and Correspondence of General Nathanael Greene* (Charleston, S.C., 1822), 1:486–88.

79. AH to Boudinot, July 5, 1778, *PAH* 1:512.

80. Williams, "Narrative of the Campaign of 1780," Johnson, *Greene*, 1:487–88.

81. *PNG* 6:513–14n; Pancake, *This Destructive War*, 104.

82. John C. Dann, ed., *Revolution Remembered: Eyewitness Accounts of the War of Independence* (Chicago, 1980), 195.

83. On Camden, see Nelson, *General Horatio Gates*, 231–36; Christopher Ward *The War of the Revolution*. 2 vols. (New York, 1952), 2:725–30; Buchanan, *Road to Guilford Court House*, 153–54, 157–70; Williams, "Narrative of the Campaign of 1780," Johnson, *Greene*, 1:494–98; Pancake, *This Destructive War*, 103–6. Cornwallis's account of the battle is in Cornwallis to Germain, Aug. 20, 21, 1780, *DAR* 18:147–51. The "bore away in the croud" remark was that of General Greene. See NG to William Greene, Sept. 5, 1780, *PNG* 6:257.

84. Williams, "Narrative of the Campaign of 1780," Johnson, *Greene*, 1:496.

85. Quoted in Buchanan, *Road to Guilford Court House*, 169.

86. AH to Duane, Sept. 6, 1780, *PAH* 2:421; AH to Elizabeth Schuyler, Sept. 6, 1780, ibid., 2:422.

87. Rivington's *Royal Gazette*, Aug. 30, 1780, in *SOS* 2:1134.

88. GW to PC, Sept. 15, 1780, *WW* 20:50.

89. GW to Rochambeau, Sept. 8, 1780, ibid., 20:16.

Chapter 18. "Southern Means and Southern Exertions": Hope and Despair, June–December 1780

1. Comte de Rochambeau, *Memoirs of the Marshall Count de Rochambeau*, M. W. E. Wright, comp., reprint (New York, 1971), 9; Clinton to Germain, June 2, Aug. 25, 1780, *DAR* 18:100–1, 152–53; Lee Kennett, *The French Forces in America, 1780–1783* (Westport, Conn., 1977), 48–51; William B. Willcox, *Portrait of a General: Sir Henry Clinton in the War of Independence* (New York, 1964), 324–32.

2. Lafayette, Memorandum to GW on Military Operations, July 16, 1780, *LLP* 3:92–95.

3. GW to Meshech Weare, June 30, 1780, *WW* 19:106; GW, Memorandum for Concerting a Plan of Operations, July 15, 1780, ibid., 19:174–76; Kennett, *French Forces in America*, 13.

4. Lafayette to GW, July 29, 31, 1780, *LLP* 3:113–15, 116–19; Lafayette to Rochambeau and Ternay, Aug. 9, 1780, ibid., 3:131, 133–34; Rochambeau to Lafayette, Aug. 12, 1780, ibid., 3:140; Rochambeau to Chevalier de La Luzerne, Aug. 14, 1780, ibid., 3:141; Kennett, *French Forces in America*, 52–53.

5. GW to Lafayette, Aug. 3, 1780, *WW* 19:314; Lafayette to GW, July 29, 1780, *LLP* 3:114.

6. Conference at Hartford, Sept. 22, 1780, *WW* 20:76–81.

7. Conference at Hartford, Sept. 22, 1780, ibid., 20:79–81; Summary of the Hartford Conference, Sept. 22, 1780, *LLP* 3:175–78; Lafayette to Adrienne de Lafayette, Feb. 2, 1781, ibid., 3:311; Lafayette to Luzane, Feb. 7, 1781, ibid., 3:317; Lafayette to Vergennes, Oct. 4, 1780, ibid., 3:188.

8. Quoted in Willard Sterne Randall, *Benedict Arnold: Patriot and Traitor* (New York, 1990), 538.

9. "Armageddon: An Interview with Sir Max Hastings," conducted by Donald A. Yerxa, in *Historically Speaking*, 6 (March/April 2005):16.

10. This account of Arnold's treason draws on Randall, *Benedict Arnold*, 453–83, 499–563; Willard Sterne Randall, "Why Benedict Arnold Did It," *American Heritage*, 41 (Sept.–Oct. 1990):60–73; Willard M. Wallace, *Traitorous Hero: The Life and Fortunes of Benedict Arnold* (Freeport, N.Y., 1964), 128–259. All quotes are from the *American Heritage* article.

11. GW to J. Laurens, April 9, 1781, *WW* 21:438; John Ferling, *The First of Men: A Life of George Washington* (Knoxville, 1988), 286; George F. Scheer, "The Sergeant Major's Strange Mission," *American Heritage* 8 (October 1957): 26–29, 98. Carl Van Doren, *Secret History of the American Revolution* (New York, 1941), 392–94.

12. William Beaumont Jr. to Samuel Daggett, Sept. 27, 1780, Dennis P. Ryan, ed., *A Salute to Courage: The American Revolution as Seen through Wartime Writings of Officers of the Continental Army and Navy* (New York, 1979), 98.

13. Charles Royster, "'The Nature of Treason': Revolutionary Virtue and American Reactions to Benedict Arnold," *WMQ* 36 (1979):163–93. The quotation is on page 189.

14. GW to TJ, June 29, Oct. 10, 1780, *WW* 19:97, 20:147; GW to James Henry, June 29, 1780, ibid., 19:92. The Rutledge quote is from James Haw, *John Edward Rutledge of South Carolina* (Athens, Ga., 1997).

15. The two Clinton quotations are in Carl P. Borick, *A Gallant Defense: The Siege of Charleston, 1780* (Columbia, S.C., 2003), 230, 233.

16. Cornwallis to Clinton, Aug. 20, 1780, *DAR* 18:145.

17. Borick, *Gallant Defense*, 231; Walter Edgar, *Partisans and Redcoats: The Southern Conflict That Turned the Tide of the American Revolution* (New York, 2001), 53–54. The quotation is from *Partisans and Redcoats*, page 54.

18. Cassandra Pybus, "Jefferson's Faulty Math," *WMQ* 62:255.

19. James Collins, *A Revolutionary Soldier* (Clinton, La., 1859), 25; Thomas Young, "Memoir of Thomas Young," *Orion* 3 (1843):85; John Buchanan, *The Road to Guilford Courthouse: The American Revolution in the Carolinas* (New York, 1997), 124; Borick, *Gallant Defense*, 237–38; Willcox, *Portrait of a General*, 321; Edgar, *Partisans and Redcoats*, 22, 54–55, 57, 91, 92, 125, 141. The quotation is from *Partisans and Redcoats*, page 55. For an excellent appraisal of the factors that made backcountry rebels and Tories, see ten provocative essays in Ronald Hoffman, Thad W. Tate, and Peter J. Albert. eds., *An Uncivil War: The Southern Backcountry during the American Revolution* (Charlottesville, Va., 1985).

20. Edgar, *Partisans and Redcoats*, 21, 39, 57–59.

21. On Sumter and Marion, see Russell F. Weigley, *The Partisan War: The South Carolina Campaign of 1780–1782* (Columbia, S.C., 1970), 10–24; Buchanan, *Road to Guilford Courthouse*,

115–19, 151–52, 299–301; Hugh Rankin, *Francis Marion: The Swamp Fox* (New York, 1973), 1–58; Robert Calhoon, *The Loyalists in the Revolutionary America, 1760–1781* (New York, 1965), 492; Henry Lee, *Memoirs of General Henry Lee*, ed. Robert E. Lee, reprint (New York, 1998), 585.

22. *PNG* 7:33n; Theodore Thayer, *Nathanael Greene: Strategist of the Revolution* (New York, 1960), 305.

23. Lee, *Revolutionary War Memoirs of General Henry Lee*, 215. See also Don Higginbotham, *The War of American Independence: Military Attitudes, Policies, and Practice, 1763–1789* (New York, 1971), 67, 364; Buchanan, *Road to Guilford Courthouse*, 141; Blackwell P. Robinson, *William R. Davie* (Chapel Hill, N.C., 1957), 27–89.

24. Borick, *A Gallant Defense*, 236; Franklin and Mary Wickwire, *Cornwallis and the War of Independence* (London, 1971), 135–36, 137, 140; Edgar, *Partisans and Redcoats*, 88.

25. Cornwallis to Clinton, Aug. 6, 1780, *CC* 1:54.

26. Edgar, *Partisans and Redcoats*, 73–87, 89. The quotations are on pages 73–74 and 85. See also the account in Robert D. Bass, *The Green Dragoon: The Lives of Banastre Tarleton and Mary Robinson* (New York, 1957), 84–94, 104–26, which spans the period from mid-1780 until the end of the year.

27. Arthur Bowler, *Logistics and the Failure of the British Army in America, 1775–1783* (Princeton, N.J., 1975), 86–91; Rankin, *Francis Marion*, 299.

28. John C. Dann, ed., *Revolution Remembered: Eyewitness Accounts of the War of Independence* (Chicago, 1980), 192, 199, 200.

29. Quoted in Wickwire and Wickwire, *Cornwallis*, 170.

30. Buchanan, *Road to Guilford Courthouse*, 131–41, 173–86; Edgar, *Partisans and Redcoats*, 90, 97–106.

31. Quoted in Wickwire and Wickwire, *Cornwallis*, 175, 179, and Edgar, *Partisans and Redcoats*, 123. See also Cornwallis to Germain, Aug. 21, 1780, *DAR* 18:151.

32. The Wemyss quote is in Edgar, *Partisans and Redcoats*, 60. The "war of desolation" remark was that of General O'Hara, though Ferguson shared his outlook. It is in Buchanan, *Road to Guilford Courthouse*, 201–2.

33. Edgar, *Partisans and Redcoats*, 136.

34. Anthony Allaire, *Diary of Lieut. Anthony Allaire*, reprint (New York, 1968), 20, 22, 24; Edgar, *Partisans and Redcoats*, 93.

35. The quotations are from Buchanan, *Road to Guilford Courthouse*, 185.

36. Cornwallis to Clinton, Aug. 6, 1780, *CC* 1:54.

37. Cornwallis to Clinton, July 14, Aug. 6, 10, 1780, ibid., 1:52, 54, 55.

38. Allaire, *Diary*, 30; Wilma Dykeman, *With Fire and Sword: The Battle of King's Mountain, 1780* (Washington, D.C., 1978), 35.

39. W. J. Wood, *Battles of the Revolutionary War, 1775–1781* (Chapel Hill, N.C., 1990), 189–94; Buchanan, *Road to Guilford Courthouse*, 219, 224; Edgar, *Partisans and Redcoats*, 116. Ferguson's edict to Shelby is in Lyman C. Draper, *King's Mountain and Its Heroes: History of the Battle of King's Mountain, October 7ᵗʰ, 1780, and the Events Which Led to It* (Cincinnati, 1881), 169.

40. Dykeman, *With Fire and Sword*, 31.

41. Young, "Memoirs," *Orion*, 3:86.

42. Collins, *A Revolutionary Soldier*, 52–53.

43. Account of Shelby, *SOS* 2:1142; Account of Campbell, ibid., 2:1142–43; Account of James Collins, ibid., 2:1143–45; Young, "Memoir," *Orion*, 3:87; Allaire, *Diary*, 31–32; Christopher Ward *The War of the Revolution*. 2 vols. (New York, 1952), 2:739–45; Wickwire and Wickwire, *Cornwallis*, 194–216; Dykeman, *Fire and Sword*, 58–76; Hank Messick, *King's Mountain: The Epic of the Blue Ridge "Mountain Men" in the American Revolution* (Boston, 1976), 107–55; Wood, *Battles of the Revolutionary War*, 196, 200–2. The "every tree bore fruit such as this" quotation can be found in North Callahan, *Royal Raiders: The Tories of the American Revolution* (Indianapolis, 1963), 218.

44. Rush to JA, Oct. 23, 1780, *PJA* 10:303; Paul David Nelson, *General Horatio Gates: A Biography* (Baton Rouge, 1976), 240–41.

45. NG to Committee of Congress, Oct. 29, 1780, *PNG* 6:441; NG to Reed, Nov. 1, 1780, ibid., 6:455; NG to PC, Oct. 27, 31, Nov. 2, 1780, ibid., 6:436, 451, 459–60; NG to GW, Nov. 13, 19, 1780, ibid., 6:479, 488; NG to TJ, Nov. 20, 1780, ibid., 6:491; NG to Sumter, Dec. 16, 1780, ibid., 6:564; NG to Carrington, Dec. 4, 1780, ibid., 6:516–17; NG to Knox, Dec. 7, 1780, ibid., 6:547.

46. Ibid., 6:xviii, 587–88; NG to Morgan, Dec. 16, 1780, ibid., 6:589–90; NG to Steuben, Dec. 28, 1780, ibid., 7:11; NG to Marion, Dec. 4, 24, 1780, ibid., 6:519–20, 607; NG to ?, Jan. 1–23, 1781, ibid., 7:175.

47. GW to Cadwalader, Oct. 5, 1780, *WW* 20:121–22; GW to PC, Oct. 11, Dec. 15, 1780, ibid., 20:158, 478; GW to Mason, Oct. 22, 1780, ibid., 20:242; GW to Board of War, Oct. 25, 1780, ibid., 20:256; GW to Clinton, Nov. 6, 1780, ibid., 20:306; GW to TJ, Nov. 20, 1780, ibid., 20:373; GW to NG, Dec. 13, 1780, ibid., 20:469.

48. Douglas Southall Freeman, *George Washington: A Biography*. 7 vols. (New York, 1948–1957), 5:236–37; Knouff, *Soldiers Revolution*, 101–2; Carl Van Doren, *Mutiny in January* (New York, 1947), 16–17.

49. GW, Circular to the New England States, Jan. 5, 1781, *WW* 21:61; GW to Clinton, Jan. 13, 1781, ibid., 21:94–95; GW to PC, Jan. 15, 1781, ibid., 21:102; GW to J. Laurens, Jan. 15, 1781, ibid., 21:107–8.

Chapter 19. Choices, 1781

1. Lovell to JA, Jan. 2, 1781, *LDC* 16:537.

2. Quoted in Alan Valentine, *Lord North* (Norman, Okla., 1967), 2:262.

3. Alan Valentine, *Lord George Germain* (Oxford., England, 1962), 414–16.

4. Lee to JA, Sept. 28, 1780, *PJA* 10:185; JA to Vergennes, July 26, 1780, ibid., 10:43; JA to PC, No. 19, Oct. 31, 1780, ibid., 313; Sullivan to John Hancock, Nov. 18, 1780, *SP* 3:205; S. Adams to R. H. Lee, Jan. 15, 1781, *LDC* 16:599; James Varnum to William Greene, Jan. 8, 1781, ibid., 16:575.

5. GW to St. Clair, Jan. 12, 1781, *WW* 21:92; GW to Wayne, Jan. 8, 1781, ibid., 21:71; Committee on the Pennsylvania Mutiny Draft Proclamation, Jan. 10, 1781, *LDC* 16:585; Committee on the Pennsylvania Mutiny to GW, Jan. 10, 13, 15, 1781, ibid., 16:587, 592, 600; James T. Flexner, *George Washington in the American Revolution* (Boston, 1967), 407; Douglas Southall Freeman, *George Washington: A Biography*. 7 vols. (New York, 1948–1957), 5:236–42.

6. GW to Howe, Jan. 22, 1781, *WW* 21:128–29; GW to Heath, Jan. 21, 1781, ibid., 21:124; GW to Sullivan, Jan. 21, 1781, ibid., 21:128; Glover to Sullivan, Nov. 19, 1780, *SP* 3:209.

7. GW to PC, Jan. 31, 1781, ibid., 21:165–66; Freeman, *George Washington*, 5:247–48.

8. E. James Ferguson, *The Power of the Purse* (Chapel Hill, N.C., 1961), 40–44.

9. Stacy Schiff, *A Great Improvisation: Franklin, France, and the Birth of America* (New York, 2005), 260–62. The quotation is on page 261.

10. The evidence concerning a congressional vote on Franklin is contradictory. The *JCC* do not mention such a vote, which is not surprising, but John Witherspoon, a congressman from New Jersey noted in his correspondence that a committee of which he was a member had agreed to request "that the Sense of the House be taken on whether Dr. Franklin shall be continued at Paris or not." See Witherspoon to William Livingston, Dec. 18, 1780, *LDC* 16:461.

11. Ibid., 16:407n; Oliver Wolcott to Jonathan Trumbull, Dec. 18, 1780, ibid., 16:461; McKean to JA, Dec. 18, 1780, ibid., 16:459.

12. GW to Laurens, Jan. 15, 1781, *WW* 21:107, 108, 110.

13. John Ferling, *A Leap in the Dark: The Struggle to Create the American Republic* (New York, 2003), 177–82, 230–32.

14. GW to J. Laurens, Jan. 15, 1781, *WW* 21:105, 110; Jack Rakove, *The Beginnings of National Politics* (New York, 1979), 289–90; Cornell to William Greene, Aug. 28, 1780, *LDC* 15:626; Alexander Hamilton, *The Continentalist*, in *PAH* 2:649–50, 664, 665. On the Nationalists long campaign to strengthen the powers of the national government, see Ferling, *A Leap in the Dark*, 123–280.

15. JA to Gerry, June 24, 1780, *PJA* 9:470; JA to PC, Dec. 14, 1780, ibid., 10:410–11; Joan Dark van der Capellen to JA, Dec. 24, 1780, ibid., 10:431; Richard B. Morris, *The Peacemakers: The Great Powers and American Independence* (New York, 1965), 179, 182; Jonathan Dull, *The French Navy and American Independence: A Study of Arms and Diplomacy, 1774–1787* (Princeton, N.J., 1975), 199–202; Edward Corwin, *French Policy and the American Alliance of 1778* (New York, 1916), 285.

16. JA to PC, April 18, 1780, June 23, 1781, *PJA* 9:151; 11:385.

17. JA to Joseph Ward, April 15, 1809, Adams Family Papers (Boston, MHS, 1954–1959), reel 118.

18. These foregoing paragraphs draw on William Stinchcombe, *The American Revolution and the French Alliance* (Syracuse, 1969), 153–59; Schiff, *A Great Improvisation*, 264–74; Morris, *Peacemakers*, 180–81; Corwin, *French Policy and the American Alliance*, 284–95; Jonathan Dull, *A Diplomatic History of the American Revolution* (New Haven, Conn., 1983), 123; Orville T. Murphy, "The View from Versailles: Charles Gravier Comte de Vergennes's Perceptions of the American Revolution," in Ronald Hoffman and Peter J. Albert, eds., *Diplomacy and Revolution: The Franco-American Alliance of 1778* (Charlottesville, Va., 1981), 140–41; Carl Van Doren, *Benjamin Franklin* (New York, 1938), 623–24; Vergennes to Lafayette, Aug. 7, 1780, April 19, 1781, *LLP* 3:129; 4:47; BF to Samuel Huntington, March 12 [–April 12], 1781, *PBF*: 34:444–45. For an account of Laurens's Atlantic crossing and his activities during his two months in France, see Gregory D. Massey, *John Laurens and the American Revolution* (Columbia, S.C., 2000), 177–88.

19. JA to PC, June 23, July 11, 1781, *PJA* 11:384, 411.

20. JA to Vergennes, July 13, 16, 18, 21, 1781, ibid., 11:413–17, 420–21, 424–29, 431–33; JA to President of Congress, July 11, 14, 15, 1781, ibid., 11:410–12, 418–20; Vergennes to JA, July 18, 1781, ibid., 11:423; Austro-Russian Proposal for Anglo-American Peace Negotiations, with John Adams Translation [July 11, 1781], ibid., 11:408–10.

21. Benedict Arnold, "Report on Present State of American Army, Navy, and Finances," Oct. 7, 1780, *DAR* 18:181–82; Germain to Clinton, Nov. 9, 1780, ibid., 18:224; Thomas Digges to JA, June 29, 1780, *PJA* 9:487.

22. Morris, *Peacemakers*, 175; Germain to Clinton, Nov. 28, 1780, *DAR* 18:237; Digges to JA, June 29, 1780, *PJA* 10:289.

23. JA to Jenings, Jan. 3, 1781, *PJA* 11:10.

24. Jean Baptiste Donatien De Vimeur, Comte de Rochambeau, *Memoirs of the Marshall Count de Rochambeau, Relative to the War of Independence of the United States*, reprint (New York, 1971), 16.

Chapter 20. "Bloody and Severe": The Pivotal Southern War, Early 1781

1. Clinton to Germain, Aug. 30, 1780, *DAR* 18:154–55; Colonel Lord Rawdon to Clinton, Oct. 28, 1780, ibid., 18:215; Leslie to Germain, Nov. 27, 1780, ibid., 18:235; John Selby, *The Revolution in Virginia, 1775–1783* (Williamsburg, Va., 1988), 216–20; William B. Willcox, *Portrait of a General: Sir Henry Clinton in the War of Independence* (New York, 1964), 348–51.

2. GW to TJ, Nov. 18, Dec. 9, 1780, *PTJ* 4:105, 195.

3. TJ to Harrison, Dec. 1780, ibid., 4:197; TJ to Clark, Dec. 25, 1780, ibid., 4:233–34; "Dairy of Arnold's Invasion," ibid., 4:258–59; "Depositions Concerning Jefferson's Conduct during Arnold's Invasion" [1796], ibid., 4:271–72; J. G. Simcoe, *Simcoe's Military Journal: A*

History of the Operations of a Partisan Corps, Called the Queen's Rangers, reprint (New York, 1998), 159–64; Clinton to Arnold, Dec. 14, 1780, *DAR* 18:256; Clinton to Germain, Dec. 16, 1780, ibid., 18:257; Selby, *Revolution in Virginia,* 222–25; Dumas Malone, *Jefferson and His Times,* 6 vols. (Boston, 1948–1981), 1:338; Willard Sterne Randall, *Benedict Arnold: Patriot and Traitor* (New York, 1990), 581–83; Richard M. Ketchum, *Victory at Yorktown: The Campaign That Won the Revolution* (New York, 2004), 72; John Ferling, "Jefferson's War," *American History* 35 (Feb. 2001):37–44.

4. Cornwallis to Tarleton, Jan. 2, 1781, *SOS* 2:1155.

5. Rawdon to Clinton, Oct. 28, 1780, *DAR* 18:216; Cornwallis to Clinton, Dec. 3, 1780, ibid., 18:244; Cornwallis to Clinton, Jan. 6, 1781, *CC* 1:80–82; W. J. Wood, *Battles of the Revolutionary War, 1775–1781* (Chapel Hill, N.C., 1990), 212; Franklin and Mary Wickwire, *Cornwallis and the War of Independence* (London, 1971), 230–48; R. Arthur Bowler, *Logistics and the Failure of the British Army in America, 1775–1783* (Princeton, N.J., 1975), 151, 200–1.

6. Don Higginbotham, *Daniel Morgan: Revolutionary Rifleman* (Chapel Hill, N.C., 1961), 121, 122, 125; Lawrence E. Babits, *A Devil of a Whipping: The Battle of Cowpens* (Chapel Hill, N.C., 1998), 31, 34, 41, 49; John Buchanan, *The Road to Guilford Courthouse: The American Revolution in the Carolinas* (New York, 1997), 302–3, 319.

7. Greene to Morgan, Jan. 13, 1781, *PNG* 7:106; Morgan to *NG,* Jan. 4, 1781, ibid., 7:51.

8. Babits, *A Devil of a Whipping,* 61.

9. James Collins, *A Revolutionary Soldier* (Clinton, La., 1859), 56.

10. Buchanan, *Road to Guilford Courthouse,* 316–17.

11. Thomas Young, "Memoirs of Thomas Young," *Orion* 3(1843):88.

12. Henry Lee, *The Revolutionary War Memoirs of General Henry Lee,* ed. Robert E. Lee, reprint (New York, 1998), 592.

13. Babits, *A Devil of a Whipping,* 81; Higginbotham, *Daniel Morgan,* 133–34.

14. Babits, *A Devil of a Whipping,* 57–58, 159.

15. Morgan to NG, Jan. 19, 1781, *PNG* 7:154.

16. Collins, *Autobiography of a Revolutionary Soldier,* 56–57.

17. Quoted in Higginbotham, *Daniel Morgan,* 137.

18. Young, "Memoirs," *Orion,* 3:100.

19. Collins, *Autobiography of a Revolutionary Soldier,* 57.

20. Young, "Memoirs," *Orion,* 3:101.

21. *PNG* 7:157n.

22. Wickwires, *Cornwallis,* 265.

23. *PNG* 7:160n; Wickwires, Cornwallis, 265.

24. Morgan to NG, Jan. 19, 1781, ibid., 7:154.

25. Collins, *Autobiography of a Revolutionary Soldier,* 57; Higginbotham, *Daniel Morgan,* 142.

26. This account of Cowpens draws on Morgan to Greene, Jan. 19, 1781, and the extensive editorial notes that accompany the document in *PNG* 7:152–55, 155–61n; Higginbotham, *Daniel Morgan,* 135–55; Babits, *A Devil of a Whipping,* 81–136; Robert D. Bass, *The Green Dragoon: The Lives of Banastre Tarleton and Mary Robinson* (New York, 1957), 152–62. Tarleton's accout of the engagement can be found in Banastre Tarleton, *Campaigns of 1780 and 1781 in the Southern Provinces,* reprint (North Stratford, N.H., 1999), 215–18. Additional secondary accounts of great merit can be found in Buchanan, *Road to Guilford Courthouse,* 319–26; Wood, *Battles of the American Revolution,* 221–26.

27. Morgan to NG, Jan. 19, 1781, *PNG* 7:153, 155, 160n.

28. "Captain Samuel Shaw's War Letters to Captain Winthrop Sargent," *PMHB* 70(1946):321.

29. Quoted in Jeremy Black, *War for America: The Fight for Independence, 1775–1783* (New York, 1991), 39.

30. Quoted in Wickwires, *Cornwallis*, 269.

31. Morgan to NG, Jan. 25, 1781, *PNG* 7:199; Wickwires, *Cornwallis*, 274; Buchanan, *Road to Guilford Courthouse*, 337–41; Christopher Ward *The War of the Revolution*. 2 vols. (New York, 1952), 2:764–65. Clinton's comment can be found in Sir Henry Clinton, *Observations on Some Parts of Earl Cornwallis's Answer to Sir Henry Clinton's Narrative* (1783), in Benjamin F. Stevens, ed., *The Campaign in Virginia, 1781: An Exact Reprint of Six Rare Pamphlets on the Clinton-Cornwallis Controversy*, 2 vols. (London, 1888), 1:103.

32. Morgan to NG, Jan. 23, 25, 28, 29, *PNG* 7:178, 200–1, 211, 215; NG to PC, Jan. 31, 1781, ibid., 7:225; Morgan to TJ, Feb. 1, 1781, *PTJ* 4:495; Higginbotham, *Daniel Morgan*, 145–48.

33. *PNG* 7:161n.

34. Lewis Morris to Abner Nash, Jan. 28, 1781, ibid., 7:209; NG to Huger, Jan. 30, 1781, ibid., 7:219; NG to PC, Jan. 31, 1781, ibid., 7:225; NG to the Officers Commanding the Militia in the Salisbury District of North Carolina, Jan. 31, 1781, ibid., 7:227–28; Morgan to NG, Jan. 23, 1781, ibid., 7:178; ibid., 7:200n, 219n; Theodore Thayer, *Nathanael Greene: Strategist of the Revolution* (New York, 1960), 308–10.

35. Thayer, *Nathanael Greene*, 311; Ward, *War of the Revolution*, 2:770–72; NG to Campbell, Jan. 30, 1781, *PNG* 7:218; NG to AH, Jan. 10, 1781, ibid., 7:90; Morgan to TJ, Feb. 1, 1781, *PTJ* 4:495–96.

36. NG to Steuben, Feb. 3, 1781, *PNG* 7:242; Higginbotham, *Daniel Morgan*, 150; Wickwires, *Cornwallis*, 278–81. The quotation is in *PNG* 7:244n.

37. Proceedings of a Council of War, Feb. 9, 1781, *PNG* 7:261–62; Higginbotham, *Daniel Morgan*, 151–52.

38. *PNG* 7:191n, 271n, 282n; NG to GW, Feb. 15, 1781, ibid., 7:294; Higginbotham, *Daniel Morgan*, 154.

39. Lee, *Revolutionary War Memoirs of General Henry Lee*, 593.

40. Terry Golway, *Washington's General: Nathanael Greene and the Triumph of the American Revolution* (New York, 2005), 251.

41. Williams to NG, Feb. 13, 1781, *PNG* 7:285; NG to Williams, Feb. 14, 7:287, 287n; NG to TJ, Feb. 15, 1781, PTJ 4:616; Ward, *War of the Revolution*, 2:770–76; Buchanan, *Road to Guilford Courthouse*, 358; Thayer, *Nathanael Greene*, 315–18.

42. *PNG* 7:287n; Ward, *War of the Revolution*, 2:777–78.

43. NG to Colonel Alexander Martin, Feb. 23, 1781, *PNG* 7:335; NG to GW, Feb. 28, 1781, ibid., 7:369–70; NG to TJ, March 10, 1781, ibid., 7:419–20; Ward, *War of the Revolution*, 2:779–80.

44. Pickens to NG, Feb. 26, 1781, *PNG* 7:358; NG to Reed, March 18, 1781, ibid., 7:449; NG to TJ, Feb. 28, 1781, *PTJ* 5:23; Buchanan, *Road to Guilford Courthouse*, 362–64.

45. NG to TJ, March 10, 1781, *PNG* 7:420; NG to Martin, Feb. 23, 1781, ibid., 7:335; NG to GW, Feb. 28, 1781, ibid., 7:369; NG to Steuben, March 1 [?], 5, 1781, ibid., 7:375, 396; NG to Edward Stevens, Feb. 19, 1781, ibid., 7:316; David Campbell to NG, Feb. 17, 1781, ibid., 7:305; Colonel John Gunby to NG, Feb. 17, 1781, ibid., 7:305; NG to TJ, Feb. 28, 1781, *PTJ* 5:23; TJ to NG, Feb. 17, 18, 1781, ibid., 4:638, 648; Wickwires, *Cornwallis*, 288–91; Buchanan, *Road to Guilford Courthouse*, 372; Thayer, *Nathanael Greene*, 326–27.

46. NG to Sumter, Jan. 8, 1781, *PNG* 7:75; NG to Robert Howe, Dec. 29, 1780, ibid., 7:17; NG to AH, Jan. 10, 1781, ibid., 7:88; NG to GW, Jan. 13, 1781, ibid., 7:111; NG to Varnum, Jan. 24, 1781, ibid., 7:188.

47. Quoted in Don Higginbotham, "American Militia," in Don Higginbotham, ed., *Reconsiderations on the Revolutionary War: Selected Essays* (Westport, Conn., 1978), 99.

48. Morgan to NG, Feb. 20, 1781, *PNG* 7:324; Wood, *Battles of the American Revolution*, 243–46; Buchanan, *Road to Guilford Courthouse*, 373.

49. *PNG* 7:437n; Buchanan, *Road to Guilford Courthouse*, 374.

50. NG to PC, March 16, 1781, *PNG* 7:434; NG to TJ, March 16, 1781, ibid., 7:441. On the debate over the performance of the North Carolina militia, see ibid., 7:439–40n.

51. Letter of Major St. George Tucker, March 18, 1781, *SOS* 2:1166.

52. Journal of Sergeant of Roger Lamb, *SOS* 2:1164–65.

53. On the Battle of Guilford Courthouse, see Ward, *War of the Revolution*, 2:784–94; Wood, *Battles of the American Revolution*, 246–56; Buchanan, *Road to Guilford Courthouse*, 374–83; Wickwires, *Cornwallis*, 305–10; Thayer, *Nathanael Greene*, 327–31. See also NG to Catherine Greene, March 18, 1781, *PNG* 7:446.

54. NG to Steuben, April 2, 1781, *PNG* 8:25.

55. NG to Governor Abner Nash, March 18, 1781, ibid., 7:448. See also ibid., 7:440–41n.

56. Both quotes can be found in Golway, *Washington's General*, 260.

57. NG to GW, March 18, 1781, *PNG* 7:452; NG to Reed, March 18, 1781, ibid., 7:450; NG to Catherine Greene, March 18, 1781, ibid., 7:447.

58. Cornwallis to General William Phillips, April 10, 1781, *CC* 1:87; Cornwallis to Germain, April 18, 23, ibid., 1:89–90, 93–94; Cornwallis to Clinton, April 23, 1781, ibid., 1:92–93; Cornwallis to Clinton, April 10, 1781, *SOS* 2:1168–69.

Chapter 21. "We Are Suspended in the Balance": Spring and Summer 1781

1. GW to NG, Feb. 2, 27, 1781, *WW* 21:171, 304; GW to William Fitzhugh, March 25, 1781, ibid., 21:376.

2. GW to NG, Jan. 9 [–11], Feb. 27, 1781, ibid., 21:87, 304; GW to Knox, Jan. 7, 1781, ibid., 21:67; GW to Lincoln, Jan. 9, 1781, ibid., 21:74–75; GW to Rochambeau, Feb. 26, 1781, ibid., 21:298; GW to PC, Feb. 26, 1781, ibid., 21:301; GW to Rochambeau and Ternay, Dec. 15, 1780, ibid., 20:480–81; Douglas Southall Freeman, *George Washington: A Biography*. 7 vols. (New York, 1948–1957), 5:265n.

3. GW to Rochambeau, Feb. 15, 1781, *WW* 21:230; GW to Lafayette, March 1, 1781, ibid., 21:322; Freeman, *George Washington*, 5:255–65; James T. Flexner, *George Washington in the American Revolution* (Boston, 1967), 410; Lee Kennett, *The French Forces in America, 1780–1783* (Westport, Conn., 1977), 83–84, 94–95.

4. Flexner, *George Washington in the American Revolution*, 414–15; Freeman, *George Washington*, 5:5:268; GW to Hancock, March 17, 1781, *WW* 21:339; GW to Schuyler, March 23, 1781, ibid., 21:361.

5. Kennett, *French Forces in America*, 99–100; GW to Alexander McDougall, March 31, 1781, *WW* 21:400; GW to Lund Washington, March 28, April 30, 1781, ibid., 21:385–86; 22:14–15; GW to J. Laurens, April 9, 1781, ibid., 21:438; GW to TJ, April 18, 1781, ibid., 21:473; ibid., 22:14n; Freeman, *George Washington*, 5:275.

6. GW to J. Laurens, April 9, 1781, *WW* 21:439; GW to Lafayette, April 14, 1781, ibid., 21:455; GW to Rochambeau, May 14, 1781, ibid., 22:86; GW to Steuben, May 16, 1781, ibid., 22:91; GW to PC, May 17, 1781, ibid., 22:97; Kennett, *French Forces in America*, 78; Freeman, *George Washington*, 5:285.

7. GW to TJ, May 16, 1781, *WW* 22:94; GW to PC, May 17, 1781, ibid., 22:97–98; Flexner, *George Washington in the American Revolution*, 418–19; Kennett, *French Forces in America*, 91, 104–5.

8. Baron Ludwig von Closen, *The Revolutionary Journal of Baron Ludwig von Closen, 1780–1783*, ed. Evelyn Acomb (Chapel Hill, N.C., 1958), 86; Blanchard, *Journal*, 104.

9. Quoted in Flexner, *George Washington in the American Revolution*, 429

10. Conference with Rochambeau, May 23, 1781, *WW* 22:105–7; GW to NG, June 1, 1781, ibid., 22:146; Edward G. Lengel, *General George Washington* (New York, 2005), 329–30; Flexner, *George Washington in the American Revolution*, 430.

11. TJ to Luzerne, April 12, 1781, *PTJ* 5:422.

12. GW to Rochambeau, April 16, June 2, 3, 7, 1781, *WW* 21:466; 22:154, 155–56, 171; GW to NG, April 19, 22, 1781, ibid., 22:477, 492.

13. GW to NG, Oct. 22, 1780, *PNG* 6:425; NG to GW, Oct. 31, Nov. 19, 1780, ibid., 6:448, 485–86; NG to TJ, Nov. 20, 1780, ibid., 6:493; NG to Steuben, Nov. 20, 1780, Feb. 3, 1781, ibid., 6:496–97; 7:243.

14. John E. Selby, *The Revolution in Virginia, 1775–1783* (Williamsburg, Va., 1988), 255–56; TJ to GW, Feb. 8, 1781, *PTJ* 4:559, 566; GW to Lafayette, Feb. 20, 1781, *LLP* 3:333–34; GW, Instructions to Lafayette, Feb. 20, 1781, ibid., 3:334–36.

15. Lafayette to GW, March 15, 1781, *LLP* 3:397.

16. Steuben, Proposal for an Expedition against Cornwallis, March 27, 1781, ibid., 3:419–20; Lafayette on Steuben's Proposed Expedition, March 27, 1781, ibid., 3:420–21; Lee to TJ, March 27, 1781, *PTJ* 5:262; Weedon to TJ, March 27, 1781, ibid., 5:267; Harry M. Ward, *Duty, Honor or Country: General George Weedon and the American Revolution* (Philadelphia, 1979), 177–82.

17. Selby, *Revolution in Virginia*, 270; *PTJ* 5:275–77n; Weedon to Steuben, April 1, 1781, ibid., 5:276n; Steuben to NG, March 30, 1781, *PNG* 8:15–16; NG to Steuben, April 6, 1781, ibid., 8:60.

18. Selby, *Revolution in Virginia*, 270–74; Christopher Ward *The War of the Revolution*, 2 vols. (New York, 1952), 2:871–72; TJ to Steuben, April 14, 1781, *PTJ* 5:453; TJ to Speaker of the House of Delegates, May 10, 1781, ibid., 5:626.

19. Weedon to Steuben, April 3, 1781, *PTJ* 5:277n; Franklin and Mary Wickwire, *Cornwallis and the War of Independence* (London, 1971), 314–25. The Cornwallis quote is on page 316.

20. Cornwallis to Clinton, April 10, 1781, *CC* 1:87–88; Wickwires, *Cornwallis*, 321.

21. NG to H. Lee, March 22, 1781, *PNG* 7:461; NG to TJ, March 27, 1781, ibid., 7:471; NG to Lafayette, March 29, 1781, ibid., 7:478; NG to GW, March 29, May 1, 1781, 7:481; 8:185; NG to Ichabod Burnet, April 5, 1781, ibid., 8:54; NG to James Emmet, April 3, 1781, ibid., 8:33; ibid., 7:482.

22. Cornwallis to Clinton, April 10, 23, 1781, Sir Henry Clinton, *Observations on Some Parts of Earl Cornwallis's Answer to Sir Henry Clinton's Narrative* (1783), in Benjamin F. Stevens, ed., *The Campaign in Virginia, 1781: An Exact Reprint of Six Rare Pamphlets on the Clinton-Cornwallis Controversy*, 2 vols. (London, 1888), 1:398, 424–25; Cornwallis to Phillips, April 24, 1781, ibid., 1:428; Cornwallis to Germain, April 18, 1781, ibid., 1:417–18; Clinton to Cornwallis, June 1, 1780, ibid., 1:213; Earl Cornwallis, *An Answer to . . . the Narrative of . . . Henry Clinton*, in ibid., 1:65, 67; Cornwallis to Phillips, April 10, 1781, *CC* 1:87; GW's "canvas wings" quotation is in William B. Willcox, "Sir Henry Clinton: Paralysis of Command," in George A. Billias, ed., *George Washington's Opponents* (New York, 1969), 85. Many, but not all, of pieces of the Cornwallis-Clinton correspondence in 1781 can also be found in *DAR*, volume 20.

23. William B. Willcox, *Portrait of a General: Sir Henry Clinton in the War of Independence* (New York, 1964), 386–88.

24. Henry Clinton, *The American Rebellion: Sir Henry Clinton's Narrative of His Campaigns, 1775–1782*, ed. William B. Willcox (New Haven, Conn., 1954), 274, 293.

25. Ibid., 284, 305–6; Willcox, "Sir Henry Clinton," in Billias, *George Washington's Opponents*, 91–92.

26. Clinton to Phillips, March 24, April 5, 11, 13, 26–30, April 30, 1781, Stevens, *Campaign in Virginia*, 1:373, 392–95, 401–5, 437–40, 450–55.

27. Cornwallis to Clinton, May 26, June 30, 1781, ibid., 1:488; 2:35–36.

28. GW to Lafayette, April 11, 21, 22, May 5, 1781, *WW* 21:444–46, 488–89, 493–96; 22:34–35; Lafayette to GW, April 8, May 4, 8, 1781, *LLP* 4:14, 82–84, 88; Lafayette to Luzerne, April 22, 1781, ibid., 4:55; Lafayette to Weedon, May 3, 1781, ibid., 4:77–78; Lafayette to NG, May 3, 1781, ibid., 4:79; J. G. Simcoe, *Simcoe's Military Journal: A History of the Operations of a*

Partisan Corps, Called the Queen's Rangers, reprint (New York, 1998), 223; Harlow Giles Unger, *Lafayette* (Hoboken, N.J., 2002), 135.

29. Lafayette to GW, May 24, 1781, *LLP* 4:130–31.

30. Ward, *War of the Revolution,* 2:873; Dumas Malone, *Jefferson and His Times,* 6 vols. (Boston, 1948–1981), 1:356–58; John Maass, "To Disturb the Assembly: Tarleton's Charlottesville Raid and the Invasion of Virginia, 1781," *Virginia Cavalcade,* (Autumn 2000):149–57.

31. Cassandra Pybus, "Jefferson's Faulty Math," *WMQ* 62:246, 256–57; George Weedon to NG, July 27, 1781, *PNG* 8:91.

32. Cornwallis to Clinton, May 26, 1781, Stevens, *Campaign in Virginia,* 1:489.

33. Wickwires, *Cornwallis,* 334–35; Ward, *War of the Revolution,* 2:875.

34. Clinton to Cornwallis, June 11, 19, 28, 1781, Stevens, *Campaign in Virginia,* 2:18–22, 26–28, 29–31.

35. Clinton, *American Rebellion,* 329.

36. Lafayette to Nelson, July 1, 1781, *LLP* 4:229.

37. Lafayette to NG, July 8, ibid., 4:236–38, 238n; Wickwires, *Cornwallis,* 341–45.

38. "Journal of Ebenezer Wild," MHS, *Proceedings,* 2d Ser., 6:144.

39. Clinton to Cornwallis, June 28, 1781, Stevens, *Campaign in Virginia,* 2:29–30.

40. Clinton to Cornwallis, May 29, June 8, 19, 1781, ibid., 1:493–98; 2:14–17, 26–28.

41. Clinton to Cornwallis, July 11, 1781, ibid., 2:62–65.

42. Cornwallis to Clinton, July 27, 1781, ibid., 2:104.

43. Cornwallis to Clinton, July 8, 1781, ibid., 2:57.

44. Willcox, "Sir Henry Clinton," in Billias, *George Washington's Opponents,* 91–92, 96; Piers Mackesy, *The War for America, 1775–1783* (Cambridge, Mass., 1965), 401–3, 405, 412.

45. NG to Steuben, April 2, 1781, *PNG* 8:24; NG to H. Lee, April [12], 1781, ibid., 8:86; NG to Nash, May 23, 1781, ibid., 8:300–1; Hugh F. Rankin, *The North Carolina Continentals* (Chapel Hill, N.C., 1971), 323.

46. Ward, *War of the Revolution,* 2:798, 800.

47. David Hackett Fischer, *Paul Revere's Ride* (New York, 1994), 284; Willcox, *Portrait of a General,* 61–62, 505; *PNG* 9:152–53n.

48. Quoted in Willcox, *Portrait of a General,* 389. See also Clinton to Cornwallis, May 29, 1781, Stevens, *Campaign in Virginia,* 1:493–95.

49. Ward, *War of the Revolution,* 2:798–801, 824–25; *PNG* 8:xii.

50. *PNG* 8:273–74n; NG to Sumter, Nov. 28, 1781, ibid., 9:634; NG to Griffith Rutherford, Oct. 18, 20, 1781, ibid., 9:452–53, 456; Burke to NG, Aug. 31, 1781, ibid., 9:272. A good account can be found in Terry Golway, *Washington's General: Nathanael Greene and the Triumph of the American Revolution* (New York, 2005), 271–76.

51. *PGN* 8:159n.

52. Ibid., 8:158–59n; NG to Reed, Aug. 6, 1781, ibid., 9:135.

53. Ward, *War of the Revolution,* 2:802–8; *PNG* 8:157–60n; NG to H. Lee, April 29, 1781, ibid., 8:173; NG to Reed, May 4, 1781, ibid., 8:201; NG to PC, April 27, 1781, ibid., 8:157; NG to Luzerne, April 28, 1781, ibid., 8:168.

54. Quoted in Golway, *Washington's General,* 284.

55. Burke to NG, July 4, 1781, *PNG* 8:491; Lafayette to NG, June 21, 1781, ibid., 8:434; NG to Burke, July 16, 1781, ibid., 9:20; NG to PC, July 17, 1781, ibid., 9:30.

56. Ibid., 9:310–11n, 338n; NG to Lafayette, Sept. 17, 1781, ibid., 9:358; NG to GW, Sept. 17, 1781, ibid., 9:362; Golway, *Washington's General,* 280–84; Ward, *War of the Revolution,* 2:823–34; John C. Dann, ed., *Revolution Remembered: Eyewitness Accounts of the War of Independence* (Chicago, 1980), 232.

57. NG to Steuben, Sept. 17, 1781, *PNG* 9:360; NG to Sumter, Oct. 3, 1781, ibid., 9:423; NG to Rutledge, Oct. 15, 1781, ibid., 9:447; NG to James Varnum, Sept. 17, 1781, ibid., 9:361; NG to Wayne, Sept. 29, 1781, ibid., 9:413.

Chapter 22. "America Is Ours": Victory at Yorktown, 1781

1. Claude Blanchard, *The Journal of Claude Blanchard, 1780–1783*, ed., Thomas Bulch, reprint (New York, 1969), 107; Lee Kennett, *The French Forces in America, 1780–1783* (Westport, Conn., 1977), 114; Ludwig von Closen, *The Revolutionary Journal of Baron Ludwig von Closen, 1780–1783*, ed. Evelyn Acomb, reprint (Chapel Hill, N.C., 1958), 91–92; "Journal of Comte de Clerment-Crèvecoueur," in Howard C. Rice Jr. and Anne S. K. Brown, eds., *The American Campaigns of Rochambeau's Army, 1780, 1781, 1782, 1783* (Princeton, N.J., 1972), 1:33.

2. Edward G. Lengel, *General George Washington* (New York, 2005), 332; GW to Rochambeau, June 13, 1781, *WW* 22:208.

3. Conference at Dobbs Ferry, July 19, 1781, *WW* 22:396–97; *DGW* 3:397, 399, 404–5; Rochambeau, *Memoirs*, 59.

4. *DGW* 3:406, 407, 409–10; Richard M. Ketchum, *Victory at Yorktown: The Campaign That Won the Revolution* (New York, 2004), 151; Lengel, *General George Washington*, 333.

5. James T. Flexner, *George Washington in the American Revolution* (Boston, 1967), 441.

6. David Syrett, *The Royal Navy in American Waters, 1775–1783* (Aldershot, England, 1989), 178, 181, 191; Ketchum, *Victory at Yorktown*, 159; Douglas Southall Freeman, *George Washington: A Biography*. 7 vols. (New York, 1948–1957), 5:315.

7. GW, General Orders, Aug. 19, 1781, *WW* 23:19; GW to Lafayette, Aug. 21, 1781, ibid., 23:34; Answers to Questions Proposed by . . . Rochambeau, Aug. 22, 1781, ibid., 23:36; *DGW* 3:413; Freeman, *General George Washington*, 5:314.

8. *DGW* 3:414–16; Thacher, *Journal*, 271; Lafayette to GW, Aug. 25, 1781, *LLP* 4:357; Ketchum, *Victory at Yorktown*, 159; Lengel, *General George Washington*, 335.

9. James Thacher, *Military Journal of the American Revolution* reprint (New York, 1969), 273–78; GW to Lafayette, Sept. 10, 1871, *WW* 23:11; Kennett, *French Army in America*, 135–37; Flexner, *George Washington in the American Revolution*, 444; Freeman, *George Washington*, 5:325–28.

10. William B. Willcox, *Portrait of a General: Sir Henry Clinton in the War of Independence* (New York, 1964), 409, 421; W. J. Wood, *Battles of the Revolutionary War, 1775–1781* (Chapel Hill, N.C., 1990), 266.

11. William B. Willcox, "Arbuthnot, Gambier, and Graves: 'Old Women' of the Navy," in George A. Billias, ed., *George Washington's Opponents* (New York, 1969), 280; Wood, *Battles of the Revolutionary War*, 272–85; John A. Tilley, *The British Navy and the American Revolution* (Columbia, S.C., 1987), 235–64; Syrett, *Royal Navy in American Waters*, 177–204.

12. Journal of St. George Tucker, *SOS* 2:1224; Ketchum, *Victory at Yorktown*, 186.

13. Franklin and Mary Wickwire, *Cornwallis and the War of Independence* (London, 1971), 358–64; Willcox, *Portrait of a General*, 428; Cornwallis to Clinton, Sept. 1, 4, 1781, Sir Henry Clinton, *Observations on Some Parts of Earl Cornwallis's Answer to Sir Henry Clinton's Narrative* (1783), in Benjamin F. Stevens, ed., *The Campaign in Virginia, 1781, An Exact Reprint of Six Rare Pamphlets on the Clinton-Cornwallis Controversy*, 2 vols. (London, 1888) 2:147, 151; Cornwallis, *An Answer*, ibid., 1:75–77.

14. Willcox, *Portrait of a General*, 427; J. G., Simcoe, *Journal. A History of the Operations of a Partisan Corps, Called the Queen's Rangers*, reprint (New York, 1998), 250.

15. Clinton to Cornwallis, Sept. 6, 1781, Stevens, *Campaign in Virginia*, 2:152–53; Cornwallis to Clinton, Sept. 16–17, 1781, ibid., 2:157; Wickwires, *Cornwallis*, 364.

16. Flexner, *George Washington in the American Revolution*, 449–50.

17. Cornwallis to Clinton, Oct. 20, 1781, Stevens, *Campaign in Virginia*, 2:205–6. The best source for understanding Yorktown's terrain, and the difficulties that Cornwallis faced in laying out a proper defense, is Jerome A. Greene, *The Guns of Independence: The Siege of Yorktown* (New York, 2005), 25.

18. For a detailed appraisal of the British defenses, see Greene, *Guns of Independence*, 41–67.

19. GW to Weedon, Sept. 20, 1781, *WW* 23:126; GW to the Officer Commanding the Infantry of Lauzun's Legion, Sept. 20, 1781, ibid., 23:125; Christopher Ward *The War of the Revolution*, 2 vols. (New York, 1952), 2:887–88; Ketchum, *Victory at Yorktown*, 198, 217.

20. Journal of Trumbull, in *SOS* 2:1227; Weedon to NG, Sept. 5, 1781, *PNG* 9:300–1.

21. Quoted in Greene, *Guns of Independence*, 70.

22. For a detailed look at the deployment of the allied armies, see ibid., 77–89.

23. St. George Tucker to his wife, Sept. 15, 1781, *SOS* 2:1224; GW to de Grasse, Sept. 25, 1781, *WW* 23:136; George Scheer, ed., *Private Yankee Doodle: Being a Narrative of Some of the Adventures, Dangers and Sufferings of a Revolutionary Soldier* (Boston, 1962), 230; Lengel, *General George Washington*, 337.

24. Scheer, *Private Yankee Doodle*. 231–32; Ketchum, *Victory at Yorktown*, 222.

25. Quoted in Greene, *Guns of Independence*, 160.

26. Scheer, *Private Yankee Doodle*, 233–34; Thacher, *Journal*, 283–284; Ketchum, *Victory at Yorktown*, 227; Lengel, *General George Washington*, 338.

27. AH to Elizabeth Hamilton, Oct. 12, 1781, *PAH* 2:678; Lengel, *General George Washington*, 339; Greene, *Guns of Independence*, 59, 61, 238; Wickwires, *Cornwallis*, 375.

28. *PAH* 2:679n.

29. John Ferling, *The First of Men: A Life of George Washington* (Knoxville, 1988), 301–2; Ketchum, *Victory at Yorktown*, 238; Wickwires, *Cornwallis*, 378–79.

30. Thacher, *Journal*, 286.

31. Quoted in Wickwires, *Cornwallis*, 385.

32. Greene, *Guns of Independence*, 283, 457n.

33. Cornwallis to GW, Oct. 17, 1781, Stevens, *Campaign in Virginia*, 2:189.

34. GW to Cornwallis, Oct. 17, 1781, *WW* 23:236–37; Greene, *Guns of Independence*, 283–84.

35. Flexner, *George Washington in the American Revolution*, 459.

36. Closen, *Journal*, 153; GW to Cornwallis, Oct. 18, 1781, *WW* 23:237–38; Cornwallis to GW, Oct. 18, 1781, Stevens, *Campaign in Virginia*, 2:195–96; Cornwallis to Clinton, Oct. 20, 1781, ibid., 2:215; Freeman, *George Washington*, 5:383; Flexner, *George Washington in the American Revolution*, 460.

37. Articles of Capitulation, Oct. 19, 1781, Stevens, *Clinton-Cornwallis Controversy*, 2:200, 201. The entire surrender document is in ibid., 2:199–203.

38. Ketchum, *Victory at Yorktown*, 244.

39. John Buchanan, *The Road to Guilford Courthouse: The American Revolution in the Carolinas* (New York, 1997), 335, 378.

40. Deposition of Sarah Osborn, John C. Dann, ed., *Revolution Remembered: Eyewitness Accounts of the War of Independence* (Chicago, 1980), 245; Scheer, *Private Yankee Doodle*, 240; Thacher, *Journal*, 298; Blanchard, *Journal*, 152, Closen, *Journal*, 153–54; Greene, *Guns of Independence*, 296.

41. State of Troops in Virginia, Under . . . Cornwallis, Oct. 1, 1781, Stevens, *Campaign in Virginia*, 2:197.

42. Scheer, "The Sergeant Major's Strange Mission," *American Heritage* 8 (Oct. 1957): 26–29, 98.

43. Henry Wiencek, *An Imperfect God: George Washington, His Slaves, and the Creation of America* (New York, 2003), 247–48, 251; Cassandra Pybus, "Jefferson's Faulty Math," *WMQ* 62:256–57; Ketchum, *Victory at Yorktown*, 256. On GW and the acquisition of his slaves, see George Washington, General Orders, Oct. 9, 25, 1781, George Washington Papers, LC. I am indebted to Gregory Urwin for directing me to GW's General Orders and to Mary Thompson at Mount Vernon, who assisted me on the matter of GW's efforts to regain the runaway slaves from his estate.

44. Ketchum, *Victory at Yorktown*, 242–55; Lengel, *General George Washington*, 343.

45. GW to PC, Oct. 19, 1781, *WW* 23:241–44; GW, General Orders, Oct. 20, 1781, ibid., 23:244–47.

46. George F. Scheer and Hugh F. Rankin, *Rebels and Redcoats* (Cleveland, 1957), 494–95.

47. Deposition of William Burnett, Dann, *Revolution Remembered*, 373–74.

Chapter 23. Choices, 1782

1. Boudinot to Hannah Boudinot, Oct. 21, 1781, *LDC* 18:151; John Ferling, *A Leap in the Dark: The Struggle to Create the American Republic* (New York, 2003), 240–41.

2. Connecticut Delegates to Jonathan Trumbull Sr., Oct. 25, 1781, *LDC* 18:165.

3. William B. Willcox, *Portrait of a General: Sir Henry Clinton in the War of Independence* (New York, 1964), 429–38, 446–47; Clinton to Germain, Oct. 29, 1781, *DAR* 20:252; Clinton to Germain, March 14, 1782, ibid., 21:44; Sir Henry Clinton, *Observations on Some Parts of Earl Cornwallis's Answer to Sir Henry Clinton's Narrative* (1783), in Benjamin F. Stevens, ed., *The Campaign in Virginia, 1781: An Exact Reprint of Six Rare Pamphlets on the Clinton-Cornwallis Controversy*, 2 vols. (London, 1888), 1: 103, 105, 111.

4. Alan Valentine, *Lord North* (Norman, Okla., 1967), 2:274.

5. Ibid. The "Burgoynishing" quote can be found in Francois Van der Kemp to JA, Nov. 26, 1781, *PJA* 12:89.

6. Piers Mackesy, *The War for America, 1775–1783* (Cambridge, Mass., 1965), 460.

7. *PH* 22:636, 680, 705–7, 723, 726, 729.

8. Germain to Clinton, Jan. 2, 1782, *DAR* 21:27; Valentine, *Lord North*, 2:282–89.

9. Solomon Lutnick, *The American Revolution and the British Press, 1775–1783* (Columbia, Mo., 1967), 192–93; Stanley Weintraub, *Iron Tears: America's Battle for Freedom, Britain's Quagmire, 1775–1783* (New York, 2005), 306–7; *PH* 22:802–3, 808, 812, 831.

10. Alan Valentine, *Lord George Germain* (Oxford, England, 1962), 442–43.

11. Richard B. Morris, *The Peacemakers: The Great Powers and American Independence* (New York, 1965), 252; Hartley to BF, Jan. 2 [–8], 1782, *PBF* 36:360, 363, 364.

12. BF to Hartley, Jan. 15, April 13, 1782, *PBF* 36:435; 37:143–44.

13. Quoted in Morris, *Peacemakers*, 254; Orville T. Murphy, *Charles Gravier, Comte de Vergennes: French Diplomacy in the Age of Revolution, 1719–1787* (Albany, 1982), 322.

14. BF to Hartley, April 13, 1782, *PBF* 37:143–44.

15. Valentine, *Lord North*, 2:292, 296; Weintraub, *Iron Tears*, 316.

16. *PH* 22:1028–48.

17. Ibid., 22:1089.

18. Ibid., 22:1076–80, 1085–90; Valentine, *Lord North*, 2:303–5.

19. The two quotations are in Valentine, *Lord North*, 314, and Carl B. Cone, *Burke and the Nature of Politics: The Age of the American Revolution* (Lexington, Ky., 1957), 394, respectively.

20. Quoted in Peter D. G. Thomas, *Lord North* (London, 1976), 132.

21. Morris, *Peacemakers*, 260, 266–69.

22. South Carolina Delegates to James Mathews, May 6, 1781, *LDC* 18:491; James Madison to Edmund Randolph, May 14, 1782, ibid., 18:510; Theodorick Bland to St. George Tucker, May 13[?], 1782, ibid., 18:505; Virginia Delegates to Benjamin Harrison, May 14, 1782, ibid., 18:516.

23. John Ferling, *John Adams: A Life* (Knoxville, 1992), 244.

24. BF to GW, April 8, 1782, *PBF* 37:116; BF to Robert Livingston, March 30, 1782, ibid., 37:71.

Chapter 24. "May We Have Peace in Our Time": Peace and Demobilization, 1782–1783

1. GW to de Grasse, Oct. 28, 1781, *WW* 23:285, 286–87; GW to PC, Oct. 27 [–29], 1781, ibid., 23:294–99; Lafayette to PC, *LLP* 4:437–38.

2. GW to Secretary of War, Jan. 20, 1782, *WW* 23:452–53.

3. Lietenant Governor William Bull to Thomas Townsend, Jan. 19, 1783, *DAR* 21:149; Governor Patrick Tonyn to Townshend, Dec. 24, 1782, ibid., 21:145; Narrative of Governor Sir James Wright, [Sept. 3, 1782], ibid., 21:116.

4. William Franklin to Galloway, May 11, 1782, ibid., 21:72–73.

5. *PNG* 11:581–82n; Gregory D. Massey, *John Laurens and the American Revolution* (Columbia, S.C., 2000), 226–27.

6. Piers Mackesy, *The War for America, 1775–1783* (Cambridge, Mass., 1965), 436–59; Christopher Lloyd, "Sir George Rodney: Lucky Admiral," in George A. Billias, ed., *George Washington's Opponents* (New York, 1969), 346–49; Shelburne to Carleton, June 5, 1782, *DAR* 21:82.

7. GW to James McHenry, July 18, 1782, *WW* 24:432; GW to NG, July 9, 1782, ibid., 24:409.

8. GW to NG, Dec. 18, 1782, ibid., 25:448; Mackesy, *War for America*, 479–84.

9. GW to Knox, May 1, 1782, *WW* 24:214n; GW to Secretary for Foreign Affairs, April 23, 1782, ibid., 24:156; GW, Memorandum, May 1, 1782, ibid., 24:199; Substance of a Conference between Comte de Rochambeau and General Washington, July 19, 1782, ibid., 24:434–35.

10. GW to BF, Oct. 18, 1782, ibid., 25:273; GW to James McHenry, Sept. 12, 1782, ibid., 25:151; GW to William Gordon, Oct. 23, 1782, ibid., 25:287; GW to NG, Sept. 23, Dec. 18, 1782, ibid., 25:195, 447–48; Lee Kennett, *The French Forces in America, 1780–1783* (Westport, Conn., 1977), 162.

11. BF to Shelburne, March 22, 1782, *PBF* 37:24–25; Shelburne to BF, April 6, 1782, ibid., 37:103–4; ibid., 24n, 102n; Shelburne to Commissioners for Restoring Peace, June 5, 1782, *DAR* 21:77; Jonathan Dull, *A Diplomatic History of the American Revolution* (New Haven, Conn., 1983), 140.

12. Dull, *Diplomatic History of the American Revolution*, 129–33, 144–48.

13. *JADA* 3:82; JA to AA, [ca. Aug. 15, 1782], Jan. 22, 1783, *AFC* 4:361; 5:74; David McCullough, *John Adams* (New York, 2001), 283, 285. For further details on the negotiations, see John Ferling, *John Adams: A Life* (Knoxville, 1992), 245–56, and John Ferling, *Setting the World Ablaze: Washington, Adams, Jefferson and the American Revolution* (New York, 2000), 256–65.

14. GW to John Armstrong, Jan. 10, 1783, *WW* 26:25–26; GW to Luzerne, March 29, 1783, ibid., 26:264; GW to Secretary of Foreign Affairs, March 29, 1783, ibid., 26:266. On the *Triumph* bringing the news of the peace, see John Mercer to William Fitzhugh and General Weedon, March 24, 1783, *LDC* 20:87.

15. Bland to Frances Tucker, March 24, 1783, *LDC* 20:79; Bland to St. George Tucker, March 24, 1783, ibid., 20:80–81; John Montgomery to Robert Magaw, March 24, 1783, ibid., 20:88.

16. Robert Calhoon, *The Loyalists in Revolutionary America, 1760–1781* (New York, 1965), 501.

17. Cassandra Pybus, "Jefferson's Faulty Math," *WMQ* 62:255–64.

18. GW to Carleton, April 9, 1783, *WW* 26:307.

19. Larry G. Bowman, *Captive Americans: Prisoners during the American Revolution* (Athens, Ohio, 1977), 109–15; Memorandum of Agreement for Liberation of British Prisoners of War. . . . , April 19, 1783, *WW* 26:341.

20. Charles H. Lesser, *The Sinews of Independence: Monthly Strength Reports of the Continental Army* (Chicago, 1976), 210–50.

21. See Richard H. Kohn, "The Inside History of the Newburgh Conspiracy: America and the Coup d'Etat," *WMQ* 27 (1970):187–220; Paul David Nelson, "Horatio Gates at Newburgh, 1783: A Misunderstood Role," ibid., 29 (1972):143–51, with Richard H. Kohn's Reply, ibid., 29 (1972):151–58. See also AH to GW, Feb. 13, 1783, *PAH* 3:253–55; GW, To the Officers of the Army, March 15, 1783, *WW* 26:222–27; JCC 24:310–11. On GW's acting skills, see Richard Brookhiser, *Founding Father: Rediscovering George Washington* (New York, 1996), 43, 151–56.

22. James Kirby Martin and Mark Edward Lender, *A Respectable Army: The Military Origins of the Republic, 1763–1789* (Arlington Heights, Ill., 1982), 195 George Scheer, ed., *Private Yankee Doodle: Being a Narrative of Some of the Adventures, Dangers and Sufferings of a Revolutionary Soldier* (Boston, 1962), 282–83, 287.

23. Benjamin Gilbert to Daniel Gilbert, [late June 1783), in John Shy, ed., *Winding Down: The Revolutionary War Letters of Lieutenant Benjamin Gilbert of Massachusetts, 1780–1783* (Ann Arbor, Mich., 1989), 108.

24. Lesser, *Sinews of Independence*, 254–55.

25. John Ferling, *The First of Men: A Life of George Washington* (Knoxville, 1988), 314–15; GW to George Clinton, Aug. 12, 1783, *WW* 27:99.

26. Douglas Southall Freeman, *George Washington: A Biography*. 7 vols. (New York, 1948–1957), 5:450n; John K. Alexander, *Samuel Adams: America's Revolutionary Politician* (New York, 2002), 196–97.

27. Return of Loyalists Leaving New York, Nov. 24, 1783, *DAR* 21:225; Judith L. Van Buskirk, *Generous Enemies: Patriots and Loyalists in Revolutionary New York* (Philadelphia, 2002), 177, 179.

28. Benjamin Talmadge, *Memoirs of Colonel Benjamin Talmadge*, ed. Henry Phelps Johnston (New York, 1904), 62–63.

29. Freeman, *George Washington*, 5:459, 458–62; Edwin G. Burrows and Mike Wallace, *Gotham: A History of New York City to 1898* (New York, 1999), 260–61.

30. These figures draw on Howard H. Peckham, *The Toll of Independence: Engagements and Battle Casualties of the American Revolution* (Chicago, 1974), 130–34.

31. For British casualty figures, see Michael Clodfelter, *Warfare and Armed Conflicts: A Statistical Reference to Casualty and Other Figures, 1618–1991* (Jefferson, N.C., 1992), 1:197–98; Neil Cantlie, *A History of the Army Medical Department* (Edinburgh, 1974), 1:156; Rodney Atwood, *The Hessians: Mercenaries from Hessen-Kassel in the American Revolution* (Cambridge, England, 1980), 255; Ernst Kipping, *The Hessian View of America, 1776–1783* (Monmouth Beach, N.J., 1971), 39; Paul H. Smith, "The American Loyalists: Notes on their Organization and Numerical Strength," *WMQ* 25 (1968): 264, 266, 268, 275n. I am grateful to Caroline Cox, Walter Dornfest, John Maass, Gregory Urwin, and Paul Kopperman who provided assistance in my search for answers regarding British casualties, and especially to Professor Kopperman, who generously shared his soon to be published findings regarding British casualties.

32. Clodfelter, *Warfare and Armed Conflicts*, 1:198.

33. Richard M. Ketchum, *Victory at Yorktown: The Campaign That Won the Revolution* (New York, 2004), 289–90.

34. Ferling, *Setting the World Ablaze*, 271.

35. James Tilton to Gunning Bedford, Dec. 25, 1783, *LDC* 21:232; James McHenry to Margaret Caldwell, Dec. 23, 1783, ibid., 21:221; TJ to Benjamin Harrison, Dec. 24, 1783, *PTJ* 6:419; GW, Address to Congress, *WW* 27:284–85; Freeman, *George Washington*, 5:469–78; John C. Fitzpatrick, ed., *Account of Expenses while Commander in Chief* (Boston, 1917).

Chapter 25. "Little Short of a Miracle": Accounting for America's Victory

1. Quoted in Maldwyn A. Jones, "Sir William Howe," in George A. Billias, ed., *George Washington's Opponents* (New York, 1969), 61.

2. GW, Farewell Orders to the Armies of the United States, Nov. 2, 1783, *WW* 27:223.

3. Piers Mackesy, *The War for America, 1775–1783* (Cambridge, Mass., 1965), 524–26; Charles H. Lesser, *The Sinews of Independence: Monthly Strength Reports of the Continental Army* (Chicago, 1976), 43–47, 58–59.

4. Cassandra Pybus, "Jefferson's Faulty Math," *WMQ* 62:249–50.

5. JA to AA, Aug. 2, 30, 1777, *AFC* 2:298, 334; Jeremy Black, *War for America: The Fight for Independence, 1775–1783* (New York, 1991), 22.

6. Eric Robson, *The American Revolution in Its Political and Military Aspects, 1763–1783* (New York, 1966), 99–100; Jones, "Sir William Howe," in Billlias, *George Washington's Generals*, 49.

7. Piers Mackesy, "British Strategy in the War of American Independence," *The Yale Review* 52 (1963):543.

8. Quoted in Black, *War for America*, 17, 168.

9. Mackesy, "British Strategy in the War of American Independence," *Yale Review*, 52:545–47.

10. The quotes can be found in Stephen Conway, "To Subdue America: British Army Officers and the Conduct of the Revolutionary War," *WMQ* 43 (1986):392.

11. For the Phillips quotation, see Mackesy, "British Strategy in the War of American Independence," *Yale Review*, 52:547.

12. The quote is in Conway, "To Subdue America," *WMQ* 43:381.

13. John Ferling, *The First of Men: A Life of George Washington* (Knoxville, 1988), 301. For an extended discussion of British problems in this war, see Robson, *American Revolution in Its Political and Military Aspects*, 93–152. See also, Mackesy, *War for America*, 17–24, 510–16.

14. JA to AA, June 3, 1776, May 22, 1777, *AFC* 2:6, 245.

15. Lafayette to Vergennes, July 19, 1780, *LLP* 3:100; Lafayette to GW, Feb. 5, 1783, ibid., 5:91; Robson, *American Revolution in Its Political and Military Aspects*, 169.

16. James T. Flexner, *George Washington in the American Revolution* (Boston, 1967), 531–52.

17. David McCullough, *1776* (New York, 2005), 293.

18. TJ, Notes on a Conversation with John Beckley and George Washington, June 7, 1793, *PTJ* 26:219–20.

19. JA to Jay, Nov. 28, 1781, *PJA* 12:93.

20. "Letters from a Hessian Mercenary," *PMHB* 62 (1938):496. The officer was named Hans Huth.

21. Robert Middlekauff, "Why Men Fought in the American Revolution," *Huntington Library Quarterly* 43 (1980):135–48; Robert Middlekauff, *The Glorious Cause: The American Revolution, 1763–1789*, rev. ed. (New York, 2005), 507–11.

22. George Scheer, ed., *Private Yankee Doodle: Being a Narrative of Some of the Adventures, Dangers and Sufferings of a Revolutionary Soldier* (Boston, 1962), 284, 288.

23. Samuel Shaw, *The Journals of Samuel Shaw, The First American Consul at Canton* (Boston, 1847), 39, 54–55.

24. Thomas Paine, *American Crisis*, in Philip S. Foner, ed., *The Complete Writings of Thomas Paine*, 2 vols., (New York, 1945) 1:57, 198.

Morgan, Daniel: Don Higginbotham, *Daniel Morgan: Revolutionary Rifleman* (Chapel Hill, N.C., 1961).

Putnam, Israel: Richard M. Ketchum, "Men of the Revolution: Israel Putnam," *American Heritage*, 24 (June 1973):26–27.

Schuyler, Philip: Martin Bush, *Revolutionary Enigma: A Re-Appraisal of General Philip Schuyler of New York* (Port Washington, N.Y., 1969); Don R. Gerlach, *Proud Patriot: Philip Schuyler and the War of Independence, 1775–1783* (Syracuse, 1987).

Scott, Charles: Harry M. Ward, *Charles Scott and the "Spirit of '76"* (Charlottesville, Va., 1988).

Stephen, Adam: Harry M. Ward, *Major General Adam Stephen and the American Liberty* (Charlottesville, Va., 1989).

Steuben, Friedrich: John McAuley Palmer, *General von Steuben* (New Haven, Conn., 1937).

Stirling, Lord (Alexander, William): Alan Valentine, *Lord Stirling* (New York, 1969).

Sullivan, John: Charles P. Whittemore, *General of the Revolution: John Sullivan of New Hampshire* (New York, 1961).

Ward, Artemas. Charles Martyn, *The Life of Artemas Ward* (New York, 1921).

Wayne, Anthony. Paul David Nelson, *Anthony Wayne: Soldier of the Early Republic* (Bloomington, Ind., 1985).

Weedon, George: Harry M. Ward, *Duty, Honor or Country: General George Weedon and the American Revolution* (Philadelphia, 1979).

Excellent essays on the leading Continental army generals can be found in George A. Billias, ed. *George Washington's Generals* (New York, 1964).

Leading British Military Figures (In Alphabetical Order)

Burgoyne, John: Richard J. Hargrove, *General John Burgoyne* (Newark, Del., 1983).

Carleton, Guy: Paul David Nelson, *General Sir Guy Carleton, Lord Dorchester: Soldier-Statesman of Early British Canada* (London, 2000).

Clinton, Henry: William B. Willcox, *Portrait of a General: Sir Henry Clinton in the War of Independence* (New York, 1964).

Cornwallis, Earl: Franklin and Mary Wickwire, *Cornwallis and the War of Independence* (London, 1971).

Gage, Thomas: John R. Alden, *General Gage in America—Being Principally a History of His Role in the American Revolution* (Baton Rouge, 1948).

The Howe Brothers: Troyer Steele Anderson, *The Command of the Howe Brothers during the American Revolution* (New York, 1936); Ira D. Gruber, *The Howe Brothers and the American Revolution* (New York, 1972).

Tarleton, Banastre: Robert D. Bass, *The Green Dragoon: The Lives of Banastre Tarleton and Mary Robinson* (New York, 1957).

Excellent essays on the leading British military figures can be found in George A. Billias, ed., *George Washington's Opponents* (New York, 1969).

Battles, Campaigns, and Events of the War (In Chronological Order)

Lexington-Concord: David Hackett Fischer, *Paul Revere's Ride* (New York, 1994); Louis Birnbaum, *Red Dawn at Lexington: "If They Mean to Have a War, Let It Begin Here"* (Boston, 1986).

Bunker Hill: Richard M. Ketchum, *Decisive Day: The Battle for Bunker Hill* (Boston, 1974).

Siege of Boston: Thomas Fleming, *Now We Are Enemies: The Story of Bunker Hill* (New York, 1960); Allen French, *The First Year of the American Revolution* (Boston, 1911); Richard Frothingham, *History of the Siege of Boston* (Boston, 1849); David McCullough, *1776* (New York, 2005).

BIBLIOGRAPHY

Bibliographic Note

Among American wars, the War of Independence is second only to the Civil War in literary output. The first histories of the war appeared shortly after the Treaty of Paris was ratified and works on Revolutionary battles and leaders have never stopped, spiking as anniversaries, centennials, and bicentennials occurred. What follows therefore is hardly a comprehensive bibliography, but a guide to what I consider the most noteworthy books for those who wish to plunge deeper into the Revolutionary War. The plethora of journals, diaries, and narratives kept by soldiers, officers, and public officials on every side that are cited in the notes have been omitted due to spatial considerations. Readers who are interested in these primary sources should consult the notes.

General Histories and Documentary Collections on the Revolutionary War

John R. Alden, *A History of the American Revolution* (New York, 1969); Jeremy Black, *War for America: The Fight for Independence* (New York, 1991); Mark M. Boatner, III, *Encyclopedia of the American Revolution* (New York, 1976); William Bell Clark, ed., *Naval Documents of the American Revolution* (Washington, D.C., 1964–); Henry Steele Commager and Richard B. Morris, eds., *The Sprit of '76: The Story of the American Revolution As Told by Participants*. 2 vols. (New York, 1958); Peter Force, ed., *American Archives: Fourth Series, Containing a Documentary History of the English Colonies in North America from the King's Message to Parliament of March 7, 1774, to the Declaration of Independence by the United States*, 6 vols. (Washington, D.C., 1837–1846); idem., *American Archives: Fifth Series, Containing a Documentary History of the United States of America from the Declaration of Independence, July 4, 1776, to the Definitive Treaty of Paris with Great Britain, September 3, 1783*, 3 vols. (Washington, D.C., 1848–1853); Christopher Hibbert, *Redcoats and Rebels: The American Revolution through British Eyes* (New York, 1990); Don Higginbotham, *The War of American Independence: Military Attitudes, Policies, and Practice,*

1763–1789 (New York, 1971); Piers Mackesy, *The War for America, 1775–1783* (Cambridge, Mass., 1965); Robert Middlekauff, *The Glorious Cause: The American Revolution, 1763–1789*, rev. ed. (New York, 2005), Marshall Smelser, *The Winning of Independence* (New York, 1972); Christopher Ward *The War of the Revolution*, 2 vols. (New York, 1952); W. J. Wood, *Battles of the Revolutionary War, 1775–1781* (Chapel Hill, N.C., 1990).

Papers and Documentary Collections

Adams, John: Robert J. Taylor, et al., eds., *Papers of John Adams* (Cambridge, Mass., 1977–???); L. H. Butterfield, et al., eds., *Adams Family Correspondence* (Cambridge, Mass., 1963–???), and L. H. Butterfield, et al., eds., *The Diary and Autobiography of John Adams*, 4 vols. (Cambridge, Mass., 1961).

British Government: K. G. Davies, ed., *Documents of the American Revolution*, 21 vols. (Dublin, 1972–1981).

Continental Congress: Worthington C. Ford, et al., eds., *The Journals of the Continental Congress*, 34 vols. (Washington, 1904–1937); Paul H. Smith, ed., *Letters of Delegates to Congress, 1774–1789*, 26 vols. (Washington, D.C., 1976–2000).

Franklin, Benjamin: Leonard W. Labaree, et al., eds., *The Papers of Benjamin Franklin* (New Haven, Conn., 1959–).

Greene, Nathanael: Richard Showman, et al., eds., *The Papers of Nathanael Greene*, 13 vols. (Chapel Hill, N.C., 1976–2005).

Hamilton, Alexander: Harold C. Syrett and Jacob E. Cooke, eds., *The Papers of Alexander Hamilton*, 27 vols. (New York, 1961–1979).

Jefferson, Thomas: Julian P. Boyd, et al., eds., *The Papers of Thomas Jefferson* (Princeton, N.J., 1950–).

Layfayette, Marquis de: Stanley J. Idzerda, et al., eds., *Lafayette in the Age of the American Revolution: Selected Letters and Papers, 1776–1790*, 5 vols. (Ithaca, N.Y., 1976–1983).

Lee, Charles: *Lee Papers, Collections of the New-York Historical Society for the Year 1871 . . . 1872 . . . 1873 . . . 1874*, 4 vols. (New York, 1871–1874).

Sullivan, John: Otis G. Hammond, ed., *Letters and Papers of Maj, General John Sullivan*, 3 vols. (Concord, N.H., 1930–1939).

Washington, George: W. W. Abbot, et al., eds., *The Papers of George Washington: Revolutionary War Series* (Charlottesville, Va., 1985–); John C. Fitzpatrick, ed., *Writings of Washington* (Washington, D.C., 1931–1944).

General Works: Peter Force, ed., *American Archives: Consisting of a Collection of Authentick Records, State Papers, Debates, and Letters and Other Notices of Public Affairs*, 4th Ser., 9 vols. (Washington, D.C., 1837–1853); Benjamin F. Stevens, ed., *Facsimiles of Manuscripts in European Archives Relating to America, 1773–1783*, 25 vols. (London, 1889–1898).

Countless additional collections of published documents—especially the diaries, journals, and later narratives left by the soldiers—can be found in the endnotes.

Biographies

Washington, George: Washington is the subject of nearly as many biographies as all the other major military figures in the Revolutionary War combined. Biographies are only the tip of the iceberg of the literature on General Washington. Numerous works exist that scrutinize Washington as a military commander. No biography compares to Douglas Southall Freeman, *George Washington: A Biography*, 7 vols. (New York, 1948–1957). Volumes 3–5 deal with the war years. For single volume biographies of the life of Washington, see Joseph J. Ellis, *His Excellency: George Washington* (New York, 2004) and John Ferling, *The First of Men: A Life of George Washington* (Knoxville, 1988). Peter Henriques's *Realistic Visionary: A Portrait of George*

Washington (Charlottesville, Va., 2006) is an excellent appraisal of Washington's career and character. Two excellent single volume works focus on Washington during the Revolutionary War: see Edward G. Lengel, *General George Washington* (New York, 2005) and James T. Flexner, *George Washington in the American Revolution* (Boston, 1967), volume two of his four volume life of the Founder. On young Washington, see Paul K. Longmore, *The Invention of George Washington* (Charlottesville, Va., 1989). For a fine character study, see Richard Brookhiser, *Founding Father: Rediscovering George Washington* (New York, 1996). Don Higginbotham, an esteemed scholar of the war, has produced several noteworthy works on Washington; see *George Washington and the American Military Tradition* (Athens, Ga., 1985); *George Washington Reconsidered* (Charlottesville, Va., 2001); and *George Washington: Uniting a Nation* (Lanham, Md., 2002).

Biographies of Other Leading American Military Figures (In Alphabetical Order)

Arnold, Benedict: James Kirby Martin, *Benedict Arnold: Revolutionary Hero* (New York, 1997); Willard Sterne Randall, *Benedict Arnold: Patriot and Traitor* (New York, 1990); Willard M. Wallace, *Traitorous Hero: The Life and Fortunes of Benedict Arnold* (Freeport, N.Y., 1964).

Davie, William: Blackwell Robinson, *William R. Davie* (Chapel Hill, N.C., 1957).

de Kalb, Johannes: A. E. Zucker, *General De Kalb, Lafayette's Mentor* (Chapel Hill, N.C., 1966).

Gates, Horatio: Paul David Nelson, *General Horatio Gates: A Biography* (Baton Rouge, 1976).

Glover, John: George A. Billias, *John Glover and His Marblehead Men* (New York, 1960).

Greene, Nathanael: Theodore Thayer, *Nathanael Greene: Strategist of the Revolution* (New York, 1960); Terry Golway, *Washington's General: Nathanael Greene and the Triumph of the American Revolution* (New York, 2005).

Hamilton, Alexander: Ron Chernow, *Alexander Hamilton* (New York, 2004);

Howe, Robert: Charles H. Bennett and Donald R. Lennon, *A Quest for Glory: Major General Robert Howe and the American Revolution* (Chapel Hill, N.C., 1991).

Jones, John Paul: Samuel Eliot Morison, *John Paul Jones: A Sailor's Biography* (Boston, 1959); Evan Thomas, *John Paul Jones: Sailor, Hero, Father of the American Navy* (New York, 2003).

Knox, Henry: North Callahan, *Henry Knox: General Washington's General* (New York, 1958).

Lafayette, Marquis de: Harlow Giles Unger, *Lafayette* (Hoboken, N.J., 2002).

Laurens, John: Gregory D. Massey, *John Laurens and the American Revolution* (Columbia, S.C., 2000),

Lee, Charles: John Alden, *Charles Lee, Traitor or Patriot?* (Baton Rouge, 1951).

Lee, Henry: Charles Royster, *Light Horse Harry Lee and the Legacy of the American Revolution* (New York, 1981).

Lincoln, Benjamin: David Mattern, *Benjamin Lincoln and the American Revolution* (Columbia, S.C., 1995).

McDougall, Alexander: Roger J. Champagne, *Alexander McDougall and the American Revolution in New York* (Schnectady, N.Y., 1975); William L. McDougall, *American Revolutionary: A Biography of General Alexander McDougall* (Westport, Conn., 1977).

McIntosh, Lachlan: Harvey H. Jackson, *Lachlan McIntosh and the Politics of Revolutionary Georgia* (Athens, Ga., 1979).

Marion, Francis: Robert Bass, *The Life and Campaigns of General Francis Marion* (New York, 1959); Hugh Rankin, *Francis Marion: The Swamp Fox* (New York, 1973).

Maxwell, William: Harry M. Ward, *General William Maxwell and the New Jersey Continentals* (Westport, Conn., 1997).

Mercer, Hugh: Joseph M. Waterman, *With Sword and Lancet: The Life of General Hugh Mercer* (Richmond, 1941).

Montgomery, Richard: Hal T. Shelton, *General Richard Montgomery and the American Revolution* (New York, 1994).

Canadian Campaign: Thomas A. Desjardin, *Through a Howling Wilderness: Benedict Arnold's March to Quebec, 1775* (New York, 2006); Gustave Lanctot, *Canada and the American Revolution* (Cambridge, Mass., 1965); George M. Wrong, *Canada and the American Revolution* (New York, 1968).

New York Campaign: John Buchanan, *The Road to Valley Forge: How Washington Built the Army That Won the Revolution* (New York, 2004); Bruce Bliven, *Under the Guns: New York, 1775–1776* (New York, 1972); Thomas Fleming, *1776: Year of Illusions* (New York, 1975); John Gallagher, *The Battle of Brooklyn, 1776* (Edison, N.J., 2002); Henry P. Johnston, *The Battle of Harlem Heights, September 16, 1776* (New York, 1897); idem, *The Campaign of 1776 around New York and Brooklyn* (Brooklyn, 1878); Arthur Lefkowitz, *The Long Retreat* (Metuchen, N.J., 1998); Barnet Schecter, *The Battle for New York: The City at the Heart of the American Revolution* (New York, 2002).

Trenton-Princeton: David Hackett Fischer, *Washington's Crossing* (New York, 2004); William M. Dwyer, *The Day Is Ours! An Inside View of the Battles of Trenton and Princeton* (New York, 1983); Richard M. Ketchum, *The Winter Soldiers: The Battle for Trenton and Princeton* (New York, 1973).

Saratoga: Richard M. Ketchum, *Saratoga: Turning Point of America's Revolutionary War* (New York, 1997); Max Mintz, *The Generals of Saratoga* (New Haven, Conn., 1990); Hoffman Nickerson, *The Turning Point of the American Revolution, or Burgoyne's Army in America* (Boston, 1928); John S. Pancake, *1777: The Year of the Hangman* (University, Ala., 1977); Gavin K. Watt, *Rebellion in the Mohawk Valley: The St. Leger Expedition of 1777* (Toronto, 2002).

Philadelphia Campaign: Stephen R. Taaffe, *The Philadelphia Campaign, 1777–1778* (Lawrence, Kan., 2003)

Valley Forge: Wayne K. Bodle, *Valley Forge Winter: Civilians and Soldiers in War* (University Park, Pa., 2002); Wayne K. Bodle and Jacqueline Thibaut, *Valley Forge Historical Research Project* (Valley Forge, Pa., 1980).

Conway Cabal: Thomas Fleming, *Washington's Secret War: The Hidden History of Valley Forge* (New York, 2005); Bernard Knollenberg, *Washington and the Revolution, a Reappraisal: Gates, Conway, and the Continental Congress* (New York, 1940).

Monmouth: William S. Stryker, and William S. Myers, *The Battle of Monmouth* (Princeton, N.J., 1927); Theodore Thayer, *Washington and Lee: The Making of a Scapegoat* (Port Washington, N.Y., 1976).

Newport: Paul F. Dearden, *The Rhode Island Campaign of 1778: Inauspicious Dawn of Alliance* (Providence, 1980).

Sullivan Expedition: Joseph R. Fischer, *A Well-Executed Failure: The Sullivan Campaign against the Iroquois, July–September 1779* (Columbia, S.C., 1997); Glenn F. Williams, *Year of the Hangman: George Washington's Campaign against the Iroquois* (Yardley, Pa., 2005).

Southern Campaign: John Buchanan, *The Road to Guilford Courthouse: The American Revolution in the Carolinas* (New York, 1997); John S. Pancake, *This Destructive War: The British Campaign in the Carolinas, 1780–1782* (University, Ala., 1985); David K. Wilson, *The Southern Strategy: Britain's Conquest of South Carolina and Georgia, 1775–1780* (Columbia, S.C., 2005).

Siege of Savannah: Alexander A. Lawrence, *Storm over Savannah: The Story of Count d'Estaing and the Siege of the Town in 1779* (Athens, Ga., 1951).

Siege of Charleston: Carl P. Borick, *A Gallant Defense: The Siege of Charleston, 1780* (Columbia, S.C., 2003).

Southern Partisan War: Walter Edgar, *Partisans and Redcoats: The Southern Conflict That Turned the Tide of the American Revolution* (New York, 2001); Russell Weigley, *The Partisan War: The South Carolina Campaign of 1780–1782* (Columbia, S.C., 1970).

King's Mountain: Lyman C. Draper, *King's Mountain and Its Heroes: History of the Battle of King's Mountain, October 7th, 1780, and the Events Which Led to It* (Cincinnati, 1881).

Cowpens: Lawrence E. Babits, *A Devil of a Whipping: The Battle of Cowpens* (Chapel Hill, N.C., 1998).

Yorktown: Jerome A. Greene, *The Guns of Independence: The Siege of Yorktown* (New York, 2005); Richard M. Ketchum, *Victory at Yorktown: The Campaign That Won the Revolution* (New York, 2004).

Newburgh Conspiracy: Richard H. Kohn, "The Inside History of the Newburgh Conspiracy: America and the Coup d'Etat," *William and Mary Quarterly*, 3d Ser., 27 (1970):187–220; Paul David Nelson, "Horatio Gates at Newburgh, 1783: A Misunderstood Role," with a Rebuttal by Richard H. Kohn. *William and Mary Quarterly*, 3d Ser., 29 (1972):143–58.

The Continental Army

Charles Bolton, *The Private Soldier under Washington* (London, 1902); Allen Bowman, *The Morale of the American Revolutionary Army* (Washington, D.C., 1943); Caroline Cox, *A Proper Sense of Honor: Service and Sacrifice in George Washington's Army* (Chapel Hill, N.C., 2004); E. Wayne Carp, *To Starve the Army at Pleasure: Continental Army Administration and American Political Culture, 1775–1783* (Chapel Hill, N.C., 1984); John Elting, *Military Uniforms in America: The Era of the American Revolution, 1755–1795* (San Rafael, Calif., 1974); Louis Clinton Hatch, *The Administration of the American Revolutionary Army* (New York, 1904); Ronald Hoffman and Peter J. Albert, eds., *Arms and Independence: The Military Character of the American Revolution* (Charlottesville, Va., 1984); James H. Huston, *The Sinews of War: Army Logistics, 1775–1783* (Washington, D.C., 1966); Victor L. Johnson, *The Administration of the American Commissariat during the Revolutionary War* (Philadelphia, 1941); Gregory T. Knouff, *The Soldiers' Revolution: Pennsylvania in Arms and the Forging of Early American Identity* (University Park, Pa., 2004); Charles M. Lefferts, *Uniforms of the American, British, French, and German Armies in the War of Independence* (New York, 1926); Arthur Lefkowitz, *George Washington's Indispensable Men: The 32 Aides Who Helped Win American Independence* (Mechanicsburg, Pa., 2003); Charles H. Lesser, *The Sinews of Independence: Monthly Strength Reports of the Continental Army* (Chicago, 1976); James Kirby Martin and Mark Edward Lender, *A Respectable Army: The Military Origins of the Republic, 1763–1789* (Arlington Heights, Ill., 1982); Holly A. Mayer, *Belonging to the Army: Camp Followers and Community during the American Revolution* (Columbia, S.C., 1996); Charles P. Neimeyer, *America Goes to War: A Social History of the Continental Army* (New York, 1996); Howard H. Peckham, *The Toll of Independence: Engagements and Battle Casualties of the American Revolution* (Chicago, 1974); Erna Risch, *Supplying Washington's Army* (Washington, D.C., 1981); Jonathan G. Rossie, *The Politics of Command in the American Revolution* (Syracuse, 1975); Charles Royster, *A Revolutionary People at War: The Continental Army and American Character, 1775–1783* (Chapel Hill, N.C., 1979); Carl Van Doren, *Mutiny in January* (New York, 1943); Harry M. Ward, *George Washington's Enforcers: Policing the Continental Army* (Carbondale, Ill., 2006); Robert Wright, *The Continental Army* (Washington, D.C., 1983).

American Militia

John R. Galvin, *The Minute Men: A Compact History of the Defenders of the American Colonies, 1645–1775* (New York, 1967); Robert Gross, *The Minutemen and Their World* (New York, 1976); Don Higginbotham, "The American Militia: A Traditional Institution with Revolutionary Responsibilities," in idem, *Reconsiderations on the Revolutionary War: Selected Essays* (Westport, Conn., 1978); Mark V. Kwasny, *Washington's Partisan War, 1775–1783* (Kent, Ohio, 1996); John Shy, "A New Look at the Colonial Militia," in idem, *A People Numerous and Armed: Reflections on the Military Struggle for American Independence* (New York, 1976).

American Prisoners of War

Larry G. Bowman, *Captive Americans: Prisoners during the American Revolution* (Athens, Ohio, 1977); Sheldon Cohen, *Yankee Sailors in British Gaols: Prisoners of War at Forton and Mill, 1777–1783* (Newark, Del., 1995).

Army Pensions and the American Memory of the War

Sarah J. Purcell, *Sealed with Blood: War, Sacrifice, and Memory in Revolutionary America* (Philadelphia, 2002); John Resch, *Suffering Soldiers: Revolutionary War Veterans, Moral Sentiment, and Political Culture in the Early Republic* (Amherst, Mass., 1999).

The British Army, Hessians, and Provincial (Loyalist) Units

Rodney Atwood, *The Hessians: Mercenaries from Hessen-Kassel in the American Revolution* (Cambridge, England, 1980); R. Arthur Bowler, *Logistics and the Failure of the British Army in America, 1775–1783* (Princeton, N.J., 1975); Edward S. Curtis, *The Organization of the British Army in the American Revolution* (New Haven, Conn., 1926); William M. Dabney, *After Saratoga: The Story of the Convention Army* (Albuquerque, 1954); Max von Eelking, *German Allied Troops in the North American War*, trans. J. G. Rosengarten (Albany, 1893); Sir John Fortescue, *A History of the British Army*, 13 vols. (London, 1899–1930); Sylvia Frey, *The British Soldier in America: A Social History of Military Life in the Revolutionary Period* (Austin, Tex., 1981); Richard Sampson, *Escape in America: The British Convention Prisoners, 1777–1783* (Chippenham, England, 1995); John Shy, *Toward Lexington: The Role of the British Army in the Coming of the American Revolution* (Princeton, N.J., 1965); Paul H. Smith, *Loyalists and Redcoats: A Study in British Revolutionary Policy* (Chapel Hill, N.C., 1964); William B. Willcox, "The British Road to Yorktown: A Study in Divided Command," *American Historical Review* 52 (1946):1–35.

The French Army and Navy

Jonathan Dull, *The French Navy and American Independence: A Study of Arms and Diplomacy, 1774–1787* (Princeton, N.J., 1975); Lee Kennett, *The French Forces in America, 1780–1783* (Westport, Conn., 1977).

America's Homefront and Wartime Politics

Richard Buel Jr., *In Iron's: Britain's Naval Supremacy and the American Revolutionary Economy* (New Haven, Conn., 1998); idem, *Dear Liberty: Connecticut's Mobilization for the Revolutionary War* (Middletown, Conn., 1980); Edmund C. Burnett, *The Continental Congress* (New York, 1941); Judith L. Van Buskirk, *Generous Enemies: Patriots and Loyalists in Revolutionary New York* (Philadelphia, 2002); E. James Ferguson, *The Power of the Purse* (Chapel Hill, N.C., 1961); John Ferling, *A Leap in the Dark: The Struggle to Create the American Republic* (New York, 2003); idem, *John Adams: A Life* (Knoxville, 1992); idem, *The Loyalist Mind: Joseph Galloway and the American Revolution* (University Park, Pa., 1977); David Freeman Hawke, *Paine* (New York, 1974); James Henderson, *Party Politics in the Continental Congress* (New York, 1974); Ronald Hoffman, Thad W. Tate, and Peter J. Albert, eds., *An Uncivil War: The Southern Backcountry during the American Revolution* (Charlottesville, Va., 1985); Merrill Jensen, *The Founding of a Nation, A History of the American Revolution, 1763–1776* (New York, 1968); idem, *The American Revolution within America* (New York, 1974); idem, *The Articles of Confederation: An Interpretation of the Social-Constitutional History of the American Revolution, 1774–1781* (Madison, Wisc., 1948); Wayne Lee, *Crowds and Soldiers in Revolutionary North Carolina: The Culture of Violence in Riot and War*

(Gainesville, Fla., 2001); Pauline Maier, *American Scripture: Making the Declaration of Independence* (New York, 1997); Jerrilyn G. Marsten, *King and Congress: The Transfer of Political Legitimacy, 1774–1776* (Princeton, N.J., 1987); David McCullough, *John Adams* (New York, 2001); John C. Miller, *The Triumph of Freedom, 1775–1783* (Boston, 1948); Edmund S. Morgan, *Benjamin Franklin* (New Haven, Conn., 2002); Jack Rakove, *The Beginnings of National Politics* (New York, 1979); Ray Raphael, *A People's History of the American Revolution: How Common People Shaped the Fight for Independence* (New York, 2001); Gordon S. Wood, *The Creation of the American Republic, 1776–1787* (Chapel Hill, N.C., 1969); idem, *The Radicalism of the American Revolution* (New York, 1992).

British Civilian Leaders and Politics

Gerald S. Brown, *American Secretary: The Colonial Policies of Lord George Germain* (Ann Arbor, Mich., 1963); Dora Mae Clark, *British Opinion and the American Revolution* (New York, 1966); Carl B. Cone, *Burke and the Nature of Politics: The Age of the American Revolution* (Lexington, Ky., 1957); Solomon Lutnick, *The American Revolution and the British Press, 1775–1783* (Columbia, Mo., 1967); Charles Ritcheson, *British Politics and the American Revolution* (Norman, Okla., 1954); Alan Valentine, *Lord George Germain* (Oxford, England, 1962); idem, *Lord North* (Norman, Okla., 1967); Stanley Weintraub, *Iron Tears: America's Battle for Freedom, Britain's Quagmire, 1775–1783* (New York, 2005); William B. Willcox, "Too Many Cooks: British Planning before Saratoga," *Journal of British Studies* 2 (1962):56–90.

Diplomacy of the War of Independence

Samuel Flagg Bemis, *The Diplomacy of the American Revolution* (New York, 1935); H. W. Brands, *The First American: The Life and Times of Benjamin Franklin* (New York, 2000); Edward Corwin, *French Policy and the American Alliance of 1778* (New York, 1916); Jonathan Dull, *A Diplomatic History of the American Revolution* (New Haven, Conn., 1983); John Ferling, *Setting the World Ablaze: Washington, Adams, Jefferson and the American Revolution* (New York, 2000); Ronald Hoffman and Peter J. Albert, eds., *Diplomacy and Revolution: The Franco-American Alliance of 1778* (Charlottesville, Va., 1981); idem, *Peace and the Peacemakers: The Treaty of 1783* (Charlottesville, Va., 1986); Richard B. Morris, *The Peacemakers: The Great Powers and American Independence* (New York, 1965); Orville T. Murphy, *Charles Gravier, Comte de Vergennes: French Diplomacy in the Age of Revolution, 1719–1787* (Albany, 1982); Stacy Schiff, *A Great Improvisation: Franklin, France, and the Birth of America* (New York, 2005); William Stinchcombe, *The American Revolution and the French Alliance* (Syracuse, 1969); Carl Van Doren, *Benjamin Franklin* (New York, 1938); Gordon S. Wood, *The Americanization of Benjamin Franklin* (New York, 2004); Esmond Wright, *Franklin of Philadelphia* (Cambridge, Mass., 1984).

The Naval War

Gardner W. Allen, *A Naval History of the American Revolution*, 2 vols. (Boston, 1913); William Bell Clark, *George Washington's Navy: Being an Account of His Excellency's Fleet in New England Waters* (Baton Rouge, 1960); Jack Coggins, *Ships and Seamen of the American Revolution: Vessels, Crews, Weapons, Gear, Naval Tactics, and Actions of the War of Independence* (Harrisburg, Pa., 1969); William M. Fowler, *Rebels under Sail: The American Navy during the American Revolution* (New York, 1976); Nathan Miller, *Sea of Glory: The Continental Navy Fights for Independence, 1775–1783* (New York, 1974); N. A. M. Rodger, *The Command of the Seas: A Naval History of Britain, 1649–1815* (New York, 2005); David Syrett, *The Royal Navy in American Waters, 1775–1783* (Aldershot, England, 1989); John A. Tilley, *The British Navy and the American Revolution* (Columbia, S.C., 1987).

The Native Americans' War

Colin G. Calloway, *The American Revolution in Indian Country* (Cambridge, England, 1995); Barbara Graymont, *The Iroquois in the American Revolution* (Syracuse, 1972); Isabel T. Kelsay, *Joseph Brant, 1743–1807: Man of Two Worlds* (Syracuse, 1984); Max M. Mintz, *Seeds of Empire: The American Revolutionary Conquest of the Iroquois* (New York, 1999); James H. O'Donnell, III, *Southern Indians in the American Revolution* (Knoxville, 1972); Alan Taylor, *The Divided Ground: Indians, Settlers, and the Northern Borderland of the American Revolution* (New York, 2006).

African Americans in the Revolutionary War

Philip Foner, *Blacks in the American Revolution* (Westport, Conn., 1975); Benjamin Quarles, *The Negro in the American Revolution* (Chapel Hill, N.C. 1961).

Weaponry

B. P. Hughes, *British Smooth-Bore: The Muzzle Loading Artillery of the Eighteenth and Nineteenth Centuries* (Harrisburg, Pa., 1969); Torsten Link, *The Flintlock: Its Origin and Development*, edited by John E. Haywood (London, 1965); George C. Neumann, *The History of the Weapons of the American Revolution* (New York, 1967); Harold L. Peterson, *Arms and Armor in Colonial America, 1526–1783* (Harrisburg, Pa., 1956); idem, *The Book of the Continental Soldier: Being a Complete Account of the Uniforms, Weapons, and Equipment with Which He Lived and Fought* (Harrisburg, 1968); idem, *Round Shot and Rammers* (Harrisburg, 1969).

INDEX